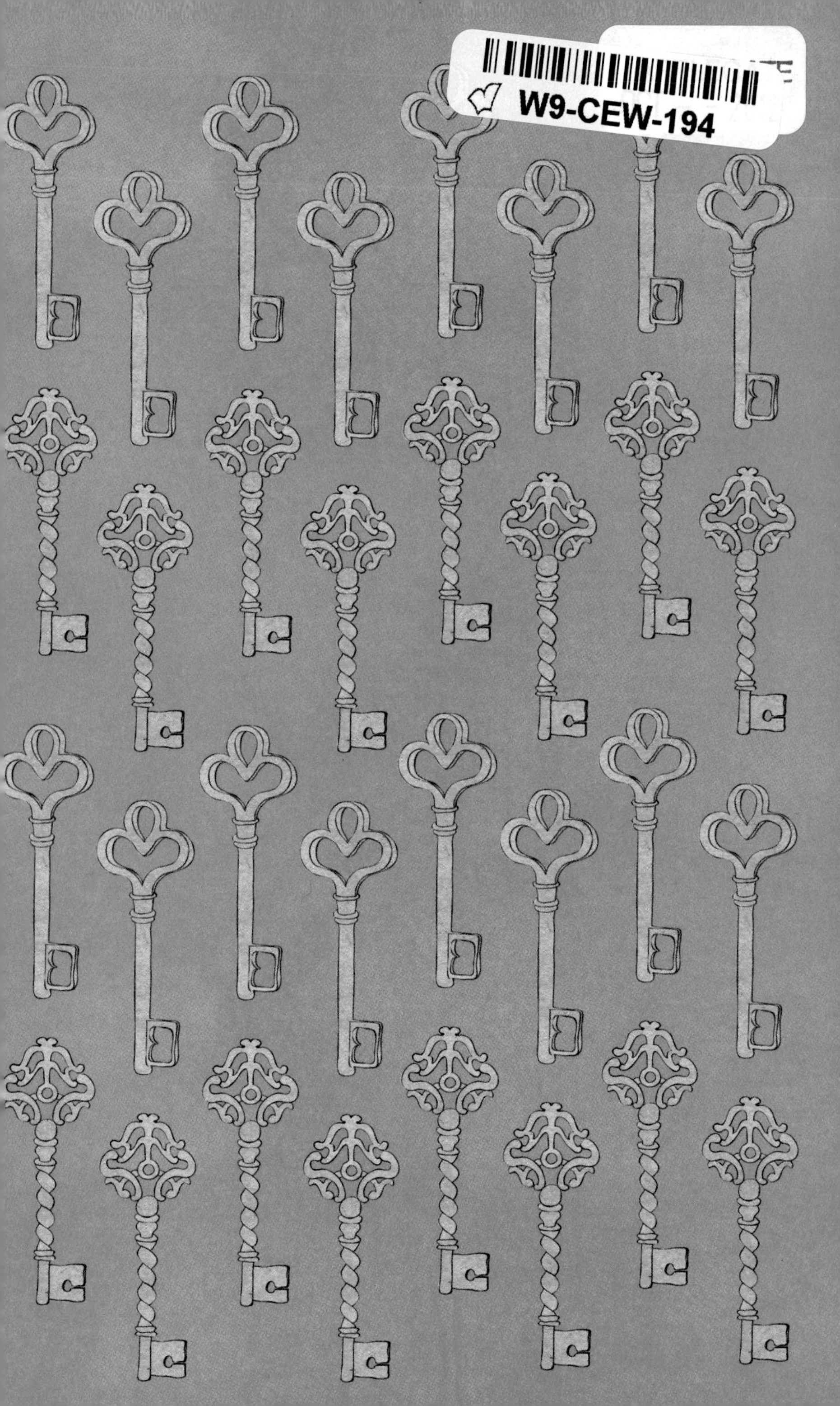
W9-CEW-194

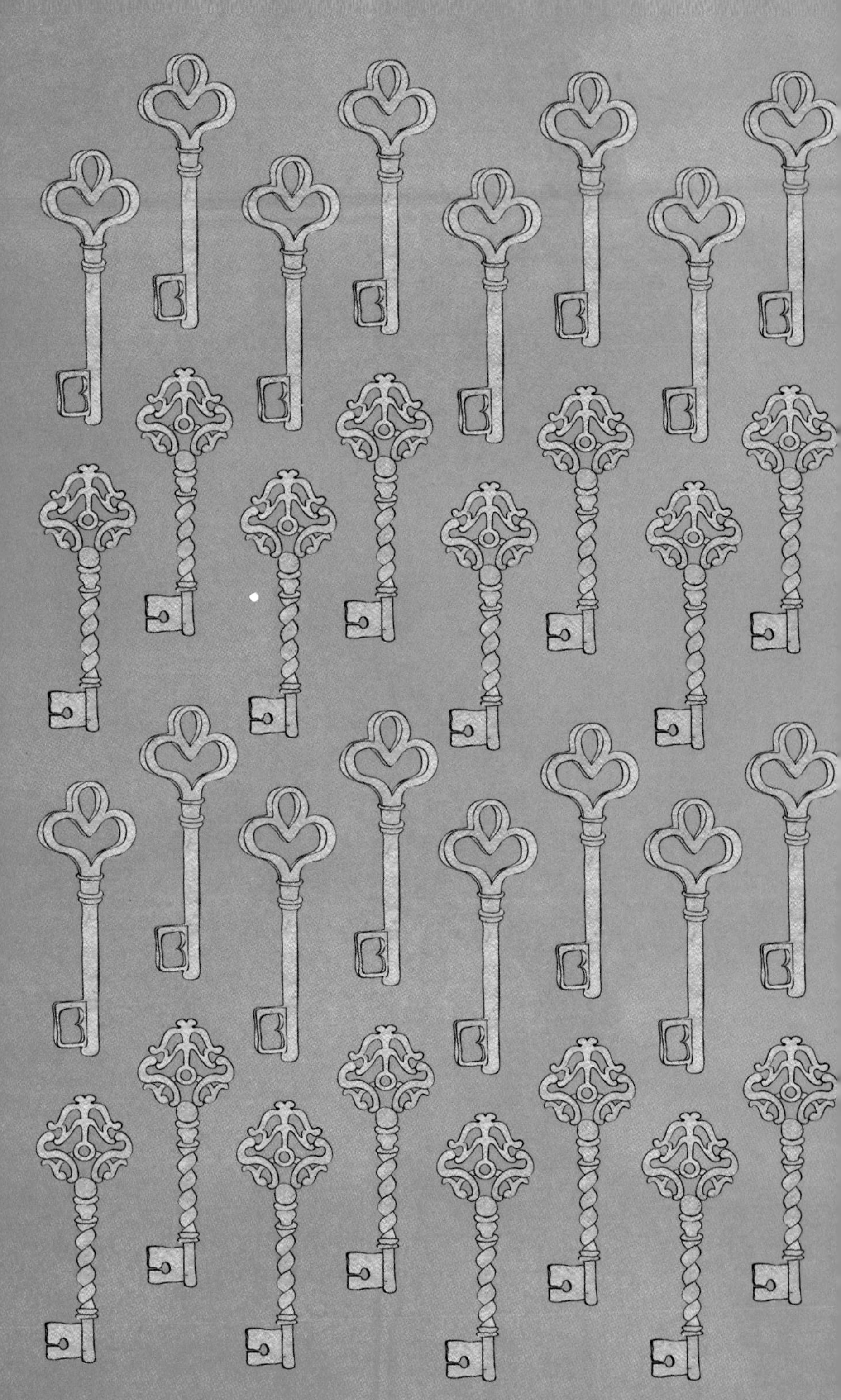

The Art of the Visit

Being the Perfect Host
Becoming the Perfect Guest

by Kathy Bertone

RUNNING PRESS
PHILADELPHIA • LONDON

Printed in the United States of America

Books published by Running Press are available at special discounts for bulk purchases in the United States by corporations, institutions, and other organizations. For more information, please contact the Special Markets Department at the Perseus Books Group, 2300 Chestnut Street, Suite 200, Philadelphia, PA 19103, or call (800) 810-4145, ext. 5000, or e-mail special.markets@perseusbooks.com.

ISBN 978-0-7624-4395-6
Library of Congress Control Number: 2012934285

E-book ISBN 978-07624-4493-9

9 8 7 6 5 4 3 2 1
Digit on the right indicates the number of this printing

Book design by Amanda Richmond
Typography: Lomba, Gotham, and Samantha Script

Running Press Book Publishers
2300 Chestnut Street
Philadelphia, PA 19103–4371

Visit us on the web!
www.runningpress.com

This book is dedicated to

MY HUSBAND CHET OBIELESKI,

WHO MAKES MY LIFE BETTER BECAUSE HE IS.

Acknowledgments

I WISH TO EXPRESS GRATITUDE TO MY FAMILY: MY FATHER, Richard, and my mother, Beverly, who taught me that good manners are best expressed by how you treat others; and to my brothers, Peter and Kurt, their wives, Joyce and Laurence, respectively, and their children, my nieces and nephews Bertone: Katherine, Cristina, Alexander, Kurt, Peter, and Zoé.

And to my dear friends: Meile Rockefeller, who, after seeing the outline assured me how valid and needed the book was and advised me to make it lighthearted and entertaining. I tried, Meile.

Karen Knab, whose contributions and continual support, through all the emotional ups and downs, were invaluable as always.

Karen Harper, best-selling author with over fifty books to her credit, who out of unselfish kindness gave encouragement when needed the most.

Jeannie and David Zook, who always had a house available to which I could go and write.

Maryann Jones, charming person and hostess after my own heart.

Thomas Troost, friend without whom I could only write.

John Douglas, editor, who gave an unknown writer her first column.

Thanks to new friends and family for whom I am so grateful: Debby and Joseph Sellitto; Pierrette DeCinti; Courtney Harden; George and Mena Gerstein; Susan Inscoe; Jennifer Burke; Christine Watts; Tammy Chase; and Madeleine Abissidan.

And my mother-in-law, Regina Obieleski, who is missed everyday.

And finally, several extraordinary people: Diane O'Connell, first editor, who expertly knew what to do with the manuscript and the nervous author; Geoffrey Stone, editor at Running Press, who encompasses all the qualities of a true gentleman and a great editor: style, ability, and kindness; production editor Cisca Schreefel; and copyeditor Martha Whitt, ladies and professionals both.

My brilliant literary agent, Deborah Ritchken, who said, "I get it" and then quickly and efficiently found it a home. Without her I would not have the honor of thanking anyone.

And because I run the risk of never being invited to anyone's home ever again I want to thank my future hosts in advance for their understanding of my intent in writing this book. You should have seen it before I was encouraged to "lighten it up."

And to you, hosts and guests everywhere, who, like me, wish to make time together with loved ones the best it can possibly be. I hope you enjoy this book. I loved writing it.

PART I

Being the Perfect Host

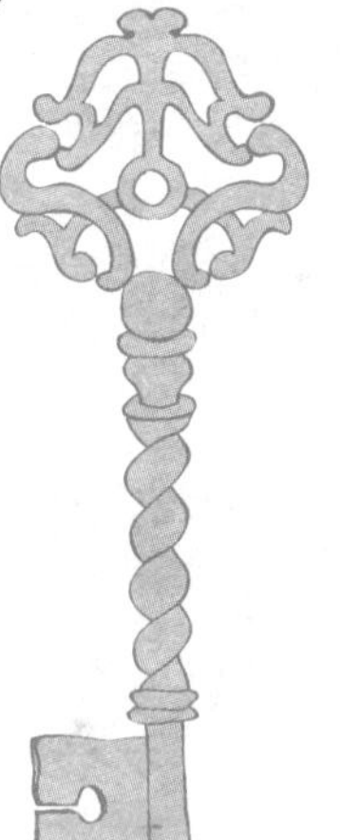

DON'T WE ALL SECRETLY WISH FOR A CURRIER & IVES–LIKE world where our homes are warm and peaceful and the people in them courteous, compassionate, loving, and happy? Although not often possible, we can, and should, try to give our guests an environment as close to that idyllic vision as possible.

E. B. White said, "I arise in the morning torn between a desire to improve the world and a desire to enjoy the world. This makes it hard to plan the day." If you substitute "my guests" for "the world" you have a good idea of the reality of hosting friends and family for an extended period of time. It is a tough job and a significant investment of time and effort.

If you are looking for the Two-Minute-Guide-to-Good-Hosting, you will not find it here. I just don't think anything done in that amount of time can be any good. Not cooking, not sex, not hosting. It took God six days to create the world and then there was the needed rest. It may take more than two minutes to prepare your home or plan meals for your guests.

The best times in our lives should be the time we spend with the people we love, but I know it often doesn't go smoothly. No matter how much we love our friends and family, even the thought of the upcoming invasion can sometimes leave us breathless. That need not be the case. The tips and suggestions included in these chapters will make you prepared, ready, and therefore relaxed and able to truly enjoy your guests, whether they are arriving alone, or with children, grandparents, or pets. So take a deep breath and know you are not alone. These chapters will help ease the anxiety of any upcoming visit whether you are having guests to your home for the first time or the five hundredth.

CHAPTER 1

Creating a Welcoming Home: Preparing the Rooms

"I hate housework! You make the beds, you do the dishes and six months later you have to start all over again."

—JOAN RIVERS

YOUR ROLE—AS THE PERFECT HOST—IS TO MAKE YOUR guests feel welcome, wanted, and at ease from the moment they walk through the door to the very last "goodbye." How your house looks and feels and how it is organized and set up plays a big part. That doesn't mean you need to prep your home as though you were hosting The Royals. But you certainly don't want to have half-empty coffee mugs, piles of papers, and used socks loitering about like desultory teens. As long as your home is relatively presentable, your guests will be more responsive to your calm, smiling face than to a picture-perfect interior, the making of which sapped you of all your enthusiasm.

No matter how far one plans ahead there is always something forgotten or undone at the last minute. But if you at least ensure all the rooms are taken care of well in advance, you have plenty of time to easily handle all the other stuff!

Let's get started.

The Bedrooms

AFTER A LONG DAY OF DRIVING TO VISIT MY FRIEND AND her family, I rolled my small suitcase into the guest room and what did my tired eyes see? A cozy room in blue and white with big fluffy pillows on the bed and a white bathrobe laid across it, fresh towels folded at the foot, and flowers on the nightstand. I immediately felt the stress of the day's travel melt away and—more importantly—I felt welcomed.

Be sure the beds have freshly laundered sheets and blankets. No matter if someone slept on the bed just once a few months ago, it is a must. I'll never forget the evening a friend came into the living room dangling a dirty, wadded up sock he had found in the guest bed. I thought that bed was clean! Good thing he was a good friend!

Provide a variety of pillows. I have four pillows on the guest beds, some hard, some soft. Your guest will appreciate having the choice. But stay away from feather pillows as many people have an allergic reaction to them. This may seem like a minor thing, but I can't sleep on too high a pillow (I know… poor baby…) as I have a painfully stiff neck in the morning! Age, not beauty, trust me.

Always have an extra blanket or throw at the foot of the bed, no matter the weather. If it is summer, and your guests get chilled because of the air conditioner, they will appreciate its presence. I have learned that some guests are warm when some are always cold, so it is best to err on the side of warmth. Your guests can always take away covers, but they can't add them without stumbling around looking for one or waking you up in the middle of the night! If you would prefer to keep them in the closet, fine, but make sure they are not so high on a shelf that Grandmother can't reach them.

VISIT WIZARD TIP If there are more guests than beds, there are alternatives to sleeping bags on the floor (which should be reserved only for people twenty years of age or under). Consider buying an inflatable mattress. They come in different sizes and store quite easily when deflated. The guest who is having a hard time sleeping with their partner, for whatever reason, can use that bed and get a good night's sleep.

Make a fan available. If you do not have ceiling fans in your guest bedrooms, keep a small table fan in the closet. If your guests are hot at night they can pull that out and place it on a table. If you really want to pamper them equip all your ceiling fans with remote control. You can either purchase them that way or set them up later if they are a type that can be so controlled. There is nothing better than being able to lie in bed and control the fan at the touch of a button.

If you prefer the kind with the hanging cord, make sure it is long enough for ancient Uncle Ralph to reach but short enough not to hit tall cousin Ronald in the head as they climb into bed. Add a decorative pull—either bought or made. See the Resources (page 271) for more ideas.

Put fresh flowers in the room. Either picked from your garden or purchased, it is still the one thing that tells your guests you care, but stay away from flowers that are heavily scented. My sister-in-law came for a long weekend with her husband to one of our homes. I had two large rose bushes on either side of the front door. I kicked myself for not cutting fresh roses for their bedroom but later was glad I did not because the next morning she told me how terribly sensitive she is to roses.

Instead, put a single flower in a small vase and place it in the bathroom or on the nightstand. It makes a good impact with little scent and minimal space consumption.

Make some space for your guests' clothes and items. Let's face it: We maximize our use of every closet in our home. But it's not good enough to simply push over your clothes hanging in the guest closet to open up a few stingy inches. Do you really think your guests will feel welcome if they have to share closet space with your out-of-season clothes or those that you *still* can't get into? Even if you have to put "the stuff" in your own closet, or in the basement, or in the backseat of the car, clean out those guest closets before the visit!

Make sure there are more than enough empty hangers in the closet. Invest in wood or plastic. Figure on at least six shirt and six pant hangers per guest for a maximum of twelve hangers per guest. Any more than that means you have permanent guests. If your closet is large, or a walk-in, stash a small ironing board and iron in it.

And if guests are staying longer than a night or two, clear out a few drawers if you don't have a dedicated dresser in the room, or buy a rolling cart with drawers that you can put in the closet. There are many styles and price ranges available. Check your local home supply store. Again, if you know your guest has no allergies, put a sachet of lightly scented lavender in one of the drawers.

Have a cleared space on the dresser for guests to put their belongings like keys, wallets, purses, medications, and so on. This space is for your guests—not for you to show off your collection of miniature whatevers. If your room looks a bit barren, that's a good thing.

VISIT WIZARD TIP Have coasters out for use on the wood dresser or end tables. People will leave rings on dressers where they put their wet glasses or where a glass perspires unbeknownst to them. It just happens. You have two options: have only furniture that can withstand that, like treated wood or glass, or consider putting a removable glass top on the piece, cut to fit. They are not as expensive as you might think.

Set up luggage racks. You can find these at kitchen and bath stores. They will make unpacking easier for your guests and save your bedspread from usually dirty luggage. You can set them up in the guest closet if space allows, as often there are some things the guest does not want to unpack but still wants to have accessible. They can move the luggage racks later if they prefer. And if your grandmother can't lift her luggage, remember to do it for her. If time or cost does not permit luggage racks, be creative. Visit the Resources section (page 271) for some ideas.

If your guests have completely emptied out their suitcases in your *empty* closet and drawers, let them know where to store their luggage, and it should not be the now-clean closet unless it is truly big enough to accommodate both suitcases and their clothes. If a better storage place for those suitcases is the garage or another room, move them for your guests.

Install decorative hooks inside your closet or on the back of the door for bathrobes or wet towels. You know your teenage guests—and some adults—are going to choose the floor, or your furniture, for their wet towels unless given an easy alternative!

Pay attention to lighting. This seems to perplex some. I actually had a friend borrow a table lamp from me to take with him to the house of the person he was visiting! Lighting on a nightstand at each side of the bed is important and should allow for each guest to read in bed should they desire. I put three-way bulbs in my lamps so if a guest wants to read and not disturb the other they can use low light. One woman emailed me this after a weekend visit with friends:

"The house was pleasant and I did think of you and your book more than once. For one thing, no bedside lights anywhere in the house. Not one! We all bitched, moaned and complained that we couldn't read! (What does this say about us, that reading was first on our list of sadly missed bedroom activities??)"

If you do use three-way bulbs in your bedroom lamps, check them. It irritates the Visit Wizard when the three-ways are—in actuality—one-way.

Night lighting is very important: Put little night-lights in rooms, halls, and bathrooms, as plain or fancy as you like. Remember that guests don't know the house like you do and the last thing you want is someone taking a fall or fumbling in the dark. I am not a big collector of anything but these are one thing with which I like to have fun. I glue seashells onto the base of night-lights and have some for different times of the year, like the fall and spring. There are some on the market now that are like miniature works of art. I also use battery-operated candles throughout the house for a warm, homey touch.

Make sure there are mirrors. Obviously important, and often overlooked in the guest room. Hang a full-length mirror behind the door or on the wall. They are not very expensive and the little mirror in the bathroom will not do! Also have a mirror, preferably with a table beneath it, either on the wall or on a stand, which can be used by your guest for hair and makeup.

Have a variety of books in the room, from novels and poetry to books of specialty interests, like gardening or travel. Books on the local area are a good choice so your guest can find things to do and places to explore. Humor books are also often welcome—as long as they're not raunchy, as some people will be offended. One of my favorite things in life is reading in bed at night, so I appreciate having new and interesting books in the room.

Put a small writing pad and pen in the bedroom, either plain or as special as you'd like. Local postcards in the room are a very special gift for guests, who can send them to friends and family back home. In days gone by, retiring to one's room to write was a usual occurrence. It gave the guest some alone time and the host a usually needed break.

Have a surge protector power strip in each guest bedroom, clearly visible. It is important that guests are able to easily charge and protect their electronic gadgets. Visible surge protectors mean that guests won't have to pull out furniture trying to find an outlet and will have comfort knowing their devices are protected.

Consider a television. I like televisions in the guest bedrooms. That is just a personal choice, you can go either way, but if a guest just has to get away for a bit, or watch one of their favorite programs that cannot be missed, they are able. However, I take out the television if a child is staying in the room.

VISIT WIZARD TIP Do not have a phone in the room unless you remember to turn the ringer off! No one wants to be awakened by your daughter's late night phone friend or when trying to enjoy the luxury of a nap in the afternoon.

Provide an alarm clock. Just don't forget to check that the alarm is off—and don't have a clock that ticks loudly, if at all. I once found a clock I had so lovingly purchased just for the guest room sitting outside it one morning. Well, that's better than having them bury it under the far end of the mattress. Yes, it did happen....

Don't forget the little things. One of my friends puts a carafe of water in the guest bedroom in the evening. How elegant. You can buy them with the little glass that fits on top. If you don't want to do the carafe, make sure there is bottled water. Although not as economical as tap, bottled is great because your guests can recap what they don't use and it won't spill or break. Don't forget the glasses, whether glass or plastic.

And don't put tap water in a bottled water container (yes, I've seen it done). A nice alternative is putting tap water in a plastic pitcher with ice and floating a lemon slice in it. Pretty, economical, and enhances the taste.

Also, make sure to put a box of tissues and a small wastepaper basket in the bedroom—with liner!

The Five-Star Treatment

"I cannot bear un-ironed pillow cases.
I iron something literally every single day. It's sort of
pleasantly mindless—which in my case is a huge plus."
—WASHINGTON, D.C., HOSTESS

EVEN THE VISIT WIZARD DOES NOT IRON SHEETS OR PILLOW cases, but it is so very, very luxurious when it is done. It truly makes one feel as if they are in a five-star hotel. After a trip to a swanky London hotel, my husband and I swore we would get the highest quality sheets and carry on this dying tradition. Right.

Consider this: A bathrobe is a necessary item for guests but it is big and bulky to pack. I have a couple of bathrobes on hand and I let my visiting family members know so they can use them if they would like to. One is special from a resort that the family frequented so that's nice, but I'm not sure if a casual friend would want to use a guest bathrobe. Use your judgment. I remember traveling to a friend's for the weekend and did not pack a bathrobe. She had one lying out on the guest bed and it was so welcoming and wonderful. That night I put it on, and three of us girls met in the living room and watched (yes, for the eighth time) that classic movie, *Gone with the Wind*. What I would have given to outfit the guest rooms at Tara.... Here are some five-star ideas:

- Have a small bowl of fruit or other goodies in the room, like a split of Champagne with glasses and an ice bucket.
- Line the curtains in your guest room with blackout lining so your guest can sleep in if desired.
- A "sleep machine" or small CD player with a few soothing, spa-like CDs is a real treat.
- A nice touch for your guests is providing a mini reading light that attaches to the books.

For those guests you either really treasure or want to impress (like your new mother-in-law—just as an example!), do this: Get a medium-sized, shallow, beautiful basket and line it with bright tissue paper. Fill it with a combination of the following and put on the night-stand or bedroom table:

- Eye shades or eye pads that you can use hot or cold (easily purchased at any drugstore) and perfect for keeping out morning light if unwelcomed
- Hotel-like slippers in cellophane
- New back scrubber for the bath
- Hand or foot cream
- Small wrapped treats like candy or mints
- Wrapped, scented exotic soaps
- Bath beads or bath milk
- Bath pillow

For the first night that your guests will be staying, consider putting a little chocolate or mint on their pillow. My mom remembers when her grandchildren put a stuffed animal on her bed so she felt welcome. That is an especially nice touch coming from the children.

Once in a while during the visit slip into your guest's bedroom, fluff up the pillows and turn down the bed. But do this only if you know them well. You don't want to be seen as intrusive. If the bed is unmade, clothes are strewn about, and there are rings on the bed side table, refer your guests to the Becoming the Perfect Guest section, page 150!

VISIT WIZARD TIP Place a personal picture that has meaning for your guest in the bedroom. I put an old picture I have of my French friend and her father in the room. She was very touched seeing it.

The Bathrooms

"A guest sees more in an hour than the host in a year."

—POLISH PROVERB

A GENTLEMAN WHO JUST COMPLETED HIS GUEST HOUSE, A stunning Mediterranean structure, complete with wrought iron balconies outside every floor, was justifiably proud of the interior and exterior design. Unfortunately, his first visitors reported the next morning they had no wastebasket in the bathroom... and no mirror!

If you have not used your guest bedroom and bathroom for any length of time *do it* for several days. No, I am not kidding. That is absolutely the best way to determine what is needed. You will be surprised at what you discover is missing!

Bath towels are big and bulky, so leave the majority of them in the linen closet. However, you want your guests to have easy access to several when they first arrive. I have a variety of clever ways to present towels.

Although too complex to describe here, visit the Resources section in this book (page 271), and no, it doesn't have anything to do with turning hand towels into animal shapes... although the monkey ones *are* cute.

And if by chance you are expecting royalty (or those who think they are), put a silk ribbon under each complete set, pull up, and tie with a bow. But just remember that nothing says tacky like towels labeled "King" and "Queen."

Be careful to leave enough vanity space for your guests to put out their personal items. Less is more when it comes to guest-bathroom decor. If you have little space, consider buying an étagère which can hold supplies, or building or buying a shelf and attaching it to the wall. Under no circumstances make this mistake, conveyed to me by a woman after returning home from an otherwise delightful visit:

> *"We go to visit these friends of ours quite often. They have a lovely house with two bedrooms for guests upstairs. Between the two rooms is a bath. The bathroom has two sinks but on each side of the sink there is barely room to lay a toothbrush! The sink tops are loaded with stuff. We must use the windowsill or the floor for our stuff or put her stuff on the floor so we can use the sink top. In the bath area there are plenty of towels but after you take a shower there is absolutely no place to hang it!"*

Have liquid hand soap, as well as soap in a dish. I suggest you put out a standard soap for daily use and face washing instead of the exotic variety, but leave the soap wrapped or in its little box. That way your guests will know it's fresh and not used by others. Don't be too concerned with brands. If your guests can't do without a certain product, they will most likely bring it. You can't be expected to stock every soap known to man. A regular guest of mine must have a certain kind of soap, one that I don't use. I used to stock this soap to make sure she had it. After a few years of doing this I now tell her to bring her own. I know. Some of you are recoiling in horror that I would suggest such a thing, but a host has to draw the line somewhere!

Provide a stand-alone small mirror, preferably one that flips for magnification. Place it on the vanity, if there is room, or under the sink or in the closet if there is not room. Your guests can use it for makeup application, eyebrow plucking, or whatever.

Place a box of tissues either on the vanity or on the toilet tank top. Speaking of toilet tank tops, it doesn't have to be yucky or cold looking. Decorate it! If things slide off, cut out a nonskid pad (the same color as the tank top) to fit and place it on top. Set a small, decorative room deodorizer spray on it. Put a colorful object d'art on it or a framed poem written by your child. There is really no other use for the darn thing, so be as creative as you like! (Just don't put towels on it. Not sanitary or visually appealing.)

Clear out the vanity cupboard so your guests can put away their items. Leave it open a crack so they can see it is empty, or better yet, when you show them the bath let them know they are free to use it. Say this in the most encouraging way possible. When the guest bathroom also serves as the main bathroom or powder room for the house this will be more important than ever.

Set out a toothbrush holder. That way your guests don't have to put their toothbrush on the vanity or in their drinking glass.

Provide a drinking cup. Most people like to have a glass in the bathroom, which is fine as long as no children are using it. For adults I take a rectangular plate or a napkin caddy and put two small nice glasses on it. Kind of like "his" and "hers." Use little plastic disposable cups for the children.

Put a handful of cotton balls and swabs in a small, pretty bowl of either glass or ceramic, or an apothecary jar made for that purpose.

Present a variety of shampoos and other necessities from which your guests can choose. They do not have to be expensive or salon-like unless you wish, but giving the guest the opportunity to try something new is a treat, and if conditioner was forgotten, well there it is.

Make sure extra toilet paper is readily available—in the bathroom! I still pale remembering one houseguest who called out to his wife from the bathroom to fetch him a roll of toilet paper.

Have a toilet brush in each bathroom in the house, for your convenience and for the convenience of guests. It is worth the expense to buy those plastic ones that come with their own holder complete with disposable heads. These are sanitary and easy for everyone to use. You'll never go back (and no more rinsing the brush under the bathtub faucet...).

Have cleaning supplies below the sink. The basics should be paper towels, glass and counter cleaner, and pop-up disinfectant wipes. The good guest will want to tidy up during the visit.

VISIT WIZARD TIP Speaking of toilets, here's a great device: the soft-close toilet seat. Thank the creator of good stuff for this one. With the mere touch of your little finger on the lid, it closes oh so slowly and quietly. No more slamming of lids and no excuses for the toilet seat to be left raised—ever.

Ensure there is a waste can with liner in sight. I went to visit for a weekend and there was no waste can in the bathroom. I was too embarrassed to point it out to my host so I snuck into the kitchen one night and grabbed some large trash bags (which were all I could find). The better idea would have been for me to ask, no matter the discomfort, but did I really want to?

And although we are recycling, don't use those thin grocery store bags as liners, at least for guests. I'm sorry, but they just don't say you care!

Install decorative hooks in the bathroom for bathrobes and after-shower towels. This will lessen the likelihood that towels will end up in a heap on the bathroom floor or refolded and put back on the rail only to remain in that damp, yucky state.

If the bathroom is large enough, have a hamper for dirty towels. I like those cute ones that have LAUNDRY clearly marked on the liner.

In the bathroom or linen closet make sure you have the following personal items:

- Toothpaste and wrapped toothbrush
- Cotton balls
- Can of shaving cream
- Tissues
- Disposable shaving razors
- Bandages
- Brush and comb
- Hair spray
- Blow dryer
- Shower cap
- Personal supplies for women

Extras:

- Sunscreen
- Bug repellent
- Ear plugs
- Nail polish remover and file
- Moisturizers
- Facial products
- Curling iron and flat iron
- Bath products

A nice (and tidy) alternative is to have these things in a basket labeled "Guest" in the bathroom or in the closet. That way your guests know they are free and welcome to use these items.

The Powder Room

Preparing the powder room is just as important and is often overlooked. ("Powder room" is an old-fashioned term I adore and is used for a small bathroom on the main floor that is used by everyone but is not a dedicated guest bathroom. In the eighteenth century it was a small room where people would have their wigs repowdered, then in more recent times, where women went to "powder their nose.")

The powder room can be both special and efficient. Here's how you can make it unique:

- Put a bowl of potpourri and a small vase with flowers on the toilet tank top.
- I put out paper "cloth" hand towels in a pretty napkin caddy on the vanity top by the sink. I just found some with GUEST written on them so I am, of course, ecstatic. They are disposable so guests aren't using the same towel.
- You can also buy a disposable cloth towel dispenser that sits on your towel rack; although more costly up front, using disposables does cut back on your laundry and keeps the powder room tidy. However if you choose to use a hand towel, fold it in thirds, then in half, and place it on the vanity by the sink. I happen to use the small finger towels—easier to keep neat and change out.
- I really like battery powered flickering "flameless" candles. The good ones look very realistic, and there is no threat of fire. There has not been one guest who has not commented on how unique they are, and of course they are much more economical and safer

than the real thing. Another good vanity or toilet tank top item!

- Have a toilet brush in here as well. As mentioned above but worth repeating, the absolute best are the ones which include a disposable head that is snapped on to the wand and disposed of in the lined wastebasket after use—the whole procedure is hands free. Smart.
- I keep a can of pretty room spray in a scent of the season. No one wants to enter a bathroom that smells of disinfectant spray. And don't forget a pretty holder for the box of tissues. Buy an inexpensive one and decorate it yourself. Fun, efficient, and it will match your décor perfectly!

VISIT WIZARD TIP A small electronic device or radio playing a sweet melody or piano number in the background is the perfect touch. It can be placed on the floor out of the way or behind a fake potted plant. Yes, I'm serious. Try it.

Small Space Solutions

JUST BECAUSE YOU ARE IN YOUR FLAT IN LONDON OR YOUR one-bedroom apartment in New York does not mean you can't provide great comfort for your guests, so don't let that deter you from inviting friends and family. The key to success is to be super-organized.

Some of the best times my husband and I had were when we packed our guests into our little condominium. The children, now teenagers, still laugh about the time their "baby bed" was in our walk-in closet (clothes mostly cleared out, of course!).

Here are some ideas for making your guests comfortable—and keeping your sanity when the guest room is also the living room.

Provide a Comfortable Sleep Space

Consider a futon sofa for your living room. These are great, as they quickly and easily flatten into a double-sized bed.

Pullout sofas are good for this, too, but it seems that you have to buy the expensive version to get a good-quality mattress, so beware of that. You can even buy an over-sized chair that pulls out to a twin-sized bed, or a cabinet that opens up with a bed hidden neatly inside.

Sleeping on a sofa is not a problem for most people for a few nights, but so much nicer if made up properly. Make it comfy by doing the following:

Make the sofa exactly like you would a bed with a tucked-in, fitted sheet, a flat sheet, and one light blanket with a heavier one at the foot. You may want to buy a sheet of plywood to put under the cushions if they are limp or if your guest has a weak back. Colorful pillows along with the normal sleeping pillow can add a festive, happy touch.

Children (and some adults) don't mind the floor for a weekend, given enough pillows and blankets or sleeping bags. My husband's family remembers fondly the times their children stretched comfortably on the floor of "Nana's" apartment—being together was the goal. Still, you may want to consider investing in a blow-up mattress. It's much more comfortable, and takes up very little room when stored.

When You Have One Bathroom

If you can get up very early to use it, well, that's a nice thing to do. That way it will be free for your guests when they awaken. Keep it as tidy as possible by putting up a liberal amount of stick-up hooks that can be taken down later without damaging the walls. For the time that your guests will be visiting, do as many bathroom chores as you can in your bedroom, like makeup application and hair styling.

Pay Attention to Lighting

Don't forget lighting for the sofa or futon. Your guests may want to read at night. A good solution is a free-standing floor lamp that can be moved about the room.

Subtle night lighting in the living room or whatever room is serving as your guest room is a must. Guests will need to get to the bathroom, refrigerator, etc., without turning on the main lights. Find an outlet for the night-light that's not so bright your guests are kept awake, but good enough for them to safely get up and move about.

VISIT WIZARD TIP Some people are very sensitive to noise and light. If you live next to a busy road or freeway consider a sound machine on very low. Show your guest how to turn it off in case they don't like it. If they are not used to "city noises," offer them earplugs. I always travel with them.

If you are going to be entertaining overnight often in a room that gets a lot of light, consider investing in a window treatment that really blocks the light. Or, do what I did and line your existing curtains with blackout liner, which is very economical and easily found in a kitchen and bath store.

Help Your Guests Stay Neat

Unless you don't mind wading through clothes and blankets on your way to the kitchen in the morning, you should take the time and effort to organize the space before your guests arrive.

Put out a large basket or plastic-tub container for the guests to put their sheets and blankets in when they awake. Have a footlocker or wonderful old trunk? Great. Use it. Let your guests know what it is for, or, better yet, label it!

Place a clothes tree or coat rack in the corner of the room so your guests can use it for their clothes and to hang their bathrobe and towels. No, your bike will not do.

Put a luggage rack against the wall for them to set their suitcases on as they will most likely be living out of it during their stay. Put a waste can with liner underneath the luggage rack so no one has to look at dirty tissues and other unpleasant disposables while in the living room, and your guests don't have to go searching for a place to throw out their stuff.

A nice addition is to have a small table or two, preferably with drawers, where they can store their belongings. Clear the top for their items. Think mini guest room.

If, after your guests are up for a decent period of time, the living room still looks like a disaster zone tell them nicely that it's time to stow their gear. Help them if necessary! Getting your place back to normal as soon as feasible will go a long way to your comfort and that of your guests.

Finally, if you have a pet, put it in another room when guests are sleeping in the living room or a common room. You don't want to give your guest a heart attack when the cat decides to attack the "lump" on the sofa. They may trip over the dog, or its snoring may keep them up. And not too many people enjoy being woken up with a cold wet nose and doggie breath.

Mind Your Rooms!

I WAS TOLD OF A WOMAN WHO ACTUALLY BRAGS THAT SHE GOES through the medicine cabinets of her hosts' homes! Outrageous. Why would anyone care? In any event, take the time to put your personal or sensitive items where your guests can't find them, and especially out of reach of children.

If you are reading a particularly racy book or have movies that may not be suitable for children or teens put them away securely. With this done, your mind will be more at rest when you are away from the house.

It should go without saying: Put weapons out of reach! And that doesn't mean just putting them up on a high shelf. The safest thing is to lock them away or, if children will be visiting, get them out of the house.

Put away any personal belongings of a sensitive nature—even in your own bedroom. Some people (and especially children, innocently enough) may find something they shouldn't. I have one friend who was mortified when her eight-year-old nephew snuck into her bedroom and discovered a baby doll teddy that he thought would look great on his six-year-old brother. So go diligently through your personal rooms and put away anything you would not want someone finding—or wearing!

So, now that your rooms are "guest ready" you can sit back and relax, right? Well... almost! The next chapter gives you seven simple steps to follow to ensure a smooth visit. Yes, simple—really!

CHAPTER 2

Seven Simple Steps to a Smooth Visit

"The ornaments of your house will be the guests who frequent it."

—AUTHOR UNKNOWN

WHEN PSYCHIATRISTS HOLMES AND RAHE CAME UP WITH their now-famous stress scale that lists life-changing events that can wreak havoc with health and well-being, they left something out: hosting out-of-town guests. If it were up to me, I would put hosting somewhere between "marriage" and "imprisonment," and it's not because I don't love hosting—obviously I do. But let's face it: Being a host can be very stressful—even if it's something you look forward to. And, okay, there are times when even I fantasize about making a run for it, even faster than one would from a shotgun wedding.

But that doesn't mean you have to let your stress run amok. If you do, you could end up making your guests feel as though they just walked into a hornet's nest rather than your lovely home.

I remember visiting a friend whom I hadn't seen in about five years. I had been having a particularly difficult time and was eagerly anticipating rekindling some of the fun and laughs we used to share. Since she had invited me, I figured she felt the same. But when I rang her bell, she greeted me with—I kid you not—a frighteningly large chef's knife in her hand, hair askew, beads of sweat on her brow, and what looked like a very surprised look on her face.

My first thought was, did I have the wrong day or time? I *had* called her from my hands-free cellular device to tell her that traffic was running smoothly and I should be arriving in an hour or so. Truth be told, I did get her voicemail, but I didn't think much of it. Turns out, she had been working herself into a frenzy preparing for our visit and had gotten totally behind. Apparently, my call came at the time she was racing through the house with the vacuum cleaner. A couple of drinks later, she admitted she had been praying I would get caught in a traffic jam. Sound familiar? We did end up having a wonderful visit, but it certainly got off to a rocky start.

As host, you are orchestra conductor, traffic cop, captain of the ship, ring leader, helper, and sometimes referee. The key to making the visit enjoyable is striking and maintaining a balance between "just going with the flow" and being a drill sergeant. You want your guests to leave on a high, looking forward to the next visit, not feeling as though they had just been through an episode of *Survivor*.

Will things go wrong? You can bet on it. I don't know of one extended visit with friends or family that has been perfect, although getting as close as possible is the goal.

Following you will find seven simple steps to help you make the visit as enjoyable as possible—for both you and your guests. You'll find tips to help you get and stay organized and establish your home as a delightful, welcoming place for your friends and family. What we do for those we care for, even when difficult and time-consuming, is truly part of the art of the visit.

Step One: Plan Events and Activities

PLANNING TRIPS, OUTINGS, AND ENTERTAINMENT FOR family and friends is something my husband and I relish. Think of it as an adventure, rather than a chore. Consider the ages and interests of your guests, what can be done in your town and in your home, and what might be new experiences for them. We sometimes make a list and email it to our guests before they come, so they are as prepared as possible and can offer any comments or concerns they might have. Good thing, too; although I still think my mother would have had a good time parasailing.

Take into consideration your guests' financial situation. Always ask before committing to expensive outings, even if it's your treat. Why? Because some people feel badly if you offer to take the crew deep-sea fishing or for some other expensive form of entertainment, while others are thrilled. It's always best to ask. Unless it is a celebration of some kind, no one really likes surprises.

Find things in your community that you can do as a group. Everyone might enjoy the zoo, the botanical gardens, local vineyards, and local sporting events. There are often free concerts and other fun things to do that cost little or no money. Taking a walk to enjoy nature or the sights and sounds of a city is free. If nothing exciting comes to mind, consult the Internet. Most communities have a website that lists upcoming events and activities.

If a guest *really* does not want to do something don't force him or make the guest feel bad about not wanting to participate. He may have secret fears or phobias, or doesn't feel well that day but doesn't want to say anything.

For example, I am terrified of both caves and heights so I will always decline a rock climbing adventure or a trip to the top of—anywhere! Once my poor husband crammed me into the body of a tiny, rickety-looking old airplane from which to view the Grand Canyon—wrong! I made my escape (just prior to the plane taxiing down the runway) and took a cab back to the hotel. Luckily, my husband was a sport about it. If he had gotten angry it would have put a damper on our trip.

Have a dressy adult dinner. Really!

The dinner does not have to be fancy; just light some candles and use name cards for a formal touch. Don't seat husbands and wives next to each other—in fact, put cranky Judy next to the most amusing guest you have, put on some soft music, and people who have bickered during the day, or are exhausted from watching the kids, may just be transformed... at least for those few hours!

If you don't want to do the more formal affair, at least have a "cocktail hour." Plan it for a specific time and your guests are likely to attend. For example, tell everyone the day before that cocktails will be served at 5 p.m. on the porch, or in the den, or even in the kitchen. It doesn't matter where. Tell them you are stirring up something enticing like martinis or retro drinks like Manhattans. Remember to do something fancy for your nondrinking friends as well, like Virgin Marys, or virgin whatever you are making..

Mr. Ward McAllister, the self-appointed guard of New York City society in the late 1800s is credited with having said the following about a formal dinner party: "You must show up. And in case you die, you must send your executor in your place." Although our modern rules are not quite as stringent, adhering to some can be not only fun for adults, but wonderful learning opportunities for children.

Cooking at home can be a fun event for everyone. You don't have to start from scratch to make pizza. Buy those little individual-sized prepared dough crusts and pizza sauce, cut up different toppings, and let everyone make their own. There are many fun meals family and friends can make together. The trick is to give everyone a specific chore that they can easily handle.

Good old games. One of my and my brothers' fondest memories is playing cards with the entire family at a lake house that we visited in the summertime. It was great fun for both children and adults. Okay, I know what you're thinking: That was back in the day when the original *Star Trek* ruled the television airways and William Shatner was thin; the latest hits were played on 45 rpm's, not downloaded; and earrings on guys was considered uncool. But trust me on this: Kids of *all* ages will appreciate the opportunity to unplug and actually interact face-to-face in real time with each other. Checkers and puzzle building are both great for this, as are just about any crafts you can share, or teach, your guest.

Get physical. If you're looking for a little more physical activity, put a badminton set out on the lawn for younger kids and older adults. If your guests are young and athletic invite them to have a tennis lesson or to engage in an activity you think they might like but have not experienced, such as yoga or Zumba. Even people who have never been in a saddle can enjoy horseback riding. From apple picking to surfing, find activities guests of different ages and abilities can enjoy. Finally, remember: Fun, relaxation, and maybe discovering something new about each other should be the goal, not how much you can cram into one day.

VISIT WIZARD TIP There is nothing wrong, toward the end of the visit, in inviting a neighbor to join you for dinner or a friend that you think your guests would like to meet. But don't do that their first night. It will make your guests feel as if they are not special enough to warrant your full attention.

Step Two: Let Your Guests Know What to Expect

Right way to let guests know what to expect:

"Hey Kathy, Could you get here about 11:00 to 11:30? That way we can all go to the airport together to pick up the girls and then right to a casual lunch at the Inn. After lunch we'll drive downtown for a bit of sightseeing and then home for drinks, dinner, and a movie. Besides that, nothing much planned for the weekend other than eating and drinking. I thought we would take a walk out in the lovely Arboretum on Saturday (bring sneakers) weather permitting, and have lunch out Saturday. Dinner at home Friday and Saturday. Please give us some movie recommendations so we can all park in the family room when we get too full to move! Any food issues? Any special drink requests? I will do pasta one night and some variety of seafood the other night. Can't wait to see you!"—Email from my host, received about one week before I took a car trip to visit her.

Wrong way to let guests know what to expect:

Your hosts pick you up at the airport after a six-hour flight, where you have to share the backseat with their tutu-wearing Chihuahua, to whom you happen to be allergic. Your hosts then inform you that you will be driving for another two hours to have dinner with their friends "who you'll just adore." When you arrive, you see that everyone is dressed to the nines. Hence the tutu-wearing Chihuahua. Through puffy, watery eyes, you finally notice how well-dressed your hosts are, and that you look like something the cat dragged in.

Although you may have some wonderful things planned, if you don't inform your guests before their arrival, you could be headed for visit disaster. So, first things first: Confirm the exact dates of the visit! Although one *assumes* this is a no-brainer, you would be surprised at how many people have told me horror stories about the guests who came and would not leave or who you thought were coming for three days and instead stayed for eight.

Call or email your guests at least a week ahead of their visit with any plans you have made so they can pack accordingly or make whatever arrangements may be necessary.

Let them know if any of the following will be happening:

Special events: Is a birthday or anniversary party or some other event planned? If so, where (at home or a restaurant or other venue) and what dress is expected or appropriate?

Formal events or dressy restaurants: Will they need to bring formal attire for a Black Tie or Black Tie Optional event? Let them know which level of dress—cocktail or business attire, for example—is appropriate.

Day trips and outings: Hiking in the woods or white-water rafting? Let them know what special clothing or gear will be needed. And no, it's not funny to watch your sister-in-law try to get into the boat while wearing Manolos.

Any unusual weather expected: Is a heat wave or unusually cold weather predicted? Will extra warm clothes or rain gear be advisable? You can email your guests the weather forecast from weather.com.

Sports or recreation activities: Should they bring jogging shoes, a bathing suit, or a tennis racket? As I was upacking one host asked me if I brought my bathing suit—I didn't even know they had a pool!

Other guests: Absolutely let your guests know what other guests—if any—will be visiting. You can try to be clever by not telling your sister that she'll be sharing the visit with your cousin Laura—whom she's had a grudge against ever since high school, when they both had a crush on the same guy, the one Laura ended up marrying, but don't blame the Visit Wizard if the time together is strained.

Remember, it is *your* responsibility to inform your guests so they may be as prepared as possible.

Consider an itinerary: If you have many guests coming for the visit and the visit is longer than a weekend, I advise you to do a preliminary itinerary and email it to each guest ahead of time. Although it does require time and thought, and, heaven forbid, planning, it is useful for a variety of reasons. Here is a simple sample for one day:

SATURDAY SUGGESTIONS:

8:00 to 9:00 a.m.: Breakfast at the house. (Assign a cook so one person does not end up cooking all the time.)

After breakfast: Family beach time (including Sam the dog and Frisbees!). For non–beach lovers, there is a shopping street just a few blocks away.

11:30: Back to the house.

12:15: Lunch at Spanky's restaurant for whoever wants to go (my treat).

1:30 to 3:00: Whatever.

3:00 to 5:00: Nine holes of golf at the course. Total fee is $45 per person. Let me know who wants to go so I can make a tee time and get carts.

5:30: Adult drinks on the patio.

7:00: Dinner served, Aunt Sally and Martha are cooking!

After dinner: Cards for the adults and a movie for the kids—yes, popcorn included!

An itinerary is a useful tool. Before you shake your head and tell me all the reasons it can't or shouldn't be done, read this:

- You are able to schedule downtime for yourself and others. Some part of every day should be set aside for you and your guests to relax. Constant activity will wear out everyone but the children.
- You will actually spend *better* quality time with your guests. Often we don't see those people who are running off here and there throughout the day, because we are stuck in the house with old Aunt Margaret who only wants to bake and talk about why you still aren't married. When beach time is scheduled you can drop the oven mitts and grab your bikini.
- You can subtly let people know who is expected to pay for what: When making your list you might say "Friday 7 p.m. dinner at Chez Françoise. My treat," or "Saturday fishing trip for those who want to participate, 7 a.m. to 11 a.m., $75 per person, paid to the captain upon arrival to the boat." So many people, especially hosts, get flustered as to who pays when and for what, but not to worry, this often sensitive issue is discussed several times in the chapters that follow.
- It offers an out for those who don't wish to go. They can find something else to do during that time or you can make an alternate suggestion. For example, I know my sister-in-law loves to shop at a certain shoe store when she comes to visit, but she is not a beach person. She hates to take time away from the group to go to the store and does not want to "put us out." This itinerary lets her know not to worry—her shoe shopping time is secure!
- You help ensure that your guests get to do those things that interest them. There may be something a guest wants to do and if so she can tell you in advance.
- Logistically it is important: If you have a tennis fanatic among

your guests, you have to reserve court time or make a tee time for your golf enthusiasts. If you know one of them loves the theater, and he confirms he wants to go, you are able to buy the tickets for that almost-sold-out show. Things like this can't wait until the day of.

- You avoid the anxiety of being uncertain if you scheduled too much or not enough. If everyone shows up with nothing planned or, conversely with too much planned, the nice visit could quickly turn into a fiasco.
- What could be nicer than to take the time to plan things that might interest your friends and family? Not much. And one more thing: It takes pressure off you *and your guests* during the visit.

By emailing the itinerary a week or so in advance of their visit your guests can confirm, or not, or suggest other things. For those people who are not interested in an activity, that's fine; they can do something else in that time. If absolutely no one is interested in an event, then scratch it. Don't make it too complicated, don't be intimidated, and don't try to please everyone. That is never going to happen, but you will please most everyone and that is part of the art of the visit.

There will always be one or two people who are grumpy or don't like planning things or just don't want to do anything. That's fine. Let them do what they want. Can plans change, get rained out, or just not work out? Of course. Hence one of the most important "Qualities" in the following chapter: The Great Host Is... Flexible!

Step Three: Ask the Right Questions Before They Arrive

EMAIL YOUR GUESTS A LIST OF QUESTIONS BEFORE THE VISIT. It just really makes life easier for you as host and saves you time and money. I have made the error time and again of buying things only to have wasted that money on soft drinks children were not allowed or other items that were not appropriate.

Here are some examples of questions you can ask your guests.

- Are they going to need any special accommodations, like cribs or child car seats that you need to get ahead of time?
- Do their children have any particular needs or specific food items that they love or cannot have, or would the parents like to discuss meals?
- Do your adult guests have any dietary restrictions? Are they vegans, semi-veggies, or gluten free?
- Ask guests if there are any specific foods they like or don't like or if they have any special requests. For example, my brother-in-law likes one particular thing for breakfast every day so I make sure I get that, and my father likes a specific brand of liquor.
- If they are traveling with an elderly person, ask what equipment might be necessary or what special needs that person might have and what he or she can or likes to eat or drink.
- Is there anything in particular they would like to do on the visit or any special place they would like to go?
- Although we assume guests are coming solely to enjoy our lovely

company, ask if this is a special occasion. Are they coming to also celebrate their anniversary or birthday? Is this their vacation? Knowing this will not only help you plan, but also understand if they say they would like to spend some romantic time alone. Know how your guests are getting to the visit (see Step Six for details).

- Let me say this about the advance purchasing of food as it seems to make some people very uptight: as host you are required to have the basics with perhaps some nice specialty items thrown in and special requests within reason. It is important that you know if a guest does not eat meat, is gluten free, or has food allergies so you can plan meals. It is good to know if little Joey can't go to sleep without a certain snack, or if Aunt Helen loves that Key lime pie at the beach, but that's about it. If your sister can only eat natural foods found in the rain forest and untouched by human hands, she can buy those things herself when she arrives. Are we clear on this? Let me put it another way: anything unusual or overly expensive is the responsibility of the guest. I have a friend who absolutely must have her morning coffee with raw organic blue agave syrup. She would never dream of sending her hosts on a royal goose chase hunting down this expensive and hard-to-find sweetener. On the other hand, if her hosts ask her what she likes to drink, she doesn't, and shouldn't, hesitate to say, "an inexpensive California chardonnay on the oaky side."

Step Four: Avoid the Run-Around—Have What You Need

ALTHOUGH NO ONE CAN THINK OF EVERYTHING . . . TRY. I can't overly stress how being prepared makes your hosting life so much easier and the visit more enjoyable. Check for the following:

Bedroom and bath basics: sheets, blankets, pillows, towels, tissues, toilet paper, soap, hangers (for complete bedroom and bath lists, see page 13 and page 25 in chapter 1 of the Being the Perfect Host section). If you have been putting off buying that new towel set to replace the threadbare ones, now is the time.

Food and drink: You can get great ideas for plan-ahead meals from my website, theartofthevisit.com, but let me say a few words about beverages. This is not the time to be frugal, so stock premium beers and wines to the best of your financial ability. Top-shelf liquors are not as important because they tend to be mixed. But if you know Uncle Stanley has to have that Premium English gin, get it if you can. If you can't afford it, no worry. Tell him you will gladly drive him to the liquor store upon his arrival.

I purchase a variety of beverages as it is impossible to know who drinks what. Be sure to have these basics: fruit juices; tonic and soda water; mixes such as Bloody Mary mix; a variety of soft drinks, including ginger ale and some diet brands; fruit nectar for those yummy martinis, and don't forget the accoutrements: olives; bitters; grenadine; fresh lemons and limes. Go online (or to the library!) for information on how to properly stock a bar.

If you have a second refrigerator or a freezer that is not already packed, keep your beer steins and martini glasses, vodka, and other liquor in there. They will be nicely chilled.

Your guests should have emailed you a list of what they need that they cannot bring with them or get when they arrive. Now is the time to go get it. Today. Not the day of their arrival. I had this habit. I would put off running around until the morning of my guests' arrival. Not smart. Causes stress level to reach DEFCON 1.

Run your errands and get done with your appointments before your guests arrive whenever possible.

VISIT WIZARD TIP Although a bit more expensive up front, those little 6-ounce cans of juices are great. When you only need to open one, for an individual drink, for example, there is no waste as there might be for a larger container that could sit and go bad in the fridge. I also buy sodas with screw-on caps for the same reason.

Step Five: Make Meals (or Reservations!) Ahead

I NOW SIT DOWN AND ACTUALLY PLAN OUT MEALS. MY attitude, prior to this enlightenment, was to buy food and cook as I wanted, which was fun, but resulted in food being wasted and, worse, my constantly asking guests for a consensus for meals. Not something I would recommend. Shouting into a crowd "Who wants what for dinner?" should rank right up there with shouting "Fire!" in a crowded theater. Or worse, your significant other comes up to you as friends and family are gathered on the porch for evening cocktails and whispers in your ear, "Honey. Have you thought about dinner?" Been there, done that. Not good.

The goal, at least for me, is to make as much ahead of time as possible, freeze it, and bring it out when needed, thereby cutting down the time one person spends in the kitchen to a manageable period. I can see a friend of mine now, hand spread across open mouth, recoiling in horror as she reads these words. Her idea of a great time when having guests is staying in the kitchen cooking all day and being as creative as possible. I shudder at the thought. And besides, how could I play with the others if I am inside all day? Here are some examples of easy meals and some basics that should satisfy most everyone:

Breakfast

Cereal and such. Have two selections for children and two for adults; bananas, sliced oranges, and berry mixture with yogurt; toast (buy both whole wheat and white bread); butter, honey, and jam.

Fruit salad. Put together a fruit salad and keep in the refrigerator. Don't buy the prepackaged kind. They never seem to be fresh, nor do they last for any length of time.

Hot oatmeal. This is nice and quick and easy in the microwave. Add some raisins, blueberries, or sliced banana on top.

Eggs. You can easily hard-boil some *free-range* chicken eggs the night before (they're no more expensive than the others and they really do taste better and chickens everywhere will thank you): Place your eggs in a small pot with cold water just enough to cover them, heat water to boiling, cover, turn off the heat and fifteen minutes later dump the hot water and run the eggs under cold water until cool enough to handle and then refrigerate. Ready to go the next morning to eat straight or use in egg salad.

Good advice from a lady who often entertains overnight guests:

"I tend to have some sort of breakfast bread that can simply stay out

at room temperature, like coffee cake or scones. I generally bake before guests arrive and freeze them—then each day just take out something from the freezer. I also try to break it up with some breakfast casserole or quiche that can be heated when the first group up is ready for breakfast, but can sit out for a few hours at room temperature. Unless it's just one couple, I stay away from omelets, cooked eggs, pancakes, etc."

Lunch

Tuna Salad. You can make this a day ahead for sandwiches, just toss with the dressing the day of. It is usually a hit with everyone but use a light hand with the mayo. Guests who prefer a little tuna with their mayo can always add more!

Hamburgers, hot dogs, or veggie burgers. On the grill or in the kitchen these are easy, especially if you buy the prepared patties. If not, get the meat, mix it with some salt, pepper, and spices, form into patties, wrap and refrigerate. That, with chips and a green salad (made in advance) is another easy lunch.

Cold Cuts. Also, have a variety of cold cuts on hand for lunches and the late-night munchies crowd. Always, always have smoked salmon in the fridge and frozen scallops in the freezer. I can't tell you how many times both have saved my bacon, pun intended.

Dinner

Make-ahead dinner. There are just too many fun (yes, really) make-ahead meals to mention in this book but here's an easy one: before guests arrive, make meat loaf or something similar, like chili, which can feed a crowd, and freeze it, ready to bring out for any dinner anytime during the visit. If I know I have a vegetarian in the group I make meatless lasagna. Delicious and if done right your meat lovers won't even notice. There are ways to prepare make-ahead meals for all your guests (including vegans). Visit my website when you get a chance.

Prepared items. When entertaining many people of various ages for longer than a weekend, it's a good idea to purchase some prepared items, like potato salad and chicken wings. Although store-bought, you can use these as quick sides or appetizers when the crew comes in hungry.

One-Pot Dishes. I like one-pot wonders for the main course, so we make a big batch of clam chowder, pasta sauce, and things that can cook low and slow in one large pot or slow cooker. Cooking at your leisure several days before your guests arrive and freezing soups in individual containers is a great way to satisfy different tastes.

Vegetarian. Don't forget your vegetarian and semi-veggie friends. I always make sure I have a fish or straight veggie alternatives. A good guest should tell you in advance if they prefer meatless dishes or have any food allergies, but in case they haven't read that chapter, or simply forget, don't make them feel badly about it, just have items like frozen jumbo shrimp handy. Easy to pop out, defrost, and cook for snacks, appetizers or served as a meal with rice or pasta.

Cooking meals ahead will save you both time and money—both of which are better spent with friends and family.

Dining Out

When making reservations for meals out, keep the cost in mind. Is one person buying or will everyone share in the expense? I make it known ahead of time that either "this is my treat" (if they don't say it is theirs) or suggest we "go Dutch." There is nothing more embarrassing than either everyone—or no one—grabbing the bill. And don't try to itemize it: If you are dividing the bill between three couples just split in it thirds.

If your guest is paying, don't order the most expensive bottle of wine on the list. Be considerate and err on the side of frugality.

Here's a smart way to handle the wine list: when presented to you at the table or you take it, open it and hold it just slightly away from your chest as you would a hand of cards at poker, and peruse the list as if you are studying it carefully. Call the wine steward or waiter over and point to the list of moderately priced wines (while he is looking over your shoulder) and ask his opinion between the two or three you are able to afford, saying something like, "of these three, which do you recommend?" Voilà! You look like you know what you are doing. You have made a selection based on his good recommendation (if he knows what he's doing), and you have picked something affordable, for you or your host. Never ask the server or steward what they recommend without using this technique unless you are willing to pay for one of the most expensive wines on the list.

In a more formal situation (like when taking your boss out to dinner if you are spending a weekend with them), go middle-of-the-road in terms of price. Too low and she may doubt your taste and sophistication. Too high and she might doubt your taste and sophistication.

Be conscious of what people can spend if *they* are treating. Don't make reservations at the swankiest new restaurant in town if it is also one of the most expensive. If you have the misfortune of hosting a very picky person, it may be in your best interest to have them peruse the menu online before picking the restaurant! I often email connoisseurs a list of restaurants complete with their website links—safer that way!

VISIT WIZARD TIP If your guests insist they are taking you to that expensive restaurant, and if you have drinks at the bar before being seated, a nice thing for you to do is pay for that bill even if they all had martinis and you only had club soda. However, if drinks are served at the table before dinner, don't ask for a separate bill. Those drinks are considered part of the dinner.

Step Six: Ensure a Smooth Arrival

NOTHING CAN START A VISIT OFF ON THE WRONG FOOT FASTER than an arrival screwup. I know. I am writing this as I sit on a hard bench while my husband is standing in the rental car pickup line. We arrived at the airport and had gotten on the bus for the god-awful twenty-minute drive to the rental car company location, when our host called our cell: "Where are you?" he wanted to know. He was back at the airport waiting for us! We told him we were on the bus. He asked why we had rented a car when he was *planning* on picking us up and taking us around! But our *plan* was to call him after we had gotten the rental car and checked into the hotel, which was where I had *planned* on putting on lipstick and maybe combing my hair before driving to their home since I had been up before dawn and looked like it! Did you send the email to him yesterday, I asked my husband. Yes, I did, he said. Did our host get it? Obviously not, he said. I would now be forced to meet our friend who would now meet us in the lobby of the hotel—with no lipstick! It's enough to irritate the Visit Wizard, I'll tell you that!

Airport Etiquette

If you are picking up your guests, whether you meet them outside the arrival gate, at baggage claim, or at the curb depends entirely on your wishes and the ease of access at the airport. At most major international airports you cannot wait in your car at the curb. You will be asked to leave by the police. Then you keep circling… and circling… and circling like some sharp-eyed bird of prey searching for its victims.

Many hosts have their guests call them on their cell phones once they have landed, and many large airports have "cell phone lots" where people wait for their arriving passengers to call; it is then just a few minutes to the arrival curb. Good all around. And bring some water for your guests. People are thirsty right off the plane.

If you or your guests do not have a cell phone, and it is a busy airport, best to meet them right at the entrance to security. Remember the days of meeting your loved ones at the gate? Even now when I disembark I see those ghosts of welcomers past who evaporate in a blink as I make my way to baggage claim. If Grandmother, Grandfather, children, or that long-lost friend from overseas is coming, it's wonderful to meet them as soon as security permits. I guess it's kind of cheesy to have a bouquet of flowers as well, but we can always hope....

VISIT WIZARD TIP Confirm and confirm again! When sending an email about something as important as arrival plans, ask your guest to confirm that she received it. If she does not, make sure you follow up with a phone call.

The easiest and most efficient way for you to pick up your guests is at the curb as they are walking out of baggage claim. Should they come out the wrong door and have you searching frantically, or have packed for three weeks instead of the weekend, smile, hold out your arms, and remember why they came and the effort they made in doing so.

If your guests are renting a car and are unfamiliar with the area, do email them directions from the airport to their destination. It can be a stressful time trying to get around in an unfamiliar environment.

When you can't be there: If you cannot be there to meet your arriving guests because of a scheduling conflict on your end, and they are not renting a car, you must offer to have a car pick them up or pay for their cab fare. They will most likely decline, but you should offer. The email could go something like this: "Hi guys! So excited you are coming but I can't pick you up at the airport as we planned. Forgot Susie has a piano lesson at that time. I feel badly and would like to reimburse you for the cab fare." Or if you have the means (or a friend who owes you a favor) arrange to have a car and driver pick them up. However, if it is their choice to come Friday afternoon and they know you are working and cannot meet them, it is their responsibility to get to your house. A subtle difference, I know, but one that lets your guests know you understood you were obligated to pick them up, but screwed up. Or, conversely, that you are working (the only reason for not being there in my opinion—you really should have thought of Susie's piano lesson before this), and it is on them.

Driving Etiquette

If your guests are driving, email them detailed directions, but make sure *you* know what route they are taking to your home. On more than one occasion I have assumed my guests were taking a certain route so I gave them directions based on that. They found us, eventually, but were inconvenienced. I know the conversation in the car went something like this: "Kathy said turn *right*!" "No! Turn left! What was she thinking? There is no *right* turn onto that street—it's one-way!" "I don't care—turn anyway!" You get the picture. Always gracious, they did arrive cool as cucumbers and laughing about it... well... at least smiling.

There is a reason ET phoned home. Don't assume they have, or let them rely on, GPS. And make sure they have the proper spelling of your street address unless you really don't want to see your in-laws. It appears that just one wrong letter or typo can spell disaster. A couple, intending to visit the island of Capri on the Mediterranean coast, typed in Carpi, and powered on until they reached an industrial town in Northern Italy some four hundred miles off track.

VISIT WIZARD TIP Make sure your guests have parking passes and amenity passes if needed and, of course, the keys to the house if you won't be there.

Step Seven: Create a Lasting Impression

ALTHOUGH YOU ARE BUSY DOING MANY THINGS AT ONCE and preparing for the next event or meal, take time to really enjoy your guests. Play with the kids, talk with the elders, sit and just visit.

The hours in the day can so easily be consumed with host chores that leave you worn out and off-sorts. You can change that.

One visit I decided that was not going to happen and I was going to take time out to play. To the dismay of some of the adults and certainly the confusion of others, I got together the four children who were visiting and we headed down to my newly finished basement/studio. I pulled out pounds of clay, buckets of water, my pottery wheel, aprons, and towels, and we went to work. We happily created the most glorious, messy masterpieces imaginable. I threw caution to the wind and cared not for time or cleanliness! Dinner could be made by others or not at all. There was clay literally on the walls and on the carpet. I taught these small children to use the potter's wheel and "throw" a bowl. The result of that chaos was great photos of me and the kids, prized bowls, and… well, things that resemble vases, or maybe spaceships. One year later they have been bisque fired in the kiln and are awaiting glazing and the second firing. That's okay. They will get done and be wonderful reminders of time well spent.

Nothing brings friends and family together and creates good memories like the old-fashioned game of cards or movies and popcorn. Keep some generic DVDs in your library. They can really come in handy on a rainy day or when the children need some downtime. Have a few children's movies as well as a few oldies or classics. Get them together and go to exciting new lands like Whoville. I can still tell you exactly where I was and with whom when I first saw *The Wizard of Oz.*

One of the fondest memories I have is of my mom with her two granddaughters, complete with my small dog, rolling around, laughing, and playing cards on one of the guest beds. My regret is that I did not join them, but instead was more concerned with whatever needed tending. My loss.

Your guests will remember what was cooked and the events for weeks or maybe months, but they will remember the personal time spent together for much longer—if you're lucky, for their whole lives.

The perfect host is a strange and wonderful blend of empathy, selfishness, generosity, and frugality, all at the same time.

It is not for the weak-spirited. You can never be everything to all people. You will be criticized by some and adored by others. When your guests are walking out your door on that last day, the one important thing is that you can honestly say you put your guests' comfort before your own and did everything you could to ensure a pleasant and loving time together. If you can, then the impression they carry away is one in which you can take pride for a job well done and time well spent. Now go finish the dishes.

CHAPTER 3

The Twelve Essential Qualities of a Great Host

"A great host is like a great cocktail. Shaken or stirred, it will come out fine, but only if quality ingredients are used in the mix."

—THE VISIT WIZARD

WHAT MAKES FOR A HAPPY, SUCCESSFUL VISIT? IT'S NOT the size of your home, or the entertainment you have planned, or the elaborate dinners you have slaved over; it's your willingness and ability to be cool under pressure, think on your feet, and adjust when necessary. The woman in the example below, for instance, would have made us feel the same had she been hosting us in a grass hut, because the truly greatest quality of a host is doing those things you don't always want to do, in a way that leaves your guests feeling like honored royalty without them ever being aware of the sometimes extraordinary effort it took to do so.

I, along with two girlfriends, was invited to spend the weekend in the mountain home of a couple whom I had never met. I didn't know what to expect. Here is what I found:

I am usually up early, and that first morning at my host's home was no exception. I entered the kitchen at the crack of dawn with great anticipation hoping to savor my one cup of coffee, which usually cleans out at least some of the cobwebs. By the look of our host's gorgeous, well-kept (okay, neat as a pin) 6,000-square-foot home, I figured they probably had a coffee maker, but how long would I have to search to find it? And heaven forbid I not know how to use that no doubt state-of-the-art device or, worse, break something!

This was going to be a task I didn't really want to conduct, so I assumed I would have to wait until everyone arose at some ungodly hour, like eight o'clock! What was I going to do? I know... but one's mind is a bit peculiar at that hour and without coffee, well, you understand. My worries were immediately squelched. On the granite kitchen island counter sat the following:

A coffeemaker with a little sticky note on the front button that said "Press me!"; beautiful white cups; saucers and spoons; sugar bowl and creamer; pastries of various kinds; homemade jams; sliced fruit... need I go on? I silently thanked my host and dove in. This charming person must have either heard me stumbling around in the guest room that morning, or had gotten up *before* dawn to set up. Either way, I was a happy girl. Not only did I get to sit out on the porch to watch the glorious sunrise with coffee and a scone, but she made me feel, for that moment in time, like a beloved princess in a wonderful fairy tale. And I had no doubt she had ground the coffee beans herself!

It gets even better:

The lower floor of this home served as the guest suite: bedrooms, bathrooms, a living room area, and a theater room the size of a small opera house, complete with tiered seating.

That evening, after dinner and an exhausting day of touring around town with our hosts, I headed downstairs, thinking I'd squeeze in a little work on my laptop. Silly me! The guest living area had been set up like an Aspen resort après ski: bottles of after-dinner liqueurs and cookies were on a tray, next to which was the remote control for the large flat-screen television with a note on how to tune into various movies; also available was a table with a puzzle on it—just barely started—and books lined the walls! What could I do but put down the laptop, grab a soft cookie, sink into the lush sofa and grab a book. It was one of the most delightful evenings I have spent in another person's home.

The next morning was Sunday and our wonderful host had announced we could do as we pleased, but brunch was at 10:30 a.m. prompt and, by the way, who wanted Mimosas? It was hard to leave.

It makes no difference if your home is a grand estate or a one-bedroom flat. Making your guests feel at home is what counts.

Can't cook brunch? Pop frozen waffles in the toaster and then add some blueberries or sliced fruit on top. Put orange juice in a Champagne or wine glass to dress it up. Heat up the maple syrup and soften the butter.

No theater room? No worries! A game of cards or a rented movie work just as well. Guest sleeping on the sofa? So what. Put out cookies and milk or liqueurs anyway.

Being a great host may seem to be a mystery that only the rich, the beautiful, the well-connected, the truly *fabulous* have solved. But the truth is, anyone can be the perfect host. Part of the secret is in knowing—and practicing—the twelve qualities every successful host possesses. Make them your own, and you will give your guests a memorable experience—for all the right reasons. And the bonus is that you'll have a wonderful (and nearly) stress-free visit yourself.

1. A Great Host Is… Welcoming

WHENEVER PEOPLE ARRIVE AT YOUR HOME THERE CAN BE a brief moment of tension, either for you or for them. That moment can seem like eternity with people you don't know very well, perhaps a new family member you are meeting for the first time or one who has been estranged. It's natural and it's your job to alleviate it. These simple tips will help calm any jittery nerves and make your home warm and welcoming.

Setting the Stage

The art of welcoming your guests starts well before they cross your threshold.

Put on tranquil, soft music. Jazz, classical, or New Age works well. It immediately sets the right tone of welcome and comfort, with a touch of sophistication thrown in. The party tunes can come later.

Have drinks prepared or ready to fix. If my guests drink alcoholic beverages, I set out a mini bar in advance so we can chat while I fix drinks. I find that adults who drink usually enjoy a cocktail or a glass of wine or beer after coming from the airport or after a long trip in the car. Just don't forget the cold water, juices, and sodas for those who don't partake in alcoholic beverages.

Prepare a light snack or appetizer. I usually have cheese, crackers, and fruit or veggies and dip all ready to go. This way they can nibble as you catch up and they get settled in. Even if dinner is only an hour away it is a simple way to show you care, and who knows? They might not have eaten in hours. What you don't want is an appetizer that you must watch like a hawk while your guests are arriving. Don't worry. The book on entertaining is coming.

Put the dog (or cat—yes, some people fear cats) away until your guests get settled. There is nothing as distracting as trying to greet your guests with a dog barking or running about, or heaven forbid, jumping on your guests. Bring the dog or cat out after your guests are a bit settled. It is really better for the animal as well, as they are not in as excited a state when they are introduced to your guests. Some children (and adults) are frightened of animals but too shy or embarrassed to say so. This simple act alleviates any stress an animal might cause your guest. There is plenty of time for hugs and play later.

Take a deep whiff. Smells are more important than we may appreciate and can just as easily repel your guests as wrap them in comfort. There is a fine line between a pleasant, wonderful aroma coming from the kitchen (like bread baking, or mulled cider simmering on the stove) and a powder room that smells like a perfume factory. When in doubt, err on the side of caution and don't over scent! Be alert to the odors in your home from pets or cooking. We grow accustomed to the scents in our own home and need to be aware of how it might smell to guests. Step outside, breath deeply and go back in. You may be glad you did.

Remember parking. If you live in a city where parking is next to impossible—and you happen to have a garage or driveway—park your car on the street and leave the private parking for your guests. Let them know ahead of time where to park their car. They'll be so much less stressed—and they won't have to schlep their bags for blocks. My car was towed one Christmas Eve because parking was not taken into account. Good thing we were all having a grand time.

Upon Arrival

As your guests walk through the door, what you do and say at that time sets the stage for the entire visit. Not an okay scenario: motioning for your guests to come in as you yak on your phone then disappear for twenty minutes, leaving only your Golden Retriever as their greeter. As host, the first important thing you do is make your guests feel welcome, wanted, and at ease the minute they walk through your door. If there are two hosts, both of you should greet your guests at the door.

Greet your guests warmly with hugs or handshakes. Remember to tell them you are happy they came! Some people are just plain bad at the initial greeting. I'm sorry, but it must be said! Bear hugs are not required, but a warm welcome is mandatory!

Help them with their bags if you are able. However, if the minivan is packed tighter than a size twelve in a pair of size-six jeans, suggest you help them with that *after* they get settled in. It will be appreciated and give you both time to greet each other and them time to relax.

Offer them that snack and drink. I have found that most people do appreciate water first, then a beverage of their choosing.

VISIT WIZARD TIP Save the house tour for after your guests are settled in and comfortable. No one can really enjoy your newly upgraded kitchen, latest baby portrait, or state-of-the art sound system if they are dirty and thirsty. Offer them something to drink and a chance to freshen up first. Remember: it is not your comfort schedule—it's theirs.

Settling In

Remember that your guests may be tired, anxious, distraught, or downright irritated by a delayed airplane, a wailing child, or sleep deprivation because of being up since dawn. Most travelers over age eighteen need some time to relax and get acclimated. Let them settle down and settle in before leading them off on the next great adventure.

Take your guests to their rooms. Don't just point up the stairs or down the hall like a traffic cop. Offer them a shower or chance to freshen up if they have been traveling some distance, and then allow them time alone to unpack and unwind.

Make sure the adults know they can take their drink to their room so they can enjoy it as they unpack. If they are carrying the luggage you carry the drinks, or vice-versa. I have some treat in the bedroom like a bowl of sweets, cookies, or fruit and cold bottled water. Make sure there are coasters in the bedroom please!

Don't just show your guests their bathroom and bedroom, take them into them. Point out where the supplies are located and that the medicine cabinet is free for their use. Invite them to use the products you put out for them. People typically will not unless you tell them they can. As host, it is extremely important that your guests know (1) where things are located; and (2) that they are free to use them.

Show your guests where and how to adjust the heat or air conditioning. Always! I am often hot at night and really appreciate being able to adjust the temperature if necessary. You don't want to hear at breakfast the next morning that your sister was "just so hot I could not sleep." You know it's hot flashes, but bite your tongue and invite her to adjust the temperature.

Explain your security system to your guests. The last thing you want is for them to accidentally set off a screeching siren when they're just looking for a little fresh air in the middle of the night.

2. A Great Host Is . . . Gracious

GRACE, WHEN THINGS ARE GOING WELL, IS A WONDERFUL attribute. You feel marvelous and generous. Grace under pressure is truly divine and requires work, patience, and empathy. Graciousness is a little-used word these days—think Audrey Hepburn in a flowing gossamer gown, smiling, nodding, and effortlessly passing the plate of canapés, all the while putting her guests' needs first.

Yes, I know that's a scene out of a Hollywood film from an era that went out with mink stoles and white gloves, but still, grace is something that should be aspired to, and can be achieved, with just a little bit of effort. Just follow these ten laws, handed down from the great Visit Wizard in the sky, or the kitchen, depending on what needs doing:

THE TEN COMMANDMENTS OF GRACIOUS HOSTING

1. **Thou shall be accessible to your guests for the majority of their visit.** This is not the time to work on cleaning out the garage or finishing that business proposal, no matter how pressing. If you do have a deadline or some major event that can't be avoided, tell your guests in advance and give them the opportunity to reschedule the visit.

2. **Thou shalt not talk constantly about yourself or be a braggart.** It's just rude, bad mannered, and does not give you any opportunity to share and learn from others. If you are a "talker" learn to zip it. It is the most boring thing you can do. Instead, get guests to open up by asking them questions about themselves and their lives—yes, even though you've known your brother from birth. Although one could eat off your floors, the house smells of just-picked flowers, the wine is chilling, and the hors d'oeuvres are a culinary sight to behold, this is not just about you.

3. **Thou shalt not be overly proper or overly casual.** Be you, only you with your best foot forward! Just because your best friend dresses like she's the latest "It Girl" on the Hollywood Red Carpet, doesn't mean you have to wear your real pearls at dinner, but you may want to switch out your favorite sweat pants with some clean khakis.

4. **Honor your guests' habits.** Just because you don't drink alcoholic beverages, for example, doesn't mean they don't, or should not, in your home unless you have some rule about it. If so, you should let them know before their visit.

   If you are a vegetarian, your guests might want meat. Know their diet and preferences and satisfy them, regardless of yours. I don't mean you should compromise your standards or needs, no indeed. Just make sure theirs are being met. And if your guests don't drink or don't eat meat don't pester or pressure them and ask why or say you think it's foolish. Respect their choices.

5. **Thou shalt not show hours of your personal travel documentaries.** We all love seeing little Bethany and Joshua playing in the park, or riding the pony—but only for just... so... long. And, really, is thirty minutes of your parasailing trip any more exciting to watch than five minutes? If you know how to use a video camera, there's really no reason you can't learn to edit your videos—or hand them off to a smart fifth-grader to do the task.

6. **Honor your guest's gift offering.** If your guest has brought a gift, you are not obligated to open it the moment they present it to you, but do so in a timely fashion. If it is a bottle of wine, you are not obligated to serve it but may do so at your discretion. You could say to the guest, "Would you mind if I open this tonight?" or words to that effect. When you are ready to open the gift, it is nice to give it the attention it deserves. You may want the children to be present, for example. Your guest has gone through the time and trouble to pick it out or make it for you, and often the hubbub and excitement of the arrival does not allow you to appreciate that. But make sure you thank them wholeheartedly and not just plunk it down, forgotten, on the table. And learn to lie convincingly: "What an adorable toilet paper caddy! How do you ever find the time to do such intricate crochet work?"

7. **Thou shalt hold thy tongue.** When you're outside grilling with your father-in-law, and he says—*again*—that his grill, car, or whatever, is

bigger or better than yours, handle his lack of grace with grace. Don't defend yourself and don't run him through with the skewer; just smile and change the subject. And later that night please, *please* don't tell your wife what an ill-mannered jerk he is. That will only make her uptight. If you really must have that type of discussion, save it for after your guests leave.

8. **Thou shalt put a nervous guest at ease.** If your guest is nervous or this is their first time visiting you, give them something to do. A simple chore (like helping you chop carrots in the kitchen or taking the dog for a walk, if they are pet savvy) will make them feel a part of the household and will do much to calm their nerves. But:

9. **Thou shalt not ask your sister-in-law to clean the basement while you fix dinner.** Unless you really need help in shortening the visit—if so, that should do it!

10. **Thou shalt be thankful.** There are people in your life who want to spend time with you, and you have the means and opportunity to provide them with a warm, welcoming home.

3. A Great Host Is . . . a Master Planner

Like Noah before the flood a good host must "think in advance" when it comes to planning. Where will everyone sleep? Who is expected to do what? What must you do if you won't be home when your guests arrive?

Sleeping Arrangements

I have heard stories of people, usually adult children visiting mom and dad, who get downright obstinate over who sleeps where. While it's true that some homes have one guest room that overlooks the ocean, complete with balcony, while the other has a window the size of a cereal box, most rooms are about equal. More typically, it is a question of who gets the pull-out sofa instead of the blow-up mattress!

So if you have the luxury of having several different guest rooms in which you can put your guests, how to decide? Whose feelings will be hurt if they don't get the room with the best view or the biggest bed? Do you decide by age? Flip a coin? It really doesn't matter which tactic you employ—just don't go by who arrives first. That is not fair and besides, once this becomes known, in the future your guests will be arriving thirty minutes early. The most important thing is to decide fairly and *before* your guests arrive. And if Gerald pouts and looks as if he is suffering the insult of all times, just smile, be gracious, and lead the way.

If your guests are unmarried but cohabitate, it is prudent to make up separate bedrooms for each person, or at least separate beds. Some hosts are uncomfortable with adults sleeping together if unmarried, while some are not. This is a personal decision that is up to you. And keep in mind that the couple themselves may feel uncomfortable sleeping with their partner in your home, which is why you should offer each their own room if possible. You could add, "but if you prefer to share a room by all means feel free."

If, on the other hand, you have limited space and your guests must share a room and are not partners, tell them ahead of time so they are aware. If they are of the opposite sex or uncomfortable sleeping together get a blow-up mattress or make some other arrangement (see chapter 1, Small Space Solutions, page 27). No matter the space restrictions, try to make sure each adult has their own bed.

Children, teens, and elders come with their own issues and concerns, which are covered in the following chapters.

Cooking Arrangements

If the visit is going to be a long one, like a week or two, make out a schedule. I know some of you are moaning, but it's really simple once you sit down and start. It may include assigning what meal which person or couple is responsible for and what days or nights you will go out for meals.

When cooking at home you can partner people up so perhaps a teen is cooking with a competent adult, or two people who wouldn't naturally cook together suddenly are. And when you do this have the "couple" responsible for the meal take it from soup to nuts—from setting the table to doing the dishes so you truly get a full night off.

Keep a record of who has any food allergies; what wine a particular guest enjoys; which guest is a vegetarian, and so on. That way when they next visit, you are even more prepared and impressive.

If You Won't Be Home When Your Guests Arrive

My husband and I flew to Europe to visit family for the first time in their new home and had a very late arrival time and did not get to the house until literally the wee hours of the morning. There were children in the house, and although the family was asleep, the host was thoughtful and had left lights on, detailed written instructions as to where we were to go, and had left out a plate of cookies and even a slow cooker filled with chili. We felt immediately at home.

First, make sure guests have a key and the code to the house alarm and leave notes... many notes. For example: where their room is; to help themselves to anything in the fridge, liquor included; instructions for the television or other electronics; your phone number; and anything they should know about the family pet, for example: "Whatever you do, don't let Buster into the laundry room, no matter how much he scratches and whines. His kibble is stored there, and he knows how to break open the bag."

And don't forget the welcoming note: "I am so glad you're here, sorry I could not be. Please make yourself at home, and call me if you have any questions or need anything" and let them know what time you plan to be home. Don't forget to have food prepared for them if you will be gone most of the day. As noted a slow cooker (crock pot) might be good for this as is something prepared ahead and kept in the fridge that they can pop in the oven (don't forget the instructions).

Leave fresh towels on their bed, have the luggage racks out, and fresh flowers or a bowl of fruit somewhere. Instead of them walking into an empty house or apartment that *feels* empty, these little things will make it warm and inviting even without your presence. They will feel special and cared for.

4. A Great Host Is… The Picture of Restraint

FOR ME, THIS IS THE HARDEST QUALITY TO LIVE BY. I KNOW I must do it, and I know why I do it—but still! It is definitely a learned skill.

If a guest offers to cook a meal, and you agree, great! But then don't stand over them watching every move, although do slide the cutting board discreetly under the veggies if you know Aunt Martha sometimes forgets. . . .

If the resulting meal is less than perfect don't criticize at the table or after. The guest may not cook often and not know that thirty minutes in the microwave is not the recommended method for skinless, boneless chicken breast! Although you could literally bounce it across the table, now is not the time to say so.

As my parents would tell us when we were children, dinnertime is not the time to discuss politics or religion. I will add: or anything of a sensitive nature, especially with family. As host you should take the responsibility of ensuring pleasant conversation at the table. If you want to discuss sensitive subjects away from the table or over dessert, perhaps, fine. Truth be told, politics and religion are great conversations to have, but this is best done in the right environment. The best advice is to know your guests. When I am with one particular friend, politics, religion, and any other ghastly, controversial topic we can think of is the most interesting!

If a heated argument is taking place behind closed doors, don't interfere in the private discussion. If you happen to walk in on two people who are in the midst of a quarrel, turn around and walk back out. No one wants to air their dirty laundry "in public" and often it only makes matters worse when others are brought into the mix.

If you see someone do something that really gets on your nerves, forget it. Don't run out of the house screaming, "I can't believe you just picked that flower from my garden!" or, "Why in the world did you just use that scrub brush on the Corian countertop!" (granted, I might freak on that one), but you get the picture. Unless it will do serious harm or injure someone, let it go. Yes, I know this is a hard one!

If your friend has the habit of smoking, doesn't want anyone to know he hasn't quit and sneaks a few out behind the garage and you know it, let it pass. If you want to mention it to him privately at some other time fine, but don't embarrass him at the moment.

One of your guests is wearing a Chanel suit and four-inch heels to a casual backyard picnic at your neighbor's. Another looks as if he just rolled out of bed, and still thinks the unshaven look rocks—at a "black tie optional" affair (and no, you are not in Hollywood). What to do? Absolutely say something if you think your guest will be uncomfortable in any situation, but only if your guest will truly be embarrassed. (Just because your sister looks stunning in that little black dress do not recommend jeans.)

You may have realized by now that I'm a little obsessive/compulsive when it comes to tidiness. And, like all of us, I do have some guests who would put Monk to shame. I really only insist that the common areas remain relatively neat for the enjoyment of all. True, I sometimes have to put one hand over my eyes when passing by their bedroom door, or with eyes closed tight, reach in and pull it shut, as my first impulse is to go in and start cleaning and organizing! Trust me, don't spend your time that way.

Your guest has kindly offered to drive everyone around one day, and as you enter the backseat of the van you step on what can only be a week-old bag of something that is now squishy, and smells. Even if you're totally grossed out, don't say some nasty or hurtful remark, like, "Good Lord, are you people some modern-day version of the Beverly Hillbillies?" Do remember that your guests have driven twelve hours with three children.

Instead, throw the offending item out at the next convenient place. Just make sure it isn't little Billy's "How-does-mold-grow?" science project.

5. A Great Host Is... Self-Caring

DOES THIS SOUND FAMILIAR? YOUR GUESTS LOOK GREAT, tan, and fresh from their day at the beach, or from lying in the outdoor hammock, or from reading for an entire stress-free afternoon in front of the fire. You, on the other hand, look like a character in a zombie movie—and there is still dinner to make!

My husband would start to see the signs of a meltdown a good day before. Heed these warnings signs:

- bags under eyes getting larger and eyes getting narrower at the same time
- a stooped, hunched-over look to the body
- a malicious head snap at the random sound
- hair not brushed
- a distant look in the eye combined with a focused stare
- standing in one spot for an extended period of time
- running the dishwasher constantly

If these symptoms describe you, it's time for some ALONE TIME! Don't neglect yourself. Things will get done and handled even if you go read or take a nap. Really! I didn't learn this until it was almost too late and knives were about to be drawn.

If the thought of making dinner has all the appeal of an IRS audit, give yourself a break. Tell everyone you are ordering pizza and get in the bathtub, or schedule a fun and relaxing activity for yourself the next day.

If you have the strength, tell an adult (not a child) where you are going and what you plan to do. If you don't they will come looking for you, so first get an ally, someone to tell the children "Aunt Kathy has left the building. She is having a time out," or whatever works.

Go for a long walk alone. Go read. Make an excuse to run an errand. Do whatever you can within reason to get some quality time for yourself. If you don't, no one will have any fun and your guests, who have come all this way and made all this effort to be in your company, will feel like they are burdens to you. It is the beginning of a downward spiral that is hard to stop.

If your guests are staying longer than two or three days don't neglect your own activities. If you play tennis every Monday at 8 a.m. or take a class after work, you must go. Your guests will survive without you as long as you give them a copy of this book and have them read chapter 6 of the Becoming the Perfect Guest section. If you don't go you will fall behind in your own life and feel badly about it when they are gone.

So your guests are spending an hour getting ready for the nice night out at the fancy restaurant while you are still in the kitchen unloading the dishwasher? Stop. It can wait. Go spend some time on yourself. You will feel better that you did—not to mention looking and smelling better, too.

Does it give you pleasure to go for a walk with your father or read a bedtime story to a little one? Do it. Don't hesitate. The chores will be there when you are done. Or, maybe you'll be pleasantly surprised and the kitchen will be clean upon your return. Well... we can always hope.

6. A Great Host Is… A Great Communicator

DON'T BE AFRAID—COMMUNICATE WITH YOUR GUESTS! LET them know what your concerns or issues are, or, for example, what rooms may be off-limits to children or pets. If necessary, mark with a sticky note that the bottle of Château Pétrus is not for consumption!

No matter how painful or petty sounding the message might be, you must speak up. Are they doing something wrong? Do you prefer they stay out of a certain area? Take their shoes off when they enter the house? Not toss M&Ms at the parrot no matter how "cute" it is when he catches them?! You must let them know!

Try not to be overly picky, but really nothing is too minor if it is going to upset you or ruin the visit—for you or for them.

You can nicely ask the teenagers and young adults to wear something appropriate for dinner. Here's a good way to do it: "Justine, I think that tube top and the ring in your belly button is interesting, but would you mind wearing something a bit more conservative at dinner? You know how old-fashioned your grandfather is." Yes, if a minor thing and done tongue-in-cheek, feel free to put the blame on others if you must. Shameless, I know, but it gets the job done! I'm sorry, but no one except other teenagers wants to see belly buttons and butt!

If you are sure clumsy Cousin Ed will knock that priceless piece of sculpture off its pedestal, put it away. Just telling him to watch it and then looking on with that painful expression on your face each time he enters the room will not do. He will sense it and be uncomfortable.

Here's what good communication can do: A friend is a wonderful host, loves to cook and care for people. On Friday night he announced when lunch would be served the following day. That morning there were people in different places, some out for a walk, some watching a sporting event on television, some out with the dogs, but all of us knew *exactly* where we were suppose to be and when. And guess what? No one was late! And everyone appreciated the chance to have a nice lunch together.

Help Your Guests Help Themselves

Unless you know your guest will eat you out of house and home or drink beer all day long, show them around the kitchen, pointing out where things are and letting them know to help themselves. I used to wait hand and foot on guests, bringing them every little thing they needed. I no longer practice this masochistic ritual. If they want a gin-and-tonic, for example, they know where the refrigerator and the liquor cabinet are located and they are free to help themselves. I don't mean to say that for the first day or so I don't go out of my way to offer these niceties, and of course fix the first G&T, but thereafter they can help themselves. It also really makes your guests feel at home.

Daily Household Chores: Who Does What, When?

Communicating well also extends to the issue of chores. I know some hosts who want to do literally everything around the house, and some who expect their guests to act like members of the family, even if they aren't. The truth, in my opinion, is somewhere in the middle. Here is how you might divvy up the responsibilities:

Suggest that your guests participate in helping out around the house if only to chop veggies, keep their bathrooms tidy, and pick up after themselves. Usually a well-placed "would you mind?..." works.

It is not wrong for you to point out what your guests can do for themselves and show them what to do, or how to do something, instead of doing it for them. An example of this is coffee. If you don't want to brew coffee or tea whenever it is wanted during the day or evening, make sure everyone knows where the supplies are kept and how to use the appropriate appliance.

You may even leave little notes about the house with instructions for things, like the washing machine or some complicated electronic gadget. So if you don't mind they use these things, or if you are away from the house, they know they are free to help themselves and do not have to always ask. Better for you both.

VISIT WIZARD TIP You are not obligated to do your guests' laundry. Don't offer unless for some reason they are unable to do it themselves due to age or injury or if you are obsessive about your new state-of-the-art baby. If you are not, then do let them know they are free to use it. Most everyone knows how to work a washing machine, and if they are older than twelve and don't, then you should probably teach them.

Some hosts insist that only they load and unload the dishwasher or hand wash the dishes. If that is your personal preference, make it known. If you ask a guest to do it don't get upset if you can't find something the next morning, or if a glass gets broken. I know someone who throws things in the dishwasher with no rhyme or reason. Her husband, however, instinctively loads the same way I do, so I try to encourage him to take on the task.

One absolute must, although a constant chore and terribly inconvenient at times, is to keep the kitchen clean. Dirty dishes piled up in the sink and left to sit not only looks bad but may leave your guests wondering as to your cleanliness in other areas. If it becomes too much of a burden for you, by all means ask for help, but the majority of the work for this is left up to you.

Your guests really do appreciate knowing what is expected, what may be a problem, or what they can do to help or assist. If you want your sister to set the dining table, ask her to do it. If you prefer the children not jump on the beds, tell them.

VISIT WIZARD TIP What creates stress is when the host has something to say but does not say it. What is most important is *how* you say it. If you keep things bottled up, what should have come out as a pleasant request will instead be a screeching entreaty.

Communicating the Right Way

Most people will respect their host's wishes or concerns when communicated in a polite manner. Don't be dictatorial, confrontational, or nasty. Communicate your wishes in a polite, controlled way and all will be well.

If necessary, recruit an ally. If you know your mother-in-law would rather hear something from her son than from you, by all means ask your husband to deliver the message. If he refuses because he is more terrified of his mother than you are, well, I'm afraid you will have to bite the bullet and get it done.

Sometimes you can disguise a request with the time-honored use of "someone else" or a "neighbor." Example: "I can't believe 'that person' took it upon herself to transplant a plant in Missy's garden, can you, Mom?" you innocently ask as you see your mother preparing to head out to the gardening shed. Or, sometimes the smallest of fibs is not out of line: "Beth, I was wondering if you would mind telling little Johnny not to jump on the bed. I know he is allowed at home but my bed has weak springs." Problem solved without your saying that her son could use a lesson in manners.

When Guests Overstay Their Welcome

I had to laugh when I received this email, quite frankly because I have heard this tale of woe many times:

"Our guests came to visit... and stayed three weeks. They were invited for two, but for some reason, still unknown to me, when I heard 'just one more?' I agreed. They said something about loving the area and wanting to house hunt—sounded exciting—at first. It ended up with me having to leave my own house just to get a break from them! I could not take one more night of these two adults sitting around like teenagers asking what was for dinner!"

Have that guest who just doesn't know that the visit is over? Well, by now you know *you* should have made the departure time known to him *before* he came, but if you did not, don't hesitate to tell him outright or, if you must, engage the small white lie. "Oh, Bill, I'm sorry I forgot to mention it, but I'm having the bathroom renovated, and the demolition begins tomorrow." But be careful when resorting to this tactic. He will want to know why the bathroom is not changed when next he visits. Just be honest. So many of you seem to worry about this because you don't want to hurt feelings. Get real! Some people take advantage of others' hospitality and big hearts. It's your house to have people in for as long, or as little, as you like.

Finally, good communication goes far beyond making requests and issuing warnings. Talk! Have a real conversation. Tell your guests what is happening with you and your family, the neighborhood, the town. People who don't live where you do usually love to hear about it and they certainly want to hear about you and hopefully exchange information. If not, then maybe you should ask yourself why they are visiting.

7. A Great Host Is... In the Moment

YOU ARE AT THE SINK WASHING POTS AND PANS AFTER A family dinner. You glance out the window and spy a male bluebird checking out the birdhouse in your backyard as a possible place to start the new family. The female is perched on a branch close by, seeing if he gives the okay. It suddenly dawns on you that your eight-year-old niece, who is now playing video games in the family room, has never seen a bluebird pair before. What do you do?

a. Wring out the sponge and go find her. The pots and pans can wait.

b. Keep washing. If the pans don't get done now, they'll never get done!

c. Yell to your sister to get her—it's her kid anyway and it's about time she knock off the blasted video games!

If you answered "a," congratulations! You know what really counts. If you answered "b," don't skip this section. If you answered "c," don't miss the Hosting Children and Young Adults chapter.

I know you have a thousand things on your mind from cooking dinner that night to wondering why the cat won't come out of the closet and how you are going to get those ink stains off the suede sofa, but guess what? You must put them out of your mind as best you can, for the moment. You must channel Scarlett O'Hara and "think about that tomorrow" or at least in an hour or two.

The little things can be handled tomorrow or next week, but this may be the only time you get to enjoy your family or friends for, perhaps, a long time. So as you are scrubbing that pan that won't come clean or having anxiety over meal preparation as little Emma comes running into the kitchen to grab your leg and beg to be lifted up, stop, put down that important thing, and hoist her lovingly into the air. *That* will be remembered, not what was for dinner, or that the pots and pans sparkled like new.

Plan and arrange meals so that you actually enjoy them, too! Conversation around the dinner table can be one of the great delights in life, but if you are jumping up and down like a pogo stick throughout you'll miss all the good stuff!

Although you enjoy talking to your neighbor or best friend on the phone for hours, don't do it while guests are visiting. It makes them feel as if they are second-rate citizens and the pleasure of their company is not what is most important to you. I can't tell you how many times I missed out because I was "too busy." Too busy trying to be perfect, too busy keeping everything in order, too busy doing laundry... let the laundry pile up for the weekend or week. It will always be there! Your guests won't.

Staying in the moment also means recognizing—and acknowledging—the present reality of your guests. One night I was watching *Frasier*, a hilarious sitcom (now in syndication) about a psychiatrist, and during one of the more serious scenes he said, "We have a tendency to freeze people in the roles in which *we* are most comfortable." I thought about this for some time and you know what? It's true! In thinking back on the absolute worst times I felt when visiting or hosting, it was because of someone's inability to perceive the other as the person they have become, instead of their notion or idea from days gone by, be that last year or when they were a teenager.

VISIT WIZARD TIP Stay in the moment (or at least in the room) during dinners: If you don't have a buffet table, set up any table in the dining area (or bring in a card table) and use it for extra drinks, water, bottle of cola or juice, bucket of ice, and keep the remaining food warm there. Your trip time to the kitchen will be cut down considerably!

8. A Great Host Is... A Skilled Ringleader

HOSTING CAN SOMETIMES FEEL LIKE A THREE-RING CIRCUS. In ring one you have guests who are behaving like contestants on a bad television reality show. In ring two is the parade, except that it's literally raining on it, and that's the reason everyone traveled to visit you in the first place, and in ring three you have a sulky teenager who is way bored and would rather be hanging out with the lowlifes at the local mall. It's enough to drive the good host crazy. You must juggle, and crack the whip as necessary, to get all the rings working smoothly.

For example, you may have to find things for your guests to do around the house. If it is apparent Sally is sulky, take her out to the garden and have her cut some flowers or plant something. Or, if two guests are not enjoying each other's company, separate them by suggesting one do some task.

Bring out a puzzle, chess board, party game, or a video game.

Is there some event that day that would be of interest? For example, the football game is on at 1 p.m. Announce that whoever wishes to watch should be in the living room at that time as Dallas vs. Washington (or Italy vs. Brazil, depending on what part of the world you watch and what you consider to be football) will be shown, complete with cold beverages and snacks!

Make up an event. You see things are dire. It's raining out, plans are ruined and someone is in bed with a cold, brought on, no doubt, by the airplane ride to your home. No time to waste! You have options: Have a cook-off if some of the adults cook—or even if they don't; put on a movie you know will be a crowd-pleaser and make popcorn—yes—even in the afternoon! Make it even more interesting by having the children find some items in the pantry or fridge to drizzle on it. When you're done the three rings are each working smoothly: One of the adults is with the older children at the movies; little Ashley is set up on the floor with a coloring book and crayons and flavored popcorn; and the remaining adults are in the kitchen making pasta sauce and martinis and yes—you are there! Until tomorrow... when it all starts lovingly again.

9. A Great Host Is... Flexible

YOU'VE MADE YOUR PRIZED LASAGNA, ONLY TO FIND OUT THAT Nancy is lactose-intolerant, Greg is a vegetarian, Alan is kosher, and Jennifer is allergic to tomatoes! So what do you do? The flexible host would laugh it off and say "I guess we're having Chinese tonight." Then save the lasagna for another time. (Remember to make guest notes for next time!)

Of all the attributes you can have as host, being flexible is one of the most important, if not the most. As host it is up to you to manage the situation. Remember the young branch that bends in the spring breeze without breaking? Yes, it is mentioned in the guest section of this book and yes, it applies to you as well.

From a conscientious host:

"My biggest flaw as host is getting worried that people are bored and trying to cajole them into activities or sightseeing. I still have trouble understanding that sometimes people just want to sit on the porch or in the home theater or hang around the kitchen and visit/read/watch movies. I am getting better, but I still get nervous when we have a group of folks who still have not left the house at 2:00 p.m. and then only reluctantly get dragged somewhere."

Remember the motto of the great host: stay cool; stay flexible. Just because a walk in the woods this afternoon was on the agenda doesn't mean you should order everyone to start putting their shoes on. They're into a good movie so let them be. I know a woman who is very good at this. Want to stay home today and just relax? Fine! Want to go for a trip somewhere? No problem! That attitude, when appropriate for the group, does put people at ease and makes the visit a relaxing, albeit a disorganized one.

And if the prima donna of the group has unexpectedly broken a nail and now, not only can't take that hiking trip, but must rush off to the manicurist, don't get upset. Let her go.

10. A Great Host Is... Cool Under Pressure

CONSIDER THIS FROM A FRIEND IN NEW YORK CITY. WHAT would you have done?

"At a very saucy Thanksgiving Day dinner party the young maid brought in the turkey platter with all the trimmings to the 'oh's and ah's' of the guests. In her anxiety she stumbled. The platter tilted and the bird and all dropped to the floor. As the guests held their collective breath, the host rose and with a wink to the maid, said, "It's all right. Pick that up, my dear, and I will go into the kitchen and help you prepare the other turkey."

Did I say being flexible was the most important attribute? Nix that: it's this one. For those of us who have enjoyed guests for years, this is an understood trait (think Mother Teresa and you're getting the picture). For those of us who are just starting down the path of welcoming family and friends into our home for extended periods, read this section twice.

If two old friends whom you have known since birth, and are as relaxed as the wilted greens in your fridge, breeze in Friday afternoon driving the new Jaguar in which they will take drives in the country, praise everything in your world, with their only desire being to take you out to dinner and perhaps a show, skip this step. Cling to them as you would a vine when swinging through the jungle of life.

Now, back to reality. Your guests are wound tighter than a pair of Spandex shorts on a sumo wrestler. Not only do they hold you personally responsible for no snow during the holidays but they have gone and insulted your decorating prowess. Smile. You are fuming inside or perhaps even outwardly shaking, but smile. No one will know. They may cock their head at you, thinking you have a temporary chemical imbalance, but it works. Your guests might even smile back, then the smoke will clear, and all will be well again.

Entertaining relatives for a weekend at our mountain home included a teenaged girl. My husband and I were appalled when she plopped down on our sofa and put her dirty feet up on my brand new Jonathan Adler needlepoint pillow without a thought, while her parents looked on saying nothing.

Expect the occasional mishap or broken object. Try not to show your emotions and certainly don't ask your guest to pay for the damage, except in unusual circumstances. However, if your guests read the Becoming the Perfect Guest section, they know they should at least offer to pay, but with an exception: If the item is a family heirloom or terribly expensive, I am afraid you will just have to bear it.

Your guests will insult you, either intentionally or not. Your neighborhood will not be as pretty as theirs or your kitchen as state-of-the-art, and their television will be bigger, flatter, and with enough pixels for one to see the real wrinkles on their favorite actress. Take it in stride and change the subject. Arguing is futile.

If your children have to be disciplined, try not to do it in front of your guests. It will only serve to make everyone uncomfortable and ensure tears from the child! Take them from the room and correct them in private. You will be doing everyone a favor.

If during the dinner festivities a family member offers to take the chicken out of the oven only to have it go skidding across the kitchen floor right into the paws of Rufus the dog, don't lash out. Remember: the food is replaceable but your friend or family member is not.

Don't tolerate bad behavior but do take into consideration that (especially at family gatherings, it seems) emotions can run high and old feelings, good or bad, can surface. There is such a fine line to walk in these situations. I make a conscious effort to be on my very best behavior when hosting relatives but am not always successful! Even the best of intentions can come up short.

When you feel temper start to rise, or the tears start to well because of an unthinking or cruel remark or a dropped piece of china, do remember that how you behave and how others behave in your home is determined by you. No one else.

Humor can be used to defuse almost any situation, but never, ever do it at someone's expense unless you're very, very good at it, in which case it will be perceived as an obvious joke, not insulting. Often you can turn around what may be an awkward or potentially ignitable situation fairly quickly if you can get people to see the humor in it. There are two people in my life who are able to do this: my maternal grandmother and my father. Although I try to remember this trick I am not always successful!

VISIT WIZARD TIP The outward appearance of cool is as important as the actual feeling . . . sometimes even more so.

11. A Great Host Is . . . A Diplomat

"When our relatives are at home, we have to think of all their good points or it would be impossible to endure them."

—GEORGE BERNARD SHAW

YOUR MOTHER-IN-LAW WILL TELL YOU THAT YOUR CAKE batter is lumpier than tapioca pudding on steroids. Your brother will diss your spouse's haircut. Your father will think your dog is stupid. All these things will happen to some extent and in some capacity. They just do when families are grouped together for an extended period of time. Try not to be easily insulted or take things personally. And try not to overreact. I don't mean to take insults, definitely not, but ask your mother-in-law what she would recommend to help your batter; tell your brother that he hurt your spouse's feelings and that you love his new hairstyle; and tell your father you enjoy your dog just the way he is. There are better ways to handle these things than demanding an apology or storming out of the room.

If a transgression arises (or two guests are yelling at each other over something that happened years—or just minutes—ago) you must step in. You set the tone and example by which your guests will conduct themselves. You are pack leader and must be the cool one. Perhaps take one outside or into the kitchen, but it is up to you to try to bring harmony and balance back into the picture. Just make sure you don't neglect your other guests while attempting to do so.

A family member has brought up a past incident that no one really wants to discuss. As host you have two options: allow it or not. As host you can control the conversation and should. It is absolutely your privilege to change the subject or just tell folks you don't want to discuss that in your home at this time. You rule. Don't be intimidated.

However, if Uncle Mark wants to take the opportunity now that the entire family is assembled to tell everyone he was terribly insulted because of X, Y, and Z that happened last year, you might decide to give him the opportunity. However, if you know he will zero in on Fred, who has been sipping wine a little too aggressively and will go ballistic, you may want to change the subject or tell him firmly that it is best talked about tomorrow. Don't worry. It most likely won't be.

I honestly go either way depending on the situation, the timing, and the people involved. Vocal purging in an intimate setting can be a good and healthy thing if there is a neutral party or referee, and as host, you are it. Do you want to take on that role at that particular time? It's entirely up to you.

As host, you must know when, and how, to say "no." The following is a great example from a very diplomatic friend:

"I have a friend I have known for years who wanted to visit me with her husband and preteen child for a weekend in the city. Wonderful, I thought! We began to make plans.

"I reminded her that my guest room had only a single bed. I told her that when they come I would give them my bedroom, the child could have the guest room, and I would sleep on the pull-out sofa. Not a problem, she said. I offered to take them out to dinner when they arrived Friday night. That would not do, she said. The child had an afternoon commitment and they would not arrive to my house until about 1 a.m.! My misgivings were beginning to surface. I then suggested dinner Saturday night. My friend then told me they were planning to meet friends that night but I could surely join them and would I mind picking the restaurant and making the reservation? I did and made reservations for five people. I got a phone call: There were going to be twelve people and would I please select a different restaurant? I don't mind being a fifth wheel at dinner but I draw the line at being the thirteenth. With conscious forbearance I suggested we go out for breakfast Saturday morning. I got another phone call: that was not going to work either, she was afraid. They had something else to do and had to leave my apartment by 7 a.m.

"I was now torn between feeling used—displaced from my bedroom and waiting to the wee hours for guests who could not find room in their schedule for time with me—and feeling guilty for letting down a friend. I agonized for a day or two and finally called them, letting them know that I thought the plans had gotten a bit cumbersome, but I would love to see them at some point, the next time they are in the city."

Instead of losing her temper, or getting in a huff at the time of the various phone calls, this lady took the time to ponder the situation and be as tactful as possible to her friend while still being true to herself and maintaining self-respect. It was handled smoothly and with aplomb.

VISIT WIZARD TIP Let's face it—there are times when you and your partner are just not getting along. If that time coincides with a visit, well, that's just too bad. Suck it up. You must never let it show or interfere with your guest's comfort. No one is comfortable when the host is not. Show appreciation, or at least civility toward your partner. No one thing will make guests more uncomfortable than tension or outright fighting between hosts, and that includes keeping your comments to yourself if your love overcooked the shrimp.

For some unknown psychological reason some couples wait to discuss those things they dislike about each other until they are in the presence of others. Change the topic quickly. Don't agree, disagree, or take sides. There is one exception: if it is a rational and tame discussion between a few adults and if you feel you can truly help or contribute in a positive way, do so. Just proceed with caution!

Old habits will creep back uninvited, old rivalries will rise from the sand of our childhood playgrounds, and we will get stuck in a time warp. Nothing is worse. As host you *must* put any negative thoughts and feelings from years ago behind you. You must see your family guests as adult friends, and your friends as family.

I will tell you a very moving story: Two couples were attending an event. The event was going much longer than expected. One of the couples wanted to leave. Badly. The other couple wanted to stay just as badly. They had all come in one car, so one couple leaving was not an option, nor was calling a cab. Well, the couple who did not want to stay did. They were the hosts and it was their duty. The man was not happy about being forced to stay and made his feelings angrily known in the car on the way back home. This led to the other man getting just as angry and making his feelings known, which of course led to the women getting very upset! It was horrible and could have caused a terrible visit with perhaps the visiting couple leaving the next day. However, here is what happened when the men stepped out of the car at the house: They embraced, apologized to each other in a sincere and loving way, and went inside for a much-needed after-event drink. All was well. What could have ended in disaster actually resulted in the two men becoming closer. One of the men made the first move. It was necessary and the right thing to do. I applaud them both. Think about this next time you have a hostile situation on your hands. Someone has to reach out and if no one does, that someone must be you.

If you know a friend or family member is easily hurt, stick up for them should that hurt occur. They will forever be your friend.

VISIT WIZARD TIP If one of your guests just happens to be someone you just don't like, do try to find *some* attribute of theirs that is agreeable. Surely there is one! Make it your mission to find it. If there are two guests who just do not get along don't try to play matchmaker, it will be too obvious, but do invite them along when you are with others as they just might make some progress.

There is always that one family member or friend who wants to talk about another family member or friend, present or not. All I can say is whatever you discuss will, most likely, get back to the person you are talking about. Michael will ask you if you agree that Sarah's new cosmetic enhancement just makes her look, well, strange. Whether you agree or not is no matter. You must as diplomatically as possible say nothing of consequence—unless a week or a month from the visit you want an angry phone call from Sarah. These things do have a way of making their way back around.

12. A Great Host Is… Able to Ensure a Happy Departure

No matter how pleasant the visit, you may be eagerly anticipating the hour—if not the minute—your guests will be saying their goodbyes. But you cannot simply issue a "Don't let the door slam on your way out" and call it a day. You owe it to your guests—and yourself—to treat them just as importantly upon their departure as you did upon their arrival.

If your guests are driving and have a ways to go, pack some refreshments for them to take on the road, like water and things they can easily snack on, like apple slices (just don't forget the tiniest drop of lemon juice on the apples to keep them from turning that unappetizing shade of brown), nuts, grapes, or carrot sticks. Don't forget napkins.

Keep handy those frozen plastic things to keep items cold, or just a bag of ice will do, enclosed in a larger baggie. Nothing fancy required, just a nice gesture.

If your guests are headed to the airport, make sure they have cold bottled water.

Walk your guests to their car or go down with them in the elevator. Let them know you enjoyed having them, even if the time was a bit stressful or full of strife. The next time won't be as bad and after a few days, or perhaps weeks, you will look back fondly on the memory.

If you are locking the door behind them and falling in a heap on the floor weeping for joy at their departure, you need to give them a copy of this book. Perfect visit or not, put your arms around each of your guests and wish them a safe trip.

If you sincerely cannot wait to have them again, and you believe they have enjoyed themselves, then you have been successful. And you can honestly tell them to "go slow... and hurry back."

CHAPTER 4

Hosting Children and Young Adults

"The truth is that hosting children is a lot like having your eyebrows waxed—not without pain, but oh, so satisfying when done right."

—THE VISIT WIZARD

AS ADULTS IT'S EASY TO FORGET HOW KIDS VIEW THE WORLD. Often, as hosts, we spend so much time agonizing and stressing over the visit that it's easy to forget that what's important to us, kids don't really care about. So the first rule of hosting children is: Think like a kid. Better yet, think back to *when* you were a kid. What did you like to do? What made you want to go hide in the closet? What did you look forward to and what did you dread? How did you view the world and the adults that inhabited it? Of course all children are different. They like—and hate—different things. But if you treat your young guests with the same respect you afford your adult guests, all should go well, or as well as possible when small tornados disguised as cute little people arrive at your door. They have to be cute or how could we tolerate them? For example,

I look really cute in a photo of me as a child making mud pies (real mud) with my great aunt. Adorable, until I added them to the cake batter my mom had out on the counter. I know some of you are laughing wishing your little ones were as well behaved.

Game Theory: Plan Interesting Activities

THE TWENTY-FIRST-CENTURY CHILD WILL MOST LIKELY ARRIVE at your door fully gadgetized for entertainment. But a visit is a time to gently ease your child guest *away* from his personal entertainment system to engage in more social activities. Don't be afraid. Just have on hand what you need, and do what you must, to make your visiting children content and otherwise happily occupied so that they gladly fork over that screaming gadget because whether you have a yard or are in a high-rise condo, there are many fun things for kids to do. It is as limitless as your (and their) imaginations.

Before your young visitor arrives, find out if he or she has an interest in any specific activity. If she loves to draw or paint, for example, you may want to set up a place for her to do that. Take it a step further and if your young guest plays the piano or is into photography, arrange for him to play piano with a talented friend or go to a photography exhibit.

Have traditional games, and if you choose, have noncontroversial, nonviolent video games for the children to play. If you don't have any, borrow some toys or games from friends or neighbors or rent movies from the library. And when Tommy tells you that the just-released *Village Beast* is a spinoff of *Beauty and the Beast*, don't believe him.

Do expose the children to new, safe adventures. Nothing wrong with going for a lead-line pony ride or to a petting zoo, but I'd stay away from sky diving or a swim in the Atlantic. And even with the normal activities they are used to doing at home, conditions could be different at your place. In driving up the mountain to our rental home, I came across a young man lying on the side of the road, skateboard in hand, blood on forehead and knees. He was visiting his grandparents and did not realize the hills here were much steeper than back home. He was fine, but lesson learned. Hopefully.

So to counter this age of high tech, low imagination, have the children build a fort out of the furniture pillows complete with a sheet roof, or help them write a play. Set up a stage in the living room. Bring in chairs and watch the show.

Of course, children don't always know what they'd actually enjoy. Sometimes you have to prod them a bit or make suggestions. When told it was time for them to play alone for a while before dinner, the two adorable little boys looked up at their host towering above them, and with huge, doe eyes asked in earnest, "But Uncle Chet, where is the play room?" When they were told there was no "playroom," but the great outdoors with its many acres was all theirs, they did not sulk or moan. The three went outside and collected sticks to build a fort. Although they had grand plans for a tree house, by the end of the day it was more like a teepee, which still suited everyone just fine. They came back tired, dirty, happy, and proud.

Sometimes you need more than a gentle prod—like maybe a cattle prod. Here's a case in point, from a dear friend, minor changes made to protect the guilty:

"A couple brought their children to my wonderful summer rental home on a beautiful weekend evening. The pain started immediately when the children refused to exit the car—they were happy watching a movie and didn't know why they had to visit me anyway!

"The swimming pool held no charm and 'I'm cold,' 'I'm tired,' 'I don't want to' was all that was heard. I even tried baking, to no avail. We decided to go to an amusement park, but they would not go on any rides. We finally convinced one to try and he loved it. We went home, a bit happier, but not by much. The last straw happened the next morning when I had arranged for a boat to go deep-sea fishing. Several of the children went below refusing to come out and the other did not want to fish. Finally, to my delight, the parents said, 'One fish or no dinner tonight.' The children changed their minds, participated, and were in the end beaming with pride and joy at catching their first fish."

Know When to Play the Clown

Is everyone gloomy? Is it raining outside and have plans been cancelled? Do the little one's little faces look as if Santa died? Even the happiest of kids can get into funks. They are bored or restless or mad at you or each other. What to do? If possible, lead the parade! Recall that most magic of doctors, Dr. Seuss, and don't be afraid to bring out "Thing 1 and Thing 2"! It doesn't much matter what you do as long as it is distracting and somewhat entertaining. Most kids—at least the ones who have not yet hit their teenage years—are just not that picky.

Were tears shed? Did someone hurt the other? One of the best attributes you can have when hosting children is the ability to find humor in situations and use it to "turn that frown upside down" as the old saying goes. I can still hear my grandmother's laugh, so infectious that you could not help but feel that bubbly sensation starting in your stomach and gurgling out your mouth when all of a sudden the trouble was magically gone. Some people seem to have that natural ability. If you don't, fake it. It can be contagious.

Don't forget to join in the play yourself. One of my fondest memories with my nieces and nephews was the time we spent in the basement with my potter's wheel and jewelry beads. We made a mess; we created masterpieces; we laughed and joked and got to know each other. The carpet had to be cleaned and, centrifugal force not to be stopped, the spinning clay splattered on the newly painted walls, but it was worth every minute. Was I guilty about leaving the "adults" upstairs to fend for themselves for many hours? Yes. Did I care? Not in the least!

Food, Glorious Food! Oliver Never Had It So Good

WE ARE FORTUNATE THAT OUR FOOD AND PREPARATION choices are extensive... or are we? Microwave, frozen, farm-fresh, organic, canned, gluten free, meat free, semi-veggie, eat-in, take-out, drive-through. What to eat tonight, what not to eat, who will eat what—it's enough to exhaust even the Visit Wizard. Not all choices are right or will work for all kids. I'm big on unprocessed foods and have been both meatless and wheatless at different times, but that doesn't mean I don't get when you have to pop the frozen whatever in the micro at the end of a long day. Been there—and still do that!

If you've gotten this far in the book, you know by now what questions to ask your visitors about their food and drink preferences before they arrive and before you go shopping.

When hosting kids, either alone or with their parental units in tow, you have to respect the parents' rules. Some parents are very concerned with what their children eat, as they should be, so best not to venture from the list of approved foods. And don't be critical of said list. Just because you practically lived on Froot Loops and Twinkies as a child doesn't mean it's okay to stock the cupboard with same.

Here are a few more questions to ask before your young guest arrives:

- Does the child have any specific dietary restrictions or needs?
- What can the child have and not have in terms of food and snacks? This question will save you bundles of time and money at the grocery store.
- Does the child have any food allergies? If they are allergic to peanuts you will want to put away the nut bowl. Also, lupin is a protein that can cause an allergic reaction in people who are allergic to peanuts. Lupin is sometimes found in food like breads, pasta, chocolate, and cakes. There are a number of different allergies that affect children, including latex, milk, egg, dairy, and wheat, which contains gluten. Gluten is a protein. It can be found in barley, rye, and wheat breads. For an example of a gluten-free menu go to glutenfree.com.

If there are several younger children visiting, consider a "kids" table in the dining room or kitchen. Make the table fun: Put a disposable paper tablecloth and crayons, similar to what some restaurants offer, on the table for the children to draw on. At each place set out those party poppers (called "crackers") filled with little fun gifts to be opened before or after the meal (some have very small parts hiding inside, so use caution), or make your own little treat. Plastic silverware in bright colors can add a festive touch and is disposable. Now let's get down to business:

Breakfast

The most important meal in a child's day.

Pancakes. I will not forget watching my brother make pancakes... for four kids and four adults. He was in the kitchen of our vacation home for several hours, demonstrating great patience and more than a little skill. A clever way to get eggs and milk into kids in a child-friendly way, no doubt. Put a few sliced strawberries, blueberries, or bananas on the pancakes (child permitting) and there you go—a veritable smorgasbord of good ingredients.

Eggs. My little niece used to ask for "smashed eggs!" so we would put into scrambled eggs whatever we could get away with, such as cheese, or a bit of lean ham—we were stopped at peas, however. Served with whole wheat or multigrain toast, what could be better?

Cereal. There are some great cereals on the market now that are loaded with good stuff. I am a fan of Kashi, and not just because of their motto: "Seven Whole Grains on a Mission," which is just so cool. Hot or cold cereal is a simple quick-fix choice.

Waffles. Frozen multigrain waffles? Perfect!

Bagels and lox. Why not do something crazy and introduce the older kids to smoked salmon with bagels and cream cheese for breakfast? Don't forget the shaved red onion and capers. No, I am not kidding!

Lunch

Lunch is pretty easy; just stay away from those fast-food places with all their fat and fried fat. I honestly don't know how those owners sleep at night. It's the twenty-first century and they are just now offering salads?

Remember that kids are totally dependent on you to keep them safe and healthy. It is a big responsibility. If they want burgers, great, get some ground beef at the store and fire up the grill or the burner. No, I won't bug you about getting ground turkey or tofu instead, but here's a really neat substitute they will love once they try:

Mushroom burgers! Get those large Portabella mushroom halves, (spoon out the gills), brush some olive oil on each side, sprinkle with a touch of salt, put your pan on medium high, and sauté (or grill) those suckers! Only about three minutes per side. Add a slice of cheese on top while it's still in the pan so the cheese melts slightly, add lettuce and sliced tomato, put between a hamburger bun, and voilà!—a really tasty, nutritious meal. These giant mushrooms have a woodsy, meaty taste just like steak—really! (And if the kids have to have ketchup on everything, that's okay, it won't hurt these.) Other ideas:

Make-ahead "MacSalad": That's macaroni salad.

Peanut butter and—honey! Try it on whole wheat bread.

Dinner

This gets a bit more complicated, but have no fear. I have room for only a few suggestions, but it's a start: Pasta can be made ahead al dente, brought out from the fridge and put in a pot of boiling water quickly and efficiently, and the tomato sauce, or just a pat of butter, can be added to finish it off. Served with sliced cucumber (to be picked up and eaten with the fingers, of course), and what child wouldn't love that. Fun with food is the way to go. My niece taught me that English cucumbers (the long thin ones wrapped in cellophane) are less tart. She's right.

Mashed potatoes as a side usually works for everyone. Here's a trick: Hide veggies in it. Boil your skinned potatoes on the stove top as usual, roast asparagus in the oven with a bit of olive oil and salt and pepper sprinkled on first (make sure to put aluminum foil in your pan for easy clean up). Drain the potatoes, cut up the asparagus, put both and some low-fat milk and a mild white cheese of your choice (easy on the cheese) into your blender or food processor, and whip up a wonderful, tasty, nutritious side that will have the kids (and the adults) asking for more.

Build a kebab or taco—all at the same time! Good for all your guests:

Put out on a plate square chunks of uncooked meat (pork or beef), and on another plate shell-less raw jumbo shrimp (for the semi-veggies); and on a BIG platter put sliced veggies like zucchini, yellow squash, mushrooms, red or green bell peppers, and cherry tomatoes (works for your vegans). Set out those store-bought hard taco shells, diced tomatoes, cilantro, limes, salsa, chopped lettuce, a "Mexican" cheese blend, sour cream, and long skewers. It's not as hard as it was to write! Then ask the crew who wants what. Let the adults (and the kids, with adult supervision) skewer those ingredients they want, and off to the grill the adult-in-charge goes. For those who just want the shrimp or meat taco, there it is! Guests young and old, meat lovers or not, get to assemble their own special dinner with just the ingredients they want. And it's fun. For everyone. (Do the ninety-second rice thing in the microwave, put out a bowl of chips and salsa, and there you have it.) You will find simple and fun make-ahead meals for kids and adults in my upcoming book on effortless entertaining.

Invest in some inexpensive plastic or coated place mats that can be wiped clean. Don't make the painfully amateurish mistake of serving pasta to children on a linen tablecloth. Yes, really....

An Ounce of Prevention: Kid-Proof Your Home

AS ADULTS, WE WANT OUR HOMES TO BE AS APPEALING TO our guests as possible. It's natural to want to show off all the care we've poured into decorating them. But be forewarned: children can wreck your home faster than a tornado in a trailer park. And just because *your* children know not to get into something does not mean your guest child won't.

Put away the heirlooms and breakables before the children arrive. Why take the chance that a running youngster could collide with your priceless whatnot and send it crashing to the floor? Very few objects, standing or lovingly placed on the cocktail table, can withstand the usually innocent, but often disastrous exuberance of children.

Check your closets for lingerie or other interesting items. If you don't want to see your undies atop some little head as your niece races through the house, your lacey corset in tow, mind these words. Some little ones do like to discover new and interesting objects in closets and drawers, and even your own children may want to show off something pretty. Put anything potentially embarrassing in a box on a high, high shelf. Knowing my two friends with their curious son were coming to stay in my house while I was gone for a few days, I put some things of a delicate nature in a small suitcase and locked it in my car. Knowing I was the only one with a key to the car gave me great comfort!

Get all firearms out of the house or locked away out of reach. I know this should go without saying, but too often, in all the hubbub of getting ready for visitors, sometimes this obvious step can get overlooked. In one of our homes we had guns, which we fired for sport on the firing range, and to shoot skeet (no, that is not some exotic bird on the endangered species watch list, as one guest thought). A nice memory for me is my young nephew learning from my brother the *right* way to fire, but more importantly, to respect guns. Since he is actually one of the most loving young men I know I am not terribly concerned that he will turn into a gun fanatic but the best idea is to get the firearms out of the house completely.

Think your home is now "child ready"? Think again. Use this checklist as a guide to all the little childproofing chores to attend to, depending on the age of the child visiting. This is the short list:

- Cover unused outlets. You can buy those little plug-in outlet covers for a reasonable price and then hand down once the little ones are grown (see the Resource section for a link).
- Pad sharp-edged furniture.
- Install baby gates in front of stairs or other dangerous places. When I was young and in my first apartment, I had to drag heavy dining room chairs in front of a stairway when a toddler was visiting. Not great, but what did I know?!
- Alarm the doors if you have a swimming pool or hot tub or other outdoor danger spots; have a fence with a gate that locks around the pool.
- Secure cabinets with locks or safety devices so there can be no access to medications, toxic chemicals, or other dangerous material.
- Lock the door leading down to the basement or out to the garage.
- Look for strings and things that hang in which a child can get tangled or choke. Check your window treatments and blinds for cords that are not secured.
- Railings are always a hazard. Never let a child alone on a balcony or porch or an open loft.
- Look at your raised, stone fireplace hearth with those child-enticing tools, sharp edges, and matches. I say no more.

Sweet Dreams: Create an Inviting Bedroom

CONSIDER WHERE THE CHILD OR CHILDREN ARE GOING TO sleep. Do you have a cot that can be set up in the parents' room? Will a crib be needed? If so, and you do not have one, look into renting one or borrowing one from a friend or neighbor. Your guest should email you a list of things she may need but will not be able to transport.

Is the child old enough to have his or her own guest room? Are children of the opposite sex too old to share a room? Depending on your space and the age of the child, prepare the room with the same care and attention to detail as you would for an adult (see the Creating a Welcoming Home chapter, page 12) but consider the following:

- Get anything sharp, fragile, precious, or that gets hot like a halogen lightbulb or that iron in the closet out of the room.
- Protect your furniture. Buy the temporary nonstick waffle pads you can get at the grocery or home supply store that can be cut to fit. These are perfect for on top of dressers to protect against childish mishaps.
- If you are fortunate enough to have a room dedicated solely as a child's guest room try this as a special treat: Let the child—supervised—paint on the walls. A woman has this in one of her guest rooms used for the children, and it is just so clever. Every time they visit, you could let the children paint something on the wall that has meaning for them. Imagine what memories that wall will hold for both the adults and the children as both age.

- Display old photographs of the family, the child's parents, and/or you and the child, all of which will be very meaningful and will allow you to discuss where you were, what you were doing, and so on. For special photos, make a copy, write on the back the people in it, the place, and the year taken and give it to the child or start an album.
- Use colorful or fanciful sheets and pillows. Back in the day there was something called tie dying. Buy plain white sheets and try it. Kids love it.
- Put out stuffed animals or dolls, but nothing so precious that if it ends up missing an eye or an arm it will bother you. As a child I absolutely loved stuffed animals and still have several from that time.
- Have a small table set up with paper and pen or crayons. Now is a great time to introduce the child to letter writing!
- Provide books suitable for the age of the child. If you don't have any simply go to the library. The young adult books are cool, but don't forget old classics like *The Nancy Drew* mysteries or *The Hardy Boys.*
- Make sure to have good lighting, as well as a night-light that can be turned on and off.
- Hang curtains or shades that block out the sun in the morning. I once had to throw dark towels over the curtain rods so the children could sleep.
- If a baby bed/playpen is needed, look for a traveling, collapsible one that can be easily stored.
- I don't think a television or telephone in the child's room is a good idea, for obvious reasons.
- Make the closet easy for kids and an inviting place to hang up clothes. I once painted the inside of the guest room closet bright green and had little hangers to match. It was pretty cool, I must say. Use those stick-up, removable hooks at a height a child can reach.

- Do make sure the child knows where you are at night and that she can come to you if she gets scared, if the parents are not along for the visit.

VISIT WIZARD TIP If the visiting child will be bunking with your child, make sure you take out anything of value that can't be replaced. Nothing gets feelings hurt quicker than the guest child breaking something of your child's.

The House Rules: Set—and Enforce—the Rules

IT'S YOUR HOUSE, SO YOU SHOULD BE COMFORTABLE IN setting the rules and letting the children's parents know what they are, either in advance, or when they first come to your home. It seems that this one topic, to me so simple, creates much angst among... well... everyone! We're not talking about a laundry list, but the basics are fine. Letting your wishes known will make you, and therefore your guests, more relaxed, which means a better visit.

Simple works. For those without children or who have not had children visit in a long while, prepare yourself... mentally. You can't pick up every time there is something left here and there. You can't expect your perfect house to stay that way. To ease yourself into the process, you many want to start by setting up some simple boundaries that are easily understood and obeyed, like "no food in the living room," and, "don't carry the dog by the tail." You should work up gradually to "let the adults speak now, children" so as not to cause too much dismay.

Take a supporting role. As host you must support whatever rules the adult guests have for their children. Yes, even if you disagree. You can talk to the parents about it later in private but not in the moment.
Ask specifically what the children are not allowed to do. What restrictions do they have to any public media, like blocked-out television channels or restriction to the Internet? That is the best way to avoid, "but Mom and Dad let me!" Let the parents know what you have planned so they can agree, or not.
If you are the only adult at the scene and in doubt—don't! The best course of action is to call one of the parents if you have any questions or concerns.
Stick to your own rules. If visiting Johnny gets to watch or play video games that you think are inappropriate for your own child, what do you do? You absolutely stay firm to your rules. Now is not the time to lower your standards or have your child up that night with nightmares after watching something beyond his understanding or maturity level.

VISIT WIZARD TIP What to do when some children are on a routine where bedtime is a certain time, but other children are able to stay up later? The parents of the children rule. Your opinion is most likely unwanted and you don't want to be seen as undermining the parent. The children will forget—the parent won't!

Be Careful with Corrections

What do you do when little Jennifer and Joshua are acting out, acting up, or are just bad actors?

Sometimes you simply have to bite your tongue. Other times you should speak up. Of course you can, and must, when the parents are not there to do it, but if they are present and not doing anything to correct the situation, what to do? I believe that if done gently, and at appropriate times, correcting a child's behavior is fine. I know many of you disagree, so no need to email. I only ask those of you who disagree to consider this: You heard the young child use foul language; you saw him pull the cat's tail; he mispronounced a word and you want to help. Are these examples of times when the host, or another family member, can correct the child? I think so, but I do recognize there are various opinions on such matters. Here is one:

> *"I would rather have the person discuss [the misbehavior] with me and then I would discipline my own child. If it is a matter of safety then I think it's good for the child to hear from someone else, as well as their parent … having one very sensitive child it was always better for me to explain things to him in a manner he could understand. I try to not discipline others' children."*

A friend doesn't mind at all when other adults she knows and trusts discipline her children. She wants her children to know that they must respect adults and the opinions and feelings of others. Another mother says correcting a child shows love for the child, and she supports her parents and other adults she trusts to correct her child, as long as it's done in a loving way, not out of anger.

Here is one point that I think *everyone* can agree on: No matter your particular parenting style, never overrule the parent, even in your own home. But if your guest says the child certainly may use your Limoges porcelain plates for her teddy bear tea party you may suggest another set. If there is a problem that can't be ignored, take the parent aside and tell her or him privately. Children shouldn't learn they can get away with something just because they are in another person's home. But don't be overly picky. That is the very best way to annoy your guest or ensure a premature departure.

Bad Behavior: Handling Tricky Situations

TWO DEFINITIONS OF TOLERANCE:

1. Showing understanding or leniency for conduct or ideas differing from or conflicting with one's own.

—MERRIAM-WEBSTER UNABRIDGED DICTIONARY

2. Knowing how long to keep one's mouth shut when other people's children are badly behaved.

—THE VISIT WIZARD

IT IS SO EASY TO JUDGE, ISN'T IT? WE ALL DO IT; I'M NO EXCEPtion. But if you want peace in the house during the visit, be as tolerant as you can be without running the risk of being committed to some institution as soon as your guests roll from the driveway.

If you find yourself wishing to flee the scene on the wings of Pegasus, it may help to think of what the poor harried parents probably went through just to get to you. They may have suffered through the agony of a six-hour car trip with squabbling siblings; a plane ride with a cranky, air-sick toddler; or a train ride with a tween who somehow managed to wander off to another car after telling her parents to "bugger off." Oh, and did I forget to mention all the gear that comes with kids? And what it must have taken to get everyone out the door on time?

So take a deep breath and remember the doctor's creed: "first, do no harm." Think what you can do to help alleviate some of your guests' pain. Following are just some of the irritants, small and large, that you may find causing you to bite your tongue:

Little Jimmy won't go to sleep unless one of his parents lies down with him? For hours, interfering with your dinner plans? Don't make a big deal of it. Put a plate in the oven for the parent. Or call the restaurant, tell them you will be late, and put out some snacks while you wait. Of course, over an hour and all bets are off! Make up a plate with a note for the parent and take care of your other guests.

Grossed out by that tattoo on your nephew's... well... *wherever?* Sure you can tell him you're not crazy about it, but remember what you did when you were his age? I say no more.

Your niece is dressed like a pole dancer? Tell her that although you think the outfit is cute for the clubs, it will not work for breakfast with Grandpa (yes, blame others when necessary and done out of earshot). Later you may joke with your sister that Dad would never have let you or your sister out of the house that way! Make your point, but do it nicely.

Little George has "eating issues"? You're all having hot dogs and hamburgers but little George will have none of it! He wants only French fries! So what do you do? If you have some, feed him French fries. Now is not the time or the place to try to correct any behavior you find offensive or force the child to do something out of the norm. If you are too busy feeding the other eight children, nicely ask his parents if they would mind making the fries. Now, if he only wants something you don't have or that would be inconvenient to try to "whip up," then a solution must be found by the parents. If you are entertaining the child sans the parents then do what you must. But bear in mind that it's *never* a good idea to try to camouflage asparagus spears with ketchup.

A rambunctious preschooler has broken a lamp... or spilled grape juice on your new sofa... or torn a foot-wide hole in your screen door. The price of having children, or any guest, in your home is that unfortunate things do happen. If the child is visibly upset, make every effort not to show (too much) concern. It will only further add to the trauma. When those things have happened in my own home I do my best to make the child know it is not "a big deal"—even if it is. I quickly retrieve the broom or whatever is called for and tell the child that accidents happen! However, just because you are acting all jovial and devil-may-care, the child's parent should offer to pay to replace or repair whatever damage was done. If you feel they should and they do not, you have only two options: forget about it, or ask the parent later, and in private, that you would like it righted. The satisfactory response from the guest, or the lack thereof, will determine when, and if, you have them back again. Just don't fight that battle in the heat of it.

Parents too lax? Is it hard to differentiate the children from the couch? Do they toss the football from the kitchen out the window in an attempt to unrest the sleeping dog on the lawn? Do they have their faces stuck in Facebook instead of their forks stuck in your meatloaf?

Tolerance is a wonderful trait, but you must know when to draw the line in the sandbox. If you don't speak up you will only remember that you gave in to unacceptable behavior, which means you will more than likely not have them back. But avoid putting them on the defensive. Instead of criticizing their behavior ("Get your lazy butt off the couch!"), give them a positive directive ("Could you set the table for me, please?").

Parents too strict? Let's say your child is used to having a sweet treat in the afternoon, but your guest has a strict no-sugar policy. Not one Gummy Bear! But the sugar-free tot looks pleadingly on, big eyes filling with tears while your child heartily chomps on his treat. There may be a perfectly good reason your guest's child is not allowed sweets. Don't judge or second-guess and—most importantly—don't let it get to you. Be tolerant of a parent's right to refuse the Gummy Bear! To be kind, you may want to give your child his treat when the other child is not present.

The visit is not the time to discuss the relative strictness or laxity of your guests' parenting style, unless it is truly a large problem. If you feel ready to call the police, by all means talk to the parent, but do it in a relaxed venue, away from the children. Do keep in mind that all parents parent differently, and each child is unique. If you learn to let the little things go, the big things—like your relationships—will flourish during the visit.

I know all this is sometimes more difficult than a Cirque du Soleil routine, but here's the bottom line: you have to respect how the parent is raising the child, but you also have to be comfortable enough with how they behave in your home to want them back. It is a fine line to walk, so if in doubt, it's always best to err on the side of biting your tongue.

Remember, the visit is only for a few days, and the most important thing is making wonderful memories for the kids, right? So don't let the small things ruffle your feathers. When things don't go as planned or just get too crazy, remember the oft-used hippie verbiage... and chill.

When Your Tolerance Is Tested Beyond Human Limits

Do you have teenage guests sleeping until noon, throwing their clothes about the house, and not leaving a tabletop unscathed? Fear not! You are not alone! This is high on the list of host complaints. You have only two options: ignore it until they go away; or, if you dare, complain directly to them or their parents.

First, cut some of your stress off at the pass by not planning that hiking trip for eight o'clock in the morning. Or, if you absolutely have to go somewhere at the crack of dawn, say ten a.m., set several alarms in your young guest's bedroom and be prepared to listen to them go off until you see the wild-haired, bleary-eyed young ones stumble from the room. If that fails, simply sneak in with the proverbial bucket of cold water, or, as my father used to do, unleash the family dogs who will lick faces, jump, and carry on until we were either up and yelling or laughing. Properly managing teenagers takes work and no small dose of courage. If not handled from the beginning of the day, the next time you see them will most likely be at dusk, in the kitchen, food and dirty dishes littering the counter, your car keys in their hands....

And whatever you do don't look around during the (hopefully short) time you are in their room. That will only add to your distress. Come in, throw water, and make a quick exit. It's really best that way.

If you choose to complain directly to them, try this approach: "You know, Matt and Doug, I was a teenager once and remember how important sleeping in was, but if you don't get your butts out of bed this morning, those great big steaks I was planning on grilling for you guys for lunch I am feeding to the dogs." Yes, bribery and threats work.

There is always the stubborn one who will not go. Who will not do. Who just—will not! Now is the time to stay cool, very, very cool. You have had this particular event planned for weeks, your last nerve is stretched tight, and now one of the little buggers refuses to go! Your best defense is a good offense. First, go find the parent. If there is no parent this visit, consider telling the uncooperative child something similar to the following: "There will be no ice cream or pony rides after dinner if you do not come with us this morning and enjoy the event."

Yes, of course he did get ice cream that evening, but it seemed that darn pony had to cancel. Oh, well.

The eight-year-old taunts the dog endlessly. She races about the place leaving chaos in her wake. Magic marker in hand, she races down the hall, using your house as her personal canvas. She refuses to eat and then wants everything you don't have. If she makes one more pass at the cat with the fly swatter you will lose it. Here is a thought: save yourself. Find other children for her to torment! Is there a playgroup you can find through your church or synagogue? A neighbor who has children? Since you will probably not be able to rent one, go to a water park or any park and look for mothers who are congregated. There you may find solace... at least for a few hours.

Jami and Kaylan are locked in the kind of preteen sibling war that knows no end. You are sure the demons of hell treat each other better. From what they do in your presence you can't imagine what they are up to when your back is turned—so you don't. You are scared to death that blood will be shed or at least your living room torn to bits. The words any adult would instantly respond to, like "Stop hitting your coworker," are lost on these two and you finally understand why the world is in the state that it is. But then, as if to add to the confusion, as soon as it started it magically stops. They end up giggling as they roll on the floor and you sigh with relief. But then one pushes a little too hard and they start at each other again. It quickly escalates out of control.

Take immediate action: divide and conquer. You take one someplace and another adult takes the other. If you are the only adult within miles, well, good luck. The threat of punishment, usually enough to stop the behavior for at least ten minutes, may not be your best course of action in this particular situation. Perhaps distraction is a more apt strategy. For best results distract with unhealthy food or video games, or as one mother put it: "Bribe with sugar."

Finally, here's a bit of advice you are *really* going to appreciate right about now: do your best not to raise your voice to the children. A friend told me they listen better if you are quieter and I think she is spot-on. Besides, it only scares the bejeebers out of everyone, including the adults.

Money Matters: Honor Your Guests' Financial Situation

NOTHING WILL BE MORE EMBARRASSING TO A GUEST THAN not being able to pay for something their child wants or is expected to do. As host you must be very attuned to this. Among family and friends there are varying levels of financial ability. No matter who has more, you or your guests, it is bound to create some anxiety at some point during the visit.

Elsewhere in this book I talk about the best way to handle monetary situations among and between host and guest and how to plan to avoid problems. But when hosting children some things are bound to come up that were not planned. So who pays? And no, the answer is not the one who can better afford it. Let's consider a few things:

You've had enough and know that everyone could use a child break, so you would like to get a baby-sitter so the adults can be free for a few hours. This luxury is on you. When you suggest it, if your guest says they absolutely demand to split the cost with you, fine, but only then. If funds are low, pick one of the more responsible teenagers to do the deed and repay them by making their favorite meal the next day or something similar.

You have made, or are making, a reservation for everyone for lunch or dinner, so *you* are treating the group. If you don't want to go out, or can't afford it, don't make the reservation.

If your guest has said they will treat, pick a moderately priced restaurant, or, if you know they are financially strapped, choose a lower-priced venue. Chances are good they are not familiar with local restaurants so it is up to you to make that decision. Err on the side of moderation unless you are certain price is no object.

Just because you can afford some expensive excursion or entertainment don't assume your guests can. The children have all decided that they just *have* to go see the Red Sox vs. the Yankees. Tickets are expensive. You could afford it, but you are quite sure your guests cannot. You have two options, and as host it is your responsibility to do one or the other:

1. *Tell the children that is not a good idea because (insert excuse here) or,*
2. *Take the parents off alone and tell them that if it's okay with them, you would like to treat everyone to the tickets. Never embarrass your guests by agreeing that everyone will go to the game before privately consulting with them, and when and if necessary, blame yourself for disappointing the children.*

Split the check: I like this idea when the parties are about evenly matched in number. It is easy to do these days, is no longer seen as tasteless, and will not have one party feel that they were always the ones that paid. It works in today's society and credit or debit cards make this a snap for the waitperson. Just hand your server both and tell him or her to evenly split the bill.

Let's assume you, as host, have no children and your guests have several. What should be expected? There are a few options:

If your guests can afford it they should pay for the entire meal out (treating you for your hosting generosities), or you can offer to split the bill equally.

You can agree that you will pay for yourself (and your partner) and they will pay for themselves and their six children.

Or, if you are better-off, you can pay for everything—that is nice to do, but not always.

Confused? Don't be. Even wealthy hosts complain that guests come with their children and assume the hosts (because they are well-off) will pay for absolutely everything the family eats, drinks, and enjoys. This upsets the Visit Wizard and it is not because it is wrong for people with lots of money to pay for people with little money. That's actually nice. No, it's because it goes against human nature. You, as host, will come to resent it. Therefore even if you can pay for everything, don't. Give your guests an opportunity to pay for something, even if it is a little something. When should visiting guests with children pay? That is addressed in the Visiting with Children and Young Adult Confidential chapter, page 216.

Let your guests know the cost of whatever it is you want to do and let them decide and always offer them an out. Giving choices is the most tactful way to handle it. For example, everyone has decided to go out to dinner that night and split the check. You might say, "We could go to the new swanky five-star restaurant that is a bit pricey, but excellent, or we could go to a more modest-priced restaurant that has a great view of the water." They can then opt for the water view without revealing it was really the price that mattered.

"Bye-Bye!": Ending on a High Note

ALTHOUGH I REPEAT MYSELF, THIS BEING ADDRESSED IN chapter 3, it is justified: how you treat your young guests upon departure is just as important, if not more so, than how you welcomed them. Why do I say this? Because everyone is usually excited and on their best behavior when the visit is just starting! Not so much at the end. People, even the youngsters, are usually tired, maybe not looking forward to that long trip home, or just mentally spent from all the activity.

If the visit did go well then this part is a breeze. If it did not, remember that bad memories fade. It's a really good human survival mechanism.

Remember that when you would rather boot them out the door than hug them goodbye.

VISIT WIZARD TIP Don't forget to get everyone together for a photo. It will make a nice gift. Best to do it in the first day or two of the visit.

So no matter how it went, hugs and kisses for the children is most important. Unless some unbelievable horror struck, in *their* eyes things were fine and it was fun. Don't let them feel otherwise. And whatever you do, don't let any gripe you may have with the grownups transfer down to the child. In adulthood some people still remember a nasty word or being treated unkindly by an adult during a visit.

Hosting children is one of the more fun things you can do, for yourself and for your own children, if you have them. All it requires is lots of patience, an abundance of love, and the ability to remember way back when.

CHAPTER 5

Hosting Older Guests

"A good head and a good heart are always a formidable combination."

—NELSON MANDELA,

who on his eighty-ninth birthday announced the formation of The Elders, a group of leaders established to contribute wisdom and leadership to address the world's toughest problems.

WITH A LITTLE LESS WORK THAN IS REQUIRED TO GAIN world peace, but just as much heart, hosting an older guest can be one of the most rewarding experiences in life. I don't think that's a stretch. Here's why:

Besides all the usual planning and logistics of the visit, there are needed other ingredients which can't be bought, borrowed, or prepared: The basic human virtues of patience, kindness, and empathy are even more important than your beautifully turned-out guest room. Part of the art of the perfect visit with elders is to remember that older people need the same emotional and physical things we all need—just doubled.

"What?!"

I can hear you now: "Not only do I have crazy Uncle Ed, the twins from hell, complete with dogs, coming for the weekend, but now you tell me hosting older guests takes—not just good house etiquette—but the milk of human kindness on steroids?" Yes! And therein lies the rewards part. To be the robust, dynamic people they still are, older people need to see and experience friends and family: to feel wanted, loved, and cared for. Loneliness and mental and physical inactivity are worse for your older loved ones than most of their ailments. Sure there are special considerations when hosting people with some minor (and not so minor) disabilities, but it will all be so much easier for you—and better for them—if you pay attention to the few, and very basic, human needs.

Reassuring Your Older Visitor

"I measure every grief I meet with narrow, probing eyes.
I wonder if it weighs like mine or has an easier side."

—EMILY DICKINSON

YOU KNOW THAT EIGHTY-NINE-YEAR-OLD AUNT EDNA IS COMING and she has a bad hip. Your aged father and mother are on their way with your brother and his children. How can you help ensure that they are comfortable, both physically *and* mentally? Let's take the mental part first: quell their fears and apprehensions. Don't worry, this is easy, but should be done before the visit.

To the extent that you can, let the older guest—and the person coming with them if they are not visiting alone—know what they will be doing. Are there any special events planned? What is the weather expected to be? You might then suggest the right style and weight of clothing. Granny, just like us all, wants to look her best for that event or dinner out and will be just as embarrassed as the 'tweeners if she does not fit in.

Unless you planned a surprise birthday party for your older guest and you are sure he will be ecstatic, let him know who else is coming to visit so there are no surprises of the negative kind, like this one:

> *"I really had no idea that after all this time those two still held a grudge, but the tension was so thick you really could cut it with a knife. We managed to get through the weekend without bloodshed but I will never have them back at the same time. Who would have known two eighty-year-olds still remembered!"*

Reassure your older guests by letting them know where they will be sleeping and that you have prepared the room for any special needs they might have.

Buy the right food and drink. Ask them what they normally drink and eat and have it stocked before their arrival. If you get the "Anything, dear!" don't buy it. Keep asking and insist they tell you, that way you can get their favorite snacks even if they are unhealthy and indulgent. Who would have known a "sweet tooth" is a curse of the young *and* old? You will benefit from knowing their likes and dislikes and they will appreciate that you care. You will alleviate their concern, as their memory is good enough to recall that you live basically on bean sprouts and tofu. Your getting what they like and are used to, and not deviating from their diet or normal eating routine is important for many reasons, some medical, some psychological.

Ask them, or confirm again, what special needs they have, such as a wheelchair or oxygen. They may have other issues since last you saw them.

Know their travel plans and make sure you have the specific details. Make any necessary arrangement with the airline or train, for example, having them met with a wheelchair. If you are concerned that your guest who is traveling alone may not be able to comfortably make it from the gate to where you are at security, most airlines will gladly assist.

Make certain your older guest has your complete contact information including cell phone number and street address and that they carry it with them.

Check what your older guests are bringing. If they are forgetful, have them make a list with you over the phone of things such as medications, clothing, and the like.

Encourage them to bring their medications in the bottles in which they came, which have the warning labels, not just a pill container with those many little compartments. Recipe for disaster, I assure you. If you meet with resistance, tell them that it's just for your own peace of mind as there are several people in the house who take meds and you want to make sure there is no mix-up. I have seen more than one older guest not able to remember what pills they took when, or indeed even how many they were supposed to be taking.

Offer to make any outside arrangements they might require before they leave their home, like having someone come in to take care of the cat or check the house while they are visiting you.

Remember to make any arrangements they may need while they are visiting you. For example, will your older guest need in-home care from a health care provider? If they are receiving some assistance at home, knowing they will have the same opportunity while staying with you will give them comfort.

Preparing Your Home

"You know you're getting old when you start putting parts of yourself on the dresser."

—EARL ZOOK,
hiking the Appalachian Trail at age eighty-nine to raise money for cancer research.

FOR DETAILED IDEAS ABOUT PREPARING YOUR HOUSE IN general, please refer to the Creating a Welcoming Home chapter starting on page 12.

Here are specific things your older guest may or may not need, but will definitely appreciate:

The Bathroom

"Age before beauty" should be the operating principle when preparing the guest bath. Your older guest could care less that your towels clash with the wall color or that the fixtures haven't been updated since the Eisenhower era. In fact, they may feel more at home. What you need to be concerned about is *function.*

Elders can have a tough time getting in and out of the tub for a bath or shower. Although walk-in showers with handrails are the best solution, not all of us can call the handyman before the visit. There are suction-mounted handles you can purchase that can help, but depending on the age and condition of your guest, you may want to offer personal assistance.

Make sure there is a good-sized anti-slip mat in the tub and shower. For folks who need even more help, a specially designed chair that fits in the bathtub and a sprayer hose attached to the tub faucet might do the trick.

A chair or small bench with feet that don't slide might be a good idea in the walk-in shower as well so the elder can sit. I can see you eyeing that dining room chair now. Not a good idea...

A raised toilet seat might also be welcome.

Walk around: If the elder uses a walker or cane, do they have enough room to maneuver in the bathroom?

Look around: Check to make sure all necessary items, such as towels and toilet tissue, are easily accessible. Would bath towels be best in a basket on the floor rather than on a high-placed shelf or hook, for example?

Make sure there is a plastic drinking cup and a place for false teeth. No one wants to put teeth on a vanity! Just a small, pretty dish for this purpose would be a nice touch.

Remove all medications that are not the older guest's from the medicine cabinet in the bathroom. Again, you want to do your best to prevent any confusion over meds.

Although said in other chapters, it is more important than ever that your guest bathroom be clutter free.

The Bedroom

Besides the niceties and necessities for a comfy bedroom listed in the Creating a Welcoming Home chapter, consider the following.

Is that antique, down-topped, giant of a bed that takes a step ladder to get into and in which a small dog can get lost the best bet for your older guest, or should you use one with an easier entry and exit? Will they need help getting into and out of bed? Avoid using steps unless they are short and sturdy.

A night-light in the room is a must for obvious reasons, and make sure their path to the bathroom is well lit and clutter free.

A bell or whistle on the nightstand within easy reach is a good idea in case they need you in the night. Remind them it is not to summon the cook, unless you really *want* to serve them breakfast in bed.

Extra blankets at the foot of the bed are a good idea. As people age their ability to tolerate cold decreases, but stay clear of the electric blanket. Some older guests might turn it on high and fail to either turn it down before falling asleep or be unable to easily reach the temperature adjuster during the night which could lead to a mishap. I make sure to ask if the bed is comfortable. Old bones need comfort and deserve it.

Having a sturdy chair in the bedroom is important so the older guest can easily get shoes and socks on and off.

If stairs are a problem, turn a downstairs room into a bedroom by putting in a cot. Just make sure you make it as comfortable as possible (see chapter 1, Small Space Solutions, on page 27). If your guest must go upstairs but has difficulty and there is a large enough landing, put a sturdy chair at the landing so she can take a break.

VISIT WIZARD TIP You may have noticed that I am big on notes. Leave a note, written in large letters, on your guest's nightstand or pillow telling her how happy you are she is visiting and encouraging her to let you know anything she might need.

Kitchen and Dining

Will your older guest be comfortable in the dining room or at the kitchen table for meals? I once saw a woman come into a restaurant with tape measure in hand, checking tables' heights for an elderly couple that were going to be her guest for dinner the following evening. I presume she was making sure the wheelchair would fit under the table. A considerate thing to do.

Pull a chair into the kitchen area so the elder can be part of the action but still comfortable. Those tall bar stools at the counter may not be the best option.

Watch for water on the floor or knives left on the counter or in the sink. Love that heavy, cut-glass pitcher for your orange juice? You may want to put it away. And if Grandmother Gurdy wears those flowing, long-sleeved gossamer gowns, best not to ask her to whip up Bananas Foster on your gas range.

In and Around the Place

View your house through "older eyes." Look at your environment like an older person would. Keep in mind that you are used to navigating around your home and don't see the danger it can pose to an elderly person. One of the most important things you can do is look down. Yes, down. Are there throw rugs to be slipped on? Does the floor go from flat wood or tile to plush carpet thereby creating a small rise that can be tripped over?

Check the halls: Are hallways doing double duty as children's closets, with toys and clothes strewn about? Are there extension cords or wires that can become entangled with a walker, or tipsy tables or umbrella stands easily upset?

Your older guest may be coming for a first visit and may not know the house, may have a difficult time adjusting, may overindulge in different food and drink, may be excited or nervous, all of which could lead to confusion or dizziness, which could lead to a loss of balance.

VISIT WIZARD TIP I know you have a lot on your plate, but preventing falls has to be a goal for the good host. Falls can result in fractures that often do not mend and the elder is reduced to bed . . . or worse.

What else do you see that is a potential hazard? While writing this I am mostly on the couch, on my back from an injury, so it's not hard for me to be in that mindset. Knees bent, laptop perched on stomach, I am in constant pain, can't bend over—you get the picture. So from this position I am looking at the sliding glass doors, too easy to accidently walk into. Put stickers on yours, or a little suction cup and hang something pretty so people know when it's closed. They're fun to make—you can coordinate them with your décor—and better than stickers as they are easy to remove when and if necessary. Do you really want cartoonlike stickers in your Louis the XIV living room? See the Resources section (page 271) for ideas. Someone accused me of having my glass *too* clean. No, really?

Whether your main gathering room is a family room or the kitchen, is there a comfortable chair either in the middle of the action or slightly apart from it? Does it have a side table where a drink or a book is within easy reach... with a view of the outdoors, perhaps, and good lighting?

As people age they require more light to see well. Now is not the time to set the dimmer switches to low, but it may be time to break out the soft music of yesteryear. Familiar, soothing sounds help people relax and often bring back fond memories.

I make a designated place for my older guest's things so they are more easily located. And if your elder wears glasses and cannot always find them, buy your guest a chain that goes around the neck to which the glasses attach. Or make them, as I do. Ideas and instructions are available. Check the Resources section (page 271). Having things organized and easy to find makes life much easier for everyone!

The Outside

Don't forget to walk around the outside of your house. Are the steps to the house difficult? Is the sidewalk cracked? Is snow or ice a concern? Is there a step up or down in the path where they could fall or catch a shoe? You may want to get some yellow duct tape or caution tape and put a strip down at that spot.

Do you have an in-ground pool? Check the ladder to make sure it is secure. Ours has a very large ladder that descends deep into the shallow end. During construction I suggested we get one smaller, more attractive, and less obvious but after some thought nixed that idea: The large ladder is better for older people to grab on to. We also have a swim-out bench in the deep end that aids in that process. We have a floating lounge chair and those long Styrofoam noodle things, but I have drawn the line at the round life preserver. Use caution if your older guest wants to use the floating devices. They are easily upended and often very difficult to get in and out of. Never leave your older guest in or around the pool alone or in the care of a young person who may not be able to get them to safety should that be necessary.

Be very mindful of the sun. While you are happily basking in the rays working on that perfect tan, your elder should be under an umbrella, cool drink in hand.

So as you examine your space and your world, imagine yourself with poor eyesight, hard of hearing, and difficulty walking. Ahh... now you've got it!

Respecting Your Elders

WEREN'T WE ALL TAUGHT AS CHILDREN TO RESPECT OUR elders? But often it's just as meaningless a concept for adults as it is for the young. As a culture we respect rock stars. We say, "Hey, man, you're a rock star!" Not, "Hey, man, you're a geezer!" (not even if we're talking Mick Jagger).

Since the older person is a guest in your home, you have to treat him or her with the same respect and courtesy as you do every other guest—and then some. Why? Because they naturally feel a bit insecure, having lost some of the moxie of youth, and may often feel in the way or unwanted.

So I give you: R-E-S-P-E-C-T, a song by Aretha Franklin and spelled out by yours truly, the Visit Wizard (still working on Rock Star status):

Make the elder ***R**elevant*: Don't forget them as they sit in the chair in the living room while you are busy with the children or your other guests. Make a conscious effort to include them as much as you can. And it has to be conscious, because naturally the loudest noise gets the most attention.

The complaining child, the barking dog or the missing cat, the demanding partner, the messy house... remember that those pressing matters of the moment will, in all likelihood, be around longer than your aged loved one, so give them as much of your ***E**nergy* as you can.

Respect them by ***S**upporting* them. They don't feel like going to the zoo with everyone else today? Don't say, suit yourself and let them sit home. Instead, support their decision and have someone else take the kids to the zoo or postpone it for another day.

Don't take away their ***P**restige*. When they were younger they were working hard, maybe running a business or working at home, raising children. Whatever they did, to some extent they were in command. They were certainly in command of their own thoughts and bodies. Now, not so much. Don't steal their power by belittling their opinions or treating them any less than the experienced, mature adults they are.

Part of how we show respect to people of any age is in how we ***E**ngage* them, even more so with your older guests. Don't talk down to an elder person and don't talk about them as if they weren't in the room. Talk to them in a calm voice—never shout. It will just create anxiety for everyone. Even when frustrated with their hearing loss, try to concentrate on the elder and what they are saying. A friend has a hundred-year-old aunt who has been going increasingly deaf, yet refuses to get a hearing aid. Here is how she gracefully handles it:

"My aunt has her reasons, and though I would love for her to be able to

hear better, I have to respect her wishes. So when I speak to her, I sidle up very close, lean in, and talk in a natural—albeit slightly louder—voice directly into her ear. She can hear me quite well this way. If she's happy, I'm happy. And—even more importantly—I listen to what she has to say."

When engaging with an elder there is nothing worse than arguing with him. It will get you absolutely nowhere and only cause you to feel bad later, especially if you've won the argument! So what if his memory is faulty or he's positive you said something you didn't? Let it go. Often older folks are more reluctant to back down from an argument or admit when they are wrong. They don't want to appear, or admit, that they can't remember.

VISIT WIZARD TIP Don't ask your older guest to reveal their age because you think your neighbor Marty will get a hoot out of knowing Aunty Gracie is ninety. It often embarrasses people of a certain generation. If Aunty Gracie wants anyone to know, she can tell them herself. It also just shows a lack of class to ask people their age—whatever their age.

Let older people know that their opinions and concerns about their life ***Count*** by hearing them, sticking to their timetable, and respecting their needs. If they have to eat by 5 p.m. it is probably for a good reason. That just means that they eat before the rest of the crowd. And, if your guest is used to eating certain things, respect that. If you want to make something different for dinner, ask them first. The last thing you want to do is set down corn-on-the-cob, not realizing there may be a false-teeth issue, which they were too embarrassed to mention.

People get used to certain things and find it hard to deviate. So don't be offended if Granny does not want to try your duck confit. Perhaps chicken soup instead. Think comfort food instead of sushi. There are always exceptions, of course, and if you have an adventurous older guest, great, just err on the side of caution. Some things may not be easily digested.

Give older folks your ***Time***. If they are the only one visiting this is not hard to do. Except if they're your partner's parent, then it seems you can become very busy doing this and that and running here and there! We are all busy. It is the way we have allowed our lives to become. We all act as if our time is never ending. Our elders know better.

Finally, treating older people with the respect they deserve (no matter how often they get cranky), which means really seeing them and really hearing them, will show your children how *you* should be treated in future.

VISIT WIZARD TIP Although this should not have to be said, don't allow anyone to pick on or joke about an elderly person. It's just a terrible thing to do. I know it's funny to the kids when they point to the car ahead on the street and roll with laughter saying that there is no one driving the car because they can't see the older person's head above the head rest, and that is harmless, I agree, but there are those among us who are mean to old people. When that happens, it makes the Visit Wizard want to take the Visit Wizard stick and bust somebody upside the head . . . in a nice way, of course.

However, respect is a two-way street. If it is one way the visit will surely be a disaster. Older people must be just as respectful to their host as the host is to them. Some elders use their age as an excuse for either engaging in bad manners or trying to get everything their way. Of course it's hard to be nice all the time when you're in pain or have to deal with all the other problems that come with old age, but don't allow your older guest to disrespect you, your family, or your home. Be firm, but in as kind a way as possible. You, after all, have a long life ahead (we assume).

Making the Visit Memorable

"...thus began my father's own private adventure... his vacation took on a life of its own. As he whiled away his afternoons on the bench, he was entertained by a snake charmer, treated to a political debate, and hit on by two hookers."

—ERMA BOMBECK

MOST OF US HAVE ELDERLY FAMILY MEMBERS WHO HAVE passed on and often we regret that we did not spend more time with them doing, well, just fun stuff. I recall the last time my parents came for a summer vacation visit. They are not elderly, but still I went out of my way to make sure they were having downright, old-fashioned fun instead of schlepping with me on mundane errands or sitting around while I worked on... whatever. We played games and did some sports, took walks, watched movies, and talked. My father and my husband had lively debates over favorite stocks and politics. We did all the cooking so Mom didn't have to set foot in the kitchen; instead, she did her best to teach me how to knit (that didn't really work, but that's not the point).

The goal is to plan activities in which your older guest can participate to the best of their abilities. The saddest thing is when elders are left alone in a chair while everyone is having a good time—unless they want to be there. But even if they claim they do, do your best to include them or get them involved in something of interest to them.

Does Grandfather play golf, or would he be more up to putt-putt golf with the kids? Would your female guest like her hair done, or can you invite some neighborhood friends of her era over for cards?

VISIT WIZARD TIP To the extent possible, clear your work and social commitments while your older guests are visiting. It is not as easy for them, as for your younger guests to independently find things to do and it's so nice when you can spend dedicated time with them.

I remember as a young person not really knowing what to do with my elderly relatives. What do you talk about with someone several times your age? As host, it is your responsibility to help. When in doubt, turn to these tried and true activities:

Simple works: Sit around the kitchen table and talk, or do some simple household task, like folding laundry together. This may sound odd, but there is fellowship and contentment found in the ordinary and routine. Remember when women used to gather at a table and make quilts together? I have a very vivid memory of my grandmother teaching me how to fold a fitted bed sheet. I still haven't mastered it, impossible to properly fold round corners if you ask me, but to this day I remember that simple chore as a loving expression of her patience with a young girl.

Games: People of almost any age can build a puzzle. No talking necessary, just good bonding. A child can get involved by helping the older person find pieces. Checkers is another good game, as is cards if your older guest still has the mental ability.

Activities with the younger ones: Having the kids show your older guests the latest cool gadgets, or having them help a child with simple activities like coloring, reading, or being read to is all good. Why not bring back some memories, or start new ones, by baking cookies or pies with the children? This is an easy task for everyone and will surely be enjoyed. Put a chair near the action so the elder can sit if necessary but still participate in the fun.

If you have a pet that is docile and well behaved, by all means introduce it to your elder guest. There is an exciting fact that older people who enjoy pets are better-off: They get more exercise; they have companionship; and stroking and loving a pet can lower blood pressure and lessen stress. See the Resources section (page 271) for information about bringing pets and older people together.

Stimulate the senses: Go to a museum or on a tour. Some museums and galleries are adding wings specifically for exhibits that your older guest might enjoy. If they are interested, a library is often a good place for activities like lectures on interesting and often historical subjects. There may be a club or senior center in your area that offers "Senior Day Care." I dislike that term. Let's call it "Elders Out" or "On-Going Elder Education" or something more respectful. But no matter what you call it, this could be a good place for the older guest to get involved in some interesting activities.

Read, or have another guest read, something aloud that the older person might like. You can find a quiet spot and once you start you may be surprised who you might attract.

Get up and get out: If your older guest is physically able, go for a walk and take the kids or dog. Some mild depression in elders, and all of us, is much improved just by light daily exercise.

Crafts: Although fun, this does not work well for all elders. They are often frustrated when they can't easily learn a new skill and sometimes feel foolish or embarrassed because of it. Unless it is something they already know how to do, or is easily mastered, avoid anything difficult. Scrapbooking is a nice thing to do that is not difficult. Ask if your guest would like to bring some old photographs and help put together an album or collage. Anything you can do that brings back happy memories and is something they can take home from the visit is great.

Your interest and hobbies: If you do something of interest, from herb growing to model ship building, by all means show off your work to your older guest. They will most likely have an interest in what you do and how you do it. I remember my mother doing this with my grandmother and the three of us laughing and having a great time over some project or another. It is the camaraderie that counts, not the finished product.

In their day: Reminisce. One great way to get the conversation started and get others involved is to ask what things were like in their day, or to talk about past events or politics. What do they remember from the past and what was it like to live through? Have them recall growing up, and the houses they lived in. Many people record the conversations for future generations. Great idea if your older guest agrees.

Teach a new skill: If they have never tried making pasta from scratch or pesto that might be fun to do together. The important thing is to enjoy it—don't worry so much how it comes out. And be prepared for the "Where is the ___?" kitchen item and "Well, *I* wouldn't do it that way!" Smile and bear it.

Take them for a slow ride on the Internet superhighway. Not at race-car speed, but show them all the fabulous things the net has to offer or help them research something important to them.

Allow for downtime: Let your older guests know that an afternoon nap is fine by you or they might not suggest it. Don't keep the schedule so full that it wears them out. Usually one outing a day is enough.

And no, mindless television watching does not count as an activity unless it's an old movie that everyone can enjoy—together.

Include your older guest, even if they aren't family: Here is a good example: My husband and I took his mother to visit my brother, sister-in-law, and their large family overseas. It was Christmas. We had opened gifts at our own home before we went to visit them. We were staying at their home through New Year's and it just seemed like the prudent thing to do. We had enough baggage to carry on a very long flight! After we happily watched the children and my brother's family open gifts for a good part of the day, I was so incredibly touched to see my brother and sister-in-law present my mother-in-law with the most wonderful gifts! And not just an after-thought or small token. These were thought-out, beautifully wrapped gifts. It was so unexpected, and so thoughtful, it is hard to convey how that made us feel. I can tell you one thing: my mother-in-law never failed to mail them a Christmas card every year and ask about them every time we spoke; she even displayed in her living room along with pictures of her own children and grandchildren a photo of all of us taken that long-ago Christmas. It was not the gifts that touched her—it was the fact that through that simple act the family conveyed that they were truly pleased she was in their home for the holidays. And what a wonderful thing to show their children. So, the first-ever "Visit Wizard Award for Gracious Hosting: Holiday Category" goes to—that family.

Finally, there is a fine line between convincing an elderly person to try something new, or join the group in some activity, and forcing the issue. I have found that some elderly people will not want to go somewhere or do something because they are hurting that day, or tired, or afraid, but they would rather strap on that parachute than tell you that. Their pride forbids it, or they may not want to ruin everyone else's good time. So, be mindful that they don't agree to something that may be harmful to them just to please you. If you can get them alone and gently probe you can sometimes discover the truth.

Use your best judgment in how much pressure you apply in your insistence they attend. If they persist in wanting to stay home, don't push it. They know best. Understand and, if possible, bring someone in to be with them when the group goes out, or have family members rotate and stay with them. And if they are able to stay home alone, make sure the phone is easily accessible and your cell number is written down. Don't expect them to remember it should they need to call you.

Understanding and Empathy

"A friend knows the song in my heart and sings it to me when my memory fails."
—DONNA ROBERTS, AUTHOR

WHEN WITH YOUR ELDER GRANDPARENT, PARENT, SIBLING, or friend you become frustrated, impatient, agitated, or tired, or when things are simply not going well and stress is the emotion of the moment, stop, take a breath, and try to imagine the way it must feel to be old:

You are tired, annoyed at your body for not doing what your mind asks of it. Often you are frightened because you are confused or unsure. Sometimes that fear translates into anger when you don't mean it to. You want to get to know the grandchildren better, but they have their own interests and are no longer interested in you. You want to help your grown child with a problem, but it is too complex. Often you feel unwanted and unworthy, dependent at best, needy at worst. Nobody really sees you anymore.

Is it any wonder our elders sometimes become irritable and demanding? Understanding their concerns and empathizing alleviates that fear and makes for a happier, less-anxious older guest—which makes for a better visit.

Understand that physical and mental abilities and interests change as we age. Let's say your grandmother was once a great cook. Don't expect or assume the same level of competence or interest now. And even if she wants to show off her knife skills, you may want to discourage it by asking her to critique yours. However, if your guest wants to help, by all means let them. Just don't tell your aged mother-in-law that you always thought her pasta sauce was bland—at least not if she has the chef's knife in hand.

Don't expect the older guest to know how that new fancy gadget or piece of equipment works. Take the time to explain. And don't rush them or confuse them: now is *not* the time to ask for assistance in creating that complicated meal for eight with each dish time critical.

The visit is not the venue to discuss anything controversial or painful, if it can possibly be avoided. If you must talk seriously about a difficult issue, it is best to do that quietly and alone. If your elderly guest starts a discussion that has the potential to be, well, deadly, like why someone isn't yet married, or when young Steve is going to get serious about school, defuse it quickly. Don't waste precious time trying to change their opinion. There are other, better, times to discuss these things, if they need to be discussed at all. If you can't avoid it, try to make light of the situation and do not side with any one party against the other. In this case your safest bet is to stay neutral.

VISIT WIZARD TIP If your older guest has a physical or mental disability, explain it to the children in terms they can understand. That way the child will be less afraid or hesitant, and the elder will feel better knowing everyone understands. Children are not as naïve as you think. They can understand and they will be better adults for the understanding. Just be open with them.

Patience Is a Virtue—Really

YOU'RE A PATIENT PERSON. I KNOW YOU ARE. BUT THE REALITY is that there is only so much the mind can take before the final thread that holds together this super-human virtue unravels faster than a string bikini in a hot tub.

But how can you have patience and compassion when the guns of hosting warfare are going off about your head? When the "impossible to please" is back again? When you haven't heard so many "I don't wanna's" since your child was six?

Next time Grandma looks for her glasses for the seventh time in the past hour, or your Aunt Betty adds one more complaint to her ever-growing list, or your uncle Todd is *still* not ready to go out... resist the urge to roll your eyes or put your hands over your ears while screaming "let's *goooo!*"

Slow down. Take a breath. Channel Gandhi. Recall that elderly people are often uncomfortable or in some degree of pain, so getting around—quickly—is just not easy. Add to that their justifiable need to feel wanted, welcomed, and not a burden, and voilà!—a potent combination.

They are a step slower, mentally and physically. They are not up for all the things they used to be. They themselves are perhaps less patient with some things and more opinionated about others. They are cautious and concerned. And the worst part? They too often try not to show it!

So laugh with the "show off." You know him. He believes that he is a twenty-something just trapped inside an old body. Be patient with him. As long as he is not about to injure himself or others, laugh and revel in his sheer tenacity and love of life. Then there is the second childhood syndrome: Some older people regress (notice I did not say digress), acting like they did when much, much younger; wanting or demanding attention and being impatient when they don't get it. Just be patient and keep in mind that most of their adult lives may have been taken up in giving to others. They are just demanding a little "me" time. Don't we all?

Put yourself in their orthopedic stockings: None of us will know what it's like to face the end of life on this planet until we face it, so give them a break. If they are withdrawn, moody, or testy, be patient. Change the scenery, crack a joke, grab a book, and show them you care. They will come out of it... and so will you.

Final Thoughts...

THROUGHOUT THE VISIT TRY TO REMEMBER THAT YOU ARE not going to be able to enjoy the elder's company forever, so really be in the moment.

An older family member would come to visit and yes we would go here and there, but how much time did we take to really get to know each other in a deeper way? Don't get so caught up in the doing that you forget that this is perhaps the most important part of the visit. What you will remember and be thankful for when you reflect on your life and theirs is not just the two extremes of great and traumatic events, but the normal, quieter times of sitting and talking, or baking apple pies in the kitchen, as I did with my mother-in-law, who became my friend. It doesn't have to be a cliché.

Finally, embrace the elder's age. Accepting older people (especially family members) for who they are *now*, today, is one of the hardest things to successfully accomplish. You remember how they were in years gone by, or how you still want, wish, or expect them to be.

It is often difficult, but showing compassion and understanding for where and who they are at this stage in their life, with all that it means, will make *you* feel as good as it will them and will absolutely mean a better, happier, and more deeply satisfying visit for everyone. And maybe you won't mind as much that new wrinkle, because looking in the mirror will just not be as frightening.

CHAPTER 6

The Absent Host: Giving Family and Friends the Use of Your Home

"An ounce, or in this case a pound, of prevention is better than losing a friend."

—THE VISIT WIZARD

"'Tis Easy to see, hard to Foresee."

—BEN FRANKLIN, THE WORD WIZARD

SO YOU'VE GOT EVERY LITTLE THING IN PLACE. THE KITCHEN IS better organized than the celebrity chef sets of The Food Network. You even splurged on that new gadget that you absolutely did not need. The walls are painted just the right color to offset, without offending, the new window treatments that you made yourself after months of painful work on the borrowed sewing machine. Life is not only good, it's right. You have dreamed since childhood of having the perfect little vacation getaway or the perfect home. It doesn't matter where it is. It doesn't matter how big it is, and it really doesn't matter if you have a hole-patched recliner with a year's worth of newspapers lovingly spread about because there is that *one more* article you still must read. It is yours and you love it. Congratulations.

But now you are leaving and others are coming. Your hand shakes as you turn your house key over to the man in the red jacket who will make the duplicate that you will mail to your friend, cousin, brother-in-law who will be staying a weekend, a week, a month.

Fear not. If this is your first time, or if you have been letting friends and family use your home for years, the Visit Wizard will be your guide to help ensure all goes as well as... humanly... possible. So grab on to the Visit Wizard stick and off we go!

First, let's be clear lest you feel guilty: you are *not* obligated to let the cousin you can't stand or the destructive duo use your home or vacation home, or anyone else for that matter. And just because you have pets does not mean you have to allow friends or family to bring theirs. It's all very much a personal decision. I enjoyed letting others use my homes and I definitely enjoy using theirs, but things can and will go wrong. Not often, but certainly once in a while. If you are a very private person, or can't take trauma, perhaps you should have guests only when you are present. Calling the house every few hours or installing cameras in rooms is just not an option.

However, if you do decide to be generous, what is imperative is that you let your guests know in advance any issues with the house, how to operate things while there, and any serious house rules. All these things should be included in *The Visit Wizard's Guide for Guests* you are going to prepare and leave at your home. Yes, really. Don't worry. It will only take a few hours.

Timing—and Who Is Coming—Is Everything

ARE PEOPLE YOU DON'T EVEN KNOW CLAMORING FOR YOUR mountaintop condo during ski season, your beach house in the summer, or your apartment in Paris... well, anytime? Some even want to stay in your adorable little Hansel and Gretel house in the woods while you are away visiting the kids for a week? If you have the great fortune to have a vacation home or a primary home that numerous people wish to use, you may want to consider having an "every-other-year" or, depending who it is, a "once-in-your-lifetime" policy. Some people so endowed have a rule that a guest who comes at a certain time one year must skip the next year to allow someone else that time. And some say that if a guest has not read this book they may not come at all. (Not completely self-serving. Someone really smart did say that.)

Further, if a friend or family member wants to use your vacation home during a time when you would normally rent it out, it is not wrong of you to expect some form of payment. That is a personal matter between you and your guest, but it is not miserly to let them know your beach condo rents for $X per week in the summer, but you are happy to let them enjoy it for half that amount, or for merely painting the baseboards. But no matter what you decide, do not charge one friend and then let another stay for free. Word will get out!

Family members (close and not) are another kettle of fish. I am not even going there. Some of you will think how horrible of me to even *consider* charging family members, and others will make the point that a mortgage has to be paid, and even if family is going to use it, they should contribute something to its cost or its upkeep!

You may want to limit the length of stay to a certain number of days or weeks. Different people have different levels of tolerance and comfort. Again, it's your personal choice.

What to do if both a friend and a family member wish to use your home at the same time? Make up a calendar a year or more in advance (yes, as noted some homes are that much in demand), block out the time you will be using it, and then those who tell you first get their requested time slot. Of course, don't agree to five years out for obvious reasons. You may hate that person by then or your dog may have gotten it in your will. Ultimately the choice is yours. If your brother and his wife are consistently poor guests, skip them this year. They'll learn!

Most importantly, have no fear and be decisive. Perhaps you think you—or your house—could use a break. Fine! You will be forever crazy if you don't put your foot down without feelings of remorse or guilt.

A Pound of Prevention

IF YOU HAVE NOT BEEN IN YOUR VACATION HOUSE FOR SOME time, go. Make a list of anything that needs repair or is not working properly. If you can't get them fixed, due to time or money constraints, let your guests know ahead of time if, say, the air conditioner in your southern home won't be working. I love a good adventure and can be happy as moss on a tree stump in the barest and most remote of places, but I wouldn't want a roof collapsing on me, nor do I much care for the great outdoors because the plumbing is on the fritz.

Check to make sure the basics are there and in good order: sheets, towels, fireplace tools, toaster, coffeemaker, you get the idea. If you want me to come have a look, let me know.

And, as if you didn't know, in a second or vacation home things can go wrong in your absence. Squirrels can have built a nest, well... anywhere! The refrigerator could have stopped working, or the driveway could have washed away. It's best to know these things before your guests use your home.

VISIT WIZARD TIP There are door locks that have a numerical lock pad instead of a key. Good solution if you have lots of guests coming and going. Easier to give out a number than a key, and easier to change!

Do's and Don'ts for the Absent Host

Don'ts

- Don't offer your home to someone you don't trust or like. I see you rolling your eyes thinking "duh!" but you would be surprised at how many people feel obligated to do just that.
- Don't expect everyone to treat your home the way you treat it. Some may treat it better.
- Don't have anything in the house that is irreplaceable, within reason. Chances are pretty good the Rembrandt will not be sold, sliced with a knife, or paint splattered, but that hand-blown vase from Italy may bite the dust.
- Don't keep extremely personal items in the house. You know what I mean.
- Don't leave drugs or medications of any kind out anywhere. Go through your medicine cabinet.

- Don't keep a gun in the house. Although you think a specific adult may be completely responsible, you must take into account all other members of the (hunting or nonhunting) party.
- Don't leave the keys to the new convertible, or the tractor, in the house unless you want your guests to use them.
- Don't say in your exuberance, "Use anything you'd like!" They will.
- Don't be embarrassed to ask that they pay for the use of the house or at least the utility bill for the period of time they will be staying.
- Don't forget to give them the garage door and the house alarm code or you will have one unhappy guest and police department.
- Don't pop in on them unexpectedly. Not fair.

Do's

- Do let your guests know they are free to use the amenities.
- Do let them know what they are *not* free to use, like the new 36-foot catamaran or your master bedroom or the crystal wine goblets you received as a wedding gift. If you don't, don't email me and complain when the cat is grounded on some rock jetty.
- Do let your guests know whatever cannot go into the dishwasher. Leave notes taped to the inside of cabinets, if necessary.
- Do buy the nonscratch pads if your countertops scratch, and leave a note for your guests to use only those.
- Do password-protect your personal computer unless you want your guest to use it freely.
- Do block out certain cable television channels if children or young adults will be visiting, if necessary.

- Do put away any personal or business papers.
- Do leave operational and instructional notes where needed. Be liberal.
- Do expect to see the occasional scratched or broken item.
- Do expect your guest to offer to pay for any scratched or broken item. Whether you take them up on the offer is up to you.
- Do ask them to do some minor task that needs doing if they are staying for any length of time. No, suggesting they chop a cord of wood that weekend is not fair.
- Do expect a thank-you card and a small token of appreciation.
- Do have a few starter logs handy if you have a fireplace. So nice if your friends come dragging in late on a cold night.
- Do pay ahead of time any people who will be doing work during your guest's visit.
- Do check that the bills are up-to-date so the guest doesn't get the power turned off some cold, wintry morning.

If young children will be visiting, see the Hosting Children and Young Adults chapter on page 100 for details about precautions you can take when having them in the house. However, there is an important difference: In that chapter I talk about things like wrapping furniture with sharp edges and locking up the cabinets. You don't have to go to those extremes when friends and family use your home or vacation house. It is the responsibility of the parents to make sure the children are protected from those types of items. You need only focus on the larger, more critical issues.

The Visit Wizard's Guide for Guests—A Sample

The Magic Is in the Details

ALTHOUGH A DETAILED LOOK AT HOW TO PROPERLY OUTFIT a home for your guests is in the Creating a Welcoming Home chapter, the needs of people who use your home while you are absent, and therefore your issues, are different. For example you have a responsibility to ensure your guests' safety and comfort to the best of your ability.

Therefore an important piece of the puzzle in having your vacation house properly prepared for guests is the three-ring binder you are going to put together and place on the cocktail table or in the kitchen. Come on. It will be fun. You can even decorate the cover.

Here's what you need:

A large, three-ring binder
8.5 x 11-inch plastic sleeves (the kind with the three precut holes down the left-hand side)
8.5 x 11-inch clear plastic business card holder
8.5 x 11-inch copy paper
A printer

It's impossible to list here all the necessary ingredients in the guide, so I have only included the major categories. The entire list is posted on my website, theartofthevisit.com.

A map of the immediate area.

Local merchant business cards. Quite easy to collect from around the area for inclusion in the business card section of the guide, and much easier than listing and writing out the same information. Get them from the local restaurants, your favorite hairdresser, the doctor's office, and so on.

House opening and operational instructions. Make sure your guests have your contact information—and that you are reachable—should they not understand or are not able to perform any of these important functions. Some of them are: the location of the water pump and hot water heater and turning on the ice maker if you had it turned off. (Don't laugh. I once ran out for a bag of ice thinking it was broken.)

Directions and phone numbers where applicable, to important places, like the grocery and liquor store, churches, and recreational places.

Phone numbers and account numbers. Account numbers and the name in which the service is listed are important for things like the power and television companies, as most service providers (at least in the United States) ask for that information before they can assist. Don't forget to list emergency services and doctors and veterinarians and other service providers like a cleaning service or handyperson.

Things to do. Include a map and/or written directions to places of interest, including parks, activities for the children, shopping areas, movie theater, the farmers' market and the health club, and of course whatever recreational activities are in the area.

Operating instructions for... The television (with a list of the channels), the remote control, DVD player and other gadgets, Internet, heat and a/c, the gas or log fireplace (don't assume!), all other major appliances like the clothes washer and dryer, the skeet machine, the gas grill, the patio heater, the pool or hot tub.

House Rules. What the guests can and can't use or do (refer back to the above "do's and don'ts" list) is a crucial part of the guide. There is nothing that will make an absent host hotter than having a guest do something the host thinks they should not have, and rightly the same for the guest. How can they be blamed if they did not know? Here are some examples:

How to properly dispose of trash and recyclables

Where to walk the dogs, if applicable

The smoking rules

No ski boots or golf shoes in the house

House closing instructions. This is one of the most important parts of the guide. If you are not going to be going to the house anytime soon after your guests' departure and don't have someone who can go check on it (which you should get, by the way), this is critical. Some examples are what the heat or a/c should be set to when the guests leave and what to do with fireplace ashes, the keys, or interior or exterior lights. Again, please visit the website for the complete list.

Extras. Write a few sentences about the restaurants you like and the price. Include their menus. Include times for religious services or interesting local history.

You can download the complete list from my website and then add whatever is applicable to your home and your area. If there is anything at all that you are squeamish about including in the guide, go ahead and add it and just blame the Visit Wizard. I can take it.

VISIT WIZARD TIP Why a three-ring binder? That way you can put each page in its own plastic sleeve so your guest can pop open the binder and take a page with them in the car and it won't matter if they spill coffee on it. Put coming home directions as well as going to directions.

I'm big on notes and so is *New York Times* best-selling author Karen Harper. Here is what she offered when I asked her if she had any tricks:

"One thing we have learned is to leave notes taped to the wall right next to things like the laundry, water heater, thermostat, humidifier, etc., about tips to operate them. Even if we are at home when guests come, we may be briefly away when they are in the house/condo during a visit. It's a mistake to assume a guest knows how to work that particular mechanical or 'easy-turn-on' item. In South Florida, where thunderstorms can be a problem and things are best sometimes left unplugged, even notes reminding the guest that 'Be sure such-and-such is unplugged after you use it' are a good idea. A friend of ours lost her laptop because she went out for a few hours while her guests were there and a big storm came up and fried the hard drive. In short, pretend you have loaned to or are sharing the house with primary school–age kids, even if a really smart couple is coming. Whether you are on site or not, make it easy for your guests to safely and correctly use your living space."

VISIT WIZARD TIP If your friends or family are using your primary home, get some 4 x 6-inch or larger frames that suit your décor and put your typewritten instructional notes in those and then hang on the walls or place around as necessary. That way they are easy to take down and put in a drawer when not needed.

At the end of the day, or in this case visit, it is you who pays the mortgage, shops for new area rugs when the red wine is spilled, and gets the frantic call when the Internet is down, and therefore you are the ultimate decision maker on who comes to visit and for how long. At least now when away you are well armed with the potent combination of legible notes placed about the house and *The Visit Wizard's Guide for Guests*. You are covered, your house is as protected as possible, and your guests are both informed and comfortable. You can relax now, able to appreciate the fact that you have a wonderful home for your loved ones to enjoy.

PART II

Becoming the Perfect Guest

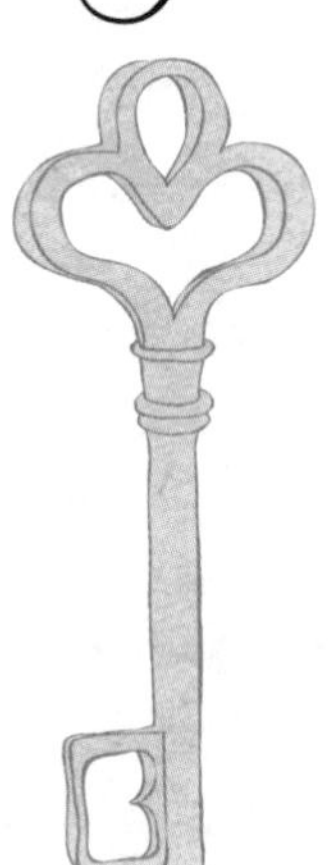

I KNOW MANY OF YOU STRUGGLE WHEN GOING TO A FRIEND or family member's home as a houseguest for any length of time. I've heard the stories and felt the frustration. You are uncomfortable either because you are unsure of what to do and how to do it, or, just as important, what not to do. Or it may simply be that you don't like or are uncomfortable with the people you are going to visit. That doesn't make you (or them) a bad person. I was the same way at one time. That is no longer the case.or

There are a few of you who are completely confident, your love for all your friends and family reciprocated in spades, you are the perfect guest and all your visits go swimmingly. Right.

As I am writing this introduction, I am watching with awe and respect the patience of a twenty-something-year-old mother as her baby throws his bottle on the floor for the fourth time. I wonder about her fears and concerns as she prepares to visit her in-laws or grandparents.

I overheard a conversation between four women as they discussed a friend who can no longer get around easily but is flying from Boston to California to visit her daughter and to see her first grandson. I know there will be issues both she and her daughter will face and I hope they both find information in these pages that will be helpful.

No human can be the perfect guest for any significant length of time, but we can try to get as close to perfection as much of the time as hosts, pets, or children will allow. Some will say, "Stop trying to obtain perfection!" But I say, why not at least strive for it? We will never reach it, of course, but trying will make our time with friends and family better, and that's what we really want because it's them we really care about.

This is not a book on how to behave at a dinner party. That's relatively easy. Watch what everyone else does with their various utensils, don't overindulge in food or drink, be charming, and don't be the last to leave.

It's sometimes complicated and sometimes picky so don't attempt to read every single chapter the night before departing on your visit. Your head will spin and you will be upset at the Visit Wizard. There is too much to digest. It would be akin to reading a Miss Manners book start to finish without stopping. It simply shouldn't be done.

And although I may be thought of as the good-guest-guru by some, and as simply fanatical by others—my only concern being tidiness, guest's comforts, and how they should behave—it's not true: I am just as concerned with the host!

I write with love and out of love, my sincere hope being that you take away from these chapters those things which will make your time with family and friends the very best it can possibly be.

CHAPTER 1

Seven Simple Steps to a Smooth Visit

"A good guest knows that the devil is in the details, that's why she beats the tar out of him with the Visit Wizard stick."

—YOU KNOW WHO

WHILE YOU'RE STRESSING OVER CHOOSING THE PERFECT gift and what to pack, your host is probably having a panic attack of her own. Sure, when you arrive, she's all smiles, the house looks like a spread from *Martha Stewart Living*, and Enya is playing softly in the background. But have you considered what it took to create this picture of "effortless" entertaining? Days spent shopping for your favorite food and drink, yanking weeds from the garden, emptying the guest room of last year's tax files, dumping the piles of junk mail from the dining room table into a tote bag and stuffing it in the closet, cooking like a contestant on *Top Chef* only to find out that the food no longer fits the suddenly miniscule refrigerator... well, you get the picture.

A recent email to the Visit Wizard perfectly captured the panic that many hosts feel:

"My old law school buddy and her husband arrive in 48 hours to stay the weekend and I must say that while I am dying to see their wonderful faces, all I can do is wince repeatedly at the state of the house. There are dog toys everywhere. There are dog bowls, dog leashes, dog hair and dog treats everywhere. For that matter, there are dogs everywhere. I wouldn't be so upset except that we're at the point where even we're sick of it and I know neither of them are dog, much less even pet, people. I just fear that they'll feel besieged and uncomfortable."

Your role—as a perfect guest—is to make the visit as low stress for your host, and thereby for you, as it can possibly be. The more you plan ahead, the more your host can avoid the last-minute scrambling and the dreaded "Do you have's?" as in: "I don't drink milk. Do you have Rice Dream?" Remember: It's not all about you; it's about the relationship and what you can and should do to help ensure you both feel as good about each other by visit's end as you felt at the beginning.

Follow these seven simple steps to avoid the deadly sins of visiting.

Step One: Make Your Needs Known in Advance

WHEN I WAS SINGLE, A FRIEND CAME TO VISIT ONE CHRISTmas with her husband and toddler. Naturally, because I was childless, I never gave a thought to the potential death trap my apartment posed to a small, wandering—and wondering—three-year-old. My apartment consisted of steep stairs, an open balcony, and furniture with edges sharp enough to cut teeth. There was not a round corner in the place. My friend and I were forced to spend the first twenty-four hours of our short weekend building barricades and taping dishtowels to the corners of the cocktail table. I was in constant fear that the child would impale himself on some corner or object I had overlooked. Whenever we were in the house all I did was walk behind him looking for obstacles real or by now imagined!

This scenario could have been easily avoided had my friend called (or now emailed) ahead and said something like, "I know you're not used to having a toddler around. Michael's at that stage where he's into everything. Here are some things you'll want to do to protect him and your stuff before we visit."

You may hesitate in making your needs known, thinking that you're placing a list of demands on your host like a celebrity politician who "must have bendable straws!" (which I actually get, by the way). But it's really just the opposite. You're taking the guesswork out of your host's preparations, and using the visit to actually enjoy each other's company—rather than spending it acting as a safety net for a toddler's tumultuous circus act.

In advance of their coming to the United States for a weeklong visit at our home, my sister-in-law had the great sense and consideration of supplying me with a list of those things her children needed—a good two weeks in advance. It included what they could (or would!) eat and drink, among other things. Rather than being offended, I was relieved. I did not buy boxes of cereal the children disliked, or sodas they were not allowed. My grocery list was whittled down considerably, and much time and money saved and frustration avoided.

The following questions will help get you thinking about what your needs might be:

If you have a young child or children... Will a crib, playpen, or high chair be necessary? If you are coming by airplane, and you know your host does not have such items, ask if a neighbor has one to borrow. There are companies that rent everything from baby monitors to car seats and even bottle warmers and sterilizers, and the great news is that some of them even deliver. Do research in advance and these items can be at your destination when you arrive. You might try babysaway.com or some similar service.

If you or your family has special needs... Be sure to tell your host if you have any medical or dietary considerations of which they should be aware. If you are a vegetarian, for example, let your host know ahead of time. If your child or anyone in your group has a food—or any other type of—allergy, make that known.

VISIT WIZARD TIP People who eat meat often don't have a clue what to serve a vegetarian. You can help your host by telling her what you do eat and offering some suggestions, or simple recipes, for main course meals everyone can enjoy. (You might want to nix the tofurky recipe.) Make sure to tell your host that if a barbeque has been planned, not to worry or fuss—you are content eating just the sides or salads, or as my husband says, the twigs and nuts!

If you are elderly or traveling with an elderly person... Will you need a wheelchair, oxygen refills, or access to a medical specialist? Internet websites list doctors and hospitals in various towns and stores where you can rent equipment if needed. (More on this subject is covered in the Hosting Older Guests chapter.)

If you are a student... Find out where the nearest library is located. If it's necessary for you to work while on your trip, bring your laptop or ask in advance if you may use your host's computer. Don't forget that you will need Internet access, so know how to configure it.

If you are financially strapped... Here is an original concept: Let your host know ahead of time if funds are low and do it unashamed!

The before visit email or phone call could go something like this: "You know business has been bad... [or "I have been fired" or "my spouse left me, closed the accounts, but I did get a postcard from the Caribbean, which was nice" or "The kids (all five of them) need braces]... but I (we) would love to come see you if you don't mind us fixing burgers on the deck and playing cards... or [would like to rent that deep sea boat but just can't do that right now]." You get the point.

The truth is that you and your host will be much more comfortable when things are known up-front, ahead of time. This truly is part of the art of the visit. We understand each other by knowing our limitations and expectations, thereby having a better chance at ensuring harmony and a more relaxed and enjoyable time together.

VISIT WIZARD TIP Never be embarrassed or apprehensive in asking your host about things (within reason) that may be important to your health and comfort while visiting them. The result will be a far more relaxed visit for you and your host.

Step Two: Be Prepared

IF YOU ARE GOING TO BE VISITING FOR MORE THAN A FEW days, go to the grocery store either right before or soon after you arrive. Purchase some supplies, but don't get anything unusual (like octopus) or that might be embarrassing to your host (like toilet paper... unless there is none—in which case, give them this book!).

If there is something you cannot live without, bring it yourself or ask your host where you can buy it. Do not expect your host to have that certain diet soda you love, or the special tea blend you drink in the morning.

If these things make your stay more comfortable, by all means bring them, but under no circumstances ask your host to make a special trip to get them after you arrive.

If visiting your boss for the weekend, before going to the store if that is in your plans, ask what brand of liquor she drinks or, if that is not appropriate, pick up a treat or dessert that you know everyone can enjoy. (Avoid chocolate or nuts as some people can't eat them.)

Step Three: If You Are Delayed—Call

THESE DAYS PEOPLE TEXT, CALL, AND TWEET OBSESSIVELY, but some don't think to use the phone when it really matters: when they're running late. And this is when you really need to be on the phone!

A friend and her companion were flying in for an extended visit and were expected "early evening." To my mind that means anywhere from 4 to 6 p.m. Foolish me! Starting at around 7 p.m. I began pacing the floor, straightened the dining room table for the fifth time, pulled the pot roast out of the oven and put it back in, popped that expensive bottle of wine I had been saving for them and poured myself a glass, stared at the clock, found a last-minute-something for my husband to do, had another glass of wine, brushed the dog, took the pot roast out of the oven and let it grow cold on the counter, called their cell phone to no avail, had one final glass of wine and fell asleep on the couch paperback in hand, to be awakened by knocking on the front door at midnight. There stood my guests smart enough to look meek and exhausted.

It was a simple matter of their international flight being delayed out of one of the connecting cities. When I called their cell phone to check, there was no service nor could they call out. I did not have their itinerary or I could have called the airline. There were errors all around that night so what could I do except pour the wine and offer them warmed over pot roast? The poor things were beat. It did my heart good to feed them and have them fall into bed, happy but tired, a valuable lesson learned.

This step seems like such a no-brainer, but I'm amazed at how many people ignore this simple, unwritten rule: Be on time. And if you can't be on time, call. And if you can't call, by all means make sure your host has your flight information for each leg of the journey.

VISIT WIZARD TIP If you're driving, call your host when you are thirty minutes to an hour away—even if you are on time. If you're flying, make sure your host has your itinerary.

This goes back to keeping your host's comfort level in mind. She may have planned for snacks or a meal to be ready, or may just be one of those people who anticipate the worst. Having your host picturing you lying in a ditch on the side of the road if you're more than fifteen minutes late is not a good way to set the tone of the visit! It doesn't matter how late you are, as long as you have the courtesy to call and let your host know what's happening, that way your hosts can do something important to them instead of just waiting around like jilted lovers.

Keeping your host informed is a sign that you value his time and respect the preparation put into this visit. Check to make sure you have your host's phone number, address, and directions handy before departing on the trip. If you are driving and don't have a cell phone or service, call from a convenience store or rest stop if possible. If your plane has been delayed, or if you are just having a hard time getting the kids ready and are running late, call. Call. Don't rely on email or a text. Your host may be (can you imagine?!) not checking the electronic device.

While we're on the subject of timing, one more thing: Arriving too *early* is just as bad as arriving late, so don't show up at your host's door before the appointed time. The last thing you want to do is surprise your host when he's still in his jockey shorts wrestling with a can of ham that refuses to open, a scenario that happened to a friend of mine when his invited guests rang the doorbell *forty-five minutes* before their scheduled arrival time! His poor wife greeted their guests at the front door, wearing a bathrobe complete with towel wrapped around head, while he pounded on the can with a hammer, trying to force the ham from its prison (the key had broken off). The guests, who were oblivious to the added trauma they had caused, simply said, "Oh, don't worry about us; we don't mind waiting."

VISIT WIZARD TIP Ask your host if she has a preference as to your arrival time. A friend of mine prefers it when guests arrive in the late afternoon or early evening. That way she can finish all planned work for the day, while the guest has time to unpack and relax before dinner.

Step Four: Pack Considerately—Not Considerably!

UNCLE EDGAR AND AUNT SUSAN WERE COMING FOR A LONG weekend. They do this a few times a year and it is mostly enjoyable, except that Uncle Edgar has a problem with decision making. That—coupled with his need to be prepared for every conceivable event and environmental oddity—and you have a guest-room-disaster in the making! How many clothes can one man stuff into a suitcase? It would shock you.

My first concern is the usual: Do I have enough hangers for the suits, trousers, and various shirts and sweaters of differing weights and styles? Will Aunt Susan have any closet or drawer space at all, or will panties and hose be spread out on top of the dresser? Will I be able to even enter the room if, heaven forbid, that becomes necessary? And finally, where do I store the unpacked luggage, under the bed? Or should we take a car out of the garage?!

If you're a pack rat and tend to dump your entire wardrobe and medicine cabinet into your super-sized luggage, remember that most people have limited closet and drawer space and the last thing your host wants to do is rush around from closet to closet pulling clothes off hangers at the last minute. Ask yourself if certain items can do double duty and make decisions about what you want to wear to certain events before you pack.

VISIT WIZARD TIP Bring several of your own hangers, just in case your host does not have enough. Better idea: Leave your clothes on your hangers when you pack. Side benefit: fewer wrinkles! And bring your own hypoallergenic pillow if necessary. . . Don't ask . . .

Maybe you've got the opposite problem: You're one of those people who never pack enough. You forget about those really crucial items, like deodorant or sleepwear, leaving it up to your host to scramble to fill in the gaps.

A particularly embarrassing moment for me was my failing to bring an appropriately warm coat on a visit to a relative. The good woman—who is smaller than I am—offered me her best coat: a rather expensive one. I should have declined but did not. To my dismay, when putting it on I ripped the armholes between the sleeves and the shoulders. Both of them! No one saw so I kept my mouth shut and we went on to the night-time outdoor event. Of course I told her the next day and took the coat to have it repaired at no small expense to myself.

Have an idea what the weather will be during your stay. Consult weather.com, which predicts weather patterns weeks out. That way you can bring whatever is needed.

Step Five: Plan for Events

I WILL NEVER FORGET A TRIP TO VISIT FRIENDS FOR A WEEKEND in the country. They failed to tell me that we would be traipsing through grassy fields to a local muddy, outdoor event. The heels and dress flats I packed were less-than-adequate to say the least, and my friend was not my size. I ended up putting Baggies over my shoes. They worked, but made me look and feel like a character out of a bad "chick lit" novel. Had I thought to ask what was on the agenda, I would have packed a pair of old sneakers.

Don't be shy about asking your host what she has planned. If you're afraid of putting her on the spot, you can say, "I want to be sure I pack everything I need. Do you have anything planned I should be aware of?"

Although they should have, don't be surprised if your hosts haven't thought of activities ahead of time, in which case refer them to the relevant Being the Perfect Host chapters. Most people tend to take where they live for granted—not seeing it through the eyes of a visitor. So do a little research on your own. If there are things you would like to do while on your visit by all means tell your host. He may even be relieved that he doesn't have to come up with plans on his own.

Would you like to have lunch or dinner at one of the restaurants overlooking the water or some other special place? If so, tell your hosts that you'd love to take them there and then make the reservation. It can always be changed later if necessary. Your thoughtfulness will be appreciated and your resourcefulness respected. And don't forget to pick up the check.

VISIT WIZARD TIP If you wish to explore the area on your own, ask your hosts if you can borrow their car. If not, and if your stay is longer than a weekend, be prepared to rent one.

Step Six: Bring a Gift

ABSOLUTELY, EVERY TIME, BRING SOMETHING FOR YOUR HOST. It does not matter if you just saw her at work on Friday or if you are staying for one night or ten days.

VISIT WIZARD TIP Don't worry about price when selecting a gift. In fact, it should not be too extravagant no matter what you can afford. Make the gift appropriate and take into consideration the length of the visit and the relationship.

A new girlfriend of mine was visiting me with her sister for the first time. We had not known each other long. It was to be a "girls' weekend" with just us three. We wanted to get to know each other and they wanted to enjoy a weekend in the country. She brought just two simple and wonderful things: a bottle of wine she knew I would enjoy and a bag of specialty bread mix. Baking the bread together in the cozy kitchen was a perfect, nonstressful way to bond.

What to Bring

If you know your host enjoys a particular activity or topic, bring something that relates to it. An interesting book or DVD on your host's favorite subject will always be appreciated. A kitchen gadget for the cook is usually welcome.

Don't discount the unusual. A French friend who visited for a week brought my husband an assortment of miniature colognes as a gift. It was something he would not have bought for himself, and because it was from France it was perfectly thoughtful and wonderful.

Let's look at some specifics:

Alcoholic beverages: You can never go wrong with a bottle of good wine or liquor provided your host drinks. If you are staying the week, bring several bottles.

Scented candles and flowers: Proceed with caution. Some people are allergic to certain flowers or can't tolerate strong smells, so make sure you know your host fairly well before selecting these.

Music: Take your host's age into consideration, but show some discretion in introducing your host to new or different music. Obviously, don't bring heavy metal for Granny, but she might enjoy being introduced to a new jazz group.

Books: This is always a great choice but play it safe: don't bring a Stephen King novel to person who fears the dark or a book on landscape gardening to a person who has paved over her backyard. There are many good, neutral choices. "Coffee table" books make lovely gifts, as well as books on entertaining family and friends.

Plants: If you bring a live plant for the garden, ask your host if you can plant it for them before you leave. If my host has a garden, large or small, or even a sunny windowsill, an herb is often what I bring. A lot of people don't cook with fresh herbs simply because they are not close at hand. Receiving one as a gift is a way for the person to experiment with fresh and different herbs.

VISIT WIZARD TIP Call a friend or another family member and ask what might make a good gift for the host. They might know something about the person that you don't and if the gift is a complete flop you can always say that it was recommended . . . but of course not by whom!

What Not to Bring

Aunt Susan loves a good birdhouse. She actually makes them... out of milk cartons. We all know this about Aunt Susan, and we laugh and on occasion it comes up in phone conversations. They actually do hold up to the elements for a season or two, although no bird has ever been seen in one. She paints them in merry colors of lime green and bright red but never quite enough to hide the name of the brand of milk—or the picture of the cow. Aunt Susan thinks every female friend and member of the family should have one; therefore, I am compelled to dig deep in the basement before her every visit.

Remember that one person's treasure can often be another person's trash. Do not bring handcrafted items unless you know your host loves those cute little sun catchers you make or that dried leaf arrangement for the door.

Here are more gifts to avoid:

Live houseplants. I once made the mistake of bringing a frail, elderly family member a rather large houseplant only to realize that it was too difficult for her to care for so I ended up taking it home when I left, but not without first embarrassing her and making myself look foolish.

Cut flowers (if you are arriving around the time dinner will be served). I know this may fly in the face of tradition, but your host may view it as yet one more chore to do. First, it means getting out the step stool, then rooting around in the nether reaches of the kitchen cabinets for the right vase, then trimming and arranging the bouquet to fit (because it never fits the vase you have on hand). If you do want to present flowers as a gift, wonderful, just have them delivered the day of, or even the day before the visit, or bring them already in a vase and ready to set down so no immediate work is required.

Homemade food items. Unless specifically requested, your "specialty" may not be exactly welcome. The host feels compelled to serve and eat it, even though it may make her feel like a contestant on *Survivor*. Further, and more serious, someone may have a food allergy of which you are unaware.

Clothes of any kind—unless you know the person's taste very well. And a person's taste, not to mention size, can change over the years. One friend of mine—a city mouse—is the recipient of the most godawful appliquéd sweaters from her country-mouse cousin whenever she comes to visit. Of course, my friend feels compelled to wear the sweater at least once during the visit—but only inside her home. It goes right to Goodwill as soon as her guests leave.

Recycled gifts. Do not bring anything that was given to you that you don't like and of which you want to be rid. "Regifting"—a term coined by the classic TV show *Seinfeld*—can always be spotted and can even result in embarrassment for you and your host. A friend told me that once during the Christmas holidays, she and her husband were rushing out the door to visit friends, when they realized they had forgotten to buy their hosts a gift. Quickly, she remembered a box that a neighbor had given to them, which the neighbor said was chocolate she had special ordered just for them. My friend was about to stuff it into her purse, when she had the brilliant idea of unwrapping it first—just to check. Good thing! The special chocolate was in the form of a greeting card: with my friends' names embossed on the bar!

VISIT WIZARD TIP Keep this in mind when selecting a gift for your host: If it requires work upon giving, perform that work. If it requires work after you leave, don't bring it.

Framed photos with a picture of you and your host. If the host does not like it or looks terrible (and what woman of a certain age doesn't think she looks terrible), she will feel compelled to display it because you brought it. It will be quickly put away when you leave, and then create angst every time you visit, as your host will have to pull it back out for fear of hurting your feelings. Better idea: Frame a truly beautiful photo of just your host or something that is dear to her. You're almost always safe giving your host a picture of her child or pet.
Other friends! A friend of mine was horrified when she got a last-minute email from a friend whom she had invited to her guest house for a weekend, asking if she could bring a friend of hers, complete with husband! My friend does not know these people. But what could be said at that point? The large house had plenty of bedrooms so the other two guests could be easily accommodated, but that is not the point. There is one simple rule here: Do not invite people to join you that your host does not know. You'll be putting her in an awkward spot. Maybe your host doesn't want the extra company, but how can she turn down your request without feeling like the bad guy? And even if they do know him, no one wants to be forced into a corner or have to say: "You know I just can't stand Jack—sorry!" or "As a surprise I had paid for the four of us to go deep sea fishing but I can't afford two more!" She is placed in the awkward position of having either to cancel plans, pay for the extra two people herself, or ask them to pay. Bad juju no matter how you shake the bones.

Step Seven: Be Complimentary

ONCE YOU ARRIVE, THE VERY FIRST THING YOU SHOULD DO is find something to compliment. Even if it doesn't appear that way, your host has most likely done her best preparing for your arrival. Your noticing will be greatly appreciated. My mother-in-law was amazing in that she noticed everything that had occurred since her last visit, and her visits were usually many months apart.

If new things have been added to the house or painting or remodeling done, be sure to mention it. That doesn't mean you have to lie, even if it looks more like a "what *not* to do" rather than your idea of an "improvement." So instead of exclaiming: "Wow! Those zebra-striped shutters really liven up your house!" or "You're so creative. I would have never thought to hang a wagon from the ceiling," smile and point out something that you truly like, even if it's only your host's new hairstyle.

Now that you are prepared for your visit, the next chapter will show you how to make your stay one that will be remembered—for all the right reasons.

CHAPTER 2

The Twelve Essential Qualities of a Great Guest

"You cannot put manners on like an overcoat, that is, only when needed. They should be like your skin, always there, if sometimes wrinkled."

—THE VISIT WIZARD

THINK OF YOUR LAST VISIT WITH FAMILY OR FRIENDS. WHICH answer best describes how it went:

a. "I was comfortable and relaxed and enjoyed my visit thoroughly."

b. "By the second day I found myself counting the hours until I could go home."

c. "A visit to the local prison seemed like a more appealing option."

Even if you've prepared well, the main event—the actual visit—is ripe for conflict and complications. It's just these times—the much-anticipated long weekend with friends in the country, the family reunion at a major holiday, or a young person's first stay with a relative—when emotions run high and nerves can be stretched tighter than Joan Rivers's face. Because more is expected of our loved ones than the occasional social acquaintance, the setting is ripe for discord and hurt feelings.

If you answered "b" or "c" to the quiz above, instead of swearing off visiting altogether, or spending your next visit with a clenched jaw and fist, you can take certain actions—and avoid certain minefields—to ensure your next visit goes smoothly.

It's easy to do all the right things when you're invited over for a dinner party at a friend's home. Let's face it: Being on your best behavior for four hours isn't exactly an Olympic event. But extend that time to twenty-four hours—or longer—and there is not a person alive on this planet who couldn't use a little help in the basic etiquette department, especially when visiting family or close friends. Long-term rifts can result and friendships can end because of misunderstandings and hurt feelings due to a simple lack of knowledge of what to do and—even more importantly—what *not* to do.

Can the Twelve Essential Qualities always be adhered to? No. Will some things just not work all the time and with everyone? Of course. Will the unexpected happen? Without a doubt. But by adhering to these good practices, the threat of upset to friends and family will be lessened and your precious time with your hosts will be more enjoyable. I can't promise that your brother won't continue to be a pain, or your nagging mother-in-law will suddenly turn into Mother Teresa, but I can promise you that by following these steps, the likelihood of you selecting "a" after your next visit will be vastly improved!

1. A Great Guest Is... Neat

I ENTERED THE ROOM WITH A SENSE OF DREAD. COLD, HALF-filled coffee cups and paper plates with unrecognizable matter clinging to them littered the family room like wounded soldiers. Three of my old college friends, down for vacation, were partially dressed in well-worn bathrobes, apparently old favorites. The women lay limply on the sofas like puppets on strings, their bare feet atop the glass cocktail table. The television was too loud and the sight was too shocking. It was noon.

Bad Host popped into my head like a rabid animal: How dare they destroy my beautiful, neat, well-thought-out family room! I don't leave a plate down for two minutes and theirs have been here two hours! Good Host gained control, and I said, "Ladies, the slumber party is over—let's get this place back in shape!" They of course smiled, leapt up, and things were back to normal in no time.

All neat people are alike, but each sloppy person is sloppy in his own way. What may seem perfectly acceptable to you (plopping down on the velvet settee in your sweat-drenched bicycle shorts... tossing your used tea bags in the brand new white porcelain farmer's sink) may give your host a meltdown. So, how do you know the difference between acceptable self-expression and just plain slovenliness? Follow these simple rules:

The Living Areas...

Before you come inside from out-of-doors, inspect your shoes and clothing. If they are dirty, take your shoes off. Brush off your clothes or go change and clean up if necessary.

Don't leave your things around the house or clutter the living areas. Use your bedroom to keep and store your belongings.

If you're sleeping on a pullout sofa, make it up as soon as you rise and try to put the bedding somewhere out of site, like in another room.

The Bedroom...

Do your best to put your items away and keep the room neat, but if the bedroom is small or there is not enough storage area, keep the door closed so passersby don't have to see the mess and you have some privacy.

When unpacking, do not put your suitcase on the bed unless you are positive it is clean, including the wheels if it is a roller style. Your host should have provided a luggage rack for this purpose. If not, lay down a towel so you don't soil the bedspread.

If you don't want the comforter or extra blankets or extra pillows on your bed, don't pile them in a corner; instead ask your host if there is a convenient place to store them.

Make your bed every morning the same way your host had it made when you arrived—or how you have edited it down—even if it means putting back those quaint little hand-crocheted pillows!

The Bathroom...

If your host has the towels folded neatly over the bar or ring, put them back that way after use. No one wants to come in to find the hand towel wadded up and thrown on the vanity. If it is your private bath and you know no one but yourself is going to use it—do it anyway!

If the medicine cabinet in your bathroom is empty, feel free to put your things in that space; the same for the clothes closet. Your host has cleared it for that purpose and appreciates your using it instead of leaving your things on the vanity.

If you are sharing a bath with another person or couple, take your own towels back to your bedroom and leave the bathroom spotless for the next person by wiping down the sink top and checking the toilet. You may want to ask your host for paper towels for this purpose, or use a washcloth or hand towel to wipe down the sink and then take it back to your room.

The Car...

If you have driven to the visit and are thoughtful enough to suggest that your car be used for touring, carting the kids, or going out to dinner, make sure it and the windows are clean! Stepping on a bag of stale Doritos when entering the backseat or not being able to see out the windows is not conducive to a nice trip. Be assured your host will not mind if you ask for glass cleaner and paper towels!

2. A Great Guest Is... Not Shy

IF AT ANY TIME YOU ARE THIRSTY OR HUNGRY, UNCOMFORTABLY hot or cold, let your host know. Don't be afraid to speak up about things like your sleeping needs and desires. Many people find it difficult to get a good night's sleep when they are not at home. If your pillow is too big or too hard, ask for another; if you are too hot at night, ask your host if he could adjust the air conditioner or if they have a table fan. If you are uncomfortable and are going to be there for a long period of time you might consider buying one and leaving it as a gift for your host. A nice thing to do since there will surely be other guests who would appreciate it.

If you're not sure where an item goes or how to do something that has been asked of you, consult your host. Don't worry about appearing stupid. A friend thought she was being thoughtful by unloading the dishwasher while I was out. Only one problem: the dishes were dirty. No, I am not joking. Although well intended, she should have asked if she thought they were not clean.

It's usually not a problem to use the clothes washer, but do ask first. Your host may still have a load in there.

And finally don't try to "over please." Don't constantly say, "Whatever you or the group wants, I'll do." That is no help and can give the impression that you really don't care. If you want to do something or go somewhere, say that. If you don't, say that, too. Your honesty will be appreciated.

If you are concerned you might have unwittingly done something wrong, don't be afraid to ask your host. Everybody makes the occasional *faux pas*. Better to get things out in the open, apologize, and move on.

3. A Great Guest Is... Flexible

YOU HAD YOUR HEART SET ON GOING TO THE MOVIES ONE afternoon but at the last minute everyone decided to take a nature walk in the mountains instead... you were looking forward to that special meal your host cooks so well, but he was exhausted from the activities of the day and could not bring himself to prepare it. So what do you do? You are as supple and bendable as the new branch in a spring breeze. You go hike the mountain and offer to run out and get pizza.

Being flexible will demonstrate to your host that you are a mature person who understands the difficulties involved with planning activities and can easily and seemingly effortlessly cope with a sudden change in plans. If you once were, you will no longer be seen as that bratty child who once pounded his foot or sulked in the corner because he could not get his way every time. Your host will greatly appreciate your selflessness and your willingness to help ease the tension of the situation rather than add even more stress.

However, that doesn't mean you always have to slavishly go along with everything. If you really, really hate fishing and one afternoon your host suggests fishing at the local lake, you have two choices: (1) speak up and tell your host not only do you get boat sick but the smell of bait makes you gag, or (2) smile, go, and make every attempt to have a good time. If you opt not to go, that's fine, you can offer to stay home and prepare something for dinner or you can suggest an alternative, like a trip to the local fish market to actually *buy* the rainbow trout.

Sometimes a bit of persuasion will do the trick. My husband will rightly say that it is often difficult to get me to go somewhere new or different, but when I am there I truly enjoy it. So, don't automatically nix a trip to the SPAM museum (the spam in the can, not in your inbox) or the alpaca farm. And more importantly, how will you really know you'll hate it unless you give it a try?

VISIT WIZARD TIP If you are on the fence or undecided about participating in some event, go. Err on the side of following the crowd's wishes. There is one exception: if an event was planned in advance you are obligated to go. Only illness or death can be used as an excuse!

4. A Great Guest Is... Grateful

I WAS VISITING A FRIEND WHO HAD A LARGE FAMILY AND THE added stress of even more family on the way. When I saw her unbelievably well-stocked walk-in pantry loaded to the brim with food and goodies, I made the unfortunate mistake of saying, "Oh, Jane, you shouldn't have bothered." Jane looked at me and said, "Kathy, please. You don't know the half of it." And she was right. What I did not realize was that she needed to have all that stocked in advance so she could enjoy some time with all of us. The lesson I learned is that you should not protest or be shocked and comment on the things a host may do to prepare for your visit. Instead, be grateful that your host thought enough of you to go to the effort.

Don't be picky. If you prefer Diet Coke but your host has only Diet Pepsi, either accept or decline graciously. Don't ask for name-brand liquors. If you ask for Johnnie Walker Blue Label and your host only has Johnnie Walker Black, what are you going to do, turn it down? Early on in my hosting life I either made sure I had absolutely everything possible on hand in all its varieties and forms, or I actually ran to the store if I did not have that one thing a person wanted. That is the way to madness, not to mention wasted time and much frustration.

VISIT WIZARD TIP Never say the following: "I came all this way and it is too _____" (fill in the blank: hot, cold, rainy, humid, or the like). Bad weather is not your host's fault. Although you expected sun, snow, or whatever condition and did not get it, complaining to your hosts only makes them feel even worse because Mother Nature did not cooperate!

5. A Great Guest Is… Helpful

I THINK THAT SOME GUESTS ASSUME THE HOST'S HOUSE IS A free bed & breakfast and that the hosts are wait staff, maids and butlers, cooks, and entertainers all rolled into one. Always offer to help. If you receive a "no" in reply, simply keep asking, but don't be a pest, as conscientious people sometimes can be. If after the third or fourth inquiry you receive a firm "no!" you can stop asking and be thankful you have a host who actually wants to do everything.

Unless you're helping to prepare a meal, ask if you can set the table. After the meal, tell your host to go away—cleanup is on you. She may balk, but nicely insist. If she really doesn't want you in the kitchen, then of course respect her wishes.

If you're all watching a movie together, make a bag of popcorn or ask your host if you can slice up some fruit or bring in drinks so they can just sit and enjoy the movie, too, instead of them popping up and down every few minutes like some children's toy gone awry.

A great way to bond or reconnect with friends and family members is in the kitchen. Ask your host for a favorite recipe, or one she's wanted to try, and volunteer to make it or assist in making it.

During one visit, a friend told me she would like to prepare dinner using a special recipe from her homeland. She then went to the store alone, bought all the ingredients, and prepared the meal start to finish. It was an unexpected delight. Prepare what you can even if it's just a basic dish, like a chicken in the oven with potatoes or scrambled eggs for breakfast. And you guys who don't cook: Don't let that stop you from trying. Nice moments are spent over the grill!

I am fortunate to have terrific brothers. On a visit by one to our mountain house, unbeknownst to me, he proceeded outside to chop almost half a cord of wood. You cannot mention a thing that needs to be done around my other brother without him immediately setting out to fix it. If you do something for the host that needs doing, it will never be forgotten. I think they learned that from my father, who on a recent visit helped my husband fell a large tree and painted what seemed like miles of baseboard that I was installing. We never asked. The best help is the volunteered kind.

6. A Great Guest Is… Generous with Time and Treasure

I HAVE HEARD STORIES LIKE THIS TOO MANY TIMES:

> *"They did not offer to take my husband and me out to dinner once, nor did they offer to help with any chores. The straw that broke this host's back: the woman would leave me her grocery list! No money with it. I literally went on strike. For the first time in my hosting life and did not really care if they were happy or attended to. I'd had enough."*

Contrast the above example with this:

My friend saw I was dragging. We had just returned from an all-day outing with the kids and I was beat. That morning I had bragged to everyone that I was going to make a lavish dinner, complete with handmade appetizers and dessert. Right. As I limped my way into the kitchen, my friend grabbed my arm, handed me a glass of wine, and told me she was off to get Chinese take-out for the gang. *Bless her*, was all I thought.

Nothing will endear you more to your host than if you see an opportunity to do something thoughtful—and then go for it. Here are some simple suggestions: pick some wildflowers on your host's property and bring them in for the table or your host's bedroom; ask your host what drink you might bring them; suggest a game of cards that everyone can play; rent a movie for everyone to enjoy; weed the garden; take the dog for a walk.

If you can afford to, take your hosts out to their favorite restaurant, or one they would like to try, and pay the bill. If they have been playing tour guide all day, ask if you can drive the car or call a taxi. If you would prefer, or if funds are low, make a night out a "night in" by going to pick up pizza or take-out food, bringing it back for your host, setting the table, and doing all those nice things a restaurant would do.

If things are tight financially, don't worry and—most importantly—don't let that stop you from enjoying your visit. Just demonstrate to your host that you are doing what you can to be generous and giving. As host, I don't care how much you spend or if you can take me to a fancy dinner. I just want to know that you care. Don't be ashamed and don't be bashful about suggesting less-expensive alternatives. One of the best times I have ever spent with a friend was when we were both broke. We microwaved popcorn, did puzzles, walked together for what seemed miles, and watched movies. Not one dinner out all weekend! It was the best time, and the one I remember the most.

If your host uses her car for touring and sightseeing, make sure you pay (or at least offer to pay) for gas. If your host resists, the best thing to do is jump out of the car first and beat her to the pump! And taking the vehicle through a car wash is an especially nice thing to do.

VISIT WIZARD TIP To make sure you and your host don't get into a tug-of-war over the check, prearrange with the server to give the check to you discreetly. Or, sometime near the end of the meal, excuse yourself for a trip to the restroom, and settle up out of sight.

7. A Great Guest Is... Mindful of Others

MY MOTHER WOULD CALL THIS QUALITY "BEING CONSIDerate." Try to be cognizant of the comfort of your hosts and other guests. A great example of this was when one of my guests saw a fellow guest, the mother of twin boys, really struggling one Sunday morning. She was exhausted and on her "last nerve" with the rambunctious kids. This thoughtful person scooped the squirming, crying boys in both arms and headed outside to play. The next thing we saw through the family room window was the three of them rolling around in the grass screaming, this time with delight. Some considerate suggestions:

If you snore, keep your door closed at night and wear one of those anti-snore nasal strips.

Do not use the "powder room" for extended bathroom chores. Use your guest bathroom or one of the bedroom bathrooms for this if you do not have a designated bathroom.

Before renting or downloading a movie, try to get everyone's opinion of what might be enjoyed. Take into consideration the age of any children and older adults. Remember that what is common now in terms of language and violence can be quite appalling to many, so best to err on the side of caution.

Do not talk during the movie. I have a friend who tends to comment excessively during movies to the annoyance of everyone (okay, it's me). I have now been "shushed" enough to have learned.

Take your cigarette smoking outside. Unless your host smokes indoors, consider it off-limits. When outside, be sure to ask for a plastic cup, or something with water in it, in which to put the ashes and butt and then dispose of it.

Never smoke cigars in the house. Even if after several drinks after dinner your host says that it's okay, don't do it. Everyone will regret it the next day! And please, please, don't smoke around children. In addition to the health concerns, you don't want them to believe it is cool or acceptable to smoke.

Know when events and meals are planned and don't be late. I have seen tempers flare and plans ruined or cancelled because a guest was late or not prepared. If that happens, it will surely make your host feel that you simply don't care enough to make the effort. If you are playing with the children, reading, or out for a walk, make sure you are ready in time for events. It can ruin a meal if a guest comes back after some activity and needs to shower and dress when dinner is about to be served. If your host does not tell you the time something is planned, ask.

VISIT WIZARD TIP Remember that your hosts actually live where you are visiting, so don't make them late for reservations or when taking you to their friend's home.

8. A Great Guest Is... Respectful of the Boundaries

HONOR YOUR FRIENDSHIPS AND YOUR FAMILY MEMBERS BY knowing when to keep quiet. Put past rivalries behind you. Let's face it: There are just some family issues best left buried. If your sister wants to bring up that old argument about who did what to whom when, in a negative or unproductive way, simply say something polite and change the subject or, if you must, leave the room, or tell her you and she can talk privately about it later. There is always one person whose behavior gets under the skin. Make the mature and very conscious decision not to allow those feelings to surface no matter what. The result will be a happier visit for everyone.

Learn how to change topics quickly and effortlessly during conversations. There is an art to making good conversation and this skill is a must! You can draw attention away from a negative subject, in midstream when necessary, without anyone being the wiser or getting offended.

Under no circumstances make suggestive jokes or tell off-color stories in mixed company. Always err on the side of caution here. No one wants to hear nasty stories or be "grossed out." What you think may be hilariously funny can easily insult or upset someone else. There is nothing that can ruin an evening faster than having someone tell a disgusting story before dinner or comment on a woman's physique at a restaurant.

It's not just what comes out of your mouth that matters; it's also what goes in. Avoid overindulging in anything. This is especially true on that weekend visit to your boss or business associate's home. Believe me, if you knock back a few too many martinis, then scarf down most of that overpriced box of truffles, it will get back to the office—and you don't want to be the topic of conversation around the old watercooler. Worse yet, your boss may be considering you for a raise or promotion and the last thing you want is to be seen as a lush or irresponsible, even if you are neither. Err on the side of moderation, and you will be thought of as a sophisticated and polished person. Your reward for a few days of restraint could be great.

9. A Great Guest Is... Present and Engaged

COME WITH ME ON THIS TRIP: FOUR ADULTS ARE IN A VERY small car on the way home from hours of sightseeing when a cell phone rings... for the third time. The call was again for one of the guests and it went on and on and on. Not only could no one else talk, but we had to listen to every word that was said! My instinct was to turn around and tell the person that if he answered it again we would put him out on the side of the road, but I held my tongue.

So, do not use your cell phone extensively in the presence of your hosts or other guests. If possible, set your phone to vibrate and if you must make or receive a call leave the room. Do your best to tell the caller you will get back to them shortly when you can get time alone.

We are in the "gadget era," and I have yet to find one I don't enjoy. Portable devices with differing forms of entertainment have their place, but use them sparingly, if at all, on the visit. The goal is to bond with other humans who are important to you—not with your machine.

And if you absolutely have to do work on the computer or conduct business during your visit, tell your host and apologize for doing so. Everyone realizes that at times work cannot wait, but to do it without explanation can appear to the host that you are simply uninterested and would prefer to entertain yourself. Your priorities should be the visit with your host, and the other guests or family members coming in second and third. When that is not possible it will be understood and tolerated but only if you handle it properly.

Do try to focus on enjoying the time with your family and friends. So many of us, these days especially, are workaholics. I am guilty. Do your best to organize your time so that you don't feel guilty about not doing the work you must, but also so you have wonderful memories of the time spent with the ones you love.

A friend told me that some hotels are offering "digital detox" specials. When you check in, you surrender all your technology. Why not try that your next visit? (Scared you there for a minute, didn't I?)

VISIT WIZARD TIP It is often better to excuse yourself from the room if you need to work. This way you are not distracting to others and you can most likely be more productive in a shorter period of time. I had an incident where a person told a group of us to be quiet as he needed to work! That simply doesn't work!

---

10. A Great Guest Is... Self-Caring

WHEN THE VISIT IS HECTIC, MOST EVERYONE CAN BENEFIT from some time alone—even the dog! I am by nature a pretty simple soul—really! Besides the love of family and friends, a good book, and limited daily exercise, I have just one simple need to be happy: time alone. This is now a running joke in my home and among my friends. Alone time helps my mind regroup and takes it out of overdrive. I begrudge no one this pleasure and have been known to even encourage it. Let's be honest: sometimes you just need to get away.

By all means go to your room and nap or read a book if you need time to yourself. The break may be good for your host as well. Just make sure to tell her what you are doing and why. Don't just disappear, leaving your host to wonder where you went or if you left out of anger or simply did not want to be around.

VISIT WIZARD TIP If you go out alone make sure you have the key, security code, or whatever you need to get back into the house without disturbing your host. And if you feel like partying until the wee hours, be sure to let your host know your plan.

11. A Great Guest Is... Cool Under Pressure

"The thing about family disasters is that you never have to wait long before the next one puts the previous one into perspective."

—ROBERT BRAULT

NO VISIT IS WITHOUT INCIDENT. AT SOME TIME OR ANOTHER you are bound to have difficulties with your host, other guests, the children, the dog....

People will be late and mess up plans; things will get broken; people (young and old) will sulk; someone will say something hurtful; someone will be lazy or careless; arguments (both minor and major) will break out for no apparent reason; someone will get up and leave the table in disgust; you will be criticized; there will be some type of mess. You name it and it has probably occurred, or is occurring, at a home near you.

So what to do? Try your best to (you guessed it) *be polite!* There are many times when I have gotten angry, hurt, bent out of shape, tired, or exacerbated by my hosts. I have heard the horror stories, both sad and funny, about such times from all of you.

Expect the occasional scratch on the furniture or broken glass. Offer to pay your host for any damage. And whatever you do, don't try to cover up a mishap. A friend told me that she found something broken when returning to her condo after having guests, and they never said a thing about it. She was understandably irritated. Had they just left a note of apology it would have been forgiven—and forgotten.

Even when at someone else's home you don't have to tolerate bad behavior, but do take into consideration that (especially during family visits, it seems) emotions can run high, and old feelings, good or bad, can surface. Despite your best efforts, you don't have control over others' behavior, and even less control when in someone else's home.

So when things do go wrong remember that just a few kind words can set a person at ease and make everything right again. Acting with grace and class will always set the right tone in your life and in the lives of others. When you feel tempers start to rise or tears start to well because of an unthinking or cruel remark, or a dropped piece of china, remember that how you behave is a choice made by you, no matter where you are and who you are with.

12. A Great Guest Is... Able to Handle the Hostiles

If you travel and visit enough, you are going to run into hostile people. Perhaps there is one family member who just doesn't like you, or there are past hurts that have not been overcome, or a jealousy in the family or among friends or their spouses. It can be very uncomfortable. Often you have to visit because your loved one wants or needs you to go, or you have an obligation that requires it. Not fun, I know, but you must do your best: stiff upper lip and all that! Find humor where you can. That always helps.

Or, just relax. Give yourself things to do. Yes, you can avoid nasty Aunt Nancy or overly touchy Thomas by taking a drive just to "see the sights," taking time out to read a book, offering to cook (alone) in the kitchen, getting that critical final report done for school or your boss, or taking the dog for a walk or the children to the park. Suggest that you take a friendly family member or friend shopping, or on some other venture while the hostiles are otherwise occupied. But beware of the fine line between taking some time for yourself, and being obvious you prefer to be elsewhere!

When you are forced to socialize with the offending party, yes, here it is again: Be polite. And if you really want to be the bigger person, be especially nice! Go overboard to engage that person and be warm and interested in them. Who knows? You may even crack through the ice or start to repair the relationship. And what could be better, really? It may be that Aunt Nancy thinks you are a self-centered little twit who cares nothing about her family or her. Prove her wrong. Don't take at face value what you have been told about others. Every person brings his or her own uniqueness to the visit. Is someone cranky because he isn't well, just got bad news, or doesn't feel welcome? I have learned to err on the side of acceptance and, as hard as it can be, understanding!

And when dealing with someone who for whatever reason turned ugly during the visit, how you depart is just as important, if not more so, than how you arrived. This is your final opportunity to right a wrong, give an honest hug, look your hosts in the eye and thank them—even if you would rather back the car into their house upon leaving!

The next chapter offers ways to end the visit with class and on a high note, regardless of whether it was delightful or dreadful. So not only will you leave feeling calm and cool, you'll be remembered as a truly great guest.

CHAPTER 3

Leaving a Lasting Impression

"I've learned that people will forget what you said, people will forget what you did, but people will never forget how you made them feel."

—MAYA ANGELOU

During the Visit, Sit and Visit

NO VISIT HAS TO BE, OR SHOULD BE, CONSTANT ACTION AND adventure. While fun and excitement is naturally part of the trip, it should not be the whole enchilada (with or without a frozen margarita, depending on how it's going).

Although the days of rocking on the front porch, sipping tea, and talking with Grandma have gone the way of the icebox, they needn't have.

Make time to just sit and talk, catch up, and get to know each other again... or perhaps really for the first time.

As gadgets increasingly take over our lives, it becomes too easy to be immersed in the cyber world of high-tech, nonverbal communication. It is often easier and less demanding than engaging one-on-one. Get off the laptop, power down the iPod, put away the e-reader, and engage. Hard—I know!

One of my personal pet peeves (I know you may be rightfully thinking I have plenty) is people who don't open up, at least a little, about themselves. I want to get to know my friends and family better. People change, evolve, and grow from the time we saw them last. We want to hear the good, the bad, and, yes, the ugly (just as long as you intersperse some good—nobody wants to be depressed for five hours). One doesn't need the complete life story, but some personal information is required! I think one of the saddest things is never really getting to know someone. To share the human experience. Why are we hiding? Why are we waiting? There are many people I can point to in my life about whom I will unfortunately be able to say—at their funeral—You know? I never really knew him. So how can you stop the cycle of silence among your own friends and family? Start at the beginning:

VISIT WIZARD TIP This section is just as important for the mother you go visit every few months, as for the boss and spouse you are visiting for that all important weekend at their beach house, with one caveat: Don't open up quite so much with them as you would with your family and close personal friends, but all else applies—in spades.

"Making conversation" was a manner taught long ago, but it is just as relevant now as it always has been, perhaps more so. Part of being polite and having good manners is knowing how to make conversation that includes everyone. But conversation is a two-way street. If you are trying to have meaningful dialog with that proverbial bump on the log who only grunts the occasional response, you will soon stop talking. Conversely, if you are talking about yourself nonstop, the other person will soon turn away.

Inquire about your host or fellow guests. Take an active interest in what others are doing. Do they have a new hobby or have they taken on a new project? Have they read a good book or seen a bad movie? How are they feeling, emotionally and physically?

The greatest flattery is asking someone about themselves. What are they up to? What is new in their lives? And if you get a "nothin'"—be persistent! Find common ground and common interests: Jeans are fitting a little snugger than usual so you've started a new diet; now that the kids are in school you are thinking about taking an adult-learning class; you have a dog behavioral problem and can't figure out how to correct it; you want to sew curtains for the kitchen window but haven't got a clue. The topics are endless but all must start with a basic premise: You are interested in another person and you wish to express that interest.

If there are children about, then one of the best times for adults to reconnect is over dinner. Sometimes it is the *only* time. When possible hire a baby-sitter for the kids and go out one night, or send them into another room with a movie, grab a bottle of wine or brew some tea, and just talk.

Although important for every healthy adult relationship, I find the communicating part of the visit particularly important for younger and older people, which is discussed in more detail in the chapters Visiting with Children and Young Adult Confidential, and Visiting with Older Guests.

VISIT WIZARD TIP Don't let the grown-up conversation be all about the children or other family members. Although these are wonderful topics, you will get closer with your friends and family as you share about yourself and they talk about themselves, what they are doing and their interests.

Be Remembered for What You Did, Not What You Didn't Do

OVER A HOLIDAY VISIT MY SISTER-IN-LAW TOOK AN INTEREST in my jewelry making. I was thrilled to have her spend several hours with me beading and making necklaces. We turned the kids over to the men in the house so we were alone to concentrate on that task. It gave us time to get close, talk just us two, and enjoy an interest we still share.

Answer this question honestly: Are you helpful when you visit or a pain in the rump roast? Pitch in! Ask what you can help with or what needs to be done. Has your host been struggling with cleaning out a closet, or are they getting on in years and can't pull weeds from the garden? If you are able, take the time to help them out. You may not ever know how your kindness was appreciated but you and the visit will be remembered fondly.

Tying Up Loose Ends

MANY PEOPLE FEEL IT NECESSARY TO CLEAN AS SOON AS guests leave, which can literally take the rest of the day and sometimes a good part of the following, depending on the number of kids . . . and/or pets! Anything you can do to lighten the load will be greatly appreciated because most hosts don't have maids who come in the back door as guests are leaving by the front. And even if they do, it is still proper to ask what you can do. If, by chance, the host's maid *is* on the way, they will tell you not to bother, but they will remember that you asked. You show respect for your host by leaving the house in good order. This is imperative if you want to be well thought of and invited back, and even if you don't.

I am told of a couple who is notorious for putting off everything until the last minute, including packing up the children's things, then rushing around like crazy people until finally one of them runs into the kitchen where the host is loading the dishwasher for the nineteenth time, while the guest, all flustered, looking pointedly at the clock, asks if there is anything he can do to help. The answer, of course, is nothing. It's too late.

So get an early start. Here's what to do:

Allow plenty of time for leave taking. Do not be in a mad rush. There is nothing worse at the end of a wonderful visit than rushing around in an unorganized frenzy of activity.

Strip the bed or sofa bed of sheets and pillowcases but don't leave the dirty sheets on the floor. Be very cool and stuff the sheets and the pillowcase into the remaining pillowcase (assuming there are two!) and take them to the laundry room; that way your host can easily dump the load into the washer. There may be the odd host who does not want you to strip the bed. Best to ask first.

Gather up the dirty towels from the bath and put all in a pile in the laundry room. If you do not know where the laundry room is, ask. Do not leave towels hanging in the bathroom. If there are clean towels you have not used, put a note on them letting your host know they are clean. Your host does not know which you have or haven't used and if there were several guest rooms and two sofas in use, she may not remember you mentioning it!

Fold the blankets (if they do not have to be washed) and place them neatly on a chair in the bedroom or on the bed.

Pull the comforter back over the mattress. No reason to leave it on the floor to wrinkle. The host may not remake the bed for some time. My husband's two nieces have a great rule, which makes even the Visit Wizard blush for not doing it: Not only does each bed get stripped, but every bed is then *remade* with clean sheets. The amount of time and effort this saves the host is immeasurable. I don't ask my guests to do that, but how super of you to offer.

Clean the bathroom: the toilet (yes, sorry), wipe down the sink and tub, and use glass cleaner on the mirror. Empty the waste can and replace the liner (why does no one replace the liner?). Put out fresh towels if they are clearly visible in the closet. If you can't find them, don't ask. Leave it as you found it—try to put things back as they were. Pull the shower curtain closed. No, not to hide the dirty tub, but because it dries better that way. Simple. These tasks should take all of five minutes and your host will be hugely impressed, not to mention relieved.

Leave the bedroom as you found it. If you had to rearrange items upon arriving, try to put them back as they were. What, you didn't take a picture when you got there?!

Take away any metal hangers *you* brought or throw them in the recycle bin.

Do ask your host about predeparture chores: For example, would your host like you to vacuum your bedroom or other areas of the house or take out the trash? The answer will most likely be no, but it is very thoughtful to ask. Anything you can do now means less labor for your host.

Leave your packed luggage in your room or in an unobtrusive area in the house until time of departure or put it in the car. One good guest I know gets up, comes down for a cup of coffee, goes back upstairs, does all the bathroom and bedroom chores and then comes down for breakfast. That way we can have a wonderful leisurely breakfast together without the last-minute scrambling and falling over luggage.

Look around diligently for your items. There are those, including yours truly, who forget glasses, laptops, and even purses. On many occasions as host, I have found multiple personal belongings that had to be mailed back to their owners. That's fine, but do remember to take the time to look around.

Pick up and put away any things your children used. This is all contingent upon your not having a 6 a.m. flight and a toddler with an ear infection, of course. If so, do what you reasonably can that morning and let your host know you are sorry you couldn't do more.

VISIT WIZARD TIP If you have a very early morning or late night flight, consider having a car service pick you up and take you to the airport if affordable. I would never have thought of it until we had guests who insisted. I did get up, bleary eyed, at 4 a.m. to fix coffee and a light breakfast and to say good-bye, but I admit that not having to drive them to the airport at that hour was wonderful. I went happily back to bed, pulled the sheet around me, and thought "what thoughtful guests.... "

The Final Farewell

THE TONE YOU USE WHEN YOU LEAVE THE HOUSE AT THE end of the visit is just as important as it was when you first arrived. Your attitude and behavior at this time can make up for mistakes, misunderstandings, and misbehavior, either real or imagined.

If you put into practice the strategies in this book I will assume your visit went pretty well. But even if it didn't, you are obliged to perform this same action:

Be vocal. Tell your host you had a wonderful (okay, you can say "nice") time, even if you didn't. If you behaved politely they won't know you were miserable, wailing behind your bedroom wall having never fully unpacked, but will always remember you were kind enough to thank them. Just don't come back when next invited.

Be warm. Now is the time for hugs and handshakes. Be sincere in your thanks. I personally remember having a less-than-perfect time with a particular friend, but as I was leaving I hugged that person, looked him in the eye and told him I loved him. He reciprocated and in that one simple act we both immediately knew all was right again.

After Words

ALWAYS, ALWAYS, ALWAYS MAIL (YES, THAT'S SNAIL MAIL) A thank-you card when you get back home. I know some of you may balk at this, thinking it an old-fashioned, unnecessary tradition, but I assure you that is not the case. And if you visited with your children have them sign it. A simple way to show them nice manners.

Friends who brought their dog when they visited did a very cute thing: the card they sent was from their dog to my dog. You can't imagine how well a simple note will be received. Yes, I admit I have been guilty of sending thank-you *emails* (sorry Miss Manners), but they are just not the same. However, a thank-you email is better than nothing!

On my Facebook page we were chatting about thank-you notes. One young woman told me it was unnecessary and she never did it and her friends never expect it. I told her to give it a shot just for fun. A few weeks later she wrote me back saying she did indeed send a thank-you note, and the recipient was so shocked that she received a thank-you note for her thank you! I, of course, was thrilled.

When "Thank You" Is a Stretch

HOWEVER, IF THINGS WENT POORLY, PEOPLE FOUGHT, OR tears were shed, someone has to be the first to reach out to the other. Someone simply must make the first move. But who, when, and how? And is it ever right *not* to get in touch and either apologize or at least make the effort to make amends? Surprisingly, yes. Read on.

The best way to communicate your hurt feelings, thoughts, or remorse is by using the power of the handwritten note, yet again. You can briefly say your piece, speak your mind, make amends thoughtfully and in your own way. If you try to do it by phone, the two-way conversation can quickly dissolve into confrontation and misunderstanding—yet again! The note is personal. It lets you form your thoughts without being reactionary. It also gives the reader time to think, accept or not, and write back or not. In these situations it is best to allow for time and distance to put the squabble into perspective.

Example of a bad note:

> *"I'm sorry our time together stunk. When I broke that vase I did not understand why you got so upset. You know I ended up crying in my room because of it! Anyway, I felt we were just distant after that and our husbands were uptight because of our behavior. If we ever do it again I will make sure I watch myself around your property!—Your sister."*

Better note:

> *"Well, we've had better visits as I know you'd agree! I am so very sorry about the vase. I had forgotten Jim had gotten it for you on your anniversary and how special it was to you. I understand you were upset, and so was I, so it just escalated. I feel bad that we both made our husbands uncomfortable. I would love to put this one behind us and get together again soon.*

Please pass my apology on to Jim. With love and hugs, Your sister."

This sister went out the next day and bought a vase and shipped it to her sister. Although not as expensive or sentimentally special as the one she broke, the gesture, and more importantly, the recognition for her actions, made all the difference.

VISIT WIZARD TIP If you are going to send the reaching-out note electronically, read it twice and walk away for a bit before you hit the send button—or you could end up making a regrettable typo like "you're a real fiend," instead of "you're a real friend."

Other times it is best to completely ignore what happened and go on as if it didn't. Here is when:

- Nothing you say or no amount of groveling is going to help or change the other's mind;
- The host honestly did not know you were offended;
- You would do irreparable harm by bringing it up;
- You would so embarrass the other person that you should just take the higher road and remain quiet.

Parting Thoughts

REMEMBER THE GOAL OF THE VISIT: WHEN YOU GET IN THE car, bus, or taxi, suitcases stowed, you should think to yourself, or turn to your partner and remark, what a great time you had and that you are anxious to return and see your hosts again.

The goal you want for your host, as they shut the door and the quiet returns, is to think what a wonderful guest you were and that they can't wait to have you back.

The lasting impression you want to leave is one of a classy, fun, team player who understands the difficulties and anxieties of hosting—yes, even people you love—especially people you love, for an extended period of time.

And for you, I wish nothing more than to hear the sound of you patting yourself on the back for making the effort and taking the time, for getting through the usual rough spots, laughing when you could have cried, joking when you could have been angry, and enjoying to the fullest extent possible those who love you most: your family and friends.

CHAPTER 4

Visiting with Children and Young Adult Confidential

"There's no such thing as fun for the whole family."

—JERRY SEINFELD

A LITTLE GIRL CAME TO SEE THE VISIT WIZARD. "VISIT WIZARD," she pleaded, "can you make my parents more relaxed? I never get to do anything fun and I always have to mind my manners." The Visit Wizard waved the VW stick and *poof!* her parents became more lenient.

Then a little boy came to see the Visit Wizard. "Visit Wizard!" he cried, "my parents let me do whatever I want and I always get yelled at by the other adults. Can you make them give me some boundaries?" The Visit Wizard waved the VW stick and *poof!* the parents of the little boy became stricter. The moral of this story? Always carry a Visit Wizard stick.

Unless you have a nanny, cook, Dr. Phil, or the Visit Wizard stick with you, visiting with children will be stressful. More planning, preparing, flexibility, patience, and skill is required than typical adult visits. And don't worry, no matter your parenting style, strict or relaxed, someone is going to find fault. The only one you can count on to be on your side is the dog. The cat really doesn't care. The only thing that is certain is that following some of these basic rules will make the visit more enjoyable for everyone (including you) and one of the best experiences in the life of your child, the memory of which will be long cherished.

A Simple Plan: Anticipate Your Needs in Advance

I WAS HEADED SOMEWHERE... OR MAYBE JUST ARRIVING HOME, I can't remember which, and it really doesn't matter. It could have been any airport, anywhere in the world. It was a Friday afternoon, it was hot, and the airport was busy. I looked up, plastic fork poised tentatively over my greasy scrambled egg something, and could only watch aghast as a young mother trudged past, pushing one of those two-children strollers that needs its own parking space, loaded down like some twenty-first-century version of the Joads from *The Grapes of Wrath*. Bags hung all over it, blankets and other items were stacked one on top of the other. The mother looked like she was on a mission from hell: Grandma's or bust! I can only assume there were two children somewhere in the pile. Coming behind was Dad, toting four pieces of baggage, two collapsible strollers tucked under one arm, shirt half in, half out, and a similarly fierce look on his face. I wanted to run over and offer help, but I knew in my heart it would do no good. I only hoped that this leg of the trip would be the tough part, but sadly I knew it was probably just the beginning.

Like this couple so literally demonstrates, children come with baggage—lots of it. Find me a parent who breezes through an airport with one suitcase and a carry-on, and I'll show you a parent who left her child at home. Good planning will mean less stress and headache for you for the entire course of the trip. There's a fine line between dragging the entire contents of your home and leaving everything to chance. You want to be prepared, but not overburdened.

So, what to bring? Let's start with the basics. I've left a few lines blank for you to fill in any special items. Go through the list and start checking off who will provide each item: you, your host, or a rental service. Yes, thankfully, there are places, easily found on the Internet, where you can rent items like cribs and car seats (even bottle sterilizers), which can be delivered to your destination.

You	Host	Rental	
_____	_____	_____	Crib or bassinet
_____	_____	_____	Playpen
_____	_____	_____	Sleeping bags
_____	_____	_____	Car seat
_____	_____	_____	Baby bottles and/ or medicines
_____	_____	_____	Specific foods/formula
_____	_____	_____	Baby monitor
_____	_____	_____	The comfy toy
_____	_____	_____	Breast-feeding equipment
_____	_____	_____	Diapers, diaper bag, baby wipes, powder, etc.
_____	_____	_____	Night-light
_____	_____	_____	Plastic sheets if your child may wet the bed
_____	_____	_____	Entertainment material
_____	_____	_____	Sports equipment, life preservers, sunglasses, lotion
_____	_____	_____	Stroller(s)

_____ _____ _____ Baby gates

_____ _____ _____ Appropriate clothes for the weather and activities planned

_____ _____ _____ Directions (written, please!)

_____ _____ _____ Contact numbers

_____ _____ _____ Your electronic communication device

_____ _____ _____ Keys to your host's house, if necessary

_____ _____ _____ Other: ____________________

_____ _____ _____ Other: ____________________

_____ _____ _____ Other: ____________________

Share with your host the items on your list you are hoping they can provide. If you're worried that your needs will sound like a list of demands from a hostage taker—don't. Most hosts will appreciate your thoughtfulness and not having to scramble to get things after you arrive. Once they know what you need, and if they don't have it, it gives them the opportunity to ask a neighbor or friend to supply something for the time you will be there. Your host will let you know what is not available. Coordinating with them in advance is the key.

Planes, Trains, and Automobiles

How you are getting to the visit makes a difference in what you can bring, or not, so know what is allowed on an airplane, bus, or train. It is always best to call ahead or check the website.

As an example, as of this writing: on US Air you're allowed one checked bag with certain specific dimensions and a maximum weight of 50 lbs/23 kg (checked-bag fees apply); one fully collapsible stroller or one child restraint device or car seat at no charge. Because airline policies change, make sure you check with your airline.

If you are driving, well, you know what to do. Just load up the minivan with as much stuff as you can possibly cram in, ready for any event or emergency. Gone are the days when you packed as perfect and orderly as Hyacinth Bucket, sorry, *Bouquet*. But if you find yourself searching the Internet for a trailer maybe it's best if you leave the baby pool and bikes at home. And the car is one place where the children's electronic gadgets may be used with impunity.

VISIT WIZARD TIP Take the time to research the place you will be visiting. Check to see where the nearest doctor, pharmacy, playground or park, theater, library, or pool is located. Although one would assume the host will know, Grandmother may not have been watersliding in some time!

Do Ask, Do Tell: Communicate with Your Host in Advance

MOST OF US ARE NOT BIG ON SURPRISES, UNLESS IT'S A birthday party at The Ritz, after which your spouse sweeps you off to Paris in a private jet for a week while your mother-in-law happily takes care of the children.... Back to reality. I believe that the more information you have—and can give—up front and *before* the visit, the better off you are going to be. For those of you too bashful or intimidated to communicate, consider this stressful arrival due solely to lack of communication on everyone's part:

"We arrived late in the day after an eight-hour drive to find nothing prepared. I mean nothing. I guessed that my two kids were sleeping with me and my husband in the one queen bed, which is okay, but our kids

are twelve and thirteen! Our hosts were at work, their kids at football practice, and I was staring into a pretty empty refrigerator. The good news is that I found a note on the counter asking me to walk the dog and would I mind starting something for dinner? Directions to a grocery would have been nice! So back into the car trudged all four of us . . . and the dog. I got what I thought everyone would eat but no way was I cooking. Frozen pizzas would have to work. As my thoughts turned to the evening all I could hope was that she had sleeping bags."

So what went wrong? Just as surely as your wireless device on a rainy day, a communication failure had occurred. The guest did not let the host know when she and her family would be arriving; the guest did not ask about sleeping arrangements; the host was not prepared no matter when the arrival time; and the guest, although asked to prepare dinner, had no idea who would eat what!

Following are some perfectly reasonable things to communicate about with your host:

Sleeping Arrangements for the Children

Will the child or children sleep with you? Are sleeping bags on a floor the best option, or will there be a guest room available? You really don't think it's a good idea for your little Susie and now older cousin Marcus to share the same room? Let your host know. The importance of nailing down who sleeps where obviously depends on the age and number of children and the size of your host's house. Obviously if you and your child have been invited to Balmoral Castle for a weekend of hunting, probably no need to inquire ahead.

Activities in the Area

Is there a pool nearby, a park, an ice skating rink, or tennis courts? If you know what activities your child might participate in, you can pack and prepare accordingly. If you would like your children to do something specific while you are visiting, tell your host. If it is significant, like a drive two states north to a ski slope, it is your responsibility to rent a car to get there. Let the host know that you are going to pay for whatever activity your child does alone and ask if it's okay. Remember, they want to see your kids... yes, really!

VISIT WIZARD TIP Although I know some of you would rip it from my clutched fingers and shred it to small pieces, I am big on itineraries. If there are several children visiting, you might want to coordinate with the other parents and your host, especially if tickets need to be bought in advance or there are expensive or unusual activities available. Plan one out (see the Seven Simple Steps to a Smooth Visit chapter) and email it around for comments.

Financial Concerns

Don't let money worries stop you from visiting. Unashamedly let your host know you need to limit activities and meals out this trip. Everyone will understand. There are not many of us who haven't been in that position and you will be more relaxed and comfortable being up-front about it. It will also stop your host from booking that expensive outing, unless it is their treat. There are many wonderful things you can do without money. Some of the best times are those spent in no outside pursuits or fancy restaurants at all, but at home doing things that can't be bought, like sharing, talking, laughing. "But what will the children *do*?" you cry!

Don't worry—they'll find something! I'm not sure when we all decided that children have to be managed like little beauty pageant contestants, their lives just not complete without unrelenting activity and attention.

It's Okay to Say No

Your host will hopefully send you a list of things they might suggest everyone do. If your host has something planned that is too expensive or too dangerous and you don't want your child to participate, let them know ahead of time. That is so much easier to do in advance, out of your child's earshot, than in the heat of the moment with cries of, "But Mommy, why *can't* we?" ringing in your ears.

Special Dietary Needs

If there are just some things your children can't or won't eat or are allergic to, let your host know. Your host will most likely go to the store to stock up on some items and will appreciate not spending time or money on things that won't be consumed. Emailing a list ahead of time is a smart and reasonable thing to do. You can always add the words, "But if you were not planning on going to the market, no worries! I am happy to go after we arrive." If your child only eats certain foods, and you are driving, bring some with you or stop at a grocery store close to the host's house. Don't expect your host to have specialty items unless you specifically requested them in advance.

Safety Concerns

If you are visiting with a toddler or an infant and your host does not have children, let them know what they can do to "childproof" the house in advance of your visit. They will not be insulted if you do it nicely and offer simple suggestions. And if they read this book you won't have to worry, as it's covered in the Hosting Children and Young Adults section!

Pets

If your child is allergic to animal dander ask your host if any pets will be in the house. If so, you may have to ask your host to board their pets if you are going to be there a short period of time. However, don't expect your host to board their pet for several weeks unless they offer.

VISIT WIZARD TIP I know some of you would rather sleep in the yard than communicate your needs and the needs of your children to your host. Don't worry. That is why the Universe invented email and the Visit Wizard. Both give you a polite, nonthreatening way to make your needs and concerns known.

High Anxiety: Reassure Your Child Before the Visit

I THINK WE TEND TO SEE CHILDREN'S ISSUES AS LESS STRESSful than ours because they are well, just kids. Relatively speaking, I believe that children have more stress in dealing with their everyday life than we do. Consider this:

ADULT	CHILD
I just lost my job.	My best friend doesn't want to be best friends anymore.
My boss wants that report on his desk by Monday.	I don't understand the homework, but worse than that, my teacher wants it tomorrow morning and there will be a test!
I swear that Joe is angling for my job.	This bully at school is threatening to take my lunch and beat me up.
My clothes are out-of-date and, worse, they don't fit me anymore.	Everyone else has the cool new shoes that I don't have so they think we are poor.

We know how to meet and greet people we have not met before. We can usually handle that gruff Uncle Bill or nagging Aunt Sally. Kids don't have those skills yet. We have to reassure and protect them.

If the cousins are picking on them, step in. Don't worry about hurting your brother's or sister's feelings. Your child is more important at that moment. As adults you can discuss what happened later.

Brush up on the basics with your children before the visit. Go through the photo album and remind them who Uncle David is; teach, or remind, young men and women the importance of shaking hands with a solid grip and looking adults in the eye. Tell them what is not allowed and what you expect in terms of their behavior, and what you hope they might enjoy during the visit. Remind them, also, of basic manners, such as saying "please" and "thank you" and "may I?" Children are much more comfortable when they know how to behave and what is expected of them.

Reassure them that you will be there to help. Tell them where they will be sleeping, who will be there, and, to the extent you can, what they might expect or what might be off-limits. For example, your host has horses and your child wants to ride. That may or may not be possible.

Talk to your child if he is fearful of dogs (or other critters) if any will be at the home you are visiting.

If they know their cousin will want to water ski but they are afraid and feel they will be forced to participate, reassure them that they don't have to, although if they would like to try you will help them.

And by all means let them bring that torn up, ugly, stained, stuffed animal that they can hug to their body when needed! There are times when we all need something to cuddle.

VISIT WIZARD TIP Help your child make or bring a gift for the host or the children of the host. Even children feel special when presenting a gift and feel proud not arriving empty-handed.

Ain't Misbehavin': Help Your Child Be on His Best Behavior

"If you want your children to improve, let them overhear the nice things you say about them to others."

—HAIM GINOTT

"If that doesn't work, put a wee bit of brandy in the sippy cup."

—THE VISIT WIZARD

YOU DON'T HAVE TO BE ATTILA THE HUN, BUT DO BE FIRM enough so that everyone enjoys the visit. How you, the visiting parent, behave toward, and with, your children in the host's home is crucial to the success of the visit. There must be limits that are communicated to the child and enforced. The children must be supervised and not left to run wild. One woman told me of a time when her guest's children happily ran through her house upsetting things and creating general mayhem while even her own children looked on with concern. The woman finally had to take matters into her own hands and ask the children directly to stop, which naturally she was embarrassed and upset to have to do. She told me it was their only visit.

Manage the children's time so the adults are not waiting for them to complete activities or sit down to a meal together. If your host says dinner is at 6 p.m. for the children, make sure your child is not late. It is irritating for everyone when parents can't, or won't, put forth the effort necessary to ensure their children adhere to the adults' schedule.

When possible, know the "house rules" in advance. Ask your host, "Do you have any house rules that we should know about?" For example, there may be big ones, like the children may not be allowed in a certain room because of breakables or because it's the host's painting studio, or in the Jacuzzi. Or little rules that bear repeating, like young Billy cannot ride the Irish Wolfhound like a pony again or jump up and down on Aunt Martha's down-stuffed comforter.

Don't break your own rules just because you're visiting. If you want your children to be in bed at a certain time, make it happen. You rule! If you don't want them to drink sodas or watch a movie you think is inappropriate for their temperament or age, don't let them. Your host should respect your rules and support them.

Do not allow your children to use electronic games or gadgets excessively. The point of the visit is to get everyone involved with each other—to be inclusive—not reclusive. Your child may fight you tooth and nail but you need to win this one. Bells and whistles going off when the adults are trying to talk is terribly distracting and not conducive to a pleasant visit. To lessen this potential stress, one woman recommends the following:

> *"The children will naturally want to play and keep in contact with their friends while away. There should be a limit, though, and not while eating. Remind the kids that visit time is a special time for them to get to know the hosts. There can be designated times set aside when the devices are allowed. Perhaps as a reward for finishing and behaving well at dinner, they can leave the table and play games and catch up on the phones. The relatives may enjoy having the kids share and teach about their technology, too, a time for both to learn and spend time together."*

If your children have to be disciplined, try not to do it in front of other guests or your hosts. It will only serve to make everyone uncomfortable and ensure tears from the child. Take them from the room and correct them in private. You will be doing everyone a favor and look like the calm, in-control parent you are. With one exception, if the children are at the dinner table with the adults, make sure they behave and are not the focal point of attention. This is a good time for parents to teach proper table manners if they (the children) have not had these experiences before.

Speaking of discipline, you are the right one to discipline your child. That's a given. But I am going to go out on that proverbial shaky limb: allow the host (or another visiting friend or family member) to comment if a child has done something wrong or is behaving badly if you are otherwise engaged or just not doing what's proper in terms of child management. It should be graciously accepted by the parent if the comment is made out of concern and is appropriate for the situation.

If you do *not* think their comment is appropriate, don't lash out hastily but do talk to the person privately after you have cooled down. All bets are off, of course, if someone abuses your child either physically or emotionally. Just pack up and leave.

Stay Flexible

Yes, your rules are important and how you rear your child is up to you. But there may be a time when being flexible is your smartest choice. I have heard many parents complain that other parents cause stress during the visit because they are overly strict with their own children. (Don't worry. I've heard just as many complaints about parents who are too lax.)

Consider these few examples and think about what you would do:

Your child is the same age as the one you are visiting, but he is allowed to stay up an hour later than your child. Might it be wise of you to make an exception for the few nights you will be visiting? That is up to you, not your host, and not your child.

You and your child were excited about doing something, or going to some event. Unfortunately, it's not going to happen for whatever reason. Instead of being bitter or communicating your disappointment, try to find an alternative that works.

Your aging father-in-law loves to take Tommy to the baseball game and fill him with hot dogs, cotton candy, and other things that you are convinced will stunt his growth and keep him back a grade in school. Tommy loves it even more. So should you be flexible...just this once? Please, Mom?

You're Not Off the Hook: Take Responsibility for Your Child

YOU MAY BE ON HOLIDAY, BUT YOU STILL HAVE TO REPORT FOR parental duty. It's up to you to take responsibility for your child's:

Meals. If your children are not eating what the adults or other children are eating, prepare their food yourself and use what is on hand to the extent that you can. Don't expect the host, who may be concentrating on preparing the main dinner, to also prepare your children's meals, unless your host has offered to prepare the meal for all the children. Clear as mud pie? Example: your eight-year-old has decided he wants to be a vegan. The host is cooking burgers on the grill for everyone. Guess what? You're on veggie duty!

Activities. Don't expect your host to act as full-time playmate or baby-sitter. As much as you may need it and unquestionably deserve it, your visit is not your vacation from the children. Even if the host *wants* to take over, allow that for a limited amount of time, or at least until you are called back for duty.

I once had the opportunity to send a visiting friend and his wife to a house I owned about thirty miles away from our vacation home, and for that weekend we took their two kids. Yippee! I was so excited and pleased to be able to do this. Then one of the children got sick—the first night the parents were away. That was okay with me, I handled the throwing-up-at-night situation, but it was apparent the next day, when the parents called to "check in," that their little second honeymoon time away that I had so eagerly planned was going to be short-lived. I doubted they even had a chance to light the scented candles by their tub.

Safety. It is important that you be with your children for any unusual or even semi-dangerous activity. The last thing a host wants is for something to happen to the children on their watch, or to inadvertently do something with the child that you might not allow. One can only shake their head in dismay at the horror stories of children happily running into the house excitedly exclaiming that Aunt Kathleen and Uncle Jim let them drive the tractor or go bungee jumping, only to leave the parents horrified. My husband volunteered to take two visiting children to a very crowded community pool and water park. I'm talking slides that would get Flipper seasick. He was confident there would be no problem, and I'm sure there probably would not have been, but I insisted that one of the children's parents accompany the kids. But, as you know, I tend to err on the side of caution.

Time. Allow everyone time with the children. Make sure one set of grandparents or one aunt or uncle do not monopolize the children's time. Others may want to spend time with your children but may feel it's not right to ask or take them away from other activities. Please step in. Your children are wonderful gifts that should be shared equally.

Mistakes. When your child spills something, or there is an accident, jump on it. Your hosts will most likely help, but the main duty falls to you. If your child breaks something you must offer to pay your host to either have it repaired or replaced. If you see something in the house that causes you fear, ask your host if it could possibly be removed temporarily. I am even now eyeing that fragile vase on the end table....

Needs. If your child needs something he or she is not getting, don't be afraid to ask your host for it or ask where you can get it. Don't let anyone suffer. Speak up.

VISIT WIZARD TIP If you see your host could use a break, volunteer to take the child or children on some little trip, or just to play outside.

Hygiene. Time to be blunt: Little guys and girls just don't have the knowledge or experience to handle some chores alone! When your younger child uses the bathroom, when possible, go behind and make sure the toilet is flushed and clean.

Do bring plastic sheets if your child has a bed-wetting problem. He or she will feel much more comfortable, and it is the polite thing for your host.

Kid's stuff. Keep your child's things as picked up as possible. I know this is a tough one but don't let it get too out of control. When your host starts creating piles of clothes and toys in different rooms of the house you know it's time to take action.

Food and fun. Finally, unless your host otherwise insists, pay for some food at the grocery store and some activities for the children. Don't expect your host to pay for everything or anything for your children, unless they have made it clear that they wish to do so. A woman I had just met asked me what I did for a living. I told her I was writing this book and was currently working on the children's chapter. Not two minutes later here is what she told me:

"My son's friend and his father came to visit for five days. The man did not offer to pay for any food, or to pick up the tab for anything in which his son participated. One day he had to write a check for an activity we all were doing because I had forgotten my checkbook at the

house. He then had the nerve to ask me to pay him back! I know the family. They are not the least bit strapped financially. They will never be invited back."

A wealthy couple told me they resent it when their children come with their grandchildren as the couple is always expected to pay for everything. Even if your hosts can afford it and do so seemingly happily, you should still make the offer.

Keep Your Cool, Keep Your Head

THIS IS THE CHALLENGING PART OF ANY VISIT. LITTLE JOHNNY gets into a fight with little cousin Tony; your friend doesn't understand why your Anne can't have any sugar; Billy throws a fit when he can't stay up late like the big kids; your child gets sick and gives it to everyone else. There are hurt feelings and crying fits. You name it or even think it, and kids can probably make it happen. Not to mention the sheer volume of activity and chores that must be done on a daily basis. It's enough to make Mother Nature herself send down lightning bolts of frustration.

Although your blood pressure may be higher than your sister Marcy's new chest, stay as calm and cool as possible for the benefit of yourself, your children, and your host. Sometimes that means you must discipline your child or take them and go off by yourselves for a bit. Do whatever you can to calm the waters and right the ship. And sometimes that means taking no obvious action:

I recall as a child using a thick black marker to draw dinosaurs on a leather recliner in our home. I thought the drawings were pretty darn good, not really knowing what ink on leather actually does, but still feeling there was something wrong with this particular art project. To this day,

I remember my fear of being punished in front of the others and thinking how fortunate I was that my mother kept her cool. But come to think of it, why didn't she go ballistic? Could it be that she just didn't see them? I did, after all, have the good sense to draw on the back of the chair....

If you do not approve of something being done to, or with, your children do not be bashful about speaking up. Privately and firmly tell your host your concerns. But try not to be *overly* paranoid or protective.

See? Isn't visiting with children simple? Which reminds me: You know that weekend at their country home in the Hamptons your childless boss has invited you and your family to enjoy? Can you say, "Call the grandparents"?

Happy Endings: Make a Smooth Exit

SO THE END HAS COME. BY THIS TIME YOU MAY NOT BE QUITE as chipper as when you first arrived and crying tears of joy, or grief, as departure time looms near. Either way you are to be congratulated. Visiting with children, although fun and great for them, is never easy for you. But take heart! Only... a... few... more... things....

An important and often overlooked nicety: Give the host (grandparent, uncle or aunt, or just dear friend) the opportunity for some quiet time with your children right before departure. So often with the wonderful chaos and confusion they bring, there is little opportunity for meaningful time together. It is important to both host and child that they spend just ten or fifteen minutes together on the couch or in the kitchen talking or just enjoying each other's company. What happens in the last few minutes is just as important, if not more than, the entire rest of the visit.

Clean up the mess. Whatever toys or other things you and/or your child may have pulled out or used, you must put away before you leave. If your child painted on the furniture, for example, try your best to get it off. Make the time to do so. Look around for objects you brought and take them with you. See the Leaving a Lasting Impression chapter on page 193 for detailed departure cleanup tips.

When you get home have the child create, or pick out from my website, a thank-you card for the host. How artistic it is makes absolutely no difference. The fact that it is handmade makes it beautiful. And the child will learn a valuable lesson from doing it. No, email will not do.

Young Adult Confidential: Your First Time Visiting Alone

SO YOU WANT TO, OR HAVE TO, VISIT WITH FRIENDS OR FAMILY for the first time sans parental units and you are concerned. You're not sure if it's right to strip the bed the day of departure and if you need something that is not provided, should you ask for it? Can you go into the refrigerator at night? (And the answer is yes, you can, but only for something necessary, not to raid the place.)

The two lads had never been invited to visit the country estate for the weekend and were as nervous as . . . well, young people getting ready to go on a trip into the unknown. Who would tell them what they needed to know?

"Did someone say guide?" The Visit Wizard appeared before the young people as they packed.

"VW. Cool. So what should we take?"

The Visit Wizard looked down her nose at the pair. "Let's start at the beginning. Do you have a gift for the host? Do you know what activities you will be doing? Have you consulted the Internet about the weather this weekend?

"Oh, all right. It's not a big deal, and you two will be the proverbial rock stars, but you must not skip anything. Understood?" Nods of appreciation. "But we must be speedy so try to keep up. Here's what you should do:"

Bring a small gift for the host. Doesn't matter what it is. Stop and pick some wildflowers along the way if you can (as long as it's legal), or make a batch of brownies before the trip or bring a card. Your hosts do not care if it was expensive or not. Really.

Pick up after yourself *everywhere*. Examples: If you are watching television one night, take your shoes or your shirt or whatever with you into your bedroom when you go to bed that night. Take your plates, cups, and glasses back into the kitchen when you are done with them. Nice touch: Offer to clear the table when a meal is done.

Keep your bedroom neat. Take a small plastic bag in which to put your dirty clothes so they are not lying about the room. Make your bed every morning or make up the sofa if that is your bed.

Offer to do things, *anything*—from sweeping the porch to running to the store. *But don't:* offer to do things in which you have no experience, such as fixing a complex computer issue. Yes, we know you probably know more about it than your ancient host, but it could lead to disaster—like your host's hard drive crashing. Not something for which you want to be responsible.

If you would like a drink or snack, just ask. Your host will be impressed and most likely tell you to help yourself. Use restraint, of course. *But don't:* down Uncle Fred's six-pack or eat half the fruit pie. Do not be afraid to ask for what you need or want in general. This is important. Naturally most of us are a bit fearful or hesitant in asking for something from someone we may not know well. Don't be. You want to be comfortable and your host wants that as well.

Be independent and self-sufficient. I don't mean you should feel as if you have to go into the kitchen and make your own dinner, but if you have a car and you want to drive into town or go sightseeing alone, fine. What's important is to strike a balance between being needy and being completely carefree.

Talk. Engage with your hosts. They want to hear your thoughts and opinions and about school or your job. Just don't talk nonstop about yourself. Ask about them.

Speak up. If your hosts want you to do something that you would prefer not to do, let them know. You have the right to say "no." (I'm talking about things like taking a tour of the local coal mine, not taking out the garbage.)

Watch your manners and mind your knickers. Be polite. Keep all low-slung items, top and bottom, to a minimum ... I mean to a maximum!

Engage with the younger kids. They love to see what you are up to and will be thrilled you are taking the time.

Thank your hosts and *mail* them a thank-you note when you get back home. Yes, the kind that requires a stamp.

And no matter what, don't:

Be offended if your hosts don't want you and your significant other sharing the same bedroom. Respect their opinions. You can wait a few days.

Sleep until all hours if everyone is up and about in the morning. Stay on the schedule of the household to a reasonable extent.

Disappear without explanation. If you are going up to read or out for a walk tell your host.

Use their things without asking if it's okay. That includes everything from the television to the pool.

Expect your hosts to have your "can't-live-withouts." If life just isn't worth living without the designer coffee you've grown attached to, bring it or get it yourself while there, but don't bring a shopping bag full of food with you. That will only insult your host.

Be late to meals—ever.

Be overly demanding. Your host is not there to wait on you. A good visit is like a two-way street with both guest and host giving and receiving.

Make long-distance calls on your host's phone without asking if you may. Not everyone has free or unlimited long distance. I know—shocking.

Corrupt the younger members of the household. *But do:* uphold their parents' rules.

Ask for money. Ever. Just don't.

VISIT WIZARD TIP It's important that you demonstrate your appreciation and good manners to your host. If you have no money with which to treat your host, ask your host if you can do something for them around the house or cook dinner one night.

"So how are you feeling now?" The Visit Wizard asked her charges.

"Wow. Much better, VW. We get it. We can do this. We might even have a pretty good time!"

"One final thought, young and fearless ones: Even if you would rather be wind surfing or rock climbing or whatever it is you people do, put it out of your head for this weekend. Your hosts really want you and are excited about you coming, so no 'I'd rather be somewhere else than here' attitude. Get over yourselves and into the visit," and with that she was gone.

CHAPTER 5

Visiting with Older Guests

"To me, fair friend, you never can be old, For as you were when first your eye I ey'd, Such seems your beauty still."

—WILLIAM SHAKESPEARE

AT THE AGE OF EIGHTY-SIX, GREAT BRITAIN'S PRINCESS ALICE, Countess of Athlone, traveled to Barbados in a banana boat (*The Book of Royal Lists*, 1982); I know an eighty-two-year-old gentleman who plays tennis twice a week and asks why his partners can't play more sets; my mother-in-law lived happily alone at ninety-two, playing cards with her girlfriends and walking to church.

Gone are the days when getting old meant rocking in a chair at the nursing home. Just because a person is *older* (which, some of you will be thrilled to hear, I am defining as a state-of-being, not an age) doesn't mean he can't be an active, productive, happy, contributing member of the party. And even if activity is becoming more difficult, that doesn't mean the elder's other attributes can't be enjoyed and that they can't have mind-and soul-fulfilling experiences.

The goal of the visit should be just that: to get our older friends and family members up and out and socializing, and bringing positive energy to them. On its face that seems easy enough, but most of our elders have several ailments of differing degrees: hearing and eyesight loss, memory loss, fragility, eating concerns, and stress when traveling and visiting. These things, as well as the many other problems associated with aging, can lead to feelings of isolation and depression if older people don't interact positively and on a regular basis.

So if the elder is physically able and if done right, a visit to friends and family can be uplifting and even downright exciting, even as he grumbles about his potential sleeping arrangements... that he's sure he won't get what he wants to eat... and that Aunt Martha's little dog has always annoyed him, although this is the first time in the ten years Aunt Martha has had the dog you've heard this.

Your generosity in helping older people experience new and interesting things in a safe and caring environment is a wonderful experience for all. One of the things we share as human beings, no matter our age, is the need to socialize, bond, and feel secure and useful. Not necessarily *be* useful, mind you, but *feel* useful. They are two different things. Taking an older person to visit is one of the most giving things you can do. That's the upside.

Here's the downside: When responsible for the visiting older guest, you are in the role of caregiver. It seemingly offers little reward—unless you look deeply. Surprisingly, it is an opportunity to grow and even overcome your own fears in a way that is akin to nothing else. Right before and then during the visit, concerns for our own selves growing old rise to the top of our consciousness as it does for most of the family. It is one of the hardest things to do in life: face the nearness of death, look it in the eye, and embrace it. Find beauty in the wrinkles.

In this part of the book, Becoming the Perfect Guest, I go into great detail about shopping issues, what to bring or not, basic good guest behavior and etiquette, and so on, so I am not going to repeat it here. Please refer to those relevant "guest" chapters for specific information.

So, in a nutshell, the art of visiting with our elders is about showing compassion, caring, and commitment to their needs. Here's how:

Getting to Your Destination

IF ONLY WE COULD CLICK OUR HEELS TOGETHER AND BE EASILY transported not just miles, but through time, how much easier life would be! But, alas, reality dictates that we must rely on more pedestrian modes of transport. Are you traveling by car, bus, train, or airplane? Simple question and decision, right? Wrong! Whatever gets us there in the shortest amount of time or is the most economical is the best choice, right? Wrong again! Well, okay, maybe. But first consider the following:

Is getting to your destination the quickest way really better than the way that allows for frequent stops and breaks? You know what I mean. With age comes a smaller bladder. Why the Creator decided this I haven't a clue, but enough already! Aren't brittle bones and memory loss ample ailments?

If medications have to be administered during the trip, how and when will you do that? No, crushing up the meds and putting them in a water bottle to be sipped en route is not the right answer.

Is a special diet required? If so, what means of transport will best allow it? If the elderly traveler has digestive concerns will rushing through that fast-food line off the freeway, or airline food (or the lack thereof), really work?

Is a wheelchair or oxygen needed? If so, what restrictions or requirements are necessary?

If your trip requires an overnight stay in a hotel, what specific accommodations will you need?

Before deciding on transportation, ask the elder and, if possible, choose what makes *him* most comfortable based on his needs and physical condition. I remember wanting, and rather insisting, that an elderly relative travel by airplane to come visit and could not understand why she insisted just as emphatically that she would not do it. It was the most logical way, after all! After some time and many questions, I finally got it: She was simply not comfortable traveling that way. That was her personal choice and I had to respect it.

First, Speak with the Doctor

Just because Grandfather saw the doctor six months ago doesn't mean you are good to go. Call his doctor's office, let them know the plan, and ask if a physical or shots, like the flu shot, is necessary or advisable before the trip. The fact that you will not be climbing Kilimanjaro is not the point. Even a trip that seems small to you is really not to someone a generation or two ahead of you. The doctor can also advise on the best mode of transportation given the older traveler's particular issues. The doctor may advise against flying, for example.

You will also need specific, written information from the doctor, as follows:

Does your older traveler have artificial implants, joints, or a pacemaker? This documentation will be necessary when going through security at the airport and is just good information to have however you travel. But if you're traveling with your in-law in some foreign country, and the paperwork somehow gets lost, and the bells and whistles of security go off, now is your golden opportunity: Deny knowing him and cruise on past!

Get a written list of medications the elder is taking and the proper dosage and the side effects of each. Make sure there are enough meds to last the trip; if not make sure there are refills available.

If the older guests are on a specific diet know what foods they can and can't eat. And don't listen to them if they try to convince you that donuts and cakes were specifically prescribed by the doctor.

Make sure you have the doctor's contact and emergency contact information.

If Traveling by Air

Get an aisle seat for the elderly traveler so he or she can more easily get up and move around when necessary. Blood clots are often a concern for older people seated for too long a time.

Let the flight attendant know of any special needs.

Check the airline's policy regarding medications or syringes onboard the aircraft.

Make sure your elder drinks water to avoid dehydration.

Get a wheelchair if necessary. Most airlines will gladly arrange for one to be at the curb when you arrive or to assist in deplaning.

If the older traveler is on oxygen, the airlines require you tell them in advance, and the tank is not permitted in the cabin of the aircraft although it can be checked if it meets requirements. Some airlines will provide oxygen during the flight for a fee. What? You expected free oxygen? Call the airline to get specific information.

Check what the airline allows to be checked or carried on, for example, required mobility devices, such as wheelchairs, canes, or crutches and required medical supplies or equipment may or may not be allowed. Some items may be carried onto the aircraft, as long as they meet size and weight restrictions. Don't forget to ask what is considered a free item and what will be subject to baggage fees.

Don't forget to pack necessary medications, extra batteries, and/or food in the *carry-on* bag, not the checked luggage. And again, keep that letter from the doctor handy.

If Traveling by Land

When going by car, bus, or train, make the older traveler as comfortable as possible. Bring a blanket and pillow, water, meds, extra batteries for hearing aids, snacks or meals, magazines or other reading material or music they might enjoy.

Take plenty of breaks along the way and get out of the car to walk around a bit.

Again, have with you that letter from the doctor outlining medical history, current conditions, and medications just in case that information becomes important on your trip.

Do your research and know where the hospitals are along your route. This may seem like a waste of time, but you will be so relieved should you need it.

Try to keep meal and sleep schedules as close to the elder's daily routine as possible, especially when traveling.

What to Take

ASK THE OLDER TRAVELERS WHAT WOULD MAKE THEIR TRIP comfortable and don't shun what they might suggest. Perhaps a pillow from home or a throw would be soothing. I have one friend who will not travel without a picture of her departed loved one.

If you are helping to pack, make sure they bring warm clothes and especially warm night wear. Your elder may not need those flannel pj's, but best to be too warm than cold. It is surprising to most adults the difference between their degree of cold tolerance and older people's. Of course pack sensible shoes for the trip and the visit. Remember falls for elders cause injury to old and brittle bones that are difficult, if not impossible, to mend. Great Aunt Sally thinks she can still pull off stilettos? I want to still be in heels in my nineties, but think one- or two-inch instead.

If the elder is visually impaired and her glasses are just not enough at times, could you bring a handheld magnifying glass so she can more easily read the menu at that dark restaurant, or a digital clock with large, lighted display for the guest room?

If they are hearing impaired there are wireless devices you can purchase online that they can comfortably wear to hear the television so it does not have to be turned up so loudly that it is uncomfortable for the others. An online search for "television listening devices" will bring up a variety of options. Models are available to use with or without hearing aids.

Or perhaps try those temporary, and in some cases quite inexpensive, hearing aids you can buy at the drugstore. That way the older guests can enjoy, and most importantly join in on, the conversations.

What food and snacks do they eat? As we age our digestive system is not what it once was. Your host may love bagels and lox for breakfast but the elder guests may prefer something more easily digested. Bring what they like, or buy it when you arrive, or let your hosts know in advance if they have offered to do the shopping. Does decaf or herbal tea in the evening bring back good memories and help the elder sleep? Get or bring it.

Bring that list and instructions from the doctor, complete with a list of any food or drug allergies. (Yes, I know I've said this three times, and no, it's not because I'm having a senior moment; it's just that important.) Basically you have to be prepared if an emergency arises that results in a trip to a doctor or hospital during the visit.

Bring any reading material and games that the older person likes. Usually the newspaper or magazines are a good choice. If the person can't read while in the car because it makes her dizzy, don't discount audio books or music. Granny may love tuning out to Frank Sinatra.

VISIT WIZARD TIP Pack earplugs (yes, I have a specific recommendation as I use them often: they are the foam square ones—not the oval) and those ear protector contraptions that one wears when firing a gun. I never visit without them (the contraptions, not the gun). They are padded so quite comfortable and perfect for when the older guest wants to retire early but the music video the kids are watching just has to be shown—one—more—time! Although neither are completely sound-deadening, they are effective enough.

And just when you thought the list was over and you could start packing, it's not: Take a spiral notebook or an electronic device. Using something that can be easily transported in your bag and kept handy is a great tool. In it you can jot down when meds need to be taken, and that they were, and other important and useful information.

Plan Ahead

THE HOSTING OLDER GUESTS CHAPTER (PAGE 117) DETAILS what your host can do to help ensure safety and comfort for the visiting elder. Here are some things you can do to help ensure that happens. Let your host know of any special needs you have well in advance, and if they can't be supplied by your host, make arrangements to get them. For example:

Preventing falls: Falling is one of the most common causes of injury for older people. It can be a result of impaired vision, medications, poor balance, alcohol intake, or even something as simple as dim lighting. Ask your host to check for things around the house that could be moved or modified to help prevent falls, like throw rugs on hardwood floors or icy front paths. For a complete list, see the Hosting Older Guests chapter.

Sleeping: Ask where your older guest will be sleeping. This is important to know so you can bring what you need or make other arrangements if you are concerned that Great Uncle Harry may end up in a sleeping bag in the kid's room. Will the older visitor be able to get in and out of a high bed easily? Will a stepstool be required?

Bathroom necessities: Ask if there is a substantial nonslip mat in the tub or shower. There are temporary suction-cup grab handles that you can buy at most bed and bath or department stores if you are concerned with tub safety, although I am sure their safety is somewhat dependent on the size or ability of the elder. If older guests have trouble getting down to or up from the commode, perhaps bringing a walker would give the assistance needed. Take a look in the bathroom your older friend or family member will be using. Are things they will need, like towels and tissue, within easy reach? Is the cabinet free of someone else's medications?

Rental items: Are there any items you could rent upon arrival that would make the visit easier for you and your elder, and your host as well, like ramps, canes, wheelchairs or scooters, or bath safety items? Consult the Internet. You will be surprised at the availability.

Look for clutter: If the elder is in a wheelchair, make sure he can maneuver around the house. And even if he does walk on his own, or with a cane or walker, check that the hallways are clear of clutter such as toys or cords. You have to take all the same precautions as you would when visiting with a young person. That is not meant to belittle an older person, but to respect them.

Food: Email your host a short list of what would be great for them to get for your elder. Offer to reimburse them for the expense. The point here is that having things on hand *when you arrive* will alleviate the stress for everyone.

Research weather patterns: Know what the weather will be during your visit. Don't assume your older friend has watched the Weather Channel or that your host knows the needs of your elderly person. I remember one visit abroad with an older in-law. Although we had some idea of what to expect, we were not prepared for the bone-chilling cold and damp. Having to buy additional hats and scarves when there, although a fun adventure, was really a waste of money when we could have easily brought what was needed. If there is the potential for severe weather like a tropical storm or a blizzard, either of which could mean loss of electrical power, best to put off the visit.

Ask about plans: If your host does not let you know before you travel, ask what events or day trips are planned. That way you can tell your host if you think it best to nix that hike, and also let them know if Grandmother would love a quiet game of croquet on the lawn, or if just sitting in front of the fire chatting is best.

The Heart of the Visit

ONE OF THE HARDEST THINGS FOR US AS ADULTS TO ACCEPT is the simple fact that our elders often view us as children—still. It is a wise and enlightened elder that sees us for the adults we are—and accepts us as we are. But what to do if your older parent or grandparent still sees you as that irresponsible little kid who needed to be reminded not to leave his bike out in the rain, or to wear an overcoat in subzero weather, or to eat her veggies?

Take responsibility for the elder—that's what you do. Your attitude to your host can't be, "Well, I brought Gramps—the rest is up to you!," unless you specifically agreed to that before you arrived at your host's home. This is a big job, but I'm sure you are up for it or you would not have volunteered.

You must do those chores that the elder needs, including bed and bath activities if needed. If you are visiting family, then an able family member should help.

Many older people are on a fixed income or have little money. Decide among your family members *before* the visit how the elder's expenses during the trip are going to be handled. There is nothing worse than embarrassing an older person by arguing in front of her over some expense. Also decide who is going to prepare meals if the elder can't eat what is prepared for the others.

VISIT WIZARD TIP If Grandma needs help getting up the stairs, why not ask one of the teenage boys or young men to assist you? This provides a good learning lesson on courtesy, respect, and empathy.

Lighten Up!

Stress during the visit is likely, either for you or the older person, and is the one thing that will hurt you and cause the elder (who is likely more uptight than you) to have a bad visit. Because it's not always easy to travel with and be responsible for an older visitor, your best alley to get you through any rough spots is... your sense of humor!

Be at your most mature even if you are still thought of as the baby of the family. I understand. All I can say is: Don't worry about it. Demonstrate your control and compassion by rising above the basic human tendency to get testy or upset when confronted with difficulties. Do as one of my favorite television characters did: Francis Urquhart in *House of Cards* and *To Play the King* would smile and reply, "You might very well think that; I couldn't possibly comment." Said sweetly and with a coy smile it usually gets the job done. So lock the old ghosts in the baggage of childhood, leave it in the guest room, and emerge triumphant.

And finally, don't always try to be right—because you're not! And even when you are, take joy in the fact that you no longer have to prove it.

Comfort and Joy

It's hard to fathom old age, because we are, well... just not at that stage in our lives. Vastly different things are important to us at this point in time. We are worried about our jobs, getting the kids educated, what time practice is, and why our friend or loved one is in a funk. We know Granny should bring a sweater and we really hope she enjoys her time with the grandkids, but that's about the extent to which we can focus right now. Our lives are full to the point of busting and we can't handle one more thing. I can hear you now: "Hey, Visit Wizard. You're lucky we're even *taking* the old folks. You can't imagine how difficult this trip is going to be with three teenagers and two adult siblings who don't get along. Of course we will do our best, and hope the folks have a good time, but that's about as much as I can promise."

Like a bad politician on a virtuous mission, I "hear you" and "feel your pain," the only difference being that I sincerely want to help. I only ask that during this flurry of young and midlife activity, you remember that your kids will grow up—you still have years with them—and there really is time to correct the rivalry between your husband and sister, but this could be the last trip with your folks. And frankly, they don't care about those petty issues anymore. It only worries and sometimes confuses them, depending on their age and mental health.

I am going to go out on that proverbial limb again and say that you should put all those things aside, to the best of your ability, and focus, to the extent that you reasonably can, on the old one's comfort and joy. Enough disclaimers? So, concentrate on what is really important for those few days you will be together. You know what might happen? By focusing on the old, and not the young, and not yourself, you—and (with luck) the entire family—may find that with selflessness comes an inner peace which is a direct result of focusing on others who are more needy and less able than us. Okay, enough. You get the picture, so just read and incorporate:

Comfort...

For older eyes. Does your host like to keep her house cool in the summer months by drawing the curtains or blinds? Suggest that on this visit you open them up and turn up the ***light***. That makes it easier for the elders to get around and they are less likely to trip. Easier for them to read, knit, or whatever they like to do. Make sure there are night-lights in the bathroom and bedroom and hall. (I actually bring my own, just in case.)

For thinner skin. You thought our skin was supposed to get tougher as we aged, right? Not so. Just the opposite, so make sure the ***temperature*** in the house is comfortable for older guests. If chilly, make sure there is an extra blanket at the foot of their bed and that they packed warm clothes.

For sensitive digestions. Keep the elder as close to their normal ***eating*** schedule as possible, even if that means you have to fix them dinner at 5 p.m. when everyone else is going to eat at 7 p.m. If everyone has a cocktail before dinner or wine with dinner, it is up to you to make sure your elder has an alternative. Older people who are not used to drinking can have a problem with loss of balance or confusion. And beware of drug interactions. Alcohol also can interfere with a good night's sleep. If the elder cannot eat what everyone else does, then you must prepare meals.

Joy...

In conversation. Although there are a million things to do while you are visiting friends and family—some fun, some not so much—one of the nicest things you can do is sit and talk with an older person and invite others to do the same. Reminiscing is an easy ice breaker for everyone. Encourage your elders to talk about their lives and ask if you can record it. Have the children gather round and ask their own questions. Questions will keep the conversation going and stimulate their memory.

First, sit up straight and don't talk with your mouth full. Second, pick a neutral subject that would be of interest to him or her. Don't discuss complicated issues or the latest fashion guru, as the older person most likely won't know or won't care. Take on topics that might have meaning for them. And remember that elders will have their own, often ingrained opinions and beliefs. Now is not the time to try to change hearts or minds or discuss sensitive issues.

In bringing the generations together. What is more fun to watch than an older person interacting with a younger one? Each can learn from the other and enjoy the time tremendously. My grandmother loved children. Even when she no longer had the ability to hold or care for them, her eyes would light up when she gazed upon a child. Still, older people can be scary to kids, so don't let little Caroline hiding behind your pants alarm you. She will come around if gently prodded.

For example, you might be surprised at the enlightened courting/young love advice an older person can give. Often an elderly lady and a teenage girl will bond beautifully if given the opportunity to discuss teenage boys! And don't butt in, unless of course, Grandma is saying she doesn't know why you won't let her granddaughter get her nose pierced!

What activities can the older person and child do together? Gardening—simply planting some flowers together; crafts—that an older person might be able to teach a child; games; puzzles; even that tame video game, believe it or not, are all good vehicles to promote what is really the most important activity: bringing the older person and the younger person together.

In respecting them. No nagging, no bossing, no treating the elderly guests like children—period. If they were respected in the past, why not now? Insist that others do the same. Never talk about anyone as if they are not present. No condescending talk or attitude. You must see to it that your elder is having the best possible time. Is he interacting with others, including children and pets? Research has found that pets greatly add to an older person's enjoyment of life, so grab Fido if he is friendly (Fido, not the elder) and introduce them.

Making Merry

IN THE HOSTING OLDER GUESTS CHAPTER (PAGE 117) THERE are many suggestions for what might be fun for the visiting elders and the entire group. But here are a few suggestions for making the visit as enjoyable for the elders as for you.

Something simple like a drive in the country or a walkabout may be just what your elder needs to feel connected and cared for. Take the older guest along with the family as often as you can. Before going and when you get to your destination, look into a senior center, which may offer day trips, some which may not require walking, like a bus tour of the local attractions.

Are there some activities or hobbies that someone can teach the older guests on the visit that they can continue with when they get home? For instance, consider taking them to your local craft or hobby store and checking things out. If your dad was a shipbuilder in earlier days, would a model airplane or ship building kit be a nice idea? If your mom did intricate needlework in her younger days would something easier, like rug hooking, be better now? Would a nice gift be an e-reader with some books downloaded that the older person could enjoy? Have all the guests make suggestions of their favorite books. Make sure you write out simple, clear instructions that the older person can keep. Keep it as simple as possible. If the elder doesn't enjoy reading, or finds it difficult, books on tape might be a good option.

Ask your host if you can have a party for the older guests, where you do all the preparations and chores for the event. It can be as simple as playing music from when they were young, everyone dressing up, and maybe a few presents to round out the event. Let them decide what is for dinner or organize a formal dinner in their honor. By the way, soothing music can lower blood pressure and release opiates and may indeed alleviate pain. Good to know for everyone!

Rent videos of movies that are from the elder's era or watch travel videos of a place they have been or have always wanted to go and get the grandkids to join in.

Is there a bingo night somewhere while you are visiting?

If the older guests desire, let them participate in children's games. I remember as a child playing easy but fun card games with my elderly grandmother.

The goal when taking elders to visit is to help them feel useful, not a burden. To engage and include them so the grandchildren can get to know them and learn from them. To do what you can to make their limited time with loved ones as wonderful as possible. I know you are most likely torn between many people during the hectic life of a visit and not one person should monopolize all of your time, but give the elders as much time as you reasonably can.

So if you just put into practice two things from this chapter it will be enough: Treat the elder person as you would like to be treated when you are their age, with respect and kindness; and forgive and forget their idiosyncrasies or occasional ill temperament.

I am a firm believer that older people often behave as they are treated. If you are upbeat, positive, and kind, they will naturally reciprocate.

I've said this before but it bears repeating: Your children will be watching and learning from the example you set when you take older guests visiting. And if you don't have children, you will be the one who will reflect back on the visit. Will it bring a sweet smile to your face, or will you recoil in horror at the memory, embarrassed that it went so badly?

My hope is that you'll smile.

CHAPTER 6

Using the Home of a Friend or Family Member

"Treat your host's home as you would like yours to be treated."

—THE GOLDEN RULE, REVISED

IT IS A LUXURY TO HAVE THE USE OF A FRIEND'S OR FAMILY member's home when they are away, to treat your family to a vacation or yourself to a getaway. I am fortunate to have friends with second homes and I often do just that. There is nothing more exciting than spending time in different places, at least for me. Using the homes of friends and family is just plain fun. In some cases it's like being in a wonderful hotel or resort for free, or very little. You are able to experience new things and a new environment, see how others live, and get exciting new ideas for your own life. When visiting the home of friends, I saw how they displayed their photographs and it was so smart I went home and did the same.

But don't be offended if a good friend (or even family member) says "no" when you ask to use their home. Everyone has their own issues regarding privacy, has hang-ups and concerns, and it may not have anything to do with you personally, or... it may! They might recall how you kept your room as a child, for example. That's okay. Let them know you have read this book and that should alleviate any concerns.

Never be afraid to ask, but ask you must. Just because a friend or family member has a vacation home, don't assume it is yours to use when and as you like. And never, *ever* just announce your intentions. A woman told me how shocked she was after she listened to a voicemail from a relative: "He just called up to let me know he would be at my house for the next two weeks! How nice of him. Well, he'll be surprised and cold because we had the power shut off!"

Yes, the lady did call him back and told him. No, he did not go.

Your conversation, in real time or not, should go something like this: "If you are not using your house next weekend (or week), I would really love to use it. It would be me (or me, my husband, three kids, and two dogs). I would be happy to pay you something for the use, but will certainly pay for all utilities for the time I am there. If there is something you would like me to do while at the house just let me know and I will be happy to."

The important points you made were:

1. You let them know how many of you would be coming;
2. You offered to pay "something" (implying less than full fare would be appreciated if they typically rent their home out); you insisted on paying the utilities, which is only fair (let them say no)
3. You made a generous offer to do something that may be needed at the house.

Your friends and family members may tell you to forget paying for anything, but you must still make the offer. Making a point to ask if there is something you can do while you are there shows you respect their needs, but if your host eagerly suggests that gutters have to be cleaned, or new carpet installed, you may want to reconsider your vacation plans. Remember that using another's home is much less expensive than renting a house or condominium for vacation, so expect to contribute something, either in labor or monetarily. You will be rewarded by being happily allowed back.

VISIT WIZARD TIP If possible email your request to use the house to your friend or family member. That gives them time to think and does not put them on the spot.

Get the Full Lowdown

YOU WILL FIND SOME HOUSES IN BETTER CONDITION THAN others, some cleaner, some better equipped, some with all the high-tech gadgets you could want and some with none. It depends on the host and the location of the house. If it's on one hundred acres in the middle of nowhere and you must have that daily trip to the gourmet coffee place, best you make other plans.

If you are a football fanatic and must have the large flat screen, better ask if there is one.

If you are a clean freak and know your sister is, well, a slob, don't go—you'll spend the whole time cleaning and she will be upset because she won't be able to find anything later.

Finally, bear in mind the house, unlike a hotel or resort, may not be ideal. This from a woman who was asked by a girlfriend if she and her elderly mother could use her vacation home in the mountains:

> *"If you go, be warned there are neighbors that you will just have to tolerate at times. The people behind our house own weapons and like to shoot them off at all hours. We have asked them nicely to keep it to a minimum and it is indeed better, but I know your mother is going to have a heart attack."*

Before you go you will need to ask some basic things:

Ask if there is a television, radio, or if the phones are turned on. In some remote areas your cell may not work and you may not find out until you are out in the hinterland with absolutely no ability to communicate with the outside world—a very scary proposition to some.

Ask if there is Internet connectivity in the house in terms of a modem, or if wireless works—again, there are some areas of the world with no, or limited, satellite reception. If it is a vacation or second home used by the owners for only a few months of the year, these things may not be supplied or even available.

Ask if there is a security alarm. You will need the code prior to getting in the house. Besides the front door, are there any passes or keys to any area or buildings that you should have, like a garage door opener or gate key? Don't let this happen to you. I know this is what my friend must have been thinking when I forgot to give her the gate key:

> *"I can't believe this! We have to park and walk, walk with suitcases and bags of groceries and frozen food, the mile up the driveway because our dear friend forgot to tell us the gate was locked! Thank goodness we took the day off from work and came up early otherwise we would have had to do the trek tonight in the dark. Not a pleasant journey in the middle of nowhere, any time of day!"*

Ask if there are any major appliances that are either nonexistent or nonoperational. Washing clothes in the tub and putting them out on the line to dry is a nice thing... for about a day.

Get directions to the nearest grocery and drugstore. If the closest one is an hour from the house and in the opposite direction from which you are coming you may want to stop on your way!

Ask about recreation in the area, like golf or tennis courts or rivers or whatever it is you like to do. If you can do an Internet search before you go, better still.

Ask about club fees. If there is a fee for any club activity, you must pay, not charge it to your host's membership.

Finally, if you are told, and you should be told in advance, that other friends or relatives will be at the house that same time, and either you don't like them or would prefer to be alone, there's nothing you can do except come up with a plausible excuse. It's fine to say that you decided to bow out because you really were looking for some alone time to finish a project or take long, solitary walks; just don't tell your host that you really can't stand being around Mary for any length of time, as they might think Mary the most delightful person on the planet.

Upon Arrival . . . Opening the House

YOU WILL NEED TO KNOW HOW TO "OPEN" AND SAFELY operate the house. Your absent host should have created, and conspicuously placed in the house, *The Visit Wizard's Guide for Guests*, which, among other juicy things, contains a list of important contact numbers, detailed opening and closing instructions, operating instructions, things to do, places to go, and so on. Read it and obey! (Please see The Absent

Host: Giving Family and Friends the Use of Your Home chapter, page 146, for examples of what should be in it.) That way you don't have to be scrambling for a pen as your host is firing off instructions over the phone or print out the ten pages she emailed at the last minute.

Upon arrival test the major appliances and electronics to make sure they are operating properly. Let your host know right away if something is not. You don't want to be falsely accused of mucking up the plumbing or causing a fire, do you?

Go to the grocery store and stock the kitchen and pantry with items you want. And if you polish off your host's supply of anything, replace it before you leave.

In addition to your personal needs, don't forget to buy the house basics so you don't use up your host's toilet paper, trash bags, paper towels, laundry detergent, dishwasher detergent, napkins, tissues, sugar, or any other basic supplies. Even if these things are in the house, it's best to buy your own so they are there for the next person or your hosts.

Do's and Don'ts

Don'ts

- Don't think your host won't notice that expensive bottle of Champagne you popped, drank, and conveniently forgot to replace!
- Don't throw out your host's Jujyfruits or the venison stew in the fridge just because it offends you.
- Don't do a major rearranging of the furniture; but if you do move a chair or two remember where they were located and put them back! I will not soon forget how my father completely

rearranged all the furniture (except for moving the bed; I guess it was just too darned heavy) in my condo when he visited in my absence. The fact that the living room did look better is not the point.

- Don't let a stranger to your host sleep in the host's bedroom. In fact, if there are plenty of guest rooms, don't use the master bedroom at all unless your host has invited you to do so.
- Don't try to cover up any damage or accident! That never works. They will see the glue marks.
- Don't throw out anything just because it looks old! That newspaper from last year may have an article about your host's son or daughter in it. Or, a cherished first newspaper article your host wrote on wildlife (I'm still sad).
- Don't snoop. Would you want someone going through your private things? Yikes.
- Don't take it upon yourself to paint the living room just that right shade of green you are absolutely convinced it should be, or shorten the living room drapes. And if you do have a design suggestion, be careful in voicing it. Your host may just love that little-boy-peeing fountain out front!
- Don't have parties loud enough for the neighbors to hear. It will get back to your hosts. Trust me on this one... not to mention the potential damage. I pale at the thought.
- Don't take the Lamborghini or motorcycle out for a test drive unless your host suggests it, and even then turn it down. Those potential dings and scratches are very costly.
- Don't put a load of wood onto the living room rug.
- Don't smoke (anything) in the house. The smell will linger.

- Don't order movies unless you pay for them, and remember your host will get the bill, so unless you want Aunt Mary to see you rented that—whatever—don't.
- Don't treat their home as if it is yours, no matter what they say. They are lying.
- Don't be so careful or paranoid that you don't have a good time!
- Don't bring pets into the house unless you first clear it with your host, and then very, very carefully. For example don't let the dog(s) alone in the house without being in a large crate or confined in one room.
- Don't let the children bang on the furniture with heavy objects or eat or drink anywhere they please.
- Don't use your host's personal computing devices unless you get permission in advance. People can be very touchy about this, so make sure it's okay. Best to bring your own laptop or mobile device.
- Don't leave personal items in the house (for your potential return visit!) unless invited by your host to do so. No one wants to come home to find a drawer full of delicates and your tennis shoes in the closet.
- Don't use your host's sports equipment unless you specifically have asked.
- Don't make any "minor" repairs about the house or grounds—although a potentially nice gesture—without first talking with your host.

Do's

- Do check the flue in the fireplace before starting a fire. Yes, I have not done this. The resulting smoke alarm blasts were just no fun.
- Do look around and make a mental note of where things were so you can put them back should you move them.
- Do let your host know right away if something is broken or not working properly.
- Do make a note of how your host folds the sheets and towels so you can do the same. While visiting a friend's home I opened the bathroom closet and smiled. Her towels not only matched, but they were in perfect order, grouped by size, of course, but also folded in a very specific way that I had not tried before. I took one or two out, dissected them, and noted the technique. That way, after use, I could fold them as she liked. I was rewarded when she called a few weeks later laughing that I was the first guest who had ever cared enough to do that. Go figure....
- Do lock up the house *every time* you leave, even if you think the house is in a completely safe neighborhood or you will only be gone a "minute." You would feel just awful if anything was stolen on your watch.
- Do throw anything out in the refrigerator if it is obviously rotten or sour. But if in doubt, don't. Just because you think the Blue Stilton cheese smells, well, wrong, does not mean it has gone bad. It's supposed to smell that way. Really....
- Do replace any item of your host's that you used.
- Do ask your host if you should turn anything down or off when you leave. For example, what should the heat or a/c be set to? If your host has completed *The Visit Wizard's Guide for Guests*

then you will know. As earlier noted, elements of the guide can be found beginning on page 146 and an exhaustive list can be found on my website.

- Do *carefully* straighten any pictures or paintings on the walls that have gone askew (I know some of you will be compelled), but don't move them because you think one would look much better on a different wall!
- Do pay for anything that you, your child, or your pet broke or damaged and for any incidental expenses, like long-distance phone calls. If you are paying for the utilities while you are using the home, pay the bill promptly after your host sends it to you.
- Do hand wash dishes, cookware, and delicate glassware when in doubt. I don't know what possessed me but I put my host's stainless steel pots and pans in the dishwasher. Yes, I did, not knowing they had never felt anything harder than a nonscratch pad and a cloth. When I pulled them out I was horrified and convinced they were ruined. These shiny pots and pans, so lovingly cared for prior to my arrival, looked like a rainy day, covered with some unknown nastiness that I hoped were hard water stains. I was horrified as I knew my host to be meticulous. The first thing that popped into my head was the ghastly price to replace them, but as I calmed I thought I could try to bring them back to their original, shiny glory. I ran to the store, bought a product made specifically for the job, and held my breath while I worked on them. Success, I am happy to report, and they looked almost new.
- Do ask your host if you can take with you that wonderful book of theirs that you were unable to finish. And then remember to return it.

- Do call or email your hosts the day before, or the morning of departure, just so they know you are leaving and all is well.

VISIT WIZARD TIP If you are given the use of your host's car during the visit, return it filled with gas and clean inside and out. However, you may want to consider a rental if the last time you drove a stick shift was when they first came out, or if your brother-in-law plays soft music in the garage as he polishes its chrome with a lint-free cloth.

Before You Leave

YOU MUST LEAVE THE HOUSE IN THE SAME CONDITION—OR better—than you found it. No one wants to walk back into their home to find unmade beds or a dirty sink. Your hosts will know you appreciated their generosity by leaving their home in good shape and letting them know how much you enjoyed it.

Cleaning and Closing the House

Allow plenty of time before your departure to do the laundry completely (sheets, towels, kitchen towels, and so on). Fold things neatly and replace them where you found them and remake all beds. If your host prefers you not do laundry she should let you know that.

If you prefer not to clean the house yourself, ask your host who you can call to have the house cleaned the day of your departure. If the owner has a person who cleans for them, hiring that person is a nice solution and a time-saver for you. If you find a housecleaner yourself, make sure you remain in the house while the work is being performed. You pay for this service, of course.

Double the time you think it will take to make a proper exit. When using a friend's second home I called my mother the morning I was leaving, as I was driving from there to her home. It was noon and I said I would be done and leaving my friend's house at about 3 p.m. It was not to be. At three I called Mom again and told her it would be two more hours. We were anxious to see each other, and my dear mother paused and said, "Kathy. Are you just being your overly picky self?" What could I say, except, "Gee Mom… could be!"

If you think I am being overly fastidious, heed this warning from someone who owns a vacation home in a resort area:

"One house guest used our condo two years straight while we were out of town. The first year he left the dirty sheets and towels on the floor because he had an early morning flight. He cleaned a little, but not well. I returned home to a dirty condo and laundry. He left no gift, only a thank-you note.

"The second year he visited I left the card of a cleaning lady and asked this same guest to call her before leaving. It did not happen, although he apologized profusely. His free vacations have ended."

If you know your host is returning in a few days, leave the perishables you bought in the refrigerator if you'd like. If they are not coming back within a week or two, do not. There is nothing like coming back to a drawer full of lettuce gone wrong. Or worse, an invasion of fruit flies arising from the rotting peaches left in the fruit bowl.

Vacuum the rugs, sweep, mop the floors.

Don't leave any trash. I have been known to drive hundreds of miles with a bag of garbage in the trunk. Sometimes you just have to. Remember, your host may not be returning for weeks or months. Put garbage in an outside container only if you are sure it is critter proof.

Diligently check the doors and windows to make certain all are locked and reset the alarm, if applicable.

When in doubt about anything, don't be afraid to call your host and ask.

If it is not listed in *The Visit Wizard's Guide for Guests*, get instructions on turning off water, turning down hot water, and any other routines for closing up the house. When you turn the water off, open the faucet briefly to make sure it is off. Some water will trickle out but then it should stop. Reclose the faucet.

Leave a small gift and thank-you card. It does not have to be much if your stay was just the weekend, but for longer periods of time, consider offering more. A pony may be too much, a stick of gum too little. One visit I purchased a kitchen digital scale for my host—having snooped deep in the bowels of the kitchen cabinets and found she didn't have one—popped it in a pretty bag with tissue paper, and left it in the kitchen with the thank-you card. It's one of those things that's nice to have, but not necessarily something that one would buy for oneself.

A spice/coffee grinder or a fancy wine bottle opener are examples of gifts that not everyone rushes out to buy but might really appreciate. However, expensive gifts are not necessary. Just buy something appropriate, or make a gift. Maybe pick some flowers from your host's garden and press them in a book, and then mount on card stock and frame. It is not the amount you spend but the thought you put into it. Truly.

Be mindful of what you do leave, as some gifts can have the opposite impact. Although I know you were just being thoughtful leaving that case of toilet paper because your host's was so thin you could see through it, she may not see it that way.

Beside the thank-you card, leave a note if necessary, to let them know what has been done, or not, or if there were any problems of which they should be aware that do not require immediate attention. Also, be sure to let your host know in the note if clean sheets are on the beds or the towels hanging in the bathroom are clean. If you don't tell them they will assume they are dirty and wash them all again.

My note to a friend was brief and said all she would need to know upon her return the following evening: "Sheets are clean, vodka's cold."

BONUS CHAPTER

Hospitality with Our Pets
Hosting Nonhumans

"Acquiring a dog may be the only opportunity a human ever has to choose a relative."

—MORDECAI SIEGAL

HOSTING PETS CAN BE A LOT OF FUN BUT BE WARNED: THEY do require as much—and sometimes more—attention than your two-legged guests. Preparing for the visit, including laying the ground rules in advance, will mean the visit will go as smoothly as humanly possible when pets, and sometimes small children, are combined under one roof for a period of time.

All homes are different but share this one trait: they all have safety and escape issues. Can a visiting pet get out or under or through something? Are there baby toys (or for that matter, a baby) around that a visiting dog may think are tasty? Are doors easily pushed open? Is there anywhere a small animal can get stuck?

So instead of throwing shoes in closets *after* they have teeth marks on the leather, or searching frantically for a water bowl for that panting Husky, tackle these things before the visit, so that you can enjoy the time instead of struggling to figure out where the Great Dane is going to sleep.

Visualize a large tail anywhere from one to three feet from the floor, happily sweeping away everything in its wake, or a feline that can jump from table to bookcase with ease, and put away the breakables. Put away anything you don't want an animal to chew or play with, like children's toys, especially stuffed animals!

Cats have an interesting physiological trait: they knead their claws on things. I personally think it quite interesting but you might find it offensive once Tiger starts on your silk-covered pillows. If you do not have a cat but a neighbor does, ask to borrow a cat scratcher mat or board.

Start saving newspapers now for the bottom of the bird cage.

Remember to secure the exit doors. If you have a "doggie door" and an inside-only cat is coming, well, you will have to get up to let Roscoe out. And if there are children running in and out of the house, best to put kitty in a room with a view during that time of the day. Better than someone always running around looking to make sure the cat is still inside.

Issue Commands

Down! Most owners of small or medium dog breeds let their pets on the sofas and chairs, at least in my world. Let your guest know the boundaries ahead of time. If you prefer their pets not be on the furniture, it's important that they know that because if their pet is not very well trained it will most likely be difficult to keep them off. The owner can then make the decision if they should bring their pet or not.

Go to bed. The days of the wolf ancestor timidly crawling toward the cave, hoping to get some shelter from the elements are long gone. Let your guest know in advance if their pet is allowed in your guest bedroom or not.

It's important the pet have its own comfortable area in which to sleep. If not, howls and yowls in the wee hours may be the result.

In any circumstances it's not a good idea to let any pet roam an unfamiliar house freely at night or you might wake to discover Roscoe in the middle of a garbage buffet or that the cat did indeed figure out how to open the canary's cage.

Out! Think about where the pet will go to the bathroom. If there is no yard or designated area, tell your guest where the pet should go, ask them to clean up after their pet, and let them know where to dispose of the "particulars."

Be aware that cats might dig in your potted plants around the house. An inexpensive precaution is to spread aluminum foil over the potting soil.

Think about where the pet will be exercised. If a dog is visiting, a nice thing to do is find out where the nearest dog-friendly park or even the doggie play group is located and when they meet. A tired pet of any kind is a more relaxed pet.

Stay out. Create pet-free zones or rooms for guests who might be allergic or afraid or if you just don't want animals in those rooms.

. . . the furniture: Knowing the cat, ferret, or other small critter will almost certainly get up on the furniture, as will the dog, of course, if he's allowed, consider covering the sofa with a slipcover if you are concerned with hair or want to protect the fabric.

. . . the kitchen: Put down a mat, or even a towel, on whatever floor surface the food and water bowls will go. Water stains on hardwood are just not pleasant, nor is slipping on water on your way to the fridge in the wee hours of the morning.

Stop and consider the trash can. Is it either behind a pantry door or covered by a secure enough lid so that Fido can't get into it? And keep those recyclables secured away as well (think bungee cord for over the top of the lids).

The best way to keep cats off kitchen counters is to keep them free of food (the counters, not the cats.) Again, if you know cats will be regular visitors, you can buy gadgets that scare them off the counters, like motion alarms.

. . . the house!: One of my favorite things on the planet are puppies, but a visiting puppy has its own set of issues. Will the owner bring a crate for the pup to get needed nap time? If not, consider putting up those expandable gates so that one room, like the laundry room or the kitchen, will confine the little ball of energy when necessary.

Put down newspapers or "wee wee pads" if house breaking, and confine when necessary.

Put away your shoes and other gnaw-able objects. I can't tell you how many of my shoes have been destroyed by those sharp little teeth. All worth it, of course.

Caution: Furniture legs may be gnawed on! Take precautions by either wrapping the legs in towels and ties or banning the puppy from that room.

. . . the critters: If you have an in-ground pool or an above-ground pool, be alert. It is easy for any animal to fall in and not be able to reach the steps to get out or even know where the steps are. Best rule:

Never allow pets around the pool unsupervised by an adult.

If you're on a farm, remember that dogs, and other animals that are unfamiliar with horses or other livestock, can cause a problem and also be kicked or otherwise injured. Let your guest know what precautions to take, like keeping their dogs on a lead.

Is there a fast moving-stream on your property, alligators in your lake, or bears in the woods? I once opened the door to our cabin not seeing the deer in the yard, only to have my five-pound Chihuahua take off like a shot, hair on back standing straight up, barking like she was possessed.

VISIT WIZARD TIP If you cannot be there when your guests and pet arrive, leave detailed instructions on where things are in terms of bowls and food, the area where the bed or cage can be set up, where the dog can be walked, etc.

"Guard!"

HOSTING A PET IS AKIN TO BABY-SITTING A CHILD. WHAT could be worse than having tragedy strike during your watch? I was horrified when reading this email from a woman who has had dogs her entire life. Even experienced dog owners can have a momentary lapse. Be doubly cautious with pet guests in your home:

VISIT WIZARD TIP Although you're not expected to pull plants from the garden or toss the Christmas poinsettia (although you may want to get a smaller one that will fit on a table), do be aware that many plants are hazardous and some even fatal to pets. Find a full list at the ASPCA website, aspca.org.

In the heat of battle, with the duties and responsibilities of hosting people, and now pets, make sure of one thing at all times: that the pet has access to water.

Mind the garbage cans. Be aware of small bones and other things an animal would love to get at and keep the garbage secure even when it is outside the house.

"No!"

KNOW WHEN TO SAY "NO." IF YOU REALLY DON'T WANT A PET IN your home you will just be miserable and so will everyone else. If you have the means and you know your guest does not, it is nice to offer to board the pet so they can still visit. And of course, if you are allergic to pet dander ask that the pet be boarded.

No sense ruining the human visiting experience. Thank Nancy Reagan and "just say no."

"Be Nice!"

SO THE DOG HAS DRUNK FROM THE TOILET BOWL AND tracked some mud into the house and stole a steak from the grill. That's not such a big deal, in the overall scheme of things. If the toilet bowl drinking bothers you, tape a note to the bathroom door asking the humans to keep it closed.

In regards to mud, water, and dirt, your guest should absolutely clean up after their pet; if they don't, ask them to—but in a *nice* way!

Is the dog on your bed when you specifically said that was not allowed? If necessary, close bedroom doors and put sticky notes on places where these crimes occur. That way you won't make yourself crazy constantly telling the ten-year-old the toilet is not a swimming pool for the lizard.

"Greet!"

IF YOUR GUEST IS ARRIVING IN A CAT CARRIER (!), BE CAUTIOUS when you let them out as they might make a mad dash under the sofa or to another room. Also, make sure the cat can't get out of the house or back out the door. Although often frightened at first, I have found that they usually come around soon enough. Make sure you show them the food and the litter box as soon as possible!

Be very careful when introducing children to pets. If the animals are not used to small children they may nip out of fear, or the child could be afraid. Tell the child to be gentle and not to touch for awhile until they get used to each other. If you have an animal that is at all aggressive or you don't know how it will react with children, best to board it or have a friend or neighbor baby-sit while your guests are visiting.

To you, and rightly so, your pets are another member of the family with whom you communicate as easily as you do with people. So how do you make your guests comfortable and still be faithful to your faithful friends? No, don't tell your guests to stay off the sofa because that is where your coach potato Greyhound likes to hang out or that they can't shower Saturday morning because that is when you give your three Shelties a bath.

Just remember that when your non-pet-loving guests are finally gone you can run and play with, hug, allow everywhere, feed with spoons, put in the bathtub, and go back to happily spoiling your pet.

Dogs jumping up on people, either your dog or your guest's dog, is just bad and annoying behavior. Try to train your dog with the "off" command. It is a relatively easy thing for your pet to learn regardless of its age.

It is going to be difficult to make sure all critters, whatever the number of legs, get along all of the time. All you can do is make certain your pet is well behaved and under control, which should be well . . . most of the time.

Now, to make the visit as enjoyable as possible, pet person or not, all you have to do is . . . you guessed it: "Obey!"

Visiting with Nonhumans

THIS IS NOT A CHAPTER ON CORRECTING BAD PET—OR human—behavior. There are animal and human behavioral experts for that. And, besides, we all know your pet is perfect just the way he is. So is mine. Visiting with pets can be either a fun, rewarding experience for all concerned . . . or it can be a disaster. Following these simple commands will mean less stress for you and your pet.

"No Begging!" Be Sure You're Welcome

ALTHOUGH THIS SEEMS LOGICAL, MAKE SURE YOU ASK YOUR host if you can bring your pet, as far in advance of the trip as possible. Don't just assume that everyone loves Teddy, your Saint Bernard, or that Zelda will be "no problem." Your host may have allergies or just not want an animal in the house.

Always respect your host's wishes and don't "forget to ask" or assume that because Aunt Julie had a cat twenty years ago she would not mind you showing up with yours now. Besides, she forgot to tell you she now has canaries!

"Speak!" Communicate with Your Host

TELL YOUR HOST IF THERE IS ANYTHING SPECIAL OR DIFFERENT about your pet that they should know before they agree and you happily dance with your little companion into their home. When you talk about cuddling "Rex" in your arms, they may be picturing a loveable little dog or cat, not your pet boa constrictor. Further, if you don't know, ask if your host has any pets, or if other guests will be bringing pets. Rex might not get along so well with your nephew's pet mice.

If your pet sleeps in your room at home, let your host know. It may or may not be okay during your visit. Your advance email to your host could go something like this: "George, Fluffy sleeps in my room at night. I am bringing her bed so she won't be on your guest bed. Is that okay?" If it is not, and you know there will be howls or yowls through the night, you have two options: don't bring her, or, prior to the trip, get her used to sleeping in another room without you.

"Ready!"
Preparing Your Friend for Travel

OUR FURRY FRIENDS ARE SOMETIMES AN AFTERTHOUGHT when it comes to travel prep. We forget to give them a bath or trim their nails or brush their teeth or make sure their shots are up to date.

Bathe, brush, comb, and clip! No matter how cute, no one wants a smelly or dirty critter in their home, so clip your pet's claws for the sake of your host's furniture and hardwood floors—not to mention their skin. Ouch!

Visit the vet to make sure your pet is current on all shots. Should some disaster strike, like a bite or an accident, or if you have to board while you are visiting, you will have that covered.

If lost or stolen. Make sure your pet has either a collar with identification tags with your home *and* cell phone number, or an identification microchip that a vet has put under the skin.

Do your research on where you are going. If your dog is used to playing with other dogs there may be a dog playgroup in the area.

And please, know the local environment! I was truly horrified when people visiting another family let their dog swim in the lake behind our home. It had two resident alligators! The dog could have been pulled under quickly. I ran to the woman and told her, but even so it took some time to get the dog out.

Beware of bitches in heat. No, I'm not talking about your sister going through menopause. You don't want to be surprised a few months later because you let your little sweetie out to play with your friend's unneutered male.

VISIT WIZARD TIP If you're traveling by car and your trip includes an overnight stay, research in advance which hotels along your route take pets. Be prepared for an additional fee. More and more hotels and motels are pet-friendly, thank goodness, including standbys like Best Western as well as some luxury hotels and resorts, like the Arizona Biltmore, part of the Hilton's Waldorf-Astoria collection; just make sure to ask ahead—often there are size restrictions.

"Behave!" Mind Your (Pet's) Manners

IS YOUR DOG A "COUNTER SURFER" OR WILL HE STEAL FOOD from the grill? Make sure your host knows and helps keep food safe! Does your cat love to lick the butter after the morning breakfast? Get it into the refrigerator pronto!

If you know your dog gets overly excited or is shy with strangers, meet your hosts outside first. That way if there's an "accident" it's easily handled.

If your pet has been out in the rain or playing in the mud, remember to wipe his paws before coming back inside. Ask your host for some old towels and a basket to store them in during use.

Are there some rooms that your host would prefer your pet not enter? Be respectful of their territory. If you know this in advance bring a child or pet gate if applicable for your pet. They may not have one and it will mean much less stress on you.

Be especially mindful of the children. Little kids are curious and don't understand the potential dangers any animal may pose. A friend told me that his dog is terrified by small children and will get aggressive out of fear. Definitely don't take a dog to a home with children unless you are absolutely sure the dog is not only good with them, but can tolerate ears and tails being pulled and the occasional paw stepped upon.

"Wanna Go for a Ride?" On the Road

TRAVELING WITH YOUR PET BY AUTO CAN BE EITHER A JOY ride . . . or hell on wheels. It all depends on the right preparation by you (and a little cooperation from your passenger).

Safety First

Although we think we can text, talk, and drive at the same time, we can't. Don't let this be about you:

The police report began, "She was last seen with what a witness says looked like a stuffed animal in the crook of her arm, administering blush with one hand, holding a cell phone in the other and steering with her knee, cigarette dangling from mouth."

I used to hold my small dog in my lap as I drove. I shamefully admit it. I finally bought a wire cage with one side that opens, large enough for her to be comfortable in (turn around, lay down, stretch out) and fit in the back seat. I put a pillow in the bottom, a blanket in the winter, and she traveled for hours. Better for her, much safer for the driver.

All pets, including cats, should be kept in cages, crates, or carriers, never let to wander free in the car. It is recommended that the carrier be in the back seat and strapped in by a safety belt. This way the carrier will stay secure around sharp corners or if an accident should occur. A cage may be impractical if you have a very big dog. In that case, use a seatbelt specifically made for dogs and have him in the back seat.

I know you think Fido loves to travel with his head out the car window but it's really not a good idea. Flying debris can get into eyes and mouth causing serious injury and some dogs can actually topple out the window, either accidentally or when going after some irresistible thing outside.

VISIT WIZARD TIP Beware of stuffing your friend into a too small carrier when traveling. They often don't get enough air and are too cramped to be comfortable. Air circulation and movement is just as important to your pet as it is to you.

Packing for Pets

Here's a list of items to take to your host's home if you are traveling by auto:

Cat litter and litter box: Unless the whiskered one is potty trained (yes, there are some cats who are that clever), this is a must even if your host has a cat.

Water and food bowls, openers, and utensils: Please don't think you can use your aunt's good china or the top of a Styrofoam coffee cup. Take a can opener, as during the trip you may need to open cans. I would take plastic utensils to feed my small dog, Pups, and a big jug of bottled water.

Doggie waste disposal bags: No matter where you are visiting, you must plan to pick up after your pet. Your host's yard is not an acceptable potty place.

Food and treats: Don't expect to use your host's pet's food. First, it's not right, and second, your pet should stay on its own diet for health reasons—especially when traveling.

Medicines: Don't assume a vet is handy at your destination for refills of meds. Take all that you need and find the phone number of the closest vet to your destination. When Pups was old and had health issues, I discovered the nearest vet was over an hour away from where we were once visiting..

Leash, collar, harness, toys, and brush: Again, bring everything you will need for you and your pet to be self-sufficient. Your pet's own toys will be better than your little nephew's favorite stuffed bunny.

Blanket: Your pet may get cold and, no, you shouldn't ask to borrow the handmade afghan.

Cage, crate, aquarium, perch, and bed: Your pet, be it dog, cat, small mammal bird, or reptile will have to have some place to call home away from home. This is important for their happiness as well as their security.

Expandable pet gate: This is very important for keeping your pet out of areas it may not be welcome and pretty much required when visiting with a puppy!

They are important for your pet's safety in the home and the comfort of your host and other guests. You don't want your pet getting into trouble in the house when everyone is out.

During the Trip

Take frequent breaks. Animals can get dehydrated quite quickly so make sure you stop every few hours to exercise your pet and offer it water. Water is important as excited dogs pant and a panting dog needs water. I recommend bottled water for both dogs and cats as who knows the water quality of places where you stop, and bottled water is easy and convenient to transport. And of course the more water they drink the more you have to take potty breaks! Try not to feed too much on your trip. If on a long voyage, talk with your vet about eating schedules.

Beware freedom! Always put your pet's leash or harness on while you are both *in* the car, if not Fido may make a break for the far tree line quicker than you can say "Dog Whisperer."

If you have to get out of the car but your pet doesn't, don't leave the windows down far enough so that a pet thief can get an arm in the window and open the door.

CAUTION! Please never ever leave a pet in a car when the temperature is even warm! The interior of a car can heat up to over 100 degrees in minutes, even with the windows partly open. I was in a store on a very hot day when a woman walked in and I heard her dogs barking in her car. She noted my look of concern and before I could get the words out of my mouth she said, "Don't worry. The car is running and the air conditioning is on!" Good woman, if bad environmentalist.

Cat Confidential

Cats deserve their own special tips, as the poor things are so reluctant to leave their kingdom, and who can blame them? They've worked hard to establish that territory and are just downright peeved you are taking them from it. Besides, they can't stand motion or making new friends, so why go?

But when they do go, here are some things to make them more comfortable:

Get them used to their carrier weeks before the trip. Have it in the house with toys inside and leave the door open. They may decide to venture in. Pretend not to care and your chances are better. Take your cat on short car trips while in the carrier, and not always just to the vet or your cat will associate the carrier with that nasty person with the needles.

Get them used to wearing a harness or collar and leash. This may be trickier but using it will allow them to have a walk during the trip or at the visit. Just be warned that some cats have been known to wiggle out of a harness, and a collar and leash can cause throat or vocal cord problems if pulled too tightly so proceed with caution, if at all.

Put familiar items in the carrier during the trip, like a beloved toy or blanket. And as you might a bird cage, drape a towel over the top of the cage, as that can soothe a cat when traveling. Just make sure to leave plenty of ventilation. If he can snuggle down into a familiar-smelling cloth, that might just do the trick.

Offer them treats during the trip. They may not take them but at least they know you are trying to make up for the indignity of them being confined.

Use disposable litter boxes. You'll be able to throw them out after your cat has used them. And when traveling in a car, just let them out of their cage to use the litter box in the car. Just make sure the doors are closed and the windows open no more than a crack.

"Sit! Stay!" The Well-Behaved Pet Guest

IF YOU'VE FOLLOWED THE PRECEDING ADVICE, YOU AND your pet should arrive to your host's home ready for a fun-and-fur-filled visit. But don't relax just yet! You've still got to be vigilant or the visit, which was a delight to get to, may be short-lived.

Make sure you supervise during feedings and treat time. Dogs may get along like best buddies, but just try leaving one out when you give the other a treat. Separate them at feeding time.

Exercise, feed, and discipline your pet just as you would, or as close to it as possible, as when you are home.

VISIT WIZARD TIP Tell Uncle Bill, nicely but firmly, that feeding your Pekingese doughnuts at breakfast will just not do. Pets' diets can get terribly upset when traveling and visiting, which leads to all kinds of problems best not described in detail. And just because he is visiting with cousin Roscoe, don't allow him into the pool if he can't do that at home.

Take great care when leaving your pet alone in a strange house or one he has not visited for some time. As previously noted, a crate when possible is a good solution, if your pet will tolerate a crate. If not, making sure he is comfortable and secure in a room may be the best choice.

You must control your pet to the requirements of the host. If your host does not want your pet in the garden or pool or wherever, respect those boundaries.

When other pets are present: Here is the "consensus": It should be no problem introducing pets to each other! Oh, no, it is a *big* problem introducing pets to each other. Cats hate each other on sight. Cats get along if given enough time. Dogs will turn on each other in a heartbeat. Dogs are fine; just let them work it out.

So, if you are unsure about your pet's reaction to other pets, it may be more responsible to not bring your pet. Use your best judgment, but never leave animals that are strangers without parental supervision.

Did your pet misbehave? Did he grab those steaks while your back was turned? Did she dig, chew, or put holes in the screen? Did your sweetie go after another pet, resulting in a vet bill? The offending party must pay for the damage. Even if your host says to forget it, don't. They don't really mean it.

If you use as much patience, care, and advance planning as with your human friends and family, your visiting and hosting experiences with our beloved pets can be just as stress-free and fun-filled.

Resources

FOR INSTRUCTIONS ON GUEST AND HOST PROJECTS, *THE ART of the Visit* specialty gifts and products—including thank-you and special-occasion cards for, and from, adults and children—and make-ahead recipes, visit theartofthevisit.com. You will also find the Visit Wizard blog where you can ask questions and join in the discussion of relationship visiting. Visit Kathy's Facebook page: facebook.com/artofthevisit and Tweet her at @artofthevisit.

Babies and Children

To rent cribs, car seats, playpens, and so on, visit baby-equipment rental.com, which gives information by state.

For child-safety items like electric outlet plug covers and cabinet door locks, visit large department stores or websites like babyearth.com.

To learn about children and food allergies, visit kidswithfood allergies.org. They have information, lists of food suppliers, and some free recipes. Also visit websites like keepkidshealthy.com.

Elders

For travel tips and information for seniors, visit the American Association of Retired Persons at aarp.org.

To rent scooters, wheelchairs, and other things for elders, start at thewheelchairsite.com. For ramp rentals try amramp.com.

Locating senior centers for recreational purposes starts at the state

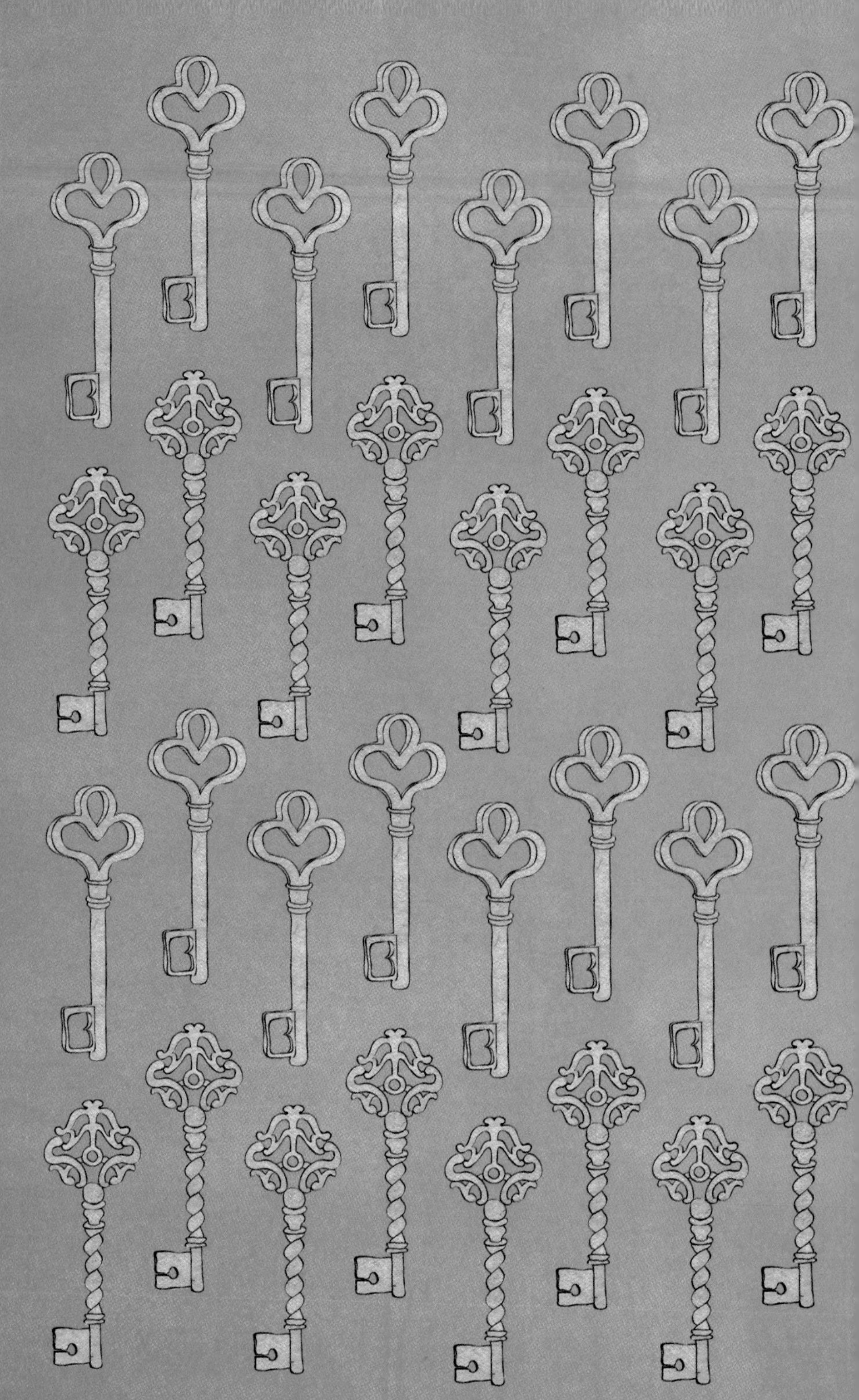

La France

LES PAYS-BAS^m
L'ANGLETERRE^f
L'ALLEMAGNE^f
LA BELGIQUE
LE LUXEMBOURG
LA MANCHE
Dunkerque
Calais
Boulogne
Lille
la Picardie
Dieppe
Amiens
Le Havre
Rouen
Cherbourg
Caen
la Normandie
la Seine
Paris
Versailles
Chartres
l'Ile-de-France^f
Reims
la Champagne
Verdun
la Lorraine
Nancy
Strasbourg
l'Alsace^f
LES VOSGES^f
Brest
la Bretagne
Rennes
Orléans
Blois
Tours
Angers
Nantes
la Loire
la Vendée
la Touraine
Bourges
Dijon
la Bourgogne
Besançon
la Saône
LE JURA
LA SUISSE
La Rochelle
le Poitou
Limoges
Clermont-Ferrand
Lyon
la Savoie
Grenoble
LES ALPES^f
L'ITALIE^f
L'OCÉAN^m ATLANTIQUE
l'Auvergne^f
Bordeaux
la Garonne
LE MASSIF CENTRAL
le Rhône
le Dauphiné
Nice
MONACO^m
Avignon
la Provence
Nîmes
Arles
Aix-en-Provence
Cannes
Montpellier
Marseille
St-Tropez
Toulouse
Biarritz
Carcassonne
LES PYRÉNÉES^f
le Languedoc
L'ESPAGNE^f
Perpignan
L'ANDORRE^f
la Corse
Ajaccio
LA MER MÉDITERRANÉE

Le français est la langue maternelle majoritaire
Le français est une des langues officielles
Le français est la langue administrative
Présence de la langue française sans statut particulier

0 50 100 150 MILLES
50 100 150 200 250 KILOMÈTRES

m = masculin f = féminin

L'Europe^f
0 50 100 200 300 400 500 MILLES
0 100 200 300 400 500 600 700 800 KILOMÈTRES
m = masculin f = féminin
Le français est la langue maternelle majoritaire
Le français est une des langues officielles
Le français est la langue administrative
Présence de la langue française sans statut particulier
Reykjavik
L'ISLANDE^f
LA SUÈDE
LA FINLANDE
LA NORVÈGE
Helsinki
St-Pétersbourg
Oslo
Tallinn
LA RUSSIE
Stockholm
L'ESTONIE^f
Moscou
L'ÉCOSSE^f
LA MER DU NORD
Riga
LA MER BALTIQUE
LA LETTONIE
L'IRLANDE DU NORD^f
LE DANEMARK
LA GRANDE-BRETAGNE
Copenhague
LA LITUANIE
L'IRLANDE^f
Dublin
Vilnius
Tver
Minsk
LE PAYS DE GALLES
L'ANGLETERRE^f
LA BIÉLORUSSIE
Amsterdam
Varsovie
Londres
LES PAYS-BAS^m
Berlin
LA BELGIQUE
L'ALLEMAGNE^f
LA POLOGNE
Kyev
Bruxelles
Bonn
Jersey
Luxembourg
Prague
L'UKRAINE^f
LE LUXEMBOURG
LA RÉPUBLIQUE TCHÈQUE
Paris
LA SLOVAQUIE
L'OCÉAN ATLANTIQUE^m
Bratislava
LA FRANCE
Vienne
LA MOLDAVIE
Budapest
Chisinau
Berne
L'AUTRICHE^f
Lausanne
LA SUISSE
LA HONGRIE
Genève
Ljubljana
Zagreb
LA ROUMANIE
le Val d'Aoste
LA SLOVÉNIE
LA CROATIE
Belgrade
L'ITALIE^f
LA BOSNIE-HERZÉGOVINE
Bucarest
LA MER NOIRE
LA MER ADRIATIQUE
Sarajevo
LA SERBIE
LA BULGARIE
L'ANDORRE^f
LE MONTÉNÉGRO
Sofia
LE PORTUGAL
La Corse
Istanbul
Madrid
Titograd
Skopje
Lisbonne
Ajaccio
Rome
L'ESPAGNE^f
Tirana
LA MACÉDOINE
L'ALBANIE^f
LA TURQUIE
LA GRÈCE
LA MER ÉGÉE
LA MER MÉDITERRANÉE
Athènes
L'AFRIQUE^f
LA CRÈTE

Débuts

An Introduction to French

H. Jay Siskin
Cabrillo College

Ann Williams-Gascon
Metropolitan State College, Denver

Thomas T. Field
University of Maryland, Baltimore County

Boston Burr Ridge, IL Dubuque, IA Madison, WI New York San Francisco St. Louis
Bangkok Bogotá Caracas Kuala Lumpur Lisbon London Madrid Mexico City
Milan Montreal New Delhi Santiago Seoul Singapore Sydney Taipei Toronto

McGraw-Hill Higher Education
A Division of The ***McGraw-Hill*** *Companies*

This is an  book.

Débuts
An Introduction to French

Published by McGraw-Hill, an imprint of The McGraw-Hill Companies, Inc., 1221 Avenue of the Americas, New York, NY 10020.

This book is printed on acid-free paper.

3 4 5 6 7 8 9 0 DOW DOW 0 9 8 7 6 5 4 3

ISBN 0-07-289754-6 (Student's Edition)
ISBN 0-07-289755-4 (Instructor's Edition)

Editor-in-chief: *Thalia Dorwick*
Publisher: *William R. Glass*
Senior sponsoring editor: *Leslie Oberhuber*
Development editor: *Peggy Potter*
Senior marketing manager: *Nick Agnew*
Senior project manager: *David M. Staloch*
Senior production supervisor: *Richard DeVitto*
Freelance design coordinator: *Michelle D. Whitaker*
Freelance interior and cover designer: *Maureen McCutcheon/McCutcheon Design*
Art editor: *Nora Agbayani*
Senior supplements producer: *Louis Swaim*
Photo research: *Judy Mason*
Compositor: *TechBooks*
Typeface: *10/12 Legacy Serif Book*
Printer and binder: *RR Donnelley & Sons*

Library of Congress Cataloging-in-Publication Data

Siskin, H. Jay
Débuts: An Introduction to French / H. Jay Siskin, Ann Williams-Gascon, Thomas T. Field. p. cm.
ISBN 0-07-289754-6
1. French language—Textbooks for foreign speakers—English. I. Williams-Gascon, Ann. II. Field, Thomas T. III. Title: Débuts: An Introduction to French

PC2129.E5 S546 2001
428.2'421—dc21

2001034554

http://www.mhhe.com

I dedicate this book to my partner, Gregory P. Trauth (1958–1999), whose life taught me the importance of generosity, integrity, and most of all, love. "Good night, sweet prince, / And flights of angels sing thee to thy rest!"

And to my family, David, Frances, and Jan Siskin, for their encouragement and support during the course of the project.

H. Jay Siskin

I dedicate this project to my son, Benjamin, a constant reminder that language opens all doors.

Ann Williams-Gascon

Thank you once again, Marie-Hélène, for your support and help.

Thomas T. Field

About the Authors

H. Jay Siskin Dr. Siskin received his Ph.D. in French and Romance linguistics from Cornell University, and has taught at Wayne State University, Northwestern University, the University of Oregon, and Brandeis University. He is currently the director of the Language Learning Center at Cabrillo College and teaches courses in both French and Spanish. He has coauthored five college-level French textbooks as well as several in Spanish.

Ann Williams-Gascon Dr. Williams-Gascon received her Ph.D. from Northwestern University and also has a Diplôme d'Études Approfondies from the Université de Lyon II. She is currently professor of French at Metropolitan State College of Denver, where she teaches courses in language, literature, and culture. She regularly presents conference papers and writes on contemporary culture, and she has coauthored two other college-level French textbooks. Dr. Williams-Gascon was the recipient of a McGraw-Hill/Glencoe Teacher of the Year award in 2001, the Excellence in Teaching Award (Golden Key Honor Society) in 1994, and Young Educator of the Year in 1991 (Colorado Congress of Foreign Language Teachers).

Thomas T. Field Dr. Field received his Ph.D. in linguistics from Cornell University. He is currently professor of Linguistics and French and Director of the Center for the Humanities at the University of Maryland, Baltimore County. Dr. Field's research is focused on Occitan sociolinguistics and the teaching of French and Francophone culture. In 1996, he was named Maryland Professor of the Year by the Carnegie Foundation for the Advancement of Teaching.

Contents

Structures

Culture / Synthèse

Vocabulaire

Chapitre

Une nouvelle vie à Paris 83

Chapitre

Secrets 107

Chapitre

Bonjour, grand-père! 129

Vocabulaire

Chapitre 7

Préparatifs 150

Chapitre 8

C'est loin, tout ça. 174

Chapitre 9

Inquiétudes 195

Structures

Culture / Synthèse

Vocabulaire

Chapitre

Chapitre

Chapitre

Structures

Culture / Synthèse

Vocabulaire

Structures

Culture / Synthèse

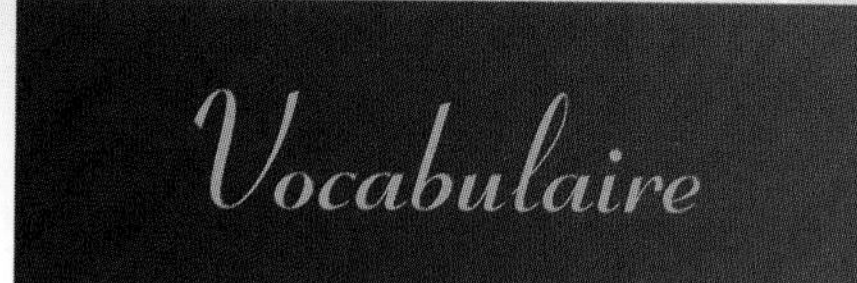

Chapitre 22

Secrets dévoilés 461

Épilogue

Le Chemin du retour 478

Preface

How often have you tried to integrate French films into your first-year French course and found the language too difficult for your students to comprehend? How many times have you been disappointed by the French videos offered with other textbooks? Would you like your students to watch a French film that they can actually understand, and one that will help them learn about French language and culture? If so, this program is for you!

The Débuts / Le Chemin du retour Program: What Is It?

The textbook, *Débuts,* and the film, *Le Chemin du retour,* are a completely integrated film-based introductory course for learning French language and culture.

A two-hour feature-length film, *Le Chemin du retour* is the story of a young television journalist, Camille Leclair, and her pursuit of the truth about her grandfather's mysterious past. Through Camille's quest, students learn language and culture in the functional context provided by the story.

Unlike other textbook/video programs, in which the video component is thematically, functionally, or grammatically driven, and thus self-consciously pedagogical, this program has been developed so that the textbook is a complement to the film. The film narrative is what drives the scope and sequence of vocabulary and grammar, the presentation of culture, and the development of reading and writing. This does not mean, however, that these items are presented in a random fashion. Rather, the screenwriter worked within the authors' pedagogical framework *but did not let it limit* his creative expression. He did a wonderful job of writing a good story while still honoring the major steps in learning the French language.

The textbook/film package grew out of the authors' conviction that language learning is more than just learning skills: it is also a process in which understanding of culture must surely occupy a central position. Therefore, *Débuts* and *Le Chemin du retour* emphasize the importance of cultural awareness and understanding, not only of the French culture, but also of the student's own culture.

Equally important, the authors strongly believe in the principles of communicative competence. *Débuts* gives students a solid foundation in the structure of the language, stressing acquisition of high-frequency grammar, vocabulary, and functional language. In addition, students come to view listening, reading, and writing as active tasks, requiring meaningful interaction as well as high-order cognitive processing.

The Goals of the Program

The overall goal in *Débuts* is to move students toward communicative competence while guiding them toward intercultural sophistication. Included in this framework are the following student objectives:

- to communicate orally and in writing in natural-sounding French and in culturally appropriate ways
- to read with comprehension both informational and literary texts taken from authentic French sources
- to understand French when spoken by a variety of people using authentic speech patterns and rates of speed
- to increase awareness and understanding of cultural institutions and culturally determined patterns of behavior
- to develop critical thinking skills as they apply to language learning
- to link language study to broader and complementary discipline areas

Understanding French

As students begin their study of French, it is important that they examine their beliefs about the nature of language and the language-learning process. They may believe that they have little difficulty understanding what they hear in their native language, yet if they reflect on their interactions with others, they will find that this is not always true. They will see, for example, that in one's native language it is not unusual to ask someone to repeat or to clarify what he or she said. People who speak rapidly or indistinctly are harder to understand than people who speak more slowly or clearly. Students should recognize that when speaking with someone who mumbles, they are probably often reluctant to ask that person to repeat over and over again. In such a circumstance, they probably rely instead on the subject or direction of the conversation to fill in the gaps in their comprehension. Although they don't understand every word, they continue to listen to get the gist of the message.

When listening in a foreign language, however, students often set the bar higher. They are eager to understand every word, and when they don't, they become frustrated or they even give up. As they begin learning French, they should remember the following hints:

- Keep your expectations realistic.
- When you don't understand, keep listening!
- Try to fill in the gaps using context to help.
- See if you can get the gist of the message.

These strategies will be particularly important as students listen to the actors in the film. From the outset, they will be hearing authentic French spoken at a natural rate of speed. It has not been artificially slowed or simplified, because this will not be their experience when they travel in the French-speaking world or listen to French radio or television. But they should not worry. They will find that although they do not understand every word of the dialogue, they will still understand the story of *Le Chemin du retour*.

Cultural Competence

Débuts had its origins in the desire to provide students with a stimulating, culturally rich set of tools for the acquisition of French. Cultural content was thus a central concern in the devising of the plot of *Le Chemin du retour*, and it has been integrated into every section of the text. Through the film, students have the opportunity for intensive exposure not only to the language and communicative habits of French speakers, but also to the visual culture of objects and nonverbal communication and to the auditory culture of music and the sounds of everyday life.

The approach to culture in *Débuts* is content-based. Themes treated in the sections specifically devoted to culture derive from the film but consistently move students toward the big questions of culture, stimulating them to consider matters that are of concern to all people, whether or not they ever travel to the French-speaking world. The authors have made culture a "hook" in this program, to generate interest in longer-term language study and to place the study of language and culture within the larger context of a humanistic education. The cultural content of *Débuts* aims to be thought-provoking and to expand students' horizons beyond simple "travelogue" facts toward understanding the roots of cultural differences.

The National Standards

With its integrated, multifaceted approach to culture, *Débuts* exemplifies the spirit of the National Standards* of foreign language education. By watching the characters in the film perform routine tasks and interactions and by grappling with complex issues of history and identity, students are exposed to a multiplicity of products, processes, and perspectives.

Through the presentation of functional language, role-play activities, and personalized activities, as well as an emphasis on listening comprehension, *Débuts* emphasizes **communication**. Documents, readings, and other exploratory activities help students make **connections** between their study of French, other discipline areas, and their own lives. As for **culture**, the *Regards sur la culture* and *Synthèse* sections in the textbook provide sustained opportunities for hypothesis and analysis, inviting students to make connections between beliefs, behaviors, and cultural artifacts. Ample opportunities are also provided for cross-cultural **comparisons** in the follow-up activities to the *Regards sur la culture* and *Synthèse* sections. Finally, web-based and experiential activities allow students to explore the many types of **communities** inherent in the French-speaking world.

Structure of Le Chemin du retour

Le Chemin du retour is available in a Director's Cut version that is the uninterrupted, full-length feature film. The instructional version of the film, however, divides the story into a preliminary episode, twenty-two story episodes, and an epilogue. Except for the **Épisode préliminaire**, which introduces students to the concept of learning French through film, each episode of *Le Chemin du retour* follows the same three-step format.

1. Students watch and participate in on-screen previewing activities.
   - **Vous avez vu...** Scenes from previous episodes are used to remind students about main events in the story that will help them understand the new episode.
   - **Vous allez voir...** Scenes previewing the upcoming episode set up the context for what students will see and hear in the episode.
   - **Paroles et images** This section, which occurs through Episode 11, introduces and practices a particular viewing strategy that students can apply to help them understand the language and events of the film.
2. Students view the complete episode.
3. Students watch and participate in on-screen postviewing activities.
   - **Vous avez compris?** Scenes from the episode are used in a variety of multiple-choice and true-false activities to help students verify their comprehension of the main ideas and the plot of the episode they've just viewed. Students who didn't understand an important point as they viewed the episode will find they understand more after doing these activities.

**Standards for Foreign Language Learning: Preparing for the 21st Century* (1996, National Standards in Foreign Language Education Project). The standards outlined in this publication were established by a collaboration of the American Council on the Teaching of Foreign Languages (ACTFL), the American Association of Teachers of French (AATF), the American Association of Teachers of Spanish and Portuguese (ASTSP), and the American Association of Teachers of German (AATG).

- **Langue en contexte** A transition back to the textbook, this section identifies for students the language functions and structures they will learn about in the textbook. Appropriate scenes from the film are subtitled in French and the targeted grammar and vocabulary are highlighted in yellow.

Using *Le Chemin du retour* in a Classroom Setting

The film, *Le Chemin du retour,* can be used as the foundation for a classroom-based beginning French course at the college level. As such, it offers several options for implementation. For example, an instructor may

- use the textbook, *Débuts,* and the film in class, assign most of the material in the Workbook and Laboratory Manual for homework, and follow up selected homework activities with discussions in class.
- use only the textbook in class, and have students view the film episodes at home, in the media center, or in the language laboratory.
- use the Student Viewer's Handbook with the film either by itself or to accompany other print materials.

Options for Using *Le Chemin du retour*

The film, *Le Chemin du retour,* can also be used

- in a distance learning course.
- as an offering for adult or continuing education students.
- as the foundation for French courses at the high school level.
- as a supplement to beginning, intermediate, or advanced courses, at all levels of instruction.
- as a resource for informal learning.
- as training materials for French-language classes in business and industry.
- as a significant addition to library movie collections.

Cast of Characters

Camille Leclair

A young television journalist who searches for the truth about her grandfather's past.

Mado Leclair

Camille's mother, who fears the truth and wants to keep her father's history hidden forever.

Bruno Gall

Camille's cohost on the morning television show "Bonjour!"

Rachid Bouhazid

A new reporter at "Bonjour!" who, with his family, must adjust to a new life in Paris.

Louise Leclair

Camille's grandmother, who encourages her granddaughter to pursue her quest for the truth.

Martine Valloton

Producer of "Bonjour!" who has to risk her job to support Camille's determination to find out about her grandfather.

Hélène Thibaut

A journalist from Quebec, and friend of Bruno and Camille.

David Girard

Historian, friend of Bruno, who researches information about Camille's grandfather.

Alex Béraud

A musician who plays in the Mouffetard Market. Friend of Louise, Mado, and Camille.

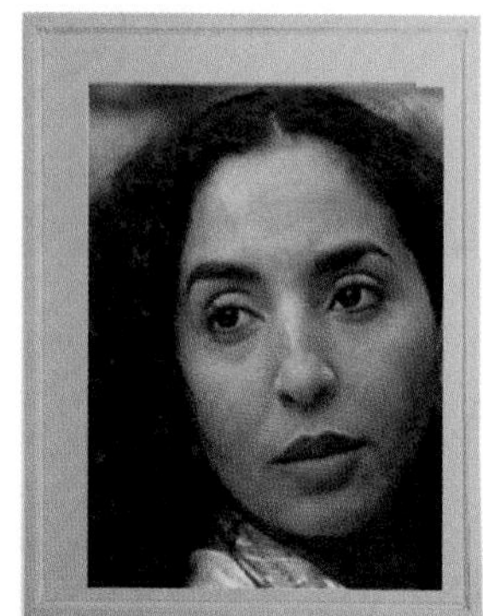

Sonia Bouhazid

Wife of Rachid and mother of their daughter, Yasmine.

Jeanne Leblanc

A woman who knew Camille's grandfather during the time of the German occupation of France.

Roland Fergus

A man who worked with Camille's grandfather during the German occupation and who holds the key to the truth.

Débuts

A Guided Tour of the Textbook

Débuts, the textbook, is clearly organized and easy to use. The chapters are coordinated with the individual episodes of the film. Each of the twenty-two main chapters consists of the following self-contained teaching modules, which maximize flexibility in course design. The preliminary chapter, containing a slightly different structure, introduces students to basic vocabulary and provides an overall framework for using the film.

Chapter Opener

Chapter learning goals prepare students for what is to come in the chapter and in the accompanying movie episode.

Vocabulaire en contexte

Thematically grouped vocabulary is presented in culturally informative contexts with drawings and scenes from the movie. It is accompanied by activities that promote vocabulary development.

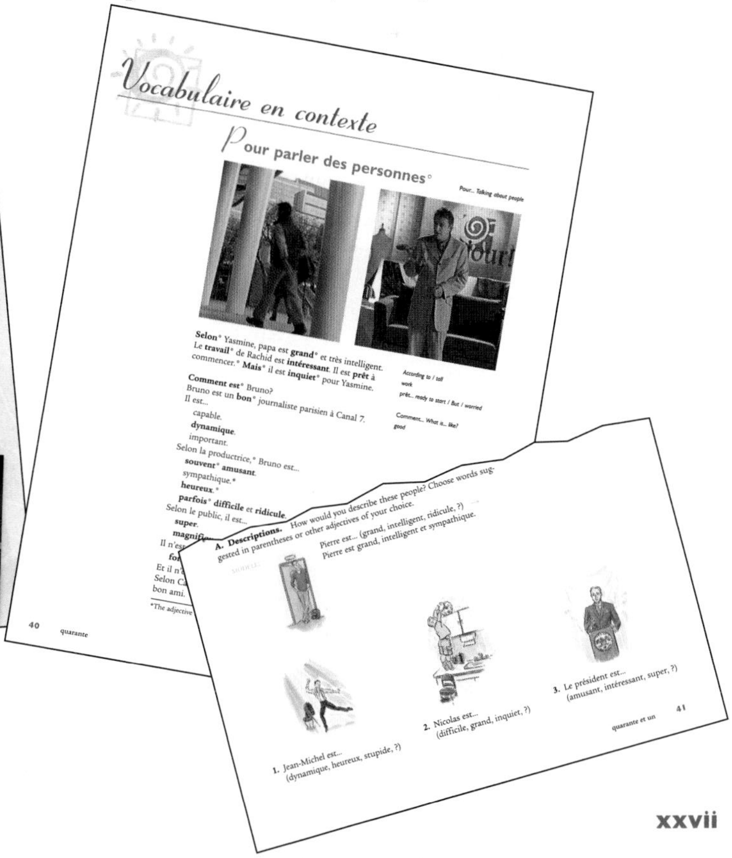

Visionnement 1

This section provides pre- and postviewing activities that supplement those found on-screen in the movie episode, as well as vocabulary needed for comprehension and questions that focus students' attention on what to watch and listen for in the story.

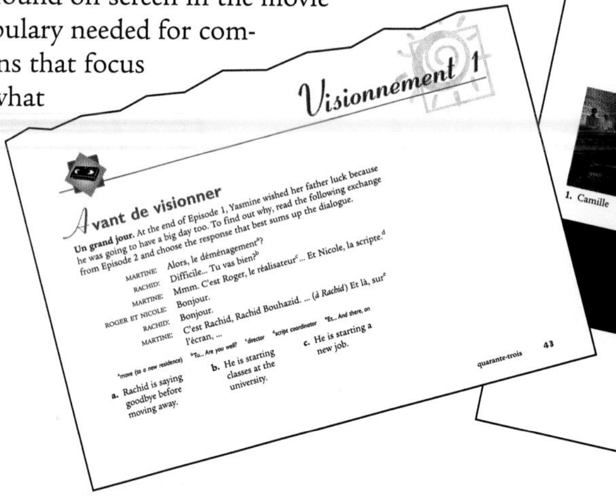

Visionnement 1

Avant de visionner

Un grand jour. At the end of Episode 1, Yasmine wished her father luck because he was going to have a big day too. To find out why, read the following exchange from Episode 2 and choose the response that best sums up the dialogue.

MARTINE: Alors, le déménagement[a]?
RACHID: Difficile... Tu vas bien?[b]
MARTINE: Mmm. C'est Roger, le réalisateur[c]... Et Nicole, la scripte.[d]
ROGER ET NICOLE: Bonjour.
RACHID: Bonjour.
MARTINE: C'est Rachid, Rachid Bouhazid. ... (*à Rachid*) Et là, sur[e] l'écran, ...

[a]move (to a new residence) [b]You... Are you well? [c]director [d]script coordinator [e]So... And there, on

a. Rachid is saying goodbye before moving away.
b. He is starting classes at the university.
c. He is starting a new job.

quarante-trois 43

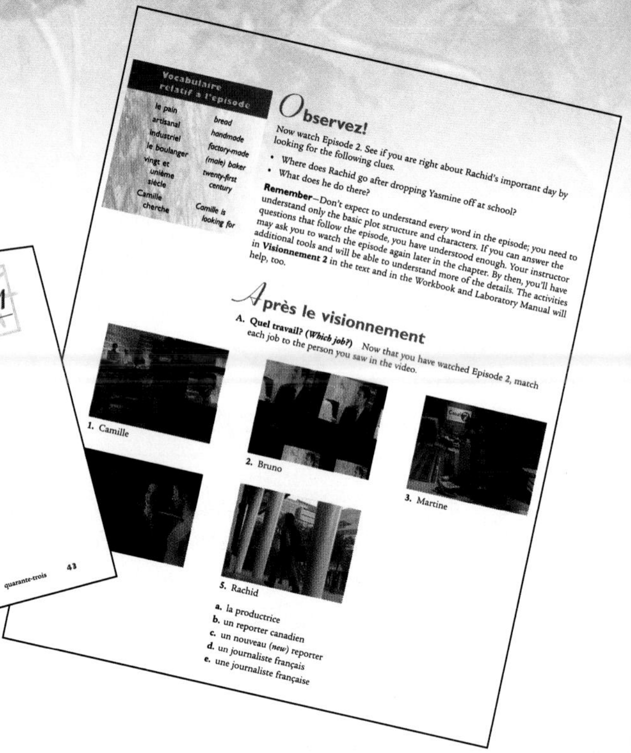

Vocabulaire relatif à l'épisode	
le pain	bread
artisanal	handmade
industriel	factory-made
le boulanger	(male) baker
vingt et unième siècle	twenty-first century
Camille cherche	Camille is looking for

Observez!

Now watch Episode 2. See if you are right about Rachid's important day by looking for the following clues.

- Where does Rachid go after dropping Yasmine off at school?
- What does he do there?

Remember—Don't expect to understand every word in the episode; you need to understand only the basic plot structure and characters. If you can answer the questions that follow the episode, you have understood enough. Your instructor may ask you to watch the episode again later in the chapter. By then, you'll have additional tools and will be able to understand more of the details. The activities in **Visionnement 2** in the text and in the Workbook and Laboratory Manual will help, too.

Après le visionnement

A. Quel travail? (*Which job?*) Now that you have watched Episode 2, match each job to the person you saw in the video.

1. Camille
2. Bruno
3. Martine
5. Rachid

a. la productrice
b. un reporter canadien
c. un nouveau (*new*) reporter
d. un journaliste français
e. une journaliste française

Structure

Three grammar points per chapter are introduced through clear and concise explanations and examples from the movie. Grammar points are accompanied by a wide range of practice, from controlled and form-focused to open-ended and creative communicative activities.

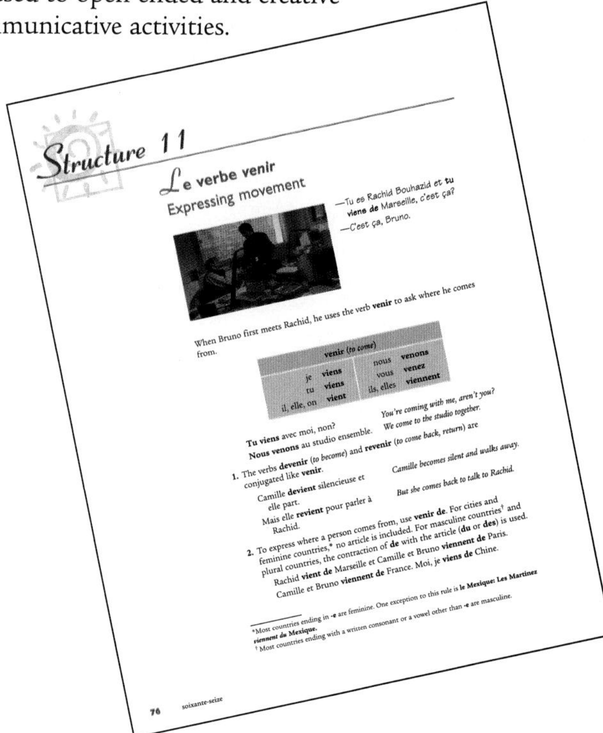

Structure 11

Le verbe venir
Expressing movement

—Tu es Rachid Bouhazid et tu **viens de** Marseille, c'est ça?
—C'est ça, Bruno.

When Bruno first meets Rachid, he uses the verb **venir** to ask where he comes from.

venir (*to come*)			
je	**viens**	nous	**venons**
tu	**viens**	vous	**venez**
il, elle, on	**vient**	ils, elles	**viennent**

Tu viens avec moi, non? — *You're coming with me, aren't you?*
Nous venons au studio ensemble. — *We come to the studio together.*

1. The verbs **devenir** (*to become*) and **revenir** (*to come back, return*) are conjugated like **venir**.

   Camille **devient** silencieuse et elle part. — *Camille becomes silent and walks away.*
   Mais elle **revient** pour parler à Rachid. — *But she comes back to talk to Rachid.*

2. To express where a person comes from, use **venir de**. For cities and feminine countries,* no article is included. For masculine countries† and plural countries, the contraction of **de** with the article (**du** or **des**) is used.

   Rachid **vient de** Marseille et Camille et Bruno **viennent de** Paris.
   Camille et Bruno **viennent de** France. Moi, je **viens de** Chine.

*Most countries ending in **-e** are feminine. One exception to this rule is **le Mexique: Les Martinez viennent du Mexique.**
†Most countries ending with a written consonant or a vowel other than **-e** are masculine.

76 soixante-seize

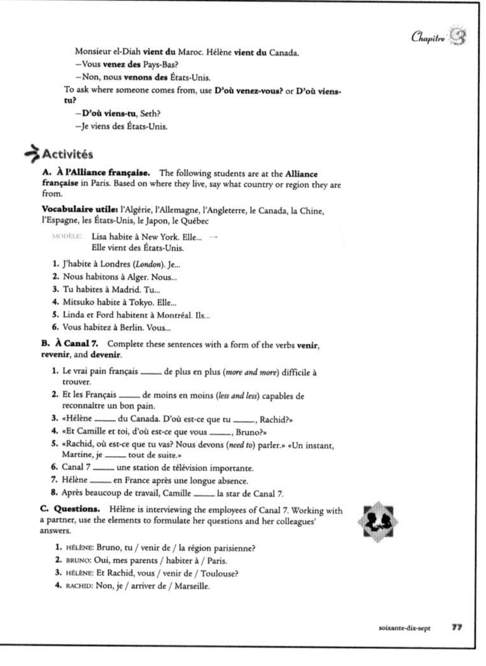

Chapitre 3

Monsieur el-Diah **vient du** Maroc. Hélène **vient du** Canada.
—Vous **venez des** Pays-Bas?
—Non, nous **venons des** États-Unis.

To ask where someone comes from, use **D'où venez-vous?** or **D'où viens-tu?**

—**D'où viens-tu**, Seth?
—Je viens des États-Unis.

Activités

A. À l'Alliance française. The following students are at the **Alliance française** in Paris. Based on where they live, say what country or region they are from.

Vocabulaire utile: l'Algérie, l'Allemagne, l'Angleterre, le Canada, la Chine, l'Espagne, les États-Unis, le Japon, le Québec

MODÈLE: Lisa habite à New York. Elle... → Elle vient des États-Unis.

1. J'habite à Londres (*London*). Je...
2. Nous habitons à Alger. Nous...
3. Tu habites à Madrid. Tu...
4. Mitsuko habite à Tokyo. Elle...
5. Linda et Ford habitent à Montréal. Ils...
6. Vous habitez à Berlin. Vous...

B. À Canal 7. Complete these sentences with a form of the verbs **venir**, **revenir**, and **devenir**.

1. Le vrai pain français _____ de plus en plus (*more and more*) difficile à trouver.
2. Et les Français _____ de moins en moins (*less and less*) capables de reconnaître un bon pain.
3. «Hélène _____ du Canada. D'où est-ce que tu _____, Rachid?»
4. «Et Camille et toi, d'où est-ce que vous _____, Bruno?»
5. «Rachid, où est-ce que tu vas? Nous devons (*need to*) parler.» «Un instant, Martine, je _____ tout de suite.»
6. Canal 7 _____ une station de télévision importante.
7. Hélène _____ en France après une longue absence.
8. Après beaucoup de travail, Camille _____ la star de Canal 7.

C. Questions. Hélène is interviewing the employees of Canal 7. Working with a partner, use the elements to formulate her questions and her colleagues' answers.

1. HÉLÈNE: Bruno, tu / venir de / la région parisienne?
2. BRUNO: Oui, mes parents / habiter à / Paris.
3. HÉLÈNE: Et Rachid, vous / venir de / Toulouse?
4. RACHID: Non, je / arriver de / Marseille.

soixante-dix-sept 77

Regards sur la culture

A cultural note and its accompanying critical thinking question deepen students' awareness and understanding of cultural issues raised in the movie episode or chapter vocabulary.

Regards sur la culture

Perceptions et réalités

Stereotypes usually tell us as much about the values and customs of the people who use them as about those whom they are supposed to describe. There are a few North American stereotypes about the French that are shared by the French themselves, but many others are not.

- French people often think of themselves as particularly interested in food and gifted at appreciating it. They are especially concerned about bread, which is truly the staple food of French cuisine. Bread is eaten along with nearly every dish at every meal, and it is the main food eaten at breakfast and for most children's snacks. Bread made in the traditional craft sense (**le pain artisanal**) has to be bought daily because it contains no preservatives and dries out quickly. Mass-produced bread (**le pain industriel**) is also available in stores. Most French people are ready at any moment to engage in animated debates about the quality of bread today.
- The French do not think of themselves as eating rich food, however, but only *good* food. When asked what the typical French meal is, most people in France would probably answer **le steak-frites** (*steak with fries*). This may not correspond to North American ideas of what French people like to eat, but it is the

50 cinquante

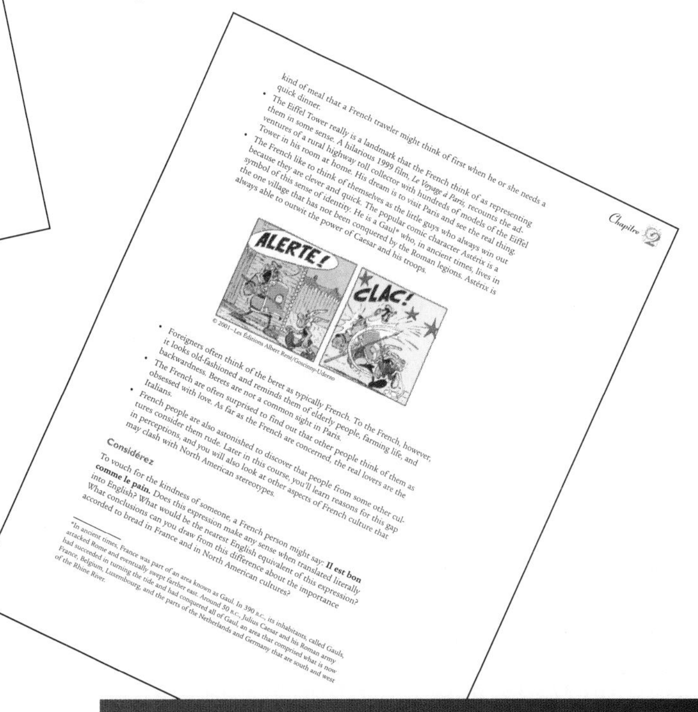

Chapitre 2

kind of meal that a French traveler might think of first when he or she needs a quick dinner.

- The Eiffel Tower really is a landmark that the French think of as representing them in some sense. A hilarious 1999 film, *Le Voyage à Paris*, recounts the adventures of a rural highway toll collector with hundreds of models of the Eiffel Tower in his room at home. His dream is to visit Paris and see the real thing.
- The French like to think of themselves as the little guys who always win out because they are clever and quick. The popular comic character Astérix is a symbol of this sense of identity. He is a Gaul* who, in ancient times, lives in the one village that has not been conquered by the Roman legions. Astérix is always able to outwit the power of Caesar and his troops.

© 2001–Les Éditions Albert René/Goscinny-Uderzo

- Foreigners often think of the beret as typically French. To the French, however, it looks old-fashioned and reminds them of elderly people, farming life, and backwardness. Berets are not a common sight in Paris.
- The French are often surprised to find out that other people think of them as obsessed with love. As far as the French are concerned, the real lovers are the Italians.
- French people are also astonished to discover that people from some other cultures consider them rude. Later in this course, you'll learn reasons for this gap in perceptions, and you will also look at other aspects of French culture that may clash with North American stereotypes.

Considérez

To vouch for the kindness of someone, a French person might say: **Il est bon comme le pain.** Does this expression make any sense when translated literally into English? What would be the nearest English equivalent of this expression? What conclusions can you draw from this difference about the importance accorded to bread in France and in North American cultures?

*In ancient times, France was part of an area known as Gaul. In 390 B.C., its inhabitants, called Gauls, attacked Rome and eventually swept farther east. Around 50 B.C., Julius Caesar and his Roman army had succeeded in turning the tide and had conquered all of Gaul, an area that comprised what is now France, Belgium, Luxembourg, and the parts of the Netherlands and Germany that are south and west of the Rhine River.

Visionnement 2

An optional second viewing section encourages students to watch the episode again, this time to concentrate on cultural information.

Visionnement 2

Avant de visionner

A. Points de repère. (*Landmarks.*) This map shows the southeastern edge of Paris and the adjacent suburbs, where the Canal 7 studios are located. This whole area, on both banks of the Seine, became rather run-down after World War II, but recently, it has been attracting new development and prestige projects like the national library (**la Bibliothèque nationale de France**).

Les environs de Canal 7

le Palais Omnisports de Bercy
le boulevard p riph rique
le zoo de Vincennes
Place de la Nation
Jardin des Plantes
Gare de Lyon
Gare d Austerlitz
Place d Italie
PARIS
la Seine
le Bois de Vincennes
CHARENTON-LE-PONT
IVRY-SUR-SEINE
la Biblioth que nationale de France
CANAL 7
l Autoroute de l Est (A4)

58 cinquante-huit

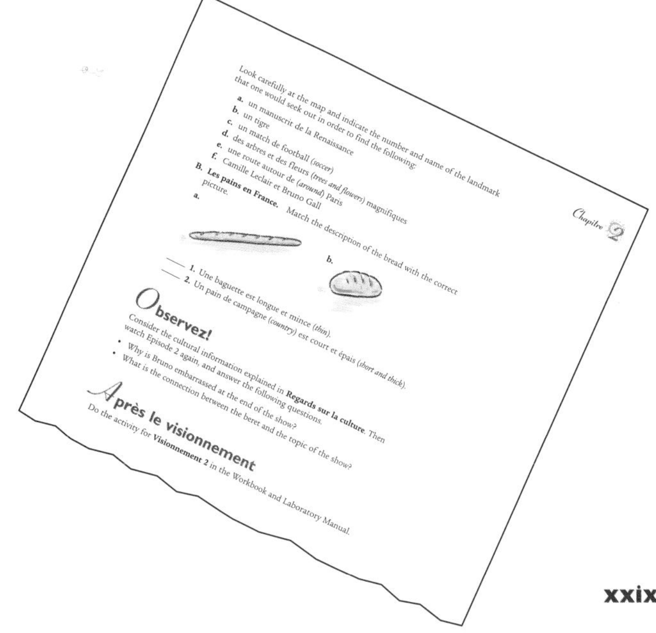

Chapitre 2

Look carefully at the map and indicate the number and name of the landmark that one would seek out in order to find the following:

a. un manuscrit de la Renaissance
b. un tigre
c. un match de football (*soccer*)
d. des arbres et des fleurs (*trees and flowers*) magnifiques
e. une route autour de (*around*) Paris
f. Camille Leclair et Bruno Gall

B. Les pains en France. Match the description of the bread with the correct picture.

a.

b.

___ **1.** Une baguette est longue et mince (*thin*).
___ **2.** Un pain de campagne (*country*) est court et épais (*short and thick*).

Observez!

Consider the cultural information explained in **Regards sur la culture**. Then watch Episode 2 again, and answer the following questions.

- Why is Bruno embarrassed at the end of the show?
- What is the connection between the beret and the topic of the show?

Après le visionnement

Do the activity for **Visionnement 2** in the Workbook and Laboratory Manual.

Synthèse

The chapter culminates in a synthesis section, which alternates between cultural presentations and readings, many of which are literary selections. Prereading strategies and postreading comprehension activities help students develop reading skills. A writing activity follows in the Workbook and Laboratory Manual.

Synthèse: Lecture

Mise en contexte

The notion of family in France has for centuries been the traditional dual-parent household and a closely knit extended family. In this tradition, husbands support the family, wives stay at home and raise the children, the whole family sits down to meals together, the children cooperate rather than compete, and so on. Marriage, children, and family are almost synonymous in this tradition, and it is, of course, a generalization.

Stratégie pour mieux lire

Recognizing cognates

Scientific texts tend to use a vocabulary that is high in cognate forms. This text draws on sociological terminology that may be familiar to you because of its similarity to English. Skim the passage, paying particular attention to familiar words and cognates. Then predict which of the following sentences will best summarize the gist of the entire text.

1. L'institution de la famille reste (*remains*) très importante pour la majorité des Français.
2. La diversité de la famille française résulte en une déstabilisation de la société.
3. La famille française assume (*takes on*) une multiplicité de configurations.

Now read the whole text through and see if your prediction is correct.

cent trois 103

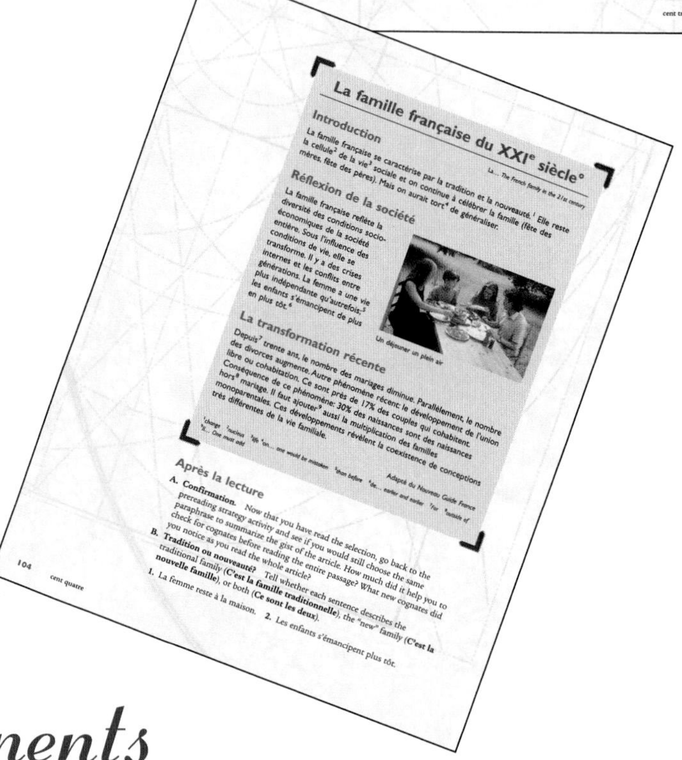

La famille française du XXIe siècle°

°La... The French family in the 21st century

Introduction

La famille française se caractérise par la tradition et la nouveauté.[1] Elle reste la cellule[2] de la vie[3] sociale et on continue à célébrer la famille (fête des mères, fête des pères). Mais on aurait tort[4] de généraliser.

Réflexion de la société

La famille française reflète la diversité des conditions socio-économiques de la société entière. Sous l'influence des conditions de vie, elle se transforme. Il y a des crises internes et les conflits entre générations. La femme a une vie plus indépendante qu'autrefois;[5] les enfants s'émancipent de plus en plus tôt.[6]

Un déjeuner un plein air

La transformation récente

Depuis[7] trente ans, le nombre des mariages diminue. Parallèlement, le nombre des divorces augmente. Autre phénomène récent: le développement de l'union libre ou cohabitation. Ce sont près de 17% des couples qui cohabitent. Conséquence de ce phénomène: 30% des naissances sont des naissances hors[8] mariage. Il faut ajouter[9] aussi la multiplication des familles monoparentales. Ces développements révèlent la coexistence de conceptions très différentes de la vie familiale.

Adapté du Nouveau Guide France

[1]change [2]nucleus [3]life [4]on... one would be mistaken [5]than before [6]de... earlier and earlier [7]For [8]outside of [9]Il... One must add

Après la lecture

A. **Confirmation.** Now that you have read the selection, go back to the prereading strategy activity and see if you would still choose the same paraphrase to summarize the gist of the article. How much did it help you to check for cognates before reading the entire passage? What new cognates did you notice as you read the whole article?

B. **Tradition ou nouveauté?** Tell whether each sentence describes the traditional family (**C'est la famille traditionnelle**), the "new" family (**C'est la nouvelle famille**), or both (**Ce sont les deux**).

1. La femme reste à la maison. 2. Les enfants s'émancipent plus tôt.

104 cent quatre

Other features

Langage fonctionnel

This feature provides useful phrases for carrying on conversations in particular situations.

Vocabulaire relatif à l'épisode

Unfamiliar vocabulary items needed for comprehension of the episode are provided in **Visionnement 1.**

Notez bien!

These marginal notes highlight important details about grammar and vocabulary that students should learn.

Pour en savoir plus

These marginal notes contain optional information about culture, vocabulary, and grammar.

Program Components

As a full-service publisher of quality educational products, McGraw-Hill does much more than just sell textbooks to students; we create and publish an extensive array of print, video, and digital supplements to support instruction on your campus. Orders of new (versus used) textbooks help us to defray the substantial cost of developing such supplements. Please consult your local McGraw-Hill representative to learn about the availability of the supplements that accompany *Débuts.*

Books and Multimedia Materials Available to Adopters and to Students

Student Edition

The *Débuts* textbook is correlated with the individual episodes in the film, *Le Chemin du retour,* and contains vocabulary presentations and activities; pre- and postviewing activities; grammar explanations and practice activities; cultural, historical, and literary readings; and pre- and postreading activities.

Listening Comprehension Audio CD or Cassette
The listening comprehension audio CD or cassette contains the vocabulary list from the end of each chapter of the textbook.

Workbook and Laboratory Manuals
The Workbook and Laboratory Manual accompanies the main textbook. Each chapter is divided into sections that follow the organization in the main textbook; and each section, as appropriate, may contain both laboratory and workbook exercises. All chapters provide practice in global listening comprehension, pronunciation, speaking, vocabulary, grammar, reading, writing, and culture.

Student Audio Program
For use with the laboratory exercises in the Workbook and Laboratory Manual, the audio CDs or audiocassettes offer hours of listening, oral communication, and pronunciation practice.

Student Viewer's Handbook
Ideal for those courses in which *Le Chemin du retour* is used to supplement other course materials than *Débuts,* the Handbook offers a variety of pre- and postviewing activities for use with the film.

Le Chemin du retour
The complete film broken into episodes, each with on-screen pre- and postviewing activities.

Director's Cut
Available in either VHS or DVD format, the entire film can be viewed uninterrupted. The DVD version allows inclusion of French or English subtitles.

Student CD-ROM
This multimedia CD-ROM allows students to interact with the film while practicing vocabulary and grammar skills, listening comprehension, and reading and writing skills in a highly interactive format.

Online Learning Center
A complete learning and teaching resource center for both students and instructors, this website brings the French and Francophone worlds to student's fingertips and allows them to work with film clips for enhanced comprehension. Instructor resources are available to aid in building a complete online French course.

Books and Multimedia Materials Available to Adopters Only

Instructor's Edition
The Instructor's Edition is identical to the Student Edition except that it contains annotated suggestions, cultural information, additional vocabulary, activity extensions and variations, and so on.

Instructor's Manual / Test Bank
The Instructor's Manual provides additional background information on the film as well as sample lessons, syllabus planning and scheduling suggestions, and an answer key for the Student Edition. It also offers suggestions for working with videos in the classroom. The Test Bank consists of two sets of tests for each chapter of *Débuts,* as well as quarter and semester exams.

Instructor's Audio Program
The Instructor's Audio Program, available on audio CD or audiocassette, contains the same material as the Student Audio Program, but the package includes an Audioscript.

Audioscript
Packaged with the Instructor's Audio Program, the Audioscript contains the complete recording script of the Audio Program.

Picture File
The Picture File contains fifty color photographs from the film and textbook and is designed to stimulate conversation in the classroom.

Distance Learning Faculty Guide
The Distance Learning Faculty Guide contains useful information on how to implement a distance learning course and how to incorporate the film and print materials in that environment.

Acknowledgments

The authors and the publisher would like to express their gratitude to the following instructors and students across the country whose valuable suggestions contributed to the preparation of this program. The appearance of their names in this list does not necessarily constitute their endorsement of the text or its methodology.

Reviewers

Elizabeth Brereton Allen, Washington University
Eileen M. Angelini, Philadelphia University
Miguel Aparicio, Santa Monica College
Daniela Elena Ascavelli, Drexel University
Patricia Eileen Black, California State University, Chico
Ruth L. Bradshaw, Truman State University
Ruth L. Caldwell, Luther College
Judith Jean Chapman, Worcester State College
Simone Clay, University of California, Davis
Dennis Conrad, Clarke College
Suzanne E. Cook, United States Air Force Academy
Véronique F. Courtois, Tufts University
Diane Griffin Crowder, Cornell College
Susan L. Dorff, Boston University
Nicole Dufresne, University of California, Los Angeles
Richard Durán, Baylor University
Karin Egloff, Western Kentucky University
Helen Gant Guillory, St. Edward's University
Hollie Harder, Brandeis University
Shawn Huffman, SUNY Plattsburgh
Madeleine Kernen, Southwest Missouri State University
Elizabeth M. Knutson, United States Naval Academy
Carolyn Gascoigne Lally, University of Nebraska at Omaha
Marc Lony, Loyola Marymount University
Amy Lorenz-Ianke, Loras College
Domenico Maceri, Allan Hancock College
Sayeeda H. Mamoon, University of South Dakota
Alain Martinossi, University of Michigan
Hassan Melehy, University of Connecticut
Mary Jo Muratore, University of Missouri, Columbia
June Hall McCash, Middle Tennessee State University
George J. McCool, Towson University
Kay Riddle McLean, Volunteer State Community College
Juliette Parnell-Smith, University of Nebraska at Omaha
Marina Peters-Newell, University of New Mexico
Denis Rochat, Smith College
Sini Prosper Sanou, University of Arizona
Joanne Schmidt, California State University, Bakersfield
Mary Ellen Scullen, University of Maryland
Dianne Elizabeth Sears, University of Massachusetts, Amherst
Elizabeth Ann Smith, Southwest Virginia Community College
Stuart Smith, Austin Community College
Karen Rhea Sorsby, California State University, Chico
Beverly Turner, Truckee Meadows Community College
Patricia Ann Umfress, Western Carolina University
Guy H. Wagener, University of Nevada, Reno
Alexandra K. Wettlaufer, University of Texas at Austin
Susan L. Wolf, University of Massachusetts, Boston

Focus Group Participants

Ali Alalou, University of Delaware
Eileen M. Angelini, Philadelphia University
Theresa A. Antes, University of Florida
Anne-Marie Bourbon, Queensborough Community College, CUNY
Véronique F. Courtois, Tufts University
Robert Davis, University of Oregon
Hilary Fisher, University of Oregon
Janet Fisher-McPeak, University of Notre Dame
Jeffrey H. Fox, College of DuPage
Mary Jane Highfield, Cornell University
John J. Janc, Minnesota State University, Mankato
Elizabeth Knutson, United States Naval Academy
Philip A. Lee, Macalester College
Kathryn M. Lorenz, University of Cincinnati
George McCool, Towson University
Pary Pezechkian, Augsburg College
Debra Popkin, Baruch College, CUNY
Laurie Postlewate, Barnard College
Pam Renna, Delta College
Sylvie Richards, Queens College, CUNY
Gail L. Riley, American University
Jean Luc Robin, University of Oregon
Arlene J. Russell, Purdue University, Calumet
Gloria Sawicki, Brooklyn College, CUNY
Mary Ellen Scullen, University of Maryland
Christina Vander Vorst, University of Oregon
Catherine Wiebe, University of Oregon
Yvette A. Guillemin Young, University of Wisconsin, Oshkosh

Student Focus Group Participants

Cabrillo College
Brian Honeywell
Megan S. Marietti
Patrick Tanner
Michelle Wonnacott
Benjamin Worden

Metropolitan State College, Denver
Tom Bustinduy
Marina Hudgens
Marie-Meredith Mangum
Ana Bel Marquez
Devin Scheinberg
Bonni Stewart
Brian Stiller
Jennifer Suihlik
Jaime Vargas

University of Maryland, Baltimore County
Dawn Brautlacht
Katie Collins
Michael Cooper
LaTonya R. Howard
Christina Lee
Justina J. Lee
Alejandro Magadán
Omorola Oluponmile
Farah Philippe
John R. Scott
John Thomas

University of Oregon
Sara Anoushirvani
John Archetro
Mark Boloens
Hadley Brown
Erin Dawson
Connor Dudley
Amy Horgan
Kelsey Kopra
Abolade Majekobaje
Larissa Rhodes
Andrea Wilcox

Tufts University
Jacqueline A. Fields
Daniel Kramer
Nannette Martinez
Reid Palmer

The authors would also like to extend very special thanks to the following organizations and individuals:

- David Murray and Ginger Cassell, of Wray Media, for their tireless work on the creation, direction, production, and final editing of *Le Chemin du retour*.
- SAME Films in France for their efforts in producing this film.
- David Lang, for a beautiful script.
- Karine Adrover, Denis Cherer, and the whole cast and crew for a highly professional production.
- Edge Productions for taking chances and for providing support to get the filming started.
- Cherie Mitschke, Austin Community College, for her endless enthusiasm and creativity in writing the on-screen pre- and postviewing activities.

Additional thanks to Catherine Coste, Claudette Pelletier Deschesnes, Marie-Hélène Le Tuan, Jean-Michel Margot, and Lise Nathan, who provided materials and consultation during the development process.

Finally, the authors wish to thank the editorial, design, and production staff at McGraw-Hill and their associates, especially Peggy Potter, Leslie Oberhuber, Thalia Dorwick, Sandra Beris, Nicole Dicop-Hineline, Veronica Oliva, Judy Mason, Jennifer Chow, Michelle Whitaker, David Staloch, Nora Agbayani, Diane Renda, Rich DeVitto, Louis Swaim, Melissa Gruzs, and Julie Melvin for all their patience and dedication to a project that was extremely complex.

Débuts

An Introduction to French

Chapitre préliminaire

Ça tourne!°

°Ça… *Action!*

OBJECTIFS

In the film, you will

- see a preview of *Le Chemin du retour*
- find out how the on-screen activities and episodes are organized

In this chapter, you will

- learn how to use this film to study French
- greet others, introduce yourself, and say good-bye in French
- count from 0 to 59 in French
- identify classroom objects and people in the classroom
- learn about French words that look or sound similar to English words
- identify people and places
- identify and specify people and things

Visionnement

*A*vant de visionner

Le film

The textbook, *Débuts,* is based on the film *Le Chemin du retour.* The film tells the story of Camille Leclair, a young TV journalist in Paris who risks her career to search for the truth about her grandfather. By following Camille's attempts to unravel the mystery surrounding her grandfather, you will learn about the culture of contemporary France and other French-speaking areas of the world, as well as historical information about France during the Second World War. *Le Chemin du retour* provides a natural, authentic context for learning to understand, speak, read, and write French.

Pour utiliser le film°

°Pour... *Using the film*

To use the film to its full advantage as a learning tool, you'll want to remember a few important pieces of advice.

- Always participate fully in the activities that precede and follow your viewing of the film. These activities are specially designed to help you understand what you see and hear on-screen.
- As a beginning student of French, don't worry about understanding every word as you watch the film. Instead, just try to understand the gist (the main idea) of what is happening. You'll discover that you can figure out quite a lot by watching the action. Watch for body language and other visual clues that may clarify what is happening. Keep an ear tuned not only for vocabulary that you already know, but also for the tone people use as they speak. If you relax and don't worry about understanding every word, you'll find that you can still understand the story. As the course progresses, you will gradually understand more and more of what you hear.
- Watch, too, for similarities and differences between French culture and that of your own country. You may be surprised at some of the ways in which people

interact, and you may see objects that you do not recognize. Think of the film as an immersion experience, like actually going to France, and pay attention to the place and to details of behavior just as carefully as you do to the plot. Many of the cultural features that you notice will be discussed in this book, but you may want to ask your instructor about others.

Pour parler du film°

Pour... *Talking about the film*

To help you talk about the film, you will learn vocabulary in each chapter of the textbook. The following activity will teach you a few terms that you may need in class discussions and in your writing. See if you can match the English meanings with the French words. Note: The words **un** and **une** mean *a*.

1. film	**a.** un acteur
2. studio	**b.** une actrice
3. scene	**c.** un cinéma
4. actress	**d.** une femme
5. actor	**e.** un film
6. story	**f.** une histoire
7. person	**g.** un homme
8. character	**h.** un personnage
9. movie theater	**i.** une personne
10. man	**j.** une scène
11. woman	**k.** un studio

How many of these words are similar in both English and French?

Visionnez!°

Watch!

Every chapter in the textbook contains previewing activities that you will do before watching the new episode of the story. In fact, you just did a previewing activity in the **Pour parler du film** section. In addition to the activities in the textbook, however, there are on-screen previewing and postviewing activities to help you understand what you see and hear in the story. Go ahead and do the on-screen lesson for this chapter now. It will introduce you to the story of *Le Chemin du retour* and show you how the on-screen activities in the episodes work.

Vocabulaire en contexte

Les salutations°

°Les... *Greetings*

When you address a person you don't know well, include the word **monsieur** (*sir*), **madame** (*madam*), or **mademoiselle** (*miss*) in your greeting. In French, using these words is considered part of everyday polite conversation. Here is a very simple conversation that shows what people might say when meeting for the first time.

—**Bonjour**, monsieur. Vous êtes Monsieur* Le Roy?	*Hello. Are you Mr. Le Roy?*
—**Oui**, madame. **Et vous?**	*Yes. And you?*
—**Je m'appelle** Chantal Lépine.	*My name is Chantal Lépine.*
—**Enchanté**, madame.	*Nice to meet you.*
—**Comment allez-vous**, monsieur?	*How are you?*
—**Très bien, merci.** Et vous?	*Very well, thank you, And you?*
—Très bien. **Au revoir**, monsieur.	*Very well. Good-bye.*
—Au revoir, madame.	*Good-bye.*

Note: If a woman wants to say *Nice to meet you,* she says **Enchantée**. This form is spelled with an extra **e**, but the word sounds the same as **Enchanté** when spoken.

Here is another conversation that includes greetings, introductions, and good-byes.

—Tu es Brigitte?	*Are you Brigitte?*
—Oui, **et toi**, tu es... ?	*Yes, and you, you are . . . ?*
—Je suis Benoît.	*I'm Benoît.*
—**Salut**, Benoît.	*Hi, Benoît!*
—Salut, Brigitte, **ça va**?	*Hi, Brigitte, how's it going?*
—**Ça va bien. Salut**, Benoît. **À bientôt!**	*Fine. 'Bye, Benoît. See you soon!*
—Oui, **à demain**! Salut, Brigitte!	*Yeah, see you tomorrow. 'Bye, Brigitte!*

What similarities do you notice between these two conversations? What differences? Can you guess why these differences occur? How do you think a child and an adult would interact? You probably noticed that two adults who don't know each other use **vous** and the titles **monsieur**, **madame**, **mademoiselle**. Children use **tu** among themselves. When a child and an adult (other than a parent or close relative) speak, the adult uses **tu** and the child uses **vous**.

*In writing, the words **Monsieur**, **Madame**, and **Mademoiselle** are capitalized only when used before a name or title. In addition, **Monsieur** is often abbreviated before a name as **M.** (with a period). **Madame** is abbreviated as **Mme** (without a period) and **Mademoiselle** as **Mlle** (without a period).

Vocabulaire en contexte

Les salutations°

Les... *Greetings*

When you address a person you don't know well, include the word **monsieur** (*sir*), **madame** (*madam*), or **mademoiselle** (*miss*) in your greeting. In French, using these words is considered part of everyday polite conversation. Here is a very simple conversation that shows what people might say when meeting for the first time.

—**Bonjour**, monsieur. Vous êtes Monsieur* Le Roy?	*Hello. Are you Mr. Le Roy?*
—**Oui**, madame. **Et vous?**	*Yes. And you?*
—**Je m'appelle** Chantal Lépine.	*My name is Chantal Lépine.*
—**Enchanté**, madame.	*Nice to meet you.*
—**Comment allez-vous**, monsieur?	*How are you?*
—**Très bien, merci.** Et vous?	*Very well, thank you, And you?*
—Très bien. **Au revoir**, monsieur.	*Very well. Good-bye.*
—Au revoir, madame.	*Good-bye.*

Note: If a woman wants to say *Nice to meet you,* she says **Enchantée**. This form is spelled with an extra **e**, but the word sounds the same as **Enchanté** when spoken.

Here is another conversation that includes greetings, introductions, and good-byes.

—Tu es Brigitte?	*Are you Brigitte?*
—Oui, **et toi**, tu es... ?	*Yes, and you, you are . . . ?*
—Je suis Benoît.	*I'm Benoît.*
—**Salut**, Benoît.	*Hi, Benoît!*
—Salut, Brigitte, **ça va**?	*Hi, Brigitte, how's it going?*
—**Ça va bien. Salut**, Benoît. **À bientôt!**	*Fine. 'Bye, Benoît. See you soon!*
—Oui, **à demain**! Salut, Brigitte!	*Yeah, see you tomorrow. 'Bye, Brigitte!*

What similarities do you notice between these two conversations? What differences? Can you guess why these differences occur? How do you think a child and an adult would interact? You probably noticed that two adults who don't know each other use **vous** and the titles **monsieur**, **madame**, **mademoiselle**. Children use **tu** among themselves. When a child and an adult (other than a parent or close relative) speak, the adult uses **tu** and the child uses **vous**.

*In writing, the words **Monsieur**, **Madame**, and **Mademoiselle** are capitalized only when used before a name or title. In addition, **Monsieur** is often abbreviated before a name as **M.** (with a period). **Madame** is abbreviated as **Mme** (without a period) and **Mademoiselle** as **Mlle** (without a period).

interact, and you may see objects that you do not recognize. Think of the film as an immersion experience, like actually going to France, and pay attention to the place and to details of behavior just as carefully as you do to the plot. Many of the cultural features that you notice will be discussed in this book, but you may want to ask your instructor about others.

Pour parler du film°

°Pour… *Talking about the film*

To help you talk about the film, you will learn vocabulary in each chapter of the textbook. The following activity will teach you a few terms that you may need in class discussions and in your writing. See if you can match the English meanings with the French words. Note: The words **un** and **une** mean *a*.

1. film	**a.** un acteur
2. studio	**b.** une actrice
3. scene	**c.** un cinéma
4. actress	**d.** une femme
5. actor	**e.** un film
6. story	**f.** une histoire
7. person	**g.** un homme
8. character	**h.** un personnage
9. movie theater	**i.** une personne
10. man	**j.** une scène
11. woman	**k.** un studio

How many of these words are similar in both English and French?

Visionnez!°

°*Watch!*

Every chapter in the textbook contains previewing activities that you will do before watching the new episode of the story. In fact, you just did a previewing activity in the **Pour parler du film** section. In addition to the activities in the textbook, however, there are on-screen previewing and postviewing activities to help you understand what you see and hear in the story. Go ahead and do the on-screen lesson for this chapter now. It will introduce you to the story of *Le Chemin du retour* and show you how the on-screen activities in the episodes work.

Structures

Culture / Synthèse

Vocabulaire

Chapitre

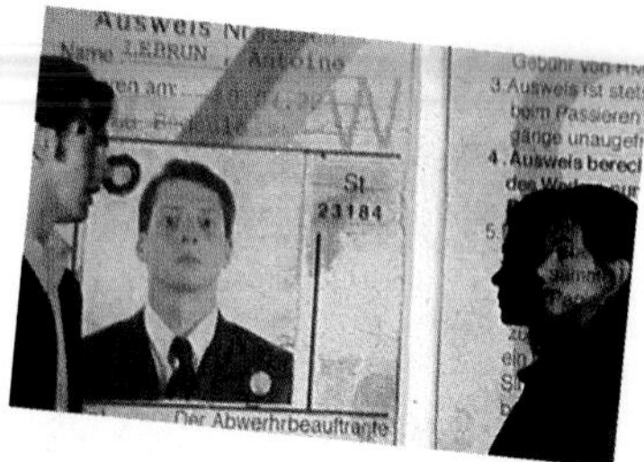

Chapitre

Chapitre

Structures	Culture / Synthèse

Vocabulaire

Activités

A. Quoi dire? (*What should they say?*) Complete each dialogue using one of the following expressions: **Au revoir, madame. / Au revoir, monsieur. / Bonjour, madame. / Salut!**

1. MME LÉPINE: Bonjour, monsieur. Je m'appelle Chantal Lépine.
   M. LE ROY: ______
2. BRIGITTE: Salut, Benoît.
   BENOÎT: ______
3. M. LE ROY: Au revoir, madame.
   MME LÉPINE: ______
4. MME LÉPINE: Au revoir, Brigitte.
   BRIGITTE: ______

B. Dans votre classe. (*In your class.*) With three other people in your classroom (one could be your instructor), greet each other, introduce yourself, and say good-bye. Depending on whom you speak to, use expressions from the appropriate column as a sort of script. Add names or the words **monsieur**, **madame**, **mademoiselle** after some phrases, as appropriate.

WITH OTHER STUDENTS	WITH YOUR INSTRUCTOR
—Bonjour.	—Bonjour,...
—Salut.	—Bonjour,...
—Je m'appelle... Et toi?	—Je m'appelle...
—Je m'appelle...	—Enchanté (Enchantée)... Et je m'appelle...
—Ça va?	—Comment allez-vous,... ?
—Oui, ça va bien, merci.	—Très bien, merci. Au revoir,...
—À bientôt...	—Au revoir,...
—Salut...	

Les nombres de 0 à 59

0	**zéro**	10	**dix**	20	**vingt**	30	**trente**
1	**un**	11	**onze**	21	**vingt et un**	31	**trente et un**
2	**deux**	12	**douze**	22	**vingt-deux**	32	**trente-deux**
3	**trois**	13	**treize**	23	**vingt-trois**	33	**trente-trois**
4	**quatre**	14	**quatorze**	24	**vingt-quatre**	34	**trente-quatre**
5	**cinq**	15	**quinze**	25	**vingt-cinq**	35	**trente-cinq**
6	**six**	16	**seize**	26	**vingt-six**	36	**trente-six**
7	**sept**	17	**dix-sept**	27	**vingt-sept**	37	**trente-sept**
8	**huit**	18	**dix-huit**	28	**vingt-huit**	38	**trente-huit**
9	**neuf**	19	**dix-neuf**	29	**vingt-neuf**	39	**trente-neuf**

40 **quarante**
41 **quarante et un**
42 **quarante-deux (...)**
49 **quarante-neuf**

50 **cinquante**
51 **cinquante et un**
52 **cinquante-deux (...)**
59 **cinquante-neuf**

Activités

A. Dans la papeterie. (***In the stationery store.***) What are the prices of the following items that you're thinking of buying in the stationery store? Use the expression **Ça coûte** (*That costs*) in your answers.

MODÈLE: → Ça coûte cinq euros.

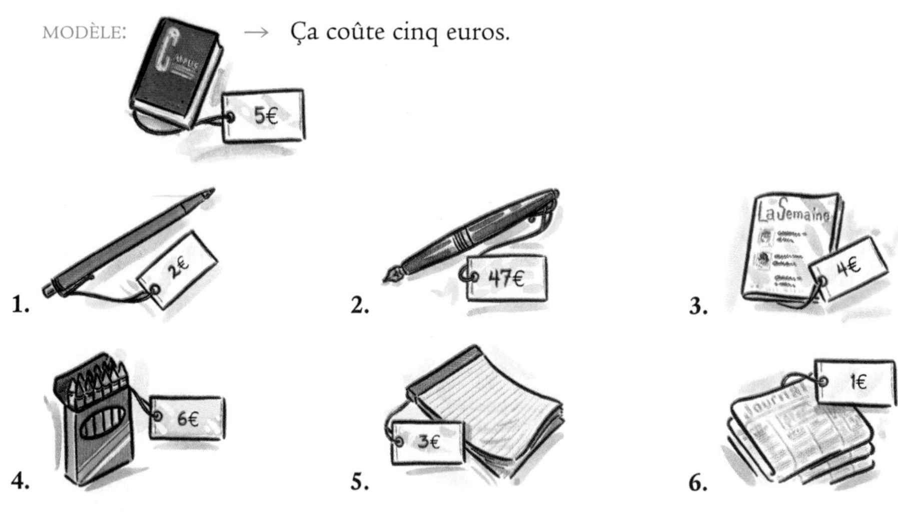

B. Les maths.

1. Comptez de (*Count from*) 0 à 20.
2. Comptez de 41 à 53.
3. Comptez de 32 à 20.
4. Comptez de 59 à 44.
5. Complétez la série: 5, 10, ____, ____, ____, 30
6. Complétez la série: 22, 24, 26, ____, ____, ____, 34
7. Complétez la série: 41, 43, 45, ____, ____, ____, 53
8. Complétez la série: 41, 39, 37, ____, ____, ____, 29

*1, 2, 3... *1, 2, 3, I'll go into the woods 4, 5, 6, to pick cherries 7, 8, 9, in a new basket. 10, 11, 12, they'll all be red, in Toulouse.*

C. La température. Read the average high Celsius temperatures in January and July for the following French-speaking cities. For temperatures below zero, use the word **moins** (for example: −8 degrees = **moins huit**).

Température maximale moyenne pour le mois de...°		
	janvier	**juillet**
Abidjan	27	25
Casablanca	12	22
Genève	0	19
Marseille	6	23
Montréal	−10	21
Paris	4	19

°Température... *Average high temperature for the month of . . .*

1. Montréal
2. Abidjan
3. Paris
4. Casablanca
5. Genève
6. Marseille

Dans la salle de classe°

Dans... *In the classroom*

Autres mots utiles

un ami	(*male*) friend
une amie	(*female*) friend
une classe	class
un laboratoire	laboratory
une université	university, college

*__Un étudiant__ is a male student; **une étudiante** is a female student. You will learn more about differences in nouns for males and females later in the chapter.

Activités

A. Combien? (*How many?*) Say how many objects you see in each drawing. Use the phrase **Il y a...** (*There is/are . . .*).

MODÈLE: 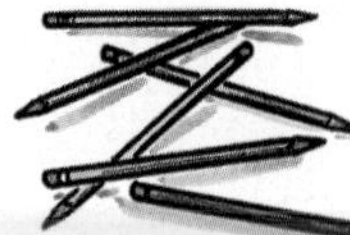 crayons → Il y a six crayons.

1. étudiants

2. étudiantes

3. salle de classe

4. livres

5. stylos

6. laboratoire

7. enfants

8. calculatrices

B. Trouvez les différences. (*Find the differences.*) With a partner, compare the two drawings and tell what the differences are.

MODÈLE: É1: Dans le dessin 1, il y a dix crayons.
É2: Et dans le dessin 2, il y a quatre crayons.

1.

2.

C. Dans votre salle de classe. (*In your classroom.*) With a partner, decide how many of the following people and things there are in your classroom. Use the expression **Il y a...** .

MODÈLE: cahiers →
É1: Il y a vingt-trois cahiers dans la salle de classe.
É2: Oui, vingt-trois. (*ou** Non, il y a vingt-cinq cahiers dans la salle de classe.)
É1: Voilà. (*ou* OK. Vingt-cinq.)

1. professeurs **2.** livres de français **3.** étudiants **4.** stylos **5.** sacs à dos **6.** tables **7.** étudiantes

Les mots apparentés et les faux amis°†

Les... *Cognates and false cognates*

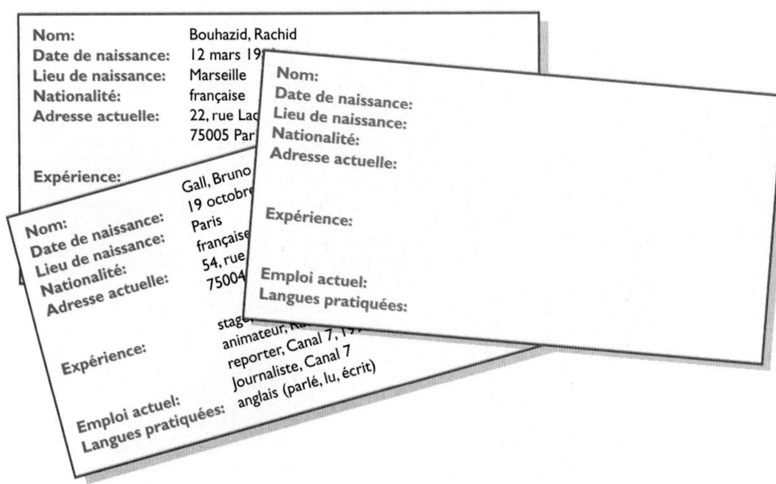

*The word **ou** mears *or.* Here it shows a possible alternative answer.

†**Les faux amis** are words that have a different meaning from the English words they resemble. Examples are **actuel(le)** (*present, current*), **crayon** (*pencil*), and **conférence** (*lecture*).

Reading in French is made easier by the large number of French and English words that are related. Thousands of French words have been borrowed into English over the past millennium (10,000 in the 12th and 13th centuries alone). These words are called "cognates." The meanings are usually very similar, if not exactly the same, in both languages, although the spellings and pronunciations may sometimes differ slightly. Ask your instructor to pronounce the following French words and contrast the sound with the sound of the corresponding English word.

FRENCH	ENGLISH
date	*date*
expérience	*experience*

In *Débuts,* unfamiliar words that are true cognates, like the preceding examples, are not translated for you. False cognates will be translated until they have been presented for active use.

Activités

A. Que veut dire... ? (*What is the meaning of . . . ?*) For each French word, say what you think the English equivalent is.

1. visite
2. lampe
3. carottes
4. téléphone
5. appartement
6. microphone
7. adresse
8. géographie
9. groupe
10. drame
11. enthousiaste
12. calme

B. Écoutez bien. (*Listen well.*) Repeat the cognates after your instructor. The second time you hear them, match them to the appropriate drawing.

1. 

2. 

3. 

4. 

5. 

6. 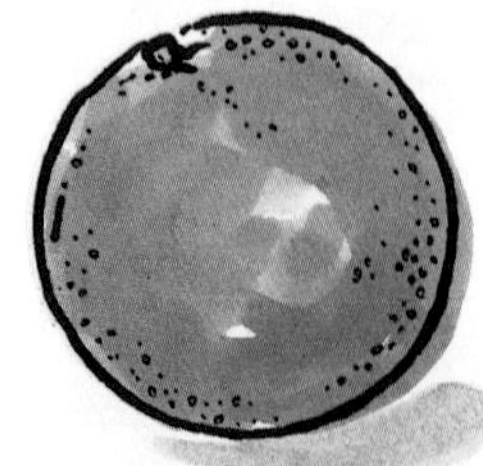

7. 

Structure 1

Est-ce... ? Qui est-ce? C'est... , Ce sont...

Identifying people and places

—**Est-ce** Suzanne Michaud?	*Is that Suzanne Michaud?*
—Oui, **c'est** Suzanne.	*Yes, it is Suzanne.*
—Et **qui est-ce**?	*And who is that?*
—**Ce sont** Paul Lemieux et Diane Coste.	*They are Paul Lemieux and Diane Coste.*
—Mais **qui est-ce** à la table?	*But who is that at the table?*
—**Je ne sais pas.**	*I don't know.*

1. To ask who a person is, use **Qui est-ce?**

   Qui est-ce? — *Who is that?*

2. Use **Est-ce... ?** to ask *Is it . . . ? / Is this . . . ? / Is that . . . ?*

   Est-ce un film français? — *Is this a French film?*
   Est-ce Serge? — *Is that Serge?*

3. Use the phrase **c'est** to make an identification. The plural of **c'est** is **ce sont**.

   C'est Paris. — *This is Paris.*
   Ce sont Serge et Chantal. — *They are Serge and Chantal.*

4. In the negative, **c'est** and **ce sont** become **ce n'est pas** and **ce ne sont pas**.

   Ce n'est pas Paul. — *This is not Paul.*
   Ce ne sont pas Suzanne et Diane. — *They are not Suzanne and Diane.*

5. To indicate that you don't know the answer, say **Je ne sais pas.**

   –Qui est-ce? Est-ce Chantal? — *Who is that? Is it Chantal?*
   –**Je ne sais pas.** — *I don't know.*

Activités

A. Qui est-ce? Ask your partner **Qui est-ce?** Your partner will answer.

MODÈLE: 

Yasmine →
É1: Qui est-ce?
É2: C'est Yasmine.

1. Camille

2. Rachid

3. Bruno et Camille

4. Rachid et Yasmine

5. Mado

6. ?

B. Négations. Look at the drawing and answer the question according to the model. Choose from the following cities: New York, Paris, Pise, Rome, San Francisco, St. Louis, Tokyo.

MODÈLE: 

Est-ce San Francisco? →
Non, ce n'est pas San Francisco. C'est St. Louis.

1. Est-ce Paris?

2. Est-ce St. Louis?

3. Est-ce New York?

4. Est-ce Boston?

C. Qui est dans la classe de français? In groups of three to five students, introduce yourselves using **Je m'appelle**. Then have conversations in which you check how well each of you remembers each name. Follow the models.

MODÈLE: É1: (*pointing to É3*) Qui est-ce?
É2: C'est Paul.
É3: Oui, je m'appelle Paul. (Non, je m'appelle Carlos.)

MODÈLE: É1: (*pointing to É3*) Est-ce Paul?
É2: Oui, c'est Paul. (Non, ce n'est pas Paul. C'est Carlos.)
É3: Oui, je m'appelle Paul. (Oui, je m'appelle Carlos.)

Now use the expressions **Est-ce... ? / Qui est-ce? / C'est... / Ce sont...** to check whom your group members know in the whole class. If you don't know who someone is when you are asked, answer with **Je ne sais pas.**

Structure 2

Qu'est-ce que c'est?, les articles indéfinis et définis et les substantifs

Identifying and specifying people and things

—**Qu'est-ce que c'est?**	*What is this?*
—C'est **un** studio de télévision. Il y a **des** techniciens dans **la** salle. Il y a **une** caméra. **Les** acteurs regardent **le** chien.	*It's a television studio. There are technicians in the room. There is a camera. The actors are watching the dog.*

In French, nouns▲ are divided into two broad categories, masculine and feminine. Gender▲ in French is a grammatical category used to classify nouns that share certain patterns. You should learn the gender of each noun as you learn the noun itself. To do this, you will need to know the articles.▲

▲Terms followed by ▲ are explained in the *Glossary of Grammatical Terms* in Appendix A.

L'article indéfini

The **indefinite article**▲ means *a* (*an*) or *some.* **Un** is used before masculine nouns, **une** before feminine nouns, and **des** before either gender of plural nouns.

	SINGULIER	PLURIEL
masculin	**un** personnage	**des** personnages
féminin	**une** caméra	**des** caméras

C'est **un** film américain. — *It is an American film.*
C'est **une** photo de Louise. — *This is a photo of Louise.*
Ce ne sont pas **des** photos d'Antoine. — *These are not photos of Antoine.*

L'article défini

The **definite article**▲ means *the.* **Le** is used before masculine nouns, **la** before feminine nouns, and **les** in the plural. Note that before a noun beginning with a vowel sound, **le** and **la** become **l'**.

	SINGULIER	PLURIEL
masculin	**le** studio **l'**acteur **l'**hôtel	**les** studios **les** acteurs **les** hôtels
féminin	**la** personne **l'**actrice **l'**histoire	**les** personnes **les** actrices **les** histoires

Voilà **le** film. — *Here's the film.*
C'est **l'**histoire de Camille Leclair. — *It is the story of Camille Leclair.*
C'est **la** vérité. — *That's the truth.*
Voilà **les** acteurs! — *There are the actors!*

Le pluriel des substantifs

1. Noun plurals are usually formed by adding an **s** to the written singular form. See the examples in the preceding article charts. This plural **-s** ending is usually silent.

   le film
   les films

   Note the following plurals of compound nouns.

   un sac à dos — deux sac**s** à dos
   un bloc-notes — deux bloc**s**-notes
   une salle de classe — deux salle**s** de classe

Notez bien!

Marginal notes called **Notez bien!** (*Note well!*) appear throughout your textbook. You should study and learn the material in all **Notez bien!** notes.

Many words that refer to people have only one gender. For example, **personne** is feminine, even when it designates a man. **Personnage** and **professeur** are masculine, even when they refer to women. In Canada, however, a distinction is made between **le professeur** and **la professeure**. In both France and Canada, the informal **le/la prof** is acceptable.

2. To ask for identification of a thing, use **Qu'est-ce que c'est?**

—**Qu'est-ce que c'est?**	*What is that? (this? it?)*
—C'est un sac à dos.	*It's a backpack.*

Activités

A. Quels articles? (*Which articles?*) Place the correct form of the indefinite and then the definite article before the following nouns.

MODÈLE: cahier → un cahier, le cahier

1. étudiante
2. stylo
3. livre
4. professeur
5. salle de classe
6. crayon
7. calculatrice
8. classe
9. ami
10. amie
11. personnage
12. personne

B. Transformez. Convert the singular to the plural or vice versa.

MODÈLES: les étudiantes → l'étudiante
un professeur → des professeurs

1. des crayons
2. le livre
3. les étudiants
4. un sac à dos
5. des dictionnaires
6. la salle de classe
7. les amies
8. une personne

C. Personnes et objets. Working with a small group, look around the room and point out at least five objects or people, asking **Qu'est-ce que c'est?** or **Qui est-ce?** Your partners will tell you what they think you're referring to, using definite and indefinite articles in the singular or plural.

MODÈLE: É1: [*Points to several female students.*] Qui est-ce?
É2: Ce sont des étudiantes.

D. Les étudiants et les professeurs. Working with a partner and using what you have learned in this chapter, use the following guidelines to play the roles of a professor and a student in French class.

1. Say hello to each other and introduce yourselves.
2. Ask each other how you are.
3. Professor: Tell the student to count from zero to ten. Use the expression **Comptez de 0 à 10.**
4. Student: Tell how many students are in the class today. Use **il y a**.
5. Student: Tell how many professors are in class.
6. Student: Ask what certain objects in the classroom are. Professor: Tell him/her what they are.
7. Discuss how many books and other things are in the classroom.
8. Talk about who other people in the class are, using **Est-ce... ?**, **Qui est-ce?**, **C'est...**, and **Je ne sais pas.**
9. Say good-bye to each other.

FRANCE

CANADA

MAROC

ALGÉRIE

SÉNÉGAL

HAÏTI

Le français dans le monde[1]

Félicitations! You are among the 100 to 110 million people outside of the Francophone world who are studying French. Not only is French one of the five official languages of the United Nations, but it is important in many ways in places all around the world. French ranks tenth worldwide in terms of the number of native speakers—70 million—and, impressively, it ranks sixth in the world in the number of people for whom it is an official language—220 million. In fact, French ranks *second* in the world, after English and before Spanish, in the number of countries where it is an official language—28 countries, located on five continents. Take a look at the maps in the front and back of your textbook to see its distribution throughout the world.

The ten countries with the largest numbers of French speakers are France, Algeria, Canada, Morocco, Belgium, Côte-d'Ivoire, Tunisia, Cameroon, the Democratic Republic of the Congo, and Switzerland. However, the official status of French varies from country to country. French is one of two or more official languages in Canada, Belgium, Cameroon, and Switzerland, and although it is spoken by many in Algeria, Morocco, and Tunisia it is not an official language at all in those countries. In Côte-d'Ivoire, however, French is the only official language and is used in some aspects of day-to-day life because there is no common African language that is used by all the people of the nation. In fact, Côte-d'Ivoire is one place in Africa where local innovations in French are giving birth to a new dialect of the language. In other countries, such as Senegal, French is again the only official language, but it is used almost exclusively in an administrative or educational context. As you can imagine, these two contexts mean a significant use of the French language there.

Numbers of speakers and status as an official language only tell part of the story of the importance of French in the world, however. Other factors must also be considered in order to appreciate fully the role of French in the community of nations. French is one of the world's major languages, not only because of the geographic spread of its speakers, but more importantly, because of the many contributions of French-speaking nations to the advancement of knowledge and artistic creation throughout the international community. France and the French language have had a profound influence on international culture in such areas as science, sociology, political theory, literature, the arts, fashion, and gastronomy. Furthermore, in the realm of international relations, France has had long historical ties with both the United States and Canada. You will explore some of these many influences in more detail throughout *Débuts*.

[1]Le... *French in the world*

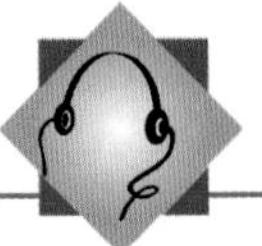

Vocabulaire

Pour parler du film

un(e) acteur/trice	actor, actress
un cinéma	movie theater
une femme	woman
une histoire	story
un homme	man
un personnage	character

MOTS APPARENTÉS: **un film, une personne, une scène, un studio**

Dans la salle de classe

un(e) ami(e)	(*male/female*) friend
un bloc-notes (des blocs-notes)	pad of paper
un cahier	notebook; workbook
une calculatrice	calculator
un(e) camarade de classe (des camarades de classe)	(*male/female*) classmate
un crayon	pencil
un(e) étudiant(e)	(*male/female*) university student
un livre	book
un sac à dos (des sacs à dos)	backpack
une salle de classe (des salles de classes)	classroom
un stylo	pen

MOTS APPARENTÉS: **une classe, un dictionnaire, un laboratoire, un professeur, une table, une université**

Articles

des	some
le, la, les	the
un, une	a (an)

Les nombres de 0 à 59

zéro, un, deux, trois, quatre, cinq, six, sept, huit, neuf, dix, onze, douze, treize, quatorze, quinze, seize, dix-sept, dix-huit, dix-neuf, vingt, vingt et un, vingt-deux, trente, quarante, cinquante

Pour identifier

est-ce... ?	is this/that/it . . . ?
Qui est-ce?	Who is this/that/it?
Qu'est-ce que c'est?	What is this/that/it?
c'est	this/that/it is
ce sont	these/those/they are
ce n'est pas	this/that/it is not
ce ne sont pas	these/those/they are not
je ne sais pas	I don't know

Salutations

À bientôt.	See you soon.	**Et vous?**	And you? (*fam. pl.; formal s. and pl.*)
À demain.	See you tomorrow.	**Je m'appelle...**	I am . . . , My name is . . .
Au revoir.	Good-bye.	**madame (Mme)**	madam, ma'am; Mrs.
Bonjour.	Hello.	**mademoiselle (Mlle)**	miss; Miss
Ça va?	How's it going?	**merci**	thank you
Ça va bien.	I'm fine., I'm well.	**monsieur (M.)**	sir; Mr.
Comment allez-vous?	How are you?	**Salut.**	Hi.; 'Bye.
Enchanté(e).	Nice to meet you., It's a pleasure.	**très bien**	very well
Et toi?	And you? (*fam. sing.*)		

Autres expressions utiles

bien	well	**non**	no
dans	in	**ou**	or
de	of; from	**oui**	yes
et	and	**très**	very
il y a	there is, there are (*for counting*)		

Chapitre 1

Un grand jour°

° Un... *A big day*

OBJECTIFS

In this episode, you will

- meet Rachid Bouhazid and his daughter, Yasmine, as they begin a new life in Paris
- learn cultural information about Paris and about French customs

In this chapter, you will

- spell words in French
- identify more classroom objects
- talk about your studies
- talk about yourselves and others
- express negative ideas
- ask simple yes/no questions
- learn about the school system in France
- learn about education in other French-speaking countries

Vocabulaire en contexte

L'alphabet français

a	a	j	ji	s	esse
b	bé	k	ka	t	té
c	cé	l	elle	u	u
d	dé	m	emme	v	vé
e	e	n	enne	w	double vé
f	effe	o	o	x	iks
g	gé	p	pé	y	i grec
h	hache	q	ku	z	zède
i	i	r	erre		

1. Spelling a word correctly in French requires using written accents, which are part of the spelling of some words. They may not be omitted.

ACCENT	NOM	EXEMPLE
´	accent aigu	éléphant
`	accent grave	scène
^	accent circonflexe	dîner
ç	cé cédille	français
¨	tréma	Noël

2. You will also need these additional terms when spelling a word aloud.

majuscule	*upper case*	apostrophe	*apostrophe*
minuscule	*lower case*	trait d'union	*hyphen*

3. To ask how to spell a French word, say **Comment s'écrit le mot... ?** (*How do you spell the word . . . ?*).

—Comment s'écrit le mot **Eiffel**?
—Le mot **Eiffel** s'écrit «e majuscule-i-deux effes-e-elle»*.
—Comment s'écrit le mot **s'aider**?
—Le mot **s'aider** s'écrit «esse apostrophe-a-i-dé-e-erre».

Activités

A. Qui sont ces personnes? (*Who are these people?*) Here are the names of some of the characters in the film. Taking turns with a partner, spell their names aloud.

*Note that double consonants are spelled using the expression **deux...** (*two. . .*): **ss** = **deux esses**.

1. Camille Leclair
2. Bruno Gall
3. Hélène Thibaut
4. Rachid Bouhazid
5. Yasmine Bouhazid

B. Informations personnelles. Spell out the following personal information. Your partner will write it down. Then trade roles.

1. votre nom (*your name*)
2. le nom de votre professeur
3. le nom d'un ami / d'une amie
4. votre ville (*city*) favorite
5. votre actrice favorite

La rentrée°

La... *Back-to-school day*

C'est **un** grand **jour**° **pour**° Brigitte.
Elle est **à l'école**°* **avec**° des amis.
Elle dit° bonjour à la maîtresse et aux élèves.
L'institutrice est très **sympa**.°
C'est **une leçon** de sciences naturelles, **alors**° la maîtresse montre une fleur **à**° la classe.

un... *a big (important) day / for*
à... *at school / with*
Elle... *She says*
nice
so
montre... *is showing a flower to*

Pour en savoir plus...

Marginal notes called **Pour en savoir plus...** (*To know more . . .*) appear throughout your textbook. The information in these notes is for general interest and understanding, but you are not required to memorize it.

In one sense, **la rentrée** designates the period when students return to school—mid-September for students ages 6 to 18 and October for universities. It also implies "back-to-work" for parents, who may have been on the traditional long (four-to-five-week) summer vacation, and in general a return to the everyday rhythms of life.

*__Une école__ is an elementary school, and the pupils are referred to as **élèves**. A secondary school is **un lycée**, and its students are also called **élèves**. Students at colleges and universities are called **étudiant(e)s**.

1. The plural forms of **le tableau** and **le bureau** are **les tableaux** and **les bureaux**, ending with **-x** instead of **-s**.
2. The words **élève** (*pupil*) and **enfant** (*child*) can be either masculine or feminine, depending on the gender of the child.
3. A male primary school teacher is called **un maître** or **un instituteur**.*

Activités

A. Chassez l'intrus! (*Find the intruder!*) Tell which item doesn't belong to the group.

1. une table, une chaise, un bureau, une horloge
2. un tableau, un ordinateur, une craie, une éponge
3. un mur, une fenêtre, une porte, une leçon
4. un étudiant, une maîtresse, un professeur, une institutrice
5. un élève, un tableau, un étudiant, un camarade de classe

B. Combien? (*How many?*) How many of each object are there? Use the expression **Il y a...**

MODÈLE:  → Il y a deux maîtresses. (Il y a deux institutrices.)

1. 

2. 

3. 

4. 

5. 

6. 

*To reinforce the status of elementary school teachers, the official term is now **un professeur des écoles**. Children, however, still do not talk about their **prof** but use the older expressions instead.

C. Qu'est-ce que c'est que ça? (*What is that?*) Your partner will tell you to point out an object in the classroom. Point to the object and say that it is there. Take turns telling each other what to point out. Don't forget that you can use vocabulary you learned in the preliminary chapter as well. Use the expressions **Montre-moi** (*Show me*), **Voilà** (*There is/are*), and **Voici** (*Here is/are*).

MODÈLE: É1: Montre-moi un tableau.
É2: [*pointing*] Voilà un tableau. Montre-moi une étudiante.

Les leçons / Les études / Les cours°

À l'école, Yasmine apprend°
- **la lecture°**
- **l'écriture°** (*f.*)
- **le français** (*f.*)
- **les mathématiques (les maths)** (*f. pl.*)
- **les sciences** naturelles (*f. pl.*)
- **la géographie** (*f.*)
- **l'histoire** (*f.*)

D'autres° élèves dans l'école apprennent **aussi°**
- **l'anglais°** (*m.*)
- **l'informatique°** (*f.*)

Les... *Lessons / Studies / Courses*
is learning
reading
penmanship, writing
Other / apprennent... *also learn*
English
computer science

Activités

A. Qu'est-ce qu'il faut? (*What's needed?*) For each lesson, name two useful classroom objects. There may be several appropriate answers. Follow the model, and vary your choices, using words from the list and other words you know.

Vocabulaire utile: un bloc-notes, un cahier, un crayon, un dictionnaire, un livre, un microscope, un ordinateur, un stylo, une calculatrice

MODÈLE: pour une leçon de géographie →
Pour une leçon de géographie? Un livre de géographie et aussi un atlas.

1. pour une leçon de maths
2. pour une leçon d'anglais
3. pour une leçon de sciences naturelles
4. pour une leçon d'histoire
5. pour une leçon d'informatique
6. pour une leçon de français

B. Associations. With which class or course do you associate the following? Answer with a complete sentence according to the model.

MODÈLE: les problèmes et les formules →
J'associe les problèmes et les formules avec les maths.

1. les continents, les océans et les nations
2. les dates, les événements du passé (*events of the past*)
3. les codes et les programmes

4. les mots (*words*) et les livres simples
5. les lettres majuscules et minuscules
6. les plantes et les animaux (*animals*)

Visionnement 1

Before you watch each new episode of *Le Chemin du retour*, you will do several activities that prepare you to understand what you will see and hear.

Avant de visionner

A. La tour Eiffel a quatre pieds. (*The Eiffel Tower has four feet.*) The film opens with children singing a **comptine**, a song somewhat like a nursery rhyme. A **comptine** often has an instructional purpose, for example, to help children learn months of the year, holidays, or telling time. **Comptines** are also used in school to help pupils improve their pronunciation. Read the following **comptine**. Later, as you hear it in the film, you can follow along.

La tour Eiffel a quatre pieds; Il en faut deux pour y monter (bis)
Et pour s'aider, on peut chanter (bis)
A...B...C...D...E...F...G...H...I...J...K...L...M...N... (bis)

The Eiffel Tower has four feet; You need two feet to climb it (repeat)
And to help, you can sing (repeat)
A...B...C...D...E...F...G...H...I...J...K...L...M...N... (repeat)

B. Moments importants. Here is a look at two important moments in Episode 1. Read the exchanges and answer the questions.

1. In this scene, a little girl named Yasmine and her father, Rachid, are arriving at school. How do you think she feels about being there?

YASMINE: C'est ma nouvelle[a] école?
PAPA: Mmm-hmm. La maîtresse est là.[b] Elle est très sympa. Regarde![c]
YASMINE: Non, papa, je ne veux pas.[d] On repart à la maison![e]

[a]ma... *my new* [b]*over there* [c]*Look!* [d]je... *I don't want to (look at her)* [e]On... *Let's go home!*

a. Yasmine est contente.
b. Yasmine est nerveuse.

2. What is the relationship between the people in this dialogue?

ISABELLE: Vous êtes Monsieur Bouhazid?
RACHID: Oui. Bonjour, madame.
ISABELLE: Monsieur. Et toi, tu es Yasmine. Je m'appelle Isabelle.

a. Isabelle et Rachid sont amis.
b. Isabelle ne connaît pas (*doesn't know*) Rachid et Yasmine.

Observez!

Now watch Episode 1. You already know that Yasmine is going to school. As you watch the film, see if you can answer these questions.

- What is Yasmine worried about?
- Why does she wish her father luck?

Remember—Don't expect to understand every word in the episode; you need to understand only the basic plot structure and characters. If you can answer the questions that follow the episode, you have understood enough. Your instructor may ask you to watch the episode again later. By then, you'll have additional tools and will be able to understand more of the details. The activities in **Visionnement 2** in the text and in the Workbook and Laboratory Manual will help, too.

Vocabulaire relatif à l'épisode

Here are a few more expressions from the film. Don't worry if you miss them as you are watching. You don't need to hear every word to understand the main idea of what is happening.

Qu'est-ce qu'il y a, ma puce?	*What's wrong, sweetheart?*
Pourquoi… ?	*Why . . . ?*
Où est… ?	*Where is . . . ?*
fatiguée	*tired*
le déménagement	*move (to a new residence)*
bonne chance	*good luck*

Après le visionnement

In this section of each chapter, you will review important information from the episode you have just watched.

A. Identifiez. Who makes the following statements to whom in Episode 1? Choose among Rachid, Yasmine, and the teacher (**l'institutrice**).

MODÈLE: La maîtresse est là. Elle est très sympa. →
Rachid parle à (*is speaking to*) Yasmine.

1. C'est ma nouvelle école?
2. Mais (*But*) où est-elle? Où est maman?
3. Au Jardin des Plantes (*To the Botanical Garden*), pour une leçon de sciences naturelles.
4. Au revoir, madame. Salut, ma chérie (*honey*)!
5. Pour toi aussi, c'est un grand jour, non?

B. Réfléchissez. (*Think.*) Read the following dialogue exchanges and answer the questions.

1. In this episode, Yasmine asks where her mother is, but Rachid seems uncomfortable discussing her.

YASMINE: Pourquoi maman n'est pas là[a]?

RACHID: C'est, euh, Maman est fatiguée à cause du déménagement. Alors, elle se repose.[b]

YASMINE: Mais où est-elle? Où est maman?

RACHID: Allez viens,[c] ma chérie. Regarde les enfants.

[a]n'est... *isn't here* [b]elle... *she's resting* [c]Allez... *Come on*

Why might Rachid feel so uncomfortable? What does this scene tell you about his relationship with his wife?

2. As Yasmine begins her first day at her new school, she wishes her father luck.

YASMINE: Bonne chance, papa! Pour toi aussi, c'est un grand jour, non?

RACHID: Oui. Salut, ma chérie.

Why might Rachid have a big day ahead of him, too?

Structure 3

Les pronoms sujets et le verbe *être*

Talking about ourselves and others

—**Vous êtes** Monsieur Bouhazid?

—Oui. Bonjour, madame.

—Monsieur. Et toi, **tu es** Yasmine.

Les pronoms sujets

Just as in English, every French verb ▲ has a subject,▲ the person or thing that performs the action of the verb. Subjects are singular or plural, as well as masculine or feminine. Sometimes the subject is not named specifically but is identified by a pronoun.▲

▲Terms followed by ▲ are explained in the *Glossary of Grammatical Terms* in Appendix A.

je	I	**nous**	we
tu	you (*fam. sing.*)	**vous**	you (*fam. pl.; formal s. and pl.*)
il	he; it (*m.*)	**ils**	they (*m.* or *m.* + *f.*)
elle	she; it (*f.*)	**elles**	they (*f.*)
on	one; you; people; we; they		

1. **Je** becomes **j'** before a verb form beginning with a vowel sound.

   J'adore Paris! — *I love Paris!*

2. French has two pronouns meaning *you;* the distinction is mostly one of politeness. **Tu** is familiar and informal. It is used with animals, young children, family, friends, and contemporaries in age and status. The plural of **tu** is **vous**.

   Tu es Yasmine? — *Are you Yasmine?*
   Vous êtes Yasmine et Benoît? — *Are you Yasmine and Benoît?*

   Vous is also used in more formal situations, to address a person with whom you are not well acquainted, who is older, or who possesses greater status (for example, a superior at work). The plural form is also **vous**.

   Vous êtes M. Bouhazid? — *Are you Mr. Bouhazid?*
   Vous êtes M. et Mme Bouhazid? — *Are you Mr. and Mrs. Bouhazid?*

   These guidelines are general and may vary according to situation, region, or social class. If you are in doubt, it is best to address a person using **vous**.

3. **Il**, **elle**, **ils**, and **elles** may refer to both people and things. (Note that French has no single equivalent of the pronoun *it.*) Use **il** or **ils** to replace masculine nouns; use **elle** or **elles** to replace feminine nouns.

   —**Le scénario** est sur la table? — *Is the script on the table?*
   —Oui, **il** est sur la table. — *Yes, it is on the table.*

   —**Les comptines** sont utiles? — *Are comptines useful?*
   —Oui, **elles** sont très utiles. — *Yes, they are very useful.*

   If you need to refer to both masculine and feminine nouns at once, use the pronoun **ils.**

   Rachid, Yasmine et Isabelle sont à l'école. **Ils** parlent ensemble. — *Rachid, Yasmine, and Isabelle are at school. They are talking.*

4. The meaning of the pronoun **on** depends on the context: *one, you, people, we, they.*

   En France, **on** aime le pain. — *In France, people like bread.*
   On va où? — *Where are we going?*

5. **Tout le monde** is a singular expression meaning *everybody.* It takes the same verb form as **il**, **elle**, **on**.

   Tout le monde est là? — *Is everybody here?*

Le verbe être

In French, the form of a verb changes depending on its subject.

Je suis Isabelle.	*I am Isabelle.*
Tu es Yasmine?	*Are you Yasmine?*
Vous êtes M. Bouhazid?	*Are you Mr. Bouhazid?*

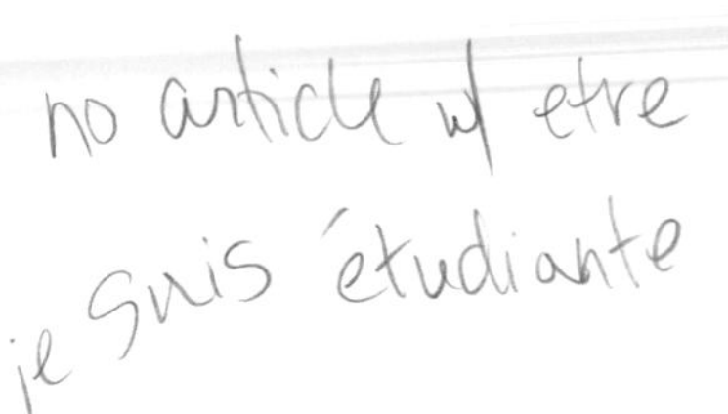

être (*to be*)			
je	**suis**	nous	**sommes**
tu	**es**	vous	**êtes**
il, elle, on	**est**	ils, elles	**sont**

1. The verb **être** can be followed by a name, a noun,▲ an adjective,▲ and many other kinds of phrases.

Je **suis** Yasmine!	*I am Yasmine!*
C'**est*** une éponge.	*That is an eraser.*
Il **est** intelligent.	*He is intelligent.*
C'**est** vrai.	*That's true.*
Vous **êtes** dans la classe?	*Are you in the class?*

2. When expressing someone's job or profession in French, the indefinite article is not used after the verb **être**.

Je suis institutrice.	*I am a school teacher.*
Il est professeur.	*He is a professor.*

Activités

A. Complétez. Here are some things people might have said on Yasmine's first day at her new school. Complete the sentences with the correct form of **être**.

1. Voilà! Nous ______ à l'école Bullier.
2. Vous ______ M. Bouhazid?
3. Je ______ Isabelle.
4. Tu ______ inquiète (*worried*), Yasmine?
5. Marie et Claire, elles ______ dans ta (*your*) classe.
6. Tout le monde ______ là?
7. On ______ maintenant (*now*) au Jardin des Plantes!
8. C' ______ vrai? Super!

B. Tu ou vous? Which pronoun would you use to address the following people: **vous** or **tu**?

1. un étudiant ou une étudiante dans la classe
2. deux étudiants dans la classe

---

*You already know the expressions **c'est** and **ce sont**, which are combinations of the verb **être** with the pronoun **ce** (*this, that, it, these, those, they*).

3. le professeur de français
4. un homme et une femme
5. une enfant

C. Questions. A friend asks you to tell about some people you know. Answer each question using the appropriate subject pronoun and form of **être** with the information in parentheses.

MODÈLE: Paul et toi (*you*)? (étudiants) → Nous sommes étudiants.

1. Charles et Robert? (à l'université)
2. Christine? (dans la salle de classe)
3. Jeanne-Marie et toi? (amis)
4. Le professeur? (fantastique)
5. Toi? (sympa)
6. Moi? (sociable)

Structure 4

Ne... pas et d'autres négations

Expressing negatives

—Non, papa, je **ne** veux **pas**.

You have already learned the negative forms of **C'est** and **Ce sont**.

Ce n'est pas vrai.	*It's not true.*
Ce ne sont pas mes parents.	*They are not my parents.*

To negate a verb in French, insert **ne** before the verb and **pas** after it.

Je suis content.	*I am happy.*
Je **ne** suis **pas** content.	*I am not happy.*

Pour en savoir plus...

When you hear rapid spoken French, you may notice that the **ne** or **n'** of the negative is sometimes not pronounced. The presence of the term **pas** identifies the sentence as negative.

CAREFUL FRENCH

Ce n'est pas Yasmine.
Ce n'est pas vrai!

RAPID, SPOKEN FRENCH

C'est pas Yasmine.
C'est pas vrai!

1. There are other negations, with special meanings, that work exactly like **ne... pas**.

ne... pas du tout	*not at all, absolutely not*
ne... pas encore	*not yet*
ne... plus	*not any more, no longer*
ne... jamais	*never, not ever*

Yasmine **n'**est **pas du tout** fatiguée.*	*Yasmine is not tired at all.*
La maman de Yasmine **n'**est **pas encore** là.	*Yasmine's mother is not there yet.*
Yasmine et Rachid **ne** sont **plus** à Marseille.	*Yasmine and Rachid are not in Marseille anymore.*
Vous **n'**êtes **jamais** calme.	*You are never calm.*

2. Note that **ne** becomes **n'** before a verb form beginning with a vowel sound.

Isabelle **n'**est pas la maman de Yasmine.	*Isabelle is not Yasmine's mother.*

Activités

A. Mais non! (*No!*) Complete the negative response to each sentence. Use **Mais non** and **ne... pas**.

MODÈLE: ÉTUDIANTE: Vous êtes dans un cours d'anglais?
ÉTUDIANTS: Mais non, nous... →
Mais non, nous ne sommes pas dans un cours d'anglais.

1. ENFANT 1: Tu es riche?
   ENFANT 2: Mais non, je...
2. BÉBÉ (*baby*): C'est une porte?
   MAMAN: Mais non, ce...
3. ENFANT 1: Je suis l'instituteur!
   ENFANT 2: Mais non, tu...
4. ÉTUDIANTE 1: Ce sont les livres pour le cours de géographie?
   ÉTUDIANTE 2: Mais non, ce...
5. ÉTUDIANTE: Vous êtes le professeur?
   HOMME: Mais non, je...
6. ÉTUDIANTE: Il est sympathique, le professeur d'histoire?
   ÉTUDIANT: Mais non, il...
7. PARENT: Les études à l'université sont ordinaires?
   ÉTUDIANT: Mais non, elles...

*The position of **du tout** is flexible. This same sentence might be expressed as **Yasmine n'est pas fatiguée du tout**.

B. On n'est pas comme ça. (***We're not like that.***) Working with a partner, take turns asking and answering the following questions. Use a variety of these expressions in your answers: **ne... pas**, **ne... pas du tout**, **ne... pas encore**, **ne... plus**, **ne... jamais**.

MODÈLE: É1: Tes (*Your*) amis sont calmes pendant (*during*) des concerts de rock?
É2: Mes (*My*) amis ne sont jamais calmes pendant des concerts de rock. (Mes amis ne sont pas du tout calmes pendant des concerts de rock.)

1. Tu es professeur? **2.** Tu es un(e) enfant? **3.** Tes amis sont dans la classe de français? (Mes amis...) **4.** Le cours de français est terminé (*finished*)? **5.** Les professeurs d'université sont toujours sympas? **6.** Les classes d'anglais sont difficiles?

Regards sur la culture

L'enseignement° en France

Education

Here are some basic facts about the public school program in France.

- Discipline, memorization, and the imitation of good models are the fundamental principles of early education in French schools. Students do a lot of very careful copying of language (the teacher's notes on the board) and of images (the teacher's model of the umbrella indicating the day's weather, for example*). They also spend quite a bit of time memorizing and reciting poetry and **comptines**.
- The French educational system is very centralized. School programs and the requirements for diplomas are usually determined by the Ministry of Education so that all citizens, no matter where they live or what their social status, have the same educational opportunities.
- Nearly all French children enter elementary school having already been in public preschools for several years. Thirty-six percent of French children are in **l'école maternelle** (preschool) at age 2, and by age 3, 99.8% of all children attend. **L'école maternelle** is free and available to all.
- When they enter elementary school (**l'école primaire**), French children usually know how to copy cursive handwriting, but not how to read. "Printing" is never learned. The first year of elementary school in France is called **le cours préparatoire**. Children enter this class around age 6. In **le cours préparatoire**, they begin to learn to read.

*Every morning in the early primary grades, many teachers draw a symbol on the board to indicate the day's weather—a sun for sunny weather, an umbrella for rain, a snowflake for snow, etc.

Âge	Écoles	Classes
17	Lycée	Terminale
16		1
15		2
14	Collège	3
13		4
12		5
11		6
10	École primaire	Cours moyen
9		
8		Cours élémentaire
7		
6		Cours préparatoire
5	École maternelle	
4		
3		
2		

Considérez

Education in the United States is controlled locally and may vary greatly from county to county and from state to state. In Canada, education is the responsibility of each province and territory. What advantages and disadvantages do you see in local control of education? Are there advantages to a centralized system like the one in France? What about a compromise like the Canadian system?

Structure 5

L'intonation et *est-ce que...*

Asking yes/no questions

—**Elle m'aime toujours? C'est promis?**

—Ben, bien sûr! Viens, ma puce.

There are two very common ways to ask yes/no questions in French.

1. The simplest way to form a question in French is to raise the pitch of your voice at the end of the sentence. A sentence ending in a period (a declarative statement) always ends in a falling tone, whereas the same sentence used as a question ends in a rising tone.

STATEMENT: C'est l'école de Yasmine. — *This is Yasmine's school.*

QUESTION: C'est l'école de Yasmine? — *Is this Yasmine's school?*

2. A statement can also be turned into a yes/no question by placing **Est-ce que** at the beginning. A rising tone is used in **Est-ce que** questions.

STATEMENT: Rachid est reporter. — *Rachid is a reporter.*

QUESTION: Est-ce que Rachid est reporter? — *Is Rachid a reporter?*

Note that **est-ce que** becomes **est-ce qu'** before a subject that begins with a vowel sound: **est-ce qu'il...** , **est-ce qu'elle...** , etc.

Activités

A. Questions sur le film. Some of these statements about the film are true and some are false. Make each one into a question. Vary the way you express the questions, using rising intonation and **est-ce que**.

1. Les enfants chantent (*sing*) une comptine. **2.** La classe est à la tour Eiffel.
3. La maîtresse de Yasmine est sympa. **4.** La maman de Yasmine est là.
5. C'est un grand jour pour Rachid.

Now work with a partner. When your partner asks the question again, answer either **Oui** or **Non**. If your answer is **oui**, restate the sentence. If it is **non**, rephrase the sentence in the negative.

B. Les professions. Working with a partner, take turns asking and answering questions about each person's profession. Follow the model.

MODÈLE: Pierre / athlète / garagiste →
É1: Est-ce que Pierre est athlète?
É2: Non, il n'est pas athlète. Il est garagiste.

1. Michel / chauffeur de taxi / journaliste
2. Midori / accordéoniste / violoniste
3. Jean-Paul / violoniste / accordéoniste
4. Barbara / garagiste / athlète
5. Chantal / institutrice / reporter
6. Isabelle / reporter / institutrice
7. Marcel / acteur / mime
8. David / journaliste / chauffeur de taxi

C. Conversation. Carry on a conversation with a partner following the guidelines.

1. Greet your partner and find out how he/she is feeling.
2. Give your name and say that you are a student.
3. Find out if your partner is a teacher.

4. Ask whether the students in the class are friends.
5. Say good-bye to each other and that you'll see each other soon.

Visionnement 2

Avant de visionner

A. Quelle classe? (*Which class?*) The public school system in France is described earlier in this chapter in **Regards sur la culture**. Considering Yasmine's age, the type of field trip the class is about to take, and the song the class is singing as they line up, what grade do you think Yasmine is entering? Choose the best answer.

a. Elle est à l'école maternelle.
b. Elle est au cours préparatoire.
c. Elle est au cours élémentaire.

Les environs de l'appartement des Bouhazid

les arènes de Lutèce
le musée de Minéralogie
le Jardin des Plantes
les universités de Paris VI et VII
la Seine
Quai Saint-Bernard
Rue Linné
Rue Lacépède
Rue Buffon
l'école de Yasmine
la Mosquée
la gare d'Austerlitz
l'appartement des Bouhazid
l'hôtel Saint-Christophe
1 2 3 4 5 6 7 8 9 10

B. Points de repère. (*Landmarks.*) Look at this map showing the part of Paris where the action in this episode takes place. It is part of the **Quartier latin** (*Latin quarter*), so named because hundreds of years ago, Latin was the language of instruction at the university there. Rachid and Yasmine also live near the **Jardin des Plantes**, a botanical garden. The area around the **Jardin des Plantes** has always been a place where groups mixed: university students, wine merchants, and, since the 18th century, the scientists who have directed the **Jardin des Plantes**. Look carefully at the map and indicate the number and the name that correspond to the following landmarks in the neighborhood near Yasmine's school.

a. un édifice (*building*) religieux **b.** une résidence **c.** des ruines romaines
d. un fleuve (*large river*) **e.** une école

Observez!

Rachid and the teacher greet each other in a typical French manner for people who don't know each other. Watch and listen to answer the following questions.

- Would you use a similar gesture when meeting a teacher for the first time?
- What level of language (formal, informal) does Rachid use when he speaks with the teacher? when he speaks with Yasmine? How do you know?

Après le visionnement

Do the activity for **Visionnement 2** in the Workbook and Laboratory Manual.

Synthèse: Culture

L'école dans le monde francophone°

°*L'école… School in the French-speaking world*

Yasmine's school uses the standard curriculum prescribed by the French Ministry of Education, and French is the language of instruction. But in most places in the French-speaking world, the decision about which language should be used in education is a difficult one. In fact, elementary school is one of the most important places in which "the politics of language" are played out.

Québec

Faced with a massive language shift to English in Montreal, the Quebec government has passed several laws that restrict access to public English-language elementary schools. Today, only those children with at least one parent who studied in an English elementary school somewhere in Canada can attend Montreal's English-language school system. This means that immigrants from other countries (including the United States) are required to enter the French system. Many feel that this is an important factor in preventing the disappearance of French in North America and that the rights of the French community to maintain its integrity occasionally have to outweigh the freedom of individual choice.

New Caledonia

In the colonial period, the entire French Empire used the same school curriculum. The children of Africa and those in New Caledonia in the south Pacific were all schooled in French, not in their native language. They studied the history of France and the building of the French nation, just as children in Paris or Marseille did. Not until the late 1980s, after violent confrontations between the French police and the native Melanesian population in New Caledonia, did local elements become a systematic part of the teaching of geography, history, and civics there. It was only then that Melanesian languages could be used in primary school. Today, about 20% of the curriculum in this French territory is devoted to learning about New Caledonia.

Louisiana

Many generations of children in Louisiana were punished for speaking French at school.* In 1968, the Council for the Development of French in Louisiana (CODOFIL) was established to change this situation and to promote the use of the language. But what form of French was to be taught in the schools? CODOFIL did not want to teach the Cajun French dialect, which it considered to be substandard, so teachers of standard European French were brought in from France. The results were not successful at first. The debates over the "Louisianification" of French teaching in Cajun country are still going on, but the use of teachers from Quebec, whose language is closer to that of the Cajuns, has improved the situation.

---

*Louisiana was a French colony until 1803. In the mid-1700s, the use of French was intensified there by the arrival of thousands of Acadians, who were deported from Nova Scotia by the British. These are the people who came to be called "Cajuns."

À vous

A. Which is more important in your family: the preservation of ethnic tradition or complete assimilation to your country's culture? In your opinion, should children of immigrants or those that are not native speakers of English be schooled in English, in their native language, or in both languages? Whose history and culture should they learn in school?

B. Imagine that you are developing the educational policy for a town in northern Quebec where most of the population speaks Cree.* In a small group, decide what language or languages you would use in the classroom and at what points in the child's development. Keep in mind that French is the official language of the province of Quebec and that English is the other official language of Canada. Would you aim to make the children bilingual or trilingual? Organize your plan using the grid below.

Age	Language of instruction	Other language(s) studied

À écrire

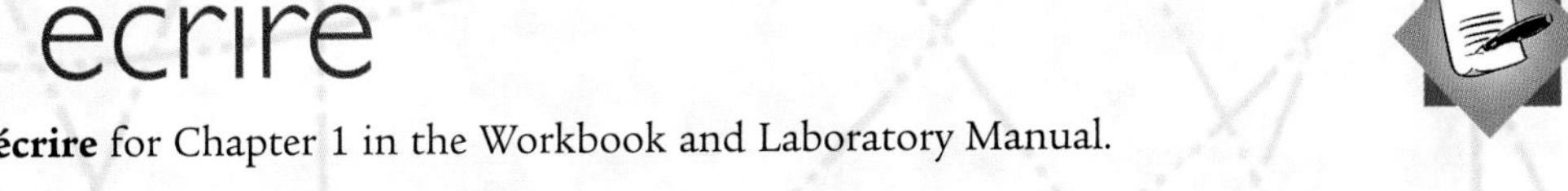

Do **À écrire** for Chapter 1 in the Workbook and Laboratory Manual.

*Cree is a Native American (Amerindian) language of the Algonquian family. Algonquian is one of the largest of Native American language groups, which also includes Ojibwa, Cheyenne, and many others.

Vocabulaire

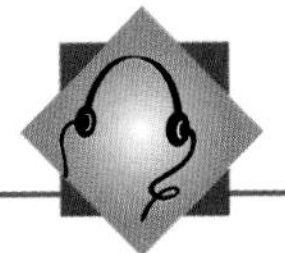

La rentrée

un bureau (des bureaux)	desk
une chaise	chair
une craie	chalk
une école	(elementary) school
un(e) élève	pupil
un(e) enfant	child
une éponge	sponge; blackboard eraser
les études (*f. pl.*)	studies
une fenêtre	window

une horloge clock
un(e) instituteur/trice elementary school teacher
un jour day
un lycée secondary school
un(e) maître/maîtresse elementary school teacher
un mur wall
un ordinateur computer
une porte door
un tableau (des tableaux) blackboard

MOTS APPARENTÉS: **un cours, une leçon**

Les leçons / Les études / Les cours

l'anglais (*m.*) English
l'écriture (*f.*) penmanship; writing
le français French
l'informatique (*f.*) computer science
la lecture reading

MOTS APPARENTÉS: **la géographie, l'histoire** (*f.*), **les mathématiques** (*fam.* **les maths**) (*f. pl.*), **les sciences (naturelles)** (*f. pl.*)

Les pronoms sujets

je I
tu you (*fam. sing.*)
il he; it (*m.*)
elle she; it (*f.*)
on one; you; people; we; they
tout le monde everyone
nous we
vous you (*fam. pl.; formal sing. and pl.*)
ils they (*m.*)
elles they (*f.*)

Verbe, question et négations

être to be
est-ce que... ? is it (*true*) that . . . ?
ne... pas not
ne... pas du tout not at all, absolutely not
ne... pas encore not yet
ne... plus not anymore
ne... jamais never, not ever

Prépositions

à to; at
avec with
pour for

Autres expressions utiles

alors so, therefore; then, in that case
aussi also
là there; here
sympathique (*fam.* **sympa**) nice
voici here is/are
voilà there is/are; here is/are (*for pointing out*)

Chapitre 2

Bonjour!

OBJECTIFS

In this episode, you will

- meet Camille Leclair and her coworkers on a Paris TV show
- watch a segment of the TV show "Bonjour!"
- learn about the French tradition of breadmaking

In this chapter, you will

- describe people and things
- use adverbs of frequency
- use expressions of agreement and disagreement
- talk about TV production
- talk about everyday actions
- learn how the French define their culture
- read about the importance of television in France

Vocabulaire en contexte

Pour parler des personnes°

Pour... *Talking about people*

Selon° Yasmine, papa est **grand**° et très intelligent.	*According to / tall*
Le **travail**° de Rachid est **intéressant**. Il est **prêt** à	*work*
commencer.° **Mais**° il est **inquiet**° pour Yasmine.	prêt... *ready to start / But / worried*
Comment est° Bruno?	Comment... *What is... like?*
Bruno est un **bon**° journaliste parisien à Canal 7.	*good*
Il est...	
capable.	
dynamique.	
important.	
Selon la productrice,° Bruno est...	*producer*
souvent° **amusant**.	*often*
sympathique.*	
heureux.°	*happy*
parfois° **difficile** et **ridicule**.	*sometimes*
Selon le public, il est...	
super.	
magnifique.	
formidable.°	*terrific*
Il n'est pas **sans**° charme.	*without*
Et il n'est jamais **ennuyeux**.°	*boring*
Selon Camille, Bruno est un **vrai** Français° et un bon ami.	vrai... *true Frenchman*

*The adjective **sympa**, which you learned in Chapter 1, is a shortened form of **sympathique**.

Langage fonctionnel

Pour exprimer l'accord / le désaccord°

Pour... *Expressing agreement/disagreement*

The following expressions can be used to express agreement or disagreement.

Pour exprimer l'accord

Bien sûr! (Bien sûr que oui!)	*Of course! (Yes, of course!)*
D'accord! (Je suis d'accord!)	*Okay! (I agree!)*
C'est vrai!	*That's true!*
Sans doute!	*Probably! No doubt!*

Pour exprimer le désaccord

Bien sûr que non!	*Of course not! Certainly not!*
Je ne suis pas d'accord.	*I don't agree.*
Ce n'est pas vrai! (Pas vrai!)	*That's not true! (Not true!)*
C'est faux.	*That's false.*

—Bruno est ridicule. *Bruno is ridiculous.*

—Non, **c'est faux**! Il est amusant. *No, that's wrong! He's funny.*

Activités

A. Descriptions. How would you describe these people? Choose words suggested in parentheses or other adjectives of your choice.

MODÈLE:

Pierre est... (grand, intelligent, ridicule, ?) →
Pierre est grand, intelligent et sympathique.

1. Jean-Michel est...
(dynamique, heureux, stupide, ?)

2. Nicolas est...
(difficile, grand, inquiet, ?)

3. Le président est...
(amusant, intéressant, super, ?)

B. Un portrait. Think of a famous male sports figure, entertainer, or politician, and describe him by completing the following sentences.

1. J'admire (Je déteste) ______.
2. Il est...
3. Il est toujours...
4. Il est souvent...
5. Il est parfois...
6. Il est rarement...
7. Il n'est pas du tout...
8. Il n'est jamais...

Notez bien!

To make your descriptions more accurate, use these five useful adverbs▲:

toujours	always
souvent	often
parfois	sometimes
rarement	rarely
ne... jamais	never

These adverbs usually precede the adjectives they modify.*

Bruno est **souvent** amusant, mais **rarement** ridicule.
Rachid est **toujours** capable et il **n'est jamais** ridicule.

C. D'accord ou pas d'accord? Use one of the expressions of agreement or disagreement to give your opinion about these statements about television.

MODÈLE: Les films à la télé† sont souvent violents. →
C'est vrai! Les films à la télé sont très souvent violents. (*ou* Je ne suis pas d'accord. Les films à la télé ne sont pas violents du tout. *ou* Ce n'est pas vrai. Les films à la télé sont rarement violents.)

1. Les Américains sont très influencés par la télé.
2. La télé est un élément important de ma vie (*my life*).
3. Le travail d'un reporter à la télé est super.
4. Les reporters à la télé sont toujours objectifs.
5. Les documentaires à la télé sont rarement éducatifs.

Les locaux et les employés de Canal 7

La régie

la productrice (Martine)

Le plateau

la journaliste (Camille) — le journaliste‡ (Bruno) — l'écran (*m.*)

▲Terms followed by ▲ are explained in the *Glossary of Grammatical Terms* in Appendix A.
*Remember also that **ne... jamais** follows the pattern of **ne... pas** for its placement with the verb.
†**La télé** is a short form of **la télévision**. It is often used in conversation.
‡Depending on the gender of the person, a job title may vary slightly: for example, **le/la journaliste**, **le producteur / la productrice**. A few job titles have only one grammatical gender even if the person doing the job is not of that gender: **Bruno est *la star* de l'émission. Hélène est *un reporter* canadien.**

Autres mots utiles

une émission	program
un reporter	reporter
la télévision (télé)	television (*the industry; the medium*)

Activité

À Canal 7. Fill in the blanks with the appropriate word from the list of useful vocabulary. Look at the preceding photos if you need to verify who has which job.

Vocabulaire utile: écran, émission, journalistes, productrice, reporter, public, télévision, studio

«Bonjour!» est une _____¹ diffusée[a] à la _____² sur Canal 7. Les _____³ de «Bonjour!» sont Camille Leclair et Bruno Gall. Martine est la _____⁴.

À Canal 7, l'émission est filmée dans le _____⁵ sur le plateau. Martine est en régie pendant[b] l'émission, et elle peut voir[c] Bruno et Camille sur l'_____⁶. «Bonjour!» est une émission populaire. Le _____⁷ adore Camille et Bruno.

[a]*broadcast* [b]*during* [c]*peut... can see*

Visionnement 1

Avant de visionner

Un grand jour. At the end of Episode 1, Yasmine wished her father luck because he was going to have a big day too. To find out why, read the following exchange from Episode 2 and choose the response that best sums up the dialogue.

MARTINE: Alors, le déménagement[a]?
RACHID: Difficile... Tu vas bien?[b]
MARTINE: Mmm. C'est Roger, le réalisateur[c]... Et Nicole, la scripte.[d]
ROGER ET NICOLE: Bonjour.
RACHID: Bonjour.
MARTINE: C'est Rachid, Rachid Bouhazid. ... (*à Rachid*) Et là, sur[e] l'écran, ...

[a]*move (to a new residence)* [b]*Tu... Are you well?* [c]*director* [d]*script coordinator* [e]*Et... And there, on*

a. Rachid is saying goodbye before moving away.

b. He is starting classes at the university.

c. He is starting a new job.

Vocabulaire relatif à l'épisode

le pain	*bread*
artisanal	*handmade*
industriel	*factory-made*
le boulanger	*(male) baker*
vingt et unième siècle	*twenty-first century*
Camille cherche	*Camille is looking for*

Observez!

Now watch Episode 2. See if you are right about Rachid's important day by looking for the following clues.

- Where does Rachid go after dropping Yasmine off at school?
- What does he do there?

Remember—Don't expect to understand every word in the episode; you need to understand only the basic plot structure and characters. If you can answer the questions that follow the episode, you have understood enough. Your instructor may ask you to watch the episode again later in the chapter. By then, you'll have additional tools and will be able to understand more of the details. The activities in **Visionnement 2** in the text and in the Workbook and Laboratory Manual will help, too.

Après le visionnement

A. Quel travail? (*Which job?*) Now that you have watched Episode 2, match each job to the person you saw in the video.

1. Camille

2. Bruno

3. Martine

4. Hélène

5. Rachid

a. la productrice
b. un reporter canadien
c. un nouveau (*new*) reporter
d. un journaliste français
e. une journaliste française

B. Qu'est-ce qui se passe? (*What's happening?*) Tell what happens in Episode 2 by choosing words from the following list to fill in the blanks in the summary of the story.

Vocabulaire utile: béret, Camille, Canal 7, content, émission, médaillon, Montréal, pain, présente, prêt, test

Rachid arrive à _____ 1. Martine, la productrice, _____ 2 ses nouveaux[a] collègues. Rachid va travailler[b] avec _____ 3 et Bruno.

Aujourd'hui,[c] pendant[d] l'émission «Bonjour!», Camille et Bruno interviewent un boulanger parisien. Il y a un _____ 4 sur le pain: pain artisanal ou pain industriel? Bruno est _____ 5 pour le test. Il identifie le _____ 6 artisanal, et il gagne[e] le _____ 7 de la semaine[f]... mais il n'est pas _____ 8.

Hélène, une amie de Bruno, arrive de _____ 9. Bruno est très content de la revoir.[g] Plus tard,[h] Camille cherche son[i] _____ 10. Où[j] est-il?

[a]*ses... his new* [b]*va... will be working* [c]*Today* [d]*during* [e]*wins* [f]*week* [g]*de... to see her again* [h]*Plus... Later* [i]*her* [j]*Where*

C. Réfléchissez. (*Think.*) Answer the following questions based on what you saw and heard in Episode 2.

1. Bruno and Camille work together as hosts of "Bonjour!" From what you have seen, would you guess that they are friends or simply coworkers? Or is it too early to tell?
2. Camille seems to have lost something. What do you think she has lost? What could its significance be?

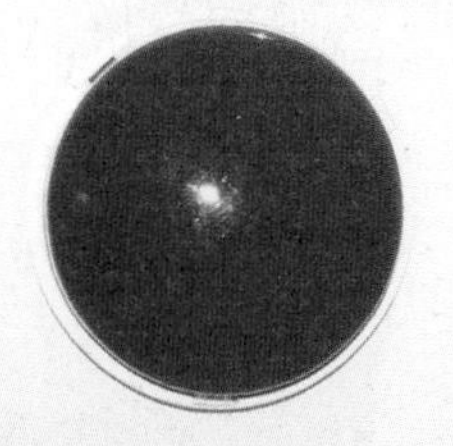

Structure 6

Les adjectifs

Describing people and things

—Les Français sont **formidables**! Au XXIe siècle, vous êtes encore **inquiets** pour le pain.

Hélène uses two adjectives▲ to describe the character and preoccupation of the French: **formidables** and **inquiets**. French adjectives agree in gender (feminine or masculine) and number (singular or plural) with the noun being described. That is, an adjective used to describe a noun will be

- masculine if the noun is masculine: **Le reporter est *intelligent.***
- feminine if the noun is feminine: **La productrice est *intelligente.***
- masculine plural if the noun is masculine plural: **Les reporters sont *intelligents.***
- feminine plural if the noun is feminine plural: **Les productrices sont *intelligentes.***

Le genre des adjectifs

Adjectives can be grouped according to the sound and spelling of their masculine and feminine singular forms.

1. Many adjectives have masculine and feminine forms that sound alike and are spelled alike.*

difficile	*difficult*	**ridicule**	*ridiculous, silly*
facile	*easy*	**sympathique**	*nice*
formidable	*terrific*	**triste**	*sad*
magnifique	*magnificent*		

*Adjectives in this group are often cognates or near-cognates to English words: **dynamique**, **stupide**, etc.

La rentrée n'est pas **facile** pour Yasmine.	*The first day of school is not easy for Yasmine.*
Bruno n'est probablement jamais **triste**.	*Bruno is probably never sad.*

2. Some adjectives have masculine and feminine forms that sound alike but have different spellings. The feminine form usually ends in **-e** whereas the masculine does not.

fatigué(e) *tired* **joli(e)** *pretty* **vrai(e)** *true* **fâché(e)** *angry*

Rachid n'est pas **fatigué**.	*Rachid is not tired.*
Sonia est **fatiguée**.	*Sonia is tired.*
Le médaillon de Camille est **joli**.	*Camille's locket is pretty.*
Yasmine est **jolie**.	*Yasmine is pretty.*

Note that the feminine forms of adjectives like **cher** and **intellectuel** have additional changes: **chère**, **intellectuelle**.

Chère maman	*Dear Mom*
Est-ce qu'Hélène est **intellectuelle**?	*Is Hélène intellectual?*

3. Many adjectives have masculine and feminine forms that are pronounced and spelled differently. A large number of these have a silent final consonant in the masculine but a pronounced final consonant in the feminine. There are several types in this group.

- Those that form the feminine by adding **-e** to the masculine are common.

amusant(e)	*amusing*	**laid(e)**	*ugly*
français(e)	*French*	**mauvais(e)**	*bad*
grand(e)	*big; tall*	**petit(e)**	*little*
intéressant(e)	*interesting*	**prêt(e)**	*ready*

Benoît n'est pas **laid**.	*Benoît isn't ugly.*
Yasmine n'est pas **laide**.	*Yasmine isn't ugly.*
Benoît est **petit**.	*Benoît is little.*
Yasmine est **petite**.	*Yasmine is little.*
Benoît est **mauvais** en arithmétique.	*Benoît is bad in arithmetic.*
Yasmine n'est pas **mauvaise** en arithmétique.	*Yasmine isn't bad in arithmetic.*

- Those with masculine forms ending in **-x** form the feminine by dropping the **-x** and adding **-se**.

heureux → **heureuse**	*happy*
ennuyeux → **ennuyeuse**	*boring*
malheureux → **malheureuse**	*unhappy*

Bruno est **heureux**. — *Bruno is happy.*
Yasmine est **malheureuse**? — *Is Yasmine unhappy?*

- Those with masculine forms ending in a nasal vowel make the feminine by denasalizing the vowel and pronouncing the final consonant. The feminine of this type ends with either **-e** or a doubled final consonant plus an **-e.** Learn each feminine spelling when you learn the adjective.

américain(e) *American*
canadien(ne) *Canadian*
bon(ne) *good*
parisien(ne) *Parisian*

Bruno est **parisien**. — *Bruno is Parisian.*
Martine est **parisienne**. — *Martine is Parisian.*

- Other adjectives have masculine and feminine forms that are spelled various ways. Learn both forms when you learn the adjective.

inquiet/inquiète *anxious, worried*
gentil(le) *nice; kind; well behaved*

Bruno est **gentil**. — *Bruno is nice.*
Camille est **gentille** aussi. — *Camille is also nice.*

4. Some adjectives end in one consonant sound in the masculine and another in the feminine.

actif/active *active*
sportif/sportive *athletic*

Rachid est **sportif**. — *Rachid is athletic.*
Est-ce que Camille est **sportive**? — *Is Camille athletic?*

Le pluriel des adjectifs

1. To form the plural of adjectives, add an **-s** to the singular, except where the singular already ends in an **-s** or an **-x**.

	Il est **sportif**.	Ils sont **sportifs**.
but	Il est **mauvais** en maths.	Ils sont **mauvais** en maths.
	Il est **ennuyeux**.	Ils sont **ennuyeux**.

2. **Sympa** is invariable for masculine and feminine, meaning its ending doesn't change for feminine nouns. It does take a plural ending. **Super** is completely invariable; its ending never changes for feminine or plural nouns.

Les institutrices sont **sympas**! — *The teachers are nice!*
Elles sont **super** aussi! — *They are also super!*

3. When describing a group of which at least one member is masculine, the masculine plural form of the adjective is used.

Yasmine, Carmen et Benoît sont **sportifs**.

Activités

A. Descriptions. Create complete statements about Episodes 1 and 2.

MODÈLE: Camille / être / heureux / aujourd'hui →
Camille est heureuse aujourd'hui.

1. l'institutrice / être / patient / et / sympathique
2. Yasmine et les autres enfants / être / petit
3. la démonstration / être / intéressant
4. les baguettes* (*f.*) / être / bon
5. Bruno / ne pas être / content
6. le béret / être / ridicule
7. Camille / être / parfois / impatient
8. l'émission «Bonjour!» / ne jamais être / ennuyeux

B. Vrai ou faux? (*True or false?*) Take turns with your partner using **est-ce que** to change the following statements about Episodes 1 and 2 into questions. The person who answers the question should use one of the expressions of agreement or disagreement.

MODÈLE: L'institutrice est inquiète. →
É1: Est-ce que l'institutrice est inquiète?
É2: Bien sûr que non! Elle est contente.

1. Camille est triste aujourd'hui.
2. Yasmine est gentille.
3. Camille est laide.
4. L'émission «Bonjour!» est intéressante.
5. Les collègues de Rachid sont sympathiques.
6. Rachid n'est pas content à Canal 7.
7. Hélène est heureuse.
8. Bruno est prêt pour le test.

C. Comment sont-ils? (*What are they like?*) Take turns with a partner describing the following people. Use the correct forms of the adjectives in the list, and create both affirmative and negative sentences when possible.

Vocabulaire utile: amusant, calme, ennuyeux, fâché, fatigué, gentil, intellectuel, intelligent, joli, laid, malheureux, riche, ridicule, sportif, stupide, triste

MODÈLE: les hommes politiques →
É1: Les hommes politiques sont intelligents.
É2: Oui, mais parfois ils ne sont pas gentils.

1. Michael Jordan
2. Julia Roberts
3. les stars (*f.*) de cinéma
4. les journalistes
5. un clown

*__Baguettes__ are long, thin loaves of French bread.

D. Parlons de... (*Let's talk about . . .*) Make a list of four famous people or things that you can describe with the following adjectives. Give your list to your partner. Then, taking turns, describe a person or thing from your list and let your partner guess the identity by choosing from your list.

Vocabulaire utile: cher, difficile, ennuyeux, fâché, facile, fatigué, grand, intéressant, laid, malheureux, mauvais, petit, ridicule, sportif, super, sympa

MODÈLE: Liste: Tiger Woods, la Cadillac, les étudiantes, les films avec *Godzilla*
É1: Elle est grande. Elle est chère.
É2: C'est la Cadillac.

Regards sur la culture

Perceptions et réalités

Stereotypes usually tell us as much about the values and customs of the people who use them as about those whom they are supposed to describe. There are a few North American stereotypes about the French that are shared by the French themselves, but many others are not.

- French people often think of themselves as particularly interested in food and gifted at appreciating it. They are especially concerned about bread, which is truly the staple food of French cuisine. Bread is eaten along with nearly every dish at every meal, and it is the main food eaten at breakfast and for most children's snacks. Bread made in the traditional craft sense (**le pain artisanal**) has to be bought daily because it contains no preservatives and dries out quickly. Mass-produced bread (**le pain industriel**) is also available in stores. Most French people are ready at any moment to engage in animated debates about the quality of bread today.
- The French do not think of themselves as eating rich food, however, but only *good* food. When asked what the typical French meal is, most people in France would probably answer **le steak-frites** (*steak with fries*). This may not correspond to North American ideas of what French people like to eat, but it is the

kind of meal that a French traveler might think of first when he or she needs a quick dinner.

- The Eiffel Tower really is a landmark that the French think of as representing them in some sense. A hilarious 1999 film, *Le Voyage à Paris,* recounts the adventures of a rural highway toll collector with hundreds of models of the Eiffel Tower in his room at home. His dream is to visit Paris and see the real thing.
- The French like to think of themselves as the little guys who always win out because they are clever and quick. The popular comic character Astérix is a symbol of this sense of identity. He is a Gaul* who, in ancient times, lives in the one village that has not been conquered by the Roman legions. Astérix is always able to outwit the power of Caesar and his troops.

- Foreigners often think of the beret as typically French. To the French, however, it looks old-fashioned and reminds them of elderly people, farming life, and backwardness. Berets are not a common sight in Paris.
- The French are often surprised to find out that other people think of them as obsessed with love. As far as the French are concerned, the real lovers are the Italians.
- French people are also astonished to discover that people from some other cultures consider them rude. Later in this course, you'll learn reasons for this gap in perceptions, and you will also look at other aspects of French culture that may clash with North American stereotypes.

Considérez

To vouch for the kindness of someone, a French person might say: **Il est bon comme le pain.** Does this expression make any sense when translated literally into English? What would be the nearest English equivalent of this expression? What conclusions can you draw from this difference about the importance accorded to bread in France and in North American cultures?

*In ancient times, France was part of an area known as Gaul. In 390 B.C., its inhabitants, called Gauls, attacked Rome and eventually swept farther east. Around 50 B.C., Julius Caesar and his Roman army had succeeded in turning the tide and had conquered all of Gaul, an area that comprised what is now France, Belgium, Luxembourg, and the parts of the Netherlands and Germany that are south and west of the Rhine River.

Structure 7

Les verbes réguliers en -er et la construction *verbe + infinitif*

Talking about everyday actions

—Tu **arrives*** de Montréal?

—Oui. Je **lance** une série de reportages sur la vie au Québec.

When Bruno and Hélène exchange remarks about her visit to Paris, they use the verbs **arriver** and **lancer**. These infinitives▲ end in **-er**. Many French verb forms are created, or conjugated,▲ like **arriver** and **lancer**.

Les verbes réguliers en *-er*

1. To use regular **-er** verbs, drop the **-er** and add these endings: **-e**, **-es**, **-e**, **-ons**, **-ez**, **-ent**.

chercher (*to look for*)			
je	cherch **e**	nous	cherch **ons**
tu	cherch **es**	vous	cherch **ez**
il, elle, on	cherch **e**	ils, elles	cherch **ent**

aimer (*to like*)			
j'	aim **e**	nous	aim **ons**
tu	aim **es**	vous	aim **ez**
il, elle, on	aim **e**	ils, elles	aim **ent**

*In the film, Bruno runs the subject and verb together, saying **T'arrives...** . This is a common occurrence in everyday French conversation when the pronoun **tu** precedes a verb that begins with a vowel.

2. Here is a list of some common regular **-er** verbs.

aimer *to like; to love*	**habiter** *to live (in a place), reside*
aimer mieux *to prefer*	**parler** *to speak; to talk*
chercher *to look for*	**penser** *to think*
dîner *to eat dinner; to dine*	**porter** *to wear*
donner *to give*	**regarder** *to watch; to look at*
écouter *to listen (to)*	**travailler** *to work*
étudier *to study*	**trouver** *to find; to consider*

As you continue your study of French, you'll recognize other regular **-er** verbs, many of which are cognates. Before doing the activities, be sure you know the meaning of the following cognate verbs: **commencer**, **identifier**, **inviter**, **présenter**, **respecter**, **visiter**.

3. The present tense verb forms in French can express three different meanings in English.

j'étudie { *I study* / *I am studying* / *I do study* }

nous travaillons { *we work* / *we are working* / *we do work* }

4. Useful expressions are **penser que** (*to think that*), **penser à** (*to think about*), and **penser de** (*to have an opinion about*).

Qu'est-ce que Bruno **pense du** béret?	*What does Bruno think of (What is Bruno's opinion of) the beret?*
Bruno **pense que** le béret est ridicule.	*Bruno thinks that the beret is ridiculous.*
Il **pense aux** personnes âgées à la campagne quand il voit un béret!	*He thinks about old people in the countryside when he sees a beret!*

Verbe + infinitif

When two verbs are used together to express an idea, the first verb is conjugated and the second remains in the infinitive form. Some verbs that can be followed by an infinitive are **adorer**, **aimer**, **désirer**, and **détester**.

Rachid **aime habiter** à Paris.	*Rachid likes to live in Paris.*
Je **désire trouver** un emploi.	*I want to find a job.*

Activités

A. Résumons. (***Let's summarize.***) Retell the story of *Le Chemin du retour* by filling in the blank with the appropriate form of the verb in parentheses.

Aujourd'hui, Rachid _____ [1] (commencer) un travail à Canal 7. Les employés de Canal 7 _____ [2] (être) très sympathiques. Bruno Gall et Camille Leclair _____ [3] (présenter) l'émission «Bonjour!». Un boulanger _____ [4] (parler) de deux sortes de pain. Bruno _____ [5] (identifier) le bon pain.

Bruno gagne° le béret d'honneur, mais il ______[6] (trouver) le béret ridicule. Nous, les Américains et les Canadiens, nous ______[7] (penser) que le béret est typiquement français. Mais en France, on ne porte pas très souvent le béret.

°wins

B. Le pour et le contre. (*Pros and cons.*) Form complete sentences from the following cues in order to present the pros and cons of a career in journalism. Some ideas are expressed by journalism students and others by a practicing journalist.

Étudiants idéalistes:

1. nous / étudier / le journalisme / avec enthousiasme
2. les journalistes / adorer / leur (*their*) travail
3. ils / dîner / dans des restaurants chers
4. ils / parler / avec des personnes intéressantes
5. tout le monde / écouter et respecter / les opinions des journalistes

Journaliste réaliste:

6. je / trouver / la vie (*life*) d'un journaliste difficile
7. le travail / ne pas être / facile
8. nous / dîner / souvent dans des restaurants fast-food
9. nous / travailler / beaucoup (*a lot*)
10. un journaliste / ne jamais donner / sa propre (*his own*) opinion

C. Préférences. Work in groups of three or four to describe your own preferences and those of your group or other people you know. You can create sentences using words from each column, or invent your own if you need to.

MODÈLE: Je n'aime pas préparer (*to study for*) les examens. J'aime mieux regarder la télévision.

je/j'	adorer	dîner à la cafétéria
tu	(ne pas) aimer	écouter de la musique classique
vous	aimer mieux	être étudiant(e)
nous	(ne pas) désirer	étudier à la bibliothèque (*library*)
le professeur	détester	habiter à la résidence universitaire
maman		parler en classe
mon (*my*) ami(e)		préparer les examens
?		regarder la télévision
		travailler
		?

D. Sondage. (*Survey.*) Interview as many classmates as you can to find out who shares your interests and habits. Jot down what you learn.

MODÈLE: regarder les comédies à la télévision →
É1: Tu regardes les comédies à la télévision?
É2: Oui, je regarde souvent les comédies. (Non, je ne regarde jamais les comédies.)

1. étudier très tard (*late*)
2. habiter à la résidence universitaire
3. chercher des amis intéressants
4. détester les films d'horreur
5. trouver [*nom d'une star de cinéma*] formidable
6. inviter le professeur à dîner
7. aimer le fast-food
8. visiter souvent des musées (*museums*)
9. écouter de la musique classique
10. penser que la politique est fascinante ou ennuyeuse

Now share your findings with the class by telling at least one thing you learned.

MODÈLE: Jon, Ashley et Greg n'habitent pas à la résidence universitaire. Ils habitent dans un appartement.

Structure 8

La place des adjectifs

Describing people and things

—Le pain, en France, est très **important**! Alors, voilà des baguettes, du pain de campagne...

—Et avec nous, aujourd'hui, un **grand** boulanger **parisien**. Bonjour, Monsieur Liégeois!

—Bonjour!

You already know that adjectives may follow the verb **être**. Remember that they must always agree in gender and number with the noun or pronoun they modify.

Maman est **fatiguée**.	*Mom is tired.*
Le **pain**, en France, est très **important**.	*Bread, in France, is very important.*
Je suis Bruno et **je** suis **prêt**.	*I'm Bruno and I'm ready.*
Vous êtes **sûrs**, Camille et Bruno?	*Are you sure, Camille and Bruno?*

1. When placed next to the noun they are describing, most adjectives follow the noun.

C'est une leçon de **sciences naturelles**.	*It's a natural science lesson.*
D'un côté, le **pain industriel**. De l'autre, le **pain artisanal**.	*On one hand, factory-made bread. On the other, handmade bread.*

2. A few adjectives usually precede the noun they describe. You already know some of these: **bon**, **cher**, **grand**, **joli**, **mauvais**, **petit**, **vrai**. Another useful one is **autre** (*other*).

Bonne chance, papa! Pour toi aussi, c'est un **grand jour**, non?	*Good luck, Daddy! It's a big day for you, too, isn't it?*
Bruno! Encore de **mauvaise humeur**?!	*Bruno! In a bad mood again?!*
Bruno choisit l'**autre pain**—le pain artisanal.	*Bruno chooses the other bread—the handmade bread.*

3. If two or more adjectives describe the same noun, they should be placed where they would normally go. If two are the type that follows the noun, the word **et** is usually placed between them.

Yasmine est une **jolie petite** enfant.	*Yasmine is a pretty little child.*
Et avec nous, aujourd'hui, un **grand** boulanger **parisien**.	*And with us, today, an important Parisian baker.*
C'est un pain **doux et moelleux**.	*This is a soft and velvety bread.*

Activités

A. Confirmations. Match the sentences from the left column with those in the right column that confirm the information given. Then identify the word(s) in column A that helped you to make the connection.

MODÈLE: Bruno est un vrai français. →
Il identifie le pain artisanal. / vrai français

1. Bruno est un vrai français.
2. Hélène trouve Bruno de mauvaise humeur.
3. Le boulanger prépare un bon pain.
4. Camille est une jolie femme.
5. Rachid commence un travail intéressant à Canal 7.
6. Hélène est un autre reporter.

a. Bruno n'est pas content à cause du (*because of the*) béret.
b. Il identifie le pain artisanal.
c. C'est un grand jour pour lui (*for him*).
d. Elle lance une série de reportages sur le Québec.
e. Ce n'est pas un pain industriel.
f. Elle n'est pas laide.

B. Un nouveau travail. (***A new job.***) Here is a position announcement for jobs at Canal 7. Fill in each blank with the correct form of the appropriate adjective in parentheses.

Canal 7 cherche un scripte et une assistante pour la productrice. Les candidats doivent avoir[a] de ____[1] (patient, bon) qualifications et une formation[b] ____[2] (excellent, mauvais). Le travail du scripte n'est pas ____[3] (vrai, difficile), mais il est ____[4] (intéressant, autre). Nous désirons une ____[5] (bon, laid) assistante ____[6] (ennuyeux, sympathique) et ____[7] (patient, impatient).

[a]doivent... *must have* [b]*education*

C. Canal 7. Rachid is describing his new workplace to Yasmine. Put the correct form of the adjective in the appropriate place.

MODÈLE: Martine, la productrice, est une professionnelle. (vrai) →
Martine, la productrice, est une vraie professionnelle.

1. Je travaille dans un bureau. (petit)
2. Camille et Bruno sont des journalistes. (formidable)
3. Camille n'est pas une femme. (triste)
4. Camille et Bruno travaillent dans un studio. (grand)
5. Il y a un reporter. C'est Hélène. (canadien)
6. «Bonjour!» est une émission. (amusant, intéressant)
7. Hélène lance une émission sur le Québec. (autre, intéressant)

D. En général. With a partner, talk about your likes and dislikes by using elements from the three columns. How similar are you?

MODÈLE: É1: J'aime les grandes universités.
É2: Moi (*Me*), j'aime mieux les petites universités. (*ou* Moi aussi, j'aime les grandes universités.)

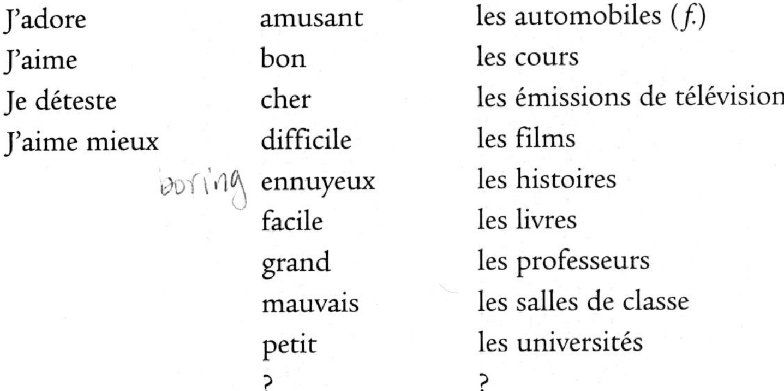

J'adore	amusant	les automobiles (*f.*)
J'aime	bon	les cours
Je déteste	cher	les émissions de télévision
J'aime mieux	difficile	les films
	ennuyeux	les histoires
	facile	les livres
	grand	les professeurs
	mauvais	les salles de classe
	petit	les universités
	?	?

Visionnement 2

Avant de visionner

A. Points de repère. (*Landmarks.*) This map shows the southeastern edge of Paris and the adjacent suburbs, where the Canal 7 studios are located. This whole area, on both banks of the Seine, became rather run-down after World War II, but recently, it has been attracting new development and prestige projects like the national library (**la Bibliothèque nationale de France**).

Les environs de Canal 7

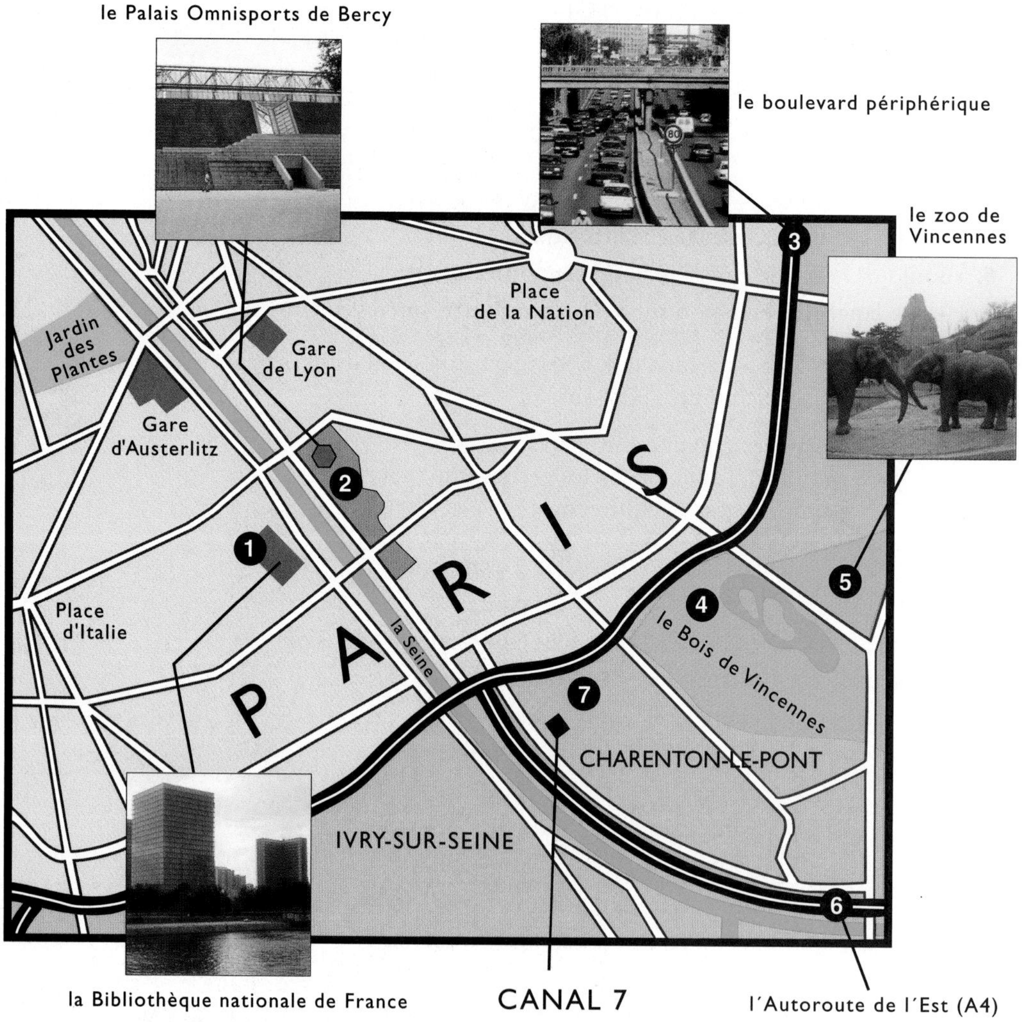

le Palais Omnisports de Bercy

le boulevard périphérique

le zoo de Vincennes

Place de la Nation

Jardin des Plantes

Gare de Lyon

Gare d'Austerlitz

PARIS

Place d'Italie

la Seine

le Bois de Vincennes

CHARENTON-LE-PONT

IVRY-SUR-SEINE

la Bibliothèque nationale de France

CANAL 7

l'Autoroute de l'Est (A4)

Look carefully at the map and indicate the number and name of the landmark that one would seek out in order to find the following:

a. un manuscrit de la Renaissance
b. un tigre
c. un match de football (*soccer*)
d. des arbres et des fleurs (*trees and flowers*) magnifiques
e. une route autour de (*around*) Paris
f. Camille Leclair et Bruno Gall

B. Les pains en France. Match the description of the bread with the correct picture.

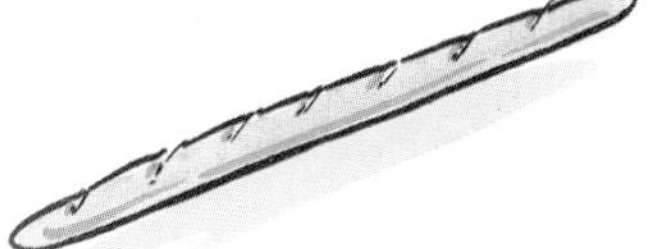

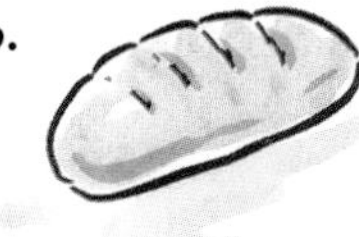

_____ **1.** Une baguette est longue et mince (*thin*).
_____ **2.** Un pain de campagne (*country*) est court et épais (*short and thick*).

Observez!

Consider the cultural information explained in **Regards sur la culture**. Then watch Episode 2 again, and answer the following questions.

- Why is Bruno embarrassed at the end of the show?
- What is the connection between the beret and the topic of the show?

Après le visionnement

Do the activity for **Visionnement 2** in the Workbook and Laboratory Manual.

Synthèse: Lecture

Mise en contexte

Public television in France is supported by an annual tax of about $100 that must be paid by every household having at least one television set.* This method of funding public television is found in most European countries. About half of French television broadcast stations (not cable) are state owned.

Commercials rarely interrupt shows in France. Rather, they are grouped at the beginning and end of programs. French television commercials have long been known as very creative and entertaining, and their style has been imitated over recent years in many North American television commercials.

Both public and private channels in France show a large number of foreign programs, usually from the United States, but also from Australia, Japan, Germany, and elsewhere. The heavy presence of American programming is of concern to some French people.

Here are statistics about the viewing audience (age 15 or older) for some of the major television channels that can be viewed nationally.

		Audience
Chaînes[a] publiques	France 2	25,0%
	France 3 (télévision régionale)	17,0%
	La cinquième (mission éducative)	1,8%
	Arte (mission européenne)	1,6%
Chaînes privées	TF1 (jeux,[b] sports, variétés, films)	34,0%
	M6 (accent sur la musique)	12,0%
Chaîne privée payante[c]	Canal Plus (films, sports)	4,6%

[a]*Networks* [b]*games* [c]Chaîne... *Private subscription channel*

Stratégie pour mieux lire

Recognizing related words

Remember—You have already learned about cognates, French words that look or sound similar to English words and that have similar meanings. Even when you can't understand every detail of a French text, you can often get a good idea of the reading's content by paying attention to cognates.

Scan the entire text that follows, and locate at least five cognates in the opening paragraphs and five more in the list. Choose the best title for this selection. Then read the whole text through and see whether your choice of title is a good one.

*This law does not apply to people over 65 years old or to handicapped people.

Des inventions importantes du XXe siècle*

Les Français aiment la télévision

La télévision et la violence

Pour les Français, les deux inventions les plus[1] importantes du XXe siècle sont la télévision et l'ordinateur. Viennent ensuite[2] la greffe du cœur,[3] les antibiotiques, le lave-linge,[4] la pilule contraceptive, le scanner (pour l'ordinateur), la pénicilline, le réfrigérateur, la carte bancaire,[5] le TGV[6] et le laser.

Au cours de sa vie,[7] un Français passe environ[8] neuf années devant[9] la télévision, mais six années au travail. Les enfants passent environ huit cents heures par an[10] à l'école—et huit cents heures devant le petit écran.

Les émissions les plus populaires, par ordre décroissant,[11] sont:

les émissions de fiction
les magazines et documentaires
les journaux télévisés[12]
la publicité[13]
les jeux
les films
les variétés
les sports
les émissions pour la jeunesse[14]
le théâtre et la musique classique

Adapté de *Francoscopie: Comment vivent les Français*

[1]*les... most* [2]Viennent... *Next come* [3]greffe... *heart transplant* [4]*washing machine* [5]carte... *bank card* [6]*high-speed train* [7]Au... *In his lifetime* [8]*about* [9]années... *years in front of* [10]huit... *800 hours per year* [11]*descending* [12]journaux... *TV news programs* [13]la... *commercials* [14]*youth*

---

*XXe means *twentieth* and is pronounced **vingtième**. **Siècle** means *century*.

Après la lecture

A. Votre titre. (*Your title.*) Now that you've read the text, do you think you chose the most appropriate title? If not, which title might be better? If you did choose correctly the first time around, which words guided you in your choice?

B. Et vous? Compare yourself to the French after studying the statistics in the article.

1. Pour les Français, les deux inventions les plus importantes du XXe siècle sont _____ et _____. Pour moi, les deux inventions les plus importantes sont _____ et _____.
2. Au cours de sa vie, un Français passe _____ années devant le petit écran. Au cours d'une journée typique (*typical day*), je passe _____ heures devant le petit écran.
3. Au cours de sa vie, un Français passe _____ années à travailler. Au cours d'une journée typique, je passe _____ heures à travailler et à étudier.
4. Les émissions favorites des Français sont _____ et _____. Moi, j'aime _____ et _____.

À écrire

Do **À écrire** for Chapter 2 in the Workbook and Laboratory Manual.

Vocabulaire

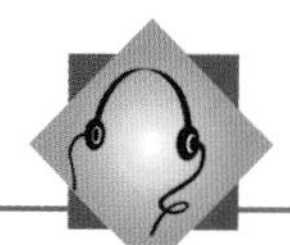

Les locaux et les employés de Canal 7

un écran	screen
une émission	program
un plateau (des plateaux)	set
un(e) producteur/trice	producer
la régie	control room
le travail	work; job

MOTS APPARENTÉS: **un(e) journaliste, un reporter, la télévision** (*fam.* **la télé**)

Verbes réguliers en *-er*

aimer	to like; to love
aimer mieux	to prefer
chercher	to look for
dîner	to eat dinner; to dine
donner	to give
écouter	to listen (to)
étudier	to study
habiter	to live (*in a place*), reside
parler	to speak; to talk
penser	to think
porter	to wear
regarder	to watch; to look at
travailler	to work
trouver	to find; to consider

MOTS APPARENTÉS: **adorer, désirer, détester**

Adjectifs pour parler des personnes

autre	other	**joli(e)**	pretty
bon(ne)	good	**laid(e)**	ugly
cher (chère)	dear; expensive	**malheureux/euse**	unhappy, miserable
ennuyeux/euse	boring	**mauvais(e)**	bad
fâché(e)	angry	**petit(e)**	small
facile	easy	**prêt(e)**	ready
fatigué(e)	tired	**sportif/ive**	athletic
faux (fausse)	false	**triste**	sad
formidable	terrific, wonderful	**vrai(e)**	true
gentil(le)	nice; kind; well behaved		
grand(e)	big; tall		
heureux/euse	happy		
inquiet/ète	anxious, worried		

MOTS APPARENTÉS: **actif/ive, amusant(e), difficile, dynamique, intellectuel(le), intéressant(e), magnifique, ridicule, super**
À REVOIR: **sympathique** (*fam.* **sympa**)

Adverbes

parfois	sometimes	**souvent**	often
rarement	rarely	**toujours**	always

Conjonction

mais — but

Pour exprimer l'accord / le désaccord

Bien sûr! (Bien sûr que oui!)	Of course! (Yes, of course!)	**D'accord! (Je suis d'accord.)**	Okay! (I agree.)
Bien sûr que non!	Of course not!	**Je ne suis pas d'accord.**	I don't agree.
C'est faux.	That's/It's false.	**Sans doute!**	Probably! No doubt!
C'est vrai.	That's/It's true.		

Autres expressions utiles

Comment est/sont... ?	What is/are . . . like?	**sans**	without
		selon	according to

Chapitre 3

Le Médaillon

OBJECTIFS

In this episode, you will

- see Camille's reaction when her locket is found
- discover new sides to Bruno's personality
- learn more about Rachid's background

In this chapter, you will

- talk about places people go
- talk about where things are located
- discuss nationalities
- express movement from place to place
- talk about what will happen soon
- ask questions using tag phrases
- learn about nonverbal communication in France
- learn about communication customs in different cultures

Vocabulaire en contexte

*L*es environs de Canal 7°

Les... *The area around Channel 7*

Le bureau de Rachid et de Bruno est dans **le bâtiment** de Canal 7, situé dans **un quartier** de **banlieue** (*f*.). Regardez bien le plan.

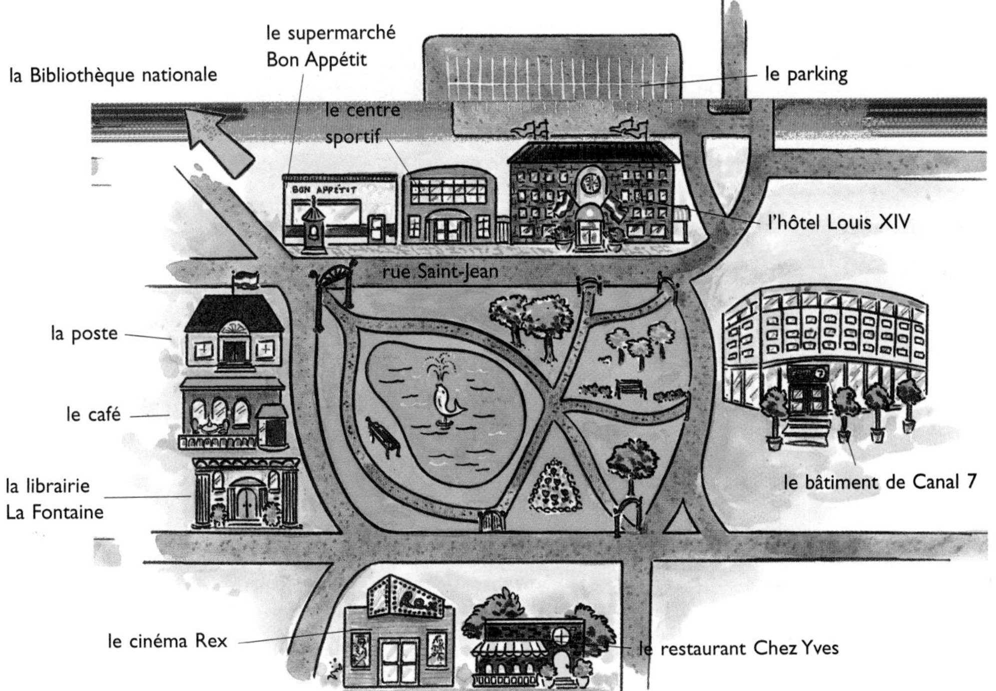

—Où° est le bâtiment de Canal 7? *Where*
—Le bâtiment de Canal 7 est **en face du** parc.

—**Où se trouve**° le restaurant Chez Yves? Où... *Where is ... located?*
—Il est **à côté du** cinéma.

Un autre restaurant se trouve **dans** le bâtiment de Canal 7.
Le centre sportif est **là, dans la rue** Saint-Jean.
Il y a un kiosque **devant** le supermarché.
Le parking est **derrière** le centre sportif et l'hôtel.
Un café est **entre** la librairie et la poste.
La Bibliothèque nationale n'est pas **loin d'ici**.° loin... *far from here*
Le supermarché est **près de** la poste.

Autres prépositions de lieu° (*m.*) *place*

au-dessous de*	below	**chez**	at the home of	**sur**	on
au-dessus de†	above, over	**sous**	under		

*The expression **en dessous de** may also be used.
†The expression **en dessus de** may also be used.

Notez bien!

Whenever **de** is used with **le** and **les,** it forms a contraction. No contraction is made with **la** or **l'**.

de + le → **du**
de + la → **de la**
de + l' → **de l'**
de + les → **des**

Le parking de Canal 7 se trouve en dessous **du** bâtiment.

Le supermarché est près **de la** poste.

Le restaurant **de l'**hôtel Louis XIV est excellent!

Le bâtiment de Canal 7 est loin **des** monuments de Paris.

Activités

A. Où? (Where?) Where might people be when they do the following activities?

MODÈLE: On filme l'émission «Bonjour!»... →
On filme l'émission «Bonjour!» dans le bâtiment de Canal 7.

1. On dîne bien...
2. Rachid regarde les carottes...
3. Bruno pratique des sports...
4. Roger gare sa moto (*parks his motorbike*)...
5. Les studios du Canal 7 se trouvent...
6. Camille envoie (*sends*) une lettre...
7. Martine regarde un film...
8. Rachid travaille...
9. Un touriste dort (*sleeps*)...

a. au cinéma
b. à la poste
c. au restaurant
d. dans son (*his*) bureau
e. à l'hôtel
f. au parking
g. au supermarché
h. au centre sportif
i. dans une banlieue de Paris

B. Où se trouve... ? Fill in each blank with a preposition to give information about classroom and student life.

1. Le bureau du professeur est _____ la classe.
2. Les livres de français sont _____ les bureaux.
3. Les sacs à dos des étudiants sont normalement _____ les bureaux ou les chaises.
4. Les lumières (*lights*) sont en général _____ bureaux.
5. Il y a souvent un(e) camarade de classe _____ moi (*me*).
6. Les étudiants habitent parfois _____ leurs (*their*) parents.

C. Où habitent-ils? Indicate where these people live, using the expressions **au-dessous de**, **au-dessus de**, **à côté de**, **dans la rue**. Use at least two expressions to situate the residents.

MODÈLE: M. Nathan habite au-dessus de M. Abdul-Hassan dans la rue Pajol.

1. Rachid et Sonia Bouhazid
2. Catherine Lapointe
3. Mohammed Abdul-Hassan
4. Isabelle Coste
5. Laurent Nathan

D. Vrai ou faux? Look at the drawing of the neighborhood of Canal 7 on page 65, and indicate whether the following statements are true or false. If the statement is true, say **C'est vrai!** and repeat the sentence. If it is false, say **C'est faux!** and correct the statement.

MODÈLES: Le bâtiment de Canal 7 est près de l'hôtel. →
C'est vrai. Le bâtiment de Canal 7 est près de l'hôtel.

Le restaurant Chez Yves est loin du cinéma. →
C'est faux. Le restaurant Chez Yves est à côté du cinéma. (C'est faux. Le restaurant Chez Yves est près du cinéma.)

1. Le parking est derrière le centre sportif.
2. Le bâtiment de Canal 7 est en face du supermarché.
3. La Bibliothèque nationale est loin de ce quartier.
4. Le centre sportif est à côté de la librairie.
5. Le restaurant Chez Yves est entre le cinéma et la librairie.

E. Sur votre campus. A new student on your campus asks you where certain buildings are. Play the roles with a partner. Then switch roles.

MODÈLE: la faculté des sciences (*school of sciences*) →
É1: Excuse-moi, où se trouve la faculté des sciences?
É2: C'est le bâtiment là-bas (*over there*), devant la bibliothèque. (Il se trouve là-bas, devant la bibliothèque.)
É1: Merci.

1. une résidence universitaire **2.** le laboratoire de langues **3.** la bibliothèque **4.** la faculté des langues étrangères (*foreign languages*) **5.** le bureau de l'administration de l'université **6.** la librairie universitaire **7.** le restaurant universitaire

Les nationalités, les origines régionales et les langues°

° *languages*

Camille et M. Liégeois sont de Paris. Ils sont **français**.

Rachid est de Marseille. Il est **français**, mais son papa est **algérien**.

Hélène est de Montréal. Elle est **canadienne**.

To talk about where people come from, you'll need to know the names of countries or regions of the world, as well as the adjectives used for those places.

Take a look at the maps in the front and back of your textbook to find out in which countries French is spoken (**les pays** (*m.*) **francophones**).

PAYS EUROPÉENS	ADJECTIFS	LANGUES OFFICIELLES
l'Allemagne° (*f.*)	allemand(e)	l'allemand (*m.*)
l'Angleterre (*f.*)	anglais(e)	l'anglais (*m.*)
l'Espagne (*f.*)	espagnol(e)	l'espagnol (*m.*)
la France	français(e)	le français
PAYS AFRICAINS		
l'Algérie (*f.*)	algérien(ne)	l'arabe (*m.*)
le Maroc	marocain(e)	l'arabe
PAYS ET RÉGIONS NORD-AMÉRICAINS		
le Canada	canadien(ne)	l'anglais, le français
les États-Unis (*m.*)	américain(e)	l'anglais
le Mexique	mexicain(e)	l'espagnol
le Québec*	québécois(e)	le français
PAYS ASIATIQUES		
la Chine	chinois(e)	le (chinois) mandarin
le Japon	japonais(e)	le japonais
le Viêtnam	vietnamien(ne)	le vietnamien

°Germany

1. The names of languages are masculine and are often formed from an adjective of nationality or regional origin. The article is omitted when the language follows **parler**, but it is otherwise required.

   On parle **mandarin** et d'autres langues chinoises en Chine.
   L'anglais est la langue officielle en Angleterre et aux États-Unis.

2. The noun referring to a person from a particular country is formed from the appropriate adjective with the first letter capitalized.

   Mais quoi, tu es magnifique comme ça! **Un** vrai **Français**.
   Les Français sont formidables!
   Hélène? C'est **une Canadienne**.

Activités

A. Nationalités. Give the nationalities of the following people.

MODÈLE: Ana María Ordoñez / Mexique →
Ana María Ordoñez est mexicaine.

1. Noriko Matsushita (*f.*) / Japon
2. Mao He (*m.*) / Chine

---

*__Le Québec__ refers to the province of Quebec in Canada. Quebec City is known in French as **Québec**. **J'aime le Québec** means *I like Quebec* (the province). **J'aime Québec** means *I like Quebec City*.

3. Mohammed Ibn-Da'ud / Algérie
4. María Losada / Espagne
5. Nick Brown / Angleterre
6. Lise Nathan / France
7. Anne Nguyen / Viêtnam
8. Monique Tremblay / Canada (Québec)
9. Ahmed el-Diah / Maroc

B. Quel pays? Identify the country being described.

MODÈLE: C'est un pays anglophone au nord (*north*) de l'Europe. La capitale est Londres. →
C'est l'Angleterre.

C'est...

1. un grand pays près du Maroc en Afrique du Nord. La capitale est Alger.
2. un pays à l'est (*east*) de la France. L'allemand est la langue officielle.
3. une ancienne (*former*) colonie française. La capitale est Ho Chi Minh Ville.
4. le pays au sud (*south*) des États-Unis. L'espagnol est la langue officielle.
5. une province francophone au Canada. Un port important est Montréal.
6. le pays situé entre le Canada et le Mexique. Un président est le chef du gouvernement. (Ce sont...)

Visionnement 1

Avant de visionner

Précisez. (*Specify.*) Which sentence best describes the dialogue? Choose from among the choices that follow the dialogue.

PRODUCTRICE: Attends,[a] Camille. Je te présente Rachid Bouhazid. C'est notre nouveau[b] reporter.

RACHID: Très heureux.

CAMILLE: Enchantée.

RACHID: «Bonjour!» est une émission très sympa. Vous êtes forts,[c] Bruno et vous!

CAMILLE: Merci.

[a]*Wait* [b]*notre... our new* [c]*strong (a good team)*

a. Rachid critique l'émission.
b. Rachid admire l'émission.
c. Rachid préfère Bruno à Camille.

Notez bien!

"Stressed" pronouns are used after **c'est**, after prepositions, and to add emphasis.

je → **moi**	nous → **nous**
tu → **toi**	vous → **vous**
il → **lui**	ils → **eux**
elle → **elle**	elles → **elles**
on → **soi**	

Tu vas travailler avec **eux**.
You'll be working with them.

Vocabulaire relatif à l'épisode

C'est à toi?	*Is this yours?*
Tu viens de	*You come from*
Tu as faim?	*Are you hungry?*

Observez!

Martine, the producer, makes an important discovery in Episode 3: she finds the locket Camille has lost. As you watch, try to answer the following questions.

- How does Camille react when Martine asks **Qui est-ce?**
- What is missing from the locket?

Après le visionnement

A. Qu'est-ce qui se passe? (*What's happening?*) Tell what happens in Episode 3 by choosing words from the list to fill in the blanks in the summary of the story.

Vocabulaire utile: le bureau, chez, l'émission, invite, jolie, pense, une photo, présente, propose, «Qui est-ce?», trouve

Martine, la productrice, _____[1] le médaillon de Camille, et il y a _____[2] dedans.[a] Martine demande _____[3], mais Camille ne répond pas.[b] Ensuite,[c] Martine _____[4] Rachid à Camille. Il aime _____[5] «Bonjour!» et _____[6] que Camille et Bruno sont forts. Bruno _____[7] à Hélène de se marier avec lui,[d] mais c'est une plaisanterie.[e] Finalement, Bruno entre dans _____[8] et rencontre[f] Rachid. Il regarde une photo de la femme[g] de Rachid et pense qu'elle est _____[9], mais Rachid ne répond pas. Pour être sociable, Bruno _____[10] Rachid à déjeuner.[h]

[a]*in it* [b]*ne... doesn't answer* [c]*Then* [d]*de... to marry him* [e]*joke* [f]*meets* [g]*wife* [h]*have lunch*

B. Les personnalités. In this episode, several characters revealed a little more of their personalities. Read these exchanges and choose which sentence best describes each person's character.

1. Quel est le caractère de Bruno?

BRUNO: Hélène?... On se marie, toi et moi?
HÉLÈNE: Eh! Quelle bonne idée! D'abord, je divorce avec Tom Cruise, OK?

a. Il aime flirter.
b. C'est un menteur (*liar*).
c. C'est un intellectuel.

2. Quel est le caractère de Camille?

MARTINE: C'est à toi... ? Le médaillon est ravissant. Qui est-ce?
CAMILLE: ... Merci, Martine. (Elle referme[a] le médaillon et part.[b])

[a]*closes* [b]*walks away*

a. Camille est heureuse.
b. Camille est discrète (*reserved*).
c. Camille est bavarde (*talkative*).

3. Quel est le caractère de Rachid?

BRUNO: Euh, excuse-moi, c'est mon[c] bureau, ici. Ton[d] bureau, il est là.
RACHID: Ah! Bon ben, pas de problème!

[c]*my* [d]*Your*

a. Rachid est ridicule.
b. Rachid n'est pas gentil.
c. Rachid est sympathique.

Structure 9

Le verbe *aller* et le futur proche

Expressing movement and intention

—On **va** où?

—Au Jardin des Plantes, pour une leçon de sciences naturelles.

Le verbe *aller*

1. The verb **aller** means *to go*. In the preceding example, Yasmine used the verb **aller** to ask where her class was going.

aller (*to go*)			
je	**vais**	nous	**allons**
tu	**vas**	vous	**allez**
il, elle, on	**va**	ils, elles	**vont**

Rachid **va** à la cantine avec ses collègues. — *Rachid goes to the cafeteria with his coworkers.*

Nicole et Hélène **vont** à la régie. — *Nicole and Hélène are going to the control room.*

Notez bien!

Whenever **à** is used with **le** and **les**, it forms a contraction. No contraction is made with **la** or **l'**.

à + le → **au**

à + la → **à la**

à + l' → **à l'**

à + les → **aux**

Camille est **au** maquillage?

Nous allons **à la** cantine.

Yasmine va **à l'**école.

Il parle **aux** reporters.

Because **aller** expresses movement *to* a place, it is often used with the preposition **à**.

Est-ce que Yasmine **va à** la maison?	*Does Yasmine go home (to the house)?*

2. You have already learned another use of **aller**—to ask and answer questions about how a person is feeling or doing.

Comment **allez-vous**, monsieur?	*How are you?*
Tu vas bien, Hélène?	*Are you well, Hélène?*
Oui, **ça va** très bien.	*Yes, everything's fine.*

Le futur proche: *Aller* + infinitif

1. To talk about what someone is going to do, you can use a conjugated form of **aller** followed by an infinitive. This is often called the "near future."

Tu **vas travailler** avec eux.	*You are going to work with them.*
Est-ce que Bruno **va identifier** le pain artisanal?	*Is Bruno going to identify the handmade bread?*

2. To make a negative statement with the near future, **ne... pas** surrounds the conjugated verb **aller**. The infinitive follows.

Je **ne vais pas choisir** le pain industriel.	*I am not going to choose the commercial bread.*

Activités

A. Après le cours. Two students are talking about where they and others are going after class. Play the roles with a partner, following the model.

MODELE: tu / la résidence universitaire / la bibliothèque →
É1: Est-ce que tu vas à la résidence universitaire?
É2: Non, je vais à la bibliothèque.

1. Michèle / le restaurant universitaire / le cours d'histoire
2. Paul et Marc / le bureau du prof / la librairie
3. vous / le centre sportif / la bibliothèque
4. Murielle / le supermarché / le bureau de l'administration
5. le professeur / la poste / le parking
6. les autres étudiants / le laboratoire / le cinéma

B. Où est-ce qu'on va? Say where each of the following people goes, based on what is told about them.

Vocabulaire utile: bibliothèque, centre sportif, cinéma, parking, poste, restaurant, supermarché

1. Je n'aime pas dîner chez moi. Je...
2. Michel cherche un roman (*novel*) de Balzac. Il...
3. Vous désirez regarder un bon film. Vous...
4. Nous cherchons notre (*our*) automobile. Nous...

5. Tu aimes jouer (*to play*) au tennis. Tu...
6. Les Robidoux vont préparer un bon dîner chez eux. Ils...

C. Et après? (*And later?*) What are the following people going to do later on? Pick phrases that seem appropriate for the characters, and use **aller** + infinitive to explain.

MODÈLE: Rachid va chercher la maman de Yasmine.

1. Rachid		travailler avec Rachid
2. Bruno et Camille		trouver son (*her*) papa après (*after*) l'école
3. Hélène	aller	lancer une série de reportages sur le Québec
4. Yasmine		regarder son médaillon
5. Camille		habiter à Paris
6. Yasmine et Rachid		chercher la maman de Yasmine

D. Et vous? Carry on a conversation with a partner, following the instructions.

Vocabulaire utile: chercher un livre, dîner, écouter la radio, étudier, parler avec des amis, regarder la télévision, travailler, visiter un musée, ?

1. Greet each other. **2.** Find out where your partner will go after this class. **3.** Find out what he/she is going to do there. **4.** Tell your partner where you are going next. **5.** Explain what you will do there and what you will not do there. **6.** Say good-bye to each other.

Structure 10

Les questions avec *n'est-ce pas? non? c'est ça? je suppose, d'accord? OK?*

Asking questions with tag phrases

—Pour toi aussi, c'est un grand jour, **non**?

—Oui. Salut, ma chérie!

You have already seen two ways of asking yes/no questions.

Rising intonation:	Tu vas bien?
Est-ce que:	Est-ce que tu vas bien?

1. A third way of formulating a yes/no question is by adding a tag at the end of the statement. Common tags are highlighted in the following examples.

Dans votre famille, on est boulanger de père en fils, **n'est-ce pas?**	*In your family, you've been bakers for generations, haven't you? (lit. ... you are bakers from father to son, isn't that so?)*
Pour toi aussi, c'est un grand jour, **non?**	*This is a big day for you too, right? (no?)*
Tu viens de Marseille, **c'est ça?**	*You come from Marseille, right? (is that so?)*
Tu es musulman, **je suppose**.	*You're Muslim, I take it. (I suppose.)*
On va à la cantine, **d'accord?**	*Let's go to the cafeteria, okay? (agreed?)*
D'abord, je divorce avec Tom Cruise, **OK?**	*First, I'll divorce Tom Cruise, okay?*

2. **N'est-ce pas? non? c'est ça?** and **je suppose** have similar functions: They simply ask for a confirmation (yes or no) of the statement that precedes the tag. **C'est ça** can be used as an answer meaning *That's right.*

—Tu viens de Marseille, **c'est ça?**	*You come from Marseille, right?*
—**C'est ça**, Bruno.	*That's right, Bruno.*

3. The function of **d'accord?** and **OK?** is to ask for agreement to do something. **D'accord** and **OK** can also be used to answer these questions.

—On va à la cantine, **OK?**	*We'll go to the cafeteria, okay?*
—**D'accord.** Pas de problème.	*Sure. No problem.*

Activité

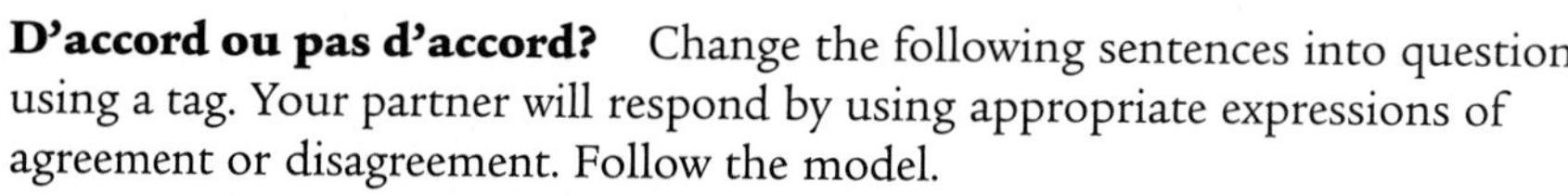

D'accord ou pas d'accord? Change the following sentences into questions using a tag. Your partner will respond by using appropriate expressions of agreement or disagreement. Follow the model.

MODÈLE: Nous allons à la bibliothèque. →
É1: Nous allons à la bibliothèque, OK?
É2: Oui. D'accord.

ou É1: Nous allons à la bibliothèque, je suppose.
É2: Bien sûr que non! Nous allons au restaurant!

1. Tu aimes les cours ce (*this*) semestre.
2. Tu vas travailler après la classe.
3. Tout le monde adore travailler.
4. Les étudiants adorent les week-ends.
5. Nous dînons au restaurant ce soir.
6. Le professeur est québécois.
7. Les émissions de télévision sont intéressantes.
8. Je suis d'origine marocaine.

Regards sur la culture

La communication non-verbale

Notice how close Martine, Rachid, and Camille stand when they are speaking. This illustrates one aspect of nonverbal communication that poses problems for many Americans and Canadians. Because we are not usually aware of our own gestures and needs for communication space, nonverbal communication can be one of the most difficult areas of adjustment when we visit another culture. Here are two examples.

- The handshake, often consisting of a single quick up-and-down movement, is an obligatory greeting in France for all colleagues and friends the first time they meet each day. It can be replaced with a quick kiss on the cheeks (two or three or four times depending on the region) between two women or between men and women, when the people involved know each other well.
- Cultures differ in how they set interpersonal distances. In English-speaking North America, the distance people maintain in day-to-day business conversations with strangers and acquaintances (sometimes called "social" distance) starts at around 4 feet. In France, social distance tends to be smaller, starting at around 0.6 meters (2 feet). When English-speaking North Americans encounter French social distances, they may back up in an attempt to reset the situation with American spacing. The French person will normally move closer so as to reestablish the space with which he or she is comfortable. More than one American or Canadian has backed all the way across a room before the end of a French conversation.

Considérez

Many people have commented that it is extremely easy to spot North Americans in France just by the way they walk and stand. If you were studying abroad, would you want to try to adjust to the nonverbal habits of the culture in which you were living, or would that be unnecessary? How hard would it be?

Structure 11

Le verbe *venir*

Expressing movement

—Tu es Rachid Bouhazid et **tu viens de** Marseille, c'est ça?
—C'est ça, Bruno.

When Bruno first meets Rachid, he uses the verb **venir** to ask where he comes from.

venir (*to come*)			
je	**viens**	nous	**venons**
tu	**viens**	vous	**venez**
il, elle, on	**vient**	ils, elles	**viennent**

Tu viens avec moi, non? — *You're coming with me, aren't you?*
Nous venons au studio ensemble. — *We come to the studio together.*

1. The verbs **devenir** (*to become*) and **revenir** (*to come back, return*) are conjugated like **venir**.

   Camille **devient** silencieuse et elle part. — *Camille becomes silent and walks away.*
   Mais elle **revient** pour parler à Rachid. — *But she comes back to talk to Rachid.*

2. To express where a person comes from, use **venir de**. For cities and feminine countries,* no article is included. For masculine countries† and plural countries, the contraction of **de** with the article (**du** or **des**) is used.

   Rachid **vient de** Marseille et Camille et Bruno **viennent de** Paris.
   Camille et Bruno **viennent de** France. Moi, je **viens de** Chine.

---

*Most countries ending in **-e** are feminine. One exception to this rule is **le Mexique: Les Martinez *viennent du* Mexique.**
† Most countries ending with a written consonant or a vowel other than **-e** are masculine.

Monsieur el-Diah **vient du** Maroc. Hélène **vient du** Canada.

—Vous **venez des** Pays-Bas?

—Non, nous **venons des** États-Unis.

To ask where someone comes from, use **D'où venez-vous?** or **D'où viens-tu?**

—**D'où viens-tu**, Seth?

—Je viens des États-Unis.

Activités

A. À l'Alliance française. The following students are at the **Alliance française** in Paris. Based on where they live, say what country or region they are from.

Vocabulaire utile: l'Algérie, l'Allemagne, l'Angleterre, le Canada, la Chine, l'Espagne, les États-Unis, le Japon, le Québec

MODÈLE: Lisa habite à New York. Elle... →
Elle vient des États-Unis.

1. J'habite à Londres (*London*). Je...
2. Nous habitons à Alger. Nous...
3. Tu habites à Madrid. Tu...
4. Mitsuko habite à Tokyo. Elle...
5. Linda et Ford habitent à Montréal. Ils...
6. Vous habitez à Berlin. Vous...

B. À Canal 7. Complete these sentences with a form of the verbs **venir**, **revenir**, and **devenir**.

1. Le vrai pain français _____ de plus en plus (*more and more*) difficile à trouver.
2. Et les Français _____ de moins en moins (*less and less*) capables de reconnaître un bon pain.
3. «Hélène _____ du Canada. D'où est-ce que tu _____, Rachid?»
4. «Et Camille et toi, d'où est-ce que vous _____, Bruno?»
5. «Rachid, où est-ce que tu vas? Nous devons (*need to*) parler.» «Un instant, Martine, je _____ tout de suite.»
6. Canal 7 _____ une station de télévision importante.
7. Hélène _____ en France après une longue absence.
8. Après beaucoup de travail, Camille _____ la star de Canal 7.

C. Questions. Hélène is interviewing the employees of Canal 7. Working with a partner, use the elements to formulate her questions and her colleagues' answers.

1. HÉLÈNE: Bruno, tu / venir de / la région parisienne?
2. BRUNO: Oui, mes parents / habiter à / Paris.
3. HÉLÈNE: Et Rachid, vous / venir de / Toulouse?
4. RACHID: Non, je / arriver de / Marseille.

5. HÉLÈNE: Est-ce que les employés de Canal 7 / venir de / loin?
6. BRUNO: Nicole / habiter dans / le quartier, mais Camille / venir de / un autre quartier.
7. HÉLÈNE: Camille, tu / venir à / le studio le week-end?
8. CAMILLE: Oui, mais je / aller à / le centre sportif après.
9. HÉLÈNE: Nous / venir tous (*all*) de / un pays francophone?
10. CAMILLE: Oui / les employés / être de / France / et de / Canada.

D. D'où viennent-ils? Ask five of your classmates from which country and city they come. Tell each of them whether or not you plan to visit their home city within the next five years.

MODÈLE: É1: D'où viens-tu?
É2: Moi, je viens du Canada—d'Ottawa, précisément (*to be precise*).
É1: Je vais visiter Ottawa l'année prochaine (*next year*)! (*ou* Je vais visiter Ottawa dans deux mois [*in two months*]. *ou* Je ne vais pas visiter Ottawa.)

Visionnement 2

Avant de visionner

***Tu* ou *vous*?** Read the following dialogues and choose the correct explanation(s) for why the highlighted pronoun **tu** or **vous** is used in that context.

1. RACHID: «Bonjour!» est une émission très sympa. **Vous** êtes forts, Bruno et vous.

   CAMILLE: Merci.

   a. C'est normal d'employer **vous** pour parler de deux personnes.
   b. Rachid vient de faire la connaissance de (*just met*) Camille.
   c. Rachid est un bon ami de Camille et de Bruno.

2. BRUNO: **Tu** es Rachid Bouhazid et **tu** viens de Marseille, c'est ça?
RACHID: C'est ça, Bruno.

a. Bruno vient de faire la connaissance de Rachid.
b. Bruno accueille (*welcomes*) Rachid avec amitié (*friendship*).
c. Bruno est beaucoup plus âgé que (*much older than*) Rachid.

Observez!

Consider the cultural information explained in **Regards sur la culture**. Then watch Episode 3 again, and answer the following questions.

- What gesture do Rachid and Bruno use when they first greet each other?
- What behaviors do you notice when people greet each other that are different from the way people act in similar situations in your country?

Après le visionnement

Do the activity for **Visionnement 2** in the Workbook and Laboratory Manual.

Pour en savoir plus...

Some people, because of their personality or training, are slow to switch from **vous** to **tu**, but others switch relatively quickly. In professions such as advertising and television, **tu** is used much more freely among coworkers. You may have noticed that Camille and Bruno use **tu** most of the time but switch to **vous** on the set to portray a more formal working relationship to the viewers.

Synthèse: Culture

La communication interculturelle

When we think about communicating with the people of another culture, we tend to focus on language. However, some researchers claim that as much as 65% of what is communicated in human interactions is not accomplished with language. This means that entering a new culture requires you to reset your expectations in dozens of areas.

Use of space

People in North African countries such as Algeria maintain social distances that are even smaller than those of the French. North Americans who have stood in line with Algerians have often remarked that "everyone was pushing."

Conceptions of time

In Togo, friends and family make regular visits to each other unannounced. It is expected that visitors will be made welcome for as long as they care to stay.

Gestures and body language

To indicate a direction in French Polynesia, people signal with their head or eyes; pointing with a finger would be considered rude.

Rules of politeness

In France, when you are at a café, it is polite to offer to pay for everyone at the table. It would be impolite, however, to let someone else pay without protesting a bit, and the expectation is that you would pay the next time.

Social attitudes

In Morocco, "white lies" are an accepted way of saving face in many circumstances; absolute truth and frankness are not as important as social connection and respect.

Facial displays of emotion

One of the most important areas of intercultural communication is the expression of emotion in the face. Certain emotions, such as happiness, universally produce particular facial displays, a smile for example. But culture complicates things. Every culture establishes its own set of "display rules" that regulate the actual production of these facial signals. For example, there are many occasions in North American culture where one is expected to amplify the smile, suggesting more pleasure than one actually feels. Take the case of Americans and Canadians greeting guests, compared to the way the French greet them. Americans and Canadians amplify their smile when greeting others; the French do not amplify the smile and, in fact, may not smile at all in this situation.

In other words, a smile does not always mean the same thing. When Rachid enters the control room in Episode 2, Martine does not really smile. In Episode 3, when Rachid and Camille meet, there are not a lot of big smiles. In France, the smile is not used as a sign of civility. Neither cashiers nor strangers of any kind will normally smile at you in France. To the North American, the French lack of a smile, in many circumstances, feels like a snub. To a French person, what seems like the eternal smile of a North American connotes hypocrisy or naïveté.

À vous

A. Choose someone in class whom you do not know well. Position yourself about two feet away from this person (the normal French distance for strangers) and carry on a short conversation in French: Start with a handshake, greet the other person, ask how he or she is doing, ask where she or he is from, etc. Then move a step closer together to simulate the Algerian distance and repeat the experiment. Discuss your comfort level in each of these experiences with the class.

B. With your partner, think of a situation in your own culture in which you are expected to amplify the facial expression of an emotion (happiness, sadness, disgust, anger) and a situation in which you are supposed to play down the emotional display. How might someone from another culture have problems interpreting what is going on? Put together a 30-second skit and perform it for the class.

À écrire

Do **À écrire** for Chapter 3 in the Workbook and Laboratory Manual.

Vocabulaire

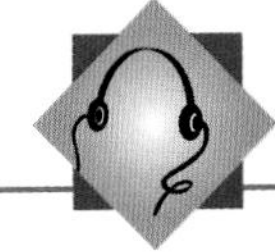

Les environs de Canal 7

une banlieue	suburb
un bâtiment	building
une bibliothèque	library
un bureau (des bureaux)	office
une librairie	bookstore
un lieu (des lieux)	place, location
la poste	post office
un quartier	neighborhood

MOTS APPARENTÉS: **un café, un centre sportif, un hôtel, un parking, un restaurant, un supermarché**

À REVOIR: **un cinéma**

Pays et régions

l'Allemagne (*f.*)	Germany
l'Angleterre (*f.*)	England
l'Espagne (*f.*)	Spain
les États-Unis (*m.*)	United States
le Maroc	Morocco
un pays	country

MOTS APPARENTÉS: **l'Algérie** (*f.*), **le Canada, la Chine, la France, le Japon, le Mexique, le Québec, le Viêtnam**

Verbes

aller	to go	**revenir**	to come back, return
devenir	to become	**venir**	to come

Nationalités et origines régionales

allemand(e)	German	**japonais(e)**	Japanese
anglais(e)	English	**marocain(e)**	Moroccan
chinois(e)	Chinese	**québécois(e)**	from Quebec
espagnol(e)	Spanish	**vietnamien(ne)**	Vietnamese
français(e)	French		
francophone	French-speaking		

MOTS APPARENTÉS: **algérien(ne), américain(e), canadien(ne), mexicain(e)**

Pronoms accentués

moi	me	**nous**	us
toi	you	**vous**	you
lui	him	**eux**	them (*m.*)
elle	her	**elles**	them (*f.*)
soi	oneself		

Prépositions de lieu

à côté de	beside	**entre**	between
au-dessous de	below	**loin (de)**	far (from)
au-dessus de	above, over	**près (de)**	near
chez	at the home of	**sous**	under
derrière	in back of, behind	**sur**	on
devant	in front of		
en face de	facing		

À REVOIR: **à, dans, de**

Questions

c'est ça?	right?, is that so?	**non?**	right?, no?
d'accord?	agreed?, okay?	**OK?**	okay?
je suppose?	I suppose?, I take it?		
n'est-ce pas?	right?, isn't that so?, aren't you?, etc.		

À REVOIR: **est-ce que... ?**

Autres expressions utiles

dans la rue [Pajol]	on [Pajol] Street	**Où se trouve... ?**	Where is . . . located?
ici	here		

À REVOIR: **là**

Chapitre 4

Une nouvelle vie à Paris

OBJECTIFS

In this episode, you will

- listen as Bruno and Rachid order lunch
- learn about Rachid's background and family

In this chapter, you will

- talk about family, marriage, and age
- use large numbers
- talk about days, months, and dates
- tell about things people just did
- talk about things you own and have
- express feelings and sensations
- practice another way to ask yes/no questions
- ask questions about where, when, why, how, how much, and how many
- learn about the diversity of France
- read about the notion of family in France

Vocabulaire en contexte

La famille de Bruno Gall (le côté paternel)°

La... *Bruno Gall's family (on his father's side)*

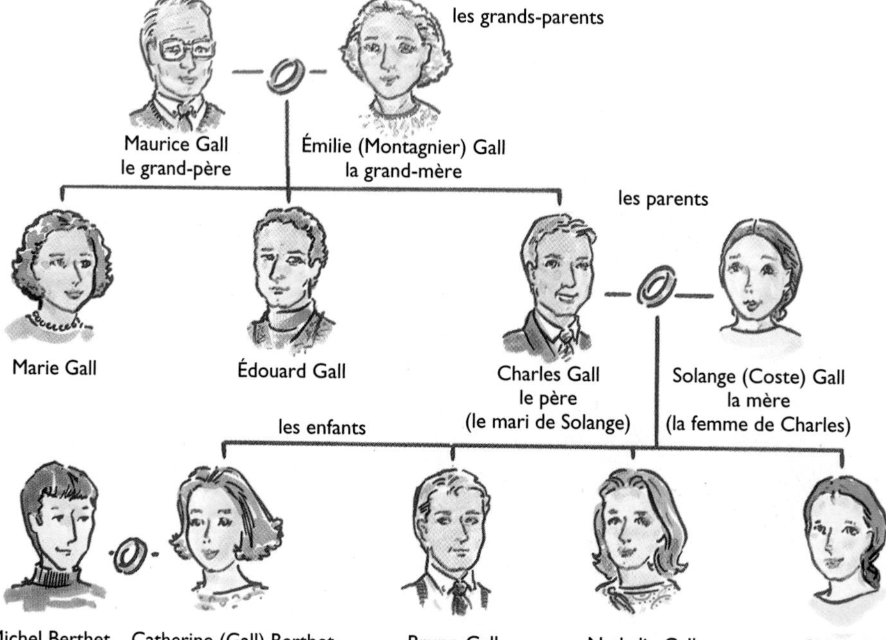

Pour en savoir plus...

Weddings in churches and synagogues are still important for some French families, but the official ceremony recognized by the French government takes place in the mayor's office. Many couples, however, choose to live together without being married, and an increasing number have children. According to INSEE (l'Institut National de la Statistique et des Études Économiques), there are now around 12 million married couples in France, whereas almost 2.4 million couples prefer a less traditional relationship. The gap has been narrowing since the late 1970s.

Bruno est **le petit-fils** de Maurice et d'Émilie. Catherine, Nathalie et Chloé sont **les petites-filles** de Maurice et d'Émilie.
Bruno est **le neveu** de Marie et d'Édouard. Ses sœurs sont **les nièces** de Marie et d'Édouard.
Marie est **la tante** de Bruno. Édouard est **l'oncle** de Bruno.
Bruno a (*has*) **une cousine**; elle **s'appelle** Chantal. Il n'a pas de **cousin**.

Les beaux-parents

le beau-père	stepfather; father-in-law
la belle-mère	stepmother; mother-in-law
le beau-frère	stepbrother; brother-in-law
la belle-sœur	stepsister; sister-in-law

L'état civil

célibataire single
marié(e) married
divorcé(e) divorced
veuf (veuve) widowed
Ils vivent en union libre. They are living together (without marriage).

The adjectives **célibataire**, **marié(e)**, **divorcé(e)**, and **veuf (veuve)** may also be used as nouns.

Mon père est mort. Ma mère est **veuve**. *My father is dead. My mother is a widow.*

Activités

A. Quelle parenté? (*What's the relationship?*) Now look at the maternal side of Bruno's family tree and explain the relationships.

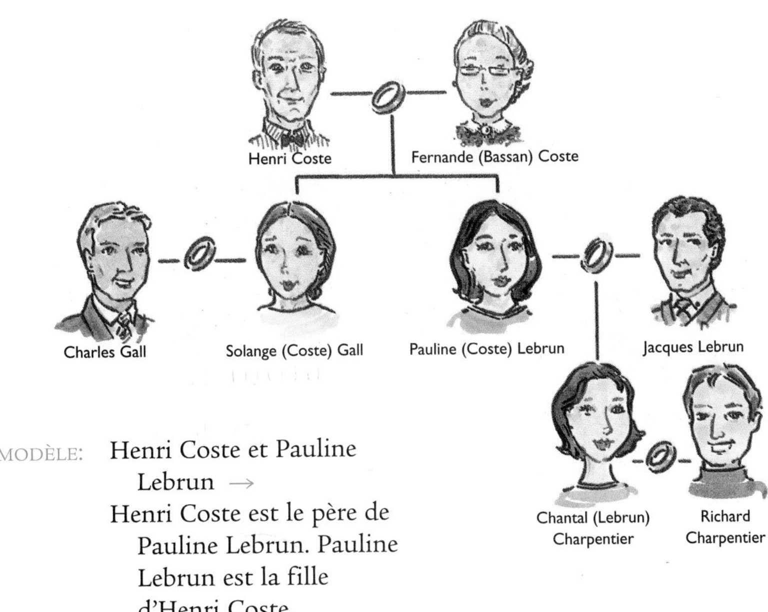

MODÈLE: Henri Coste et Pauline Lebrun →
Henri Coste est le père de Pauline Lebrun. Pauline Lebrun est la fille d'Henri Coste.

1. Solange Gall et Pauline Lebrun **2.** Chantal Charpentier et Richard Charpentier **3.** Chantal Charpentier et Fernande Coste **4.** Henri Coste et Jacques Lebrun **5.** Henri Coste et Solange Gall

B. Marié ou non? Give the marital status of these individuals.

1. un homme dont (*whose*) la femme est morte (*dead*): C'est un...
2. un homme dont le mariage est terminé: Il est...
3. une femme qui (*who*) n'est pas encore mariée: C'est une...
4. un couple qui vit ensemble (*lives together*) mais qui n'est pas marié: Ils vivent...

C. Une famille. Show a photo of your family or one that you invent using a picture from a magazine. Identify several family members to your partner, giving their names and relationships. Then your partner will ask you follow-up questions.

MODÈLE: É1: Voilà Charles. Charles est le frère de John et le fils de David.
É2: Et qui est cette (*this*) personne?
É1: Cette personne s'appelle Monique. C'est la sœur de David.
É2: Comment est-elle?
É1: Elle est petite et un peu (*a little*) bizarre, mais très sympathique.

Les nombres à partir de 60°

° *à... from 60 on*

60	**soixante**	80	**quatre-vingts**
61	**soixante et un**	81	**quatre-vingt-un**
62	**soixante-deux**	82	**quatre-vingt-deux**
63	**soixante-trois**	83	**quatre-vingt-trois**
70	**soixante-dix**	90	**quatre-vingt-dix**
71	**soixante et onze**	91	**quatre-vingt-onze**
72	**soixante-douze**	92	**quatre-vingt-douze**
73	**soixante-treize**	93	**quatre-vingt-treize**

100	**cent**	200	**deux cents**	300	**trois cents**
101	**cent un**	201	**deux cent un**	301	**trois cent un**
102	**cent deux**	202	**deux cent deux**	302	**trois cent deux**

999	**neuf cent quatre-vingt-dix-neuf**
1.000	**mille**
1.001	**mille un**
2.000	**deux mille**
1.000.000	**un million**
1.000.000.000	**un milliard**

un/une
milliardaire

Pour en savoir plus...

In this episode, Bruno asks Rachid if he is **musulman** (*Muslim*). Here is a list of some world religions and the corresponding adjectives.

le bouddhisme	bouddhiste
le catholicisme	catholique
l'islam (*m.*)	musulman(e)
le judaïsme	juif (juive)
le protestantisme	protestant(e)

Here are the most prevalent religions in France today.

Environ (*About*)
45.000.000 des Français sont catholiques baptisés.
4.000.000 sont musulmans.
1.000.000 sont protestants.
600.000 sont juifs.
500.000 sont bouddhistes.

1. In **quatre-vingts** and in the plural form **cents**, the **s** is dropped when immediately followed by another number.

	quatre-vingt**s**		deux cent**s**
but	quatre-vingt-un	*but*	deux cent un

2. **Mille** is invariable. It does not add **s** in the plural.

   trois mille   onze mille

3. French uses a period for writing larger numbers, where a comma is used in English.

   French: **1.000.000**   English: 1,000,000

   Conversely, French uses a comma for decimals, where English uses a period.

   French: **10,5% (dix virgule cinq pour cent)**   English: 10.5%

4. Larger numbers are written out and spoken as shown in the following examples. In dates, the spelling **mil** is used rather than **mille**.

1789	mil sept cent quatre-vingt-neuf
1954	mil neuf cent cinquante-quatre
2002	deux mil deux
800.550	huit cent mille cinq cent cinquante
2.152.333	deux millions cent cinquante-deux mille trois cent trente-trois

Activités

A. Dans un guide touristique. A well-known tourist guide tells how far each city is from certain other cities. Here are the listings for Marseille and for Alès, a town in the Cévennes region. Tell how many kilometers are between these cities and the others listed.

MODÈLE: Marseille—Paris: 773 km →
Marseille est à sept cent soixante-treize kilomètres de Paris.

MARSEILLE

1. Lyon: 314 km
2. Nice: 191 km
3. Torino: 373 km
4. Toulon: 64 km
5. Toulouse: 405 km

ALÈS

6. Paris: 708 km
7. Albi: 227 km
8. Avignon: 72
9. Montpellier: 70 km
10. Nîmes: 46 km

B. Lisez. (*Read.*) According to *Francoscopie* (*1999*), these are the average readership figures for certain French newspapers and magazines. Read each title and number aloud.

1. *Paris Match:* 4.783.000
2. *Le Figaro:* 1.200.000
3. *Femme actuelle:* 8.834.000
4. *Le Monde:* 1.513.000
5. *Prima:* 4.753.000
6. *Le Nouvel Observateur:* 2.760.000

Pour en savoir plus...

The French use the metric system for measurement. Here are some equivalencies that might be useful for talking about lengths or distances in France.

un millimètre = *.04 inch*
un centimètre = *.4 inch*
un mètre = *3.3 feet*
un kilomètre = *.62 mile*

Les jours de la semaine, les mois de l'année et les dates°

°Les... *Days of the week, months of the year, and dates*

Les jours (*m.*) de la semaine

octobre 2002						
lundi	mardi	mercredi	jeudi	vendredi	samedi	dimanche
	1	2	3	4	5	6
7	8	9	10	11	12	13
14	15	16	17	18	19	20
21	22	23	24	25	26	27
28	29	30	31			

1. On a French calendar, the week begins with Monday (**lundi**) and ends with Saturday and Sunday, which together are referred to as **le week-end**. The word for *today* is **aujourd'hui**.
2. The days of the week begin with a lowercase letter in French.
3. To talk about an event that takes place regularly on the same day each week, use the definite article.

J'ai cours de français **le** lundi. — *I have French class on Mondays.*
Le week-end, je ne travaille pas. — *I don't work on the weekend (on weekends).*

Les mois (*m.*) de l'année

Months, like days of the week, begin with a lowercase letter in French.

janvier	**avril**	**juillet**	**octobre**
février	**mai**	**août**	**novembre**
mars	**juin**	**septembre**	**décembre**

You may have noticed there are two words for *year* in French: **l'an** (*m.*) and **l'année** (*f.*). **An** emphasizes discrete units of time (**deux ans**), whereas **année** emphasizes the duration of time. (**Il passe** [*is spending*] **l'année en France.**) For now, just use examples in the textbook as your guide.

Notez bien!

To say that something happens in a particular month, use **en**.

Je commence mes études **en septembre**. *I begin my studies in September.*

Les dates (*f.*)

Dates in French are expressed with the number first, then the month. Use **le premier** (*the first*) for the first of a month. Other dates are expressed with the cardinal number.

C'est **le premier janvier**! — *It's the first of January!*

Mon anniversaire, c'est **le deux avril**. — *My birthday is on April second.*

Langage fonctionnel

Pour parler du jour et de la date

Pour parler du jour

Quel jour sommes-nous aujourd'hui?	*What day is it today?*
Aujourd'hui, c'est (lundi).	*Today is (Monday).*
Nous sommes aujourd'hui (lundi).	*Today is (Monday).*

Pour parler de la date

Quelle est la date (aujourd'hui, de ton anniversaire, etc.)?	*What is the date (today, of your birthday, etc.)?*
Nous sommes le combien aujourd'hui?	*What's the date today?*
Aujourd'hui, c'est le (deux février).	*Today is (February 2nd).*
La date (de mon anniversaire), c'est le (dix-neuf octobre).	*The date (of my birthday) is October 19th.*
Nous sommes le (quinze juin) aujourd'hui.	*Today is (June 15th).*

To talk about when a person was born, say **Il est né (Elle est née)** and add the date. To talk about when a person died, say **Il est mort (Elle est morte)** and add the date.

Le grand-père **est mort** en 1999.	*The grandfather died in 1999.*
Sa femme **est morte** le 5 juin, 2000.	*His wife died on June 5, 2000.*
Brigitte **est née** le 7 juillet, 2000.	*Brigitte was born on July 7, 2000.*

Activités

A. Identifiez. Identify the dates.

MODÈLE: your birthday →
C'est le 2 avril 1982.

1. your birthday
2. tomorrow
3. the date of your next exam
4. the beginning and ending dates of your next school vacation
5. an important date in your life

B. Quelle date? On what date and day of the week do the following events fall this year? Use a calendar for this school year, and work with a partner. Follow the model.

MODÈLE: É1: Quelle est la date de la fête nationale des États-Unis?
É2: C'est le 4 juillet. Ça tombe (*It falls on*) un mardi.

Quelle est la date

1. de votre anniversaire (*birthday*)?
2. de la fin (*end*) du semestre ou du trimestre?
3. de l'anniversaire d'un ami / d'une amie
4. de l'anniversaire de Martin Luther King, Jr.?
5. du nouvel an (*New Year*)?
6. aujourd'hui?

C. Détails biographiques. Here are the birth and death dates for some famous French figures. Read the dates. Follow the model.

MODÈLE: Claude Debussy: 22.8.1862–25.3.1918 →
Claude Debussy est né le vingt-deux août mil huit cent soixante-deux.
Il est mort le vingt-cinq mars mil neuf cent dix-huit.

1. Marie Curie: 7.11.1867–4.7.1934
2. Louis Pasteur: 27.12.1822–28.9.1895
3. Voltaire: 21.11.1694–30.5.1778
4. Charles de Gaulle: 22.11.1890–9.11.1970
5. René Descartes: 31.3.1596–11.2.1650

D. Rendez-vous et activités. (*Meetings and activities.*) Ask your partner questions to find out the following information.

1. what day of the week it is today
2. whether he/she has any meetings (**rendez-vous**) today
3. what meetings or activities he/she has during (**pendant**) the week
4. if he/she has any meetings or activities on weekends
5. which day of the week he/she prefers

Visionnement 1

Notez bien!

You have already learned that **aller** + infinitive means *to be going to do something.*

Je **vais appeler**. *I'm going to call.*

The construction **venir de** + infinitive works the same way but means *to have just done something.* This is sometimes referred to as the immediate past.

Hélène **vient d'arriver**. *Hélène (has) just arrived.*

Martine **vient de trouver** le médaillon. *Martine (has) just found the locket.*

Avant de visionner

Qu'est-ce que cela veut dire? (*What does it mean?*) In Episode 4, Rachid has the following conversation with Martine. Read the dialogue and then choose the most probable meaning of each of the sentences containing the word **appeler**, which means *to call.*

MARTINE: Ta femme vient d'appeler.
RACHID: Ma femme?
MARTINE: Oui... Il y a un problème?
RACHID: Sonia n'aime pas Paris. ...
MARTINE: (*donne son téléphone portable à Rachid*) Appelle ta femme.

1. Ta femme vient d'appeler.
   - **a.** Your wife is going to call.
   - **b.** Your wife just called.
   - **c.** Your wife is coming to the studio.
2. Appelle ta femme.
   - **a.** Are you going to call your wife?
   - **b.** Your wife is calling.
   - **c.** Call your wife.

Observez!

Now watch Episode 4. As you watch, try to fill in more details about Rachid.

- Where do Rachid's parents come from?
- What is Rachid's father's religion? What might Rachid's mother's religion be?

Vocabulaire relatif à l'épisode

le jarret de porc aux lentilles	*ham hocks with lentils*
l'alcool	*alcohol*
le cochon	*pig; pork*
le jambon	*ham*
des nouvelles	*news*
tu l'attends	*you'll wait for her*

Après le visionnement

A. Un résumé. Fill in the blanks to finish the summary of events in Episode 4.

Vocabulaire utile: arrive, la cafétéria, l'école, la femme, un hamburger, lui, le mari, n'aime pas, séparés

Rachid et Bruno sont à _____[1]. Le chef de cuisine recommande le jarret de porc, mais Rachid commande[a] _____[2]. Martine _____[3] et annonce que _____[4] de Rachid vient d'appeler. Rachid explique que[b] Sonia _____[5] Paris. Rachid et

[a] *orders* [b] explique... *explains that*

Sonia sont ______[6]. À la fin de la journée,[c] Rachid va chercher Yasmine à ______[7]. Camille va avec ______[8].

[c]À… At the end of the day

B. Réfléchissez. (*Think.*) What type of relationship exists between Martine and Rachid? Is it professional (**un rapport professionnel**) or personal (**un rapport personnel**)? Explain your answer in French, using examples from the episode. Combine appropriate sentence fragments to form your examples.

MODÈLE: Martine et Rachid ont un rapport…
Par exemple, Martine…

	donne un conseil (*gives advice*) à	
	est la productrice de l'émission	
	montre (*shows*) son intérêt pour	«Bonjour!»
Martine	parle de sa (*his*) famille avec	Camille
Rachid	parle de soucis (*worries*) personnels à	Martine
	pose (*asks*) des questions à	Rachid
	présente le nouveau reporter, Rachid, à	
	travaille pour	

Structure 12

Les adjectifs possessifs; la possession avec de

Expressing possession

—Tu es musulman, je suppose? Pas d'alcool, pas de cochon…

—**Mon** père est algérien et musulman. Et **ma** mère est bretonne et elle adore le jambon! Comme ça, il y a les deux côtés.

When Rachid describes his family, he uses possessive adjectives▲ to designate his father and his mother.

Pour en savoir plus…

France is divided into a number of provinces that represent administrative divisions and that each have their own distinct history and traditions. Some provinces you may have heard of are **l'Alsace** (*f.*), **la Bretagne**, **la Normandie**, and **la Provence**. The corresponding adjectives are **alsacien(ne)**, **breton(ne)**, **normand(e)**, and **provençal(e)**.

Les adjectifs possessifs

mon	père	**ma**	mère	**mes**	parents	*my*
ton	père	**ta**	mère	**tes**	parents	*your*
son	père	**sa**	mère	**ses**	parents	*his/her/its/one's*
notre	père	**notre**	mère	**nos**	parents	*our*
votre	père	**votre**	mère	**vos**	parents	*your*
leur	père	**leur**	mère	**leurs**	parents	*their*

1. The form of the possessive adjective (**mon** or **ma**, for example) depends on the gender and number of the noun it modifies. When Rachid says *my father,* he uses **mon** (because he is referring to **le père**, a masculine noun); when he says *my mother,* he uses **ma** (because **la mère** is a feminine noun).

Appelle **ta** femme.	*Call your wife.*
Je vais chercher **ma** fille à l'école Bullier.	*I'm going to pick up my daughter at the Bullier School.*
Ton bureau, il est là.	*Your desk is over there.*

2. Before a feminine noun beginning with a vowel sound, the forms **mon**, **ton**, **son** are used.

C'est **mon** amie Yasmine.	*This is my friend Yasmine.*
Est-ce que c'est **ton** école?	*Is that your school?*
Jeanne raconte **son** histoire et Fergus raconte **son** histoire.	*Jeanne tells her story and Fergus tells his story.*

La possession avec *de*

Another way of expressing possession is by joining two nouns with **de**.

le bureau **de** Bruno	*Bruno's desk (literally, the desk of Bruno)*
le médaillon **de** Camille	*Camille's locket*
la régie **du** studio	*the studio's control room*

Activités

A. Précisions sur l'Épisode 4. Tell about Rachid's day at Canal 7 using possessive adjectives to complete the sentences.

Bruno regarde la photo sur _____[1] bureau. C'est la photo de la femme de Rachid et de _____[2] enfant. _____[3] famille est petite. À la cafétéria, Rachid dit[a] à Bruno: « _____[4] père est algérien et musulman. Et _____[5] mère est bretonne...» À table, Martine dit à Rachid: « _____[6] femme vient d'appeler.» Rachid est surpris. Il explique que Sonia n'aime pas Paris. _____[7] ville préférée est Marseille parce que[b] _____[8] amis et _____[9] famille habitent à Marseille. Après, Camille invite Rachid à rentrer[c] à Paris dans _____[10] auto (*f.*).

[a]*says* [b]parce... *because* [c]*return*

B. Possessions. Answer the following questions according to the model.

MODÈLE: Est-ce que tes cousines aiment tes livres? Non, elles... →
Non, elles aiment leurs livres.

1. Est-ce que vous regardez la télévision de vos cousins?
   Non, nous...
2. Est-ce que tu écoutes les CD de tes parents?
   Non, j'...
3. Est-ce que j'emploie l'ordinateur de mon frère?
   Non, tu...
4. Est-ce que nous avons besoin du livre de notre grand-mère?
   Non, vous...
5. Est-ce que vous cherchez les calculatrices du professeur?
   Non, nous...
6. Est-ce que les étudiants aiment le professeur d'une autre classe?
   Non, ils...

C. À qui est-ce? (*Whose is it?*) Your partner will ask a question and you will answer. Follow the model, using words from the vocabulary list.

MODÈLE: le hamburger / Camille / Rachid →
É1: Est-ce le hamburger de Camille?
É2: Non, c'est le hamburger de Rachid. C'est son hamburger.

1. les deux bureaux / Bruno et Camille / Bruno et Rachid
2. le sac à dos / Rachid / Yasmine
3. le médaillon / Bruno / Camille
4. les microphones / Bruno et Rachid / Bruno et Camille
5. le téléphone portable / Camille / Sonia
6. la femme / Bruno / Rachid
7. l'amie / Yasmine / Bruno et Camille

Structure 13

Le verbe *avoir*; *il y a* et *il n'y a pas de*; expressions avec *avoir*

Expressing possession and physical conditions

—Sonia n'aime pas Paris. Elle **a** froid. Elle n'**a** pas sa famille...

In this episode, Rachid explains why his wife, Sonia, doesn't like Paris. The highlighted words in what he says are a form of the verb **avoir**, which means *to have.* It is also used in idiomatic expressions, for example, **avoir froid** (*to be cold*).

Le verbe *avoir*

avoir (*to have*)			
j'	**ai**	nous	**avons**
tu	**as**	vous	**avez**
il, elle, on	**a**	ils, elles	**ont**

1. The most common use of **avoir** means *to have.*

   Vous **avez** un ordinateur? — *Do you have a computer?*

2. After a negative form of **avoir**, the indefinite articles **un**, **une**, **des** all become **de** (**d'** before a vowel sound).

   Sonia **n'a pas de** famille à Paris. — *Sonia doesn't have any family in Paris.*

   Désolé! Nous **n'avons pas d'**ordinateur. — *Sorry! We don't have a computer.*

Pour en savoir plus...

In rapid, spoken French, **il y a** becomes **i' y a**; **il n'y a pas** may be heard as **i' y a pas** or even **y a pas**.

Il y a et *il n'y a pas de*

1. You already know that the expression **il y a** means *there is, there are.*

   Il y a des studios et une cantine à Canal 7. — *There are studios and a cafeteria at Channel 7.*

   Est-ce qu'**il y a** des salles de répétition aussi? — *Are there also rehearsal rooms?*

2. In the negative, **il y a** becomes **il n'y a pas**, and **un**, **une**, **des** become **de/d'**.

Non, **il n'y a pas de** salles de répétition à Canal 7.	*No, there are no rehearsal rooms at Channel 7.*
Il **n'y a pas de** boutique non plus.	*There is no small store either.*
Il **n'y a pas d'**ordinateur ici?	*There's no computer here?*

Expressions avec *avoir*

1. Some common idiomatic expressions with **avoir** are the following.

avoir chaud	*to be hot*	On **a** souvent **chaud** en juillet.
avoir froid	*to be cold*	Hélène **a froid** à Montréal en janvier.
avoir faim	*to be hungry*	Camille **a faim**, alors (*so*) elle va dans un restaurant.
avoir soif	*to be thirsty*	Rachid **a soif**. Il désire de l'eau (*water*).
avoir honte (de)	*to be ashamed (of)*	Est-ce que Camille **a honte** de sa famille?
avoir peur (de)	*to be afraid (of)*	Yasmine **a peur** d'aller à l'école.
avoir besoin de	*to need*	Rachid **a besoin** d'un téléphone pour appeler sa femme.
avoir envie de	*to feel like, want*	Yasmine **a envie de** rentrer à la maison.
avoir l'air	*to look, seem*	La maîtresse **a l'air** sympa.
avoir... ans	*to be . . . years old*	Yasmine **a six ans**.

2. **Avoir besoin de** and **avoir envie de** can be followed by either an infinitive or a noun. **Avoir honte** and **avoir peur** can be used either alone or with **de** + infinitive or **de** + noun.

Bruno **n'a pas envie de travailler**.	*Bruno doesn't feel like working.*
Il **a besoin de vacances**.	*He needs a vacation.*
Il va avec sa cousine parce qu' **elle a peur de voyager** seule.	*He's going with his cousin because she's afraid of traveling alone.*

3. To ask for someone's age in French, use the question **Quel âge avez-vous?** (**a-t-il? ont-elles?** etc.).

Quel âge a Camille?	*How old is Camille?*
Elle **a vingt-sept ans**.	*She's twenty-seven years old.*

Pour en savoir plus...

To talk about a person's age in comparison to his or her brothers and sisters, you can use the following nouns.

l'aîné(e)	*eldest*
le cadet / la cadette	*youngest*
le jumeau / la jumelle	*twin*

Catherine est **l'aînée** et Chloé est **la cadette**. Bruno et Natalie sont **jumeaux**. *Catherine is the eldest and Chloé is the youngest. Bruno and Natalie are twins.*

Activités

A. On a... et on n'a pas... ! Tell what the following people have and don't have using the correct forms of **avoir**.

MODÈLE: Yasmine / sac à dos / ordinateur →
Yasmine a un sac à dos. Elle n'a pas d'ordinateur.

1. Camille et Bruno / table / chaises
2. Bruno / béret / livres

3. Camille / microphone / médaillon
4. Rachid / ordinateur / crayon

B. Des photos. Two students are looking at a photo album. With a partner, create their dialogue by making complete sentences with the elements given. Follow the model.

MODÈLE: —Sur cette photo, il y / avoir / nos cousins. Ils / avoir / seize ans et douze ans.
—Est-ce que vous / avoir / des cousines aussi? →
É1: Sur cette photo, il y a nos cousins. Ils ont seize ans et douze ans.
É2: Est-ce que vous avez des cousines aussi?

1. —Sur cette photo, je / avoir / peur.
   —Pourquoi? Qu'est-ce qu'il y / avoir? (*Why? What's the matter?*)
2. —Ma mère / avoir / deux sœurs.
   —Est-ce que ses sœurs / avoir / des enfants aussi?
3. —Voici mon grand-père. Il / avoir / 86 ans.
   —Est-ce que tu / avoir / encore (*still*) ta grand-mère?
4. —Sur cette photo, nous / avoir / chaud.
   —Je suppose que vous / avoir / envie de nager (*to swim*)?

C. La vie des étudiants. (*Students' lives.*) Use one of the **avoir** expressions to talk about the following situations. There is often more than one possible answer.

MODÈLE: Melissa a une mauvaise note (*grade*) en géographie. →
Elle a honte. (Elle a besoin d'étudier.)

1. Paul cherche un coca.
2. Cinquante étudiants sont dans une petite salle de classe en août.
3. Nous allons à la bibliothèque.
4. Carole étudie le français.
5. Anne et Isabelle ne sont pas de bonnes étudiantes.
6. Vous étudiez au Canada en janvier.
7. Les étudiants vont au restaurant universitaire.
8. Un homme demande l'âge d'un enfant. Il dit...

Pour en savoir plus...

A number of adjectives that end in **-eux/-euse** are cognates of English adjectives that end in *-ous*.

généreux/euse	*generous*
nerveux/euse	*nervous*
sérieux/euse	*serious*

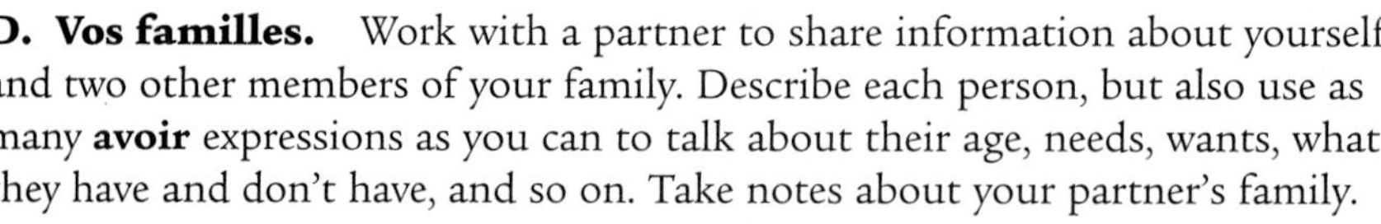

D. Vos familles. Work with a partner to share information about yourself and two other members of your family. Describe each person, but also use as many **avoir** expressions as you can to talk about their age, needs, wants, what they have and don't have, and so on. Take notes about your partner's family.

MODÈLE: Mon frère, Mike, a vingt-trois ans. Il est sympa, mais il n'est pas généreux. Il a honte de travailler dans un petit restaurant, mais c'est un bon job pour lui, parce qu'il a toujours faim. Il a envie d'aller à l'université, mais il a peur des professeurs et il n'a pas d'argent (*money*)!

When you have finished taking notes on your partner's family, describe them to another pair of students.

Regards sur la culture

La diversité de la France

Foreigners often have a view of France and French culture that doesn't actually match the truth; for them, Paris tends to represent the whole of France. In fact, the great diversity of the country makes it rather difficult to generalize about any aspect of culture.

- Geographically, France is one of the most diverse countries in Europe. It has warm Mediterranean coasts, the highest mountains on the continent, a range of extinct volcanoes, vast plains, deep canyons, and even landscapes that look like Arizona. Paris has a damp climate that is influenced by the Atlantic Ocean, whereas Marseille, located on the Mediterranean, in some ways is more like southern California than it is like Paris.

Cirque de Gavarnie, Pyrénées

Pointe du Raz, Bretagne

Èze-sur-Mer, Côte d'Azur

- This geographical diversity helps to explain the cultural diversity of France. Agriculture, architecture, and local traditions vary along with the landscapes. It is often clear when one has traveled from one province to the next, because the structure of the farm buildings, the layout of the villages, and the shapes of the fields have changed.

La Beauce

Le Périgord

L'Alsace

- The cuisine of the different regions of France varies, too. In the Southwest of France, food is traditionally cooked with goose fat, whereas in Normandy, butter is the essential cooking ingredient, and in Provence, it is olive oil.
- Recent immigration to France has added another level of diversity. The largest groups to arrive in France over the past fifty years have been the Spanish, the Portuguese, and, most recently, people from the Maghreb, which are the former French colonies of Morocco, Algeria, and Tunisia. Although these North Africans are Muslims, many of them have begun to assimilate into French society just as earlier groups did.

Considérez

Try to explain why the two farms pictured in this section would probably not be located in the regions that are represented in the photographs of the Pyrenees, Brittany, and the Riviera. Think about building materials, the layout of the farms, and the kind of agriculture that is possible in these places.

Structure 14

Questions avec inversion et avec où, *quand, pourquoi, comment, combien de*

Asking for specific information

—Les Français aujourd'hui **sont-ils** capables de reconnaître un bon pain?

—**Pourquoi** maman n'est pas là?

—C'est, euh, maman est fatiguée à cause du déménagement. Alors, elle se repose.

—Mais **où est-elle? Où est maman?**

Questions avec inversion

In a French declarative sentence, as in English, the subject is placed before the verb. The verb may or may not be followed by a complement.

SUJET	VERBE	COMPLÉMENT
Elle	vient.	
Tu	aimes	ta fille.

This word order is maintained in the three types of yes/no questions you have studied.

		SUJET	VERBE	COMPLÉMENT	
Rising intonation		Elle	vient?		
		Tu	aimes	ta fille?	
Est-ce que	Est-ce qu'	elle	vient?		
	Est-ce que	tu	aimes	ta fille?	
Tag		Elle	vient,		n'est-ce pas?
		Tu	aimes	ta fille,	je suppose?

1. Another way of asking yes/no questions is to place the verb before the subject, joined by a hyphen. This change in word order is known as *inversion*.

VERBE	SUJET	COMPLÉMENT
Vient-	elle?	
Aimes-	tu	ta fille?
Parlez-	vous	de Sonia?

2. In the **il/elle/on** form, when the verb ends in a vowel, **-t-**, is inserted between the verb and the subject.

Parle-t-il français?	*Does he speak French?*
Va-t-elle au cinéma?	*Is she going to the movies?*

3. Inversion is not made with a noun. Instead, it is made with the corresponding pronoun. Thus, the subject is mentioned twice, once as a noun before the verb, and then as a pronoun after the verb.

Camille **regarde-t-elle** les spectateurs?	*Is Camille watching the spectators?*
Bruno et Rachid **ont-ils** le même bureau?	*Do Bruno and Rachid have the same office?*

4. For yes/no questions with verb + infinitive contructions, inversion is performed on the first verb and the infinitive follows.

Aimez-vous habiter à Marseille? — *Do you like living in Marseille?*
Déteste-t-il porter un béret? — *Does he hate wearing a beret?*
Va-t-il identifier le pain artisanal? — *Will he identify the handmade bread?*
Vient-elle d'arriver? — *Did she just arrive?*

Questions avec *où, quand, pourquoi, comment, combien de*

Up until now, you have studied yes/no questions. Another type of question asks for information.

où	*where*
quand	*when*
pourquoi	*why*
comment	*how*
combien de	*how much; how many*

Information questions are normally formed with either **est-ce que** or inversion. Study the word order in these model sentences.

1. Information questions with **est-ce que**

MOT(S) INTERROGATIF(S)		SUJET	VERBE	COMPLÉMENT
Où	est-ce que	tu	vas?	
Quand	est-ce que	tu	invites	ton ami à dîner?
Pourquoi	est-ce qu'	elle	vient?	
Comment	est-ce que	tu	viens?	
Combien d'étudiants	est-ce qu'	il	y a	dans la classe?

2. Information questions with inversion

MOT(S) INTERROGATIF(S)	VERBE	SUJET	COMPLÉMENT
Où	vas-	tu?	
Quand	invites-	tu	ton ami à dîner?
Pourquoi	vient-	elle?	
Comment	viens-	tu?	
Combien d'étudiants	y a-t-	il	dans la classe?

Pour en savoir plus...

Information questions with rising intonation are characteristic of informal spoken French. It is recommended that you not use this form, but you have heard the following examples in the film.

On va où? *Where are we going?*
Elle est où? *Where is she?*

Note that with information questions (except with **pourquoi**), inversion may be made with a proper noun, if that noun is at the end of the sentence.

Où est Camille? — *Where's Camille?*
Comment va Bruno? — *How is Bruno doing?*

Activités

A. À la cantine. (*In the cafeteria.*) Using inversion, transform the following statements about the cafeteria scene in Episode 4 into yes/no questions.

MODÈLE: Bruno parle au chef de cuisine. →
Bruno parle-t-il au chef de cuisine?

1. Rachid et Bruno sont devant le chef de cuisine. **2.** Rachid a soif. **3.** Martine vient d'arriver. **4.** Martine a un petit pain. **5.** Sonia regarde son téléphone. **6.** Camille et Rachid vont chercher Yasmine à l'école.

B. La bonne question. (*The right question.*) Use **où**, **quand**, **pourquoi**, **comment**, or **combien de** to form a question that would prompt the italicized part of each given answer. Be careful about changing pronouns where necessary.

MODÈLE: Notre professeur est *au restaurant* maintenant. →
Où est votre professeur maintenant?

1. Les cours commencent *en septembre*. **2.** Je viens à l'université *en autobus*. **3.** Il y a *vingt étudiants* dans notre classe. **4.** Nous aimons parler en classe *parce que le sujet est intéressant*. **5.** J'aime ce (*this*) cours *parce que les étudiants sont sympathiques*. **6.** Nous avons cinq grandes tables *dans la salle de classe*. **7.** *Le lundi*, nous allons au cinéma. **8.** Les étudiants travaillent *à la bibliothèque*.

Notez bien!

The answer to a question asking **pourquoi** often includes the expression **parce que** (*because*).

—Pourquoi est-ce que tu viens en autobus?	*Why do you come by bus?*
—**Parce que** c'est trop loin pour venir à pied.	*Because it's too far to come on foot.*

C. Parent et enfant. A child just arrived home from school and is asking his/her parent lots of questions. Play the roles in pairs. Use inversion with **aller** + infinitive to ask questions and use **venir** + **de** + infinitive for the answers.

MODÈLE: nous / visiter le Jardin des Plantes →
ENFANT: Allons-nous visiter le Jardin des Plantes?
PARENT: Non, chérie, nous venons de visiter le Jardin des Plantes hier.

1. tu / parler avec grand-mère
2. tu / regarder mon livre
3. grand-père / écouter un reportage à la radio
4. mon ami Benoît / téléphoner
5. tu / donner un bisou (*a kiss*) à grand-mère
6. grand-mère et toi / téléphoner à tante Anne

D. Un étudiant / Une étudiante typique? Use question words and inversion to interview your partner.

1. Find out why he/she is studying French.
2. Find out how many courses he/she has.
3. Find out when (which days) he/she goes to class.
4. Find out how he/she likes to spend weekends.
5. Find out where he/she works and when.
6. Find out whether he/she likes to do something you like to do.
7. Find out whether he/she dislikes something you dislike.
8. What else can you find out?

When you have finished interviewing, present your partner to the class. Tally the information. What are the most typical responses? Are you typical?

Visionnement 2

Avant de visionner

A. J'ai faim! Bruno and Rachid decide to have lunch in the cafeteria. Here is their conversation with the chef. Stage instructions are included to portray the chef's reactions. Read the dialogue and then answer the question.

CUISINIER: Alors, pour aujourd'hui, en plat principal,[a] du jarret de porc aux lentilles! Vachement[b] bon, hein!

BRUNO: Ah bien, bien. Ça marche![c]

RACHID: Un hamburger, c'est possible?

CUISINIER (*se rembrunit*[d]): Oh. D'accord! (*Il grommelle en s'éloignant.*[e])

[a]*en... as a main course* [b]*Very* [c]*Ça... That works (for me)* [d]*se... frowning* [e]*Il... He grumbles as he walks off.*

Pourquoi le cuisinier se rembrunit-il et grommelle-t-il? Il y a 2 ou 3 raisons.

a. Préparer un hamburger, c'est beaucoup (*a lot*) de travail.
b. Il pense que Rachid n'apprécie pas ses efforts culinaires.
c. Il est toujours de mauvaise humeur (*in a bad mood*).
d. Il pense que Rachid préfère un plat américain à un plat français.
e. Certains Français sont parfois impatients avec les gens (*people*) d'origine étrangère.

B. La culture musulmane? After ordering, Rachid and Bruno discuss their food preferences. Read their exchange and reflect on the cultural information it contains. Then answer the questions.

RACHID: Bonjour. Un verre d'eau,[a] s'il vous plaît. Merci.

BRUNO: Tu es musulman, je suppose? Pas d'alcool, pas de cochon...

RACHID: Mon père est algérien et musulman. Et ma mère est bretonne[b] et elle adore le jambon[c]!...

[a]*Un... A glass of water* [b]*Breton, from Brittany (a region in the northwestern part of France)* [c]*ham*

1. Pourquoi Bruno pense-t-il que Rachid est musulman?
2. Quelles viandes et boissons (*Which meats and drinks*) ne sont probablement pas permises (*permitted*) pour une personne musulmane?

Observez!

Consider the cultural information explained in **Regards sur la culture**. Then watch Episode 4 again, and answer the following questions.

- Why does Sonia not like Paris? What difference(s) between Marseille and Paris are implied by this explanation?

- Listen for the name and location of Yasmine's school. Locate the neighborhood on a map of Paris or on the map in **Visionnement 2** in Chapter 1. Which monuments and institutions are found near the school?

Après le visionnement

Do the activity for **Visionnement 2** in the Workbook and Laboratory Manual.

Synthèse: Lecture

Mise en contexte

The notion of family in France has for centuries been the traditional dual-parent household and a closely knit extended family. In this tradition, husbands support the family, wives stay at home and raise the children, the whole family sits down to meals together, the children cooperate rather than compete, and so on. Marriage, children, and family are almost synonymous in this tradition, and it is, of course, a generalization.

Stratégie pour mieux lire
Recognizing cognates

Scientific texts tend to use a vocabulary that is high in cognate forms. This text draws on sociological terminology that may be familiar to you because of its similarity to English. Skim the passage, paying particular attention to familiar words and cognates. Then predict which of the following sentences will best summarize the gist of the entire text.

1. L'institution de la famille reste (*remains*) très importante pour la majorité des Français.
2. La diversité de la famille française résulte en une déstabilisation de la société.
3. La famille française assume (*takes on*) une multiplicité de configurations.

Now read the whole text through and see if your prediction is correct.

La famille française du XXIe siècle°

La... The French family in the 21st century

Introduction

La famille française se caractérise par la tradition et la nouveauté.[1] Elle reste la cellule[2] de la vie[3] sociale et on continue à célébrer la famille (fête des mères, fête des pères). Mais on aurait tort[4] de généraliser.

Réflexion de la société

La famille française reflète la diversité des conditions socio-économiques de la société entière. Sous l'influence des conditions de vie, elle se transforme. Il y a des crises internes et les conflits entre générations. La femme a une vie plus indépendante qu'autrefois;[5] les enfants s'émancipent de plus en plus tôt.[6]

Un déjeuner un plein air

La transformation récente

Depuis[7] trente ans, le nombre des mariages diminue. Parallèlement, le nombre des divorces augmente. Autre phénomène récent: le développement de l'union libre ou cohabitation. Ce sont près de 17% des couples qui cohabitent. Conséquence de ce phénomène: 30% des naissances sont des naissances hors[8] mariage. Il faut ajouter[9] aussi la multiplication des familles monoparentales. Ces développements révèlent la coexistence de conceptions très différentes de la vie familiale.

Adapté du *Nouveau Guide France*

[1]*change* [2]*nucleus* [3]*life* [4]*on... one would be mistaken* [5]*than before* [6]*de... earlier and earlier* [7]*For* [8]*outside of* [9]*Il... One must add*

Après la lecture

A. Confirmation. Now that you have read the selection, go back to the prereading strategy activity and see if you would still choose the same paraphrase to summarize the gist of the article. How much did it help you to check for cognates before reading the entire passage? What new cognates did you notice as you read the whole article?

B. Tradition ou nouveauté? Tell whether each sentence describes the traditional family (**C'est la famille traditionnelle**), the "new" family (**C'est la nouvelle famille**), or both (**Ce sont les deux**).

1. La femme reste à la maison.
2. Les enfants s'émancipent plus tôt.

3. L'union libre est fréquente. **4.** Les fêtes familiales sont célébrées. **5.** La famille monoparentale est ordinaire. **6.** La famille est la cellule de la vie sociale.

C. **Expliquez.** Name three factors that explain the evolution of the French family.

D. **Jugements.** What is the author's attitude toward the evolution of the French family? Does he/she approve of the "new" family, disapprove, or remain neutral? Explain.

À écrire

Do **À écrire** for Chapter 4 in the Workbook and Laboratory Manual.

Vocabulaire

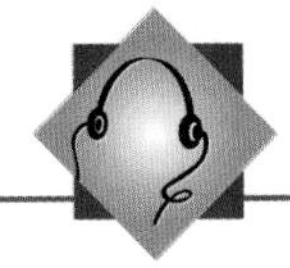

Les parents

le beau-frère (les beaux-frères)	stepbrother, brother-in-law
le beau-père (les beaux-pères)	stepfather; father-in-law
la belle-mère (les belles-mères)	stepmother; mother-in-law
la belle-sœur (les belles-sœurs)	stepsister; sister-in-law
la femme	wife
la fille	daughter
le fils	son
le frère	brother
la grand-mère (les grands-mères)	grandmother
le grand-père (les grands-pères)	grandfather
le mari	husband
la mère	mother
le neveu	nephew
la nièce	niece
l'oncle (*m.*)	uncle
les parents (*m. pl.*)	parents; relatives
le père	father
la petite-fille (les petites-filles)	granddaughter
le petit-fils (les petits-fils)	grandson
la sœur	sister
la tante	aunt

MOTS APPARENTÉS: **le cousin, la cousine, les grands-parents**

À REVOIR: **les enfants** (*m., f.*)

L'état civil

célibataire	single
Ils vivent en union libre.	They are living together (without marriage).
veuf (veuve)	widowed

MOTS APPARENTÉS: **marié(e), divorcé(e)**

Les nombres à partir de 60

soixante, soixante-dix, quatre-vingts, quatre-vingt-dix, cent, mille, un million, un milliard

L'année

janvier, février, mars, avril, mai, juin, juillet, août, septembre, octobre, novembre, décembre

un an	year	**un anniversaire**	birthday
une année	year	**un mois**	month

La semaine

lundi, mardi, mercredi, jeudi, vendredi, samedi, dimanche

aujourd'hui	today	**la semaine**	week

MOT APPARENTÉ: **le week-end**

Les adjectifs possessifs

mon, ma, mes	my	**notre, notre, nos**	our
ton, ta, tes	your	**votre, votre, vos**	your
son, sa, ses	his; her; its; one's	**leur, leur, leurs**	their

Verbes

avoir	to have
avoir... ans	to be . . . years old
avoir besoin de	to need
avoir chaud	to be hot
avoir envie de	to feel like, want
avoir faim	to be hungry
avoir froid	to be cold
avoir honte (de)	to be ashamed (of)
avoir l'air	to look, seem
avoir peur (de)	to be afraid (of)
avoir soif	to be thirsty
il n'y a pas de	there is/are not any
Quel âge avez-vous (a-t-il, etc.)?	How old are you (is he, etc.)?

À REVOIR: **il y a**

Questions

où	where	**comment**	how
quand	when	**combien de**	how many; how much
pourquoi	why		

À REVOIR: **Est-ce que... ?, je suppose?, n'est-ce pas?**

Autres expressions utiles

il/elle s'appelle	his/her name is	**le premier**	first (*of a month*)
parce que	because		

Chapitre 5

Secrets

OBJECTIFS

In this episode, you will

- meet Camille's mother
- learn more about Camille's family

In this chapter, you will

- describe houses, rooms, and furnishings
- tell time
- express and respond to apologies
- talk about everyday activities
- ask about and identify specific people and things
- learn more about the gender of nouns and how to form the plural of some nouns
- learn about common French family customs and their diversity from region to region

Vocabulaire en contexte

La maison: les pièces et les meubles°

La... *The house: Rooms and furniture*

Voici **l'appartement** (*m.*) de Camille.

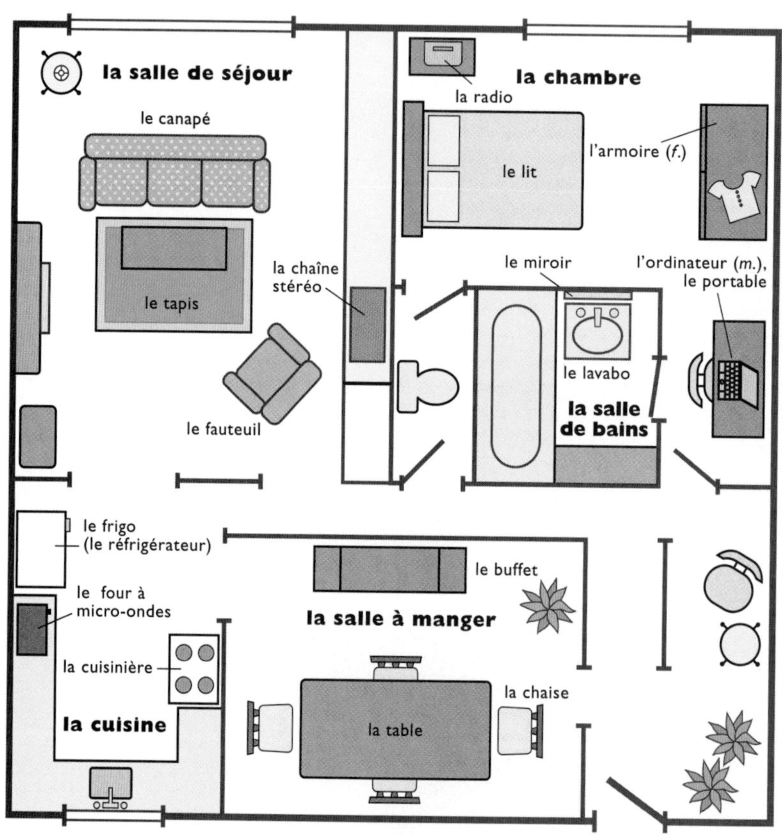

Pour en savoir plus...

To gain access to a French apartment building, you often need to enter a code into an electronic security box. When guests are invited, they must be given the code in order to enter on their own. When you enter a French building, you are on the ground floor, **le rez-de-chaussée**. The next floor up is **le premier étage** (*the first floor*), the next is **le deuxième étage** (*the second floor*), and so on.*

L'appartement de Camille se trouve au **rez-de-chaussée** d'**un immeuble** parisien. C'est un deux-pièces.†

Activités

A. Identifiez. Identify two or three pieces of furniture or other objects you have in different rooms. If your residence doesn't have one of those rooms, use your imagination.

MODÈLE: salle de bains →
Dans la salle de bains, j'ai un lavabo et un miroir.

*You will learn ordinal numbers (first, second, and so on) in Chapter 11.

†Apartments are identified by the number of bedrooms they have in addition to a living area. **Un studio** has no bedroom, **un deux-pièces** has a living area and one bedroom, and so on.

1. salle de séjour
2. chambre
3. cuisine
4. salle à manger
5. sous-sol (*m.*) (*basement*)

B. Où? Complete the following sentences with the name of the appropriate location, based on the drawing of Camille's apartment.

MODÈLE: Camille écoute la radio... →
Camille écoute la radio dans la chambre.

1. Elle parle avec ses amis...
2. Elle prépare des spaghettis...
3. Elle dîne...
4. Ses vêtements (*clothes*) sont...
5. Elle se lave (*washes up*)...

C. Un château en Espagne. Describe your ideal dwelling to your partner. Tell what type of living space it is, where it is located, how many rooms it has, and what type of furniture is in each room.

Vocabulaire utile: à la campagne (*in the country*), en ville, une cheminée (*fireplace*), un lave-vaisselle (*dishwasher*), une piscine (*swimming pool*)

un lave-linge
un sèche-linge
un ascanseur
elevator
une baignoire

MODÈLE: Ma maison idéale est à la campagne. C'est une maison à deux pièces. Il y a une chambre avec un grand lit et deux fenêtres et une salle de séjour avec une cheminée, un canapé et trois fauteuils confortables. En plus, il y a une salle à manger avec une grande table et douze chaises et une grande cuisine avec un frigo, une cuisinière et une table.

Le studio de Chloé Gall

Voici l'appartement de Chloé Gall, la sœur de Bruno. Elle habite **un studio**. Tous° **les meubles** (*m.*) sont dans **la même**° **pièce**.

All / same

Chloé a un vélo, mais elle a aussi **une voiture** dans le garage. C'est une Citroën.*

*A Citroën is a French-made automobile.

Activités

A. Quel appareil? Identify the object that Chloé uses to perform the following activities.

MODÈLE: pour parler à ses amis →
Chloé utilise (*uses*) le téléphone pour parler à ses amis.

1. pour écouter de la musique
2. pour écouter ses messages téléphoniques
3. pour regarder un film
4. pour aller au bureau
5. pour prendre (*to take*) des photos

B. Objets personnels. What objects might be in the apartments of the following people? Name at least two or three items, using vocabulary from this or earlier chapters.

MODÈLE: Mme Renée est actrice. →
Dans son appartement, il y a une grande affiche et des cassettes vidéo avec son nom dessus (*with her name on them*).

1. M. Rodriguez est musicien.
2. M. Armstrong est cycliste.
3. Mme Lumière est photographe.
4. M. Plume est écrivain (*writer*).
5. Mlle Nathan est étudiante.

C. Êtes-vous matérialiste? Tell your partner what you must have in your home to be comfortable and what you can do without. Who is the more materialistic?

MODÈLE: Pour être bien chez moi, j'ai absolument besoin d'un magnétoscope, d'un téléphone et d'un ordinateur. Un appareil photo n'est pas essentiel.

Quelle heure est-il?°

Quelle... *What time is it?*

La journée° typique de Camille et Bruno commence.

day

Il est sept heures:
Camille au maquillage°

Il est **sept heures dix**:
Bruno au maquillage

Il est **sept heures et quart**:
Techniciens sur le plateau°

make-up / set

Il est **sept heures et demie**:
Productrice à la régie°

Il est **huit heures moins le quart**:
Bruno exerce sa voix°

control room / exerce... does voice exercises

Il est **huit heures moins cinq**:
Bruno et Camille sur le plateau

Il est **huit heures**:
Début° de «Bonjour!»

°Beginning

—**À quelle heure** Camille arrive-t-elle sur le plateau?
—Elle arrive sur le plateau **à huit heures moins cinq**.

Il est dix heures **du matin**.

Il est **midi**.

Il est cinq heures **de l'après-midi**.

Quelle heure est-il?

Il est dix heures **du soir**.

Il est **minuit**.

1. To tell someone the time, add minutes to the hour for the first half hour. After the half hour, deduct minutes from the next hour.

Il est **une heure vingt-quatre**.	*It's 1:24 (twenty-four minutes past one).*
Il est **deux heures moins vingt-quatre**.	*It's 1:36 (twenty-four minutes to two).*

2. Special expressions are often used for the quarter hour and half hour.

Il est midi **et demi**.	*It's half past noon.*
Il est une heure **moins le quart**.	*It's a quarter to one.*
Il est une heure **et quart**.	*It's a quarter past one.*

3. The spelling **et demie** is used in most time-related expressions because the word **heure** is feminine. The masculine spelling **et demi** is used for **midi** and **minuit**.

Il est cinq heures **et demie**.	*It's five thirty.*
Il est midi **et demi**.	*It's twelve thirty.*

4. Whereas English uses a colon to show hours and minutes, French uses the abbreviation **h**, standing for **heure(s)**.

8 **h** 20 *8:20* 9 **h** *9:00*

Notez bien!

Three words in French can mean *time*. They are used in different ways.

L'heure (*f.*) is used for the time of day and punctuality.

Quelle **heure** est-il? *What time is it?*

Le train arrive toujours à **l'heure**. *The train always arrives on time.*

La fois is used for how many times something happens.

Je mange trois **fois** par jour. *I eat three times a day.*

Le temps is used for the broader concept of time or the availability of time.

Je n'ai pas **le temps** de parler maintenant. *I don't have time to talk now.*

5. French uses the twenty-four hour clock for train schedules, event times, and appointments. Hours are counted consecutively from 0 h (= **minuit** = *12:00 A.M.*) to 23 h 59 (= 11 h 59 **du soir** = *11:59 P.M.*). Thus, because no ambiguity is possible, the expressions **du matin**, **de l'après-midi**, **du soir**, **midi**, and **minuit** are not necessary.

onze heures du matin	=	11 h	*11:00 A.M.*
onze heures du soir	=	23 h	*11:00 P.M.*

In the 24-hour system, minutes are added to the hour up to the following hour. The quarter hours and half hours are expressed in minutes as well.

3 h 08	trois heures huit	3 h 40	trois heures quarante
3 h 15	trois heures quinze	3 h 45	trois heures quarante-cinq
3 h 30	trois heures trente	3 h 59	trois heures cinquante-neuf

6. To say an event occurs between two times, use **de... à...** .

Le musée est ouvert **de** 10 h **à** 20 h. — *The museum is open from 10:00 A.M. till 8:00 P.M.*

7. Three expressions are used to talk about punctuality.

en avance *early* **à l'heure** *on time* **en retard** *late*

Pierre est **en retard**. — *Pierre is late.*

Langage fonctionnel

Pour exprimer le regret et s'excuser°

°Pour... *Expressing regret and apologizing*

Here are some common ways of expressing regret and excusing yourself.

Expressions de regret ou d'excuse

Excusez-moi. / Excuse-moi.	*Excuse me.*
Pardon.	*Pardon (me).*
(Je suis) désolé(e).	*(I'm) sorry.*

Réponses possibles

Ce n'est pas grave.	*It's okay.*
Ne vous inquiétez pas. / Ne t'inquiète pas.	*Don't worry. Forget it.*
Pas de problème.	*No problem.*

—**Désolé** d'être en retard. *Sorry for being late.*
—**Ne t'inquiète pas.** *Don't worry about it.*

Activités

A. Quelle heure est-il? The following times are shown in English. Your partner will ask you what time it is, using the word **maintenant** (*now*). Answer by saying the time in French.

MODÈLE: 3:20 P.M. →
É1: Quelle heure est-il maintenant?
É2: Il est trois heures vingt de l'après-midi.

1. 8:45 P.M.
2. 6:15 A.M.
3. 12:30 P.M.
4. 4:55 P.M.
5. 12:00 midnight
6. 12:00 noon
7. 11:30 A.M.
8. 1:20 P.M.

B. Les musées. Read aloud the opening and closing times of the following museums for the days indicated. Use the chart to find the correct information.

MODÈLE: le Louvre / lundi →
Le Louvre est ouvert (*open*) lundi de 9 heures à 18 heures.

1. le Mémorial du Martyr Juif Inconnu / mardi
2. le Musée de l'Homme / jeudi
3. le Musée d'Orsay / vendredi
4. l'Institut du Monde Arabe / dimanche
5. le Musée du Vin / samedi
6. le Centre national d'art et de culture Georges Pompidou / mercredi

	L	M	M	J	V	S	D
Louvre	9 h–18 h	–	9 h–21 h 45	9 h–18 h	9 h–18 h	9 h–18 h	9 h–18 h
Mémorial du Martyr Juif Inconnu	10 h–13 h, 14 h–18 h	10 h–13 h, 14 h–18 h	10 h–13 h, 14 h–18 h	10 h–13 h, 14 h–18 h	10 h–13 h, 14 h–16 h 30	–	10 h–13 h, 14 h–18 h
Musée de l'Homme	9 h 45–17 h 15	–	9 h 45–17 h 15	9 h 45–17 h 15	9 h 45–17 h 15	9 h 45–17 h 15	9 h 45–17 h 15
Musée d'Orsay	–	10 h–18 h	10 h–18 h	10 h–21 h 45	10 h–18 h	10 h–18 h	9 h–18 h
Institut du Monde Arabe	–	10 h–18 h	10 h–18 h	10 h–18 h	10 h–18 h	10 h–18 h	10 h–18 h
Musée du Vin	–	10 h–18 h	10 h–18 h	10 h–18 h	10 h–18 h	10 h–18 h	10 h–18 h
Centre... Georges Pompidou	12 h–22 h	–	12 h–22 h	12 h–22 h	12 h–22 h	10 h–22 h	10 h–22 h

C. Fois? Temps? Heure? Fill in the blanks in a logical manner. Use **fois**, **temps**, or **heure(s)**, with an article if necessary.

1. Neuf heures! Les enfants, c'est _____ d'aller au lit!
2. Je suis en avance, alors j'ai _____ de lire un magazine.
3. Paul regarde toujours deux _____ ses films préférés.
4. À quelle _____ dînez-vous d'habitude?
5. Notre _____ est précieux!
6. C'est la première _____ que je mange des escargots!

D. Questions personnelles. Ask your partner questions about what time he/she does things.

Demandez à (*Ask*) votre partenaire à quelle heure il/elle

1. vient à l'université **2.** dîne **3.** travaille **4.** regarde la télévision
5. va en boîte (*goes to a club*)

Demandez-lui aussi s'il / si elle arrive généralement aux rendez-vous à l'heure, en retard ou en avance. Combien de minutes de retard sont acceptables?

E. Allons au cinéma! Using the movie schedule, ask a partner if he/she would like to go to a particular film. Your partner will accept or refuse, and may also use an expression of regret. If your partner refuses and/or apologizes, respond appropriately and try to negotiate another film, time, or date.

MODÈLE: É1: Tu as envie d'aller au cinéma aujourd'hui? Il y a «Cités de la plaine» qui passe au MK2-Beaubourg.
É2: C'est vrai? À quelle heure y a-t-il des séances (*showings*)?
É1: Il y a une séance à dix-neuf heures cinquante.
É2: Désolé. Ça ne marche pas.
É1: Pas de problème. Demain, c'est possible? etc.

FILM	DESCRIPTION	OÙ ET QUAND?
Les âmes perdues (***Lost Souls***)	Film fantastique[a] américain avec Winona Ryder, Ben Chaplin, John Hurt	Georges-V (en VO [version originale])—Tlj[b] à 10 h 35, à 12 h 45, à 15 h, à 19 h 40, à 22 h
Cités de la plaine	Drame français avec Ben, Bernard Trolet	MK2 Beaubourg—Tlj à 11 h 30, à 13 h 30, à 15 h 35, à 17 h 15, à 19 h 50, à 22 h 05
Duos d'un jour	Comédie américaine avec Gwyneth Paltrow, Andre Braugher	Megarama (en VF)—Sam, Dim à 11 h 30; Tlj à 14 h, à 16 h 30, à 19 h 15, à 22 h
Esperanza et ses saints	Comédie mexicaine avec Dolores Heredia	Latina (en VO)—Mer, Ven, Sam, Dim, Lun à 14 h; Tlj à 16 h, à 18 h, à 20 h, à 22 h
Selon Matthieu	Comédie dramatique française avec Benoît Magimel, Natalie Baye, Jeanne Moreau	UGC-Ciné Cité des Halles—Tlj à 11 h 30, à 13 h 40, à 15 h 50, à 18 h, à 20 h 10, à 22 h 20

[a]*fantasy* [b]Tlj = Tous les jours *every day*

Visionnement 1

Avant de visionner

Qu'est-ce que cela veut dire? (*What does that mean?*) In this episode, Rachid admires something in Camille's apartment. Read the following exchange and then answer the questions.

RACHID: Écoute, ce livre est vraiment,[a] euh... Il est vraiment magnifique!
CAMILLE: C'est un cadeau[b] de ma grand-mère... Tu aimes les Cévennes?
RACHID: Ah oui, beaucoup[c]... beaucoup.

[a]*truly* [b]*gift* [c]*a lot*

1. Qu'est-ce que Rachid admire? **2.** Qui a donné cette chose (*this thing*) à Camille? **3.** Est-ce que Rachid aime les Cévennes?

Observez!

In Episode 5, Rachid goes to Yasmine's school and finds his wife there. Later on he meets Camille's mother. As you watch, answer the following questions.

- What does Rachid say to Yasmine's mother? What is her reaction?
- How does the attitude of Camille's mother, Mado, change during the episode?

Après le visionnement

A. Moments clés. (*Key moments.*) Here are some key moments from Episode 5. Fill in the blanks with the name of the appropriate person or thing.

1. Rachid rencontre (*meets*) _____ dans la cour (*courtyard*) de son école. **2.** _____ demande pardon à Sonia. **3.** _____ invite Rachid et Camille à dîner. **4.** Rachid admire _____ sur les Cévennes. **5.** Il examine _____ de la grand-mère de Camille. **6.** Mado ne veut pas parler de _____. **7.** _____ se méfie de (*distrusts*) Rachid.

B. Réfléchissez. (*Think.*) Answer the following questions about Camille's mother, Mado, according to your impressions from the episode.

1. Comment l'attitude de Mado change-t-elle envers (*toward*) Rachid dans cet épisode?

   Vocabulaire utile: aimable, content(e), cynique, horrifié(e), hostile, méfiant(e) (*suspicious*)

   - Au début (*At the beginning*)...
   - Pendant (*During*) la visite de Rachid...
   - À la fin (*At the end*)...

Pour en savoir plus...

The **Cévennes,** a mountainous area in the southeast of France, is known for its magnificent scenery and its biodiversity. The region is quite isolated and relatively empty of young people, because many have moved away to find work. Lately, however, a diversified economic base, an influx of population, and the establishment of a national park in 1970 have brought more prosperity to the area.

Vocabulaire relatif à l'épisode

Je ne me rappelle jamais.	*I never remember (it).*
J'apporte tout ce qu'il faut	*I'll bring everything that's needed*
Je peux t'emprunter le livre?	*May I borrow the book from you?*
De quoi se mêle-t-il?	*What business is it of his?*

2. Pourquoi son attitude change-t-elle, à votre avis (*in your opinion*)? Choissisez (*Choose*) **a**, **b** ou **c**.

  a. Rachid n'accepte pas son invitation à dîner et part vite (*leaves quickly*).
  b. Mado a un secret de famille et Rachid pose trop de (*too many*) questions.
  c. Rachid est impoli avec Camille et Mado n'aime pas cela.

Structure 15

Le verbe *faire*; des expressions avec *faire*

Talking about everyday activities

—Mais qu'est-ce que **tu fais** là?

Le verbe *faire*

faire (*to do; to make*)			
je	**fais**	nous	**faisons**
tu	**fais**	vous	**faites**
il, elle, on	**fait**	ils, elles	**font**

Because **faire** has the general meaning of *to do* or *to make*, when you are asked a question with **faire**, you may need to use a different verb in your answer.

—Qu'est-ce que **tu fais**? — *What are you doing?*
—**Je vais chercher** ma fille à l'école. — *I'm going to pick up my daughter at school.*

Expressions avec *faire*

Faire is a high-frequency verb found in many common expressions that describe everyday activities.

faire attention (à) *to pay attention (to)*
faire la connaissance de *to make the acquaintance of*
faire les courses *to do errands*
faire la cuisine *to cook, make a meal*
faire les devoirs *to do homework*
faire la fête *to have a party*
faire la lessive *to do the laundry*

faire le lit *to make the bed*
faire le ménage *to do housework*
faire une promenade *to take a walk*
faire la queue *to stand in line*
faire du shopping *to go shopping*
faire du sport *to play/do a sport*
faire la vaisselle *to do the dishes*
faire un voyage *to take a trip*

Activités

A. Qui travaille fort? (*Who is working hard?*) Form complete sentences from the cues. After you say each one, tell whether or not the people are working hard.

MODÈLE: tu / faire une promenade dans le parc →
Tu fais une promenade dans le parc. Tu ne travailles pas fort.

1. Anne / faire la lessive pour sa famille
2. vous / faire les courses au marché
3. nous / faire la cuisine pour notre soirée (*party*)
4. je / faire un voyage au Japon
5. tu / faire la queue au cinéma
6. Christelle et Brigitte / faire du shopping
7. mon frère et moi / faire la connaissance d'un nouvel ami
8. les étudiants / faire attention en classe
9. mes amis et moi / faire la fête

B. Activités de tous les jours. (*Everyday activities.*) Your partner will ask you what the people in the drawings are doing. Answer, using expressions with **faire**, remembering to change the pronoun as necessary.

MODÈLE:

vous →
É1: Que faites-vous?
É2: Nous faisons la vaisselle.

1. tu

2. Émilie / Magalie

3. vous

4. les Truffaut

5. Chantal

6. Robert et Ahmed

C. Vos activités de tous les jours. Using the expressions with **faire**, interview a partner to find out when he/she usually does those activities.

MODÈLE: É1: À quelle heure fais-tu tes devoirs généralement?
É2: Je fais mes devoirs à 9 h du soir.
É1: Quand fais-tu le ménage généralement?
É2: Je fais le ménage le samedi matin.

Structure 16

L'adjectif interrogatif *quel* et l'adjectif démonstratif ce

Asking and identifying which person or thing

—Alors, **quel** est le plat du jour?

—Écoute, **ce** livre est vraiment, euh… Il est vraiment magnifique!

L'adjectif interrogatif *quel*

	SINGULIER	PLURIEL
masculin	**quel**	**quels**
féminin	**quelle**	**quelles**

1. You have already seen forms of the interrogative adjective▲ **quel** in several common questions.

Quel âge avez-vous?	*How old are you?*
Quelle est la date aujourd'hui?	*What is today's date?*
Quel jour sommes-nous?	*Which day of the week is it?*
Quelle heure est-il?	*What time is it?*

2. **Quel** (or a preposition + **quel**) can be placed directly before the noun. **Quel** can also be separated from the noun by the verb **être**. In either case, because it is an adjective, it must agree in gender and number with the noun it modifies.

Quel est **le nom** de cette émission?	*What is the name of this show?*
Quelle émission regardez-vous à 8 h?	*Which show do you watch at 8:00?*
Quels journalistes sont les animateurs de «Bonjour!»?	*Which journalists are the hosts of "Bonjour!"?*
Quelles sont **les émissions** diffusées sur Canal 7?	*Which shows are broadcast on Channel 7?*
À **quelle heure** viens-tu?	*(At) what time are you coming?*
Dans **quel immeuble** habitez-vous?	*In which building do you live?*

Pour en savoir plus...

Quel is also often used in exclamations and compliments.

Quelle chance! *What luck!*

Quel joli médaillon! *What a pretty locket!*

L'adjectif démonstratif ce

	SINGULIER	PLURIEL
masculin	**ce (cet)**	**ces**
féminin	**cette**	**ces**

1. To point out or designate things, use a form of the demonstrative adjective▲ **ce** (*this, that, these, those*). Because it is an adjective, the form of **ce** must agree in gender and number with the noun it modifies. The plural is the same for both masculine and feminine.

Écoute, **ce** livre est vraiment, euh... Il est vraiment magnifique.	*Hey, this book is really, um . . . It's really wonderful.*
Cette photo est de la grand-mère de Camille.	*That photo is of Camille's grandmother.*
Mado ne parle pas de **ces** secrets.	*Mado doesn't talk about those secrets.*
...pourquoi s'intéresse-t-il à **ces** photos?	*. . . why is he interested in these photos?*

2. The form **cet** is used before a masculine singular noun beginning with a vowel sound.

Mado habite dans **cet** immeuble.	*Mado lives in this apartment building.*
Comment s'appelle **cet** homme?	*What is that man's name?*

3. The forms of **ce** mean either *this* (*these*) or *that* (*those*). To make this distinction explicit, **-ci** (indicating nearness) and **-là** (indicating remoteness) can be attached to the noun.

ce livre-**ci**	*this book* (= *the one here*)
cette photo-**là**	*that photo* (= *the one over there*)
ces femmes-**là**	*those women* (= *those over there*)

Activités

A. Un client indécis. M. Martin is looking for a gift for his boss. His indecision leads him to ask his wife her opinion about each gift idea. Choose the correct form of **quel** or **ce** to complete their conversation.

MODÈLE: Chérie, quelle vidéo (*f.*) est-ce qu'il aimerait (*would he like*)? Ce film classique ou ce concert (*m.*)?

1. Chérie, _____ livre est-ce qu'il aimerait? _____ album (*m.*) de photos ou _____ collection (*f.*) d'essais?
2. Et _____ stylo est-ce qu'il aimerait? _____ beau stylo Waterman ou _____ élégant stylo Mont Blanc?
3. _____ cassettes (*f.*) est-ce qu'il aimerait? _____ cassettes des symphonies de Beethoven ou _____ cassette de Piaf?
4. _____ CDs (*m.*) est-ce qu'il aimerait? _____ CD de musique populaire française ou _____ collection (*f.*) de raï?
5. Finalement, _____ gadget (*m.*) est-ce qu'il aimerait? _____ micro-ordinateur ou _____ calculatrice?

B. Le Chemin du retour. What questions with **quel** must you ask to find out the italicized information about *Le Chemin du retour?* Use a preposition before **quel** when necessary.

MODÈLE: La profession de Martine, c'est «*productrice*». →
Quelle est la profession de Martine? (*ou* Quelle profession Martine a-t-elle? *ou* Quelle profession a Martine?)

1. Le nom de la chaîne de télévision est *Canal 7.*
2. «Bonjour!» commence à *08 h 00.*
3. Bruno aime le pain *artisanal.*
4. Yasmine va à l'école *Bullier.*
5. Le code de l'immeuble de Mado est *A456.*
6. La photo *du grand-père* n'est pas dans le médaillon de Camille.

C. Pour faire connaissance. Interview a classmate to find out what he/she prefers in the following categories. Also say whether or not you like the same thing. Then switch roles.

MODÈLE: livre →
É1: Quel est ton livre préféré?
É2: *Les Misérables* est mon livre préféré.
É1: Je n'aime pas ce livre. (*ou* J'aime ce livre.)

1. possession
2. classe
3. film
4. émissions de télévision
5. acteurs
6. professeur
7. actrice
8. jour
9. pièce (de la maison)

Regards sur la culture

La famille

As you noticed in this segment, Mado tries to discourage Camille from talking about family matters with Rachid. Although there is a very particular reason for this in the film (one that has not yet been made clear), it is also true that the family and its affairs are generally felt to be very private matters for French people.

- Unless the friendship is strong and well established, it is rather unusual for a visitor to France to be invited as a guest to the home of a French family. The home is a private domain, and even when one does enter a home in France, the visit is normally limited to the living room and dining room. One would almost never visit the entire house the way people do in North America. In addition, a French home is generally closed to the outside by a fence or wall and by shutters on the windows.
- French people often feel that they need to know something about a person's family in order to evaluate him/her. They sometimes judge an individual in part on the basis of the family's reputation or social standing within the community. Of course, because reputations are based partly on hearsay, the French know that such evaluations are only approximate.
- Meals are extremely important family affairs in France. It would be very unusual for a French person to schedule an event that would interfere with the family mealtime.

Un grand repas familial

- Competition between siblings is very strongly discouraged in France. North Americans tend to be surprised at how well French siblings appear to get along.
- To a greater extent than in North America, French children are discouraged from engaging in activities that would take them away from their families. Except in large urban areas, it is often expected that they will eventually find a job that will allow them to settle down relatively close to their parents.
- In France, it is traditionally considered shameful to the family if an elderly person ends his/her life in a retirement home or a hospital, rather than at home with the family.

Considérez

Why might a newcomer to a small town initially have a more difficult time assimilating in France than in Canada or the United States? Can you explain the origins of this difference?

Structure 17

Le genre de certains substantifs et quelques pluriels spéciaux
Guessing genders and spellings

—C'est **un cadeau** de ma grand-mère.

Le genre de certains substantifs

It is sometimes possible to identify the gender of a noun by its ending. Although this is not a foolproof system—you should always memorize the gender along with each noun you learn—the following chart will give you some hints.

IF A NOUN ENDS IN...	IT IS PROBABLY...	EXAMPLES	IMPORTANT EXCEPTIONS
-eau	masculine	bureau, cadeau, jumeau, tableau	eau (*water*)
-isme	masculine	catholicisme, impressionnisme	
-ment	masculine	appartement, bâtiment, visionnement	
-sion	feminine	émission, télévision	
-tion	feminine	attention, gratification	
-ie	feminine	Algérie, géographie, librairie	
-té	feminine	université, liberté, égalité, fraternité	côté

Quelques pluriels spéciaux

Some nouns form the plural in special ways. Check the following chart for a few general rules for vocabulary you've already seen.

IF A NOUN ENDS IN...	ITS PLURAL PROBABLY ENDS IN...	EXAMPLES
-al -ail	-aux	hôpital → hôpitaux travail → travaux
-eu -eau	-x	neveu → neveux tableau → tableaux
-s	-s	fils → fils
-x	-x	époux (*husband*) → époux
-z	-z	nez (*nose*) → nez

You already know that the plurals of some compound nouns (**des salle*s* de classe**, **des sac*s* à dos**) are formed by making the first noun in the compound plural. In compound words for family members, because one part is an adjective and the other is a noun, the plural ending is added to both parts: **grand*s*-mère*s***, **grand*s*-père*s***, **petit*s*-fils**, **petite*s*-fille*s***, **belle*s*-mère*s***, **beau*x*-père*s***, **belle*s*-sœur*s***, **beau*x*-frère*s***.

Activités

A. Est-ce important? Indicate whether or not you think each of the following is important. Follow the model. Then compare your answers with those of a partner.

MODÈLE: géographie →
La géographie est importante. (La géographie n'est pas importante.)

1. réalisme **2.** télévision **3.** liberté **4.** tableau de la salle de classe **5.** sentiments **6.** université **7.** cadeaux d'anniversaire (*birthday presents*) **8.** biologie **9.** ménage **10.** faire attention en classe

B. Quelle chance! Sophie is a very rich woman with lots of family and possessions. Marie, who always wants to seem better, says she has more. What does each woman say?

MODÈLE: voiture de sport (*sports car*) →
SOPHIE: J'ai une voiture de sport.
MARIE: Moi, j'ai deux voitures de sport.

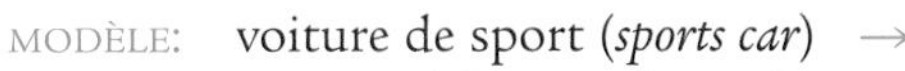

1. grand-père généreux **2.** bureau Louis XV **3.** cheval (*horse*) **4.** fils brillant **5.** neveu **6.** tableau impressionniste **7.** château **8.** ex-époux (*ex-husband*) riche **9.** travail

C. Ressemblances. Interview as many classmates as necessary to find someone who has or does three things like you. Note the similarities.

MODÈLE: Qui a une télévision dans la même (*same*) pièce que vous? →
É1: Dans quelle pièce as-tu une télévision?
É2: Dans la salle de séjour.
É1: Moi aussi. (*ou* Ma télévision est dans ma chambre.)

1. Qui fait ses devoirs dans la même pièce que vous?
2. Qui a un lecteur CD dans la même pièce que vous?
3. Qui fait le ménage le même jour que vous?
4. Qui a une voiture de la même marque (*brand*) que vous?
5. Qui fait un voyage le même mois que vous?
6. Qui a un four à micro-ondes dans la même pièce que vous?
7. Qui fait du shopping dans le même magasin (*store*) que vous?

Visionnement 2

Avant de visionner

Les environs de l'appartement de Camille

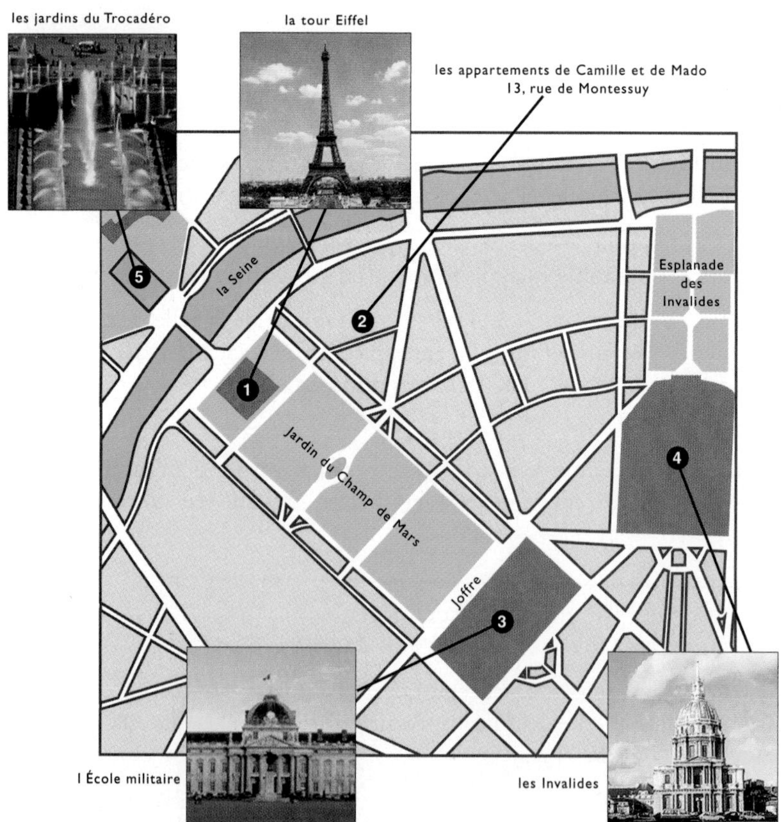

A. Visites dans le quartier. This map shows the elegant area of Paris in which Mado and Camille live. It wasn't until the time of Louis XIV, the Sun King, in the late 1600s, that this part of Paris began to be built. Louis XIV constructed **les Invalides**, an enormous complex of buildings, as a hospital and retirement home for the veterans of his many wars. Napoleon studied at the **École militaire**, and in 1840, nearly twenty years after his death, his remains were buried in the **Église du Dôme** at **les Invalides**. The **Champ de Mars** was the site of important ceremonies during the Revolutionary period in the late eighteenth century. But most of the buildings in this area date from the late nineteenth century, when the **tour Eiffel** was built. The **jardins du Trocadéro** are a reminder of the 1937 World's Fair.

Mado likes taking historical walks in her neighborhood. Indicate the number and name of the landmark that corresponds to each description.

a. un ensemble architectural de 1676
b. un bâtiment de 1773
c. un tombeau (*tomb*) de 1840
d. une construction de 1889
e. des fontaines de 1937

B. Les relations familiales. What do you remember about Episode 5?

1. Comment est la relation entre Camille et sa mère, Mado?
   a. Mado traite (*treats*) sa fille comme une enfant.
   b. Camille s'occupe de (*takes care of*) sa mère.
   c. Mado et Camille ont une vie (*life*) indépendante l'une de l'autre (*the other*).

2. Selon les observations de **Regards sur la culture** dans ce chapitre, est-ce qu'il est normal que Mado invite Rachid à dîner? Expliquez.

Observez!

Consider the cultural information explained in **Regards sur la culture**. Then watch Episode 5 again, and answer the following questions.

- What does Mado do to make Rachid feel welcome?
- What behaviors exhibited by Rachid might not conform to Mado's cultural expectations of a guest?

Après le visionnement

Do the activity for **Visionnement 2** in the Workbook and Laboratory Manual.

Synthèse: Culture

La famille, source de culture

Family relationships are the first and most important sources of culture. The kinds of interactions one has with one's parents, grandparents, and siblings are very closely related to the values and behaviors that one carries through life. Thus, different ways of raising children, or of treating the elderly, for example, determine different cultures in a very real sense.

Quelques générations d'une famille à l'occasion d'un mariage aux années 40.

You saw in Chapter 4 that even within France there is enormous cultural variety. This diversity carries over into the realm of family structures. Of course, the many immigrant groups in France have widely varying kinds of families. For example, Jewish families of Algerian origin, most of whom arrived in France over the second half of the twentieth century, are more likely to live as extended families (grandparents, parents, and children together) than many other groups.

Even the traditional rural French family is not the same in the various French provinces. De Gaulle is famous for having said that a country that makes 246 cheeses is impossible to govern. The differences in traditional family structures are a very real difficulty hinted at by de Gaulle's comment.

The two most important traditional rural family types are

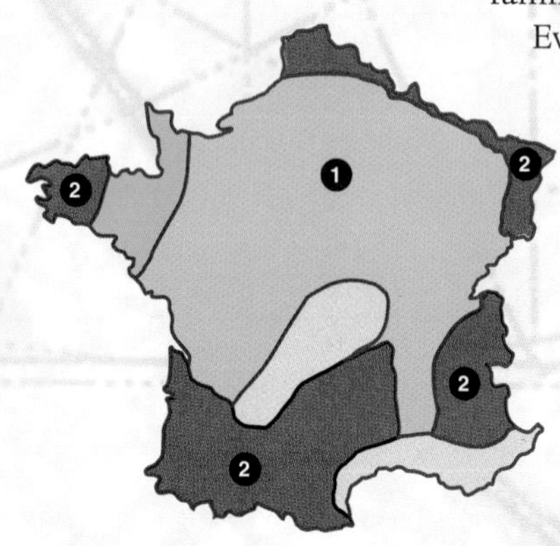

Type 1: Each child marries and founds a separate, independent household. The parents' property is divided up equally, either before or after the death of the parents.

Type 2: One child marries and inherits the parents' property, remaining under the authority of the father as long as he lives. The others leave home and find work elsewhere or remain unmarried as "uncles" or "aunts" on the farm.

Although these traditions of family structure play no role in urban environments and are disappearing even in the countryside, their presence over the centuries has left traces in the attitudes and mind-sets of the different regions of France. In type 1 families, the values of equality and independence are fundamental. In type 2, family cohesion is most important, and values such as authority and inequality are basic.

À vous

In groups, discuss the values upon which your own family relationships are based. Consider the following factors: degree of equality, independence vs. community, strong vs. weak authority, and cooperation vs. individualism. In what ways has your family structure determined your values and attitudes?

À écrire

Do **À écrire** for Chapter 5 in the Workbook and Laboratory Manual.

Vocabulaire

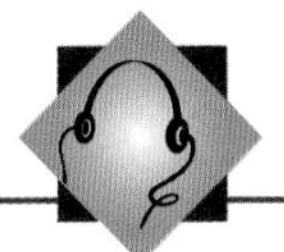

Résidences

un appartement	apartment	**une maison**	house
un immeuble	apartment building	**le rez-de-chaussée**	ground floor

Pièces d'une maison

une chambre	bedroom	**une salle à manger**	dining room
une cuisine	kitchen	**une salle de bains**	bathroom
une pièce	room	**une salle de séjour**	living room

Meubles et possessions

une affiche	poster	**un fauteuil**	armchair
un appareil photo	camera	**un four (à micro-ondes)**	(microwave) oven
une armoire	armoire, wardrobe (*furniture*)	**un réfrigérateur** (*fam.* **un frigo**)	refrigerator
un canapé	sofa	**un lavabo**	bathroom basin
une chaîne stéréo	stereo		
une cuisinière	stove		

un lecteur de CD	CD player
un lit	bed
un magnétoscope	videocassette recorder (VCR)
un meuble	(piece of) furniture
un miroir	mirror
un portable	laptop computer
un répondeur	answering machine
un tapis	rug
un vélo	bicycle
une voiture	automobile

MOTS APPARENTÉS: **un buffet, une guitare, un piano, une radio, un téléphone**

À REVOIR: **une chaise, un ordinateur, une table**

L'heure

l'heure (*f.*)	hour; (clock) time
Quelle heure est-il?	What time is it?
il est... heure(s)	it's . . . o'clock
midi (*m.*)	noon
minuit (*m.*)	midnight
et quart	quarter past
et demi(e)	half past
moins	before (the hour); less; minus
moins le quart	quarter to
à quelle heure... ?	at what time . . . ?
à... heure(s)	at . . . o'clock
de... à...	from . . . to . . .
du matin	in the morning
de l'après-midi	in the afternoon
du soir	in the evening
à l'heure	on time
en avance	early
en retard	late
une fois	one time, occasion
le temps	time

Verbes

faire	to do; to make
faire attention	to pay attention
faire la connaissance de	to make the acquaintance of
faire les courses	to do errands
faire la cuisine	to cook, make a meal
faire les devoirs	to do homework
faire la fête	to have a party
faire la lessive	to do the laundry
faire le lit	to make the bed
faire le ménage	to do housework
faire une promenade	to take a walk
faire la queue	to stand in line
faire du shopping	to go shopping
faire du sport	to play/do a sport
faire la vaisselle	to do the dishes
faire un voyage	to take a trip

Autres expressions utiles

ce (cet, cette)	this; that
maintenant	now
même	same
quel (quelle)	which

Chapitre 6

Bonjour, grand-père!

OBJECTIFS

In this episode, you will

- watch a segment of "Bonjour!" on the subject of fashion
- find out how Camille feels about a discovery Rachid makes

In this chapter, you will

- describe types and colors of clothing
- use shopping terminology
- express your abilities and say what you want
- talk about everyday activities
- ask questions about people and things
- learn about French clothing and fashion
- read reviews of French fashion shows

Vocabulaire en contexte

La mode°

La... *Fashion*

Paris est toujours la capitale de la mode. Et la mode, c'est l'image éternelle de la France...

Et n'**oublions** pas° **les vêtements** (*m.*) de sport et les accessoires de sport.

n'oublions... let's not forget

Activités

A. Décrivez. (***Describe.***) What clothing are people wearing in this episode? What else are they probably wearing that is not shown in the picture? Name one thing each is not wearing.

1. 

2. 

3. 

B. Qu'est-ce que tu portes? (***What do you wear?***) Using the verb **porter**, ask your partner ten questions about his/her clothing habits. For negative answers, your partner should provide the correct information.

MODÈLE: É1: D'habitude, est-ce que tu portes une veste en cours?
É2: Non, d'habitude, je porte un tee-shirt.

des bottes et un chapeau	au centre sportif
une écharpe	à un concert de rock
un jean	en cours
des lunettes de soleil	à l'opéra
un maillot de bain	à la piscine (*swimming pool*)
un short	au sauna
un sweatshirt	au théâtre
un tailleur	au centre commercial
une veste	à une soirée habillée
?	?

Les couleurs

Le nouveau[a] pull-over Maxichaud.
80% laine,[b] 20% cachemire.[c]

Des[d] foulards en soie.[e]
Coloris fantaisistes.

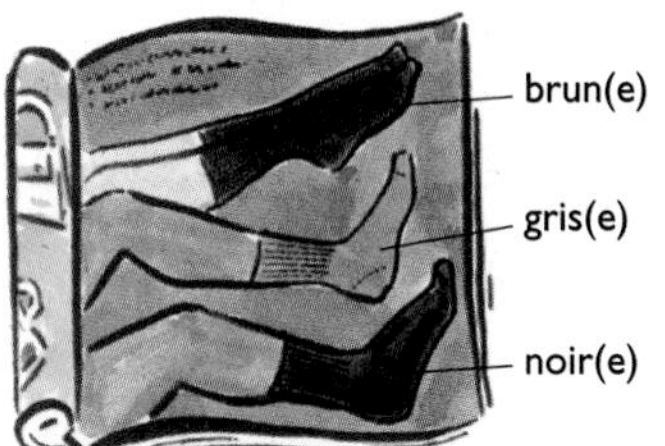

Nos chaussettes en coton et acrylique.

[a]*new* [b]*wool* [c]*cashmere* [d]*some* [e]*silk*

When colors are used as adjectives, most follow the standard rules for feminine and plural forms. The feminine forms of **violet** and **blanc** are **violette** and **blanche**.

Ce pantalon est **brun** et **violet**. Ces chapeaux sont **gris** et **blancs**.

Cette cravate est **brune** et **violette**. Ces chaussettes sont **grises** et **blanches**.

The colors **marron** (*chestnut*) and **orange** are invariable.

des yeux **marron**	*chestnut eyes*
des cravates **orange**	*orange ties*

Pour en savoir plus...

Popular fabrics for clothing include **le coton** (*cotton*), **le cuir** (*leather*), **la laine** (*wool*), and **la soie** (*silk*). To say something is made of one of these fabrics, you may use either **en** or **de**.

J'aime mon écharpe **en laine** rouge. *I like my red wool scarf.*

C'est une ceinture **de cuir** noir. *It is a black leather belt.*

Langage fonctionnel

Pour parler de la mode

Pour demander une opinion sur la mode

Ça me va?	*Does it look good on me?*
Vous l'aimez? (Tu l'aimes?)	*Do you like it?*

Pour faire des compliments

Quel beau... ! / Quelle belle... !	*What a beautiful . . . !*
Ce/Cette... vous (te) va bien.	*This . . . suits you.*
Vous êtes (Tu es) très chic.*	*You look very stylish.*

Pour exprimer des réservations

Je n'aime pas le motif.	*I don't like the pattern.*
C'est un peu trop serré.	*It's a little too tight.*
C'est un peu trop large.	*It's a little too big.*

—**Quelle belle** jupe! *What a pretty skirt!*
—Moi, je pense qu'elle est **un peu trop large**. *I think it's a little too big.*

Activités

A. Un ensemble bien assorti. Use colors to create well-matched outfits.

MODÈLE: un jean / bleu / une chemise →
Un jean bleu va bien avec une chemise blanche.

1. une chemise / orange / un pull-over
2. un pantalon / noir / une veste
3. une jupe / violet / un chemisier
4. un complet / bleu / des chaussures
5. une robe / marron / un foulard
6. des chaussettes / gris / un costume
7. un tailleur / brun / des chaussures
8. un pantalon / vert / une ceinture
9. un manteau / rouge / des bottes
10. un maillot de bain / rose / des lunettes de soleil

*L'adjectif **chic** est invariable: *Elles sont très chic.*

B. Qui est-ce? Think of a student in your class. Your partner will ask questions about the student's clothing to try to find out who it is. A maximum of five questions is allowed.

MODÈLE: É1: Je pense à un étudiant dans la classe.
É2: Est-ce qu'il porte un pantalon gris?
É1: Oui. Il porte un pantalon gris.
É2: Est-ce qu'il porte une ceinture noire?
É1: Non. Pas de ceinture noire.
É2: Porte-t-il une chemise bleue?
É1: Oui.
É2: Alors, c'est Jacques, n'est-ce pas?
É1: C'est ça! C'est Jacques.

Dans un grand magasin°

Dans... *In a department store*

Quand on a de **l'argent**° (*m.*), on fait parfois du shopping. On achète° des vêtements dans une boutique ou dans **un grand magasin**. Voici un grand magasin.

money / buys

Pour en savoir plus...

Customers buying clothes in France often request the services of the clerk before trying anything on, particularly in small shops or boutiques. In many small shops, if a person expresses interest in an item, there is an underlying assumption that he/she will probably buy it. But in French department and discount stores, the shopping behavior more closely resembles that of North America.

Le client paie **en espèces**°? Non, il paie **par chèque**.

La cliente paie **par carte de crédit**? Non, elle paie **par carte bancaire**.°

en... *in cash*
carte... *debit card*

en espèces = in cash
par carte bancaire = debit card

Activités

A. Dans un grand magasin. Fill in the blanks with an appropriate word.

1. Aujourd'hui, j'ai de l'_____ dans ma poche (*pocket*).
2. Je fais des achats (*make purchases*) dans un grand magasin. Je suis _____.

3. Pour acheter (*To buy*) un costume, je vais au _____ mode homme.
4. J'ai une question, alors je demande (*so I ask*) au _____.
5. Je paie à _____.
6. Le magasin n'accepte ni (*neither*) cartes de crédit ni (*nor*) chèques, alors je paie en _____.

B. Interview. Find out about your partner's shopping habits by asking him/her the following questions.

Demandez-lui s'il / si elle

1. aime faire du shopping.
2. préfère aller dans des grands magasins ou des petites boutiques.
3. pose beaucoup de (*asks a lot of*) questions au vendeur / à la vendeuse.
4. accepte souvent les conseils (*advice*) du vendeur / de la vendeuse.
5. paie en général par carte de crédit ou par carte bancaire.

Visionnement 1

Avant de visionner

Qu'est-ce que cela veut dire? (*What does that mean?*) In this episode, Rachid tries to learn more about Camille's family. After two or three questions, Camille responds with the following remark.

Rachid, tu es gentil, tu me poses des questions, tu t'intéresses à ma famille... Mais, tu as peut-être autre chose à faire? Ton reportage, par exemple?

Match each of Camille's phrases to the most appropriate interpretation.

1. ...tu me poses des questions...
2. ...tu t'intéresses à ma famille...
3. ...tu as peut-être autre chose à faire...

a. ...tu dois (*must*) faire ton travail...
b. ...tu trouves ma grand-mère et mon grand-père intéressants...
c. ...tu es indiscret...

Vocabulaire relatif à l'épisode

Du calme.	*Stay calm.*
coupée	*cut*
de l'autre côté	*on the other side*
le marié	*bridegroom*
vivante	*alive, living*

Observez!

Two photographs are important to the story in Episode 6. As you watch, see if you can answer the following questions.

- Where does Rachid find a picture of Camille's grandmother?
- What is unusual about the picture?
- What other photograph is important?

Après le visionnement

A. Vous avez compris? (*Did you understand?*) Summarize the episode by completing the paragraph with the correct word from the parentheses.

Au début de l'épisode, Camille est au _____[1] (plateau, maquillage) et Bruno devient _____[2] (ridicule, impatient). Aujourd'hui, le sujet de l'émission «Bonjour!» est _____[3] (la mode, la cuisine). Rachid trouve _____[4] (une photo, une carte) dans le livre sur les Cévennes. Selon[a] Camille, c'est une photo de Louise, le jour de _____[5] (ses fiançailles,[b] son mariage). La photo n'est pas entière. Elle est _____[6] (coupée, floue[c]). À la fin de l'épisode, Camille utilise _____[7] (un ordinateur, un rétroprojecteur) pour agrandir[d] une autre photo de sa grand-mère. Elle trouve son _____[8] (père, grand-père) sur cette photo.

[a]*According to* [b]*engagement* [c]*blurry* [d]*to enlarge*

B. Réfléchissez. (*Think.*) Choose what you think might be the most likely answer to each question. Explain your choice (in French).

1. Pourquoi Rachid pose-t-il beaucoup de (*many*) questions?
   - **a.** Il aime bavarder (*to gossip*).
   - **b.** Il s'intéresse à la famille de Camille et désire aider Camille.
   - **c.** Il aime les mystères comme la photo coupée.
2. Qu'est-ce qui explique (*What explains*) la réponse de Camille quand Rachid pose des questions sur la photo?
   - **a.** Camille désire parler de sa famille, mais l'histoire est trop (*too*) longue.
   - **b.** Rachid pose des questions troublantes pour Camille.
   - **c.** Camille s'impatiente parce que Rachid néglige (*is neglecting*) son travail.

C. Imaginez. In your opinion, what link might there be between the book on the Cévennes and the picture that Rachid finds in it? Use the expressions in two or three columns to form possible answers.

MODÈLE: Louise s'est mariée dans les Cévennes, peut-être.

Camille	aime voyager	dans les Cévennes
le grand-père de Camille	est mort(e) (*died*)	de noces (*wedding*)
le livre	est né(e) (*was born*)	des Cévennes
Louise	est un cadeau (*gift*)	du mari de Louise
Mado	est un ensemble de photos	
	habite	
	s'est mariée (*got married*)	
	vient	

Pour en savoir plus...

Learn to recognize the following adverbs.▲ They occur frequently in *Le Chemin du retour* and in your textbook.

TIME: aujourd'hui, demain (*tomorrow*), plus tard (*later*)

FREQUENCY: encore (*again; still*), parfois, rarement, souvent, toujours

MANNER: bien, franchement (*frankly*), peut-être (*perhaps*), très, vachement (*very*), vite (*quickly, fast*)

PLACE: ici, là

Structure 18

Les verbes *pouvoir* et *vouloir*

Expressing ability and what you want

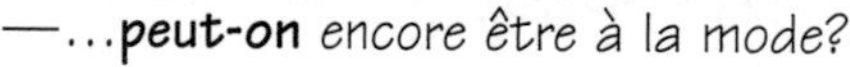

—...**peut-on** encore être à la mode?

—Non, papa, **je ne veux pas**. On repart à la maison!

Bruno uses the verb **pouvoir** to ask whether people *are able* to be stylish anymore. Yasmine uses the verb **vouloir** to tell her father she doesn't *want* to look at the teacher and children at school.

Le verbe *pouvoir*

pouvoir (*to be able, can; to be allowed*)			
je	**peux**	nous	**pouvons**
tu	**peux**	vous	**pouvez**
il, elle, on	**peut**	ils, elles	**peuvent**

Je **peux** t'emprunter le livre sur les Cévennes? — *May I borrow your book about the Cévennes?*

Est-ce que vous **pouvez** venir chez moi ce soir? — *Can you come to my house tonight?*

Pouvoir is usually followed by an infinitive.

Où **peut-on acheter** au meilleur marché? — *Where can we buy (clothing) at bargain prices?*

Le verbe *vouloir*

vouloir (*to want*)			
je	**veux**	nous	**voulons**
tu	**veux**	vous	**voulez**
il, elle, on	**veut**	ils, elles	**veulent**

Vous voulez autre chose? | *Do you want anything else?*

1. **Vouloir** can be followed by a noun or by an infinitive.

   Je veux **un hamburger**. — *I want a hamburger.*
   Voulez-vous **venir**? — *Do you want to come?*

2. When making a request, it is more polite to use the expression **je voudrais**.

   Je voudrais le jarret de porc aux lentilles, s'il vous plaît. — *I would like the ham hocks with lentils, please.*

3. Two useful expressions are **vouloir dire** (*to mean*) and **vouloir bien** (*to be glad/willing* [*to do something*]).

   Que **voulez-vous dire**? — *What do you mean?*
   Camille **veut bien** prêter son livre à Rachid. — *Camille is glad to lend her book to Rachid.*

La location de voitures, c'est simple comme : "Bonjour, je voudrais louer une voiture." Alors, nous avons mis tout en œuvre pour vous simplifier la location. Nombreux forfaits, tous types de voitures. Nous sommes présents dans plus de 75 pays à travers le monde (dont 40 pays européens) et nous avons plus de 250 points de vente en France.

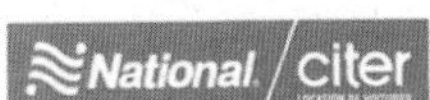

Nous ne sommes pas là pour vous compliquer la vie

Activités

A. Mini-dialogues. Complete the following mini-dialogues by replacing the blanks with the correct form of either **pouvoir** or **vouloir**.

HÔTESSE: Vous _____[1] une coupe de champagne?
INVITÉ 1: Oui. Je _____[2] bien!
INVITÉ 2: Désolé, je ne _____[3] pas. Ma famille m'attend (*is waiting for me*).

TOURISTES: Pardon, monsieur. Nous _____[4] acheter une robe française pour notre fille. Où est-ce qu'on _____[5] faire de bonnes affaires (*find bargains*) dans cette ville?
HABITANT: Ce n'est pas difficile. Les acheteurs malins (*clever shoppers*) _____[6] faire des affaires partout. Vous _____[7] commencer par demander à une vendeuse dans la petite boutique au coin.

B. Situations. Complete the sentence for each situation by choosing from the phrases provided. Be sure to use the correct form of the verb.

Vocabulaire utile:

ne pas vouloir faire la vaisselle
ne plus pouvoir regarder la télévision
ne pas pouvoir écouter de la musique
pouvoir aller à Guadeloupe
pouvoir entrer
pouvoir parler français
pouvoir travailler pour Microsoft

vouloir bien
vouloir dîner avec moi
vouloir dire qu'il est bizarre
vouloir étudier à la bibliothèque
vouloir trouver mes chaussures
vouloir un sandwich
vouloir une robe bleue

MODÈLE: Deux enfants regardent trop de (*too much*) télévision. Leur mère dit (*says*): «Vous... » →
Vous ne pouvez plus regarder la télévision.

1. Une étudiante veut entrer dans la salle de classe. Un(e) camarade dit: «Oui, tu... »
2. La vaisselle est dans l'évier (*sink*). Les enfants disent (*say*): «Nous... »
3. Un homme invite une femme au restaurant. Il dit: «Est-ce que vous... »
4. Un étudiant a besoin d'étudier. Il...
5. Une jeune fille (*girl*) cherche ses chaussures. Elle dit: «Je... »
6. Trois femmes aiment l'informatique (*computer science*). Elles...
7. Une femme est dans un grand magasin au rayon mode femme. Elle...
8. Vous demandez à votre camarade de vous prêter (*lend*) son pull. Il dit: «Oui, d'accord, je... »
9. Un étudiant dit que son professeur est «différent». Son ami demande: «Tu... ?»
10. Une personne sourde (*deaf*)...
11. Deux jeunes hommes ont très faim. Ils...
12. Un couple veut aller en vacances (*vacation*). Le mari suggère: «Nous... »

B. Journal universitaire. (*University newspaper.*) You are writing an article on student life for your school newspaper. Interview three classmates to find out about the coming week. Ask them one thing they want to do, one thing they don't want to do, one thing they can do, and one thing they cannot do. Follow the model.

MODÈLE: É1: Qu'est-ce que tu veux faire cette semaine?
É2: Je veux dîner dans un bon restaurant.
É1: Qu'est-ce que tu ne veux pas faire cette semaine?
É2: Je ne veux pas aller au supermarché.
É1: Qu'est-ce que tu peux faire cette semaine?
É2: Je peux étudier avec mes amis.
É1: Qu'est-ce que tu ne peux pas faire cette semaine?
É2: Je ne peux pas aller au cinéma.

Now summarize your findings for the class.

MODÈLE: Mark et Katie veulent aller au cinéma, mais Ann ne veut pas. Elle veut...

Les verbes avec changement d'orthographe°

changement... *spelling changes*

Talking about everyday activities

—...où peut-on **acheter** au meilleur marché?

Some **–er** verbs are called "spelling-change" (or stem-change) verbs because the stem from the infinitive changes its spelling slightly in certain persons of the conjugation.

Verbes comme *commencer* et *manger*

Verbs that end in **-cer** and **-ger** exhibit a spelling change in the stem of the **nous** form.

commencer (*to begin*)	
je	commence
tu	commences
il, elle, on	commence
nous	commençons
vous	commencez
ils, elles	commencent

manger (*to eat*)	
je	mange
tu	manges
il, elle, on	mange
nous	mangeons
vous	mangez
ils, elles	mangent

Another verb like **commencer** is **lancer** (*to launch*).
Other verbs like **manger** are **changer** (*to change*), **encourager** (*to encourage*), **partager** (*to share*), and **voyager** (*to take a trip*).

L'émission **commence** dans trois minutes!	*The show starts in three minutes!*
Nous voyageons en Europe.	*We are traveling in Europe.*

Verbes comme *préférer*

Verbs like **préférer** change the **é** before the final consonant of the infinitive stem to **è** for all singular forms and for **ils/elles**.

préférer (*to prefer*)			
je	préfère	nous	préférons
tu	préfères	vous	préférez
il, elle, on	préfère	ils, elles	préfèrent

Other verbs like **préférer** are **espérer** (*to hope*) and **répéter** (*to repeat*).

J'espère pouvoir reconnaître le bon pain. — *I hope I can recognize the good bread.*

Est-ce que **vous préférez** la personnalité de Camille ou de Bruno? — *Do you prefer the personality of Camille or of Bruno?*

Verbes comme *payer*

Verbs like **payer** change **y** to **i** at the end of the infinitive stem for all singular forms and for **ils/elles**.

payer (*to pay*)			
je	paie	nous	payons
tu	paies	vous	payez
il, elle, on	paie	ils, elles	paient

Other verbs like **payer** are **employer** (*to use; to employ*), **envoyer** (*to send*), and **essayer** (*to try*).

Rachid **envoie** Yasmine vers le groupe d'enfants. — *Rachid sends Yasmine toward the group of children.*

Essayer is followed by **de** when used with an infinitive.

Rachid **essaie de** rassurer Yasmine. — *Rachid tries to reassure Yasmine.*

Verbes comme *appeler*

Verbs like **appeler** double the final consonant of the stem for all singular forms and for **ils/elles**.

appeler (*to call*)			
j'	appelle	nous	appelons
tu	appelles	vous	appelez
il, elle, on	appelle	ils, elles	appellent

Sonia **appelle** Rachid à Canal 7. — *Sonia calls Rachid at Channel 7.*

Verbes comme *acheter*

Verbs like **acheter** change the **e** before the final consonant of the infinitive stem to **è** for all singular forms and for **ils/elles**.

acheter (*to buy*)			
j'	achète	nous	achetons
tu	achètes	vous	achetez
il, elle, on	achète	ils, elles	achètent

Est-ce que Camille **achète** une robe? *Is Camille buying a dress?*

Activités

A. Un bon ou un mauvais mariage? (*A good or a bad marriage?*) Complete each sentence with the correct form of the appropriate verb in parentheses.

1. Nous _____ tout le travail à la maison. (partager, acheter)
2. Tu _____ faire la cuisine, et je _____ faire la vaisselle. (préférer, encourager)
3. Je _____ mon nouveau travail bientôt. (appeler, commencer)
4. Tu _____ mon indépendance. (voyager, encourager)
5. Tu _____ tes parents tous (*all*) les samedis. (essayer, appeler)
6. J' _____ trop de (*too many*) chaussures. (acheter, espérer)
7. Nous _____ aussi trop de disques compacts. (payer, acheter)
8. Nous _____ changer nos mauvais traits de caractère. (essayer de, employer)
9. Mais en réalité, nous ne _____ jamais. (changer, employer)
10. Nous _____ pendant (*during*) les vacances. (voyager, répéter)
11. Tu _____ toujours les achats en espèces. (partager, payer)
12. Nos parents _____ parfois de petits cadeaux. (préférer, envoyer)
13. Tu ne _____ pas mes secrets à nos amis. (répéter, lancer)
14. Nous _____ passer le week-end ensemble. (espérer, payer)
15. Nous _____ à apprécier nos différences. (envoyer, commencer)

B. Le shopping. Find out about the clothing purchases and preferred styles of your partner and be prepared to report to the class. Use the **vocabulaire utile** or other verbs you know.

Vocabulaire utile: acheter, employer, espérer, essayer, partager, payer, préférer

Ask your partner

1. where he/she buys clothes and why
2. if he/she tries things on before buying them
3. what kinds of clothing he/she buys
4. which colors he/she prefers
5. whether he/she uses a credit card, a check, or cash when buying things
6. whether he/she and his/her friends share their clothing
7. whether he/she hopes to be chic

Regards sur la culture

Les habits et la mode°

Les... *Clothing and fashion*

In this chapter, Bruno and Camille present a segment of "Bonjour!" devoted to fashion. The significance of clothing in French culture is very great and has been so for centuries. Clothing expresses a person's wealth and status, of course, and it may also serve as an indication of age group and ethnic origin. In addition, however, clothing expresses attitudes, including, in France, a concern for elegance and "good taste."

La mode «américaine» chez les enfants

- As a general rule, appearance is more overtly valued in France than in North America. In fact, most French children are taught that how they appear to other people (in clothing, in actions, in language) is extremely important.
- French people tend to comment explicitly on the way others dress. It would not be shocking or unusual for someone in France to say that so-and-so is attractive but badly dressed (**mal habillé**).
- French people pay a lot of attention to how they dress, but may not actually own very large wardrobes. The care with which items of clothing are combined is more important than the variety of items worn.
- French children spend much of their time dressed in what North Americans might think is rather fancy clothing. They are expected not to get dirty when they are playing.
- In North America, French clothing is usually associated with elegance and high style: classic fashion like Chanel or modern styles like those of Jean-Paul Gaultier, for example. In France, however, young people love North American clothing for casual wear. In fact, there are several "imitation" American clothing companies in France. Chevignon, for example, was founded in 1979 and has created a very successful "American" style based on U.S. clothing of the 1950s.

La mode au masculin

Considérez

Someone who is passionately interested in clothing might be considered superficial by certain people in North America. This would not be the case in France. Do Americans or Canadians feel the same way about someone who has a passion for good food or for fancy cars? If not, what do you think is the difference?

Structure 20

Les pronoms interrogatifs

Asking questions

—**Qu'est-ce qu'**il y a, ma puce?

—**Qui** est-ce?

—**De quoi** se mêle-t-il?

There are two kinds of interrogative pronouns▲: those that ask questions about people and those that ask about things.

1. **Qui** (*who, whom*) asks questions about people. It can be the subject or object▲ of a verb or the object of a preposition.

Subject:	**Qui** parle?	*Who is talking?*
Object:	**Qui** est-ce que tu vois?	*Whom do you see?*
Object of a preposition:	À **qui** envoies-tu cette lettre?	*To whom are you sending that letter?*

2. **Que** (*what*) asks questions about things. For now, you will learn its use as the object of a verb. Two patterns are possible: **Que** + verb + subject (inversion) or **Qu'** + **est-ce que** + subject + verb. You already know the **Qu'est-ce que** form.

Object:	**Que** fais-tu?	*What are you doing?*
	Qu'est-ce que tu fais?	

When *what* is the object of a preposition, it is expressed with the word **quoi**. It too can be used with inversion or with **est-ce que**.

Object of a preposition:	**De quoi** parlez-vous? **De quoi est-ce que** vous parlez?	*What are you talking about?*

Activités

A. Dans le film. Using an interrogative pronoun (and a preposition if necessary), ask the question that is answered by the word or phrase in parentheses. Follow the model.

MODÈLE: ______ est-ce un grand jour? (pour Yasmine et Rachid) →
Pour qui est-ce un grand jour?

1. ______ est-ce que Yasmine adore? (son père)
2. ______ veut sa maman? (Yasmine)
3. ______ Martine travaille-t-elle en régie (*control room*)? (avec Roger et Nicole)
4. ______ Martine trouve? (le médaillon de Camille)
5. ______ Martine présente-t-elle Camille? (à Rachid)
6. ______ Rachid admire? (l'émission «Bonjour!»)
7. ______ a un parent algérien? (Rachid)
8. ______ fait le téléphone de Sonia? (Il sonne. [*It is ringing.*])
9. ______ Rachid s'intéresse-t-il? (aux Cévennes)
10. ______ Rachid emprunte (*borrows*) à Camille? (un livre sur les Cévennes)
11. ______ appelle Paris la capitale de la mode? (Bruno)
12. ______ porte Camille? (une jolie robe)
13. ______ trouve une photo dans le livre? (Rachid)
14. ______ est la photo? (de la grand-mère de Camille)
15. ______ est la photo sur l'ordinateur de Camille? (du grand-père de Camille)

B. Interview. Working in pairs, use the cues to prepare a series of interview questions. Then imagine the answers that a famous person might give, and perform your interview for the class.

Demandez à cette personne...

1. d'identifier qui il/elle admire
2. en qui il/elle a beaucoup de confiance
3. ce qu'il/elle fait pendant son temps libre
4. de quoi il/elle a peur
5. ce qu'il/elle préfère porter
6. de quoi il/elle a besoin pour être heureux/heureuse
7. à qui il/elle parle souvent
8. ce qu'il/elle veut faire dans l'avenir (*the future*)
9. ?

C. Questions personnelles. Interview three classmates, asking the same questions you asked in Activity B. Write down their names and their answers. Then work in small groups to see which answers are most common or most uncommon.

Visionnement 2

Avant de visionner

La culture de la mode. In his introduction to the fashion segment, Bruno says:

> ...Mais, pour beaucoup d'entre nous, la mode reste un rêve. Eh oui, c'est cher, très cher! Alors, aujourd'hui, la question que l'on se pose, c'est: peut-on encore être à la mode? Est-ce que c'est possible? Combien ça coûte? Et surtout, où peut-on acheter au meilleur marché?

Reflect on what you have read in **Regards sur la culture**. What cultural assumptions about the importance of appearance does Bruno express?

Observez!

Consider the cultural information explained in **Regards sur la culture**. Then watch Episode 6 again, and answer the following questions.

- What compliment does Bruno give to Camille?
- What is her response? How might an American respond to this compliment?

Après le visionnement

Do the activity for **Visionnement 2** in the Workbook and Laboratory Manual.

Synthèse: Lecture

Mise en contexte

For more than two centuries, Paris has been considered the world center for high fashion. Twice a year, major designers exhibit their new creations for prestigious guests and the press. These highly orchestrated productions generate much attention and discussion. Although the new designs might appear outlandish or suitable only for special occasions, they influence the "off-the-rack" (**prêt-à-porter**) clothing found in major department stores and designer boutiques. Indeed, designer labels such as Lapidus and Saint Laurent are very important to many fashion-conscious people throughout the world.

Stratégie pour mieux lire
Using visuals to facilitate comprehension

Before reading a text, examining the accompanying photos, graphs, and charts can facilitate your comprehension of the passage. Such visuals complement the written word and allow you to anticipate content or predict meaning.

You are going to read a report about the designs of Olivier Lapidus. Here is a quotation from it. Look at the photo that accompanies that part of the text and then answer the question, using the photo to help you guess the meaning of the unfamiliar expression.

> «Olivier Lapidus... incorpore le téléphone mobile au vêtement, incrusté dans la manche, et le petit écran à la robe.»

L'expression **incrusté dans** veut dire

a. sewn into　　b. crushed by　　c. hidden in

Did looking at the photo help you see that **incrusté dans** probably means *sewn into*? Now, read the newspaper report about four designer shows. Refer to the photographs to help you understand unfamiliar words. In addition, try to figure out how the critics and the public reacted to each show.

La haute couture du millénaire[1]

Olivier Lapidus: Vidéo mode

C'est l'an[2] 2000. Le téléphone portable et la vidéo font partie de la vie.[3] Autant les inclure dans la mode! Olivier Lapidus, avec la participation enthousiaste de Sony et de Nokia, incorpore le téléphone mobile au vêtement, incrusté dans la manche, et le petit écran à la robe. La haute couture fait ainsi[4] son entrée dans la mode moderne. Ce mariage de la haute technologie avec la mode jeune, jolie et charmante nous rassure pour demain. La mode a un beau futur devant elle.

Le miracle Chanel

Hier, midi. Chanel défile.[5] Karl Lagerfeld métamorphose et relance le tailleur familier des années 50, mais cette fois-ci «moderne» avec une nouvelle ampleur de jupes. Les dames clientes sont enchantées de retrouver une mode classique et embellissante.[6]

[1]La... *High fashion at the turn of the millennium* [2]*year* [3]*life* [4]*thus* [5]*walks down the runway* [6]*flattering*

La magie Saint Laurent

Mantille, dentelle noire… Yves Saint Laurent rappelle l'Espagne à sa façon[7] brillante et imaginaire. Le grand air de *Carmen* joue pendant le défilé des belles Andalouses.* «Bravo!» applaudissent les spectateurs, séduits[8] par la fantaisie romantique de la vieille Andalousie.

Dior, c'est fou![9]

À faire son jogging sous les ponts[10] de Paris, John Galliano y découvre[11] les clochards et les ramène[12] chez Dior. Drôle d'idée! Ses thèmes unissent le monde des SDF[13] à l'univers psychiatrique. Sa collection divise la presse et les clientes affolées[14] mais fascinées par le spectacle bizarre. Certains crient au scandale, d'autres trouvent le psycho-drame remarquable. Où va-t-il en finir?[15]

[7]à… *in his style* [8]*seduced* [9]*crazy* [10]*bridges* [11]*discovers* [12]les… *brings them back* [13]*homeless people* (SDF = sans domicile fixe = *without permanent address*) [14]*panicking, wild* [15]Où… *What will he think of next?*

Adapté du *Figaro* (janvier, 2000)

Après la lecture

A. Avez-vous compris? How well were you able to use the photo to help you guess the meaning of the following unfamiliar expressions?

1. Lapidus: L'expression **Autant les inclure** veut dire
   - **a.** They are excluded as well
   - **b.** Might as well include them
   - **c.** Useless to include
2. Chanel: Le mot **ampleur** veut dire
   - **a.** fullness **b.** short length **c.** prominence
3. Saint Laurent: Le mot **dentelle** veut dire
   - **a.** feathers **b.** lace **c.** trim
4. Dior: Le mot **clochards** veut dire
   - **a.** joggers **b.** bells **c.** street people

B. Classez. Classify these designers' fashions according to the listed categories, based on how the reporter says people reacted to the designs. You may use several categories if you wish.

1. Lapidus **2.** Chanel **3.** Saint Laurent **4.** Dior

Catégories: bizarre, fantaisiste, futuriste, original, ridicule, romantique, traditionnel

*****Andalousie** is a region in southern Spain. A woman from Andalousia is called an **Andalouse**.

C. À vous le choix. (***Your choice.***) In your opinion, which of the fashions described in the reading would be most appropriate to wear for the following occasions? Which would not be appropriate at all? Choose from the fashions in the following list.

- la mode vidéo d'Olivier Lapidus
- la mantille et la dentelle de Saint Laurent
- le tailleur de Chanel
- les ensembles de Dior

MODÈLE: pour aller au restaurant →
Le tailleur de Chanel convient (*is suitable*) pour aller au restaurant. Les ensembles de Dior ne conviennent pas du tout pour aller au restaurant.

1. pour aller à une soirée habillée
2. pour aller à un entretien d'embauche (*job interview*)
3. pour aller à la discothèque
4. pour aller à un bal
5. pour aller au cinéma
6. pour aller sous les ponts de Paris

À écrire

Do **À écrire** for Chapter 6 in the Workbook and Laboratory Manual.

Vocabulaire

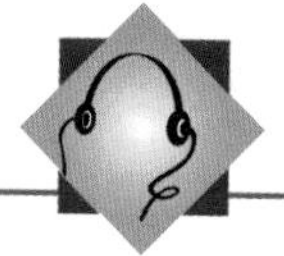

Les vêtements

une botte	boot
une ceinture	belt
un chapeau	hat
une chaussette	sock
une chaussure	shoe
une chemise	shirt
un chemisier	blouse
un costume; un complet	(man's) suit
une cravate	tie
une écharpe	scarf
un foulard	lightweight scarf
une jupe	skirt
des lunettes (*f. pl.*) **de soleil**	sunglasses
un maillot de bain	bathing suit
un manteau	overcoat
un pantalon	pants, trousers
une robe	dress
un tailleur	(woman's) suit

une veste	sports coat, jacket
un vêtement	(article of) clothing

MOTS APPARENTÉS: **un jean, un pull-over** (*fam.* **un pull**), **un short, un sweatshirt** (*fam.* **un sweat**), **un tee-shirt**

Dans un grand magasin

l' argent (*m.*)	money
la caisse	checkout
une carte bancaire	bank (*debit*) card
en espèces (*f. pl.*)	in cash
un (grand) magasin	(department) store
un rayon	department (*in a store*)
un(e) vendeur/euse	salesclerk

MOTS APPARENTÉS: **une carte de crédit, un chèque, un(e) client(e)**

Les couleurs

blanc(he)	white
brun(e)	brown
gris(e)	gray
jaune	yellow
marron	chestnut brown
noir(e)	black
rose	pink
rouge	red
vert(e)	green

MOTS APPARENTÉS: **bleu(e), orange, violet(te)**

Verbes

acheter	to buy
appeler	to call
employer	to use; to employ
envoyer	to send
espérer	to hope
essayer	to try
lancer	to launch
manger	to eat
oublier	to forget
partager	to share
pouvoir	to be able, can; to be allowed
vouloir	to want
vouloir bien	to be glad, willing (*to do something*)
vouloir dire	to mean

MOTS APPARENTÉS: **changer, commencer, encourager, payer, préférer, répéter, voyager**

Pronoms interrogatifs

que	what
qu'est-ce que	what
qui	who; whom
quoi	what

Autres expressions utiles

je voudrais	I would like
par	by; per

Chapitre 7

Préparatifs°

Preparations

OBJECTIFS

In this episode, you will

- watch Camille as she shops for food in an outdoor market
- learn more about Camille's family

In this chapter, you will

- learn the names of food merchants, their stores, and their merchandise
- learn how to express quantities
- learn to avoid repetition by using indirect object pronouns
- talk about everyday actions
- learn about how French people buy and prepare food
- read about common foods in France and other French-speaking countries

Vocabulaire en contexte

*A*u marché Mouffetard°

Au... *At the Mouffetard market*

Camille fait des courses au **marché** Mouffetard.
Elle va **chez le boucher** pour acheter un kilo de **bœuf** (*m.*).
Elle va **chez la marchande** de légumes pour acheter des **carottes** (*f.*), des **oignons** (*m.*) et des **pommes*** **de terre** (*f.*).
Elle va **chez le marchand** de fruits pour acheter des **pommes** (*f.*), des **cerises** (*f.*), des **citrons** (*m.*) et du[†] **raisin**.
Elle va chez le marchand de vin pour acheter du **vin rouge** (un Côtes-du-Rhône) et du **champagne**.

Pour en savoir plus...

Although more and more French people now shop in supermarkets, which have become quite common, many also continue to shop at outdoor markets, particularly for fresh fruit and vegetables. By talking to the merchants, they can learn more about the quality of a product, its origin, and how to prepare it. Many larger towns also have enclosed markets (**les halles**), where individual vendors set up their merchandise.

Autres mots utiles

un aliment	food
les haricots[‡] (*m.*) **verts**	green beans
le maïs	corn
les petits pois (*m.*)	peas
une tomate	tomato
le vin (rouge, blanc, rosé)	(red, white, rosé) wine

Pour en savoir plus...

The French use the metric system for weights. Here are some equivalencies that might be useful if you're buying food in France.

un kilo (1000 grammes)
= about $2\frac{1}{4}$ pounds

un demi-kilo
(500 grammes)
= about 1 pound

250 grammes
= about $\frac{1}{2}$ pound

*Compound nouns (nouns made from more than one word) often form their plurals by adding **s** to the main noun in the compound. You can tell which is the main noun because it usually comes first and because the rest of the compound describes it in some way: ***pomme(s)* de terre**, ***sac(s)* à dos**.

[†]Nouns preceded by **du** are masculine; those preceded by **de la** are feminine. The genders of plural nouns are shown in parentheses.

[‡]There are two kinds of **h** in French. The **h muet** (*mute h*) is not pronounced and allows liaison and elision before it: **l'histoire, les/z/histoires**. The **h aspiré** (*aspirate h*) is not pronounced either, but liaison and elision are not used before it: **le haricot, les haricots**.

Activités

A. Vrai ou faux. Dites si les phrases suivantes sont vraies (**C'est vrai.**) ou fausses (**C'est faux.**). Corrigez les phrases fausses. (*Say whether the following sentences are true or false. Correct the false sentences.*)

MODÈLE: Les cerises sont vertes. →
C'est faux. Les cerises sont rouges. (Les petits pois sont verts.)

1. On peut acheter de la viande au marché en plein air (*open air*).
2. On va chez le boucher pour acheter des cerises.
3. Une pomme est un fruit acide (*sour*).
4. Une pomme de terre est un fruit sucré (*sweet*).
5. On trouve souvent des tomates et des carottes dans une salade.
6. Pour acheter du champagne, on peut aller chez la marchande de légumes.
7. On emploie des petits pois pour faire du vin.
8. Le maïs est populaire dans les repas (*meals*) américains.

B. Descriptions. Identifiez...

MODÈLE: un légume orange → Une carotte est un légume orange.

1. un fruit sucré
2. un fruit jaune
3. un vin pétillant (*sparkling*)
4. un légume vert
5. un légume qui a une odeur forte
6. un légume jaune

C. Interview. Demandez (*Ask*) à votre partenaire...

1. s'il / si elle est végétarien(ne) ou s'il / si elle mange de la viande
2. combien de fois par jour il/elle mange des fruits
3. quel légume et quel fruit il/elle préfère
4. s'il / si elle aime les choux de Bruxelles et les brocolis
5. s'il / si elle préfère les fruits ou le chocolat

Les environs de la rue Mouffetard

Il y a des magasins dans les environs de la rue Mouffetard. **Chaque**° magasin a sa spécialité. On va à **la boulangerie**° pour acheter du **pain** et des croissants, mais on va à **la pâtisserie**° pour des **pâtisseries** (*f.*): des **tartes** (*f.*) et des éclairs, par exemple.

Each / (bread) bakery
pastry shop

À **la boucherie**,° on peut acheter du bœuf et du **poulet**.° À **la charcuterie**, on achète du **jambon**,° du **porc**, des **saucisses**° (*f.*) et du pâté. On va à **la poissonnerie**° pour acheter du **poisson** et des **fruits de mer**:° du **saumon**, de la sole et des **crevettes**° (*f.*).

butcher shop / chicken
ham / sausages
fish store
fruits... seafood / shrimp

On va à **la crémerie**° pour acheter de **la crème**, du **beurre**° et du **fromage**:° du camembert, du brie et du chèvre, par exemple. À **l'épicerie** (*f.*), on achète du **sucre**,° de **l'eau**° (*f.*) **minérale gazeuse** et **plate**, de **la confiture**,° des boîtes de **thon**° (*m.*), etc.

dairy shop / butter
cheese
sugar / water
jam / tuna

Notez bien!

To say you are at or going to one of these shops, you may use **à** before the name of a shop (**je vais à la boucherie**) or **chez** before the title of the shopkeeper (**je vais chez le boucher**).

Autres mots utiles

un(e) boucher/ère	butcher
un(e) boulanger/ère	(bread) baker
un(e) épicier/ière	grocer
un(e) pâtissier/ière	(pastry) baker

Langage fonctionnel

Pour faire des achats°

Pour… *Making purchases*

Here are some expressions that are frequently used in making purchases.

Pour saluer le client / la cliente

Qu'est-ce que je vous sers, monsieur/madame/mademoiselle?	*What can I get you, sir/madam/miss?*
Vous désirez?	*What would you like?*

Pour demander un service

Je voudrais regarder… / acheter… / essayer…, s'il vous plaît.	*I would like to see . . . / buy . . . / try on (a piece of clothing), please.*

Pour parler du prix et pour payer

Combien est-ce que ça coûte?	*How much does it cost?*
C'est cher / raisonnable / bon marché / en solde.	*It's expensive / reasonable / inexpensive / on sale.*
Vous payez comment?	*How will you pay?*

Derniers° mots — Last

Merci.	*Thank you.*
Bonne journée.	*Have a nice day.*

—Bonjour, madame. **Vous désirez**?
—**Je voudrais acheter** un kilo de bœuf, s'il vous plaît.
—Bien sûr, madame.
—**Combien est-ce que ça coûte**?
—15,09 euros, madame. **Vous payez comment**?
—Par chèque, s'il vous plaît.
—Très bien. Voilà. **Bonne journée**, madame.

Activités

A. Catégories. Indiquez à quelle catégorie correspond chacun (*each one*) des articles mentionnés.

1. la crème
2. l'eau
3. le fromage
4. le jambon
5. une pâtisserie
6. un poisson
7. le porc
8. le saumon
9. le sucre
10. le thon

A. des aliments sucrés
B. des produits laitiers (*dairy products*)
C. des produits de la mer
D. des produits à base de viande de porc
E. une boisson (*drink*) pure

B. Où va-t-on? Voici une liste de provisions. Dites où on va pour les acheter (*to buy them*).

MODÈLE: du jambon →
Pour acheter du jambon, on va à la charcuterie.

1. une tarte aux pommes
2. de la confiture
3. du pain
4. du poulet
5. des saucisses
6. des crevettes
7. du beurre

Répondez encore une fois aux questions 1–5, et utilisez les noms des marchands.

MODÈLE: du jambon →
Pour acheter du jambon, on va chez le charcutier.

C. Jeu de rôle. (*Role play.*) Vous passez l'année à Paris et vous décidez de préparer un repas typiquement américain pour votre famille d'accueil (*host family*). Vous passez au marché Mouffetard pour acheter les ingrédients. Demandez aux marchands si les ingrédients sont disponibles (*available*). Jouez la scène avec deux ou trois camarades de classe en utilisant les expressions de la note **Pour faire des achats**.

Visionnement 1

Avant de visionner

La réponse logique. Choisissez la phrase qui suit (*follows*) logiquement l'expression donnée.

1. LOUISE: Alex. Tu m'achètes du champagne? Une bonne bouteille,[a] s'il te plaît!

   ALEX: ______

   a. Oui, d'accord, mais chez moi!
   b. Tu fais la fête[b] ce soir?
   c. Vous en prenez[c] un kilo?

2. MARCHANDE DE LÉGUMES: Qu'est-ce que je vous sers, mademoiselle?

   CAMILLE: ______

   a. Euh, des carottes, s'il vous plaît.
   b. Non, juste deux ou trois...
   c. Est-ce que vous pouvez me le couper en petits morceaux?[d]

[a]*bottle* [b]*party* [c]*take* [d]Est-ce... *Can you cut it into little pieces for me?*

Observez!

Dans l'Épisode 7, Camille va dîner avec quelqu'un (*someone*). Regardez l'épisode et essayez de trouver les réponses aux questions suivantes (*following*).

- Où va Camille et qu'est-ce qu'elle achète?
- Quel est l'état physique de la femme à qui Camille rend visite (*whom Camille visits*)?

Vocabulaire relatif à l'épisode

ensemble	*together*
vous en prenez un kilo?	*will you take a kilo (of them)?*
je vais prendre...	*I'll take . . .*
du premier choix	*top quality*
tu as l'air en forme	*you seem to be doing well*
tu refermes... ?	*will you close . . . ?*

Après le visionnement

Notez bien!

To talk about doing something with someone else, you can often use the word **ensemble** (*together*). Camille uses it to invite her grandmother to have dinner with her.

On dîne **ensemble** ce soir?
Shall we have dinner together tonight?

A. Identifiez. Qui dit (*says*) les phrases suivantes? Est-ce Camille, Louise (la grand-mère), Alex, le boucher ou la marchande de légumes?

MODÈLE: On dîne ensemble ce soir? →
C'est Camille.

1. Oui, d'accord, mais chez moi!
2. Je fais la cuisine!
3. Tu m'achètes du champagne? Une bonne bouteille, s'il te plaît!
4. D'accord, mais vous signez un autographe!
5. Qu'est-ce que je vous sers, mademoiselle?
6. Tu vas bien? Tu as l'air en forme!

Maintenant, pensez à ces identifications pour raconter (*tell the story of*) l'Épisode 7. Commencez avec les phrases suivantes.

Camille invite sa grand-mère à dîner. La grand-mère invite Camille chez elle, et Camille propose de faire la cuisine...

B. Réfléchissez. (*Think.*) Répondez.

1. Faites une liste des produits que Camille achète. Qu'est-ce qu'elle prépare, probablement—une quiche lorraine? un poulet rôti (*roasted*)? un bœuf bourguignon? des crêpes?
2. Pourquoi est-ce que Camille invite Louise à dîner? Est-ce qu'il y a une raison particulière, à votre avis? Expliquez.

Structure 21

L'article partitif et les expressions de quantité

Talking about quantities

—Alex. Tu m'achètes **du champagne**? **Une** bonne **bouteille**, s'il te plaît!

Nouns can be divided into two classes: those you can count using cardinal numbers (*one* apple, *two* eclairs, *ten* carrots, etc.) and those that cannot be counted (*some* beef, *too much* wine, *a pound of* butter, *a glass of* water, etc.). Nouns in the second group are sometimes referred to as "mass" nouns.

You have already learned to use definite and indefinite articles with nouns.

le légume	*the (particular) vegetable*	**un** légume	*one/a vegetable*
la saucisse	*the (particular) sausage*	**une** saucisse	*one/a sausage*
les légumes	*the/all vegetables*	**des** légumes	*some vegetables*
les saucisses	*the/all sausages*	**des** saucisses	*some sausages*

The indefinite article **des** expresses an indefinite quantity of count nouns.

L'article partitif

The partitive article▲ indicates an indefinite amount of mass nouns. The forms are **du** and **de la**.

du vin (*m.*) — *(some) wine*
de la viande (*f.*) — *(some) meat*

1. If a noun begins with a vowel sound, **de l'** is used in place of both **du** and **de la**.

   de l'argent (*m.*) — *(some) money*
   de l'eau (*f.*) — *(some) water*

2. The partitive can be expressed in English as *some* or *any,* but it is often omitted. In French, however, the notion of indefinite quantity must always be expressed.

   Avez-vous **de l'**eau? — *Do you have (some, any) water?*

3. In a negative statement, the partitive article becomes **de** (**d'**), unless it follows the verb **être**.

   Nous n'avons pas **de** champagne. — *We don't have any champagne.*
   Je ne veux pas **de** salade. — *I don't want any lettuce.*
   but Ce n'est pas **du** champagne. — *It's not champagne.*
   Ce n'est pas **de la** salade. — *It's not lettuce.*

4. In some contexts, such as when ordering in restaurants, nouns that are usually preceded by a partitive article may be preceded by a number instead.

   Un vin et **deux** cafés, s'il vous plaît. — *One wine and two coffees, please.*

5. After verbs of preference (**adorer**, **aimer**, **détester**, **préférer**, etc.), the definite article is used because it expresses a generality about all of something.

   Louise aime **le** champagne. — *Louise likes champagne.*
   Rachid préfère **l'**eau. — *Rachid prefers water.*

Expressions de quantité

There are two kinds of expressions of quantity.

1. For *unspecified* quantities, the following expressions may be used with both singular and plural nouns.

trop (de)	*too much; too many*
beaucoup (de)	*much; many; a lot of*
assez (de)	*enough*
(un) peu (de)	*(a) little; (a) few*

Bruno mange **beaucoup de** bœuf.	*Bruno eats a lot of beef.*
Camille achète **assez de** viande et de légumes.	*Camille buys enough meat and vegetables.*
Peut-on manger **trop de** crevettes?	*Can one (ever) eat too many shrimp?*

2. To *specify* quantities, expressions of measure such as the following can be used.

une boîte (de)	*a can (of); a box (of)*
une bouteille (de)	*a bottle (of)*
un demi-kilo (de)	*one-half kilogram (of)*
une douzaine (de)	*a dozen*
un kilo (de)	*a kilogram (of)*
une livre (de)*	*a pound (of); a half-kilogram (of)*
un morceau (de)	*a piece (of)*

Alex achète **une bouteille de** champagne à Louise.	*Alex buys a bottle of champagne for Louise.*
...et **une livre de** pommes de terre.	*. . . and a pound of potatoes.*

3. Expressions of quantity always include **de** (**d'**) when they precede a noun.

beaucoup d'amis	*many friends*
un peu d'argent	*a little money*
une bouteille de vin	*a bottle of wine*
une boîte de thon	*a can of tuna*

4. **Peu de** is used to describe both singular and plural nouns. **Un peu de**, however, may only be used to quantify singular mass nouns.

Bruno a **peu de** nourriture chez lui.	*Bruno has little food at home.*
Camille achète très **peu de** carottes et juste **un peu de** viande.	*Camille buys very few carrots and only a little meat.*

Pour en savoir plus...

Beaucoup and the other nonspecific expressions of quantity may be used without **de** to modify verbs.

Est-ce que Bruno flirte **trop** avec Camille et Hélène?

Rachid aime **beaucoup** les Cévennes.

*Selon les régions, on utilise les termes **un demi-kilo** ou **une livre** pour désigner un poids (*weight*) de cinq cent grammes. Dans les marchés en plein air, le terme **livre** est plus courant.

Activités

A. Faire les courses en France. Vous faites les courses pour la semaine au supermarché *Super-U.* Choisissez un produit de chaque (*each*) rayon.

MODÈLE: Au rayon crémerie, j'achète du camembert.

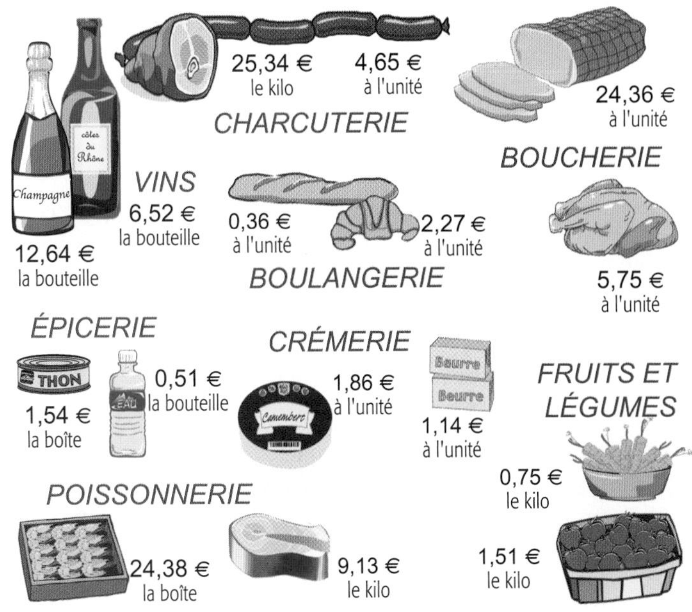

B. Un bon régime. (*A healthy diet.*) Nommez trois choses que ces personnes achètent ou n'achètent pas au marché.

MODÈLE: Un musulman pratiquant (*practicing Muslim*) achète du poulet et des tomates au marché. Il n'achète certainement pas de porc.

1. un végétarien
2. une personne qui n'aime pas le sucre
3. un athlète qui s'entraîne (*in training*)
4. une personne allergique aux produits laitiers
5. une personne qui a trop de cholestérol

C. Souvenirs du film. (*Memories of the film.*) Mettez l'article indéfini (**un/une/des**), l'article défini (**le/la/les**), l'article partitif (**du/de la/de l'**) ou **de/d'**.

MODÈLE: Bruno prend (*has*) de la salade (*f.*) verte. Rachid ne prend pas de salade verte.

1. Le chef cuisinier propose _____ jarret (*m.*) de porc aux lentilles, mais Rachid veut _____ hamburger et _____ eau.
2. Le père de Rachid ne mange pas _____ porc, mais sa mère adore _____ jambon.
3. Martine va manger _____ pain.
4. Camille aime _____ champagne. Rachid ne veut pas _____ champagne.

5. Louise dit (*says*): «Alex. Tu m'achètes _____ champagne? _____ bonne bouteille, s'il te plaît.»
6. Camille dit: «J'aimerais _____ kilo _____ bœuf, s'il vous plaît.»
7. Camille dit: «Je vais prendre aussi _____ oignons et _____ livre de pommes de terre.»

D. Une vie difficile? Utilisez des expressions de quantité et les substantifs (*nouns*) de la liste pour parler des gens suivants.

argent	crevettes	livres	responsabilités
beurre	croissants	oranges	saumon
bœuf	enfants	pain	travail
champagne	légumes	problèmes	vêtements (chic, de sport)

MODÈLE: Une femme qui prépare une fête achète... →
Une femme qui prépare une fête achète un kilo de saumon, une livre de crevettes, un demi-kilo de beurre et beaucoup de pain.

1. Un étudiant qui fait des études de yoga achète...
2. Un journaliste qui parle à la télé a...
3. Un enfant qui n'aime pas la viande mange...
4. Une mère de douze enfants met... sur la table le matin.
5. Un père de quinze enfants a...
6. Un jeune homme pauvre a...
7. Une femme riche a...
8. Un professeur a... dans son bureau.
9. Une femme qui prépare une fête achète...

E. Ressemblances. Regardez la liste suivante et notez en quelle quantité vous achetez toutes ces choses chaque mois. Ensuite (*Then*), interviewez des camarades de classe pour trouver quelqu'un (*someone*) qui achète les mêmes quantités que vous. Notez son nom.

Vocabulaire utile: du, de la, de l', un, une, des, de, d', beaucoup de, un peu de, peu de, trop de, une bouteille de, une boîte de, un demi-kilo de

MODÈLE: É1: J'achète peu de pain chaque mois.
É2: Moi aussi, j'achète peu de pain chaque mois. (*ou* Moi, j'achète trois kilos de pain chaque mois.; Moi, j'achète beaucoup de pain chaque mois.)
É1: Super! Comment t'appelles-tu? (*ou* Zut! [*Rats!*])

1. le pain
2. la viande
3. l'eau minérale
4. les pâtisseries
5. les crevettes
6. le vin
7. les petits pois
8. les pommes

Structure 22

Le complément d'objet indirect

Avoiding repetition

—Qu'est-ce que je **vous** sers, mademoiselle?

Le complément d'objet indirect

There are three broad grammatical functions in a sentence: the subject (the doer of the action); the verb (the action); and the complement (a word or phrase that "completes" what is said about another element of the sentence).

Martine	donne	le médaillon	à Camille.
sujet	**verbe**	**complément**	**complément**

In this sentence, the complement consists of two nouns. The first, **le médaillon**, is the thing that is given. It is called the direct object▲ (**le complément d'objet direct**) because the verb acts directly upon it. The second noun, **Camille**, is the person to whom the locket is given. She is the indirect object▲ (**le complément d'objet indirect**), the person for whom (or to whom) the action was done.

Les pronoms complément d'objet indirect

Pronouns are words that stand in place of nouns in sentences so that the nouns themselves do not have to be constantly repeated. They make speech and writing flow more smoothly and sound more natural. In this lesson, you will learn the forms and uses of pronouns that serve as the indirect object.

me (m')	*to/for me*	**nous**	*to/for us*
te (t')	*to/for you*	**vous**	*to/for you*
lui	*to/for him/her*	**leur**	*to/for them*

1. Here are some verbs that are frequently used with an indirect object.

acheter (à quelqu'un)	*to buy* (*for someone*)
demander* (à quelqu'un) (**si**)	*to ask* (*someone*) (*if, whether*)
donner (à quelqu'un)	*to give* (*to someone*)
montrer (à quelqu'un)	*to show* (*to someone*)
parler (à quelqu'un)	*to speak* (*to someone*)
téléphoner* (à quelqu'un)	*to call* (*someone*) *on the telephone*

Camille téléphone **à Louise**. → Camille **lui** téléphone.
Camille calls her.

Rachid parle **à Bruno et Camille**. → Rachid **leur** parle.
Rachid talks to them.

2. The indirect object pronoun precedes the verb.

Louise dit: «Alex. Tu **m'**achètes du champagne?»
Louise says, "Alex. Will you buy some champagne ***for me****?"*
Louise says, "Alex. Will you buy ***me*** *some champagne?"*

Martine cherche Camille et **lui** montre le médaillon.
Martine looks for Camille and shows the locket ***to her****.*
Martine looks for Camille and shows ***her*** *the locket.*

3. Because **lui** and **leur** can refer to both masculine and feminine nouns, the context is important for understanding exact meaning.

Bruno? Je **lui** donne un cadeau. Et Camille... Je **lui** donne un cadeau aussi. — *Bruno? I'm giving* ***him*** *a present. And Camille . . . I'm giving* ***her*** *a present too.*

4. In the negative, the pronoun still directly precedes the verb.

Tu ne **me** donnes jamais de cadeaux. — *You never give me presents.*

5. In verb + infinitive constructions, the pronoun precedes the infinitive, even in the negative.

Je vais **lui** téléphoner aujourd'hui. — *I'm going to call him/her today.*
Je ne veux pas **lui** parler. — *I don't want to talk to him/her.*

Activités

A. La journée de Camille. Camille parle de sa journée. Complétez les phrases avec les pronoms complément d'objet indirect qui conviennent (*are appropriate*).

Je vais au travail. Bruno et moi préparons l'émission de jeudi avec deux chefs de cuisine. Nous _____[1] (lui, leur) demandons de préparer un dessert délicieux.

*Les verbes **demander** et **téléphoner** sont accompagnés d'un complément d'objet indirect en français. *Je téléphone* ***à mes parents*** *toutes les semaines. Je demande* ***à mon ami*** *s'il veut venir avec moi.*

Ils _____[2] (nous, vous) proposent une mousse au chocolat, mais Bruno n'aime pas le chocolat. Les chefs _____[3] (lui, te) demandent ce qu'il préfère. Alors, ils vont _____[4] (vous, nous) préparer une tarte aux pommes américaine.

L'après-midi, je pense à ma grand-mère et je _____[5] (te, lui) téléphone. On va dîner ensemble ce soir. Au marché, le boucher _____[6] (me, lui) demande de signer un autographe. La marchande de légumes demande: «Qu'est-ce que je _____[7] (vous, te) sers, mademoiselle?» Quand j'arrive chez grand-mère, je _____[8] (me, nous) prépare un bœuf bourguignon. Après le dîner, je _____[9] (lui, leur) dit: «Je veux _____[10] (vous, te) montrer quelque chose. C'est une surprise.»

B. Questions et réponses. Votre partenaire va poser des questions. Utilisez des pronoms complément d'objet indirect pour répondre.

MODÈLE: Est-ce que tu parles à tes parents (tes enfants) de tes problèmes? → Non, je ne leur parle jamais de mes problèmes. (Oui, je leur parle parfois de mes problèmes.)

1. Est-ce que tu téléphones souvent à tes amis d'enfance? **2.** Est-ce que tu achètes une vidéo de son film préféré à ton ami? **3.** Est-ce que tu donnes une pomme à ton professeur? **4.** Est-ce que tu nous montres ton livre? **5.** Est-ce que tu téléphones à tes parents (tes enfants) tous les jours (*every day*)? **6.** Est-ce que tu demandes s'ils sont mariés à tes professeurs? **7.** Est-ce que tu me parles?

C. Tu es de la police? Votre partenaire vous pose des questions personnelles en utilisant les éléments suivants. Répondez avec un pronom complément d'objet indirect.

MODÈLE: É1: Quand est-ce que tu achètes des fleurs à une amie?
É2: Je lui achète des fleurs quand elle n'est pas heureuse. (Je ne lui achète jamais de fleurs.)

	acheter des fleurs	des étudiants dans la classe
	acheter une carte	moi
	demander un rendez-vous	nous (les autres étudiants et moi)
	donner les devoirs	tes amis
Pourquoi	montrer des photos de vacances	tes parents
Quand	montrer un examen	toi
	parler	vous (les autres étudiants et toi)
	parler de politique	ton professeur
	parler de religion	un(e) camarade de classe
	téléphoner	une amie

Regards sur la culture

Le marché et la cuisine°

Le... *The market and cooking*

In this chapter, you have seen Camille pick up a few items at an outdoor market as she prepares to make dinner for her grandmother. Food has a very high priority in French culture, and many social relations are maintained around home-cooked meals.

Un marché en plein air

Un supermarché

- One advantage of the traditional market is its appeal to the various senses. The displays are set up to highlight color and aesthetic appeal, and the mix of sounds (vendors calling, boxes being stacked) and smells (flowers, fruit, meat, cheese, fish) contributes to the experience. But for many people, the most important part of shopping at the market is the socializing that goes on.
- Another advantage to the traditional market is that the vendor typically prepares the products to order for the customer, cutting the meat into particular sized pieces, for example, or slicing off just the right amount of cheese.
- In markets and in neighborhood grocery stores, customers do not pick out individual pieces of fruit or vegetables. They tell the vendor what they want, and the vendor picks out the produce. More than one North American has been thought to be shoplifting when picking out an apple from a market display.
- Most French shoppers are very concerned about the quality of the food they buy, and they are often careful to buy pesticide-free products. They may want to know where the vegetables and beef come from or what kind of feed the chicken ate.
- Meals at home play a crucial role in family relationships. In addition, it is almost obligatory to treat guests to a meal consisting of three or more courses. Thus, having a large dining room is relatively important for French families, and one of the first pieces of furniture that many young couples purchase is a large dining table so that they can entertain family and friends appropriately.
- A French meal without some kind of first course is unusual. Even the simplest meal usually begins with the **entrée**—a few slices of salami, a bowl of soup, or a serving of marinated mushrooms—before the main dish (**le plat principal**) arrives. The distinction between **une entrée** and **un hors-d'œuvre** is based mostly on how many courses are served with the meal and whether the dish is served as part of the meal or before it begins.

Considérez

In France, **bien manger** means to eat delicious, refined food. What does *to eat well* mean in North America? Why the difference?

Structure 23

Les verbes *prendre, mettre, boire*

Talking about everyday actions

—...**Vous** en **prenez** un kilo?

—Non, juste deux ou trois...

—D'accord. Et avec ça?

—Euh, je vais **prendre** aussi des oignons et une livre de pommes de terre.

Le verbe *prendre*

prendre (*to take*)			
je	**prends**	nous	**prenons**
tu	**prends**	vous	**prenez**
il, elle, on	**prend**	ils, elles	**prennent**

Vous en **prenez** un kilo? — *Will you take a kilo of them?*

1. **Prendre** is used in several idiomatic expressions: **prendre du temps** (*to take [a long] time*), **prendre un verre** (*to have a drink*), **prendre du jambon/du pain/etc.** (*to have some ham/some bread/etc.*), and **prendre une décision** (*to make a decision*).

   Ce travail **prend du temps**! — *This work takes a long time!*
   Tu **prends un verre** avec moi? — *Will you have a drink with me?*
   Je vais **prendre** du jambon. — *I'll have some ham.*

2. Other verbs conjugated like **prendre** are **apprendre** (*to learn*) and **comprendre** (*to understand*). To say you are learning to do something, the expression is **apprendre à** + infinitive.

   Nous **apprenons** le français. — *We are learning French.*
   Nous **apprenons à parler** français. — *We are learning to speak French.*
   Tu **comprends** la leçon? — *Do you understand the lesson?*

Le verbe *mettre*

mettre (*to put*)			
je	**mets**	nous	**mettons**
tu	**mets**	vous	**mettez**
il, elle, on	**met**	ils, elles	**mettent**

Vous mettez la bouteille dans le frigo?	*Are you putting the bottle in the refrigerator?*

1. Common expressions are **mettre un vêtement** (*to put on a piece of clothing*), **mettre la table** (*to set the table*), **mettre la radio/télé/lumière** (*to turn on the radio/TV/light*), and **mettre du temps à** (*to spend time on*).

Pourquoi **tu mets ce béret** ridicule?	*Why are you putting on that ridiculous béret?*
Tu **mets la table**, Camille?	*Are you setting the table, Camille?*
Rachid **met la radio** pour écouter de la musique raï.	*Rachid turns on the radio to listen to raï music.*
Ils **mettent du temps à** trouver la vérité.	*They spend time finding the truth.*

2. Other verbs like **mettre** are **permettre (à)** (*to permit, allow* [*someone*]) and **promettre (à)** (*to promise* [*someone*]). With an infinitive, you have to use **permettre de** + infinitive and **promettre de** + infinitive.

Mado ne permet pas à Camille **de parler** de son grand-père.	*Mado doesn't let Camille talk about her grandfather.*
Je promets de te **téléphoner** demain.	*I promise to call you tomorrow.*

Le verbe *boire*

boire (*to drink*)			
je	**bois**	nous	**buvons**
tu	**bois**	vous	**buvez**
il, elle, on	**boit**	ils, elles	**boivent**

—Tu **bois** quelque chose, Rachid?	*Are you drinking anything, Rachid?*
—Non, les musulmans pratiquants ne **boivent** pas d'alcool.	*No, practicing Muslims don't drink alcohol.*

Activités

A. Habitudes. (*Habits.*) Complétez les phrases avec la forme correcte d'un des verbes indiqués.

PRENDRE, APPRENDRE, COMPRENDRE

1. Tu _____ un verre avec moi?
2. Est-ce ton frère et toi _____ le train pour aller au travail?
3. Nous _____ la leçon, mais nous ne pouvons pas l'expliquer en français.
4. J' _____ à faire la cuisine.
5. Nos classes _____ du temps.
6. Est-ce que vous _____ cette décision importante?

METTRE, PERMETTRE, PROMETTRE

7. Pourquoi est-ce que tu _____ un pantalon vert et une chemise rose?
8. Est-ce que vous _____ de revenir?
9. Je _____ la télé pour regarder un débat politique.
10. Nous ne _____ pas à nos enfants de mettre la télé avant le dîner.
11. Les femmes _____ du temps à s'habiller (*to get dressed*) avant d'aller à une soirée.
12. Tu _____ la table pour le dîner, s'il te plaît?

BOIRE

13. Tu _____ trop de coca.
14. Je _____ de l'eau minérale.
15. Nous ne _____ pas d'alcool parce que nous sommes musulmans.
16. Les étudiants _____ beaucoup de café avant les examens.

Apprendre une langue étrangère: Les méthodes les plus efficaces!

B. Enquête. (*Survey.*) Demandez à trois camarades de classe ce qu'ils (*what they*) boivent et ce qu'ils mangent normalement au dîner. Ensuite, demandez ce qu'ils ne boivent pas et ce qu'ils ne mangent pas. Prenez des notes et présentez les résultats de votre enquête à la classe en utilisant les verbes **prendre** et **boire**. Quelles boissons et quels repas sont populaires?

C. Que font-ils? Décrivez (*Describe*) chaque photo. Utilisez des éléments de chaque colonne.

Rachid		la photo sur le bureau
Sonia	(ne... pas) prendre	le portable dans son sac
Rachid et Camille	(ne... pas) mettre	de l'eau / d'eau
Camille	(ne... pas) boire	le portable de Martine
		la photo de la main (*hand*) de Bruno
		du vin / de vin
		le bus

MODÈLE: Rachid prend la photo de la main de Bruno.

1. 

2. 

3. 

4. 

5. 

6. 

Visionnement 2

Le Quartier latin. (*The Latin Quarter.*) The area represented on the map is the southern part of the **Quartier latin**, which was first built up in the 12th and 13th centuries as the home of the great Parisian schools, renowned across all of Europe. **La Sorbonne**, originally a center of theological studies, today is just one part of the University of Paris. Many of the students who attend the numerous schools and universities of the Latin Quarter spend evenings in the restaurants and bars of the **rue Mouffetard**. **Le jardin du Luxembourg** is a large public park. The building that houses the French Senate, **le palais du Luxembourg**, is located within it. **Le Panthéon**, completed in 1789, honors great men and women of France. Among those buried there are Voltaire, Rousseau, Victor Hugo, Marie Curie, Louis Braille, and Jean Moulin, one of the most famous heroes of the Resistance. **L'Institut national des Jeunes Sourds**, founded in 1760, was a pioneering institution in the education of the deaf and is closely connected with the origins of American Sign Language.

Les environs de l'appartement de Louise

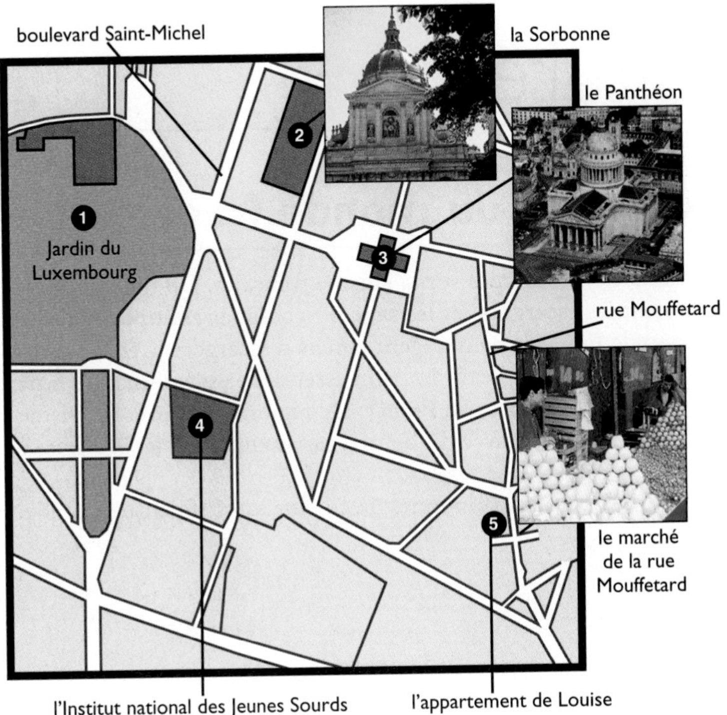

Un étudiant parle de sa journée. Complétez chaque phrase avec le nom de l'endroit qui convient.

1. Ce matin j'ai un cours (*class*) d'anthropologie à...
2. Après, j'ai un cours de la langue des signes française à...
3. À midi, je vais manger un sandwich en plein air (*outdoors*) dans...
4. Avec mon cousin, qui s'intéresse à l'histoire, je vais visiter...
5. Le soir, nous allons chercher un bon petit restaurant dans la rue...

Observez!

Considérez les aspects culturels expliqués dans **Regards sur la culture**. Ensuite, regardez l'Épisode 7 encore une fois, et répondez aux questions suivantes.

- Quelles expressions Camille et les marchands emploient-ils pour montrer leur souci (*concern*) pour la qualité des produits?
- Que fait et que dit Camille au marché Mouffetard? Comparez ce marché avec un marché près de chez vous.

Après le visionnement

Faites l'activité pour le **Visionnement 2** dans le cahier.

Synthèse: Culture

Cuisines du monde francophone

Il y a beaucoup de stéréotypes sur la cuisine française. On dit souvent que les Français aiment les escargots[1] et les sauces riches, par exemple. Mais la vérité est que beaucoup de Français ne mangent jamais d'escargots. L'élément de base de la cuisine française est le blé,[2] et la boisson essentielle est le vin, mais à part cela[3] on mange des choses très variées en France. De région en région, la cuisine change: en Normandie, on cuisine avec du beurre, par exemple, et en Provence avec de l'huile[4] d'olive.

Dans les autres pays francophones, la cuisine est différente. Voici deux exemples.

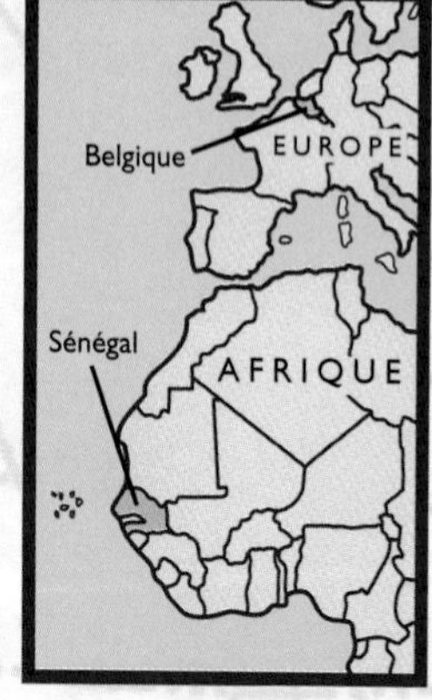

La Belgique

L'élément de base de la cuisine = la pomme de terre
La boisson essentielle = la bière

La Belgique est située à la frontière des cultures germanique et latine. Certains éléments de sa cuisine sont d'origine allemande, d'autres sont d'origine française. Les Belges mangent beaucoup de moules[5] et de frites.[6] Le chocolat est une autre grande spécialité de la Belgique.

Des aliments typiquement belges

Un repas belge

Le jambon des Ardennes

•••

La carbonnade flamande

du bœuf, des pommes de terre et des oignons cuisinés dans une sauce à la bière

Les choux de Bruxelles

•••

La tarte à la rhubarbe

[1]*snails* [2]*wheat* [3]*à… besides that* [4]*oil* [5]*mussels* [6]*fries*

Le Sénégal

L'élément de base traditionnel = le mil[7]; aujourd'hui = le riz[8]
La boisson essentielle = le thé à la menthe

Le Sénégal est situé sur l'Atlantique, dans l'ouest de l'Afrique. Son climat est influencé par le Sahara. Dans la cuisine sénégalaise, il y a aujourd'hui des influences françaises. Par exemple, en ville, les Sénégalais mangent du pain comme en France. Et le riz, introduit au Sénégal par la France, est maintenant un aliment[9] essentiel.

Un repas typiquement sénégalais

Un repas sénégalais

Le poulet au yassa
du poulet mariné
avec des citrons verts[10] et des piments,[11]
cuisiné avec des oignons
dans de l'huile de cacahuète[12]
Le riz
•••
Le lakh
du mil bouilli[13] servi avec du lait caillé[14] et du sucre

[7]*millet (a grain that thrives in dry climates)* [8]*rice* [9]*food* [10]citrons... *limes* [11]*pimento* [12]*peanut* [13]*boiled* [14]lait... *a dairy product like sour cream*

À vous

Un repas francophone. In groups of three or four, plan a meal that would illustrate the diversity of cooking in the Francophone world. It should be designed to be appetizing as well as to educate someone who knows nothing about the countries where French is spoken. Choose from among the dishes just mentioned and others presented in this book or that you know about (from Louisiana, for example). Once you have established the menu for your meal, have one person present it to the class, along with an explanation of why each of the dishes was chosen and what the overall menu communicates.

À écrire

Faites **À écrire** pour le Chapitre 7 dans le cahier.

Vocabulaire

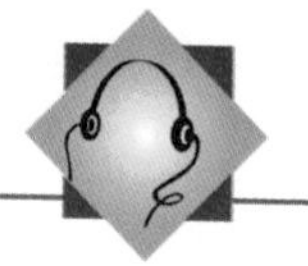

Vendeurs

un(e) boucher/ère	butcher
un(e) boulanger/ère	(bread) baker
un(e) épicier/ière	grocer
un(e) marchand(e)	merchant
un(e) pâtissier/ière	(pastry) baker

Magasins

une boucherie	butcher shop
une boulangerie	(bread) bakery
une charcuterie	pork butcher shop; delicatessen
une crémerie	dairy product store
une épicerie	grocery store
une pâtisserie	(pastry) bakery
une poissonnerie	fish store

MOT APPARENTÉ: **un marché**

À REVOIR: **un magasin**

Provisions

un aliment	food
le beurre	butter
le bœuf	beef
une cerise	cherry
un citron	lemon
la confiture	jam
des crevettes (*f.*)	shrimp
l'eau (*f.*) **(minérale, gazeuse, plate)**	(mineral, carbonated, noncarbonated) water
le fromage	cheese
des fruits (*m.*) **de mer**	seafood
des haricots (*m.*) **verts**	green beans
le jambon	ham
un légume	vegetable
le maïs	corn
le pain	bread
une pâtisserie	pastry
des petits pois (*m.*)	peas
un poisson	fish
une pomme	apple
une pomme de terre	potato
le poulet	chicken
du raisin	grapes
une saucisse	(link) sausage
le saumon	salmon
le sucre	sugar
une tarte	pie
le thon	tuna
la viande	meat
le vin (rouge, blanc, rosé)	(red, white, rosé) wine

MOTS APPARENTÉS: **une carotte, le champagne, la crème, un fruit, un oignon, le porc, une tomate**

L'article partitif

du, de la	some

Expressions de quantité

une boîte (de) can (of); box (of)
une bouteille (de) bottle (of)
une livre (de) pound (of)
un morceau (de) piece (of)
(un) peu (de) (a) little; (a) few
assez (de) enough
beaucoup (de) much; many; a lot of
trop (de) too much; too many

MOTS APPARENTÉS: **un demi-kilo (de), une douzaine (de), un kilo (de)**

Pronoms complément d'objet indirect

me to/for me
te to/for you
lui to/for him/her
nous to/for us
vous to/for you
leur to/for them

Verbes

apprendre to learn
boire to drink
comprendre to understand
demander (si) to ask (if, whether)
mettre to put
  mettre du temps à to spend time on
  mettre la radio/télé/lumière to turn on the radio/TV/light
  mettre la table to set the table
  mettre un vêtement to put on a piece of clothing
montrer to show
permettre to permit, allow
prendre to take
  prendre du temps to take (a long) time
  prendre du jambon/du pain/etc. to have some ham/some bread/etc. (*to eat*)
  prendre une décision to make a decision
  prendre un verre to have a drink
promettre to promise

MOT APPARENTÉ: **téléphoner**
À REVOIR: **acheter, donner, parler**

Autres expressions utiles

chaque each
ensemble together
si if, whether

À REVOIR: **chez**

Chapitre 8

C'est loin, tout ça.°

°C'est... *All that was long ago.*

OBJECTIFS

In this episode, you will

- witness the Leclair family's reluctance to talk about past events
- learn more about Camille's relationship with Mado

In this chapter, you will

- talk about meals and dining habits
- talk about everyday activities
- give commands and make suggestions
- learn how the French conduct conversations
- read the poem "Familiale," by Jacques Prévert

Vocabulaire en contexte

Les repas en France°

Les... *Meals in France*

Le matin, on prend **le petit déjeuner**. On peut manger et boire

L'après-midi, entre midi et 14 heures, on **déjeune**.° Voilà **quelques** possibilités.

has lunch

Comme° **entrée** (*f.*), on peut prendre, par exemple,

As

Après l'entrée, comme **plat** (*m.*) **chaud** (le **plat principal**), on peut prendre, par exemple,

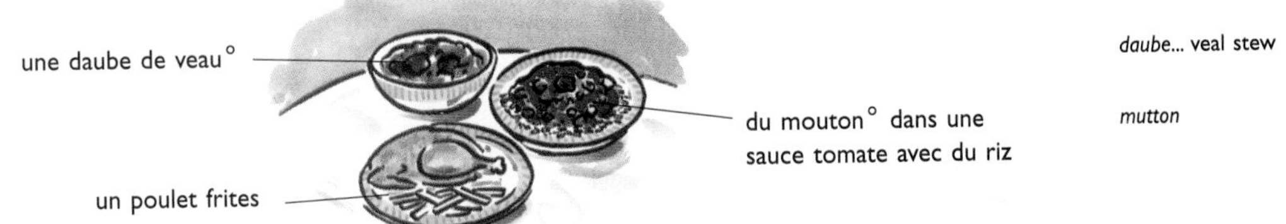

daube... veal stew

mutton

Comme **boisson** (*f.*), on peut prendre

On prend du pain avec le plat chaud, et du fromage **avant le dessert**. Comme dessert, on peut prendre quelque chose° de **sucré**. quelque... *something*

Il y a aussi des gens° qui mangent **du fast-food**: **un hamburger** et **un coca**, par exemple. D'autres prennent **une pizza** ou **un sandwich**. *people*

Pour en savoir plus...

Eating habits are gradually changing in France. Although lunch typically remains the day's heaviest meal, involving a warm dish, vegetables, and a salad, some people are now taking lighter noon meals and heavier evening meals. The French are also consuming less bread and wine than in the past. Drinking orange juice at breakfast has recently begun to gain popularity.

Le soir, entre 19 heures et 21 heures, on dîne. En général, c'est un repas **léger**. Voici quelques possibilités. On peut manger et boire

Après, on peut prendre du fromage ou un dessert.

Qu'est-ce que vous aimez manger? Quelles **choses**° est-ce que vous trouvez particulièrement délicieuses? *things*

Autres mots utiles

le déjeuner	dinner
le dîner	lunch
le poivre	pepper
le sel	salt
la salade	lettuce

Activités

A. Quelle catégorie? Classez les aliments selon (*according to*) les catégories suivantes: **une entrée**, **un plat chaud**, **une boisson**, **un dessert**, **du fast-food**.

1. une daube de veau
2. une mousse au chocolat
3. du thé
4. du saucisson
5. du fromage
6. du jus d'orange

7. du coca
8. un fruit
9. de la charcuterie
10. du mouton
11. de la glace
12. un hamburger

B. Quel repas? Dites (*Say*) à quel repas on mange probablement ces choses en France.

MODÈLE: du pain →
On mange du pain au petit déjeuner, au déjeuner ou au dîner.

1. de la soupe
2. de l'eau minérale
3. du café au lait
4. du mouton
5. du riz
6. un croissant
7. de la tarte
8. un petit pain
9. un poulet frites
10. un sandwich
11. un verre de vin rouge
12. une omelette
13. une pizza
14. une salade
15. une tartine

Maintenant, dites si on mange ou boit ces choses avant, après ou avec d'autres parties (*parts*) du repas.

MODÈLE: du pain →
On mange du pain avec le plat principal.

C. Correspondances. Identifiez un plat qui correspond aux descriptions suivantes.

1. une boisson caféinée
2. un plat riche en calories et en cholestérol
3. un plat léger
4. un plat sucré
5. deux condiments
6. un plat que vous avez envie d'essayer
7. un plat que vous n'avez pas envie d'essayer

D. Sondage. (*Survey.*) Demandez à votre partenaire

1. ce qu'il/elle prend comme petit déjeuner.
2. ce qu'il/elle mange pour le déjeuner.
3. ce qu'il/elle mange pour le dîner.
4. combien de fois par semaine il/elle mange de la viande.
5. quelles sortes de légumes il/elle mange et combien de fois par semaine.
6. s'il / si elle mange beaucoup de pâtes (*pasta*) ou de pommes de terre.
7. combien de boîtes de coca il/elle boit par semaine.
8. s'il / si elle prend un dessert tous les jours (*every day*).
9. ce qu'il/elle mange entre les repas.

Maintenant, présentez vos résultats à la classe. En général, est-ce que les étudiants de la classe ont un régime alimentaire sain (*healthy diet*)? Est-ce qu'ils consomment trop de matières grasses (*fat*)? de calories? de sucreries (*sweets*)?

À table

Pour mettre la table, on y° met les choses suivantes. *there*

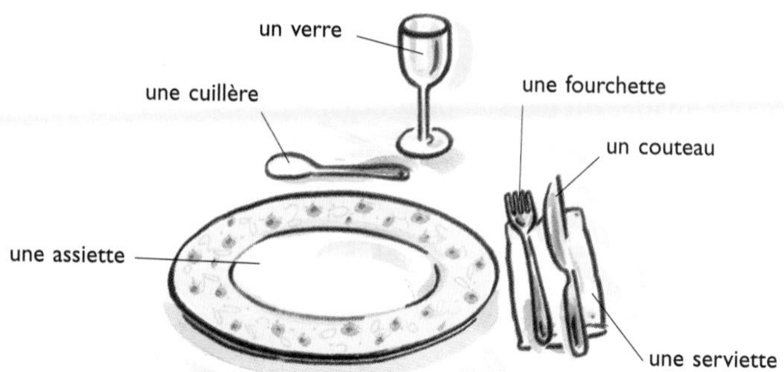

Autres mots utiles

une nappe	tablecloth
une tasse	cup

Quelques conseils°

advice

- Tenez° le couteau dans la main droite° pour couper° la viande; tenez la fourchette dans la main gauche° pour porter le morceau à la bouche.° *Hold / la... the right hand / cut* *left* *mouth*
- Rompez° votre morceau de pain; ne coupez pas le pain! *Break*
- Mettez votre pain sur la table à côté de votre assiette.
- Ne mangez pas le pain avant le repas. Mangez le pain avec le repas.
- Pliez les feuilles° de la salade. Ne les coupez pas. *Fold the leaves*
- Ne parlez pas la bouche pleine°! *full*

Langage fonctionnel

Pour parler du repas

The following expressions are often used at meals.

Pour souhaiter un bon repas

Bon appétit.	*Enjoy your meal.*
À votre santé! / Et à la vôtre! (À la tienne!)	*To your health! / And to yours!*

Pour demander quelque chose

Est-ce que vous pourriez (tu pourrais) me passer... ?	*Could you please pass . . . ?*

Pour offrir encore quelque chose

Encore du (de la, des)... ?	*(Would you like) more ... ?*
Je vous (te) ressers de... ?	*May I serve you more ... ?*
Vous pouvez (Tu peux) en reprendre un peu.	*You could have a little more.*

Pour accepter ou refuser une offre

Avec plaisir!	*With pleasure!*
Merci. (Non, merci.)	*No, thank you.*
Volontiers!	*Gladly!*

Pour faire un compliment

C'est (C'était) délicieux.	*It is (was) delicious.*
J'ai très bien mangé.	*I've had a very good meal.*

—**Je te ressers** du rôti?	*May I serve you more roast?*
—**Merci. C'était délicieux.**	*No, thank you. I've had a very good meal.*

Activités

A. Qu'est-ce qui ne va pas? (*What's not right?*) Quelles choses ne sont pas bien placées sur la table? Quels conseils ne sont pas suivis (*followed*) par les personnes à table?

B. À table. Vous êtes à table. Quelle expression pouvez-vous utiliser dans chaque (*each*) situation?

1. Tout le monde est à table. Votre hôtesse vous invite à manger. Vous dites...
2. Avant de manger, vous levez (*raise*) votre verre de vin et vous dites...
3. Vous voulez des carottes. Vous dites...
4. On vous demande si vous voulez encore du vin. Vous acceptez. Vous dites...
5. On vous offre encore du poulet. Vous refusez mais vous faites un compliment. Vous dites...

Visionnement 1

Avant de visionner

In this episode, you will hear examples of two new verb tenses: The **passé composé** (in **boldface** type) is used to talk about past events; the ***imparfait*** (in ***bold italic*** type) is used to talk about past conditions or states of mind, and ongoing action in the past. You will learn to form and use these tenses in Chapters 10, 11, and 12, but for now, just learn to recognize them so you can understand Episode 8.

Vous comprenez? Essayez de comprendre les deux extraits (*extracts*) du film.

Camille pose une question à sa grand-mère, Louise.

CAMILLE: C'***était***[a] quand, la dernière[b] fois qu'il t'**a contactée**[c]?

LOUISE: En 1943. Il ***était*** dans les Cévennes. Il m'**a envoyé** une lettre... pour l'anniversaire de ta maman. Elle ***avait*** quatre ans.

Plus tard,[d] Mado parle à Camille.

MADO: D'où sort-elle[e] cette photo?! Pourquoi tu **as montré** ça à ta grand-mère?

[a]*It was* [b]*last* [c]*il... he contacted you* [d]*Plus... Later* [e]*D'où... Where does it come from*

Maintenant, indiquez si les phrases suivantes sont vraies ou fausses. Corrigez les phrases qui sont fausses.

1. Quelqu'un (*Someone*) contacte Louise pour la dernière fois en 1940.
2. Il est à Paris.
3. Il envoie une lettre pour l'anniversaire de Mado.
4. Mado a quarante ans à cette époque (*at that time*).
5. Mado demande pourquoi Camille montre une photo à sa grand-mère.

Notez bien!

Two new words are useful for talking about the film.

la guerre war

raconter to tell (about)

Camille uses them both when she asks her grandmother . . .

Tu me **racontes** son histoire pendant **la guerre**? *Will you tell me his story during the war?*

Vocabulaire relatif à l'épisode

La guerre, c'est moche!	*War is awful!*
En es-tu sûr(e)?	*Are you sure about that?*
Mais qu'est-ce que tu as?	*What's wrong with you?*
On ne réveille pas les morts.	*Nobody should disturb the dead.*
Tu mérites une gifle!	*You deserve a slap!*
Ça suffit!	*That's enough!*

Observez!

Dans cet épisode, Camille cherche des informations sur le rôle de son grand-père pendant (*during*) la Deuxième Guerre mondiale (*Second World War*).

- Comment Louise réagit-elle (*does Louise react*) à la demande de Camille?
- Comment réagit Mado? Pourquoi?

Après le visionnement

A. Vrai ou faux? Indiquez si les phrases suivantes sont vraies ou fausses. Corrigez les phrases fausses.

1. Camille montre une lettre d'Antoine à Louise.
2. Louise aime parler de son mari.

3. Louise raconte la visite de son mari dans les Cévennes.
4. Mado est furieuse parce que Camille a montré la photo à Louise.
5. Mado pense qu'on ne doit pas (*should not*) parler de son père.

B. Réfléchissez. (*Think.*) Répondez aux questions.

1. Quels mots et expressions montrent que Louise et Mado considèrent encore Camille comme une enfant?
2. Comment Camille essaie-t-elle de montrer son indépendance?

Structure 24

Les verbes réguliers en -re

Talking about everyday activities

—Tu **perds** la tête... !

—Et cesse de me **répondre**. Tu mérites une gifle!!

The verbs **perdre** (*to lose*) and **répondre** (*to answer*) are examples of a class of verbs that are all conjugated in the same way. They are sometimes referred to as regular **-re** verbs.

1. To use regular **-re** verbs in the present tense, drop the **-re** ending and add the endings **-s**, **-s**, —, **-ons**, **-ez**, **-ent**. Notice that no ending is added for the **il/elle/on** form.

répondre (*to answer*)			
je	répond**s**	nous	répond**ons**
tu	répond**s**	vous	répond**ez**
il, elle, on	répond	ils, elles	répond**ent**

Quand le prof pose une question, **nous répondons**. — *When the professor asks a question, we answer.*

Louise **répond** au téléphone. — *Louise answers the telephone.*

2. Here is a list of some common regular **-re** verbs.

attendre	*to wait (for)*	**rendre**	*to return (something); to render, make*
descendre	*to descend, go (get) down*	**répondre**	*to answer*
entendre	*to hear*	**vendre**	*to sell*
perdre	*to lose*		

Tu descends du train.	*You get out of the train.*
L'argent **rend-il** les gens heureux?	*Does money make people happy?*

3. **Attendre** does not take a preposition before an object as *wait* does in English.

Bruno **attend** Camille.	*Bruno waits for Camille.*

4. **Perdre** usually takes an article or a possessive adjective before the thing that is lost. The idiomatic expression **perdre la tête** (*to lose one's mind*) follows this pattern; the expression **perdre patience** (*to lose patience*) does not.

	Camille **perd son médaillon**.	*Camille loses her locket.*
	Tu **perds la tête**... !	*You're losing your mind . . . !*
but	Mado **perd patience** avec Camille.	*Mado loses patience with Camille.*

5. When **rendre** means *to return something,* it takes a direct object.▲ To talk about *returning something* ***to someone,*** an indirect object pronoun or the preposition **à** + indirect object noun is needed.

Rachid **rend** le livre **à Camille**.	*Rachid returns the book to Camille.*
Il **lui rend** le livre.	*He returns the book to her.*

An idiomatic expression with **rendre** is **rendre visite à** (*to visit*). It is used only for visiting people, not places. Use **visiter** for visiting a place.

Camille **rend visite à** Louise.	*Camille visits Louise.*
Nous **visitons** Marseille.	*We're visiting Marseilles.*

6. **Répondre** can be used alone or with an indirect object (meaning *to answer something or someone*). If an object is required, use **répondre à**. Remember that for a person as object, you can use an indirect object pronoun.

Louise **répond au téléphone**.	*Louise answers the telephone.*
Yasmine **répond à Rachid**.	*Yasmine answers Rachid.*
Elle **lui répond**.	*She answers him.*

Activités

A. La journée typique de Nicole. Nicole, la scripte (*script coordinator*) à Canal 7, décrit (*describes*) sa journée typique. Utilisez les éléments donnés pour compléter sa description. Attention: It faut ajouter (*You have to add*) la préposition **à** dans deux des phrases.

MODÈLE: à 7 h 30, je / attendre / mon amie pour prendre un café →
À 7 h 30, j'attends mon amie pour prendre un café.

1. à 8 h, nous / entendre / les enfants dans l'appartement au-dessus.
2. ils / descendre / les escaliers (*the stairs*) pour aller à l'école
3. on / nous / vendre / des tickets de bus dans la station de métro
4. à 8 h 30, nous / attendre / le bus
5. les gens / perdre / patience quand le bus est en retard
6. Roger et moi, nous / répondre / les questions de Martine
7. parfois nous / entendre / les plaintes (*complaints*) de Bruno ou de Camille
8. à midi, je / rendre visite / ma sœur dans le quartier
9. ma sœur / attendre / toujours ma visite avec impatience
10. je / perdre / parfois ma clé quand je rentre (*return*) à la maison

B. Deux enfants. Répondez à Jojo et Jean-Pierre. Suivez le modèle, en utilisant **tu** ou **vous** et un des verbes suivants: **attendre**, **descendre**, **perdre**, **rendre**, **rendre visite à**, **répondre**, **vendre**.

MODÈLE: JOJO: Ma maman fait du shopping et je veux rentrer chez moi.
VOUS: Mais tu attends ta mère avec patience, n'est-ce pas?

1. JOJO ET JEAN-PIERRE: Notre maîtresse nous pose (*asks*) des questions.
   VOUS: Vous lui ____ toujours, naturellement.
2. JOJO: J'ai un livre de la bibliothèque.
   VOUS: Quand est-ce que tu ____ le livre à la bibliothèque?
3. JOJO ET JEAN-PIERRE: Notre grand-mère est triste parce qu'elle habite seule.
   VOUS: Est-ce que vous ____ vos grands-parents de temps en temps (*from time to time*)?
4. JOJO: Quand je saute (*jump*) sur le canapé, maman n'est pas contente.
   VOUS: Alors, tu ____ du canapé, non?
5. JOJO ET JEAN-PIERRE: Notre sœur à une poupée (*a doll*) très chère et nous avons besoin d'argent.
   VOUS: Vous ne ____ pas la poupée de votre sœur!
6. JOJO: Mon père attend un coup de téléphone (*phone call*) très important.
   VOUS: Alors, tu ne ____ pas au téléphone, d'accord?

C. Réactions. Que faites-vous dans les situations suivantes? Votre partenaire va poser la question. Répondez avec un des verbes réguliers en **-re**.

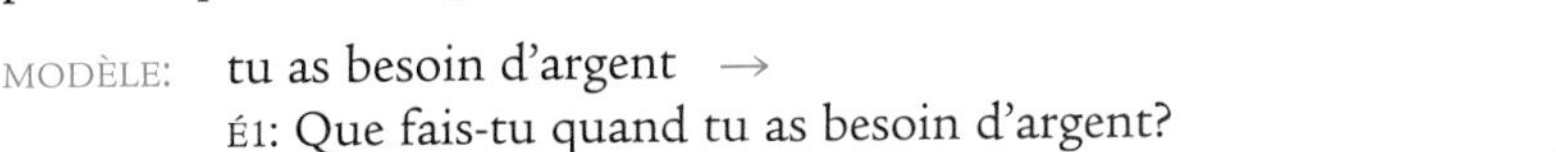

MODÈLE: tu as besoin d'argent →
É1: Que fais-tu quand tu as besoin d'argent?
É2: Je vends mes disques compacts. (Je rends visite à ma grand-mère!)

1. le professeur pose une question
2. une amie est triste
3. ton/ta camarade de chambre (ton fils, ta fille) joue (*plays*) de la guitare à deux heures du matin
4. le semestre est terminé
5. un film commence en retard
6. le téléphone sonne (*rings*)
7. tu vas à un concert
8. tes livres sont à rendre (*due*) à la bibliothèque

Structure 25

L'impératif

Giving commands and advice

—Ne **parle** jamais de lui à ta grand-mère!

The imperative is used for giving orders and advice and for making suggestions. There are three forms: **tu**, **vous**, and **nous**.

Pour en savoir plus...

Depending on the social context, the imperative may be considered too forceful and impolite in French. To "soften" a request or advice, use (1) **je voudrais**, (2) the present tense, and/or (3) **s'il te plaît** or **s'il vous plaît**.

Je voudrais parler à M. Gall, **s'il vous plaît**. *I would like to speak to Mr. Gall, please.*

Tu rentres chez toi et **tu** l'**attends**. *You should just go home and wait for her.*

Tu me **racontes** son voyage dans les Cévennes? **S'il te plaît?** *Will you tell me about his trip to the Cévennes? Please?*

1. The **tu** and **vous** imperatives are the **tu** or **vous** forms of the present tense, used without the pronoun. Note, however, that regular **-er** verbs and **aller** drop the final **s** of the **tu** form.

INFINITIF	(TU)	(VOUS)
regarder	Regarde... !	Regardez... !
répondre	Réponds... !	Répondez... !
aller	Va... !	Allez... !
boire	Bois... !	Buvez... !
faire	Fais... !	Faites... !
mettre	Mets... !	Mettez... !
prendre	Prends... !	Prenez... !
venir	Viens... !	Venez... !

Répondez à ma question! — *Answer my question!*
Et **cesse** de me répondre. — *And stop talking back to me.*
Viens, papa! **Viens**... — *Come on, Daddy! Come . . .*
Va me chercher du sucre, s'il te plaît. — *Go get me some sugar, please.*

The verbs **être** and **avoir** have irregular imperative forms.

INFINITIF	(TU)	(VOUS)
être	Sois... !	Soyez... !
avoir	Aie... !	Ayez... !

Sois prudent, Bruno. — *Be careful, Bruno.*
Ayez un peu de patience! — *Have a little patience!*

2. To make suggestions that include yourself, use the **nous** form of the imperative, which is, of course, the **nous** form of the present tense used without the pronoun. **Être** and **avoir** again have irregular forms: **soyons** and **ayons**.

Allons au marché.	*Let's go to the market.*
Prenons un café.	*Let's get some coffee.*
Soyons prudents.	*Let's be careful.*
Ayons un peu de patience!	*Let's have a little patience!*

3. To say not to do something in any of the three forms, place **ne** before the verb and **pas** after it.

Ne faites **pas** ça.	*Don't do that.*
Ne parle **jamais** de lui à ta grand-mère!	*Never speak of him to your grandmother!*
N'ayez **pas** peur!	*Don't be afraid!*
N'attendons **pas**. Je suis en train de perdre patience.	*Let's not wait. I'm getting impatient.*

4. To use an indirect object pronoun with a *negative* imperative, place the pronoun before the verb, just as in a declarative sentence.

DECLARATIVE	Tu ne lui rends pas visite.	*You don't visit him/her.*
IMPERATIVE	Ne **lui** rends pas visite!	*Don't visit him/her.*

For an *affirmative* imperative, however, place the pronoun after the verb, attached with a hyphen. The pronouns **me** and **te** become **moi** and **toi** in this situation.

Téléphone-**lui** immédiatement.	*Call him/her immediately!*
Réponds-**moi**!	*Answer me!*

Pour en savoir plus...

The imperative of **écouter** is often used as an interjection that in English might be translated as *Say!* or *Hey!* and sometimes as *Listen!* or *Look!*

Écoute, ce livre est vraiment, euh... Il est vraiment magnifique!

Écoute, Rachid... tu es gentil... Mais, tu as peut-être autre chose à faire?

Activités

A. De la régie. Martine donne des indications à l'équipe (*team*) de «Bonjour!». Mettez l'infinitif à la forme impérative.

MODÈLE: Bruno/ regarder / la caméra
Bruno, regarde la caméra!

1. Camille / parler / lentement (*slowly*), s'il te plaît
2. Attention, les techniciens / attendre / un instant
3. Les éclairagistes (*lighting crew*) / vérifier / les lumières
4. Camille et Bruno / venir / me parler, s'il vous plaît
5. Camille / répéter / tes lignes
6. L'équipe / faire (*let's make*) / un bon effort
7. Bruno / faire attention

B. Conseils. (*Advice.*) Les personnages dans *Le Chemin du retour* donnent souvent des ordres et des suggestions. Utilisez le verbe entre parenthèses pour compléter leurs phrases.

MODÈLE: RACHID À YASMINE: «_____ les enfants!» (regarder) →
Regarde les enfants!

1. RACHID À YASMINE: «Ben, bien sûr! _____, ma puce.» (venir)
2. M. LIÉGEOIS À CAMILLE: «_____ (*Let's hope*) que les Français peuvent identifier un bon pain.» (espérer)
3. CAMILLE À BRUNO: «Eh bien, _____ un test ensemble.» (faire)
4. MARTINE À CAMILLE: «_____, Camille. Je te présente Rachid Bouhazid.» (attendre)
5. BRUNO À RACHID: «Euh, _____ -moi, c'est mon bureau ici. Ton bureau, il est là.» (excuser)
6. LOUISE À CAMILLE: «_____ me chercher du sucre, s'il te plaît.» (aller)
7. MADO À CAMILLE: «Ne _____ jamais de lui à ta grand-mère!» (parler)

C. Le week-end. Suggérez (*Suggest*) à votre partenaire une activité pour le week-end. Votre partenaire n'aime pas votre idée; il/elle va suggérer autre chose.

MODÈLE: dîner à la maison ce soir / manger au restaurant →
É1: Dînons à la maison ce soir.
É2: Non, ne dînons pas à la maison ce soir! Mangeons au restaurant.

1. étudier dans nos chambres / travailler à la bibliothèque
2. préparer une salade / partager cette pizza surgelée (*frozen*)
3. aller à un concert de rock / écouter la radio
4. regarder la télé / faire les courses
5. commencer à parler français / parler anglais
6. mettre des vêtements chic pour sortir (*go out*) avec des amis / porter des vêtements confortables

Maintenant, regardez de nouveau (*again*) les numéros 1 à 4, et imaginez d'autres réponses pour ces situations.

D. La politesse à table. Vous êtes un(e) expert(e) sur la politesse en France. Faites des phrases impératives (à l'affirmatif ou au négatif) pour donner des conseils. Soyez logique (et consultez les conseils à la page 178 si nécessaire).

MODÈLE: faire beaucoup de bruit (*noise*) →
Ne faites pas beaucoup de bruit.

1. mettre votre pain sur la table
2. prendre la place de votre hôtesse à table
3. manger un morceau de pain avant le repas
4. couper la salade avec un couteau
5. être toujours poli(e)
6. boire trop de vin

Maintenant, donner d'autres conseils logiques en remplaçant les mots en italique par un pronom complément d'objet indirect.

MODÈLE: acheter des fleurs *à l'hôtesse* →
Achetez-lui des fleurs.

7. téléphoner *à l'hôtesse* si vous êtes en retard d'une heure
8. parler *à vos voisins* la bouche pleine
9. répondre *à l'hôtesse* quand elle vous pose une question
10. montrer les photos de tous vos cousins et cousines *aux autres invités*
11. demander *à l'hôtesse* de vous donner du sel pour le plat principal

E. Situations difficiles. À l'aide de la liste, donnez une suggestion pour résoudre (*resolve*) les problèmes suivants.

Vocabulaire utile: attendre, ne pas avoir peur, boire du jus d'orange, étudier avec des camarades de classe, être patient(e), manger des hamburgers, mettre un manteau, prendre le bus, rendre visite à, téléphoner à, venir souvent

MODÈLE: Nous ne comprenons pas ce chapitre. →
Étudiez avec des camarades de classe.

1. J'ai froid. **2.** J'ai peur de parler en classe. **3.** Nous avons faim. **4.** J'apprends lentement (*slowly*). **5.** J'ai soif. **6.** Mon ami est en retard! **7.** Nos professeurs aiment beaucoup parler. **8.** Je n'ai pas de voiture.

Regards sur la culture

Principes de conversation

When people are angry with each other, they tend to use confrontational language, as Camille and Mado do in this episode. In this case, Mado is extremely angry, but in France, argument and debate can also be a normal part of any conversation. In fact, there are several aspects of French conversational practices that North Americans in France generally have to adjust to.

- A conversation between two French people may sometimes sound aggressive to North Americans. This impression is partly due to the lively tone of French dialogue, and it is partly because conversation in France is an art that requires some degree of expertise in argument and disagreement. This approach to conversation may surprise English-speaking North Americans who expect exchanges to sound calm even when disagreement is involved. Some North American conversations may feel spiritless and uninteresting to French people, who are accustomed to defending their own point of view in a lively way.
- In a French conversation, it may be more important for a participant to state his/her point of view and to defend it well than it is to come to an agreement or compromise on the subject being discussed.
- It is also typical in French conversation to be critical. Criticism of food and of people's physical appearance in France may seem especially striking to North Americans, who sometimes find such comments impolite. The French, on the other hand, think of criticism as something constructive and tend to find the

Une conversation animée

North American hesitation to be frank about these things insincere or even hypocritical.

- Being a conversational partner is serious business in France! A French child learns early to speak in a lively and interesting manner.
- In the English-speaking parts of North America, conversational etiquette requires a slight pause between speakers' turns. In France, such pauses would be unusual: One begins talking just as the preceding speaker is finishing his/her turn. The result is that some North Americans find it quite challenging to get a word in when they are communicating with a group of French people: They are waiting for a tiny pause so that they can politely begin to speak, and often, the pause never arrives!
- In public places, French people tend to talk more quietly than North Americans. In France, the ideal is to speak in such a way that conversations cannot be overheard by others. North American groups often stand out in France because they tend to talk more loudly than the French in restaurants and shops.
- Conversations between strangers are rather unusual in France. It would be quite normal to spend several hours on a train face to face with three or four French people and never exchange a word with them.*

Considérez

How would you react if you arrived in France for the first time and soon faced contradiction and opposition to your point of view from conversational partners? What do you think you could learn in order to cope with these new patterns of dialogue? Do you think you could learn to enjoy or appreciate these practices? How would these new practices help you improve the way you express your ideas?

Structure 26

Quelques verbes comme *sortir*

Talking about more everyday activities

—D'où **sort**-elle, cette photo?!

*Some European trains are different from North American trains in that travelers may be seated in compartments rather than rows. Each compartment is like a small room with two seats facing each other. Several people can fit on each seat and they face the people across from them for the duration of their trip.

Mado uses the verb **sortir** to ask Camille where she found the photograph of Antoine. Her use of **sortir** is slightly idiomatic; usually **sortir** means *to go out.*

1. **Sortir** uses one stem (**sor-**) for the singular forms and another stem (**sort-**) for the plural forms. The endings are **-s**, **-s**, **-t**, **-ons**, **-ez**, **-ent**.

sortir (*to go out*)			
je	sors	nous	sort**ons**
tu	sors	vous	sort**ez**
il, elle, on	sort	ils, elles	sort**ent**

Bruno **sort** de Canal 7 avec Hélène. — *Bruno leaves Channel 7 with Hélène.*

2. Here is a list of verbs conjugated like **sortir**. Each one uses one stem for the singular and another for the plural.

dormir *to sleep*
mentir *to lie,*
partir *to leave (a place)*
sentir *to smell*
servir *to serve*

Camille **part** pour le studio à 6 h 30. — *Camille leaves for the studio at 6:30 A.M.*
Je **sors** avec des amis ce soir. — *I'm going out with friends tonight.*
Nous **dormons** bien. — *We sleep well.*
Les serveurs **servent** les repas. — *The waiters serve the meals.*

3. The imperative is formed in the normal way.

Ne **mens** pas. Je sais la vérité. — *Don't lie. I know the truth.*
Partez. Elle ne veut pas vous parler! — *Leave. She doesn't want to talk to you!*
Sortons par cette porte. — *Let's go out by this door.*

Notez bien!

The verb **quitter** also means *to leave,* but it always requires a direct object.

Camille **part**. Elle **quitte** le studio à 15 h. *Camille leaves. She leaves the studio at 3:00 P.M.*

Activités

A. Légendes. (*Captions.*) Utilisez les verbes **dormir**, **partir**, **sentir**, **servir**, et **sortir** pour expliquer les actions des personnages ou pour compléter les paroles des personnages.

MODÈLE: «D'où __sort__-elle, cette photo?»

1. Le pain _____ bon.

2. À la cafétéria, les cuisiniers _____ des salades.

3. Rachid et Martine _____ du travail.

4. Mado _____ du champagne.

5. Rachid vient de partir. Mado dit: «Pourquoi _____ -il aussi vite?»

6. Louise _____.

B. Et vous? Quand, où et pourquoi est-ce que les étudiants de votre classe font les choses suivantes? Interviewez trois camarades de classe. Utilisez le modèle et les suggestions comme inspiration.

MODÈLE: É1: Où est-ce que tu sens des croissants?
É2: Je sens des croissants à la boulangerie.

		au sujet de...
		(avec) vos amis
		(à) vos amis
	dormir	(à) vos professeurs
À quelle heure	mentir	chez moi
Où	partir	(de) la classe
Pourquoi	quitter	(de) la maison
Quand	sentir	(de) la pizza
	servir	des croissants
	sortir	du café
		en classe
		le campus

Maintenant, posez cinq questions à un groupe d'étudiants ou à votre professeur en utilisant le pronom **vous**.

Visionnement 2

Observez!

Considérez les aspects culturels expliqués dans **Regards sur la culture**. Ensuite (*then*), regardez l'Épisode 8 encore une fois et répondez aux questions suivantes.

- Est-ce que la conversation entre Mado et Camille est un échange vif (*intense*) mais normal, ou est-ce que les deux femmes sont fâchées?
- Quelles expressions Mado emploie-t-elle pour indiquer son attitude?
- Est-ce que Camille répond à sa mère calmement ou avec colère (*with anger*)?

Après le visionnement

Faites l'activité pour le **Visionnement 2** dans le cahier.

Synthèse: Lecture

Mise en contexte

During his life, the poet Jacques Prévert (1900–1977) witnessed the horrors of two world wars that decimated Europe. The work of this prolific writer includes screenplays, short stories, and volumes of poetry, including *Paroles,* published in 1943, which contains the poem "Familiale" ("*Family Life*").

Pour mieux lire

Understanding syntax and punctuation

Poets often "play" with language to create special effects and to enrich expression. You are already familiar with techniques such as rhythm and rhyme.

In this poem, Prévert uses language creatively. One way is by changing the word order (syntax) that you have come to expect in declarative sentences (subject-verb-object). Read through the first four lines of the poem, and try to identify the subject of each sentence. How many times does it occur? In what form? In what position?

La mère fait du tricot
Le fils fait la guerre
Elle trouve ça tout naturel la mère
Et le père qu'est-ce qu'il fait le père?

The first two lines use the normal syntax, but in the third line, the subject occurs twice, once at the beginning of the line of verse, as **elle**, and again at the end as **la mère**. In the fourth line, the subject (**le père**) is mentioned twice in noun form and once as a pronoun.

As you read these lines of the poem, you probably also noticed that for the most part, the verses lack punctuation. Working with a partner, reread the stanza and punctuate it. Does the addition of punctuation help your understanding? How does punctuation change the flow of the verse?

Now, read the entire poem carefully. Pay particular attention to the syntax, and imagine punctuation where you think it will clarify meaning. What message has Prévert tried to convey?

Familiale

La mère fait du tricot[1]
Le fils fait la guerre
Elle trouve ça tout naturel la mère
Et le père qu'est-ce qu'il fait le père?
Il fait des affaires[2]
Sa femme fait du tricot
Son fils la guerre
Lui des affaires
Il trouve ça tout naturel le père
Et le fils et le fils
Qu'est-ce qu'il trouve le fils?
Il ne trouve rien[3] absolument rien le fils
Le fils sa mère fait du tricot son père des affaires lui la guerre
Quand il aura fini[4] la guerre
Il fera[5] des affaires avec son père
La guerre continue la mère continue elle tricote
Le père continue il fait des affaires
La fils est tué[6] il ne continue plus
Le père et la mère vont au cimetière[7]
Ils trouvent ça naturel le père et la mère
La vie[8] continue la vie avec le tricot la guerre les affaires
Les affaires la guerre le tricot la guerre
Les affaires les affaires et les affaires
La vie avec le cimetière.

Jacques Prévert (*Paroles*, 1943)

[1]*knitting* [2]*des... business* [3]*nothing* [4]*Quand... When he has finished* [5]*will do* [6]*killed* [7]*cemetery* [8]*life*

Après la lecture

A. Vérifiez! En groupes de deux, comparez vos analyses de la syntaxe du poème. Où avez-vous mis des signes de ponctuation?

B. Les personnages. Décrivez les personnages en précisant leurs activités.

1. Que fait la mère?
2. Que fait le père?
3. Et le fils, qu'est-ce qu'il fait? Qu'est-ce qui lui arrive (*happens to him*)?

C. Le sens. (***The meaning.***) Répondez aux questions suivantes.

1. Quelle est l'attitude de cette famille face à la vie? Leurs journées sont-elles variées ou monotones?
2. Selon vous, les parents sont-ils conscients (*aware*) ou inconscients des événements (*events*) dans leur vie?
3. Quelle est la réaction du pere et de la mère à la mort (*death*) de leur fils? Sont-ils surpris? fâchés? indifférents?
4. Quelle idée Prévert essaie-t-il de communiquer? Choisissez parmi (*Choose among*) les suggestions suivantes, ou donnez votre propre (*own*) interprétation.
   - **a.** Lutter (*To fight*) pour son pays, c'est un acte patriotique.
   - **b.** La guerre est devenue (*has become*) un événement banal.
   - **c.** En temps de guerre, la vie ne compte pas beaucoup.
   - **d.** Les parents devraient être fiers (*should be proud*) d'avoir un fils qui fait la guerre.
   - **e.** Il faut (*One must*) faire des sacrifices pendant une guerre.

À écrire

Faites **À écrire** pour le Chapitre 8 dans le cahier.

Vocabulaire

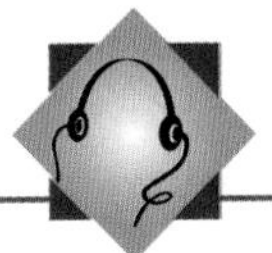

Les repas

une boisson	drink	**un plat (chaud, principal)**	(hot, main) dish
le déjeuner	lunch	**un repas**	meal
une entrée	first course	MOTS APPARENTÉS: **un dessert, le dîner**	
le petit déjeuner	breakfast		

Des provisions

le café (au lait)	coffee (with an equal amount of milk)
la charcuterie	delicatessen (pork) products
une chose	thing
les frites (*f.*)	French fries
la glace	ice cream
le jus (d'orange)	(orange) juice
le lait	milk
le mouton	mutton
un œuf (dur mayonnaise) (des œufs)	egg (hard-boiled with mayonnaise)
un petit pain	bread roll
le poivre	pepper
un poulet frites	chicken with fries
le riz	rice
la salade; une salade	lettuce; salad
le saucisson	sausage
le sel	salt
une tartine	piece of French bread with butter and jam
le thé	tea
le veau	veal

MOTS APPARENTÉS: **le chocolat, un coca, un croissant, le fast-food, un hamburger, la mousse (au chocolat), une omelette, une pizza, un sandwich, une sauce, la soupe**

À REVOIR: **l'eau** (*f.*), **un fruit, un poulet, une tarte, une tomate, le vin**

À table

une assiette	plate
un couteau	knife
une cuillère	spoon
une fourchette	fork
une nappe	tablecloth
une serviette	napkin
une tasse	cup
un verre	glass

Pour parler de la guerre

la guerre	war

Verbes

attendre	to wait (for)
déjeuner	to have lunch
descendre	to descend; to go (get) down
dormir	to sleep
entendre	to hear
mentir	to lie
partir	to leave (a *place*)
perdre	to lose
perdre la tête	to lose one's mind
perdre patience	to lose one's patience
quitter	to leave (*a place, someone*)
raconter	to tell (about)
rendre	to return (*something*); to render, make
rendre visite à	to visit (*a person*)
répondre	to answer
sentir	to smell
servir	to serve
sortir	to go out
vendre	to sell
visiter	to visit (*a place*)

Autres expressions utiles

après	after
avant	before
comme	as; like
léger (légère)	light
quelques	several, some, a few
sucré(e)	sweet

Chapitre 9

Inquiétudes°

Worries

OBJECTIFS

In this episode, you will

- learn more about Louise, Camille's grandmother
- see Hélène interview Camille for her show in Montreal

In this chapter, you will

- talk about health and parts of the body
- use direct object pronouns to avoid repetition
- talk about daily routines and activities
- discuss duties and obligations
- learn about health care in France

Vocabulaire en contexte

Les parties du corps°

Les... *Parts of the body*

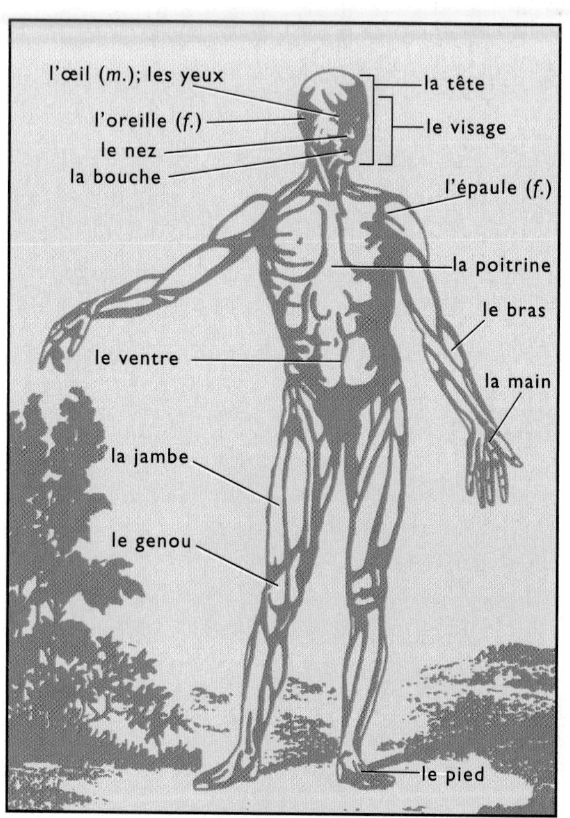

Le corps

Pour en savoir plus...

The first anatomical drawing is based on the one in the 18th-century *Encyclopédie ou Dictionnaire raisonné des sciences, des arts et des métiers.* The goal of the *Encyclopédie* was to gather together the sum of human knowledge. This massive work, directed and in part written by the French philosopher and writer Denis Diderot, was published between 1751 and 1766. Other contributors included Montesquieu, Voltaire, and Rousseau, all very important writers and thinkers during that period.

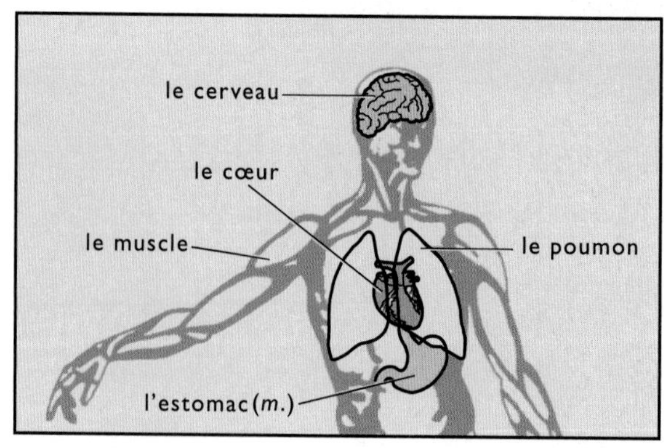

Autres mots utiles

les cheveux (*m.*)	hair	**le dos**	back
la dent	tooth		

Activités

A. Identifiez. Identifiez la partie du corps.

MODÈLE: extrémité du corps qui porte le cerveau et où on trouve les cheveux, les oreilles et d'autres organes des sens →
C'est la tête.

1. organes de la respiration
2. partie arrière (*back*) du corps, du torse (*torso*) en particulier
3. organe central du système circulatoire
4. partie de la tête où on trouve la bouche, le nez et les yeux
5. organe du système digestif
6. partie du bras où il s'attache (*is attached*) au torse

B. Dans la salle de musculation. Faites-vous de la gymnastique? Combien de fois par semaine? Quels muscles sont développés par les machines et les exercices suivants?

MODÈLE: le rameur (*the rowing machine*) →
Le rameur développe les muscles du bras et des jambes.

1. les pectoraux
2. les abdos (*sit-ups*)
3. le stepper
4. les flexions biceps
5. les squats
6. les pompes (*push-ups*)
7. les relevés (*lifts*) de jambes
8. les exercices aérobiques
9. les haltères (*free weights*)

C. Quelle partie du corps? Quelles parties du corps sont impliquées dans chacune (*each one*) des actions suivantes? Utilisez un verbe de la liste et une partie du corps pour chaque réponse.

Vocabulaire utile: boire, danser, écouter, entendre, essayer, faire, goûter (*to taste*), jouer (*to play*) au football américain, manger, montrer, parler, penser, porter, prendre, regarder, sentir, servir, tenir (*to hold*), toucher (*to touch*)

MODÈLE: aller à un concert →
On écoute avec les oreilles. On regarde les musiciens avec les yeux. On montre son appréciation avec les mains.

1. apprécier un bon repas
2. aller en boîte (*to a nightclub*)
3. aller au cinéma
4. aller chez le chiropracteur
5. visiter un parc
6. acheter des vêtements
7. faire la cuisine avec des amis
8. aller à une conférence (*lecture*)
9. aller à un institut de beauté

La santé°

La... *Health*

Michel est **malade**. Il a **un rhume**. Il **tousse** beaucoup et il **a mal à la gorge**.° C'est pourquoi il a une boîte de **pastilles**. En plus, il a **le nez qui coule**, alors il a besoin de beaucoup de **mouchoirs en papier**.° Michel reste à la maison et boit des jus de fruits.

throat

mouchoirs... *tissues*

Nathalie n'est pas du tout **en bonne forme**; elle a **une grippe**. Elle a de **la fièvre**. Elle **a mal au** ventre et elle a des **douleurs**° musculaires. **Le médecin** lui conseille° de dormir et de prendre de **l'aspirine**. Il lui donne aussi **une ordonnance**° pour **des comprimés**.°

aches, pains
advises
prescription
tablets

Autres expressions utiles

une femme médecin	(*female*) doctor
un hôpital	hospital
un(e) infirmier/ière	nurse
un médicament	medicine, drug
avoir mal à	to have a pain/ache in; to have a sore . . .

avoir mal au cœur	to feel nauseated
avoir mal au ventre	to have a stomachache
être en (bonne, pleine) forme	to be in (good, great) shape
tomber malade	to become sick

Activités

A. Identifiez. Identifiez la personne ou la chose.

MODÈLE: l'endroit où vont les malades pour guérir (*to be cured*) →
C'est l'hôpital.

1. une personne qui a fait des études en médecine
2. un morceau de papier qu'on donne au pharmacien pour obtenir (*to obtain*) un médicament
3. une température élevée
4. un médicament qui réduit la douleur (*reduces pain*)
5. une maladie dont (*whose*) les symptômes sont la fièvre et des douleurs musculaires
6. une sorte de bonbon qui calme une gorge irritée

B. Maladies et remèdes. (*Illnesses and remedies.*) Pour les maladies ou conditions suivantes, décrivez (*describe*) les symptômes.

MODÈLE: Michel a un rhume. →
Il a le nez qui coule. Il tousse beaucoup. Il a mal à la gorge.

1. Brigitte a une migraine.
2. Thomas a mal au cœur.
3. Caroline a une bronchite (*bronchitis*).
4. David a une grippe.
5. Anne n'est pas en bonne forme.
6. Marguerite est stressée.

Maintenant, suggérez des remèdes possibles.

Vocabulaire utile: acheter des médicaments, aller voir le médecin, boire de l'eau, éviter (*to avoid*) l'alcool, faire du sport, prendre de l'aspirine, prendre des comprimés, prendre du repos, rester au lit

MODÈLE: Michel a un rhume. →
Restez au lit, Michel. Buvez beaucoup d'eau. Prenez de l'aspirine.

C. Une interview. Posez à votre partenaire des questions sur sa santé. Demandez-lui...

1. s'il / si elle a mal quelque part. Demandez-lui d'expliquer les symptômes.
2. ce qu'il/elle fait quand il/elle a un rhume.
3. s'il / si elle va régulièrement chez le médecin et avec quelle fréquence. Si sa réponse est négative, demandez-lui d'expliquer.
4. quelles maladies sont fréquentes chez les étudiants.
5. ce qu'on peut faire pour éviter ces maladies.
6. ce qu'il/elle pense des traitements comme l'homéopathie et l'acuponcture.

Visionnement 1

Avant de visionner

Qu'est-ce qui se passe? Voici des extraits du dialogue du film. Choisissez la réponse qui explique le dialogue.

1. LOUISE: Oh, chérie!

CAMILLE: Grand-mère, à quoi tu joues...°? Tu veux me faire peur?

LOUISE: Je suis en pleine forme!

°*à... are you playing games?*

a. Camille est inquiète pour la santé de sa grand-mère.
b. Camille est fascinée par le jeu (*game*) de sa grand-mère.
c. Camille est contente de voir sa grand-mère.

2. HÉLÈNE: Bon ben, voilà, c'était[a] Hélène Thibaut, sur les bords[b] de la Seine, avec Camille Leclair à mes côtés. Avec un temps radieux,[c] mais un «Bientôt à Montréal» à tous.[d] Ciao!

[a]*I'm* (lit., *this was*) [b]*sur... on the banks* [c]*Avec... With great weather* [d]*everyone*

a. Hélène va quitter Paris pour rentrer (*return*) à Montréal.
b. Hélène aime Paris et ne rentre pas à Montréal.
c. Hélène fait un reportage sur les monuments du Québec.

3. CAMILLE: On va au restau? J'ai faim!

BRUNO: Tu as faim? Je ne le crois pas... !?[a] Eh! Eh oh! Appelez les photographes! Là, vite,[b] j'ai un scoop! Camille arrête son régime,[c] elle va faire un vrai repas! Ce n'est pas un scoop, ça?!

[a]*Je... I don't believe it . . . !?* [b]*quickly* [c]*arrête... is going off her diet*

a. Bruno ne veut pas aller au restaurant avec Camille.
b. Bruno taquine (*teases*) Camille, parce que d'habitude (*usually*) elle mange très peu.
c. Bruno est surpris parce que Camille préfère en général manger chez elle.

Vocabulaire relatif à l'épisode

un malaise	*weakness, fainting spell*
Vous devez	*You must*
Tu connais... ?	*Do you know . . . ?*
inutile	*useless*
au plus mal	*very ill*
Tout va bien.	*Everything's fine.*
Ne t'inquiète pas.	*Don't worry.*

Observez!

La grand-mère Louise figure dans l'Épisode 9. Regardez l'épisode et répondez à ces questions.

- À quel sujet Mado ment-elle à Camille? Qu'est-ce qu'elle dit (*say*)?
- Qu'est-ce que Louise suggère à Camille de faire avec elle?

Après le visionnement

A. Vous rappelez-vous? (*Do you remember?*) Complétez le paragraphe pour résumer l'Épisode 9. Choisissez une expression de la liste pour remplir chaque blanc (*to fill each blank*).

Vocabulaire utile:

à l'hôpital	en France	sa mère est au plus mal
à Montréal	ment	elle est en pleine forme
au lit	va bien	près de la cathédrale Notre-Dame
au restaurant	va mieux	
dans la chambre	ce n'est pas vrai	
dans la rue Mouffetard		
dans les Cévennes		

L'épisode commence _____[1] de Louise. Elle est _____[2], et le médecin l'examine.[a] Il encourage Louise à aller _____[3]. Elle refuse et dit[b] à Camille qu' _____[4]. Camille voit[c] que _____[5]. Louise demande à Camille si Alex est là _____[6]. Camille dit oui et elle va dans la rue pour lui parler. Pourquoi? Le médecin dit à Mado que _____[7]. Mais Mado _____[8] à Camille et dit que tout[d] _____[9].

Hélène interviewe Camille au bord de la Seine _____[10]. C'est pour une émission _____[11]. Camille dit qu'elle vit[e] bien _____[12], et que la famille est très importante pour elle.

Quand Louise _____[13], elle invite Camille à faire un voyage _____[14]. Camille est très heureuse et elle invite Bruno à venir avec elle _____[15].

[a]*is examining her* [b]*says* [c]*sees* [d]*everything* [e]*lives*

B. Réfléchissez. Répondez aux questions suivantes. Choisissez parmi les idées suggérées, ou formulez (*make up*) votre propre (*own*) hypothèse.

1. Pourquoi est-ce que Louise envoie Camille parler à Alex (l'homme avec l'accordéon)?
   - **a.** Louise cherche un prétexte pour terminer sa conversation avec Camille.
   - **b.** Louise veut entendre une chanson familière pour la réconforter (*comfort*).
   - **c.** Camille et Alex sont comme frère et sœur.
2. Pourquoi Mado ment-elle quand Camille demande l'opinion du médecin?
   - **a.** Mado et Camille n'ont pas une relation très ouverte.
   - **b.** Mado ne veut pas faire peur à Camille.
   - **c.** Mado a du mal à parler de la maladie et de la mort.

3. Pourquoi Louise veut-elle faire un voyage aux Cévennes?

   a. Elle cède (*gives in*) toujours aux demandes de Camille.
   b. Elle veut montrer la région à Camille, qui ne la connaît pas.
   c. Elle veut apprendre plus de détails sur l'histoire de son mari.

Structure 27

Le complément d'objet direct

Avoiding repetition

—Je **te** remercie beaucoup.

Le complément d'objet direct

You have already studied indirect objects as one type of verb complement. Another verb complement is the direct object.▲ A direct object is something that is acted on by a verb (that is, it answers the question *what?* or *whom?*).

Direct object nouns are not preceded by a preposition.

Vous attendez le prince charmant?

Nous regardons l'émission «Bonjour!»

Martine donne le médaillon à Camille.

Bruno présente Rachid à Camille.

Les pronoms complément d'objet direct

me (m')	*me*	**nous**	*us*
te (t')	*you*	**vous**	*you*
le (l')	*him/it*	**les**	*them (m., f.)*
la (l')	*her/it*		

1. Direct object pronouns refer to or replace direct object nouns in a sentence. Use of either **le** or **la** depends on whether the direct object is masculine or feminine. Use of **me**, **te**, **nous**, and **vous** depends on whether you are referring to yourself or to the person or people you are talking to.

Martine trouve le médaillon. Martine **le** trouve. *Martine finds it.*	Martine regarde la photo. Martine **la** regarde. *Martine looks at it.*
Je **t'**aime, grand-mère. Et tu **m'**aimes aussi, n'est-ce pas?	*I love you, Grandmother. And you love me too, don't you?*

2. Like indirect object pronouns, the direct object pronoun directly precedes the verb in both affirmative and negative sentences (except in the affirmative imperative).

Je **te** remercie beaucoup, Camille.	*I thank you very much, Camille.*
Tu as faim? Je ne **le** crois pas... !	*You're hungry? I don't believe it . . . !*

3. In the negative imperative, word order follows the normal rule (i.e., the pronoun precedes the verb), but in the affirmative imperative, the pronoun follows the verb and is attached with a hyphen. **Me** becomes **moi** and **te** becomes **toi**.

	Ne **la** regarde pas!	*Don't look at her/it!*
	Ne **m'**attendez pas!	*Don't wait for me!*
but	Regarde-**la!**	*Look at her/it!*
	Attendez-**moi!**	*Wait for me!*

4. In verb + infinitive constructions, the pronoun again directly precedes the verb for which it is the object (usually the infinitive). If the sentence is negative, the negation surrounds the conjugated verb, not the infinitive.

Elle va **l'**interviewer sur les bords de la Seine.	*She is going to interview her on the banks of the Seine.*
Elle **ne** va **pas l'**interviewer à Canal 7.	*She is not going to interview her at Channel 7.*
Nous voulons **vous** inviter.	*We want to invite you.*
Vous **ne** pouvez **pas m'**entendre?	*You can't hear me?*
Il **ne nous** invite **pas** à sortir.	*He doesn't ask us to go out.*

5. Some verbs that take a direct object in French take an indirect object in English. Among them are the following:

attendre *to wait for (someone, something)*
écouter *to listen to (someone, something)*
regarder *to look at (someone, something)*

Bruno **attend** Camille sur le plateau.	*Bruno waits for Camille on the set.*

Activités

A. Les personnages. Faites des questions avec les éléments donnés, puis (*then*) répondez aux questions à l'affirmatif ou au négatif avec un pronom sujet et un pronom complément d'objet direct.

MODÈLE: Yasmine / regarder / la télévision (non) →
É1: Est-ce que Yasmine regarde la télévision?
É2: Non, elle ne la regarde pas.

1. une employée de l'hôtel / apporter (*to bring*) / le dîner d'Hélène (non)
2. Bruno / mange / sa salade (oui)
3. la femme du boucher / regarder / l'émission (oui)
4. Camille / aller finir / son dessert (non)
5. Rachid / préparer / ses reportages (oui)
6. il / vouloir montrer / ses reportages à Martine (oui)
7. Yasmine / mettre / son pyjama (oui)
8. Rachid / mettre / sa cravate (non)
9. Hélène / aller quitter / l'hôtel (non)

B. Dialogues. Complétez les dialogues selon le modèle. Les réponses sont toujours au négatif.

MODÈLE: Est-ce que vous (*s.*) m'écoutez? →
Non, je ne vous écoute pas.

1. Est-ce que tu me regardes?
2. Est-ce que vous (*pl.*) nous attendez?
3. Est-ce que tu me cherches?
4. Est-ce que vous (*s.*) nous respectez?
5. Est-ce que vous (*pl.*) me trouvez magnifique?
6. Est-ce que tu m'aimes?

Maintenant, refaites cette activité et donnez des résponses affirmatives.

C. J'adore... Je déteste... Benoît, un camarade de classe de Yasmine, a des opinions arrêtées (*definite*). Imaginez les réponses de sa mère. Utilisez un impératif négatif ou affirmatif selon la logique de la situation.

Verbes utiles: acheter, attendre, écouter, finir, manger, mettre, prendre, regarder

MODÈLES: BENOÎT: Je déteste *cette émission.*
SA MÈRE: Ne la regarde pas, alors!

BENOÎT: J'adore *cette chanson* (*song*).
SA MÈRE: Alors écoute-la!

1. Je n'aime pas *ce poisson.*
2. J'aime *cette musique.*
3. Je n'aime pas *ce pantalon ridicule.*
4. Je déteste *ces devoirs.*
5. Je veux *ce CD de rock.*
6. Je ne veux pas *ce médicament.*
7. Je veux regarder *cette émission sur les dinosaures.*
8. Je ne veux pas *t'*attendre.

D. Questions et réponses. Posez des questions en utilisant les éléments des trois colonnes. Votre partenaire va vous répondre.

MODÈLE: É1: Est-ce que tes parents écoutent les concerts de rock?
É2: Non, ils ne les écoutent pas.

tu	aimer	le bus
tes amis	attendre	un café le matin
tes amis et toi	comprendre	les concerts de rock
tes parents	écouter	les devoirs avant la classe
ta classe	faire	la télé le week-end
nous	finir	me
	prendre	nous
	regarder	ton professeur
		la radio

Regards sur la culture

La santé en France

The United Nations has consistently placed France at or near the top of its world ratings based on access to health care. We tend to think of health as a rather objective matter, but cultural attitudes and traditions always play a large role in people's sense of what is healthful and what is not and in the development of policies for health care delivery.

- In part, culture determines what we think makes us healthy or sick. North Americans think of apples as especially healthful. In France, apples are considered hard to digest. On the other hand, many French people consider nearly any moving air a draft (**un courant d'air**) and a threat to one's health.
- Many common digestive complaints are referred to in France as **une crise de foie** (literally, *a liver attack*). Doctors even use this term in their diagnoses. The **crise de foie**, from which so many French people suffer, does not correspond to any single Anglo-American illness.
- French doctors make house calls, even in the middle of the night when necessary. They tend to prescribe larger numbers of different medicines than do their counterparts in North America. In fact, the French consume more medicine than any other nationality in Europe, though the government is now urging doctors to prescribe less. French doctors are also relatively generous in prescribing long hospital stays and time off from work.

Le médecin examine Louise chez elle.

- The French system of **Sécurité sociale**, established in 1945, reimburses about 72 percent of health care expenses, and about 70 percent of prescription medicine costs, although the average patient is expected to pay the doctor or pharmacist at time of service. However, many people in France take out additional insurance policies so that nearly all of their expenses are covered. Prenatal care, as prescribed by French Social Security, is virtually free and is considered a world-class model by most professionals.
- French pharmacists have a good deal of medical training and are often consulted for common health problems. They are also expected to be able to examine mushrooms collected in the woods to indicate if they are edible or not. The Health Code limits the number of pharmacies that may be opened, through a licensing process. In a city of over 30,000 people, for example, there may be only one pharmacy for every 3000 inhabitants. One of the functions of such limits is to protect the integrity and prestige of the profession.

Considérez

The French Social Security system was founded on the explicit need for maintaining "national solidarity." This is related to the notion of **fraternité** that was one of the founding principles of the French Revolution. In what ways do the health care systems in North America relate to general cultural and political principles?

Structure 28

Les verbes pronominaux

Talking about daily routines

—Maman est fatiguée à cause du déménagement. Alors, **elle se repose.**

—Alors, qu'est-ce que vous attendez? **Vous vous embrassez?**

A set of French verbs, called pronominal verbs,▲ are conjugated with a personal pronoun in addition to the subject. You have already heard or seen a few pronominal verbs in *Le Chemin du retour* and in your textbook.

Je **m'appelle** Isabelle.

Où **se trouve** la bibliothèque?

1. In pronominal verbs, the pronoun corresponds to the subject. It directly precedes the verb in both affirmative and negative uses (except in the affirmative imperative). In negative sentences, the **ne** precedes the pronoun and **pas** (**jamais**, etc.) follows the verb.

se laver (*to wash*)			
je **me**	lave	nous **nous**	lavons
tu **te**	laves	vous **vous**	lavez
il, elle, on **se**	lave	ils, elles **se**	lavent

	Je ne me rappelle jamais.	*I never remember.*
	Pourquoi **s'intéresse-t-il** à ces photos?	*Why is he interested in these photos?*
	Ne *t'*inquiète pas.	*Don't worry.*
but	**Lavez-*vous*!**	*Get washed!*

Notice that when **me**, **te**, and **se** precede a verb that begins with a vowel sound, they become **m'**, **t'**, and **s'**.

2. Here are some common pronominal verbs.

s'amuser	*to have a good time*
s'appeler*	*to be named*
se brosser (les dents, les cheveux)	*to brush (one's teeth, one's hair)*
se casser	*to break (a limb)*
se coucher	*to go to bed*
se dépêcher	*to hurry*
se disputer	*to argue*
s'embrasser	*to kiss (each other)*
s'endormir	*to fall asleep*
s'entendre (bien/mal) (avec)	*to get along (well, poorly) (with)*
se fâcher (contre)	*to become angry (with)*
s'habiller (en)	*to get dressed (in)*
s'inquiéter† (de, pour)	*to worry (about)*
s'intéresser à	*to be interested in*
se laver	*to get washed, wash up*

*conjugated like **appeler: je m'appelle, nous nous appelons**

†conjugated like **préférer: je m'inquiète, nous nous inquiétons**

se lever*	*to get up (out of bed); to stand up*
se maquiller (les yeux, les lèvres)	*to put on makeup, to make up (one's eyes, one's lips)*
se passer	*to happen*
se peigner (les cheveux)	*to comb (one's hair)*
se promener*	*to take a walk*
se rappeler†	*to remember*
se raser	*to shave*
se rendre compte (de)	*to realize*
se reposer	*to rest*
se réveiller	*to wake up*
se souvenir‡ **(de)**	*to remember*
se tromper (de)	*to make a mistake, be mistaken (about)*

3. In the negative imperative, the word order follows the normal rule. However, in the affirmative imperative, the pronoun follows the verb and is attached with a hyphen. **Te** becomes **toi**.

	Ne **t'**inquiète pas.	*Don't worry.*
	Ne **nous** disputons pas.	*Let's not argue.*
but	Dépêchons-**nous**!	*Let's hurry up.*
	Réveille-**toi**!	*Wake up!*

4. In verb + infinitive constructions, where the pronominal verb is usually the infinitive, the pronoun precedes the infinitive. If the sentence is negative, the negation surrounds the conjugated verb, not the infinitive.

Yasmine et moi, **on va *se* promener** un petit peu.	*Yasmine and I are going to take a little walk.*
Mado ***ne* peut *pas* se rappeler** le code.	*Mado can't remember the code.*

5. When a pronominal verb is used to talk about actions that affect a part of the body, the definite article is used before the body part.

Camille se brosse **les** dents et **les** cheveux, et elle se maquille **les** yeux et **les** lèvres.	*Camille brushes her teeth and her hair, and she puts makeup on her eyes and lips.*

6. Pronominal verbs sometimes have a *reciprocal* sense: They describe an action that two or more people do for or to each other.

Camille et Louise **se téléphonent**.	*Camille and Louise call each other.*
Nous **nous parlons** les samedis.	*We speak to each other on Saturdays.*
On **se marie**, toi et moi?	*Want to get married?*

---

*conjugated like **acheter: je me lève, nous nous levons**

†conjugated like **appeler: je me rappelle, nous nous rappelons**

‡conjugated like **venir: je me souviens de, nous nous souvenons de**

Activités

A. Qu'est-ce qui se passe? Complétez la phrase avec la forme correcte d'un verbe de la liste.

Vocabulaire utile: s'amuser, se coucher, se disputer, s'embrasser, s'habiller, s'intéresser, se lever, se parler, se passer, se regarder, se reposer, se souvenir

MODÈLE: Camille et Bruno _____ . →
Camille et Bruno se regardent.

1. Le soleil (*sun*) _____ au début de «Bonjour!»

2. Camille _____ bien pour l'émission sur la mode.

3. Louise _____ de son mari, Antoine.

4. Camille et Mado _____.

5. Selon le médecin, Louise a besoin de _____.

6. Mado et le médecin _____ de la santé de Louise.

7. Yasmine (à ses parents): «Alors, qu'est-ce que vous attendez? Vous _____ ?»

8. Camille: «Rachid, tu es gentil, tu me poses des questions, tu _____ à ma famille... »

9. Qu'est-ce qui _____ ? Les deux enfants _____ au marché.

B. Ce qu'on fait. Utilisez un verbe pronominal pour exprimer la suite (*outcome*) logique des situations suivantes. Plusieurs réponses sont possibles, à l'affirmatif et au négatif.

MODÈLE: Nous sommes le couple parfait. Nous... →
Nous ne nous disputons pas. Nous nous embrassons. Nous nous entendons bien.

1. Marie Dupont prend le nom de son mari, Christian Martel. Maintenant, elle...
2. Il est 7 h du matin. Les étudiants...
3. Tu as les mains sales (*dirty*). Tu...
4. Paul et Virginie s'aiment. Ils...
5. Vous allez à une soirée élégante. Vous...
6. Mes parents n'ont pas assez d'argent. Ils...
7. Nous parlons des vacances (*vacations*) passées. Nous...
8. Magalie a envie d'aller au parc. Elle...
9. La classe commence à 8 h, mais tu es en retard et tu arrives à 8 h 30. Tu...
10. J'ai les cheveux en désordre. Je...
11. Pierre tombe quand il fait du ski. Il...
12. Je vais au cinéma, mais le film que je veux voir (*see*) ne passe plus (*is no longer playing*). Je...

C. Conseils. (*Advice.*) Utilisez la forme affirmatif ou négatif de l'impératif des verbes utilisés dans les phrases suivantes pour donner des conseils aux personnages. Suivez le modèle.

MODÈLE: Paul se réveille à 11 h 30. →
Réveille-toi à 6 h 30! (Ne te réveille pas à 11 h 30!)

1. Christian et Anne s'embrassent souvent en public.
2. Monique se maquille en conduisant (*while driving*).
3. Carole et Jean-Pierre se disputent tout le temps.
4. Nicole se dépêche tous les matins.
5. Magalie se couche à 2 h du matin.
6. Chantal et François ne se parlent pas.
7. Myriam et David se promènent au centre-ville à minuit.

D. La routine. Parlez avec votre partenaire de votre routine quotidienne (*daily*). Comparez vos habitudes et préparez ensemble un compte rendu (*essay*) des similarités et des différences en utilisant au moins cinq verbes pronominaux. Présentez ensuite (*then*) ce compte rendu à la classe.

MODÈLE: É1: À 6 heures et demie, je me réveille. Et toi?
É2: Moi, je me réveille à 6 heures, mais je me lève à 6 heures et demie.

Le verbe devoir

Talking about duties and obligations

—Vous **devez** aller à l'hôpital.

devoir (*to have to, must; to owe*)			
je	**dois**	nous	**devons**
tu	**dois**	vous	**devez**
il, elle, on	**doit**	ils, elles	**doivent**

1. The verb **devoir** expresses obligation or probability when followed by the infinitive.

   Quelqu'un **doit** rester près d'elle. — *Someone should stay close to her.*
   Louise **doit** parler au médecin. — *Louise must (has to) speak to the doctor.*
   Alex **doit** avoir environ 20 ans. — *Alex must be about 20 years old.*

2. When used with a noun, **devoir** means *to owe*.

   Nous **devons** beaucoup de respect à nos collègues. — *We owe a lot of respect to our colleagues.*
   Je lui **dois** 500 euros. — *I owe him 500 euros.*

Activités

A. Quand ça ne va pas. (*When you're not feeling well.*) Complétez les phrases avec la forme correcte du verbe **devoir**.

1. Quand on a le bras cassé, on _____ aller chez le médecin.
2. Quand vous avez mal à la tête, vous _____ prendre de l'aspirine.
3. Quand j'ai une grippe, je _____ boire beaucoup d'eau.
4. Quand les enfants sont malades, ils ne _____ pas aller à l'école.
5. Quand nous consultons un spécialiste, nous lui _____ beaucoup.
6. Quand tu as mal aux yeux, tu _____ mettre des lunettes de soleil.

B. Obligations. Qu'est-ce que les personnes suivantes doivent faire dans les situations décrites?

MODÈLE: Vous comparaissez (*appear*) devant un tribunal. →
Je dois dire la vérité.

1. Vos amis ont trouvé un sac contenant (*containing*) mille dollars.
2. Vos parents et vous, vous vous disputez souvent.
3. Votre amie a trouvé un chat perdu (*lost cat*) dans la rue.
4. Vous allez arriver en retard pour un rendez-vous important.
5. Vous avez vu un de vos camarades de classe qui a triché (*cheated*) à un examen.

C. Responsabilités et désirs. Posez à votre partenaire des questions sur les responsabilités et les désirs des personnes suivantes. Essayez d'utiliser des verbes pronominaux après **devoir**, **vouloir**, **avoir envie de**, etc.

MODÈLE: É1: Est-ce que votre père doit se lever à huit heures du matin?
É2: Non, il doit se lever à six heures.
É1: Qu'est-ce qu'il veut faire?
É2: Il veut se recoucher (*go back to bed*).

ta mère (tes enfants, etc.)	à 6 h (8 h, 10 h 30, etc.) du matin
ton/ta meilleur(e) (*best*) ami(e)	à midi
ton professeur	à 15 h (16 h 30, 17 h, etc.)
tu	le week-end
tes amis et toi	pendant la semaine
nous	pendant les vacances (*vacation*)

Visionnement 2

Observez!

Considérez les aspects culturels expliqués dans **Regards sur la culture**. Ensuite, regardez l'Épisode 9 encore une fois, et répondez aux questions suivantes.

- Quelle pratique particulière aux médecins français voit-on dans cet épisode?
- Parlant de la France avec Hélène, Camille dit: «C'est un pays que j'aime. On y vit bien.» Dans cet épisode, et dans le film en général, qu'est-ce qui montre qu'on vit bien en France?

Après le visionnement

Faites l'activité pour le **Visionnement 2** dans le cahier.

Synthèse: Culture

La médecine et la culture

Dans le monde francophone, la médecine moderne est toujours présente. Au Canada et en Belgique, le gouvernement assure l'accès aux soins médicaux,[1] comme en France. Mais dans beaucoup de pays, il n'y a pas assez de médecins. Par exemple, au Maroc, il y a seulement[2] un médecin pour 5.000 personnes. Dans ces pays, la médecine moderne coexiste avec la médecine ancienne ou traditionnelle.

Les médecines douces[3]

En France et dans les autres pays francophones, il y a aussi des personnes qui guérissent[4] les malades avec des plantes, des mouvements de la main et d'autres méthodes anciennes. Ces «médecines traditionnelles» sont souvent très efficaces.[5] En 1999, l'Organisation Mondiale de la Santé[6] a recommandé l'intégration de la médecine traditionnelle dans les systèmes modernes de santé en Afrique.

En France, on appelle ces médecines «les médecines douces».

Le thermalisme

Le thermalisme, c'est l'utilisation de l'eau de source[7] dans la médecine. En Amérique du Nord, le thermalisme n'est pas très important dans la médecine aujourd'hui, mais en France, son rôle est considérable. Les médecins recommandent souvent des «cures». Faire une cure, c'est passer un certain nombre de jours dans une station thermale.

L'Auvergne est une région française particulièrement importante pour le thermalisme. Située dans le centre de la France, c'est une région volcanique. L'eau d'une station thermale contient[8] souvent beaucoup de minéraux. Elle est souvent chaude ou gazeuse. Et quelquefois elle est radioactive. Les stations thermales ont des spécialités. Voici quelques détails sur la station de Saint-Nectaire, en Auvergne.

La station thermale Vichy

Saint-Nectaire

Agent thérapeutique

Il y a plus de 40 sources. L'eau de la station de Saint-Nectaire est chaude et gazeuse. Elle est riche en lithium et en autres minéraux.

Indications

- les maladies urinaires
- les maladies métaboliques (obésité, diabète, hypertension artérielle, etc.)
- le stress

[1]soins... *health care* [2]*only* [3]Les... *Alternative medicine* [4]*heal* [5]*effective* [6]Organisation... *World Health Organization* [7]l'eau... *spring water* [8]*contains*

Soins proposés	**Autres activités proposées**
• la cure de boisson • le bain thermal • le bain d'algues[9] • le bain de boue[10] • la douche au jet[11] • les massages • l'aquagym[12]	• le tennis • le mini-golf • la pêche[13] • les promenades dans la montagne • les promenades au lac Chambon • la visite des églises[14] médiévales • les concerts • le casino • la cuisine traditionnelle d'Auvergne

[9]*seaweed* [10]*mud* [11]douche… *high-pressure shower* [12]*pool gymnastics* [13]*fishing* [14]*churches*

À vous

Une cure. Imagine that you have won a free stay of one night and one day at the spa in Saint-Nectaire. This prize includes four treatment sessions, three meals, and free access to all other activities. You want to take advantage of this prize to reduce your stress level, and so you plan a program for the day. List your activities for the day, starting at 8 A.M. and ending at 9 P.M., when you return home.

À écrire

Faites **À écrire** pour le Chapitre 9 dans le cahier.

Vocabulaire

Les parties du corps

la bouche	mouth
le bras	arm
le cerveau	brain
les cheveux (*m. pl.*)	hair
le cœur	heart
le corps	body
la dent	tooth
le dos	back
l'épaule (*f.*)	shoulder
le genou	knee
la gorge	throat
la jambe	leg
la main	hand
le nez	nose
l'œil (*m.*) **(les yeux)**	eye
l'oreille (*f.*)	ear
le pied	foot
la poitrine	chest
le poumon	lung
la tête	head
le ventre	belly; abdomen
le visage	face

MOTS APPARENTÉS: **l'estomac** (*m.*), **le muscle**

La santé

un comprimé	tablet
une douleur	ache, pain
une grippe	influenza (flu)
un(e) infirmier/ière	nurse
un(e) médecin / femme médecin	doctor
un médicament	medicine, drug
un mouchoir en papier	facial tissue
le nez qui coule	runny nose
une ordonnance	prescription
une pastille	cough drop, lozenge
un rhume	common cold
la santé	health
avoir mal à	to have pain / an ache in; to have a sore . . .
avoir mal au cœur	to feel nauseated
avoir mal au ventre	to have a stomachache
être en (bonne, pleine) forme	to be in (good, great) shape; to feel good
tomber malade	to become sick
tousser	to cough
malade	sick

MOTS APPARENTÉS: **une aspirine, une fièvre, un hôpital**

Pronoms complément d'objet direct

me	me
te	you
le, la	him; her; it
nous	us
vous	you
les	them

Verbes

s'amuser	to have a good time
s'appeler	to be named
se brosser (les dents, les cheveux)	to brush (one's teeth, one's hair)
se casser	to break (*a limb*)
se coucher	to go to bed
se dépêcher	to hurry
devoir	to have to, must; to owe
se disputer	to argue
s'embrasser	to kiss (each other)
s'endormir	to fall asleep
s'entendre (bien, mal) (avec)	to get along (well, poorly) (with)
se fâcher (contre)	to become angry (with)
s'habiller (en)	to get dressed (in)
s'inquiéter (de, pour)	to worry (about)
s'intéresser à	to be interested in
se laver	to get washed, wash up
se lever	to get up (*out of bed*); to stand up
se maquiller (les yeux, les lèvres)	to put on makeup, to make up (one's eyes, one's lips)
se passer	to happen
se peigner (les cheveux)	to comb (one's hair)
se promener	to take a walk
se rappeler	to remember
se raser	to shave
se rendre compte (de)	to realize
se reposer	to rest
se réveiller	to wake up
se souvenir (de)	to remember
se tromper (de)	to make a mistake, be mistaken (about)

Autre expression utile

mal	badly

Chapitre 10

Rendez-vous au restaurant

OBJECTIFS

In this episode, you will

- watch Camille and Bruno order dinner
- listen to banter between the husband and wife who own the restaurant
- learn more about Camille's and Bruno's family life

In this chapter, you will

- talk about things to do in the city
- discuss the weather
- learn how to order a meal
- talk about past events and when they happened
- talk about what you see and what you believe
- learn about French cafés and restaurants
- read about World War II in France

Vocabulaire en contexte

Les distractions en ville°

Les... *Recreational activities in the city*

La vie° **urbaine** offre beaucoup de **distractions** (*f.*), le jour et **la nuit.**°
On peut aller, par exemple,

life / night

On peut aussi faire

Pour en savoir plus...

French cities often have free or inexpensive publications that list upcoming movies and cultural and sporting events. In Paris, two of the most popular are *Pariscope* and *L'Officiel des spectacles. Pariscope* has a site on the Web.

Tickets for major events may be purchased at the box office, at the FNAC (a chain of book, music, video, and electronics stores), or by Minitel.

The Minitel is a small computer terminal connected by phone to an online database. A user can obtain telephone numbers and schedules, as well as access to many other services. The Minitel will be explained in more detail in Chapter 13.

Notez bien!

To say you play a sport or a game, use **jouer à** + sport or game.

Tu aimes **jouer au base-ball?** *Do you like playing baseball?*

To say you play a musical instrument, use **jouer de** + instrument.

Mon ami **joue du piano.** *My friend plays the piano.*

A more generic expression is **faire de** + sport, game, instrument.

Je **fais du jogging** tous les jours. *I jog every day.*

Il **fait du piano.** *He is playing the piano.*

Et on peut
jouer° au billard.
jouer au volley-ball.

play

Les fanatiques du sport aiment aussi aller aux **matchs** (*m.*) **de foot° (football)** ou à **des matchs de boxe**, par exemple. Le **football américain°** n'est pas très pratiqué en France, mais il est de plus en plus° populaire grace à° la télévision.

soccer
football... *football*
de... *more and more* / grace... *thanks to*

Autres mots utiles

un jeu (des jeux)	game
une ville	city
assister à	to attend (*an event*)

Langage fonctionnel

Pour commander un repas°

Pour... *Ordering a meal*

Here are some expressions that are useful when dining in a restaurant in France.

Le serveur / La serveuse

Vous prenez un apéritif?	*Would you like an aperitif?*
Vous avez choisi?	*Have you decided?*
Qu'est-ce que vous désirez comme entrée?	*What would you like for the first course?*
Et comme plat principal?	*And as a main dish?*
Et à boire?	*And to drink?*
C'est terminé?	*Will that be all?*
Bon appétit.	*Enjoy your meal.*
Tout va comme vous voulez?	*Is everything to your liking?*

Vous

Je voudrais... / Je vais prendre...	*I'd like . . . / I'll take . . .*
le menu à [20] euros	*the [20] euro meal*
L'addition, s'il vous plaît.	*May I have the check, please?*

—**Vous avez choisi**, madame?
—Oui. **Je vais prendre** le menu à 12 euros.

Activités

A. Loisirs. (*Leisure.*) Qu'est-ce que ces personnes vont faire aujourd'hui? Basez vos réponses sur leurs personnalités.

MODÈLE: M. Coste: Il adore les Impressionnistes.
M. Coste va aller au musée.

1. Mlle Matt: Le soir, elle adore sortir et danser avec d'autres jeunes.
2. Mlle Regolo: Elle apprécie beaucoup la musique classique.

3. Mme Senty: Elle aime essayer les cuisines exotiques.
4. M. Sollier: Il attend avec impatience le prochain (*next*) film de Bruce Willis.
5. M. Albe: C'est un fanatique du football.

B. Une soirée au restaurant. Vous allez au restaurant avec un ami / une amie. En groupes de trois, jouez les rôles des clients et du serveur.

1. Le serveur / La serveuse vous accueille (*welcomes*) et vous annonce les spécialités de la maison.
2. Vous consultez le menu à 20 euros. N'oubliez pas de poser des questions au serveur / à la serveuse si vous voulez savoir la préparation d'un plat ou si vous n'êtes pas certain(e) de la boisson à choisir.
3. Vous choisissez et le serveur / la serveuse répond.
4. Pendant le repas, le serveur / la serveuse vous demande si tout va comme vous voulez. Ensuite, vous parlez des raisons pourquoi vous aimez ce restaurant.
5. À la fin du repas, vous demandez l'addition.

Restaurant Chez Paul

Menu à 20€

Les Entrées

Assiette anglaise (jambon cru,[a] jambon cuit,[b] saucisson[c])
Le pâté du chef
Tomates et mozzarella
Quiche

Les Plats principaux

Riz à l'espagnole (riz, porc, poivrons,[d] crevettes, tomates)
Couscous à l'agneau[e]
Poulet rôti[f] avec haricots verts
Cassoulet (haricots blancs, saucisses, sauce tomate)
Spaghettis bolognaises (spaghettis, sauce tomate à la viande)
Steak-frites
Côte[g] de porc avec purée de pommes de terre
Filets de sardine en marinade orientale

Le Plateau[h] de fromages

La Salade verte

Les Desserts

Tarte aux pommes
Crème caramel
Mousse au chocolat
Sorbet aux fruits
Bananes flambées[i] à la crème Chantilly[j]
Riz au lait maison

Les Boissons

Vin rouge, rosé ou blanc (carafe, bouteille, demi-bouteille)
Eau minérale
Bière[k]
Café, Thé

[a]*smoked* [b]*cooked* [c]*salami* [d]*green peppers* [e]*lamb* [f]*roasted* [g]*Cutlet* [h]*Platter* [i]*flaming* [j]*crème... whipped cream* [k]*Beer*

C. Distractions. Posez les questions suivantes à votre partenaire. Demandez-lui...

1. combien de fois par semaine il/elle va au restaurant.
2. s'il / si elle fait souvent de la musculation. Sinon (*If not*), avec quelle fréquence (parfois, rarement, jamais)?
3. s'il / si elle aime aller au musée. Si oui, quelle sorte de musée préfère-t-il/elle?
4. s'il / si elle est fanatique du sport. Si oui, quel(s) sport(s) aime-t-il/elle? Va-t-il/elle voir des matchs?
5. combien de fois par mois il/elle va au cinéma ou au théâtre.
6. s'il / si elle joue d'un instrument. De quel instrument? Joue-t-il/elle bien ou mal?
7. à quels sports ou jeux il/elle aime jouer.

Temperature in France and Canada is measured in degrees Celsius. Compare some common Celsius temperatures to their close equivalents in the Fahrenheit scale used in the United States.

0°C is the same as 32°F and is the freezing point of water.

10°C is about 50°F.

20°C is about 68°F.

34°C is about 90°F.

100°C is the same as 212°F and is the boiling point of water.

Le temps et les saisons°

Le… *Weather and seasons*

Quel temps fait-il aujourd'hui? Quelles sont **les températures** (*f.*)? Consultons **la météo**.

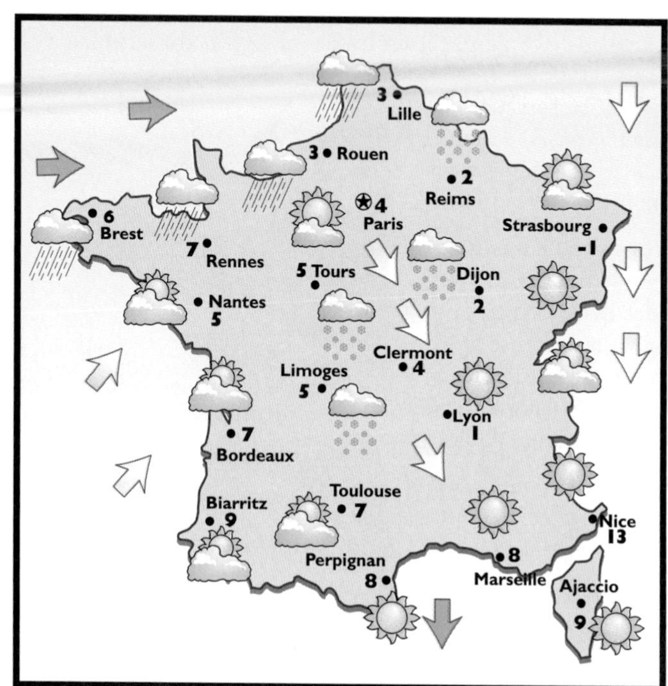

Pour en savoir plus...

The islands of Guadeloupe and Martinique are overseas departments (like states) of France in the Caribbean Sea. They have two seasons.

- The dry season, from December to May, is known as **le carême antillais**.
- The rainy season is known as **l'hivernage**, which, despite its name, actually corresponds to summer, in the months from June to November. This is the season for hurricanes and cyclones.

Le 16 janvier. **Le temps** est **nuageux** au nord de la Loire. **Le ciel est couvert** dans la région nord-ouest.° **Il fait froid**. **Il neige** à l'intérieur des terres° et **il pleut** de la Bretagne à la Normandie. Il va **faire du vent** près des côtes. Dans le Sud-Est, **le ciel est clair** et **il fait du soleil**.

northwest

intérieur… *center of the country*

Les quatre saisons (*f.*) de Paris

l'hiver (*m.*)**:** Les nuits sont longues. Il fait souvent froid, il pleut souvent et parfois il neige.

le printemps: Les jours sont plus longs.[a] **Il fait** plus **doux**.[b] Il pleut, mais **il fait** rarement **mauvais**.

[a]plus… *longer* [b]plus… *milder*

l'été (*m.*): **Il fait** souvent **beau** et **chaud.**[c] Il y a parfois **un orage**[d] en fin de journée.[e]

[c]*hot* [d]*thunderstorm* [e]*en... at the end of the day*

l'automne (*m.*): **Il fait frais**[f] et il pleut souvent.

[f]*cool*

Un seul printemps
dans l'année...,
et dans la vie
une seule jeunesse.

Simone de Beauvoir

Activités

A. Des cartes postales. Voici des cartes postales de diverses régions de la France. Quel temps fait-il dans ces scènes? De quelle saison s'agit-il?

1.

2.

3.

4.

B. La météo. Voici une carte météorologique du Canada. Parcourez (*Scan*) les maxima et les minima et regardez les dessins. De quelle saison s'agit-il? Faites des prévisions (*forecasts*) pour les villes données.

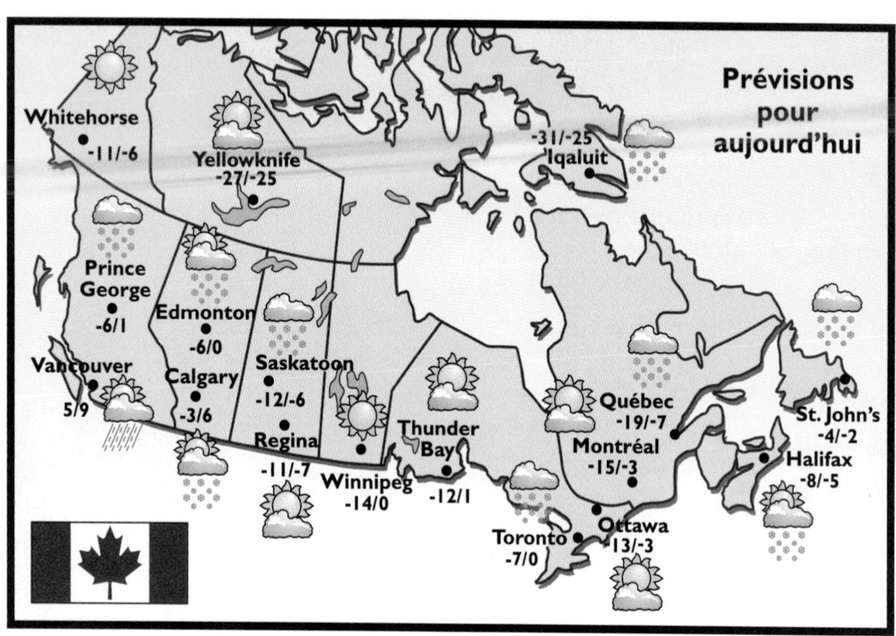

MODÈLE: À Whitehorse, il va faire très froid. On prévoit une température minimale de moins 11 et une température maximale de moins 6. Il va faire du soleil.

C. Les saisons. Décrivez (*Describe*) les saisons dans votre région.

MODÈLE: J'habite dans la Caroline-du-Sud. En été, il fait très chaud, mais en hiver, il fait doux. Ma saison préférée est le printemps, parce que...

Visionnement 1

Avant de visionner

Histoire de couples. Dans cet épisode, vous allez voir Camille et Bruno et le patron et la patronne du restaurant, un couple marié. Lisez (*Read*) le dialogue entre ces deux derniers (*latter two*), et choisissez la phrase qui résume la scène.

1. PATRONNE: Tu as vu ça?[a] C'est étonnant[b]!

PATRON: Quoi?

PATRONNE: Ils sont à nouveau ensemble[c], ces deux-là?

PATRON: Ben, apparemment, oui. Il faut croire.[d]

[a]Tu... *Did you see that?* [b]*amazing* [c]à... *together again* [d]Il... *It looks like it.*

a. Le patron et la patronne connaissent déjà (*already know*) Bruno et Camille.
b. Le patron et la patronne n'aiment pas bien Bruno et Camille.
c. C'est la première fois que Camille et Bruno viennent dans ce restaurant.

2. PATRONNE: Tu regardes trop de sitcoms à la télévision!
PATRON: Mais, je ne regarde que toi, mon amour!
PATRONNE: Regarde plutôt[a] ta sauce! Elle brûle[b]!
PATRON: Oh, nom d'un chien![c]

[a]Regarde... *Better look at* [b]*is burning* [c]nom... *damn!*

a. La patronne critique son mari.
b. Le patron et la patronne se taquinent (*are teasing each other*).
c. Le patron et la patronne ne s'aiment plus.

Notez bien!

The phrase **ne... que** means *only*. The **ne** precedes the verb and **que** precedes the person or thing that is restricted or limited.

Je **ne regarde que** toi.
I look only at you.

Camille **ne parle de son père qu'**à Bruno. *Camille speaks only to Bruno about her father.*

Observez!

Dans cet épisode, vous allez apprendre quelques détails supplémentaires sur la relation de Camille et Bruno. Ces deux personnages vont aussi révéler des détails sur leur famille.

- Est-ce que Bruno se considère comme un bon fils? Pourquoi ou pourquoi pas?
- Est-ce que Camille se considère comme une bonne fille? Pourquoi ou pourquoi pas?
- Quelle sorte de rapport Camille et Bruno avaient-ils (*did they have*) avant? Quelle sorte de rapport semblent-ils avoir (*do they seem to have*) maintenant?

Vocabulaire relatif à l'épisode

dragueur	*pick-up artist*
tellement	*quite, somewhat*
depuis quelque temps	*for some time*
comme d'habitude	*as usual*
à part la nôtre, évidemment	*except for ours, obviously*

Après le visionnement

A. Avez vous compris? (*Did you understand?*) Faites un résumé de l'épisode en complétant chacune (*each one*) des phrases suivantes avec une des options de la colonne de droite (*on the right*).

1. Le patron est étonné de voir Camille et Bruno...
2. Bruno n'est pas marié...
3. Camille n'est pas une bonne fille...
4. Comme plat principal, Bruno commande...
5. Comme vin, Bruno choisit...
6. Selon la patronne, son mari regarde trop de...
7. Mais il ne regarde pas...

a. parce qu'elle est nerveuse et impatiente.
b. des œufs en meurette.
c. sa sauce. Elle brûle.
d. parce qu'il ne les a pas vus (*hasn't seen them*) depuis quelque temps.
e. sitcoms à la télé.
f. parce qu'un bon fils ne devient pas toujours un bon mari.
g. du vin rouge.

B. Hypothèses. Réfléchissez aux questions suivantes.

1. Selon vous, est-ce que le patron et la patronne sont mariés depuis longtemps? Comment peut-on décrire leur relation?
2. Est-ce qu'on découvre un nouveau côté de Bruno dans cet épisode? Expliquez.

Structure 30

Le passé composé

Talking about past events

—Le décor **n'a pas changé**, hein...

To talk about the past in French, you will need to learn several past tenses. You have already seen examples of two of these tenses. Here is an exchange from the film that you read in Chapter 8.

Camille pose une question à sa grand-mère, Louise.

CAMILLE: C'*était* quand, la dernière fois qu'il t'**a contactée**?

LOUISE: En 1943. Il *était* dans les Cévennes. Il m'**a envoyé** une lettre... pour l'anniversaire de ta maman. Elle *avait* quatre ans.

Plus tard, Mado parle à Camille.

MADO: D'où sort-elle, cette photo?! Pourquoi tu **as montré** ça à ta grand-mère?

The verb forms in **bold type** are examples of the **passé composé**; you will learn the forms and uses of this tense in this section. The *italicized* verbs in the dialogue are examples of the **imparfait**, another past tense, which is presented in Chapter 12.

1. The **passé composé** is used for talking about a completed past event or a sequence of completed past events.

   Mado **a invité** Camille et Rachid à dîner. Ensuite, elle **a servi** du champagne. Rachid n'**a** pas **bu** de champagne. — *Mado invited Camille and Rachid to have dinner with her. Then she served champagne. Rachid didn't drink any champagne.*

2. As you can see, the **passé composé** is a compound tense, consisting of two parts: (1) an auxiliary verb▲ in the present tense and (2) a past participle.▲ The auxiliary verb is usually **avoir**.

   Bravo, Bruno! Vous **avez gagné** le béret de la semaine! — *Bravo, Bruno! You have won the beret of the week!*

3. The past participle of regular verbs is formed by dropping the infinitive ending and adding **é** (for **-er** verbs) or **u** (for **-re** verbs).

regarder →	regard + **é** →	**regardé**
attendre →	attend + **u** →	**attendu**

The past participles of **dormir**, **mentir**, **sentir**, and **servir** are formed by adding **i** to the infinitive stem.*

dormi **menti** **senti** **servi**

Some verbs have irregular past participles.

avoir	**eu**	être	**été**	pouvoir	**pu**
boire	**bu**	faire	**fait**	prendre	**pris**
devoir	**dû**	mettre	**mis**	vouloir	**voulu**

4. To make a **passé composé** form negative, place **ne** before the auxiliary and the second part of the negation (**pas**, **jamais**, etc.) after the auxiliary (and before the past participle).

Il **n'a pas contacté** sa femme? *He didn't contact his wife?*

5. Yes/no questions can be asked in the **passé composé** using **est-ce que**, rising intonation, or inversion. Notice that inversion occurs with the auxiliary verb and the subject pronoun.

Est-ce qu'elle a montré une photo à sa grand-mère?
Elle a montré une photo à sa grand-mère?
A-t-elle montré une photo à sa grand-mère?

For information questions, the most common patterns are the following:

- question word + **est-ce que** + subject + auxiliary + past participle

  Quand est-ce que Camille a trouvé la photo?
  Où est-ce qu'elle a trouvé la photo?

- question word + inversion of auxiliary verb and subject pronoun + past participle

  Où a-t-elle trouvé la photo?

6. Object pronouns precede the auxiliary in the **passé composé**.

DIRECT OBJECT: Camille a arrêté son régime. → Camille **l'**a arrêté.
INDIRECT OBJECT: Tu as parlé à Bruno? → Tu **lui** as parlé?

To make a sentence with an object pronoun negative, place **ne** before the object pronoun.

NEGATION WITH OBJECT PRONOUN: Tu n'as pas parlé à Bruno? → Tu **ne** lui as **pas** parlé?

Attention—When a *direct* object—either a noun or a pronoun—precedes the past participle, the past participle agrees with it in gender and number. In the

Notez bien!

To express how long *ago* an action took place, you can use the **passé composé + il y a** + unit of time.

Camille a trouvé une photo de son grand-père **il y a** trois jours. *Camille found a photograph of her grandfather three days ago.*

*You will learn the passé composé of **partir** and **sortir** in Chapter 11.

following example, **les** refers to a feminine plural direct object (**les photos**), therefore **-es** is added to the past participle **regardé** to make it agree in both gender and number.

> Camille a regardé les photos. (*direct object follows the past participle*)
> Camille **les** a regardé**es**. (*direct object precedes the past participle*)

In the next example, the direct object noun precedes the past participle, requiring agreement.

> **Les photos** que Camille a regardé**es** sont intéressantes.

Activités

A. Vous souvenez-vous? Regardez la photo et complétez chaque phrase avec la forme affirmative ou négative du passé composé d'un des verbes donnés à droite.

MODÈLES: Martine *a donné* son téléphone à Rachid.
Rachid *a téléphoné* à sa femme.
Sonia *n'a pas répondu*.

donner
ne pas répondre
téléphoner

1. Bruno ____ le pain artisanal.
2. Camille ____ un béret qui était (*was*) derrière la table.
3. Elle a dit (*said*): «Vous ____ le béret de la semaine!»

gagner (*to win*)
identifier
prendre

4. Bruno ____ Camille avant l'émission.
5. Soudain, il ____ peur et il ____ «Où est Camille?»
6. Mais Camille ____ apparaître (*to appear*) à l'heure.

attendre
avoir
demander
pouvoir

7. Louise et Camille ____ ensemble.
8. Camille ____ la cuisine et elle ____ la table.
9. Elle ____ de la viande et des légumes.
10. Elles ____ du café après le dîner.

boire
dîner
faire
mettre
servir

11. Louise ____ un malaise.
12. Le médecin ____ expliquer à Mado que Louise était (*was*) au plus mal.
13. Mado ____ parler de la gravité de la maladie de Louise avec Camille.
14. Elle lui ____.

avoir
devoir
mentir
ne pas vouloir

15. Bruno et Camille ____ de dîner ensemble.
16. Ils ____ longtemps au restaurant avant de commander.
17. Camille a dit: «Le décor ____, hein... »

attendre
ne pas changer
décider

18. La patronne ____ Bruno et Camille par le judas (*peephole*).
19. Elle a dit: «Ils ____ fiancés (*They got engaged*), non?»
20. Son mari ____ que les histoires d'amour finissent (*love stories end*) toujours mal.

être
regarder
répondre

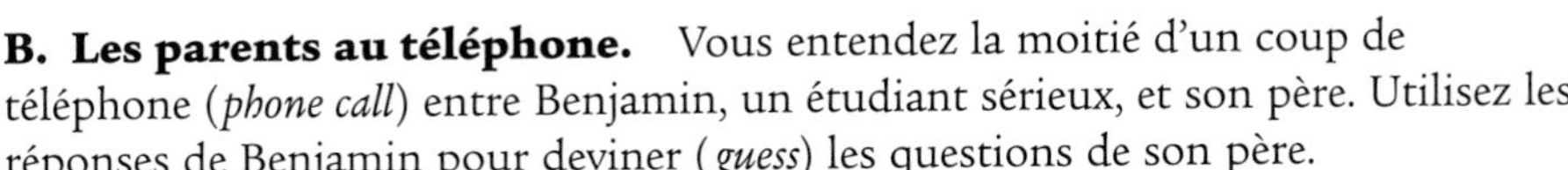

B. Les parents au téléphone. Vous entendez la moitié d'un coup de téléphone (*phone call*) entre Benjamin, un étudiant sérieux, et son père. Utilisez les réponses de Benjamin pour deviner (*guess*) les questions de son père.

MODÈLE: BENJAMIN: Non, nous n'avons pas regardé de film avant l'examen. →
QUESTION DU PÈRE: Tes amis et toi, est-ce que vous avez regardé un film avant l'examen?

1. Oui, j'ai étudié à la bibliothèque. **2.** Non, nous n'avons pas parlé anglais dans le cours de japonais. **3.** Non, mes amis ne m'ont pas téléphoné à minuit. **4.** Oui, ma sœur m'a rendu visite. **5.** Non, je n'ai pas bu trop de café. **6.** Oui, mon professeur m'a donné une bonne note. **7.** Oui, j'ai mis mon manteau quand il a neigé. **8.** Oui, nous avons joué au football après l'examen. **9.** Non, mes amies n'ont pas fait de roller dans la rue. **10.** Oui, j'ai pu travailler le week-end.

Maintenant, avec un(e) partenaire, imaginez que le père téléphone à sa fille Karine, qui est beaucoup moins sérieuse que Benjamin. Posez les mêmes questions une deuxième fois en utilisant l'inversion. Votre partenaire va répondre le contraire de ce que Benjamin a dit.

MODÈLE: QUESTION DU PÈRE: Tes amis et toi, avez-vous regardé un film avant l'examen? →
KARINE: Oui, nous avons regardé un film avant l'examen.

C. Camarades de classe curieux. Posez les questions suivantes à votre partenaire. Il/Elle va répondre en utilisant (*using*) un pronom complément d'objet. Demandez-lui...

MODÈLE: combien de fois il/elle a rendu des devoirs à son prof cette semaine. →
É1: Combien de fois as-tu rendu des devoirs à ton prof cette semaine?
É2: Je lui ai rendu des devoirs trois fois.

1. combien de fois il/elle a téléphoné à ses parents cette semaine.
2. s'il / si elle a donné un cadeau (*gift*) à un ami cette année.
3. s'il / si elle a attendu son professeur pendant plus de 20 minutes.
4. combien de fois il/elle a rendu visite à ses amis ce mois-ci.

5. s'il / si elle a perdu son livre de français aujourd'hui.
6. s'il / si elle a téléphoné au prof cette semaine.

D. Maman, maman! Les enfants Dufour posent beaucoup de questions à leur maman. Jouez le rôle des enfants, qui posent des questions, et de leur maman, qui répond en utilisant des pronoms complément d'objet direct. Attention à l'accord du participe passé.

MODÈLE: prendre / ma guitare →
É1: Maman, as-tu pris ma guitare?
É2: Oui, je l'ai prise.

1. acheter / les pommes pour le pique-nique
2. mettre / ma veste dans la voiture
3. prendre / mes chaussures de sport
4. inviter / ma cousine à la maison
5. faire / la pizza pour ma soirée
6. laver / mes vêtements de sport

E. Trouvez quelqu'un qui... (*Find someone who . . .*) Faites une liste de cinq choses que vous avez faites la semaine dernière (*last week*). Transformez ces phrases en questions et posez-les à trois camarades de classe. Qui a fait les mêmes choses que vous?

MODÈLE: J'ai mangé au restaurant. (élément de la liste)
As-tu mangé au restaurant? (question)
Non, je n'ai pas mangé au restaurant. (Oui, j'ai mangé au restaurant.) (réponse)

Notez les réponses et préparez un petit compte rendu (*report*) pour la classe.

Structure 31

La place des expressions de temps

Talking about time

—Vous prenez un apéritif?

—Non, non, merci. C'est **déjà** fait.

The placement of adverbs in French sentences is somewhat flexible. Many times, placement depends on which element of the sentence the speaker wants to emphasize. Nevertheless, here are some broad generalizations for placement of adverbs of time.

1. The following expressions tend to come at the beginning of a sentence.

d'abord	*first, first of all, at first*	**d'habitude**	*usually, normally*
ensuite	*next, then*	**maintenant**	*now*
puis	*then*		
enfin*	*at last; finally*		

D'abord, Camille trouve une photo. **Ensuite**, elle pose des questions à sa mère. — *First, Camille finds a photo. Then she asks her mother some questions.*

D'habitude, Bruno commande du vin rouge. — *Usually, Bruno orders red wine.*

2. The following expressions can come either at the beginning or at the end of a sentence.

après	*afterward*	**demain**	*tomorrow*
aujourd'hui	*today*	**hier**	*yesterday*
autrefois	*formerly; in the past*	**plus tard**	*later*
avant	*beforehand*	**quelquefois**	*sometimes*
bientôt	*soon*	**tous les jours**	*every day*
de temps en temps	*from time to time*		

Bientôt, elle va sortir avec Bruno. (Elle va sortir avec Bruno **bientôt**.) — *Soon, she'll go out with Bruno.*

De temps en temps, Camille prépare le dîner pour sa grand-mère. (Camille prépare le dîner pour sa grand-mère **de temps en temps**.) — *From time to time, Camille makes dinner for her grandmother.*

Tu étudies **encore**? — *You're still studying?*

3. Some expressions usually follow the conjugated verb.

déjà	*already; ever; yet*	**souvent**	*often*
encore	*again; still*	**tard**	*late*
jusqu'à	*until*	**tôt**	*early*
longtemps	*(for) a long time*	**toujours**	*always; still*
parfois	*sometimes*	**tout de suite**	*right away*
rarement	*rarely*		

Camille arrive **toujours** à l'heure. Elle passe **souvent** quarante minutes au maquillage. — *Camille always arrives on time. She often spends forty minutes in make-up.*

Puis, ils dînent **tard**. — *Then they dine late.*

***Enfin** is also an interjection that means *Well, In short:* **Et... *enfin*, pour le moment on est séparés./Ton grand-père! *Enfin*... Où est-il?/Non, merci... *enfin*, pas ce soir. On m'attend...**

Jusqu'à is followed by a time or an event.

Bruno et Camille travaillent **jusqu'à** quatorze heures.	*Bruno and Camille work until 2:00 P.M.*

Attention— Adverbs that follow the verb in the present tense usually follow the auxiliary in the **passé composé**. However, the adverbs **encore**, **jusqu'à**, **tard**, **tôt**, and **tout de suite** follow the past participle.

	Mado m'a **souvent** dit de ne pas parler de mon grand-père.	*Mado often told me not to talk about my grandfather.*
	Martine a **déjà** trouvé le médaillon.	*Martine already found the locket.*
but	Bruno et Camille ont dîné **tard**.	*Bruno and Camille dined late.*
	Ils ont parlé **encore** d'Antoine.	*They talked again about Antoine.*

4. Notice the following relationships.

ne... pas encore	is the negation of	**déjà**
ne... plus	is the negation of	**encore**, **toujours** (meaning *still*)
ne... jamais	is the negation of	**toujours** (meaning *always*), **souvent**, **parfois**, **quelquefois**, **de temps en temps**, **rarement**

Activités

A. Une journée en ville. Votre ami parle de ses passe-temps préférés. Vous avez des goûts (*tastes*) différents. Exprimez votre point de vue en suivant le modèle.

Vocabulaire utile: autrefois, avant, déjà, hier, ne... jamais, ne... plus, parfois, plus tard, rarement, souvent, toujours, tous les jours

MODÈLE: AMI 1: Je visite souvent le musée d'art moderne.
AMI 2: Moi, je le visite rarement.

1. Je veux toujours aller aux expositions d'art.
2. À la sortie (*opening*) d'un nouveau film, je prends des places tout de suite.
3. D'habitude, je fais du bowling le soir.
4. Je ne fais jamais de roller.
5. Je n'ai pas encore assisté à une pièce (*play*) de théâtre.
6. Il est dix-huit heures. Je veux aller au restaurant maintenant.
7. Je vais toujours dans des boîtes de nuit.
8. J'aime faire du jogging après le dîner.

B. La scène au restaurant. Pour rétablir (*re-establish*) la chronologie de l'histoire, mettez les phrases dans l'ordre 1 à 5 et ajoutez (*add*) les adverbes **d'abord**, **puis**, **ensuite**, **après**, **enfin**.

a. Bruno commande des œufs en meurette.
b. Camille remarque que le décor n'a pas changé.
c. Le patron leur demande s'ils veulent un apéritif.
d. Bruno et Camille arrivent au restaurant.
e. Le patron et la patronne parlent de Bruno et de Camille.

C. Vos distractions. Avec un(e) partenaire, jouez les rôles d'un fanatique du sport et d'un cinéphile (*movie lover*). À l'aide des adverbes, comparez vos centres d'intérêt passés, présents et futurs.

MODÈLE: FANATIQUE DU SPORT: J'ai déjà fait du sport trois fois cette semaine.
CINÉPHILE: Je ne fais jamais de sport, mais je vais souvent au cinéma.

Après le jeu de rôles, parlez ensemble de vos distractions préférées. Qu'est-ce que vous faites souvent, parfois, rarement, tous les jours, etc.? Expliquez.

Regards sur la culture

Les cafés et les restaurants

In this episode, Camille and Bruno have dinner in what is a rather typical French restaurant. As we have already seen, food is very important in France, and the experience of eating out is somewhat different there from what we know in North America. Cafés, for example, have a different function in France from restaurants, even though it is possible to get something simple to eat in many of them.

- The average French restaurant is family-owned and operated. There are very few large chain restaurants in France. This means that the owners or chefs are likely to know some of their customers quite well and may come out to speak with them.
- When French people go to a restaurant, they are looking forward to real culinary pleasure: something unusual to eat, or something that is difficult to make at home. The notion of going to a place that serves "homestyle cooking" would not be appealing to the French. They often say that there is no point in going to a restaurant if you could eat just as well at home.
- Because the focus on the quality of the food is so strong, a restaurant's décor is less important in France than it is in North America. Although successful restaurants tend to be very comfortable, French people delight in finding a place **qui ne paie pas de mine** (that is not much to look at), but that serves wonderful food.
- Waiting on tables in France is a professional (and usually male-dominated) activity. Service is expected to be efficient and unobtrusive. No French waiter will ever introduce himself. Professionalism and courtesy are more important to the French than the "friendliness" of the service.
- French people spend lots of time looking for good restaurants, and comparing notes on restaurants is a big part of everyday conversation. The average French person judges an establishment on the basis of the cost and apparent quality of the "menus" that it serves. A **menu** in France is a fixed-price meal with at least two courses. These menus are always posted outside the restaurant door.

Bruno et Camille dînent au restaurant.

- In contrast to restaurants, the focus in cafés is not so much on the food or drink as it is on the social scene. Every café has its own particular clientele. In university towns, for example, law students might have a café where they meet and where students of philosophy, for example, would never go. Their gathering place would be another café where law students would not go.

Un café à Paris

- Because one can order just a simple drink at a café and then stay seated for quite a long time, people use the café as a meeting place. They may read, write, or study at a café table. They may simply want to watch people going by (staring at others is not nearly as impolite in France as it is in North America). They may sit down and order a coffee in order to rest in the middle of a long walk.
- The social functions of the café have declined somewhat over the past 30 years, particularly in the evening. Many French people feel that having a drink at a café has become too expensive. Probably more important is the fact that people tend to stay home at night and watch television, rather than go out to socialize at the café.

Considérez

Why do you think there aren't many establishments in North America that serve the functions cafés do in France? Where in North America does café-style socializing exist?

Structure 32

Les verbes *voir, croire* et *recevoir*

Talking about everyday activities

—Et vous, Bruno?

—Moi?... Oui, oui, oui! **Je crois.** Oui!

—Eh bien, faisons un test.

—Ah! Maman, pardon si je me trompe, hein? (les yeux bandés) Il y a une panne d'électricité, là? **Je** ne **vois** plus rien du tout.

Le verbe *voir*

voir (*to see*)			
je	**vois**	nous	**voyons**
tu	**vois**	vous	**voyez**
il, elle, on	**voit**	ils, elles	**voient**
passé composé: j'**ai vu**			

Je ne le **vois** pas depuis le divorce. — *I haven't seen him since the divorce.*

Another verb like **voir** is **revoir** (*to see again*).

Et je n'ai aucune envie de le **revoir**. — *And I don't have any desire to see him again.*

Le verbe *croire*

croire (*to believe*)			
je	**crois**	nous	**croyons**
tu	**crois**	vous	**croyez**
il, elle, on	**croit**	ils, elles	**croient**
passé composé: j'**ai cru**			

1. **Croire** can be accompanied by a direct object or by a clause beginning with **que**.

   Vous me **croyez**, n'est-ce pas? — *You believe me, don't you?*

   Tu as faim? Je ne le **crois** pas... !? — *You're hungry? I don't believe it.*

   Mado **croit** que Camille est encore une enfant. — *Mado believes that Camille is still a child.*

2. **Croire à** means *to believe in.*

   Je **crois au** Père Noël. — *I believe in Santa Claus.*

Le verbe *recevoir*

recevoir (*to receive*)			
je	**reçois**	nous	**recevons**
tu	**reçois**	vous	**recevez**
il, elle, on	**reçoit**	ils, elles	**reçoivent**
passé composé: j'**ai reçu**			

Notice the use of **ç** in the **je**, **tu**, **il/elle/on**, and **ils/elles** forms and in the past participle: When **c** is followed by **a**, **o**, or **u**, it needs the cedilla to keep the sound of a soft *c*.

Camille **a reçu** le livre sur les Cévennes de sa grand-mére. — *Camille received the book about the Cévennes from her grandmother.*

Activités

A. Au présent. Faites des phrases au temps présent avec les expressions et les pronoms donnés.

MODÈLE: croire que le musée est ouvert (*open*) aujourd'hui (je) →
Je crois que le musée est ouvert aujourd'hui.

1. croire que cette boîte de nuit est fantastique (ils)
2. ne plus croire au Père Noël (tu)
3. croire que votre ami a fait du jogging ce matin (*this morning*) (vous)
4. ne pas voir de bonne pièce de théâtre tous les jours (on)
5. ne pas revoir mes anciens (*former*) profs (je)
6. voir que vous aimez jouer au billard (nous)
7. ne jamais recevoir de bonnes notes (elles)
8. recevoir déjà les billets pour le cirque (vous)
9. recevoir beaucoup de cadeaux d'anniversaire (tu)

B. Au passé composé. Faites des phrases au passé composé avec les éléments donnés.

1. est-ce que / vous / voir / la cathédrale Notre-Dame / à Paris
2. nous / recevoir / vos cartes postales
3. je / ne jamais revoir / ce pays
4. est-ce que / tu /ne jamais voir / un match de foot
5. mon frère / me croire / quand je lui / donner / la preuve (*proof*)
6. qu'est-ce que / ils / recevoir / pour Noël

C. Le passage des saisons. Parfois les saisons qui changent poussent à (*lead to*) la réflexion. Que voyez-vous quand on passe de l'hiver au printemps? Que croyez-vous? Que recevez-vous? Avec un(e) partenaire, parlez du passage des quatre saisons en pensant à ces questions.

MODÈLE: Quand l'hiver arrive, je vois qu'il neige, je crois qu'on va skier, et je reçois des invitations pour les fêtes (*holidays*).

Visionnement 2

Le Quartier des Halles. Bruno and Camille have gone to dinner in another part of Paris, on the right bank of the Seine. This area housed the central market of Paris until 1969; it was both picturesque and run-down. The district was redeveloped in the 1970s and '80s. The **Centre Pompidou**,* completed in 1977, was built to house the National Museum of Modern Art and other cultural services. It has remained a controversial piece of architecture. **Le Forum des Halles**

*__Le Centre national d'art et de culture Georges Pompidou__ porte le nom de Georges Pompidou (1911–1974), qui a été Premier ministre (1962–1968) sous le Président Charles de Gaulle et président de 1969 à 1974.

is a complex of shops, movie theaters, and restaurants, rising in tiers from a sunken patio. Much of the rest of the old market area is occupied by gardens. Nearby stands the **église Saint-Eustache**, where Richelieu* was baptized and where Molière's† funeral was held. It is probably the best architectural example of a French Renaissance church in Paris. Near the Seine, the **Hôtel de Ville**, the city hall of Paris, is a replica of the 17th-century building that was burned down when the army put down a revolutionary government that had taken over Paris in 1871.

Les environs du restaurant préféré de Camille et Bruno

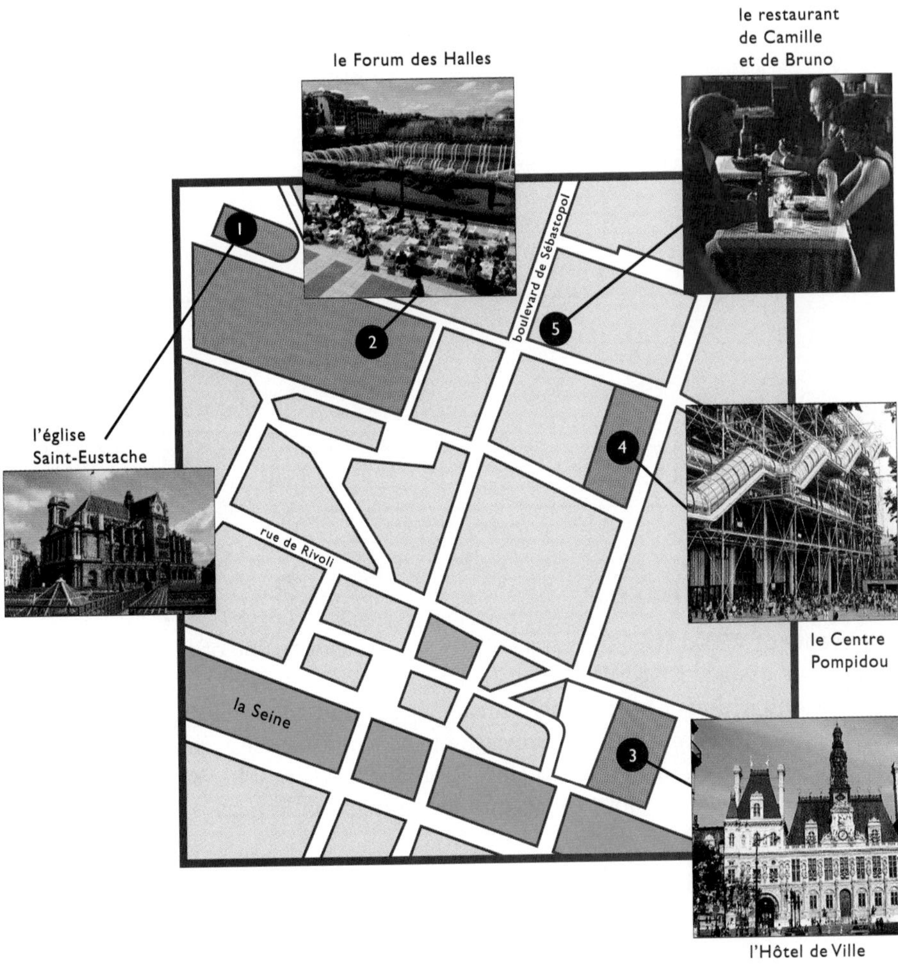

Vous recherchez une atmosphère particulière. Indiquez où vous voulez aller. Plusieurs (*Several*) réponses sont possibles.

MODÈLE: la tranquillité et les plaisirs gastronomiques
Je veux aller au restaurant où vont Camille et Bruno.

a. des souvenirs historiques
b. une ambiance esthétique
c. une atmosphère mouvementée
d. une ambiance de méditation
e. la solitude

*Le cardinal Richelieu (1585–1642), grand homme d'État, ministre de Louis XIII. Il a fondé l'Académie française pour créer un dictionnaire de la langue française.
†Molière (1622–1673), auteur célèbre de nombreuses pièces de théâtre comiques.

Observez!

Considérez les aspects culturels dans **Regards sur la culture**. Ensuite, regardez l'Épisode 10 encore une fois, et répondez aux questions suivantes.

- Comment est le décor du restaurant? Selon vous, quelle sorte de clientèle fréquente ce restaurant?
- Comment peut-on qualifier le rapport entre Bruno, Camille et le serveur? Le serveur est-il froid? réservé? respectueux? familier? trop familier? Expliquez son comportement (*behavior*).

Après le visionnement

Faites l'activité pour le **Visionnement 2** dans le cahier.

Synthèse: Lecture

Mise en contexte

The events of World War II form a backdrop to the story line of *Le Chemin du retour*. This destructive conflict is still an open wound for many in French society. The role and actions of the French during this period are being critically examined even today. The many stories of heroism, generosity, and self-sacrifice have been tempered by tales of collaboration and atrocities. In the reading for this chapter, you will learn about the war and its impact on France.

Stratégie pour mieux lire
Guessing meaning from context

You may be able to predict the meaning of an unknown word by using cues from the surrounding context. For example, read the following sentence and use it to figure out the meanings of the words in bold print.

1. Le gouvernement allemand prend des mesures d'exclusion **contre** les races **dites** «inférieures».

contre:	**a.** counter	**b.** against	**c.** with
dites:	**a.** that are	**b.** ditto	**c.** said to be

Did you correctly guess "b. against" and "c. said to be"? Try out this skill with some more sentences from the reading passage. Try to identify the meaning of the French words in **bold** print on the next page.

2. Hitler lance un programme d'agression. L'Autriche est **envahie**.

   envahie: a. envisioned b. invaded c. afraid

3. Un **appel** à la résistance est lancé de Londres par le général Charles de Gaulle.

   appel: a. call b. criticism c. apple

4. La Résistance s'organise en divers groupes non centralisés. Elle publie des **journaux** clandestins, **cache** des Juifs, donne des **renseignements** aux Alliés, **exécute** des sabotages.

journaux:	a. magazines	b. newspapers	c. journals
cache:	a. hides	b. catches	c. searches for
renseignements:	a. help	b. reassigns	c. information
exécute:	a. stops	b. carries out	c. kills

Now read the whole text through. Be sure to make use of context to facilitate the reading task. If you didn't get all meanings from the context in items 2–4, you may still be able to figure them out with the help of the greater context of the full passage. Also, pay attention to which events are results of other conditions or events.

La Deuxième Guerre mondiale,[1] les Français et l'occupation

- janvier 1933–1938

Hitler est nommé chancelier d'Allemagne après une crise économique et politique. Une dictature totalitaire s'établit en Allemagne. Le gouvernement allemand prend des mesures d'exclusion contre les races dites «inférieures».

- 1938–1940

Hitler lance un programme d'agression. L'Autriche est envahie, puis la Pologne. La France et l'Angleterre déclarent la guerre à l'Allemagne en 1939. L'armée française lutte[2] contre les forces allemandes en Europe. L'Allemagne envahit la France.

- juin 1940

Paris est occupée. La France cède. L'Allemagne contrôle les deux tiers[3] de la France. Un appel à la résistance est lancé de Londres par le général Charles de Gaulle. La Résistance est formée. Le maréchal Pétain, chef du gouvernement «libre[4]» à Vichy, signe l'armistice. La France est coupée en deux—la zone occupée, au nord, et la «zone libre», au sud sur la façade atlantique.

- 1940–1942

Le régime autoritaire de Pétain collabore avec les Allemands. Les élections, les partis politiques et les syndicats[5] sont supprimés.[6] L'État français édicte «le statut des Juifs» et participe à leur arrestation et déportation. Deux millions de Français sont faits prisonniers et envoyés en Allemagne.

[1]Deuxième… *Second World War* [2]*fights* [3]les… *two thirds* [4]*free* [5]*unions* [6]*eliminated*

La Résistance s'organise en divers groupes non centralisés. Elle publie des journaux clandestins, cache des Juifs, donne des renseignements aux Alliés, exécute des sabotages. La milice[7] française lutte contre les résistants.

- 1942–1944

Les troupes allemandes envahissent la zone libre de la France. La Résistance s'accentue. Le régime de Vichy organise la «Révolution nationale» destinée à redresser la France. La main-d'œuvre française est au service de l'Allemagne. La devise du pays devient «Travail, Famille, Patrie[8]».

- juin–septembre 1944

Les Alliés débarquent en Normandie et avancent progressivement vers l'intérieur du pays. Après un second débarquement des Alliés en Provence, Paris est libéré. La retraite des troupes allemandes s'accompagne de massacres de civils. La majeure partie du territoire français est libéré.

- 1945

Les prisonniers des camps d'extermination en Allemagne sont libérés. Hitler se suicide. La guerre en Europe est finie.

[7]*militia* [8]*Fatherland*

Après la lecture

A. Avez-vous compris? (*Did you understand?*) Quelle est la signification de chaque mot en caractères **gras**?

1. Le régime de Vichy organise la «Révolution nationale» destinée à **redresser** la France.

   a. punish **b.** rebuild **c.** reconfirm

2. La **main-d'œuvre** française est au service de l'Allemagne.

   a. manpower **b.** main people **c.** handiwork

3. La **devise** du pays devient «Travail, Famille, Patrie».

   a. device **b.** loss **c.** motto

4. Les Alliés **débarquent** en Normandie.

   a. land **b.** debase **c.** attack

B. Cause et effet. Quelle est la conséquence des actes et des événements (*events*) suivants?

MODÈLE: Il y a une crise économique et politique en Allemagne. → Hitler est nommé chancelier.

1. Hitler lance un programme d'agression. Il envahit l'Autriche et la Pologne.
2. La France est attaquée.
3. Le général de Gaulle lance un appel à la résistance.
4. Le régime de Vichy organise la «Révolution nationale».

À écrire

Faites **À écrire** pour le Chapitre 10 dans le cahier.

Vocabulaire

Les distractions en ville

une boîte de nuit	nightclub
le cirque	circus
la course à pied	running race
les distractions (*f.*)	leisure activities
une exposition d'art	art exhibit
un(e) fanatique du sport	sports fan
le football (*fam.* **le foot**)	soccer
le footing	running (*not in a race*)
un jeu (des jeux)	game
un match (de foot, de boxe)	(soccer, boxing) match
la musculation	weight training
un musée (d'art, de sciences naturelles)	museum (of art, of natural science)
la nuit	night
le roller	roller-skating
le skate	skateboarding
la vie (urbaine)	(urban, city) life
la ville	city

MOTS APPARENTÉS: **le base-ball, le billard, le bowling, le football américain, le jogging, le tennis, le théâtre, le volley-ball**

À REVOIR: **un restaurant, un cinéma**

Les saisons

l'hiver (*m.*)	winter
le printemps	spring
l'été (*m.*)	summer
l'automne (*m.*)	autumn, fall

MOT APPARENTÉ: **la saison**

Le temps qu'il fait

la météo	weather report, forecast
un orage	thunder and lightning storm
le temps	weather
le ciel (est couvert, clair)	sky (is cloudy, clear)
Quel temps fait-il?	What's the weather like?
il fait beau	it's nice out
il fait chaud	it's hot out
il fait doux	it's mild out
il fait du soleil	it's sunny out
il fait du vent	it's windy out
il fait frais	it's cool out
il fait froid	it's cold out
il fait mauvais	it's bad weather
il neige	it's snowing
il pleut	it's raining
nuageux/euse	cloudy

MOT APPARENTÉ: **la température**

Verbes

assister à	to attend (*an event*)	**revoir**	to see again
croire	to believe	**voir**	to see
jouer (à, de)	to play		
recevoir	to receive		

À REVOIR: **faire**

Des adverbes et des expressions de temps

autrefois	formerly; in the past	**longtemps**	(for) a long time
bientôt	soon	**plus tard**	later
d'abord	first, first of all, at first	**puis**	then
déjà	already; ever	**quelquefois**	sometimes
demain	tomorrow	**tard**	late
de temps en temps	from time to time	**tôt**	early
d'habitude	usually, normally	**toujours**	always; still
encore	again; still	**tous les jours**	every day
enfin	at last, finally; well; in short	**tout de suite**	right away
ensuite	next, then		
hier	yesterday		
il y a (dix ans)	(ten years) ago		
jusqu'à	until		

À REVOIR: **après, aujourd'hui, avant, maintenant, ne... jamais, ne... pas encore, ne... plus, parfois, rarement, souvent**

Autre expression utile

ne... que	only

Chapitre 11

De quoi as-tu peur?

OBJECTIFS

In this episode, you will

- learn more about Antoine's activities during the war
- find out how Bruno may be able to help Camille

In this chapter, you will

- discuss occupations
- talk about holidays, festivals, and celebrations
- use ordinal numbers (*first, second,* and so on)
- narrate events in the past
- talk about when things happened and for how long
- talk about everyday actions
- learn about the relationship between the sexes
- read about important historical events in Quebec and Haiti

Vocabulaire en contexte

Les métiers° et les professions

Les... Trades

Comment trouver **un emploi**,° **un métier, une profession**? — *work, employment*

Pour un emploi **à mi-temps** ou à temps partiel, on peut regarder **le tableau d'affichage** à l'université. Là, on trouve **des postes**° (*m.*). Parfois les gens° recherchent — *positions, jobs / people*

- **un(e) baby-sitter**
- **un(e) garde-malade**° — *garde... nurse's aide*
- **un(e) gardien(ne) d'immeuble**

Famille cherche baby-sitter
3 enfants: 3, 5, 6 ans
Tél. 01.45.54.30.85

Pour un emploi à mi-temps ou **à plein temps**,° on peut consulter **les petites annonces**° dans le journal ou chercher **sur Internet**. Par ces intermédiaires, on recrute, par exemple,... — *à... full time*; *petites... classified ads*

- **un agent (de sécurité)**
- **un(e) avocat(e)**° — *lawyer*
- **un(e) cadre**° — *executive*
- **un(e) comptable**° — *accountant*
- **un(e) conservateur/trice (de musée)**° — *(museum) curator*
- **un(e) cuisinier/ière**° — *cook*
- **un(e) employé(e) de fast-food**
- **un(e) fonctionnaire**°* — *civil servant*
- **un(e) ingénieur**° / **femme ingénieur** — *engineer*
- **un(e) interprète**
- **un(e) ouvrier/ière**° — *manual laborer*
- **un(e) patron(ne)**° **(d'un bar, d'un restaurant)** — *owner; boss*
- **un(e) secrétaire**

75 agents de sécurité
Débutants hommes/femmes.
Stage d'emploi. Gardiens d'immeuble Tél. 01.43.78.96.58

Jeune femme 25 ans recherche emploi stable à plein temps. Secrétaire 5 ans expérience. Word et Works Tél. 01.26.82.64.47

Est-ce qu'on trouve les emplois suivants dans les petites annonces?

- **un(e) agriculteur/trice**° — *farmer*
- **un(e) artisan(e)**° — *craftsman, artisan*
- **un(e) écrivain**° / **femme écrivain** — *writer*
- **un(e) musicien(ne)**
- **un(e) peintre**° / **femme peintre** — *painter*

On peut travailler dans...

- **les affaires**° (*f. pl.*) — *business*
- **le commerce (international)**
- **la gestion**° — *management*
- **le marketing**

Un étudiant peut faire **un stage**° dans **une société**° internationale ou nationale. — *internship / company*

*Le mot **fonctionnaire** est un terme générique pour les gens qui travaillent pour le gouvernement: les facteurs (*mail carriers*), les agents de police, les instituteurs et institutrices, etc.

Activités

A. Qui est-ce? Quel est le métier ou la profession de la personne décrite?

MODÈLE: Anne Leduc aide (*helps*) une personne qui est malade. →
C'est une garde-malade.

1. Mme Robert défend des clients devant un juge (*judge*).
2. M. Fourny travaille pour l'État. Il passe toute la journée derrière un guichet (*window*) à la préfecture de police.
3. Mme Bassan vient de finir son chef-d'œuvre: un tableau qui s'appelle «Le soleil couchant à Roissy». Sun set
4. Jackie travaille chez Quick où il sert des hamburgers et des frites.
5. Le père de Jackie prépare des repas dans un restaurant élégant: la Tour d'Argent.
6. M. Gascon est doué (*talented*) pour les chiffres (*numbers*). Il est responsable des comptes (*accounting*) d'une grande société.
7. Mlle Corbet est l'assistante d'un cadre. Elle envoie des lettres, répond au téléphone, etc.

B. À la recherche d'un emploi. (*Job hunting.*) À quel emploi les personnes suivantes se préparent-elles?

MODÈLE: Serge étudie la gestion et le marketing. →
Il va travailler comme cadre. (Il va travailler dans le commerce.)

1. Claude fait un stage dans une société internationale.
2. Thomas va travailler dans la ferme (*farm*) familiale.
3. Laurence organise des expositions au musée.
4. Robert fait ses études de mathématiques.
5. Michel fait des études d'anglais et d'allemand.
6. Nicole lit (*reads*) beaucoup de livres par des auteurs célèbres.

C. Identifiez. Utilisez la liste pour identifier des emplois qui correspondent aux descriptions.

Vocabulaire utile: agent de sécurité, artisan, avocat, baby-sitter, écrivain, employé de fast-food, gardien d'immeuble, ingénieur, musicien, ouvrier, patron d'un bar, peintre

Un emploi qui exige (*requires*)...

1. une bonne connaissance (*knowledge*) d'un bâtiment ou d'un appartement
2. de la créativité
3. des connaissances techniques
4. de l'amour pour les enfants
5. une personnalité extravertie
6. de la logique
7. du rythme

Un emploi...

8. qui n'est pas très prestigieux
9. qui paie mal
10. pour quelqu'un qui aime la solitude
11. que vous trouvez ennuyeux (*boring*)
12. qui est idéal pour vous (expliquez pourquoi!)

Notez bien!

To say someone has a certain profession, use **je suis (tu es, il est**, etc.) + profession (with no article).

Je suis avocate. *I am a lawyer.*
Vous êtes criminel. *You are a criminal.*
Elle est professeur. *She is an instructor.*
Ils sont étudiants. *They are students.*

For the third person (**il, elle, ils, elles**), you can also use **c'est (ce sont)** + indefinite article + profession.

C'est un professeur. *She is an instructor.*
Ce sont des étudiants. *They are students.*

D. Interview. Demandez à votre partenaire...

1. s'il / si elle a un emploi en ce moment et si c'est un travail à mi-temps ou à plein temps.
2. d'identifier son emploi.
3. à quelle profession il/elle se prépare à l'université et quelles qualités sont nécessaires pour exercer (*to practice*) cette profession.
4. s'il / si elle a déjà fait un stage et pour quelle entreprise.
5. ce qu'un candidat à un emploi doit porter ou ne pas porter pour un entretien (*interview*).
6. ce qu'on ne doit pas faire pendant un entretien.
7. de faire le portrait du patron idéal.

Les jours fériés et les fêtes°

Les... *Legal holidays and festivals*

QUELQUES JOURS FÉRIÉS EN FRANCE

le nouvel an	C'est le premier janvier. On fête le réveillon le 31 décembre.	
la fête du travail	C'est le premier mai. On organise des défilés.°	*parades*
la fête nationale	C'est le 14 juillet. On commémore la prise de la Bastille en 1789 avec des défilés et des feux d'artifice.°	feux... *fireworks*

QUELQUES FÊTES RELIGIEUSES

la pâque	C'est une fête juive qui a lieu° en mars ou avril; la date exacte varie selon l'année. On fait un repas spécial avec du pain sans levain.°	a... *takes place*; *yeast*
Pâques* (*m. s., f. pl.*)	C'est une fête chrétienne qui a lieu un dimanche en mars ou avril. La date exacte varie selon l'année. On va à la messe.°	*mass*
le ramadan	C'est le neuvième mois du calendrier musulman. On jeûne° pendant la journée.	*fasts*
la Toussaint	C'est une fête chrétienne qui a lieu le premier novembre. On va au cimetière.°	*cemetery*
Hannukah	C'est une fête juive qui dure° huit jours en décembre. La date exacte varie selon l'année. On allume des bougies° et on donne des cadeaux° aux enfants.	*lasts*; *candles*; *gifts*
Noël (*m.*)	C'est une fête chrétienne qui a lieu le 25 décembre. On va à la messe, et on offre des cadeaux à la famille et aux amis.	

DEUX FÊTES FAMILIALES

un anniversaire (de naissance) **un anniversaire de mariage**	Les dates varient selon les personnes.

***Pâques** (*Easter*) et **Noël** (*Christmas*) sont des fêtes nationales en France.

Activités

A. Identifiez. Identifiez une fête...

MODÈLE: qui a lieu en hiver →
Le nouvel an a lieu en hiver.

1. qui a lieu au printemps.
2. qui commémore un événement (*event*) historique.
3. où on jeûne.
4. où on prépare un repas spécial.
5. où on offre des cadeaux.
6. qui a lieu en hiver.
7. où on fête le réveillon.
8. où on participe à un défilé.
9. quand on va au cimetière.

B. Interview. Demandez à votre partenaire...

1. quelle est la date de son anniversaire.
2. comment il/elle aime fêter son anniversaire.
3. quels sont les jours fériés dans son pays et quelles sont les dates de ces jours fériés cette année.
4. quelle est sa fête préférée et pourquoi.
5. quelles fêtes religieuses il/elle observe.

Les nombres ordinaux°

Les... *Ordinal numbers*

You have already learned the cardinal numbers, which are used for counting. Ordinal numbers (*first, second, third,* etc.) are used for ordering and sequencing.

premier/ière	**troisième**	**cinquième**	**septième**	**neuvième**
deuxième	**quatrième**	**sixième**	**huitième**	**dixième**

1. **Premier** (*m.*) and **première** (*f.*) mean *first.*

   C'est la **première** fois que je mange du couscous. — *It's the first time I've eaten couscous.*

2. Most other ordinal numbers are formed by adding the suffix **-ième** after the final consonant of the cardinal number. Three ordinal numbers have a slightly irregular formation.

   quatre − **e** + ième → **quatrième**
   cinq **+ u** + ième → **cinquième**
   neuf **− f + v** + ième → **neuvième**

3. Ordinal numbers can be made from compound numbers.

   le **dix-neuvième** siècle — *the nineteenth century*
   le **vingt et unième** siècle — *the twenty-first century*

4. Remember that except for **le premier**, ordinal numbers are *not* used when expressing a date in French.

   le **quatorze** juillet — *July fourteenth*
   le **vingt-cinq** décembre — *December twenty-fifth*

Pour en savoir plus...

Ordinal numbers can be abbreviated as follows.

1e 2e 3e 4^e^

Centuries are designated using roman numerals.

XXIe siècle — *21st century*

Royalty are designated using cardinal roman numerals.

Louis XIV (quatorze) — *Louis the fourteenth*

Activités

A. Dans quel quartier? Dans quel arrondissement de Paris se trouvent les monuments suivants (*following*)?

MODÈLE: la basilique (*basilica*) du Sacré-Cœur →
La basilique du Sacré-Cœur est dans le dix-huitième arrondissement.

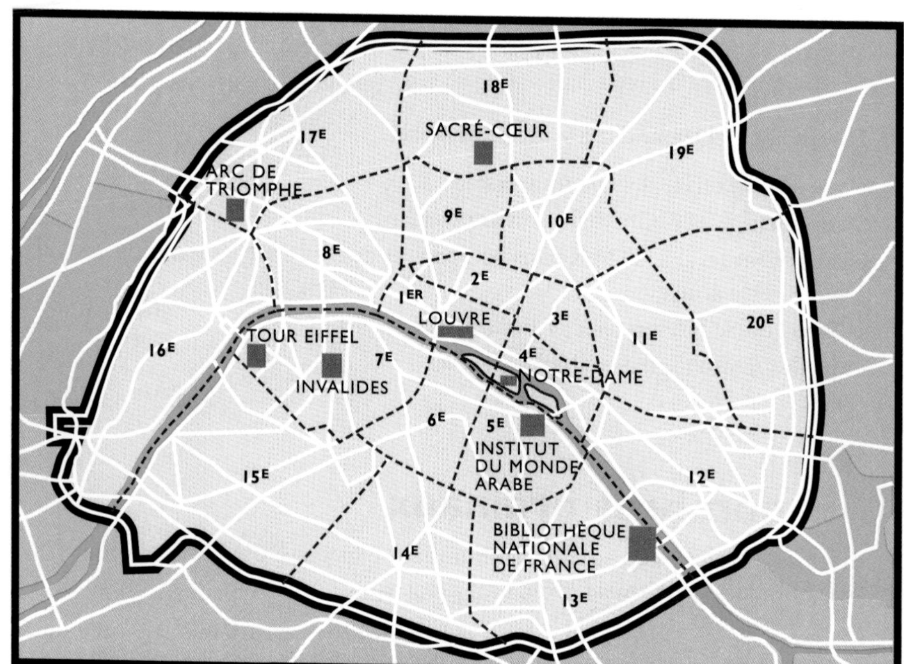

1. le Louvre
2. l'Arc de Triomphe
3. la Bibliothèque nationale de France
4. l'Institut du monde arabe
5. la cathédrale Notre-Dame de Paris
6. les Invalides

B. Personnages historiques. Quelles sont les dates de la naissance et de la mort des personnages suivants? En quel(s) siècle(s) ont-ils vécu (*lived*)?

MODÈLE: Louis XIV: 1638–1715 →
Louis quatorze est né (*was born*) en mil six cent trente-huit et il est mort (*died*) en mil sept cent quinze. Il a vécu aux dix-septième et dix-huitième siècles.

1. Edgar Degas: 1834–1917
2. Pierre de Ronsard: 1524–1585
3. Simone de Beauvoir: 1908–1986
4. Napoléon Ier: 1769–1821
5. Molière: 1622–1673

Pour en savoir plus...

Les Français célèbres qui sont nommés dans l'Activité B ont contribué beaucoup à l'histoire et à la culture françaises.

Louis XIV: roi de France de 1643 à 1715. Roi soleil (*sun*).

Edgar Degas: peintre, pastelliste, graveur et sculpteur impressionniste.

Pierre de Ronsard: poète, auteur de *Odes, Amours, Bocages, Hymnes*, etc.

Simone de Beauvoir: femme de lettres, auteur d'essais (*le Deuxième Sexe*), de romans, de pièces de théâtre, et de mémoires.

Napoleon Ier: empéreur. Il a établi (*established*) le Code civil, des universités, la Légion d'honneur, etc.

Molière: auteur de pièces de théâtre comiques—*le Misanthrope, l'Avare, le Bourgeois gentilhomme*, etc.

Visionnement 1

Avant de visionner

A. Révision du passé composé. Dans cet épisode, il y a beaucoup d'exemples de verbes au passé composé. Lisez les phrases suivantes et donnez l'infinitif de chaque (*each*) verbe.

Verbes utiles: disparaître (*to disappear*), écrire (*to write*), faire, pouvoir, raconter (*to tell*), revoir, surprendre (*to surprise*), voir

1. Et il a disparu de tous (*all*) les albums-photos?
2. Et qu'est-ce qu'on t'a raconté sur lui?
3. Et pendant la guerre (*during the war*), qu'est-ce qu'il a fait?
4. Toute petite, à l'âge de sept ou huit ans, j'ai surpris une conversation entre ma grand-mère et ma mère.
5. Il a écrit une lettre pour le quatrième anniversaire de sa fille.
6. Il a disparu. Louise ne l'a jamais revu. (deux verbes)
7. Ça fait longtemps que je ne l'ai pas vu. (*I haven't seen him for a long time.*)

B. Les dates et les événements. Lisez les dialogues suivants et ensuite, donnez la date qui correspond aux événements mentionnés.

Bruno parle avec Camille de son grand-père.

BRUNO: Et maintenant, Camille, raconte-moi ton histoire. Ton grand-père est toujours vivant[a]?

CAMILLE: Non, il est mort[b]... pendant la guerre, en 1943.

[a]*alive* [b]*il... he died*

Plus tard...

BRUNO: Ta grand-mère a toujours habité le quartier Mouffetard?

CAMILLE: Oui, à partir de[c] 1938, avec son mari.

BRUNO: Antoine? Et quel âge a-t-il à cette époque-là[d]?

CAMILLE: 20 ans.

BRUNO: Il a déjà son atelier d'ébéniste[e]?

CAMILLE: Oui, il en a hérité[f] de son père. Les affaires marchent[g] bien. Il a trois employés avec lui.

BRUNO: Et ta mère? Elle est déjà née[h]?

CAMILLE: Pas encore. Elle est venue au monde[i] en septembre 1939.

BRUNO: Oh. 1939? La déclaration de guerre contre[j] les Allemands...

[c]*à... beginning in* [d]*à... at that time* [e]*atelier... cabinetmaker's workshop* [f]*il... he inherited it* [g]*are going* [h]*born*
[i]*est... came into the world* [j]*against*

1. Louise et Antoine s'installent dans la rue Mouffetard.
2. date de naissance de Mado
3. date de la déclaration de guerre aux Allemands
4. date de la mort d'Antoine

Vocabulaire relatif à l'épisode

presque	*almost, practically*
non plus	*neither*
juif	*Jewish*
personne n'envoie	*nobody sends*
Que Dieu te protège	*May God protect you*
Prenez soin de vous	*Take care of yourself*
ce qui est juste	*what is right*
plus rien	*nothing more*
est-ce qu'il vit toujours	*is he still living*

Observez!

Dans l'Épisode 11, Camille parle à Bruno des expériences de ses grands-parents pendant la guerre. Pendant votre visionnement du film, essayez de trouver les réponses aux questions suivantes.

- Qui est Samuel Lévy? Où va-t-il et pourquoi?
- Que fait Antoine?
- De quoi est-ce qu'Antoine est accusé?
- Comment Bruno offre-t-il d'aider Camille?

Après le visionnement

A. Un résumé. Faites un résumé de l'histoire d'Antoine pendant la guerre en complétant le paragraphe suivant.

Vocabulaire utile: 1939, a trahi (*betrayed*), dans les Cévennes, la déclaration de guerre, ébéniste (*cabinetmaker*), en Amérique, un historien, juif, quatrième, dans la rue Mouffetard, trois, vingt

À partir de 1938, Antoine et Louise habitent _____[1]. À l'époque, Antoine a _____[2] ans. Il travaille comme _____[3] avec _____[4] employés. Sa fille, Mado, naît[a] en _____[5]. C'est une année importante, parce qu'elle marque _____[6] aux Allemands. Un des employés d'Antoine—Samuel Lévy—est _____[7]. Hitler veut exterminer les Juifs, alors, Samuel part _____[8] pour rejoindre[b] sa femme.

Antoine va _____[9]. Il écrit une carte pour le _____[10] anniversaire de sa fille. Ensuite, on perd sa trace. Le bruit court[c] qu'il _____[11] son pays. Bruno connaît _____[12] et espère qu'il peut aider Camille à découvrir la vérité.[d]

[a]*is born* [b]*to join* [c]*Le... Rumor has it* [d]*découvrir... to discover the truth*

B. Questions. Faites une liste de questions dont (*whose*) les réponses peuvent éclaircir (*shed light on*) ce mystère familial. Utilisez les mots **où**, **quand**, **pourquoi**, **comment**, **combien de**, **qu'est-ce que**, etc.

MODÈLE: Pourquoi Antoine va-t-il dans les Cévennes?

Ensuite, essayez de répondre aux questions de vos camarades de classe. À quelles questions est-ce qu'on ne peut pas encore répondre?

Structure 33

*L*e passé composé avec l'auxiliaire être

Narrating in the past

—Ton grand-père est toujours vivant?

—Non, il **est mort**... pendant la guerre, en 1943.

Some verbs—generally those that express motion or a change of state—use the present tense of **être** as their auxiliary in the **passé composé**. When Camille says **Non, il est mort**, she is using the **passé composé** of the verb **mourir** (*to die*).

1. Verbs that use **être** as their auxiliary include

INFINITIVE		PAST PARTICIPLE
aller	*to go*	**allé**
arriver	*to arrive*	**arrivé**
descendre	*to go/get down*	**descendu**
devenir	*to become*	**devenu**
entrer	*to enter*	**entré**
monter	*to go up, climb*	**monté**
mourir*	*to die*	**mort**
naître†	*to be born*	**né**
partir	*to leave*	**parti**
passer (par)	*to pass (by)*	**passé**
rentrer	*to come/go back (home)*	**rentré**
rester	*to stay*	**resté**
retourner	*to return*	**retourné**
revenir	*to come back*	**revenu**
sortir	*to go out*	**sorti**
tomber	*to fall*	**tombé**
venir	*to come*	**venu**

Où Antoine **est**-il **allé** pendant la guerre? — *Where did Antoine go during the war?*

Antoine **est parti** dans les Cévennes. — *Antoine left for the Cévennes.*

Antoine **n'est jamais revenu** à Paris. — *Antoine never returned to Paris.*

Notez bien!

When used with a direct object in the **passé composé**, the verbs **descendre**, **monter**, **passer**, and **sortir** take **avoir** as their auxiliary. Used this way, three of these verbs change their meanings slightly:

descendre *to go down; to take down*

monter *to go up; to raise, lift*

sortir *to take out*

Louise **a descendu l'album-photo** de l'étagère. *Louise got the photo album down from the shelf.*

Camille **a sorti la photo** de l'album. *Camille took the photo out of the album.*

---

*La conjugaison du présent de **mourir** est: **je meurs, tu meurs, il/elle/on meurt, nous mourons, vous mourez, ils/elles meurent. Je meurs de faim/soif/peur.**

†La conjugaison du présent de **naître** est rarement utilisée et n'est pas présentée dans ce cours.

Pour en savoir plus...

The pronoun in a pronominal verb can function as a direct object or an indirect object. When the pronoun serves as a direct object, the past participle must agree with it (this is the normal rule for a preceding direct object). However, if the pronoun serves as an indirect object, the past participle does not agree with it.

Camille s'est **lavée**.

Camille s'est **lavé** les cheveux.

Pourquoi se sont-ils **séparés**?

Pourquoi se sont-ils **téléphoné**?

2. When a verb is conjugated with **être** in the **passé composé**, the past participle agrees in gender and number with the subject of the verb.

Bruno est **arrivé** à l'heure.	*Bruno arrived on time.*
Camille est **venue** en retard.	*Camille came late.*
Bruno et Rachid sont **allés** déjeuner.	*Bruno and Rachid went to eat lunch.*
Mado et Camille sont **parties**.	*Mado and Camille left.*

This agreement does not usually affect pronunciation, but feminine agreement of the past participle **mort** causes the pronunciation of the final **t**.

Antoine est **mort** en 1943.

but La mère de Louise est **morte** à l'âge de 85 ans.

3. All pronominal verbs are also conjugated with **être** in the **passé composé**.

Qu'est-ce qui **s'est passé** dans les Cévennes? — *What happened in the Cévennes?*

Activités

A. Premiers jours. Comment sont les premiers jours après la naissance d'un enfant? Choisissez (*choose*) le verbe qui convient et mettez-le au passé composé.

MODÈLE: La mère _____ (sortir, aller) à l'hôpital. →
La mère est allée à l'hôpital.

1. Un jour, une petite fille _____ (naître, ne pas retourner).
2. Les parents et l'enfant _____ (arriver, partir) de l'hôpital.
3. Le papa _____ (ne pas retourner, naître) au travail.
4. La maman _____ (tomber, rester) à la maison aussi.
5. Un jouet (*toy*) du bébé _____ (venir, tomber) par terre.
6. Les grands-parents _____ (sortir, arriver) pour garder le bébé.
7. Les parents _____ (sortir, rester) ensemble au restaurant, tout contents.
8. Après le départ des grands-parents, les baby-sitters _____ (venir, aller) deux fois par mois.

B. La tragédie de l'occupation. Samuel Lévy, l'ami et l'employé d'Antoine, parle de la situation à Paris en 1940. Mettez les verbes en italique au passé composé avec **avoir** ou **être**.

Les Nazis *arrivent*[1] à Paris en 1940. Ils *viennent*[2] après la défaite de l'armée française où deux de mes amis de l'atelier *meurent*.[3] Ma femme *part*[4] tout de suite en Amérique. Mes amis *vont*[5] dans le sud de la France.

Un jour, je *descends*[6] du bus près de l'atelier d'Antoine. Antoine *passe*[7] dans la rue et nous nous *parlons*.[8] «Qu'est-ce qui se passe?» je lui *demande*[9]. Il me *répond*:[10] «Tu dois quitter Paris. La vie *devient*[11] trop dangereuse pour les Juifs et mes autres amis juifs *partent*.[12]»

Alors Antoine *rentre*[13] chez lui. Je *reste*[14] dans la rue et je *deviens*[15] de plus en plus inquiet. Finalement, je *monte*[16] l'escalier pour aller chez Antoine et *j'entre*[17] dans l'appartement. Nous *restons*[18] près de la porte pour parler. Puis, nous nous *embrassons*[19] et je *sors.*[20]

Quand je *reviens*[21] chez moi, la gardienne de mon immeuble me *voit.*[22] Elle me *dit:*[23] «Heureusement vous *sortez*[24] de chez vous. Des policiers *viennent*[25] ici et *entrent*[26] dans votre appartement.» Je *fais*[27] une valise et je *pars*[28] de Paris pour toujours.

C. Interview d'une personne célèbre. Avec votre partenaire, jouez les rôles. Un(e) journaliste pose à une célébrité six questions personnelles sur la journée (*day*) qu'elle a passée hier. La «célébrité» va répondre.

Questions utiles: à quelle heure, à qui, avec qui, combien de, comment, où, pourquoi, quand

MODÈLE: JOURNALISTE: Mel Gibson, à quelle heure est-ce que vous vous êtes levé hier?
MEL GIBSON: Je me suis levé à 7 h.
JOURNALISTE: Êtes-vous resté à la maison toute (*all*) la journée?
MEL GIBSON: Non, je suis parti au studio pour tourner un nouveau (*new*) film.

Maintenant, comparez la journée de la personne célèbre avec la vôtre (*yours*).

Structure 34

Depuis et pendant

Talking about time

—Je sais, oui, je viens souvent ici **depuis** quelques mois.

—Et **pendant** la guerre, qu'est-ce qu'il a fait?

Depuis

1. To ask about the *duration* of an action that began in the past and is still continuing in the present, use **Depuis combien de temps** + present tense.

   Depuis combien de temps est-ce que Louise habite dans la rue Mouffetard? — ***How long** has Louise been living on the Rue Mouffetard?*

   To answer this type of question, use present tense + **depuis** + unit of time. Notice that French uses the present tense where English uses a past tense.

   Louise habite dans la rue Mouffetard **depuis** soixante ans. — *Louise has been living on the Rue Mouffetard **for** sixty years.*

   In negatives, French uses the **passé composé** + **depuis** + unit of time.

   Antoine **n'a pas habité** dans la rue Mouffetard **depuis** soixante ans. — *Antoine has not lived on the Rue Mouffetard **for** sixty years.*

2. To ask about the *beginning time* of an action that began in the past and is still continuing in the present, use **Depuis quand** + present tense.

   Depuis quand est-ce que Louise habite dans la rue Mouffetard? — ***Since when** has Louise been living on the Rue Mouffetard?*

   To answer this type of question, use a present tense verb + **depuis** + date (or a word designating an event).

   Louise habite dans la rue Mouffetard **depuis** 1938. — *Louise has been living on the Rue Mouffetard **since** 1938.*

   Camille cherche son médaillon **depuis** l'émission ce matin. — *Camille has been looking for her locket **since** the show this morning.*

Pendant

1. To ask about the *duration* of an action, you can also use **pendant combien de temps**. It can be followed by any tense, depending on the meaning of the question.

   Pendant combien de temps Bruno et Camille parlent-ils? — ***How long** do Bruno and Camille talk?*

   Pendant combien de temps Bruno et Camille ont-ils parlé? — ***How long** did Bruno and Camille talk?*

   To answer this type of question, use **pendant** + unit of time.

   Ils parlent (ont parlé) **pendant** trois heures. — *They talk (talked) **for** three hours.*

2. **Pendant** can mean *during* when followed by a noun.

   Pendant le repas, Bruno pose des questions à Camille. — ***During** the meal, Bruno asks Camille questions.*

   Pendant la guerre, Antoine a habité dans les Cévennes. — ***During** the war, Antoine lived in the Cévennes.*

Pour en savoir plus...

Pour means *for* when used to express time intended.

Je vais m'absenter **pour** deux semaines. *I'm going away for two weeks.*

However, it should not be used to express duration. For that meaning of *for*, use **pendant**.

J'ai été absent **pendant** deux semaines. *I was away for two weeks.*

Activités

A. Le journal intime de Martine. (*Martine's diary.*) Martine commence un journal intime aujourd'hui. Lisez ce paragraphe et répondez aux questions. Utilisez les expressions avec **pendant** et **depuis**.

MODÈLE: Depuis quand est-ce que Martine parle de sa vie dans un journal intime? →
Elle parle de sa vie intime dans son journal depuis aujourd'hui.

J'ai habité (*lived*) à Besançon entre 1959 et 1979, puis je suis venue dans la région parisienne pour étudier. J'ai commencé à travailler avec le groupe Canal 7 en 1996 et j'ai eu l'idée de l'émission en 1998. Du point de vue personnel, j'ai épousé (*married*) Philippe il y a vingt ans et notre fils est né il y a quinze ans. Nous avons aussi une fille qui est née quatre ans après le garçon (*boy*). Nous avons déménagé (*moved*) il y a un mois et maintenant nous habitons au centre de Paris. Notre fils est entré dans son nouveau lycée il y a trois semaines. Comme je vais toujours au bureau vers 7 h 00, Philippe aide les enfants le matin avant de partir à son travail à 8 h 30. C'est vraiment une vie de rêve.

1. Pendant combien de temps est-ce qu'elle a habité à Besançon?
2. Depuis quand est-ce qu'elle travaille avec le groupe Canal 7?
3. Depuis combien de temps est-ce qu'elle est mariée?
4. Pendant combien de temps est-ce qu'elle a été mariée mais sans enfant?
5. Pendant combien de temps est-ce que Patrick a été fils unique?
6. Depuis quand est-ce que Martine habite au centre de Paris?
7. Depuis combien de temps est-ce que Patrick est dans son nouveau lycée?
8. Pendant combien de temps Philippe aide-t-il les enfants chaque matin?

B. Pour faire connaissance. Interviewez trois camarades de classe pour découvrir (*discover*) certains détails de leur passé et de leur vie actuelle. Posez des questions en utilisant les expressions **depuis quand**, **depuis combien de temps** et **pendant combien de temps**.

MODÈLE: habiter la même maison →
É1: Pendant combien de temps as-tu habité la même maison?
É2: J'ai habité la même maison pendant dix ans.

1. étudier le français
2. habiter cette ville
3. aller à cette université
4. sortir avec les mêmes ami(e)s que maintenant
5. boire du café
6. aller au lycée
7. jouer avec des jouets d'enfant
8. croire au Père Noël

Maintenant, comparez la vie de vos camarades avec votre propre (*your own*) vie.

Regards sur la culture

Le couple

In this segment of the film, we see Louise and Antoine together as a young couple. The other important couple in the story, Camille and Bruno, is linked by a somewhat ambiguous relationship, although it is clear that the two Canal 7 reporters share very strong emotional ties. Their interactions illustrate some differences between France and North America in the relations between the sexes.

- French children are usually brought up to be very happy about their sex. Both males and females are taught that they have many advantages being the sex that they are.
- In adolescence, there is no such thing as "dating." Rather than engage in the kind of one-on-one formalized "trial" relationship that is common in North America, French young people usually go out in groups. If two people do become a couple, they still may prefer to go most places with friends, rather than by themselves.
- Adolescent boys in France sometimes utter exaggerated compliments or engage in mock boasting about their sex appeal in front of girls their own age. These girls learn very young how to appreciate the attention but to deflate the pretensions of the male. Some of this male-female sparring continues later in life. Young North American women who encounter it are often at a loss about how to react. An uncomfortable smile is often the result, just the opposite of the culturally appropriate reaction.
- Anthropologist Raymonde Carroll has stated that French couples tend to manifest their relationship through the kinds of verbal interactions they have: They tease each other in front of friends and may argue, say, about politics or the choice of a restaurant. In fact, she claims that French people might be suspicious of a couple who is always in agreement, thinking that there is no "spark" in the relationship.
- The partners in a French couple tend to maintain more independence than do those in North America. They continue to frequent their own friends individually.
- Even when there is no question of a romantic or sexual relationship, French people enjoy trying to be attractive to the opposite sex. They do not find this demeaning. One might even speak of "the game between the sexes" in France, in opposition to the North American "war between the sexes."

Yves Montand et Simone Signoret, un couple célèbre

Considérez

What possible conflicts could emerge in an intercultural relationship between a mainstream North American and a French person?

Structure 35

Les verbes réguliers en *-ir*

Talking about everyday actions

—Les histoires d'amour **finissent** toujours mal.

In earlier chapters, you learned how to conjugate two large classes of regular French verbs: those ending in **-er** and those ending in **-re**. The verb **finir** (*to finish, end*) is an example of another large class of verbs that are all conjugated the same way. They are usually referred to as regular **-ir** verbs.

1. To use regular **-ir** verbs in the present tense, drop the **-ir** ending and add the endings **-is**, **-is**, **-it**, **-issons**, **-issez**, **-issent**. To form the past participle, drop the **-ir** and add **i**.

finir (*to finish*)			
je	fin **is**	nous	fin **issons**
tu	fin **is**	vous	fin **issez**
il, elle, on	fin **it**	ils, elles	fin **issent**
passé composé: j'**ai fini**			

Bruno et Camille **finissent** l'émission à neuf heures.	*Bruno and Camille finish the show at nine o'clock.*
Ils **ont fini** leur soirée à vingt-trois heures.	*They finished their evening at eleven o'clock.*

2. Here is a list of some common regular **-ir** verbs and their past participles.

INFINITIVE		PAST PARTICIPLE
applaudir	*to applaud*	**applaudi**
choisir	*to choose*	**choisi**
finir	*to finish*	**fini**
obéir (à)	*to obey*	**obéi**
réfléchir (à)	*to reflect (on), think (about)*	**réfléchi**
réussir (à)	*to succeed; to pass (a course or exam)*	**réussi**

Yasmine **obéit** à ses parents.	*Yasmine obeys her parents.*
Les Français **choisissent** généralement le pain artisanal.	*French people usually choose handmade bread.*

3. When **choisir** and **finir** are used with an infinitive, they are followed by the preposition **de**. When **réfléchir** and **réussir** are used with an infinitive, they are followed by **à**.

Camille **choisit de** dîner avec Bruno.	*Camille chooses to eat dinner with Bruno.*
Martine **réussit à** trouver le médaillon.	*Martine succeeds in finding the locket.*

4. When **obéir**, **réfléchir**, and **réussir** are used with a noun, they are followed by **à**.

Camille **n'obéit pas à** sa mère.	*Camille doesn't obey her mother.*
Elle **réfléchit à** l'histoire de son grand-père.	*She thinks about her grandfather's story.*

Notez bien!

A question using **quel** with one of these verbs must begin with the preposition **à**.

À quel problème réfléchissez-vous? *What problem are you thinking about?*

À quels cours est-ce que vous réussissez? *In what courses are you doing well?*

Activités

A. Au travail et aux études. Faites des phrases complètes au temps présent avec les éléments donnés. Utilisez une préposition (**de** ou **à**) si nécessaire.

MODÈLE: Marc / réfléchir / questions financières. →
Marc réfléchit aux questions financières.

1. Jacques / choisir / aider les gens malades chez eux
2. Paul et René / ne pas obéir / leurs professeurs de droit (*law*)
3. vous / réussir / tous vos cours de langues orientales
4. nous / finir / nos cours d'histoire de l'art
5. les gens / applaudir / après mes concerts

6. Patricia / réfléchir / problèmes de la ferme de son père
7. Danielle / choisir / travailler pour un cadre
8. tu / ne jamais finir / tes études
9. je / obéir / toutes les instructions de mon prof
10. tu / réussir / bien parler chinois et japonais
11. vous / ne pas réussir / trouver un travail intéressant

B. Explications. (*Explanations.*) Deux anciens (*former*) étudiants parlent de la situation dans leurs universités respectives. Avec votre partenaire, complétez le dialogue en utilisant le passé composé des verbes indiqués.

finir

É1: Nous ______[1] nos cours en mai. Quand est-ce que vous ______[2] dans ton université?

É2: Les étudiants de mon université ______[3] en juin.

choisir

É1: Est-ce que tout le monde ______[4] des cours faciles?

É2: Beaucoup d'étudiants ______[5] des cours difficiles. Moi, je (j') ______[6] des cours intéressants. Ils étaient° parfois faciles.

° *were*

réussir

É1: À quels cours est-ce que tu ______[7]?

É2: Moi, je (j') ______[8] aux cours de maths et de sciences naturelles. Et toi?

É1: Mes amis et moi, nous aimions° les cours d'histoire. Alors, nous ______[9] à ces cours.

° *liked*

réfléchir

É2: Est-ce que tu ______[10] à ton avenir° pendant tes années à l'université?

É1: Non. Je (J') ______[11] aux examens et à mes études!

° *future*

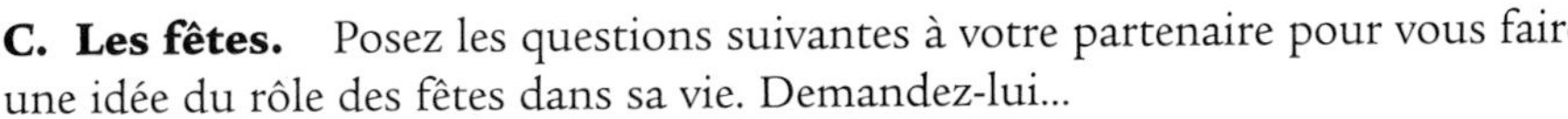

C. Les fêtes. Posez les questions suivantes à votre partenaire pour vous faire une idée du rôle des fêtes dans sa vie. Demandez-lui...

1. quelle est la fête la plus importante dans sa famille
2. s'il / si elle finit d'habitude toutes les préparations pour cette fête à temps (*in time*) (avec un exemple de son passé)
3. s'il / si elle réussit à se relaxer pendant les fêtes de famille
4. depuis combien de temps il/elle choisit des cadeaux pour ses amis
5. s'il / si elle obéit aux traditions pendant les fêtes
6. à quelles questions il/elle réfléchit le jour du nouvel an
7. s'il / si elle réussit à faire des changements (*changes*) dans sa vie chaque année après le nouvel an

Visionnement 2

Observez!

Regardez l'Épisode 11 encore une fois, et répondez aux questions suivantes.

- Pourquoi Samuel Lévy et sa femme ont-ils décidé de quitter la France?
- Est-ce que les Allemands sont les seuls à vouloir exterminer les Juifs?

Après le visionnement

Faites l'activité pour le **Visionnement 2** dans le cahier.

Synthèse: Culture

L'histoire et le mythe

Dans tous les pays, certains moments historiques prennent un aspect mythique. Ces moments sont souvent des épisodes très dramatiques qui ont déterminé un changement important dans l'histoire. Souvent aussi, ce sont des moments qui aident à expliquer[1] des problèmes qui existent encore ou des tensions sociales qui persistent. C'est pour ces raisons que l'occupation est encore une obsession pour beaucoup de Français et la Révolution française aussi. Dans d'autres pays francophones, il y a aussi des moments historiques mythiques.

Québec: La Conquête

Samuel de Champlain a fondé la ville de Québec en 1608. Cela[2] a été la naissance de la Nouvelle[3] France, qui allait[4] devenir le Canada. Mais dans les guerres entre l'Angleterre et la France, les troupes anglaises ont attaqué cette colonie. Le moment décisif a été la bataille[5] des plaines d'Abraham, devant les murs de Québec, en 1759. La ville est située sur un plateau. Pendant la nuit, les troupes anglaises sont arrivées en bateau[6] et sont montées secrètement sur le plateau. Elles ont surpris les Français. La bataille a duré[7]

[1]*explain* [2]*That* [3]*New* [4]*was going* [5]*battle* [6]*ship* [7]*lasted*

15 minutes! Mais le général anglais, Wolfe, et le général français, Montcalm, sont morts tous les deux. Cette bataille a marqué le début de la fin[8] pour le Canada français. En 1763, tout le Canada est devenu anglais. Les «Canadiens» ont considéré que la France les avait abandonnés.[9] Ils sont devenus minoritaires dans leur pays. Cela a été un moment très important de l'histoire canadienne. Pour les Canadiens français, «une conquête est une défaite[10] permanente».

La mort de Montcalm à la bataille d'Abraham
(Watteau de Lille)

Aujourd'hui, le slogan du Québec est «Je me souviens». Les Québécois se souviennent de la défaite de 1759, des difficultés que cette défaite a causées et de leurs traditions françaises. La bataille des plaines d'Abraham reste un grand symbole pour eux. En 1995, 49% des Québécois ont voté pour l'indépendance du Québec.

Haïti: La Révolution

En 1789, au début de la Révolution en France, Saint-Domingue, le futur Haïti, était[11] une colonie extrêmement riche. Avec l'arrivée des principes de liberté, d'égalité et de fraternité»,* les blancs (5% de la population) et les gens de couleur (5%) ont vu la possibilité de devenir libres[12] et plus riches.[13] Mais les esclaves[14] (90% de la population) ont fait la révolte. Après une guerre extrêmement cruelle, une invasion anglaise et la destruction d'une grande partie du pays, les noirs, sous leur général Toussaint Louverture, ont obtenu[15] la liberté; une nouvelle constitution a été proclamée le 16 juillet 1801. La Révolution haïtienne a fait d'Haïti la deuxième nation moderne dans le Nouveau Monde,[16] après les États-Unis, et la première république noire du monde.

Toussaint Louverture
(Delpich)

[8]*end* [9]*avait... had abandoned* [10]*defeat* [11]*was* [12]*free* [13]*plus... richer* [14]*slaves* [15]*obtained* [16]*Nouveau... New World*

***Liberté, égalité, fraternité** (*Liberty, equality, brotherhood*) est la devise (*motto*) de la Révolution française de 1789.

Mais cette révolution a aussi isolé Haïti. Les Haïtiens n'ont pas été acceptés dans le monde des nations, dans un monde d'économies basées sur l'esclavage ou le racisme. Aujourd'hui encore, le pays souffre de violence et d'injustice. Mais cette révolution reste un moment très important pour tous les Haïtiens aujourd'hui. Elle correspond à l'abolition de l'esclavage, à la décolonisation, à l'égalité des races, et elle représente un moment d'héroïsme et d'espoir.[17]

[17]*hope*

À vous

Un événement mythique. In groups of three or four people, create a list of five characteristics that often make a historical event "mythical." Choose from such things as heroism, insurmountable obstacles, fundamental values in conflict, and so on. Then select two events in your own people's history that have the kind of legendary status that we find in the battle of the Plains of Abraham or the Haitian Revolution.

À écrire

Faites **À écrire** pour le Chapitre 11 dans le cahier.

Vocabulaire

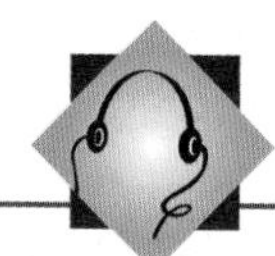

Le monde du travail

les affaires (*f. pl.*)	business
un emploi	work, employment
la gestion	management
un métier	trade
une petite annonce	classified ad
un poste	position, job
une société	company
un stage	internship
un tableau d'affichage	bulletin board

MOTS APPARENTÉS: **le commerce (international), le marketing, sur Internet, une profession**

Les métiers et les professions

un(e) agent(e) de sécurité	security guard
un(e) agriculteur/trice	farmer
un(e) artisan(e)	craftsman, artisan
un(e) avocat(e)	lawyer
un(e) cadre	executive
un(e) comptable	accountant
un(e) conservateur/trice (de musée)	curator (of a museum)

un(e) cuisinier/ière	cook
un(e) écrivain/ femme écrivain	writer
un(e) fonctionnaire	civil servant
un(e) garde-malade	nurse's aide
un(e) gardien(ne) d'immeuble	building superintendent
un(e) ingénieur/ femme ingénieur	engineer
un(e) interprète	interpreter
un(e) ouvrier/ière	manual laborer
un(e) patron(ne) (d'un bar, d'un restaurant)	owner; boss (of a bar, of a restaurant)
un(e) peintre/ femme peintre	painter

MOTS APPARENTÉS: **un(e) baby-sitter, un(e) employé(e) de fast-food, un(e) musicien(ne), un(e) secrétaire**

À REVOIR: **un(e) acteur/trice, un(e) boucher/ère, un(e) boulanger/ère, un(e) épicier/ière, un(e) infirmier/ière, un(e) instituteur/trice, un(e) journaliste, un(e) maître/tresse, un(e) marchand(e), un(e) médecin / femme médecin, un(e) pâtissier/ière, un(e) producteur/trice, un professeur, un reporter, un(e) vendeur/euse**

Les jours fériés et les fêtes

un anniversaire de mariage	wedding anniversary
une fête	holiday; festival; party, celebration
la fête du travail	Labor Day
la fête nationale	national holiday
un jour férié	legal holiday
le Noël	Christmas
le nouvel an	New Year's Day
la pâque	Passover
les Pâques (*m. s., f. pl.*)	Easter
la Toussaint	All Saints' Day

MOTS APPARENTÉS: **le ramadan, Hannukah**

À REVOIR: **un anniversaire (de naissance)**

Les nombres ordinaux

premier/ière, deuxième, troisième, quatrième, cinquième, sixième, septième, huitième, neuvième, dixième, vingtième, vingt et unième

Verbes

choisir	to choose
finir	to finish
monter	to go up, climb
mourir	to die
naître	to be born
réfléchir (à)	to reflect (on), think (about)
rentrer	to come/go back (home)
rester	to stay
réussir (à)	to succeed; to pass (*a course or exam*)
tomber	to fall

MOTS APPARENTÉS: **applaudir, arriver, entrer, obéir (à), passer (par), retourner**

À REVOIR: **aller, descendre, devenir, partir, revenir, sortir, venir**

Expressions de temps

depuis	for; since
pendant	during; while

Autres expressions utiles

à mi-temps	half-time
à plein temps	full-time

Chapitre 12

C'est à propos de Louise.°

°C'est... *It's about Louise.*

OBJECTIFS

In this episode, you will

- find out more about Louise
- find out more about where Camille's grandfather was during World War II

In this chapter, you will

- discuss life's milestones
- talk about popular media
- tell about what you used to do
- describe actions with adverbs
- discuss daily activities such as speaking, reading, and writing
- learn the lyrics to a French song that is mentioned in *Le Chemin du retour*

Vocabulaire en contexte

Les étapes de la vie°

Les... *Stages of life*

Voici une feuille d'un album de photos. Ce sont **les étapes** (*f.*) de la vie d'Adèle.

La naissance d'Adèle. C'est **un bébé** content.

Une jolie **jeune fille**, mais son **enfance** (*f.*) n'est pas heureuse. **La jeunesse**° n'est pas toujours facile. Qu'est-ce que **l'adolescence** (*f.*) lui réserve?

La... *Youth*

Le mariage d'Adèle et son mari. C'est un **événement joyeux**.

Adèle **dans la cinquantaine**.° Elle **a divorcé** il y a dix ans.

Adèle à quatre-vingts ans. C'est maintenant une personne **du troisième âge**,° mais **la vieillesse** n'est pas un handicap!

dans... *in her fifties*

du... *elderly*

Autres mots et expressions

un(e) adolescent(e) (*fam.* **un[e] ado**)	adolescent
un(e) adulte	adult
l'enterrement (*m.*)	burial
un garçon	boy
jeune	young
la mort	death
un(e) retraité(e)	retiree, retired person
prendre sa retraite	to retire

Activités

A. Qui est-ce? Complétez ces descriptions avec des termes appropriés.

1. Une personne qui (*who*) ne travaille plus est un(e)... **2.** Une fille de 15 ans est une... **3.** Si on a à peu près (*about*) 40 ans, on est... **4.** Je suis né il y a 6 ans. Je suis un petit... **5.** Le nouveau membre de la famille, âgé de 3 mois, est...

B. Quelle étape? Décidez à quelle étape de la vie on fait allusion dans chacune (*each one*) de ces descriptions.

1. C'est une période de rébellion. **2.** On commence à parler. **3.** On a eu beaucoup d'anniversaires, on se souvient du passé. **4.** On n'a pas encore 30 ans. **5.** On commence ses études au lycée.

C. Un portrait. Faites votre portrait à l'époque actuelle (*present time*). Vous êtes à quelle étape de votre vie? Quels sont vos espoirs (*hopes*)? vos déceptions (*disappointments*)? Quel est le moment idéal de la vie, selon vous?

D. Confirmations. Choisissez les phrases de la colonne de droite (*right*) qui renforcent le sens des phrases de la colonne de gauche (*left*).

MODÈLE: Bruno est un vrai Français. →
Il identifie le pain artisanal.

1. Bruno est un vrai Français.
2. Camille n'est pas une vieille femme.
3. Bruno est un bel homme.
4. Yasmine est dans une nouvelle école.
5. Le boulanger prépare un beau pain.
6. Hélène trouve Bruno de mauvaise humeur.
7. Rachid est un nouvel employé de Canal 7.
8. Le déménagement à Paris n'est pas un événement joyeux pour Sonia.

a. Elle est jeune.
b. Elle n'habite plus à Marseilles.
c. Ce n'est pas un pain industriel.
d. Il identifie le pain artisanal.
e. Il se fâche contre Camille.
f. C'est un grand jour pour lui.
g. Elle a froid et elle n'a pas sa famille.
h. Il n'est pas laid.

Notez bien!

Three common adjectives have irregular forms: **beau** (*beautiful, good-looking*), **nouveau** (*new*), and **vieux** (*old*).

m. s.	**beau**	**nouveau**	**vieux**
	(bel)	**(nouvel)**	**(vieil)**
f. s.	**belle**	**nouvelle**	**vieille**
m. pl.	**beaux**	**nouveaux**	**vieux**
f. pl.	**belles**	**nouvelles**	**vieilles**

Rachid est assez **beau.** *Rachid is rather handsome.*

C'est ma **nouvelle** école? *Is this my new school?*

Louise est **vieille.** *Louise is old.*

Notice that these three adjectives precede the noun. The special masculine singular forms are used when the adjective precedes a noun that begins with a vowel sound.

un **bel** homme *a good-looking man*

un **nouvel** emploi *a new job*

un **vieil** ordinateur *an old computer*

E. En général. Avec un(e) partenaire, décrivez des choses que vous aimez et que vous n'aimez pas en utilisant des éléments des trois colonnes. Indiquez si vous êtes d'accord avec votre partenaire ou non.

MODÈLE É1: J'aime les vieux films.
É2: Je ne suis pas d'accord! J'aime mieux les nouveaux films.

	beau	les voitures
J'adore	jeune	les classes
J'aime	mauvais	les émissions de télévision
Je déteste	nouveau	les films
J'aime mieux	petit	les histoires
	vieux	les livres
	vrai	les professeurs

Les médias

Le journal et ses rubriques (*f.*)

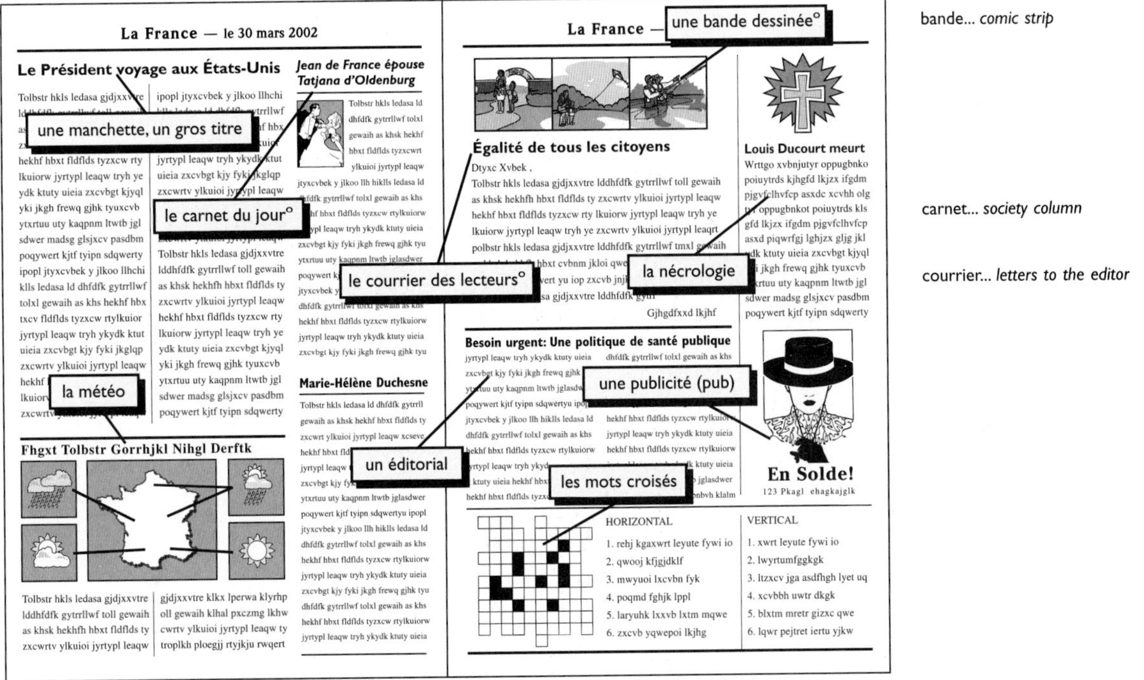

bande... *comic strip*

carnet... *society column*

courrier... *letters to the editor*

La télévision

TF1

6.05 Des filles dans le vent. Le secret. 9929425 6.30 TF1 info 3983926 6.40 TF1 jeunesse: Salut les toons 3495128 8.30 Téléshopping 5277452 9.05 La joyeuse tribu 9399443 10.05 Le siècle des intellectuels 6010094 11.15 Chicago Hope, la vie à tout prix Mort d'un brave chien. 4714471 12.05 Tac O Tac TV 9372094 12.10 Etre heureux comme 9371365 12.15 Le juste prix 7327471 12.50 A vrai dire 765704

13.00 Journal 39510

13.42 Bien Jardiner 209818568
Magazine.

13.50 Les feux de l'amour
Feuilleton. Etats-Unis. Inédit
Comme Paul sort de l'hôpital. Christine vient l'aider à faire sa valise. Sharon se défend d'avoir provoqué Matt qui la considère comme responsable. 6030297

14.45 Arabesque 5138100
Série.

15.40 Sydney Police 4087100
Série.

TF1

16.40 Sunset Beach
Série. Etats-Unis. Inédit
A peine rentrée à Sunset Beach, Olivia trouve Gregory au lit avec Annie. Betty découvre le corps d'Eddie. Cole fait la connaissance de son père. 1860988

17.35 Melrose Place
Série. Etats-Unis.
Retour de bâton.
Amanda et Billy poursuivent leur liaison. Alison démissione. Peter et Michael partent en week-end pour participer à un concours de beauté. 9302549

18.25 Les amis 299181

19.05 Le bigdil 6701487

19.57 Clic et net
Conquête spatiale. 205129297

20.00 Journal 61365

20.35 Le journal de la Coupe du monde 9518907

20.50 Le juste prix 4413839
Jeu.

Autres mots utiles

à la une	on the front page
une chaîne	(*television*) station; network
une publicité	commercial, advertisement
une station (de radio)	(radio) station

Activités

A. Qu'est-ce que c'est? Donnez le mot qui correspond à la définition.

DANS LE JOURNAL

1. C'est la rubrique du journal où on annonce les naissances et les mariages.
2. C'est un jeu où il s'agit de trouver le mot correct.
3. C'est la partie du journal où on annonce les enterrements.
4. C'est un forum où les lecteurs du journal peuvent exprimer leurs opinions.
5. Ce sont des histoires amusantes en images que les enfants aiment beaucoup.

À LA TÉLÉVISION

6. Ce sont des mélodrames à la télé.
7. On regarde cette émission pour apprendre les actualités.
8. C'est une histoire en plusieurs épisodes.

B. C'est quoi? Complétez la phrase avec le mot juste (*right*).

DANS LE JOURNAL

1. Une ____ et un ____ sont la même chose. On les trouve au début d'un article.
2. Chaque journal exprime son opinion dans l'____.
3. Si le président fait un voyage important, on le rapporte ____.

À LA TÉLÉVISION

4. Les petits enfants aiment beaucoup les ____ de Disney.
5. Il y a des ____ scientifiques sur la chaîne des sciences.
6. Aimez-vous les ____ comme *Friends* et *Frasier*?
7. Quel ____ était le plus amusant (*most fun*) à la télévision—*Qui veut être un millionnaire* ou *Tic-tac-toe de Hollywood*?
8. Chaque année, les chaînes américaines lancent de nouvelles ____.

C. Interview. Demandez à votre partenaire...

1. comment il/elle se tient au courant (*stays up to date*) des actualités.
2. quels journaux ou magazines il/elle préfère lire (*read*).
3. quelle rubrique du journal il/elle préfère et pourquoi.
4. s'il / si elle aime faire les mots-croisés dans le journal et pourquoi (pas).
5. quelle(s) émission(s) il/elle préfère regarder à la télévision.
6. quelle publicité récente à la télévision il/elle aime bien et pourquoi.
7. s'il / si elle aime les dessins animés et lequel (*which one*) il/elle préfère.
8. quelle station de radio il/elle aime et pourquoi.

Visionnement 1

Avant de visionner

Pour parler du passé. Vous avez déjà appris le **passé composé**. Mais en français, on utilise aussi un autre temps—l'**imparfait**—pour parler du passé. Vous allez apprendre l'imparfait dans ce chapitre. Mais maintenant, pour comprendre l'Épisode 12, lisez (*read*) les phrases suivantes et faites attention au sens (*meaning*).

Elle **était**[a] très calme...
Ses yeux **brillaient**,[b] comme les yeux d'un enfant à Noël...
Je **voulais**[c] discuter avec elle.

[a]*was* [b]*were shining* [c]*wanted*

Regardez encore une fois les verbes en caractères **gras**. Quels verbes décrivent (*describe*) des émotions? Quels verbes décrivent une action qui continue dans le passé?

Observez!

Dans l'Épisode 12, Camille apprend un autre détail important sur son grand-père. Pendant votre visionnement, essayez de trouver la réponse aux questions suivantes.

- Pourquoi Mado s'impatiente-t-elle contre Camille?
- Quelle est l'importance du titre de la chanson (*song*) préférée de Louise, *Mon Amant de Saint-Jean*?

Vocabulaire relatif à l'épisode

elle a souri	*she smiled*
un drôle de...	*a funny, strange . . .*
doucement	*gently*
qui a déchiré	*who tore up*
au moins	*at least*
une bourgade	*village*

Après le visionnement

A. Les détails. Qu'est-ce qu'on apprend dans cet épisode sur l'histoire de la famille Leclair? Répondez **vrai** si on trouve cette information dans l'épisode. Répondez **faux** si on ne la trouve pas.

Dans cet épisode, on apprend...

1. qui a déchiré les photos d'Antoine.
2. l'état d'esprit (*state of mind*) de Louise au moment de sa mort.
3. où Antoine est allé dans les Cévennes.
4. pourquoi on a déchiré les photos d'Antoine.
5. pourquoi *Mon Amant de Saint-Jean* était la chanson préférée de Louise.
6. où on a enterré (*buried*) Louise.

B. Réfléchissez. Selon vous, pourquoi Mado a-t-elle révélé le nom du village où Antoine est allé en 1943? Est-ce qu'elle se prépare à raconter l'histoire d'Antoine à Camille? Essaie-t-elle d'apaiser (*appease*) Camille? Ou y a-t-il une autre explication?

Structure 36

L'imparfait

Narrating in the past

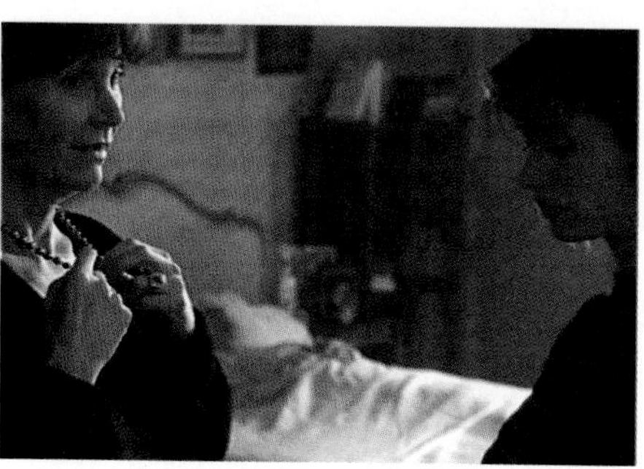

—Ses yeux **brillaient**, comme les yeux d'un enfant à Noël...

The term *tense* means "time." There are several past tenses in French—that is to say, there are several ways of expressing past time. The **passé composé** is used to talk about past events that are completed before the time or at the time being discussed. The imperfect, **l'imparfait**, has a complementary function: It is used to describe conditions, emotions, states of mind, ongoing actions, and habitual actions in the past.

1. To form the **imparfait** of all verbs except **être**, drop the **-ons** ending from the **nous** form of the present tense and then add the endings **-ais**, **-ais**, **-ait**, **-ions**, **-iez**, **-aient** to the stem.

regarder (*nous regardons*)			
je	regard **ais**	nous	regard **ions**
tu	regard **ais**	vous	regard **iez**
il, elle, on	regard **ait**	ils, elles	regard **aient**

Camille **finissait** sa toilette quand Alex est arrivé. — *Camille was finishing getting dressed when Alex arrived.*

Je **voulais** discuter avec elle. — *I wanted to talk with her.*

Elle **avait** à peu près mon âge, à cette époque... — *She was about my age, at that time . . .*

For verbs like **commencer** and **manger**, the **ç** and **ge** of the present tense **nous** form are changed to **c** and **g** for **nous** and **vous** in the **imparfait** because the endings begin with **i**.

PRESENT TENSE		IMPARFAIT
nous commen**ç**ons	→	je commen**ç**ais, *but* nous commen**c**ions, vous commen**c**iez
nous man**ge**ons	→	je man**ge**ais, *but* nous man**g**ions, vous man**g**iez

2. The **imparfait** of **être** uses the stem **ét-** and the **imparfait** endings.

être (ét-)			
j'	ét **ais**	nous	ét **ions**
tu	ét **ais**	vous	ét **iez**
il, elle, on	ét **ait**	ils, elles	ét **aient**

C'**était** un petit village. — *It was a small village.*

3. The **imparfait** is used to describe conditions, emotions, and states of mind in the past.

Louise **était** jeune en 1939. — *Louise was young in 1939.*
Elle **était** très calme, tu sais. — *You know, she was very calm.*
Je **voulais** discuter avec elle. — *I wanted to talk with her.*

4. The **imparfait** is also used to express ongoing actions in the past. This usage often can be thought of as meaning *was/were doing.*

Ses yeux **brillaient**, comme les yeux d'un enfant à Noël... — *Her eyes were shining, like a child's eyes at Christmas . . .*
Nous **pensions** à un voyage dans les Cévennes. — *We were thinking of (making) a trip to the Cévennes.*

5. Finally, the **imparfait** is used to express habitual past action, corresponding to the English *used to do.*

Elle **demandait** toujours cette chanson à Alex. — *She always used to ask Alex for that song.*
Camille **sortait** souvent avec Bruno. — *Camille used to go out often with Bruno.*
but Hier, elle **a demandé** à Alex de jouer cette chanson. — *Yesterday, she asked Alex to play that song.*
Camille **est sortie** avec Bruno hier. — *Camille went out with Bruno yesterday.*

Activités

A. Une matinée difficile. Alex parle du jour où Louise est morte. Mettez les verbes entre parenthèses à l'imparfait.

Je ______[1] (manger) un croissant dans un café quand le médecin est sorti de chez Louise. La patronne du café m'______[2] (apporter) un deuxième café quand le médecin m'a demandé de monter voir Mado. Louise ______[3] (être) là, sur son lit, et Mado la ______[4] (regarder) en silence. Elle ______[5] (ne pas pouvoir) parler.

Je lui ai dit: «C'______[6] (être) une femme extraordinaire, votre mère. Vous ______[7] (avoir) de la chance d'avoir une mère si gentille. Elle ______[8] (aimer) tous les gens du quartier, et nous l'______[9] (adorer) aussi.»

Je _____[10] (vouloir) vraiment faire quelque chose pour aider Mado. Nous _____[11] (parler) de sa mère quand Mado m'a pris les mains. Elle m'a demandé si je _____[12] (pouvoir) aller chez Camille pour lui dire (*tell*) la triste nouvelle en personne. Quand je suis arrivé chez Camille, elle _____[13] (faire) sa toilette. Elle _____[14] (se peigner) et elle _____[15] (porter) une vieille chemise. Elle a bien vu que j'_____[16] (avoir) une mauvaise nouvelle.

Quand j'ai laissé Camille à la porte de l'immeuble de Louise, elle _____[17] (essayer) de se calmer, mais je _____[18] (comprendre) bien que la journée _____[19] (aller) être difficile, très difficile.

B. Quand j'avais ton âge. Un adolescent parle de sa vie. Qu'est-ce qu'un vieil homme ou une vieille femme dirait (*would say*) pour parler de sa propre (*own*) jeunesse? Soyez logique.

MODÈLE: Je danse toute (*all*) la nuit. (avoir ton âge) →
Quand j'avais ton âge, je dansais aussi toute la nuit. (Quand j'avais ton âge, je ne dansais pas toute la nuit.)

1. Je parle avec mes amis. (être jeune)
2. Mes amis et moi, nous mangeons au restaurant. (avoir de l'argent)
3. Mes parents ne me comprennent pas. (faire des bêtises [*silly things*])
4. Tous mes amis regardent la télévision. (être jeunes)
5. Nous sortons dans des boîtes de nuit. (avoir 16 ans)
6. Je dois utiliser ma Carte bleue.* (faire mes achats)
7. Mes amis font du roller tous les vendredis soirs. (être jeunes)
8. On boit beaucoup de coca. (avoir soif)
9. Ma grand-mère veut toujours me voir. (avoir 10 ans)
10. Ma petite amie étudie l'informatique. (avoir ton âge)
11. Nous réfléchissons à l'environnement. (être adolescents)

C. Trouvez quelqu'un qui... Interviewez trois camarades de classe (ou votre professeur) pour savoir qui avait les mêmes activités que vous (et qui ne faisait pas les mêmes choses) il y a 5 ans. Vous pouvez utiliser les éléments des listes suivantes si vous voulez.

EXPRESSIONS INTERROGATIVES: à quel(le)(s), à qui, avec qui, de quel(le)(s), où, quand, quel(le)(s), qu'est-ce que

VERBES: chanter (*to sing*), danser, dessiner (*to draw*), étudier, jouer à... , jouer de... , prendre des photos, sortir le soir, travailler, parler, ???

MODÈLE: É1: De quel instrument jouais-tu?
É2: Je jouais de la flûte.

Maintenant, comparez les réponses avec le reste de la classe. Y a-t-il des choses que tout le monde faisait? que peu de gens faisaient? que votre professeur faisait?

---

*La Carte bleue est une carte bancaire.

Structure 37

La forme et la place des adverbes

Describing actions

—Tu le retrouves pour moi?
Rapidement?

Adverbs can modify verbs, adjectives, and other adverbs. In Chapter 6, you saw an overview of some common French adverbs and in Chapter 10, you practiced using adverbs of time. In this chapter, you learn about the formation and placement of many useful adverbs, especially adverbs of manner.

La forme des adverbes

1. Many adverbs are formed by adding **-ment** to the feminine form of an adjective. These adverbs often correspond to English adverbs ending in *-ly*. Here is a list of some useful adjectives and the adverbs formed from them. If you know the adjectives, you'll also know the adverb.

actuel(le)	*current, present*	**actuellement**	*currently*
discret/ète	*discreet; reserved*	**discrètement**	*discreetly; with reserve*
doux (douce)	*gentle*	**doucement**	*gently*
exact(e)	*exact, accurate*	**exactement**	*exactly, accurately*
franc(he)	*frank*	**franchement**	*frankly*
immédiat(e)	*immediate*	**immédiatement**	*immediately*
lent(e)	*slow*	**lentement**	*slowly*
rapide	*fast*	**rapidement**	*quickly*
seul(e)	*alone; sole*	**seulement**	*only*
sûr(e)	*sure*	**sûrement**	*surely*
tel(le)	*such; like*	**tellement**	*so (very), so much*

Je suis **tellement**... nerveuse, impatiente!	*I'm so . . . tense, impatient.*
Elle s'est endormie **doucement**.	*She fell asleep gently.*
Actuellement, il ne donne pas de cours.	*Currently, he's not teaching any classes.*

2. If the masculine form of an adjective ends with **i**, **é**, or **u**, the adverb is formed from the masculine adjective. The adjective **fou** (*crazy, mad*), however, builds the adverb from its feminine form, **folle**.

	vrai(e)	*true*	**vraiment**	*truly*
	absolu(e)	*absolute*	**absolument**	*absolutely*
but	**fou (folle)**	*crazy, mad*	**follement**	*madly, wildly*

Tu es **vraiment** un grand dragueur.	*You're really quite the pick-up artist.*
Camille veut **absolument** connaître la vérité.	*Camille absolutely wants to know the truth.*

3. To derive adverbs from adjectives ending in **-ant** or **-ent** in the masculine form, change these endings to **-amment** or **-emment**.

apparent(e)	*apparent*	**apparemment**	*apparently*
élégant(e)	*elegant*	**élégamment**	*elegantly*
évident(e)	*evident*	**évidemment**	*evidently, obviously*

Camille était habillée **élégamment**.	*Camille was dressed elegantly.*
Ben, **apparemment**, oui. Il faut croire!	*Well, apparently, yes. It looks like it!*
Oui, euh, à part la nôtre, **évidemment**.	*Yes, uh, except for ours, obviously.*

4. To form an adverb from **gentil**, drop the final **-l** of the masculine form and add **-ment**.

gentil → **gentiment** *nicely*

Rachid parle **gentiment** à sa fille. — *Rachid talks nicely to his daughter.*

5. Some adverbs, such as **bien** and **mal**, are not derived from adjectives at all. Another is **vite** (*fast, quickly*).

Pourquoi part-il aussi **vite**? — *Why is he leaving so fast?*

La place des adverbes

1. In the present tense or **imparfait**, adverbs of manner usually follow the verb they modify.

Camille **cherche nerveusement** dans son sac.	*Camille searches nervously in her purse.*
Pourquoi **part**-il aussi **vite**?	*Why is he leaving so fast?*
Mado **parlait furieusement** à Camille.	*Mado was speaking furiously to Camille.*

Notez bien!

Peut-être (*perhaps, maybe*) is not formed from an adjective. It usually follows the word it modifies. In the **passé composé**, it follows the auxiliary verb.

Il peut **peut-être** t'aider... *Maybe he can help you.*

Antoine est **peut-être** devenu un traître. *Maybe Antoine became a traitor.*

Peut-être may also begin a sentence, in which case it is followed either by **que** or by inversion of the subject and verb.

Peut-être qu'il peut t'aider. / **Peut-être** peut-il t'aider. } *Maybe he can help you.*

2. In the **passé composé**, adverbs of manner usually follow the past participle.

Mado a parlé **sévèrement** à sa fille.	*Mado spoke harshly to her daughter.*

Several common short adverbs, however, follow the auxiliary verb and precede the past participle.

Camille a **vite** répondu que ça ne la regardait pas.	*Camille quickly answered that it was none of her business.*
Elle a **bien** compris la situation.	*She understood the situation well.*
Mado a **trop** parlé.	*Mado spoke too much.*

Activités

A. Comment? Dites comment on fait les actions suivantes en ajoutant (*by adding*) l'adverbe qui correspond à l'adjectif entre parenthèses.

MODÈLE: Je parle de mes amis. (discret) →
Je parle discrètement de mes amis.

1. Je parle anglais avec les étrangers. (lent)
2. J'ai parlé à mon ami. (indiscret)
3. J'ai parlé à mes parents. (méchant [*nasty*])
4. Je travaille. (rapide)
5. Je m'habille quand je sors avec mes amis. (mauvais)
6. J'ai préparé tous mes examens. (bon)
7. Je vais recevoir de bonnes notes. (sûr)
8. Je joue avec les enfants. (patient)
9. Je ne joue jamais avec les enfants. (violent)

Maintenant, pour chaque phrase, formulez une autre phrase qui exprime le contraire.

MODÈLE: Je parle de mes amis. (discret) →
Je parle indiscrètement de mes amis.

B. Une amie de Louise. Mettez les adverbes logiques à leur place pour compléter ce récit d'une amie de Louise.

Adverbes utiles: absolument, actuellement, apparemment, malheureusement, peut-être, sûrement, tellement

J'ai rencontré Louise quand j'avais 15 ans. ______[1], j'ai 81 ans et elle, elle avait le même âge. J'étais ______[2] triste d'apprendre sa mort la semaine dernière. ______[3], elle voulait partir en voyage avec sa petite-fille et pensait qu'elle avait ______[4] le temps de le faire avant de mourir. Elle voulait ______[5] parler avec la petite. ______[6], elle est morte trop tôt.

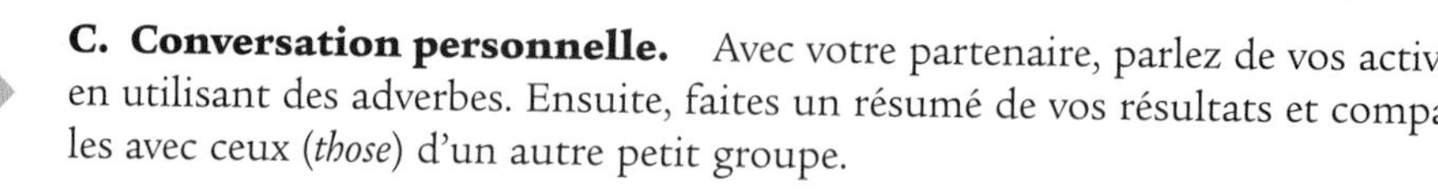

C. Conversation personnelle. Avec votre partenaire, parlez de vos activités en utilisant des adverbes. Ensuite, faites un résumé de vos résultats et comparez-les avec ceux (*those*) d'un autre petit groupe.

Vocabulaire utile: changer d'amis, danser, s'endormir, étudier, faire la cuisine, s'habiller, se lever, manger, parler à mes parents, parler français, partager mes possessions avec mes amis, travailler, voyager, etc.

MODÈLE: É1: Moi, je m'endors facilement pendant le cours de maths.
É2: Eh bien moi, je dors mal après trop de café. (*ou* Moi, je m'endors rapidement devant la télé.)

Regards sur la culture

Les étapes de la vie

Louise's death in this episode upsets Camille and seems to dash her hopes of finding out about what happened to her grandfather during World War II. It also modifies the relationship between Mado and Camille in subtle but important ways. In every culture, deaths, like births and marriages, are treated in special ways.

- French people don't give baby showers. A birth announcement is usually sent to family and friends, and many of these people visit the new baby, bringing gifts of the kind that North Americans give at a shower.
- Most French people see having a child as a major investment of time, energy, and affection. Children are looked after very closely all the way through childhood. As a result, many French families have only one child, and there is no particular sense that being an only child is a disadvantage. People who have many children are sometimes jokingly accused of being clumsy or of wanting to take advantage of the additional Social Security payments that they receive.
- French marriages take place in two parts. The civil ceremony is obligatory and is usually carried out complete with flowers and bridal gown. A religious ceremony is optional and in itself is not sufficient to legalize a marriage. This dual ceremony is the result of the separation of church and state that was mandated in early 20th-century France. The wedding reception usually consists of a huge dinner: As many as twelve or thirteen courses are presented over 5 hours or so, with dish after dish being commented on and appreciated. The meal is punctuated by individual speeches, toasts, and songs, and often is followed by dancing.

Un mariage civil à la mairie

- Career choice is often class-related. Since World War II, young people have often been discouraged by their families from entering agriculture, blue-collar jobs, and crafts. Another very important criterion in the choice is security. Finding a permanent, secure job (**une situation**) has traditionally been an obsession with French people. Most look for a job they can keep all their lives. This often means trying very hard to get a civil service job (anything from staff positions in government offices to teaching). Another criterion is location: Most people expect to find a job near home and family and to stay in it.
- **Ambition** is a word that has mainly negative connotations in France. It is impolite, at best, to be **ambitieux**. But for the French, ambition is not really necessary: French education and the system of competitive examinations are oriented toward finding people exactly the kind of job they should have.
- The average retirement age in France is 60. Most people receive 60 to 70% of their salary in retirement benefits. Many consider it selfish not to plan for an inheritance for one's children.
- Nearly every French person dreads the idea of dying in a hospital. People want to die at home, where friends and loved ones can watch over them and come to pay their last respects. Funerals and the clinical procedures surrounding death and burial are far simpler in France than they are in North America.

Considérez

Contrast French attitudes toward having children with those of your culture. What different values are involved? Why might this be? What might be the outward signs of these differences?

Structure 38

Les verbes *dire, lire et écrire*

Talking about everyday activities

—Maman? Que **dit** le médecin?

The verbs **dire**, **lire**, and **écrire** all have to do with communication. **Décrire** (*to describe*) is conjugated like **écrire**.

dire (*to say; to tell*)	**lire** (*to read*)	**écrire** (*to write*)
je **dis**	je **lis**	j' **écris**
tu **dis**	tu **lis**	tu **écris**
il, elle, on **dit**	il, elle, on **lit**	il, elle, on **écrit**
nous **disons**	nous **lisons**	nous **écrivons**
vous **dites**	vous **lisez**	vous **écrivez**
ils, elles **disent**	ils, elles **lisent**	ils, elles **écrivent**
passé composé: j'**ai dit**	passé composé: j'**ai lu**	passé composé: j'**ai écrit**

Yasmine **dit**: «C'est ma nouvelle école?»	*Yasmine says: "Is this my new school?"*
Elle **lit** sur l'écran de l'ordinateur.	*She reads on the computer screen.*
Les auteurs **écrivent** chaque jour.	*Authors write every day.*
Dites à David de venir tout de suite.	*Tell David to come right away.*
Il **a écrit** une lettre pour le quatrième anniversaire de sa fille.	*He wrote a letter for his daughter's fourth birthday.*
Des amis **ont lu** que la grand-mère de Camille était morte.	*Friends read that Camille's grandmother had died.*
Camille **décrit** la situation de ses grands-parents en 1939.	*Camille describes her grandparents' situation in 1939.*

Activités

A. Les médias. Faites des phrases avec les éléments donnés. N'oubliez pas d'utiliser **de** ou **que**, si nécessaire.

MODÈLE: nous / ne pas lire / le courrier des lecteurs tous les jours
Nous ne lisons pas le courrier des lecteurs tous les jours.

1. les journalistes / ne pas écrire / toujours clairement
2. la télévision / décrire / la misère humaine trop en détail
3. les jeunes / ne pas dire / les feuilletons sont intelligents
4. hier, je / lire / le président est à l'hôpital
5. tu / ne pas dire / toujours la vérité
6. le reporter / relire / son reportage très attentivement
7. quand vous / décrire / votre jeu télévisé préféré, qu'est-ce que vous / dire?
8. nous / dire / à nos enfants / jouer gentiment

B. Ce n'est pas vrai! Un étudiant et sa petite amie sont fâchés l'un avec l'autre. L'un(e) dit ce qu'il/elle pense. Jouez le rôle de l'autre en répondant au passé composé avec **dire**, **lire**, **décrire** ou **écrire**.

MODÈLE: Je t'écris toujours des poèmes. (ne... jamais) →
Tu ne m'as jamais écrit de poèmes.

1. Je dis toujours la vérité (*truth*). (ne... pas / hier)
2. Mes parents écrivent une lettre chaque (*each*) semaine. (ne... pas / la semaine dernière)
3. Tu lis mon journal intime (*diary*). (ne... jamais)
4. Tes amis et toi, vous dites que je suis laide. (ne... jamais)
5. Tes amis lisent toutes mes lettres. (ne... pas)
6. Vous me décrivez comme si j'étais un idiot. (ne... jamais)

C. Quand ce journaliste était jeune... . Un étudiant en journalisme pose des questions à un vieux journaliste sur sa vie. Avec un(e) partenaire, jouez les deux rôles. Utilisez des éléments des trois colonnes pour former des questions à l'imparfait.

MODÈLE: ÉTUDIANT: Est-ce que votre femme était jalouse de votre travail?
JOURNALISTE: Non. Elle travaillait avec moi. (Oui, elle pensait que je travaillais trop.)

vous	lire	vos articles
votre rédacteur en chef	écrire	votre travail
vos collègues	aimer	une vie intéressante
votre femme	avoir	jaloux/ouse de votre travail
	être	content(e)(s) de vous

Visionnement 2

Observez!

Considérez les aspects culturels expliqués dans **Regards sur la culture**. Ensuite, regardez l'Épisode 12 encore une fois, et répondez aux questions suivantes.

- Louise meurt dans son lit, chez elle. Est-ce que cette scène reflète une situation typique en France ou non?
- Camille a-t-elle tort de vouloir parler de son grand-père juste après l'enterrement de Louise?

Après le visionnement

Faites l'activité pour le **Visionnement 2** dans le cahier.

Synthèse: Lecture

Mise en contexte

The **valse musette** is a blend of folk music from the Auvergne region and light Parisian music from the 19th century. It developed into its current form during the 1930s, under the influence of Italian immigrants. The **valse musette** is accompanied by an accordion; indeed, the term **musette** refers to a small, bagpipe-like instrument, played especially in the Auvergne. Louise's favorite song, *Mon Amant de Saint-Jean,* is a **valse musette** written during the Second World War and popularized by Lucienne Delyle. Louise probably associated the song's title with her longing to see her husband, who had gone to Saint-Jean de Causse.

Stratégie pour mieux lire
Understanding the structure of a song's lyrics

When you hear a song, you can readily perceive its musicality: You hear the changes in pitch, the rhythm, and the rhyme. But you may not be able to distinguish all the lyrics or the nuances of meaning in them, because they may be delivered rapidly or indistinctly.

The song *Mon Amant de Saint-Jean* tells a story that is narrated in the past. It is divided into three verses, each consisting of three stanzas, or groups of lines. Skim the verses and identify which stanza in each advances the story. Which stanzas are repeated from verse to verse? What is different about the last verse?

When you've identified the overall structure, read the lyrics more carefully. How would you summarize the story and the narrator's feelings at the end?

Mon Amant[1] de Saint-Jean

Je ne sais pourquoi j'allais danser
À Saint-Jean au musette
Mais il m'a suffi d'un seul baiser[2]
Pour que mon cœur soit[3] prisonnier.

[1]*Lover* [2]*il... one kiss was enough* [3]*Pour... To make my heart*

Comment ne pas perdre la tête
Serrée[4] par des bras audacieux
Car l'on croit[5] toujours
Aux doux mots d'amour
Quand ils sont dits avec les yeux.
Moi qui l'aimais tant[6]
Je le trouvais le plus beau de Saint-Jean
Je restais grisée[7]
Sans volonté[8]
Sous ses baisers.

Sans plus réfléchir, je lui donnais
Le meilleur de mon être[9]
Beau parleur chaque fois qu'il mentait
Je le savais, mais je l'aimais.
Comment ne pas perdre la tête
Serrée par des bras audacieux
Car l'on croit toujours
Aux doux mots d'amour
Quand ils sont dits avec les yeux.
Moi qui l'aimais tant
Je le trouvais le plus beau de Saint-Jean
Je restais grisée
Sans volonté
Sous ses baisers.

Mais hélas,[10] à Saint-Jean comme ailleurs[11]
Un serment n'est qu'un leurre[12]
J'étais folle de croire au bonheur
Et de vouloir garder[13] son cœur.
Comment ne pas perdre la tête
Serrée par des bras audacieux
Car l'on croit toujours
Aux doux mots d'amour
Quand ils sont dits avec les yeux.
Moi qui l'aimais tant
Mon bel amour, mon amant de Saint-Jean,
Il ne m'aime plus
C'est du passé
N'en parlons plus.

Musique: Émile Carrara
Paroles: Léon Agel
1945: Éditions Méridian

[4]*Held tight* [5]Car… *For one believes* [6]qui… *who loved him so much* [7]*intoxicated* [8]Sans… *Without will* [9]Le… *The best of my being* [10]*alas* [11]*elsewhere* [12]Un… *An oath is only a deception* [13]*to keep*

Après la lecture

A. Le bon résumé. Choisissez le bon résumé de la chanson parmi les possibilités suivantes.

a. Un homme essaie de séduire (*seduce*) une femme. Au début, elle résiste, parce qu'elle ne croit pas à ses doux mots d'amour. Enfin, elle tombe amoureuse de lui, mais il la trompe (*deceives her*) et la quitte.

b. Une femme tombe amoureuse d'un homme qu'elle connaît depuis longtemps. Mais il reste froid et distant. Elle est trop intoxiquée par son amour pour remarquer son indifférence. Finalement, elle se rend compte de sa folie.

c. Un homme séduit une femme par des baisers et des doux mots d'amour. Elle ne résiste pas, elle devient intoxiquée par son amour. Mais finalement, elle apprend qu'il mentait et qu'il ne l'aime pas.

B. Un portrait. Faites le portrait de la narratrice et de son amant. Au début, quel était l'état d'esprit de la narratrice? Était-elle optimiste, sincère, cynique, impuissante (*helpless*)? Pourquoi était-elle susceptible aux désirs de l'amant? Qui a trompé qui? Comment l'attitude de la narratrice a-t-elle changé à la fin?

C. La chanson. Lisez les paroles à haute voix (*aloud*). Comment imaginez-vous la chanson? La musique est-elle gaie? rythmée? triste? lugubre (*gloomy*)?

À écrire

Faites **À écrire** pour le Chapitre 12 dans le cahier.

Vocabulaire

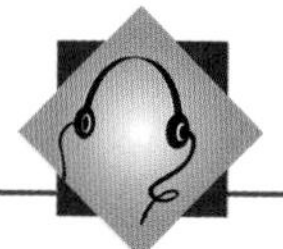

Les étapes de la vie

l'enfance (*f.*)	childhood
l'enterrement (*m.*)	burial
une étape	stage
un événement	event
un garçon	boy
une jeune fille	girl
la jeunesse	youth
la mort	death
la naissance	birth
un(e) retraité(e)	retiree, retired person
la vieillesse	old age
dans la trentaine (quarantaine, cinquantaine, soixantaine)	in one's thirties (forties, fifties, sixties) (*age*)

MOTS APPARENTÉS: **l'adolescence** (*f.*), **un(e) adolescent(e)** (*fam.* **un[e] ado**), **un(e) adulte, un bébé, le mariage**

À REVOIR: **la vie**

Les médias

les actualités (*f. pl.*) news; news program
une bande dessinée comic strip
le carnet du jour society column
une chaîne (*television*) station; network
le courrier des lecteurs letters to the editor
un dessin animé animated cartoon
un feuilleton soap opera
un gros titre headline
les informations (*f. pl.*) news; news program
un journal (des journaux) newspaper
une manchette headline
les mots (*m.*) **croisés** crossword puzzle
la nécrologie obituary column; obituary
une publicité commercial, advertisement
une rubrique section, column

MOTS APPARENTÉS: **un documentaire, un éditorial (des éditoriaux), un magazine, les médias** (*m. pl.*), **une série, une sitcom, une station (de radio)**
À REVOIR: **un jeu (des jeux), la météo**

Adjectifs

actuel(le) current, present
beau (bel, belle) beautiful, good-looking
discret/ète discreet; reserved
doux (douce) gentle
exact(e) exact, accurate
fou (folle) crazy, mad
franc(he) frank
jeune young
joyeux/euse joyous, joyful
lent(e) slow
nouveau (nouvel, nouvelle) new
seul(e) alone; sole
tel(le) such; like
vieux (vieil, vieille) old

MOTS APPARENTÉS: **absolu(e), apparent(e), élégant(e), évident(e), immédiat(e), rapide, sûr(e)**
À REVOIR: **gentil(le), vrai(e)**

Verbes

décrire to describe
dire to say; to tell
écrire to write
lire to read
prendre sa retraite to retire

MOT APPARENTÉ: **divorcer**

Adverbes

peut-être perhaps
seulement only
tellement so (very), so much
vite fast, quickly

À REVOIR: **bien, mal**

Autres expressions utiles

à la une on the front page
au/du troisième âge elderly, in old age

Chapitre 13

Documents

OBJECTIFS

In this episode, you will

- see how Bruno follows up on his offer to Camille
- find out more about Camille's grandfather, Antoine

In this chapter, you will

- talk about technology and methods of communication
- talk about university studies
- practice narration using the **passé composé** and the **imparfait** together
- discuss what and whom you know
- express the ideas of *nobody* and *nothing*
- learn about higher education in France
- read about communication technologies in France and Quebec

Vocabulaire en contexte

Comment communiquer?

Des **gens**° (*m. pl.*) différents communiquent différemment.

Des... *People*

Émilie écrit **une lettre**.

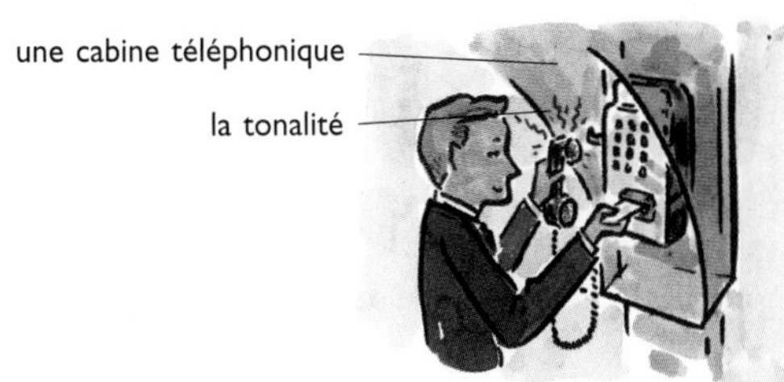

Benjamin **décroche** le combiné,° introduit sa carte, entend la tonalité et **compose**° le numéro. Il **laisse**° un message très long au répondeur, et enfin il **raccroche**.° Cet homme est **bavard**!°

décroche... *lifts the receiver*
dials
leaves
hangs up
talkative

Béatrice est **internaute**. Elle aime **naviguer (surfer) sur le Web**, et elle a **une page perso**.* Elle vient d'écrire un **mél**.† Maintenant, elle **clique** sur l'icone pour envoyer son message. Pour elle, **le courrier électronique semble** avoir **remplacé**° la poste.

semble... *seems to have replaced*

Autres expressions utiles

une boîte aux lettres électronique	electronic mailbox
une page d'accueil	home page
un portable	portable (cell) phone; laptop computer
un signet	bookmark
un site Web	website
un(e) technophobe	person who is afraid of technology

*C'est une locution familière qui signifie **une page personnelle**.
†La terme **mél** est utilisé en France. Les Canadiens disent **un courriel**.

Activités

A. Un dessin. Que font les personnes dans le dessin?

B. Qu'est-ce que c'est? Donnez le mot qui correspond à la définition.

1. C'est la première page d'un site Web.
2. C'est une personne qui navigue sur Internet.
3. Quand on est dans la rue, on peut téléphoner de cet endroit.
4. Pour ouvrir un document à l'ordinateur, on fait cette action.
5. C'est un ordinateur qu'on peut utiliser quand on voyage.
6. Pour pouvoir téléphoner, il faut attendre ce son.
7. C'est un message électronique qu'on envoie par Internet.
8. C'est l'endroit où on trouve son courrier électronique.
9. C'est une description d'une personne qui parle beaucoup.

C. Réflexions. Interviewez votre partenaire. Demandez-lui...

1. dans quelles circonstances il/elle écrit une lettre et ce dont (*what*) il/elle a besoin pour l'écrire
2. les démarches (*steps*) qu'il/elle fait pour téléphoner à quelqu'un (*someone*).
3. s'il est recommandé d'utiliser un portable au restaurant, au théâtre, en voiture.
4. s'il / si elle préfère le courrier électronique au téléphone. Demandez-lui d'expliquer (*to explain*).
5. s'il / si elle aime surfer sur le Web et quel est son site préféré.
6. pour quels sites il/elle a fait un signet, et pourquoi.
7. s'il / si elle a une page perso et, si oui, quelles informations il/elle met sur cette page. Demandez-lui si sa page est utile à son avis (*in his/her opinion*).
8. combien de fois par jour il/elle vérifie sa boîte aux lettres électronique.
9. pourquoi, à son avis, certaines personnes sont technophobes.
10. si Internet lui semble une invention utile, dangereuse, etc.

Les cours à l'université

Dans l'Épisode 13 du film, on cherche l'ami historien de Bruno. Il **enseigne** l'histoire contemporaine à l'université de Paris, mais en ce moment, il écrit sa **thèse de doctorat**. Un cousin d'Hélène donne des cours à l'université du Québec à Trois-Rivières. Voici **un plan** du campus de cette université canadienne.

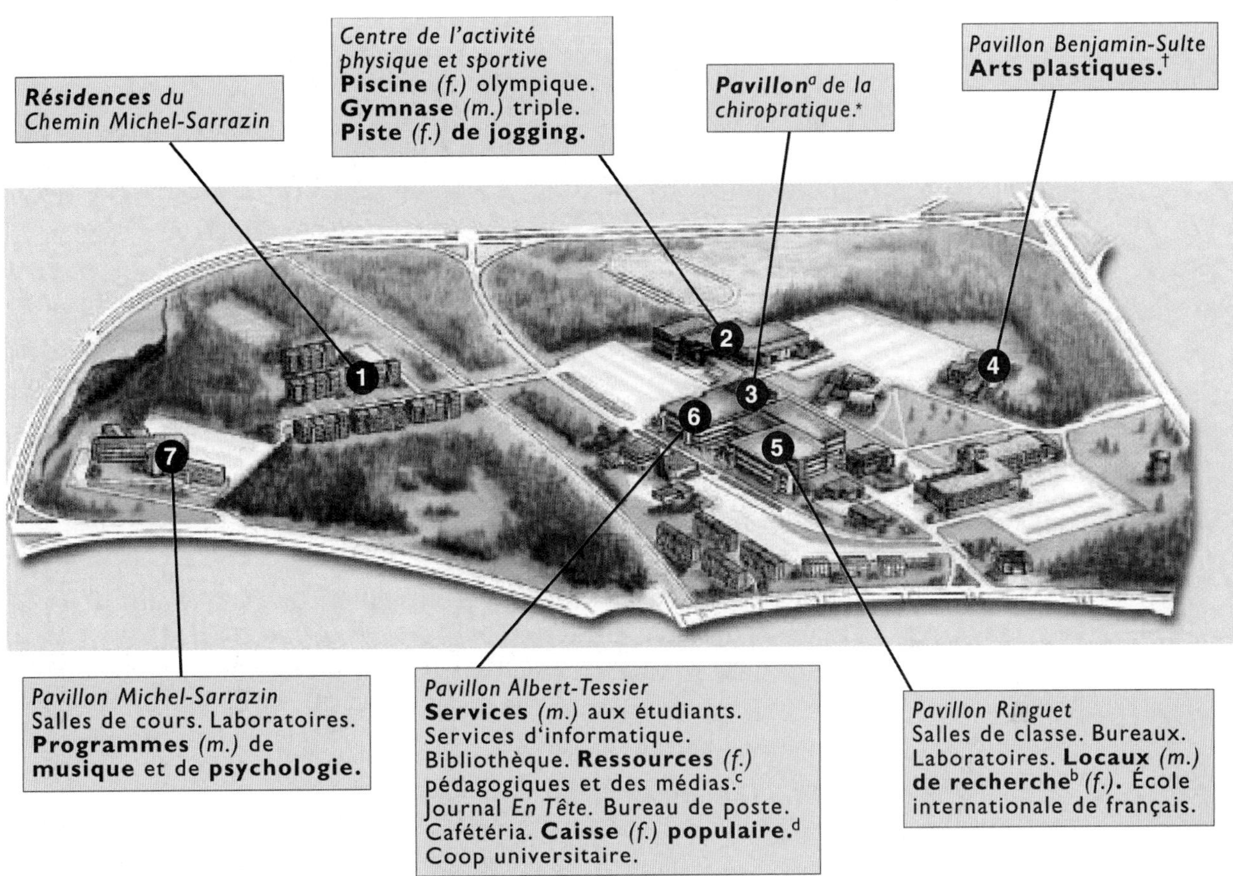

[a]*Pavillon, building* [b]Locaux... *Research facilities* [c]Ressources... *Teaching and media resources* [d]Caisse... *Credit union*

Quelles autres **matières**° (*f.*) sont offertes° par cette université? On peut **faire des études** ou **se spécialiser** en *subjects / offered*

- **administration** (*f.*) **des affaires**
- **arts** (*m.*) **dramatiques**
- **biochimie** (*f.*)
- **biologie** (*f.*)
- **chimie**° (*f.*) *chemistry*
- **économie** (*f.*) **de gestion**° *business economics*

---

*En France on dit **la chiropraxie** ou **la chiropractie**. La personne est **un chiropracteur** ou **un(e) chiropracticien(ne)**. Plus fréquent en France est **la kinésithérapie** (*massage therapy*), pratiquée par **un(e) kinésithérapeute**.

†Les arts plastiques sont les arts visuels comme la peinture (*painting*) et la sculpture.

- **enseignement**° (*m.*) **des langues**° (*f.*) **secondes*** — *teaching / languages*
- **enseignement secondaire**
- études françaises (études **littéraires** / études **langue** et communication)
- **génie**° (*m.*) (chimique, électrique, industriel, mécanique) — *engineering*
- **philosophie** (*f.*)
- **physique**° (*f.*) — *physics*
- **traduction**° (*f.*) — *translation*

Autre terme utile

le droit law

Activités

A. Où? Où va-t-on sur votre campus ou ailleurs (*elsewhere*) pour faire les choses suivantes?

1. pour obtenir des renseignements sur les activités organisées pour étudiants sur le campus
2. pour faire du jogging
3. pour étudier à fond (*in depth*) une question
4. pour faire une expérience (*experiment*)
5. pour réduire (*reduce*) le stress
6. pour voir des expositions d'arts plastiques
7. pour se coucher
8. pour trouver un bâtiment qu'on ne connaît pas sur le campus
9. pour faire de l'exercice ou pour nager (*swim*)
10. pour emprunter de l'argent

B. Trouvez la matière. Vous entendez des bribes (*bits*) de conversation dans le café. En quelle matière est-ce que chaque étudiant se spécialise?

MODÈLE: MARIE: ...la respiration des mammifères et des autres vertébrés... → Marie fait des études de biologie.

1. PIERRE: ...les cantates de Bach, «La Mer (*The Sea*)» de Debussy...
2. PHILIPPE: ...j'étudie le calcul des probabilités...
3. BENJAMIN: ...j'adore les romans (*novels*) de Marcel Proust...
4. NELLY: ...l'énergie électrostatique du condensateur...
5. LAURA: ...on fait des études sur les capacités cognitives...
6. NATHALIE: ...je lis les œuvres (*works*) de Sophocle et d'Euripide...
7. SYLVAIN: ...le code civil français n'a pas d'équivalent aux États-Unis...
8. DELPHINE: ...la combustion du carbone dans l'oxygène...
9. ANAÏS: ...l'inflation est causée par un excès de la demande...

*On peut aussi dire **des langues étrangères** (*foreign languages*).

C. Spécialisations. Quelle est l'opinion de la classe? Quelle spécialisation

1. exige (*requires*) une thèse de doctorat? **2.** exige une personnalité extravertie? **3.** exige beaucoup de réflexion abstraite? **4.** exige des connaissances (*knowledge*) en statistique? **5.** exige des connaissances en langues étrangères?

D. En quoi te spécialises-tu? Demandez à six étudiants en quoi ils se spécialisent.

MODÈLE: En quoi est-ce que tu te spécialises? →
Je fais des études de biologie. (Je ne sais pas encore.)

Pour discuter° des études universitaires

discuss

Voici des questions utiles pour une conversation sur les études universitaires.

Tu fais tes études à quelle université?
En quelle année es-tu?
Quels cours est-ce que tu suis°*? — *are taking*
En quoi est-ce que tu te spécialises?
En général, est-ce que tu as de bonnes ou de mauvaises **notes**° (*f.*)? — *grades*
Est-ce que **tu as** déjà **échoué° à un cours**? — *failed*
Est-ce que **tu sèches°† tes cours** de temps en temps? — *skip, play hooky from*
Est-ce que **tu as préparé la leçon/l'examen** pour demain?
Est-ce que tu as fait tes devoirs?
Est-ce que **tu as passé un examen°** récemment? — **passé...** *taken an exam*
Quand vas-tu recevoir ton **diplôme**?

Activité

Une interview. Interviewez votre partenaire pour en savoir plus (*to learn more*) sur sa vie à l'université.

Demandez-lui...

1. quelle est sa spécialisation.
2. quels cours il/elle suit (*takes*) pour sa spécialisation.
3. s'il / si elle apprend des choses intéressantes et s'il / si elle a de bonnes notes.
4. s'il / si elle s'inquiète avant les examens et comment il/elle prépare généralement un examen.
5. s'il / si elle trouve les services réservés aux étudiants adéquats, et pourquoi (ou pourquoi pas).
6. de parler de l'équipement et des installations disponibles (*available*) dans les salles de cours, les laboratoires et au centre des sports, par exemple.
7. si, en général, il/elle a une bonne ou une mauvaise opinion de l'université.

---

*C'est le verbe **suivre**. Une réponse possible à cette question: **Je suis** un cours de (biologie).
†**Sécher** se conjugue comme **préférer**: je sèche, nous séchons.

Visionnement 1

Avant de visionner

Les actes de parole. Lisez les extraits suivants du scénario de l'Épisode 13. Ensuite, analysez les phrases en italique. Quelles sont leurs fonctions? Choisissez parmi les possibilités suivantes.

demander une opinion	exprimer la reconnaissance (*gratitude*)
demander une précision	exprimer les condoléances
exprimer l'accord	faire un compliment
exprimer l'incrédulité	faire une demande

1. RACHID: Et je fais quoi, là-bas?
   CAMILLE: Interroge les gens sur la vie du village, pendant la guerre. Surtout les années 1942–43.
   RACHID: *D'accord.*
2. PRODUCTRICE: *Je suis désolée pour ta grand-mère.*
3. CAMILLE: L'autre jour, tu m'as parlé d'un ami historien, non?
   BRUNO: Je ne sais pas où il est, Camille. J'ai téléphoné, mais il a déménagé (*moved*).
   CAMILLE: *Dépêche-toi de le retrouver, s'il te plaît.*
4. HÉLÈNE: (après la mort de Louise) *Camille! Camille, je suis de tout cœur avec toi.*
5. CAMILLE: Au revoir. Merci, Bruno. Et toi aussi, Hélène. *Je suis contente de vous avoir comme amis.*
6. BRUNO: Alors? *Qu'est-ce que tu penses de... de David?* Un peu bizarre, non?
   HÉLÈNE: Non. *Non, il est plutôt* (rather) *bel homme... Hmmm?*
   BRUNO: *Bel homme? David?*

Vocabulaire relatif à l'épisode

type étrange	*strange guy*
vous avez découvert quelque chose	*you discovered something*
ont été détruites	*were destroyed*
partout	*throughout, everywhere*
aussi bien... que	*just as easily . . . as*
la preuve	*proof*
indice sérieux	*serious indication, clue*

Observez!

Dans l'Épisode 13, Hélène et Bruno essaient de trouver l'historien qui peut aider Camille. Pendant le visionnement, essayez de trouver la réponse aux questions suivantes.

- Où est-ce que Camille demande à Rachid d'aller? dans les Cevennes
- Quelles méthodes de communication utilise-t-on pour trouver l'historien? Est-ce qu'on réussit?
- Qu'est-ce qui semble impliquer Antoine dans un acte de trahison (*treason*)?

laissez-passer

Après le visionnement

A. Vrai ou faux? Vérifiez votre compréhension de l'épisode en indiquant si les phrases suivantes sont vraies ou fausses. Répondez **incertain** si l'épisode ne vous donne pas l'information nécessaire.

1. Rachid va à Alès pour parler aux gens du grand-père de Camille.
2. Bruno a du mal à trouver son ami historien.
3. Hélène trouve des renseignements sur Antoine Leclair aux Archives nationales.
4. Les Allemands et certains Français ont détruit beaucoup d'archives à la fin de la guerre.
5. Le laissez-passer (*pass*) que possédait (*possessed*) Antoine était contrefait (*counterfeit*).
6. Le laissez-passer a été signé par un officier allemand.
7. Il était normal de posséder un laissez-passer comme celui (*the one*) qu'avait Antoine.

B. Réfléchissez. Selon l'historien, le laissez-passer n'est pas preuve de la culpabilité d'Antoine, mais c'est un indice sérieux. À votre avis, y a-t-il d'autres scénarios qui pourraient (*that could*) expliquer le laissez-passer? Voici quelques possibilités. Quelle explication est la plus convaincante?

1. Antoine a contrefait (*counterfeited*) le laissez-passer pour obtenir des renseignements sur les activités des Allemands.
2. Les Allemands ont fabriqué ce laissez-passer pour faire croire aux Français (*to make the French believe*) qu'Antoine était un collaborateur.
3. Tous les résistants avaient un laissez-passer contrefait pour les protéger (*to protect them*) au cas où ils seraient arrêtés (*in case they were arrested*) par la Gestapo.

Avez-vous une autre idée?

Structure 39

Ne... rien, ne... personne et ne... aucun(e)

Expressing the concepts of *nothing, nobody,* and *not any*

—Il **n'**y a **rien** aux Archives à propos d'Antoine Leclair. Et toi, tu as trouvé ton ami historien?

—Non. Non, je **n'**ai **rien** trouvé. Non. Il a déménagé et **personne ne** connaît sa nouvelle adresse.

You have been using several French negations since Chapter 1: **ne... pas** (*not*), **ne... pas du tout** (*not at all*), **ne... pas encore** (*not yet*), **ne... jamais** (*never*), and **ne... plus** (*no longer*). Three other negations are also very useful.

ne... rien	*nothing, not anything*
ne... personne	*nobody, no one, not anyone*
ne... aucun(e)	*no, not a, not any*

Ne... rien et ne... personne

Ne... rien and **ne... personne** can act as the subject or object of a verb or as the object of a preposition. The positions of the two parts of the expression depends on how they are being used.

1. When used as the subject of a sentence, **rien** and **personne** precede **ne** directly, just before the verb.

Rien ne peut le justifier.	*Nothing can justify that.*
Là-bas, **personne n'**envoie les Juifs en prison.	*Nobody sends Jews to prison there.*

2. When used as the object of a verb, the negations work just like **ne... pas**, that is with **ne** before the verb and **rien** and **personne** after the verb.

Il **n'**y a **rien** aux Archives.	*There's nothing in the Archives.*
Bruno **ne** voit **personne** sur le plateau.	*Bruno doesn't see anyone on the set.*

When used as the object of a verb in the **passé composé, ne... rien** surrounds the auxiliary verb. **Ne... personne**, however, places **personne** after the past participle.

Je **n'**ai **rien** trouvé.	*I didn't find anything.*
Nous **n'**avons trouvé **personne**.	*We didn't find anyone.*

3. When a verb is followed by a preposition, **ne** is before the verb, and **rien** and **personne** follow the preposition.

Il **n'**a besoin de **rien**.	*He doesn't need anything.*
Elle **ne** parle à **personne**.	*She doesn't talk to anyone.*

4. **Rien** and **personne** can be used alone to answer a question.

—Qui va sortir avec toi?	*Who is going out with you?*
—**Personne.**	*Nobody.*
—Qu'est-ce que tu vas faire?	*What are you going to do?*
—**Rien.**	*Nothing.*

5. **Ne... rien** and **ne... personne** are related to the affirmative expressions **quelque chose** (*something*) and **quelqu'un** (*someone*).

—**Quelqu'un** a appelé?	*Did somebody call?*
—Non, **personne n'**a appelé.	*No, nobody called.*
—Tu as trouvé **quelque chose**?	*Did you find something?*
—Non, je **n'**ai **rien** trouvé.	*No, I didn't find anything.*

Ne... aucun(e)

1. **Ne... aucun(e)** acts like an adjective and agrees in gender with the noun it modifies. It precedes the noun.

Je **n'**ai **aucun** doute.	*I have no doubt.*
Je **n'**ai **aucune** envie de le revoir.	*I have no desire to see him again.*

2. **Ne... aucun(e)** is related to the adjective **quelques**. In a response to a question using **quelques**, the noun becomes singular if **aucun** is used.

—Tu as reçu **quelques** lettres?	*Did you receive some letters?*
—Non, je **n'**ai reçu **aucune** lettre.	*No, I didn't receive any letters.*

Pour en savoir plus...

Note that French routinely combines negatives within a sentence. When Bruno was blindfolded, he said

—Je **ne** vois **plus rien du tout**! *I no longer see anything at all!*

Activités

A. Problèmes de couple. Une femme n'est pas d'accord avec son mari et elle le contredit (*contradicts*). Utilisez les expressions négatives **ne... rien**, **ne... personne** et **ne... aucun(e)** pour donner les réponses négatives de la femme.

MODÈLE: Tout le monde nous croit le couple parfait. →
Personne ne nous croit le couple parfait.

1. Nous faisons quelque chose ce week-end.
2. Nous sortons avec nos amis, n'est-ce pas?
3. Tu aimes tout le monde dans ma famille. (Je...)
4. Tout (*Everything*) va bien chez nous.
5. Je parle de beaucoup de choses quand nous sommes ensemble. (Tu...)
6. Je t'envoie plusieurs méls quand je suis au travail. (Tu...)
7. Tout le monde nous invite à dîner.
8. Tu a beaucoup de preuves (*f.*) (*proofs*) de mon amour. (Je...)

B. À la recherche de la vérité. Faites des phrases négatives pour parler du film en utilisant les éléments donnés et en mettant les verbes au passé composé.

MODÈLE: Camille / apprendre / sur la mort de son grand-père / rien →
Camille n'a rien appris sur la mort de son grand-père.

1. Bruno / trouver / trace (*f.*) de son ami David / aucun
2. Bruno / parler / qui savait (*knew*) l'adresse de David / à personne
3. personne / trouver / la vérité pour Camille
4. Camille / trouver / document (*m.*) sur son grand-père / aucun
5. rien / être / facile pour Bruno

C. Dans ma vie. Interviewez votre partenaire. S'il / Si elle veut répondre à la forme négative, il/elle peut employer une négation de la liste. Soyez prêt(e) à donner des détails sur la vie de votre partenaire à la classe pour comparer les réponses.

Vocabulaire utile: ne... aucun(e), ne... jamais, ne... pas du tout, ne... pas encore, ne... personne, ne... plus, ne... rien

Demandez-lui

1. s'il / si elle a beaucoup de diplômes universitaires.
2. s'il / si elle a fait la connaissance de quelqu'un juste avant le cours aujourd'hui.
3. s'il / si elle a des arrière-grands-parents (*great-grandparents*) encore vivants (*living*).
4. s'il / si elle habite toujours la ville de sa naissance.
5. s'il / si elle a un crocodile chez lui/elle.
6. s'il / si elle trouve les émissions à la télévision à 3 h du matin intéressantes.
7. si quelqu'un va lui acheter une Ferrari.

Structure 40

Les verbes *savoir* et *connaître*

Talking about what and whom you know

—Il a déménagé et personne ne **connaît** sa nouvelle adresse.

—Il est professeur à l'université?

—Oui, oui. Seulement, actuellement, il ne donne pas de cours. Et puis **tu sais**, c'est un type étrange, un peu bizarre, très solitaire… **Je ne sais pas** quoi faire.

There are two verbs meaning *to know* in French: **savoir** and **connaître**. Each has its own special uses.

Savoir

1. The verb **savoir** means *to know* (*a fact*). You have already used it in **Je ne sais pas**.

savoir (*to know*)			
je	**sais**	nous	**savons**
tu	**sais**	vous	**savez**
il, elle, on	**sait**	ils, elles	**savent**
passé composé: **j'ai su**			
impératif: **sache, sachons, sachez**			

2. **Savoir** can take a direct object or it can be followed by a subordinate clause beginning with **que**, **comment**, **quand**, **pourquoi**, **combien de**, **où**, **qui**, etc.

Camille **sait son texte** par cœur.	*Camille knows her lines by heart.*
Je **sais que** Bruno et Camille sont deux bons professionnels.	*I know that Bruno and Camille are two good professionals.*
Camille veut **savoir comment et pourquoi** Antoine a disparu.	*Camille wants to know how and why Antoine disappeared.*

3. When followed by an infinitive, **savoir** means *to know how* (*to do something*).

Rachid **sait faire un reportage intéressant**.	*Rachid knows how to do an interesting report.*

Connaître

1. **Connaître** means *to know* in the sense of *to be acquainted with.*

connaître (*to know*)			
je	**connais**	nous	**connaissons**
tu	**connais**	vous	**connaissez**
il, elle, on	**connaît**	ils, elles	**connaissent**
passé composé: **j'ai connu**			

2. **Connaître** always takes a direct object: a person, a place, or something else that one might be familiar with, such as a song, a story, a road, and so on.

Je connais bien **le quartier**!	*I know the neighborhood well!*
Tu connais **quelqu'un** aux Archives nationales?	*Do you know anyone at the National Archives?*

3. Other verbs conjugated like **connaître** are **reconnaître** (*to recognize*), **paraître** (*to seem, appear*), **apparaître** (*to appear*), and **disparaître** (*to disappear*).

Vous le **reconnaissez**?	*Do you recognize him?*
Antoine **a disparu** pendant la guerre.	*Antoine disappeared during the war.*
Il **paraît** qu'Antoine était traître.	*It seems that Antoine was a traitor.*

Activités

A. Que savent-ils faire? Parlez de ces personnes. Que savent-elles faire?

MODÈLE: une bonne boulangère →
Elle sait faire un bon pain.

1. une étudiante en littérature
2. un professeur d'informatique
3. un internaute
4. les journalistes à la télévision
5. vous, les professeurs de français
6. vos camarades de classe et vous

B. L'université du Québec à Trois-Rivières. Deux étudiantes américaines sont arrivées à Trois-Rivières au Québec pour faire des études. Elles ne connaissent pas encore le campus de l'université. Utilisez une forme du verbe **connaître** pour compléter leur conversation avec Isabelle, une autre étudiante.

KATHY: _____[1]-tu bien ce campus?

ISABELLE: Oui, je le _____[2] assez bien. Vous le _____[3] aussi, n'est-ce pas?

ANGELA: Non, nous _____[4] déjà un peu la ville de Trois-Rivières, et Kathy _____[5] un des professeurs, mais le campus, non.

KATHY: Au fait, je veux _____[6] l'adresse du bâtiment de psychologie.

ISABELLE: Je suis désolée! Je ne la _____[7] pas, mais j'ai deux amis qui étudient la psychologie. Ils _____[8] certainement l'adresse. Je peux leur téléphoner.

C. Café Internet. Regardez ce dépliant (*brochure*). Dites ce que vous savez, ce que vous ne savez pas, ce que vous connaissez et ce que vous ne connaissez pas à propos de ce cybercafé à Paris.

MODÈLE: son numéro de fax →
Je sais son numéro de fax.
C'est le 33 (0) 1 40 51 84 40.

1. les horaires d'ouverture (*hours when it is open*)
2. où il se trouve
3. le nom du cybercafé
4. si on peut y (*there*) boire du café
5. l'adresse Internet
6. combien coûtent 15 minutes en ligne
7. la station R.E.R.
8. où on peut envoyer un mél
9. son propriétaire (*owner*)

D. L'épisode 13. Utilisez **apparaître**, **disparaître**, **paraître** et **reconnaître** pour compléter ce récit. Employez le passé composé (p.c.) s'il est indiqué.

Tout le monde à Canal 7 ____[1] que Camille est triste, et on veut l'aider. Bruno dit que l'historien est un type bizarre qui ____[2] de temps en temps, mais il essaie de le trouver. Selon Rachid, il ____[3] que les traces d'Antoine ____[4] (p.c.) de Saint-Jean de Causse. Enfin, l'historien ____[5] au bureau avec Bruno. Camille ____[6] contente. Malheureusement, des documents ____[7] souvent pendant les guerres, et David n'a trouvé que le laissez-passer incriminant.

E. Interview. Interviewez votre partenaire pour savoir ce qu'il/elle sait et ce qu'il/elle ne sait pas, ainsi que (*as well as*) les gens et les endroits (*places*) qu'il/elle connaît. Votre partenaire doit aussi parler d'autres personnes. Que savent-ils, qui connaissent-ils, etc.?

Vocabulaire utile: faire du ski, faire la cuisine, parler une autre langue, faire des recherches sur Internet, ?

MODÈLE: É1: Est-ce que tu sais chanter (*to sing*)?
É2: Je ne sais pas bien chanter, mais je sais jouer du piano.
É1: Connais-tu quelqu'un qui sait bien chanter?
É2: Ma sœur sait bien chanter. Elle a une belle voix (*voice*).
É1: Alors, connaît-elle Carnegie Hall?
É2: Oui, elle connaît cet endroit (*place*), parce qu'elle habite New York. Moi, je ne le connais pas.
É1: Sais-tu pourquoi ta sœur habite New York et non pas Chicago? etc.

Maintenant, présentez à la classe un compte rendu (*report*) sur votre partenaire.

Regards sur la culture

L'enseignement supérieur°

L'enseignement... *Higher education*

In this episode, Bruno locates David, the college history professor. He is not teaching at the moment because he is writing his thesis. A North American would probably expect a college professor to have finished writing his thesis before getting a job in higher education. In fact, French higher education is different in many ways from the North American model.

- Almost everyone who receives a higher education in France attends public institutions, which are very inexpensive. The curricula are supervised by the Ministry of Education. Anyone who has earned the **baccalauréat*** may study at a public university.
- Students at the university are called **étudiant(e)s**. This is seen as a social, and almost a professional, category in France. College students have many advantages (reduced prices at the movies, for example) and generally enjoy a rich social life by taking advantage of the services of the city where their university is located.
- College courses revolve around the end-of-year examinations. Some (not all) students rarely go to class and work only in the late spring before exams.
- Relationships between students and professors at the university in France are usually impersonal and distant compared with those in North America.
- Some college professors or researchers work on **le doctorat d'État**, a degree that requires two theses. Many finish this at age 40 or even later. David, in the film, is working on a **doctorat d'État**.
- Some young people (around 10%) hope to enter one of France's **grandes écoles**, which is an entirely different educational track. Entry into one of these institutions requires two years of very stressful preparatory studies beyond the **baccalauréat**, followed by extremely difficult competitive examinations called **concours** that involve both written and oral tests. Only a small number of positions are available in the **grandes écoles**, and those with the best scores in the **concours** get them. Students on this track do very little but study. If they gain entry into a **grande école**, they are guaranteed a salary, great social prestige, and a very useful social network. Those who are not accepted start university studies from scratch.

Une cérémonie à l'École polytechnique

*The **baccalauréat** is a comprehensive examination of general knowledge and studies done in high school. It is taken in two parts: the first at the end of the next-to-last year of high school, the second at the end of the final year. The **bac** is essential for many jobs in France. About 77% of high school students pass it.

Considérez

Compare the system of higher education in France with that of your own country. What are some of the advantages of each? What do you think are some of each system's weaknesses?

Structure 41

Le passé composé et l'imparfait

Narrating in the past

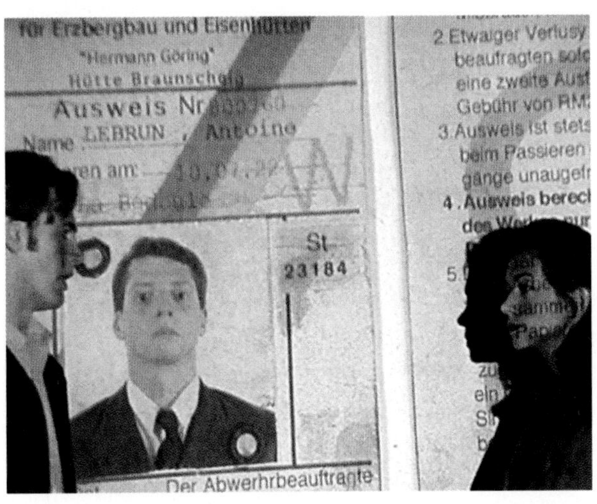

—Ce document **était** un laissez-passer spécial. Avec ça, on **pouvait** voyager partout en France. Aussi bien dans la zone occupée par les Allemands que dans la zone libre.

—Et beaucoup de gens **avaient** ce document?

—Non. Ce laissez-passer **a été** signé sur l'ordre d'un officier supérieur. Un officier allemand… Et ça, c'**était** assez rare.

—Alors, Antoine **a** peut-être **collaboré** ou **travaillé** avec les Allemands?

Both the **passé composé** and the **imparfait** are past tenses, although, as you have already seen, they are used to express different aspects of past time. These differences are summarized in the following chart.

Passé Composé	**Answers the Question . . .**
Past events or sequences of events	What happened?
Imparfait	**Answers the Question . . .**
Descriptions in the past	What were the circumstances? What was someone's state of mind?
Ongoing past action	What was happening?
Habitual past action	What used to happen?

1. When the two tenses are used in the same sentence, the **passé composé** expresses an event that interrupts the ongoing action expressed by the **imparfait**. In other words, the **imparfait** sets the scene for the event in the **passé composé**.

Camille **se brossait** les cheveux quand Alex **a frappé** à la porte.	*Camille was brushing her hair when Alex knocked at the door.*

2. Surrounding words, especially adverbs, sometimes give a good indication of the tense required. Words that indicate the precise time or number of repetitions of an action generally accompany the **passé composé**, and words that indicate habituality generally accompany the **imparfait**.

WORDS THAT SIGNAL THE *PASSÉ COMPOSÉ*	WORDS THAT SIGNAL THE *IMPARFAIT*
l'an dernier / l'année dernière	autrefois
le mois dernier	d'habitude
la semaine dernière	dans le temps (*in the past*)
lundi (dernier), etc.	de temps en temps
hier	le lundi, etc.
un jour	le week-end
un week-end	parfois
soudain (*suddenly*)	rarement
	souvent
	toujours
	tous les jours

D'habitude, Louise téléphonait à Mado **tous les jours**.	*Louise usually called Mado every day.*
La semaine dernière, Camille a préparé le dîner pour Louise.	*Last week, Camille prepared dinner for Louise.*

3. **Savoir** and **connaître** are normally used in the **imparfait** for past meanings. They have subtle differences in meaning when they are used in the **passé composé**.

IMPARFAIT	PASSÉ COMPOSÉ
Bruno **connaissait** l'historien.	Camille **a connu** l'historien.
*Bruno **knew** the historian.*	*Camille **met** the historian.*
Louise ne **savait** pas la vérité sur Antoine.	Louise **n'a pas su** la vérité sur Antoine.
*Louise didn't **know** the truth about Antoine.*	*Louise **didn't find out** the truth about Antoine.*

The verb **devoir** can mean *supposed to* in the **imparfait** and either *had to* or *probably* (*must have*) in the **passé composé**.

IMPARFAIT	PASSÉ COMPOSÉ
On **devait** faire un voyage ensemble.	On **a dû** faire un voyage ensemble.
*We **were supposed to** (**planned to**) make a trip together.*	*They **probably** took (**must have** taken) a trip together.*

Notez bien!

You have already learned about some adverbs of sequence that are used to order events in a narration: **avant, d'abord, puis, ensuite, après, enfin.** You have also seen some adverbs and expressions that refer to the past, present, or future: **déjà, hier, bientôt, demain, tout de suite, plus tard.** Other expressions that are used to tell when something happened or will happen include

l'an, l'année, le mois, la semaine dernier/ière last year, month, week

l'an, l'année, le mois, la semaine prochain(e) next year, month, week

ce matin this morning

ce soir this evening

cet après-midi this afternoon

le lendemain the next day

Je pars au Canada **le mois prochain.** *I am going to Canada next month.*

J'ai étudié **ce matin.** *I studied this morning.*

Le lendemain, Rachid est allé dans les Cévennes. *The next day, Rachid went to the Cévennes.*

These adverbs and expressions can come at the beginning or end of a sentence.

Activités

A. L'histoire, c'est fantastique. Comment est-ce que David est devenu historien? Mettez les phrases au passé composé ou à l'imparfait selon le sens. Utilisez les mots clés et le contexte pour vous aider.

MODÈLE: Quand j'avais (avoir) 13 ans, je ne comprenais pas (ne pas comprendre) l'histoire.

1. Un jour mon père _____ (trouver) un beau livre d'histoire à la bibliothèque.
2. Ce jour-là, nous _____ (regarder) toutes les images et nous _____ (parler) des hommes et des femmes importantes.
3. Une semaine après, mon père _____ (retourner) à la bibliothèque et j'y _____ (aller) avec lui.
4. Ce jour-là, nous _____ (décider) d'étudier l'histoire ensemble.
5. Parfois, quand j'_____ (avoir) des problèmes avec toutes les dates, mon père m'_____ (aider) à les apprendre.
6. D'habitude, nous _____ (aller) à la bibliothèque le samedi matin, mais un jour nous _____ (visiter) le Musée de l'Homme.
7. Ce jour-là, au musée, je (j') _____ (comprendre) que l'histoire est le sujet le plus passionnant (*exciting*) et je (j') _____ (prendre) une décision importante. Je (J') _____ (choisir) ma profession!

B. La recherche continue... Utilisez les verbes au passé composé ou à l'imparfait pour expliquer où Camille en est dans ses recherches.

MODÈLE: Camille / donner / la photo d'Antoine à Louise →
Camille a donné la photo d'Antoine à Louise.

1. Louise / ne jamais vouloir / parler de son mari, mais elle / dire / certaines choses
2. «il / être / dans les Cévennes»
3. «il / me / envoyer / une lettre»
4. Camille et Louise / aller / partir ensemble quand Louise / mourir
5. un jour, Camille / expliquer / à sa mère qu'elle / avoir envie de / parler avec Louise
6. «on / devoir / faire un voyage dans les Cévennes»
7. «je / vouloir / discuter avec elle»
8. Mado / refuser toujours / d'en parler (*to talk about it*), / alors un soir Camille / demander / à Bruno de retrouver son ami historien
9. l'historien / ne pas donner / de cours ce semestre-là et Bruno / ne pas pouvoir / le trouver
10. heureusement, Hélène / utiliser / fréquemment Internet et elle / pouvoir / aider Bruno
11. «tu / ne pas penser / à Internet»
12. ensemble, ils / trouver David, qui / venir / parler avec Camille
13. Camille / être / très impatiente et elle / poser / tout de suite des questions
14. «alors, Antoine/collaborer/avec les Allemands?»
15. nous / comprendre / qu'Antoine / avoir / un laissez-passer
16. qu'est-ce que vous / apprendre / sur ce laissez-passer?

C. Une année difficile. Chantal parle de son école préparatoire et du concours. Mettez les verbes à l'imparfait ou au passé composé, selon le cas (*depending on the case*).

Le premier jour, je ____[1] (ne pas descendre) du bus là où je ____[2] (devoir) et je ____[3] (me perdre). Je ____[4] (ne pas pouvoir) trouver mon école. Quand je ____[5] (aller) au bureau principal, il y ____[6] (avoir) trente élèves qui ____[7] (attendre) l'arrivée de la secrétaire. Je ____[8] (ne connaître personne). Nous ____[9] (commencer) à nous impatienter quand elle ____[10] (arriver enfin), mais elle nous ____[11] (faire) attendre encore un quart d'heure. Nous ____[12] (être) furieux. En plus, quand c'était mon tour, elle ____[13] (me dire): «Vous ____[14] (arriver) trop tard. Revenez demain.» Encore plus furieuse, je ____[15] (retourner) au bureau le lendemain. Enfin, je ____[16] (s'inscrire) pour l'école préparatoire.

Pendant l'année, nous ____[17] (travailler) tous les jours comme des fous. Nous ____[18] (avoir) trois heures de maths par jour et à côté de ça, les deux heures de philo ____[19] (sembler) faciles. Enfin, je ____[20] (ne que faire) étudier pendant toute l'année. Je ____[21] (savoir) que le concours ____[22] (aller) être difficile.

Enfin le jour du concours ____[23] (arriver)! Les cinquante candidats ____[24] (se trouver) dans une salle et nous ____[25] (avoir) tous peur. Mais quand le pion (*assistant*) ____[26] (nous donner) le sujet pour l'écrit, nous ____[27] (comprendre) que nous ____[28] (être) bien préparés. Merci, les professeurs!

D. Mon premier jour à la fac. (*My first day at university.*) Interviewez votre partenaire sur ce qui est arrivé pendant son premier jour à l'université. Utilisez les catégories suivantes pour vous guider dans vos questions.

Catégories:

une description (le temps, l'aspect physique du campus, l'ambiance sur le campus, etc.)

le matin	les étudiants	les professeurs	les cours
le déjeuner	l'après-midi	la fin de la journée	les classes

MODÈLE: É1: Fais-moi une description de ton premier jour à la fac.
É2: Mon premier jour était super. Il faisait beau et tous les étudiants étaient en short.

É1: As-tu bien trouvé tes classes?
É2: J'ai trouvé ma première classe sans problème...

Après votre conversation, faites un petit compte rendu sur le premier jour à la fac de votre partenaire.

MODÈLE: Michel m'a dit que son premier jour à la fac était super. Il faisait beau et tout le monde était en short. Michel a trouvé la classe pour son premier cours sans problème...

Visionnement 2

Observez!

Considérez les aspects culturels expliqués dans **Regards sur la culture**. Ensuite, regardez l'Épisode 13 encore une fois, et répondez aux questions suivantes.

- À votre avis, est-ce que David va finir sa thèse de doctorat bientôt? Pourquoi (pas)?
- Selon Hélène, pourquoi est-ce que Bruno est «un vrai Français»? Qu'est-ce qu'elle veut dire en ce qui concerne les Français et Internet?

Après le visionnement

Faites l'activité pour le **Visionnement 2** dans le cahier.

Synthèse: Culture

Les technologies de la communication

Dans le film, Hélène dit à Bruno qu'il est «un vrai Français» parce qu'il n'a pas pensé à utiliser Internet pour chercher David. Pourquoi dit-elle cela?

La France est le pays de Blaise Pascal (1623–1662), constructeur du premier ordinateur. Et la France a eu le premier réseau informatique[1] national disponible au grand public: le système *Minitel*.

Le Minitel a été lancé en 1981 par la compagnie téléphonique France Télécom. C'était une nouvelle expérience. Le terminal Minitel était distribué gratuitement[2]

[1]réseau... *computer network* [2]*for free*

au début. Maintenant il faut[3] payer, mais ce n'est pas cher. Aujourd'hui, il y a plus de 25.000 services. C'est un service de texte seulement. Ce n'est pas très esthétique, mais c'est efficace.[4] Le Minitel remplace l'annuaire téléphonique.[5] On peut, par son intermédiaire, contacter sa banque, acheter des livres, obtenir des renseignements, planifier des voyages et contacter des amis.

Le Minitel est un système centralisé, créé et surveillé[6] par le gouvernement. Pour cette raison, on considère que les informations qu'on y trouve sont en général crédibles. D'autres pays, comme la Tunisie, ont adopté le Minitel.

vtx.mctel.fr/3SUISSES

Les Bonnes Affaires 3 Suisses

BOUTIQUE HOMME		PAGES CAT. ETE	ANCIEN PRIX*		NOUVEAU PRIX*
* Prix à partir de, selon taille					
1	LA CHEMISE	567(E)	22,69€	=>	15,07€
2	LE T-SHIRT	568(A)	15,07€	=>	10,51€
3	LE PANTALON	570(E)	30,30€	=>	21,16€
4	LE T-SHIRT	587(B)	15,07€	=>	10,51€
5	LE PULL	610(A)	34,87€	=>	24,36€
6	LA CHEMISE	610(C)	21,16€	=>	13,55€
7	LE SWEAT	612(D)	30,30€	=>	21,16€
8	LE POLO	631(G)	15,07€	=>	10,51€
9	LE PULL	631(H)	44,00€	=>	30,76€
10	LE T-SHIRT	568(F)	19,64€	=>	13,70€
11	LE BLOUSON	634(C)	37,91€	=>	26,49€
12	LE GILET	647(E)	37,91€	=>	26,49€
13	LA VESTE	630(A)	91,21€	=>	63,80€
14	LE PANTALON	630(C)	45,53€	=>	30,30€
15	LA CHEMISE	631(I)	27,26€	=>	19,64€

Descriptif article:N°.. + ENVOI
Autres boutiques ou commander SOMMAIRE

Cx/Fin
Guide
Répétition
Annulation
Correction
Sommaire
Retour
Suite
Envoi
VTX-Plug MC-TEL

Une page Minitel

Dans les années 90, l'utilisation d'Internet s'est répandue[7] en Amérique du Nord. Le Québec était un des centres de ce développement. Aujourd'hui, Montréal est une des grandes villes du monde pour les technologies de la communication. Le magazine américain *Wired* appelle Montréal un «global high-tech hot spot». Le pourcentage d'emplois dans le domaine de la haute technologie est très élevé dans cette ville et ce sont d'ailleurs[8] des entreprises de Montréal qui produisent 80% des effets spéciaux pour le cinéma—comme pour le film *Gladiator* en 2000.

Le Québec a adopté Internet avec enthousiasme, mais la France a hésité. Le Minitel marchait bien. On le connaissait bien. On ne savait pas si Internet allait réussir. On ne savait pas si les informations sur Internet étaient toujours crédibles. Aujourd'hui, les Français utilisent les services Internet, mais ils n'ont pas abandonné le Minitel.

[3]il... *one must* [4]*effective* [5]annuaire... *telephone book* [6]créé... *created and managed* [7]s'est... *has spread* [8]*moreover*

À vous

Le shopping. Study the Minitel screen. *Les Trois Suisses* is a famous French mail order company; its catalogue has been a standard part of French life since 1932. In groups of three, decide how you would spend 200 euros at this sale. How would you look for descriptions of these items?

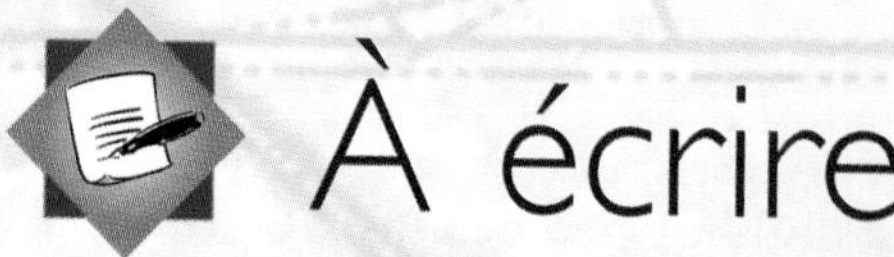

À écrire

Faites **À écrire** pour le Chapitre 13 dans le cahier.

Vocabulaire

La communication

une boîte aux lettres électronique electronic mailbox
le courrier électronique e-mail
une feuille (de papier) leaf; sheet (of paper)
des gens (*m. pl.*) people
un(e) internaute Internet user
un mél e-mail message
une page d'accueil home page
un portable portable (cell) phone; laptop computer
un signet bookmark
un(e) technophobe person who is afraid of technology
un timbre stamp
la tonalité dial tone

MOTS APPARENTÉS: **une cabine téléphonique, une enveloppe, un icone, une lettre, une page perso, un site Web**

Pour parler de la communication

composer (un numéro) to dial (a number); to compose
décrocher to pick up (*the telephone receiver*)
raccrocher to hang up (*the telephone receiver*)

MOTS APPARENTÉS: **cliquer, naviguer (surfer) sur le Web**

À l'université

une caisse populaire credit union
un gymnase gymnasium
un local (des locaux) facility
une note grade (on an exam, an assignment)
une piscine swimming pool
une piste (de jogging) (jogging) trail, track
un plan map (*subway, city, region*)
la recherche research
une ressource resource
une thèse thesis, dissertation

MOTS APPARENTÉS: **un diplôme, un doctorat, un programme, une résidence (universitaire), un service**

Les cours universitaires

l'administration (*f.*) **des affaires** business administration
les arts (*m. pl.*) **plastiques** visual arts (sculpture, painting, etc.)
la biochimie biochemistry
la chimie chemistry
le droit law
l'économie (*f.*) **de gestion** business economics
l'enseignement (*m.*) **(secondaire, des langues étrangères)** teaching (of secondary school, of foreign languages)
le génie (chimique, électrique, industriel, mécanique) (chemical, electrical, industrial, mechanical) engineering
une langue (étrangère) (foreign) language

une matière (*school*) subject
la physique physics
la traduction translation

MOTS APPARENTÉS: **les arts** (*m. pl.*) **dramatiques, la biologie, la chiropraxie, la musique, la philosophie, la psychologie**

Pour discuter des études universitaires

discuter de to discuss
échouer (à un cours, à un examen) to fail (a course, an exam)
enseigner to teach
faire des études en to major in, study (*a subject*)
passer un examen to take an exam
préparer (une leçon, un examen) to study for (a lesson, an exam)
sécher un cours to skip, cut class
se spécialiser en to major in

Autres verbes

apparaître to appear
connaître to know, be acquainted with
disparaître to disappear
laisser to leave; to allow
paraître to seem, appear
reconnaître to recognize
remplacer to replace
savoir to know (*a fact*)
sembler to seem

Négations

ne… aucun(e) not one, not any
ne… personne nobody, no one
ne… rien nothing

À REVOIR: **ne… jamais, ne… pas, ne… pas du tout, ne… pas encore, ne… plus**

Expressions de temps

ce matin this morning
ce soir this evening
cet après-midi this afternoon
le lendemain the next day

À REVOIR: **après, avant, bientôt, d'abord, déjà, demain, enfin, ensuite, hier, plus tard, puis, tout de suite**

Adjectifs

bavard(e) talkative
dernier/ière last
littéraire literary
prochain(e) next

Autres expressions utiles

quelque chose something
quelqu'un someone
Quels cours est-ce que tu suis? What courses are you taking?

Chapitre 14

Une lettre

OBJECTIFS

In this episode, you will

- watch as Camille finds a lead for her search
- learn what happened to all the photos of Antoine

In this chapter, you will

- talk about traveling by train, plane, and car
- learn about getting around in Paris
- use **tout** to express totality
- use the present participle to express simultaneous actions and manner
- talk about going *to* and *from* cities, countries, provinces, and states
- learn about various modes of transportation in France
- read correspondence from a sailor in World War II

Vocabulaire en contexte

Pour voyager

Pour aller de Paris dans les Cévennes, il y a **plusieurs**° possibilités. Choisissez votre **moyen** de transport préféré.

several

En train (*m.*)

De **la gare**° à Paris, prenez **le TGV**.°

Vous pouvez obtenir **un billet**° au **guichet**,° par Minitel, sur Internet ou à un distributeur automatique. Il faut° préciser si vous désirez un **aller simple** ou un **aller-retour** et si vous voulez voyager en première classe ou en seconde. Attention: Vous devez réserver **une place** à l'avance. Vous pouvez choisir **un wagon fumeurs**° ou **non-fumeurs**, **un siège couloir**° ou fenêtre.

Tous les **passagers**° (*m.*) doivent **composter** leur billet° avant de monter—les composteurs se trouvent à l'entrée des **quais**° (*m.*).

Descendez à Nîmes, où vous pouvez prendre un train TER° en **correspondance**° (*f.*). Pour faire le voyage de Paris aux Cévennes, vous allez mettre entre 5 et 8 heures.

station / Train à Grande Vitesse
ticket / window
Il... *It is necessary to*
wagon... *smoking car*
siège... *aisle seat*
passengers
composter... *punch their ticket*
platforms
Transport Express Régional / *transfer*

En avion° (*m.*)

De **l'aéroport** (*m.*) Orly-ouest, il y a plusieurs **vols**° (*m.*) par jour à Nîmes. Par exemple, il y a un vol à 9 h qui arrive à Nîmes à 10 h 10. De Nîmes à Alès, vous pouvez prendre **un autocar**° ou **louer**° une voiture.

En avion, vous êtes limité à deux **valises** (*f.*) et un sac à main. Vous devez arriver à l'aéroport une heure avant **le départ** de l'avion, pour **enregistrer**° vos valises, passer au poste de contrôle de sécurité et trouver **la porte d'embarquement**.°

airplane
flights
tour bus / rent
check
porte... *gate*

En voiture

Prenez **l'autoroute** (*f.*) A7 jusqu'à Orange. **La limite de vitesse**° sur l'autoroute: 120 km/h.* Ensuite, suivez° la A9 jusqu'à **la sortie**° 19 direction Alès. Suivez **la route** D981 jusqu'à Alès.

Suggestion: Évitez° **les heures de pointe**° et les grandes vacances° car° **la circulation**° est mauvaise et il y a des risques **d'embouteillages**° (*m.*).

limite... *speed limit*
follow / exit
Avoid / heures... *rush hour*
grandes... *summer vacation / since / traffic / traffic jams*

---

*km/h = kilomètres à l'heure

Comme Alès est en France, les Français n'ont pas besoin de **passer la douane**° et ils n'ont besoin ni° d'**un passeport**, ni° d'**un visa**.

customs / neither
nor

Autre mot utile

l'arrivée (*f.*) arrival

Activités

A. Quel moyen de transport? Quel moyen de transport—**le train**, **l'avion** ou **la voiture**—associez-vous aux mots suivants? Attention: parfois, il y a plusieurs possibilités.

MODÈLE: un vol → l'avion

1. une gare
2. enregistrer
3. un quai
4. un billet
5. composter
6. une correspondance
7. la limite de vitesse
8. un wagon non-fumeurs
9. une porte d'embarquement
10. un embouteillage
11. passer la douane

B. Avantages et inconvénients. Trouvez un avantage et un inconvénient des moyens de transport suivants.

AVANTAGES	INCONVÉNIENTS
a des sièges confortables	n'a pas de siège confortable
est bon(ne) pour la santé	est désagréable quand il pleut/neige
est économe	est cher (chère)
est non-polluant(e)	est polluant(e)
est pratique	n'est pas pratique
est rapide	est lent(e)
est toujours à l'heure	est souvent en retard
évite la circulation mauvaise	est désagréable aux heures de pointe
laisse plus de liberté au voyageur	a une heure de départ inflexible

MODÈLE: le vélo → Le vélo est bon pour la santé, mais il est lent.

1. la voiture
2. le train
3. l'avion
4. l'autocar
5. le taxi
6. le cheval (*horse*)

C. Un voyage. Racontez un voyage que vous avez fait. Quel mode de transport avez-vous choisi? Pourquoi? Quels préparatifs avez-vous faits avant le départ? Le voyage s'est-il bien passé?

MODÈLE: Le week-end dernier, mes amis et moi, on est allés à San Francisco pour assister à un concert. On a pris la route de bonne heure (*early*) pour éviter les embouteillages. On a mis deux heures pour arriver au stade où avait lieu le concert (*where the concert took place*). Le voyage s'est bien passé.

Circuler° à Paris

Il est très agréable de se promener à Paris. Mais si on est **pressé**,° il n'est pas toujours pratique d'aller d'**un endroit**° à l'autre **à pied**.° La solution? **Le métro**.

To travel around

in a hurry

place / à... by foot

En métro

Le **réseau du métro**° dessert° toute la ville de Paris; on n'est jamais loin d'une station. Quel est le mode d'emploi du métro? Regardez le plan.

réseau... subway system / serves

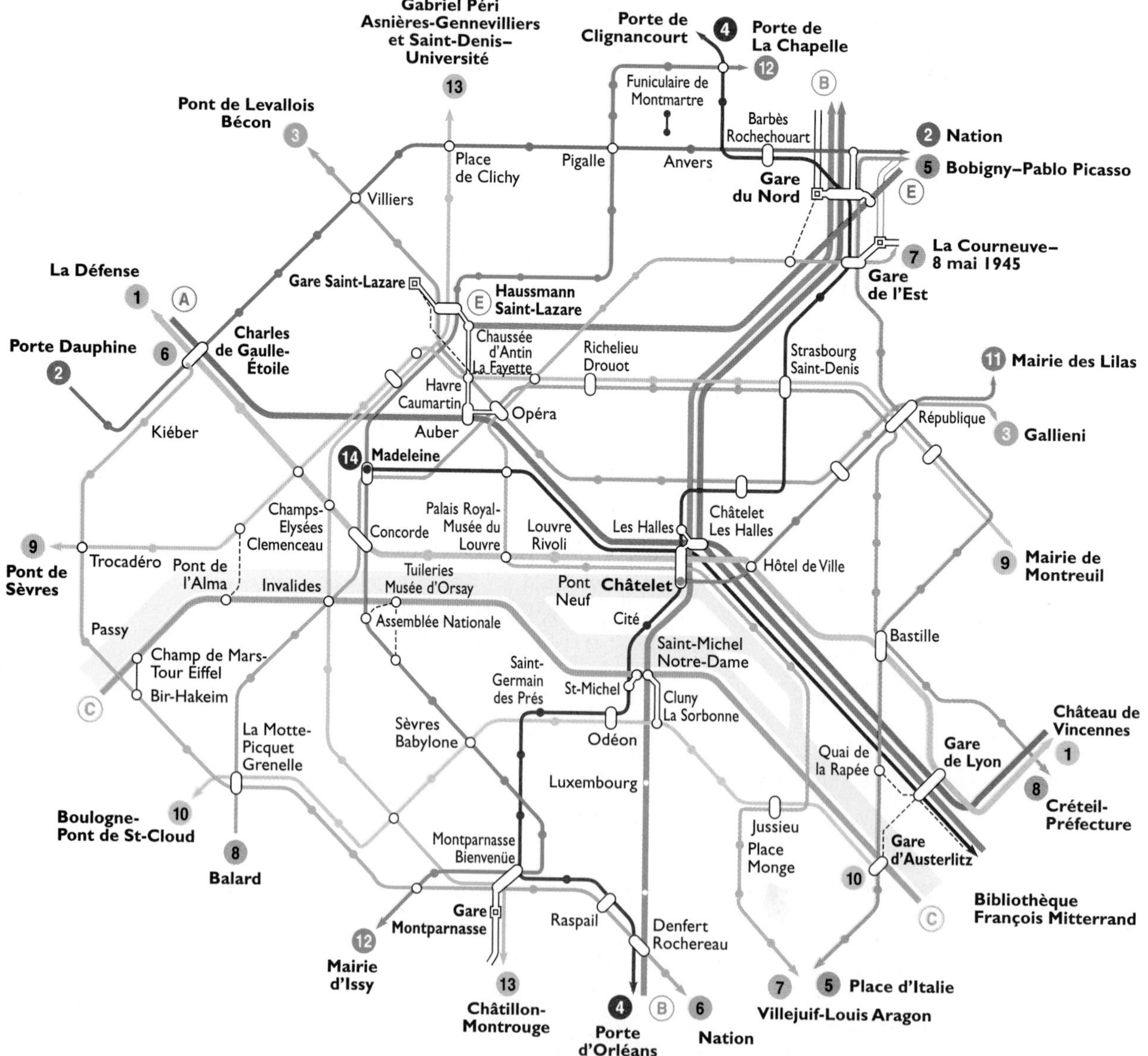

Quand Camille va de chez elle (métro Champ de Mars-Tour Eiffel) à l'appartement de Louise (métro Place Monge), elle prend la ligne 6 **direction** (*f.*) Nation (c'est **le terminus** de la ligne). Elle descend à La Motte-Picquet Grenelle pour prendre sa correspondance sur la ligne 10, direction Gare d'Austerlitz. Elle descend à Jussieu et prend la correspondance sur la ligne 7, direction Villejuif-Louis Aragon. Elle descend à **l'arrêt**° suivant pour aller à pied chez Louise. *stop*

En bus

Pour mieux° connaître les quartiers de la ville, on peut prendre **le bus**. Comme ça, on peut même **rencontrer**° des gens qui y habitent. Parfois, les embouteillages ralentissent° la circulation.

better / *meet* / *slow down*

En voiture

Il est **déconseillé**° de circuler en voiture. **Stationner**° dans la rue est souvent impossible, et les **parkings**° sont parfois **complets**.°

not advisable / *Parking* / *parking lots* / *full*

Activités

A. C'est le... Précisez le moyen ou les moyens de transport décrit(s) dans les phrases suivantes. Est-ce **aller à pied**, **le métro**, **le bus** ou **la voiture**?

1. Ce n'est pas un moyen de transport très rapide.
2. C'est un moyen de transport souterrain (*underground*).
3. Les stations ne sont pas loin les unes des autres.
4. Il est difficile de stationner dans la rue, et les parkings sont souvent complets.
5. Il faut repérer (*locate*) le terminus pour choisir sa direction.
6. C'est un moyen de transport agréable, mais pas pratique quand on est pressé.
7. Il est déconseillé de choisir ce moyen de transport pour circuler dans Paris.
8. Ils circulent jour et nuit.

B. Prenons le métro! Vous faites du tourisme à Paris et vous voulez voir les monuments principaux. Vous choisissez de vous déplacer (*to get around*) en métro. Consultez le plan du métro parisien et dites comment vous allez...

MODÈLE: de votre hôtel (métro Odéon) à la tour Eiffel (métro Bir-Hakeim)? Je prends la ligne 10, direction Boulogne-Pont de St-Cloud, et je descends à La Motte-Picquet Grenelle. Puis je prends la correspondance sur la ligne 6, direction Charles de Gaulle-Étoile. Je descends à la station Bir-Hakeim.

1. de la tour Eiffel (métro Bir-Hakeim) à l'Arc de Triomphe (métro Charles de Gaulle-Étoile)?
2. de l'Arc de Triomphe à Sacré-Cœur (métro Anvers)?
3. de Sacré-Cœur à la cathédrale Notre-Dame (métro Cité)?
4. de Notre-Dame au Louvre (métro Palais Royal-Musée du Louvre)?
5. du Louvre à votre hôtel (métro Odéon)?

Visionnement 1

Avant de visionner

La répétition. Parfois, la même idée est répétée dans une phrase sous des formes différentes. Il s'agit de paraphrases ou d'explications du mot-clé. Analysez les phrases suivantes. Les mots en *italique* ont le même sens ou renforcent le sens des mots en caractères **gras**. Que signifient les mots en italique?

1. CAMILLE: Regarde. Louise a gardé[a] cette photo **intacte**. Elle *ne l'a pas déchirée*, comme les autres.
2. CAMILLE: Elle aimait son mari. Elle l'a **toujours** aimé, *jusqu'à la fin de sa vie*.
3. MADO: J'avais 10 ou 11 ans. Un jour, à l'école, mes camarades *m'ont surnommée* la fille du traître. D'autres **disaient** la «fille du pourri[b]», la «fille du collabo».

[a]a... *kept* [b]*rotten pig*

Notez bien!

The word **traître** means *traitor*. Camille didn't know the rumors about her grandfather and never understood the reason for her mother's shame until recently.

Observez!

Dans cet épisode, Camille et Mado apprenent des détails importants sur la vie d'Antoine pendant la guerre. Pendant votre visionnement de l'Épisode 14, essayez de trouver les réponses aux questions suivantes.

- Qu'est-ce que Rachid a appris pendant son voyage?
- Qu'est-ce que Mado et Camille ont trouvé dans le coffret (*little box*) de Louise?
- À quel sujet Mado a-t-elle changé d'avis (*changed her mind*)?
- Qui a découpé les photos de Louise avec son mari? Pourquoi?

Vocabulaire relatif à l'épisode

la serrure	*latch*
verrouillé(e)	*locked*
Il faut chercher la vérité.	*We must look for the truth.*
en courant	*running*
des ciseaux	*scissors*

Après le visionnement

A. Un résumé. Complétez le résumé de l'Épisode 14 en mettant dans chaque cas un des deux verbes proposés au passé composé ou à l'imparfait.

Rachid revient de son voyage dans les Cévennes. Il y _____¹ (rencontrer,[a] rentrer) des gens intéressants, mais il _____² (ne rien apprendre, ne rien comprendre) sur le grand-père de Camille.

Plus tard, chez Mado, Camille _____³ (cacher,[b] trouver) un coffret qui _____⁴ (rendre, appartenir) à sa grand-mère. Dans ce coffret, Mado a découvert[c] les bijoux[d] de sa mère. Le coffret _____⁵ (contenir, vouloir) aussi

[a]*to meet, run into* [b]*to hide* [c]a... *discovered* [d]*jewelry*

Notez bien!

The verb **tenir** (*to hold*) is conjugated like **venir**.

je	**tiens**
tu	**tiens**
il, elle, on	**tient**
nous	**tenons**
vous	**tenez**
ils, elles	**tiennent**

Verbs like **tenir** are **appartenir** (*to belong to*), **contenir** (*to contain*), and **obtenir** (*to obtain, get*). All of these verbs use the auxiliary *avoir in the passé composé.*

une lettre d'Antoine. Il avait écrit[e] cette lettre en 1943, quand il _____[6] (travailler, habiter) dans les Cévennes, chez Pierre et Jeanne Leblanc.

Le coffret _____[7] (tenir, contenir) également une photo de Louise avec Antoine. Louise _____[8] (garder, mentir) cette photo intacte; elle _____[9] (ne pas la montrer, ne pas la déchirer[f]).

De toute façon,[g] ce n'était pas Louise qui avait découpé[h] les photos; c'était Mado. Pourquoi? Parce qu'à l'école, tout le monde l'_____[10] (acheter, appeler) la «fille du collabo». Elle _____[11] (avoir honte, avoir froid). Alors,[i] elle _____[12] (décider, savoir) de «tuer» son père en découpant les photos avec des ciseaux.

[e]avait... *had written* [f]*to rip up* [g]De... *In any case* [h]avait... *had cut up* [i]*So*

B. Réfléchissez. Répondez aux questions suivantes.

1. Au début, Mado n'a pas voulu entendre parler de son père. Maintenant, elle encourage Camille à trouver la vérité à son sujet. Selon vous, pourquoi Mado a-t-elle changé d'avis (*changed her mind*)? Est-ce à cause de la mort de sa mère? du contenu du coffret? de l'insistance de Camille?
2. Mado a voulu «tuer» son père en découpant ses photos. Est-ce que cette action l'a aidée à surmonter sa honte? Expliquez.

Structure 42

Tout comme adjectif et pronom

Expressing the idea of totality

—**Tout** va comme vous voulez?

L'adjectif *tout*

As an adjective, **tout** (*all, every, each, the whole, the entire*) is usually followed by an article (**le**, **un**, etc.), a possessive adjective (**mon**, **ton**, etc.), or a demonstrative adjective (**ce**, **cet**, **cette**, **ces**). Both **tout** and the word that follows it agree in gender and number with the noun they modify.

As-tu visité **tout** le village?	*Did you see the whole village?*
Louise a passé **toute** la guerre à Paris.	*Louise spent the entire war in Paris.*
Et il a disparu de **tous** les albums?	*And he disappeared from all the albums?*
L'historien a cherché dans **toutes** les archives.	*The historian looked in all the archives.*

Le pronom *tout*

In the singular, the pronoun **tout** (*everything*) is an indefinite pronoun. If used as a direct object in the **passé composé**, **tout** is placed between the auxiliary and the past participle.

Tout va comme vous voulez?	*Is everything as you wish?*
Camille a **tout** compris.	*Camille understood everything.*

In the plural, **tous** and **toutes** (*all* [*of them*], *every one, each one*) refer to something or someone specific. The pronoun agrees in gender with the noun it replaces.

Tous les reportages de Rachid sont bien préparés.	*All of Rachid's reports are well prepared.*
Tous sont bien préparés.	*All of them are well prepared.*
Louise a gardé toutes les lettres.	*Louise kept all of the letters.*
Louise les a **toutes** gardées.	*Louise kept all of them.*

Attention—Whereas **tous** has a silent **s** when it is an adjective, the **s** is pronounced in the pronoun.

Tou~~s~~ mes amis aiment la télé.	*All my friends like TV.*
but **Tous** aiment la télé.	*All* (*of them*) *like TV.*

Pour en savoir plus...

Tout can also be used as an adverb to mean *entirely, completely, very, quite, so.* The **tout** form is used in most cases, but **toute** or **toutes** is used before a feminine adjective that begins with a consonant sound.

Rachid semble **tout** content. *Rachid seems quite happy.*

Yasmine est **tout** heureuse aussi. *Yasmine is quite happy too.*

Oui, mon cher ami, **tout** simplement. *Yes, my dear friend, very simply.*

but

Toute petite, à l'âge de 7 ou 8 ans… *(When I was) Very little, about 7 or 8 years old…*

Camille à Mado: «Tu as l'air **toute** pâle.» *Camille to Mado: "You look so pale."*

Elles sont **toutes** folles! *They are completely crazy!*

The expression **tout à fait** means *completely.*

Activités

A. Souvenirs de Louise. Une vieille amie de Louise raconte le jour de son mariage avec Antoine. Complétez l'histoire en mettant **tout** aux formes appropriées.

Oui, elle était heureuse. ______[1] ses amis et ______[2] sa famille étaient là, et elle savait qu'Antoine l'aimait de ______[3] son cœur. Ils avaient ______[4] leur vie devant eux et leurs amis voulaient les féliciter.[a] ______[5] sont venus leur dire «au revoir» à la gare quand ils sont partis en voyage de noces.[b] ______[6] était vraiment parfait.

[a]*to congratulate* [b]voyage… *honeymoon*

B. La vie change. Utilisez une forme du pronom **tout** pour montrer comment l'histoire de Camille évolue.

MODÈLE: Avant, aucune des femmes dans la famille ne parlait d'Antoine.
Maintenant, toutes parlent d'Antoine.

1. Avant, Mado ne voulait rien savoir sur son père.
2. Avant, Camille ne comprenait rien de l'attitude de sa mère.
3. Avant, aucun des amis de Camille ne l'aidait avec ses recherches.
4. Avant, rien n'était clair dans l'histoire des photos découpées.
5. Avant, Camille ne pouvait rien dire à sa mère.
6. Avant, Mado ne voyait (*saw*) rien dans le coffret de Louise.

C. Des contrôleurs tout différents. (*Very different conductors.*) M. Diop, un contrôleur, fait très bien son travail, mais son collègue, M. Dupré, est tout à fait différent. Remplacez les mots en italique avec une expression avec **tout**, **toute**, **tous** ou **toutes** pour montrer ces différences.

MODÈLE: M. Dupré *ne parle pas aux gens.*
M. Diop parle à tous les gens.

1. M. Dupré *ne regarde aucun billet.*
2. M. Dupré *n'aide pas les vieilles dames* avec leurs valises.
3. M. Dupré *ne connaît aucune des gares* à Paris.
4. M. Dupré *ne passe pas son temps* avec ses collègues.
5. Hier, M. Dupré *n'a pas dit aux touristes* où ils pouvaient trouver les composteurs.
6. L'autre jour, M. Dupré *n'a rien compris* quand on lui a parlé en anglais.
7. M. Dupré *n'a aucune chance* de promotion.

D. Tu exagères! Vous voulez provoquer une dispute en parlant des stéréotypes. Avec votre partenaire, utilisez une forme de l'adjectif **tout** pour exagérer les caractéristiques des groupes suivants. Votre partenaire va vous contredire. Suivez (*Follow*) le modèle en utilisant seulement des phrases affirmatives.

Adjectifs utiles:

beau / laid
calme / nerveux
discret / indiscret
grand / petit
heureux / malheureux
intéressant / ennuyeux
jeune (*young*) / vieux
lent / rapide
malhonnête (*dishonest*) / honnête
méchant (*mean*) / sympathique
pauvre (*poor*) / riche
ridicule / élégant
snob / ouvert d'esprit (*open-minded*)
stupide / intelligent

MODÈLE: É1: Tous les professeurs sont méchants!
É2: Mais non, tous sont sympas.

1. les hommes
2. les femmes
3. les enfants
4. les personnes âgées
5. les avocats
6. les journalistes

Structure 43

Le participe présent

Expressing manner and simultaneity

—Moi, j'ai eu honte. Je suis partie en **courant**.

La forme du participe présent

To form the present participle, remove the **-ons** ending from the **nous** form of the present tense and add **-ant.**

sort~~ons~~	→	+ ant	→	**sortant**
lis~~ons~~	→	+ ant	→	**lisant**

En **sortant** de la gare, Rachid a souri à Camille. — *Coming out of the station, Rachid smiled at Camille.*

Mado était au bord des larmes en **lisant** la lettre. — *Mado was on the verge of tears as she read the letter.*

There are only three irregular present participles.

avoir → **ayant**   être → **étant**   savoir → **sachant**

En **ayant** de la patience, Camille va découvrir la vérité. — *By having patience, Camille will discover the truth.*

Est-ce qu'elle va être plus contente en la **sachant**? — *Will she be happier knowing it?*

L'usage du participe présent

1. The present participle, when preceded by the preposition **en**, is used

   - to tell how someone does something.

     Je suis partie **en courant**. — *I took off at a run.*

     C'est **en écoutant** qu'on apprend le plus. — *It is by listening that one learns the most.*

- to express a circumstance or an action that happens at the same time or immediately before or after another.

Il grommelle **en s'éloignant**.	*He grumbles as he walks away.*
En ouvrant son sac, elle en sort une photo.	*Opening her purse, she takes out a photo.*

2. When a present participle takes an object pronoun, the pronoun precedes the participle. This includes the pronouns of pronominal verbs.

Bruno retient l'homme **en l'interrogeant** à nouveau.	*Bruno stops the man, asking him more questions.*
En s'embrassant, Rachid et Sonia ont rassuré leur fille.	*With a kiss, Rachid and Sonia reassured their daughter.*

Activités

A. Dans l'appartement de Louise. Après la mort de Louise, Camille a mis les affaires en ordre dans l'appartement. Parlez de ce qu'elle a fait en mettant le participe présent du verbe entre parenthèses à la place indiquée.

1. Camille est entrée dans l'appartement en _____ tristement à sa grand-mère. (penser)
2. Elle a écouté les disques (*records*) de sa grand-mère tout en _____ que cela (*that*) allait la rendre triste. (savoir)
3. En _____ la chanson «Mon Amant de Saint-Jean», elle a pensé à son grand-père. (entendre)
4. Elle a préparé une tasse de café en _____ encore de Louise. (se souvenir)
5. En _____ son café, elle a cassé une tasse en porcelaine. (faire)
6. Elle a pensé au dîner avec Louise en _____ son café. (boire)
7. En _____ dans la chambre de Louise, elle a senti le parfum de sa grand-mère. (aller)
8. Elle a regardé, en _____, une robe de sa grand-mère. (pleurer [*to cry*])
9. Elle a trouvé le coffret de Louise en _____ dans le placard (*cupboard*). (chercher)
10. Tout en _____ envie de l'ouvrir (*open it*), elle a décidé d'attendre. (avoir)
11. Elle a quitté l'appartement en _____ doucement la porte. (fermer [*to close*])
12. En _____ à l'appartement, elle a tout de suite vu le coffret et a décidé de l'ouvrir. (rentrer)

B. Histoires de voyages. Utilisez **en** + participe présent pour lier (*combine*) ces deux phrases de façon logique. Utilisez un pronom complément si nécessaire.

MODÈLE: Nous attendions l'arrivée du train. Nous avons rencontré un ami d'enfance. →
En attendant l'arrivée du train, nous avons rencontré un ami d'enfance. (Nous avons rencontré un ami d'enfance en attendant l'arrivée du train.)

1. Nous avons perdu nos valises. Nous les avons laissées dans le taxi. **2.** Paul a quitté l'autoroute à la sortie 23. Il s'est perdu. **3.** J'ai réservé une place dans le train. J'ai téléphoné à l'avance. **4.** Anne roulait trop vite pendant les heures de pointe. Elle a eu un accident de voiture. **5.** Abdul a pris une très bonne décision. Il a choisi une place dans le wagon non-fumeurs. **6.** Le douanier (*customs official*) nous a rendu nos passeports. Il a dit «Passez». **7.** Diane a composté son billet. Elle l'a mis dans le composteur.

C. En même temps. Avec votre partenaire, parlez des activités que les gens peuvent faire en même temps et des choses qu'ils ne doivent pas faire en même temps. Utilisez les sujets et les verbes donnés.

MODÈLE: on / manger →
On peut manger en regardant la télévision. On ne doit pas manger en conduisant (*driving*).

1. les étudiants / faire leurs devoirs
2. une étudiante / étudier
3. un professeur / noter (*to grade*) les examens
4. un jeune homme / marcher (*to walk*) dans la rue
5. je / travailler
6. on / ?

Regards sur la culture

Les transports et la société

When Rachid tells Camille how to get to Saint-Jean de Causse, he assumes that she will take the train, not drive there. Even in the area of transportation, French cultural attitudes differ greatly from those of North Americans.

- In France, nearly everyone uses the train. Although the network of rail lines has diminished since World War II, with many smaller and out-of-the-way places now linked to the rest of France by bus, people can get to most places quickly and easily by rail. The **Société nationale des chemins de fer français** (SNCF) is a public service known for its efficiency.

Le Train à Grande Vitesse (TGV)

- The **SNCF** is also known for its advanced technology. The **TGV** is a model of modern rail technology. In fact, Amtrak's high-speed train Acela, introduced in late 2000 on the East Coast, uses an electric propulsion system developed for the TGV. Designed by the French, the trains were built by a company in Quebec, Bombardier, which also invented the snowmobile.

- The **SNCF** is one of the leading employers in France. It also has one of the largest budgetary deficits of any French organization, but no government administration would dream of radically cutting rail services in order to balance the budget. Transportation is one of the services that the French expect from the government in return for their taxes.
- For many years, French experts downplayed the need for limited-access highways—**les autoroutes**. The Ministry of Transportation wanted to promote train travel and discourage long-distance car and truck use; this is one reason for the long delays in the development of the **autoroute** system in France as compared with Germany or Italy, for example. Although the attitude has changed in recent years, many large cities are still not linked to nearby urban areas by **autoroute**.
- The French sometimes find the North American atittude toward the automobile peculiar. They are surprised that people may prefer to live far from their place of work, take the car for the slightest errand, and often treat their cars with something akin to affection.
- In French cities, modes of transportation vary. There is a subway system—**le métro**—in cities such as Paris, Toulouse, Lyon, and Marseille. The Paris **métro**, opened in 1900, is famous for its completeness and ease of use. Its Art Nouveau entryways are considered artistic masterpieces.
- Most French cities did away with their tram lines in the 1950s, and bus transportation became the norm. Today, bus service is usually extensive and efficient in French cities. Like the trains, the buses often run at a deficit but are nonetheless considered an essential public service.
- In recent years, many French cities have reintroduced tram lines (**les tramways**), partly for ecological reasons, because trams do not pollute the way buses do. Lyon reintroduced the tram in 2000, and several other French cities, including Bordeaux, have plans to do the same thing by 2005.

Une entrée de métro à Paris

Considérez

In what ways do French cultural attitudes toward transportation differ from those in North America? Why did the automobile replace other forms of transportation in North America so much more than in Europe? How do you feel about government support for and control over transportation systems?

Structure 44

Les prépositions avec les noms géographiques

Locating places and people

—Ben, tu vas jusqu'à Alès. **À Alès**, tu loues une voiture et tu montes dans la montagne.

You already learned in Chapter 3 how to express where people come from. This section reviews that information and also tells you how to express where people live and where they go.

Le genre des lieux géographiques

1. First of all, you need to be able to tell whether place names are masculine or feminine.
   - Most continents are feminine: **l'Afrique**, **l'Europe**, **l'Asie**, **l'Australie**, **l'Amérique du Nord**, **l'Amérique du Sud**. *But* **l'Antarctique** (*m.*).
   - Countries, states, and provinces that end in **-e** are feminine: **l'Algérie**, **l'Allemagne**, **l'Angleterre**, **la Caroline-du-Nord**, **la Chine**, **l'Espagne**, **la Floride**, **la France**, **la Louisiane**, **la Nouvelle-Écosse** (*Nova Scotia*), **Terre-Neuve** (*Newfoundland*), **la Virginie-Occidentale** (*West Virginia*), etc. One major exception is **le Mexique**.
   - Countries, states, and provinces that end in other letters are masculine: **le Canada**, **les États-Unis**, **le Japon**, **le Québec**, **le Texas**, **le Viêtnam**, etc.
2. When used as the subject of a sentence or as object of a verb such as **visiter** or **quitter**, place names need the correct definite article. Two exceptions are **Israël** and **Terre-Neuve**, which have no article. Most city names do not have an article either, but if a city name begins with a definite article, you should include it (the article is capitalized).

   Marseilles, **Lyon** et **Le Havre** sont de grandes villes en France.

   L'été prochain, je vais visiter **le Québec**.

   La France a une longue histoire, mais **Israël** est un pays assez jeune.

   L'Asie est un continent qui a aussi un passé riche.

D'où venez-vous?

To express where a person comes *from* or is arriving *from,* use **de**.

1. For cities, for continents, and for countries, states, and provinces that are feminine or that start with a vowel sound, use **de** or **d'**.*

    Hélène arrive **de** Montréal et Ian arrive **de** Nouvelle-Écosse. Ils viennent **d'**Amérique du Nord.

    Camille et Bruno viennent **de** France, **de** Paris exactement.

    Ce reporter vient **d'**Israël.

2. For masculine countries, states, or provinces, and for plural countries, **de** forms a contraction with the article.

    Le père de Rachid vient **du** Maroc. Mon père vient **des** États-Unis.

Où habitez-vous? Où êtes-vous? Où allez-vous?

To express the idea of *in, at,* or *to,* the preposition depends on the gender of the place name that follows it.

1. For cities, use **à**.

    Hélène habite **à** Montréal.†

    Camille habite **à** Paris.

2. For continents, and for countries, states, and provinces that are feminine or that start with a vowel sound, use **en**.

    Hélène arrive **en** Europe en avion. Elle fait un reportage **en** France.

    Le reporter qui vient de Jerusalem rentre **en** Israël.

3. For masculine countries, states, or provinces, and for plural countries, use **à** and form a contraction with the article.

    Hélène habite **au** Canada. Elle n'habite pas **aux** États-Unis.

	On vient... On arrive...	**On habite... On va...**
continent	de	en
pays / état / province féminins	de	en
pays / état / province masculins qui commence par une voyelle ou h muet	de	en
pays / état / province masculins qui commence par une consonne	du	au
pays pluriel	des	aux
ville	de	à

*City names that include an article include **Le Caire**, **Le Havre**, **La Nouvelle-Orléans**, **La Haye**. Always use the article with these names and form a contraction when necessary: *Elle vient **de La** Nouvelle-Orléans. Il vient **du** Havre.*

†Again, city names that contain a definite article must include the article or a contraction: *Elle va **à La** Nouvelle-Orléans. Il va **au** Havre.*

Activités

Voyages Internationaux

12 PRIX BAS ÉTÉ 2002

BRÉSIL 1178,63 €
CANADA 654,01 €
CHINE 1044,28 €
ÉGYPTE 525,95 €
ISRAËL 685,05 €
MADRID 129,58 €
MEXIQUE 1065,62 €
PORTUGAL 278,98 €
THAÏLANDE 745,48 €
TUNISIE 318,62 €
TURQUIE 320,14 €
FLORIDE 593,03 €

A. Destinations. Quel est le prix d'un voyage à chaque pays mentionné dans cette brochure?

MODÈLE: On paie 525,95 euros pour visiter l'Égypte.

B. Villes, pays et continents. Dans quel pays et sur quel continent se trouvent les villes suivantes? Regardez les cartes dans votre livre pour les villes que vous ne connaissez pas.
Pays utiles: Algérie, Belgique, Côte-d'Ivoire, États-Unis, Guyane, Laos, Mali, Maroc, Sénégal, Suisse

MODÈLE: Tombouctou → Tombouctou se trouve au Mali. C'est en Afrique.

1. Abidjan
2. Alger
3. Berne
4. Bruxelles
5. Casablanca
6. Cayenne
7. Dakar
8. La Nouvelle-Orléans

C. C'est logique. Faites une phrase avec les éléments donnés. Ensuite, utilisez un des verbes et un des pays donnés pour expliquer chaque situation. Attention aux temps des verbes!

Verbes utiles: aller, arriver, partir, venir, visiter

Pays et états utiles: Allemagne, Angleterre, Chine, Espagne, États-Unis, Japon, Maroc, Mexique, Texas

MODÈLE: Marta / danser / le flamenco. Elle...
Marta danse le flamenco. Elle vient d'Espagne.

1. l'avion de Paul / quitter / Denver International Airport. Paul...
2. la semaine dernière, Nadia / acheter / un beau livre en arabe. Elle...
3. dans 10 minutes, le train de Martin / rentrer/ dans la gare de Berlin. Martin...
4. Yoko / naître / Tokyo en 1980. Elle...
5. Catherine / naître / Dallas en 1977. Elle...
6. le mois dernier, Abdul /monter / sur une pyramide maya. Il...
7. Karine / regarder / Big Ben la semaine prochaine. Elle...

D. Vos voyages. Avec votre partenaire, discutez des voyages que vous avez faits et de ceux (*those*) que vous voulez faire un jour. Parlez de ce que vous avez fait pendant vos voyages et de ce que vous voulez faire pendant votre voyage de rêve (*dream*). Utilisez les éléments suivants pour vous inspirer.

VERBES	ENDROITS
aller	un continent
explorer	un état ou une province
partir	un monument
rester	un musée
visiter	un pays
voyager	un site touristique
	une ville

Visionnement 2

Avant de visionner

La gare de Lyon. In this episode, Rachid comes back to Paris with his report on Saint-Jean de Causse. Because he has been in the Cévennes, he comes into the **gare de Lyon**, where the trains from southeastern France arrive. The following map shows the area around this train station. Just across the Seine is the **gare d'Austerlitz**, named for a great victory in the Napoleonic wars. This is the station that serves southwestern France (Bordeaux, the Pyrenees, the Basque Country, etc.). You may recall from Chapter 1 that the **gare d'Austerlitz** is close to the **Jardin des Plantes** and Yasmine's school. Just to the north of the **gare de Lyon** is the **place de la Bastille**, former site of the infamous prison. Visitors to the square today see a monument to the July Revolution of 1830 and the new buildings of the **Opéra Bastille**. The outline of the now demolished Bastille is inscribed in the pavement of the square. South of the **gare de Lyon** is the **Ministère de l'Économie, des Finances et de l'Industrie**, one of the last great public building projects of the 20th century in Paris. In Chapter 2, you saw that Canal 7 is located not too far away, just down the right bank of the Seine, beyond the city limits.

Maintenant, regardez le plan à la page 322, et donnez le nom du bâtiment célèbre (*famous*) qui est en question dans les phrases suivantes.

1. Sylvie veut aller à Lourdes dans les Pyrénées. Vers quel bâtiment doit-elle aller?
2. Philippe veut voir *Carmen*. Vers quel bâtiment doit-il aller?
3. Bruno et Camille vont des Studios Canal 7 à la gare de Lyon. Quel bâtiment vont-ils voir en route?
4. Rachid va de la gare de Lyon à l'école de sa fille. Quel bâtiment va-t-il voir en route?
5. Hélène va de la gare de Lyon à la place de la Bastille. Quel bâtiment moderne va-t-elle voir en passant?

Les environs de la gare de Lyon

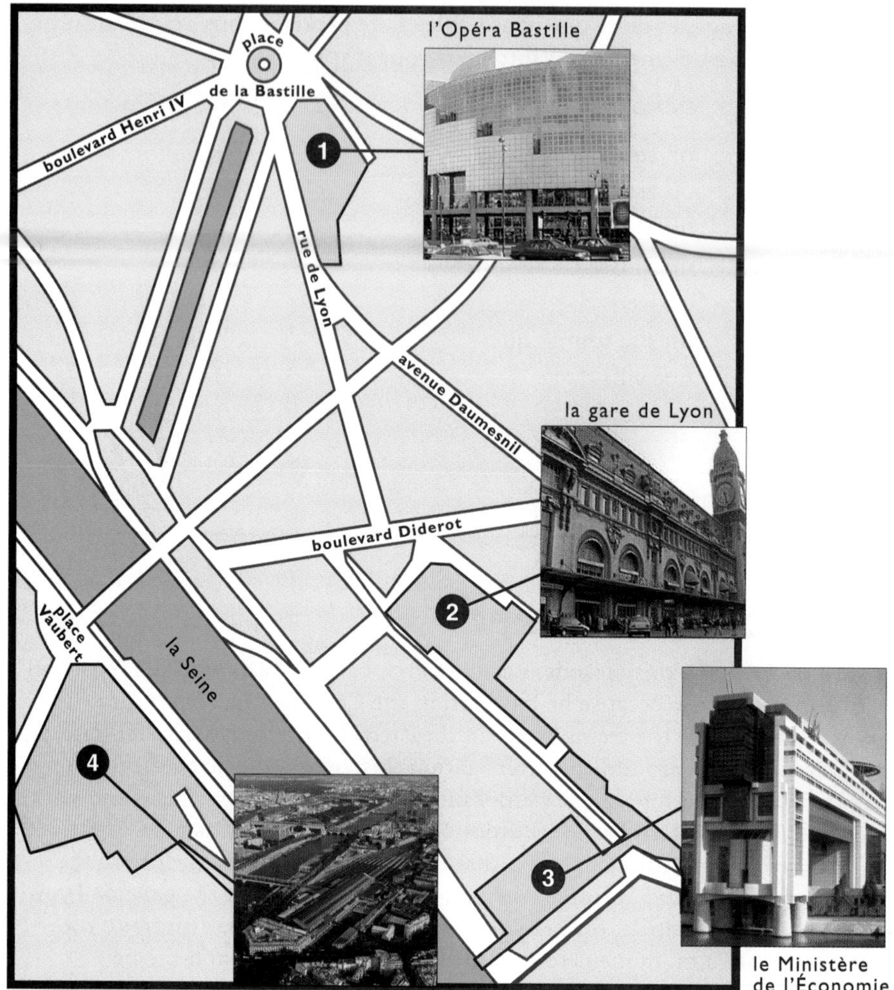

Observez!

Considérez les aspects culturels expliqués dans **Regards sur la culture**. Ensuite, regardez l'Épisode 14 encore une fois, et répondez aux questions suivantes.

- Quand Camille voit Rachid à la gare après son retour à Paris, il semble reposé et de bonne humeur. Que peut-on en conclure sur la qualité du service des trains en France?
- Enfant, Mado a été tourmentée par ses camarades à cause de son père. Que peut-on en conclure sur l'attitude des Français vis-à-vis des collaborateurs après la guerre?

Après le visionnement

Faites l'activité pour le **Visionnement 2** dans le cahier.

Synthèse: Lecture

Mise en contexte

During World War II, many soldiers sought penpals as a way of relieving the rigors of military life. These **correspondantes** provided comfort and support to men who were separated from their families and who risked their lives daily. As the penpals became acquainted, they began to address each other as **marraine** (*godmother*) and **filleul** (*godson*). These terms were simply signs of friendship and did not denote any family relationship.

In 1939, Yolande Pelletier, an 18-year-old Québécoise, began a correspondence with Carmen Pischella, a sailor from Corsica. After Yolande's death many years later, her daughter, Claudette Pelletier Deschênes, found Carmen's letters. You will be reading a few excerpts from them.

Mise en scène

Skim the following introduction to the letters. It is written by Yolande's daughter. What parallels do you see between her discovery of these letters and Camille's discovery of Antoine's letter in Episode 14. What parallels are there between Carmen and Antoine and their circumstances?

«Je savais depuis mon enfance que maman avait un correspondant pendant la guerre 39–45, j'ai toujours été curieuse de savoir les secrets que ces lettres contenaient. Maman gardait précieusement toutes les lettres de cet ami lointain[a] et elle nous refusait toujours la permission de les lire. Elle les gardait cachées et sous clé, pour une raison qu'elle ne nous a jamais dévoilée.[b] Nous pensions qu'elle considérait probablement ces lettres comme des lettres d'amour. … Quelques mois avant sa mort en 1983, elle a donné à ma nièce Julie un petit coffret de cèdre[c] contenant ses précieuses lettres avec l'instruction de les conserver en bon état.»

[a]*faraway* [b]ne… *never revealed to us* [c]coffret… *cedar box*

Stratégie pour mieux lire
Anticipating content

What kinds of information would you expect to find in the first letters from a penpal—name, address, age? What else? What other details? What might the person write about later? As you read, see if you accurately predicted the contents of Carmen's letters.

Marraine de Guerre

*Correspondance d'un matelot[1] corse à une jeune Canadienne pendant la Deuxième Guerre mondiale**

TOULON, le 18 mars 1939
Chère mademoiselle,

À présent je vais passer à ce qui vous préoccupe fort[2]: ma description. Je viens d'avoir, il y a douze jours, vingt ans et demi. Je ne suis pas originaire de Toulon, ville que vous ne connaissez pas, mais d'Ajaccio qui est plus petit mais dont vous devez certainement avoir entendu parler[3] comme ville où est né Napoléon Bonaparte.

J'ai eu ma première partie du Baccalauréat, je connais l'anglais assez passablement pour pouvoir l'écrire, avec quelques fautes, et me faire comprendre.[4] Je parle et j'écris parfaitement l'italien étant Corse et l'ayant étudié durant sept ans d'études secondaires.

J'ai encore deux ans et dix mois à faire dans la marine nationale, qui en France est la base de toute carrière civile.

J'oubliais de vous dire que je mesure en hauteur un mètre soixante et onze centimètres.

Je repars mardi prochain en Espagne où nous faisons le contrôle des armes[5] et d'où nous serons de retour[6] le vingt.

Amicalement,
Carmen

TOULON, le 7 mai 1939
Chère mademoiselle,

J'ai reçu votre gentille lettre le vingt-quatre avril, alors que j'étais bien loin de France où nous ne sommes rentrés que ce matin dimanche sept mai.

[1]*sailor* [2]*greatly* [3]dont... *of which you must have heard* [4]me... *make myself understood* [5]contrôle... *arms inspection* [6]serons... *will be back*

*Ces lettres représentent des extraits (*extracts*) de la correspondance entre Carmen et Yolande. Étant donné l'étendue (*given the length*) de la correspondance, on n'a pas pu reproduire le texte intégral.

Vous devez avoir appris par le journal que les événements étaient très graves en Europe, particulièrement entre la France et notre ennemie de toujours, l'Allemagne. Pour cette raison on nous envoie à Gibraltar qui est la porte de la Méditerranée, pour que, au cas où il se produirait quelque chose[7] nous soyons[8] prêts à en interdire l'entrée ou la sortie.[9] C'est pour cela seul que je vous fais réponse treize jours en retard. ...

Je vous serre cordialement la main.
Carmen

AJACCIO, le 16 avril 1940
Chère Marraine,
Il fait un temps splendide, le soleil brille à longueur de journée, demain ou après demain j'irai[10] avec quelques amis à la pêche puis nous ferons[11] une bonne bouillabaisse sur les rochers. Sais-tu ce qu'est la bouillabaisse? C'est une soupe de poisson mais il faut[12] savoir la préparer et comme cuisine je ne sais faire que cela, je suis certain que si tu sais ce que c'est, l'eau t'en viendra à la bouche,[13] rien que d'y penser.[14] ...
en t'embrassant bien affectueusement. Carmen

[.....], le 12 novembre 1942
Très chère amie,

Ces quelques mots pour te dire que je suis encore vivant et en très excellente santé.

Où je suis? Sur le paquebot[15] «Ville d'Ajaccio» comme timonier signaleur,[16] depuis deux mois. Je pense que tu as entendu parler et que tu te seras même beaucoup intéressée[17] à la libération de la Corse, j'étais à Ajaccio à ce moment là et j'y ai participé.[18]

Et toi que deviens-tu? Peut-être es-tu mariée à l'heure actuelle, si oui je te souhaite[19] tout le bonheur que tu désires et tu le sais, c'est sincère. J'écris quand même à ton adresse de jeune fille[20] et j'espère que la lettre te parviendra.[21]

Je vais te quitter en espérant une prompte réponse et t'embrassant bien, bien fort. Ton petit. Carmen

[7]*pour... so that in case something happens* [8]*would be* [9]*à... we are ready to forbid entrance or exit to it (the Mediterranean)* [10]*will go* [11]*will make* [12]*it's necessary to* [13]*l'eau... your mouth will water* [14]*rien... just to think of it* [15]*ocean liner* [16]*timonier... helmsman-signaler* [17]*tu... you will have even been very interested* [18]*j'y... I participated in it* [19]*je... I wish you* [20]*de... unmarried* [21]*will reach*

Après la lecture

A. Avez-vous bien anticipé? Quels éléments anticipés avez-vous trouvés dans les lettres du matelot? Quels autres thèmes avez-vous découverts? Donnez les renseignements (*information*) que vous avez trouvés.

1. son nom **2.** son adresse **3.** son âge **4.** autres thèmes que vous avez anticipés **5.** autres thèmes que vous n'avez pas anticipés. Nommez-en trois (*Name three of them*) si possible.

Maintenant, décrivez le matelot en résumant les renseignements qu'il a donnés à Yolande dans ses lettres.

B. L'éducation sentimentale. Quels détails dans ces lettres indiquent que les deux correspondants deviennent de plus en plus intimes?

C. L'histoire. Quels faits historiques sont mentionnés dans les lettres? Quel rôle Carmen a-t-il joué dans ces événements?

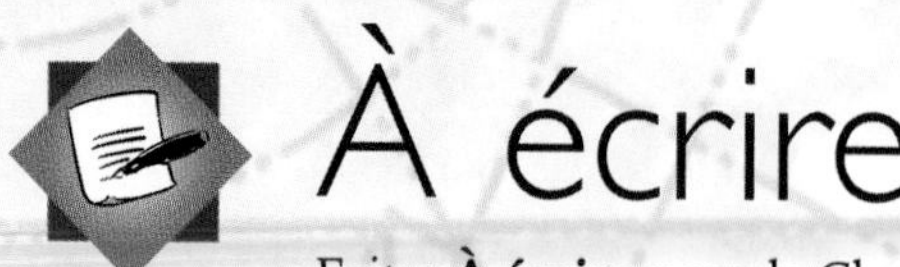

À écrire

Faites **À écrire** pour le Chapitre 14 dans le cahier.

Vocabulaire

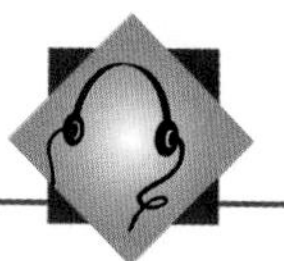

Pour voyager

un billet (aller simple, aller-retour)	(one-way, round trip) ticket	**circuler**	to get around
un endroit	place, location	**passer la douane**	to go through customs
un(e) passager/ère	passenger	**prendre une correspondance**	to transfer
une place	(*reserved*) seat		
un siège (couloir, fenêtre)	(aisle, window) seat		
à pied	on foot		

MOTS APPARENTÉS: **une arrivée, un départ, un passeport, une valise, un visa**

PRÉPOSITIONS À REVOIR: **à, de, en**

Pour voyager en train

une gare	train station	**un wagon (fumeurs, non-fumeurs)**	(smoking, nonsmoking) train car
un quai	platform	**composter**	to punch (*a ticket*)
un train à grande vitesse (*fam.* **un TGV**)	high-speed train		

MOT APPARENTÉ: **un train**

Pour voyager en avion

un avion	airplane	**un vol**	flight
une porte d'embarquement	gate	**enregistrer (une valise)**	to check (a suitcase)

MOT APPARENTÉ: **un aéroport**

Pour voyager en métro et en bus

un arrêt	(*station*) stop	**le métro**	subway
un autocar	(*long distance, tour*) bus	**un réseau (du métro)**	(subway) system, network
un bus	(*short distance, city*) bus		
un guichet	ticket window		

MOTS APPARENTÉS: **la direction, un terminus**

Pour voyager en voiture

la circulation	traffic	**complet/ète**	full
un embouteillage	traffic jam	**louer**	to rent
les heures (*f.*) **de pointe**	rush hour	**stationner**	to park
la limite de vitesse	speed limit		
une sortie	exit		

MOTS APPARENTÉS: **une autoroute, une route**
À REVOIR: **un parking**

Substantifs

un moyen	means; method; mode	**un(e) traître / traîtresse**	traitor

Adjectifs

plusieurs	several	**tout (toute, tous, toutes)**	all, every, the whole
pressé(e)	in a hurry		

Pronoms

tout	everything	**tous, toutes**	all (of them)

Verbes

appartenir	to belong to	**obtenir**	to obtain
contenir	to contain	**rencontrer**	to meet; to run into
déconseiller	to advise against	**tenir**	to hold

Les continents

l'Afrique (*f.*), **l'Amérique** (*f.*) **du Nord, l'Amérique** (*f.*) **du Sud, l'Antarctique** (*m.*), **l'Asie** (*f.*), **l'Australie** (*f.*), **l'Europe** (*f.*)

Un pays

Israël

Chapitre 15

Une piste!°

°Une... *A lead!*

OBJECTIFS

In this episode, you will

- find out what Rachid learned in Saint-Jean de Causse
- learn more about Rachid's and Sonia's backgrounds

In this chapter, you will

- talk about popular foods in various parts of the world
- talk about countries and nationalities
- talk about everyday activities
- use the pronouns **y** and **en** to refer to places and things
- read about how immigration has affected French culture

Vocabulaire en contexte

La cuisine maghrébine*

Voici **un** bon **couscous maghrébin** et ses ingrédients.

DES ÉPICES° (*f.*) ET DES CONDIMENTS — *spices*

la cannelle	cinnamon
la coriandre	coriander
le persil	parsley
le/la quatre-épices	allspice

Mettre le coucous dans le couscoussier° et **faire cuire à la vapeur**° pendant 15 minutes.
Dans l'évier,° **verser**° sur le couscous 1 litre d'eau.
Laisser égoutter° pendant 15 minutes.
Ensuite verser le coucous dans un très grand plat creux.°
Ajouter° une cuillère à café de sel et 2 cuillères à soupe d'huile et **mélanger.**°
Laisser reposer 20 minutes.

couscous cooker
faire... steam
kitchen sink / pour
drain
plat... deep dish
Add
mix

Pour lire **une recette,**° les termes suivants sont aussi utiles. — *recipe*

une casserole	saucepan
couvrir	to cover
faire bouillir	to boil
faire cuire (quelque chose) **au four**	to bake
faire frire	to fry
(ré)chauffer	to (re)heat

*Le terme **le Maghreb** et l'adjectif **maghrébin(e)** se réfèrent aux pays de l'Afrique du Nord: principalement le Maroc, l'Algérie et la Tunisie.

Activités

A. Quels ingrédients? En utilisant le vocabulaire presenté, ainsi que (*as well as*) d'autres mots que vous connaissez, identifiez les ingrédients principaux dans les plats suivants.

MODÈLE: un ragoût (*stew*) de bœuf →
Dans un ragoût de bœuf, on met du bœuf, des pommes de terre, des carottes, des oignons...

1. une salade (du chef) **2.** une pizza **3.** une soupe aux légumes **4.** une omelette **5.** des crudités (*raw vegetables*)

B. Méthodes de cuisson. (*Cooking methods.*) Identifiez la méthode de cuisson pour les plats suivants.

MODÈLE: des spaghettis → On fait bouillir les spaghettis.

1. des frites **2.** une tarte **3.** du riz **4.** un hamburger **5.** une pizza **6.** des brocolis

C. Une recette. Dites à la classe le nom de votre plat favori. Les autres étudiants vont vous poser des questions sur les ingrédients, la préparation, etc. Ensuite, plusieurs étudiants vont donner leur opinion sur ce plat.

MODÈLE: VOUS: Mon plat favori, c'est la soupe à l'oignon.
LA CLASSE: Quels sont les ingrédients principaux? Comment est-ce qu'on prépare cette soupe? Est-ce que tu manges ce plat au petit déjeuner, au déjeuner ou au dîner? Cela a l'air délicieux / trop piquant / immangeable.

Spécialités du monde entier

Vallée du Kashmir
Visitez le Pakistan et l'Inde!
spécialités pakistanaises et indiennes
Tandoori au charbon de bois
Agneau,[a] poulet ou crevettes
dans une sauce curry
Riz basmati
Menu 9€ (midi seulement), 15€/25€.
Carte environ 12€/16€.
Ouvert 7/7. Service jusqu'à 23 h 30.
3, place de Vauban (7e)
01.45.85.86.73

Les Pakistanais et les Indiens aiment **le curry**, **le yaourt**, **les lentilles** (*f.*) et **la cardamome**.

La citronnelle[d] et la coriandre sont très populaires au Viêtnam. Les Chinois aiment **la sauce de soja**, **le gingembre**,[e] l'oignon vert et l'huile de sésame.

[a]*lamb* [b]Canard... *Peking duck* [c]*prawns* [d]*lemongrass* [e]*ginger*

La cuisine russe utilise **les betteraves**[g] (*f.*), les pommes de terre, **les champignons**[h] (*m.*) et la crème fraîche.

Les Italiens aiment **les pâtes**[i] (*f. pl.*) de toutes sortes, les courgettes, les tomates, le poisson et **l'ail**[j] (*m.*).

AUTRES CUISINES ET INGRÉDIENTS TYPIQUES

israélienne: les pois chiches, les salades, **le pain pita**

thaïlandaise: les **cacahouètes**[k] (*f.*), la **noix de coco**,[l] les pâtes

[f] *candles* [g] *beets* [h] *mushrooms* [i] *pasta* [j] *garlic* [k] *peanuts* [l] noix… *coconut*

Activités

A. Des ingrédients. Voici des ingrédients propres à (*characteristic of*) certaines cuisines nationales. Identifiez la nationalité et le pays.

MODÈLE: la coriandre →
C'est la cuisine maghrébine. Elle vient du Maroc ou de l'Algérie.
(*ou* C'est la cuisine vietnamienne. Elle vient du Viêtnam.)

1. les lentilles **2.** la citronnelle **3.** le gingembre **4.** le curry **5.** les pâtes **6.** les pois chiches **7.** la sauce de soja **8.** le yaourt **9.** les betteraves

B. Présentez-vous! Décrivez-vous à la classe. Parlez de la nationalité de votre famille et de vos préférences alimentaires. Avez-vous des talents culinaires?

MODÈLE: Je m'appelle Thomas Trauth. Mes parents sont d'origine italienne et allemande,* mais je suis américain. J'aime la cuisine italienne parce que j'adore les pâtes et parce que l'ail est bon pour la santé.

C. Une interview. Interviewez votre partenaire pour déterminer ses goûts alimentaires. Demandez-lui…

1. quels ingrédients il/elle aime dans un plat, et quels ingrédients il/elle déteste.
2. s'il / si elle préfère la cuisine piquante (*spicy*) ou les plats qui ne sont pas très épicés.
3. quel est son restaurant préféré et le plat qu'il/elle commande le plus fréquemment dans ce restaurant.
4. quels plats il/elle aime servir à l'occasion d'une fête.
5. la cuisine régionale (de son pays) qu'il/elle préfère.

*Le mot **origine** est un substantif féminin, alors il prend la forme féminine de l'adjectif.

Visionnement 1

Avant de visionner

Un dialogue incomplet. Voici l'extrait d'un dialogue entre Camille et Rachid, où on parle du voyage de Rachid dans les Cévennes. Complétez le passage en choisissant les mots logiques.

CAMILLE: _____[1] (Personne, Rien) ne t'a parlé de la guerre, apparemment?

RACHID: Les vieux sont discrets. Ils _____[2] (veulent, ne veulent pas) s'exprimer[a] devant une caméra. Et les jeunes n'ont pas _____[3] (connu, su) cette période.

CAMILLE: Comment faire pour _____[4] (retrouver, retourner) la trace de mon grand-père?

RACHID: 60 ans après la guerre, c'est _____[5] (utile, difficile).

CAMILLE: _____[6] (Pourquoi, Où) tu dis ça? On sait aujourd'hui comment vivait l'homme du Néandertal.[b] Et c'était _____[7] (quand, où)? Il y a 75.000 ans!

RACHID (*sourit*): Tu n'es jamais _____[8] (encouragée, découragée), hein?

[a]*to express themselves* [b]l'homme… *Neanderthal Man (ancient human ancestor)*

Vocabulaire relatif à l'épisode

y a séjourné	*stayed there*
une petite goutte	*a little drop*
as-tu rencontré	*did you meet*
C'est comme ça que ça s'écrit?	*Is that how it's spelled?*
c'est génial	*that's fantastic*
surtout pas	*definitely not*

Observez!

Dans l'Épisode 15, Camille pose des questions à Rachid sur son voyage dans les Cévennes. Pendant votre visionnement, essayez de trouver les réponses aux questions suivantes.

- À quels obstacles Rachid doit-il faire face dans ses recherches?
- De quelle piste est-ce que Camille parle?

Après le visionnement

A. Racontez l'épisode! Un étudiant donne une phrase qui commence le résumé. Un autre étudiant reprend le récit, jusqu'à ce que tout l'épisode soit (*is*) reconstitué.

B. Réfléchissez. Répondez aux questions suivantes.

1. Pourquoi les vieux de Saint-Jean de Causse sont-ils «discrets»? Pourquoi ne veulent-ils pas parler de la guerre? Est-ce qu'ils veulent oublier les événements tragiques? Est-ce qu'ils ont quelque chose à cacher (*to hide*)? Se méfient-ils des inconnus (*Do they mistrust strangers*)?
2. Pourquoi Camille ne veut-elle pas appeler les Leblanc tout de suite? A-t-elle peur d'apprendre la vérité? Veut-elle réfléchir avant d'agir (*before acting*)?

Structure 45

Les verbes comme *ouvrir*

Talking about everyday actions

—**J'ai découvert** les Cévennes. C'est somptueux.

The verb **ouvrir** (*to open*) is conjugated like a regular **-er** verb in the present tense, but the past participle is irregular.

ouvrir (*to open*)			
j'	**ouvre**	nous	**ouvrons**
tu	**ouvres**	vous	**ouvrez**
il, elle, on	**ouvre**	ils, elles	**ouvrent**
passé composé: j'ai **ouvert**			

1. Other verbs conjugated like **ouvrir** are

couvrir	*to cover*	**offrir**	*to offer; to give*
découvrir	*to discover*	**souffrir**	*to suffer*

Tu mets les ingrédients dans une casserole et puis **tu** la **couvres**.	*You put the ingredients in a saucepan and then you cover it.*
Mado **a** beaucoup **souffert** des injures de ses camarades.	*Mado suffered a great deal because of her classmates' insults.*

2. The opposite of **ouvrir** is **fermer** (*to close*). **Fermer** is a regular **-er** verb.

Tu **fermes** les fenêtres, petite? J'ai horreur des courants d'air.	*Will you close the windows, dear? I hate drafts.*

Activités

A. Découvertes culturelles. Complétez les paragraphes en utilisant correctement les verbes entre parenthèses. Utilisez le temps présent sauf (*except*) où vous devez mettre le passé composé (p.c. = passé composé).

1. Dans mon pays l'Algérie, on _____ (souffrir, p.c.) pendant la guerre entre 1954 et 1963. Nous _____ (découvrir, p.c.) que notre culture peut résister à tout, même si les gens _____ (souffrir) toujours des conflits internes violents.
2. Je _____ (découvrir) en ce moment beaucoup de choses sur l'Algérie. Mes parents m'_____ (offrir, p.c.) un livre sur les cultures maghrébines pour mon anniversaire. Il _____ (couvrir) toute l'histoire de ces pays.
3. Les Français _____ (découvrir) la culture algérienne grace à (*thanks to*) la cuisine. Récemment, mon frére _____ (ouvrir, p.c.) un restaurant algérien, et je travaille pour lui. Nous _____ (offrir) toutes sortes de couscous et de la chorba'dess, une soupe aux lentilles. Je _____ (découvrir) beaucoup de recettes similaires dans nos deux pays, et ça m'_____ (ouvrir) vraiment les yeux.
4. Tu nous _____ (offrir) un repas au restaurant? Comme ça (*that way*), nous allons découvrir nous-mêmes (*ourselves*) cet aspect de ta culture!
5. Ah vous, les Français, vous _____ (découvrir) tout à travers (*through*) la gastronomie.

B. Résultats. (*Results.*) Pour chaque situation, il y a plusieurs résultats possibles. Utilisez les verbes de la présentation avec une des phrases suivantes pour indiquer des résultats logiques.

Vocabulaire utile: les/des allergies, un bon plat aux courgettes et aux tomates, la chaleur (*heat*), un chapitre du livre par jour, les/des fenêtres, les/des fleurs (*flowers*), un nouveau restaurant, le froid, un mal de tête, les pâtes et des sauces avec beaucoup d'ail

Verbes utiles: couvrir, découvrir, fermer, offrir, ouvrir, souffrir

MODÈLE: L'hiver arrive. La vieille dame... →
É1: L'hiver arrive, donc (*so*) la vieille dame couvre les fleurs.
É2: L'hiver arrive, donc la vieille dame n'ouvre pas les fenêtres.

1. C'est le printemps. Nous...
2. C'est l'été. Vous...
3. C'est mon anniversaire. Mon ami...
4. Je vais dans un restaurant végétarien. Je...
5. Ce cours avance vite. Le professeur...
6. Les étudiants voyagent en Italie. Ils...
7. La cuisine indienne est très à la mode. M. Desai...

Structure 46

Les pronoms y et en

Avoiding repetition

—Vous prenez un peu de vin, Camille?

—Non, merci, non. J'**en** ai beaucoup trop bu! Mais toi, tu n'**en** bois pas?

—Jamais, non. Mais tu peux **en** reprendre un peu! Une petite goutte?

Le pronom y

1. **Y** is used in place of a prepositional phrase of location (**au Maroc**, **en Italie**, or **dans les Cévennes**). It is often translated as *there.*

—Yasmine est née **à Marseille**?	*Was Yasmine born in Marseille?*
—Oui, elle **y** est née.	*Yes, she was born there.*

Attention—The verb **aller** always takes a complement. If it has no other complement, **y** must be used.

—Tu **vas *à la soirée*** avec nous?	*Are you going to the party with us?*
—Oui, j'***y*** **vais**.	*Yes, I'm going.*

2. **Y** can also be used in place of a thing after a verb that requires **à** before a noun. Verbs such as **répondre à**, **obéir à**, **réfléchir à**, **penser à**, and **jouer à** can thus be used with **y**.

—Est-ce que Camille réfléchit **au mystère de son grand-pere**?	*Does Camille think about the mystery of her grandfather?*
—Oui, elle **y** réfléchit.	*Yes, she thinks about it.*

Attention—**Y** is not used with people. When referring to people, these verbs take an indirect object pronoun. **Penser** takes **à** + stressed pronoun.

—Tu réponds **au professeur**?	*Do you answer the professor?*
—Naturellement je **lui** réponds.	*Of course I answer him.*
—Tu penses **à Camille**?	*Are you thinking of Camille?*
—Oui, je pense **à elle**.	*Yes, I'm thinking of her.*

3. **Y**, like the object pronouns, usually precedes the conjugated verb; in the **passé composé**, this means the auxiliary. Negations surround **y** + conjugated verb.

J'**y** allais tous les jours.	*I used to go there every day.*
Ton grand-père **y** a séjourné?	*Your grandfather spent time there?*
Mado n'**y** répond pas.	*Mado doesn't answer them [the questions].*
Elle n'**y** a pas bien réfléchi.	*She didn't think it over well.*

4. In verb + infinitive constructions, **y** is placed before the verb to which it is related (usually the infinitive).

Je vais **y** voyager un jour.	*I'm going to take a trip there some day.*

5. As with other pronouns, **y** follows the verb in the affirmative imperative but precedes it in the negative imperative.

Allez-**y**!	*Go ahead!*
N'**y** pense pas.	*Don't think about it.*

Attention—The **-s** in the **tu** form of **-er** verbs is restored in the affirmative imperative when **y** or **en** is used.

Reste**s**-y.	*Stay there.*
Achète**s**-en plusieurs, d'accord?	*Buy a few of them, okay?*

Le pronom *en*

1. **En** is used in place of a phrase containing an indefinite article, a partitive article, or an expression of quantity (**un bon couscous**, **des navets**, **du vin**, **quelques courges**, **un peu de quatre-épices**).

—Tu veux **des légumes**?	*Do you want any vegetables?*
—Oui, j'**en** veux.	*Yes, I'd like some.*

When a measurement (**un peu**, **une bouteille de**, **un kilo de**, etc.) or a number (**un**, **deux**, **trois**) would be indicated in a phrase using the noun, it must also be used with the pronoun **en**, following the conjugated verb.

—Tu veux encore **du vin**?	*Do you want some more wine?*
—Non, merci, j'**en** ai **trop** bu.	*I've drunk too much (of it).*
—Vous avez **trois sœurs**?	*Do you have three sisters?*
—C'est ça. J'**en** ai **trois**.	*That's right. I have three (of them).*

2. **En** can also be used with a verb that requires **de** before a noun. Verbs such as **avoir besoin/envie/honte/peur de**, **être content(e) de**, **parler de**, **penser de**, and **jouer de** can thus be used with **en**.

—Que penses-tu **de cette histoire**?	*What do you think of this story?*
—Qu'est-ce que tu **en** penses, toi?	*What do you think of it, yourself?*

Attention—**En** is not usually used to refer to people. When these verbs refer to people, they take **de** + stressed pronoun after the verb.

—Que penses-tu **de l'historien**?	*What do you think of the historian?*
—Qu'est-ce que tu penses **de lui**?	*What do you think of him?*

3. **En**, like **y** and the object pronouns, usually precedes the conjugated verb; in the **passé composé**, this means the auxiliary. Negations surround **en** + conjugated verb.

J'**en** *buvais* tous les jours.	*I used to drink some every day.*
Camille n'**en** *veut* pas.	*Camille doesn't want any.*
Elle n'**en** *a* pas souvent parlé.	*She didn't talk about it often.*

4. In verb + infinitive constructions, **en** is placed before the verb to which it is related (usually the infinitive).

Je vais **en** acheter deux.	*I'm going to buy two of them.*

5. Again, as with other pronouns, **en** follows the verb in the affirmative imperative but precedes it in the negative imperative.

Prends-**en**!	*Take some!*
N'**en** parlons pas.	*Let's not talk about it.*

Activités

A. Chez Lorenzo. Regardez cette publicité pour un restaurant parisien et répondez aux questions suivantes. Utilisez **y** dans vos réponses.

MODÈLE: Pensez-vous qu'on mange bien ou mal dans ce restaurant? → Je pense qu'on y mange bien. (Je pense qu'on y mange mal.)

1. Quelle sorte de cuisine mange-t-on dans ce restaurant? **2.** Peut-on aller à l'Arc de Triomphe à pied? **3.** Est-ce que vous vous êtes déjà promené(e) dans ce quartier? **4.** Pensez-vous que le chef de cuisine habite à Marseille? **5.** Quels repas peut-on prendre dans ce restaurant—le petit déjeuner? le déjeuner? le dîner? **6.** À votre avis (*In your opinion*), est-ce que le chef de cuisine réfléchit à son menu chaque jour?

B. Un repas spécial. Deux camarades de chambre ont invité des amis pour un repas vietnamien ce soir, mais ils sont mal organisés. Le premier parle. Quelles sont les réponses du deuxième? Utilisez le pronom **en** dans chaque réponse.

MODÈLE: Tu as choisi des recettes pour ce soir, non? / Non, je... → Non, je n'en ai pas encore choisi.

1. Tu as acheté du vin? / Oui, j'...
2. Mais tu sais que Zaki et Irène ne boivent pas de vin. / C'est vrai, ils...
3. Alors, tu vas prendre une bouteille d'eau minérale? / D'accord, je...
4. Tu peux acheter des crevettes? / Oui, je...
5. Nous sommes quatre à manger, donc prends un kilo de crevettes. / OK, je...
6. Tu vas trouver un peu de gingembre? / Pas de problème, je...
7. Tu n'as pas peur de cette recette compliquée? / Non, je...
8. Est-ce que nos amis vont être contents de la soirée chez nous? / Bien sûr, ils...

C. Dans le film. Vous rappelez-vous ces événements importants dans le film? Répondez aux questions en utilisant **y** ou **en**, ou un pronom accentué (*stressed pronoun*). Justifiez votre réponse.

MODÈLE: Est-ce que Rachid habite toujours à Marseille? → Non, il n'y habite plus. Il habite à Paris.

1. Est-ce que Camille pense à la guerre? **2.** Est-ce qu'elle a envie de trouver des renseignements (*information*) sur son père? **3.** Est-ce que Rachid part en Allemagne? **4.** Est-ce que Camille a parlé de son grand-père avec Bruno?

5. Est-ce que Rachid est allé à Saint-Jean de Causse? **6.** Est-ce qu'Antoine a habité chez les Leblanc en 1943? **7.** Est-ce que les gens du village ont parlé d'Antoine? **8.** Est-ce que Louise et Camille sont allées dans les Cévennes? **9.** Est-ce que Camille est contente du dîner chez Rachid? **10.** Est-ce que Mado a peur de la vérité?

D. Pour faire une ratatouille. Richard veut faire une ratatouille et sa femme, Marie, est tout à fait d'accord avec tout ce qu'il dit! Que dit Marie? Faites une phrase à l'impératif en utilisant les pronoms **y** ou **en**.

MODÈLE: RICHARD: Je veux faire une ratatouille.
MARIE: Alors, fais-en une.

1. Je dois d'abord acheter des aubergines, des courgettes et des poivrons. **2.** Je ne dois pas acheter de vin. **3.** Je vais aller à l'épicerie pour les herbes. **4.** Je dois trouver ensuite quatre tomates. **5.** Je dois mettre l'huile d'olive dans la casserole. **6.** Je vais mettre beaucoup d'ail, aussi. **7.** Je ne veux pas ajouter beaucoup de persil. **8.** Je dois mettre la casserole sur la plaque électrique (*the burner*).

E. Les restaurants. Posez des questions à deux camarades de classe. Ils/Elles vont vous répondre en utilisant **y** ou **en**. Prenez des notes pour pouvoir faire un compte rendu (*report*) à la classe. Demandez-lui

1. s'il / si elle aime dîner au restaurant.
2. le nom d'un bon restaurant.
3. s'il / si elle est allé(e) dans ce restaurant récemment.
4. s'il / si elle essaie des plats qu'il/elle ne connaît pas. (par exemple?)
5. s'il / si elle va au restaurant seul(e). (sinon, avec qui?)
6. s'il / si elle boit du vin avec les repas. (pourquoi ou pourquoi pas?)
7. s'il / si elle pense aller dans un restaurant bientôt. (où et quand?)

Regards sur la culture

Transformations de la culture en France

Les éléments du couscous

In this episode, Rachid and Sonia have prepared **couscous**, a traditional North African dish, for Camille. In fact, **couscous** is one of a number of cultural elements from the Maghreb that are becoming assimilated into French culture. Immigration often changes the host society.

- People of North African origin are now the largest immigrant cultural group in France. Originating in Morocco, Tunisia, and especially Algeria, many of these people originally arrived in hopes of finding temporary work.
- At the time of Algeria's independence in 1962, nearly 1.5 million French citizens who had lived their entire lives in North Africa arrived en masse in France. These people included the **pieds-noirs**,

who were descendants of European settlers; Algerian Jews, whose ancestors had lived in North Africa for centuries; and North African Muslims.

- Among the customs brought by these people are a number of culinary specialities: **merguez** (a kind of spicy beef or lamb sausage), **méchoui** (a way of preparing a whole lamb on a spit over open coals), and **couscous**.
- Couscous is based on semolina wheat, which is steamed with the vapor from a stew of meat (usually lamb) and vegetables. At the table, one generally helps oneself to the couscous grain itself, the vegetables, the bouillon, and chickpeas out of separate serving dishes. One can then add **harissa**, a hot pepper sauce.
- Because of recent immigration patterns, Islam is now the second-largest religion in France after Roman Catholicism, with more adherents than Judaism or Protestantism. The children of North African immigrants, often called **beurs**, may or may not follow Islamic traditions.
- The wearing of the veil among certain Muslim groups has been a very touchy issue in France, because French public schools have traditionally forbidden the wearing of any outward religious symbol.
- The presence of **pieds-noirs** and, more recently, of **beurs** in French entertainment has brought a new accent to the culture. The most striking recent development has been the rising popularity among French young people of **raï**, the distinctive popular music of Algeria.

Considérez

What immigrant groups have succeeded in bringing changes to your own culture in recent times? What kinds of changes are these—food? games? music? something else?

Structure 47

Les verbes *vivre* et *suivre*

Talking about everyday actions

—On sait aujourd'hui comment **vivait** l'homme du Néandertal.

Two verbs, **vivre** (*to live*) and **suivre** (*to follow; to take* [*a course*]), are conjugated in the same way in the simple tenses, but their past participles differ.

vivre (*to live*)	**suivre** (*to follow; to take* [*a course*])
je **vis**	je **suis**
tu **vis**	tu **suis**
il, elle, on **vit**	il, elle, on **suit**
nous **vivons**	nous **suivons**
vous **vivez**	vous **suivez**
ils, elles **vivent**	ils, elles **suivent**
passé composé: j'ai **vécu**	passé composé: j'ai **suivi**

Le père de Camille **vit** à Londres. — *Camille's father lives in London.*

Actuellement, nous ne **suivons** pas de cours. Nous faisons des recherches. — *Currently, we aren't taking any courses. We're doing research.*

1. **Survivre** (*to survive*) is conjugated like **vivre**. **Poursuivre** (*to pursue*) is conjugated like **suivre**.

Le grand-père de Camille **a**-t-il **survécu**? — *Did Camille's grandfather survive?*

Camille **a poursuivi** sa quête. — *Camille followed her quest.*

2. **Vivre** can be used in the same sense as **habiter** (*to inhabit, reside in, live in*), but it can also mean *to be alive, to live* in the sense of existing or having a certain lifestyle.

J'**habite** dans la rue Mouffetard. — *I live on the rue Mouffetard.*

Le père de Camille **vit** à Londres. — *Camille's father lives in London.*

but Elle **vit** encore? — *Is she still alive?*

Nous **vivons** bien en France. — *We live well in France.*

Activités

A. Qu'est-ce qu'on étudie dans chaque pays? Selon l'endroit où on vit, on suit parfois des cours différents. Mettez la forme correcte de **vivre** ou **suivre** pour parler de ces stéréotypes.

1. Je ______ en France, alors je ______ des cours de littérature française.
2. Nous ______ des cours d'histoire américaine parce que nous ______ aux États-Unis.
3. Les jeunes ______ des cours très difficiles s'ils ______ au Japon.
4. On ______ un cours de littérature portugaise si on ______ au Brésil.
5. Vous ______ en Italie, alors vous ______ un cours sur les poètes italiens.
6. Masha ______ en Russie, alors elle ______ un cours sur les arts dramatiques russes.

52, 58
C + F

B. Deux histoires de la Résistance. Mettez les verbes suivants au passé composé ou à l'imparfait pour compléter les deux histoires.

Pendant la guerre, les résistants _____[1] (survivre) parce qu'ils _____[2] (vivre) en communauté. Jean Moulin, un célèbre résistant, _____[3] (vivre) entre 1899 et 1943. Il _____[4] (suivre) Charles de Gaulle en Angleterre en 1941. Quand il est retourné en France, les Nazis le/l'_____[5] (poursuivre). En 1943, la Gestapo _____[6] (suivre) un autre résistant à une réunion avec Jean Moulin. Ils ont arrêté Jean Moulin qui (*who*) _____[7] (survivre) à deux mois de torture sans rien révéler. Mais il est mort au cours de (*during*) son transfert en Allemagne.

Yves Salaun avait 16 ans en 1942. Il _____[8] (poursuivre) des études au Lycée de St-Brieuc pendant l'Occupation. Tristes de voir leur pays occupé, deux de ses camarades et lui _____[9] (suivre) les résistants plus âgés. Ils _____[10] (vivre) ensemble pendant deux ans. Malheureusement, ils n'ont pas _____[11] (survivre) longtemps. Les Nazis les _____[12] (poursuivre) et les ont attrapés. Ils ont été fusillés (*shot*) en 1944.

C. La vie des gens. Mettez les éléments des trois colonnes ensemble pour faire des phrases logiques. Conjuguez les verbes aux temps convenables (*appropriate*).

A	B	C
je	(ne... pas) habiter	dans la ville de _____
mes parents	(ne... pas) vivre	au XVIIe siècle (*century*)
Louis XIV		à Versailles
mon ami(e)		bien
mes grands-parents		encore
les étudiants		dans un appartement (dans une maison, à la cité universitaire [*dormitory*])

D. La moyenne. (*The average.*) Utilisez les éléments suivants pour poser des questions à quatre camarades de classe. Faites attention aux temps des verbes. Notez les noms et les réponses sur une feuille de papier et calculez les moyennes.

MODÈLE: depuis combien de temps / être / dans cette université →
VOUS: Depuis combien de temps es-tu dans cette université?
PAUL: Depuis un an.
ANN: Depuis un an.
MARCOS: Depuis six mois.
ASTRID: Depuis un an et demi.
VOUS: La moyenne est un an.

1. depuis quand / vivre / ici **2.** combien de cours / suivre / maintenant **3.** pendant combien de temps / suivre / des cours au lycée **4.** combien de personnes / habiter / chez vous quand vous aviez 12 ans **5.** combien de personnes dans cette classe / suivre / un autre cours avec vous **6.** depuis combien de temps / vivre / dans ce pays

Visionnement 2

La ville de Paris

As you followed the lives of the characters through the first fifteen episodes of *Le Chemin du retour*, you examined six areas of Paris in some detail. Each of these is indicated by a chapter designation in a box on the map. As you can see, most of the action of the film has taken place near the center of Paris. Because the scene is about to shift to other parts of France, this is a good time to consolidate your knowledge about Paris.

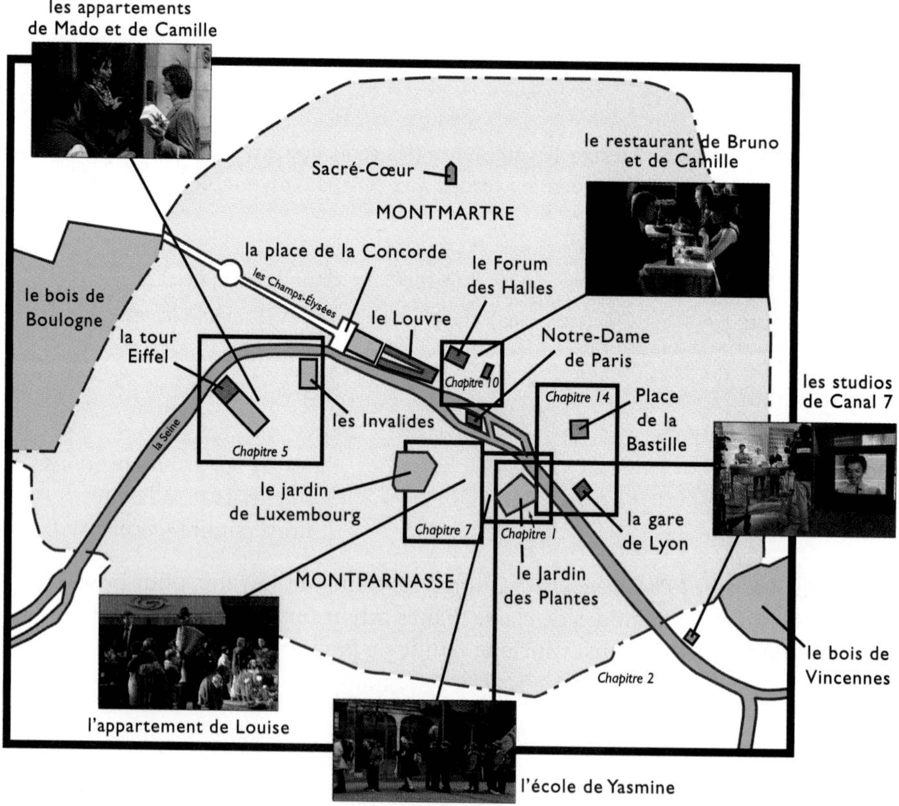

Vous souvenez-vous? Composez des phrases pour situer les endroits de la liste A par rapport (*with respect to*) aux endroits de la liste B.

Vocabulaire utile: près de, loin de, au nord de, au sud de, à l'est de, à l'ouest de

MODÈLES: Le Jardin des Plantes est près de l'école de Yasmine.
La place de la Concorde est loin des studios de Canal 7.
Montmartre est au nord du restaurant de Bruno et de Camille.

A	B
la Seine	l'appartement de Louise
la tour Eiffel	l'appartement de Mado
le Louvre	l'école de Yasmine
Montmartre	les studios de Canal 7
Notre-Dame de Paris	le restaurant de Bruno et de Camille
les Champs-Élysées	
Montparnasse	
la place de la Concorde	
le Jardin des Plantes	
la gare de Lyon	

Observez!

Considérez les aspects culturels expliqués dans **Regards sur la culture**. Ensuite, regardez l'Épisode 15 encore une fois, et répondez aux questions suivantes.

- Comment le couscous est-il présenté? Qu'est-ce qu'il y a dans un grand bol et qu'est-ce qu'il y a dans plusieurs petits bols?
- Quelle sorte de musique Rachid met-il à la radio? Pourquoi, à votre avis?

Après le visionnement

Faites l'activité pour le **Visionnement 2** dans le cahier.

Synthèse: Culture

Immigration et nationalité

Dans le film, Rachid et Sonia sont certainement de nationalité française, parce qu'ils sont nés à Marseille. Le père de Rachid et les parents de Sonia n'ont peut-être jamais pris la nationalité française, mais ils ont tous les avantages sociaux des Français.

Étrangers[1] en France

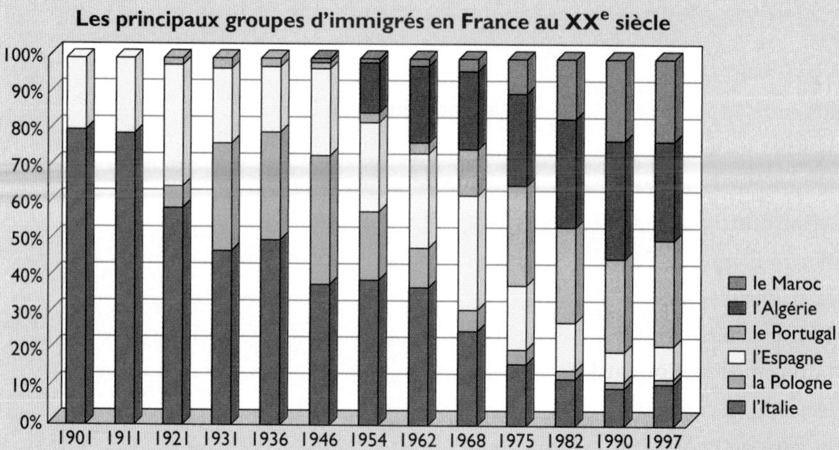

La France est depuis longtemps un pays d'immigration et un pays d'asile[2] politique. Cela signifie qu'il y a toujours beaucoup d'étrangers qui habitent en France. Certains de ces étrangers deviennent Français. Leurs enfants qui sont nés en France sont automatiquement Français. En plus, il est relativement facile pour les réfugiés politiques d'obtenir la nationalité française.

Dans certaines villes françaises, les étrangers qui y travaillent peuvent voter aux élections municipales. Et, depuis 1992, les citoyens[3] d'autres pays de l'Union européenne qui habitent en France peuvent voter lors des[4] élections municipales françaises.

La majorité des Français sont contents que la France reste un pays d'asile. Mais certains Français trouvent qu'il est trop facile d'obtenir la nationalité française. Ils pensent qu'on ne doit pas la donner aux enfants de personnes qui ne sont en France que pour le travail. Le Front national, un parti politique de droite,[5] pense qu'il faut renvoyer ces familles[6] dans leurs pays d'origine. Ces opinions s'intensifient en période de difficultés économiques. Mais le Front national ne représente qu'une petite minorité de la population—5 à 15% des votes. Les autres partis politiques veulent maintenir les droits[7] des immigrés.

[1]*Foreigners* [2]*asylum* [3]*citizens* [4]*lors... at the time of the* [5]*right (conservative)* [6]*il... these families should be forced to return (to their native country)* [7]*rights*

À vous

L'immigration. Choose one year from the graph. Imagine you are hiring a social worker in a French city in that year to deal with the foreign-born population. List the kinds of expertise you want in that person and the kinds of problems that person will have to help immigrants handle.

À écrire

Faites **À écrire** pour le Chapitre 15 dans le cahier.

Vocabulaire

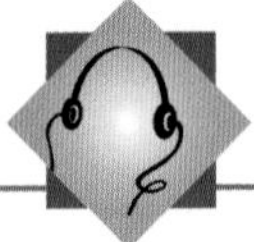

Aliments

l'ail (*m.*)	garlic
une aubergine	eggplant
une betterave	beet
une cacahouète	peanut
la cannelle	cinnamon
un champignon	mushroom
la citronnelle	lemongrass
la coriandre	coriander
une courge	squash
une courgette	zucchini
une épice	spice
le gingembre	ginger
l'huile (*f.*) **(d'olive, de sésame)**	(olive, sesame) oil
un navet	turnip
une noix de coco	coconut
des pâtes (*f. pl.*)	pasta
le persil	parsley
des pois (*m.*) **chiches**	chick-peas
le/la quatre-épices	allspice
des raisins (*m.*) **secs**	raisins
le yaourt	yogurt

MOTS APPARENTÉS: **la cardamome, le couscous, le curry, les grains** (*m.*) **de couscous, des lentilles** (*f.*), **le pain pita, la sauce de soja**

À REVOIR: **une carotte, des haricots** (*m.*) **verts, un oignon (vert), une pomme de terre, une tomate**

Pour faire la cuisine

une casserole	saucepan
une recette	recipe
chauffer	to heat
faire bouillir	to boil
faire cuire (à la vapeur, au four)	to cook (to steam, to bake)
faire frire	to fry
mélanger	to mix
réchauffer	to reheat
verser	to pour

Pays et nationalités

l'Inde (*f.*)	India
le Maghreb	the Maghreb (Morocco, Algeria, Tunisia)
maghrébin(e)	from the Maghreb
russe	Russian

MOTS APPARENTÉS: **indien(ne), israélien(ne), l'Italie** (*f.*), **italien(ne), le Pakistan, pakistanais(e), la Russie**

À REVOIR: **la Chine, chinois(e), le Viêtnam, vietnamien(ne)**

Verbes

ajouter	to add
couvrir	to cover
découvrir	to discover
fermer	to close
offrir	to offer; to give (*a gift*)
ouvrir	to open
poursuivre	to pursue
souffrir	to suffer
suivre	to follow
suivre un cours	to take a class
survivre	to survive
vivre	to live, to be alive

À REVOIR: **aller, avoir besoin/envie/honte/peur (de), être content(e) (de), habiter, jouer à, jouer de, obéir à, parler de, penser à, penser de, réfléchir à, répondre à**

Pronoms

en	some; any; of/from it/them/there
y	there

Chapitre 16

Le départ

OBJECTIFS

In this episode, you will

- find out what Camille does about Rachid's discovery in Saint-Jean de Causse

In this chapter, you will

- talk about leisure activities in the Cévennes
- talk about vacation activities in Brittany
- compare and contrast actions and things
- ask questions using interrogative pronouns
- learn about the French concept of friendship
- read maxims about friendship and love written by famous French writers

Vocabulaire en contexte

Les loisirs° dans les Cévennes

Les... *Leisure activities*

Les **loisirs** (*m. pl.*) dans les Cévennes sont nombreux, **surtout**° les activités **en plein air**.°

especially / en... *outdoors*

°*summertime*

Autres expressions utiles

un camping	campground
des patins (*m.*)	ice skates
une piste	trail; track; ski run
des vacances (*f. pl.*)	vacation
faire de la spéléologie	to explore caves, go spelunking
jouer au hockey	to play hockey
patiner, faire du patin à glace	to ice skate
prendre une photo	to take a photograph

*cueillir (*to pick, gather*)—je cueille, tu cueilles, il/elle/on cueille, nous cueillons, vous cueillez, ils/elles cueillent. *Passé composé:* j'ai cueilli. Un autre verbe qui se conjugue comme **cueillir** est **accueillir** (*to welcome*).

†VTT = vélo tout terrain (*mountain bike*).

Notez bien!

Voilà quelques noms **d'animaux** (*m.*).

un cerf	deer, stag
un chat	cat
un cheval	horse
un chien	dog
un lapin	rabbit
un oiseau	bird
un ours	bear
un poisson	fish
une souris	mouse

Le terme **une souris** est utilisé aussi pour l'ordinateur.

Activités

A. Qu'est-qu'on fait? Indiquez à quel sport ou à quelle activité correspond chacun (*each one*) des termes suivants.

MODÈLE: un panier (*basket*) → cueillir des champignons

1. un cheval
2. des skis
3. une tente
4. une grotte
5. un ours
6. un sac à dos
7. une corde
8. un snowboard (une planche à neige)
9. un fusil (*gun*)
10. un oiseau

B. Pour les amateurs de sport. Quelles activités peut-on faire aux endroits suivants? Formez des phrases complètes.

MODÈLE: en montagne →
On peut faire du vélo en montagne. (On peut faire du surf de neige en montagne.)

1. sur une piste **2.** en l'air **3.** dans une forêt **4.** sur une pente (*slope*)

Pour en savoir plus...

Les salariés français ont un minimum de cinq semaines de congés (*time off*) payés. Certaines entreprises sont fermées pendant tout le mois d'août pour permettre à tout le monde de partir en vacances, car (*since*) pour la plupart des (*most*) Français, rester chez soi pour se reposer, ce n'est pas vraiment des vacances.

La fermeture annuelle

Les gloires° de la Bretagne

°Les... *Glories*

Les gens qui vont **en vacances** en Bretagne peuvent y faire des activités bien variées.

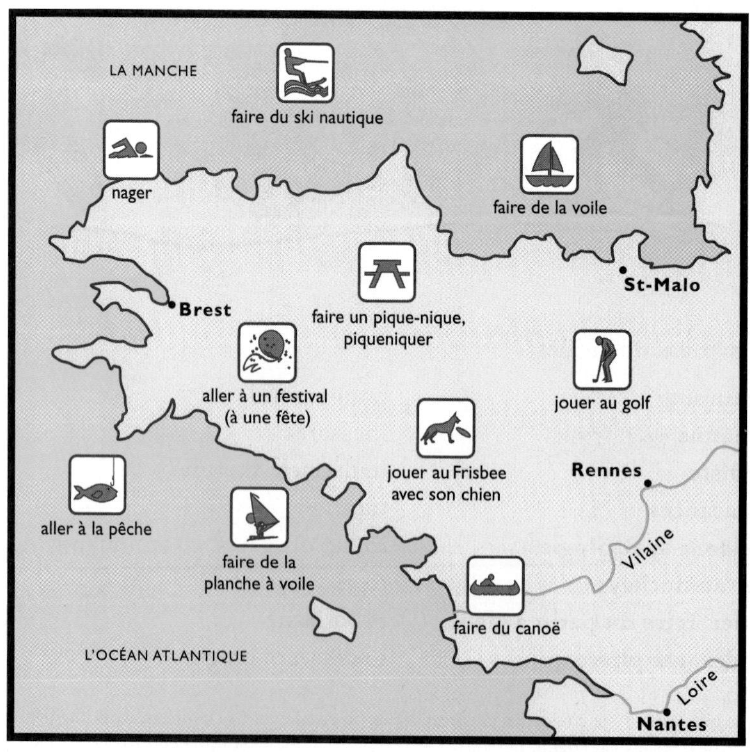

Autres mots utiles

une balle	ball (*not inflated with air*)
un ballon	ball (*inflated with air*)
un bateau (à voile)	(sail)boat
une équipe	team
un panier	basket
une plage	beach
jouer à la pétanque (aux boules)	to play lawn bowling

Activités

A. Soyez bien équipé(e)! Identifiez une activité qui correspond à l'équipement ou aux endroits suivants.

MODÈLES: un court de tennis → On joue au tennis sur un court de tennis.
une balle → On joue au golf avec une balle.

1. des boules **2.** un terrain de golf **3.** un ballon **4.** un bateau **5.** des patins **6.** une planche à voile **7.** une nappe et un panier de provisions

B. Les préférences sportives. Identifiez quelques activités que vous aimez faire dans les situations ou aux endroits indiqués.

MODÈLE: comme sport d'hiver →
Comme sport d'hiver, je préfère faire du ski de fond et du patin à glace.

1. à la plage **2.** au centre sportif **3.** dans un pays où il fait très froid **4.** à la mer (*sea*) **5.** sur un lac (*lake*) **6.** à la piscine **7.** en équipe **8.** seul(e) **9.** avec des amis

C. Interview. Demandez à votre partenaire...

1. s'il / si elle est plutôt sportif/ive ou sédentaire.
2. à quels sports il/elle aime jouer.
3. combien de fois par semaine il/elle fait du sport.
4. quelle est la meilleure (*best*) équipe de l'université, selon lui/elle.
5. quels sports sont populaires dans sa région d'origine.

D. Racontez. Avec votre partenaire, parlez des vacances que vous avez passées en plein air (ou imaginez vos vacances idéales en plein air).

1. Où êtes-vous allé(e)?
2. Comment est-ce que vous avez voyagé?
3. Combien de temps votre voyage a-t-il duré?
4. Combien de temps avez-vous passé dans cette région?
5. Qu'est-ce que vous faisiez pendant la journée? la soirée?
6. Est-ce que vous vous êtes bien amusé(e?)
7. Dans quel état d'esprit (*frame of mind*) étiez-vous en partant?

Pour en savoir plus...

L'histoire de la Bretagne a commencé 6.000 ans avant l'ère chrétienne, mais ce n'est qu'après le départ des Romains au Ve siècle (*century*) que de nombreux Celtes de Grande-Bretagne ont immigré en Bretagne. La Bretagne est restée un état indépendant jusqu'en 1532. Un million de personnes parlent encore aujourd'hui l'ancienne langue bretonne.

La côte bretonne

Visionnement 1

Avant de visionner

Une discussion. Voici des lignes tirées de l'Épisode 16. C'est une conversation entre Camille et Martine, la productrice de «Bonjour!». Considérez l'histoire jusqu'ici et essayez de déterminer si c'est Camille ou la productrice qui parle.

1. Je pars en vacances aujourd'hui! **2.** Tu es folle? Tu penses à l'émission? **3.** Mais remplace-moi [...]! J'ai besoin de partir! **4.** Inutile (*It's pointless* [*to insist*]). J'ai pris ma décision... **5.** Tu es une professionnelle! Tu dois respecter ton contrat! **6.** Je suis mal en ce moment et j'ai besoin de repos (*rest*), tu peux comprendre ça? **7.** Incroyable (*Unbelievable*)! Cette fille a perdu la tête.

Vocabulaire relatif à l'épisode

deux semaines de congé	*two weeks of vacation*
C'est si grave que ça?	*Is it as serious as that?*
le plus vite possible	*as soon as possible*
je tiens à toi	*I care about you*
elle a des soucis	*she has worries*
le moindre problème	*the slightest problem*

Observez!

Camille et la productrice se disputent dans l'Épisode 16. Essayez de répondre aux questions suivantes pendant votre visionnement de l'épisode.

- Qu'est-ce que Camille veut faire absolument?
- Quelle solution trouvent-elles pour régler (*resolve*) leur problème?

Après le visionnement

A. Une vive discussion. (*An intense discussion.*) Martine n'est pas contente de la décision de Camille de partir en vacances. Voici quelques-unes de ses objections. Comment est-ce que Camille y répond? Choisissez parmi les possibilités données.

1. MARTINE: Tu ne peux pas partir! C'est impossible...
CAMILLE: Pourquoi?
MARTINE: Tu es la vedette° de l'émission!
CAMILLE: a. Tu plaisantes!
b. Elle a des soucis!
c. Personne n'est irremplaçable.

°*star*

2. MARTINE: Camille, tu as des responsabilités.
CAMILLE: a. C'est le plus mauvais jour de ma vie.
b. Inutile. J'ai pris ma décision.
c. Tu es le meilleur.

3. MARTINE: Tu as signé un contrat avec moi! Tu es une professionnelle! Tu dois respecter ton contrat!
CAMILLE: a. Pourquoi?
b. Vraiment? C'est si grave que ça?
c. Peut-être, mais il est essentiel de vivre, aussi!

B. Les subtilités de l'amour. Quelle sorte de relation existe entre Camille et Bruno, selon vous? Est-ce un rapport d'amitié, d'amour, ou est-ce un mélange des deux? Considérez les scènes suivantes avant de répondre.

Structure 48

Le comparatif

Comparing and contrasting

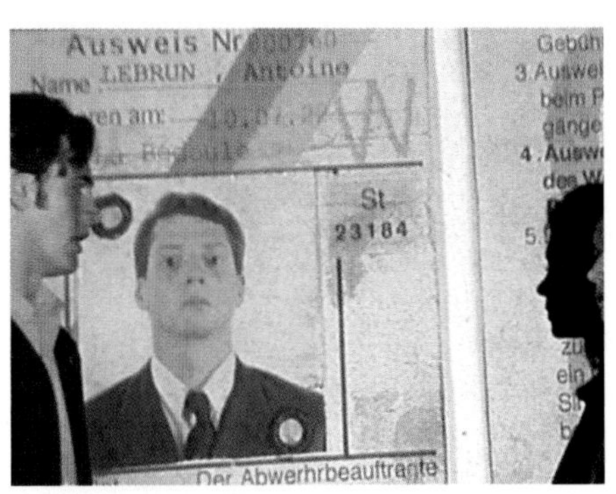

—Ce document était un laissez-passer spécial. Avec ça, on pouvait voyager partout en France. **Aussi bien** dans la zone occupée par les Allemands **que** dans la zone libre.

Comparisons in French are created using the comparison words **plus** (*more*) and **moins** (*less; fewer*). The words **aussi** (*as*) and **autant** (*as much; as many*) are used to express equality.

Comparatif des adjectifs and des adverbes

1. To use adjectives and adverbs in comparisons, use the following constructions.

plus **aussi** **moins**	+	adjective adverb	(+ **que**)

A phrase beginning with **que** is included if you need to clarify whom or what is being compared. In place of the name of a person, a stressed pronoun can be used after **que**.

Mado pense que Camille est **plus impulsive qu'**elle.	*Mado thinks that Camille is more impulsive than she is.*
Le bureau de Rachid est **aussi grand que** le bureau de Bruno.	*Rachid's desk is as big as Bruno's desk.*
Rachid est **moins égocentrique que** Bruno.	*Rachid is less self-centered than Bruno.*

2. **Bon** and **bien** have irregular comparatives: **meilleur(e)** (adjective) and **mieux** (adverb).

Camille dit que Bruno est un **meilleur** journaliste qu'elle.	*Camille says Bruno is a better journalist than she is.*
Ça va **mieux** aujourd'hui?	*Is it going better today?*

Comparatif des quantités

1. To compare quantities of nouns, use the following constructions.

plus de **autant de** **moins de**	+	noun	(+ **que**)

Camille a **autant d'**énergie que Bruno.	*Camille has as much energy as Bruno.*
Bruno a **moins de** patience que Martine.	*Bruno has less patience than Martine.*

2. To compare quantities of activity, use **plus**, **autant**, or **moins** after a verb.

Yasmine danse **plus** que ses parents.	*Yasmine dances more than her parents.*
Camille voyage **autant** qu'Hélène.	*Camille travels as much as Hélène.*

Activités

A. Comment les imaginez-vous? Comparez les personnages et les endroits du film en utilisant **plus**, **moins**, **aussi** ou **autant** et les éléments donnés. Faites tous les changements nécessaires.

MODÈLE: le boulanger / avoir un grand rôle / Bruno →
Le boulanger a un moins grand rôle que Bruno.

1. Martine / être malheureux / Camille
2. Camille / être joli / Martine
3. Bruno / être égoïste / Yasmine
4. Rachid / être un bon journaliste / Sonia
5. Saint-Jean de Causse / être important pour l'histoire d'Antoine / Paris

6. on / aller souvent à la pêche à Paris / dans les Cévennes
7. on / aller difficilement de Paris à Alès en autocar / en train
8. Camille / penser sérieusement à «Bonjour!» / Martine

B. Qu'est-ce qu'ils ont? Imaginez la vie des personnages du film et comparez les éléments suivants.

1. Hélène a _____ amies canadiennes _____ Camille.
2. Louise avait _____ souvenirs d'Antoine _____ Mado.
3. Sonia a _____ énergie _____ Hélène.
4. Rachid a _____ expérience professionnelle _____ Camille.
5. Camille a _____ responsabilités _____ Bruno pendant l'émission.
6. Rachid a _____ expérience _____ Bruno.
7. Quand Camille part, Martine a _____ soucis _____ Nicole, la scripte.
8. Rachid a _____ problèmes de famille _____ Camille.

C. Deux générations différentes. Imaginez Bruno à l'âge de 16 ans. Les activités qu'il préfère et celles que préfère son grand-père sont indiquées dans les listes suivantes. Comparez les activités de Bruno avec celles de son grand-père.

MODÈLE: Bruno joue moins à la pétanque que Papy.

	BRUNO	PAPY
1. aller à la plage	trois fois par an	trois fois par an
2. jouer à la pétanque	deux fois par an	deux fois par semaine
3. jouer au golf	jamais	une fois par semaine
4. nager	deux fois par moi en été	jamais
5. pêcher	jamais	une fois par mois
6. skier	tous les jours pendant les vacances de ski	un week-end par an

D. Généralisations. Avec un(e) partenaire, comparez les personnes et les choses suivantes, en utilisant un des mots entre parenthèses.

MODÈLE: les grandes villes / les petits villages (activités, cher, ?) →
É1: Les grandes villes ont plus d'activités pour les jeunes que les petits villages.
É2: D'accord. Mais les petits villages sont plus avantageux parce qu'on y trouve des maisons moins chères que dans les grandes villes. (*ou* Peut-être. Mais les petits villages ont autant d'avantages que les grandes villes, pour des raisons différentes.)

1. les étudiants / les professeurs (livres, danser, ?)
2. les films français / les films américains (violence, difficile à comprendre, ?)
3. les voitures d'aujourd'hui / les voitures des années 70 (rouler vite, bon, ?)
4. les champions de golf / les champions de tennis (jeune, jouer bien, ?)
5. les grands supermarchés / les petits magasins (les produits, ouvrir tôt, ?)
6. les hommes / les femmes (parler, bon, ?)

Maintenant, faites part de (*share*) vos opinions à la classe et discutez-en avec vos camarades qui ne sont pas d'accord avec vous.

Structure 49

Le superlatif

Comparing and contrasting

—Super! C'est **le plus mauvais** jour de ma vie!

Superlatives, like comparisons, use **plus** and **moins**, **meilleur** and **mieux**, but the definite article (**le**, **la**, **les**) is added.

Superlatif des adjectifs

1. To form the superlative of adjectives, use **le**, **la**, or **les** before the comparative.

C'est **le plus mauvais** jour **de** ma vie.	*This is the worst day of my life.*

2. With adjectives, the superlative expression will precede or follow the noun, depending on the usual position of the adjective. If the superlative precedes the noun, the definite article appears only once, but if it follows the noun, the definite article is repeated.

Yasmine est **le** personnage **le moins âgé** de l'histoire.	*Yasmine is the youngest character in the story.*
Camille est **la meilleure** amie de Bruno.	*Camille is Bruno's best friend.*

Attention—A possessive adjective can replace a **de** phrase that expresses possession.

Camille est **sa meilleure** amie.	*Camille is his best friend.*

Superlatif des adverbes

Use **le plus** (*the most*) or **le moins** (*the least*) before the adverb to create a superlative. A superlative adverb follows the verb.

Rachid travaille **le plus diligemment de** tous les reporters.	*Rachid works the most diligently of all the reporters.*
Dans sa famille, Rachid parle **le mieux** arabe.	*In his family, Rachid speaks Arabic the best.*

Superlatif des quantités

To express superlative quantities, use **le plus de** (*the most*) + noun for the largest quantity and **le moins de** (*the least/fewest*) + noun for the smallest quantity. For superlatives of verbs, put **le plus** or **le moins** after the verb.

Dans la famille, c'est Camille qui a **le plus d'**amis.	*In her family, Camille has the most friends.*
C'est Camille qui travaille **le plus**.	*It's Camille who works the most.*

Activités

A. Réussir votre visite à Saint-Jean de Causse. Il y a plusieurs hôtels et restaurants près de Saint-Jean de Causse. Évaluez-les, puis faites deux phrases qui contiennent un superlatif. Suivez le modèle.

MODÈLE:
restaurant / grand →
Le plus grand restaurant est le Self Select. Le moins grand restaurant est Au Vieux Moulin.

1. hôtel / luxueux
2. restaurant / cher
3. logement / vieux
4. service / bon
5. hôtel / beau
6. cuisine / bon

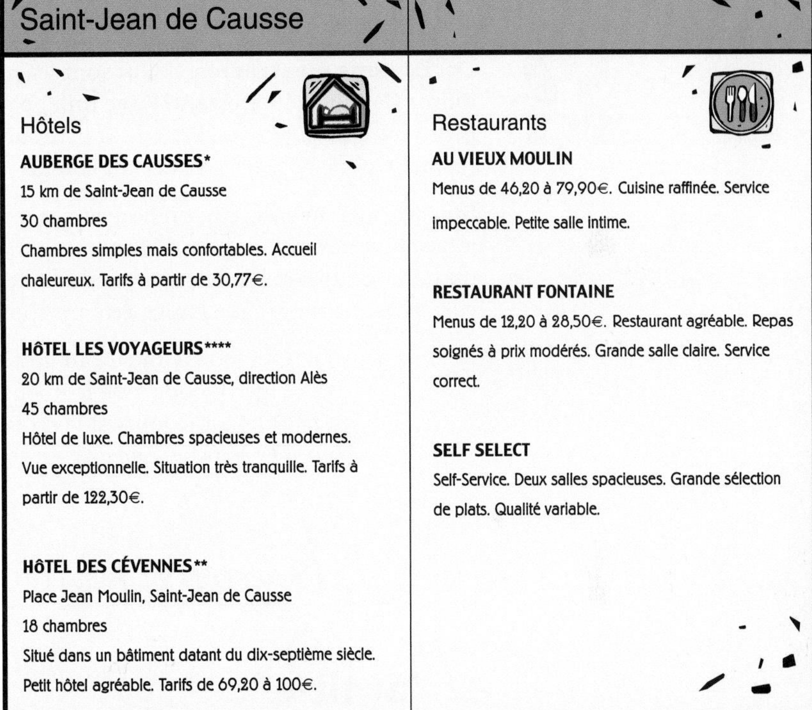
Saint-Jean de Causse

Hôtels

AUBERGE DES CAUSSES*
15 km de Saint-Jean de Causse
30 chambres
Chambres simples mais confortables. Accueil chaleureux. Tarifs à partir de 30,77€.

HÔTEL LES VOYAGEURS****
20 km de Saint-Jean de Causse, direction Alès
45 chambres
Hôtel de luxe. Chambres spacieuses et modernes. Vue exceptionnelle. Situation très tranquille. Tarifs à partir de 122,30€.

HÔTEL DES CÉVENNES**
Place Jean Moulin, Saint-Jean de Causse
18 chambres
Situé dans un bâtiment datant du dix-septième siècle. Petit hôtel agréable. Tarifs de 69,20 à 100€.

Restaurants

AU VIEUX MOULIN
Menus de 46,20 à 79,90€. Cuisine raffinée. Service impeccable. Petite salle intime.

RESTAURANT FONTAINE
Menus de 12,20 à 28,50€. Restaurant agréable. Repas soignés à prix modérés. Grande salle claire. Service correct.

SELF SELECT
Self-Service. Deux salles spacieuses. Grande sélection de plats. Qualité variable.

B. Identifiez. Pour chacune des actions suivantes, indiquez qui, parmi (*among*) vos connaissances, représente chaque extrême. Suivez le modèle.

MODÈLE: travailler sérieusement →
Mon amie Lisa travaille le plus sérieusement. Mon frère John travaille le moins sérieusement.

1. faire régulièrement du sport
2. aller souvent en boîte
3. écouter patiemment vos problèmes
4. vous conseiller logiquement
5. s'habiller élégamment
6. parler vite
7. manger bien

C. Êtes-vous matérialiste? Posez des questions à trois membres de la classe. Ensuite, comparez les réponses. Pouvez-vous déterminer qui est l'étudiant le plus matérialiste de la classe?

MODÈLE: voitures →
VOUS: Combien de voitures avez-vous?
JOHN: J'en ai deux.
LISA: J'en ai deux aussi.
SETH: Moi, je n'en ai pas.
VOUS: John a autant de voitures que Lisa, mais Seth a le moins de voitures. Il n'en a aucune.

1. ordinateurs
2. CD
3. paires de chaussures
4. montres
5. appareils photo
6. téléphones portables

D. Parlons d'extrêmes. Qui sont les meilleurs acteurs du monde? Quel est le journal le moins intéressant? Avec un(e) partenaire, posez des questions de ce genre sur cinq sujets (*subjects*) de la liste suivante. Prenez des notes sur ses réponses pour pouvoir en faire un compte rendu (*report*).

Sujets: jouer au golf, être un bon acteur, être une ville agréable à vivre, être un journal intéressant, gagner de l'argent, jouer au football américain, chanter, être un bon restaurant, parler en cours de français, être une personne connue de votre ville, être une montagne haute, être un sport bien payé, être une bonne profession

MODÈLE: É1: Qui joue le mieux au golf?
É2: Tiger Woods joue le mieux au golf.
É2: Quel est le journal le moins intéressant?
É1: *The National Enquirer* est le journal le moins intéressant.

Regards sur la culture

L'amitié°

quiz + movie

°Friendship

In Episode 16, Bruno reminds Camille that she can always count on him, that he is ready to join her immediately in the Cévennes if she should encounter any problem at all. Camille recognizes that Bruno is her best friend.

- French people generally have only a few friends, because friendship to them is a deep relationship and one that makes serious demands on one's time and attention. They check up on a friend nearly every day, and they expect to go out of their way frequently to do good turns for a friend. In short, a friend in France would expect you to participate fairly intensely in his or her life.
- Friends are not expected to agree on everything. The pleasures of debate and argument are a normal part of friendship.
- Married people in France, both men and women, may maintain friendships that they do not share with their spouses.

- Neighbors in France, whether in single-family homes or in apartments, do not expect to be friends. Proximity does not inspire friendship; shared interests and personal trust do.
- In France, people do not usually invite acquaintances to their homes. They might go out to dinner with people they know casually, but only good friends are invited into the closed domain of the home. Many North Americans who live in France are frustrated at not being invited home by the people they know. In the South, however, people tend to meet with friends in less planned, more spontaneous ways than in the North.
- Even good friends would normally not consider that they have the right to go beyond a few areas of a friend's home. They would probably not go into the kitchen, for example, and might not ever see the bedrooms. French people are shocked at the freedom that visitors seem to have in North American homes. The idea of serving oneself something from the refrigerator is anathema to the French!
- Most French people who visit North America are thrilled to find that they make many friends so quickly. They comment favorably on the openness and kindness of Americans and Canadians. However, those who stay for more than a couple of weeks are often bitterly disappointed when they find out that what seemed like "friendships" to them in fact have none of the depth and intensity that they expect of such a relationship in France.

Considérez

What is your reaction to the French notion of friendship? Would you prefer to have just a few very intense friendships, or maintain a larger number of less committed relationships? Why? What are the advantages and disadvantages of each custom?

Structure 50

Les pronoms interrogatifs (*suite*)

Asking questions

—**Qu'est-ce qui** s'est passé dans les Cévennes?

In Chapter 6, you learned to recognize the forms and meanings of most interrogative pronouns.

Qui est parti dans les Cévennes?
À quoi s'intéresse-t-elle?
Qu'est-ce qu'elle cherche?
Avec qui veut-elle parler?
Que fait elle pour trouver cette personne?
De quoi est-ce qu'elle a besoin?

Here is a complete chart of the interrogative pronouns. You already saw most of them in Chapter 6. The two new ones are the subject forms **qui est-ce qui** and **qu'est-ce qui**.

	PERSONNES	CHOSES
sujet	**qui**	—
	qui est-ce qui	**qu'est-ce qui**
objet	**qui**	**que**
objet d'une préposition	préposition + **qui**	préposition + **quoi**

Qui est-ce qui a parlé à Rachid? — *Who spoke to Rachid?*
Qu'est-ce qui inquiète Camille? — *What is worrying Camille?*

Remember—As objects, **qui**, **que**, and **quoi** can be followed by verb + subject (inversion) or by **est-ce que** + subject + verb.

De quoi Camille a-t-elle besoin?
De quoi est-ce que Camille a besoin?
} *What does Camille need?*

Activités

A. Rester chez moi? Jamais! On fait l'interview d'une vieille dame sportive. Indiquez à quelle question correspond chacune des réponses.

MODÈLE: Qu'est-ce que vous aimez faire le week-end? → J'aime faire des randonnées.

1. Qu'est-ce que vous aimez faire le week-end?
2. De quoi avez vous besoin pour vos randonnées?
3. Qui est-ce que vous rencontrez (*meet*) pendant vos randonnées?
4. Qu'est-ce qui se passe (*happens*) quand vous vous rencontrez?
5. Qu'est-ce qu'ils vous demandent?
6. Que pensez-vous de leur question?
7. Qu'est-ce qui vous empêche (*prevents*) d'aller en randonnée?
8. À qui est-ce que vous dites où vous allez?

a. Je le dis à mon petit-fils. Sinon (*Otherwise*), il s'inquiète.
b. Je rencontre des jeunes (*young people*).
c. J'ai besoin de mes chaussures de marche.
d. Ils veulent savoir mon âge.
e. Nous nous parlons.
f. Je ne pars pas quand il fait trop froid.
g. J'aime faire des randonnées.
h. Je la trouve normale. J'ai 86 ans!

Maintenant, identifiez l'expression interrogative dans chaque question et la partie de la réponse qui y correspond.

B. Un voyage important. Imaginez une conversation entre Mado et Camille. Camille explique (*explains*) son voyage dans les Cévennes. Complétez chaque question avec la forme interrogative (**qui**, **qui est-ce qui**, **qu'est-ce qui**, **que**, **quoi**) qui correspond à la réponse. Utilisez une préposition si c'est nécessaire.

MODÈLE: MADO: Qu'est-ce qui t'a donné l'idée de partir?
CAMILLE: La lettre d'Antoine m'a donné l'idée de partir.

1. MADO: _____ t'a donné l'adresse de Mme Leblanc?
   CAMILLE: Rachid m'a donné son adresse.
2. MADO: _____ a-t-il parlé quand il était à Saint-Jean?
   CAMILLE: Il a parlé avec le petit-fils de Mme Leblanc.
3. MADO: _____ est-ce que tu penses quand tu penses au voyage?
   CAMILLE: Je pense à ce village où mon grand-père a disparu.
4. MADO: _____ est-ce que tu penses de moi, avec cette histoire de photos découpées (*cut*)?
   CAMILLE: Je pense que tu étais une petite fille qui souffrait beaucoup.
5. MADO: _____ vas-tu faire en arrivant à Saint-Jean?
   CAMILLE: Je vais visiter le village.
6. MADO: _____ est-ce que tu vas voir après?
   CAMILLE: Je vais voir le petit-fils de Mme Leblanc.
7. MADO: _____ t'accompagne à la gare de Lyon?
   CAMILLE: Bruno m'accompagne à la gare.
8. CAMILLE: _____ t'inquiète, maman?
   MADO: Peut-être vas-tu apprendre que mon père était vraiment un traître.
9. MADO: _____ est-ce que tu as besoin pour le voyage?
   CAMILLE: J'ai simplement besoin de ton amour (*love*).

C. Les étudiants et les vacances. Imaginez que vous travaillez pour une agence de voyages qui se spécialise en vacances pour les étudiants. Posez cinq questions à deux étudiant(e)s. Ils/Elles doivent vous répondre en donnant leur propres opinions.

MODÈLE: É1: Qu'est-ce qui intéresse les étudiants?
É2: Les sports en plein air intéressent les étudiants.

	aimer faire
À/Avec/De qui	avoir peur
À/Avec/De quoi	devoir penser avant le voyage
Qu'est-ce qui	inquiéter les parents
Qu'est-ce que	intéresser les étudiants
Qui est-ce qui	vouloir voyager
	?

Visionnement 2

Observez!

Considérez les aspects culturels expliqués dans **Regards sur la culture**. Ensuite, regardez l'Épisode 16 encore une fois, et répondez aux questions suivantes.

- Pourquoi Martine laisse-t-elle partir Camille? Est-ce une décision basée sur des critères professionnels ou sur une amitié personnelle?
- Comment Bruno montre-t-il son amitié pour Camille?

Après le visionnement

Faites l'activité pour le **Visionnement 2** dans le cahier.

Synthèse: Lecture

Mise en contexte

In the **Regards sur la culture** section of this chapter, you learned a few things about the French notion of friendship. This **Synthèse** section contains a few maxims—short, pithy observations about people and society—formulated by some well-known French writers over the centuries.* Although some were written over three hundred years ago, many people feel that they are still relevant today.

Stratégie pour mieux lire
Paraphrasing

Good maxims are finely crafted and concise. Still, restating the idea in a different language, or paraphrasing, may enable you to understand the nuances of their observations. For example, which paraphrase best explains this maxim?

> «Nous aimons toujours ceux qui (*those who*) nous admirent, et nous n'aimons pas toujours ceux que (*those whom*) nous admirons.»
>
> La Rochefoucauld (1613–1680)

*The French writers quoted are novelists (Balzac, Colette), playwrights (Molière, d'Harleville), and other men and women of letters (Chamfort, La Rochefoucauld, Mme de Staël).

a. We often mistake self-interest for friendship.

b. We like people who look up to us and not those whom we look up to.

As you read the following **maximes** about friendship and love, formulate a paraphrase in English that you think approximately expresses the meaning of each one. Also think about which one (if any) expresses your own observations about friendship or love.

L'amitié et l'amour

«Un ami est long à trouver et prompt à perdre.»
Anonyme

«Nous pardonnons aisément[2] à nos amis les défauts[3] qui ne nous regardent[4] pas.»
La Rochefoucauld (1613–1680)

«On est aisément dupé[5] par ce qu'on aime.»
Molière (1622–1673)

«Dans le monde, vous avez trois sortes d'amis: vos amis qui vous aiment, vos amis qui ne se soucient[6] pas de vous, et vos amis qui vous haïssent.[7]»
Chamfort (1741–1794)

«Il faut[8] aimer les gens, non pour soi, mais pour eux.»
Collin d'Harleville (1755–1806)

«L'amour est un égoïsme[9] à deux.»
Mme de Staël (1766–1817)

«On n'est point[10] l'ami d'une femme lorsqu'on[11] peut être son amant.[12]»
Honoré de Balzac (1799–1850)

«Quand on est aimé, on ne doute de rien. Quand on aime, on doute de tout.»
Colette (1873–1954)

[1]*displeases* [2]*easily* [3]*faults* [4]*concern* [5]*fooled* [6]*se... care* [7]*hate* [8]*Il... One must* [9]*selfishness* [10]*absolutely not* [11]*when one* [12]*lover*

Colette

Après la lecture

A. Avez-vous compris? Les phrases suivantes sont des paraphrases des maximes. Pour chacune, notez la maxime qui convient (*fits*).

1. Pourquoi rester ami si on peut devenir amant?
2. Il est facile de pardonner les actions d'un ami si ces actions ne vous blessent (*injure, hurt*) pas.
3. Ceux qui (*Those who*) se disent votre ami ne le sont pas tous.

4. L'amitié est une chose fragile.
5. On est aveuglé (*blinded*) par l'amitié.
6. Pour être l'ami de quelqu'un, il faut abandonner l'égoïsme.
7. Il est plus facile de se sentir (*feel*) sûr de soi quand on reçoit des preuves (*proof*) d'amour que quand on en donne.
8. L'amour entre deux personnes exclut les autres.

B. Réfléchissez. Répondez aux questions suivantes.

1. Choisissez une maxime qui exprime vos propres (*own*) idées sur le thème de l'amitié ou de l'amour. S'il n'y en a pas, créez (*create*) votre propre maxime.
2. Quelle maxime trouvez-vous la moins vraie?
3. Quelle maxime réflète le mieux une caractéristique de l'amitié qui existe entre Bruno et Camille? Est-ce que leur amitié contredit une des maximes? Laquelle (*Which one*)?

À écrire

Faites **À écrire** pour le Chapitre 16 dans le cahier.

Vocabulaire

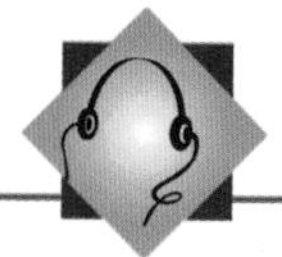

Les loisirs

aller à la pêche	to go fishing
chasser	to hunt
cueillir (des fleurs, des champignons)	to pick (flowers, mushrooms)
faire de la planche à voile	to windsurf
faire de la spéléologie	to explore caves
faire de la voile	to sail
faire de l'escalade	to go rock climbing
faire du parapente	to hang glide
faire du patin à glace	to ice skate
faire du ski de fond	to cross-country ski
faire du ski nautique	to waterski
faire du surf de neige	to snowboard
faire du vélo	to bike
faire du VTT	to mountain bike
faire une randonnée	to hike
jouer à la pétanque (aux boules)	to play lawn bowling
monter à cheval	to ride a horse
nager	to swim
patiner	to ice skate

MOTS APPARENTÉS: **faire de la photographie, faire du camping, faire du canoë, faire du ski, faire un pique-nique, jouer au Frisbee, jouer au golf, jouer au hockey, piqueniquer, prendre une photo, skier**

L'équipement et les lieux pour les loisirs

une balle ball (*not inflated with air*)
un ballon ball (*inflated with air*)
un bateau (à voile) (sail)boat
un camping campground
une équipe team
des loisirs (*m. pl.*) leisure activities
un panier basket
des patins (*m.*) ice skates
une piste trail; track; ski run
une plage beach
des vacances (*f. pl.*) vacation

MOTS APPARENTÉS: **un festival (des festivals), un frisbee**
À REVOIR: **une fête**

Les animaux

un cerf deer, stag
un chat cat
un cheval horse
un chien dog
un lapin rabbit
un oiseau bird
un ours bear
une souris mouse; computer mouse

MOTS APPARENTÉS: **un animal (des animaux)**
À REVOIR: **un poisson**

Autre Verbe

accueillir to welcome

Expressions interrogatives

qui est-ce qui who (*subject of sentence*)
qu'est-ce qui what (*subject of sentence*)

À REVOIR: **qui, que, quoi**

Pour faire des comparaisons

aussi... que as . . . as
autant (de...) que as much/many (. . . as)
meilleur(e)(s) (que) better (than)
mieux (que) better (than)
moins (de...) less/fewer (. . .)
moins (que) less/fewer (than)
plus (de...) more (. . .)
plus (que) more (than)
le/la/les meilleur(e)(s) (de) the best (of)
le mieux (de) the best (of)
le/la/les moins (de) the least (of)
le/la/les plus (de) the most (of)

Autres expressions utiles

en plein air outdoors
en vacances on vacation
une fleur flower
surtout especially

Chapitre 17

Je cherche la trace d'un homme.

OBJECTIFS

In this episode, you will

- learn the possible consequences of Camille's "vacation" from the show
- meet a new character who helps Camille move forward in her quest

In this chapter, you will

- talk about geographical features
- ask and give directions
- talk about the future
- use direct object and indirect object pronouns in the same sentence
- use **c'est** and **il/elle est** in different situations
- learn about the causes of population shifts in France and in Africa during the 20th century

Vocabulaire en contexte

Le relief° de la France

La France a **un relief** varié. Le pays se divise en deux parties: l'une, au **nord** et à l'**ouest**, a des reliefs faibles°; l'autre, au **sud** et à l'**est**, a des reliefs élevés.° Le Massif central est **un** vaste **ensemble** de **hauteurs**° et de dépressions aux aspects **divers**.

Le… The topography …

low / high

elevations, heights

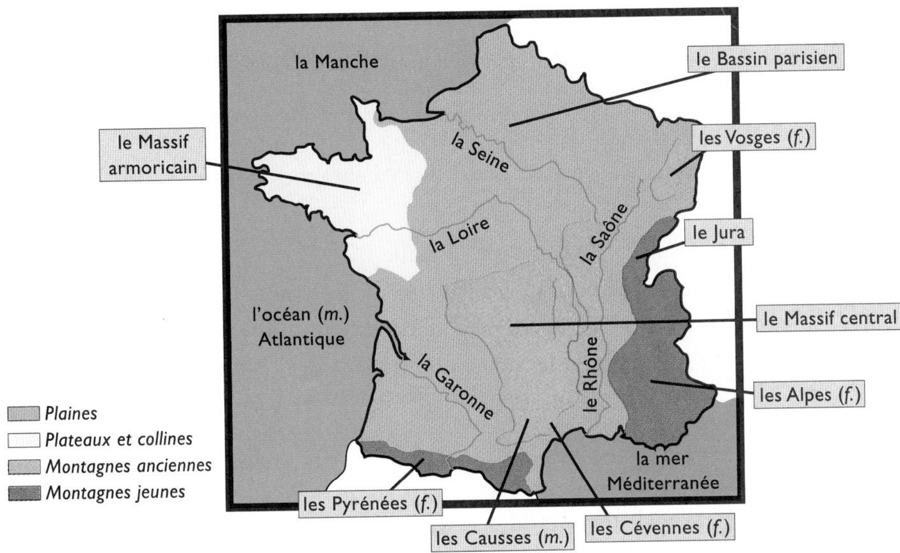

Lexique géographique

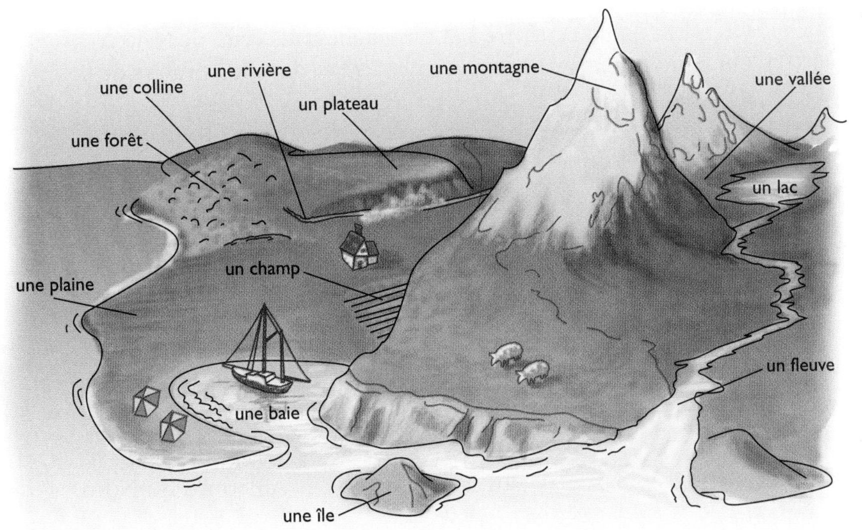

Autres expressions utiles

une côte	coast
au bord de	on the banks (shore, edge) of
à la campagne	in the country

Activités

A. Le connaissez-vous? La liste suivante identifie des endroits très connus. Indiquez le terme géographique qui les décrit.

MODÈLE: Alpes, Rocheuses → Ce sont des montagnes.

1. Guam, Hawaii, Martinique, Porto Rico
2. Adriatique, Baltique, des Caraïbes, Méditerranée
3. Amazone, Mississippi, Saint-Laurent, Seine
4. Everest, Kilimandjaro, McKinley, Rainier
5. Baffin, Biscayne, Chesapeake, d'Hudson
6. Érié, Supérieur, Tahoe, Victoria

B. Repérez. Regardez la carte d'Europe au début de votre livre et situez les pays en suivant le modèle.

MODÈLE: la France / l'Allemagne / l'Espagne / la Grande-Bretagne →
La France se trouve à l'ouest de l'Allemagne, au nord de l'Espagne et au sud de la Grande-Bretagne.

1. la Suisse / la France / l'Allemagne / l'Italie
2. la Belgique / le Luxembourg / les Pays-Bas / la France
3. l'Espagne / la France / le Portugal / la mer Méditerranée
4. la Pologne / l'Allemagne / la Slovaquie / l'Ukraine
5. le Danemark / la Grande-Bretagne / la Norvège / l'Allemagne

C. Poursuite triviale géographique. Inventez des questions sur la géographie de votre pays et posez-les à votre partenaire. Vous pouvez utiliser les verbes **se trouver** et **se situer**, des adjectifs comme **grand**, **vaste** et **vieux** et les indications données. Vous pouvez aussi utiliser vos propres (*own*) idées.

MODÈLES: Quelle grande chaîne de montagnes se trouve dans l'ouest du Canada et des États-Unis? →
Les Rocheuses se trouvent dans l'ouest du Canada et des États-Unis.

Où est-ce qu'on peut être à la campagne dans l'état de New York? →
On peut être à la campagne au centre et dans le nord-est de l'état de New York.

une baie	au bord de l'océan Atlantique
des champs de blé (*wheat*)	au bord de l'océan Pacifique
des collines	au centre des États-Unis / du Canada
un fleuve / une rivière	dans l'est des États-Unis / du Canada
une forêt	dans le nord des États-Unis / du Canada
une île / des îles	dans l'ouest des États-Unis / du Canada
un lac / des lacs	dans le sud des États-Unis / du Canada
des montagnes	dans l'état / la province de...
un plateau	sur la côte est de l'Amérique du Nord
une vallée	sur la côte ouest de l'Amérique du Nord
à la campagne	?

Demander et donner le chemin°

Demander... *Asking and giving directions*

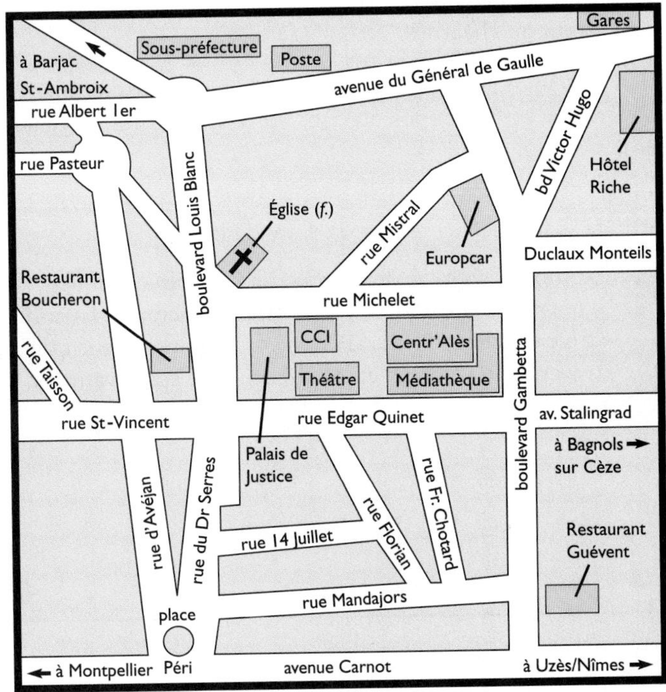

Camille arrive à Alès et veut louer une voiture pour aller à Saint-Jean de Causse. Comment trouve-t-elle l'agence de location° Europcar?

agence... *rental agency*

CAMILLE: Pardon, monsieur, **est-ce que vous pourriez° m'indiquer le chemin pour aller à** une agence de location de voitures?

could

HOMME: Bien sûr, mademoiselle. **Descendez l'avenue** du Général de Gaulle, en allant **vers°** la poste. **Tournez à gauche°** à la deuxième rue, le boulevard Gambetta, et allez **tout droit.°** L'agence Europcar est au **coin°** de la rue Mistral.

toward / à... *to the left*
tout... *straight ahead*
corner

CAMILLE: Et pour aller à Saint-Jean de Causse, s'il vous plaît?

HOMME: **Remontez° l'avenue** du Général de Gaulle. Après **le** deuxième **feu,°** vous allez voir **un poteau indicateur°** pour la D904 direction Saint-Ambroix. Continuez jusqu'à la sortie pour la D906. Prenez la D906 direction Villefort.

Go back up / *traffic light*
poteau... *sign(post)*

Autres expressions utiles

à droite to/on the right **une carte** map **traverser** to cross

Activités

A. À Alès. Comment va-t-on...

1. du Palais de Justice à la poste?
2. de l'église au restaurant Guévent?

3. de la médiathèque à la place Péri?
4. du coin de l'avenue Carnot et du boulevard Gambetta au Centr'Alès?
5. du Centr'Alès à la sous-préfecture?
6. de la rue Pasteur au théâtre?

B. Chez vous. Demandez à votre partenaire de vous dire comment aller d'un endroit à un autre sur votre campus ou dans votre ville. Votre partenaire doit vous indiquer le chemin.

Vocabulaire utile: le bâtiment de l'administration, la bibliothèque, la cafétéria, le centre sportif, le gymnase, le parking, la piste de jogging

MODÈLE: É1: Comment va-t-on de la cafétéria à la bibliothèque?
É2: Tu sors de la cafétéria par l'entrée principale. Tu continues tout droit vers le gymnase. Tu vas voir le parking sur ta gauche. Tu traverses le parking, et la bibliothèque est devant toi.

Visionnement 1

Avant de visionner

A. Le contexte. À la fin de l'Épisode 16, Camille est partie pour Saint-Jean de Causse. Martine n'était pas contente. Lisez cette conversation téléphonique qui introduit l'Épisode 17. Utilisez le contexte pour deviner (*guess*) la signification des mots en italique.

BRUNO: En fait,[a] tu sais, on a des problèmes ici, hein...
CAMILLE: Tu m'as choisi une remplaçante[b]? Comment est-elle?
BRUNO: Non, Camille. Je ne plaisante pas,[c] là! Je suis vraiment très *embêté*...
CAMILLE: Un problème d'argent. Combien te faut-il,[d] cette fois-ci?
BRUNO: Mais non, ce n'est pas ça! En fait, le problème, Camille, c'est toi, voilà! Ton absence est très mal acceptée par le président, et...
CAMILLE: Ah! Qu'est-ce qu'il a dit?
BRUNO: Ben,[e] officiellement, rien, mais, euh, il y a des rumeurs, hein! On parle d'un *licenciement* possible...
CAMILLE: Quoi, le président me met à la porte?!
BRUNO: *Méfie-toi*, il en est capable, tu sais!
CAMILLE: *Je m'en fiche!*
BRUNO: Quoi... ?
CAMILLE: Je m'en fiche, Bruno! Ce voyage est très important pour moi. Tu comprends, c'est pff![f]

[a]En... *In fact* [b]*replacement* [c]Je... *I'm not joking* [d]te... *do you need* [e]*Well* [f]c'est... *the rest is nothing!*

B. Quel ton? Regardez encore une fois le dialogue dans l'Activité A. De quel ton Bruno et Camille doivent-ils dire chacune (*each one*) des phrases dans cette scène?

d'un ton compatissant (*caringly*)
d'un ton fâché
d'un ton grave
d'un ton impatient
d'un ton incrédule (*incredulously*)
d'un ton indifférent
d'un ton inquiet
d'un ton sérieux
en plaisantant (*jokingly*)

MODÈLE: En fait, tu sais, on a des problèmes ici, hein... →
Bruno dit ça d'un ton inquiet. (Bruno dit ça d'un ton sérieux.)

Observez!

Dans l'Épisode 17, Camille arrive à Saint-Jean de Causse. Regardez l'épisode, et trouvez les réponses aux questions suivantes.

- Qui est Éric? Qu'apprenez-vous sur sa famille et sur l'endroit où il habite?
- Est-ce que les attitudes de Louise et de Jeanne Leblanc envers (*toward*) la guerre se ressemblent?

Vocabulaire relatif à l'épisode

à peine	*hardly*
j'ai hérité de la ferme	*I inherited the farm*
il a disparu	*he disappeared*
ne vous le dira pas	*won't tell you*
son mari était un résistant	*her husband was a resistance fighter*
l'ont tué	*killed him*

Après le visionnement

A. Pourquoi? Expliquez pourquoi les personnages du film font les actions suivantes dans l'Épisode 17.

1. Pourquoi Bruno téléphone-t-il à Camille?
2. Pourquoi Camille semble-t-elle indifférente à l'idée d'un licenciement éventuel?
3. Pourquoi Camille ne veut-elle pas téléphoner au président?
4. Pourquoi Camille cherche-t-elle à parler avec Éric?
5. Pourquoi y a-t-il peu de jeunes dans le village?
6. Pourquoi est-ce qu'Éric tient particulièrement à (*is fond of*) sa grand-mère?
7. Pourquoi Camille veut-elle parler avec la grand-mère d'Éric?
8. Pourquoi, selon Éric, est-ce que sa grand-mère ne va pas parler avec Camille?

B. Réfléchissez. Répondez aux questions suivantes.

1. Comprenez-vous l'attitude du président envers Camille? Est-ce qu'il a tort?
2. Bruno suggère à Camille de parler avec le président. Elle refuse, disant qu'elle ne le connaît pas. Prend-elle la bonne décision, ou non?

Notez bien!

To say that you miss someone or something, use the verb **manquer à**. In French, the person or thing missed is the subject of the sentence; an indirect object is used to identify the person who misses.

Tu **me manques**. *I miss you.*
Antoine **manque à** Louise. Il **lui manque**. *Louise misses Antoine. She misses him.*

Structure 51

Le futur

Narrating

—En été, avec la nouvelle route, les touristes **pourront** monter plus facilement jusqu'au village.

Le temps futur

1. To form the future tense, add the endings **-ai**, **-as**, **-a**, **-ons**, **-ez**, **-ont** to the infinitive. In the case of **-re** verbs, the **e** of the infinitive ending is dropped before adding the ending.

	regarder	répondre	réussir
je	regarder**ai**	répondr**ai**	réussir**ai**
tu	regarder**as**	répondr**as**	réussir**as**
il, elle, on	regarder**a**	répondr**a**	réussir**a**
nous	regarder**ons**	répondr**ons**	réussir**ons**
vous	regarder**ez**	répondr**ez**	réussir**ez**
ils, elles	regarder**ont**	répondr**ont**	réussir**ont**

Mais ma grand-mère ne vous le **dira** pas. *But my grandmother will not tell you.*

2. All verbs in the future tense have the same endings, but some verbs have irregular stems.

INFINITIF	RADICAL	FUTUR AVEC *JE*
aller	**ir-**	j'irai
avoir	**aur-**	j'aurai
cueillir	**cueiller-**	je cueillerai
devoir	**devr-**	je devrai
envoyer	**enverr-**	j'enverrai
être	**ser-**	je serai
faire	**fer-**	je ferai
pouvoir	**pourr-**	je pourrai
recevoir	**recevr-**	je recevrai
savoir	**saur-**	je saurai
venir	**viendr-**	je viendrai
voir	**verr-**	je verrai
vouloir	**voudr-**	je voudrai

Allez tout droit et vous **verrez** le monument aux morts devant vous. — *Go straight ahead and you will see the war memorial right in front of you.*

3. Some spelling-change verbs have an irregular stem in the future.

VERBES COMME...	RADICAL	FUTUR AVEC *JE*
acheter	**achèter-**	j'achèterai
appeler	**appeller-**	j'appellerai
payer	**paier-**	je paierai

Tu m'**achèteras** une bonne bouteille de champagne? — *Will you buy me a good bottle of champagne?*

However, verbs like **préférer** don't have a spelling change in the future.

Quel film est-ce que tu **préféreras** voir? — *Which movie will you prefer to see?*

Les phrases avec *si* et *quand*

1. To say that something will happen *if* another event occurs, use **si** + present tense for the possible event and the future tense for what will happen. The two clauses can appear in either order.

Si Camille **parle** à Mme Leblanc, est-ce qu'elle **apprendra** la vérité? — *If Camille talks to Mme Leblanc, will she learn the truth?*

Camille **apprendra** la vérité **si** elle **parle** à Mme Leblanc. — *Camille will learn the truth if she talks to Mme Leblanc.*

2. To say that something will happen *when* another event occurs, use **quand** + future tense for the upcoming event and another future tense verb for what will happen when the first event occurs. The two clauses can appear in either order.

Quand elle **arrivera** chez Mme Leblanc, Éric **sera** à la porte.	*When she arrives at Mme Leblanc's house, Éric will be at the door.*
Éric **sera** à la porte **quand** elle **arrivera** chez Mme Leblanc.	*Éric will be at the door when she arrives at Mme Leblanc's house.*

Activités

A. Qu'est-ce qui va se passer? Les personnages du film veulent faire certaines choses. Est-ce qu'ils réussiront? Transformez les phrases suivantes en utilisant le futur simple et mettez-les à l'affirmatif ou au négatif selon vos prédictions.

MODÈLE: Camille veut rencontrer Mme Leblanc. →
Camille rencontrera Mme Leblanc. (Camille ne rencontrera pas Mme Leblanc.)

1. Camille veut savoir la vérité.
2. Camille veut aller chez Jeanne Leblanc.
3. Camille veut voir Mme Leblanc.
4. Camille veut apprendre des détails sur son grand-père.
5. Mme Leblanc ne veut pas lui répondre.
6. Bruno veut appeler Camille chaque jour.
7. Bruno veut venir rejoindre (*to join*) Camille à Saint-Jean de Causse.
8. Camille veut finir par trouver la trace de son grand-père.
9. Camille veut comprendre sa mère.
10. Mado veut avoir l'amour de sa fille.

B. Une visite en France. Michel parle de ce qu'il fera avec ses amis quand ils viendront en France.

Mon ami Paul _____[1] (arriver) en juin avec sa nouvelle femme. Ils _____[2] (ne pas pouvoir) rester chez moi, parce qu'il y _____[3] (avoir) déjà un autre ami chez moi. Il _____[4] (venir) avec nous en voyage. Le premier soir, je _____[5] (préparer) un dîner où tout le monde _____[6] (pouvoir) faire connaissance.

Ils ne le savent pas encore, mais nous _____[7] (partir) vers le sud de la France, à Nice, où nous _____[8] (voir) la mer et la montagne. Ce _____[9] (être) super. On _____[10] (se lever) tard, on _____[11] (aller) à la plage, et on _____[12] (faire du roller). Je _____[13] (prendre) probablement un coup de soleil.° Paul et

°coup… *sunburn*

sa femme ______[14] (acheter) certainement des souvenirs et il les ______[15] (payer) cher. Nous ______[16] (visiter) ensuite des villages de la vallée du Rhône où nous ______[17] (boire) du bon vin et où nous ______[18] (manger) des plats régionaux.

Nous ______[19] (devoir) retourner à Paris avant la fin du mois, mais je suis sûr que mes amis ______[20] (être) contents du voyage, et je pense que nous ______[21] (vouloir) passer d'autres vacances ensemble.

C. La vie des gens dans la classe. Terminez les phrases à votre façon (*in your own way*). Ensuite, comparez vos réponses avec celles de deux autres étudiant(e)s.

1. Si je suis fatigué(e) ce soir,...
2. Les étudiants iront au cinéma quand...
3. Si ma famille et moi nous voyageons en France l'année prochaine,...
4. Quand mon professeur visitera un pays francophone,...
5. Si j'ai le temps ce week-end,...
6. J'aurai de bonnes notes en cours quand...

D. Âmes sœurs. (*Kindred spirits.*) Interviewez trois camarades de classe pour savoir où ils/elles seront dans cinq ans, quelle sera leur routine quotidienne, et ce qu'ils/elles feront pour s'amuser. Est-ce que vous trouverez une âme sœur dans la classe?

Structure 52

Les pronoms complément d'objet direct et indirect

Avoiding repetition

—Mais ma grand-mère ne **vous le** dira pas.

You have already learned how to place direct object pronouns and indirect object pronouns in a sentence. Now you will learn how to use them at the same time.

1. When there is more than one object pronoun in a declarative sentence, they are positioned in the following order.

me				
te	**le**	**lui**		
se	**la**		**y**	**en**
nous	**les**	**leur**		
vous				

—Rachid donne-t-il l'adresse à Camille?	*Does Rachid give Camille the address?*
—Oui, il **la lui** donne.	*Yes, he gives it to her.*

In negative sentences, the pronouns follow **ne** and precede the verb.

—Tu ne conseilles pas cet hôtel?	*You don't recommend this hotel?*
—C'est ça. Je ne **te le** conseille pas.	*That's right. I don't recommend it to you.*

Remember—**Y** is never used to refer to people. To represent a phrase containing **à** + person, use an indirect object pronoun (**à Camille → lui**). **En** cannot be used to refer to **de** + person. In that case, use **de** + stressed pronoun after the verb (**de Camille → d'elle**). **En** can be used, however, to represent a person that is a direct object introduced by an indefinite article, partitive article, or expression of quantity (**Vous avez un enfant? Oui, j'en ai un.**)

2. The same rules for the placement of object pronouns apply for two pronouns as for one. In simples tenses (the present, the **imparfait**, and the future), object pronouns precede the verb. In compound tenses (the **passé composé**), object pronouns precede the auxiliary verb. In the **futur proche**, object pronouns precede the verb of which they are an object, usually the infinitive.

Tu me choisis une remplaçante? → Tu **m'en** choisis une?

Tu m'as choisi une remplaçante? → Tu **m'en** a choisi une?

Tu vas me choisir une remplaçante? → Tu vas **m'en** choisir une?

Remember—In the **passé composé** with the auxiliary verb **avoir**, the past participle must agree with a preceding direct object pronoun.

La photo? Je **te** l'ai trouvée.	*The photo? I found it for you.*

3. In the negative imperative, both object pronouns precede the verb.

Ne **lui en** parle pas!	*Don't talk to him about it!*

In the affirmative imperative, the object pronouns follow the verb and are joined to the verb by hyphens. **Me** and **te** become **moi** and **toi**, except when they come before **en**.The order of the pronouns with an affirmative imperative is as follows:

objet direct	objet indirect	y	en

Donne l'adresse à Camille! → Donne-**la-lui**. *Give it to her.*
Montrez-moi la photo! → Montrez-**la-moi**. *Show it to me.*
Conseille-moi un hôtel! → Conseille-**m'en** un. *Recommend one to me.*

Activités

A. Interactions. Répondez aux questions en remplaçant les mots soulignés par des compléments d'objet direct et indirect ou **y** ou **en**.

MODÈLE: Est-ce que Bruno donne des conseils à Camille? →
Oui, il lui en donne.

1. Bruno parle-t-il à Camille des problèmes?
2. Est-ce que Camille trouve des noms sur le monument aux morts?
3. Camille pose-t-elle des questions aux joueurs de pétanque?
4. Camille demande-t-elle des renseignements (*information*) à la patronne du bar?
5. Est-ce que la patronne du bar parle à Camille de la famille Leblanc?
6. Est-ce que la patronne montre Éric à Camille?
7. Camille parle-t-elle à Éric de son grand-père?
8. Est-ce qu'Éric donne l'adresse (*f.*) à Camille?

B. C'est déjà fait. Magali, Danielle et Carine organisent un week-end à la montagne. Magali suggère quelques préparatifs aux deux autres, mais elles ont déjà tout fait! Suivez le modèle.

MODÈLE: MAGALI: Empruntez (*Borrow*) les sacs à dos à vos frères.
DANIELLE ET CARINE: Nous les leur avons déjà empruntés.

1. Parlez de notre itinéraire (*m.*) à vos parents.
2. Donnez-moi l'argent pour la tente.
3. Mettez des chaussures de randonnée dans le sac.
4. Apportez-moi (*Bring me*) les provisions que vous avez achetées.
5. Cherchez une carte de la région dans le placard (*cupboard*).
6. Trouvez-moi mon appareil photo.
7. Expliquez notre itinéraire à mon frère.
8. Prenez de l'essence (*gasoline*) pour la voiture à la station service.

C. Un adolescent mal élevé. Paul n'est pas gentil. Il refuse de faire ce que sa mère veut. Aidez sa mère à lui dire ce qu'il doit faire immédiatement. Suivez le modèle.

MODÈLE: PAUL: Je ne veux pas montrer mes livres à ma petite cousine!
SA MÈRE: Montre-les-lui maintenant!

1. Je refuse de donner le café à papa.
2. Je ne veux pas te parler de ma petite amie.
3. Je refuse de donner des cadeaux à mes grands-parents.

4. Je ne veux pas manger de la salade à la cantine.
5. Je ne veux pas écrire la lettre à tante Élisabeth.
6. Je n'ai pas envie de me regarder dans le miroir.
7. Je refuse de vous présenter mes amis de l'école.
8. Je ne veux pas parler de mes problèmes au psychiatre.

Maintenant, imaginez que la mère de Paul s'exaspère. Donnez les mêmes ordres au négatif en commençant par «Bon, très bien... »

MODÈLE: PAUL: Je ne veux pas montrer mes livres à ma petite cousine!
SA MÈRE: Bon, très bien, ne les lui montre pas!

D. Êtes-vous un bon ami / une bonne amie? Posez les questions suivantes à votre partenaire qui répondra en utilisant deux pronoms. Ensuite, analysez les réponses. Pensez-vous que votre partenaire a les traits d'un bon ami / d'une bonne amie?

MODÈLE: É1: Racontes-tu des mensonges (*lies*) à tes ami(e)s?
É2: Non, je ne leur en raconte pas. (Oui, je leur en raconte de temps en temps.)

Demandez à votre partenaire...

1. s'il / si elle parle de ses problèmes personnels à son meilleur ami / sa meilleure amie.
2. s'il / si elle offre parfois des cadeaux (*gifts*) à ses amis.
3. s'il / si elle cache (*hides*) ses émotions aux autres.
4. s'il / si elle oublie parfois d'envoyer une carte à son meilleur ami / sa meilleure amie pour son anniversaire.
5. s'il / si elle excuse les défauts (*faults*) de caractère à ses ami(e)s.
6. s'il / si elle ne répète pas les secrets intimes de ses amis aux autres.

Regards sur la culture

Le déclin de la campagne

Camille notices that there are not many people around in Saint-Jean de Causse. Éric tells her, however, that a new road has been built to the village and that this will certainly bring in many tourists during the summer months. The situation of Saint-Jean de Causse is similar to that of many other villages in France.

- Paris has long been the undisputed center of France. In French, one is by definition either **Parisien** or **provincial**. Even those who live in large cities such as Lyon or Marseille are "provincials."
- At the same time, the villages of rural France are the backbone of many French people's vision of their country. Many urban dwellers speak of a rural region as their family's place of origin, even if they have lived their whole lives in the city.

- At the time of the Second World War, a very high percentage of France's population did work in agriculture as compared with other developed countries such as Britain and Germany. But today, fewer than 30% of the farms of that period are still active. This relatively rapid depopulation of rural France has been called **l'exode rural**.

Ancien village de Conques, Aveyron

- The economic shift away from agricultural work since the Second World War has also been a cultural shift, as young people moved to the cities. Young women were in the forefront of this movement, and, for the past forty years, young men who wanted to maintain the family farm were sometimes unable to find wives.
- Along with the decline of traditional agriculture, France is experiencing the decline and loss of many regional traditions that had their roots in rural populations, including the daily use of languages such as Breton, Basque, and Occitan.
- Villages such as Saint-Jean de Causse in the Cévennes that today might have fifty or sixty inhabitants could have had as many as five hundred in 1880. Two institutions seem to symbolize to local people the survival of a living village community: the local grocery store and the elementary school. The closing of the school is always a particularly dramatic—and sad—event.

Dans les Pyrénées

- One result of the rural exodus is the existence of abandoned or nearly abandoned villages, particularly in areas that are difficult to reach. These places are often extraordinarily picturesque, and, in some cases, have been bought up by Europeans from other countries or by wealthy Parisians to serve as vacation sites.
- Despite this dramatic decline in rural populations and traditional farming, France is still a very important power in agriculture: It produces 21.4% of the agricultural output of the European Union, by far the largest percentage of any of the members (the next highest is Italy, with 16%).

Considérez

French attitudes toward farming as a career have been relatively negative for quite a long time. Today, a young person who decides to go into farming often feels a bit defensive. Why would this be? What perceptions and attitudes related to farming as an occupation are there in your culture?

Structure 53

L'emploi de *il/elle est* et de *c'est*

Identifying and describing

—Peut-être, mais **il est** essentiel de vivre, aussi! Je suis mal en ce moment et j'ai besoin de repos, tu peux comprendre ça?...

The constructions **il est** and **c'est** can be used in a variety of ways.

1. To describe or make a judgment about an *action,* the construction **il est** + adjective + **de** + infinitive is used. In this usage, **il** is impersonal and is translated as *it.* **Il** "announces" an upcoming topic.

Il est important de découvrir ses origines.	*It is important to find one's roots.*
Il n'est pas facile de cacher son émotion.	*It isn't easy to hide one's emotions.*

2. To describe or make a judgment about an *idea* or a *situation* that was already mentioned, the construction **c'est +** adjective (+ **à** + infinitive) is used. **Ce** refers back to the idea or situation that was already mentioned.

Un traître? **C'est difficile à croire.**	*A traitor? That's hard to believe.*
Préparer un bon pain, **c'est difficile**.	*Making a good bread is difficult.*

3. You have already learned some other uses of **il est**, **elle est**, and **c'est** that refer to actual people and things (not actions, ideas, or situations).

   - **Il/elle est** and **ils/elles sont** can be followed by an adjective, an adverb, or by a profession, nationality, religion, or political affiliation (with no article and no modifying adjective).

...et votre bordeaux, **il est parfait**.	*. . . and your bordeaux, it's perfect.*
Le troisième a peur. **Il est juif.**	*The third is afraid. He's Jewish.*

For Tues.

C'est ta femme? **Elle est jolie!**	*Is that your wife? She's pretty!*
Ton bureau, **il est là**.	*Your desk, it's there.*
Ton ami. **Il est professeur** à l'université?	*Your friend. Is he a professor at the university?*

- **C'est**, **ce sont**, and **est-ce** can be followed by a stressed pronoun, a name, or a noun preceded by a marker such as an article or a possessive adjective.

En fait, le problème, Camille, **c'est toi**!	*In fact, the problem is you, Camille!*
Camille, **c'est Bruno**!	*Camille, it's Bruno!*
C'est un cadeau de ma grand-mère...	*It's a gift from my grandmother . . .*
C'est le grand brun là, qui joue au flipper.	*He's the tall brown-haired guy playing pinball over there.*
C'est ta femme?	*Is that your wife?*

Activités

A. Camille à Saint-Jean de Causse. Utilisez **c'est**, **ce sont**, **il est**, **elle est**, **ils sont** ou **elles sont** pour compléter le résumé de l'Épisode 17.

D'abord, Camille rencontre quelqu'un. ______1 une petite fille. ______2 très gentille. Camille regarde ensuite le monument aux morts. ______3 triste parce qu'elle y voit une liste des gens qui sont morts pendant la guerre. ______4 des soldats et des civils. ______5 difficile d'imaginer l'horreur de la guerre.

Puis, Camille voit des joueurs de pétanque. ______6 des gens du village. ______7 impossible d'en être sûr, mais ______8 peut-être communistes, comme beaucoup de vieux dans des villages. ______9 une tradition politique dans certaines régions.

Après cela,[a] Camille rencontre une femme dans le bar des Cévennes. ______10 la patronne. ______11 une femme travailleuse,[b] mais ______12 sympathique. ______13 probablement catholique, mais ______14 difficile à dire. ______15 elle qui explique[c] qu'Éric est le petit-fils de Pierre Leblanc. Éric? ______16 très sérieux. ______17 un homme qui ne parle pas beaucoup, mais ______18 prêt à aider Camille dans son enquête.[d]

[a]*that* [b]*hardworking* [c]*explains* [d]*investigation*

B. Mon ami(e). Décrivez deux de vos amis à votre partenaire. Vous pouvez les décrire comme ils sont maintenant et comme ils étaient dans le passé. Utilisez le présent et l'imparfait de **c'est** ou **il/elle est** autant que possible. Votre partenaire peut poser des questions.

MODÈLE: É1: Mon ami Louis? C'est un homme intellectuel et sportif. Il était socialiste mais maintenant il est plus conservateur.
É2: Est-ce qu'il est marié?

C. Où irez-vous? Imaginez que vous partez en vacances. Choisissez trois endroits de la liste suivante et dites ce que vous y ferez. Votre partenaire vous donnera ses réactions et ses propres idées. Utilisez les structures que vous avez apprises dans le Chapitre 17.

Endroits possibles: à la campagne, à la mer, à la montagne, au bord d'un lac, dans une forêt, dans une grande plaine, dans une île, en ville

MODÈLE: É1: J'irai dans une forêt. Je m'y promènerai, j'y ferai un pique-nique et j'écouterai les oiseaux. Ce seront des vacances tranquilles.
É2: Ce genre de vacances, ce n'est pas pour moi. J'aime mieux les activités aquatiques. J'irai à la mer où je ferai de la voile toute la journée.

Visionnement 2

Les Cévennes. In order to get to Saint-Jean de Causse, Camille rode the train down the Rhône Valley and over to Nîmes. There, she changed to a local train that took her to Alès, a former center of silkworm breeding that lies in the plains near the edge of the Cévennes mountains. From Alès, Camille drove a rented car up to Saint-Jean de Causse. This is a region of rocky soils that has always been poor and isolated from the rest of France. It is one of the areas that has lost the largest percentage of its population over the past half century.

The Cévennes were a center of the Resistance in World War II, but the area's history of resistance goes much further back. In the early 1700s, it was a hotbed of Protestant revolt against royal authority. One tourist attraction in the Cévennes is the village of Le Mas Soubeyran (*The Upper Hamlet* or *Farm* in the Occitan language). It is the location of the house of the Protestant chief Roland and a museum dedicated to the Protestant resistance.

Imaginez que vous allez passer une journée dans les Cévennes. Complétez les phrases suivantes à l'aide de la carte.

Demain, nous ferons une excursion dans le Massif central. Nous prendrons le train de nuit. Il passera à Avignon, mais il ne s'y arrêtera pas.[a] Nous descendrons à ____[1] pour prendre le train régional jusqu'à ____[2].

[a]ne... *will not stop there*

Là, nous louerons une voiture et nous monterons vers les ______[3]. Nous nous arrêterons pendant une heure au ______[4], parce que nous voulons comprendre l'histoire du protestantisme en France. Ensuite, nous monterons voir le village de ______[5], pour visiter la ferme de Jeanne Leblanc. Plus tard, nous irons faire du bateau dans les ______[6]. Et après, nous descendrons vers la Méditerranée pour passer la soirée[b] dans la ville de ______[7].

[b]*evening*

Les Cévennes

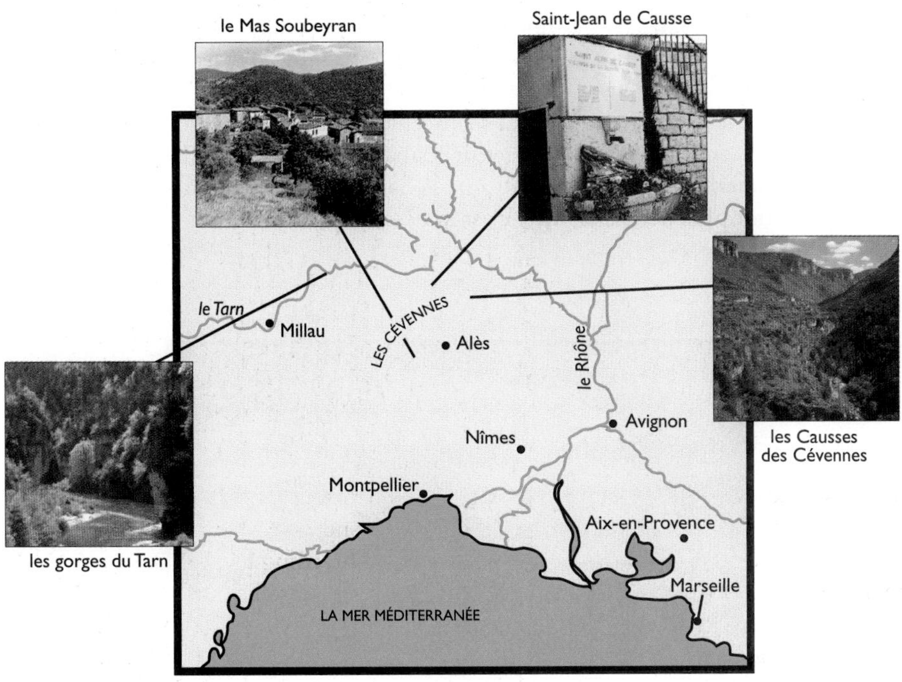

Observez!

Considérez les aspects culturels expliqués dans **Regards sur la culture**. Ensuite, regardez l'Épisode 17 encore une fois, et répondez aux questions suivantes.

- Est-ce qu'il y a beaucoup de jeunes dans le bar des Cévennes? Quel rôle le bar semble-t-il jouer dans ce petit village?
- Est-ce qu'il y a beaucoup de chômage dans cette région? Quel était le métier traditionnel dans cette région? Qu'est-ce qui va le remplacer?

Après le visionnement

Faites l'activité pour le **Visionnement 2** dans le cahier.

Synthèse: Culture

L'écologie et les mouvements de population

Au Québec, en France, au Sénégal, partout[1] dans le monde[2] francophone on observe un mouvement des populations de la campagne vers les villes. Mais, pour des raisons écologiques, ce mouvement est plus dramatique dans certaines régions du monde. Par exemple, en Haïti et à Madagascar, la disparition[3] des forêts a provoqué une migration vers les villes.

Le Sahel, c'est une vaste région d'Afrique qui sépare le Sahara des zones tropicales. Dans le Sahel, il y a huit mois par an sans pluie.[4] On cultive le millet pendant la saison des pluies, et on élève[5] des troupeaux[6] de bœufs, de moutons et de chameaux.[7]

Il y a eu[8] dans le passé des périodes de sécheresse[9] extrême dans le Sahel. Alors, les populations souffrent de famine et de maladies. Aujourd'hui, la sécheresse semble permanente. Certains pensent que le Sahara avance et que les terres[10] du Sahel ne seront plus jamais fertiles: c'est la désertification.

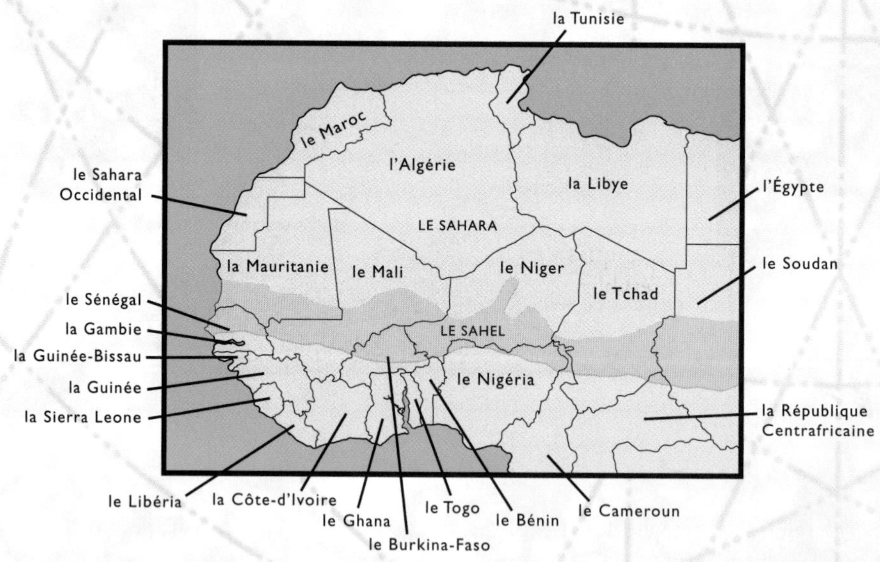

«Il y avait de la pluie et de l'eau partout. Nous cultivions et récoltions[11] et nous avions tout. Aujourd'hui, nous n'avons rien. Parfois, nous passons dix jours, vingt jours sans manger. Nos enfants meurent de faim.»
(Citation d'une Malienne, victime de la désertification)

[1]*everywhere* [2]*world* [3]*disappearance* [4]*rain* [5]*raises* [6]*herds* [7]*camels* [8]*Il... There were* [9]*drought* [10]*soils* [11]*harvested*

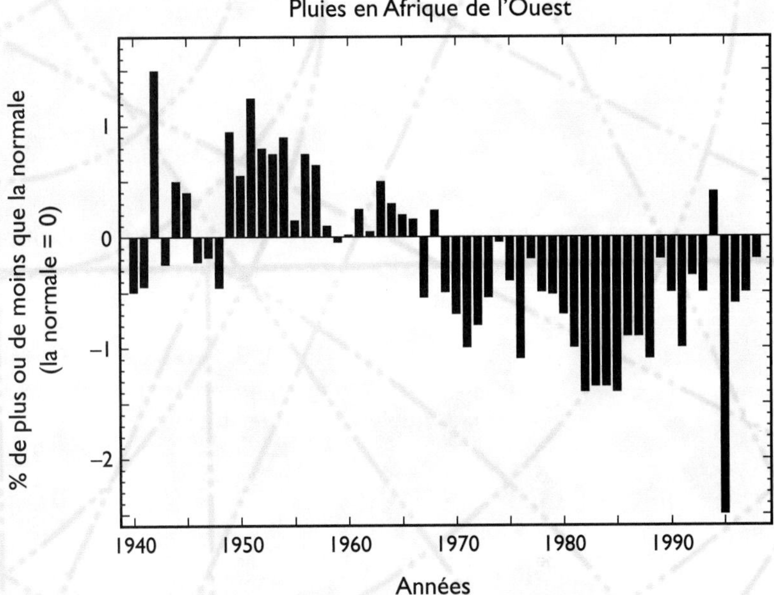

Les causes de la désertification sont souvent discutées: il y a sans doute des changements climatiques, mais il y a aussi des abus de ressources naturelles (la monoculture intensive de certaines plantes, par exemple) et l'augmentation excessive de la population.

La désertification provoque des migrations vers les villes ou vers des régions plus fertiles. Elle provoque aussi des antagonismes ethniques. Un exemple: la Mauritanie. En 1965, 70% des Mauritaniens étaient des nomades et vivaient comme leurs ancêtres depuis des siècles.[12] Aujourd'hui, avec la désertification du pays, il y a seulement 7% de nomades. Tous ces gens sont allés vers des villes: ce sont des «réfugiés écologiques». En général, ils restent très pauvres[13] et vivent dans des quartiers misérables, parce que leurs connaissances ne sont pas adaptées à la vie urbaine.

[12]*centuries* [13]*poor*

À vous

Le problème de la désertification. Why do you think the Sahel desertification problem is of particular importance in the French-speaking world? Look at the map and list the French-speaking countries that lie in the Sahel region. What other countries are probably also affected?

À écrire

Faites **À écrire** pour le Chapitre 17 dans le cahier.

Vocabulaire

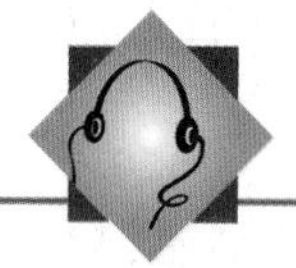

Le relief géographique

un champ field
une colline hill
une côte coast
un fleuve large river
une hauteur elevation, height
une île island
la Manche English Channel
un massif old, rounded mountain range
une mer sea
un relief topography, relief

MOTS APPARENTÉS: **une baie, un bassin, une forêt, un lac, une montagne, un océan, une plaine, un plateau, une rivière, une vallée**

Les points cardinaux

l'est (*m.*) east
le nord north
l'ouest (*m.*) west
le sud south

Demander et indiquer le chemin

une carte map
le chemin route, way
un coin corner
une église church
un feu traffic light; fire
un poteau indicateur sign(post)

Est-ce que vous pourriez m'indiquer le chemin pour aller à... Could you show me the way to . . .

monter/descendre une rue to go up/down a street
à droite to/on the right
à gauche to/on the left
tout droit straight
vers toward

MOTS APPARENTÉS: **indiquer, tourner**

Autres expressions utiles

un ensemble collection, group
à la campagne in the country
au bord de on the banks (shore, edge) of
manquer à to be missed by (*someone*)
traverser to cross

MOT APPARENTÉ: **divers(e)**

Chapitre 18

Histoires privées

OBJECTIFS

In this episode, you will

- learn more about what Antoine did during the German occupation of France

In this chapter, you will

- talk about farm life
- discuss environmental issues
- describe people and things using relative clauses
- use verbs to talk about actions
- learn about how country life and city life relate to the geography of France
- read a folktale from the Cévennes

Vocabulaire en contexte

L'agriculture

Si les agriculteurs sont de moins en moins **nombreux**° en France, les techniques agricoles se sont cependant° transformées. Il en résulte une productivité considérablement augmentée.

numerous
nevertheless

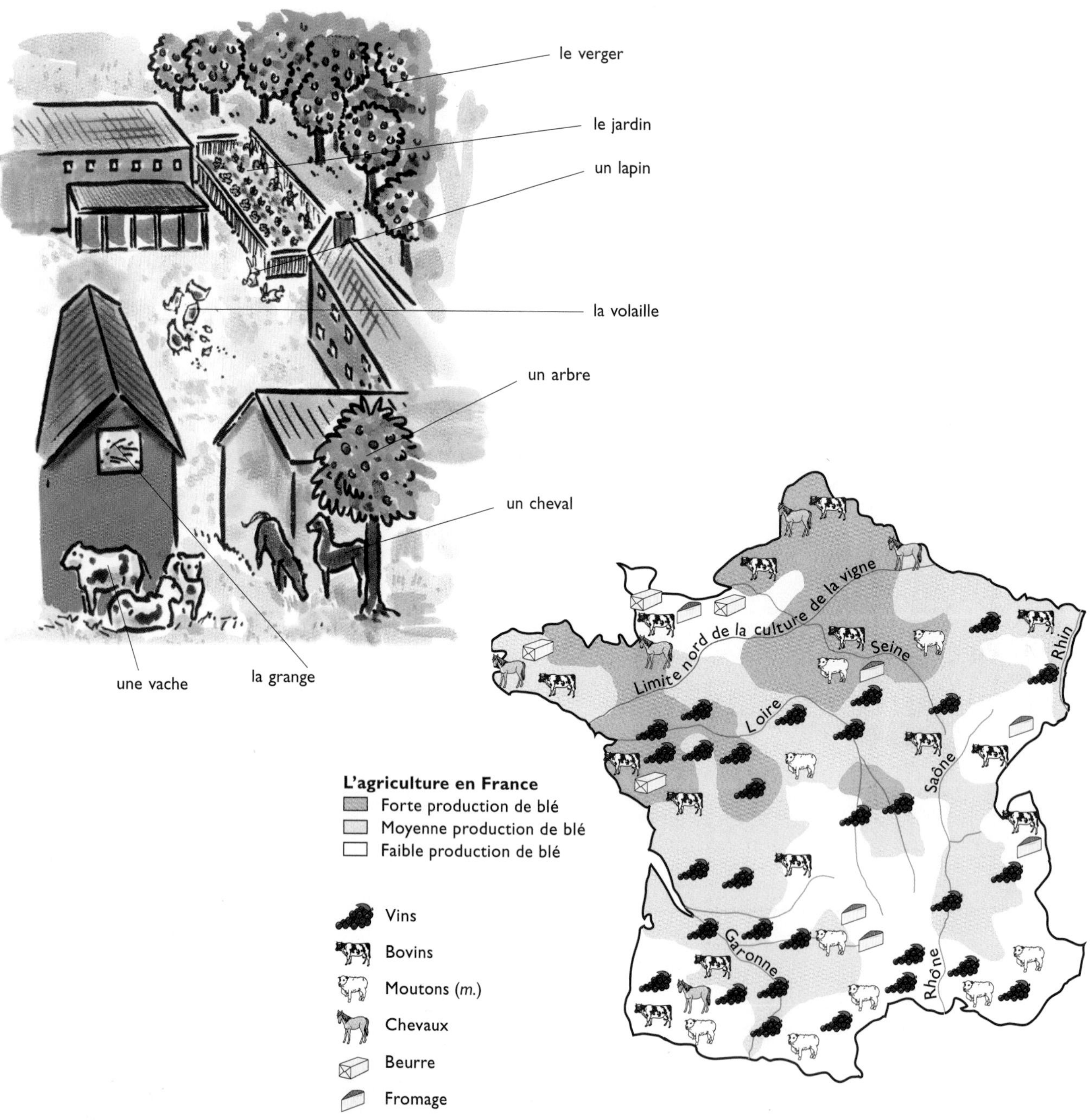

Les céréales° (*f.*)

Les... *Grains*

Le blé° est **cultivé presque partout**° en France. L'agriculteur **plante** le blé au printemps et le **récolte** en automne. **Les fermes** (*f.*) françaises produisent aussi d'autres **céréales**: l'avoine,° l'orge,° le maïs et le riz.

Wheat / presque... almost everywhere

oats / barley

La viticulture°

La... *Wine growing*

Les Français sont **fiers**° de leurs vins. **Les vignobles**° (*m.*) du Bordelais, de la Bourgogne et de la vallée du Rhône produisent des vins connus dans **le monde**° entier.

proud / vineyards

world

L'élevage°

(Animal) Breeding

Les vaches donnent leur lait, qui sert surtout à faire du fromage: tomme de Savoie, gruyère du Jura, cantal du Massif central. Le lait de **brebis**° (*f.*) des Causses donne un fromage célèbre, le roquefort. **Les fermiers** élèvent souvent aussi **des porcs** (*m.*), de la volaille et des lapins.

ewes

Autres mots utiles

une cheminée	fireplace; chimney
une marmite	large iron cooking pot
un(e) paysan(ne)	country dweller
la récolte	harvest; crop
la terre	earth; soil
une vigne	vine
un village	village
pousser	to grow; to push
ramasser	to pick (up), gather (up)

Couchon

Activités

A. Produits. De quel animal, quelle céréale ou quelle plante les produits suivants proviennent-ils?

MODÈLE: le pain → Le pain provient du blé.

1. le vin
2. le gruyère
3. le roquefort
4. des œufs
5. le cidre
6. le lait
7. le jambon

B. Une petite compétition. Mettez-vous en groupes de trois. Une personne posera les questions suivantes aux deux autres. La personne qui répondra le plus vite avec une réponse correcte obtiendra un point.

MODÈLE: Comment appelle-t-on la personne qui travaille la terre? → C'est un agriculteur. (C'est un fermier.)

1. Où est-ce qu'on cultive du raisin?
2. Quel produit est cultivé presque partout en France?

3. Quel est l'endroit où on garde (*keeps, stores*) le blé?
4. Quelles plantes poussent dans une forêt et donnent à la forêt son caractère?
5. Quelle tâche (*task*) l'agriculteur fait-il en automne?
6. Quels animaux les fermiers élèvent-ils souvent?
7. Quel est l'endroit où les fleurs sont nombreuses et où on va pour les cueillir?
8. Où les agriculteurs plantent-ils des graines (*seeds*)?

C. Chez nous. Quel est le rôle de l'agriculture dans votre pays? Répondez aux questions suivantes.

1. Quelles sont les activités agricoles principales de votre pays?
2. Dans quelle(s) région(s) de votre pays cultive-t-on les céréales?
3. Y a-t-il une région où la viticulture est importante? Quelle région? Avez-vous déjà bu des vins de cette région? Les aimez-vous?
4. Quelles régions sont connues pour leur production de fromage? Est-ce que ce fromage est fait à partir de lait de vache, de chèvre (*goat*) ou de brebis?
5. Dans quelles régions l'élevage est-il important? Quels animaux y sont élevés?

L'environnement

Les Français s'inquiètent de plus en plus pour **l'environnement** (*m.*) de la France et du monde. Le gouvernement fait de nombreux efforts pour réduire° **la pollution** de l'eau et de l'air. Il a lancé un système de **recyclage** (*m.*) et une politique de **conservation** (*f.*) pour faire baisser° **la consommation de l'essence**° (*f.*) et des ressources naturelles. Les Verts sont **un parti politique** qui joue un rôle important. Ils pensent beaucoup à **l'avenir**° (*m.*) et cherchent des moyens **efficaces**° pour réduire **l'effet** (*m.*) **de serre**,° et pour convaincre° le public de **consommer** moins et de **recycler** plus.

reduce
faire... to lower / gasoline
the future
efficient
l'effet... the greenhouse effect / convince

Activités

A. Conseils. Quels conseils peut-on donner aux personnes suivantes? Mettez vos phrases à l'impératif.

Verbes utiles: conserver, consommer, devenir, penser, recycler, réduire

MODÈLE: Jean-François pense que les partis politiques traditionnels négligent la question de l'environnement. →
Devenez vert. (Faites partie du parti des Verts. Adhérez aux Verts.)

1. Nathalie met tout dans la poubelle (*garbage can*).
2. Lise adore faire du shopping; elle achète beaucoup de choses inutiles.
3. Laurent laisse toutes les lumières allumées (*lit*) dans son appartement. Sa note d'électricité est très élevée; il s'en inquiète.
4. Le pot d'échappement (*exhaust pipe*) de la voiture de Michel ne marche pas du tout; il ne purifie absolument pas le gaz d'échappement.
5. Valérie utilise trop d'eau.

B. Et vous? Découvrez si votre partenaire s'inquiète de l'environnement. Demandez-lui...

1. s'il / si elle fait des efforts pour protéger l'environnement, s'il / si elle fait du recyclage et s'il / si elle essaie de consommer moins.
2. ce qu'il/elle peut faire pour réduire encore sa consommation de l'essence. Est-ce que les transports en commun représentent une solution pratique pour lui/elle? le vélo? le covoiturage (voyager en voiture avec des camarades)?
3. quel est le sujet écologique le plus important en ce moment, selon lui/elle: l'effet de serre, le recyclage, la conservation des ressources naturelles ou autre chose? Demandez-lui d'expliquer.
4. s'il / si elle est optimiste ou pessimiste en ce qui concerne l'avenir de la planète et si, selon lui/elle, les habitants de son pays font le maximum pour protéger l'environnement.
5. si le mouvement écologiste est important dans sa région et s'il est efficace, selon lui/elle.
6. s'il / si elle est engagé(e) dans le mouvement écologiste et, si oui, quelles sont les activités principales de son groupe.

Visionnement 1

Avant de visionner

La narration de Jeanne Leblanc. Dans cet épisode, Jeanne Leblanc raconte le séjour (*stay*) d'Antoine dans sa famille. Sa narration est au passé. Complétez le dialogue avec le passé composé ou l'imparfait. Justifiez votre choix en vous rappelant la fonction de chaque temps du verbe: le passé composé s'emploie pour raconter des événements achevés dans le passé; l'imparfait s'emploie pour des descriptions des circonstances et des situations, pour des actions habituelles et pour des actions en train de se dérouler (*unfolding*).

JEANNE: [Antoine] _____[1] (vouloir) faire de la Résistance. Pierre l'_____[2] (accueillir) avec sympathie, et très vite ils _____[3] (devenir) copains[a]...

CAMILLE: Il _____[4] (habiter) dans cette maison?

JEANNE: Oui... Pierre lui _____[5] (faire) visiter la région. Puis il lui _____[6] (présenter) nos amis résistants. Antoine _____[7] (être) serviable,[b] sympathique.

CAMILLE: Il vous _____[8] (parler) souvent de sa femme?

JEANNE: Oui, et de sa fille aussi, qui _____[9] (être) encore toute petite. Antoine _____[10] (s'inquiéter) beaucoup pour elles. Il les _____[11] (savoir) seules à Paris. Elles n'_____[12] (avoir) pas d'argent...

CAMILLE: Mais alors, il _____[13] (lutter[c]) dans la Résistance avec votre mari?

JEANNE (*acquiesce*): Oui. Il y _____[14] (avoir) quatre copains avec eux. Ils détruisaient des ponts et des voies de chemin de fer.[d] Il _____[15] (être) essentiel de retarder les troupes allemandes... Mais Antoine _____[16] (être) impatient. Il _____[17] (dire) à mon mari: «Il faut frapper plus fort![e]».

CAMILLE: Plus fort?

JEANNE: Oui. Il _____[18] (vouloir) monter des opérations plus importantes! Et je vous le dis, Camille, notre malheur _____[19] (venir) de là!

[a]*friends* [b]*willing to help* [c]*to fight* [d]détruisaient... *destroyed bridges and railroads* [e]Il... *We have to strike harder!*

Vocabulaire relatif à l'épisode

Tenez!	*Take this!*
C'est une lettre qu'a écrite mon grand-père.	*It's a letter my grandfather wrote.*
la vérité	*truth*
cacher	*to hide*
Asseyez-vous	*Sit down*
l'aligot	*regional potato-and-cheese soup*
de la part d'un ami	*on the recommendation of a friend*
c'était de la folie	*it was madness*

Observez!

Dans l'Épisode 18, Camille essaie d'apprendre plus de détails sur Antoine. Écoutez la conversation entre Camille et Jeanne, en réfléchissant aux questions suivantes.

- Quel rapport s'établit (*is established*) entre Jeanne Leblanc et Camille?
- Pourquoi Antoine est-il allé dans les Cévennes? Comment a-t-il fait la connaissance de Pierre et Jeanne Leblanc?

Après le visionnement

A. Le carnet de Camille. (*Camille's notebook.*) Avant de rencontrer Jeanne, Camille a préparé une liste de questions qu'elle voulait lui poser. Voici les questions tirées de son carnet. Quelles réponses a-t-elle reçues?

1. Quand est-ce que mon grand-père Antoine est arrivé chez vous? **2.** Est-ce qu'il habitait dans votre maison? **3.** Est-ce qu'il vous parlait souvent de sa femme ou de sa fille? **4.** Quel était son état d'esprit quand il parlait de sa famille? Pourquoi? **5.** Est-ce qu'il a vraiment lutté dans la Résistance avec votre mari? **6.** Les opérations se sont-elles bien passées?

B. Réfléchissez. Répondez aux questions suivantes.

1. Quelle sorte de personne est Jeanne? Est-elle généreuse? contente? amère (*bitter*)? Expliquez, en donnant des exemples de l'épisode. **2.** Est-ce qu'elle mène (*leads*) une vie moderne ou plutôt (*rather*) traditionnelle? Justifiez votre réponse. **3.** Selon vous, pourquoi Jeanne décide-t-elle de raconter l'histoire d'Antoine à Camille?

Structure 54

Les pronoms relatifs

Combining related ideas

—Il vous parlait souvent de sa femme?

—Oui, et de sa fille aussi, **qui** était encore toute petite.

Relative pronouns join two related sentences or ideas into one longer sentence. When the two ideas are combined, one becomes dependent or "relative" to the other.

Three useful relative pronouns are **qui**, **que**, and **où**. The choice of which one to use depends on whether it will be the subject or object of the verb in the relative clause▲ or whether it refers back to a time or place mentioned in the independent clause.▲

Le pronom relatif *qui*

The relative pronoun **qui** can refer to either people or things. It serves as the *subject* of the verb in the relative clause and is followed by that verb. It makes no elision when it is followed by a word beginning with a vowel.

Il parlait de **sa fille**. **Sa fille** était encore toute petite. →
Il parlait de sa fille, **qui** était encore toute petite.
*He spoke about his daughter **who** was still very little.*

Selon Jeanne, Antoine a monté **des opérations**. **Les opérations** ont causé la mort de Pierre. →
Selon Jeanne, Antoine a monté des opérations **qui** ont causé la mort de Pierre.
*According to Jeanne, Antoine organized operations **that** caused Pierre's death.*

Antoine est arrivé en 1943. **Antoine** a vite rencontré des résistants. →
Antoine, **qui** est arrivé en 1943, a vite rencontré des résistants.
*Antoine, **who** arrived in 1943, soon met members of the Resistance.*

In these examples, **qui** is the *subject* of the verb in the relative clause.

Le pronom relatif *que*

The relative pronoun **que** can also refer to either people or things. It serves as the *object* of the verb in the relative clause and is followed by a noun or pronoun subject and the verb. **Que** makes elision if it is followed by a word beginning with a vowel.

Camille rencontre **la femme**. Rachid a trouvé **la femme**. →
Camille rencontre la femme **que** Rachid a trouvée.
*Camille meets the woman **whom** Rachid located.*

C'est un **pays**. On aime ce **pays**. →
C'est un pays **qu'**on aime.
*It's a country **that** people love.*

In these examples, **que** becomes the *direct object* of the verb in the relative clause.

Le pronom relatif *où*

The relative pronoun **où** refers to places or times mentioned in the main clause. It is followed by a noun or pronoun subject and the verb of the relative clause.

PLACE: Camille s'approche du bar des Cévennes. Quelques hommes jouent à la pétanque **devant le bar des Cévennes**. →
Camille s'approche du bar des Cévennes **où** quelques hommes jouent à la pétanque.
*Camille approaches the bar des Cévennes **where** several men are playing pétanque.*

Pour en savoir plus...

You learned in Chapter 10 that the past participle of a verb conjugated with **avoir** agrees in number and gender with a direct object that precedes it. Because **que** has the grammatical function of a direct object in the relative clause and precedes the verb of which it is the object, the past participle must agree.

C'est **une lettre**. Mon grand-père a écrit **une lettre**. →
C'est une lettre **que** mon grand-père a écrite en 1943.*
*It's a letter **that** my grandfather wrote in 1943.*

---

*In the film, Camille actually says, **C'est une lettre *qu'*a écrit*e* mon grand-père en 1943.** This inversion of the subject and verb in the relative clause is a permissible stylistic variation. Notice that the past participle still agrees with its preceding direct object.

TIME: **À l'époque**, Antoine faisait de la Résistance dans les Cévennes. **À l'époque**, Louise et Mado vivaient à Paris. →
À l'époque **où** Antoine faisait de la Résistance dans les Cévennes, Louise et Mado vivaient à Paris.
*At the time **when** Antoine was a member of the Resistance in the Cévennes, Louise and Mado were living in Paris.*

The following chart summarizes the use of relative pronouns.

GRAMMATICAL FUNCTIONS OF NOUN	PRONOUN
subject	**qui**
object	**que**
place or time	**où**

Activités

A. Histoires privées. Employez le pronom relatif approprié pour compléter le commentaire sur l'Épisode 18.

Saint-Jean de Causse est le village ____¹ Antoine a passé les derniers jours de sa vie. C'est la vérité ____² intéresse Camille. La situation ____³ Camille se trouve est délicate. Elle veut parler d'un sujet ____⁴ Mme Leblanc n'aime pas. C'est un sujet ____⁵ est très difficile pour tout le monde. La guerre est quelque chose ____⁶ personne ne peut oublier[a] et ____⁷ touche encore beaucoup de gens.

Pendant qu'elles parlent, Mme Leblanc prépare une recette ____⁸ vient de sa grand-mère et ____⁹ Camille trouve très bonne. Mme Leblanc sort une vieille boîte ____¹⁰ contient des photos ____¹¹ quelqu'un a prises pendant la guerre. Ce sont des images ____¹² montrent Pierre Leblanc et Antoine. C'étaient des copains ____¹³ s'aimaient beaucoup au moment ____¹⁴ on a pris cette photo. Malheureusement, c'est une amitié[b] ____¹⁵ a mal fini pour tout le monde.

[a] *forget* [b] *friendship*

B. Le monde rural. Liez les deux phrases à l'aide d'un pronom relatif.

1. Autrefois, les agriculteurs vivaient dans un monde. Ce monde était plus traditionnel qu'au XXIe siècle.
2. C'est une situation compliquée. Beaucoup de jeunes agriculteurs ne comprennent pas cette situation.
3. Les jeunes continuent à travailler dans les champs. Leurs grands-parents ont travaillé dans ces champs.
4. Des fermes industrielles remplacent les petites fermes. Ces petites fermes appartiennent à des familles.

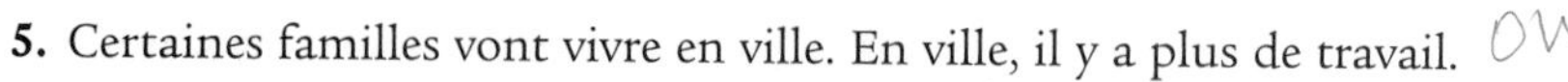

5. Certaines familles vont vivre en ville. En ville, il y a plus de travail.
6. Le gouvernement essaie d'aider les fermes. Les familles veulent protéger (*protect*) ces fermes.
7. Il y a des lois européennes concernant l'agriculture. Ces lois n'aident pas tous les agriculteurs.

C. Vos études. Avec un(e) partenaire, parlez de votre situation à l'université. Complétez les descriptions suivantes en ajoutant une phrase qui commence avec **qui**, **que** ou **où** pour clarifier votre position.

MODÈLE: Dans notre université, il y a des gens qui/que... →
É1: Dans notre université, il y a des gens qui travaillent beaucoup. Ils sont très sérieux.
É2: Il y a aussi des gens que les professeurs admirent. Ce sont de bons étudiants.

1. _____ est une matière qui/que...
2. _____ est un lieu sur le campus qui/que/où...
3. _____ est un restaurant qui/que/où...
4. Mon dernier cours était un cours de _____. C'était un cours qui/que/où...
5. Dans mon cours de _____, il y avait une personne intéressante. C'était une personne qui/que...
6. La semaine dernière, j'ai étudié _____ (un endroit). C'est un endroit qui/que/où...
7. Dans notre université, il y a des professeurs qui/que...

Structure 55

Les verbes comme *conduire*

Talking about everyday actions

—Oui. Il y avait quatre copains avec eux. Ils **détruisaient** des ponts et des voies de chemin de fer.

The verb **conduire** (*to drive*) is irregular in the present tense, and it has an irregular past participle. The formation of the **futur** and the **imparfait** are regular.

conduire (*to drive*)			
je	**conduis**	nous	**conduisons**
tu	**conduis**	vous	**conduisez**
il, elle, on	**conduit**	ils, elles	**conduisent**
passé composé: j'**ai conduit**			

Other verbs conjugated like **conduire** are

construire	*to construct*
détruire	*to destroy*
produire	*to produce*
réduire	*to reduce*
traduire	*to translate*

L'historien **a traduit** le laissez-passer en français.	*The historian translated the pass into French.*
On **construit** une nouvelle autoroute.	*They're building a new highway.*
Sans Camille, il est difficile de **produire** «Bonjour!».	*Without Camille, it's difficult to produce "Bonjour!"*

Activités

A. Qui dit quoi? Complétez chaque phrase en mettant un des verbes suivants au présent.

Verbes: conduire, construire, détruire, produire, réduire, traduire

MODÈLE: Est-ce que vous traduisez des documents pour les Nations Unies?

1. Est-ce que tu ______ la voiture de tes parents?
2. Notre usine (*factory*) ______ des sacs en papier recyclables. Et nous ne ______ pas d'arbres!
3. Je ______ les lettres de Camus de français en anglais.
4. Je voudrais une interview sur ce que (*what*) vous ______ dans votre usine.
5. Les armées ennemies ______ des villages. Et des gens du Corps de la Paix ______ de nouveaux villages.
6. Je ______ ce taxi depuis dix ans et je n'ai jamais eu de problème.
7. Nous sommes fiers de notre usine. Nous ______ la pollution un peu chaque année. Nous ______ beaucoup moins de pollution qu'avant.
8. Mon ami Marc ______ sa propre (*own*) voiture.
9. Quand tu lis en français, est-ce que tu ______ le texte dans ta tête?
10. Attention! Vous ______ trop vite. Vous allez avoir un accident de voiture.

B. Rêves et réalités. (*Dreams and realities.*) Complétez les phrases avec la forme correcte d'un des verbes sur la liste. Attention aux temps des verbes.

Vocabulaire utile: conduire, construire, détruire, produire, réduire, traduire

Dans le passé, on _____[1] régulièrement les vieux bâtiments et les gens _____[2] des bâtiments plus modernes à la place. Dans votre ville, est-ce que les gens _____[3] beaucoup de nouveaux bâtiments récemment? Est-ce que votre famille _____[4] une nouvelle maison?

Dans le monde d'aujourd'hui, nous ne _____[5] pas la pollution de l'air parce que les gens _____[6] leurs voitures tous les jours. De plus, on ne _____[7] pas beaucoup de voitures électriques qui polluent moins. Et vos amis et vous, _____[8]-vous tous les jours?

Certains étudiants ne _____[9] pas de français en anglais dans leur tête. Est-ce que vous _____[10] de français en anglais quand vous lisez?

Dans le monde de demain, la vie sera parfaite.[a] Les régions agricoles _____[11] assez de céréales pour nourrir[b] le monde entier. Ainsi,[c] on _____[12] le nombre de gens qui ont faim. À votre avis, quel pays _____[13] le plus de nourriture dans ce monde idéal?

[a]*perfect* [b]*feed* [c]*In this way*

C. Interview. Formez des questions avec les éléments suivants. Interviewez trois camarades de classe pour obtenir des réponses à ces questions. Ensuite, comparez ces réponses avec celles de la classe.

MODÈLE: combien de fois par semaine / tes parents (tes enfants) / conduire / la voiture →
É1: Combien de fois par semaine est-ce que tes parents (tes enfants) conduisent la voiture?
É2: Ils conduisent la voiture au moins (*at least*) dix fois par semaine.

1. quand tu / lire / en français / traduire / tous les mots (*words*)
2. les agriculteurs de ton pays / produire / quelque chose de spécial
3. quel type de voiture / ton meilleur ami (ta meilleure amie) / conduire
4. quand / tu / ne... pas conduire
5. comment / tu / réduire / personnellement la pollution de l'air dans ta ville l'année dernière
6. quel type de bâtiment / ton université / construire / récemment

D. L'environnement, hier et aujourd'hui. Avec un(e) partenaire, jouez les rôles d'une jeune personne qui interviewe une personne âgée. La jeune personne veut savoir comment on pensait à l'environnement autrefois par rapport à aujourd'hui.

MODÈLE:	LE/LA JEUNE:	Aujourd'hui, on réduit la pollution de l'air avec des voitures moins polluantes.
	LA PERSONNE ÂGÉE:	Autrefois, nous ne pensions pas à ce problème. Nous ne réduisions pas la pollution.

conduire
recycler (les journaux, le verre, le plastique, etc.)
conserver les ressources naturelles (les forêts, l'eau, etc.)
réduire la pollution de l'air (de l'eau, de la terre)
détruire de vieux bâtiments
réduire la consommation d'essence (d'électricité, de gaz naturel, d'énergie nucléaire)
produire (des voitures plus petites, des produits recyclables, etc.)

Regards sur la culture

La vie en ville et à la campagne

As you saw in this episode, Camille eventually finds the house in Saint-Jean de Causse where her grandfather spent part of the war. Jeanne and her grandson seem to have a fairly comfortable life.

Le village de Sainte-Engrâce dans les Pyrénées

- A farmhouse in the Cévennes would usually have the stable and barn on the ground floor. The family would live on the second floor, which would have an exterior stone staircase leading up to it. The roof would be covered with rough stone tiles. Jeanne's house is more elaborate and southern-looking. It has certainly been modified as the family became more prosperous. However, like most village homes in France, it is filled with a curious mix of traditional and modern elements.
- French people, both urban and rural, are very much attached to certain local traditions. For example, in the Central **Pyrénées**, everyone wants to be able to enjoy **la garbure** (a thick stew of cabbage, pork, rye bread, and preserved goose meat). And on special occasions, for example at a wedding dinner, everyone will sing the song "Aqueras montanhas" (*Those Mountains*) in Occitan, the traditional language of southern France.

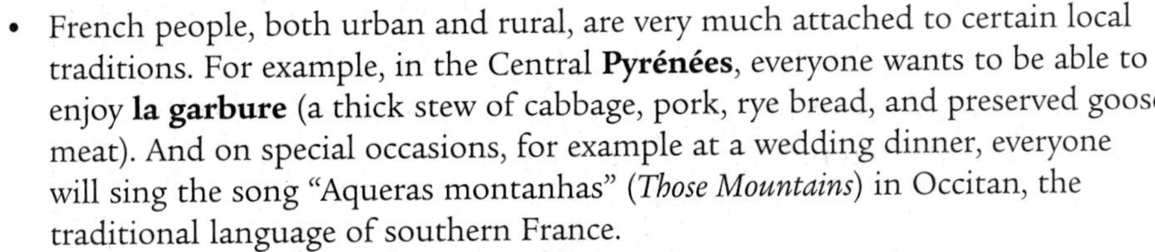

- Until the 1970s or 1980s, the borders separating city from country were very distinct in most areas of France. Except for the special cases of a few very large cities, urban sprawl was absent. The past few decades, however, have seen the development of huge supermarkets and malls around even small towns.
- At the same time, the desire for North American–style suburban living is growing, not among the wealthiest people, who prefer urban environments, but in the middle class. Hosts of large **lotissements** (*developments*) are

appearing all over France. More and more people want to have their own **pavillon** (*small single-family home*), with garden and lawn.

- Today, the major cities of France are developing very specific looks and personalities. Lille, in the north, aims to promote a modern image, with its Euralille district and high-tech public transportation. Montpellier, on the Mediterranean coast, has renovated its 18th-century center and has linked it to what is probably the most ambitious postmodern architectural development in France. Though they differ considerably one from the other, cities in France are in general very livable and intensely lived in. The North American city that is in large part emptied of its inhabitants at night is a shock to the French.

Lyon la nuit

Considérez

The majority of French people would probably prefer to live in a city. Why do you think that this is true when so many North Americans would rather live in the suburbs or in the country?

Structure 56

La construction *verbe* + *préposition* + *infinitif*

Talking about everyday actions

—Tenez, s'il vous plaît. **Demandez**-lui simplement **de lire** ceci.

All verbs that follow a conjugated verb are in the infinitive form. You have been using these verb + infinitive constructions since Chapter 2.

Tu **vas travailler** avec eux.	*You're going to work with them.*
Je ne **sais** pas quoi **faire**.	*I don't know what to do.*
Je **veux** simplement **savoir** la vérité, pour moi.	*I only want to find out the truth, for me.*
Il **a voulu monter** des opérations plus importantes!	*He wanted to organize larger operations!*

1. Verbs that can take an infinitive directly after them include

adorer	désirer	espérer	savoir
aimer (mieux)	détester	pouvoir	vouloir
aller	devoir	préférer	

2. Some verbs use a preposition (usually **à** or **de**) before an infinitive. You've already learned some of these as well. These two categories of verbs include

VERBE + **à** + INFINITIF
apprendre à *to learn to* (*do*)
arriver à *to succeed in* (*doing*)
commencer à *to begin to* (*do*)
continuer à *to continue to* (*do*)
encourager (quelqu'un) à *to encourage* (*someone*) *to* (*do*)
hésiter à *to hesitate to* (*do*)
inviter (quelqu'un) à *to invite* (*someone*) *to* (*do*)
réfléchir à *to think about* (*doing*)
réussir à *to succeed in* (*doing*)

VERBE + **de** + INFINITIF
accepter de *to accept* (*doing*)
cesser de *to stop* (*doing*)
choisir de *to choose to* (*do*)
décider de *to decide to* (*do*)
demander (à quelqu'un) de *to ask* (*someone*) *to* (*do*)
se dépêcher de *to hurry to* (*do*)
dire (à quelqu'un) de *to tell* (*someone*) *to* (*do*)
essayer de *to try to* (*do*)
finir de *to finish* (*doing*)
permettre (à quelqu'un) de *to allow* (*someone*) *to* (*do*)
promettre de *to promise to* (*do*)
refuser de *to refuse to* (*do*)
venir de *to have just* (*done*)

Je vous **invite à dîner**...	*I'm inviting you to dine . . .*
Écoute, n'**hésite** pas **à** m'**appeler**.	*Look, don't hesitate to call me.*
Dépêche-toi de le **retrouver**.	*Hurry and find him.*
...et **tu** lui **dis de venir** tout de suite!	*. . . and you tell him to come right away!*

Activités

A. Jeanne et Camille. Créez des phrases complètes avec les éléments suivants. N'oubliez pas la préposition si nécessaire.

1. Éric / dire / à Camille / partir
2. Camille / demander / à Éric / montrer / la lettre d'Antoine à Jeanne
3. Jeanne / accepter / parler à Camille
4. Camille / commencer / parler à Jeanne de sa quête
5. Jeanne / ne pas hésiter / montrer les photos à Camille

6. Jeanne / décider / expliquer / comment Pierre et Antoine se sont connus
7. Camille / encourager / Jeanne / parler
8. Jeanne / essayer / raconter son histoire calmement
9. Camille / inviter / Jeanne / s'asseoir (*to sit down*)
10. Jeanne / permettre / Camille / l'aider

a de

B. Au contraire. Vincent et Véronique sont des jumeaux (*twins*), mais ils ne se ressemblent pas. Complétez la première partie de la phrase avec une préposition et utilisez un verbe de la liste (avec une préposition, si nécessaire) pour terminer la phrase. Montrez que ces deux personnes n'agissent pas de la même façon.

Verbes utiles: arriver, choisir, commencer, continuer, hésiter, refuser

MODÈLE: Véronique cesse de fumer, mais Vincent commence à fumer.

1. Véronique accepte _____ parler aux gens, mais Vincent...
2. Véronique réussit _____ se faire des amis (*to make friends*), mais Vincent ne...
3. Véronique a fini _____ faire des bêtises (*silly things*) à l'âge de 12 ans, mais Vincent...
4. Véronique se dépêche _____ aider les gens, mais Vincent...
5. Véronique refuse _____ critiquer les gens, mais Vincent...

C. Actions et opinions. Terminez chaque phrase avec une construction qui utilise un verbe à l'infinitif. N'oubliez pas la préposition, si nécessaire.

1. Je refuse...
2. Cette année, mon meilleur ami / ma meilleure amie va commencer...
3. Mes camarades de classe finissent...
4. J'adore parfois...
5. Les professeurs détestent...
6. Cette année, j'ai appris...
7. Mes amis me promettent...

Visionnement 2

Observez!

Considérez les aspects culturels expliqués dans **Regards sur la culture**. Ensuite, regardez l'Épisode 18 encore une fois, et répondez aux questions suivantes.

- De quelle région de la France la famille de Jeanne vient-elle?
- Quelle est l'attitude de Jeanne envers son héritage régional? Que fait-elle dans cet épisode pour vous donner cette idée?

Après le visionnement

Faites l'activité pour le **Visionnement 2** dans le cahier.

Synthèse: Lecture

Mise en contexte

The reading selection in this chapter is a folktale that dates back to the Middle Ages.* Numerous versions have been found throughout France. It is also found in the Grimm† collection, which may explain its increased popularity in the late 19th and early 20th centuries. This version originated in the Cévennes region.

Stratégie pour mieux lire
Understanding oral tradition in written folktales

Folktales are transmitted orally and are addressed to a local audience. For this reason, they sometimes contain samples of regional dialect and exhibit characteristics of unplanned, spoken speech, such as repetition, incomplete sentences, exclamations, and a more flexible word order. Look at this example from the story that illustrates an oral style.

C'était un vilain,‡ un serf, quoi, et alors il voulait être riche.	*There was a villein, a serf, see, and, well, he wanted to be rich.*

Notice how the narrator refines his choice of vocabulary as he goes along and how he uses the expressions **quoi** and **alors** as interjections to give him time to think of what he will say next. Both of these are stylistically more like spoken narration than traditional written narration. Now look at another example.

Alors un jour, le diable, il y dit...	*So one day, the devil, he says to him . . .*

Here, the subject, **le diable**, is repeated in the pronoun **il**, and as an indication of dialect, **y** is used in place of **lui**. Again, these are indications of an oral presentation of the story.

---

*The Middle Ages refers to the period in European history often dated from 476 (fall of the Western Roman Empire) to 1453 (when Constantinople was conquered by the Turks).

†The German brothers Jakob Grimm (1785–1863) and Wilhelm Grimm (1786–1859) are known for their collection of folksongs and folktales. Between 1812 and 1822, they published these stories and songs in *Grimm's Fairy Tales* and other books.

‡Vilein: a vile, brutish peasant; originally "feudal serf." A serf was a member of the lowest feudal class in medieval Europe, bound to the land and owned by a lord.

Now read the whole folktale. What is the moral of the story? What does it illustrate?

Le partage[1] de la récolte

C'était un vilain, un serf, quoi, et alors il voulait être riche. Alors il se plaignait[2] toujours:

—Oh! Moi si je savais! J'invoquerais[3] le diable! Même si… S'agit que j'aie des sous, quoi.[4]

Alors un jour, le diable, il y dit:

—Écoute, tu m'as invoqué. Je peux te venir en aide, seulement à une condition: nous allons partager la moitié[5] de tes récoltes. Alors, qu'est-ce que tu plantes cette année?

—Eh ben, je plante des pommes de terre…

—Ah! alors le diable y dit, ben écoute: tu plantes des pommes de terre, moi je me réserverai ce qui[6] sortira du champ.

—Bon, ça va. Moi je prendrai ce qui est dans la terre.

Alors quand la récolte arrive, pardi,[7] le diable se présente, et il est obligé de prendre la fane[8] des pommes de terre. Et lui, le paysan lui, il ramasse ce qu'il y avait dans la terre. Mais c'est tout des pommes de terre.

—Oooh! le diable dit, cette année tu m'as trompé! Mais l'année prochaine! Moi je veux prendre ce qui restera dans la terre!

Alors l'année d'après il sème[9] du blé, le bonhomme. Alors là, le diable arrive, quand c'est la fenaison,[10] là, et pardi bien sûr, le bonhomme, il ramasse la cime[11] du blé, quoi, ce qui est sorti de terre et le diable a été obligé de ramasser l'éteule,[12] les racines, ce qui restait, quoi. Ça, c'était le diablotin trompé par un vilain…

[1]*sharing* [2]*se… complained* [3]*I would invoke* [4]*S'agit… I need some money, see?* [5]*half* [6]*ce… that which* [7]*of course* [8]*useless part (the leaves)* [9]*sows* [10]*harvest time* [11]*top* [12]*roots*

Après la lecture

A. Qui est-ce? Identifiez la personne qui a fait les actions suivantes. S'agit-il du paysan ou du diable?

1. Il a besoin d'argent.
2. Il est obligé de prendre la fane des pommes de terre.
3. Il ramasse des pommes de terre.
4. Il invoque le diable.
5. Il vient en aide.
6. Il plante du blé.
7. On l'a trompé.

B. La narration orale d'un conte. Voici quelques phrases tirées du texte. Quelles indications ont-elles de la narration orale de ce conte?

Possibilités:

répétition	expressions dialectales
exclamations	ordre flexible des éléments de la phrase
phrases incomplètes	expressions utilisées pour gagner du temps

1. Ah, alors, le diable y dit, ben, écoute.
2. Et lui, le paysan lui, il ramasse ce qu'il y avait dans la terre.
3. Alors là, le diable arrive, quand c'est la fenaison, là, et pardi, bien sûr, le bonhomme, il ramasse la cime du blé, quoi…

C. Réflexions. Réfléchissez aux questions suivantes.

1. D'habitude, quels traits associe-t-on avec un paysan? avec le diable? Est-ce que leurs portraits dans cette histoire correspond à vos idées?
2. Quelles autres histoires ou fables connaissez-vous où une personne ou un animal redoutable (*fearsome*) est trompé par quelqu'un qui est moins puissant (*powerful*)?
3. Quelle est la morale du conte? Quelles particularités du caractère humain illustre-t-il?

À écrire

Faites **À écrire** pour le Chapitre 18 dans le cahier.

Vocabulaire

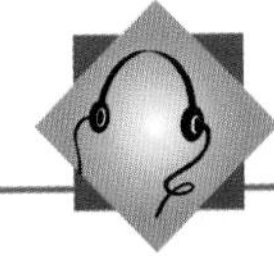

L'agriculture

un arbre	tree
le blé	wheat
une brebis	ewe
une céréale	grain
une cheminée	fireplace; chimney
l'élevage (*m.*)	(animal) breeding
une ferme	farm
un(e) fermier/ière	farmer
une grange	barn
un jardin	garden
une marmite	large iron cooking pot
un mouton	sheep
un(e) paysan(ne)	country dweller
un porc	pig
la récolte	harvest; crop
la terre	earth; soil
une vache	cow
un verger	apple orchard
une vigne	vine
un vignoble	vineyard
la viticulture	wine growing
la volaille	poultry
pousser	to grow; to push
ramasser	to pick (up), gather (up)
récolter	to harvest

MOTS APPARENTÉS: **l'agriculture** (*f.*)**, cultiver, planter, un village**

À REVOIR: **un(e) agriculteur/trice, le beurre, un cheval, le fromage, un lapin, le vin**

L'environnement

l'avenir (*m.*)	future
la consommation	consumption, usage
l'effet (*m.*) **de serre**	greenhouse effect
l'essence (*f.*)	gasoline
le monde	world
consommer	to consume

MOTS APPARENTÉS: **la conservation, l'environnement** (*m.*)**, un parti politique, la pollution, le recyclage, recycler**

Pronoms relatifs

que	whom, that, which
qui	who, that, which
où	where, when

Autres verbes utiles

arriver (à)	to succeed in (doing)
cesser (de)	to stop (doing)
conduire	to drive
construire	to construct
détruire	to destroy
produire	to produce
réduire	to reduce
traduire	to translate

MOTS APPARENTÉS: **accepter (de), continuer (à), décider (de), hésiter (à), inviter (quelqu'un) à, refuser (de)**

À REVOIR: **adorer, aimer, aller, apprendre (à), choisir (de), commencer (à), demander (à quelqu'un) (de), se dépêcher (de), désirer, détester, devoir, dire (à quelqu'un) (de), encourager (quelqu'un) (à), espérer, essayer (de), finir (de), permettre (à quelqu'un) (de), pouvoir, préférer, promettre (de), réfléchir (à), réussir (à), savoir, venir de, vouloir**

Adjectifs

efficace	efficient
faible	weak
fier (fière)	proud
fort(e)	strong; significant
moyen(ne)	moderate; average
nombreux/euse	numerous

Autres expressions utiles

partout	everywhere
presque	almost, nearly

Chapitre 19

Un certain Fergus

OBJECTIFS

In this episode, you will

- hear Jeanne tell what happened the night her husband was killed
- find out where Camille will go next on her quest

In this chapter, you will

- talk about war-time events
- discuss hypothetical situations and conditions
- use demonstrative pronouns to refer to specific things and people
- learn more about the Resistance movement in France during the Second World War
- read about Martinique and New Caledonia

Vocabulaire en contexte

Un reportage° sur la Résistance

report

Le S

le 20 décembre 1943

MORT DE RÉSISTANTS

Alès—Les **résistants** continuent leur effort pour **retarder l'avance**° des **troupes** allemandes. Ils **frappent** plus **fort***,° détruisant des **ponts**° et **des voies de chemin de fer.**°

La nuit du 17 décembre, sept résistants sont tombés dans **un piège**° tendu° par l'ennemi. Ils **ont attaqué** un train où les Allemands avaient entreposé° des **armes**—un train qu'ils croyaient **gardé** par seulement deux ou trois **soldats.** Les résistants sont passés un à un **silencieusement**° dans l'ombre° des wagons, mais **soudain†**,° la porte d'un wagon s'est ouverte et des soldats allemands **ont tiré sur**° les résistants. Ils ont été tous **tués.**°

Un résistant, grièvement blessé,° a pu **s'échapper**° et **se réfugier**° sous un wagon, mais il est mort le lendemain, le 18 décembre. Comme tous ses camarades, il est mort pour **la patrie.**°

En fait, les résistants attendaient **un camion**° pour transporter les armes. **Le conducteur,**° un certain Antoine **Lebrun‡**, les avait poussés° à attaquer le train. Comme° ce camion n'est jamais arrivé, la Résistance **accuse** Antoine Lebrun de **trahison**° et le **recherche** activement. De son côté,° l'ennemi a commencé une campagne° de désinformation et a lancé des représailles:° plusieurs **otages**° ont déjà été **fusillés.**°

Dabes
a voll
mesd
af bre
cei kj
lod n

Casdr
sisdah
jesdyl
cemr
sakln

Xenl
safba
arrb j
vabdl
dib dr
I flas
a lkd j
menb
a fesd

Qclc
daldfj

retarder... *to slow the advance*
frappent... *are striking harder / bridges*
voies... *railroad tracks*
trap / set
stored
silently
shadow / suddenly
ont... *fired on / killed*
grièvement... *seriously wounded / to escape*
se... *to hide*
la... *his country*
truck
driver
avait... *had pushed*
As
treason
De... *For its part*
campaign
reprisals / hostages
shot

Activités

A. Définitions. Voici des définitions de certains mots utilisés dans le reportage sur la Résistance. Donnez le mot convenable (*fitting*).

1. une sorte de prisonnier **2.** une personne qui participe au combat pendant une guerre **3.** le pays d'origine d'une personne **4.** les membres d'un groupe clandestin qui se battent contre (*fight against*) l'ennemi **5.** la personne qui conduit un véhicule **6.** un groupe de soldats **7.** la conséquence fatale d'une attaque

---

*Rappelez-vous que **fort(e)** est aussi un adjectif: **On devient fort quand on fait régulièrement de la musculation.**

†**Soudain(e)** est aussi un adjectif: **Il a eu une crise cardiac soudaine.**

‡Antoine Lebrun est le nom pris par Antoine Leclair pour s'identifier sur son laissez-passer.

B. Événements d'une guerre. Complétez chaque phrase avec un des termes de la liste. Conjuguez les verbes au temps approprié et faites l'accord des substantifs et des adjectifs lorsque (*when*) c'est nécessaire.

Vocabulaire utile: accuser, attaquer, camion, fort, frapper, fusiller, piège, rechercher, retarder, silencieusement, soudain, voie de chemin de fer

1. L'ennemi a déjà envahi (*invaded*) plusieurs pays. Comment peut-on _____ son avance?
2. Ils _____ la ville et l'ont complètement détruite.
3. Personne n'attendait cette attaque. Ça a été un événement _____.
4. Les résistants ont perdu cette bataille (*battle*). L'ennemi était plus _____ qu'eux.
5. Les soldats _____ les résistants dans la forêt, mais ils ne les ont pas trouvés.
6. Pour tromper la Résistance, les troupes ont quitté la ville. Mais c'était un _____. Ils étaient cachés (*hidden*) près de la ville.
7. Les soldats ont avancé sans faire aucun bruit (*noise*). Ils ont avancé _____.
8. Les _____ roulaient sur les routes, chargés (*loaded*) d'armes et de bombes.
9. Les résistants ont voulu _____ plus fort contre l'ennemi.
10. Pour empêcher la livraison (*prevent the delivery*) des armes par train, les résistants ont détruit les _____.
11. On _____ un des résistants de trahison.

C. Qu'est-ce qu'ils font? Avec votre partenaire, inventez deux légendes pour chacun des dessins suivants. Une des légendes décrit le dessin, l'autre décrit ce qui se passera après. Mettez les substantifs au pluriel si nécessaire. Vous pouvez utiliser d'autres mots si vous voulez.

Substantifs utiles: Allemands, armes, camion, otage, piège, pont, résistant, soldat, train, voie de chemin de fer, wagon

Verbes utiles: accuser, attaquer, détruire, s'échapper, frapper, garder, rechercher, se réfugier, retarder, tirer sur, tuer

1.

2.

3.

4.

Visionnement 1

Avant de visionner

Jeanne raconte son histoire. Dans le passage suivant, Jeanne raconte les événements de la nuit du 17 décembre 1943. À votre avis, qu'est-ce que les résistants allaient faire ce soir là? Qu'est-ce qui ne s'est pas passé comme prévu (*as planned*)?

Mon mari est arrivé le premier, avec les autres résistants. Antoine était en retard. Il devait le rejoindre[a] avec un camion, pour transporter les armes. Pierre était nerveux. Il savait qu'il risquait sa vie et celle[b] de ses camarades. Mais mon mari avait confiance[c]: Il croyait qu'Antoine était son ami. Et Antoine leur avait assuré[d] qu'il y aurait[e] très peu de soldats ce soir-là.

[a]*meet* [b]*that* [c]*avait... trusted him* [d]*leur... had assured them* [e]*il... there would be*

Vocabulaire relatif à l'épisode

il faut les empêcher de combattre	*we have to keep them from fighting*
un type	*guy*
nous saisirons ces armes	*we'll seize these arms*
tout s'est précipité	*everything began happening quickly*
se traîner	*to move slowly, with difficulty; to crawl*
il a disparu	*he disappeared*
le chagrin	*pain, sorrow*

Observez!

Regardez l'épisode pour répondre aux questions suivantes.

- Qui était Fergus? Quelle «preuve» (*proof*) a-t-on de sa trahison?
- Qui a accusé Antoine de trahison? Pourquoi?

Après le visionnement

A. Ordre chronologique. Classez les événements suivants par ordre chronologique de 1 à 10.

_____ **a.** Pierre est arrivé le premier au rendez-vous, avec les autres résistants.
_____ **b.** Antoine a voulu frapper plus fort.
_____ **c.** Éric donne une photo de Fergus à Camille.
_____ **d.** Pierre a été grièvement blessé.
_____ **e.** Fergus a demandé à Pierre de réunir (*gather together*) tous ses amis résistants.
_____ **f.** Pierre s'est traîné jusque chez lui.
_____ **g.** Fergus est arrivé de Paris.
_____ **h.** Jeanne a soigné (*took care of*) Pierre.
_____ **i.** Pierre a accusé Antoine de trahison.
_____ **j.** Pierre a pu s'échapper.

B. Réfléchissez. Répondez aux questions suivantes.

1. À la fin de l'épisode, Jeanne demande à Camille de partir. Selon vous, regrette-t-elle sa décision d'accueillir Camille? Est-ce que le récit des événements de la nuit du 17 décembre 1943 a été trop pénible (*painful; difficult*) pour elle? Jeanne ressent-elle de la haine (*does she feel hatred*) envers Camille, la petite-fille d'Antoine?
2. Jeanne demande à Éric de donner la photo de Fergus à Camille. Est-ce que les remarques de Camille l'ont incitée à revoir sa façon de penser en ce qui concerne l'histoire d'Antoine? Veut-elle savoir elle-même la vérité?

Structure 57

Le conditionnel

Being polite and talking about possibilities

Où **serait** la France sans l'effort des résistants, des héros de la guerre?

You have already studied the use of verbs in two verbal moods▲: the **indicative** (present, *passé composé, imparfait,* and future) and the **imperative**.

The **conditional** is another mood. It is used to make polite requests, to offer advice politely, and to talk about things that might happen.

1. To form the conditional, use the same stem as in the future tense but add the endings of the **imparfait**.

	regarder	répondre	réussir
je	regarder**ais**	répondr**ais**	réussir**ais**
tu	regarder**ais**	répondr**ais**	réussir**ais**
il, elle, on	regarder**ait**	répondr**ait**	réussir**ait**
nous	regarder**ions**	répondr**ions**	réussir**ions**
vous	regarder**iez**	répondr**iez**	réussir**iez**
ils, elles	regarder**aient**	répondr**aient**	réussir**aient**

Camille explique qu'elle **aimerait** rencontrer la grand-mère d'Éric. — *Camille explains that she would like to meet Éric's grandmother.*

Verbs with irregular future stems have the same stems in the conditional. The endings are always regular.

Je **serais** contente de voir votre grand-mère. — *I would be happy to see your grandmother.*

Auriez-vous une photo des résistants? — *Would you have a photo of the resistance fighters?*

2. You have already seen examples of the conditional of *politeness*, a form used to soften a request or a piece of advice.

   - Requests made with the present tense are not considered as polite as those made using the conditional.

     David, est-ce que vous **pourriez** m'aider dans mes recherches? — *David, could you help me with my research?*

   - Advice can be given using the conditional of **devoir** + infinitive or by beginning with the expression **À ta (votre) place.**

     Tu **devrais** appeler le président, Camille. — *You should call the president, Camille.*

     À ta place, Camille, j'**abandonnerais** cette idée. — *If I were you, Camille, I would give up that idea.*

3. The conditional expresses a hypothetical occurrence. It can stand alone in sentences about hypothetical situations such as a description of a perfect world. It can also follow the expression **au cas où** (*in case, in the event that*) to set up a circumstance in which something else should happen.

   Dans un monde parfait, il n'y **aurait** plus jamais de guerre. — *In a perfect world, there would be no more war.*

   Au cas où vous **trouveriez** Fergus, demandez-lui des preuves de son innocence. — *In case you find Fergus, ask him for proof of his innocence.*

Activités

A. Une université parfaite. Complétez les phrases avec un verbe au conditionnel pour indiquer comment les choses seraient dans une université parfaite.

MODÈLE: Les professeurs _____ (ne pas donner) d'examens. →
Les professeurs ne donneraient pas d'examens.

1. On _____ (avoir) du bon café dans toutes les salles de classe.
2. La librairie _____ (vendre) les livres pour un dollar.
3. Vous _____ (réussir) à tous vos examens sans préparer.

4. Je _____ (pouvoir) me lever tard le matin.
5. Les professeurs _____ (faire) les devoirs pour les étudiants (et pas le contraire).
6. Tu _____ (venir) sur le campus une fois par semaine.
7. Je _____ (ne pas travailler) à la bibliothèque tous les soirs.
8. Vous _____ (finir) tous vos cours à midi.
9. Nous _____ (recevoir) nos diplômes après un an d'études.

B. À votre place... / Vous devriez... Antoine Leclair donne des conseils à Pierre Leblanc et leur ami résistant David Berg. Quels sont les conseils? Commencez les phrases avec **À votre place, je...**

MODÈLE: contacter tous les résistants de la région →
À votre place, je contacterais tous les résistants de la région.

1. essayer de tout faire pour prendre les armes des Allemands
2. aller à la voie de chemin de fer
3. prendre les armes qui sont dans le train
4. ne rien dire à vos femmes
5. faire très attention

Pierre donne des conseils à Antoine aussi. Commencez les phrases avec **À ta place, je...**

6. être très prudent (*careful*)
7. ne pas parler tout de suite de ce projet
8. attendre encore un peu

Maintenant, donnez les mêmes conseils en utilisant **vous** ou **tu** avec le verbe **devoir** au conditionnel. Suivez le modèle.

MODÈLE: contacter tous les résistants de la région →
Vous devriez contacter tous les résistants de la région.

C. Dans un monde de rêve. Avec un(e) partenaire, parlez d'un monde où tout serait parfait parce que les gens feraient ou ne feraient pas certaines choses. Suivez le modèle et utilisez votre imagination.

MODÈLE: mes parents →
Dans un monde de rêve, mes parents me donneraient beaucoup d'argent. (Dans un monde de rêve, mes parents ne se disputeraient pas.)

1. mes parents / mes enfants
2. mon meilleur ami / ma meilleure amie
3. je
4. mon professeur de _____ (*sujet*)
5. les étudiants de cette classe
6. les jeunes en général
7. le président du pays
8. les célébrités

Structure 58

Les phrases avec *si*

Expressing hypothetical situations and conditions

Si Camille ne **poursuivait** pas la vérité, elle ne la **saurait** jamais.

You have already learned that in order to say something *will* happen *if* another event occurs, you should use **si** + present + future. You also know that the two clauses can appear in either order.

Si Camille ne **retourne** pas immédiatement à Canal 7, **sera**-t-elle licenciée?	*If Camille does not return to Channel 7 immediately, will she be fired?*
Est-ce que Camille **abandonnera** sa quête **si** elle ne **trouve** pas Fergus?	*Will Camille abandon her quest if she doesn't find Fergus?*

1. To say that something *would probably* happen *if* another event occurred, the construction **si** + **imparfait** + conditional is used. The two clauses can appear in either order.

Si Louise **était** encore vivante, elle **ferait** le voyage avec Camille.	*If Louise were still living, she would make the trip with Camille.*
Est-ce que le président **accepterait** l'absence de Camille **si** Martine **était** moins convaincante?	*Would the president accept Camille's absence if Martine were less convincing?*

Sometimes the **si** clause is understood but not expressed.

Tu **ferais** ça pour moi?	*You would do that for me?*

2. **Si j'étais toi (vous)** + conditional can be used to give advice. Used this way, it plays the same role as **À ta (votre) place.**

Si j'**étais** toi, Camille, j'**abandonnerais** cette idée.	*If I were you, Camille, I would give up that idea.*

Pour en savoir plus...

The structure **si** + **imparfait** can be used alone to make suggestions or invitations.

Si on **allait** au restaurant ce soir? *How about going out to eat tonight?*

Si nous **prenions** un pot ensemble? *What about having a drink together?*

Activités

A. Le Vercors. Le Vercors, une région pas loin des Alpes, était comme les Cévennes un lieu important pour la Résistance. On y trouve aujourd'hui le *Site national historique de la Résistance en Vercors.* Faites des phrases avec les éléments donnés en utilisant l'imparfait et le conditionnel pour faire des hypothèses.

Site national historique de la Résistance en Vercors

Les chemins de la Liberté

1. si nous / aller à cet endroit, / nous / visiter / un site national
2. je / trouver / facilement le Mémorial / si je / passer / par le village de Vassieux-en-Vercors
3. nous / ne pas avoir / le temps de visiter le Mémorial / si nous / arriver après 17 h
4. si les gens / venir / un dimanche en mai, / ils / pouvoir / visiter le Mémorial
5. si vous / voir / cet endroit, / vous / être sans doute touché(e) par l'héroïsme des résistants
6. si les Français / ne pas comprendre / l'importance de l'histoire, / ils / ne pas construire / des sites comme cela

B. Situations communes et situations absurdes. Terminez les phrases suivantes avec une proposition contenant un verbe au présent, au futur, à l'imparfait ou au conditionnel, selon le sens de la phrase.

1. Si j'ai le temps ce soir...
2. Si j'avais un crocodile...
3. Mes amis et moi, nous mangerions au restaurant si...
4. Si mon ami(e) ne trouve pas de travail après les études...
5. Si mes parents étaient des extra-terrestres...
6. Si mes amis oublient mon anniversaire...
7. Je serais triste si...
8. Si mon professeur nous donnait des examens faciles...
9. Si les étudiants avaient moins de travail...
10. Les étudiants parleraient bien français si...
11. Si j'avais trois pieds...
12. Si je trouvais cent dollars dans la rue...

C. Que ferait-on? Interviewez trois camarades de classe pour savoir ce qu'ils/elles feraient seul(e)s et ce qu'ils feraient ensemble dans votre région par les temps indiqués. Faites attention aux temps et aux modes des verbes.

MODÈLES: automne / il pleut →
É1: Que ferais-tu en automne s'il pleuvait?
É2: S'il pleuvait, je visiterais le musée d'art.
É1: Que feriez-vous ensemble en automne s'il pleuvait?
É1, 2, 3 ENSEMBLE: S'il pleuvait, nous danserions dans la rue.

1. hiver / il fait du soleil
2. été / il fait très chaud
3. printemps / il fait mauvais et il pleut
4. automne / il fait frais mais beau
5. hiver / il neige

Regards sur la culture

La Résistance

Antoine avec ses camarades de la Résistance

During the years immediately following the Second World War, those who had served in the Resistance were seen as heros and saviors of France.

- In 1940, shortly after the French defeat, General Charles de Gaulle made a radio broadcast from London, encouraging the French nation not to cooperate with the German victors or their French allies but rather to fight to free France. By this act, he became the leader of the Free French forces.
- The Resistance movement that emerged little by little in occupied France engaged in secret military action (sabotage, assassinations, etc.), intelligence missions, medical service, and political contact. It had its own underground newspapers and periodicals. With the Resistance fighting both the German occupiers and the French Vichy government, World War II became a French civil war.
- After Germany turned against Russia in 1941, many well-organized French Communist groups became active members of the Resistance. The participation of these people made the movement far more effective.
- Much of the Resistance operated out of remote areas in the French countryside. Many groups were centered in rural southern France, where they came to be known as **maquisards** after the region's scrubby vegetation, **le maquis**.
- By the time of the Allied landings in Normandy in 1944, many who had originally supported Vichy started considering themselves members of the Resistance. By the end of the war, the number of **résistants** had multiplied considerably.
- A number of well-known French writers joined the Resistance through the underground **Comité national des écrivains**. Among these were Camus, Aragon, Éluard, and Malraux. One of the most important outcomes of this period was the tendency for intellectuals to become **engagés**, in other words, to be political activists. Many joined the French Communist Party. For nearly 25 years after the war, famous literary figures, like Jean-Paul Sartre, were significant political opinion makers.

Considérez

In 1940, France was defeated and partly occupied, but there was a French government operating from Vichy, with a popular man (le Maréchal Pétain) at its head. Why might some people have joined the Resistance when it seemed like a doubtful cause and when it made them traitors to the existing government?

Structure 59

Les pronoms démonstratifs

Avoiding repetition

—Il savait qu'il risquait sa vie et **celle** de ses camarades.

Demonstrative pronouns▲ are used to mean *this/that* (*one*) or *these/those* (*ones*).

1. The four demonstrative pronouns correspond in gender and number to the noun they represent.

	SINGULIER	PLURIEL
masculin	celui	ceux
féminin	celle	celles

2. Demonstrative pronouns must be followed by one of the following constructions.

- **-ci** (to indicate proximity) or **-là** (to indicate distance)

—Dans **quel train** les Allemands ont-ils entreposé des armes?	*In which train did the Germans store weapons?*
—Il en ont entreposé dans **celui-ci**.	*They stored some in this one.*
—**Quels hommes** ont fait partie de la Résistance?	*Which men were in the Resistance?*
—**Ceux-là!**	*Those!*

- **de** + noun (to express possession)

—Savait-il qu'il risquait **la vie** de ses camarades?	*Did he know he was risking his buddies' lives?*
—Oui. Il savait qu'il risquait sa vie et **celle** de ses camarades.	*Yes. He knew he was risking his life and those of his buddies.*

- a relative clause introduced by **qui**, **que**, or **où** (to give more information)

—**Quel camion** attendaient-ils?	*Which truck were they waiting for?*
—Ils attendaient **celui** qu'Antoine conduisait.	*They were waiting for the one that Antoine was driving.*

Activités

A. Vous rappelez-vous les personnages? Utilisez un pronom démonstratif pour lier (*join*) logiquement les éléments de la colonne de gauche avec ceux de la colonne de droite.

MODÈLE: Hélène est celle qui vient du Québec

1. David est	**a.** qui aide Camille à comprendre le laissez-passer
2. Roger et Nicole sont	**b.** que Pierre a vu avec un uniforme nazi
3. Pierre et Antoine sont	**c.** qui ont organisé l'attaque contre le train
4. Roland Fergus est	**d.** qui travaillent avec Martine à la régie
5. Mado et Louise sont	**e.** qui aiment Camille de tout leur cœur

B. Comparaisons. Mettez-vous par groupes de trois ou quatre. Comparez-vous à un ou plusieurs membre(s) de votre groupe. Vos camarades vont vous dire s'ils / si elles sont d'accord avec vous. Utilisez les catégories suivantes.

MODÈLE: cheveux →

É1: Mes cheveux sont plus courts que ceux de Suzanne.

É2: Je ne suis pas d'accord. Tes cheveux sont plus longs que ceux de Suzanne. (*ou* D'accord. Ceux de Suzanne sont plus longs.)

1. voiture	**3.** famille	**5.** études	**7.** yeux
2. travail	**4.** cours	**6.** vêtements	**8.** oreilles

Visionnement 2

Observez!

Considérez les aspects culturels expliqués dans **Regards sur la culture**. Ensuite, regardez l'Épisode 19 encore une fois, et répondez aux questions suivantes.

- Comment la Résistance a-t-elle essayé d'infiltrer les Allemands?
- Dans quel quartier de Marseille Fergus habitait-il avant la guerre?

Après le visionnement

Faites l'activité pour le **Visionnement 2** dans le cahier.

Synthèse: Culture

Deux îles françaises loin de la France

En 1939, l'empire français était vingt-deux fois plus grand que la France métropolitaine, c'est-à-dire que la France elle-même. Il y avait des colonies aux Caraïbes,[1] en Afrique, dans l'océan Indien, en Indochine et dans le Pacifique. La Deuxième Guerre mondiale et la période 1945–1960 ont transformé la situation. Beaucoup de colonies sont devenues indépendantes; d'autres sont restées françaises.

La Martinique

La population:

- Traditionnellement ouvriers et paysans, **les Noirs** sont aujourd'hui souvent de la classe moyenne aussi.
- Les blancs des grandes familles traditionnelles (l'élite de la population) sont **les Békés**.
- Les personnes de race mixte, **les Mulâtres** sont en général de la classe moyenne.
- **Les Blancs créoles**, nés dans l'île, sont souvent des artisans et des commerçants.
- Les Français de France (professeurs, policiers, administrateurs) sont surnommés **les Métros**.

Un marché à Fort-de-France en Martinique

En 1940, la Martinique, aux Antilles, était dominée par douze grandes familles, «les Békés», c'est-à-dire les blancs qui possédaient les grandes plantations. Au moment de la Deuxième Guerre mondiale, ces familles sont restées fidèles[2] au gouvernement de Vichy. Mais beaucoup de Noirs sont partis à la Dominique, l'île située au nord, pour rejoindre l'armée de Charles de Gaulle.

En 1945, les Martiniquais ont voté pour l'union politique avec la France. Aujourd'hui, l'île est un «département d'outre-mer» (DOM)[3] de la France et les Martiniquais sont donc des citoyens[4] français. La situation économique de la Martinique est difficile. La ressource traditionnelle était la canne à sucre, mais l'agriculture ne prospère plus aujourd'hui. Plus de 50% des salaires dans l'île sont payés par le gouvernement. Cependant,[5] avec l'assistance de la France, la Martinique est plus prospère que les autres pays de la région.

[1]*Caribbean* [2]*loyal* [3]*overseas department (state)* [4]*citizens* [5]*Nevertheless*

La Nouvelle-Calédonie

Un village kanak en Nouvelle-Calédonie

La population:

- Les Mélanésiens, **les Kanaks**, étaient les premiers habitants de l'île. Ouvriers et paysans, ils habitent en général à la campagne.
- Les blancs qui sont nés sur l'île, **les Caldoches**, vivent sur leurs terres ou dans les villes.
- Les Français de France (professeurs, policiers, administrateurs, ingénieurs) sont surnommés **les Zozos**.

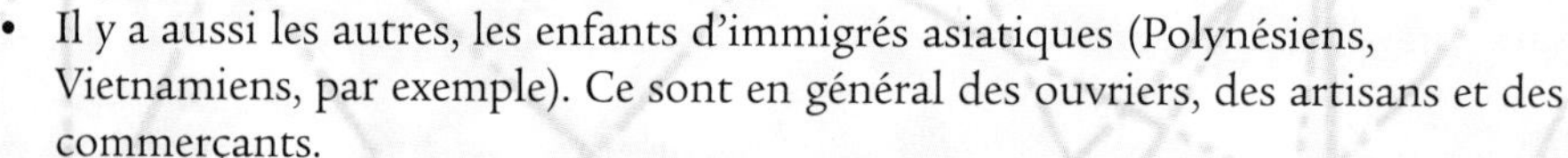

- Il y a aussi les autres, les enfants d'immigrés asiatiques (Polynésiens, Vietnamiens, par exemple). Ce sont en général des ouvriers, des artisans et des commerçants.

En 1940, le gouvernement de Vichy n'a pas pu contrôler toutes les colonies: la Nouvelle-Calédonie a déclaré son soutien[6] pour de Gaulle et les Forces françaises libres. Les partisans de Vichy sont partis à Saïgon, au Viêtnam. Après l'attaque contre Pearl Harbor, la Nouvelle-Calédonie est devenue une base importante pour les troupes américaines. Les militaires sont arrivés avec beaucoup d'argent. Ils ont construit des aéroports, des hôpitaux et des routes. Beaucoup de Kanaks ont vu pour la première fois des bulldozers et des jeeps. Ils ont vu aussi que certains des soldats américains étaient noirs. Cette présence américaine a transformé les mentalités.

Après la guerre, la Nouvelle-Calédonie est devenue un «territoire d'outre-mer» (TOM)* de la France et ses habitants sont devenus citoyens français. La prospérité est arrivée après 1960 avec l'exploitation du minerai nickel. L'île a 40% des ressources du monde en nickel. Mais les Kanaks n'ont pas autant profité des avantages de cette expansion économique et les années 80 ont vu une montée du mouvement indépendantiste kanak. Entre 1984 et 1988 il y a eu une période de violence anti-française. Aujourd'hui, la situation est plus calme, mais les Kanaks sont toujours beaucoup plus pauvres que les Caldoches. Et maintenant, ils sont minoritaires dans l'île.

[6]*support*

À vous

Un reportage. En petits groupes, préparez une présentation orale où vous comparerez la Martinique et la Nouvelle-Calédonie. Utilisez les suggestions suivantes.

1. ...une colonie française...
2. ...la société est dominée par...
3. ...les plus pauvres sont...
4. ...on appelle les gens qui représentent la France...
5. ...pendant la guerre de 39–45...
6. ...les ressources naturelles...
7. ...est près de pays pauvres/riches...
8. ...il y a eu de la violence...

---

*Les DOM sont plus intégrés au système politique français que les TOM. Les habitants des DOM ont les mêmes droits (*rights*) et les mêmes devoirs que les citoyens français en France. Les TOM diffèrent entre eux par leurs lois (*laws*) et par leurs relations avec la France.

À écrire

Faites **À écrire** pour le Chapitre 19 dans le cahier.

Vocabulaire

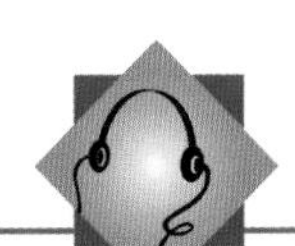

La guerre

une arme (*f.*)	weapon, arm
un camion	truck
un(e) conducteur/trice	driver
un otage	hostage
la patrie	homeland
un piège	trap
un pont	bridge
un soldat	soldier
la trahison	treason
une voie de chemin de fer	railroad tracks

MOTS APPARENTÉS: **un résistant, des troupes** (*f.*)

Verbes

s'échapper	to escape
frapper	to strike, hit
fusiller	to execute (*somebody*) by shooting
garder	to guard; to keep
rechercher	to search for; to research
se réfugier	to hide, take refuge
retarder l'avance	to slow the advance
tirer sur	to fire on, shoot at
tuer	to kill

MOTS APPARENTÉS: **accuser, attaquer**

Les pronoms démonstratifs

celui, celle; ceux, celles	this/that; these/those

Adjectifs et adverbes

fort	with strength; with effort
silencieusement	silently
soudain	suddenly
soudain(e)	sudden

À REVOIR: **fort(e)**

Autres expressions utiles

à ta (votre) place	in your place, if I were you
au cas où	in case, in the event that

À REVOIR: **-ci, -là, si**

Chapitre 20

Risques

OBJECTIFS

In this episode, you will

- find out what Martine says to the station president about Camille
- watch as Camille looks for Roland Fergus

In this chapter, you will

- talk about the city of Marseille
- discuss the world of work and money
- express judgments, necessity, and obligation using infinitives
- express obligation and will, using the subjunctive
- learn about workplace customs in France
- read an excerpt of a story by Jules Verne

Vocabulaire en contexte

La ville de Marseille

Marseille: 807.000 **habitants** (*m.*), deuxième ville de France.

La situation géographique de Marseille, premier **port** en France, a favorisé **au cours des siècles**° (*m.*) l'implantation sur son sol° de différentes nationalités avec une forte proportion d'**immigrés** (*m.*) des pays d'Afrique du Nord, mais aussi des Italiens, des Turcs, des Espagnols et des Portugais.

au... *through the centuries* / *soil*

L'accent marseillais, rendu si populaire dans les films de Marcel Pagnol, est **célèbre** dans le monde entier. Les Marseillais sont **réputés** pour **la chaleur**° de leur **accueil** (*m.*) et leur **joie** (*f.*) **de vivre**.°

warmth

joie... *joyful attitude (towards life)*

Marseille est divisé en seize **arrondissements**° (*m.*) dont° plusieurs quartiers et **sites** (*m.*) **touristiques** comme

districts / *including*

- *Le Vieux-Port:* port de plaisance,° hôtels, restaurants, cafés, boutiques
- *Le Panier:* quartier aux **ruelles**° **étroites**° anciennement **délabrées**° mais maintenant en pleine **rénovation**, boutiques, **galeries** (*f.*)
- *Notre-Dame-de-la-Garde:* basilique° du XIXe siècle, perchée sur une colline qui **donne sur**° le port
- *Le cours Julien:* **rue piétonne**,° **antiquaires**° (*m., f.*), librairies, cafés, restaurants

port... *marina*

alleyways / *narrow* / *dilapidated*

basilica (large Roman Catholic church)

donne... *overlooks*

rue... *pedestrian street* / *antique dealers*

Pour en savoir plus...

L'écrivain et cinéaste Marcel Pagnol (1895–1974) est très connu pour sa description du paysage et des habitants de la Provence, y compris (*including*) la célèbre trilogie marseillaise *Marius*, *Fanny* et *César*. Il décrit sa jeunesse dans la région dans ses deux films *La Gloire de mon père* (1957) et *Le Château de ma mère* (1958), qui ont été refaits par le cinéaste Yves Robert en 1991.

Activités

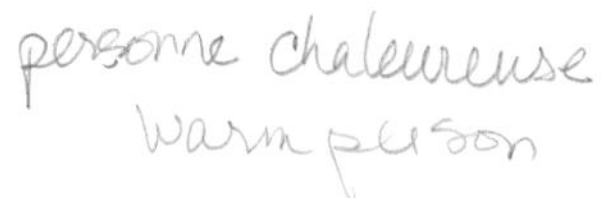

A. Définitions. Donnez le mot qui correspond aux définitions suivantes. Attention: Faites des phrases complètes!

MODÈLE: un commerçant qui vend des objets devenus plus précieux au cours des années →
Un antiquaire est un commerçant qui vend des objets devenus plus précieux au cours des années.

1. un étranger qui s'installe dans un nouveau pays **2.** une division administrative d'une ville **3.** une zone où la circulation automobile est interdite (*prohibited*) **4.** une période de cent ans **5.** un endroit où les bateaux arrivent **6.** un adjectif qui décrit un bâtiment qui a besoin d'être rénové

Pour en savoir plus...

Voici quelques mots du dialecte marseillais. Leur origine est la langue occitane (le provençal). Leur équivalent dans le langage «standard» est indiqué.

bazarette = une personne qui parle beaucoup, un(e) bavard(e)
fada = fou ou passionné de quelqu'un ou de quelque chose
pitchoun ou **pitchon** = petit enfant
Qu'es aco? = Qu'est-ce que c'est?
testard = têtu (*stubborn*)

B. Chez vous. Identifiez une ville...

1. où il y a une cathédrale célèbre. De quel siècle date cette cathédrale?
2. où il y a un port. Est-ce un port de plaisance ou un port maritime (*shipping*)?
3. qui est réputée pour la chaleur de son accueil. Comment sont ses habitants?
4. qui est célèbre dans le monde entier. Quels sites touristiques y trouve-t-on? Quelles galeries? Quelles boutiques?
5. où il y a un accent particulier. Cet accent est-il lent? rythmé? prestigieux?
6. qui accueille beaucoup d'immigrés. Quel(s) groupe(s) d'immigrés y trouve-t-on?

C. Une annonce publicitaire. Avec un(e) partenaire, créez une annonce publicitaire pour votre ville ou région. Suivez le modèle donné dans la présentation sur Marseille, et décrivez, par exemple, des rues piétonnes ou des ruelles pittoresques, des bâtiments ou de grandes maisons qui donnent sur des jardins, des ports de plaisance, des sites touristiques célèbres, la joie de vivre des habitants, etc.

Le monde du travail et de l'argent

Quand Martine, la productrice à Canal 7, a **engagé**° Camille, les deux ont signé **un contrat**. Avec son équipe, Martine a **formé**° Camille, qui est bientôt devenue **la vedette**° de l'émission «Bonjour!». Maintenant Camille reçoit **un** très bon **salaire**. Chaque mois, elle **dépose**° un chèque d'un **montant** important° sur son **compte**° à **la banque**.

Camille décide de prendre **un congé**° de deux semaines sans en parler à Martine. Le président de Canal 7 n'en est pas du tout content. Il va peut-être **licencier**° Camille. Bruno a peur qu'il le fasse° et que Camille se retrouve **au chômage**.°

a... *hired*
a... *trained*
star
deposits
montant... *large amount* / *account*
time off
to fire
le... *might do it*
au... *unemployed*

Autres expressions utiles

un carnet de chèques	checkbook
faire un chèque	to write a check
toucher un chèque	to cash a check

Langage fonctionnel

Pour trouver un emploi

Expressions pour parler de la recherche d'un emploi

rédiger/soumettre son curriculum vitæ (C.V.)	*to write/submit one's CV (resumé)*
poser sa candidature	*to apply, submit one's candidacy*
avoir un entretien d'embauche	*to have a job interview*
être payé(e) [10 dollars] de l'heure	*to be paid [10 dollars] per hour*
un(e) chômeur/euse	*unemployed person*

Questions souvent posées à un entretien d'embauche

Pourquoi avez-vous répondu à notre annonce?	*Why did you respond to our ad?*
Pourquoi avez-vous quitté votre dernier emploi?	*Why did you leave your last job?*
Quelles sont vos qualifications?	*What are your qualifications?*
Que savez-vous de notre société?	*What do you know about our company?*

Quand je cherche un nouvel emploi, je **rédige mon curriculum vitæ** et je **pose ma candidature** dans plusieurs entreprises. Quand j'obtiens **un entretien d'embauche**, on me demande parfois de parler de **mes qualifications**.

Activités

A. Le monde du travail. Complétez les phrases suivantes par le mot ou l'expression qui convient. S'il s'agit d'un verbe, conjuguez-le au temps convenable. Si c'est un substantif, mettez l'article si nécessaire.

1. Camille est l'animatrice la plus connue et la plus aimée de Canal 7. C'est _____ (congé, vedette) de «Bonjour!»
2. Quand Martine l'a engagée, Camille avait très peu d'expérience. Martine la (l') _____ (former, licencier) et maintenant, c'est la meilleure journaliste.
3. Camille reçoit un bon _____ (argent, salaire). Chaque mois, elle _____ (déposer un chèque, être au chômage) d'un montant important.
4. Pour des raisons personnelles, Camille a pris _____ (congé, contrat) et sera absente pour deux semaines.
5. Le président n'est pas content de l'absence de Camille. Après tout, elle a signé _____ (chèque, contrat).
6. Si le président ne se calme pas, il va sûrement _____ (former, licencier) Camille. Elle n'aura plus d'emploi à Canal 7.

B. Questions personnelles. Posez les questions suivantes à votre partenaire. Demandez-lui...

1. s'il / si elle préfère travailler en équipe ou seul(e). Quels sont les avantages et les inconvénients de chaque situation?
2. s'il / si elle préférerait gagner un bon salaire en faisant un travail qu'il/elle n'aime pas ou un salaire médiocre en faisant un travail qui l'intéresse.
3. ce qu'il/elle ferait s'il / si elle pouvait interrompre (*interrupt*) ses études ou son travail et prendre des congés.
4. ce qu'une personne qui est au chômage devrait faire pour trouver un emploi.
5. s'il / si elle pense que Camille va être licenciée. Pourquoi ou pourquoi pas?

C. Comment trouver un emploi. Expliquez quelles démarches (*steps*) vous devez faire pour trouver un emploi. Utilisez les adverbes **d'abord**, **ensuite**, **puis** et **enfin**.

MODÈLE: D'abord, je rédige mon curriculum vitæ. Ensuite,...

Visionnement 1

Avant de visionner

Vocabulaire relatif à l'épisode

elle était censée être...	*she was supposed to be . . .*
elle a changé d'avis	*she changed her mind*
démissionner	*to quit, resign*
rédactrice	*editor*
faites-lui confiance	*trust her*
Vous êtes de passage...	*Are you traveling through . . .*

Confrontation professionnelle. Dans l'Épisode 20, la productrice, Martine, doit parler avec le président de Canal 7. Il est furieux à cause de l'absence de Camille. Voilà quelques paroles du président. À votre avis, qu'est-ce que Martine pourrait répondre?

1. Martine, vous me connaissez depuis longtemps. Je n'accepte pas les caprices. L'attitude de Camille est intolérable!
2. Personne n'a le droit (*right*) de déserter son poste. Rien ne peut le justifier.
3. C'est nous qui l'avons découverte, formée et rendue célèbre. Elle nous doit quelque chose, n'est-ce pas?
4. Je lui accorde (*I'll give her*) deux jours. Pas un jour de plus!

Observez!

Dans cet épisode, Martine est convoquée (*summoned*) chez le président. Ils discutent les actions de Camille. Maintenant, regardez l'Épisode 20 et répondez aux questions suivantes.

- Quel effet a l'absence de Camille sur les indices d'audience (*ratings*) de Canal 7?
- À quelle solution de compromis est-ce que Martine et le président arrivent à la fin de leur discussion?
- Que fait Camille pour essayer de trouver Roland Fergus?

Après le visionnement

A. Reconstituez. Mettez les répliques du dialogue dans l'ordre logique.

DIALOGUE A: MARTINE ET BRUNO

_____ MARTINE: À Marseille. Qu'est-ce qu'elle va faire à Marseille?

_____ MARTINE: Elle a changé d'avis. Et pourquoi?

_____ MARTINE: Est-ce que quelqu'un a des nouvelles de Camille?

_____ BRUNO: Oui. Elle a appelé. Elle est à Marseille.

_____ BRUNO: Elle a peut-être changé d'avis!

DIALOGUE B: LE PATRON DU BAR ET CAMILLE

_____ PATRON: Alors, vous êtes de passage à Marseille?

_____ PATRON: Fergus... ? Fergus... ? Je connais tout le monde dans cette ville.

_____ PATRON: Oui. Je vous trouve son adresse pour demain matin.

_____ CAMILLE: C'est vrai?

_____ CAMILLE: Je cherche cet homme. Il s'appelle Roland Fergus... . Autrefois, son père avait un garage sur le Vieux-Port.

B. Réfléchissez. À votre avis, est-ce que le président est trop sévère envers Camille ou a-t-il raison? Justifiez votre réponse.

Structure 60

Les expressions impersonnelles + infinitif

Expressing judgments, necessity, and obligation

—La vérité... Savez-vous qu'**il n'est pas** toujours **bon de** la **connaître**?

—Peut-être. Mais **il n'est jamais bon de** la **cacher**, surtout à un enfant.

Impersonal expressions are those that have no specific person as the subject. In English, they are usually expressed as *It is important to . . . , One needs to . . . ,* and so on.

Pour en savoir plus...

The impersonal expression **il vaut mieux** (*it is better*) can also be used before an infinitive to express a judgment.

Il vaut mieux savoir la vérité. *It is better to know the truth.*

It is also sometimes used in the future and the conditional.

Il vaudra mieux... *It will be better . . .*

Il vaudrait mieux... *It would be better . . .*

1. The construction **Il est** + adjective + **de** + infinitive can be used to express judgments about situations and circumstances. Adjectives such as **bon**, **essentiel**, **important**, **impossible**, **inutile**, **juste** (*right*), **préférable**, **triste**, and **utile** can be used in this way. The verb **être** can be in almost any tense. The phrase **il est** may be omitted in certain expressions.

Il sera essentiel de retarder les troupes allemandes...	*It will be essential to slow the German troops . . .*
Il était triste de penser aux événements de la guerre.	*It was sad to think about the events of the war.*
Il est juste de chercher la vérité.	*It is right to look for the truth.*
Inutile de vous **mentir**, madame.	*It's no use lying to you, ma'am.*

2. Impersonal expressions can also be used before an infinitive to talk about obligation or necessity. Three common expressions are

il faut	+ infinitive	*it is necessary to; one must*
il est nécessaire de	+ infinitive	*it is necessary to*
il suffit de	+ infinitive	*it is enough to, all that is necessary is to*

Pour en savoir plus...

It is useful to learn to recognize **il faut** and **il suffit** in other tenses.

PASSÉ COMPOSÉ: **il a fallu, il a suffi**

IMPARFAIT: **il fallait, il suffisait**

FUTUR: **il faudra, il suffira**

CONDITIONNEL: **il faudrait, il suffirait**

In English, these impersonal expressions are sometimes expressed with personal pronoun subjects.

Il est nécessaire de chercher la vérité sur mon père.	***We*** *need to look for the truth about my father.*
Il faut frapper plus fort.	***We*** *need to strike harder.*
Il suffit de tromper l'ennemi.	*All* ***you*** *need to do is to trick the enemy.*

Attention—**Il ne faut pas** means (*someone*) *should not.* Use **il n'est pas nécessaire de** to mean *it is not necessary to.*

Il ne faut pas mentir à un enfant.	*You shouldn't lie to a child.*
Il n'est pas nécessaire de mentir à un enfant.	*It's not necessary to lie to a child.*

3. You have already learned a few other constructions that can also be used with an infinitive to express judgment and necessity. In such cases, the infinitive has the same subject as the conjugated verb.

JUDGMENT: Camille **est heureuse d'avoir** Bruno comme ami.
Es-tu **content de voir** ces indices d'audience?

NECESSITY: Camille **a besoin d'aller** à Marseille.
Martine **doit parler** au président de Canal 7.

Activités

A. Marseille, une ville au service de ses habitants. Imaginez que les personnes suivantes se trouvent à Marseille. Pour chaque personne, indiquez quels services publics sont importants, essentiels, inutiles, etc., en utilisant une expression impersonnelle.

Vocabulaire utile: bon, essentiel, important, impossible, indispensable, inutile, préférable, triste, utile

MODÈLE: Pour un jeune de 16 ans sans voiture, il est essentiel d'avoir un plan du métro. Il est inutile de connaître le parking du Vieux-Port.

PERSONNES

1. un jeune de 16 ans sans voiture
2. un touriste qui ne connaît pas la ville
3. une employée qui téléphone aux restaurants pour réserver
4. un homme d'affaires qui conduit une voiture mais qui n'a pas d'enfants
5. un instituteur qui veut enseigner l'importance de la protection des eaux
6. une dame avec des enfants qui veulent nager
7. un père célibataire avec une petite fille
8. un couple qui veut ajouter un garage à la maison

SERVICES PUBLICS

a. avoir un plan du métro
b. visiter le centre pédagogique de la mer
c. utiliser les pages jaunes
d. demander un permis de construire
e. trouver l'Office du Tourisme et des Congrès
f. pouvoir consulter le site Internet «Marseille et ses plages»
g. connaître le parking du Vieux-Port
h. contacter les services de la Direction de la Petite Enfance

B. Pour trouver un bon poste. Utilisez les expressions **il faut**, **il ne faut pas**, **il est nécessaire de**, **il n'est pas nécessaire de**, **il suffit de** et **il ne suffit pas de** pour expliquer comment trouver un bon travail.

MODÈLE: savoir négocier un bon salaire →
Il faut savoir négocier un bon salaire.

1. répondre à l'annonce
2. connaître le patron
3. donner des cadeaux au patron
4. poser sa candidature
5. envoyer son dossier
6. rédiger son curriculum vitæ
7. faire une demande d'emploi par téléphone
8. s'habiller en short pour l'entretien d'embauche
9. parler de ses qualifications
10. engager un avocat

Structure 61

Le subjonctif

Expressing obligation and necessity

Il faut que Camille attende jusqu'au lendemain pour obtenir l'adresse de Roland Fergus.

Up until now, the tenses you have learned are in verbal moods▲ called the *indicative*, the *imperative*, and the *conditional.* The subjunctive is another verbal mood that is used in very predictable and specific instances.

In this section, you will learn the formation of the present tense of the subjunctive and a set of expressions that trigger its use.

1. To form the subjunctive of all regular verbs, use the **ils/elles** form of the present indicative as the stem and add the endings **-e**, **-es**, **-e**, **-ions**, **-iez**, **-ent**.

	travailler	attendre	finir
que je	travaill**e**	attend**e**	finiss**e**
que tu	travaill**es**	attend**es**	finiss**es**
qu'il, qu'elle, qu'on	travaill**e**	attend**e**	finiss**e**
que nous	travaill**ions**	attend**ions**	finiss**ions**
que vous	travaill**iez**	attend**iez**	finiss**iez**
qu'ils, qu'elles	travaill**ent**	attend**ent**	finiss**ent**

Il faut que Camille finisse sa quête. *Camille has to finish her quest.*

The following verbs also form the subjunctive this way: **connaître**, **dire**, **écrire**, **lire**, **mettre**, and all verbs conjugated like **conduire**, **ouvrir**, **sortir**, and **vivre**.

Il est important que Mme Leblanc **lise** la lettre d'Antoine. *It is important that Mme Leblanc read the letter from Antoine.*

2. The verb + infinitive construction that you have already seen is used when a generalization is being made or when the subject of the infinitive is understood. But the infinitive has to be turned into a clause with the subjunctive when the following two things are *both* true:

- an expression that triggers the subjunctive (such as **il faut**) is used
- there are different subjects for the two verbs

ONE SUBJECT	Il faut **frapper** plus fort.
TWO SUBJECTS	Il faut **que vous frappiez** plus fort.
ONE SUBJECT	Il suffit de **lire** la lettre.
TWO SUBJECTS	Il suffit **qu'elle lise** la lettre.

Activités

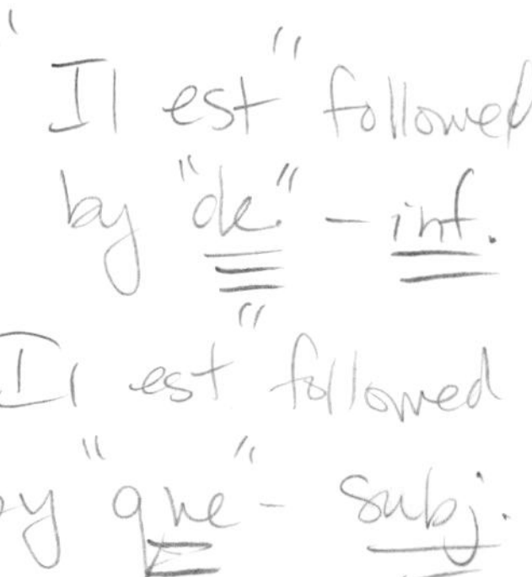

A. Pour changer sa vie. Quand on veut changer sa vie, il faut prendre beaucoup de décisions. Transformez les phrases pour les rendre plus personnelles en utilisant le subjonctif et en faisant les autres changements nécessaires.

MODÈLE: Il faut penser à ses problèmes (nous) →
Il faut que nous pensions à nos problèmes.

1. Il ne faut pas oublier ses amis. (vous)
2. Il est essentiel de poser beaucoup de questions. (je)
3. Il n'est pas nécessaire de changer radicalement. (tu)
4. Il suffit de choisir un nouveau style de vie. (on)
5. Il est important de regarder le monde avec beaucoup d'attention. (les gens)
6. Il est très important de mettre fin aux activités nuisibles (*harmful*). (vous)
7. Il faut réfléchir longuement. (nous)
8. Il est nécessaire d'attendre le bon moment pour changer sa vie. (je)

Maintenant, parlez avec un(e) camarade de classe pour décider les trois activités essentielles pour changer sa vie.

B. Une audition ratée. (*A failed audition.*) Votre ami est allé passer une audition à Canal 7. Malheureusement, il l'a complètement ratée. Il vous raconte les critiques de la productrice. Conseillez-lui en vous inspirant des idées suivantes et en utilisant des expressions d'obligation + le subjonctif.

se calmer	se laver les cheveux	porter un nouveau costume
lire des notes	réfléchir avant de parler	choisir des sujets intéressants
parler moins vite	bien connaître les sujets	dire au caméraman de faire attention

MODÈLE: Elle n'aime pas mes vêtements. →
Il faut que tu portes un nouveau costume.

1. Elle dit que je suis difficile à comprendre quand je parle. **2.** Elle trouve que mes cheveux ne sont pas beaux. **3.** Elle dit que les spectateurs n'aimeront pas les sujets de l'émission. **4.** J'ai oublié le nom de mon invité. **5.** Elle pense probablement que je ne suis pas très intelligent. **6.** Elle dit que j'ai l'air nerveux. **7.** Elle dit que les spectateurs ne peuvent pas me voir clairement.

Regards sur la culture

Le monde du travail

You have probably noticed that the working relationships between Camille, Bruno, Rachid, and Martine are quite informal. In this segment, however, you see that the president of Canal 7 maintains a somewhat different connection with those who work there.

Martine parle avec le président de Canal 7

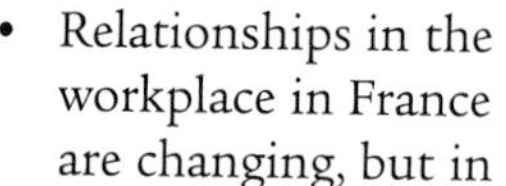

- Relationships in the workplace in France are changing, but in most cases they are more formal than in North America. The fact that Martine addresses her boss as **Monsieur le président**, even in an industry like broadcasting where informal relationships are more common, would not surprise French people. Coworkers rarely call each other by their first names, unless they have become friends outside of work. Familiarity in the world of work is not equated with friendship.
- Adhering to schedules is not as important in the French workplace as it is in North America, probably because people expect to be taking care of several things at once and know that new obligations may easily take precedence over old ones.* There is also a sense that relationships need to be maintained even at the expense of deadlines and promptness for appointments.
- It is usually considered rude in a meeting to "get down to business" right away. The French expect a certain amount of time to be spent on general conversation, making the personal relationships work, before real work can get done.
- The French are raised to be individualists. They do not join clubs and organizations nearly as much as North Americans do and sometimes consider that those who do are unacceptably conformist. As a result, French people in the workplace often resist teamwork, preferring to do their jobs separately.
- At the same time, however, the French have a long tradition of joining together for the defense of their professions and jobs. The power and appeal of labor unions in France is much greater than it is in North America, partly because

*Edward Hall, an anthropologist particularly interested in nonverbal communication, has called this approach "polychronic." He contrasts French attitudes with respect to time to the "monochronic" approach of North Americans, for whom fixed deadlines are a fairly serious matter.

social class is perceived to be a more important factor in one's identity in France.

- Just as authority is centralized in the French political system (although that is changing slowly), control tends to be vested in a few individuals in the workplace. Decisions made by the central power source seem more natural to French workers than attempts at creating consensus, which are often felt to be a waste of time.
- Mealtimes are usually considered more important than any normal work obligations. Traditionally, French businesses and offices were closed for two hours between 12:00 and 2:00 P.M., so that employees could go home for lunch and relaxation. This is still considered the norm, although the situation is slowly changing. The expression **la journée continue** describes business situations where this lunch break is not taken.
- July and August are vacation time in France, and, because everyone has at least five weeks of paid vacation, many businesses simply shut down for several weeks during this period.

Considérez

Few people in France would admit to being workaholics. What differences in priorities regarding work do you see when you compare the French situation with that in your culture?

Structure 62

Les formes subjonctives irrégulières et le subjonctif de volonté

Expressing wishes and desires

—Bonjour, petite! **Vous voulez que je vous serve** quelque chose?

Les formes subjonctives irrégulières

Irregular verbs in the subjunctive can be classified according to the number of stems used in their conjugation. All of them use the standard endings, except **avoir** and **être**.

1. Verbs with one subjunctive stem: **faire**, **pouvoir**, **savoir**

	faire	pouvoir	savoir
	fass-	*puiss-*	*sach-*
que je	**fasse**	**puisse**	**sache**
que tu	**fasses**	**puisses**	**saches**
qu'il, qu'elle, qu'on	**fasse**	**puisse**	**sache**
que nous	**fassions**	**puissions**	**sachions**
que vous	**fassiez**	**puissiez**	**sachiez**
qu'ils, qu'elles	**fassent**	**puissent**	**sachent**

2. Verbs with two subjunctive stems (one irregular, one derived from the present indicative **nous** form): **aller**, **vouloir**

	aller	vouloir
	aill-; all-	*veuill-; voul-*
que je (j')	**aille**	**veuille**
que tu	**ailles**	**veuilles**
qu'il, qu'elle, qu'on	**aille**	**veuille**
que nous	**allions**	**voulions**
que vous	**alliez**	**vouliez**
qu'ils, qu'elles	**aillent**	**veuillent**

3. Verbs with two subjunctive stems (one derived from the present indicative **ils/elles** form, one derived from the present indicative **nous** form): **boire**, **croire**, **devoir**, **prendre**, **recevoir**, **venir**

	boire	croire	devoir	prendre	recevoir	venir
	boiv-; buv-	*croi-; croy-*	*doiv-; dev-*	*prenn-; pren-*	*reçoiv-; recev-*	*vienn-; ven-*
que je	**boive**	**croie**	**doive**	**prenne**	**reçoive**	**vienne**
que tu	**boives**	**croies**	**doives**	**prennes**	**reçoives**	**viennes**
qu'il, qu'elle, qu'on	**boive**	**croie**	**doive**	**prenne**	**reçoive**	**vienne**
que nous	**buvions**	**croyions**	**devions**	**prenions**	**recevions**	**venions**
que vous	**buviez**	**croyiez**	**deviez**	**preniez**	**receviez**	**veniez**
qu'ils, qu'elles	**boivent**	**croient**	**doivent**	**prennent**	**reçoivent**	**viennent**

4. Only two verbs have both irregular stems and irregular endings: **avoir**, **être**.

	avoir	être
	ai-; ay-	*soi-; soy-*
que je (j')	**aie**	**sois**
que tu	**aies**	**sois**
qu'il, qu'elle, qu'on	**ait**	**soit**
que nous	**ayons**	**soyons**
que vous	**ayez**	**soyez**
qu'ils, qu'elles	**aient**	**soient**

Le subjonctif de volonté

Besides being used after verbs that express judgment and necessity, the subjunctive is used after verbs that express desire or will, for example **désirer**, **exiger** (*to demand; to require*), and **vouloir**. Once again, if there is no change of subject, an infinitive can follow the expression of will. But if there is a change of subject, the second verb will be in the subjunctive in a dependent clause introduced by **que**. Compare the following examples.

ONE SUBJECT Je voudrais **savoir** la vérité.
TWO SUBJECTS Je voudrais **que tu saches** la vérité.

ONE SUBJECT Camille ne désire pas **revenir** à Paris.
TWO SUBJECTS Le président désire que Camille **revienne** tout de suite à Paris.

Activités

A. Une visite de Marseille. Dominique, une jeune Marseillaise, explique à deux touristes, Thérèse et Paul, ce qu'il faut faire pour profiter de sa ville. Choisissez un verbe qui convient, et mettez-le au subjonctif pour compléter les phrases. Plus d'un verbe est parfois logique.

Vocabulaire utile: aller, avoir, boire, comprendre, croire, être, faire, pouvoir, prendre, savoir, venir

1. Il n'est pas nécessaire que vous _____ du pastis.*
2. Je veux que Paul _____ visiter le Château d'If. Il peut y aller demain s'il fait beau.
3. Je voudrais que nous _____ au musée d'Archéologie méditerranéenne ensemble.
4. Thérèse, il faut que tu _____ le temps d'acheter du tissu provençal dans une des boutiques «Les Olivades».

*__Le pastis__ est une boisson alcoolisée à l'anis, qui sent le réglisse (*licorice*). On prononce le **s** final de **pastis** et d'**anis**.

5. Paul, je veux que tu _____ comment aller au Vieux-Port. Il faut prendre le métro ligne 1 à la gare.
6. Il ne faut pas que vous _____ peur de vous promener le soir dans les rues piétonnes.
7. Il n'est pas nécessaire que vous _____ la langue provençale. Mais il faut comprendre l'accent marseillais.
8. Je voudrais que l'Opéra de Marseille _____ ouvert pendant votre visite.
9. J'exige que vous _____ chez moi pour dîner demain.
10. Thérèse, il faut que tu _____ du vin de pays pendant ta visite.

B. Les problèmes de Camille. Faites des phrases complètes avec les éléments donnés pour imaginer des bribes (*snatches*) de conversation entre Camille et Bruno quand elle lui téléphone de Marseille.

MODÈLES: BRUNO: le président/ exiger / tu / être / au travail demain →
Le président exige que tu sois au travail demain.
CAMILLE: Je / ne pas vouloir / être / au travail demain. →
Je ne veux pas être au travail demain.

1. BRUNO: Martine / vouloir / je / te parler / sérieusement
   CAMILLE: d'accord / je / accepter de / te parler / sérieusement
2. CAMILLE: je / ne pas vouloir / revenir / tout de suite
   BRUNO: nous / désirer vraiment / tu / revenir
3. BRUNO: je / vouloir / tu / savoir / le numéro de mon portable
   CAMILLE: je / vouloir / aussi / savoir / le numéro de ton portable
4. BRUNO: Martine / aller / voir le président
   CAMILLE: je / ne pas vouloir / Martine / aller / voir le président
5. BRUNO: le président / vouloir / recevoir / tes excuses pour ce «caprice»
   CAMILLE: je / vouloir simplement / il / comprendre / que cette absence est importante pour moi
6. CAMILLE: je / vouloir / tu / faire / une chose pour moi
   BRUNO: je / désirer vraiment / faire / quelque chose pour toi
7. CAMILLE: à mon retour, je / vouloir / nous / prendre / un verre ensemble
   BRUNO: je / vouloir / te revoir / le plus vite possible
8. BRUNO: je / vouloir / tu / croire / à ma sincérité
   CAMILLE: bien sûr, je / pouvoir / croire / à ta sincérité
9. BRUNO: je / vouloir / tu / avoir confiance en moi
   CAMILLE: bien sûr, je / pouvoir / avoir confiance en toi

C. Pour réussir. Avec un(e) partenaire, jouez les rôles d'un conseiller universitaire et d'un étudiant / d'une étudiante qui a des difficultés. Utilisez des éléments des deux colonnes et changez de rôle après avoir donné cinq conseils.

MODÈLE: ÉTUDIANT: Qu'est-ce qu'il faut que je fasse pour réussir aux examens?
CONSEILLER: Je veux que vous veniez plus souvent en classe.

ÉTUDIANT(E)	CONSEILLER
1. pour réussir aux examens	vouloir bien participer
2. pour avoir de bonnes notes	finir tous les cours
3. pour finir mes études cette année	venir plus souvent en classe
4. pour comprendre le livre	aller à la bibliothèque
5. pour mieux étudier	faire tous les devoirs
6. pour parler en classe	écrire les réponses dans le cahier
	arrêter (*stop*) de regarder la télé
	lire attentivement

Visionnement 2

Observez!

Considérez les aspects culturels expliqués dans **Regards sur la culture**. Ensuite, regardez l'Épisode 20 encore une fois, et répondez aux questions suivantes.

- Écoutez le français du patron du bar. En quoi son accent est-il différent du français que vous avez entendu jusqu'ici?
- D'après ce que dit le patron du bar, qu'est-ce qui indiquerait que Marseille a certaines caractéristiques d'une petite ville?

Après le visionnement

Faites l'activité pour le **Visionnement 2** dans le cahier.

Synthèse: Lecture

Mise en contexte

Jules Verne (1828–1905) is often considered the father of science fiction. He wrote sixty-six novels—including ***Le Tour du monde en 80 jours*** (*Around the World in 80 Days*), ***Vingt mille lieues sous les mers*** (*20,000 Leagues Under the Sea*), and ***Voyage au centre de la terre*** (*Journey to the Center of the Earth*)—short stories, a geography of

France, theatrical works, and an essay on Edgar Allen Poe. The United States fascinated Verne and twenty-three of his novels took place there. This story was published in 1910, after his death, in a collection of previously unpublished works.

In this excerpt, Jules Verne imagines a day in the life of Francis Bennett, director of the newspaper *The Earth Herald* in the year 2890. Bennett, **roi des journalistes** (*king of journalists*), is the latest in the line of newspaper magnates descended from Gordon Bennett, who, twenty-five generations earlier, founded the *New York Herald*. Since that time, the American capital has been transferred from Washington, D.C., to Universal City, capital of the United Americas. Although this is a fictional account of a workplace very distant in time and set in America, can you find any parallels with the French workplace described in **Regards sur la culture**?

Stratégie pour mieux lire
Understanding the passé simple

In this passage, Verne uses a tense called the **passé simple** to narrate the events. The **passé simple** is used primarily in literary and historical contexts but is otherwise equivalent to the **passé composé**; both are used to talk about completed past actions.

You do not need to learn to use the forms of the **passé simple** to understand this passage; you need to recognize and understand only the **il/elle** form. The **il/elle** form is usually made up of the infinitive stem and an ending. For **-er** verbs, the ending is **-a**, and for **-re** and **-ir** verbs, the ending is **-it**.

gagner	il gagna la salle de rédaction	*he entered the editing room*
répondre	il répondit	*he answered*
finir	il finit	*he finished*

Some verbs are irregular in the **passé simple**. In this excerpt, you will see only one example.

voir	il vit	*he saw*

Stratégie pour mieux lire
Discerning the author's point of view

As Verne imagines the future, he also expresses his social vision and attitudes toward change. For example, read the following sentence, in which he begins to describe a new invention used in the offices of *The Earth Herald*. Try to identify which elements in the sentence represent the author's point of view on the new invention.

> Grâce à[a] un ingénieux système, d'ailleurs,[b] une partie de cette publicité se propage[c] sous une forme absolument nouvelle....
>
> [a]Grâce... *Thanks to* [b]*moreover* [c]se... *spreads*

Phrases such as **Grâce à**, **ingénieux**, and **absolument nouvelle** express Verne's admiration, even awe, for this mechanical advance.

As you read, look for other phrases that reflect Verne's attitude toward life in the 29th century. Does he think that society is always just? How do people and nature interact?

Au XXIXe siècle ou La journée d'un journaliste américain en 2890

Francis Bennett poursuit son inspection et pénètre dans la salle de reportage. Ses quinze cents reporters, placés alors devant un égal[1] nombre de téléphones, communiquaient aux abonnés[2] les nouvelles reçues pendant la nuit des quatre coins du monde. L'organisation de cet incomparable service a été souvent décrite. Outre[3] son téléphone, chaque reporter a devant lui une série de commutateurs,[4] permettant d'établir la communication avec telle ou telle[5] ligne téléphotique.[6] Les abonnés ont donc non seulement le récit,[7] mais la vue des événements, obtenue par la photographie intensive.

Francis Bennett interpelle[8] un des dix reporters astronomiques, attachés à ce service, qui accroîtra[9] avec les nouvelles découvertes opérées dans le monde stellaire.

—Et bien, Cash, qu'avez-vous reçu?...

—Des phototélégrammes de Mercure, de Vénus et de Mars, monsieur.

—Intéressant, ce dernier?...

—Oui! une révolution dans le Central Empire, au profit des démocrates libéraux contre les républicains conservateurs.

—Comme chez nous, alors. Et de Jupiter?

—Rien encore! Nous n'arrivons pas à comprendre les signaux des Joviens.[10] Peut-être les nôtres[11] ne leur parviennent[12]-ils pas?

—Cela vous regarde,[13] et je vous en rends responsable, Monsieur Cash! répondit Francis Bennett, qui, fort mécontent, gagna la salle de rédaction scientifique.

«Cela vous regarde, et je vous en rends responsable, Monsieur Cash!»

La salle adjacente, vaste galerie longue d'un demi-kilomètre, était consacrée[14] à la publicité, et l'on[15] imagine aisément[16] ce que doit être la publicité d'un journal tel que le *Earth Herald*. Elle rapporte en moyenne[17] trois millions de dollars par jour. Grâce à un ingénieux système, d'ailleurs, une partie de cette publicité se propage sous une forme absolument nouvelle, due à un brevet[18] acheté au prix de trois dollars à un pauvre diable qui est mort de faim. Ce sont d'immenses affiches, réfléchies par les nuages, et dont la dimension est telle que l'on peut les apercevoir[19] d'une contrée toute entière.

De cette galerie, mille projecteurs étaient sans cesse occupés à envoyer aux nues,[20] qui les reproduisaient en couleur, ces annonces démesurées.[21]

[1]*equal* [2]*users* [3]*In addition to* [4]*switches* [5]telle... *any* [6]ligne... *an invention imagined by Verne that reproduces the image at the other end of the line* [7]*words* [8]*calls out to* [9]*will grow* [10]*inhabitants of Jupiter* [11]*ours* [12]*reach* [13]Cela... *It's your business* [14]*devoted* [15]= on [16]*easily* [17]rapporte... *brings in on average* [18]*patent* [19]*see* [20]*clouds* [21]*excessive, outsized*

Mais, ce jour-là, lorsque[22] Francis Bennett entra dans la salle de publicité, il vit que les mécaniciens se croisaient les bras auprès de[23] leurs projecteurs inactifs. Il s'informe... Pour toute réponse, on lui montre le ciel d'un bleu pur.

—Oui!... du beau temps, murmure-t-il, et pas de publicité aérienne possible! Que faire? S'il ne s'agissait que de pluie,[24] on pourrait la produire! Mais ce n'est pas de la pluie, ce sont des nuages qu'il nous faudrait!...

—Oui... de beaux nuages bien blancs, répondit le mécanicien-chef.

—Eh bien! Monsieur Samuel Mark, vous vous adresserez à la rédaction scientifique, service météorologique. Vous lui direz de ma part qu'elle s'occupe activement de la question des nuages artificiels. On ne peut vraiment pas rester ainsi[25] à la merci du beau temps.

Jules Verne
Illustration de Georges Roux

[22]*when* [23]auprès... *near* [24]S'il... *If it were only rain* [25]*like this*

Après la lecture

A. Avez-vous compris? Répondez aux questions suivantes.

1. Comment M. Bennett passe-t-il sa journée?
2. Quelles sont les deux inventions décrites? Est-ce qu'elles marchent bien?
3. Quelle est l'attitude de M. Bennett devant un problème? Est-il défaitiste (*defeatist*)? réfléchi (*thoughtful*)? prêt à agir (*act*)?

B. Le point de vue de l'auteur. Avec un(e) partenaire, analysez le texte pour trouver...

1. une remarque de l'auteur qui indique que les riches exploitent les pauvres.
2. des expressions qui expriment l'attitude de l'auteur envers la nouvelle technologie.
3. un exemple où l'auteur envisage que l'homme peut dompter (*overcome*) la nature.

C. Le lieu de travail. Comment est le lieu de travail décrit par Verne? Est-ce qu'on travaille en équipe ou seul? Y a-t-il une hiérarchie dans cette entreprise? Comment est le rapport patron-travailleur?

À écrire

Faites **À écrire** pour le Chapitre 20 dans le cahier.

Vocabulaire

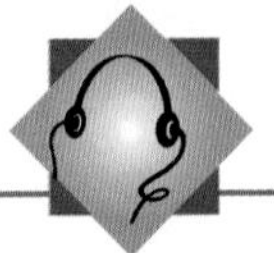

La ville de Marseille

l'accueil (*m.*)	welcome; greeting
un(e) antiquaire	antique dealer
un arrondissement	district
un(e) habitant(e)	inhabitant
une ruelle	alleyway
une rue piétonne	pedestrian street

MOTS APPARENTÉS: **une galerie, un(e) immigré(e), la joie de vivre, un port, la rénovation, un site touristique**

Le monde du travail

un congé	holiday, time off
une vedette	star (*of a show, movie*)
engager	to hire
former	to train; to form
licencier	to fire
au chômage	unemployed

MOTS APPARENTÉS: **un contrat, un salaire**

Le monde de l'argent

une banque	bank
un carnet de chèques	checkbook
un compte (en banque)	(bank) account
un montant	amount (*of a check or sale*)
déposer un chèque	to deposit a check
faire un chèque	to write a check
toucher un chèque	to cash a check

Expressions d'opinion, de nécessité, d'obligation et de volonté

il est bon	it is good
il est juste (injuste)	it is right (not right)
il est triste	it is sad
il est utile (inutile)	it is useful (useless, no use)
il faut	it is necessary; (one) must, should
il ne faut pas	(one) must not, should not
il suffit	it is enough, all it takes is

MOTS APPARENTÉS: **il est essentiel (important, impossible, nécessaire, préférable), il n'est pas nécessaire**

Substantifs

la chaleur	warmth; heat
un siècle	century

Verbes

donner sur (le port)	to overlook, have a view of (the port)
exiger	to demand; to require

À REVOIR: **désirer, vouloir**

Adjectifs

célèbre	famous
délabré(e)	dilapidated
étroit(e)	narrow
réputé(e)	well known

Autres expressions utiles

au cours de	throughout (*time*)

Chapitre 21

D'où vient cette photo?

OBJECTIFS

In this episode, you will

- see Camille pursue leads in Marseille
- meet a band of musicians who play raï music

In this chapter, you will

- talk about art, music, and other cultural opportunities in Marseille
- use the subjunctive to talk about emotions
- use the subjunctive to talk about doubt and uncertainty
- use the subjunctive in other contexts
- learn about museums as institutions in French society
- read about cultural policy in Quebec

Vocabulaire en contexte

Spectacles et manifestations culturelles° à Marseille

Spectacles… *Entertainment and cultural events*

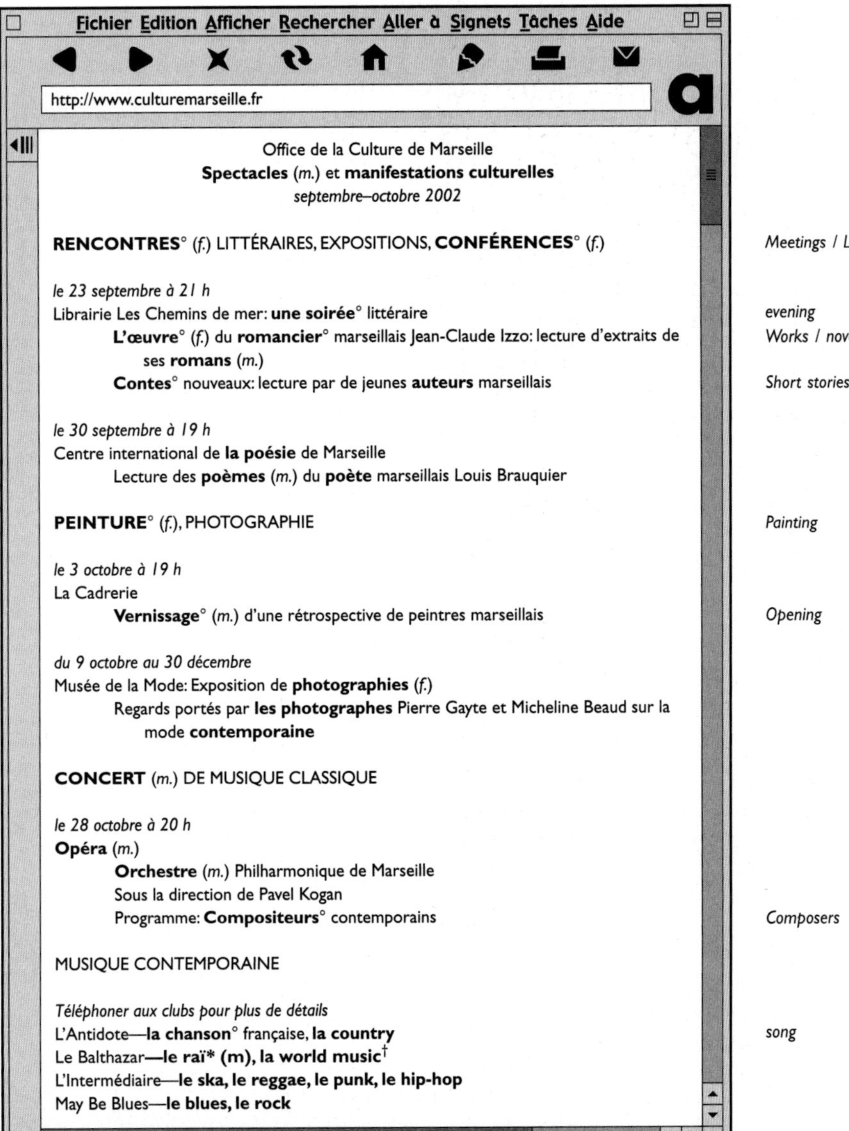
Fichier Edition Afficher Rechercher Aller à Signets Tâches Aide

http://www.culturemarseille.fr

Office de la Culture de Marseille
Spectacles (*m.*) et **manifestations culturelles**
septembre–octobre 2002

RENCONTRES° (*f.*) LITTÉRAIRES, EXPOSITIONS, **CONFÉRENCES**° (*f.*)

le 23 septembre à 21 h
Librairie Les Chemins de mer: **une soirée**° littéraire
L'œuvre° (*f.*) du **romancier**° marseillais Jean-Claude Izzo: lecture d'extraits de ses **romans** (*m.*)
Contes° nouveaux: lecture par de jeunes **auteurs** marseillais

le 30 septembre à 19 h
Centre international de **la poésie** de Marseille
Lecture des **poèmes** (*m.*) du **poète** marseillais Louis Brauquier

PEINTURE° (*f.*), PHOTOGRAPHIE

le 3 octobre à 19 h
La Cadrerie
Vernissage° (*m.*) d'une rétrospective de peintres marseillais

du 9 octobre au 30 décembre
Musée de la Mode: Exposition de **photographies** (*f.*)
Regards portés par **les photographes** Pierre Gayte et Micheline Beaud sur la mode **contemporaine**

CONCERT (*m.*) DE MUSIQUE CLASSIQUE

le 28 octobre à 20 h
Opéra (*m.*)
Orchestre (*m.*) Philharmonique de Marseille
Sous la direction de Pavel Kogan
Programme: **Compositeurs**° contemporains

MUSIQUE CONTEMPORAINE

Téléphoner aux clubs pour plus de détails
L'Antidote—**la chanson**° française, **la country**
Le Balthazar—**le raï* (m), la world music**†
L'Intermédiaire—**le ska, le reggae, le punk, le hip-hop**
May Be Blues—**le blues, le rock**

Meetings / Lectures
evening
Works / novelist
Short stories
Painting
Opening
Composers
song

Notez bien!

Many nouns designating artists have clear masculine and feminine forms; for example,

un(e) chanteur/euse singer
un(e) compositeur/trice composer
un(e) musicien(ne) musician
un(e) photographe photographer
un(e) romancier/ière novelist

Female painters, poets, and authors can be called either by the masculine forms **un peintre, un poète, un auteur** or by the feminine forms **une femme peintre, une femme poète, une femme auteur**.

***Le raï** est une sorte de musique qui est populaire dans les pays maghrébins.
†Le terme **world music** désigne les différentes musiques du Tiers Monde (*Third World*) et des groupes minoritaires dans les pays développés. Il s'agit en général de styles qui combinent la tradition de ces régions avec des éléments du rock occidental (*western*).

Pour en savoir plus...

La ville de Marseille a beaucoup d'espaces (*venues*) consacrés aux événements musicaux. Les spectacles d'opéra et de musique symphonique ont lieu à l'Opéra municipal. De grands concerts de musique contemporaine ont lieu au Théâtre National de Marseille, la Criée. Il existe aussi d'autres endroits, plus petits, où on peut écouter de la musique populaire, tels que *L'Antidote*, *L'Intermédiaire* et *Le Balthazar*. Le programme culturel du *Balthazar*, qui se déclare «Ouvert à toutes les musiques et à toutes les rencontres artistiques», reflète la diversité de la ville de Marseille.

Autres expressions utiles

une pièce (de théâtre)	play
un tableau	painting (*picture*)
avoir lieu	to take place

Langage fonctionnel

Pour parler des spectacles

Pour parler de votre réaction à une chanson, un film, une pièce de théâtre, une exposition d'art, etc., utilisez les éléments suivants.

J'ai adoré...	*I loved . . .*
Je n'ai pas du tout aimé...	*I didn't like . . . at all.*
J'ai détesté...	*I hated . . .*
C'est un navet.*	*It's awful (terrible, a flop).*

Je le/la trouve	bien (mal) interprété(e).	*I find it*	*well (badly) performed.*
	bien (mal) joué(e).		*well (badly) acted.*
Il/Elle est	génial(e).	*It is*	*brilliant, inspired.*
	médiocre.		*mediocre, dull.*
	passionnant(e).		*fascinating, gripping.*
	sans intérêt.		*uninteresting.*
	très réussi(e).		*very well done.*
	un succès.		*a success.*

—**J'adore** les films de Polanksi. Et toi?	*I love Polanski's films. Do you?*
—J'en ai vu un récemment et **je l'ai trouvé** tout à fait **médiocre**!	*I saw a one recently and thought it was really dull!*
—Mais non! Il faut que tu voies un de ses chefs-d'œuvre: Polanski est vraiment **génial**!	*Not at all! You must see one of his masterpieces: Polanski is really brilliant.*

Activités

A. L'artiste et son œuvre. Quelle est la spécialité de chaque artiste? Suivez le modèle, et faites des phrases complètes.

MODÈLE: Un poète... → Un poète écrit de la poésie.

1. Un peintre...
2. Une photographe...
3. Une romancière...
4. Une musicienne...
5. Un chanteur...
6. Une compositrice...

---

*Utilisez cette expression seulement pour les films.

B. Une visite à Marseille. Vous passez quelques semaines à Marseille. Divisez en trois groupes les activités culturelles présentées dans le vocabulaire précédent.

- «les musts»: celles auxquelles (*at which*) il faut assister à tout prix
- les activités que vous ferez si vous avez le temps
- les activités qui ne vous intéressent pas du tout

Organisez votre itinéraire et présentez-le à la classe. Expliquez votre classement.

MODÈLE: Il faut absolument que j'aille au Balthazar, parce que j'adore le raï.

C. Une interview. Posez les questions suivantes à votre partenaire pour déterminer plus précisément ses intérêts culturels. Demandez-lui

1. quelles sorties culturelles il/elle a faites récemment.
2. quelle activité culturelle il/elle aime le mieux.
3. quelle activité culturelle il/elle trouve la plus ennuyeuse et pourquoi.
4. quel genre de musique il/elle préfère et quel est son musicien préféré.
5. si ses goûts culturels sont les mêmes ou différents de ceux de ses parents et de ses amis.
6. ses opinions sur un film (un roman, une pièce) récent(e).

Visionnement 1

Avant de visionner

Vrai ou faux? Lisez le dialogue. Ensuite, lisez les phrases qui suivent et dites si elles sont vraies ou fausses. Si elles sont fausses, corrigez-les (*correct them*).

—Cet homme, Roland Fergus, qui est-il exactement? Vous savez quelque chose sur lui?

—Je sais qu'il est marseillais et qu'il a quitté la ville au début de la guerre pour se rendre dans les Cévennes.

—Ici, nous conservons les photos qui sont de provenance[a] incertaine ou douteuse.

—C'est-à-dire?[b]

—Nous avons reçu beaucoup de photos. Impossible de tout exposer[c]! Alors, nous avons écarté[d] les photos des gens que nous ne pouvions pas identifier.

—Ceux qui ont collaboré avec les Allemands?

—Pas seulement... Marseille a beaucoup souffert de la guerre. Des familles entières sont mortes. Des milliers de personnes.

[a]*origin* [b]*c'est... Which means?* [c]*exhibit* [d]*set aside*

1. Cette scène se passe probablement dans un bar.
2. Il y a des photos dont (*of which*) personne ne sait l'origine.
3. On a exposé toutes les photos.
4. On a exposé des photos de ceux qui ont collaboré avec les Allemands.
5. Beaucoup de Marseillais ont souffert pendant la guerre.

Vocabulaire relatif à l'épisode

vous longez les quais	*you walk along the docks*
déçu(e)	*disappointed*
40 ter	*40c (in a street address)*
vous squattez ce local?	*are you squatters here?*
l'accord de la mairie	*approval of the mayor's office*
ce mec	*this guy*
une piste	*lead, clue*

Observez!

Dans cet épisode, Camille trouve l'adresse du garage de Fergus et de son père. Maintenant, regardez l'Épisode 21, et cherchez les réponses aux questions suivantes.

- Comment Camille trouve-t-elle le garage de Fergus?
- Où va-t-elle ensuite pour s'informer?
- Qu'est-ce que Camille apprend de plus sur Fergus?
- Est-ce qu'on établit l'identité de Fergus comme collaborateur?

Après le visionnement

A. De qui s'agit-il et quelle est la réponse? Lisez les extraits du dialogue et déterminez qui parle avec qui: Camille, le patron du bar, un musicien, la conservatrice du musée. Choisissez ensuite la réplique correcte.

1. _____: Vous voyez? Mon bar est ici. Vous prenez à gauche... Vous longez les quais. Vous tournez à droite... jusqu'au boulevard de la Corderie, et c'est là.

_____: **a.** J'ai peur que vous soyez déçue, vous savez.
b. Où est-ce?
c. Je peux garder cette carte?

2. _____: Vous squattez ce local?

_____: **a.** Il a travaillé dans la Résistance.
b. Non, non. On a l'accord de la mairie...
c. Le propriétaire? Personne ne l'a jamais vu.

3. _____: Alors, nous avons écarté les photos des gens que nous ne pouvions pas identifier.

_____: **a.** Des familles entières sont mortes. Des milliers de personnes.
b. Du Maroc. Il y a bien ce nom, Fergus.
c. Ceux qui ont collaboré avec les Allemands?

4. _____: Mais c'est lui! C'est lui! C'est Roland Fergus. D'où vient cette photo?

_____: **a.** Regardez ceci...
b. Du Maroc. Il y a bien ce nom, Fergus. Et il y a une adresse à Casablanca.
c. Nous avons reçu beaucoup de photos.

B. Réfléchissez. Les musiciens expliquent à Camille qu'ils squattent le garage avec la permission de la mairie. À votre avis, pourquoi veulent-ils utiliser le garage pour leur répétitions?

Structure 63

Le subjonctif d'émotion et d'opinion

Expressing emotion and opinion

—**J'ai peur que vous soyez** *déçue*, vous savez.

In Chapter 20, you saw that the subjunctive is used after verbs of obligation, necessity, and will, when the subject of the verb in the subordinate clause is different from the subject of the independent clause.

1. The subjunctive is also used after expressions of emotion as long as a *second* subject occurs in the subordinate clause. Expressions of emotion include the following:

   avoir peur que
   être content (**heureux, ravi** [*thrilled*]) **que**
   être fâché (**furieux**) **que**
   être surpris (**étonné** [*astonished*]) **que**
   être triste (**désolé** [*sorry*]) **que**
   il est bon (**bizarre**, **dommage** [*too bad*], **incroyable** [*incredible*], **formidable**, **ridicule**) **que**
   préférer que
   regretter que
   souhaiter (*to wish, hope*) **que**

Le patron du bar **souhaite que** Camille **ait** de la chance.	*The bartender hopes that Camille will have good luck.*
Camille **est ravie que** les musiciens lui **donnent** une piste.	*Camille is delighted that the musicians give her a lead.*
Mado **est contente que** Camille **fasse** ce voyage.	*Mado is happy that Camille is making this trip.*

Il est dommage que Camille ne **puisse** pas trouver Fergus. — *It's a shame that Camille can't find Fergus.*

Remember—When only one subject is involved in the action, use **de** + infinitive after these expressions. In the case of **préférer** and **souhaiter**, the infinitive follows the conjugated verb directly.

Camille **a peur de perdre** la trace de Fergus. — *Camille is afraid of losing track of Fergus.*

Les musiciens **souhaitent jouer** au *Balthazar.* — *The musicians hope to play at the Balthazar.*

2. One verb of emotion, **espérer**, is followed by the indicative (present, future, etc.), not the subjunctive.

Le patron du bar **espère que** Camille **aura** de la chance. — *The bartender hopes that Camille will have good luck.*

However, with only one subject, **espérer** is followed by the infinitive.

Elle **espère apprendre** la vérité sur son grand-père. — *She hopes to find out the truth about her grandfather.*

Activités

A. Au Conservatoire National de Région de Marseille. Il y a beaucoup de perceptions en ce qui concerne le Conservatoire National de Région de Marseille. Exprimez-les à l'aide du subjonctif, de l'indicatif ou de l'infinitif des verbes entre parenthèses.

MODÈLE: Il est incroyable que cette école _____ (pouvoir) enseigner la musique à 16.000 jeunes. →
Il est incroyable que cette école *puisse* enseigner la musique à 16.000 jeunes.

1. Alexandre regrette qu'il y _____ (avoir) si peu de cours d'improvisation.
2. Annie a peur de _____ (faire) son récital en public.
3. Il est triste que le Premier Prix du Conservatoire _____ (être) si difficile à obtenir.
4. Benjamin préfère que les cours de jazz _____ (finir) avant 6 h.
5. M. Goya sera ravi de _____ (découvrir) un jeune guitariste avec du talent.
6. Certains parents espèrent que la musique _____ (ne pas devenir) trop importante pour leurs enfants.
7. Beaucoup d'enfants souhaitent _____ (aller) au Conservatoire.
8. Il est dommage que ce jeune homme ne _____ (réussir) pas à tous ses cours.
9. Les jeunes musiciens sont étonnés que les études _____ (pouvoir) prendre près de quinze ans.
10. Beaucoup de jeunes musiciens espèrent _____ (jouer) dans une des nouvelles salles de concerts au conservatoire.
11. Il est bon que le Conservatoire _____ (offrir) beaucoup de cours intéressants aux jeunes musiciens.

B. Le Festival d'Avignon. Parlez du festival qui se passe chaque été en Avignon en complétant chaque phrase avec les choix suggérés entre parenthèses. Faites l'élision avec **qu'** si nécessaire.

MODÈLE: Les commerçants de la ville sont contents que les gens achètent beaucoup de souvenirs.

1. Les commerçants de la ville sont contents que... (a, f)
2. Les metteurs en scène sont ravis que... (e, h)
3. Le jeune spectateur est triste que... (b, c)
4. Il est dommage que... (b, c, i)
5. Le directeur du Centre Acanthes pour la création musicale est surpris que... (d, j)
6. Une actrice est furieuse que... (c, g, i)
7. Il est ridicule que... (b, c, i)
8. Il est formidable que... (a, d, f, h, j)

a. il y avoir / beaucoup de touristes pendant le festival
b. les places au théâtre / être / si chères
c. les auteurs / ne pas pouvoir / toujours venir aux lectures de leurs pièces
d. beaucoup de jeunes / vouloir / étudier la musique contemporaine
e. tant de spectateurs / aller / à leurs pièces
f. les gens / acheter / beaucoup de souvenirs
g. son rôle / être / trop petit
h. une femme auteur / faire / une lecture publique de sa pièce
i. un journaliste / dire / de mauvaises choses sur la pièce
j. les danseurs allemands / venir / en Avignon pour présenter leur création

C. Camille continue ses recherches. Voilà quelques commentaires sur le film. En vous basant sur le modèle, créez de nouvelles phrases pour dire que la deuxième personne partage les sentiments de la première. Utilisez les pronoms complément d'objet direct et indirect si possible.

MODÈLE: Le patron du bar est content de savoir l'ancienne adresse de Fergus. (Camille) → Et Camille est contente qu'il la sache.

1. Camille a peur de ne pas pouvoir trouver le garage. (le patron du bar)
2. Camille est surprise de reconnaître le visage de Fergus sur l'une des photos. (la conservatrice)
3. Le patron du bar est heureux de donner la carte à Camille. (Camille)
4. Camille est contente d'entendre la chanson de raï. (les musiciens)
5. La conservatrice est ravie de trouver l'adresse au dos de la photo. (Camille)
6. Un musicien est heureux d'avoir une piste. (Camille)
7. La conservatrice regrette de ne pas avoir plus d'informations. (Camille)

D. Vous, vos amis et vos vies. Terminez chaque phrase. Utilisez un verbe au subjonctif ou à l'indicatif selon le cas.

MODÈLES: Dans cinq ans, j'espère que mon meilleur ami... →
Dans cinq ans, j'espère que mon meilleur ami aura un bon travail.

Mes amis souhaitent que... →
Mes amis souhaitent que je vienne chez eux pendant les vacances.

1. Je regrette que mes amis...
2. Mes amis ont peur que leurs cours...
3. Nous, les étudiants, sommes désolés que les professeurs...
4. Mon meilleur ami espère que je...
5. Les professeurs sont toujours contents que les étudiants...
6. Ma meilleure amie préfère que son travail...
7. Les jeunes souhaitent...
8. Il est bizarre que les professeurs...

Structure 64

Le subjonctif de doute, d'incertitude et de possibilité

Expressing doubt, uncertainty, and possibility

Camille **n'est pas certaine que** la conservatrice du musée **puisse** l'aider.

1. The subjunctive is also used after expressions of doubt, uncertainty, or possibility as long as a second subject occurs in the subordinate clause. Expressions of doubt and uncertainty include the following:

douter (*to doubt*) **que**	**il est incertain que**
être incertain que	**il est peu probable** (*unlikely*) **que**
il est douteux (*doubtful*) **que**	**il est possible que**
il est impossible que	**il se peut** (*it could be*) **que**

Le patron du bar doute que Fergus soit toujours à Marseille.	*The bartender doubts that Fergus is still in Marseille.*
Mais **il se peut que les musiciens aient** une piste.	*But it could be that the musicians have a lead.*

2. Some expressions are followed by the subjunctive only when they are in the negative.

ne pas être certain (sûr) que

ne pas croire que

ne pas penser que

Je ne crois pas qu'il soit un collaborateur.	*I don't believe he is a collaborator.*

3. Used in questions, **croire que**, **penser que**, and **être certain (sûr) que** are followed by the subjunctive when the issue is questionable, vague, or uncertain or when the questioner considers it as such.

Croyez-vous que ce soit une photo de Roland Fergus?	*Do you think that this is a photo of Roland Fergus?*

4. The indicative is used in affirmative statements after **croire que**, **penser que**, **être certain (sûr) que**, and **il est probable (clair**, **évident**, **vrai**, **certain**, **sûr) que** because the element of doubt is not present in these expressions. Instead, they imply probability or certainty. This is also true of **ne pas douter que**.

Il est clair que Camille essaiera de trouver Fergus à tout prix.	*It's clear that Camille will try to find Fergus at any cost.*
Rachid **ne doute pas que Camille poursuivra** sa quête.	*Rachid doesn't doubt that Camille will continue her quest.*

Remember—When there is only one subject involved in the action, use **de** + infinitive after these expressions. In the case of **ne pas croire** and **ne pas penser**, the infinitive follows the conjugated verb directly.

Je **ne crois pas** savoir l'adresse.	*I don't believe I know the address.*
Il **ne pense pas** avoir envie d'y aller.	*He doesn't think he feels like going.*
Il est impossible de tout exposer.	*It is impossible to exhibit everything.*

Activités

A. Malik Musique. Un site Internet propose toutes sortes de musique arabe à écouter et à acheter. Mettez les verbes au mode indiqué.

INDICATIF PRÉSENT OU CONDITIONNEL, SELON LE CAS

1. Je pense qu'on _____ (pouvoir) y trouver le CD «Sahara» de Naima Ababsa.
2. Il est certain qu'on _____ (entendre) beaucoup de raï sur ce site.
3. Je n'y trouve pas le CD «La Musique judéo-arabe» de Leïla Sfez. Mais je crois qu'il _____ (être) facile à trouver sur d'autres sites.
4. Je suis sûr que cela _____ (prendre) des heures si on voulait écouter toutes les chansons sur le site!

SUBJONCTIF

5. Il est impossible que nous _____ (écouter) toutes les chansons sur ce site.
6. Nous doutons que le site _____ (vendre) des CD de Madonna.
7. Il est peu probable que nous _____ (trouver) le CD «Alger, Alger» de Lili Boniche dans la catégorie «musique tunisienne».
8. Pensez-vous que ce site _____ (vouloir) annoncer des concerts de musique sénégalaise? Ou croyez-vous qu'il _____ (faire) de la publicité pour des chants berbères?
9. Je ne crois pas que le webmestre _____ (mettre) beaucoup de musique techno sur son site. Mais est-il possible qu'il _____ (dire) aux clients où ils peuvent trouver d'autres sites sur la musique?

B. Conseils à un entrepreneur. Jacques décide de lancer une «start-up». Après le «e-krach» (*crash of technology stocks*), est-ce une bonne idée? Faites des phrases avec les éléments donnés pour découvrir les conseils de ses amis, Philippe et Nicole. Mettez les verbes à l'indicatif (présent ou futur), à l'infinitif ou au subjonctif, selon le cas.

MODÈLE: NICOLE: «Écoute, Jacques, je / ne pas être sûre que / cette start-up / être / une bonne idée.» →
Écoute, Jacques, je ne suis pas sûre que cette start-up soit une bonne idée.

1. JACQUES: «Je / être sûr de / trouver / un grand public, mais j'aurai besoin d'une équipe.»
2. NICOLE ET PHILIPPE: «Nous / ne pas penser que / les amis / vouloir / y participer.»
3. NICOLE: «Il / être douteux que / les internautes / choisir / d'acheter en ligne, surtout après le krach.»
4. PHILIPPE: «Il / se pouvoir que / tu / avoir / quelques clients...
5. ... mais il / être probable que / ce projet / finir / mal.»
6. JACQUES: «Je / ne pas croire que / vous / bien comprendre / l'e-commerce.»
7. NICOLE ET PHILIPPE: «Au contraire, il est clair que / les gens / préférer / les entreprises brique et mortier (*brick and mortar*).»
8. JACQUES: «Alors, vous / croire que / la netéconomie / être en train de / perdre son attrait?»

C. Devant un nouveau musée d'art. Mettez-vous à trois et jouez les rôles suivants: un(e) journaliste, quelqu'un qui pense que l'art est très important dans la vie et une autre personne qui pense que l'art n'est pas important du tout. Le/La journaliste doit poser cinq questions et les deux autres se contredisent, en suivant le modèle.

MODÈLE: vous pensez / ce musée / être / important pour la ville →
É1: Pensez-vous que ce musée soit important pour la ville?
É2: Oui, je pense qu'il est très important.
É3: Moi, je ne pense pas qu'il soit important.

1. il est vrai / les enfants / venir souvent au musée
2. il est évident / ces tableaux / avoir / beaucoup de valeur
3. vous pensez / les statuettes africaines / être / intéressantes
4. il est possible / l'aquarelle berbère / devoir / être protégée (*protected*) du soleil
5. il est incertain / la boutique du musée / vendre / des CD-ROM sur l'art

Regards sur la culture

La notion du musée

Camille's search leads her to the **Musée de la Résistance**, a historical museum of the type that one could find anywhere in Europe or North America.

- The modern concept of the museum developed out of the Enlightenment and came into its own in the 19th century, when the notion of educating the masses for participation in democracy began to dominate the thinking of Euro-American intellectuals. The Louvre itself, originally made up of the confiscated collections of the monarchy, opened in 1793, in the middle of the French Revolution. It stood for the new order of things, where works of beauty could be admired not just by the wealthy, but by the common people as well.

Le musée d'Orsay à Paris

- The typical museum has thus aimed to provide examples of beauty and moments of instruction. In Marseille, there are museums that display works of art, archeological finds, and other historically significant objects. Larger museums, such as the Louvre, often display a combination of all three, with objects ranging from the Code of Hammurabi (18th c. B.C.E.) to **la Joconde** (*Mona Lisa*) by Leonardo da Vinci (16th c.) and the Crown Jewels of France.
- Over the two centuries since the founding of the Louvre, the notion of the museum has developed and expanded in many ways. Museums of technology and of natural history were developed very early on and continue to be popular. As time has gone by, more and more kinds of phenomena have found their way into specific sorts of museums, often for educational rather than

aesthetic goals. Paris, for example, has a **Musée de la Contrefaçon** (*Counterfeiting*).

La place Stravinsky à Paris

- For tourists, the many churches, palaces, and other historic buildings of France are museums in a sense, too. The Palace of Versailles is one of the most heavily visited buildings in Europe, and most people move through it and view it just as they would an art museum.
- There are even whole villages, towns, and cities in France that are thought of as **villes-musées**. For example, the walled city of Carcassonne, the ruins of Roman cities such as Vaison-la-Romaine, and the parts of Avignon that lie inside the medieval ramparts, are felt to be museum-like and are treated so by visitors.
- European museums usually have an aesthetic and instructional goal, but American and Canadian museums have been particularly concerned about combining instruction and entertainment. Science museums in particular are usually more didactic in France than they are in North America. The point of view that the museum can be a place of entertainment is not particularly common in France.

Considérez

Most museums in France are publicly funded, whereas the majority of North American museums are private. How might this difference relate to the higher entertainment value found in North American museums? What are the advantages and disadvantages of the two systems?

Structure 65

Autres usages du subjonctif

Un musicien donne une piste à Camille **pour qu'elle puisse** trouver Roland Fergus.

1. Certain conjunctions▲ must be followed by the subjunctive when the two clauses in the sentence have different subjects.

afin que	*in order that, so that*
avant que	*before*
bien que	*although*
jusqu'à ce que	*until*
pour que	*in order that, so that*
sans que	*unless; without*

Camille fait ce voyage **pour que son grand-père soit** innocenté.	*Camille is making this trip so that her grandfather will be vindicated.*
Le président ne sera pas content **jusqu'à ce que Camille revienne**.	*The president won't be happy until Camille returns.*

2. When only one subject is involved in both actions, the conjunctions **bien que** and **jusqu'à ce que** still take the subjunctive, but the other conjunctions are replaced by the following prepositions + infinitive.

afin de
avant de
pour
sans
} + infinitive

Bien que Camille ait l'adresse, elle ne connaît pas le chemin.	*Although Camille has the address, she doesn't know how to get there.*
Camille continuera **jusqu'à ce qu'elle sache** la vérité.	*Camille will continue until she knows the truth.*
Que faisait Camille **avant de travailler** pour nous?	*What did Camille do before working for us?*
Il a quitté la ville **pour se rendre** dans les Cévennes.	*He left the city to go to the Cévennes.*
Martine plaisante **sans sourire**.	*Martine jokes without smiling.*

3. When only one subject is involved in both actions, you can use **après** and the *past infinitive.* The past infinitive consists of the infinitive form of **avoir** or **être** followed by a past participle.

Après avoir parlé aux musiciens, Camille est allée au musée.	*After having spoken to the musicians, Camille went to the museum.*
Fergus s'est installé à Casablanca **après avoir quitté** Marseille.	*Fergus moved to Casablanca after leaving Marseille.*

Pour en savoir plus...

The subjunctive can also be used in a clause beginning with **que** to express a wish. Louise used it this way in Episode 11, when she said good-bye to Samuel Lévy.

—Que Dieu te **protège**.	*May God protect you.*

Activités

A. Avec la conservatrice du musée. Choisissez la bonne conjonction ou préposition de la liste pour faire des phrases complètes. Il y a parfois deux possibilités.

Conjonctions: afin que, avant que, bien que, jusqu'à ce que, pour que, sans que
Prépositions: afin de, après, avant de, pour, sans

1. ____ rencontrer la conservatrice, Camille commence à perdre l'espoir (*hope*).
2. La conservatrice vient vers Camille ____ l'aider.
3. Camille parle à la conservatrice ____ elle comprenne la situation.
4. La conservatrice s'excuse ____ aller chercher une boîte de photos ____ savoir s'il y a une photo de Fergus.
5. ____ il y ait beaucoup de photos, elles trouvent celles qu'elles cherchent.
6. ____ partir, Camille comprend qu'il faut aller au Maroc.
7. ____ Camille puisse trouver Fergus, la conservatrice lui donne l'adresse à Casablanca.
8. Camille ne va pas parler à ses collègues à Paris. Elle va partir au Maroc ____ le président de Canal 7 le sache.
9. Camille cherchera Fergus ____ elle le trouve.
10. ____ avoir quitté le musée, Camille a plus d'espoir.

B. Quelques conseils. Complétez chaque conseil en utilisant une des constructions suivantes: **apres** + substantif, **après** + infinitif passé, **avant** + substantif, **avant de** + infinitif, **avant que** + subjonctif.

MODÈLE: avant / se mettre au lit / ne regardez pas la télévision. →
Avant de vous mettre au lit, ne regardez pas la télévision.

Pour une bonne nuit de sommeil

1. Ne buvez pas de caféine / après / 16 h 00.
2. Gardez du temps pour vous détendre / avant / aller au lit.
3. Il est important de prendre un léger goûter / avant / vous / se coucher.
4. Apprenez à pratiquer les techniques de relaxation avant / dîner / et avant / l'heure où vous vous couchez d'habitude.
5. Pour aider à vous détendre, / prenez un bain chaud une heure / avant / se mettre au lit.
6. Après / se reposer, vous vous sentirez bien.

Pour éviter le décalage horaire

7. Quelques semaines / avant / le départ, / essayez d'établir un horaire fixe.
8. Les médecins conseillent de cesser de boire du café trois jours / avant / vous / partir.
9. Après / votre arrivée, / ne faites pas de sieste; la sieste retarde votre adaptation au nouveau fuseau horaire.
10. Après / arriver, / sortez le plus possible au soleil. Cela stimulera votre horloge biologique.
11. Après / quelques jours, / vous rétablirez votre rythme habituel.

C. Les musées d'histoire. Quel est le rôle d'un musée d'histoire? Avec un(e) partenaire, parlez de ce rôle en utilisant les phrases suivantes comme point de départ. Suivez le modèle.

MODÈLE: Les gens gardent des objets du passé afin de / afin que... →
É1: Les gens gardent des objets du passé afin de se souvenir des événements.
É2: Et ils les gardent aussi afin que les jeunes puissent mieux comprendre l'histoire.

1. Ces musées doivent exister pour que... / pour...
2. Les gens ne peuvent pas les visiter sans... / sans que...
3. On montre des images horrifiants afin que... / afin de...
4. Les jeunes ne comprennent pas l'histoire avant... / avant que...
5. Nous devons tous étudier l'histoire jusqu'à ce que... / bien que...

Visionnement 2

La ville de Marseille.
Marseille est la ville la plus ancienne de France. Fondée par les Grecs vers 600 avant J.-C.,* elle était célèbre pour son port magnifique. Aujourd'hui on trouve des cafés et des restaurants autour du Vieux-Port. Il y a aussi un marché aux poissons tous les matins.

Marseille est très different de Paris: c'est une ville méditerranéenne qui ressemble un peu à Naples ou à Alger. Dans le quartier du Panier, on voit de petites rues étroites qui montent et qui descendent comme en Italie. La Canebière est la grande rue où les Marseillais aiment se promener. L'église Notre-Dame-de-la-Garde domine la ville et semble la protéger.

La ville de Marseille

*avant J.-C. = avant Jésus-Christ. En anglais, on écrit B.C. ou B.C.E. (*before the common era*). 600 B.C.

La ville de Marseille

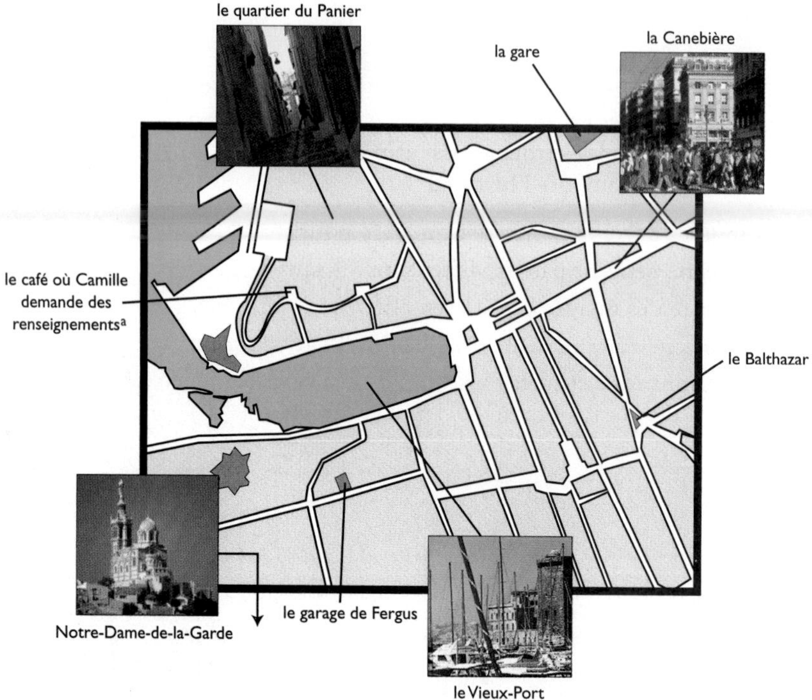

Complétez le paragraphe à l'aide de la carte et de la lecture à la page 455.

Camille a pris le train à Nîmes, et elle est arrivée dans la ville de Marseille à _____[1]. Elle est allée à pied jusqu'au grand boulevard qui s'appelle _____[2] et où tout le monde se promène. Elle a continué dans cette rue, et elle est arrivée au _____[3], où elle a vu le marché aux poissons. Mais elle était pressée. Dans le quartier du _____[4], elle est entrée dans un petit _____[5] pour demander des renseignements. Le patron du bar lui a dit de revenir le lendemain matin, alors le soir elle est peut-être allée s'amuser au _____[6].

Le lendemain, elle est retournée au _____[7] et le patron du bar lui a dit qu'il fallait chercher le boulevard de la Corderie de l'autre côté du _____[8]. Elle y est allée, mais le _____[9] avait disparu[b]: le bâtiment était vide.[c] Elle y a trouvé des musiciens qui jouaient de la musique raï. Est-elle montée sur la colline pour voir _____[10], qui domine la ville? Non, elle s'est dépêchée d'aller au musée de la Résistance.

[a]des... *information* [b]avait... *had disappeared* [c]*empty*

Observez!

Considérez les aspects culturels expliqués dans **Regards sur la culture**. Ensuite, regardez l'Épisode 21 encore une fois, et répondez aux questions suivantes.

- Quelles expressions le patron du bar utilise-t-il pour expliquer à Camille comment aller au garage de Fergus? Quelles expressions utilisez-vous quand vous indiquez le chemin dans votre ville? Trouvez-vous des différences entre l'usage français et l'usage nord-américain?
- Dans le film, à quoi devine-t-on le mélange de cultures qui caractérise la ville de Marseille?

Après le visionnement

Faites l'activité pour le **Visionnement 2** dans le cahier.

Synthèse: Culture

La politique culturelle au Québec

Dans le monde francophone, la culture est un sujet politique important, et les problèmes linguistiques dominent souvent dans les débats politiques. Par exemple, pendant longtemps la France, comme les États-Unis, n'avait pas de langue officielle. Mais en 1992, après des débats très difficiles, la constitution a été modifiée et le français est devenu la langue officielle de la République. C'était une réaction, en partie, contre la domination de l'anglais dans les sciences et dans la politique internationale.

Au Québec, les problèmes linguistiques ont beaucoup d'importance. Les francophones sont une minorité au Canada, et l'environnement nord-américain est dominé par l'anglais, qui est en expansion.

Les drapeaux canadien et québécois

Année	Population du Canada	% de Francophones
1951	14.010.000	29%
1996	28.528.000	23%

La situation en 1971

En 1971, beaucoup de Québécois parlaient français et anglais. Mais le bilinguisme mène[1] à l'assimilation, et presque toutes les communautés francophones de l'ouest du Canada et de la Nouvelle-Angleterre sont devenues progressivement anglophones.

L'anglais était la langue des affaires et de l'industrie au Québec. Les anglophones étaient souvent à la tête des entreprises. Les immigrés préféraient envoyer leurs enfants dans les écoles anglophones. En 1971, 79% des enfants des immigrés étaient dans une école anglophone. Depuis la Conquête,* le français canadien adoptait beaucoup de mots anglais. Dans les régions anglophones, on avait peu de respect pour le français nord-américain. À Toronto, à Vancouver, même dans les écoles anglophones du Québec, on apprenait généralement le français de Paris.

1977: La charte de la langue française

La «charte de la langue française» était un acte de politique culturelle unique au monde. Son but[2] était d'assurer à la langue française le premier rôle dans la société québécoise et de permettre au français de survivre en Amérique du Nord.

PROVISIONS DE LA CHARTE

1. Le français est obligatoire dans l'administration de la province (dans les bureaux, pour les contrats, sur les routes, etc.).
2. Le français est la langue ordinaire des entreprises qui ont une importance publique (le téléphone, les transports, l'électricité, etc.). Les documents peuvent contenir aussi une traduction en anglais.
3. Le français est la langue officielle des relations du travail. La communication officielle dans les entreprises doit être en français.
4. Les affiches, les inscriptions sur les produits doivent être en français. Une traduction en anglais est possible, mais le texte français doit dominer.
5. L'accès aux écoles anglophones est limité. Les enfants des immigrés doivent aller à l'école française.

Aujourd'hui

Après 1977, certaines grandes entreprises ont quitté Montréal pour Toronto pour protester contre ces mesures. Mais aujourd'hui, le Québec est transformé, surtout à Montréal. Plus de 70% des enfants d'immigrés sont à l'école française. La plupart[3] des anglophones sont devenus bilingues, et le français domine partout.

Malheureusement, bien que le français se stabilise au Québec, la langue continue à décliner dans le reste du Canada.

[1]*leads* [2]*goal* [3]La... *Most*

*La Conquête se réfère à la victoire de l'Angleterre au moment de la bataille des plaines d'Abraham à Québec en 1759. Voir *Synthèse: Culture* dans le Chapitre 11.

À vous

Une petite ville francophone en Louisiane. Mettez-vous par groupes de quatre. Imaginez que vous êtes le conseil municipal d'une petite ville cajun dans le sud-ouest de la Louisiane. On vous a suggéré d'adopter une politique linguistique pour protéger le français dans votre ville. Décidez quelle sera votre politique linguistique. Considérez les domaines suivants: l'administration de la ville, les contrats locaux, la signalisation routière (*road signs*), les affiches, l'école. Présentez votre «charte» à la classe.

Expressions utiles: on peut; on doit; il faut que

À écrire

Faites **À écrire** pour le Chapitre 21 dans le cahier.

Vocabulaire

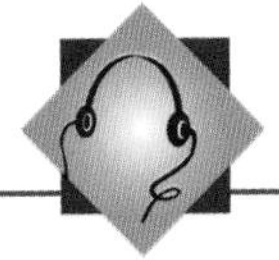

Les beaux-arts

la peinture painting (*action, art*)
un(e) photographe photographer
une photographie (*fam.* une photo) photograph
un tableau painting (*picture*)
un vernissage opening, preview

À REVOIR: **un(e) conservateur/trice, un(e) peintre / femme peintre**

La musique

une chanson song
un(e) chanteur/euse singer
un(e) compositeur/trice composer

MOTS APPARENTÉS: **le blues, un concert, la country, le hip-hop, un opéra, un orchestre, le punk, le raï, le reggae, le rock, le ska, la world music**

À REVOIR: **un(e) musicien(ne)**

La littérature et le théâtre

un(e) auteur / femme auteur author
un conte short story
une pièce (de théâtre) play
la poésie poetry
un roman novel
un(e) romancier/ière novelist

MOTS APPARENTÉS: **un poème, un(e) poète / femme poète**

Substantifs

une conférence	lecture	**une rencontre**	meeting, encounter
une manifestation (culturelle)	(cultural) event; (*public, political*) demonstration	**une soirée**	evening
une œuvre	literary or art work, musical composition	**un spectacle**	entertainment, show

Adjectif

contemporain(e)	contemporary

Expressions d'émotion et d'opinion

être désolé(e) que	to be sorry that
être étonné(e) que	to be astonished that
être ravi(e) que	to be thrilled that
il est dommage que	it is too bad that
il est incroyable que	it is incredible that
souhaiter que	to wish, hope that

MOTS APPARENTÉS: **être furieux/euse (surpris[e]) que, il est bizarre que, regretter que**

À REVOIR: **avoir peur que, espérer que, être content(e) (fâché[e], heureux/euse, triste) que, il est bon (formidable, ridicule) que, préférer que**

Expressions de doute et d'incertitude

douter que	to doubt that
il est douteux que	it is doubtful that
il est peu probable que	it is unlikely that
il se peut que	it could be that, it is possible that

MOTS APPARENTÉS: **être incertain(e) que, il est incertain que, ne pas être certain(e) que**

À REVOIR: **il est impossible (possible) que, ne pas croire que, ne pas être sûr(e) que, ne pas penser que**

Expressions de probabilité et de certitude

il est clair que	it is clear that
ne pas douter que	not to doubt that

MOTS APPARENTÉS: **être certain(e) que, il est certain (probable) que**

À REVOIR: **croire que, être sûr(e) que, il est évident (sûr, vrai) que, penser que**

Conjonctions

afin que	so that, in order that	**pour que**	so that, in order that
avant que	before	**sans que**	unless; without
bien que	although		
jusqu'à ce que	until		

Prépositions

afin de	in order to
avant de	before

À REVOIR: **après, pour, sans**

Autre expression utile

avoir lieu	to take place

Chapitre 22

Secrets dévoilés

OBJECTIFS

In this episode, you will

- meet the person who reveals the truth to Camille

In this chapter, you will

- talk about traveling to other countries
- express ownership using possessive pronouns
- narrate stories that include events at various points in the past
- learn to understand indirect discourse in narration
- learn about the culture of Casablanca
- read about a boy of Algerian descent who learns something about his heritage

Vocabulaire en contexte

En voyage à Casablanca

Aperçu° de la ville

Métropole cosmopolite, Casablanca est une ville de contrastes: un côté oriental—**arabe** et **berbère**°*—et un côté occidental, les habitants **riches** et leurs **voisins**° **pauvres,** la vie traditionnelle et les développements modernes. On voit des voitures de luxe et des chariots,° des femmes **en décolleté**° et robe **courte**° et des femmes musulmanes qui s'habillent **dignement**° en djellabas† (*f.*) ou qui portent des foulards sur la tête.

Comme **la plupart des**° villes marocaines, Casablanca comporte° deux parties distinctes. **La médina**° offre un spectacle **étonnant**°; un labyrinthe de ruelles **sombres**° et d'impasses étroites, où on découvre des **mosquées** (*f.*), des hammams° et des marchés. **À l'écart** (*m.*) **de**° la médina, le vingtième siècle a donné naissance à un nouveau type de ville: le long de **larges**° avenues, les bâtiments officiels alternent avec des commerces. À l'arrière, ce sont des villas° qu'on trouve **au milieu des**° jardins.

General survey
Berber
neighbors
carts / en... *in low-cut clothing*
short
with dignity
la... *most of the*
includes
old city
amazing
dark
baths / À... *Apart from*
wide
(detached) houses / au... *in the middle of*

Activités

A. Familles de mots. Identifiez le mot ou la phrase du vocabulaire qui est de la même famille que l'expression donnée. Puis, dites si la réponse est un substantif, un adjectif, un adverbe ou une phrase prépositionnelle.

MODÈLE: écarté (*separated*) → à l'écart de (phrase prépositionnelle)

1. un Berbère
2. le décolleté
3. la dignité
4. un Arabe
5. l'étonnement (*m.*) (*astonishment*)
6. le voisinage (*neighborhood*)
7. le milieu
8. la pauvreté
9. la richesse

*Les Berbères sont un groupe ethnique nord-africain (distincts des Arabes).

†Une djellaba est un vêtement (une robe) long à manches (*sleeves*) et à capuchon (*hood*), porté par les hommes et les femmes, en Afrique du Nord.

B. Associations. Avec quel côté de la ville de Casablanca associez-vous les expressions suivantes—le côté moderne et occidental ou le côté traditionnel et oriental?

MODÈLE: une mosquée →
J'associe une mosquée avec le côté traditionnel et oriental de Casablanca.

1. des bâtiments officiels
2. des femmes en robes courtes
3. des hommes en djellabas
4. les ruelles sombres de la médina
5. des villas et de larges avenues
6. des femmes habillées dignement

C. Pour découvrir une ville. Interviewez votre partenaire pour découvrir ses souvenirs d'une ville à l'étranger (*abroad*). Il/Elle peut imaginer un voyage à Marseille ou à Casablanca s'il / si elle n'est jamais allé(e) à l'étranger.

Demandez à votre partenaire...

1. quelle ville il/elle a visitée et pourquoi il/elle a décidé d'y aller.
2. si cette ville ressemblait à la plupart des villes qu'il/elle connaissait déjà. Demandez-lui d'expliquer pourquoi ou pourquoi pas.
3. s'il / si elle a pu distinguer des quartiers différents dans la ville et en quoi ils étaient distincts. Demandez-lui de décrire les quartiers résidentiels.
4. ce qu'il/elle a vu d'intéressant (d'étonnant, de fabuleux).
5. ce qu'il/elle a aimé le plus dans cette ville.
6. s'il / si elle voudrait retourner dans cette ville pour une visite plus longue ou pour y habiter. Demandez-lui d'expliquer sa réponse.

Visionnement 1

Avant de visionner

Étude de vocabulaire. Parfois, on peut deviner (*guess*) la nouvelle signification d'un mot en analysant son emploi dans des contextes familiers. D'abord, lisez les phrases que vous avez déjà rencontrées dans le film. Ensuite, lisez la phrase où le nouvel emploi apparaît, et essayez de préciser le sens du nouvel usage.

1. **Famille *prendre***

   Il rentre à Paris, il retrouve sa femme, *reprend* son travail...

   Mais tu peux en *reprendre* un peu! Une petite goutte?

   NOUVEL EMPLOI: Les Allemands ***ont repris*** cette rumeur à leur compte (*to their advantage*)!

2. **Famille *lancer***

   Je *lance* une série de reportages sur la vie au Québec.

   NOUVEAUX EMPLOIS: C'est lui qui ***a lancé*** la rumeur...
   C'était un bon prétexte pour ***lancer*** des représailles.

3. **Famille *rendre***

Dans quelle ville *s'est-il rendu*?

Donc, c'est nous qui l'avons découverte, formée et *rendue* célèbre.

Je sais qu'il est Marseillais et qu'il a quitté la ville au début de la guerre pour *se rendre* dans les Cévennes.

NOUVEAUX EMPLOIS: La Résistance avait ***rendez-vous*** avec Antoine et moi.
Mais aujourd'hui, croyez-vous qu'il est possible de ***rendre justice*** à... ?

4. **Famille *mettre***

Quoi, le président me *met* à la porte?!

On y *met* de la tomme fraîche du Cantal.

Elle aussi, elle est désolée de vous *avoir mise* à la porte.

NOUVEAUX EMPLOIS: *J'**avais mis*** un uniforme...
La Résistance ***a mis*** des mois à ***s'en remettre***.

Vocabulaire relatif à l'épisode

Puis-je vous être utile?	*Can I help you?*
Il a demandé qu'on ne le dérange pas.	*He asked not to be disturbed.*
Inutile d'insister.	*There's no use insisting.*
C'est ce que tout le monde était censé croire.	*That's what everyone was supposed to believe.*
On ne peut pas abandonner les copains!	*We can't abandon our friends!*
crever	*to die (slang)*
les avait aperçus	*had caught sight of / seen them*

Observez!

Dans l'Épisode 22, Camille rencontre Fergus, l'homme mystérieux qu'elle cherche depuis sa visite avec Jeanne Leblanc. Regardez l'épisode, et essayez de trouver les réponses aux questions suivantes.

- Comment l'histoire racontée par Fergus diffère-t-elle de celle racontée par Jeanne Leblanc? Quels détails ajoute-t-il?
- Pourquoi Fergus a-t-il quitté la France pour vivre à Casablanca?

Après le visionnement

A. **Le récit de Fergus.** Dans cet épisode, Roland Fergus et son fils Thomas racontent les événements du 17 décembre 1943 du point de vue de Fergus père. Classez les actions dans l'ordre chronologique de 1 à 5.

_____ ROLAND FERGUS: Les Allemands ont repris cette rumeur à leur compte! Ils ont dit que nous travaillions pour eux et que c'est la Résistance qui avait tué[a] Antoine.

_____ ROLAND FERGUS: Antoine a vu que ses amis étaient tombés[b] dans un piège. Les Allemands les tuaient un à un, comme des lapins!

_____ THOMAS FERGUS (FILS): Un résistant, un certain Pierre Leblanc, les avait aperçus. Il avait vu votre grand-père, Antoine, avec mon père qui portait un insigne nazi. C'est lui qui a lancé la rumeur...

_____ ROLAND FERGUS: Antoine voulait rejoindre les résistants. Mais j'ai vu que ce combat était perdu.

_____ ROLAND FERGUS: C'était un bon prétexte pour lancer des représailles et pour commencer une campagne de désinformation! Ils ont pris vingt-cinq hommes au hasard,[c] dans la région, et ils les ont fusillés[d]! La Résistance a mis des mois à s'en remettre.

[a]avait... *had killed* [b]étaient... *had fallen* [c]au... *at random* [d]les... *shot them*

B. De graves malentendus. Qu'est-ce que Pierre Leblanc a vu qui l'a mené (*led*) à la conclusion que Fergus et Antoine étaient des traîtres? En quoi s'était-il trompé (*had he been mistaken*)?

Structure 66

Les pronoms possessifs

Avoiding repetition

—Et c'est ainsi qu'Antoine est mort, le 17 décembre 1943. Pour sauver ma vie, il a donné **la sienne**.

You have been using possessive adjectives since very early in *Débuts,* and you have heard a number of them in Episode 22.

Fergus est **mon** ancien nom.	*Fergus is **my** former name.*
Oui, vous avez **ses** yeux!	*Yes, you have **his** eyes!*

Now you will learn to use possessive pronouns▲ to say *mine, yours, theirs,* and so on.

1. A possessive pronoun is used in place of a possessive adjective + noun. It reflects the gender and number of the noun it replaces.

MASCULIN SINGULIER	FÉMININ SINGULIER	MASCULIN PLURIEL	FÉMININ PLURIEL
un livre	*une table*	*des livres*	*des tables*
le mien	**la mienne**	**les miens**	**les miennes**
le tien	**la tienne**	**les tiens**	**les tiennes**
le sien	**la sienne**	**les siens**	**les siennes**
le nôtre	**la nôtre**	**les nôtres**	**les nôtres**
le vôtre	**la vôtre**	**les vôtres**	**les vôtres**
le leur	**la leur**	**les leurs**	**les leurs**

Pour sauver ma vie, il a donné *sa vie*.	*To save my life, he gave his life.*
Pour sauver ma vie, il a donné **la sienne**.	*To save my life, he gave his (own).*

Ben, à *notre santé* et à *ta santé*, ma puce!	*Well, to our health and to your health, sweetheart!*
Ben, à **la nôtre*** et à **la tienne**, ma puce!	*Well, to ours (our health) and yours, sweetheart!*

2. The prepositions **à** and **de** contract with the masculine singular and plural forms of the possessive pronouns.

   Camille parle de son grand-père. → Elle parle **du** sien.
   Fergus réfléchit à ses amis résistants. → Il réfléchit **aux** siens.

Activités

A. Ce qu'il faut pour voyager. Un groupe d'amis part pour un séjour (*trip*) de trois semaines. Marie veut vérifier que les autres n'ont rien oublié. Utilisez le pronom possessif approprié pour compléter ce qu'elle dit. Attention: Utilisez une préposition s'il le faut!

MODÈLE: J'ai pris mes lunettes de soleil. Avez-vous pris les vôtres?

1. J'ai apporté mon foulard. As-tu apporté ______?
2. J'ai changé mes euros (*m.*) en dirhams marocains. Paul a-t-il déjà changé ______?
3. J'ai pris mes médicaments avec moi. As-tu pris ______?
4. J'ai lu mes guides (*m.*) du Maroc. Jacques et Anne ont-ils lu ______?
5. J'ai fait ma valise. Anne a-t-elle fait ______?
6. J'ai vérifié mon passeport. Avez-vous vérifié ______?
7. J'ai étudié mon lexique français-arabe. Paul et Anne ont-ils étudié ______?
8. Tu as ton billet d'avion? J'ai ______ dans mon sac.
9. As-tu téléphoné à tes amis marocains? J'ai téléphoné ______.
10. J'aimerais écouter une cassette de musique arabe pendant le voyage. Est-ce que tu as besoin ______? Je ne trouve pas ______.
11. Vous n'avez pas choisi d'hôtel? Anne et moi, nous pourrons peut-être vous trouver une chambre dans ______.

B. Les gens qu'on connaît. Avec un(e) partenaire, parlez des choses que vous aimez ou détestez. Demandez à votre partenaire l'opinion de quelqu'un d'autre.

MODÈLE: ma voiture / tes parents →
É1: J'aime beaucoup ma voiture. (Je n'aime pas du tout ma voiture.) Et tes parents?
É2: Ils aiment la leur. (Ils n'aiment pas la leur.)

1. mes cours / toi **2.** ma vie / toi **3.** mon travail / ta meilleure amie **4.** mes disques compacts / tes amis et toi **5.** ma ville natale / tes amis et toi **6.** mes examens de fin de semestre / tes amis et toi **7.** ma patrie / tes voisins **8.** mes dernières vacances / ton meilleur ami **9.** mes grands-mères / tes amis et toi **10.** mon professeur de ______ / tes camarades de classe

*The toast **à votre santé** in all its forms (**ta**, **notre**, etc.) is so widely used that people often shorten it to just the possessive pronoun, as in this phrase used by Rachid in the film.

Structure 67

Le plus-que-parfait

Narrating

—Oui. Mais je ne travaillais pas pour les nazis! J'**avais mis** un uniforme pour tromper l'ennemi.

—Antoine a vu que ses amis **étaient tombés** dans un piège.

You have already learned to use the **passé composé** and the **imparfait**. In this section, you will learn another past tense, the **plus-que-parfait**, which is useful in narrating a series of past events.

1. The **plus-que-parfait** is formed by conjugating the auxiliary—**avoir** or **être**—in the **imparfait** and adding the past participle.

répondre			
j'	**avais répondu**	nous	**avions répondu**
tu	**avais répondu**	vous	**aviez répondu**
il, elle, on	**avait répondu**	ils, elles	**avaient répondu**

aller			
j'	**étais allé(e)**	nous	**étions allé(e)s**
tu	**étais allé(e)**	vous	**étiez allé(e)(s)**
il, elle, on	**était allé(e)**	ils, elles	**étaient allé(e)s**

2. The **plus-que-parfait** is used to talk about an action that occurred before another past action. It occurs frequently in longer narrations in past time, where multiple events are recounted in sequence.

Nous n'avons jamais su qui nous **avait trahis**.	*We never found out who (had) betrayed us.*
Antoine **avait donné** rendez-vous aux résistants.	*Antoine had set up a meeting with the resistance fighters.*

Activités

A. Pour connaître le Maroc. À la fin (*end*) de leur cours sur la culture marocaine, les étudiants se sont rendu compte de toutes les activités auxquelles (*in which*) ils avaient participé au courant du semestre. Formez des phrases selon le modèle. Attention aux auxiliaires.

MODÈLE: le professeur / inviter / la classe à étudier le Maroc →
Le professeur avait invité la classe à étudier le Maroc.

1. un ami marocain du professeur / venir / pour nous parler de son enfance
2. les étudiants / apprendre / certaines expressions en arabe
3. Anne / décrire / ses vacances à Marrakech de l'année précédente
4. nous / regarder / des photos de Fès et de Marrakech
5. nous / chercher / des sites Internet sur le Maroc
6. tu / lire / un livre de Tahar Ben Jelloun*
7. je / recevoir / une carte postale d'un étudiant à Casablanca
8. les étudiants / apporter / des CD de raï en classe
9. vous / découvrir / la musique berbère
10. vous / rester / après le cours pour écouter plus de musique
11. nous / préparer / des loukoums† en classe
12. les étudiants / aller / dans un restaurant marocain
13. je / manger / un couscous délicieux
14. tu / boire / du thé à la menthe (*mint*)

B. Imaginez. Que s'était-il passé avant? Avec votre partenaire, considérez les actions et les situations des personnes suivantes et imaginez des actions ou des situations qui les avaient précédées.

MODÈLE: Marta a bu un grand verre d'eau. →
É1: Avant, elle avait couru un marathon.
É2: Avant, elle était restée au soleil pendant trois heures.

1. Jean-Philippe a préparé un grand repas pour ses amis.
2. Vous avez passé un examen difficile.
3. J'ai acheté une nouvelle voiture.
4. Le patron a fermé le bar.
5. Magalie était très fatiguée le matin.
6. Nous avons choisi un concert.
7. L'étudiant avait mal à la tête le matin.
8. Nous avons réussi à nos examens.
9. J'ai rendu une rédaction (*composition*) en cours d'anglais.

---

*Tahar Ben Jelloun est un écrivain marocain de langue française, né à Fès en 1944.
†**Le loukoum** est une sorte de bonbon du moyen orient qui est populaire au Maroc.

Regards sur la culture

La culture à Casablanca

When Camille decides to go to Casablanca, she does not seem bothered by the intercultural difficulties that such a trip will involve. It is true that the city has one of the largest populations of French citizens of any outside Europe. Still, Morocco is very different from Europe, despite its many historical connections with Spain and France.

La tradition et la modernité à Casablanca

- Morocco is only 8 miles (13 kilometers) from Europe and has had close historical links with both Spain and France. The country became a French protectorate in 1912. Although theoretically France was responsible only for maintaining order, it also directed foreign and economic policy. As Morocco became something very much like a French colony, it also underwent a process of modernization and Europeanization. During World War II, the sultan supported the Allies but met secretly with Churchill and Roosevelt in an attempt to build support for independence. Morocco finally did become independent in 1956. The French presence had an enormous impact, however, and is still a source of conflict and disagreement among Moroccans.
- The city of Dar el-Beida (*White House*)—best known abroad by its Spanish name, Casablanca—is the largest city in the entire Maghreb region (Morocco, Algeria, Tunisia) and the fourth largest city in Africa. The harbor of Casablanca, which was developed by the French in the early 20th century, has made the city the economic center of the country.
- Casa, as it is sometimes called in French, is considered a loud, aggressive, and cosmopolitan city. Parts of it look very modern and European, with restaurants, cafés, banks, and luxury stores. Other parts, like the Old Medina, resemble the traditional Muslim cities that have dominated the landscape of North Africa for centuries. On the outskirts are shantytowns, where country people, attracted by the economic dynamism of the city, often locate after moving to the city. Outsiders feel about Casablanca much as they do about Marseille or New York.
- Although it is situated on the Atlantic, Casablanca has a kind of Mediterranean climate. The weather is generally mild. Average temperatures range from 12 degrees Celsius (54 Fahrenheit) in January to 23 degrees C (73 F) in August.

- The official language in Morocco today is Arabic. But many Moroccan families have relatives living and working in France, and the constant communication back and forth maintains some knowledge of French at all levels of society.
- There has been a strong Jewish presence in the Maghreb since Roman times. In 1950, the Jewish population of Morocco was estimated at 300,000, but in recent years, many of the old Jewish communities have dwindled and disappeared, as their inhabitants moved to Israel or France. Today, there are only about 8,000 Moroccan Jews, and most of them live in Casablanca.
- Among the most important sights of Casablanca is the largest mosque and Islamic cultural center outside Saudi Arabia. The Hassan II Mosque, named for the late King of Morocco, was completed in 1988. It was built with contributions from Moroccans all over the world.

Considérez

If you were planning to go to Casablanca on business, what kinds of information and training would you want to have before going? Think about questions of language, religion, social customs, relations between the sexes, etiquette, work habits, food and drink, and so on.

Structure 68

Le discours indirect

Telling what others said

—Les Allemands ont repris cette rumeur à leur compte! Ils ont dit **que nous travaillions pour eux** et **que c'est la Résistance qui avait tué Antoine.**

Important—The information in this section is meant to help you understand when people tell what someone else said. You do not need to learn to create sentences like this, but you should learn to understand them when others use them.

Le discours direct

Direct discourse quotes a speaker's exact words. Sometimes, the quote is accompanied by a verb of communication such as **dire** and **demander**.

Jeanne Leblanc m'a dit: «Il n'était pas supposé être à ce rendez-vous.» — *Jeanne Leblanc told me, "He wasn't expected to be at that meeting."*

Camille demande à l'employé: «Est-ce que M. Fergus est là?» — *Camille asks the employee, "Is Mr. Fergus here?"*

Le discours indirect

Indirect discourse tells what somebody said without using a direct quotation.

1. A speaker's statement is reported in a subordinate clause beginning with **que**. Just as in indirect discourse in English, pronouns change as necessary. Jeanne Leblanc used the pronoun **il** to refer to Fergus in the previous example of direct discourse. Hence, Camille uses **vous** when reporting the comment to Fergus himself in this example:

   Jeanne Leblanc m'a dit **que vous** n'**étiez** pas supposé être là. — *Jeanne Leblanc told me you weren't expected to be there.*

   Yes/no questions are reported indirectly in a subordinate clause beginning with **si**. Questions are phrased as statements, so question marks are not used.

   Camille demande à l'employé **si** M. Fergus est là. — *Camille asks the employee if Mr. Fergus is there.*

2. When the verb of communication (**dire**, **demander**, etc.) in indirect discourse is in the *present* tense, the tense of the verb in the subordinate clause is the same as in direct discourse.

   DIRECT DISCOURSE Bruno demande à Camille: «Est-ce que tu **vas** au bureau aujourd'hui?»

   INDIRECT DISCOURSE Bruno demande si Camille **va** au bureau aujourd'hui.

3. When the verb of communication in indirect discourse is in a *past* tense, the tense in the subordinate clause changes, according to certain rules.

DIRECT DISCOURSE VERB		INDIRECT DISCOURSE SUBORDINATE CLAUSE VERB
present	→	imparfait
passé composé	→	plus-que-parfait

DIRECT DISCOURSE La conservatrice a dit: «Fergus **est** à Casablanca.»

INDIRECT DISCOURSE La conservatrice a dit que Fergus **était** à Casablanca.

DIRECT DISCOURSE Fergus a dit: «J'**ai mis** l'uniforme nazi pour tromper l'ennemi.»

INDIRECT DISCOURSE Fergus a dit qu'il **avait mis** l'uniforme nazi pour tromper l'ennemi.

Pour en savoir plus...

You already know several verbs that are often used to introduce indirect discourse: **ajouter**, **demander**, **dire**, **écrire**, **indiquer**, and **répondre**. A few others that you may have seen or heard are

annoncer	*to announce*
déclarer	*to declare*
expliquer	*to explain*
préciser	*to specify*
rapporter	*to report*

Activités

A. Qui dit... ? Choisissez le personnage qui dit chaque chose. Ensuite, transformez chaque phrase indirecte en phrase directe, en faisant tous les changements nécessaires. Suivez le modèle.

Personnages: l'employé, Thomas Fergus (fils), Roland Fergus, Camille

MODÈLE: L'employé dit que M. Fergus est absent. «Monsieur Fergus est absent.»

1. _____ explique que M. Fergus est malade.
2. _____ répond qu'elle est la petite fille d'Antoine Leclair.
3. _____ annonce que M. Fergus veut bien la recevoir chez lui.
4. _____ demande à la femme si elle a dit à M. Fergus qu'elle était arrivée.
5. _____ explique que Fergus est son ancien nom.
6. _____ dit que les autres membres de la Résistance avaient rendez-vous avec Antoine et lui.
7. _____ explique qu'à la Libération son père a voulu rétablir la vérité.

B. Qu'est-ce qu'ils ont dit? Plusieurs étudiants qui ont vu *Le Chemin du retour* ont parlé du film. Transformez les phrases indirectes en phrases directes en faisant tous les changements nécessaires.

MODÈLES: Le professeur a demandé si les étudiants avaient aimé le film. →
«Est-ce que vous avez aimé le film?»

Chris a dit qu'il aimait tous les films français. →
«J'aime tous les films français.»

1. Esmeralda a demandé si tout le monde avait compris le film.
2. Lori a expliqué que le film était un peu difficile mais très intéressant.
3. Tamara a ajouté que parfois les acteurs parlaient un peu vite.
4. Corey a demandé si les autres avaient aimé le jeu des acteurs.
5. Chris et Mark ont dit que les acteurs étaient très bons.
6. Corey a dit qu'il n'avait jamais vu les Cévennes avant.
7. Courtney a annoncé qu'elle avait reconnu le quartier Mouffetard.
8. Tamara a déclaré qu'elle préférait la scène à Casablanca.
9. Mark a demandé si la classe pouvait voir tout le film à la fin du semestre.
10. Le professeur a dit que c'était une excellente idée.
11. Brandon a ajouté qu'il préférait regarder le film au lieu de passer un examen de fin de semestre!

Maintenant, donnez votre propre opinion en ce qui concerne les questions et les commentaires que vous venez de lire.

MODÈLES: Le professeur a demandé si les étudiants avaient aimé le film. →
Oui, j'ai aimé le film. (Non, je n'ai pas aimé le film.)

Chris a dit qu'il aimait tous les films français. →
Moi aussi, j'aime tous les films français. Ils sont tellement différents des films américains. (Moi, non. Je n'aime pas la plupart des films français. Ils sont ennuyeux.)

Visionnement 2

Le Maroc. Camille arrive à l'aéroport international Mohammed V de **Casablanca**, qui est la ville où vivent la majorité des juifs marocains et la plupart des Français. Mais le Maroc est très varié. Chacune (*Each one*) de ses villes a une réputation différente. **Rabat**, la capitale, est une ville élégante et calme. On y trouve des quartiers historiques, mais aussi des ambassades, le Palais Royal et l'université. **Marrakech**, la ville la plus importante du sud, a conservé un caractère traditionnel. C'est le point de rencontre des populations de la montagne de l'Atlas et du désert. **Fès** est le centre religieux et intellectuel traditionnel du Maroc, où des gens de toutes origines se rencontrent. La ville a la réputation d'être la plus raffinée du Maroc.

Le Maroc

Casablanca: une ruelle

Fès: une école islamique du XIVe siècle

Marrakech: la place Jemaa el Fna

Rabat: quartier des ambassades

Indiquez la ville que vous choisiriez pour faire les choses suivantes.

MODÈLE: voir la capitale → Si je voulais voir la capitale, j'irais à Rabat.

1. regarder l'océan **2.** faire une promenade dans la montagne de l'Atlas **3.** voir une école islamique médiévale **4.** visiter une synagogue **5.** aller à l'ambassade américaine **6.** voir un grand port **7.** connaître les traditions intellectuelles marocaines **8.** voir le palais du roi (*king's palace*)

Pour en savoir plus...

Le thé, symbole d'hospitalité

Le thé au sucre et à la menthe fait partie intégrale de la vie marocaine: il est caractéristique de tous les milieux, à toute heure, dans toutes les circonstances. Sa préparation comporte de nombreux gestes (*movements*) traditionnels. À la fin, il est versé en tenant la théière (*teapot*) de plus en plus haut: on le boit avec les doigts écartés parce que le verre est très chaud.

Observez!

Considérez les aspects culturels expliqués dans **Regards sur la culture**. Ensuite, regardez l'Épisode 22 encore une fois, et répondez aux questions suivantes.

- Comment conseille-t-on à Camille de s'habiller pour aller voir Fergus?
- Comment est-ce qu'on accueille Camille quand elle arrive chez Fergus?

Après le visionnement

Faites l'activité pour le **Visionnement 2** dans le cahier.

Synthèse: Lecture

Mise en contexte

Azouz Begag, a first-generation French citizen of Algerian descent, was born outside of Lyon in 1957. In this autobiographical work, he describes the poverty of his childhood. After many years in a slum, his family moves to state-subsidized housing (**une HLM***). This change has profound effects on the cultural identity of his family. In the excerpt you will be reading, his high school French teacher, M. Loubon, a **pied-noir** who grew up in Algeria, tries to raise Azouz's awareness of an Algeria he has never known.

Stratégie pour mieux lire

Identifying pronoun referents

This scene contains two voices: the narrator (Azouz) and his teacher (M. Loubon). Azouz alternately addresses M. Loubon and the reader. In order to follow the direction of the narrative, it is especially important to understand the various pronoun references.

The following sentences are taken from the text. Try to identify the person to whom each italicized pronoun refers. Is it Azouz, M. Loubon, Azouz's parents, or the reader?

1. —Azouz! *Vous* savez comment on dit «le Maroc» en arabe?, *me* demande tout à coup M. Loubon...
2. Depuis maintenant de longs mois, le prof a pris l'habitude de *me* faire parler en classe, de moi, de ma famille...
3. Savez-*vous* comment on dit les allumettes (*matches*) chez *nous,* par exemple? Li zalimite.

***HLM** = Habitation à loyer (*rent*) modéré

4. —Ah non, m'sieur. Mon père et ma mère, *ils* disent jamais ce mot. Pour appeler un Marocain, *ils* disent Marrocci.
5. Puis *il* reprit son cours pendant quelques minutes avant de s'adresser à nouveau à *moi*...
6. *Il* me dit: —*Vous* ne savez pas qu'en arabe on appelle le Maroc le «pays du soleil couchant»?

Now read the entire text, paying close attention to the identity of the speaker and to whom the pronouns refer. Think, too, about M. Loubon's motivation in calling on Azouz.

M. Loubon

—Azouz! Vous savez comment on dit «le Maroc» en arabe?, me demande tout à coup[1] M. Loubon alors qu'il était en train d'écrire au tableau quelques phrases de style conjuguées au subjonctif.

La question ne me surprend pas. Depuis maintenant de longs mois, le prof a pris l'habitude de me faire parler en classe, de moi, de ma famille, de cette Algérie que je ne connais pas mais que je découvre de jour en jour avec lui.

À la maison, l'arabe que nous parlons ferait certainement rougir de colère un habitant de La Mecque.[2]* Savez-vous comment on dit les allumettes chez nous, par exemple? Li zalimite. C'est simple et tout le monde comprend. Et une automobile? La taumobile. Et un chiffon[3]? Le chiffoun. Vous voyez, c'est un dialecte particulier qu'on peut assimiler aisément lorsque[4] l'oreille est suffisamment entraînée.[5] Le Maroc? Mes parents ont toujours dit el-Marroc, en accentuant le *o*. Alors je réponds à M. Loubon:

—Le Maroc, m'sieur, ça se dit el-Marroc!

D'abord, il paraît un peu stupéfait, puis il poursuit:

—On ne dit pas el-Maghreb?

—Ah non, m'sieur. Mon père et ma mère, ils disent jamais ce mot. Pour appeler un Marocain, ils disent Marrocci.

M. Loubon reprend, amusé:

—En arabe littéraire,[6] on dit el-Maghreb et ça s'écrit comme ça.

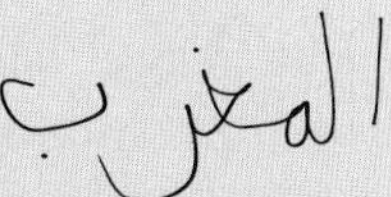

Il dessine quelques lettres arabes au tableau sous les regards ébahis[7] des élèves. Je précise pendant qu'il écrit:

—J'ai déjà entendu mes parents prononcer ce mot.

Il me dit:

—Vous ne savez pas qu'en arabe on appelle le Maroc le «pays du soleil couchant»?

[1]tout... *suddenly* [2]ferait... *would certainly cause an inhabitant of Mecca to grow red with anger* [3]*rag* [4]*when* [5]*trained* [6]arabe... *classical Arabic* [7]*dumbfounded*

*La Mecque est une ville sainte en Arabie Saoudite, le but (*goal*) du pèlerinage (*pilgrimage*) musulman appelé «le hajj». Ce pèlerinage est une des obligations des musulmans pratiquants.

—Non, m'sieur.»

Puis il reprit[8] son cours pendant quelques minutes avant de s'adresser à nouveau à moi:

—Vous savez ce que cela veut dire? me relance-t-il en dessinant des hiéroglyphes.

J'ai dit non. Que je ne savais pas lire ni écrire l'arabe.

—Ça c'est alif, un *a*. Ça c'est un *l* et ça c'est un autre *a*, explique-t-il. Alors, qu'est-ce que ça veut dire?

J'hésite un instant avant de réagir:

—Ala! dis-je mais sans saisir la signification de ce mot.

—Pas Ala, dit M. Loubon. Allah! Vous savez qui c'est Allah?...

Je souris[9] légèrement de son accent berbère:

—Oui, m'sieur. Bien sûr. Allah, c'est le Dieu des musulmans!

Azouz Begag (*Le gone du Chaâba*, 1986)

[8]*continued* [9]*smile*

Après la lecture

A. Analyse des pronoms. Relisez le passage en réfléchissant aux questions suivantes.

1. À qui se réfèrent les pronoms de la première personne (*je*, *me*, *nous*)?
2. Qui est le *il* du récit?
3. Entre quelles personnes s'emploie le pronom *vous*? Pourquoi?
4. Quel autre usage du pronom *vous* y a-t-il? À qui se réfère ce pronom?

B. Réfléchissez. Réfléchissez à l'histoire pour répondre aux questions suivantes.

1. Qui connaît mieux l'arabe littéraire et écrit? Est-il fier de cette connaissance?
2. Qui connaît mieux l'arabe parlé? Est-il fier de son dialecte?
3. Azouz sait-il lire et écrire l'arabe? Et ses parents?
4. Azouz a-t-il une formation (*education*, *upbringing*) religieuse?
5. Avec qui Azouz se sent-il confortable—avec ses parents? M. Loubon? le lecteur? Comment ce sentiment se montre-t-il sur le plan linguistique?
6. Pourquoi M. Loubon pose-t-il ces questions à Azouz? Pourquoi montre-t-il comment écrire ces deux mots en arabe?

À écrire

Faites **À écrire** pour le Chapitre 22 dans le cahier.

Vocabulaire

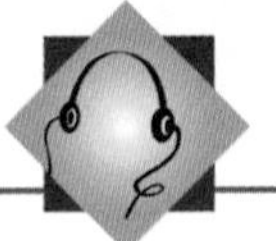

Au Maroc

une médina	old portion of an Arab city

MOT APPARENTÉS: **arabe, berbère, une mosquée**

Substantif

un(e) voisin(e)	neighbor

Adjectifs

court(e)	short
étonnant(e)	surprising, amazing, shocking
large	wide
pauvre	poor
sombre	dark

MOT APPARENTÉ: **riche**

Adverbe

dignement	with dignity

Pronoms possessifs

le mien, la mienne, les miens, les miennes	mine
le tien, la tienne, les tiens, les tiennes	yours
le sien, la sienne, les siens, les siennes	his/hers/its
le nôtre, la nôtre, les nôtres	ours
le vôtre, la vôtre, les vôtres	yours
le leur, la leur, les leurs	theirs

Autres expressions utiles

à l'écart de	apart from
au milieu de	in the middle of
en décolleté	in low-cut clothing
la plupart de	most (of)

Épilogue

Le Chemin du retour

OBJECTIFS

In this episode, you will

- get hints about the direction Camille's life may take now that she has learned the truth

In this chapter, you will

- talk about the characters in the film and predict their future
- learn about the history and characteristics of French filmmaking

Visionnement 1

Avant de visionner

A. Analyse. En visionnant *Le Chemin du retour* jusqu'ici, vous avez eu l'occasion d'analyser les actions et le caractère des personnages. En groupes de trois, discutez des questions suivantes.

1. Quel est le caractère de Camille? de Bruno? de Mado?
2. Quel est le rapport entre Camille et Bruno? entre Camille et Mado?

B. Changements. Maintenant, lisez les échanges suivants, extraits de l'Épilogue du film. D'après (*Based on*) ces dialogues, est-ce que le caractère de ces personnages a changé depuis qu'on les a rencontrés au début du film? Leurs rapports les uns avec les autres ont-ils changé?

1. Considérez d'abord Bruno.

BRUNO: Euh, excusez-moi. Quelqu'un sait où est Camille? (*vers la régie*) Euh, la régie? Quelqu'un peut me dire où se trouve Camille?

PRODUCTRICE: (*off*) Ne t'affole pas,[a] Bruno! Elle arrive!

BRUNO: Je suis sûr qu'elle est encore au maquillage!... C'est dingue,[b] ça! Non, mais qu'est-ce qu'on lui fait, un lifting[c] peut-être?

Et encore...

BRUNO: Excuse-moi, Camille. Excuse-moi. J'ai été ridicule, comme d'habitude. Au fond, je suis un type[d] banal, tu sais, un journaliste sans talent, sans avenir. Je comprends que tu ne veuilles pas de moi!

[a]Ne... *Don't get upset* [b]*crazy* [c]*facelift* [d]*guy*

Est-ce le même Bruno dont (*of whom*) on a fait la connaissance au début du film ou est-ce un Bruno transformé par les événements de l'histoire?

2. Maintenant, lisez les réflexions de Mado.

MADO: J'ai été tellement stupide pendant toutes ces années, tellement lâche.° Maintenant, c'est fini, c'est trop tard... Je ne veux pas te perdre!

°*cowardly*

Le caractère de Mado a-t-il changé?

3. Finalement, lisez l'échange suivant.

MADO: Je n'ai pas le souvenir d'un seul jour où tu n'aies été impatiente avec moi, nerveuse.

CAMILLE: (*réfléchit une seconde*) C'est vrai. Mais maintenant, c'est fini. Ça va changer!

MADO: Vraiment? Tu ne pousseras plus de soupirs[a] à chaque fois que je parle?

[a]Tu... *You won't sigh any more*

CAMILLE:	Non!
MADO:	Tu ne lèveras plus les yeux au ciel?
CAMILLE:	Jamais plus!
MADO:	(*pour elle*[b]) Oh, c'est sûrement un rêve,[c] mais c'est tellement bon à entendre!

[b]*pour... to herself* [c]*dream*

Le rapport entre Mado et Camille a-t-il changé? Expliquez.

Vocabulaire relatif à l'épisode

libérée d'un poids	*freed from a burden*
sa femme l'a pleuré	*his wife mourned him*
ils se réuniront	*they will be meeting*
décerné(e)	*awarded*
Ça, je vous fais confiance	*I trust you on that*
déranger	*to disturb*
me gronder	*scold me*
s'il y a bien une chose dont on n'a pas à avoir peur	*if there's anything one doesn't need to fear*

Observez!

Camille a découvert la vérité sur son grand-père, Antoine. Qu'est-ce qui va se passer maintenant? Pendant votre visionnement de l'Épilogue, essayez de trouver la réponse aux questions suivantes.

- Quel moment de l'épisode est le plus difficile pour Camille? le plus satisfaisant?
- À la fin de l'épisode, peut-on dire que Camille est une «nouvelle» femme? Justifiez votre réponse.

Après le visionnement

A. Avez-vous compris? Dites si les phrases suivantes sont vraies ou fausses et corrigez celles qui sont fausses.

1. En rentrant de son voyage, Camille téléphone immédiatement à Mado pour lui raconter les nouvelles.
2. À l'occasion de leur première rencontre, Camille et Bruno se disputent.
3. Bruno s'impatiente parce que Camille arrive en retard pour l'émission «Bonjour!».
4. David explique à Camille qu'un comité a refusé de revoir le cas d'Antoine.
5. Camille est très mécontente des nouvelles que David lui donne.
6. À la fin, Camille et Mado s'entendent bien.

B. Le passé... et l'avenir. Répondez aux questions suivantes.

1. Quelle est la réaction de Bruno quand il entend les nouvelles de Camille à propos d'Antoine? Comment Camille répond-elle aux remarques de Bruno?
2. Pourquoi David apporte-t-il des fleurs à Camille? A-t-il peut-être une autre motivation que celle qu'il annonce?
3. Selon vous, quel sera l'avenir de Camille et David? de Camille et Bruno? de Camille et Mado? de Camille et ses supérieurs? Est-ce que leurs rapports vont changer?

C. Hypothèses. Selon vous, pourquoi Camille a-t-elle persisté dans ses efforts pour trouver la vérité? Qu'est-ce qui l'a encouragée pendant les moments difficiles?

Regards sur la culture

Le cinéma français

Vous voilà arrivés maintenant à la fin du *Chemin du retour*, et c'est le moment de réfléchir au cinéma en général et à sa relation avec la culture française. Le cinéaste[1] de ce film est américain, mais le scénariste[2] et les acteurs sont français. Le film a donc[3] un caractère interculturel.

- Le cinéma, tel que[4] nous le connaissons aujourd'hui, est l'invention de deux Français: les frères Louis et Auguste Lumière. Ils ont organisé la première présentation publique du cinéma en 1895 au Grand Café de Paris. L'originalité de leur conception (par rapport à celle de Thomas Edison, par exemple) se trouve dans l'idée d'une projection publique sur grand écran. C'est ce qui a déterminé le caractère social du cinéma, une caractéristique qui existe encore aujourd'hui, plus de cent ans plus tard.
- Le cinéma s'est développé rapidement en France. Le premier film de fiction a été créé[5] par Georges Méliès en 1897. C'est Méliès aussi qui a créé *Le Voyage dans la lune*[6] (1902), un film bien connu des amateurs du cinéma aujourd'hui. En réalité, la France a dominé le monde du cinéma jusqu'à la Première Guerre mondiale. Plus tard, c'est l'industrie américaine qui a pris la première place.

Une scène du *Voyage dans la lune* de Méliès

- En ce qui concerne le nombre de films produits par an, la France est en cinquième position (après l'Inde, les États-Unis, le Japon et la Chine). Mais l'influence du cinéma français est primordial.[7] Le Festival du film de Cannes symbolise le rôle important joué par la France dans cette industrie.
- Beaucoup de Français prennent le cinéma très au sérieux. Les jeunes assistent souvent à des séances[8] de ciné-club, où l'on[9] visionne et discute de films exceptionnels ou expérimentaux. De nombreux jeunes Français connaissent suffisament l'histoire du cinéma pour pouvoir comparer et évaluer les œuvres des grands cinéastes français et américains.
- La politique culturelle française prend le cinéma au sérieux aussi. L'État finance la Cinémathèque, qui conserve et restaure les films anciens et organise la projection de toutes sortes de films. L'État finance aussi la formation[10] des professionnels du cinéma et essaie de favoriser la promotion et la diffusion du cinéma français dans le monde.
- L'influence internationale du cinéma français a été particulièrement importante à la fin des années 50, quand la Nouvelle Vague (*New Wave*) est née. Ce mouvement, qui représentait une nouvelle spontanéité dans la création cinématographique, a accordé une grande importance au cinéaste en tant qu'«auteur»[11] de son film. Le caractère innovateur et expérimental des œuvres de la Nouvelle Vague—les films de François Truffaut et de Jean-Luc Godard, par exemple—a influencé des cinéastes dans le monde entier.

Le cinéaste François Truffaut au travail

- Puisque[12] les spectateurs nord-américains n'aiment pas beaucoup les films doublés[13] ou sous-titrés, il n'est pas rare qu'un film français soit refait en version américaine. Ces films, qu'on appelle «*remakes*» en anglais, ont souvent

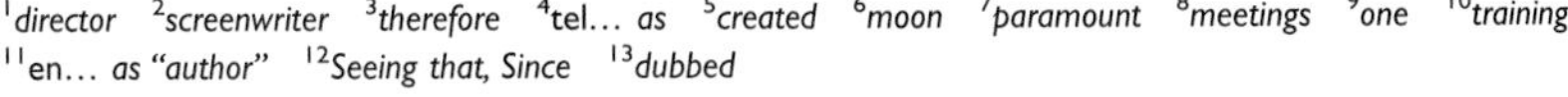

[1]*director* [2]*screenwriter* [3]*therefore* [4]tel... *as* [5]*created* [6]*moon* [7]*paramount* [8]*meetings* [9]*one* [10]*training* [11]en... *as "author"* [12]*Seeing that, Since* [13]*dubbed*

eu beaucoup de succès en Amérique du Nord, et quelquefois en France aussi, où le public peut donc voir la même histoire sous deux formes différentes. Mais les spécialistes du cinéma considèrent souvent que ces films américains n'ont pas la qualité artistique des versions d'origine. Quelques exemples de films français et de leurs versions américaines:

Boudu sauvé des eaux (Renoir, 1932) — *Down and Out in Beverly Hills* (Mazursky, 1986)
Diabolique (Clouzot, 1955) — *Diabolique* (Chechik, 1996)
À bout de souffle (Godard, 1959) — *Breathless* (McBride, 1983)
Cousin Cousine (Tacchella, 1976) — *Cousins* (Schumacher, 1989)
La Cage aux folles (Molinaro, 1978) — *The Birdcage* (Nichols, 1996)
Trois Hommes et un couffin (Serreau, 1985) — *Three Men and a Baby* (Nimoy, 1987)
Les Visiteurs (Poiré, 1993) — *Just Visiting* (Gaubert, 2001)

La Cage aux folles de Molinaro

The Birdcage de Nichols

Considérez

Réfléchissez aux différences culturelles entre la France et l'Amérique du Nord que vous avez eu l'occasion d'observer dans ce cours. Ensuite, choisissez un de vos films nord-américains préférés et essayez de déterminer ce qu'on changerait pour en faire une version française. Considérez les éléments suivants:

- l'environnement (urbain ou rural, bâtiments, etc.)
- les relations familiales qui sont illustrées dans le film
- la conception de l'amitié dans le film
- le rôle de la nourriture, des voitures et d'autres objets
- les valeurs morales des personnages
- le ton ou le contenu moral du film
- la fin du film

Visionnement 2

À présent, regardez le film encore une fois, sans interruption. Vous allez voir que vous comprenez maintenant toute l'histoire et une grande partie du dialogue. Et après le visionnement, n'oubliez pas de vous offrir une petite récompense pour tous vos efforts. Bravo!

Appendice A

Glossary of Grammatical Terms

ADJECTIVE (ADJECTIF, *m.*) A word that describes a noun or a pronoun. It agrees in number and gender with the word it modifies.	
demonstrative adjective (adjectif démonstratif) An adjective that points out a particular noun.	**ce** garçon, **ces** livres ***this** boy, **these** books*
interrogative adjective (adjectif interrogatif) An adjective used to form questions.	**Quelles** affiches cherchez-vous? ***Which** posters are you looking for?*
possessive adjective (adjectif possessif) An adjective that indicates possession or a special relationship.	**leur** voiture, **ma** sœur ***their** car, **my** sister*
ADVERB (ADVERBE, *m.*) A word that describes an adjective, a verb, or another adverb.	Il écrit **très bien**. *He writes **very well**.* Elle est **plus** efficace. *She is **more** efficient.*
AGREEMENT (ACCORD, *m.*) Nouns in French are marked for gender and number: any word that modifies a noun must reflect that noun's gender and number. This principle is known as agreement. Adjectives, articles, and past participles of verbs conjugated with **être** show agreement, for example.	C'est **une femme indépendante**. *She is an independent woman.* **Elles sont arrivées** à temps. *They arrived in time.*
ARTICLE (ARTICLE, *m.*) A word that signals an upcoming noun.	
definite article (article défini) An article that indicates a specific noun or a noun used in a generic or abstract sense.	**le** pays, **la** chaise, **les** femmes ***the** country, **the** chair, **the** women*
indefinite article (article indéfini) An article that indicates an unspecified noun or an unspecified quantity of a count noun.	**un** garçon, **une** ville, **des** carottes ***a** boy, **a** city, (**some**) carrots*
partitive article (article partitif) In French, an article that indicates an unspecified quantity of a mass (noncount) noun.	**du** chocolat, **de la** tarte, **de l'**eau *(**some**) chocolate, (**some**) pie, (**some**) water*

CLAUSE (PROPOSITION, *f.*) A construction that contains a subject and a verb.	
independent (main) clause (proposition principale) A clause that stands on its own and expresses a complete idea.	**Je cherche la femme** qui joue au tennis. ***I'm looking for the woman** who plays tennis.*
relative clause (proposition relative) A subordinate clause that refers back to a person, thing, place, or time mentioned in the main clause.	Je cherche la femme **qui joue au tennis**. *I'm looking for the woman **who plays tennis**.*
subordinate clause (proposition subordonnée) A clause that cannot stand on its own because it does not express a complete idea.	Je la cherche **parce que j'ai besoin d'elle**. *I'm looking for her **because I need her**.*
COMPARATIVE (COMPARATIF, *m.*) An expression used to compare two adjectives, adverbs, nouns, or actions.	Léa est **moins** bavarde **que** Julien. *Léa is **less** talkative **than** Julien.* Elle court **plus** vite **que** lui. *She runs **faster than** he does.*
CONDITIONAL (CONDITIONNEL, *m.*)	See **Mood**.
CONJUGATION (CONJUGAISON, *f.*) The different forms of a verb for a particular tense or mood. A present indicative conjugation:	je parle — *I speak* tu parles — *you speak* il, elle, on parle — *he, she, it, one speaks* nous parlons — *we speak* vous parlez — *you speak* ils, elle parlent — *they speak*
CONJUNCTION (CONJONCTION, *f.*) An expression that connects words, phrases, or clauses.	Christophe **et** Diane sont sérieux **mais** sympas. *Christophe **and** Diane are serious **but** nice.*
GENDER (GENRE, *m.*) A grammatical category of words. In French, there are two genders: feminine and masculine. Gender applies to nouns, articles, adjectives, and pronouns.	*m.* / *f.* articles and nouns: **le** disque / **la** cassette adjectives: **lent, beau** / **lente, belle** pronouns: **il, celui** / **elle, celle**
IMPERATIVE (IMPÉRATIF, *m.*)	See **Mood**.
IMPERFECT (IMPARFAIT, *m.*) A verb tense that expresses habitual past actions, past descriptions, or ongoing actions in the past.	Nous **nagions** souvent. *We **used to swim** often.*
INDIRECT DISCOURSE (DISCOURS INDIRECT, *m.*) The reporting of what someone said using a subordinate clause.	Elle a dit **que la chanson était super**. *She said **that the song was terrific**.*

INFINITIVE (INFINITIF, *m.*)	See **Mood**.
MOOD (MODE, *m.*) A set of categories for verbs that indicates the speaker's attitude toward what he/she is saying.	
conditional mood (mode conditionnel) A verb form conveying possibility.	J'**irais** si j'avais le temps. *I* ***would go*** *if I had time.*
imperative mood (mode impératif) A verb form expressing a command.	**Allez**-y! ***Go*** *ahead!*
indicative mood (mode indicatif) A verb form denoting actions or states that are considered facts.	Je **vais** à la bibliothèque. *I* ***am going*** *to the library.*
infinitive mood (mode infinitif) A verb form introduced in English by *to*.	**jouer, vendre, venir** ***to play, to sell, to come***
subjunctive mood (mode subjonctif) A verb form, uncommon in English, used primarily in subordinate clauses after expressions of obligation, desire, doubt, or emotion. French constructions with the subjunctive have many possible English equivalents.	Je veux que vous y **alliez**. *I want you to go there.*
NOUN (NOM, *m.* ou SUBSTANTIF, *m.*) A word that denotes a person, place, thing, or idea. Proper nouns are capitalized names.	**avocat, ville, journal, Louise** ***lawyer, city, newspaper, Louise***
NUMBER (NOMBRE, *m.*) A grammatical category of words. It indicates whether a noun, article, adjective, or pronoun is singular or plural.	singulier Le fromage est bon. pluriel Les fromages sont bons.
OBJECT (OBJET, *m.*) A noun that follows a verb or a preposition, or a pronoun that takes the place of or refers to this noun.	
direct object (objet direct) A noun that follows the verb directly, i.e., without an intervening preposition, and that receives the action of that verb. It could also be a pronoun that refers to this noun. It answers the questions *What?* or *Whom?*	J'ai vu **le film**. Tu **l'**as vu aussi. *I saw* ***the film****. You saw* ***it*** *too.* Est-ce que tu connais **cette femme**? *Do you know* ***that woman****?*
indirect object (objet indirect) A noun, designating a person, that follows the verb and is introduced by the preposition **à**, or a pronoun that refers to this noun.	Tu téléphones souvent à **tes amis**? *Do you call your friends often?* Oui, je **leur** parle tous les jours. *Yes, I talk to them every day.*
PASSÉ COMPOSÉ (*m.*) In French, a verb tense that expresses a past action with a definite ending. It consists of the present indicative of the auxiliary verb (**avoir** or **être**) and the past participle of the conjugated verb.	j'**ai mangé** *I* ***ate****, I* ***did eat****, I* ***have eaten*** elle **est tombée** *she* ***fell****, she* ***did fall****, she* ***has fallen***

PAST PARTICIPLE (PARTICIPE PASSÉ, *m.*) The form of a verb used in a compound tense (like the **passé composé**) with forms of *to have* in English, and with **avoir** and **être** in French.	**mangé, fini, perdu** ***eaten, finished, lost***
PLUS-QUE-PARFAIT (*m.*) A tense that denotes an action that took place before another past action.	Quand je suis arrivé, mes parents **étaient** déjà **partis**. *When I arrived, my parents **had** already **left**.*
PREPOSITION (PRÉPOSITION, *f.*) A word or phrase that specifies the relationship of one word (usually a noun or a pronoun) to another. The relationship is usually spatial or temporal.	**près de** l'aéroport, **avec** lui, **avant** 11 h ***near** the airport, **with** him, **before** 11:00*
PRESENT PARTICIPLE (PARTICIPE PRÉSENT, *m.*) A verb form used to express near simultaneity and/or how an action is performed. French constructions with the present participle have many possible English equivalents.	En **entrant**, il a remarqué le changement du décor. *As he entered, he noticed the change in décor.* Elle travaille en **écoutant** la radio. *She listens to the radio while she works.*
PRONOUN (PRONOM, *m.*) A word used in place of one or more nouns.	
demonstrative pronoun (pronom démonstratif) A pronoun that singles out a particular person or thing.	Voici deux livres: **celui-ci** est intéressant, mais **celui-là** est ennuyeux. *Here are two books: **this one** is interesting, but **that one** is boring.*
interrogative pronoun (pronom interrogatif) A pronoun used to ask a question.	**Qui** parle? ***Who** is speaking?* **Qu'est-ce que** vous voulez? ***What** do you want?*
object pronoun (pronom complément d'objet) A pronoun that replaces a direct object noun or an indirect object noun.	direct: Je vois Alain. Je **le** vois. *I see Alain. I see **him**.* indirect: Je donne le livre à Daniel. Je **lui** donne le livre. *I give the book to Daniel. I give **him** the book.*
possessive pronoun (pronom possessif) A pronoun that represents an object belonging to someone.	Quel stylo est **le mien**? *Which pen is **mine**?*
reflexive pronoun (pronom réfléchi) A pronoun that represents the same person as the subject of the verb.	Je **me** regarde dans le miroir. *I am looking at **myself** in the mirror.*
relative pronoun (pronom relatif) A pronoun that introduces a subordinate clause and denotes a noun already mentioned.	On parle à la femme **qui** habite ici. *We're talking to the woman who lives here.* C'est le stylo **que** vous cherchez? *Is this the pen (**that**) you are looking for?*
stressed pronoun (pronom accentué ou pronom disjoint) In French, a pronoun used for emphasis, after **C'est**, or as the object of a preposition.	**Toi**, tu es incroyable! *You are unbelievable!* C'est **moi**! *It's me! (It's I!)* Je travaille avec **lui**. *I work with **him**.*

subject pronoun (pronom sujet) A pronoun representing the person or thing performing the action of the verb.	**Ils** travaillent bien ensemble. *They work well together.*
SUBJECT (SUJET, *m.*) The word(s) denoting the person, place, or thing performing an action or existing in a state.	**Mon ordinateur** est là-bas. ***My computer** is over there.* **Marc** arrive demain. ***Marc** arrives tomorrow.*
SUBJUNCTIVE (SUBJONCTIF, *m.*)	See **Mood**.
SUPERLATIVE (SUPERLATIF, *m.*) An expression used to compare more than two adjectives, adverbs, nouns, or actions.	Elle a choisi la robe **la plus chère**. *She chose **the most expensive** dress.* Béatrice court **le plus vite**. *Béatrice runs **the fastest**.*
VERB (VERBE, *m.*) A word that reports an action or state.	Elle **est arrivée** hier. *She **arrived** yesterday.* Elle **était** fatiguée. *She **was** tired.*
auxiliary verb (verbe auxiliaire) A verb used in conjunction with an infinitive or a participle to convey distinctions of tense and mood. In French, the main auxiliaries are **avoir** and **être**.	J'**ai** fait mes devoirs. *I did my homework.* Nous **sommes** allés au cinéma. *We went to the movies.*
impersonal verb (verbe impersonnel) A verbal expression introduced by the impersonal pronoun **il**.	**Il fait** beau aujourd'hui. ***It is** nice today.* **Il faut** travailler fort. ***One has** to work hard.*
pronominal verb (verbe pronominal) A verb conjugated with a pronoun (**me**, **te**, **se**, **nous**, **vous**) that corresponds to the subject pronoun. A pronominal verb may express reflexive or reciprocal action, or it may be idiomatic in usage.	**se souvenir, je me souviens** *to remember, I remember* **Il se coupe** quand **il se rase**. ***He cuts himself** when **he shaves** (**himself**).*

Appendice B

Verbes

Verbes réguliers

INFINITIF ET PARTICIPE PRÉSENT	PRÉSENT	PASSÉ COMPOSÉ	IMPARFAIT	FUTUR	CONDITIONNEL	SUBJONCTIF	IMPÉRATIF
1. **chercher** cherchant	je cherche tu cherches il/elle/on cherche nous cherchons vous cherchez ils/elles cherchent	j' ai cherché tu as cherché il/elle/on a cherché nous avons cherché vous avez cherché ils/elles ont cherché	je cherchais tu cherchais il/elle/on cherchait nous cherchions vous cherchiez ils/elles cherchaient	je chercherai tu chercheras il/elle/on cherchera nous chercherons vous chercherez ils/elles chercheront	je chercherais tu chercherais il/elle/on chercherait nous chercherions vous chercheriez ils/elles chercheraient	que je cherche que tu cherches qu' il/elle/on cherche que nous cherchions que vous cherchiez qu' ils/elles cherchent	cherche cherchons cherchez
2. **répondre** répondant	je réponds tu réponds il/elle/on répond nous répondons vous répondez ils/elles répondent	j' ai répondu tu as répondu il/elle/on a répondu nous avons répondu vous avez répondu ils/elles ont répondu	je répondais tu répondais il/elle/on répondait nous répondions vous répondiez ils/elles répondaient	je répondrai tu répondras il/elle/on répondra nous répondrons vous répondrez ils/elles répondront	je répondrais tu répondrais il/elle/on répondrait nous répondrions vous répondriez ils/elles répondraient	que je réponde que tu répondes qu' il/elle/on réponde que nous répondions que vous répondiez qu' ils/elles répondent	réponds répondons répondez
3. **finir** finissant	je finis tu finis il/elle/on finit nous finissons vous finissez ils/elles finissent	j' ai fini tu as fini il/elle/on a fini nous avons fini vous avez fini ils/elles ont fini	je finissais tu finissais il/elle/on finissait nous finissions vous finissiez ils/elles finissaient	je finirai tu finiras il/elle/on finira nous finirons vous finirez ils/elles finiront	je finirais tu finirais il/elle/on finirait nous finirions vous finiriez ils/elles finiraient	que je finisse que tu finisses qu' il/elle/on finisse que nous finissions que vous finissiez qu' ils/elles finissent	finis finissons finissez
4. **se laver*** (se) lavant	je me lave tu te laves il/on se lave elle se lave nous nous lavons vous vous lavez ils se lavent elles se lavent	je me suis lavé(e) tu t'es lavé(e) il/on s'est lavé elle s'est lavée nous nous sommes lavé(e)s vous vous êtes lavé(e)(s) ils se sont lavés elles se sont lavées	je me lavais tu te lavais il/on se lavait elle se lavait nous nous lavions vous vous laviez ils se lavaient elles se lavaient	je me laverai tu te laveras il/on se lavera elle se lavera nous nous laverons vous vous laverez ils se laveront elles se laveront	je me laverais tu te laverais il/on se laverait elle se laverait nous nous laverions vous vous laveriez ils se laveraient elles se laveraient	que je me lave que tu te laves qu' il/on se lave qu' elle se lave que nous nous lavions que vous vous laviez qu' ils se lavent qu' elles se lavent	lave-toi lavons-nous lavez-vous

*All pronominal verbs are conjugated with **être** in the compound tenses.

Verbes Réguliers Avec Changements Orthographiques

INFINITIF ET PARTICIPE PRÉSENT	PRÉSENT		PASSÉ COMPOSÉ	IMPARFAIT	FUTUR	CONDITIONNEL	SUBJONCTIF	IMPÉRATIF	*AUTRES VERBES*
1. **commencer** commençant	je commence tu commences il/elle/on commence	nous commen**ç**ons vous commencez ils/elles commencent	j'ai commencé	je commen**ç**ais nous commencions	je commencerai	je commencerais	que je commence que nous commencions	commence commen**ç**ons commencez	divorcer, lancer, remplacer
2. **manger** mangeant	je mange tu manges il/elle/on mange	nous mang**e**ons vous mangez ils/elles mangent	j'ai mangé	je mang**e**ais nous mangions	je mangerai	je mangerais	que je mange que nous mangions	mange mang**e**ons mangez	changer, encourager, engager, exiger, mélanger, nager, partager, voyager
3. **préférer** préférant	je préf**è**re tu préf**è**res il/elle/on préf**è**re	nous préférons vous préférez ils/elles préf**è**rent	j'ai préféré	je préférais	je préférerai	je préférerais	que je préf**è**re que nous préférions	préf**è**re préférons préférez	espérer, répéter, s'inquiéter, sécher
4. **payer** payant	je pa**i**e tu pa**i**es il/elle/on pa**i**e	nous payons vous payez ils/elles pa**i**ent	j'ai payé	je payais	je pa**i**erai	je pa**i**erais	que je pa**i**e que nous payions	pa**i**e payons payez	employer, envoyer, essayer
5. **appeler** appelant	j' appe**ll**e tu appe**ll**es il/elle/on appe**ll**e	nous appelons vous appelez ils/elles appe**ll**ent	j'ai appelé	j'appelais	j'appe**ll**erai	j'appe**ll**erais	que j'appe**ll**e que nous appelions	appe**ll**e appelons appelez	s'appeler, se rappeler
6. **acheter** achetant	j' ach**è**te tu ach**è**tes il/elle/on ach**è**te	nous achetons vous achetez ils/elles ach**è**tent	j'ai acheté	j'achetais	j'ach**è**terai	j'ach**è**terais	que j'ach**è**te que nous achetions	ach**è**te achetons achetez	se lever, se promener

Verbes Irréguliers

INFINITIF ET PARTICIPE PRÉSENT	PRÉSENT		PASSÉ COMPOSÉ	IMPARFAIT	FUTUR	CONDITIONNEL	SUBJONCTIF	IMPÉRATIF	*AUTRES VERBES*
1. **aller*** allant	je vais tu vas il/elle/on va	nous allons vous allez ils/elles vont	je suis allé(e)	j'allais	j'irai	j'irais	que j'aille que nous allions	va allons allez	
2. **avoir** ayant	j' ai tu as il/elle/on a	nous avons vous avez ils/elles ont	j'ai eu	j'avais	j'aurai	j'aurais	que j'aie que nous ayons	aie ayons ayez	
3. **boire** buvant	je bois tu bois il/elle/on boit	nous buvons vous buvez ils/elles boivent	j'ai bu	je buvais	je boirai	je boirais	que je boive que nous buvions	bois buvons buvez	
4. **conduire** conduisant	je conduis tu conduis il/elle/on conduit	nous conduisons vous conduisez ils/elles conduisent	j'ai conduit	je conduisais	je conduirai	je conduirais	que je conduise que nous conduisions	conduis conduisons conduisez	construire, détruire, produire, réduire, traduire
5. **connaître** connaissant	je connais tu connais il/elle/on connaît	nous connaissons vous connaissez ils/elles connaissent	j'ai connu	je connaissais	je connaîtrai	je connaîtrais	que je connaisse que nous connaissions	connais connaissons connaissez	apparaître, disparaître, paraître, reconnaître
6. **croire** croyant	je crois tu crois il/elle/on croit	nous croyons vous croyez ils/elles croient	j'ai cru	je croyais	je croirai	je croirais	que je croie que nous croyions	crois croyons croyez	
7. **cueillir** cueillant	je cueille tu cueilles il/elle/on cueille	nous cueillons vous cueillez ils/elles cueillent	j'ai cueilli	je cueillais	je cueillerai	je cueillerais	que je cueille que nous cueillions	cueille cueillons cueillez	accueillir, recueillir
8. **devoir** devant	je dois tu dois il/elle/on doit	nous devons vous devez ils/elles doivent	j'ai dû	je devais	je devrai	je devrais	que je doive que nous devions	dois devons devez	
9. **dire** disant	je dis tu dis il/elle/on dit	nous disons vous dites ils/elles disent	j'ai dit	je disais	je dirai	je dirais	que je dise que nous disions	dis disons dites	
10. **écrire** écrivant	j' écris tu écris	nous écrivons vous écrivez	j'ai écrit	j'écrivais	j'écrirai	j'écrirais	que j'écrive que nous écrivions	écris écrivons	décrire

Verbs followed by an asterisk are conjugated with **être** in the compound tenses.

Verbes Irréguliers (continued)

INFINITIF ET PARTICIPE PRÉSENT	PRÉSENT		PASSÉ COMPOSÉ	IMPARFAIT	FUTUR	CONDITIONNEL	SUBJONCTIF	IMPÉRATIF	*AUTRES VERBES*
11. **être** étant	je suis tu es il/elle/on est	nous sommes vous êtes ils/elles sont	j'ai été	j'étais	je serai	je serais	que je sois que nous soyons	sois soyons soyez	
12. **faire** faisant	je fais tu fais il/elle/on fait	nous faisons vous faites ils/elles font	j'ai fait	je faisais	je ferai	je ferais	que je fasse que nous fassions	fais faisons faites	
13. **falloir**	il faut		il a fallu	il fallait	il faudra	il faudrait	qu'il faille	—	
14. **lire** lisant	je lis tu lis il/elle/on lit	nous lisons vous lisez ils/elles lisent	j'ai lu	je lisais	je lirai	je lirais	que je lise que nous lisions	lis lisons lisez	
15. **mettre** mettant	je mets tu mets il/elle/on met	nous mettons vous mettez ils/elles mettent	j'ai mis	je mettais	je mettrai	je mettrais	que je mette que nous mettions	mets mettons mettez	permettre, promettre
16. **mourir*** mourant	je meurs tu meurs il/elle/on meurt	nous mourons vous mourez ils/elles meurent	je suis mort(e)	je mourais	je mourrai	je mourrais	que je meure que nous mourions	meurs mourons mourez	
17. **naître*** naissant	je nais tu nais il/elle/on naît	nous naissons vous naissez ils/elles naissent	je suis né(e)	je naissais	je naîtrai	je naîtrais	que je naisse que nous naissions	nais naissons naissez	
18. **ouvrir** ouvrant	j' ouvre tu ouvres il/elle/on ouvre	nous ouvrons vous ouvrez ils/elles ouvrent	j'ai ouvert	j'ouvrais	j'ouvrirai	j'ouvrirais	que j'ouvre que nous ouvrions	ouvre ouvrons ouvrez	couvrir, découvrir, offrir, souffrir
19. **partir*** partant	je pars tu pars il/elle/on part	nous partons vous partez ils/elles partent	je suis parti(e)	je partais	je partirai	je partirais	que je parte que nous partions	pars partons partez	dormir, mentir, s'endormir,* sentir, servir, sortir*

*Verbs followed by an asterisk * are conjugated with **être** in the compound tenses.

Verbes Irréguliers (continued)

INFINITIF ET PARTICIPE PRÉSENT	PRÉSENT		PASSÉ COMPOSÉ	IMPARFAIT	FUTUR	CONDITIONNEL	SUBJONCTIF	IMPÉRATIF	*AUTRES VERBES*
21. **pouvoir** pouvant	je peux** tu peux il/elle/on peut	nous pouvons vous pouvez ils/elles peuvent	j'ai pu	je pouvais	je pourrai	je pourrais	que je puisse que nous puissions	—	
22. **prendre** prenant	je prends tu prends il/elle/on prend	nous prenons vous prenez ils/elles prennent	j'ai pris	je prenais	je prendrai	je prendrais	que je prenne que nous prenions	prends prenons prenez	apprendre, comprendre
23. **recevoir** recevant	je reçois tu reçois il/elle/on reçoit	nous recevons vous recevez ils/elles reçoivent	j'ai reçu	je recevais	je recevrai	je recevrais	que je reçoive que nous recevions	reçois recevons recevez	
24. **savoir** sachant	je sais tu sais il/elle/on sait	nous savons vous savez ils/elles savent	j'ai su	je savais	je saurai	je saurais	que je sache que nous sachions	sache sachons sachez	
25. **suivre** suivant	je suis tu suis il/elle/on suit	nous suivons vous suivez ils/elles suivent	j'ai suivi	je suivais	je suivrai	je suivrais	que je suive que nous suivions	suis suivons suivez	poursuivre
26. **venir*** venant	je viens tu viens il/elle/on vient	nous venons vous venez ils/elles viennent	je suis venu(e)	je venais	je viendrai	je viendrais	que je vienne que nous venions	viens venons venez	appartenir, contenir, devenir,* obtenir, revenir,* tenir
27. **vivre** vivant	je vis tu vis il/elle/on vit	nous vivons vous vivez ils/elles vivent	j'ai vécu	je vivais	je vivrai	je vivrais	que je vive que nous vivions	vis vivons vivez	survivre
28. **voir** voyant	je vois tu vois il/elle/on voit	nous voyons vous voyez ils/elles voient	j'ai vu	je voyais	je verrai	je verrais	que je voie que nous voyions	vois voyons voyez	revoir
29. **vouloir** voulant	je veux tu veux	nous voulons vous voulez	j'ai voulu	je voulais	je voudrai	je voudrais	que je veuille que nous voulions	veuille veuillons	

If **je peux is inverted to form a question, it becomes **puis-je… ?**

*Verbs followed by an asterisk * are conjugated with **être** in the compound tenses.

Lexique français-anglais

This end vocabulary provides contextual meanings of French words used in this text. It does not include proper nouns (unless presented as active vocabulary or unless the French equivalent is quite different in spelling from English), most abbreviations, exact cognates, most near cognates, past participles used as adjectives if the infinitive is listed, or regular adverbs formed from adjectives listed. Adjectives are listed in the masculine singular form; feminine endings or forms are included. An asterisk (*) indicates words beginning with an aspirate *h*. Active vocabulary is indicated by the number of the chapter in which it is activated.

Abbreviations

ab.	abbreviation	*indef.*	indefinite	*p.p.*	past participle
adj.	adjective	*inf.*	infinitive	*prep.*	preposition
adv.	adverb	*interj.*	interjection	*pron.*	pronoun
art.	article	*interr.*	interrogative	*Q.*	Quebec usage
colloq.	colloquial	*inv.*	invariable	*rel.*	relative
conj.	conjunction	*irreg.*	irregular	*s.*	singular
fam.	familiar or colloquial	*m.*	masculine noun	*s.o.*	someone
f.	feminine noun	*n.*	noun	*s.th.*	something
Gram.	grammatical term	*pl.*	plural	*v.*	verb

à *prep.* to; at (1); in; **à bientôt** see you soon (P); **à coté de** next to, beside (3); **à demain** see you tomorrow (P); **à droite (gauche)** to/on the right (left) (17); **à haute voix** aloud; **à la campagne** in the country (17); **à la une** on the front page (12); **à l'heure** on time (5); **à mi-temps** part-time (11); **à nouveau** again; **à Paris** in Paris; **à pied** on foot (14); **à table** at the table; **à temps partiel** part-time; **à votre (ta) place** if I were you (19)
abandonner to abandon, desert
abolition *f.* abolition
abonné(e) *m., f.* user, subscriber
abord: d'abord *adv.* first, first of all, at first (10)
absence (de) *f.* absence (from)
absent(e) *adj.* absent
absolu(e) *adj.* absolute (12)
abstrait(e) *adj.* abstract
absurde *adj.* absurd; silly
abus *m.* abuse, misuse
Académie Française *f.* French Academy (*official body that rules on language questions*)
accent *m.* accent; emphasis; accent mark; **accent aigu (grave, circonflexe)** acute (grave, circumflex) accent
accentuer to emphasize; **s'accentuer** to grow stronger
acceptable *adj.* acceptable
accepter (de) to accept (*to do s.th.*) (18)
accès *m.* access
accessoire *m.* accessory
accident *m.* accident
accompagner to accompany, go along (with)
accord *m.* approval; agreement; **d'accord (je suis d'accord)** okay; agreed (I agree) (2)
accorder to give
accordéon *m.* accordion
accordéoniste *m., f.* accordionist
accroître (*p.p.* **accru**) *irreg.* to grow, increase
accueil *m.* welcome, greeting (20); **famille** (*f.*) **d'accueil** host family; **page** (*f.*) **d'accueil** home page (13)
accueillir (*like* **cueillir**) *irreg.* to welcome (16)
accuser (de) to accuse (*of s.th.*); to blame (19)
achat *m.* purchase; **faire des achats** to make purchases
acheter (j'achète) to buy (6); **acheter à quelqu'un** to buy for someone
acide *adj.* sour; tart
acrylique *adj.* acrylic
acte *f.* act; action
acteur/trice *m., f.* actor/actress (P)
actif/ive *adj.* active (2)
action *f.* action, deed
activité *f.* activity
actualités *f. pl.* news; news program (12)
actuel(le) *adj.* current, present (12)
acuponcture *f.* acupuncture
adapté(e) *adj.* adapted
addition *f.* check, bill (*in a restaurant*)
adéquat(e) *adj.* adequate
adhérer to join (*a political party*)
adjacent(e) *adj.* adjacent
adjectif *m., Gram.* adjective
administrateur/trice *m., f.* administrator; manager
administratif/ive *adj.* administrative
administration *f.* administration; management; **administration des affaires** business administration (13)
admirer to admire
adolescence *f.* adolescence (12)
adolescent(e) (*fam.* **ado**) *m., f.* adolescent, teenager (12)
adopter to adopt; to take up
adorer to love, adore (2)
adresse *f.* address
adresser: s'adresser à to address, speak to
adulte *m., f.* adult (12)
adverbe *m., Gram.* adverb
adversité *f.* adversity
aérien(ne) *adj.* aerial
aéroport *m.* airport (14)
affaire *f.* affair; subject; **affaires** (*f. pl.*) business (11); **homme (femme)** (*m., f.*) **d'affaires** businessman (woman)
affichage: tableau (*m.*) **d'affichage** bulletin board (11)

affiche *f.* poster (5)
affirmatif/ive *adj.* affirmative
affoler to panic; **ne t'affole pas** don't get upset
afin de *prep.* in order to (21)
afin que *prep.* in order that, so that (21)
africain(e) *adj.* African; **Africain(e)** *m., f.* African (*person*)
âge *m.* age; **au troisième âge** in old age (12); **quel âge avez-vous (as-tu) (a-t-il,** *etc.*)? how old are you (is he, etc.)?
âgé(e) *adj.* old; elderly
agence *f.* agency; **agence de location** car rental agency; **agence de voyages** travel agency
agent(e) *m., f.* agent; **agent(e) de police** police officer; **agent(e) de sécurité** security guard (11)
agir to act; **il s'agit de** it's a question of, it's about
agneau *m.* lamb
agrandir to enlarge
agréable *adj.* pleasant, nice
agression *f.* aggression
agricole *adj.* agricultural
agriculteur/trice *m., f.* farmer (11)
agriculture *f.* agriculture, farming (18)
ah bien *interj.* well then
aide *f.* help, assistance; **à l'aide de** with the help of
aider to help
aigu: accent (*m.*) **aigu** acute accent (**é**)
ail *m.* garlic (15)
ailleurs *adv.* elsewhere; **d'ailleurs** moreover, besides
aimable *adv.* lovable
aimer to like; to love (2); **aimer bien** to like; **aimer mieux** to prefer (2); **j'aimerais** I would like; **s'aimer** to love each other
ainsi *conj.* thus, in this way, like this; **ainsi que** as well as
air *m.* air; tune; **avoir l'air** to look, seem (4); **courant** (*m.*) **d'air** breeze, draft; **en plein air** outdoors (16)
aisément *adv.* easily
ajouter to add (15)
album-photo *m.* photo album
alcool *m.* alcohol
alcoolisé(e) *adj.* alcoholic (*beverage*)
Algérie *f.* Algeria (3)
algérien(ne) *adj.* Algerian (3); **Algérien(ne)** *m., f.* Algerian (*person*)
algue *f.* seaweed
aligot *m.* regional potato-and-cheese soup
aliment *m.* food (7)
alimentaire *adj.* alimentary, pertaining to food
Allemagne *f.* Germany (3)
allemand(e) *adj.* German (3); **Allemand(e)** *m., f.* German (*person*) (3)
aller *irreg.* to go (3); **aller** + *inf.* to be going (*to do s.th.*) (3); **aller à la pêche** to go fishing (16); **billet** (*m.*) **aller-retour** roundtrip ticket (14); **billet** (*m.*) **aller simple** one-way ticket (14); **allez-y!** go ahead!; **ça va?** how's it going? (P); **ça va bien** I'm fine (P); **comment allez-vous (vas-tu)?** how are you? (P)
allergie *f.* allergy
allergique *adj.* allergic
alliance *f.* alliance, union
alliés *m. pl.* allies
allumer to light
allumette *f.* match
allusion *f.*: **faire allusion à** to make reference to
alors *adv.* so; then, in that case
alphabet *m.* alphabet
alsacien(ne) *adj.* Alsatian; **Alsacien(ne)** *m., f.* Alsatian (*person*)
amant(e) *m., f.* lover
amateur de *m.* fan of, enthusiast of
ambassade *f.* embassy
ambiance *f.* atmosphere, ambiance
ambitieux/euse *adj.* ambitious
ambition *f.* ambition
âme *f.* soul; **âme sœur** kindred spirit; **âmes perdues** lost souls
amère *adj.* bitter
américain(e) *adj.* American (3); **Américain(e)** *m., f.* American (*person*); **football** (*m.*) **American** football (10)
Amérique (*f.*) **du Nord** North America (14)
Amérique (*f.*) **du Sud** South America (14)
ami(e) *m., f.* friend (P); **faux ami** false cognate; **petit(e) ami(e)** *m., f.* boyfriend (girlfriend); **se faire des amis** to make friends
amicalement *adv.* amicably
amitié *f.* friendship
amour *m.* love; **lettre** (*f.*) **d'amour** love letter
amoureux/euse *adj.* in love; **tomber amoureux/euse** to fall in love
amphithéâtre (*fam.* **amphi**) *m.* amphitheater, lecture hall
ampleur *f.* fullness
amusant(e) *adj.* amusing, funny (2)
amuser: s'amuser (à) to have a good time (9)
an *m.* year (4); **j'ai (il a,** *etc.***) (vingt) ans** I am (he is, *etc.*) (twenty) years old (4); **nouvel an** New Year's Day (11)
analyse *f.* analysis
analyser to analyze
ancêtre *m., f.* ancestor
ancien(ne) *adj.* ancient; old; former
anglais(e) *adj.* English (3); **anglais** *m.* English (*language*) (1); **Anglais(e)** *m., f.* English person (3)
Angleterre *f.* England (3)
anglophone *adj.* English-speaking
animal *m.* animal (16)
animateur/trice *m., f.* television anchor
animé(e) *adj.* animated; **dessin** (*m.*) **animé** animated cartoon (12)
anis *m.* anise
année *f.* year (4); **année prochaine (dernière)** next (last) year
anniversaire *m.* birthday (4); **anniversaire de mariage** wedding anniversary (11)
annonce *f.* advertisement; **petites annonces** classified ads (11)
annoncer (nous annonçons) to announce; to state
annuaire *m.* telephone book
anonyme *adj.* anonymous
antagonisme *m.* antagonism
Antarctique *m.* Antarctica (14)
anthropologie *f.* anthropology
antibiotique *m.* antibiotic
anticiper to anticipate, expect
antidote *m.* antidote
antillais(e) *adj.* West Indian; **Antillais(e)** *m., f.* West Indian (*person*)
antiquaire *m., f.* antiques dealer (20)
août *m.* August (4)
apaiser to appease
apercevoir (*like* **recevoir**) *irreg.* to see; to notice
apéritif *m.* cocktail
apostrophe *m.* apostrophe
apparaître (*like* **connaître**) *irreg.* to appear (13)
appareil photo *m.* camera (5)
apparent(e) *adj.* apparent (12)
apparenté(e) *adj.* related, similar; **mots** (*m. pl.*) **apparentés** cognates
appartement *m.* apartment, flat (5)
appartenir (*like* **tenir**) (*irreg.*) **à** to belong to (14)
appel *m.* call
appeler (j'appelle) to call (6); **il (elle) s'appelle** his (her) name is (4); **je m'appelle** my name is (P); **s'appeler** to be named (9)
appétit *m.* appetite; **bon appétit** enjoy your meal
applaudir to applaud (11)
apporter to bring
appréciation *f.* appreciation
apprécier to appreciate
apprendre (*like* **prendre**) *irreg.* to learn (7)
approcher to approach, draw near; **s'approcher (de)** to approach (*s.th.*)
approprié(e) *adj.* appropriate, fitting

après *prep.* after (8); **après que** after (21); **d'après** based on, according to
après-demain *adv.* day after tomorrow
après-midi *m. or f.* afternoon (5); **cet après-midi** this afternoon (13); **de l'après-midi** in the afternoon (5)
aquarelle *f.* watercolor
aquatique *adj.* aquatic
arabe *adj.* Arab (22); **Arabe** *m., f.* Arab (*person*); **arabe** (*m.*) **littéraire** classical Arabic
arbre *m.* tree (18)
arc *m.* arch
archéologie *f.* archeology
architectural(e) *adj.* architectural
archives *f. pl.* archives
arène *f.* arena
argent *m.* money (6)
arithméthique *f.* arithmetic
armée *f.* army
arme *f.* arm, weapon (19)
armistice *m.* armistice
armoire *f.* armoire, wardrobe (*furniture*) (5)
arrestation *f.* arrest
arrêt *m.* (station) stop (14)
arrêter (de) to stop, cease; to arrest; **des opinions** (*f. pl.*) **arrêtées** definite opinions; **s'arrêter** to stop (*oneself*)
arrière *adv.* (in the) back; **arrière-grand-parent** *m.* great-grandparent; **arrière plan** *m.* background
arrivée *f.* arrival (14)
arriver (à) to arrive (11); to happen; to succeed in (doing) (18); **qu'est-ce qui lui arrive?** what's going on with him?
arrondissement *m.* district (20)
art *m.* art (10); **arts dramatiques** dramatic arts (13); **arts plastiques** visual arts (sculpture, painting, etc.) (13); **beaux-arts** fine arts
arteriel(le) *adj.* arterial
article *m., Gram.* article
artifice: feux (*m. pl.*) **d'artifice** fireworks
artisan(e) *m., f.* craftsman, artisan (11)
artisanal(e) *adj.* hand-crafted; **pain** (*m.*) **artisanal** hand-crafted bread
artiste *m., f.* artist
artistique *adj.* artistic
ascenseur *m.* elevator
asiatique *adj.* Asian; **Asiatique** *m., f.* Asian (*person*)
Asie *f.* Asia (14)
asile *m.* asylum; **asile politique** political asylum
aspect *m.* aspect, feature
aspiré(e) *adj.* spoken, aspirated; **h aspiré** letter *h* not allowing liaison or elision
aspirine *f.* aspirin (9)
asseoir (*p.p.* **assis**) *irreg.* to seat; **asseyez-vous (assieds-toi)** sit down; **s'asseoir** to sit down
assez *adv.* rather, somewhat, quite; **assez de** *adv.* enough (7); **assez jeune** quite young
assiette *f.* plate (8)
assimilation *f.* assimilation
assimiler to assimilate
assistance *f.* assistance, help
assistant(e) *m., f.* assistant
assister à to attend (*an event*) (10)
associer to associate
assorti(e) *adj.* matching; **bien assorti(e)** well-matched
assumer to take on
assurer to ensure
astronomique *adj.* astronomical
atelier *m.* workshop
athlète *m., f.* athlete
atmosphère *f.* atmosphere
attacher to attach; **s'attacher à** to become attached to (*s.th.*)
attaque *f.* attack
attaquer to attack (19)
attendre to wait (for) (8)
attention *f.* attention; **attention!** *interj.* watch out!; **faire attention (à)** to pay attention (to) (5)
attentivement *adv.* attentively
attitude *f.* attitude
attraper to trap
aubergine *f.* eggplant (15)
au revoir *m.* good-bye (P)
aucun(e): ne... aucun(e) *adj.* no, not one, not any (13)
audacieux/euse *adj.* audacious
audience *f.* audience; **indices** (*m. pl.*) **d'audience** ratings
augmentation *f.* increase; rise
augmenter to increase
aujourd'hui *adv.* today (4); nowadays; **nous sommes le combien aujourd'hui?** What date is it?
auprès de *prep.* near, close to
aussi *adv.* also (1); as; so; **aussi... que** as . . . as (16); **aussi bien que** just as easily as
Australie *f.* Australia (14)
autant; autant de + *noun* + **que** *adv.* as much/many + *noun* + as (16); **autant que** as much as (16)
auteur (femme auteur) *m., f.* author (21); **en tant qu'auteur** as author
autocar *m.* (tour) bus (14)
autographe *m.* autograph
automatique *adj.* automatic
automne *m.* autumn (10)
automobile (*fam.* **auto**) *f.* automobile
autoritaire *adj.* authoritarian
autoroute *f.* highway (14)
autour de *prep.* around
autre *adj., pron.* other, another (2); **autre chose?** something else?; **l'autre / les autres** the other(s)
autrefois *adv.* formerly, in the past (10)
auxiliaire *m., Gram.* auxiliary (*verb*)
avance *f.* advance; **en avance** early (5); **retarder l'avance** to slow the advance (19)
avancer (nous avançons) to advance
avant *adv.* before (in time) (8); *prep.* before, in advance of; **avant de** before (21); **avant que** *conj.* before (21)
avantage *m.* advantage, benefit
avantageux/euse *adj.* advantageous; profitable
avare *m., f.* miser
avec *prep.* with (1)
avenir *m.* future (18)
avenue *f.* avenue; **monter l'avenue** to go up the avenue (17)
aveugle *adv.* blind
avion *m.* airplane (14); **billet** (*m.*) **d'avion** airplane ticket; **en avion** by airplane
avis *m.* opinion; **à votre (ton) avis** in your opinion; **changer d'avis** to change one's mind
avocat(e) *m., f.* lawyer (11)
avoine *f.* oats
avoir (*p.p.* **eu**) *irreg.* to have (4); **avoir (vingt) ans** to be (twenty) years old; **avoir besoin (de)** to need (4); **avoir chaud** to feel hot (4); **avoir confiance en** to have confidence in; **avoir du mal (à)** to have a hard time (*doing s.th.*); **avoir envie de** to be in the mood for (4); **avoir faim** to be hungry (4); **avoir froid** to be cold (4); **avoir honte (de)** to be ashamed (of) (4); **avoir horreur de** to hate, detest; **avoir l'air** to look, seem (4); **avoir lieu** to take place (21); **avoir l'occasion** to have the chance; **avoir mal à** to have pain, an ache in; to have a sore . . . (9); **avoir mal au cœur** to feel nauseated (9); **avoir peur (de)** to be afraid (of) (4); **avoir raison** to be right; **avoir soif** to be thirsty (4); **avoir sommeil** to be sleepy; **avoir tort** to be wrong, to be mistaken
avril *m.* April (4)

baccalauréat *m.* (*fam.* **bac**) high school diploma
baby-sitter *m., f.* babysitter (11)
baguette *f.* French bread, baguette
baie *f.* bay (17)
baignoire *f.* bathtub
bain *m.* bath; **bain thermal** spa bath (*spring water*); **maillot** (*m.*) **de bain** swimsuit (6); **salle** (*f.*) **de bains** bathroom (5)

baiser *m.* kiss
baisser to lower
balle *f.* ball (*not inflated with air*) (16)
ballon *m.* ball (*inflated with air*) (16)
banal(e) *adj.* trite, superficial, banal
bande (*f.*) **dessinée** comic strip (12)
bandé(e) *adj.*: **yeux** (*m. pl.*) **bandés** blindfolded
banlieue *f.* suburb (3)
bancaire: carte (*f.*) **bancaire** bank (*debit*) card (6)
banque *f.* bank (20); **banque de données** database
baptisé(e) *adj.* baptized, christened
bar *m.* bar, pub
base *f.* basis; base (*military*); **à base de** based on, from
base-ball *m.* baseball (10)
baser to base; **baser sur** to base on
bassin *m.* basin (17)
bataille *f.* battle
bateau *m.* boat; **bateau à voile** sailboat (16); **en bateau** by boat; **faire du bateau** to go sailing
bâtiment *m.* building (3)
bavard(e) *adj.* talkative (13)
bavarder to gossip; to talk a lot
beau (bel, belle [*pl.* **beaux, belles**]) *adj.* handsome; beautiful (12); **beau temps** nice weather; **il fait beau** it's nice (weather) out (10)
beaucoup (de) *adv.* much, many, a lot (of) (7); **beaucoup plus** much more, many more
beau-frère *m.* stepbrother; brother-in-law (4)
beau-père *m.* stepfather; father-in-law (4)
beauté *f.* beauty; **institut** (*m.*) **de beauté** beauty parlor
bébé *m.* baby (12)
belle-mère *f.* stepmother; mother-in-law (4)
belle-sœur *f.* stepsister; sister-in-law (4)
ben *interj. fam.* well
berbère *adj.* Berber (22)
béret *m.* beret
besoin *m.* need; **avoir besoin de** to need (4)
bêtise *f.* foolishness; **faire des bêtises** to make mistakes; to do silly things
betterave *f.* beet (15)
beurre *m.* butter (7)
bibliothèque *f.* library (3)
bien *adv.* well, good (P); **bien payé** well paid; **bien que** although (21); **bien sûr que non** of course not (2); **bien sûr (que oui)** (yes), of course; (2); **ça va bien** I'm fine, I'm well (P); **s'entendre bien (avec)** to get along well (with) (9); **très bien** very well (P); **vouloir bien** to be glad, willing (*to do s.th.*) (6)
bientôt *adv.* soon (10); **à bientôt** *interj.* see you soon (P)
bière *f.* beer
bijoux *m. pl.* jewelry
bilingue *adj.* bilingual
bilinguisme *m.* bilingualism
billiard *m.* billiards (10)
billet *m.* ticket (14); **billet aller-retour** roundtrip ticket (14); **billet aller simple** one-way ticket (14); **billet d'avion** airplane ticket
biochimie *f.* biochemistry (13)
biographique *adj.* bibliographical
biologie *f.* biology (13)
bisou *m. fam.* kiss (*child's language*)
bizarre *adj.* weird, strange (21)
blanc *m.* blank; space; **remplir les blancs** to fill in the blanks
blanc(he) *adj.* white (6)
blé *m.* wheat (18)
bled *m. fam.* small village
blesser to wound, injure
bleu(e) *adj.* blue (6); **carte** (*f.*) **bleue** bank card
bloc-notes *m.* pad of paper (P)
blues *m. s. inv.* blues music (21)
bœuf *m.* beef (7); **les bœufs** oxen
boire (*p.p.* **bu**) *irreg.* to drink (7)
bois *m.* woods, wooded area
boisson *f.* beverage, drink (8)
boîte *f.* box, can (7); **boîte aux lettres électronique** electronic mailbox (13); **boîte de nuit** nightclub (10)
bol *m.* bowl
bombe *f.* bomb
bon(ne) *adj.* good (2); **bon appétit** enjoy your meal; **bon ben** *interj.* all right then; **bonne chance** good luck (1); **bonne humeur** good mood; **bonne journée** have a good day; **en bonne forme** in good shape (9)
bonbon *m.* piece of candy
bonjour *interj.* hello, good day (P)
bord *m.* edge; bank; **au bord de** on the banks (shore, edge) of (17)
bordelais(e) *adj.* from Bordeaux (*region*)
botte *f.* boot (6)
bouche *f.* mouth (9)
boucher/ère *m., f.* butcher (7)
boucherie *f.* butcher shop (7)
bouddhisme *m.* Buddhism
bouddhiste *adj.* Buddhist
boue *f.* mud
bougie *f.* candle
bouillabaisse *f.* fish soup
bouillir (je bous) *irreg.* to boil; **faire bouillir** to boil (*food*) (15)
boulanger/ère *m., f.* (bread) baker (7)
boulangerie *f.* (bread) bakery (7)
boule *f.* bowling ball; **jouer aux boules** to play lawn bowling
boulevard *m.* boulevard
bourgade *f.* village
bourgeois(e) *adj.* bourgeois, middle-class
bourguignon(ne) *adj.* from Burgundy (*region*)
bout *m.* end; **à bout de souffle** out of breath, breathless
bouteille *f.* bottle 7
boutique *f.* small shop, boutique
bowling *m.* bowling (10)
boxe *f.* boxing; **match** (*m.*) **de boxe** boxing match (10)
bras *m.* arm (9); **se croiser les bras** to cross one's arms
brebis *f.* ewe (18)
breton(ne) *adj.* from Brittany (*region*)
brevet *m.* patent
bribes *f. pl.* snatches; bits
brie *m.* Brie cheese
briller to shine
brocoli *m.* broccoli
bronchite *f.* bronchitis; bad cough
brosser to brush; **se brosser (les cheveux, les dents)** to brush (one's hair, teeth) (9)
bruit *m.* noise; **le bruit court** rumor has it
brûler to burn
brun(e) *adj.* brown (6)
buffet *m.* buffet; sideboard (5)
bureau *m.* desk (1); office (3); **bureau de poste** post office building
bus *m.* (city) bus (14)
but *m.* goal

ça *pron.* this, that, it; **ça marche** that works for me; **ça me va?** does it suit me?; **ça va?** how's it going? (P); **ça va bien** I'm fine, I'm well (P); **c'est ça?** is that right? (3); **qu'est-ce que c'est que ça?** what is that? (P)
cabine *f.* cabin; booth; **cabine téléphonique** telephone booth (13)
cacahouète *f.* peanut (15)
cacher to hide
cachemire *m.* cashmere
cadeau *m.* gift
cadre *m., f.* executive (11)
café *m.* coffee (8); café; **café au lait** coffee with milk (8)
caféteria *f.* cafeteria
cage *f.* animal cage
cahier *m.* notebook, workbook (P)
caillé: lait (*m.*) **caillé** curdled milk (*similar to sour cream*)
caisse *f.* checkout (6); **caisse populaire** credit union (13)
calcul *m.* calculus
calculatrice *f.* calculator (P)

calendrier *m.* calendar
calme *adj.* calm
calmer to calm; **se calmer** to calm down
calorie *f.* calorie
camarade *m., f.* friend; **camarade de classe** classmate (P)
camembert *m.* Camembert cheese
caméra *f.* movie camera
cameraman (*pl.* **cameramen**) *m.* cameraman
camion *m.* truck (19)
camp *m.* camp
campagne *f.* country(side); campaign (*publicity, military*); **à la campagne** in the country (17); **pain** (*m.*) **de campagne** country-style wheat bread
camping *m.* campground (16); **faire du camping** to go camping (16)
campus *m.* campus
Canada *m.* Canada (3)
canadien(ne) *adj.* Canadian (3); **Canadien(ne)** *m., f.* Canadian (*person*)
canal *m.* channel
canapé *m.* sofa (5)
canard *m.* duck; **canard laqué** Peking duck
candidat(e) *m., f.* candidate
candidature *f.* candidacy; **poser sa candidature** to submit one's application
canne (*f.*) **à sucre** sugarcane
cannelle *f.* cinnamon (15)
canoë *m.* canoe; **faire du canoë** to go canoeing (16)
cantate *f.* cantata
cantine *f.* cafeteria
capable *adj.* capable; **il en est capable** he can do it
capacité *f.* skill
capitale *f.* capital (city)
caprice *m.* caprice, whim
capuchon *m.* hood
car *conj.* for, because, since
caractère *m.* character (*personal quality*); **charactères gras** boldface type
caractériser to characterize; **se caractériser (par)** to be characterized (by)
caractéristique *f.* caracteristic
carbone *m.* carbon
carbonnade (*f.*) **flamande** regional meat stew
cardamome *f.* cardamom (15)
cardiaque *adj.* cardiac; **crise** (*f.*) **cardiaque** heart attack
cardinal(e) (*pl.* **cardinaux**) *adj.* essential, cardinal
carême *m.* Lent
carnet *m.* notebook; **carnet de chèques** checkbook (20); **carnet du jour** society column (12)
carotte *f.* carrot (7)
carrière *f.* career
carte *f.* map (17); (greeting) card; menu; **carte bancaire** bank (*debit*) card (6); **carte bleue** bank card; **carte de crédit** credit card (6); **carte météorologique** weather map; **carte postale** postcard; **par carte de crédit** by credit card
cas *m.* case; **au cas où** in case, in the event that (19); **selon le cas** as the case may be
casser to break; **se casser** to break (*a limb*) (9)
casserole *f.* saucepan (15)
cassette *f.* cassette
catégorie *f.* category
cathédrale *f.* cathedral
catholicisme *m.* Catholicism
catholique *adj.* Catholic
cause *f.* cause; **à cause de** because of
causer to cause
CD *m.* compact disk (CD)
ce (cet, cette, *pl.* **ces)** *adj.* this, that, these, those (5); **ce (c')** *pron.* it, this, that; **ce matin** this morning (13); **ce soir** this evening (13); **c'est** this/that/it is (P); **cet après-midi** this afternoon (13); **n'est-ce pas?** isn't that right? (3)
ceci *pron.* this
céder (je cède) to give in
cédille *f.* cedilla (**ç**)
cèdre *m.* cedar
ceinture *f.* belt (6)
cela (ça) *pron.* that; **à part cela (ça)** besides that; **c'est pour cela seul** it's only for that reason; **cela (ne) vous regarde (pas)** that is (not) your problem
célèbre *adj.* famous (20)
célébrer (je célèbre) to celebrate
célébrité *f.* fame; celebrity
célibataire *adj.* unmarried, single (4)
celle *pron. f. s.* the/this/that one (19)
celles *pron. f. pl.* these/those (ones) (19)
cellule *f.* nucleus
celte *adj.* Celtic; **Celte** *m., f.* Celtic (*person*)
celui *pron. m. s.* this/that one (19)
censé(e) *adj.*: **être censé(e) faire** to be supposed to do (*s.th.*)
cent *adj.* hundred (4); **pour cent** percent
centimètre *m.* centimeter
central(e) *adj.* central; primary
centralisé(e) *adj.* centralized
centre *m.* center; **centre commercial** shopping center; **centre sportif** sports center (3); **centre-ville** (*m.*) downtown
cependant *adv.* nevertheless
céréale *f.* grain (18)
cerf *m.* deer, stag (16)
cerise *f.* cherry (7)
certain(e) *adj.* certain; sure (21)
certitude *m.* certainty
cerveau *m.* brain (9)
cesser (de) to stop (*doing*) (18)
c'est-à-dire *conj.* that is to say, I mean
ceux *pron. m. pl.* these/those ones (19)
chacun(e) *pron.* each (one), every one
chagrin *m.* sorrow
chaîne *f.* (television, radio) station; network (12); **chaîne privée payante** private subscription channel
chaîne stéréo *f.* stereo system (5)
chaise *f.* chair (1)
chaleur *f.* warmth (20); heat
chambre *f.* bedroom (5); **camarade** (*m., f.*) **de chambre** roommate
chameau *m.* camel
champ *m.* field (17)
champagne *m.* champagne (7)
champignon *m.* mushroom (15)
champion *m.* champion
chance *f.* luck; **avoir de la chance** to be lucky; **bonne chance** good luck (1)
chancelier *m.* chancellor
chandelle *f.* candle
changer (nous changeons) to change (6); **changer d'avis** to change one's mind
changement *m.* change
chanson *f.* song (21)
chant *m.* chant, song
chanter to sing
chanteur/euse *m., f.* singer (21)
chapeau *m.* hat (6)
chaque *adj.* each, every (7)
charcuterie *f.* pork butcher shop (7); delicatessen (7); pork products (8)
charcutier/ière *m., f.* butcher
chargé(e) *adj.* loaded (*weapon*)
charmant(e) *adj.* charming
charte *f.* charter; chart
chasser to hunt (16)
chat *m.* cat (16)
château (*pl.* **châteaux**) *m.* castle; **châteaux en Espagne** castles in the air
chaud(e) *adj.* warm, hot; **avoir chaud** to feel hot (4); **il fait chaud** it's hot (weather) out (5)
chauffer to heat (15); **réchauffer** to reheat (15)
chauffeur *m.* driver
chaussée *f.* pavement; **rez-de-chaussée** (*m.*) ground floor
chaussette *f.* sock (6)
chaussure *f.* shoe (6); **chaussures de marche** walking shoes
chef *m.* chief; chef
chef-d'œuvre (*pl.* **chefs-d'œuvre**) *m.* masterpiece
chemin *m.* route, way (17); **chemin de fer** railroad; **est-ce que vous pourriez m'indiquer le chemin pour aller à... ?** could you show me the way to . . . ? (17); **voie** (*f.*) **de chemin de fer** railroad tracks (19)

cheminée *f.* fireplace; chimney (18)
chemise *f.* shirt (6)
chemisier *m.* blouse (6)
chèque *m.* check (6); **carnet** (*m.*) **de chèques** checkbook (20); **déposer un chèque** to deposit a check (20); **faire un chèque** to write a check (20); **par chèque** by check; **toucher un chèque** to cash a check (20)
cher (chère) *adj.* dear; expensive (2)
chercher to look for (2)
chéri(e) *m., f.* dear, darling, honey
cheval (*pl.* **chevaux**) *m.* horse (16); **monter à cheval** to go horseback riding (16)
cheveux *m. pl.* hair (9); **se brosser les cheveux** to brush one's hair (9)
chèvre *m.* goat; goat cheese
chez *prep.* at the home (establishment) of (3); **chez moi** at my place
chic *adj.* chic
chiches: pois (*m.*) **chiches** chickpeas
chien *m.* dog (16); **nom** (*m.*) **d'un chien!** *interj.* darn it!
chiffon *m.* rag
chiffre *m.* number
chimie *f.* chemistry (13)
chimique *adj.* chemical; **genie** (*f.*) **chimique** chemical engineering (13)
Chine *f.* China (3)
chinois(e) *adj.* Chinese (3); **Chinois(e)** *m., f.* Chinese person
chiropracteur/ticienne *m., f.* chiropractor
chiropractie *f.* chiropractic
chiropratique *f. Q.* chiropractic
chiropraxie *f.* chiropractic (13)
chocolat *m.* chocolate (8); **mousse** (*f.*) **au chocolat** chocolate mousse (8)
choisir to choose (11)
choix *m.* choice; **à vous le choix** your choice; **premier choix** top quality
cholestérol *m.* cholesterol
chômage *m.* unemployment; **au chômage** *adj.* unemployed (20)
chômeur/euse *m., f.* unemployed person
chose *f.* thing (8); **autre chose** something else; **quelque chose** something (13)
choux de bruxelles *m. pl.* brussels sprouts
chrétien(ne) *adj.* Christian
christianisme *m.* Christianity
chronologie *f.* chronology
chronologique *adj.* chronological
cidre *m.* cider
ciel *m.* sky (10); **le ciel est couvert (clair)** the sky is cloudy (clear) (10)
cimetière *m.* cemetery
cinéaste *m., f.* filmmaker
ciné-club *m.* film club
cinéma *m.* movie business; movie theater (P)
cinémathèque *f.* film store, film library
cinématographe *m., f.* cinematographer
cinéphile *m., f.* movie lover
cinq *adj.* five (P)
cinquantaine *f.*: **dans la cinquantaine** in one's fifties (*age*) (12)
cinquante *adj.* fifty (P)
cinquième *adj.* fifth (11)
circonflexe: accent (*m.*) **circonflexe** *Gram.* circumflex accent (**â**)
circonstances *f. pl.* circumstances
circulation *f.* traffic (14)
circulatoire *adj.* circulatory
circuler to travel around (14)
cirque *m.* circus (10)
ciseaux *m. pl.* scissors
cité *m.* area in a city; **cité universitaire** dormitory
citoyen(ne) *m., f.* citizen
citron *m.* lemon (7)
citron vert *m.* lime
citronnelle *f.* lemongrass (15)
civil *m.* general public; civilian; **civil(e)** *adj.* public; **état** (*m.*) **civil** civil status
clair(e) *adj.* clear (10, 21); **le ciel est clair** the sky is clear (10)
clandestin(e) *adj.* clandestine
clarifier to clarify
classe *f.* class (P); **camarade** (*m., f.*) **de classe** classmate (P); **classe moyenne** middle class; **salle** (*f.*) **de classe** classroom (P)
classement *m.* classification
classer to classify
classique *adj.* classic; classical
clé *f.* key; **moments** (*m. pl.*) **clés** key moments; **mot-clé** *m.* key word; **sous clé** under lock and key
client(e) *m., f.* client (6)
clientèle *f.* clientele
climat *m.* climate
climatique *adj.* pertaining to climate
cliquer (sur) to click (on) (13)
clochard(e) *m., f.* hobo, tramp
clown *m.* clown
club *m.* club (*social*); **ciné-club** *m.* film club
coca *m.* Coca Cola (8)
cochon *m.* pig; pork
coco: noix (*f.*) **de coco** coconut (15)
code *m.* numerical code; **code civil** civil code, common law
cœur *m.* heart (9); **avoir mal au cœur** to feel nauseous (9); **savoir par cœur** to know by heart; **de tout cœur** with all one's heart; **greffe** (*f.*) **du cœur** heart transplant
coexistence *f.* coexistence
coexister to coexist
coffret *m.* little box
cognitif/ive *adj.* cognitive
cohabitation *f.* cohabitation
cohabiter to live together
coin *m.* corner (17); **les quatres coins du monde** the four corners (far reaches) of the world
coïncidence *f.* coincidence
colère *f.* anger
collaborateur/trice (*fam.* **collabo**) *m., f.* collaborator
collaborer to collaborate
collection *f.* collection
collègue *m., f.* colleague
colline *f.* hill (17)
colonne *f.* column
coloris *m.* coloring
combat *m.* combat, fighting
combattre (*like* **battre**) *irreg.* to fight (*against*)
combien (de) *adv.* how much? how many? (4); **depuis combien de temps?** how long?; **nous sommes le combien aujourd'hui?** what date is it today?
combiné *m.* (telephone) receiver
combustion *f.* combustion
comédie *f.* comedy
comique *adj.* comic
comité *m.* committee
commander to give orders; to order (*in a restaurant*)
comme *adv.* as, like (8); **comme ça** this way; **comme d'habitude** as usual; **comme prévu** as expected
commémorer to commemorate
commencer (nous commençons) to begin (6)
comment *adv.* how (4); **comment allez-vous (vas-tu)?** (P); **comment est/sont... ?** what is/are . . . like? (2)
commentaire *m.* commentary
commerçant(e) *m., f.* tradesperson
commerce *m.* commerce (11); **commerce international** international commerce (11)
commercial(e) *adj.* commercial; **centre** (*m.*) **commercial** shopping center
commun(e) *adj.* common
communauté *m.* community
communication *f.* communication
communiquer to communicate
communiste *m., f.*; *adj.* communist
commutateur *m.* switch
compagnie *f.* company, business
comparaison *f.* comparison
comparatif/ive *adj.* comparative
comparer to compare
compatissant(e) *adj.* caring
compétition *f.* competition
complément *m.* complement; **pronom complément d'objet direct (indirect)** *Gram.* direct (indirect) object pronoun

complet *m.* man's suit (6)
complet/ète *adj.* full (14)
compléter (je complète) to complete
compliment *m.* compliment
compliqué(e) *adj.* complicated
comportement *m.* behavior
comporter to involve, include
composé(e) *adj.* composed; **passé** (*m.*) **composé** compound past tense
composer to compose (13); **composer un numéro** to dial a (telephone) number (13)
compositeur/trice *m., f.* composer (21)
composter to punch (*a ticket*) (14)
composteur *m.* dating stamp; ticket puncher
compréhension *f.* understanding
comprendre (*like* **prendre**) *irreg.* to understand (7); to include
comprimé *m.* tablet (9)
compris(e) *adj.* included
compromis *m.* compromise
comptable *m., f.* accountant (11)
compte *m.* account; **à leur compte** to their advantage; **compte en banque** bank account (20); **compte rendu** report; **se rendre compte (de)** to realize (9)
conception *f.* conception
concerner to concern; **en ce qui concerne** concerning (*s.o. or s.th.*)
concert *m.* concert (21)
conclure to conclude
conclusion *f.* conclusion
concours *m.* competitive examination
conçu(e) *adj.* conceived, designed
condensateur *m.* condenser
condiments *m. pl.* condiments
condition *f.* condition
conditionnel *m., Gram.* conditional (*verb tense*)
condoléances *f. pl.* condolences
conducteur/trice *m., f.* driver (19)
conduire (*p.p.* **conduit**) *irreg.* to drive (18)
conférence *f.* lecture (21)
confiance *f.* confidence; **avoir confiance en** to have confidence in; **faire confiance (à)** to trust (*s.o.*)
configuration *f.* configuration
confirmation *f.* confirmation
confiture *f.* jam (7)
conflit *m.* conflict; dispute
confortable *adj.* comfortable
confrontation *f.* confrontation
congé *m.* holiday, time off (20); **prendre du congé** to take time off
congrès *m.* congress
conjonction *f., Gram.* conjunction
conjugaison *f., Gram.* conjugation
conjuguer to conjugate
connaissance *f.* knowledge; acquaintance; **faire la connaissance de** to meet (*a new person*) (5)
connaître (*p.p.* **connu**) *irreg.* to know, be acquainted with (13)
conquête *f.* conquest
consacré(e) *adj.* devoted
conscient(e) *adj.* aware
conseil *m.* advice; **donner des conseils** to give advice
conseiller to advise; **conseiller/ère** *m., f.* counselor
conséquence *f.* consequence
conservateur/trice *m., f.* curator (11); *adj.* (politically) conservative
conservation *f.* conservation (18)
conservatoire *m.* conservatory
conserver to conserve
considérable *adj.* considerable
considérer (je considère) to consider; **se considérer** to believe oneself to be
console *f.* console
consommation *f.* consumption (18)
consommer to consume, use (18)
consonne *f.* consonant
constitution *f.* constitution
constructeur *m.* manufacturer
construction *f.* construction
construire (*like* **conduire**) *irreg.* to construct (18)
consultation *f.* consultation
consulter to consult
contacter to contact
conte *m.* short story (21)
contemporain(e) *adj.* contemporary (21)
contenir (*like* **tenir**) *irreg.* to contain (14)
content(e) *adj.* happy
contenu *m.* content
contexte *m.* context
continent *m.* continent
continuer to continue (18)
contraceptive *adj.*: **pilule** (*f.*) **contraceptive** contraceptive pill
contraire *m.* opposite; **au contraire** on the contrary
contrat *m.* contract (20)
contre *prep.* against; **le pour et le contre** pros and cons
contredire (*like* **dire**) *irreg.* to contradict
contrée *f.* homeland; region
contrefaçon *f.* counterfeiting
contrefait(e) *adj.* counterfeit
contribuer to contribute
contrôler to control
contrôleur/euse *m., f.* ticket collector; conductor
convaincre (*p.p.* **convaincu**) *irreg.* to convince
convaincant(e) *adj.* convincing
convenable *adj.* fitting, appropriate
convenir (*like* **venir**) *irreg.* to suit, be suitable for
conversation *f.* conversation
convoqué(e) *adj.* summoned
copain (copine) *m., f. fam.* friend, pal
corde *f.* rope
cordialement *adv.* cordially
cordialité *f.* cordiality
coriandre *f.* coriander (15)
corps *m.* body (9); **Corps de la paix** Peace Corps; **extrémité** (*m.*) **du corps** limb; **partie** (*f.*) **du corps** part of the body
correct(e) *adj.* correct
correspondance *f.* correspondence; transfer, change (of trains); **faire/prendre, une correspondance** to transfer (14)
correspondant(e) *m., f.* correspondent
correspondre to correspond
corse *adj.* Corsican; **Corse** *m., f.* Corsican (*person*)
costume *m.* man's suit (6)
costumier/ière *m., f.* wardrobe-keeper
côte *f.* coast (17)
côté *m.* side; **à côté de** beside (3); **d'un côté** on the one hand
coton *m.* cotton
coucher to put to bed; **se coucher** to go to bed (9)
couler to flow; **avoir le nez qui coule** to have a runny nose (9)
couleur *f.* color
couloir *m.* hallway; **siège** (*m.*) **couloir** aisle seat (14)
country *f.* country music (21)
coup *m.* blow; **coup de soleil** sunburn; **coup de téléphone** telephone call; **tout à coup** suddenly
couper to cut
couple *m.* couple
cour *f.* courtyard
courant *m.* current; **courant d'air** breeze, draft; **tenir au courant** to keep up to date
courge *f.* squash (15)
courgette *f.* zucchini (15)
courir (*p.p.* **couru**) *irreg.* to run; **le bruit court** rumor has it
courrier *m.* mail; **courrier des lecteurs** letters to the editor (12); **courrier électronique** e-mail (13)
cours *m.* class; course (1); **au cours de** throughout (*time*) (20); **au cours des siècles** through the centuries; **échouer à un cours** to fail a course (13); **quels cours est-ce que vous suivez (tu suis)?** what courses are you taking? (13); **sécher un cours** to cut a class (13)

course *f.* errand; **course à pied** running race (10); **faire les courses** to do errands (5)
court(e) *adj.* short (22)
couscous *m.* couscous (15); **grains** (*m. pl.*) **de couscous** grains of couscous (15)
cousin(e) *m., f.* cousin (4)
coûter to cost; **combien est-ce que ça coûte?** how much does it cost?
couteau *m.* knife (8)
couture *f.* sewing; **haute couture** high fashion
couvert(e) *adj.* covered; **le ciel est couvert** the sky is cloudy
couvrir (*like* **ouvrir**) *irreg.* to cover (15)
craie *f.* chalk (1)
cravate *f.* tie (6)
crayon *m.* pencil (P)
création *f.* creation
crédit *m.* credit; **carte** (*f.*) **de crédit** credit card (6)
créer to create
crème *f.* cream (7)
crémerie *f.* dairy store (7)
créole *adj.* creole
crêpe *f.* crepe
crever (je crève) *fam.* to die
crevettes *f. pl.* shrimp (7)
criée *f.* auction
crier to shout, yell; **crier au scandale** to call it a scandal
crise *f.* attack; **crise cardiaque** heart attack; **crise de foie** queasy feeling
critère *m.* criteria
critique *m., f.* critic; *f.* criticism
critiquer to criticize
crocodile *m.* crocodile
croire (*p.p.* **cru**) *irreg.* to believe (10); **croire à** to believe in (*s.th.*); **il faut croire** it looks as if, it seems like it
croiser to cross; **mots** (*m. pl.*) **croisés** crossword puzzle (12); **se croiser les bras** to cross one's arms
croissant *m.* croissant, crescent roll (8)
croustillant(e) *adj.* crusty
crudités *f. pl.* raw vegetables
cruel(le) *adj.* cruel
cueillir *irreg.* to pick, collect (*flowers*) (16)
cuillère *f.* spoon (8)
cuir *m.* leather
cuire to cook; **faire cuire à la vapeur** to steam (15); **faire cuire au four** to bake (15)
cuisine *f.* food; kitchen (5); **faire la cuisine** to cook (5)
cuisiner to cook
cuisinier/ière *m., f.* cook (11)
cuisinière *f.* stove (5)
cuisson *f.* cooking; **méthodes** (*f. pl.*) **de cuisson** cooking methods
culinaire *adj.* culinary
culpabilité *f.* guilt
cultiver to cultivate, grow, raise (18)
culture *f.* culture
culturel(le) *adj.* cultural; **manifestation** (*f.*) **culturelle** cultural event (21)
curieux/euse *adj.* curious
curriculum vitæ *m.* resumé, CV
curry *m.* curry (15)
cybercafé *m.* cybercafe
cycliste *m., f.* cyclist
cynique *adj.* cynical

d'abord *adv.* first, first of all, at first (10)
d'accord *interj.* okay, agreed (2); **d'accord?** okay? (3); **je suis d'accord** I agree (2)
d'ailleurs *adv.* moreover, besides
dame *f.* lady
dangereux/euse *adj.* dangerous
dans *prep.* in (P); within; **dans cinq ans** in five years; **dans la rue...** on . . . Street (3)
danser to dance
danseur/euse *m., f.* dancer
date *f.* date (*time*)
dater de to date from
daube *f.*; **daube de veau** veal stew
de *prep.* of; from (P); **de... à** from . . . to (5); **de l'après-midi** in the afternoon (5); **de nouveau** again; **de plus en plus** more and more; **de temps en temps** from time to time (10)
débarquement *m.* landing
débarquer to land
débat *m.* debate
début *m.* beginning; **au début (de)** in/at the beginning (of)
décembre *m.* December (4)
déception *f.* disappointment
décerner to award
décevoir (*p.p.* **déçu**) *irreg.* to disappoint
déchirer to tear up
décider (de) to decide (to) (18)
décision *f.* decision; **prendre une décision** to make a decision (7)
déclaration *f.* declaration
déclarer to declare
déclin *m.* decline
décliner to decline
décolleté: en décolleté in low-cut clothing (22)
décolonisation *f.* decolonization
déconseiller to advise against (14)
décor *m.* decor; (stage) set
découper to cut (up)
découragé(e) *adj.* discouraged
découvrir (*like* **ouvrir**) *irreg.* to discover (15)
décrire (*like* **écrire**) *irreg.* to describe (12)
décrocher to pick up (*the telephone receiver*) (13)
décroissant(e) *adj.* descending
dedans *adv.* inside (it)
défaite *f.* defeat
défaitiste *adj.* defeatist
défaut *m.* fault (*character*)
défendre to defend
défilé *m.* parade
défiler to walk in procession, march
défini: article (*m.*) **défini** *Gram.* definite article
définition *f.* definition
degré *m.* degree
déjà *adv.* already; ever (10); yet
déjeuner to have lunch (8); *m.* lunch (8); **petit déjeuner** *m.* breakfast (8)
délabré(e) *adj.* dilapidated (20)
délicat(e) *adj.* delicate
délicieux/euse *adj.* delicious; **cela a l'air délicieux** that looks delicious
demain *adv.* tomorrow (10); **à demain** see you tomorrow (P)
demande *f.* demand
demander (si) to ask (if, whether) (7)
démarche *f.* step
déménagement *m.* move (*to a new residence*)
déménager to move (*to a new residence*)
démesuré(e) *adj.* excessive
demi(e) *adj.* half; **et demie** half-past (*the hour*) (5); **un an et demi** a year and a half
demi-kilo *m.* half-kilogram (7)
démissioner to quit, resign
démocrate *adj.* democrat
démonstratif/ive *adj.* demonstrative; **pronom (adjectif)** (*m.*) **démonstratif** *Gram.* demonstrative pronoun (adjective)
dent *f.* tooth (9); **se brosser les dents** to brush one's teeth (9)
dentelle *f.* lace
départ *m.* departure (14); **point** (*m.*) **du départ** starting point
département *m.* department; **département d'outre-mer (DOM)** overseas department
dépêcher: se dépêcher (de) to hurry up (*to do s.th.*) (9)
déplacer: se déplacer (nous nous déplaçons) to move around; to travel
déplaire (*like* **plaire**) *irreg.* to displease
dépliant *m.* brochure
déportation *f.* deportation
déposer to deposit; **déposer un chèque** to deposit a check (20)
dépression *f.* depression, low area
depuis *prep.* for; since (11); **depuis combien de temps?** how long?; **depuis quand?** since when?; **depuis six ans** for the past six years
déranger (nous dérangeons) to disturb, bother

dernier/ière *m., f.; adj.* last (13); latter; **ces deux derniers** the latter two; **la semaine dernière** last week
dérouler: se dérouler to unfold, happen
derrière *adv.* in back of, behind (3)
désaccord *m.* disagreement
désagréable *adj.* unpleasant
descendre (de) to descend; to get down (*from s.th.*) (8); **descendre une rue** to go down a street (17)
description *f.* description
désert *m.* desert
déserter to desert
désertification *f.* desertification
désigner to designate
désinformation *f.* misinformation
désir *m.* wish, desire
désirer to want, desire (2)
désolé(e) *adj.* sorry (21)
désordre *m.* disorder; **en désordre** disorderly
dessert *m.* dessert (8)
desservir to serve
dessin *m.* drawing; **dessin** (*m.*) **animé** animated cartoon (12)
dessiné(e): bande (*f.*) **dessinée** comic strip (12)
dessiner to draw
dessous: au-dessous (de), en dessous (de) *prep.* below (3)
dessus: au-dessus (de), en dessus (de) *prep.* above, over (3)
déstabilisation *f.* destabilization
destination *f.* destination
destruction *f.* destruction
détail *m.* detail
déterminer to determine; to figure out
détester to detest, hate (2)
détruire (*like* **conduire**) *irreg.* to destroy (18)
deux *adj.* two (P)
deuxième *adj.* second (11)
deux-pièces *m.s.* one-bedroom apartment
devant *prep.* in front of (3)
développement *m.* development
développer: se développer to develop, expand
devenir (*like* **venir**) *irreg.* to become (3)
deviner to guess
devise *f.* motto
dévoiler to reveal
devoir (*p.p.* **dû**) *irreg.* to have to, must; to owe (9); *m.* homework; duty; **faire les devoirs** to do homework (5)
dévoué(e) *adj.* devoted
d'habitude *adv.* usually, normally (10); **comme d'habitude** as usual
diable *m.* devil
dialectal(e) *adj.* dialectal
dialecte *m.* dialect
dialogue *m.* dialogue
dictature *f.* dictatorship
dictionnaire *m.* dictionary (P)
dieu *m.* god
différence *f.* difference
différent(e) *adj.* different
différer (je diffère) (de) to differ (from)
difficile *adj.* difficult (2)
difficulté *f.* difficulty
diffusé(e) *adj.* broadcast
diffusion *f.* broadcasting
digestif/ive *adj.* digestive
dignement *adv.* with dignity (22)
diligemment *adv.* diligently
dimanche *m.* Sunday (4)
dimension *f.* dimension, size
diminuer to diminish
dîner to dine, eat dinner (2); *m.* dinner (8)
dingue *adj., fam.* crazy
dinosaure *m.* dinosaur
diplôme *m.* diploma (13)
dire (*p.p.* **dit**) *irreg.* to tell; to say (12); **c'est-à-dire** that is to say; **dire à quelqu'un** to tell someone; **vouloir dire** to mean (6)
direct(e) *adj.* direct; **pronom** (*m.*) **complément d'object direct** *Gram.* direct object pronoun
directeur/trice *m., f.* director, manager
direction *f.* direction (14)
discothèque *f.* discotheque
discours *m.* discourse, speech; **discours direct (indirect)** *Gram.* direct (indirect) speech
discret/ète *adj.* discreet; reserved (12)
discussion *f.* discussion
discuter to discuss (13)
disparaître (*like* **connaître**) *irreg.* to disappear (13)
disparition *f.* disappearance
disponible *adj.* available
dispute *f.* dispute
disputer: se disputer to argue (9)
disque *m.* record; **disques compacts** compact disks
distant(e) *adj.* distant
distinct(e) *adj.* distinct; separate
distinguer to distinguish, tell apart
distractions *f. pl.* leisure activities (10); entertainment, amusement
distribuer to distribute
distributeur (*m.*) **automatique** (ticket) vending machine
divers(e) *adj.* various; diverse (17)
diversité *f.* diversity
diviser to divide; **se diviser (en)** to divide / be divided (into)
division *f.* division
divorce *m.* divorce
divorcé(e) *adj.* divorced (4)
divorcer (nous divorçons) to get a divorce (12)
dix *adj.* ten (P); **dix-huit** eighteen (P); **dix-neuf** nineteen (P); **dix-sept** seventeen (P)
dixième *adj.* tenth (11)
doctorat *m.* doctorate (13); **thèse** (*m.*) **de doctorat** doctoral dissertation
document *m.* document
documentaire *m.* documentary (12)
domaine *m.* domain, field
dôme *m.* dome
domicile *m.* domicile, residence; **sans domicile fixe** homeless
domination *f.* domination
dominer to dominate
dommage *m.*: **il est dommage que** it's too bad that (21)
dompter to overcome
donc *conj.* therefore; thus; so
donner to give (2); **donner des conseils** to give advice; **donner sur (le port)** to have a view of, overlook (the port) (20)
dont *pron.* whose, of which; including
dormir (je dors) *irreg.* to sleep (8)
dos *m.* back (9); **sac** (*m.*) **à dos** backpack (P)
dossier *m.* resumé; papers
douane *f.* customs; **passer la douane** to go through customs (14)
douanier/ière *m., f.* customs officer
double *adj.* double
doublé(e) *adj.* dubbed; **film** (*m.*) **doublé** dubbed film
douche *f.* shower; **douche au jet** high-pressure shower
doué(e) *adj.* talented, gifted
douleur *f.* ache, pain (9)
doute *m.* doubt; **sans doute** probably, no doubt; **sans aucun doute** without a doubt
douter que to doubt that (21)
douteux/euse *adj.* doubtful (21)
doux (douce) *adj.* gentle (12); soft; sweet; **doux mots** (*m. pl.*) **d'amour** sweet nothings; **il fait doux** it's mild (weather) out (10); **médecine** (*f.*) **douce** alternative medicine
douzaine (de) *f.* dozen (of) (7)
douze *adj.* twelve (P)
dragueur *m.* flirt
dramatique *adj.* dramatic; **arts** (*m. pl.*) **dramatiques** performing arts
drame *m.* drama; **psycho-drame** psychological drama
droit *m.* law (13); (*legal*) right
droit(e) *adj.* right; straight; **tout droit** *adv.* straight ahead (17)
droite *f.* right (side), right-hand side; **à droite** to/on the right (17)

drôle *adj.* odd; comical, funny; **drôle d'idée** *f.* odd idea
du (de la) *art. Gram.* some (7); **du matin** in the morning (5); **du soir** in the evening (5)
dû (due) à owing to
duo *m.* duet
dupé(e) *adj.* duped
dur(e) *adj.* hard; **œuf** (*m.*) **dur mayonnaise** hard-boiled egg with mayonnaise (8)
durant *prep.* during
durer to last
dynamique *adj.* dynamic (2)

eau *f.* water (7); **eau de source** spring water; **eau minérale gazeuse (plate)** carbonated (noncarbonated, flat) mineral water (7); **l'eau t'en viendra à la bouche** your mouth will water
eaux *f. pl.* bodies of water
ébahi(e) *adj.* dumbfounded
ébéniste *m., f.* cabinet maker
écart *m.*: **à l'écart de** apart from (22)
écarter to set aside
échange *m.* exchange
échappement *m.* exhaust; **gaz** (*m.*) **d'échappement** exhaust fumes; **pot** (*m.*) **d'échappement** exhaust pipe
échapper: s'échapper to escape (19)
écharpe *f.* scarf (6)
échouer to fail (13); **échouer à un cours (à un examen)** to fail a course (an exam) (13)
éclair *m.* eclair (*pastry*)
éclairagiste *m., f.* lighting engineer
éclaircir to shed light on
école *f.* (elementary) school (1); **école maternelle** preschool, nursery school; **école primaire** elementary school
écologie *f.* ecology
écologique *adj.* ecological
écologiste *m., f.* ecologist; *adj.* ecological
économe *adj.* thrifty, economical
économie *f.* economy; **économie de gestion** business economics (13)
économique *adj.* economic
écouter to listen (to); **écouter la radio** to listen to the radio (2)
écran *m.* screen (*film, computer*) (2); **petit écran** television
écrire (*p.p.* **écrit**) *irreg.* to write (12); **comment s'écrit... ?** how do you spell . . . ?
écrit *m.* written examination
écriture *f.* penmanship (1)
écrivain (femme écrivain) *m., f.* writer (11)
édicter to enact
édifice *m.* building
éditeur/trice *m., f.* publisher
édition *f.* edition
éditorial *m.* editorial (12)
éducatif/ive *adj.* educational
éducation *f.* training
effet *m.* effect; **effet de serre** greenhouse effect (18)
efficace *adj.* effective; efficient (18)
effort *m.* effort; **faire un effort** to try, make an effort
égal(e) *adj.* equal
égalité *f.* equality
église *f.* church (17)
égocentrique *adj.* self-centered
égoïsme *m.* selfishness
égoïste *adj.* selfish; egotistical
élection *f.* election
électricité *f.* electricity; **panne** (*f.*) **d'électricité** power outage
électrique *adj.* electric; **genie** (*f.*) **électrique** electrical engineering (13); **plaque** (*f.*) **électrique** burner (*on a stove*)
électronique *adj.* electronic; **boîte** (*f.*) **aux lettres électronique** electronic mailbox (13); **courrier** (*m.*) **électronique** e-mail (13); **message** (*m.*) **électronique** e-mail message
électrostatique *adj.* electrostatic
élégant(e) *adv.* elegant (12)
élément *m.* element
élémentaire *adj.* elementary
éléphant *m.* elephant
élevage *m.* animal breeding (18)
élève *m., f.* pupil (1)
élevé(e) *adj.* high
élision *f., Gram.* elision
élite *f.* elite
éloigner: s'éloigner to walk off, move away
elle *pron.* she, it; her (1, 3); **elle-même** herself
elles *pron.* they; them (1, 3)
émanciper: s'émanciper to become independent
embarquement *m.*: **porte** (*f.*) **d'embarquement** (*airport*) gate (14)
embauche: entretien (*m.*) **d'embauche** job interview
embaucher to hire
embellissant(e) *adj.* flattering
embêté(e) *adj.* upset
embouteillage *m.* traffic jam (14)
embrasser: s'embrasser to kiss (each other) (9)
émission *f.* program (*television*) (2)
émotion *f.* emotion
empêcher to hinder, prevent
empereur *m.* emperor
empire *m.* empire
emploi *m.* work; employment; job (11); **emploi à mi-temps** part-time job; **mode** (*f.*) **d'emploi** directions for use
employé(e) *m., f.* employee; *adj.* employed; **employé(e) de fast-food** fast-food worker (11)
employer to employ; to use (6); **s'employer** to be used
emprunter to borrow
en *prep.* in; by; while; *pron.* of/from it/them/there; some; any (15); **en avance** early (5); **en bonne (pleine) forme** in good (great) shape; feeling good (9); **en décolleté** in low-cut clothing (22); **en espèces** in cash (6); **en face de** opposite, facing (3); **en plein air** outdoors (16); **en plus** in addition; **en réalité** in fact, actually; **en retard** late (5); **en solde** on sale; **en train** by train; **être en train de** to be in the process of; **en vacances** on vacation (16)
enchaîner: s'enchaîner to be linked
enchanté(e) *adj.* delighted; it's nice to meet you (P)
encore *adv.* again; still (10); more; **encore une fois** once again; **ne... pas encore** not yet (1)
encourager (nous encourageons) to encourage (6)
endormir: s'endormir (*like* **dormir**) *irreg.* to fall asleep (9)
endroit *m.* place, location (14)
énergie *f.* energy
enfance *f.* childhood (12)
enfant *m., f.* child (1)
enfin *adv.* at last, finally (10); *interj.* well; in short (10)
engager (nous engageons) to hire (20)
ennemi(e) *m., f.* enemy
ennuyeux/euse *adj.* boring (2); annoying, tiresome
enquête *f.* investigation; survey
enregistrer to register, check (in) (14); **enregister une valise** to check a suitcase (14)
enseignement *m.* teaching, education (13); **enseignement des langues étrangères** foreign language teaching (13); **enseignement secondaire** secondary school teaching (13); **enseignement supérieur** higher education
enseigner to teach
ensemble *adv.* together (7); *m.* collection, group (17)
ensuite *adv.* next, then (10)
entendre to hear (8); **s'entendre (bien, mal) (avec)** to get along (well, badly) (with) (9)
enterrement *m.* burial (12)

enterrer to bury
enthousiasme *m.* enthusiasm
enthousiaste *adj.* enthusiastic
entier/ière *adj.* entire, whole
entraîner: s'entraîner to train, be in training
entre *prep.* between (3); among
entrée *f.* first course (*meal*) (8); entrance (*to a building*)
entreposer to warehouse, store
entreprise *f.* business
entrer to enter (11)
entretien *m.*: **entretien d'embauche** job interview
envahir to invade
enveloppe *f.* envelope (13)
envers *prep.* toward
envie *f.*: **avoir envie de** to feel like, want (4)
environ *adj.* about
environnement *m.* environment (18)
environs *m., f.* surroundings
envisager to envisage, imagine
envoyer (j'envoie) to send (6)
épais(e) *adj.* thick
épaule *f.* shoulder (9)
épice *f.* spice (15); **quatre-épices** *m., f. s.* allspice
épicé(e) *adj.* spicy
épicerie *f.* grocery store (7)
épicier/ière *m., f.* grocer (7)
épilogue *m.* epilogue
épisode *m.* episode
éponge *f.* sponge; blackboard eraser (1)
époque *f.* period; era; **à l'époque** at that time
épouser to marry
époux (épouse) *m., f.* husband (wife); **ex-époux (ex-épouse)** ex-husband (ex-wife)
équipe *f.* team (16)
équipement *m.* equipment
équiper to equip
équivalent(e) *m.* equivalent
escalade *f.*: **faire de l'escalade** to go rock climbing (16)
escalier *m.* flight of stairs
escargot *m.* snail
esclavage *m.* slavery
esclave *m., f.* slave
espace *m.* space; venue
Espagne *f.* Spain (3); **châteaux** (*m. pl.*) **en Espagne** castles in the air
espagnol(e) *adj.* Spanish (3); **Espagnol(e)** *m., f.* Spaniard
espèce *f.*: **en espèces** in cash (6)
espérer (j'espère) to hope (6)
espoir *m.* hope
esprit *m.* spirit; mind; **état** (*m.*) **d'esprit** state of mind; **ouvert(e) d'esprit** open-minded
essai *m.* essay, composition
essayer (j'essaie) to try (6)
essence *f.* gasoline (18)
essentiel(le) *adj.* essential (20)
est *m.* east
esthéthique *adj.* esthetic
estival(e) *adj.* summertime
estomac *m.* stomach (9)
et *conj.* and (P); **et demi(e)** half-past (*the hour*) (5); **et quart** quarter past (*the hour*) (5); **et toi?** (*fam. s.*) and you? (P); **et vous?** (*fam. pl.; formal s. and pl.*) and you? (P)
établir to establish; **s'établir** to be established, evolve
étage *m.* floor (*of building*); **premier étage** first floor (*above ground floor*)
étagère *f.* shelf
étape *f.* stage (12)
état *m.* state; **état civil** civil status; **état d'esprit** state of mind
États-Unis *m. pl.* United States (3)
été *m.* summer (10)
éternel(le) *adj.* eternal
étonné(e) *adj.* astonished, surprised (21)
étonnant(e) *adj.* amazing, surprising, shocking (22)
étrange *adj.* strange; odd
étranger/ère *adj.* foreign; unfamiliar *m., f.* foreigner; stranger; **à l'étranger** abroad; **langue** (*f.*) **étrangère** foreign language (13)
être (*p.p.* **été**) *irreg.* to be, **ce ne sont pas** these/those/they are not (P); **ce n'est pas** this/that/it is not (P); **c'est...** this/that/it is . . . (P); **c'est ca?** is that right? (3); **comment est/sont... ?** what is/are . . . like? (2); **est-ce... ?** is this/that . . . ? (P); **est-ce que... ?** is it so (*true*) that . . . ? (1); **il est (cinq) heures** it is (five) o'clock (5); **être de passage** to be passing through; **être de retour** to be back
étroit(e) *adj.* narrow (20)
études *f. pl.* studies (1); **faire des études en** to major in (13)
étudiant(e) *adj.* (male/female) university student (P)
étudier to study (2)
euh... *interj.* uh . . .
euro *m.* euro
Europe *f.* Europe (14)
européen(ne) *adj.* European
eux *pron., m. pl.* them (3); **eux-mêmes** themselves
évaluer to evaluate
événement *m.* event (12)
éventuel(e) *adj.* possible
évidemment *adv.* evidently, obviously
évident(e) *adj.* evident (12)
évier *m.* (kitchen) sink
éviter to avoid
évoluer to evolve
exact(e) *adj.* exact, accurate (12)
exagérer (j'exagère) to exaggerate
examen (*fam.* **exam**) examination, test; **échouer à un examen** to fail an exam (13); **passer un examen** to take an exam (13); **réussir à un examen** to pass a test (11)
examiner to examine
excellent(e) *adj.* excellent
exceptionnel(le) *adj.* exceptional
excès *m.* excess
exclusion *f.* exclusion; **mesure** (*f.*) **d'exclusion** segregation policy
excursion *f.* excursion, trip
excuser: s'excuser to excuse oneself; to apologize; **excusez-moi** excuse me
exemple *m.* example; **par exemple** for example
ex-époux (ex-épouse) *m., f.* ex-husband (ex-wife)
exercer (nous exerçons) to practice (*a profession*)
exiger (nous exigeons) to demand, require (20)
exister to exist
exode *m.* exodus
exotique *adj.* exotic
expansion *f.* expansion
expérience *f.* experience; experiment
expérimental(e) *adj.* experimental
expert(e) *adj.* expert
explication *f.* explanation
expliquer to explain
exploiter to exploit
explorer to explore
exposer to exhibit
exposition (*f.*) **d'art** art exhibit (10)
express *adj. inv.* express; **transport** (*m.*) **express régional** regional express train
expression *f.* expression
exprimer to express; **s'exprimer** to express oneself
extermination *f.*: **camp** (*m.*) **d'extermination** concentration camp
exterminer to exterminate
extrait *m.* extract
extraordinaire *adj.* extraordinary
extra-terrestre *m., f.* extraterrestrial
extraverti(e) *adj.* extroverted
extrème *adj.* extreme
extrémité *f.* extremity; **extrémité du corps** limb

fable *f.* fable
fabriquer to build
fabuleux/euse *adj.* fabulous; amazing

façade *f.* façade; side
face *f.* side; **en face de** opposite, facing (3); **face à** in the face of, facing; **faire face à** to face, confront
fâché(e) *adj.* angry (2)
fâcher: se fâcher (contre) to become angry (with) (9)
facile *adj.* easy (2)
façon *f.* manner, way; **à sa façon** in his (her) own way; **de façon sérieuse** in a serious way; **de toute façon** in any case
facteur *m.* letter carrier
faculté (*fam.* **fac**) *f.* faculty (*university department for a specific field of study*)
faible *adj.* weak (18); low
faim *m.* hunger; **avoir faim** to be hungry (4)
faire (*p.p.* **fait**) *irreg.* to make; to do (5); **faire allusion** to make reference to; **faire attention (à)** to pay attention (to) (5); **faire beau (il fait beau)** to be nice out (10); **faire bouillir** to boil (15); **faire chaud (il fait chaud)** to be hot out (10); **faire confiance à** to trust (*s.o.*); **faire cuire à la vapeur** to steam (15); **faire cuire au four** to bake (15); **faire de la photographie** to take photographs (16); **faire de la planche à voile** to windsurf (16); **faire de la spéléologie** to go spelunking (explore caves) (16); **faire de la voile** to go sailing (16); **faire de l'escalade** to go rock climbing (16); **faire des achats** to make purchases; **faire des bêtises** to make mistakes, do silly things; **faire des études (en)** to major in (13); **faire des recherches** to do research; **faire doux (il fait doux)** to be mild out (10); **faire du bateau** to go sailing; **faire du camping** to go camping (16); **faire du canoë** to go canoeing (16); **faire du jogging** to go jogging; **faire du parapente** to hang glide (16); **faire du patin à glace** to go ice skating (16); **faire du roller** to roller-skate; **faire du shopping** to go shopping (5); **faire du ski** to go skiing (16); **faire du ski de fond** to cross-country ski (16); **faire du ski nautique** to waterski (16); **faire du soleil (il fait du soleil)** it's sunny out (10); **faire du sport** to play sports; **faire du surf de neige** to snowboard (16); **faire du tourisme** to go sightseeing; **faire du tricot** to knit; **faire du vélo (du VTT)** to bike (mountain bike) (16); **faire du vent (il fait du vent)** to be windy (10); **faire face à** to face, confront; **faire frais (il fait frais)** to be chilly (10); **faire frire** to fry (15); **faire froid (il fait froid)** to be cold out (10); **faire la connaissance** to meet (*a new person*) (5); **faire la cuisine** to cook (5); **faire la fête** to have a party (5); **faire la lessive** to do the laundry (5); **faire la queue** to stand in line (5); **faire la vaisselle** to do the dishes (5); **faire le lit** to make the bed (5); **faire le ménage** to do housework (5); **faire les courses** to run errands (5); **faire les devoirs** to do homework (5); **faire mauvais (il fait mauvais)** to be bad weather (10); **faire partie de** to be a part of; to belong to; **faire peur (à)** to frighten; **faire sa toilette** to wash up; **faire un chèque** to write a check (20); **faire une correspondance** to transfer (14); **faire un effort** to try, make an effort; **faire une promenade** to take a walk (5); **faire une randonnée** to hike, go hiking (16); **faire un pique-nique** to have a picnic (16); **faire un reportage** to prepare/give a report (*TV*); **faire un stage** to do an internship; **faire un voyage** to take a trip (5); **je ne sais pas quoi faire** I don't know what to do; **se faire des amis** to make friends; **se faire mal (à)** to hurt (a part of one's body) (9)
fait *m.* fact, **tout à fait** completely
falloir (*p.p.* **fallu**) *irreg.* to be necessary; **il fallait** it was necessary to; **il faut** it is necessary (to); one must, one should (20); **il ne faut pas** one must (should) not (20)
familial(e) *adj.* relating to the family
familier/ière *adj.* familiar
famille *f.* family
famine *f.* famine
fanatique: fanatique (*m., f.*) **du sport** sports fan (10)
fantaisie *f.* fantasy
fantaisiste *adj.* fanciful
fantastique *adj.* fantastic; **c'est fantastique** it's fantastic; **film** (*m.*) **fantastique** fantasy film
fascinant(e) *adj.* fascinating
fasciné(e) *adj.* fascinated
fast-food *m.* fast food (8)
fatal(e) (*pl.* **fatal(e)s**) *adj.* fatal
fatigué(e) *adj.* tired (2)
faut: il faut it is necessary (to); one must, one should (20)
faute *f.* fault; mistake
fauteuil *m.* armchair (5)
faux (fausse) *adj.* false (2); **c'est faux** that's wrong (2); **faux ami** *m.* false cognate; **vrai ou faux?** true or false?
favori(te) *adj.* favorite
favoriser to favor
fax *m.* fax
félicitations *f. pl.* congratulations
féliciter to congratulate
féminin(e) *adj.* feminine
femme *f.* woman (P); wife (4); **femme écrivain** (woman) writer (11); **femme ingénieur** (woman) engineer (11); **femme médecin** (woman) doctor (9); **femme peintre** (woman) painter (11); **femme poète** (woman) poet (21); **femme sculpteur** woman sculptor
fenêtre *f.* window (1); **siège** (*m.*) **fenêtre** window seat (14)
fer *m.* iron; **chemin** (*m.*) **de fer** railroad; **voie** (*f.*) **de chemin de fer** railroad tracks (19)
férié(e) *adj.*: **jour** (*m.*) **férié** legal holiday (11)
ferme *f.* farm (18)
fermer to close (15)
fermier/ière *m., f.* farmer (18)
fertile *adj.* fertile
festival (*pl.* **festivals**) *m.* festival (16)
fête *f.* celebration; festival; Saint's day; party (11); **fête des mères** Mother's Day; **fête du travail** Labor Day (11); **faire la fête** to have a party (5); **fête nationale** national holiday (11)
feu *m.* traffic light; fire (17); **feux d'artifice** fireworks
feuille *f.* leaf; **feuille (de papier)** sheet (of paper) (13)
feuilleton *m.* soap opera (12)
février *m.* February (4)
fiançailles *f. pl.* engagement
fiancer: se fiancer (nous nous fiançons) to get engaged
ficher: je m'en fiche *fam.* I don't care
fiction *f.* fiction
fier (fière) *adj.* proud (18)
fièvre *f.* fever (9)
figurer (dans) to figure (in)
fille *f.* girl; daughter (4); **jeune fille** girl (12); unmarried woman; **petite fille** granddaughter (4)
filleul *m.* godson
film *m.* film (P)
filmer to film
fils *m.* son (4); **fils unique** only son; **petit-fils** *m.* grandson (4)
fixe *adj.*: **sans domicile fixe** homeless
fin *f.* end; **en fin de journée** at the end of the day; **mettre fin à** to put an end to
finalement *adv.* finally
financer (nous finançons) to finance
financier/ière *adj.* financial
finir to finish (11)
flamand(e) *adj.* Flemish; **Flamand(e)** *m., f.* Flemish person; **carbonnade** (*f.*) **flamande** Flemish regional stew
flamenco *m.* flamenco
fleur *f.* flower (16)

fleuve *m.* large river (17)
flexible *adj.* flexible
flipper *m.*: **jouer au flipper** to play pinball
flirter to flirt
flou(e) *adj.* blurry
flûte *f.* flute
foie *m.* liver; **crise** (*f.*) **de foie** queasy feeling
fois *f.* time (*occasion*) (5); **encore une fois** once again
folie *f.* madness
follement *adv.* madly, wildly
fonction *f.* function
fonctionnaire *m., f.* civil servant, government worker (11)
fonctionnel(le) *adj.* functional, useful
fonctionner to function
fond *m.* bottom; back; background; **à fond** in depth; **au fond** basically; **faire du ski de fond** to cross-country ski (16)
fontaine *f.* fountain
football (*fam.* **foot**) *m.* soccer (10); **football américain** football (10); **match** (*m.*) **de foot** soccer match (10)
footing *m.* jogging, running (10)
forces *f. pl.* (armed) forces
forêt *f.* forest (17)
formation *f.* education, training; upbringing
forme *f.* form; **en bonne (pleine) forme** in good (great) shape; feeling good (9)
former to train; to form (20)
formidable *adj.* terrific, wonderful (2)
formule *f.* formula
formuler to formulate
fort(e) *adj.* strong; significant (18); *adv.* with strength, with effort (19); **frapper plus fort** to strike harder
forum *m.* forum
fou (folle) *adj.* crazy, mad (12)
foulard *m.* lightweight scarf (6)
four *m.* oven (5); **faire cuire au four** to bake (15); **four à micro-ondes** microwave oven (5)
fourchette *f.* fork (8)
fragile *adj.* fragile
frais (fraîche) *adj.* cool; fresh; **il fait frais** it's chilly out (10)
franc (franche) *adj.* frank (12)
français(e) *adj.* French (1); *m.* French (*language*) (1); **Français(e)** *m., f.* French person (3)
France *f.* France (3)
francophone *adj.* French-speaking (3); **monde** (*m.*) **francophone** French-speaking world
frapper to strike, hit (19); **frapper plus fort** to strike harder
fraternité *f.* brotherhood
fréquence *f.* frequency
fréquent(e) *adj.* frequent
fréquenter to frequent
frère *m.* brother (4); **beau-frère** stepbrother, brother-in-law (4)
frigo *m., fam.* fridge, refrigerator (5)
frire: faire (*irreg.*) **frire** to fry (15)
Frisbee *m.* Frisbee (16)
frites *f. pl.* French fries (8); **poulet-frites** *m.* chicken with French fries (8); **steak-frites** *m.* steak with French fries
froid *m.* cold; **avoir froid** to feel cold (4); **il fait froid** it's cold out (10)
fromage *m.* cheese (7)
Front national *m.* National Front (*political party*)
frontière *f.* border
fruit *m.* fruit (7); **fruits de mer** seafood (7)
fumer to smoke
fumeurs: wagon (*m.*) **fumeurs (non-fumeurs)** smoking (nonsmoking) train car (14)
furieux/euse *adj.* furious (21)
fusil *m.* gun
fusiller to execute (somebody) by shooting (19)
futur(e) *adj.* future; **futur** *m., Gram.* future tense; **futur proche** *Gram.* near future

gagner to earn; to win
gai(e) *adj.* cheerful, happy
galerie *f.* (art) gallery (2)
garage *m.* garage
garagiste *m., f.* garage owner
garçon *m.* boy (12)
garde-malade *m., f.* nurse's aide (11)
garder to guard; to keep (19)
gardien(ne) *m., f.* attendant; **gardien(ne) d'immeuble** building superintendent (11)
gare *f.* train station (14)
garer to park
gastronomie *f.* gastronomy
gastronomique *adj.* gastronomical
gauche *adj.* left; *f.* left (side), left-hand side; **à gauche** to/on the left (17)
gaz *m.* gas; **gaz d'échappement** exhaust fumes
gazeux/euse *adj.* carbonated; **eau** (*f.*) **minerale gazeuse** carbonated mineral water (7)
général(e) *adj.* general; **en général** in general
générale *f.* dress rehearsal
généralisation *f.* generalization
généraliser to generalize
génération *f.* generation
généreux/euse *adj.* generous
générique *adj.* generic
génial(e) *adj.* brilliant, inspired; fantastic
génie *m.* engineering (13); **génie chimique (électrique, industriele, mécanique)** chemical (electrical, industrial, mechanical) engineering (13)
genou *m.* knee (9)
genre *m.* type
gens *m. pl.* people (13)
gentil(le) *adj.* nice, kind; well-behaved (2)
gentilhomme *m.* gentleman
gentillesse *f.* kindness
géographie *f.* geography (1)
géographique *adj.* geographical
germanique *adj.* Germanic
gestapo *f.* Gestapo
gestion *f.* management (11); **économie** (*f.*) **de gestion** business economics (13)
gifle *m.* slap
gingembre *m.* ginger (15)
glace *f.* ice cream (8); ice; **faire du patin à glace** to ice skate (16)
gloire *f.* glory
golf *m.* golf (16); **mini-golf** *m.* miniature golf
gorge *f.* throat (9); **avoir mal à la gorge** to have a sore throat (9)
goût *m.* taste
goûter to taste
goutte *f.* little drop
gouvernement *m.* government
grâce à *prep.* thanks to
grain *m.* grain; **grains de couscous** couscous grains (15)
graine *f.* seed
gramme *m.* gram
grand(e) *adj.* large, big; tall (2); **grandes vacances** *f. pl.* summer vacation; **grand magasin** *m.* department store; **grand-mère** *f.* grandmother (4); **grand-père** *m.* grandfather (4); **grands-parents** *m. pl.* grandparents; **train** (*m.*) **à grande vitesse (TGV)** French high-speed train (14)
grange *f.* granary, barn (18)
gras(se) *adj.* fatty; thick; **en caractères** (*m. pl.*) **gras** in boldface type; **matières** (*f. pl.*) **grasses** (*meat*) fat
gratuitement *adv.* for free
grave *adj.* serious, grave; **accent** (*m.*) **grave** *Gram.* grave accent (**è**)
graveur *m.* engraver
gravité *f.* gravity
greffe *f.* graft; **greffe du cœur** heart transplant
grièvement *adv.* gravely
grippe *f.* flu, influenza (9)
gris(e) *adj.* grey (6)
grisé(e) *adj.* intoxicated
grommeller (nous grommelons) to grumble
gronder to scold

gros(se) *adj.* large, big; fat; **gros titre** *m.* headline (12)
grotte *f.* cave
groupe *m.* group
gruyère *m.* Gruyere (Swiss) cheese
guérir to cure; to heal
guerre *f.* war (8); **Deuxième Guerre mondiale** Second World War
guichet *m.* ticket window (14)
guide *m.* guidebook
guider to guide
guitare *f.* guitar (5)
guitariste *m., f.* guitar player
gymnase *m.* gymnasium (13)
gymnastique *adj.* gymnastic

habillé(e) *adj.* dressed; **mal (bien) habillé(e)** badly (well) dressed
habiller: s'habiller (en) to get dressed (in) (9)
habit *m.* clothing, dress
habitant(e) *m., f.* inhabitant (20)
habitation *f.* dwelling, residence; **habitation à loyer modéré (HLM)** low-income housing
habiter to live (in a place), reside (2)
habitude *f.* habit; **comme d'habitude** as usual; **d'habitude** usually, normally (10)
***haine** *f.* hatred
***haïr (je hais)** to hate
***halle** *f.* covered market
***hamburger** *m.* hamburger
***handicap** *m.* handicap
***Hannukah** *m.* Hannukah (11)
***haricot** *m.* bean; **haricots verts** green beans (7)
***hasard** *m.* chance; **au hasard** by chance, accidentally
***haut(e)** *adj.* high; **à haute voix** aloud **haute couture** *f.* high fashion; **haute technologie** *f.* high tech
***hauteur** *f.* elevation, height (17)
***hein?** *interj. fam.* eh?; all right?
***hélas** *interj.* alas
herbe *f.* grass; herb
héritage *m.* inheritance; heritage
hériter (de) to inherit (*s.th.*)
***héroïsme** *m.* heroism
hésiter (à) to hesitate (*to do s.th.*) (18)
heure *f.* hour; time (*on a clock*) (5); **à... heure(s)** at . . . o'clock (5); **à l'heure** on time (5); **à quelle heure?** at what time? (5); **à toute heure** at any time; **de bonne heure** early; **heures de pointe** rush hour (14); **il est... heure(s)** it is . . . o'clock (5); **kilomètres** (*m. pl.*) **à l'heure** kilometers per hour; **quelle heure est-il?** what time is it? (5)
heureux/euse *adj.* happy (2)
hier *adv.* yesterday (10)
***hiérarchie** *f.* hierarchy
***hiéroglyphe** *m.* hieroglyphic
***hip-hop** *m.* hip-hop music (21)
histoire *f.* story (P); history (1); **histoire naturelle** natural history
historien(ne) *m., f.* historian
historique *adj.* historical
hiver *m.* winter (10); **sports** (*m.*) **d'hiver** winter sports
hivernage *m.* rainy season
***hockey** *m.* hockey (16)
homéopathie *f.* homeopathy
homme *m.* man (P); **homme d'affaires** businessman
honnête *adj.* honest
honneur *m.* honor
***honte** *f.* shame; **avoir honte (de)** to be ashamed (of) (4)
hôpital *m.* hospital (9)
horaire *m.* schedule, timetable; **horaires d'ouverture** hours when open
horloge *f.* clock (1)
horreur *f.* horror; **avoir horreur de** to hate, detest; **j'ai horreur de** I can't stand
***hors (de)** *adj.* outside (of)
hospitalité *f.* hospitality
hostile *adj.* hostile
hôtel *m.* hotel
hôtesse *f.* hostess
huile *f.* oil (15); **huile d'olive (de sésame)** olive (sesame) oil (15)
***huit** eight (P)
***huitième** *adj.* eighth (11)
humain(e) *adj.* human
humeur *f.* mood; **de bonne (mauvaise) humeur** in a good (bad) mood
humide *adj.* humid
hymne *m.* hymn
hypertension (*f.*) **artérielle** high blood pressure
hypothèse *f.* hypothesis

ici *adv.* here (3)
icone *m.* computer icon (13)
idéal(e) *adj.* ideal
idéaliste *adj.* idealistic
idée *f.* idea; **drôle d'idée** odd idea
identification *f.* identification
identifier to identify
identité *f.* identity
idiot(e) *adj.* idiot
il *pron.* he, it (1); **il y a** there is / there are (*for counting*) (P); **il y a (dix ans)** (ten years) ago (10)
île *f.* island (17)
illustration *f.* illustration
illustrer to illustrate; to exemplify
ils *pron.* they (1); **ils vivent en union libre** they are living together (without marriage) (4)
image *f.* picture; image
imaginaire *adj.* imaginary
imagination *f.* imagination
imaginer to imagine
immangeable *adj.* uneatable, inedible
immédiat(e) *adj.* immediate (12)
immense *adj.* immense
immeuble *m.* apartment building (5); **gardien(ne)** (*m., f.*) **d'immeuble** building superintendant (11)
immigration *f.* immigration
immigré(e) *m., f.* immigrant (20)
immigrer to immigrate
imparfait *m., Gram.* imperfect (*verb tense*)
impatience *f.* impatience
impatient(e) *adj.* impatient
impatienter: s'impatienter to become impatient
impératif/ive *adj.* imperative; **impératif** *m., Gram.* imperative; command
impersonnel(le) *adj.* impersonal
implantation *f.* planting
impliquer to implicate
impoli(e) *adj.* impolite
importance *f.* importance
important(e) *adj.* important; big (20)
impossible *adj.* impossible (20)
impressionné(e) *adj.* impressed
impressionnisme *m.* impressionism
impressionniste *m., f.* impressionist
improvisation *f.* improvisation
improviste: à l'improviste *adv.* unexpectedly
impuissant(e) *adj.* helpless
impulsif/ive *adj.* impulsive
inactif/ive *adj.* inactive
incertain(e) *adj.* uncertain (21)
incertitude *f.* indecision
inciter to prompt
inclure (*p.p.* **inclu**) *irreg.* to include
incomparable *adj.* incomparable
incomplet/ète *adj.* incomplete
inconnu(e) *adj.* unknown
inconscient(e) (de) *adj.* unaware (of)
inconvénient *m.* inconvenience
incorporer to include
incrédule *adj.* incredulous; **d'un ton incrédule** incredulously
incrédulité *f.* disbelief
incroyable *adj.* unbelievable (21)
incrusté(e) *adj.* inlaid
Inde *f.* India (15)
indécis(e) *adj.* indecisive
indéfini(e) *adj.* indefinite; **article** (*m.*) **indéfini** *Gram.* indefinite article
indépendance *f.* independence

indépendant(e) *adj.* independent
indépendantiste *adj.* separatist
indicateur/trice *adj.*: **poteau** (*m.*) **indicateur** signpost
indicatif *m., Gram.* indicative (*verb tense*)
indice *m.* indication; **indices d'audience** ratings
indien(ne) *adj.* Indian (15); **Indien(e)** *m., f.* Indian (*person*)
indifférence *f.* indifference
indifférent(e) *adj.* indifferent
indiquer to show, indicate (17); **est-ce que vous pourriez m'indiquer le chemin pour aller à... ?** could you show me the way to . . . ? (17)
indirect(e) *adj.* indirect; **discours** (*m.*) **indirect** *Gram.* indirect speech; **pronom** (*m.*) **complément d'objet indirect** *Gram.* indirect object pronoun
indiscret/ète *adj.* indiscreet
indispensable *adj.* indispensable
industrie *f.* industry
industriel(le) *adj.* commercial; **genie** (*f.*) **industrielle** industrial engineering (13)
inférieur(e) *adj.* inferior
infiltrer to infiltrate
infinitif *m., Gram.* infinitive
infirmier/ière *m., f.* nurse (9)
inflation *f.* inflation
inflexible *adj.* inflexible
influence *f.* influence
influencer (nous influençons) to influence
information *f.* information; data
informations *f. pl.* news; news program (12)
informatique *f.* computer science (1); **réseau** (*m.*) **informatique** computer network
informer: s'informer to find out, become informed
ingénieur (femme ingénieur) *m., f.* engineer (11)
ingénieux/euse *adj.* ingenious
ingrédient *m.* ingredient
injuste *adj.* unjust, not right (20)
innocence *f.* innocence
innocent(e) *adj.* innocent
innovateur/trice *adj.* innovating
inquiet (inquiète) *adj.* anxious, worried (2)
inquiéter: s'inquiéter (de, pour) (je m'inquiète) to worry (about) (9)
inquiétude *f.* worry, anxiety
inscription *f.* inscription; writing
inscrire: s'inscrire (*like* **écrire**) *irreg.* to register
insigne *m.* badge, insignia
insistance *f.* insistence, tenacity
insister to insist
inspiration *f.* inspiration
inspirer to inspire
installer: s'installer to settle, set up (*house*)
instant *m.* instant, moment
institut *m.* institute; **institut de beauté** beauty parlor
instituteur/trice *m., f.* elementary school teacher (1)
instruction *f.* instruction, education
instrument *m.* (musical) instrument; **jouer d'un instrument** to play a musical instrument
intacte *adj.* intact
intégrant(e) *adj.* essential; **partie** (*f.*) **intégrante** essential/integral part
intégration *f.* integration
intellectuel(le) *adj.* intellectual (2)
intelligent(e) *adj.* intelligent
intensif/ive *adj.* intensive
intensifier: s'intensifier to intensify
interculturel(le) *adj.* intercultural
interdire (*like* **dire,** *but* **vous interdisez**) *irreg.* to forbid
interdit(e) *adj.* prohibited
intéressant(e) *adj.* interesting (2)
intéresser to interest; **s'intéresser à** to be interested in (9)
intérêt *m.* interest; concern; **sans intérêt** of no interest
intérieur(e) *adj.* interior; **intérieur** *m.* interior; **à l'intérieur des terres** in the center of the country
interjection *f., Gram.* interjection
intermédiaire *m.* intermediary
international(e) *adj.* international
internaute *m., f.* Internet user (13)
interne *adj.* internal
interpeller to call out to
interprétation *f.* interpretation
interprète *m., f.* interpreter (11)
interrogatif/ive *adj., Gram.* interrogative
interroger (nous interrogeons) to question
interrompre (*like* **rompre**) *irreg.* to interrupt
interruption *f.* interruption
interview *f.* interview
interviewer to interview
intime *adj.* intimate; personal; **journal** (*m.*) **intime** diary
intolérable *adj.* intolerable
intonation *f.* intonation
intoxiqué(e) *adj.* intoxicated
introduction *f.* introduction
introduire (*like* **conduire**) *irreg.* to introduce
intrus(e) *m., f.* intruder
inutile *adj.* useless, no use (20)
invasion *f.* invasion
inventer to invent
invention *f.* invention
inversion *f.* reversal
invitation *f.* invitation
inviter (à) to invite (*s.o.*) (to) (18)
invoquer to invoke, call upon
ironique *adj.* ironic
irrégulier/ière *adj., Gram.* irregular
irremplaçable *adj.* irreplaceable
irrité(e) *adj.* irritated
islamique *adj.* Islamic
isoler to isolate
Israël *m.* Israel (15)
israëlien(ne) *adj.* Israeli (15); **Israëlien(ne)** *m., f.* Israeli (*person*)
Italie *f.* Italy (15)
italien(ne) *adj.* Italian (15); **Italien(ne)** *m., f.* Italian (*person*)
italique *m.*: **en italique** in italic type
itinéraire *m.* itinerary

jamais *adv.* never; **jamais plus** never again; **ne... jamais** never, not ever (1)
jambe *f.* leg (9)
jambon *m.* ham (7)
janvier *m.* January (4)
Japon *m.* Japan (3)
japonais(e) *adj.* Japanese (3); **Japonais(e)** *m., f.* Japanese (*person*)
jardin *m.* garden (18); **jardin des plantes** botanical garden
jarret (*m.*) **de porc** ham hocks
jaune *adj.* yellow (6); **pages** (*f. pl.*) **jaunes** yellow pages
jazz *m.* jazz
je *pron.* I (1); **J'ai (vingt) ans** I'm (twenty) years old (4); **je m'appelle...** my name is . . . (P); **je ne sais pas** I don't know (P); **je (ne) suis (pas) d'accord** I (don't) agree (2); **je suppose** I suppose (3); **je voudrais** I would like (6)
jean *m. s.* jeans (6)
jeep *m.* jeep
jet *m.*: **douche** (*f.*) **au jet** high-pressure shower
jeter (je jette) to throw
jeu (*pl.* **jeux**) *m.* game (10); **jeu de rôle** role play
jeudi *m.* Thursday (4)
jeune *adj.* young; **jeune fille** *f.* girl (12); unmarried woman
jeûner to fast
jeunesse *f.* youth (12)
job *m.* job
Joconde: la Joconde *f.* Mona Lisa (*painting*)
jogging *m.* jogging (10); **faire du jogging** to go jogging; **piste** (*f.*) **de jogging** jogging trail (13)
joie *f.* joy; **joie de vivre** joy in living (20)

joindre (je joins, nous joignons) *irreg.* to join
joli(e) *adj.* pretty (2)
jouer to play (10); to act; **jouer à un sport/un jeu** to play a sport/game (10); **jouer d'un instrument** to play a musical instrument (10)
jouet *m.* toy
joueur/euse *m., f.* player
jour *m.* day (1); **carnet du jour** society column; **jour férié** legal holiday (11); **par jour** per day; **plat** (*m.*) **du jour** today's special; **quel jour sommes-nous?** what day is it today?; **tous les jours** every day (10)
journal (*pl.* **journaux**) *m.* newspaper (12); **journal intime** diary; **journal universitaire** college newspaper
journalisme *m.* journalism
journaliste *m., f.* journalist (2)
journée *f.* (*whole*) day; **bonne journée** have a good day; **en fin** (*f.*) **de journée** at the end of the day; **toute la journée** all day
jovien(ne) *m., f.* inhabitant of Jupiter
joyeux/euse *adj.* joyous, joyful (12)
judaïsme *m.* Judaism
judas *m.* peephole
judéo-arabe *adj.* Judeo-Arab
juge *m.* judge
jugement *m.* judgment
juif (juive) *adj.* Jewish
juillet *m.* July (4)
juin *m.* June (4)
jumeau (jumelle) *m., f.* twin
jupe *f.* skirt (6)
jus *m.* juice; **jus d'orange** orange juice (8)
jusque (jusqu'à, jusqu'en) *prep.* up to; as far as; until; **jusqu'à** until (10); **jusqu'à ce que** until (21)
juste *adj.* just; fair (20)
justice *f.* justice; **rendre justice à** to do justice to
justifier to justify

kilo *m.* kilogram (7); **demi-kilo** half kilogram (7)
kilomètre (km) *m.* kilometer; **kilomètres à l'heure** kilometers per hour
kinésithérapeute *m., f.* massage therapist
kinésithérapie *f.* massage therapy
kiosque *m.* kiosk

la (l') *art., f. s.* the (P); *pron., f. s.* her, it (9)
là *adv.* there (1); **là-bas** over there
laboratoire *m.* laboratory (P)
lac *m.* lake (17); **au bord d'un lac** on a lake shore
lâche *adj.* cowardly
laid(e) *adj.* ugly (2)
laine *f.* wool
laisser to leave (13); to allow (13)
laissez-passer *m.* security pass
lait *m.* milk (8); **café** (*m.*) **au lait** coffee with milk; **lait caillé** curdled milk (*similar to sour cream*)
laitier/ière *adj.* dairy; **produits** (*m. pl.*) **laitiers** dairy products
lampe *f.* lamp
lancer (nous lançons) to launch (6)
langage *m.* language, speech
langue *f.* language; **langue étrangère** foreign language (13); **langue seconde** second/foreign language
lapin *m.* rabbit (16)
large *adj.* wide (22)
larme *f.* tear; **au bord des larmes** on the verge of tears
latin(e) *adj.* Latin; **quartier** (*m.*) **latin** Latin quarter
lavabo *m.* bathroom sink (5)
lave-linge *m.* washing machine
laver: se laver to get washed, wash up (9); **se laver les cheveux (les mains)** to wash one's hair (hands)
lave-vaisselle *f.* dishwasher
le (l') *art., m. s.* the (P); *pron., m. s.* him, it (9)
leçon *f.* lesson (1)
lecteur *m.* reader; **courrier des lecteurs** letters to the editor (12); **lecteur de CD** CD player (5)
lecture *f.* reading (1)
légende *f.* caption
léger/ère *adj.* light (*weight*) (8)
légion (*f.*) **d'honneur** legion of honor
légume *m.* vegetable (7)
lendemain *m.* next day (13)
lent(e) *adj.* slow (12)
lentilles *f. pl.* lentils (15)
lequel (laquelle, lesquels, lesquelles) *pron.* who; whom; which
les *art., m., f., pl.* the (P); *pron., m., f., pl.* them (9)
lessive *f.* laundry; **faire la lessive** to do the laundry (5)
lettre *f.* letter (13); **boîte** (*f.*) **aux lettres electronique** electronic mailbox; **lettre d'amour** love letter
leur (*pl.* **leurs**) *adj.* their (4); **leur** *pron. m., f., pl.* to/for them (7); **le/la/les leur(s)** *pron.* theirs (22)
levain *m.* yeast
lever: se lever (je me lève) to get up (*out of bed*); to stand up (9)
lèvres *f. pl.* lips; **se maquiller les lèvres** to put on lipstick (9)
lexique *m.* glossary
liaison *f., Gram.* liaison
libéral(e) *adj.* liberal
libération *f.* liberation
libéré(e) *adj.* liberated
liberté *f.* liberty
librairie *f.* bookstore (3)
libre *adj.* free; **ils vivent en union libre** they are living together (without marriage) (4); **zone** (*f.*) **libre** free zone
licenciement *m.* dismissal, firing (*from a job*)
licencier to fire (*from a job*) (20)
lifting *m.* facelift
lier to link, join
lieu (*pl.* **lieux**) *m.* place, location (3); **au lieu de** instead of; **avoir lieu** to take place (21); **lieu de naissance** birthplace
lieue *f.* league (*unit of measure*)
ligne *f.* line; **ligne téléphonique** telephone line
limite *f.* limit; **limite de vitesse** speed limit (14)
limiter to limit, restrict
linge *m.* laundry; **lave-linge** *m.* washing machine
linguistique *adj.* linguistic
lire (*p.p.* **lu**) *irreg.* to read (12)
lit *m.* bed (5); **faire le lit** to make the bed (5)
lithium *m.* lithium
littéraire *adj.* literary (13); **arabe littéraire** classical Arabic
littérature *f.* literature
livraison *f.* delivery
livre *m.* book (P)
livre *f.* pound (*approx. half kilo*) (7)
local (*pl.* **locaux**) *m.* premises; business; facility (13); **local de recherche** research facility
location *f.* rental; **agence** (*f.*) **de location** car rental agency
logement *m.* lodging; place of residence
logique *f.* logic; *adj.* logical
loi *f.* law
loin *adv.* far; **loin de** *prep.* far from (3)
lointain *adj.* faraway, distant
loisirs *m. pl.* leisure activities (16)
long(ue) *adj.* long
longer (nous longeons) to walk along
longtemps *adv.* (for) a long time (10)
longueur *f.* length
lors de *prep.* at the time of
lorsque *conj.* when
lôtissement *m.* (housing) development
louer to rent (14)
loyer *m.* rent; **habitation** (*f.*) **à loyer modéré (HLM)** low-income housing
lugubre *adj.* gloomy
lui *pron., m., f.* him; to/for him/her (7)
lumière *f.* light; **mettre la lumière** turn on the light (7)
lundi *m.* Monday (4)
lune *f.* moon
lunettes *f. pl.* glasses; **lunettes de soleil** sunglasses (6)

leurre *m.* deception
lutter to fight
luxueux/euse *adj.* luxurious
lycée *m.* secondary school (1)

ma *adj.* my
machine (*f.*) **à laver** washing machine
madame (*ab.* **Mme**) (*pl.* **mesdames**) *f.* madam; ma'am (*ab.* Mrs.) (P)
mademoiselle (*ab.* **Mlle**) (*pl.* **mesdemoiselles**) *f.* miss (*ab.* Miss) (P)
magasin *m.* store; **grand magasin** department store (6)
magazine *m.* magazine (12)
Maghreb *m.* Maghreb (Morocco, Algeria, Tunisia) (15)
maghrébin(e) *adj.* from the Maghreb (15)
magie *f.* magic
magnétoscope *m.* videocassette recorder (VCR) (5)
magnifique *adj.* magnificent, great (2)
mai *m.* May (4)
maillot (*m.*) **de bain** swimsuit (6)
main *f.* hand (9); **sac** (*m.*) **à main** handbag
main-d'œuvre *f.* manpower, workforce
maintenant *adv.* now (5)
mairie *f.* mayor's office
mais *conj.* but (2)
maïs *m.* corn (7)
maison *f.* house (5); **maison particulière** private home; **rentrer à la maison** to go home
maître (maîtresse) *m., f.* elementary school teacher (1)
majeur(e) *adj.* major
majorité *f.* majority
majuscule *adj., Gram.* uppercase (*alphabet letter*)
mal *adv.* badly (9); **au plus mal** very ill; **avoir du mal (à)** to have a hard time (*doing s.th.*); **avoir mal (à)** to have pain / an ache (in); to have a sore... (9); **avoir mal au cœur** to feel nauseated (9); **avoir mal au ventre** to have a stomachache (9); **se faire mal (à)** to hurt (a part of one's body) (9)
malade *adj.* sick (9); *m., f.* sick person; patient; **garde-malade** *m., f.* nurse's aide (11); **tomber malade** to fall ill (9)
maladie *f.* illness
malaise *m.* weakness, fainting spell
malentendu *m.* misunderstanding
malheur *m.* unhappiness, misery
malheureux/euse *adj.* unhappy, miserable (2)
malhonnête *adj.* dishonest
malien(ne) *adj.* from Mali; **Malien(ne)** *m., f.* person from Mali
maman *f., fam.* mommy
mammifère *m.* mammal
manche *f.* sleeve; **La Manche** *f.* English Channel (17)
manchette *f.* headline (12)
mandarin(e) *adj.* Mandarin
manger (nous mangeons) to eat (6); **salle** (*f.*) **à manger** dining room (5)
manifestation *f.* (*public, political*) demonstration; outward sign; **manifestation culturelle** cultural event (21)
manquer à to be missed by (*s.o.*); **tu me manques** I miss you
manteau *m.* overcoat (6)
mantille *f.* mantilla
manuscrit *m.* manuscript
maquillage *m.* makeup; makeup room
maquiller: se maquiller to put on makeup; **se maquiller les yeux (les lèvres)** to make up one's eyes (one's lips)
maquis *m.* scrub, bush; French Resistance
maquisard(e) *m., f.* French Resistance fighter
marathon *m.* marathon race
marchand(e) *m., f.* merchant (7)
marché *m.* market (7); **bon marché** cheap; **supermarché** *m.* supermarket (3)
marcher to walk; to work (properly); **ça marche** that works for me
mardi *m.* Tuesday (4)
maréchal *m.* marshal, field marshal
mari *m.* husband (4)
mariage *m.* marriage (12); **anniversaire** (*m.*) **de mariage** wedding anniversary (11)
marié(e) *adj.* married (4)
marier: se marier to get married
marine nationale *f.* Marines
maritime *adj.* maritime
marketing *m.* marketing (11)
marmite *f.* large iron cooking pot (18)
Maroc *m.* Morroco (3)
marocain(e) *adj.* Moroccan (3); **Marocain(e)** *m., f.* Moroccan (*person*) (3)
marque *f.* brand
marquer to mark
marraine *f.* godmother
marron *adj., inv.* chestnut brown (6)
mars *m.* March (4)
marseillais(e) *adj.* from Marseille; **Marseillais(e)** *m., f.* person from Marseille
martiniquais(e) *adj.* from Martinique; **Martiniquais(e)** *m., f.* person from Martinique
martyr *m.* martyr
masculin(e) *adj.* masculine
massacre *m.* massacre
massage *m.* massage
massif *m.* old rounded mountain range (17)
match *m.* **(de foot, de boxe)** (soccer, boxing) match (10)
matelot *m.* sailor
matérialiste *adj.* materialistic
maternel(e) *adj.* maternal; **école** (*f.*) **maternelle** nursery school, preschool
mathématiques (*fam.* **maths**) *f. pl.* mathematics (1)
matière *f.* (school) subject (13); substance; **matières grasses** (*meat*) fat
matin *m.* morning (5); **ce matin** this morning (13); **du matin** in the morning (5)
matinée *f.* morning (*duration*)
mauritanien(ne) *adj.* Mauritanian; **Mauritanien(ne)** *m., f.* Mauritanian (*person*)
mauvais(e) *adj.* bad (2); **de mauvaise humeur** in a bad mood; **il fait mauvais** it's bad weather (10)
maxichaud(e) *adj., fam.* extremely warm
maxima *f.* maximum
maximal(e) *adj.* highest
maxime *f.* maxim, saying
maximum *m.* maximum
mayonnaise *f.* mayonnaise; **œuf** (*m.*) **dur mayonnaise** hard-boiled egg with mayonnaise (8)
me *pron.* me; to/for me (7, 9)
mec *m., fam.* guy
mécanicien(ne) *m.* mechanic
mécanique *adj.* mechanical; **génie** (*f.*) **mécanique** mechanical engineering (13)
méchant(e) *adj.* mean, nasty
méchoui *m.* whole lamb roasted on a spit over open coals
mécontent(e) *adj.* displeased
mecque: La Mecque *f.* Mecca
médaillon *m.* locket
médecin (femme médecin) *m., f.* doctor (9)
médecine *f.* medicine (*profession*); **médecine douce** alternative medicine
médias *m. pl.* media (12)
médiathèque *f.* media library
médical(e) (*pl.* **médicaux, médicales**) *adj.* medical; **soins** (*m. pl.*) **médicaux** health care
médicament *m.* medicine, drug (9)
médiéval(e) *adj.* medieval
médina *f.* old portion of an Arab city (22)
médiocre *adj.* mediocre; dull
méditation *f.* meditation
méditerranéen(ne) *adj.* Mediterranean
méfiant(e) *adj.* suspicious
méfier: se méfier to distrust
meilleur(e) *adj.* **(que)** better (than) (16); **le/la/les meilleur(e)(s)** the best
mél *m.* e-mail message (13)
mélanésien(ne) *adj.* Melanesian; **Mélanésien(ne)** *m., f.* Melanesian (*person*)

mélange *m.* mixture
mélanger (nous mélangeons) to mix (15)
mélodrame *m.* melodrama
membre *m.* member
même *adj.* same (5); **elle-même** herself; **même chose** *f.* same thing; **nous-mêmes** ourselves
mémoires *m. pl.* memoires
mémorial (*pl.* **mémoriaux**) *m.* memorial
ménage *m.* housekeeping; **faire le ménage** to do housework (5)
mener (je mène) (à) to lead (to)
mensonge *m.* lie
mentalité *f.* mindset, attitude
menteur/euse *m., f.* liar
menthe *f.* mint; **thé** (*m.*) **à la menthe** mint tea
mentionné(e) *adj.* mentioned
mentir (*like* **sortir**) *irreg.* to lie (8)
menu *m.* menu
mer *f.* sea (17); **département** (*m.*) **d'outre-mer (DOM)** overseas department; **fruits** (*m. pl.*) **de mer** seafood (7); **territoire** (*m.*) **d'outre-mer (TOM)** overseas territory
merci *interj.* thank you (P)
mercredi *m.* Wednesday (4)
mercure *m.* Mercury
mère *f.* mother (4); **belle-mère** *f.* stepmother; mother-in-law (4); **fête** (*f.*) **des mères** Mother's Day; **grand-mère** *f.* grandmother (4)
mériter to deserve
mes *adj.* my
message *m.* message; **message électronique** e-mail message
messe *f.* mass
mesure *f.* measure; **mesure d'exclusion** segregation policy
mesurer to measure
métabolique *adj.* metabolical
métamorphoser to change
météo *f., fam.* weather report, forecast (10)
météorologique *adj.* meteorological; **carte** (*f.*) **météorologique** weather map
méthode *f.* method; **méthodes de cuisson** cooking methods
métier *m.* skilled trade (11)
métro *m.* subway (14); **plan** (*m.*) **du métro** subway map; **réseau** (*m.*) **du métro** subway system (14)
métropolitain(e) *adj.* metropolitan
metteur en scène *m.* director (*theatrical*)
mettre (*p.p.* **mis**) *irreg.* to put (on); to turn on (7); **mettre du temps à** to spend time on (7); **mettre en ordre** to put in order; **mettre fin à** to put an end to; **mettre la radio/télé/lumière** to turn on the radio/TV/light (7); **mettre la table** to set the table (7); **mettre un vêtement** to put on a piece of clothing (7)
meuble *m.* piece of furniture (5)
meurette: en meurette in wine sauce
mexicain(e) *adj.* Mexican (3); **Mexicain(e)** *m., f.* Mexican (*person*)
Mexique *m.* Mexico (3)
micro-ondes: four à micro-ondes *m.* microwave oven (5)
micro-ordinateur *m.* personal computer
microphone *m.* microphone
microscope *m.* microscope
midi *m.* noon (5); **cet après-midi** *m.* this afternoon (13); **de l'après-midi** in the afternoon (5); **il est midi** it is noon
mien: le/la/les mien(ne)(s) *pron.* mine (22)
mieux *adv.* **(que)** better (than) (16); **aimer mieux** to prefer (2); **ça va mieux?** are you feeling better?
migraine *f.* migraine (headache)
migration *f.* migration
mil *m.* millet
milice *f.* militia
milieu *m.* environment; middle; **au milieu de** in the middle of (22)
militaire *adj.* military; *m. pl.* the military
mille *adj.* thousand (4)
millénaire *m.* millennium
milliard *m.* one billion (4)
millier *m.* (around) a thousand
millimètre *m.* millimeter
million *m.* one million (4)
millionaire *m.* millionaire
mime *m., f.* mime
mince *adj.* thin
minérai *m.* ore; **exploitation** (*f.*) **du minérai** mining of the ore
minéral(e) *adj.* mineral; **eau** (*f.*) **minérale gazeuse (plate)** carbonated (noncarbonated, flat) mineral water (7)
minéralogie *f.* mineralogy
minéraux *m. pl.* minerals
mini-golf *m.* miniature golf
minima *f.* minimum
minimal(e) *adj.* minimal
minimum *m.* minimum
ministère *m.* ministry
ministre *m.* minister; **premier ministre** prime minister
Minitel *m.* Minitel (*French personal communications system*)
minoritaire *adj.* minority
minorité *f.* minority
minuit *m.* midnight (5)
minuscule *adj., Gram.* lowercase (*alphabet letter*)
minute *f.* minute
miroir *m.* mirror (5)
misanthrope *m.* misanthrope
mise *f.* putting; placing; **mise en contexte** putting into context; **mise en scène** (theatrical) production
misérable *adj.* miserable
mi-temps *f. inv.*: **à mi-temps** part-time (11)
mixte *adj.* mixed
mobile *adj.* mobile
moche *adj., fam.* awful; ugly
mode *f.* fashion
mode *m.* method; *Gram.* mood; **mode d'emploi** directions for use
modèle *m.* model
modéré(e) *adj.* moderate; **habitation** (*f.*) **à loyer modéré (HLM)** low-income housing
moderne *adj.* modern
moelleux/euse *adj.* smooth, velvety
moi *pron., s.* me; I (*emphatic*) (3); **à moi** mine; **chez moi** at my place; **excusez-moi** excuse me
moindre *adj.*: **le moindre problème** the slightest problem
moins *adv.* less; minus; before (the hour) (5); fewer (16); **au moins** at least; **de moins en moins** less and less; **le moins** + *adv.* the least + *adv.* (16); **le/la/les moins** + *adj.* the least + *adj.* (16); **le/la/les moins de** + *n.* the least/fewest + *n.* (16); **moins** + *adj./adv.* + **que** less + *adj./adv.* + than (16); **moins de** + *n.* + **que** less/fewer + *n.* + than (16); **moins le quart** quarter to (the hour) (5); *v.* + **le moins** *v.* + the least (16); *v.* + **moins que** *v.* + less than (16)
mois *m.* month (4)
moitié *f.* half
moment *m.* moment; **moments clés** key moments
mon *adj.* my
monde *m.* world (18); **les quatre coins** (*m. pl.*) **du monde** the far reaches of the world, the four corners of the world; **monde du travail** work world; **monde francophone** French-speaking world; **tout le monde** everyone (1)
mondial(e) *adj.* worldwide; **Deuxième Guerre** (*f.*) **mondiale** Second World War
monoculture *f.* monoculture
monoparental(e) *adj.* single-parent
monotone *adj.* monotonous
monsieur (*ab.* **M.**) (*pl.* **messieurs**) *m.* sir; mister (*ab.* Mr.) (P)
mont *m.* mount; mountain
montagne *f.* mountain (17)
montant *m.* amount (*of a check or sale*) (20)
montée *f.* climb; ascendancy
monter to go up; to climb (11); **monter à cheval** to go horseback riding (16); **monter une rue** to go up a street (17)

montréalais(e) *adj.* from Montreal; **Montréalais(e)** *m., f.* person from Montreal
montrer to show (7)
monument *m.* monument
moral(e) *adj.* moral
morale *f.* moral (*philosophy*)
morceau *m.* piece (7)
mort *f.* death (12)
mosquée *f.* mosque (22)
mot *m.* word; **doux mots d'amour** sweet nothings; **le mot juste** the right word; **mot-clé** *m.* key word; **mot apparenté** cognate; **mots croisés** crossword puzzle (12)
motivation *f.* motivation
moto *f., fam.* motorcycle
mouchoir *m.* handkerchief; **mouchoir en papier** facial tissue (9)
moules *f. pl.* mussels
moulin *m.* mill
mourir (*p.p.* **mort**) *irreg.* to die (11)
mousse *f.* mousse; **mousse au chocolat** chocolate mousse
mouton *m.* sheep; mutton (8)
mouvement *m.* movement
mouvementé(e) *adj.* lively
moyen *m.* means, method, mode (14); **moyen de transport** means of transportation
moyen(ne) *adj.* moderate, average (18); **classe** (*f.*) **moyenne** middle class; **en moyenne** on average
mulâtre *adj.* mulatto, of mixed race
multiplication *f.* multiplication
multiplicité *f.* multiplicity
municipal(e) (*pl.* **municipaux**) *adj.* municipal
mur *m.* wall (1)
muscle *m.* muscle (9)
musculaire *adj.* muscular
musculation *f.* weight training (10)
musée *m.* museum (10); **conservateur/trice** (*m., f.*) **de musée** museum curator; **musée d'art (de sciences naturelles)** art (natural science) museum (10)
musical(e) (*pl.* **musicaux**) *adj.* musical
musicien(ne) *m., f.* musician (11)
musique *f.* music (13)
musts *m. pl.* things one must do or have
musulman(e) *adj.* Muslim
mystère *m.* mystery
mystérieux/euse *adj.* mysterious
mythe *m.* myth
mythique *adj.* mythical

nager (nous nageons) to swim (16)
naissance *f.* birth (12); **anniversaire** (*m.*) **de naissance** birthday; **date** (*f.*) **de naissance** birth date; **lieu** (*m.*) **de naissance** birthplace
naître (*p.p.* **né**) *irreg.* to be born (11)
nappe *f.* tablecloth (8)
narrateur/trice *m., f.* narrator
narration *f.* narrative, account
natal(e) *adj.* native; **ville** (*f.*) **natale** birthplace
nation *f.* nation
national(e) (*pl.* **nationaux**) *adj.* national; **fête** (*f.*) **nationale** national holiday (11)
nationalisme *m.* nationalism
nationalité *f.* nationality
nature *f.* nature
naturel(le) *adj.* natural; **histoire** (*f.*) **naturelle** natural history; **sciences** (*f. pl.*) **naturelles** natural science (1)
nautique *adj.* nautical; **faire du ski nautique** to waterski (16)
navet *m.* turnip (15); **c'est un navet** it's awful, terrible, a flop
naviguer to navigate; **naviguer le Web** to surf the Web (13)
nazi *adj.* Nazi
ne (n') *adv.* no; not; **ce n'est pas** this/that/it is not (P); **ce ne sont pas** these/those/they are not (P); **il n'est pas nécessaire** it is not necessary (20); **ne... aucun(e)** not any (13); **ne... jamais** not ever, never (1); **ne... ni... ni...** neither . . . nor; **ne... pas** not (1); **ne... pas du tout** not at all, absolutely not (1); **ne... pas encore** not yet (1); **ne... personne** no one, nobody (13); **ne... plus** not anymore, no longer (10); **ne... point** absolutely not; **ne... que** only (10); **ne... rien** nothing (13); **n'est-ce pas?** isn't that right? (3)
néandertal *m.*: **homme** (*m.*) **du Néandertal** Neanderthal man
nécessaire *adj.* necessary (20); **si nécessaire** if necessary
nécessité *f.* necessity
nécrologie *f.* obituary column; obituary (12)
négatif/ive *adj.* negative
négation *f., Gram.* negative
négliger (nous négligeons) to neglect
négocier to negotiate
neige *f.* snow; **faire du surf de neige** to snowboard (16); **planche** (*f.*) **à neige** snowboard
neiger to snow; **il neige** it's snowing (10)
nerveux/euse *adj.* nervous, high-strung
neuf *adj.* nine (P); **dix-neuf** nineteen (P)
neuf (neuve) *adj.* new
neuvième *adj.* ninth (11)
neveu *m.* nephew (4)
nez *m.* nose (9); **nez qui coule** runny nose (9)
ni *conj.* neither, nor; **ne... ni... ni...** neither . . . nor
nièce *f.* niece (4)
noces *f. pl.* wedding; **voyage** (*m.*) **de noces** honeymoon
Noël *m.* Christmas (11); **père** (*m.*) **Noël** Santa Claus
noir(e) *adj.* black (6); **pieds-noirs** *m. pl.* French people born in North Africa
noix *f.* nut; **noix de coco** coconut (15)
nom *m.* name; **nom d'un chien!** *interj.* darn it!
nomade *m., f.* nomad
nombre *m.* number; **nombres ordinaux** ordinal numbers
nombreux/euse *adj.* numerous (18)
nommer to name
non *interj.* no (P), not; **bien sûr que non!** of course not! (2); **non?** isn't that right? (3); **non plus** neither, not either
non-fumeur: wagon non-fumeur nonsmoking train car (14)
non-polluant(e) *adj.* nonpolluting
nord *m.* north (17)
normal(e) *adj.* normal; **il est normal** it's to be expected
nos *adj.* our (4)
note *f.* grade (*on a school paper*) (13); note; **bloc-notes** (*pl.* **blocs-notes**) *m.* pad of paper (P); **prendre des notes** to take notes
noter to take note (of); to notice; to grade (*papers*); **notez bien** take note
notre *adj.* our (4)
nôtre: le/la/les nôtre(s) *pron.* ours (22)
nourrir to feed
nourriture *f.* food
nous *pron.* we; us; to/for us (3, 7, 9); **nous-mêmes** ourselves
nouveau (nouvel, nouvelle [*pl.* **nouveaux, nouvelles**]) *adj.* new (12); **à/de nouveau** again; **le nouvel an** New Year's Day (11)
nouveauté *f.* novelty; change
nouvelle *f.* piece of news
novembre *m.* November (4)
nuage *m.* cloud
nuageux/euse *adj.* cloudy (10)
nucléaire *adj.* nuclear
nue *f.* cloud
nuisible *adj.* harmful
nuit *f.* night (10); **boîte** (*f.*) **de nuit** nightclub (10); **bonne nuit** good night
numéro *m.* number; **composer un numéro** dial a (phone) number (13)

obéir (à) to obey (11)
obésité *f.* obesity
objectif *m.* objective
objectif/ive *adj.* objective
objection *f.* objection

objet *m.* object; **pronom** (*m.*) **complément d'objet direct (indirect)** *Gram.* direct (indirect) object pronoun
obligation *f.* obligation
obligatoire *adj.* obligatory
obligé(e) *adj.* obligated
observateur/trice *m., f.* observer
observation *f.* observation
observer to observe
obstacle *m.* obstacle
obtenir (*like* **tenir**) *irreg.* to obtain (14)
occasion *f.* opportunity; occasion; **à l'occasion de** at the time of; **avoir l'occasion** to have the chance
occidental(e) (*pl.* **occidentaux**) *adj.* western
occitan(e) *adj.* of the Provençal language
occupation *f.* occupation
occuper to occupy; **s'occuper de** to take care of
océan *m.* ocean (17)
octobre *m.* October (4)
ode *f.* ode
odeur *f.* odor, smell
œil (*pl.* **yeux**) *m.* eye (9)
œuf *m.* egg; **œuf dur mayonnaise** hard-boiled egg with mayonnaise (8); **œufs en meurette** eggs in wine sauce
œuvre *f.* work (of art, literature, music); body of work (21); **chef-d'œuvre** (*pl.* **chefs-d'œuvre**) *m.* masterpiece; **main d'œuvre** *f.* manpower, workforce
office *m.* office
officiel(le) *adj.* official
officier *m.* officer
offrir (*like* **ouvrir**) *irreg.* to offer; to give (15)
oignon *m.* onion (7); **oignon vert** green onion; **soupe** (*f.*) **à l'oignon** French onion soup
oiseau *m.* bird (16)
O.K.? *interj.* okay? (3)
olive *f.* olive; **huile** (*f.*) **d'olive** olive oil (15)
olympique *adj.* olympic
omelette *f.* omelet (8)
on *pron.* one; we, they, people, you (1)
oncle *m.* uncle (4)
onde *f.* wave; **four** (*m.*) **à micro-ondes** microwave oven (5)
onze *adj.* eleven (P)
opéra *m.* opera (21)
opération *f.* operation; tactic
opéré(e) *adj.* operated
opinion *f.* opinion
optimiste *adj.* optimistic
option *f.* option
orage *m.* thunderstorm (10)
oral(e) *adj.* oral
orange *adj., inv.* orange (6); *m.* orange (*color*); *f.* orange (*fruit*); **jus** (*m.*) **d'orange** orange juice (8)
orchestre *m.* orchestra (21); band
ordinaire *adj.* ordinary; regular
ordinal(e) *adj.* ordinal; **nombres** (*m. pl.*) **ordinaux** ordinal numbers
ordinateur *m.* computer (1)
ordonnance *f.* prescription (9)
ordre *m.* order; **mettre en ordre** to put in order
oreille *f.* ear (9)
organe *m.* organ (*body part*)
organisation *f.* organization
organiser to organize; **s'organiser** to organize oneself
orge *f.* barley
oriental(e) (*pl.* **orientaux**) *adj.* oriental, eastern
originaire (*adj.*) **de** originating from
originalité *f.* originality
origine *f.* origin
orthographe *f.* spelling
otage *m., f.* hostage (19)
ou *conj.* or (P)
où *adv., pron.* where (4); when: in/on which (18); **où se trouve...** ? where is . . . ? (3)
oublier to forget (6)
ouest *m.* west (17); **sud-ouest** *m.* southwest
oui *interj.* yes (P); **bien sûr que oui!** yes, of course! (2)
ours *m.* bear (16)
outre *prep.* besides, over and above; **département** (*m.*) **d'outre-mer (DOM)** overseas department; **outre-mer** *adv.* overseas; **territoire** (*m.*) **d'outre-mer (TOM)** overseas territory
ouvert(e) *adj.* open; **ouvert(e) d'esprit** open-minded
ouverture *f.* opening; **horaires** (*m. pl.*) **d'ouverture** hours when open
ouvrier/ière *m., f.* manual laborer (11)
ouvrir (*p.p.* **ouvert**) *irreg.* to open (15)
oxygène *m.* oxygen

page *f.* page; **page d'accueil** home page (13); **page perso** personal home page (13); **pages jaunes** yellow pages
pain *m.* bread (7); **pain artisanal** hand-crafted bread; **pain de campagne** country-style wheat bread; **petit pain** bread roll (8)
paire *f.* pair
paix *f.* peace; **Corps** (*m.*) **de la paix** Peace Corps
Pakistan *m.* Pakistan (15)
pakistanais(e) *adj.* Pakistani (15); **Pakistanais(e)** *m., f.* Pakistani (*person*)
palais *m.* palace; **palais du roi** king's palace
pâle *adj.* pale
panier *m.* basket (16)
panne *f.* breakdown (*mechanical*); **panne d'électricité** power outage
pantalon *m. s.* pants, trousers (6)
papa *m., fam.* papa, daddy
papeterie *f.* stationery store
papier *m.* paper; **feuille** (*f.*) **de papier** sheet of paper (13); **mouchoir** (*m.*) **en papier** facial tissue (9)
papy *m., fam.* grandpa
pâque *f.* Passover (11)
paquebot *m.* ocean liner
Pâques *m. s., f. pl.* Easter (11)
par *prep.* by; per (6); **par chèque (carte de crédit)** by check (credit card); **par cœur** by heart; **par exemple** for example; **par jour** (**semaine,** *etc.*) per day (week, *etc.*); **par rapport à** with respect to; **par train** (**avion,** *etc.*) by train (plane, *etc.*); **passer par** to pass by (13)
paragraphe *m.* paragraph
paraître (*like* **connaître**) *irreg.* to seem, appear (13)
parallèlement *adv.* in parallel, at the same time
parapente *m.***: faire du parapente** to hang glide (16)
paraphrase *f.* paraphrase
parc *m.* park
parcourir (*like* **courir**) *irreg.* to scan
pardon *interj.* pardon me
pardonner to excuse
parenté *f.* kinship, relationship; **quelle parenté?** what's the relationship?
parenthèse *f.* parenthesis; **entre parenthèses** in parentheses
parents *m. pl.* relatives; parents (4); **arrière-grands-parents** great-grandparents; **grands-parents** grandparents
parfait(e) *adj.* perfect
parfois *adv.* sometimes (2)
parfum *m.* perfume
parisien(ne) *adj.* Parisian; **Parisien(ne)** *m., f.* Parisian (*person*)
parking *m.* parking lot, parking garage (3)
parler to talk; to speak (2); **se parler** to talk to oneself
parmi *prep.* among
parole *f.* word
part *f.*: **à part cela** besides that; **de ma part** on my behalf; as for me, in my opinion; **quelque part** *adv.* somewhere
partage *m.* sharing
partager (nous partageons) to share (6)
partenaire *m., f.* partner
parti *m.*: **parti politique** political party (18)
participation *f.* participation
participe *m., Gram.* participle
participer to participate
particularité *f.* particularity
particulier/ière *adj.* particular; **en particulier** in particular; **maison** (*f.*) **particulière** private home

partie *f.* part (9); **faire partie de** to be a part of, belong to; **partie du corps** part of the body; **partie intégrante** essential/integral part
partiel(le) *adj.* partial; **à temps partiel** part-time
partir (*like* **dormir**) *irreg.* to leave (*a place*) (8); **à partir de** beginning, starting from; **partir en voyage (vacances)** to go on a trip (vacation)
partisan(e) *m., f.* partisan, follower
partitif/ive *adj., Gram.* partitive
partout *adv.* everywhere (18); **presque partout** almost everywhere
parvenir (*like* **venir**) *irreg.* to reach
pas: ne... pas *adv.* not (1); **ce n'est pas** this/that it is not (P); **ne... pas du tout** not at all, absolutely not (1); **ne... pas encore** not yet (1); (21); **pas de problème** no problem; **pourquoi pas?** why not?
passablement *adv.* fairly well
passage *m.* passage; **être de passage** to be passing through
passager/ère *m., f.* passenger (14)
passé *m.* past; **passé composé** *Gram.* compound past tense
passeport *m.* passport (14)
passer to pass; to spend; to be showing (*a film*); **en passant** in passing; **laissez-passer** *m.* security pass; **passer la douane** to go through customs (14); **passer le week-end** to spend the weekend; **passer par** to pass by (11); **passer un examen** to take an exam (13); **qu'est-ce qui se passe?** what's going on?; **se passer** to take place, to happen (9)
passionant(e) *adj.* fascinating, gripping, exciting
passionné(e) *adj.* crazy/mad about
pastelliste *m., f.* artist who works in pastels
pastille *f.* lozenge, cough drop (9)
pastis *m.* aperitif made with anise
pâté *m.* liver paste; pâté
paternel(le) *adj.* paternal
pâtes *f. pl.* pasta (15)
patience *f.* patience; **perdre patience** to lose patience (8)
patient(e) *adj.* patient
patin *m.* ice skate; **faire du patin à glace** to ice skate (16)
patiner to ice skate (16)
patisserie *f.* pastry bakery (7); pastry (7)
patissier/ière *m., f.* pastry baker (7)
patrie *f.* one's country, homeland (19)
patriotique *adj.* patriotic
patron(ne) *m., f.* owner; boss (11)
pauvre *adj.* poor (22); *m., f.* poor person
pavillon *m.* large building; private house
payant(e) *adj.* for which one must pay, not free; **chaîne** (*f.*) **privée payante** private subscription channel
payer (je paie) to pay (6)
pays *m.* country (3)
paysage *m.* landscape; scenery
paysan(ne) *m., f.* country dweller (18); peasant, farmer
pêche *f.* fishing; **aller à la pêche** to go fishing (16)
pêcher to fish
pédagogique *adj.* pedagogical
peigner: se peigner to comb one's hair (9)
peine *f.* punishment; **à peine** hardly
peintre (femme peintre) *m., f.* painter (11)
peinture *f.* painting (21)
pèlerinage *m.* pilgrimage
pendant *prep.* during; while (11); **pendant (cinq) heures** for (five) hours; **pendant combien de temps... ?** for how long . . . ?; **pendant les vacances** during vacation
pénétrer to enter, penetrate
pénible *adj.* painful; difficult
penicilline *f.* penicillin
penser to think (2); **penser à** to think about; **penser de** to think of, to have an opinion about; **penser que** to think that
pente *f.* slope
perception *f.* perception
perché(e) *adj.* perched
perdre to lose (8); **perdre la tête** to lose one's mind (8); **perdre patience** to lose patience (8); **se perdre** to get lost
perdu(e) *adj.* lost; **âmes** (*f. pl.*) **perdues** lost souls
père *m.* father (4); **beau-père** *m.* father-in-law, stepfather (4); **grand-père** *m.* grandfather (4); **père Noël** Santa Claus
période *f.* period (*of time*); **en période de** during times of
périphérique *adj.* peripheral
permanent(e) *adj.* permanent
permettre (*like* **mettre**) *irreg.* to permit, allow (7)
permis *m.* permit
permission *f.* permission
persil *m.* parsley (15)
persistent(e) *adj.* persistent
persister to persist, perservere
perso: page (*f.*) **perso** personal home page (13)
personnage *m.* character (P)
personnalité *f.* personality
personne *f.* person (P); **ne... personne** *pron. indef.* nobody, no one (13)
personnel(le) *adj.* personal
pessimiste *adj.* pessimistic
pétanque: jouer à la pétanque to play lawn bowling (16)
pétillant(e) *adj.* sparkling; fizzy; **vin** (*m.*) **pétillant** sparkling wine
petit(e) *adj.* small (2); **petit(e) ami(e)** *m., f.* boyfriend (girlfriend); **petit déjeuner** *m.* breakfast (8); **petit écran** *m.* small screen (TV); **petite-fille** *f.* granddaughter (4); **petites annonces** *f. pl.* classified ads (11); **petit-fils** *m.* grandson (4); **petit pain** *m.* bread roll (8); **petits pois** *m. pl.* peas (7); **tout(e) petit(e)** very little; at a young age
peu *adv.* little; few (7); hardly; **à peu près** about, nearly; **il est peu probable que** it is unlikely that (21); **un peu(de)** a little (of), a few (of) (7)
peur *f.* fear; **avoir peur (de)** to be afraid (of) (4); **faire peur à** to frighten
peut-être *adv.* perhaps (12)
pharmacien(ne) *m., f.* pharmacist
phénomène *m.* phenomenon
philosophie (*fam.* **philo**) *f.* philosophy (13)
photographie (*fam.* **photo**) *f.* photograph (21); **album-photo** *m.* photo album; **appareil photo** *m.* camera (5); **faire de la photographie** to take photographs (16); **prendre une photo** to take a photograph (16)
photographe *m., f.* photographer (21)
phrase *f.* sentence
physique *f.* physics (13); *adj.* physical
piano *m.* piano (5)
pièce *f.* room (5); **deux-pièces** *m. s.* one-bedroom apartment **pièce de théâtre** play (21)
pied *m.* foot (9); **à pied** on foot (14); **course** (*f.*) **à pied** running race (10); **pieds-noirs** *pl.* French people born in North Africa
piège *m.* trap (19)
piéton(ne) *m., f.* pedestrian; **rue** (*f.*) **piétonne** pedestrian street (20)
pilule (*f.*) **contraceptive** contraceptive pill
piment *m.* pimento, hot pepper
pion *m.* assistant (*in a school*)
piquant(e) *adj.* spicy
pique-nique *m.* picnic; **faire un pique-nique** to have a picnic (16)
piqueniquer to have a picnic (16)
piscine *f.* swimming pool (13)
piste *f.* trail, track (13); ski run (16); lead; **piste de jogging** jogging trail (13)
pita *m.* pita (bread) (15)
pittoresque *adj.* picturesque
pizza *f.* pizza (8); **pizza surgelée** frozen pizza
placard *m.* cupboard

place *f.* place; (reserved) seat (14); public square; **à votre (ta) place** if I were you (19)
plage *f.* beach (16)
plaindre: se plaindre (nous nous plaignons) to complain
plaine *f.* plain (17)
plainte *f.* complaint
plaire (*p.p.* **plu**) *irreg.* to please; **s'il vous (te) plaît** *interj.* please
plaisance *f.*: **port** (*m.*) **de plaisance** marina
plaisanter to joke/kid around
plaisanterie *f.* joke
plaisir *m.* pleasure; **avec plaisir** with pleasure, gladly
plan *m.* map (*subway, city, region*) (13); plane; **arrière plan** background; **plan du métro** subway map; **sur le plan linguistic** linguistically
planche *f.* board; **faire de la planche à voile** to windsurf (16); **planche à neige** snowboard
planète *f.* planet
planifier to plan
plantation *f.* planting
plante *f.* plant; **jardin** (*m.*) **des plantes** botanical garden
planter to plant (18)
plaque *f.*: **plaque électrique** burner (*on a stove*)
plastique *m., adj.* plastic; **arts** (*m. pl.*) **plastiques** visual arts (sculpture, painting, etc.) (13)
plat *m.* dish (8); **plat (chaud, principal)** (hot, main) dish (8); **plat du jour** today's special
plat(e) *adj.* flat; **eau** (*f.*) **minérale plate** noncarbonated (flat) mineral water (7)
plateau (*pl.* **plateaux**) *m.* plateau (17); set, stage (*cinema, television*) (2)
plein(e) *adj.* full; **à plein temps** full-time (11); **en plein air** outdoors (16); **en pleine forme** in great shape (9)
pleut: il pleut it's raining (10)
pleurer to cry
pleuvoir (*p.p.* **plu**) *irreg.* to rain; **il pleut** it's raining (10)
plier to fold
pluie *f.* rain
plupart *f.*: **la plupart (de)** most (of), the majority (of) (22)
pluriel *m., Gram.* plural
plus *adv.* more (16); **au plus mal** very ill; **beaucoup plus** much more; **de plus en plus** more and more; **de plus en plus tôt** earlier and earlier; **en plus** in addition; **le plus** + *adv.* the most + *adv.* (16); **le/la/les plus** + *adj.* the most + *adj.* (16); **le/la/les plus de** + *n.* the most + *n.* (16); **ne... plus** not any more, no longer (10); **non plus** neither; **plus** + *adj./adv.* + **que** more + *adj./adv.* + than (16); **plus de** + *n.* + **que** more + *n.* + than (16); **plus rien** nothing more; **plus tard** later (10); *v.* + **le plus** *v.* + the most (16); *v.* + **plus que** *v.* + more than (16)
plusieurs *adj., indef. pron.* several (14)
plûtot *adv.* rather; instead
poche *f.* pocket
poème *m.* poem (21)
poésie *f.* poetry (21)
poète (femme poète) *m., f.* poet (21)
poids *m.* weight
point *m.* point; **ne... point** *adv.* absolutely not; **point de départ** starting point; **point de repère** landmark; **point de vue** point of view
pointe: heures de pointe *f. pl.* rush hour (14)
pois *m. pl.* peas; **petits pois** green peas (7); **pois chiches** chickpeas (15)
poisson *m.* fish (7); **soupe** (*f.*) **de poisson** fish soup
poissonnerie *f.* fish store (7)
poitrine *f.* chest (9)
poivre *m.* pepper (8)
poivron *m.* bell pepper
poli(e) *adj.* polite
police *f.* police; **agent(e)** (*m., f.*) **de police** police officer
policier/ière *m., f.* police officer
politesse *f.* courtesy, good manners
politique *f.* politics; policy; *adj.* political; **parti** (*m.*) **politique** political party (18)
polluant(e) *adj.* polluting
polluer to pollute
pollution *f.* pollution (18)
pomme *f.* apple (7); **pomme de terre** potato (7); **tarte** (*f.*) **aux pommes** apple pie
ponctuation *f.* punctuation
pont *m.* bridge (19)
populaire *adj.* popular; **caisse** (*f.*) **populaire** credit union (13)
population *f.* population
porc *m.* pork (7); pig (18); **jarret** (*m.*) **de porc** ham hocks
porcelaine *f.* porcelain
port *m.* port (20); **port de plaisance** marina; **port maritime** shipping port
portable *m.* laptop computer (5); portable (cell) phone (13)
porte *f.* door (1); **porte d'embarquement** (*airport*) gate (14)
porter to wear (2); to carry; **prêt-à-porter** off-the-rack/ready-to-wear clothing
portrait *m.* portrait
portugais(e) *adj.* Portuguese; **Portugais(e)** *m., f.* Portuguese (*person*)
poser: poser sa candidature to submit one's application; **poser une question** to ask a question
position *f.* position; place
posséder (je possède) to possess
possessif/ive *adj.* possessive
possession *f.* possession
possibilité *f.* possibility
possible *adj.* possible; **autant que possible** as much as possible (16); **il est possible (que)** it is possible (that); **le plus vite possible** as soon as possible
postal(e) *adj.* postal; **carte** (*f.*) **postale** postcard
poste *f.* mail (3); post office; **bureau** (*m.*) **de poste** post office building
poste *m.* position, job (11)
pot *m.*: **prendre un pot** to have a drink; **pot d'échappement** exhaust pipe
poteau (*m.*) **indicateur** signpost (17)
poubelle *f.* garbage can
poulet *m.* chicken (meat) (7); **poulet-frites** *m.* chicken with French fries (8)
poumon *m.* lung (9)
poupée *f.* doll
pour *prep.* for (1); **c'est pour cela** it's for that reason; **le pour et le contre** the pros and cons; **pour cent** percent; **pour que** so that, in order that (21); **s'inquiéter pour** to worry about
pourcentage *m.* percentage
pourquoi *adv., conj.* why (4); **pourquoi pas?** why not?
pourri(e) *m., f.* rotten person
poursuivre (*like* **suivre**) *irreg.* to pursue (15)
pousser to grow; to push (18); **pousser des soupirs** to sigh
pouvoir (*p.p.* **pu**) *irreg.* to be able, can; to be allowed (6); **est-ce que vous pourriez m'indiquer le chemin pour aller à... ?** could you show me the way to . . . ? (17); **il se peut que** it is possible that (21)
pratiquant(e) *adj.* practicing
pratique *f.* practice; *adj.* practical
pratiquer to practice
précédent(e) *adj.* preceding
précieux/euse *adj.* precious
précipiter: se précipiter to happen quickly
précisement *adv.* precisely, to be precise
préciser to specify
précision *f.* clarification
prédiction *f.* prediction
préfecture *f.* prefecture
préférable *adj.* preferable (20)
préférer (je préfère) to prefer (6)
préférence *f.* preference
premier/ière *adj.* first (11); **le premier** *m.* the first of the month (4); **premier**

choix *m.* top quality; **premier étage** *m.* first floor (*above ground level*)
prendre (*p.p.* **pris**) *irreg.* to take (7); to have (*something to eat/drink*) (7); **prendre des notes** to take notes; **prendre du temps** to take a long time (7); **prendre sa retraite** to retire (12); **prendre un congé** to take time off; **prendre une correspondance** to transfer; **prendre une décision** to make a decision (7); **prendre une photo** to take a photograph; **prendre un verre (un pot)** to have a drink (7); **prenez soin de vous** take care of yourself
préoccuper to preoccupy
préparatif *m.* preparation
préparation *f.* preparation
préparatoire *adj.* preparatory
préparer to prepare; **préparer (une leçon, un examen)** to study for (a lesson; a test) (13); **se préparer** to get ready
préposition *f., Gram.* preposition
près (de) *adv.* near (3); **à peu près** about, nearly
présence *f.* presence
présent *m.* present (*time*); **à présent** now, currently
présentation *f.* presentation
présent(e) *adj.* present
présenter to present; to introduce; **se présenter** to introduce oneself
président(e) *m., f.* president
presque *adv.* almost, nearly (18); **presque partout** almost everywhere
presse *f.* news media; press
pressé(e) *adj.* in a hurry (14)
prestigieux/euse *adj.* prestigious
prêt(e) *adj.* ready (2); **prêt-à-porter** *m.* off-the-rack/ready-to-wear clothing
prêter to lend
prétexte *m.* pretext
preuve *f.* proof
prévision *f.* forecast
prévoir (*like* **voir**) *irreg.* to foresee, anticipate; **comme prévu** as expected
primaire *adj.* primary; **école** (*f.*) **primaire** elementary school
primordial(e) *adj.* paramount
prince *m.* prince
principal(e) *adj.* principal, main; **plat** (*m.*) **principal** main course (8)
principe *m.* principle
printemps *m.* spring (10)
prison *f.* prison
prisonnier/ière *m., f.* prisoner
privé(e) *adj.* private; **chaîne** (*f.*) **privée payante** private subscription channel; **vie** (*f.*) **privée** private life
prix *m.* price; prize; **à tout prix** at all costs
probabilité *f.* probability
probable *adj.* probable (21)
problème *m.* problem; **le moindre problème** the slightest problem; **pas de problème** no problem
prochain(e) *adj.* next (13); **la semaine (l'année,** *etc.***) prochaine** next week (year, etc.)
proche (de) *adj., adv.* near, close; **futur** (*m.*) **proche** *Gram.* near future
proclamer to proclaim
producteur/trice *m., f.* producer (2)
production *f.* production
productivité *f.* productivity
produire (*like* **conduire**) *irreg.* to produce (18)
produit *m.* product; **produits laitiers** dairy products
professeur *m.* professor (P); **professeure** *f. Q.* female professor (2); **prof** *m., f. fam.* professor (2)
profession *f.* profession (11)
professionnel(le) *adj., m., f.* professional
profit *m.* profit; **au profit de** at the expense of
profiter to take advantage of; to profit from
programme *m.* program (13)
progressivement *adv.* progressively
projecteur *m.* projector
projection *f.* projection
projet *m.* project
promenade *f.* walk; **faire une promenade** to take a walk (5)
promener: se promener to take a walk (9)
promettre (*like* **mettre**) *irreg.* to promise (7)
promotion *f.* promotion
prompt(e) *adj.* prompt
pronom *m., Gram.* pronoun; **pronom complément d'objet direct (indirect)** direct (indirect) object pronoun; **pronom (démonstratif, possessif, relative)** (demonstrative, possessive, relative) pronoun
pronominal *adj., Gram.* pronominal; **verbe** (*m.*) **pronominal** *Gram.* pronominal (reflexive) verb
prononcer (nous prononçons) to pronounce
propager: se propager (nous nous propageons) to be disseminated, spread
proportion *f.* proportion
propos *m.*: **à propos de** about, concerning
proposer to propose, suggest
propre *adj.* own; **propre à** characteristic of; **sa propre opinion** *f.* his (her) own opinion
propriétaire *m., f.* owner
prospère *adj.* prosperous
prospérer (je prospère) to prosper
prospérité *f.* prosperity
protection *f.* protection
protéger (je protège, nous protégeons) to protect
protestant(e) *adj.* Protestant; **Protestant(e)**, *m., f.* Protestant (*person*)
protestantisme *m.* Protestantism
protester to protest
provenance *f.*: **de provenance** originating in/from
provençal(e) *adj.* from Provence (*region*)
provenir (*like* **venir**) *irreg.* to come from, to originate in
province *f.* province
provincial(e) *adj.* provincial
provision *f.* provision; *pl.* food (*supplies*)
provoquer to provoke
prudent(e) *adj.* careful
psychiatre *m., f.* psychiatrist
psychiatrique *adj.* psychiatric
psycho-drame *m.* psychological drama
psychologie *f.* psychology (13)
public *m.* public; **en public** in public
public (publique) *adj.* public
publicitaire *adj.* commercial
publicité *f.* commercial, advertisement (12)
publier to publish
puce *f.* flea; **ma puce** *fam.* sweetheart
puis *adv.* then (10)
puisque *conj.* since, seeing that
puissant(e) *adj.* powerful
pull-over (*fam.* **pull**) *m.* pullover (*sweater*) (6)
punk *m.* punk music (21)
pur(e) *adj.* pure
purifier to purify
pyjama *m.* pyjamas
pyramide *f.* pyramid

quai *m.* platform (14); dock
qualification *f.* qualification
qualifier to characterize
qualité *f.* quality
quand *adv., conj.* when (4); **depuis quand?** since when?
quantité *f.* quantity
quarantaine *f.*: **dans la quarantaine** in one's forties (*age*) (12)
quarante *adj.* forty (P)
quart *m.* quarter, fourth; quarter of an hour; **et quart** quarter past (*the hour*) (5); **moins le quart** quarter to (*the hour*) (5)
quartier *m.* neighborhood, area of town (3); **Quartier latin** Latin Quarter
quatorze *adj.* fourteen (P)
quatre *adj.* four (P); **quatre-vingt-dix** ninety (4); **quatre vingts** eighty (4)
quatre-épices *m., f.* allspice
quatrième *adj.* fourth (11)

que (qu') *conj.* that; than; as; *interr. pron.* what (6); *rel. pron.* whom, that, which (18); **ne... que** only (10); **pour que** in order to (21); **qu'est-ce que** what (*object*) (6); **qu'est-ce que c'est?** what is it/this/that? (P); **qu'est-ce qui** what (*subject*) (16)
Québec *m.* Quebec (3)
québécois(e) *adj.* from Quebec (3); **Québécois(e)** *m., f.* person from Quebec
quel(le)(s) *interr. adj.* what?, which? (5); **quel âge avez-vous (as-tu)(a-t-il,** *etc.***)?** how old are you (is he, etc.)? (4); **quel jour sommes-nous?** what day is it today?; **quel temps fait-it?** what's the weather like? (10); **quelle heure est-il?** what time is it? (5); **quels cours est-ce que vous suivez (tu suis)?** what courses are you taking? (13)
quelque(s) *indef. adj.* several, some (8); **quelque chose** *indef. pron.* something (13); **quelque part** *adv.* somewhere
quelquefois *adv.* sometimes (10)
quelques-uns/unes *indef. pron., pl.* some, a few
quelqu'un *indef. pron.* someone (13)
question *f.* question; **poser une question** to ask a question
quête *f.* quest
queue *f.* queue, line; **faire la queue** to stand in line (5)
qui *interr. pron.* who, whom (6); *rel. pron.* who, that, which (18); **qui est-ce?** who is it? (P); **qui est-ce que** whom (*object*); **qui est-ce qui** who (*subject*) (16)
quinze *adj.* fifteen (P)
quitter to leave (*s.o. or someplace*) (8)
quoi *pron.* what (6); **à quoi tu joues?** are you playing games?; **de quoi parlez-vous (parles-tu)?** what are you talking about? **je ne sais pas quoi faire** I don't know what to do
quotidien(ne) *adj.* daily

raccrocher to hang up (*the telephone receiver*) (13)
race *f.* race (*ethnicity*)
racine *f.* root
racisme *m.* racism
raconter to tell (about) (8)
radicalement *adv.* radically
radieux/euse *adj.* glorious, radiant
radio *f.* radio (5); **écouter la radio** to listen to the radio; **mettre la radio** to turn on the radio (7); **station** (*f.*) **de radio** radio station (12)
radioactif/ive *adj.* radioactive
raffiné(e) *adj.* refined
ragoût *m.* stew
raï *m.* raï music (21)
raisin *m.*: **du raisin** grapes (7); **raisin sec** raisin (15)
raison *f.* reason; **avoir raison** to be right
raisonnable *adj.* reasonable
ralentir to slow down
ramadan *m.* Ramadan (11)
ramasser to pick (up), gather (up); to dig up (18)
randonnée *f.* hike; **faire une randonnée** to hike (16)
rap *m.* rap music
rapide *adj.* fast, rapid (12)
rapidité *f.* speed
rappeler: se rappeler (je me rappelle) to remember (9)
rappeur *m.* rap musician
rapport *m.* relation; **par rapport à** with respect to
rapporter to report; to bring in; to bring back
rare *adj.* rare
rarement *adv.* rarely (2)
raser: se raser to shave (9)
rassurer to reassure, comfort
ratatouille *f.* ratatouille
ravi(e) *adj.* thrilled (21)
ravissant(e) *adj.* beautiful, delightful
rayon *m.* department (*in a store*) (6)
réaction *f.* reaction
réagir to react
réalisateur/trice *m., f.* director
réalisme *adj.* realism
réaliste *adj.* realistic
réalité *f.* reality; **en réalité** in fact, actually
rébellion *f.* rebellion
récent(e) *adj.* recent
recette *f.* recipe (15)
recevoir (*p.p.* **reçu**) *irreg.* to receive (10)
réchauffer to reheat (15)
recherche *f.* research (13); **à la recherche de** in search of; **faire des recherches** to do research; **local** (*m.*) **de recherche** research facility
rechercher to search for; to research (19)
récit *m.* narrative, story
récolte *f.* harvest, crop (18)
récolter to harvest (18)
recommander to recommend
récompense *f.* recompense
reconforter to comfort
reconnaissance *f.* gratitude
reconnaître (*like* **connaître**) *irreg.* to recognize (13)
reconstituer to restore
recoucher: se recoucher to go back to bed
recueillir (*like* **cueillir**) *irreg.* to collect (16)
recyclable *adj.* recyclable
recyclage *m.* recycling (18)
recycler to recycle (18)
rédacteur/trice *m., f.* editor
rédaction *f.* composition; **salle** (*f.*) **de rédaction** editing room
rédiger (nous rédigeons) to write, compose
redoutable *adj.* fearsome
redresser to rebuild
réduire (*like* **conduire**) *irreg.* to reduce (18)
refait(e) *adj.* remade (*movie*)
référer: se référer (je me réfère) to refer (back) to
refermer to close again
réfléchi(e) *adj.* thoughtful
réfléchir à to reflect (on), think (about) (11)
refléter (je reflète) to reflect, mirror
réflexion *f.* reflection; thought
refrigérateur (*fam.* **frigo**) *m.* refrigerator (fridge) (5)
réfugié(e) *m., f.* refugee
réfugier: se réfugier to take refuge (19)
refuser (de) to refuse (*to do s.th.*) (18)
regard *m.* look, glance
regarder to watch, look at (2); **cela (ne) vous regarde (pas)** that is (not) your problem; **regarder la télé** to watch TV
reggae *m.* reggae music (21)
régie *f.* control room (2)
régime *m.* regime; diet
région *f.* region
régional(e) *adj.* regional
régler (je règle) to resolve, settle
réglisse *m.* licorice
regret *m.* regret, remorse
regretter to regret, be sorry; **regretter que** to be sorry that (21)
régulier/ière *adj.* regular
rejoindre (*like* **craindre**) *irreg.* to join; to meet
relatif/ive *adj.* relative; **pronom** (*m.*) **relatif** *Gram.* relative pronoun
relation *f.* relationship
relativement *adv.* relatively
relief *m.* topography, relief (17)
religieux/euse *adj.* religious
religion *f.* religion
relire (*like* **lire**) *irreg.* to reread
remarquable *adj.* remarkable
remarque *f.* remark, comment
remarquer to notice
rembrunir: se rembrunir to become somber/disgruntled/darker; to cloud over
remède *m.* remedy, treatment, fix
remercier to thank
remettre: se remettre (*like* **mettre**) *irreg.* to recover
remonter to go back (up)
remplaçant(e) *m., f.* replacement
remplacer (nous remplaçons) to replace (13)
remplir to fill out (*a form*); **remplir les blancs** to fill in the blanks

renaissance: la renaissance *f.* the Renaissance
rencontre *f.* meeting, encounter (21)
rencontrer to meet; to run into, encounter (14)
rendez-vous *m.* meeting; appointment
rendre to return (*s.th.*); to render, make (8); **rendre justice** (*f.*) **à** to do justice to; **rendre visite à** to visit (*s.o.*) (8); **se rendre à** to go to; **se rendre compte (de)** to realize (9)
renforcer (nous renforçons) to reinforce
rénovation *f.* renovation (20)
renseignements *m. pl.* information
rentrée *f.* back-to-school day
rentrer to come/go back (home) (11); **rentrer à la maison** to go home
renvoyer (je renvoie) to send back, return
répandre: se répandre to spread
repartir (*like* **partir**) *irreg.* to leave again
repas *m.* meal (8); **commander un repas** to order a meal
repère: point (*m.*) **de repère** landmark
repérer (je repère) to locate
répéter (je répète) to repeat (6)
répétition *f.* rehearsal
réplique *f.* response
répondeur *m.* answering machine (5)
répondre to answer, respond (8)
réponse *f.* response
reportage *m.* report; **faire un reportage** to prepare/give a report (*TV*)
reporter *m.* reporter (2)
repos *m.* rest
reposé(e) *adj.* rested
reposer: se reposer to rest
reprendre (*like* **prendre**) *irreg.* to take up again, continue; to take more (*food*)
représailles *f. pl.* reprisals
représenter to represent
réproduire (*like* **conduire**) *irreg.* to reproduce
républicain(e) *m., f.* Republican
république *f.* republic
réputation *f.* reputation
réputé(e) *adj.* well known (20)
réseau *m.* network (14); system; **réseau du métro** subway system (14); **réseau informatique** computer network
réserver to reserve
résidence *f.* residence (13); **résidence universitaire** dormitory building (13)
résidentiel(le) *adj.* residential
résistance *f.* resistance
résistant(e) *m., f.* French Resistance fighter (19)
résister to resist
résoudre (*p.p.* **résolu**) *irreg.* to resolve
respecter to respect
respectif/ive *adj.* respective
respectueux/euse *adj.* respectful
respiration *f.* breathing
responsabilité *f.* responsibility
responsable *adj.* responsible
ressemblance *f.* resemblance
ressentir (*like* **dormir**) *irreg.* to feel
resservir (*like* **dormir**) *irreg.* to serve again (*food*)
ressource *f.* resource (13); **ressources naturelles** natural resources
restaurant (*fam.* **restau**) *m.* restaurant (3)
rester to stay (11)
résultat *m.* result
résulter (en) to result in
résumé *m.* summary
résumer to summarize
rétablir to reestablish
retard *m.* delay; **en retard** late (5)
retarder to slow; **retarder l'avance** to slow the advance (19)
retour *m.* return; **être de retour** to be back
retourner to return; to turn around (11)
retraite *f.* retirement (12); **prendre sa retraite** to retire (12)
retraité(e) *m., f.* retiree (12)
retroprojecteur *m.* overhead projector
retrouver to find (again); **se retrouver** to find oneself
réunion *f.* meeting
réunir to gather together; **se réunir** to get together
réussir (à) to succeed (11); to pass (*a course or an exam*) (11)
rêve *m.* dream
réveiller to wake (*s.o.*); **se réveiller** to wake up (9)
réveillon *m.* Christmas Eve; New Year's Eve
révéler (je révèle) to reveal
revenir (*like* **venir**) *irreg.* to come back, return (3)
révision *f.* review
revoir (*like* **voir**) *irreg.* to see again (10); **au revoir** good-bye (P)
révolte *f.* revolt
révolution *f.* revolution
rez-de-chaussée *m.* ground floor (5)
rhubarbe *f.* rhubarb
rhume *m.* common cold (9)
rhythme *m.* rhythm
rhythmé(e) *adj.* rhythmic
riche *adj.* rich (22)
richesse *f.* wealth
ridicule *adj.* ridiculous (2)
ridiculiser to make fun of, mock
rien; ne... rien *indef. pron.* nothing (13); **plus rien** nothing more
ringard(e) *adj.* out-of-date
risque *m.* risk
risquer to risk
rivière *f.* small river (17)
riz *m.* rice (8)
robe *f.* dress (6)
rocher *m.* rock
rocheux/euse *adj.* rocky
rock *m.* rock music (21)
roi *m.* king; **palais** (*m.*) **du roi** king's palace
rôle *m.* role; **jeu** (*m.*) **de rôle** role play
roller *m.* roller skating (10); **faire du roller** to roller-skate
romain(e) *adj.* Roman
roman *m.* novel (21)
romancier/ière *m., f.* novelist (21)
romantique *adj.* romantic
rompre (*p.p.* **rompu**) *irreg.* to break
roquefort *m.* Roquefort cheese
rose *adj.* pink (6)
rosé(e) *adj.* rosy; **vin** (*m.*) **rosé** rosé wine
rôti *m.* roast; **rôti(e)** *adj.* roasted
rouge *adj.* red (6)
rougir to blush
rouler to travel (*in a car*); to roll (along)
route *f.* road, highway (14); **en route** on the way
routier/ière *adj.* pertaining to the road; **signalisation** (*f.*) **routière** road signs
routine *f.* routine
royal(e) *adj.* royal
rubrique *f.* section, column (*in a newspaper*) (12)
rue *f.* street; **dans la rue...** on . . . Street (3); **descendre une rue** to go down a street (17); **monter une rue** to go up a street (17); **rue piétonne** pedestrian street (20)
ruelle *f.* alleyway (20)
ruine *f.* ruin
rumeur *f.* rumor
rural(e) *adj.* rural
russe *adj.* Russian (15); **Russe** *m., f.* Russian (*person*)
Russie *f.* Russia (15)

sa *adj.* his, her, its, one's (4)
sac *m.* bag; **sac à dos** backpack (P); **sac à main** handbag
sacré(e) *adj.* sacred
sacrifice *m.* sacrifice
sage *adj.* well-behaved
saint(e) *m., f.* saint
saisir to seize; to grasp
saison *f.* season (10)
salade *f.* lettuce; salad (8); **salade verte** green salad
salaire *m.* salary (20)
salarié(e) *m., f.* full-time employee
sale *adj.* dirty
salle *f.* room; **salle à manger** dining room (5); **salle de bains** bathroom (5); **salle**

de classe classroom (P); **salle de rédaction** editing room; **salle de séjour** living room (5)
saluer to greet
salut *interj.* hi; bye (P)
salutations *f.* greetings
samedi *m.* Saturday (4)
sandwich *m.* sandwich (8)
sans *prep.* without (2); **sans aucun doute** without a doubt; **sans domicile fixe** homeless; **sans doute** probably, no doubt (2); **sans intérêt** of no interest; **sans que** unless; without (21)
santé *f.* health (9)
satisfaisant(e) *adj.* satisfying
sauce *f.* sauce (8); **sauce de soja** soy sauce (15)
saucisse *f.* sausage link (7)
saucisson *m.* sausage
sauf *prep.* except
saumon *m.* salmon (7)
sauna *m.* sauna
sauter to jump
sauver to save
savoir (*p.p.* **su**) *irreg.* to know (*a fact*) (13); **je ne sais pas** I don't know (P); **je ne sais pas quoi faire** I don't know what to do
scandale *m.* scandal; **crier au scandale** to call it a scandal
scanner *m.* scanner
scénario *m.* script; scenario
scénariste *m., f.* screenwriter
scène *f.* scene (P); **metteur en scène** director (*theatrical*); **mise** (*f.*) **en scène** (*theatrical*) production
science *f.* science; **sciences naturelles** natural science (1)
scientifique *adj.* scientific
scoop *m.* scoop (*news*)
scripte *m.* script
script *m., f.* script coordinator
sculpteur (femme sculpteur) *m., f.* sculptor
sculpture *f.* sculpture
se (s') *pron.* oneself; himself; herself, itself, themselves; to oneself, etc.; each other
séance *f.* meeting; showing (*of a film*)
sec (sèche) *adj.* dry; **raisin** (*m.*) **sec** raisin (15)
sécher (je sèche) to dry; **sécher un cours** to cut a class (13)
sécheresse *f.* drought
séchoir *m.* dryer
secondaire *adj.* secondary; **enseignement** (*m.*) **secondaire** secondary school teaching (13)
seconde *f.* second (*sixtieth of a minute*); **second(e)** *adj.* second; **langue** (*f.*) **seconde** second/foreign language
secret *m.* secret
secrétaire *m., f.* secretary (11)
secrètement *adv.* secretly
sécurité *f.* security; **agent (e)** (*m., f.*) **de sécurité** security guard (11)
sédentaire *adj.* sedentary
séduire (*like* **conduire**) *irreg.* to seduce, charm
seize *adj.* sixteen (P)
séjour *m.* stay; trip; **salle** (*f.*) **de séjour** living room (5)
séjourner to stay (*in a place*)
sel *m.* salt (8)
self-sélect *m.* self-service restaurant
selon *prep.* according to (2); **selon le cas** depending on the case; **selon vous** in your opinion
semaine *f.* week (4); **par semaine** per week; **la semaine dernière (prochaine)** last (next) week
sembler to seem (13)
semer (je sème) to sow
semestre *m.* semester
sénégalais(e) *adj.* Senegalese; **Sénégalais(e)** *m., f.* Senegalese (*person*)
sens *m.* meaning
sentiment *m.* sentiment, emotion
sentimental(e) *adj.* sentimental
sentir (*like* **dormir**) *irreg.* to smell, to feel (8); **se sentir** to feel (*an emotion*)
séparer to separate
sept *adj.* seven (P)
septembre *m.* September (14)
septième *adj.* seventh (11)
serf *m.* serf
série *f.* series (12)
sérieux/euse *adj.* serious
serre *f.* greenhouse; **effet** (*m.*) **de serre** greenhouse effect (18)
serré(e) *adj.* tight
serrure *f.* latch
serveur/euse *m., f.* waiter/waitress
serviable *adj.* willing (*to do s.th.*)
service *m.* service (13); department; **station** (*f.*) **service** service station
serviette *f.* napkin (8)
servir (*like* **dormir**) *irreg.* to serve (8)
ses *adj.* his, her, its, one's
sésame *m.* sesame; **huile** (*f.*) **de sésame** sesame oil (15)
seul(e) *adj.* alone; sole (12); **c'est pour cela seul** it's only for that reason
seulement *adv.* only (12)
sévère *adj.* severe
sexe *m.* sex
shopping *m.* shopping; **faire du shopping** to go shopping (5)
short *m.* shorts (6)
si *adv.* so (very); so much; yes (*response to negative question*); **si (s')** *conj.* if, whether (7); **s'il vous (te) plaît** *interj.* please
SIDA *m.* AIDS
siècle *m.* century (20); **au cours des siècles** through the centuries
siège *m.* seat (14); **siège couloir (fenêtre)** aisle (window) seat (14)
sien: le/la/les sien(ne)(s) *pron.* his, hers (22)
signaleur *m.* signalman; **timonier** (*m.*) **signaleur** helmsman-signalman
signalisation *f.* signage; **signalisation routière** road signs
signe *m.* sign
signer to sign
signet *m.* bookmark (13)
signification *f.* significance
signifier to mean, signify
silence *f.* silence
silencieux/euse *adj.* silent
silencieusement *adv.* silently (19)
similaire *adj.* similar
similarité *f.* similarity
simple *adj.* simple
sincère *adj.* sincere
sincérité *f.* sincerity
singulier/ière *adj.* singular; *m., Gram.* singular (*form*)
sinon *prep.* if not, otherwise
site *m.* site; **site touristique** tourist site (20); **site web** website (13)
situation *f.* situation; placement
situer to situate; **se situer** to be located
six *adj.* six (P)
sixième *adj.* sixth (11)
ska *m.* ska music (21)
skate *m.* skateboarding (10)
ski *m.* skiing; ski; **faire du ski** to go skiing (16); **faire du ski de fond (ski nautique)** to cross-country ski (waterski) (16)
skier to ski (16)
snob *m.* snob
sociable *adj.* friendly
social(e) *adj.* social
socialiste *adj.* socialist
société *f.* company (11); society, organization
socio-économique *adj.* socioeconomic
sœur *f.* sister (4); **âme** (*f.*) **sœur** kindred spirit; **belle-sœur** *f.* sister-in-law, stepsister (4)
soi (soi-même) *pron.* oneself, herself, himself, itself (3); **sûr de soi** self-confident
soie *f.* silk
soif *f.* thirst; **avoir soif** to be thirsty (4)
soigner to take care of, nurse
soin *m.* care, treatment; **prenez soin de vous** take care of yourself; **soins médicaux** health care
soir *m.* evening (5); **ce soir** this evening (13); **du soir** in the evening (5)

soirée *f.* evening (21); party
soixantaine *f.*: **dans la soixantaine** in one's sixties (*age*) (12)
soixante *adj.* sixty (4)
soixante-dix *adj.* seventy (4)
soja *m.* soy; **sauce** (*f.*) **de soja** soy sauce (15)
sol *m.* ground; **sous-sol** *m.* basement
soldat *m.* soldier (19)
solde *f.* sale; **en solde** on sale
soleil *m.* sun; **coup** (*m.*) **de soleil** sunburn; **il fait du soleil** it's sunny out (10); **lunettes** (*f. pl.*) **de soleil** sunglasses (6)
solitaire *adj.* solitary
solitude *f.* solitude
solution *f.* solution
sombre *adj.* dark (22)
sommeil *m.* sleep; **avoir sommeil** to be sleepy
somptueux/euse *adj.* sumptuous
son *adj.* his, her, its, one's (4)
sondage *m.* survey
sonner to ring (*telephone, bell*)
sorte *f.* sort, type
sortie *f.* exit (14)
sortir (*like* **dormir**) *irreg.* to go out (8); **sortir avec** to go out with (*s.o.*)
soucier: se soucier de to care about
souci *m.* worry, concern
soudain *adv.* suddenly (19); **soudain(e)** *adj.* sudden (19)
souffle *m.* breath; **à bout de souffle** out of breath, breathless
souffrir (*like* **ouvrir**) *irreg.* to suffer (15)
souhaiter (que) to wish, hope (that) (21)
soumettre (*like* **mettre**) *irreg.* to hand in; to submit
soupe *f.* soup (8); **soupe à l'oignon** French onion soup; **soupe de poisson** fish soup
soupir *m.* sigh; **pousser des soupirs** to sigh
source *f.* source; **eau** (*f.*) **de source** spring water
sourd(e) *adj.* deaf; *m., f.* deaf person
sourire to smile
souris *f.* mouse; computer mouse (16)
sous *prep.* under (3); **sous clé** under lock and key; **sous-préfecture** *f.* subprefecture; **sous-sol** *m.* basement; **sous-titre** *m.* subtitle
souterrain(e) *adj.* underground
soutien *m.* support
souvenir *m.* memory
souvenir: se souvenir (*like* **venir**) *irreg.* **de** to remember (9)
souvent *adv.* often (2)
spaghettis *m. pl.* spaghetti
spécial(e) *adj.* special
spécialisation *f.* (*educational*) major
spécialiser: se spécialiser en to major in
spécialiste *m., f.* specialist, expert
spécialité *f.* specialty
spectacle *m.* entertainment; show (21)
spectateur/trice *m., f.* spectator
spéléologie *f.* spelunking; **faire de la spéléologie** to go spelunking (explore caves) (16)
splendide *adj.* splendid, wonderful
spontanéité *f.* spontaneity
sport *m.* sports; **faire du sport** to play sports; **fanatique** (*m., f.*) **du sport** sports fan (10); **sports d'hiver** winter sports; **voiture** (*f.*) **de sport** sportscar
sportif/ive *adj.* athletic (2); **centre** (*m.*) **sportif** sports center (3)
squatter to squat (*claim a residence*)
stabiliser: se stabiliser to become stable
stade *m.* stadium
stage *m.* internship (11); **faire un stage** to do an internship
standard *m.* standard
star *f.* star (*celebrity*)
station *f.* station; **station de radio** radio station (12); **station service** service station; **station thermale** spa, health resort
stationner to park (14)
statistique *f.* statistics
statuettes *f.* statuette
statut *m.* statute
steak-frites *m.* steak with French fries
stéréo *adj.* stereo; **chaîne** (*f.*) **stéréo** stereo system (5)
stéréotype *m.* stereotype
stratégie *f.* strategy
stress *m.* stress
stressé(e) *adj.* stressed
structure *f.* structure
studio *m.* studio (P); studio apartment
stupéfait(e) *adj.* stupefied, dumbfounded
stupide *adj.* stupid
style *m.* style
stylo *m.* pen (P)
subjonctif *m., Gram.* subjunctive (*mood*)
substantif *m., Gram.* noun
subtilité *f.* subtlety
succès *m.* success
sucre *m.* sugar (7); **canne** (*f.*) **à sucre** sugarcane
sucré(e) *adj.* sweet (8)
sucrerie *f.* sweets
sud *m.* south (17); **sud-ouest** southwest
suffisamment *adv.* sufficiently
suffire to suffice; **ça suffit** that's enough; **il suffit** it's enough (20)
suggérer (je suggère) to suggest
suggestion *f.* suggestion
suicider: se suicider to commit suicide
suite *f.* outcome; **tout de suite** right away (10)
suivant(e) *adj.* following
suivre (*p.p.* **suivi**) *irreg.* to follow; to take (*a class*) (15)
sujet *m.* subject; **au sujet de** concerning
super *adj.* super, great (2)
supérieur(e) *adj.* superior; **enseignement** (*m.*) **supérieur** higher education
superlatif *m., Gram.* superlative
supermarché *m.* supermarket (3)
supplémentaire *adj.* supplementary, extra
supposer to suppose; **je suppose?** I suppose? (3)
supprimer to eliminate, abolish
sur *prep.* on, on top of (3); **donner sur** to overlook, have a view of (20); **sur Internet** on the Internet (11); **tirer sur** to fire on, to shoot at (19)
sûr(e) *adj.* sure, certain (12); **bien sûr, bien sûr que oui (non)!** of course (not)! (2); **sûr de soi** self-confident
surf de neige *m.* snowboarding; **faire du surf de neige** to snowboard (16)
surfer (le Web) to surf (the Web) (13)
surgelé(e) *adj.* frozen; **pizza** (*f.*) **surgelée** frozen pizza
surmonter to overcome
surnommer to name, call; to nickname
surprendre (*like* **prendre**) *irreg.* to surprise
surpris(e) *adj.* surprised (21)
surprise *f.* surprise
surtout *adv.* especially (16); above all; **surtout pas** definitely not
surveillé(e) *adj.* managed
survivre (*like* **vivre**) *irreg.* to survive (15)
susceptible *adj.* susceptible
sweatshirt (*fam.* **sweat**) *m.* sweatshirt (6)
symbole *m.* symbol
symboliser to symbolize
sympathie *f.* friendliness, liking
sympathique (*fam.* **sympa**) *adj.* nice (1)
symphonie *f.* symphony
symptôme *m.* symptom
synagogue *f.* synagogue
syndicat *m.* union
syntaxe *f.* syntax
synthèse *f.* synthesis
système *m.* system

ta *adj.* your (4)
table *f.* table (P); **à table** at the table; **mettre la table** to set the table (7)
tableau (*pl.* **tableaux**) *m.* blackboard (1); painting (*picture*) (21); **tableau d'affichage** bulletin board (11)
tâche *f.* task
tailleur *m.* woman's suit (6)
talent *m.* talent
tant *adj.* so much; so many; **en tant qu'auteur** as author; **tant de spectateurs** so many spectators
tante *f.* aunt (4)

tapis *m.* rug (5)
taquiner to tease
tard *adv.* late (10); **plus tard** later (10)
tarte *f.* pie (7); **tarte aux pommes** apple pie
tartine *f.* bread with butter and jam (8)
tasse *f.* cup (8)
taxi *m.* taxi
te (t') *pron., s., fam.* you; to/for you (7, 9); **combien te faut-il?** how much do you need?; **s'il te plaît** please
technicien(ne) *m., f.* technician
technique *adj.* technical
technologie *f.* technology; **haute technologie** high tech
technophobe *m., f.* technophobe (13)
tee-shirt *m.* T-shirt (6)
tel(le) *adj.* such; like (12); **tel(le) ou tel(le)** this or that; **tel que** like, such as
télé *fam.* TV (2)
téléphone *m.* telephone (5); **coup** (*m.*) **de téléphone** phone call; **téléphone portable** mobile (cell) phone (13)
téléphoner (à) to phone (*s.o.*) (7)
téléphonique *adj.* telephone; **annuaire** (*f.*) **téléphonique** phone book; **cabine** (*f.*) **téléphonique** phone booth (13); **ligne** (*f.*) **téléphonique** telephone line
télévisé(e) *adj.* televised
télévision (*fam.* **télé**) *f.* television (TV) (2); **mettre la télé** to turn on the TV (7); **regarder la télé** to watch TV
tellement *adv.* so (very), so much (12)
température *f.* temperature (10)
temps *m.* time (5); weather (10); *Gram.* tense; **à mi-temps** part-time (11); **à temps partiel** part-time; **beau temps** nice weather; **dans le temps** in the past; **de temps en temps** from time to time (10); **depuis combien de temps?** how long?; **il fait un temps splendide** it's a gorgeous day; **mettre du temps à** to spend time on (7); **prendre du temps** to take a long time (7); **quel temps fait-il?** what's the weather like? (10)
tenir (*p.p.* **tenu**) *irreg.* to hold (14); to keep; **je tiens à toi** I care about you; **tenir au courant** to stay up to date
tennis *m.* tennis (10)
tension *f.* tension
tente *f.* tent
terme *m.* term
terminal *m.*: **terminal Minitel** Minitel terminal (*French personal communication system*)
terminal(e) *adj.* terminal, final
terminer to finish; **c'est terminé?** are you finished?
terminus *m.* terminus, last stop (14)
terrain *m.* ground; **terrain de golf** golf course; **vélo** (*m.*) **tout terrain** (*fam.* **VTT**) mountain bike (16)
terre *f.* earth; soil; land (18); **à l'intérieur des terres** in the center of the country; **pomme** (*f.*) **de terre** potato (7); **par terre** to/on the ground
terrestre *adj.* earthly; **extra-terrestre** *m., f.* extraterrestrial
terrible *adj.* terrible, awful
territoire *m.* territory; **territoire d'outre-mer (TOM)** overseas territory
tes *adj.* your
test *m.* test
tête *f.* head (9); **avoir mal à la tête** to have a headache; **perdre la tête** to lose one's mind (8)
têtu(e) *adj.* stubborn
texte *m.* text
TGV (train à grande vitesse) *m.* French high-speed train (14)
thailandais(e) *adj.* Thai; **Thailandais(e)** *m., f.* Thai (*person*)
thé *m.* tea (8); **thé à la menthe** mint tea
théâtre *m.* theater (10); **pièce** (*f.*) **de théâtre** play (21)
théière *f.* teapot
thème *m.* theme, subject
thérapeutique *adj.* therapeutic
thermal(e) *adj.* thermal; **bain** (*m.*) **thermal** spa bath (*hot spring water*); **station** (*f.*) **thermale** spa, health resort
thermalisme *m.* science of therapeutic baths
thèse *f.* thesis, dissertation (13); **thèse de doctorat** doctoral dissertation
thon *m.* tuna (7)
tien: le/la/les tien(ne)(s) *pron.* yours (22)
tiers *m.* third; **deux-tiers** two-thirds
tigre *m.* tiger
timbre *m.* stamp (13)
timonier-signaleur *m.* helmsman-signalman
tiré(e) *adj.* **de** taken from, excerpted from
tirer sur to fire on, shoot at (19)
tissu *m.* fabric
titre *m.* title; **gros titre** headline (12); **sous-titre** *m.* subtitle
tofu *m.* tofu
toi *pron., s., fam.* you; **et toi?** and you? (P)
toilette *f.*: **faire sa toilette** to wash up, get ready to go out; *pl.* restroom
tomate *f.* tomato (7)
tomber to fall (11); **ça tombe un mardi** that falls on a Tuesday; **tomber amoureux/euse** to fall in love; **tomber malade** to fall ill (9)
tomme *f.* regional cheese
ton *adj.* your (4)
ton *m.* tone
tonalité *f.* dial tone (13)
torse *m.* torso
tort *m.* wrong; **avoir tort** to be wrong, to be mistaken
torture *f.* torture
tôt *adv.* early (10); **de plus en plus tôt** earlier and earlier
totalitaire *adj.* totalitarian
touché(e) *adj.* touched; moved
toucher to touch; **toucher un chèque** to cash a check (20)
toujours *adv.* always (2); still (10); **est-ce qu'il vit toujours?** is he still living?
tour *f.* tower; *m.* walk; turn; **c'était mon tour** it was my turn
tourisme *m.* tourism; **faire du tourisme** to go sightseeing
touriste *m., f.* tourist
touristique *adj.* tourist; **site** (*m.*) **touristique** tourist site (20)
tourmenté(e) *adj.* tormented
tourner to turn (17); to film (*a movie*); **tournez** (tourne) **à droite** turn right
Toussaint *f.* All Saints' Day (11)
tousser to cough (9)
tout(e) (*pl.* **tous, toutes**) *adj., indef. pron.* all, every (one), the whole (14); very; **à toute heure** at any time; **à tout prix** at all costs; **ne... pas du tout** not at all, absolutely not (1); **tous les jours** every day (10); **tout à coup** suddenly; **tout à fait** completely; **tout de suite** right away (10); **tout droit** straight ahead (17); **tout heureux/euse** very happy; **toute la journée** all day; **tout le monde** everyone (1)
trace *f.* trace
tradition *f.* tradition
traditionnel(le) *adj.* traditional
traduction *f.* translation (13)
traduire (*like* **conduire**) *irreg.* to translate (18)
tragédie *f.* tragedy
tragique *adj.* tragic
trahir to betray
trahison *f.* treason (19)
train *m.* train (14); **en train** by train; **en train de** to be in the process of; **par train** by train; **train à grande vitesse** (*fam.* **TGV**) French high-speed train (14)
traîner: se traîner to move slowly, with difficulty; to crawl
trait *m.* trait, feature; **trait d'union** hyphen
traitement *m.* treatment
traiter to treat, behave toward

traître/tresse *m., f.* traitor (14)
trajet *m.* journey (14)
tramway *m.* tramway, trolley car
tranquille *adj.* calm, peaceful
tranquillité *f.* calm, tranquillity
transformation *f.* transformation
transformer to change, transform
transport *m.* transportation; **moyen** (*m.*) **de transport** means of transportation; **transport express régional** regional express train
travail *m.* work; job (2); **au travail** at work; **fête** (*f.*) **du travail** Labor Day (11); **monde** (*m.*) **du travail** work world
travailler to work (2)
travailleur/euse *adj.* hardworking
travers: à travers *prep.* through
traverser to cross (17)
treize *adj.* thirteen (P)
tréma *m.* umlaut (ë)
trentaine *f.*: **dans la trentaine** in one's thirties (*age*) (12)
trente *adj.* thirty (P)
très *adv.* very (P); **très bien** very well (P)
tricot *m.* knitting; **faire du tricot** to knit
tricoter to knit
trilogie *f.* trilogy
trimestre *m.* trimester
triomphe *f.* triumph
triple *adj.* triple
triste *adj.* sad (2)
trivial(e) *adj.* commonplace
trois *adj.* three (P)
troisième *adj.* third (11); **au/du troisième âge** elderly, in old age (12)
tromper to deceive, trick; **se tromper** to make a mistake, be mistaken (9)
trop (de) *adv.* too much (of), too many (of) (7); **trop tard** too late
tropical(e) *adj.* tropical
troublant(e) *adj.* troubling
troupe *f.* group; troop (19)
troupeau *m.* herd; flock
trouver to find; to consider (2); **où se trouve... ?** where is . . . ? (3); **se trouver** to be located (situated; found)
tu *pron.* you (1)
tuer to kill (19)
tunisien(ne) *adj.* Tunisian; **Tunisien(ne)** *m., f.* Tunisian (*person*)
turc (turque) *adj.* Turkish; **Turc (Turque)** *m., f.* Turk (*person*)
type *m.* type, kind; *fam.* guy
typique *adj.* typical

un(e) (*pl.* **des**) *indef. art.* a, an (P); *inv. adj.* one (P); *pron.* one; **à la une** on the front page (12); **les uns avec les autres** with each other; **un peu (de)** a little (of); a few (of) (7)
uni(e) *adj.* united
unième: vingt et unième *adj.* twenty-first
uniforme *m.* uniform
union *f.* union; **ils vivent en union libre** they're living together (without marriage) (4); **trait** (*m.*) **d'union** hyphen
unique *adj.* sole, only; **fils** (*m.*) **unique** only son
unir to unite
univers *m.* universe
universitaire *adj.* (*of or belonging to the*) university; **cité** (*f.*) **universitaire** dormitory; **journal** (*m.*) **universitaire** college newspaper; **résidence universitaire** dormitory building (13)
université *f.* university (P)
urbain(e) *adj.* urban; **vie** (*f.*) **urbaine** city life (10)
urinaire *adj.* urinary
usage *m.* use; *Gram.* usage
utile *adj.* useful (20)
utilisation *f.* use
utiliser to use

vacances *f. pl.* vacation (16); **grandes vacances** summer vacation; **partir en vacances** to go on vacation (16); **pendant les vacances** during vacation; **vacances de Noël** Christmas vacation
vache *f.* cow (18)
vachement *adv., fam.* very, tremendously
vague *f.* wave; **Nouvelle Vague** New Wave (*films*)
vaisselle *f.* dishes; **faire la vaisselle** to do the dishes (5); **lave-vaisselle** *f.* dishwasher
valeur *f.* value
valise *f.* suitcase (14); **enregistrer une valise** to check a suitcase (14)
vallée *f.* valley (17)
valse *f.* waltz
vapeur *f.* steam; **faire cuire à la vapeur** to steam (*food*) (15)
varié(e) *adj.* varied, diverse
varier to vary
variété *f.* variety show
vaste *adj.* vast
veau *m.* veal (8); calf; **daube** (*f.*) **de veau** veal stew
vedette *f.* star (*of a show, movie*) (20)
végétarien(ne) *adj.* vegetarian
véhicule *m.* vehicle
vélo *m.* bicycle (5); **faire du vélo (du VTT)** to bike (mountain bike) (16); **vélo tout terrain (VTT)** mountain bike (16)
vendeur/euse *m., f.* sales clerk (6)
vendre to sell (8)
vendredi *m.* Friday (4)
venir (*p.p.* **venu**) *irreg.* to come (3); **venir de** + *inf.* to have just (*done s.th.*) (4)
vent *m.* wind; **il fait du vent** it's windy (10)
ventre *m.* belly (9); stomach; **avoir mal au ventre** to have a stomachache
verbe *m.* verb; **verbe pronominal** *Gram.* pronominal (reflexive) verb
verger *m.* orchard (18)
vérifier to check; to verify
vérité *f.* truth
vernissage *m.* opening; preview (21)
verre *m.* glass (8); **prendre un verre** to have a drink (7); **verre d'eau** glass of water
verrouillé(e) *adj.* locked
vers *prep.* toward (17)
verser to pour (15)
version *f.* version; **version originale** original-language version, not dubbed (*film*); **version française** French-language version (*film*)
vert(e) *adj.* green (6); **citron** (*m.*) **vert** lime; ***haricots** (*m. pl.*) **verts** green beans (7); **oignon** (*m.*) **vert** green onion; **salade** (*f.*) **verte** green salad
vertébré *m.* vertebrate
veste *f.* sports coat (6)
vêtement *m.* piece of clothing (6); *pl.* clothes; **mettre un vêtement** to put on a piece of clothing (7)
veuf (veuve) *adj.* widowed (4)
viande *f.* meat (7)
vice-versa *adv.* vice versa
victime *f.* victim (*male or female*)
victoire *f.* victory
vide *adj.* empty
vidéo *f.* videotape; *adj.* video
vidéotext *adj.* on-screen text
vie *f.* life (10); **étape** (*f.*) **de la vie** stage of life; **vie privée** private life; **vie urbaine** city life (10)
vieillesse *f.* old age (12)
Viêtnam *m.* Vietnam (3)
vietnamien(ne) *adj.* Vietnamese (3); **Vietnamien(ne)** *m., f.* Vietnamese (*person*)
vieux (vieil, vieille [*pl.* **vieux, vieilles**]) *adj.* old (12); *m., f.* old man, old woman; *m. pl.* the elderly
vif (vive) *adj.* lively; spirited; intense
vigne *f.* vine (18)
vignoble *m.* vineyard (18)
vilain *m.* brutish peasant
villa *f.* single-family house; villa
village *m.* village (18)
ville *f.* city (10); **centre-ville** *m.* downtown; **en ville** in the city; **ville natale** birthplace
vin *m.* wine (7); **vin pétillant** sparkling wine; **vin rouge (blanc, rosé)** red (white, rosé) wine (7)

vingt *adj.* twenty (P); **vingt et un** (**vingt-deux,** etc.) twenty-one (twenty-two, etc.); **vingt et unième** twenty-first (11)
vingtième *adj.* twentieth (11)
violence *f.* violence
violent(e) *adj.* violent
violet(te) *adj.* purple (6)
violoniste *m., f.* violinist
virgule *m.* comma
vis-à-vis *adv.* with respect to
visa *m.* visa (14)
visage *m.* face (9)
visionnement *m.* viewing
visionner to watch, view
visite *f.* visit; **rendre visite à** to visit (*s.o.*) (8)
visiter to visit (*a place*) (8)
visiteur/euse *m., f.* visitor
vite *adv.* fast, quickly (12)
vitesse *f.* speed; **limite** (*f.*) **de vitesse** speed limit; **train** (*m.*) **à grande vitesse (TGV)** French high-speed train
viticulture *f.* wine growing (18)
vitre *f.* pane of glass; windowpane
vivant(e) *adj.* alive, living
vivre (*p.p.* **vécu**) *irreg.* to live, be alive (15); **est-ce qu'il vit toujours?** is he still living; **joie** (*f.*) **de vivre** joy in living (20); **ils vivent en union libre** they're living together (without marriage) (4)
vocabulaire *m.* vocabulary
voici *prep.* here is/are (1)
voie *f.* road, lane; **voie de chemin de fer** railroad tracks (19)
voilà *prep.* there is/are, here is/are (*for pointing out*) (1)
voile *f.* sail; **bateau à voile** sailboat (16); **faire de la planche à voile** to windsurf (16); **faire de la voile** to sail (16)
voir (*p.p.* **vu**) *irreg.* to see (10)
voisin(e) *m., f.* neighbor (22)
voiture *f.* car (5); **voiture de sport** sportscar
voix *f.* voice; **à haute voix** aloud
vol *m.* flight (14)
volaille *f.* poultry; group of chickens (18)
volcanique *adj.* volcanic
volley-ball *m.* volleyball (10)
volonté *f.* will
volontiers *adv.* willingly, gladly
vos *adj.* your
vote *m.* vote
voter to vote
votre *adj.* your (4)
vôtre: le/la/les vôtre(s) *pron.* yours (22)
vouloir (*p.p.* **voulu**) *irreg.* to want (6); **je voudrais** I would like (6); **vouloir bien** to be glad, to be willing (*to do s.th.*) (6); **vouloir dire** to mean (6)
vous *pron.* you; to/for you (1, 3, 7, 9); **comment allez-vous?** how are you? (P); **et vous?** and you? (P); **quel âge avez-vous?** how old are you? (4)
voyage *m.* trip; **agence** (*f.*) **de voyages** travel agency; **faire un voyage** to take a trip (5); **partir en voyage** to go on a trip; **voyage de noces** honeymoon
voyager to take a trip, travel (6)
voyageur/euse *m., f.* traveler
voyelle *f.* vowel
vrai(e) *adj.* true (2); **c'est vrai** that's true (2); **vrai ou faux?** true or false?
vraiment *adv.* truly
VTT (vélo tout terrain) *m.* mountain bike (16)
vue *f.* view; panorama; **point** (*m.*) **de vue** point of view

wagon *m.* (train) car (14); **wagon fumeurs (non-fumeurs)** smoking (nonsmoking) train car (14)
Web *m.* World Wide Web; **site** (*m.*) **Web** website (13); **sur le Web** on the Web; **surfer le Web** to surf the Web (13); **webmestre** *m.* webmaster
week-end *m.* weekend (4); **passer le week-end** to spend the weekend
world music *f.* world music (21)

y *pron.* there, to/about it/them (15); **il y a** there is / there are (*for counting*) (P); **il y a (dix ans)** (ten years) ago (10)
yaourt *m.* yogurt (15)
yeux (*pl. of* **œil**) *m. pl.* eyes (9); **les yeux bandés** blindfolded; **se maquiller les yeux** to put on eye makeup (9)
yoga *m.* yoga

zéro *m.* zero (P)
zone *f.* zone; **zone libre** free zone
zoo *m.* zoo
zut! *interj.* rats!

Lexique anglais-français

This English-French end vocabulary includes the words in the active vocabulary lists of all chapters. See the introduction to the *Lexique français-anglais* for a list of abbreviations used.

abdomen ventre *m.* (9)
able: to be able pouvoir *irreg.* (6)
above au-dessus de (3)
absolute absolu(e) (12)
absolutely: absolutely not ne... pas du tout (1)
accept accepter (de) (18)
according to selon (2)
account: bank account compte *m.* en banque (20)
accountant comptable *m., f.* (11)
accurate exact(e) (12)
accuse accuser (19)
ache: douleur *f.* (9); **to have an ache in** avoir (*irreg.*) mal à (9)
acquaintance: to make the acquaintance of faire (*irreg.*) la connaissance de (5)
active actif/ive (2)
actor acteur/trice *m., f.* (P)
ad: classified ad petite annonce *f.* (11)
add ajouter (15)
adolescence adolescence *f.* (12)
adolescent adolescent(e) (*fam.* ado) *m., f.* (12)
adore adorer (2)
adult adulte *m., f.* (12)
advertisement publicité *f.* (12)
advise against déconseiller (14)
afraid: to be afraid of avoir (*irreg.*) peur de (4)
Africa Afrique *f.* (14)
after après (8); après que (21)
afternoon après-midi *m., f.* (5); **in the afternoon** de l'après-midi (5); **this afternoon** cet après-midi (13)
again encore (10)
age âge (*m.*); **in old age** au/du troisième âge (12); **old age** vieillesse *f.* (12)
ago: ten years ago il y a dix ans (10)
agree: I (don't) agree je (ne) suis (pas) d'accord (2)
agriculture agriculture *f.* (18)
airplane avion *m.* (14)
airport aéroport *m.* (14)
aisle seat siège (*m.*) couloir (14)
Algeria Algérie *f.* (3)
Algerian *adj.* algérien(ne) (3)
alive: to be alive vivre (15)
all tout, toute, tous, toutes (14); **all it takes is** il suffit de (20); **All Saints' Day** Toussaint *f.* (11)
alleyway ruelle *f.* (20)
allow permettre *irreg.* (7); laisser (13); **to be allowed** pouvoir (6)
allspice quatre-épices *m., f.* (15)
almost presque (18)
alone seul(e) (12)
already déjà (10)
also aussi (1)
although bien que (21)
always toujours (2)
amazing étonnant(e) (22)
American *adj.* américain(e) (3); **American football** football (*m.*) américain (10)
amount (*of check or sale*) montant *m.* (20)
amusing amusant(e) (2)
and et (P); **and you?** et vous (toi)? (P)
angry fâché(e) (2); **to get angry** se fâcher (9)
animal animal *m.* (*pl.* animaux) (16); **animal breeding** élevage *m.* (18)
animated cartoon dessin (*m.*) animé (12)
anniversary (*wedding*) anniversaire (*m.*) de mariage (11)
answer *v.* répondre (8)
answering machine répondeur *m.* (5)
Antarctica Antarctique *m.* (14)
antique dealer antiquaire *m., f.* (20)
anxious inquiet (inquiète) (2)
any *pron.* en (15); **there is/are not any** il n'y en a pas (de) (4)
apart from à l'écart de (22)
apartment appartement *m.* (5); **apartment building** immeuble *m.* (5)
apparent apparent(e) (12)
appear apparaître *irreg.* (13); paraître *irreg.* (13)
applaud applaudir (11)
apple pomme *f.* (7)
April avril *m.* (4)
Arab *adj.* arabe (22); **old portion of an Arab city** médina *f.* (22)
argue se disputer (9)
arm bras *m.* (9); (*weapon*) arme *f.* (19)
armchair fauteuil *m.* (5)
armoire armoire *f.* (5)
arrival arrivée *f.* (14)
arrive arriver (11)
artisan artisan(e) *m., f.* (11)
as comme (8); **as . . . as** aussi... que (16); **as many/much (. . .) as** autant (de...) que (16)
ashamed: to be ashamed (of) avoir (*irreg.*) honte (de) (4)
Asia Asie *f.* (14)
ask demander (7)
asleep: to fall asleep s'endormir *irreg.* (9)
aspirin aspirine *f.* (9)
astonished: to be astonished that être (*irreg.*) étonné(e) que (21)
at à (1); **at . . . o'clock** à... heure(s) (5); **at first** d'abord (10); **at last** enfin (10); **at the home of** chez (3); **at what time?** à quelle heure? (5)
athletic sportif/ive (2)
attack *v.* attaquer (19)
attend (*an event*) assister à (10)
attention: to pay attention faire (*irreg.*) attention (5)
August août *m.* (4)
aunt tante *f.* (4)
Australia Australie *f.* (14)
author auteur / femme auteur *m., f.* (21)
automobile voiture *f.* (5)
autoroute autoroute *f.* (14)
autumn automne *m.* (10)
average *adj.* moyen(ne) (18)

baby bébé *m.* (12)
babysitter baby-sitter *m., f.* (11)
back dos *m.* (9); **to go back home** rentrer (11); **in back of** derrière (3)
backpack sac à dos *m.* (P)
bad mauvais(e) (2); **it's bad weather** il fait mauvais (10); **it is too bad that** il est dommage que (21)
badly mal (9)
bake faire (*irreg.*) cuire au four (15)
baker (*of bread*) boulanger/ère (7); **pastry baker** patissier/ière (7)
bakery (*for bread*) boulangerie *f.* (7); **pastry shop** patisserie *f.* (7)
ball (*inflated with air*) ballon *m.* (16); (*not inflated with air*) balle *f.* (16)
bank banque *f.* (20); **bank account** compte (*m.*) en banque (20); **bank (debit) card** carte (*f.*) bancaire (6)

banks: on the banks of au bord de (17)
bar bar *m.* (11)
barn grange *f.* (18)
baseball base-ball *m.* (10)
basin bassin *m.* (17); **bathroom basin** lavabo *m.* (5)
basket panier *m.* (16)
bathing suit maillot (*m.*) de bain (6)
bathroom salle (*f.*) de bains (5); **bathroom basin** lavabo *m.* (5)
bay baie *f.* (17)
be être *irreg.* (1); **there is/are** (*counting*) il y a (P); **there is/are, here is/are** (*pointing out*) voilà (1); **these/those/they are (not)** ce (ne) sont (pas) (P); **to be alive** (*to live*) vivre (15); **to be mistaken (about)** se tromper (de) (9); **to be named** s'appeler (9); **to be (twenty) years old** avoir (vingt) ans (4)
beach plage *f.* (16)
beans: green beans haricots (*m. pl.*) verts (7)
bear ours *m.* (16)
beautiful beau (bel, belle, beaux, belles) (12)
because parce que (4)
become devenir *irreg.* (3); **to become angry (with)** se fâcher (contre) (9); **to become sick** tomber malade (9)
bed lit *m.* (5); **to go to bed** se coucher (9); **to make the bed** faire (*irreg.*) le lit (5)
bedroom chambre *f.* (5)
beef bœuf *m.* (7)
beet betterave *f.* (15)
before avant (8); avant de (21); avant que (21); **before** (*the hour*) moins (5)
begin commencer (6)
behaved: well-behaved gentil(le) (2)
behind derrière (3)
believe croire *irreg.* (10)
belly ventre *m.* (9)
belong to appartenir (*irreg.*) à (14)
below au-dessous de (3)
belt ceinture *f.* (6)
Berber berbère (22)
beside à côté de (3)
best: the best *adj.* le/la/les meilleur(e)(s) (16); *adv.* le mieux (16)
better *adj.* meilleur(e) (16); *adv.* mieux (16)
between entre (3)
bicycle vélo *m.* (5); **to go bicycling (to bike)** faire (*irreg.*) du vélo (16); **to mountain bike** faire (*irreg.*) du VTT (16)
big grand(e) (2)
billiards billiard *m.* (10)
billion milliard *m.* (4)
biochemistry biochimie *f.* (13)
biology biologie *f.* (13)
bird oiseau *m.* (16)
birth naissance *f.* (12)
birthday anniversaire *m.* (4)
black noir(e) (6)
blackboard tableau *m.* (*pl.* tableaux) (1); **blackboard eraser** éponge *f.* (1)
blouse chemisier *m.* (6)
blue bleu(e) (6); **blues** (*music*) blues *m.* (21)
board: blackboard tableau *m.* (*pl.* tableaux) (1); **bulletin board** tableau d'affichage (11)
boat bateau *m.* (16); **sailboat** bateau à voile (16)
body corps *m.* (9); **body of work** œuvre *f.* (21)
boil faire (*irreg.*) bouillir (15)
book livre *m.* (P)
bookmark signet *m.* (13)
bookstore librairie *f.* (3)
boot botte *f.* (6)
booth: telephone booth cabine (*f.*) téléphonique (13)
boring ennuyeux/euse (2)
born: to be born naître *irreg.* (11)
boss patron(ne) *m., f.* (11)
bottle bouteille *f.* (7)
bowling bowling *m.* (10)
box boîte *f.* (7)
boy garçon *m.* (12)
brain cerveau *m.* (9)
bread pain *m.* (7); **bread roll** petit pain *m.* (8); **bread with butter and jam** tartine *f.* (8)
break (*a limb*) se casser (9)
breakfast petit déjeuner *m.* (8)
breeding: animal breeding (*farming*) l'élevage *m.* (18)
bridge pont *m.* (19)
brother frère *m.* (4); **brother-in-law, stepbrother** beau-frère *m.* (*pl.* beaux-frères) (4)
brown brun(e) (6); **chestnut brown** marron *inv.* (6)
brush (one's teeth, hair) se brosser (les dents, les cheveux) (9)
buffet buffet *m.* (5)
building bâtiment *m.* (3); **apartment building** immeuble *m.* (5) **building superintendent** gardien(ne) (*m., f.*) d'immeuble (11)
bulletin board tableau (*m.*) d'affichage (11)
burial enterrement *m.* (12)
bus: short distance, city bus bus *m.* (14); **long distance, tour bus** autocar *m.* (14)
business affaires *f. pl.* (11); **business administration** administration (*f.*) des affaires (13); **business economics** économie (*f.*) de gestion (13)
but mais (2)
butcher boucher/ère *m., f.* (7); **butcher shop** boucherie *f.* (7)
butter beurre *m.* (7)
buy *v.* acheter (6)
by par (6)
'bye salut (P)

café café *m.* (3)
calculator calculatrice *f.* (P)
call *v.* appeler (6)
camera appareil photo *m.* (5)
campground camping *m.* (16)
camping: to go camping faire (*irreg.*) du camping (16)
can (to be able) pouvoir *irreg.* (6)
can (*container*) boîte *f.* (7)
Canada Canada *m.* (3)
Canadian *adj.* canadien(ne) (3)
canoeing: to go canoeing faire (*irreg.*) du canoë (16)
car voiture *f.* (5); **train car** wagon *m.* (14)
carbonated *adj.* gazeux/euse (7)
card carte *f.* (6); **credit card** carte de crédit (6); **bank (debit) card** carte bancaire (6)
cardamom cardamome *m.* (15)
carrot carotte *f.* (7)
cartoon: animated cartoon dessin (*m.*) animé (12)
case: in case au cas où (19); **in that case** alors (1)
cash: in cash en espèces (6); **to cash a check** toucher un chèque (20)
cat chat *m.* (16)
cave: to explore caves faire (*irreg.*) de la spéléologie (16)
CD player lecteur (*m.*) de CD (5)
celebration fête *f.* (11)
cell phone portable *m.* (13)
century siècle *m.* (20)
certain certain(e) (21); sûr(e) (12)
chair chaise *f.* (1)
chalk craie *f.* (1)
champagne champagne *m.* (7)
change *v.* changer (6)
character (*in a story*) personnage *m.* (P)
check chèque *m.* (6); **to cash a check** toucher un chèque (20); **to check a suitcase** enregistrer une valise (14); **to deposit a check** déposer un chèque (20); **to write a check** faire (*irreg.*) un chèque (20)
checkbook carnet (*m.*) de chèques (20)
checkout caisse *f.* (6)
cheese fromage *m.* (7)
chemistry chimie *f.* (13)
cherry cerise *f.* (7)
chest poitrine *f.* (9)
chestnut brown marron *inv.* (6)
chicken poulet *m.* (7); **chicken with French fries** poulet frites *m.* (8); **poultry, group of chickens** volaille *f.* (18)
chick peas pois (*m. pl.*) chiches (15)

child enfant *m., f.* (1)
childhood enfance *f.* (12)
chimney cheminée *f.* (18)
China Chine *f.* (3)
Chinese chinois(e) *adj.* (3)
chiropractic chiropraxie *f.* (13)
chocolate chocolat *m.* (8); **chocolate mousse** mousse (*f.*) au chocolat (8)
choose choisir (11)
Christmas Noël *m.* (11)
church église *f.* (17)
cinnamon cannelle *f.* (15)
circus cirque *m.* (10)
city ville *f.* (10); **city life** vie (*f.*) urbaine (10); **old portion of an Arab city** médina *f.* (22)
civil servant fonctionnaire *m., f.* (11)
class classe *f.* (P); **to cut a class** sécher un cours (13)
classified ad petite annonce *f.* (11)
classmate camarade (*m., f.*) de classe (P)
classroom salle (*f.*) de classe (P)
clear clair(e) (10); **the sky is clear** le ciel est clair (10)
click (on) cliquer (sur) (13)
client client(e) *m., f.* (6)
climb *v.* monter (11)
clock horloge *f.* (1)
close *v.* fermer (15)
clothing (*article*) vêtement *m.* (6); **to put on a piece of clothing** mettre (*irreg.*) un vêtement (7)
cloudy nuageux/euse (10); **the sky is cloudy** le ciel est couvert (10)
coast côte *f.* (17)
coat: overcoat manteau (*m.*) (6); **sports coat** veste *f.* (6)
Coca Cola coca *m.* (8)
coconut noix (*f.*) de coco (15)
coffee café *m.* (8); **coffee with an equal amount of milk** café au lait (8)
cold: to be cold avoir (*irreg.*) froid (4); **it's cold out** il fait froid (10); **common cold** rhume *m.* (9)
collection ensemble *m.* (17)
column (*newspaper*) rubrique *f.* (12); **society column** carnet (*m.*) du jour (12)
comb (one's hair) se peigner (les cheveux) (9)
come venir *irreg.* (3); **to come back** revenir *irreg.* (3), rentrer (11); **to come home** rentrer (11)
comic strip bande (*f.*) dessinée (12)
commerce commerce *m.* (11)
commercial publicité *f.* (12)
company société *f.* (11)
compose composer (13)
composer compositeur/trice *m., f.* (21)
composition (*literary, artwork, musical*) œuvre *m.* (21)
computer ordinateur *m.* (1); **computer mouse** souris *f.* (16); **computer science** informatique *f.* (1); **laptop computer** portable *m.* (5)
concert concert *m.* (21)
conservation conservation *f.* (18)
consider (*s.o., s.th.*) **to be** trouver (2)
construct *v.* construire (18)
consume consommer (18)
consumption consommation *f.* (18)
contain contenir *irreg.* (14)
contemporary contemporain(e) (21)
continue continuer (18)
contract contrat *m.* (20)
control room régie *f.* (2)
cook cuisinier/ière *m., f.* (11); **to cook** (*s.th.*) faire (*irreg.*) cuire (15) **to cook (make) a meal** faire (*irreg.*) la cuisine (5)
cooking pot (*large, iron*) marmite *f.* (18)
cool: it's cool out il fait frais (10)
coriander coriandre *f.* (15)
corn maïs *m.* (7)
corner coin *m.* (17)
cough *v.* tousser (9); **cough drop** pastille *f.* (9)
could you show me the way to . . . ? est-ce que vous pourriez m'indiquer le chemin pour aller à... ? (17)
country pays *m.* (3); **country dweller** paysan(ne) *m., f.* (18); **country music** country *f.* (21); **in the country** à la campagne (17)
course cours *m.* (1); **first course** (*meal*) entrée *f.* (8); **of course** bien sûr (que oui) (2); **of course not** bien sûr que non (2); **to fail a course** échouer à un cours (13); **to pass a course** réussir à un cours (11); **to take a course** suivre un cours (15); **What courses are you taking?** Quels cours est-ce que tu suis? (13)
couscous couscous *m.* (15); **couscous grains** grains (*m. pl.*) de couscous (15)
cousin cousin(e) *m., f.* (4)
cover *v.* couvrir *irreg.* (15)
cow vache *f.* (18)
craftsperson artisan(e) *m., f.* (11)
crazy fou (folle) (12)
cream crème *f.* (7)
credit: credit card carte (*f.*) de crédit (6); **credit union** caisse (*f.*) populaire (13)
croissant croissant *m.* (8)
crop récolte *f.* (18)
cross *v.* traverser (17)
cross-country: to cross-country ski faire du ski de fond (16)
crossword puzzle mots (*m. pl.*) croisés (12)
cultivate cultiver (18)
cup tasse *f.* (8)
curator (of a museum) conservateur/trice *m., f.* (de musée) (11)
current *adj.* actuel(le) (12)
curry curry *m.* (15)
customs douane *f.* (14); **to go through customs** passer la douane (14)

dairy product store crémerie *f.* (7)
dark *adj.* sombre (22)
daughter fille *f.* (4)
day jour *m.* (1)
dear cher (chère) (2)
death mort *f.* (12)
December décembre *m.* (4)
decide (to do) décider (de) (18)
decision: to make a decision prendre (*irreg.*) une décision (7)
deer cerf *m.* (16)
delicatessen charcuterie *f.* (7)
demand *v.* exiger (20)
demonstration (*public, political*) manifestation *f.* (21)
department (*in a store*) rayon *m.* (6); **department store** grand magasin *m.* (6)
departure départ *m.* (14)
deposit *v.*: **deposit a check** déposer un chèque (20)
descend descendre (8)
describe décrire *irreg.* (12)
desire *v.* désirer (2)
desk bureau *m.* (*pl.* bureaux) (1)
dessert dessert *m.* (8)
destroy détruire *irreg.* (18)
detest détester (2)
dial (a phone number) composer un numéro (13); **dial tone** tonalité *f.* (13)
dictionary dictionnaire *m.* (P)
die *v.* mourir *irreg.* (11)
difficult difficile (2)
dignity: with dignity dignement (22)
dilapidated délabré(e) (20)
dine dîner (2)
dining room salle (*f.*) à manger (5)
dinner dîner *m.* (8); **to eat dinner, to dine** dîner (2)
diploma diplôme *m.* (13)
direction direction *f.* (14)
disappear disparaître *irreg.* (13)
discover découvrir *irreg.* (15)
discreet discret/ète (12)
discuss discuter (13)
dish: hot dish plat (*m.*) chaud; **main dish** plat (*m.*) principal (8); **to do the dishes** faire (*irreg.*) la vaisselle (5)
dissertation thèse *m.* (13)
district arrondissement *m.* (20)
diverse divers(e) (17)
divorce *v.* **(to get divorced)** divorcer (12); **divorced** divorcé(e) (4)

do faire *irreg.* (5); **to do errands** faire les courses (5); **to do homework** faire les devoirs (5); **to do housework** faire le ménage (5); **to do the dishes** faire la vaisselle (5); **to do the laundry** faire la lessive (5)
doctor médecin / femme médecin *m., f.* (9)
doctorate doctorat *m.* (13)
documentary documentaire *m.* (12)
dog chien *m.*(16)
door porte *f.* (1)
doubt *v.* douter (21); **it is doubtful that** il est douteux que (21); **no doubt** sans doute (2)
down: to get/go down descendre (8); **to go down a street** descendre une rue (17)
dozen douzaine *f.* (7)
dramatic arts arts (*m. pl.*) dramatiques (13)
dress robe *f.* (6); **to get dressed (in)** s'habiller (en) (9)
drink boisson *f.* (8); **to drink** boire *irreg.* (7); **to have a drink** prendre un verre (7)
drive conduire *irreg.* (18)
driver conducteur/trice *m., f.* (19)
drug (medicine) médicament *m.* (9)
during pendant (11)
dynamic dynamique (2)

each chaque (7)
ear oreille *f.* (9)
early en avance (5); tôt (10)
earth terre *f.* (18)
east est *m.* (17)
Easter Pâques *m. s., f. pl.* (11)
easy facile (2)
eat manger (6); **to eat dinner** dîner (2)
economics: business economics économie (*f.*) de gestion (13)
edge: on the edge of au bord de (17)
editor: letters to the editor courrier (*m.*) des lecteurs (12)
editorial éditorial *m.* (*pl.* éditoriaux) (12)
efficient efficace (18)
effort: with effort fort (19)
egg œuf *m.*; **hard-boiled egg with mayonnaise** œuf dur mayonnaise (8)
eggplant aubergine *f.* (15)
eight huit (P)
eighteen dix-huit (P)
eighth huitième (11)
eighty quatre-vingts (4)
elderly au/du troisième âge (12)
electronic mailbox boîte (*f.*) aux lettres électronique (13)
elegant élégant(e) (12)
elevation (*height*) hauteur *f.* (17)
eleven onze (P)
e-mail courrier (*m.*) électronique (13); **e-mail message** mél *m.* (13)
employ *v.* employer (6)
encounter rencontre *f.* (21)
encourage encourager (6)
engineer ingénieur / femme ingénieur *m., f.* (11)
engineering génie *m.* (13); **chemical (electrical, industrial, mechanical) engineering** génie chimique (électrique, industriel, mécanique) (13)
England Angleterre *f.* (3)
English *adj.* anglais(e) (3); (*language*) anglais *m.* (1)
English Channel Manche *f.* (17)
enough assez (de) (7); **it is enough** il suffit (20)
enter entrer (11)
entertainment (*show*) spectacle *m.* (21)
envelope enveloppe *f.* (13)
environment environnement *m.* (18)
eraser gomme *f.*; **blackboard eraser** éponge *f.* (1)
errands: to do errands faire (*irreg.*) les courses (5)
escape *v.* s'échapper (19)
especially surtout (16)
essential: it is essential il est essentiel (20)
Europe Europe *f.* (14)
evening soir *m.* (5); soirée *f.* (21); **in the evening** du soir (5); **this evening** ce soir (13)
event événement *m.* (12); **cultural event** manifestation (*f.*) culturelle (21); **in the event that** au cas où (19); **special event** spectacle *m.* (21)
ever déjà (10)
every tout, toute, tous, toutes (14); **every day** tous les jours (10)
everyone tout le monde (1)
everywhere partout (18)
evident évident(e) (12)
ewe brebis *f.* (18)
exact exact(e) (12)
exam examen *m.* (13); **to fail an exam** échouer à un examen (13); **to pass an exam** réussir à un examen; **to study for an exam** préparer un examen (13); **to take an exam** passer un examen (13)
execute (s.o.) **by shooting** fusiller (19)
executive cadre *m., f.* (11)
exhibit: art exhibit exposition (*f.*) d'art (10)
exit sortie *f.* (14)
expensive cher (chère) (2)
explore caves faire de la spéléologie (16)
eye œil *m.* (*pl.* yeux) (9)

face visage *m.* (9)
facial tissue mouchoir (*m.*) en papier (9)
facility local *m.* (*pl.* locaux) (13)
facing en face de (3)
fail échouer (13); **to fail a course (an exam)** échouer à un cours (à un examen) (13)
fall *v.* tomber (11); (*season*) automne *m.* (10) **to fall asleep** s'endormir *irreg.* (9)
false faux (fausse) (2); **that's (it's) false (wrong)** c'est faux (2)
famous célèbre (20)
far (from) loin (de) (3)
farm ferme *f.* (18)
farmer agriculteur/trice *m., f.* (11); fermier/ière *m., f.* (18)
fast *adj.* rapide (12); *adv.* vite (12); **fast food** fast-food *m.* (8); **fast-food worker** employé(e) (*m., f.*) de fast-food (11)
father père *m.* (4); **father-in-law, stepfather** beau-père *m.* (*pl.* beaux-pères) (4)
February février *m.* (4)
feel: to feel like (*doing*) avoir envie de (4); **to feel nauseated** avoir mal au cœur (9)
festival festival *m.* (*pl.* festivals) (16); fête *f.* (11)
fever fièvre *f.* (9)
few peu (de) (7); **a few** quelques (8); un peu (de) (7)
fewer (. . .) than moins (de...) que (16)
fewest: the fewest le moins (de) (16)
field champ *m.* (17)
fifteen quinze (P)
fifth cinquième (11)
fifty cinquante (P); **in one's fifties** (*age*) dans la cinquantaine (12)
film film *m.* (P)
finally enfin (10)
find *v.* trouver (2)
fine: I'm fine ça va bien (P)
finish *v.* finir (11)
fire feu *m.* (17); **to fire** licencier (20); **to fire on** tirer sur (19)
fireplace cheminée *f.* (18)
first *adj.* premier/ière (11); **at first, first (of all)** *adv.* d'abord (10); **first course** (*meal*) entrée *f.* (8); **first of the month** premier *m.* (4)
fish poisson *m.* (7); **fish store** poissonnerie *f.* (7); **to go fishing** aller (*irreg.*) à la pêche (16)
five cinq (P)
flight vol *m.* (14)
flower fleur *f.* (16)
flu grippe *f.* (9)
follow suivre *irreg.* (15)
food aliment *m.* (7)
foot pied *m.* (9); **on foot** à pied (14)
football (American) football (*m.*) américain (10)
for pour (1); (*time*) depuis (11)
forest forêt *f.* (17)
foreign *adj.* étranger/ère (13); **foreign language** langue (*f.*) étrangère (13)

forget oublier (6)
fork fourchette *f.* (8)
form *v.* former (20)
formerly autrefois (10)
forty quarante (P); **in one's forties** (*age*) dans la quarantaine (12)
four quatre (P)
fourteen quatorze (P)
fourth quatrième (11)
France France *f.* (3)
frank franc(he) (12)
French français(e) (3); (*language*) français *m.* (1); **French fries** frites *f. pl.* (8); **French-speaking** francophone (3)
Friday vendredi *m.* (4)
friend ami(e) *m., f.* (P)
Frisbee Frisbee *m.* (16)
from de (P); **from . . . to . . .** de... à... (5); **from time to time** de temps en temps (10)
front: in front of devant (3); **on the front page** (*newspaper*) à la une (12)
fruit fruit *m.* (7)
fry faire (*irreg.*) frire (15)
full complet/ète (14); **full-time** à plein temps (11)
funny amusant(e) (2)
furious furieux/euse (21)
furniture (piece of) meuble *m.* (5)
future avenir *m.* (18)

gallery galerie *f.* (20)
game jeu *m.* (*pl.* jeux) (10)
garden jardin *m.* (18)
garlic ail *m.* (15)
gasoline essence *f.* (18)
gate (*airport*) porte (*f.*) d'embarquement (14)
gather (*flowers*) cueillir *irreg.* (16); **to gather up** (*toys, etc.*) ramasser (18)
gentle doux (douce) (12)
geography géographie *f.* (1)
German *adj.* allemand(e) (3)
Germany Allemagne *f.* (3)
get: to get along well (poorly) (with) s'entendre bien (mal) (avec) (9); **to get around** circuler (14); **to get down** descendre (8); **to get dressed (in, as)** s'habiller (en) (7); **to get up** se lever (9)
ginger gingembre *m.* (15)
girl jeune fille *f.* (12)
give *v.* donner (2); **to give a gift** offrir un cadeau (15)
glad: to be glad to vouloir (*irreg.*) bien (6)
glass verre *m.* (8)
go aller *irreg.* (3); **to go back (home)** rentrer (11); **to go camping** faire (*irreg.*) du camping (16); **to go canoeing** faire (*irreg.*) du canoë (16); **to go down** descendre (8); **to go down (up) a street** descendre (monter) une rue (17); **to go fishing** aller à la pêche (16); **to go horseback riding** monter à cheval (16); **to go out** sortir *irreg.* (8); **to go rock climbing** faire de l'escalade (16); **to go shopping** faire (*irreg.*) du shopping (5); **to go through customs** passer la douane (14); **to go to bed** se coucher (9) **to go up** monter (11)
golf: to play golf jouer au golf (16)
good bon(ne) (2); **good-bye** au revoir (P); **good-looking** beau (bel, belle, beaux, belles) (12); **good luck** bonne chance; **to have a good time** s'amuser (9)
grade (*on a paper*) note *f.* (13)
grain céréale *f.* (18)
granddaughter petite-fille *f.* (*pl.* petites-filles)(4)
grandfather grand-père *m.* (*pl.* grands-pères) (4)
grandmother grand-mère *f.* (*pl.* grands-mères) (4)
grandparents grands-parents *m. pl.* (4)
grandson petit-fils *m.* (*pl.* petits-fils) (4)
grape raisin *m.* (7)
great super (2); magnifique (2)
green vert(e) (6); **green beans** haricots (*m. pl.*) verts (7)
greenhouse effect effet (*m.*) de serre (18)
greeting accueil *m.* (20)
gray gris(e) (6)
grocer épicier/ière *m., f.* (7); **grocery store** épicerie *f.* (7)
ground floor rez-de-chaussée *m.* (5)
group ensemble *m.* (17)
grow pousser (18)
guard *v.* garder (19); **security guard** agent(e) *m., f.* de sécurité (11)
guitar guitare *f.* (5)
gymnasium gymnase *m.* (13)

hair cheveux *m. pl.* (9)
half: half-kilogram demi-kilo *m.*, (7); **half-past** (*the hour*) et demi(e) (5); **half-time** à mi-temps (11)
ham jambon *m.* (7)
hamburger hamburger *m.* (8)
hand main *f.* (9)
handkerchief: paper handkerchief mouchoir (*m.*) en papier (9)
handsome beau (bel, belle, beaux, belles) (12)
hang glide faire (*irreg.*) du parapente (16)
hang up (*the telephone receiver*) *v.* raccrocher (13)
Hannukah Hannukah (11)
happen se passer (9)
happy heureux/euse (2)
harvest récolte *f.* (18); **to harvest** récolter (18)
hat chapeau *m.* (6)
hate *v.* détester (2)
have avoir (*irreg.*) (4); **to have** (*s.th. to eat*) prendre (*irreg.*) (7); **to have a drink** prendre un verre (7); **to have a good time** s'amuser (9); **to have a party** faire la fête (5); **to have a picnic** faire un pique-nique, piqueniquer (16); **to have a stomachache** avoir mal au ventre (9); **to have a view of (the port)** donner sur (le port) (20); **to have lunch** déjeuner (8); **to have pain, an ache in, to have a sore . . .** avoir (*irreg.*) mal à (9); **to have to** (*must*) devoir *irreg.* (9)
head tête *f.* (9)
headline gros titre *m.* (12); manchette *f.* (12)
health santé *f.* (9)
hear entendre (8)
heart cœur *m.* (9)
heat *v.* chauffer (15); *n.* chaleur *f.* (20)
height (*elevation*) hauteur *f.* (17)
hello bonjour (P)
here ici (3); là (1); **here is (here are)** voici (1)
hesitate (*to do*) hésiter (à) (18)
hi salut (P)
hide se réfugier (19)
high-speed train train à grande vitesse (*fam.* TGV) *m.* (14)
highway autoroute *f.* (14)
hike *v.* faire (*irreg.*) une randonnée (16)
hill colline *f.* (17)
hip-hop music hip-hop *m.* (21)
hire engager (20)
history histoire *f.* (1)
hit *v.* frapper (19)
hockey: to play hockey jouer au hockey (16)
hold *v.* tenir (*irreg.*) (14)
holiday congé *m.* (20); fête *f.* (11); **legal holiday** jour (*m.*) férié (11)
home: at the home of chez (3); **home page** page (*f.*) d'accueil (13); **personal home page** page (*f.*) perso (13); **to come home** rentrer (11)
homeland patrie *f.* (19)
homework devoir *m.* (5); **to do homework** faire (*irreg.*) les devoirs (5)
hope *v.* espérer (6); souhaiter (21)
horse cheval *m.* (16); **to go horseback riding** monter à cheval (16)
hospital hôpital *m.* (9)
hostage otage *m.* (19)
hot: to feel hot avoir (*irreg.*) chaud (4); **it's hot out** il fait chaud (10)
hotel hôtel *m.* (3)
hour heure *f.* (5); **rush hour** heures (*f. pl.*) de pointe (14)
house maison *f.* (5)

housework: to do the housework faire (*irreg.*) le ménage (5)
how comment (4); **how are you?** comment allez-vous? (vas-tu?) (P); **how many, how much** combien de (4); **how old are you (is he,** *etc.***)?** quel âge avez-vous (a-t-il, *etc.*)? (4); **How's it going?** Ça va? (P)
hundred cent (4)
hungry: to be hungry avoir (*irreg.*) faim (4)
hunt *v.* chasser (16)
hurry *v.* se dépêcher (9); **in a hurry** pressé(e) (14)
husband mari *m.* (4)

ice cream glace *f.* (8)
ice skate *n.* patin *m.* (16); *v.* patiner (16); faire [*irreg.*] du patin à glace (16)
icon (computer) icone *m.* (13)
if si (7); **if I were you** à ta (votre) place (19)
immediate immédiat(e) (12)
immigrant immigré(e) *m., f.* (20)
important important(e) (20)
impossible impossible (20)
in dans (P); **in a hurry** pressé(e) (14); **in back of** derrière (3); **in case, in the event that** au cas où (19); **in cash** en espèces (6); **in front of** devant (3); **in good (great) shape** en bonne (pleine) forme (9); **in old age** au troisième âge (12); **in one's thirties** (*age*) dans la trentaine (12); **in order to/that** afin de/que (21), pour que (21); **in short** *interj.* enfin (10); **in that case** alors (1); **in the afternoon** de l'après-midi (5); **in the country** à la campagne (17); **in the evening** du soir (5); **in the middle of** au milieu de (22); **in the morning** du matin (5); **in the past** autrefois (10); **in your place** à ta (votre) place (19)
incredible incroyable (21)
India Inde *f.* (15)
Indian *adj.* indien(ne) (15)
indicate indiquer (17)
inhabitant habitant(e) *m., f.* (20)
intellectual intellectuel(le) (2)
interesting intéressant(e) (2); **to be interested in** s'intéresser à (9)
Internet: Internet user internaute *m., f.* (13); **on the Internet** sur Internet (11)
internship stage *m.* (11)
interpreter interprète *m., f.* (11)
invite inviter (18)
is: to be être (1); **is it so** (*true*) **that . . .** Est-ce que... (1); **isn't that right?** n'est-ce pas? (3); non? (3); **is that right?** c'est ça? (P); **is this (that, it) . . . ?** est-ce... ? (P); **it could be that, it is possible that** il se peut que (21)
island île *f.* (17)
Israel Israël *m.* (14)
Israeli *adj.* israëlien(ne) (15)
it: it could be that il se peut que (21); **it is . . .** c'est... (P); **it is not . . .** ce n'est pas... (P); **it's (ten) o'clock** il est (dix) heures (5); **It's a pleasure** (*to meet you*). Enchanté(e). (P)
Italian italien(ne) *adj.* (15)
Italy Italie *f.* (15)

jam confiture *f.* (7)
January janvier *m.* (4)
Japan Japon *m.* (3)
Japanese *adj.* japonais(e) (3)
jeans jean *m., s.* (6)
job emploi *m.* (11); poste *m.* (11); travail *m.* (2)
jogging jogging *m.* (10); **jogging trail** piste (*f.*) de jogging (13)
journalist journaliste *m., f.* (2)
joyful, joyous joyeux/euse (12); **joyful attitude** (*toward life*) joie (*f.*) de vivre (20)
juice (orange) jus *m.* (d'orange) (8)
July juillet *m.* (4)
June juin *m.* (4)
just: to have just (*done something*) venir (*irreg.*) de + *inf.* (4)

keep garder (19)
kill *v.* tuer (19)
kilogram kilo *m.* (7); **half kilogram** demi-kilo *m.* (7)
kind *adj.* gentil(le) (2)
kiss (each other) *v.* s'embrasser (9)
kitchen cuisine *f.* (5)
knee genou *m.* (9)
knife couteau *m.* (8)
know: to be acquainted with connaître (*irreg.*) (13); **I don't know** je ne sais pas (P); **to know** (*a fact*) savoir (*irreg.*) (13)

Labor Day fête (*f.*) du travail (11)
laboratory laboratoire *m.* (P)
laborer: manual laborer ouvrier/ière *m., f.* (11)
lake lac *m.* (17)
language langue *f.* (13); **foreign language** langue étrangère (13); **foreign language teaching** enseignement (*m.*) des langues étrangères (13)
laptop computer portable *m.* (5)
last *adj.* dernier/ière (13); **at last** enfin (10); **last stop** terminus *m.* (14)
late en retard (5); tard (10)
later plus tard (10)
launch *v.* lancer (6)
laundry: to do the laundry faire (*irreg.*) la lessive (5)
law droit *m.* (13)
lawn bowling: to play lawn bowling jouer à la pétanque (aux boules) (16)
lawyer avocat(e) *m., f.* (11)
leaf feuille *f.* (13)
learn apprendre (*irreg.*) (7)
least: the least le/la/les moins (16)
leave partir *irreg.* (8); **to leave** (*s.o., a place*) quitter (8); **to leave** (*s.th. somewhere*) laisser (13)
lecture conférence *f.* (21)
left: to/on the left à gauche (17)
leg jambe *f.* (9)
legal holiday jour (*m.*) férié (11)
leisure activities distractions *f. pl.* (10); loisirs *m. pl.* (16)
lemon citron *m.* (7)
lemongrass citronnelle *f.* (15)
lentil lentille *f.* (15)
less moins (5); **less (. . .)** moins (de...) (16); **less (than)** moins (que) (16)
lesson leçon *f.* (1); **to study for a lesson** préparer une leçon (13)
let laisser (13)
letter lettre *f.* (13); **letters to the editor** courrier (*m.*) des lecteurs (12)
lettuce salade *f.* (8)
library bibliothèque *f.* (3)
lie *v.* mentir (*irreg.*) (8)
life vie *f.* (10); **city life** vie urbaine (10)
light: to turn on the light mettre (*irreg.*) la lumière (7); **traffic light** feu *m.* (17)
light (*weight*) léger (légère) (8)
like *prep.* comme (8); *adj.* tel(le) (12)
like: *v.* aimer (2); **I would like** je voudrais (6)
likely: it is (un)likely that il est (peu) probable que (21)
line: to stand in line faire (*irreg.*) la queue (5)
listen (to) écouter (2)
literary littéraire (13)
little peu (de) (7); **a little** un peu (de) (7)
live *v.* (*reside*) habiter (2); **live** (*to be alive*) vivre (15); **they are living together (without marriage)** ils vivent en union libre (4)
living: joy in living joie (*f.*) de vivre (20); **living room** salle (*f.*) de séjour (5)
location endroit *m.* (14); lieu *m.* (*pl.* lieux) (3)
long time: for a long time longtemps (10)
look (at) regarder (2); **to look for** chercher (2); **to look (like)** avoir (*irreg.*) l'air (4)
lose perdre (8); **to lose one's mind** perdre la tête (8); **to lose patience** perdre patience (8)
lot: a lot (of) beaucoup (de) (7)
love *v.* aimer (2)
low-cut: in low-cut clothing en décolleté (22)
lozenge (*cough drop*) pastille *f.* (9)

lunch déjeuner *m.* (8); **to have lunch** déjeuner *v.* (8)
lung poumon *m.* (9)

madam (Mrs.) madame (Mme) (P)
magazine magazine *m.* (12)
Maghreb Maghreb *m.* (15); **from the Maghreb** maghrébin(e) (15)
magnificent magnifique (2)
mail *n.* poste *f.* (3); (*letters, etc.*) courrier *m.* (12)
major in se spécialiser en (13); faire (*irreg.*) des études en (13)
make faire *irreg.* (5), rendre (8); **to make a decision** prendre (*irreg.*) une décision (7); **to make a meal** faire (*irreg.*) la cuisine (5); **to make a mistake (about)** se tromper (de) (9); **to make the acquaintance of** faire (*irreg.*) la connaissance de (5); **to make the bed** faire (*irreg.*) le lit (5); **to make up one's eyes (one's lips)** se maquiller les yeux (les lèvres) (9)
makeup: to put on makeup se maquiller (9)
man homme *m.* (P)
management gestion *f.* (11)
manual laborer ouvrier/ière *m., f.* (11)
many beaucoup (de) (7); **how many** combien de (4); **too many** trop (de) (7)
map carte *f.* (17); (*subway, city, region*) plan *m.* (13)
March mars *m.* (4)
market marché *m.* (7)
marketing marketing *m.* (11)
marriage mariage *m.* (12)
married marié(e) (4)
match (soccer, boxing) match *m.* (de foot, de boxe) (10)
mathematics (math) mathématiques (maths) *f. pl.* (1)
May mai *m.* (4)
meal repas *m.* (8); **to cook a meal** faire la cuisine (5)
mean *v.* vouloir (*irreg.*) dire (6)
means moyen *m.* (14)
meat viande *f.* (7)
medicine médicament *m.* (9)
media médias *m. pl.* (12)
meet *v.* rencontrer (14) **Nice to meet you** Enchanté(e) (P)
meeting rencontre *f.* (21); (*business*) réunion *f.*
merchant marchand(e) *m., f.* (7)
method moyen *m.* (14)
Mexican mexicain(e) (3)
Mexico Mexique *m.* (3)
microwave oven four (*m.*) à micro-ondes (5)
middle: in the middle of au milieu de (22)
midnight minuit *m.* (5)
mild: it's mild out il fait doux (10)
milk lait *m.* (8)
million million *m.* (4)
mind: to lose one's mind perdre la tête (8)
mineral water eau (*f.*) minérale (7)
minus moins (5)
mirror miroir *m.* (5)
miserable malheureux/euse (2)
Miss mademoiselle (Mlle) (P)
miss: to be missed by (*s. o.*) manquer à (17); **I miss you** tu me manques
mistake: to make a mistake, be mistaken (about) se tromper (de) (9)
mix *v.* mélanger (15)
mode moyen *m.* (14)
moderate moyen(ne) (18)
Monday lundi *m.* (4)
money argent *m.* (6)
month mois *m.* (4)
more: more (. . .) plus (de) (16); **more (than)** plus (que) (16)
morning matin *m.* (5); **in the morning** du matin (5); **this morning** ce matin (13)
Moroccan *adj.* marocain(e) (3)
Morocco Maroc *m.* (3)
mosque mosquée *f.* (22)
most (of) la plupart (de) (22); **the most (of)** le/la/les plus (de) (16)
mother mère *f.* (4); **mother-in-law, stepmother** belle-mère *f.* (*pl.* belles-mères) (4)
mountain montagne *f.* (17); **mountain bike** vélo *m.* tout terrain (VTT) (16); **old rounded mountain range** massif *m.* (17)
mouse souris *f.* (16); **computer mouse** souris *f.* (16)
mousse: chocolate mousse mousse (*f.*) au chocolat (8)
mouth bouche *f.* (9)
movie theater cinéma *m.* (P)
much beaucoup (de) (7); **how much** combien de (4); **so much** tellement (12); **too much** trop (de) (7)
muscle muscle *m.* (9)
museum musée *m.* (10); **art (natural science) museum** musée d'art (de sciences naturelles) (10); **museum curator** conservateur/trice (*m., f.*) de musée (11)
mushroom champignon *m.* (15)
music musique *f.* (13)
musician musicien(ne) *m., f.* (11)
must: one must (not) il (ne) faut (pas) (20); **must (to have to)** devoir *irreg.* (9)
mutton mouton *m.* (8)
my name is je m'appelle (P)
name: to be named s'appeler (9); **his (her) name is** il (elle) s'appelle (4); **my name is** je m'appelle (P)
napkin serviette *f.* (8)
narrow étroit(e) (20)
national holiday fête (*f.*) nationale (11)
nauseated: to feel nauseated avoir (*irreg.*) mal au cœur (9)
near près (de) (3)
nearly presque (18)
necessary: it is necessary il est nécessaire (20), il faut (20); **it is not necessary** il n'est pas nécessaire (20)
need: to need avoir (*irreg.*) besoin de (4)
neighbor voisin(e) *m., f.* (22)
neighborhood quartier *m.* (3)
nephew neveu *m.* (4)
network (*system*) réseau *m.* (14); **television network** chaîne *f.* (12)
never ne... jamais (1)
new nouveau (nouvel, nouvelle, nouveaux, nouvelles) (12); **New Year's Day** nouvel an *m.*(11)
news actualités *f. pl.* (12), informations *f. pl.* (12); **news program** actualités *f. pl.* (12), informations *f. pl.* (12)
newspaper journal *m.* (*pl.* journaux) (12); **newspaper section, column** rubrique *f.* (12)
next *adj.* prochain(e) (13); *adv.* ensuite (10); puis (10); **the next day** le lendemain *m.* (13)
nice (*person*) gentil(le) (2); sympathique (*fam.* sympa) (1); (*weather*) beau (10); **it's nice out** il fait beau (10); **Nice to meet you** Enchanté(e) (P)
niece nièce *f.* (4)
night nuit *f.* (10); **nightclub** boîte (*f.*) de nuit (10)
nine neuf (P)
nineteen dix-neuf (P)
ninety quatre-vingt-dix (4)
ninth neuvième (11)
no non (P); **no doubt** sans doute (2); **no one** ne... personne (13)
nobody ne... personne (13)
noncarbonated *adj.* plat(e) (7)
nonsmoking (train) car wagon (*m.*) non-fumeurs (14)
noon midi *m.* (5)
normally d'habitude (10)
north nord *m.* (17)
North America Amérique (*f.*) du Nord (14)
nose nez *m.* (9); **runny nose** le nez qui coule (9)
not ne... pas (1); **not anymore** ne... plus (1); **not at all, absolutely not** ne... pas du tout (1); **not ever** ne... jamais (1); **not one, not any** ne... aucun(e) (13); **not yet** ne... pas encore (1)

notebook cahier *m.* (P)
nothing ne... rien (13)
novel roman *m.* (21)
novelist romancier/ière *m., f.* (21)
November novembre *m.* (4)
now maintenant (5)
numerous nombreux/euse (18)
nurse infirmier/ière *m., f.* (9); **nurse's aide** garde-malade *m., f.* (11)

obey obéir (à) (11)
obituary nécrologie *f.* (12); **obituary column** nécrologie *f.* (12)
obtain obtenir (*irreg.*) (14)
ocean océan *m.* (17)
o'clock: it's (five) o'clock il est (cinq) heures (5); **at (five) o'clock** à (cinq) heures (5)
October octobre *m.* (4)
of de (P); **of course** bien sûr (que oui) (2); **of course not** bien sûr que non (2); **of it/them/there** en (15)
offer *v.* offrir (*irreg.*) (15)
office bureau *m.* (*pl.* bureaux) (3)
often souvent (2)
oil (olive, sesame) huile *f.* (d'olive, de sésame) (15)
okay d'accord (2); **I'm okay** ça va; **okay?** d'accord? (3); OK? (3)
old vieux (vieil, vieille, vieux, vieilles) (12); **elderly, in old age** au/du troisième âge (12); **old age** vieillesse *f.* (12); **old portion of an Arab city** médina *f.* (22)
omelet omelette *f.* (8)
on sur (3); **on foot** à pied (14); **on the street** dans la rue (3); **on the banks (shore, edge) of** au bord de (17); **on the front page** à la une (12); **on the Internet** sur Internet (11); **on the left/right** à gauche/droite (17); **on time** à l'heure (5); **on vacation** en vacances (16)
one (*numeral*) un; (*number, amount*) un(e) (P)
onion oignon *m.* (7)
only ne... que (10); seulement (12)
open *v.* ouvrir (*irreg.*) (15)
opening (*of an art exhibit*) vernissage *m.* (21)
opera opéra *m.* (21)
or ou (P)
orange *adj.* orange *inv.* (6)
orchard verger *m.* (18)
orchestra orchestre *m.* (21)
order: in order that afin que (21); pour que (21); **in order to** afin de (21)
other autre (2)
out: to go out sortir (8)
outdoors en plein air (16)
oven four *m.* (5); **microwave oven** four à micro-ondes (5)
over au-dessus de (3)
overcoat manteau *m.* (6)
overlook (the port) donner sur (le port) (20)
owe devoir (*irreg.*) (9)
owner (*of a bar, restaurant*) patron(ne) *m., f.* (11)

pad of paper bloc-notes *m.* (P)
page page *f.* (13); **home page** page d'accueil (13); **on the front page** à la une (12); **personal home page** page perso (13)
pain douleur *f.* (9); **to have pain in** avoir (*irreg.*) mal à (9)
painter peintre / femme peintre *m., f.* (11)
painting (*action, art*) peinture *f.* (21); (*picture*) tableau *m.* (21)
Pakistan Pakistan *m.* (15)
Pakistani *adj.* pakistanais(e) (15)
pants pantalon *m. s.* (6)
paper: pad of paper bloc-notes *m.* (P); **paper handkerchief** mouchoir (*m.*) en papier (9); **sheet of paper** feuille (*f.*) de papier
parents parents *m., pl.* (4)
park *n.* parc *m.*; *v.* stationner (14)
parking lot, parking garage parking *m.* (3)
parsley persil *m.* (15)
part partie *f.* (9)
party fête *f.* (11); **to have a party** faire (*irreg.*) la fête (5); **political party** parti (*m.*) politique (18)
pass (by) passer (par) (11); **to pass a course (exam)** réussir à un cours (à un examen) (11)
passenger passager/ère *m., f.* (14)
Passover pâque *f.* (11)
passport passeport *m.* (14)
past: in the past autrefois (10)
pasta pâtes *f. pl.* (15)
pastry pâtisserie *f.* (7); **pastry baker** pâtissier/ière *m., f.* (7); **pastry shop** pâtisserie *f.* (7)
patience: to lose patience perdre patience (8)
pay payer (6); **to pay attention** faire (*irreg.*) attention (5)
peanut cacahouète *f.* (*alt. spelling* cacahuète) (15)
peas petits pois *m. pl.* (7); **chick-peas** pois (*m. pl.*) chiches (15)
pedestrian street rue (*f.*) piétonne (20)
pen stylo *m.* (P)
pencil crayon *m.* (P)
penmanship écriture *f.* (1)
people gens *m. pl.* (13)
pepper poivre *m.* (8)
per par (6)
permit *v.* permettre (7)
perhaps peut-être (12)
person personne *f.* (P); **person who is afraid of technology** technophobe *m., f.* (13)
philosophy philosophie *f.* (13)
phone: See **telephone.**
photograph: photographie (*fam.* photo) *f.* (21); **to take photographs** faire (*irreg.*) de la photographie (16); **to take a photograph** prendre (*irreg.*) une photo (16)
photographer photographe *m., f.* (21)
physics physique *f.* (13)
piano piano *m.* (5)
pick (*flowers*) cueillir (*irreg.*) (16); **to pick up** (*toys, etc.*) ramasser (18); **to pick up** (*the telephone receiver*) décrocher (13)
picnic: to have a picnic faire (*irreg.*) un pique-nique (16), piqueniquer (16)
pie tarte *f.* (7)
piece (of) morceau *m.* (de) (7)
pig porc *m.* (18)
pink rose (6)
pita (bread) (pain) pita *m.* (15)
pizza pizza *f.* (8)
place (*location*) endroit *m.* (14); lieu *m.* (*pl.* lieux) (3); **in your place** à ta (votre) place (19); **to take place** avoir (*irreg.*) lieu (21)
plain *n.* plaine *f.* (17)
plant *v.* planter (18)
plate assiette *f.* (8)
plateau plateau *m.* (17)
platform quai *m.* (14)
play *v.* jouer (10); *n.* pièce *f.* (de théâtre) (21); **to play** (*a sport*) jouer à (10); faire du sport (5); **to play** (*a musical instrument*) jouer de (10)
pleasure: It's a pleasure (*to meet you*) Enchanté(e) (P)
poem poème *m.* (21)
poet poète / femme poète *m., f.* (21)
poetry poésie *f.* (21)
political party parti (*m.*) politique (18)
pollution pollution *f.* (18)
pool (*swimming*) piscine *f.* (13)
poor pauvre (22)
pork porc *m.* (7); **pork butcher shop (delicatessen)** charcuterie *f.* (7); **pork products** charcuterie *f.* (8)
port port *m.* (20)
position (*job*) poste *m.* (11)
possible: it is possible that il est possible que (21); il se peut que (21)
poster affiche *f.* (5)
pot: large iron cooking pot marmite *f.* (18)
potato pomme (*f.*) de terre (7)
poultry volaille *f.* (18)

pound (*approx. half kilo*) livre *f.* (7)
pour verser (15)
prefer aimer mieux (2); préférer (6); **it is preferable** il est préférable (20)
prescription ordonnance *f.* (9)
pretty joli(e) (2)
preview (*of an art exhibit*) vernissage *m.* (21)
probable probable (21)
probably sans doute (2)
produce *v.* produire *irreg.* (18)
producer producteur/trice *m., f.* (2)
profession profession *f.* (11)
professor professeur *m.* (P)
program émission *f.* (2); programme *m.* (13)
promise *v.* promettre *irreg.* (7)
proud fier (fière) (18)
psychology psychologie *f.* (13)
pullover pull-over (*fam.* pull) *m.* (6)
punch (*a ticket*) composter (14)
punk music punk *m.* (21)
pupil élève *m., f.* (1)
purple violet(te) (6)
pursue poursuivre *irreg.* (15)
push *v.* pousser (18)
put mettre *irreg.* (7); **to put on a piece of clothing** mettre (*irreg.*) un vêtement (7); **to put on makeup, to make up (one's eyes, one's lips)** se maquiller (les yeux, les lèvres) (9)

quarter: quarter past (*the hour*) et quart (5); **quarter to** (*the hour*) moins le quart (5)
Quebec Québec *m.* (3); **from Quebec** québécois(e) (3)
quickly vite (12)

rabbit lapin *m.* (16)
race: running race course (*f.*) à pied (10)
radio radio *f.* (5); **to put/turn on the radio** mettre (*irreg.*) la radio (7); **radio station** station (*f.*) de radio (12)
raï music raï *m.* (21)
railroad tracks voie (*f.*) de chemin de fer (19)
rain: it's raining il pleut (10)
raisin raisin (*m.*) sec (15)
Ramadan ramadan *m.* (11)
rapid rapide (12); **rapidly** rapidement (12); vite (12)
rarely rarement (2)
read lire *irreg.* (12)
reading lecture *f.* (1)
ready prêt(e) (2)
realize se rendre compte (9)
receive recevoir *irreg.* (10)
recipe recette *f.* (15)
recognize reconnaître *irreg.* (13)
recycle recycler (18); **recycling** recyclage *m.* (18)
red rouge (6)
reduce réduire *irreg.* (18)
reflect (on) réfléchir (à) (11)
refrigerator réfrigérateur (*fam.* frigo) *m.* (5)
refuge: to take refuge se réfugier (19)
refuse (to do) refuser (de) (18)
reggae music reggae *m.* (21)
register (check in) *v.* enregistrer (14)
regret regretter (21)
reheat réchauffer (15)
relatives parents *m., pl.* (4)
relief (*topography*) relief *m.* (17)
remember se rappeler (9); se souvenir *irreg.* (de) (9)
render (*make*) rendre (8)
renovation rénovation *f.* (20)
rent *v.* louer (14)
repeat répéter (6)
replace remplacer (13)
reporter reporter *m.* (2)
require exiger (20)
research recherche *f.* (13); **to research** rechercher (19)
reserved (*person*) discret/ète (12)
reside habiter (2)
residence résidence *f.* (13); **university dormitory** résidence universitaire (13)
Resistance fighter résistant(e) *m., f.* (19)
resource ressource *f.* (13)
rest *v.* se reposer (9)
restaurant restaurant *m.* (3)
retire prendre (*irreg.*) sa retraite (12)
retiree (*person*) retraité(e) *m., f.* (12)
return (*something*) rendre (8); **to return** retourner (11)
rice riz *m.* (8)
rich riche (22)
ride: ride a horse monter à cheval (16)
ridiculous ridicule (2)
right: to/on the right à droite (17); **it is right (not right)** il est juste (injuste) (20); **is that right?** c'est ça? (3); **isn't that right?** n'est-ce pas? (3), Non? (3); c'est ca? (3); **right away** tout de suite (10)
river: rivière *f.* (17); **large river** fleuve *m.* (17)
rock: to go rock climbing faire (*irreg.*) de l'escalade (16)
rock music rock *m.* (21)
roll (*bread*) petit pain *m.* (8)
roller skating roller *m.* (10); **to roller skate** faire du roller
room (*in a home*) pièce *f.* (5); **bathroom** salle (*f.*) de bains (5); **bedroom** chambre *f.* (5); **classroom** salle (*f.*) de classe (P); **dining room** salle (*f.*) à manger (5); **living room** salle (*f.*) de séjour (5)
route chemin *m.* (17); route *f.* (14)
rug tapis *m.* (5)
run: to run into (*meet*) rencontrer (14)
running (*jogging*) footing *m.* (10) jogging *m.* (10); **running race** course (*f.*) à pied (10)
runny nose le nez qui coule (9)
rush hour heures (*f. pl.*) de pointe (14)
Russia Russie *f.* (15)
Russian *adj.* russe (15)

sad triste (2); **it is sad** il est triste (20)
sail *v.* faire (*irreg.*) de la voile (16)
sailboat bateau (*m.*) à voile (16)
saint's day fête *f.* (11)
salad salade *f.* (8)
salary salaire *m.* (20)
salesclerk vendeur/euse *m., f.* (6)
salmon saumon *m.* (7)
salt sel *m.* (8)
same même (5)
sandwich sandwich *f.* (8)
Saturday samedi *m.* (4)
sauce sauce *f.* (8)
saucepan casserole *f.* (15)
sausage saucisson *m.* (8); **link sausage** saucisse *f.* (7)
say dire *irreg.* (12)
scarf écharpe (6); (*lightweight*) foulard (6)
scene scène *f.* (P)
school: elementary school école *f.* (1); **secondary school** lycée *m.* (1)
science: natural science sciences (*f. pl.*) naturelles (1)
screen écran *m.* (2)
sea mer *f.* (17)
seafood fruits (*m. pl.*) de mer (7)
search for rechercher (19)
season saison *f.* (10)
seat siège *m.* (14); **aisle (window) seat** siège (*m.*) couloir (fenêtre) (14); **(reserved) seat** place *f.* (14)
second deuxième (11)
secretary secrétaire *m., f.* (11)
section (*newspaper*) rubrique *f.* (12)
security guard agent(e) (*m., f.*) de sécurité (11)
see voir *irreg.* (10); **see you soon** à bientôt (P); **see you tomorrow** à demain (P); **to see again** revoir *irreg.* (10)
seem avoir (*irreg.*) l'air (4); sembler (13); paraître *irreg.* (13)
sell vendre (8)
send envoyer (6)
September septembre *m.* (4)
series série *f.* (12)
serve servir *irreg.* (8)
service service *m.* (13)
set (*TV, theater, cinema*) plateau *m.* (2); **to set the table** mettre (*irreg.*) la table (7)
seven sept (P)
seventeen dix-sept (P)
seventh septième (11)

seventy soixante-dix (4)
several plusieurs (14); quelques (8)
shape: in good (great) shape en bonne (pleine) forme (9)
share *v.* partager (6)
shave *v.* se raser (9)
sheep mouton *m.* (18)
sheet (of paper) feuille *f.* (de papier) (13)
shirt chemise *f.* (6)
shocking étonnant(e) (22)
shoe chaussure *f.* (6)
shoot at tirer sur (19)
shopping: to go shopping faire du shopping (5)
shore: on the shore of au bord de (17)
short court(e) (22); **in short** *interj.* enfin (10)
short story conte *m.* (21)
shorts short *m. s.* (6)
should: one should (you should, etc.) (not) il (ne) faut (pas) (20)
shoulder épaule *f.* (9)
show *v.* montrer (7); indiquer (17); *n.* spectacle *m.* (21); **could you show me the way to** est-ce que vous pourriez m'indiquer le chemin pour aller à (17)
shrimp crevettes *f. pl.* (7)
sick malade (9); **to become sick** tomber malade (9)
sideboard buffet *m.* (5)
significant fort(e) (18)
signpost poteau (*m.*) indicateur (17)
silently silencieusement (19)
since (*time*) depuis (11)
singer chanteur/euse *m., f.* (21)
single (*unmarried*) célibataire (4)
sir (Mr.) monsieur (M.) (P)
sister sœur *f.* (4); **sister-in-law, stepsister** belle-sœur *f.* (*pl.* belles-sœurs) (4)
site site *m.* (13); **touriste site** site touristique (20); **website** site Web (13)
situation comedy (sitcom) sitcom *f.* (12)
six six (P)
sixteen seize (P)
sixth sixième (11)
sixty soixante (4); **in one's sixties** (*age*) dans la soixantaine *f.* (12)
ska music ska *m.* (21)
skateboarding skate *m.* (10)
ski *v.* skier, faire (*irreg.*) du ski (16); **ski run** piste *f.* (16); **to cross-country ski** faire (*irreg.*) du ski de fond (16)
skip: to skip class sécher un cours (13)
skirt jupe *f.* (6)
sky ciel *m.* (10); **the sky is cloudy (clear)** le ciel est couvert (clair) (10)
sleep dormir *irreg.* (8)
slow lent(e) (12); **to slow the advance** retarder l'avance (19)
small petit(e) (2)
smell *v.* sentir *irreg.* (8)
smoking (nonsmoking) train car wagon (*m.*) fumeurs (non-fumeurs) (14)
snow: it's snowing il neige (10)
snowboard *v.* faire (*irreg.*) du surf de neige (16)
so *conj.* alors (1); **so** (*very*) tellement (12); **so that** afin que (21); **pour que** (21)
soap opera feuilleton *m.* (12)
soccer football (*fam.* foot) *m.* (10)
society column carnet (*m.*) du jour (12)
sock chaussette *f.* (6)
sofa canapé *m.* (5)
soil terre *f.* (18)
soldier soldat *m.* (19)
sole seul(e) (12)
some des (P); quelques (8); *pron.* en (15)
someone quelqu'un (13)
something quelque chose (13)
sometimes parfois (2); quelquefois (10)
son fils *m.* (4)
song chanson *f.* (21)
soon bientôt (10); **see you soon** à bientôt (P)
sore: to have a sore . . . avoir mal (*irreg.*) à (9)
sorry: to be sorry (that) être (*irreg.*) désolé(e) (que) (21)
soup soupe *f.* (8)
south sud *m.* (17)
South America Amérique *f.* du Sud (14)
soy sauce sauce (*f.*) de soja (15)
Spain Espagne *f.* (3)
Spanish *adj.* espagnol(e) (3)
speak parler (2)
special event spectacle *m.* (21)
speed limit limite (*f.*) de vitesse (14)
spend: to spend time on mettre du temps à (7)
spice épice *f.* (15)
sponge éponge *f.* (1)
spoon cuillère *f.* (8)
sport: play/do sports faire du sport (5)
sports center centre (*m.*) sportif (3)
sports coat veste *f.* (6)
sports fan fanatique (*m., f.*) du sport (10)
spring printemps *m.* (10)
squash courge *f.* (15)
stage (*in a process*) étape *f.* (12); (*theater*) scène *f.*
stamp timbre *m.* (13)
stand: to stand up se lever (9); **to stand in line** faire (*irreg.*) la queue (5)
star (*of a show, movie*) vedette *f.* (20)
station: (*bus, métro*) **station stop** arrêt *m.* (14); **radio station** station (*f.*) de radio (12); **television station** chaîne *f.* (12); **train station** gare *f.* (14)
stay *v.* rester (11)
steam *v.* faire (*irreg.*) cuire à la vapeur (15)
step: stepbrother beau-frère *m.* (4); **stepfather** beau-père *m.* (4); **stepmother** belle-mère *f.* (4); **stepsister** belle-sœur *f.* (4)
stereo chaîne (*f.*) stéréo (5)
still encore (10); toujours (10)
stomach estomac *m.* (9); **to have a stomachache** avoir mal au ventre (9)
stop *v.* cesser (de) (18); **stop** (*bus métro*) arrêt *m.* (14); **last stop** terminus *m.* (14)
store magasin *m.* (6); **bread store** boulangerie *f.* (7); **butcher shop** boucherie *f.* (7); **dairy products store** crémerie *f.* (7); **department store** grand magasin *m.* (6); **fish store** poissonnerie *f.* (7); **grocery store** épicerie *f.* (7), supermarché *m.* (3); **pastry shop** pâtisserie *f.* (7); **pork butcher shop** charcuterie *f.* (7)
storm (*thunder and lightning*) orage *m.* (10)
story histoire *f.* (P); **short story** conte *m.* (21)
stove cuisinière *f.* (5)
straight (ahead) tout droit (17)
street: on (Mouffetard) street dans la rue (Mouffetard) (3); **on the street** dans la rue (3); **pedestrian street** rue (*f.*) piétonne (20)
strength: with strength fort (19)
strike *v.* frapper (19)
strong fort(e) (18)
student (*university*) étudiant(e) *m., f.* (P)
studies études *f. pl.* (1)
studio studio *m.* (P)
study *v.* étudier (2); **to study** (*a subject*) faire (*irreg.*) des études en (13); **to study for (a lesson, an exam)** préparer (une leçon, un examen) (13)
subject (*school*) matière *f.* (13)
suburb banlieue *f.* (3)
subway métro *m.* (14); **subway system** réseau (*m.*) du métro (14)
succeed réussir (à) (11); **to succeed in (doing)** arriver à (18)
such tel(le) (12); **such a** un(e) tel(le) (12)
sudden soudain(e) (19)
suddenly soudain (19)
suffer souffrir *irreg.* (15)
sugar sucre *m.* (7)
suit (*man's*) costume *m.* (6), complet *m.* (6); (*woman's*) tailleur *m.* (6)
suitcase valise *f.* (14)
summer été *m.* (10)
Sunday dimanche *m.* (4)
sunglasses lunettes (*f. pl.*) de soleil (6)
sunny: it's sunny out il fait du soleil (10)
superintendent: building superintendent gardien(ne) (*m., f.*) d'immeuble (11)
supermarket supermarché *m.* (3)
suppose: I suppose je suppose (3)

sure sûr(e) (12); certain(e) (21)
surf: to surf the Web naviguer (surfer) le Web (13)
surprised surpris(e) (21)
surprising étonnant(e) (22)
survive survivre *irreg.* (15)
sweatshirt sweatshirt (*fam.* sweat) *m.* (6)
sweet sucré(e) (8)
swim *v.* nager (16)
swimming pool piscine *f.* (13)
system (*network*) réseau *m.* (14); **subway system** reseau du métro (14)

table table *f.* (P); **to set the table** mettre (*irreg.*) la table (7)
tablecloth nappe *f.* (8)
tablet (*medicinal*) comprimé *m.* (9)
take prendre *irreg.* (7); **all it takes is** il suffit de (20); **I take it** je suppose (3); **to take a course** suivre un cours (15); **to take (a long) time** prendre du temps (7); **to take a trip** faire (*irreg.*) un voyage (5), voyager (6); **to take a walk** faire (*irreg.*) une promenade (5), se promener (9); **to take an exam** passer un examen (13); **to take a photograph** prendre (*irreg.*) une photo (16); **to take photographs** faire (*irreg.*) de la photographie (16); **to take place** avoir (*irreg.*) lieu (21); **to take refuge** se réfugier (19)
talk *v.* parler (2)
talkative bavard(e) (13)
tall grand(e) (2)
tea thé *m.* (8)
teach enseigner
teacher (*elementary school*) instituteur/trice *m., f.* (1), maître (maîtresse) *m., f.* (1)
teaching enseignement *m.* (13); **foreign language teaching** enseignement des langues étrangères (13); **secondary school teaching** enseignement secondaire (13)
team équipe *f.* (16)
telephone téléphone *m.* (5); **cell phone** portable *m.* (13); **telephone booth** cabine (*f.*) téléphonique (13); **to telephone** téléphoner (à) (7)
television télévision (*fam.* télé) *f.* (2); **television station** chaîne *f.* (12); **to put/turn on the television** mettre (*irreg.*) la télévision (7)
tell dire (12); **to tell about** raconter (8)
temperature température *f.* (10)
ten dix (P)
tennis tennis *m.* (10)
tenth dixième (11)
terminus terminus *m.* (14)
terrific formidable (2)
thank you merci (P)
that *adj.* ce, cet, cette (5); *rel. pron.* que (18); *rel. pron.* qui (18); **that is** c'est (P); **that is not** ce n'est pas (P); **that (one)** celle, celui (19)
theater théâtre *m.* (10)
then ensuite (10); puis (10); alors (1)
there *adv.* là (1); *pron.* y (15); **there is/are** (*pointing out*) voilà (1); (*counting*) il y a (P); **there is/are not** il n'y a pas de (4)
therefore alors (1)
these *adj.* ces (5); *pron.* celles, ceux (19); **these are (not)** ce (ne) sont (pas) (P)
thesis thèse *m.* (13)
they are (not) ce (ne) sont (pas) (P)
thing chose *f.* (8)
think penser (2); **to think (about)** réfléchir (à) (11)
third troisième (11)
thirsty: to be thirsty avoir (*irreg.*) soif (4)
thirteen treize (P)
thirty trente (P); **in one's thirties** (*age*) dans la trentaine (12)
this *adj.* ce, cet, cette (5); **this is** c'est (P); **this is not** ce n'est pas (P); **this (one)** celle, celui (19)
those *adj.* ces (5); *pron.* celles, ceux (19); **those are (not)** ce (ne) sont pas (P)
thousand mille (4)
three trois (P)
thrilled ravi(e) (21)
throat gorge *f.* (9)
throughout (*time*) au cours de (20)
thunder and lightening storm orage *m.* (10)
Thursday jeudi *m.* (4)
ticket billet *m.* (14); **one-way (round trip) ticket** billet aller simple (aller-retour) (14) **ticket window** guichet *m.* (14)
tie cravate *f.* (6)
time fois *f.* (5); temps *m.* (5); heure *f.* (5); **at what time . . . ?** à quelle heure... ? (5); **from time to time** de temps en temps (10); **for a long time** longtemps (10); **full-time** à plein temps (11); **half-time** à mi-temps (11); **on time** à l'heure (5); **time off** congé *m.* (20); **to have a good time** s'amuser (9); **to spend time on** mettre (*irreg.*) du temps à (7); **to take (a long) time** prendre du temps (7); **what time is it?** quelle heure est-il? (5)
tired fatigué(e) (2)
tissue (*facial*) mouchoir (*m.*) en papier (9)
to à (1); en (14)
today aujourd'hui (4)
together ensemble (7)
tomato tomate *f.* (7)
tomorrow demain (10); **see you tomorrow** à demain (P)
too: too much, too many trop (de) (7); **that's too bad** c'est dommage; **it is too bad that** il est dommage que (21)
tooth dent *f.* (9)
topography relief *m.* (17)
tourist site site (*m.*) touristique (20)
toward vers (17)
track piste *f.* (16); **railroad tracks** voie (*f.*) de chemin de fer (19)
trade (*craft*) métier *m.* (11)
traffic circulation *f.* (14); **traffic jam** embouteillage *m.* (14); **traffic light** feu *m.* (17)
trail piste *f.* (16)
train train *m.* (14); **high-speed train** train à grande vitesse (*fam.* TGV) (14); **train car** wagon *m.* (14); **train station** gare *f.* (14); **to train** (*teach*) former (20)
traitor traître/tresse *m., f.* (14)
transfer *v.* faire/prendre (*irreg.*) une correspondance (14)
translate traduire *irreg.* (18)
translation traduction *f.* (13)
trap piège *m.* (19)
treason trahison *m.* (19)
tree arbre *f.* (18)
trip voyage *m.* (5); **to take a trip** faire (*irreg.*) un voyage (5), voyager (6)
troops troupes *f. pl.* (19)
trousers pantalon *m. s.* (6)
truck camion *m.* (19)
true vrai(e) (2); **is it true that . . . ?** est-ce vrai que... ? (1); **that is (it's) true** c'est vrai (2)
try essayer (6)
T-shirt tee-shirt *m.* (6)
Tuesday mardi *m.* (4)
tuna thon *m.* (7)
turn *v.* tourner (17); **turn around** retourner (11); **turn on the radio (TV, light)** mettre (*irreg.*) la radio (télé, lumière) (7)
turnip navet *m.* (15)
twelve douze (P)
twentieth vingtième (11)
twenty vingt (P)
twenty-first vingt et unième (11)
two deux (P)

ugly laid(e) (2)
uncertain incertain(e) (21)
uncle oncle *m.* (4)
under sous (3)
understand comprendre *irreg.* (7)
unemployed au chômage (20)
unhappy malheureux/euse (2)
United States États-Unis *m. pl.* (3)
university université *f.* (P); **university residence** (*dormitory*) résidence (*f.*) universitaire (13); **university student** étudiant(e) *m., f.* (P)
unless sans que (21)
unlikely: it is unlikely (that) il est peu probable (que) (21)

until jusqu'à (10); jusqu'à ce que (21)
up: to get up, stand up se lever (9); **to go up** monter (11)
use *v.* employer (6)
useful utile (20)
useless (*no use*) inutile (20)
usually d'habitude (10)

vacation vacances *f. pl.* (16); **on vacation** en vacances (16)
valley vallée *f.* (17)
veal veau *m.* (8)
vegetable légume *m.* (7)
very très (P); **very well** très bien (P)
videocassette recorder (VCR) magnétoscope *m.* (5)
Vietnam Viêtnam *m.* (3)
Vietnamese *adj.* vietnamien(ne) (3)
view: to have a view of (the port) donner sur (le port) (20)
village village *m.* (18)
vine vigne *f.* (18)
vineyard vignoble *m.* (18)
visa visa *m.* (14)
visit: to visit (*a person*) rendre visite à (8); **to visit** (*a place*) visiter (8)
visual arts arts (*m. pl.*) plastiques (13)
volleyball volley-ball *m.* (10)

wait (for) attendre (8)
wake up se réveiller (9)
walk: to take a walk faire (*irreg.*) une promenade (5), se promener (9)
wall mur *m.* (1)
want avoir (*irreg.*) envie de (4); vouloir *irreg.* (6)
war guerre *f.* (8)
wardrobe (*furniture*) armoire *f.* (5)
warmth chaleur *f.* (20)
wash: to get washed, wash up se laver (9)
watch *v.* regarder (2)
water eau (*f.*) (7); **(carbonated, noncarbonated) mineral water** eau minérale (gazeuse, plate) (7)
waterski *v.* faire (*irreg.*) du ski nautique (16)
way route *f.* (14); chemin *m.* (17); **could you show me the way to** est-ce que vous pourriez m'indiquer le chemin pour aller à (17)
weak faible (18)
weapon arme (*f.*) (19)
wear porter (2)
weather temps *m.* (10); **weather report** météo *f.* (10); **what's the weather?** quel temps fait-il? (10)
website site (*m.*) Web (13)
wedding anniversary anniversaire (*m.*) de mariage (11)
Wednesday mercredi *m.* (4)
week semaine *f.* (4)
weekend week-end *m.* (4)
weight training musculation *f.* (10)
weird bizarre (21)
welcome accueil *m.* (20); **to welcome** accueillir *irreg.* (16)
well *adv.* bien (P); **I'm well.** Ça va bien. (P); **very well** très bien (P); **well** *interj.* enfin (10); **well behaved** gentil(le) (2); **well known** réputé(e) (20)
west ouest *m.* (17)
what *interr. pron.* que (6); qu'est-ce que (6); qu'est-ce qui (16); quoi (6); **at what time?** à quelle heure? (5); **what courses are you taking?** quels cours est-ce que tu suis (vous suivez)? (13); **what is it/this/that?** qu'est-ce que c'est? (P); **what is/are . . . like?** comment est/sont... ? (2); **what's the weather?** quel temps fait-il? (10); **what time is it?** quelle heure est-il? (5)
wheat blé *m.* (18)
when quand (4); *rel. pron.* où (18)
where *adv.* où (4); *rel. pron.* où (18); **where is . . . ?** où se trouve... ? (3)
whether si (7)
which *interr. adj.* quel (quelle, quels, quelles) (5); *rel. pron.* que (18); qui (18)
while pendant (11)
white blanc(he) (6)
who *interr. pron.* qui (6); qui est-ce qui (16); *rel. pron.* qui (18) **who is it/this/that?** qui est-ce? (P)
whole: the whole . . . tout le / toute la... (14)
whom *interr. pron.* qui (6); *rel. pron.* que (18)
why pourquoi (4)
wide large (22)
widowed veuf (veuve) (4)
wife femme *f.* (4)
willing: to be willing vouloir (*irreg.*) bien (6)
window fenêtre *f.* (1); **ticket window** guichet *m.* (14); **window seat** siège (*m.*) fenêtre (14)
windsurf faire (*irreg.*) de la planche à voile (16)
windy: it's windy out il fait du vent (10)
wine vin *m.* (7); **red (white, rosé) wine** vin rouge (blanc, rosé) (7); **wine growing** viticulture *f.* (18)
winter hiver *m.* (10)
wish *v.* souhaiter (21)
with avec (1); **with dignity** dignement (22); **with strength, with effort** fort (19)
without sans (2); sans que (21)
woman femme *f.* (P)
wonderful formidable (2)
work travail *m.* (2); **to work** travailler (2); **work (of art, literature, music); body of work** œuvre *f.* (21)
workbook cahier *m.* (P)
world monde *m.* (18)
world music world music *f.* (21)
worried inquiet/inquiète (2)
worry (about) *v.* s'inquiéter (de, pour) (9)
write écrire *irreg.* (12); **to write a check** faire (*irreg.*) un chèque (20)
writer écrivain/femme écrivain) *m., f.* (11)
wrong faux/fausse (2)

year an *m.* (4); année *f.* (4); **to be (twenty) years old** avoir (vingt) ans (4)
yellow jaune (6)
yes oui (P); **yes, of course!** bien sûr que oui! (2)
yesterday hier (10)
yogurt yaourt *m.* (15)
you: and you? et vous (toi)? (P)
youth jeunesse *f.* (12)

zero zéro (P)
zucchini courgette *f.* (15)

Index

This index has four sections: Grammar, Culture, Vocabulary, and Reading Strategies. Topics treated within the Grammar index are cross-referenced. The Culture, Vocabulary, and Reading Strategies indexes are short; their contents are, for the most part, not cross-referenced. Page references followed by "n" refer specifically to footnotes.

Note: No references are given to the appendices. Appendice A (pp. A1-A5) provides definitions of grammatical terms, with examples. Appendice B (pp. A6-A10) is a table of verb forms and conjugations for active verbs in this text.

Grammar

Culture

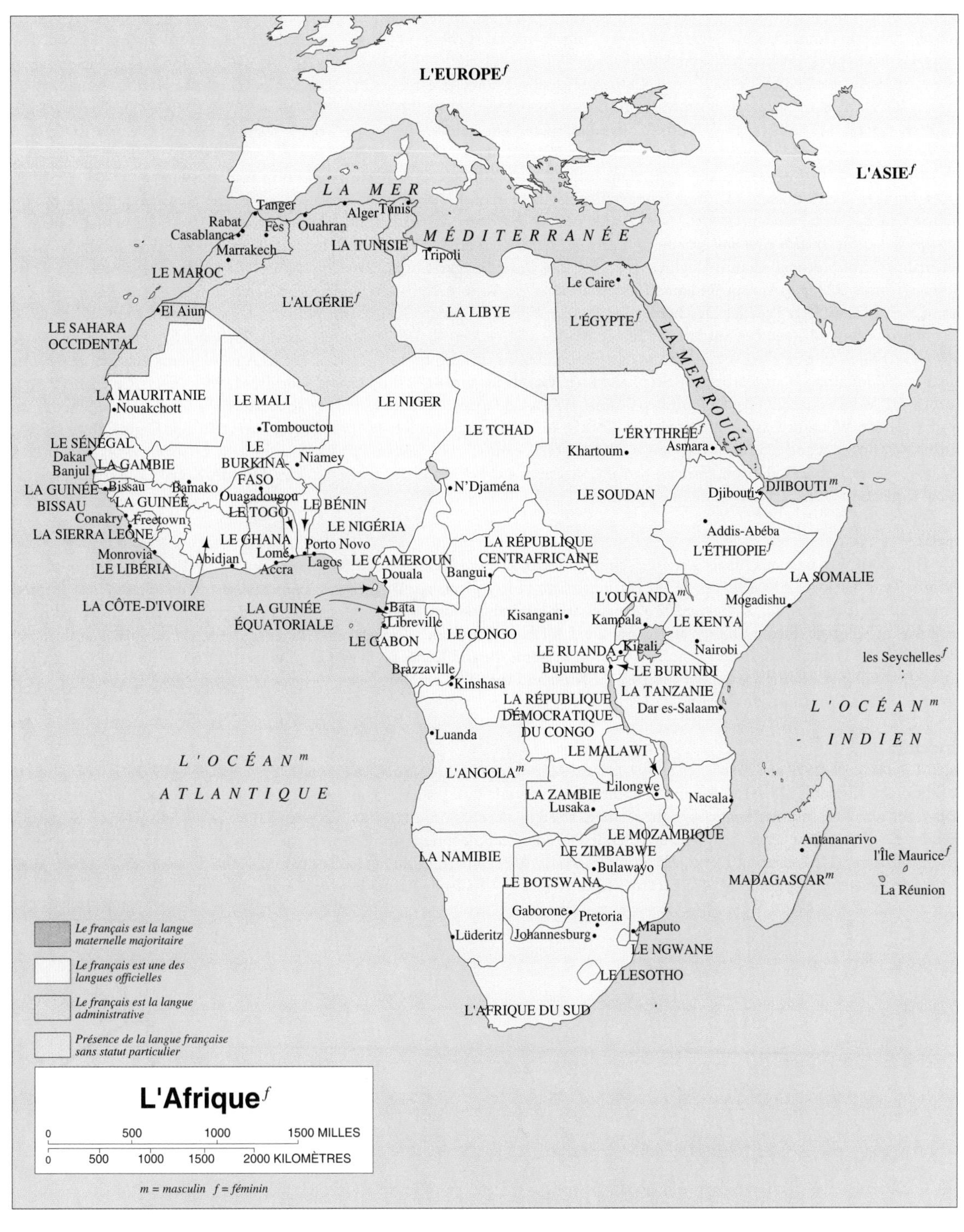
L'EUROPE^f
L'ASIE^f
LA MER MÉDITERRANÉE
Tanger
Rabat
Casablanca
Fès
Ouahran
Alger
Tunis
LA TUNISIE
Tripoli
Marrakech
LE MAROC
L'ALGÉRIE^f
LA LIBYE
Le Caire
L'ÉGYPTE^f
LA MER ROUGE
El Aiun
LE SAHARA OCCIDENTAL
LA MAURITANIE
Nouakchott
LE MALI
LE NIGER
LE TCHAD
Tombouctou
L'ÉRYTHRÉE^f
Asmara
Khartoum
LE SÉNÉGAL
Dakar
Banjul
LA GAMBIE
LE BURKINA-FASO
Niamey
N'Djaména
LA GUINÉE BISSAU
Bissau
Bamako
Ouagadougou
LA GUINÉE
LE TOGO
LE BÉNIN
LE SOUDAN
Djibouti
DJIBOUTI^m
Conakry
Freetown
LA SIERRA LEONE
LE NIGÉRIA
Addis-Abéba
L'ÉTHIOPIE^f
LE GHANA
Porto Novo
LA RÉPUBLIQUE CENTRAFRICAINE
Monrovia
LE LIBÉRIA
Abidjan
Lomé
Accra
Lagos
LE CAMEROUN
Bangui
Douala
LA SOMALIE
L'OUGANDA^m
Mogadishu
LA CÔTE-D'IVOIRE
LA GUINÉE ÉQUATORIALE
Bata
Libreville
Kisangani
Kampala
LE KENYA
LE GABON
LE CONGO
LE RUANDA
Kigali
Nairobi
les Seychelles^f
Brazzaville
Bujumbura
LE BURUNDI
Kinshasa
LA TANZANIE
LA RÉPUBLIQUE DÉMOCRATIQUE DU CONGO
Dar es-Salaam
L'OCÉAN^m INDIEN
Luanda
LE MALAWI
L'OCÉAN^m ATLANTIQUE
L'ANGOLA^m
Lilongwe
LA ZAMBIE
Lusaka
Nacala
LE MOZAMBIQUE
Antananarivo
LA NAMIBIE
LE ZIMBABWE
l'Île Maurice^f
Bulawayo
MADAGASCAR^m
LE BOTSWANA
La Réunion
Gaborone
Pretoria
Lüderitz
Johannesburg
Maputo
LE NGWANE
LE LESOTHO
L'AFRIQUE DU SUD
Le français est la langue maternelle majoritaire
Le français est une des langues officielles
Le français est la langue administrative
Présence de la langue française sans statut particulier
L'Afrique^f
0 500 1000 1500 MILLES
0 500 1000 1500 2000 KILOMÈTRES
m = masculin f = féminin

Credits

Photos

Page 34 (*top left*) Beryl Goldberg, (*top right*) Franz-Marc Freil/Corbis, (*bottom right*) © Ann Williams-Gascon; *36* (*top*) Robert Fried/Stock Boston, (*bottom*) Philippe Giraud/Corbis Sygma; *50* Becky Luigart-Stayner/Corbis; *58* (*clockwise from top left*) © Ann Williams-Gascon, Toutain Dorbec Pierre/Corbis Sygma, Hekimian/Corbis Sygma, Ann Williams-Gascon; *97* (*clockwise from top left*) Walter Rapho/The Liaison Agency, Michael A. Dwyer/Stock Boston, Nik Wheeler/Corbis, Catherine Ursillo/Photo Researchers Inc., Lee Snider/The Image Works, James Andanson/Corbis Sygma; *104* David Simson/Stock Boston; *121* R. Lucas/The Image Works; *124* (*clockwise from top left*) © Corbis, Corbis, Ann Williams-Gascon, Bill Ross/Corbis; *126* © Thomas T. Field; *142* (*top and bottom*) Lee Snider/The Image Works; *146* (*left*) François Bouchon/*Le Figaro*, (*right*) J.-J. Ceccarini/*Le Figaro*; *147* (*left and right*) J.-J. Ceccarini/*Le Figaro*; *164* (*top*) Owen Franken/Stock Boston, (*bottom*) R. Lucas/The Image Works; *169* (*top left*) © Ann Williams-Gascon, (*top right*) Yann Arthus-Bertrand/Corbis, *(bottom right)* © Ann Williams-Gascon; *170* OPT, M. Schneider; *171* Owen Franken/Stock Boston; *187* Steve Raymer/Corbis; *213* Michael Nicholson/Corbis; *221* (*clockwise from top left*) Joanna B. Pinneo/Aurora/Picture Quest, Owen Franken/Corbis, Owen Franken/Corbis, Robert Aschenbrenner/Stock Boston; *232* (*top*) Catherine Karnow/Corbis; *235* (*top left*) © Corbis, (*middle right and bottom right*) Ann Williams-Gascon, (*left*) Stefano Bianchetti/Corbis; *254* Farrell Grehan/Corbis; *259* (*top*) Bettmann/Corbis, (*bottom*) Gianni Dagli Orti/Corbis; *274* Dean Conger/Corbis; *296* Chip Hires/The Liaison Agency; *316* © Corbis; *317* Robert Holmes/Corbis; *322 (top)* © Ann Williams-Gascon, (*bottom left*) Yann Arthus-Bertrand/Corbis, (*bottom right*) Art on File/Corbis; *324* Used by permission of Claudette Pelletier Deschênes; *344* © Ann Williams-Gascon; *348* © Ann Williams-Gascon; *349* © Ann Williams-Gascon; *361* Bettmann/Corbis; *377* (*top*) Lee Snider/The Image Works; *377* (*bottom*) © Ann Williams-Gascon; *381* (*top left*) Michel Caby, Musée du Désert; (*bottom left*) Michael Busselle/Corbis, (*bottom right*) Bob Gibbons, Eye Ubiquitous/Corbis; *388* © Ann Williams-Gascon; 389 © Ann Williams-Gascon; *397* Jonathan Blair/Corbis; *398* Stephane Ruet/Corbis Sygma; *417* Philip Gould/Corbis; *418* Jack Fields/Corbis; *451* Macduff Everton/Corbis; *452* Mike Southern, Eye Ubiquitous/Corbis; *455* Pascal Parrot/Corbis Sygma; *456* (*clockwise from top right*) Jean Marc Charles/Corbis Sygma, © Ann Williams-Gascon, Chris Hellier/Corbis; *457* Wolfgang Kaehler; *462* (*top*) Pascal Parrot/Corbis Sygma, (*bottom*) Roger Wood/Corbis; *469* Roger Wood/Corbis; *473* (*top right*) The Purcell Team/Corbis, (*bottom left*) Wolfgang Kaehler, (*bottom right*) Robert Holmes/Corbis; *481* (*top*) Melies/Kobal Collection, (*bottom*) Kobal Collection; *482* (*left*) Prods. Artistes Associes/DA MA/Kobal Collection, (*right*) United Artists/Kobal Collection.

Realia

Page 51 © 2001, Les Éditions Albert René/Goscinny-Uderzo; *92 Histo Magazine; 126* Based on Emmanuel Todd, *The Explanation of Ideology,* Oxford: Basil Blackwell Ltd, 1985, p. v.; *137* National/Citer; *285* Université du Québec à Trois Rivières; *220 Le Figaro; 222* adapted from map at www.weatheroffice.com; *265 Le Figaro; 302* 3 Suisses and Minitel; *308* based on map of the Paris metro, RATP; *383* Adapted from Eugene M. Rasmusson, "Global Climate Change and Variability," Michael Glantz, ed., *Drought and Hunger in Africa*, Cambridge: Cambridge University Press, 1987. Additional data from Nicholson, Sharon E; Some, B; and Kone, B. 2000. "An Analysis of Recent Rainfall Conditions in West Africa, Including the Rainy Seasons of the 1997 El Niño and the 1998 La Niña Years," *Journal of Climate 13:2628–2640; 413* Site national historique de la Résistance en Vercors

Literature

Page 61 Francoscopie 1997 and *Francoscopie 1999*, Gérard Mérmet; *146* Janie Samet, *Le Figaro*; *192* «Familiale» in *Paroles* by Jacques Prévert. © Éditions Gallimard; *278* «Mon Amant de Saint-Jean» by Émile Carrara and Léon Agel. © 1945 by Les Nouvelles Éditions Méridian. Copyright renewed, international copyright secured. Used by permission. All rights reserved; *324* Photos and text used by permission of Claudette Pelletier Deschênes, daughter of Yolande Dionne. Complete texts and research can be found at: http://www.geocities.com/Heartland/Acres/3561/carmen01.htm. All rights reserved.; *402* «Le partage de la récolte» from *Le conte populaire en Cévennes,* Jean-Noël Pelen, © Éditions Payot et Rivages 1994; *475* Excerpts from *Le gone du Chaâba* de Azouz Begag, © Éditions Seuil 1986.

Reading Strategies

Vocabulary

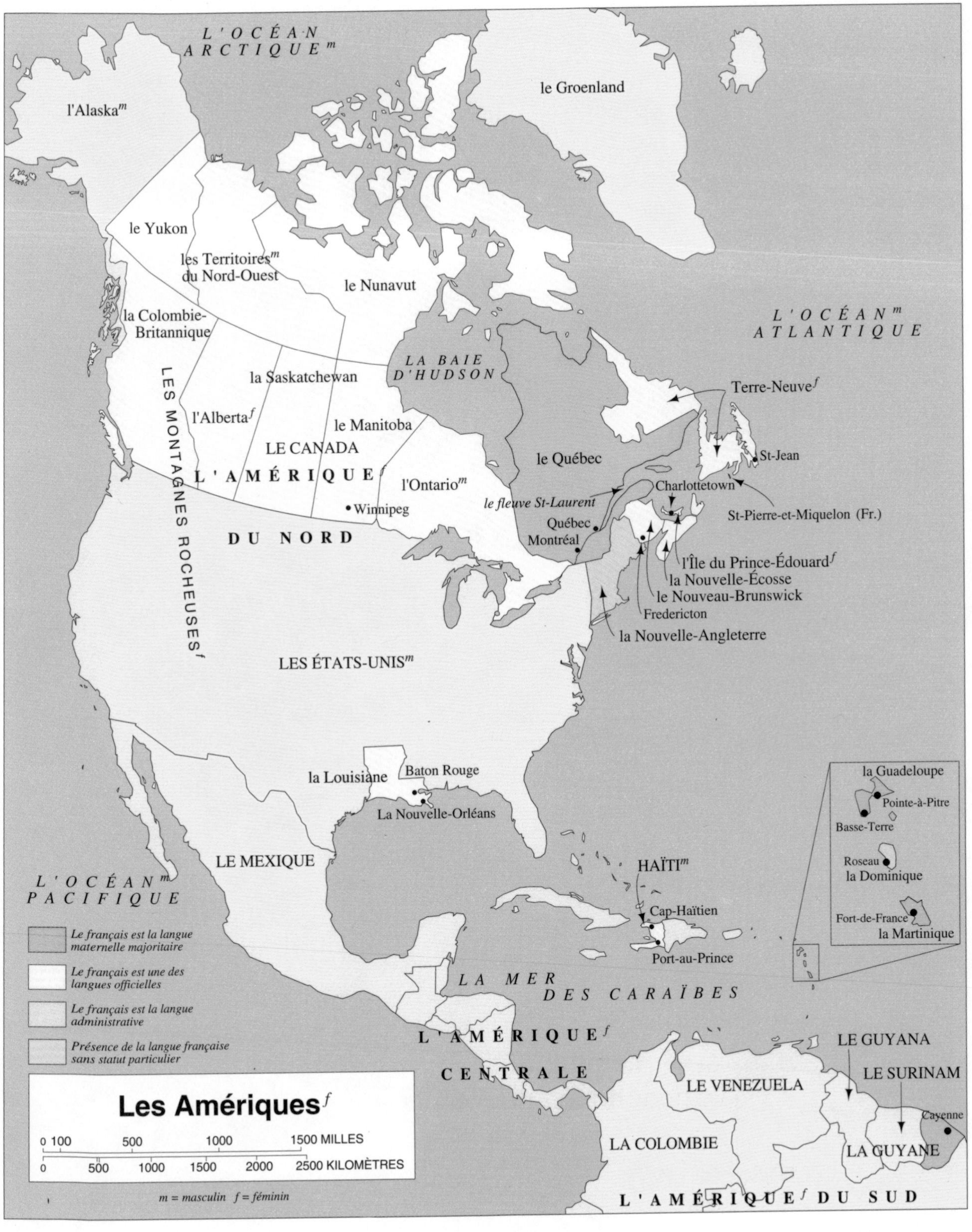
L'OCÉAN ARCTIQUE m
le Groenland
l'Alaska m
le Yukon
les Territoires m du Nord-Ouest
le Nunavut
L'OCÉAN m ATLANTIQUE
la Colombie-Britannique
LA BAIE D'HUDSON
la Saskatchewan
Terre-Neuve f
l'Alberta f
le Manitoba
LES MONTAGNES ROCHEUSES f
LE CANADA
le Québec
St-Jean
L'AMÉRIQUE f
l'Ontario m
Charlottetown
le fleuve St-Laurent
Winnipeg
St-Pierre-et-Miquelon (Fr.)
Québec
DU NORD
Montréal
l'Île du Prince-Édouard f
la Nouvelle-Écosse
le Nouveau-Brunswick
Fredericton
la Nouvelle-Angleterre
LES ÉTATS-UNIS m
la Guadeloupe
la Louisiane
Baton Rouge
Pointe-à-Pitre
La Nouvelle-Orléans
Basse-Terre
LE MEXIQUE
HAÏTI m
Roseau
la Dominique
L'OCÉAN m PACIFIQUE
Cap-Haïtien
Fort-de-France
la Martinique
Port-au-Prince
Le français est la langue maternelle majoritaire
Le français est une des langues officielles
LA MER DES CARAÏBES
Le français est la langue administrative
Présence de la langue française sans statut particulier
L'AMÉRIQUE f
LE GUYANA
CENTRALE
LE SURINAM
LE VENEZUELA
Les Amériques f
Cayenne
0 100 500 1000 1500 MILLES
LA COLOMBIE
LA GUYANE
0 500 1000 1500 2000 2500 KILOMÈTRES
m = masculin f = féminin
L'AMÉRIQUE f DU SUD

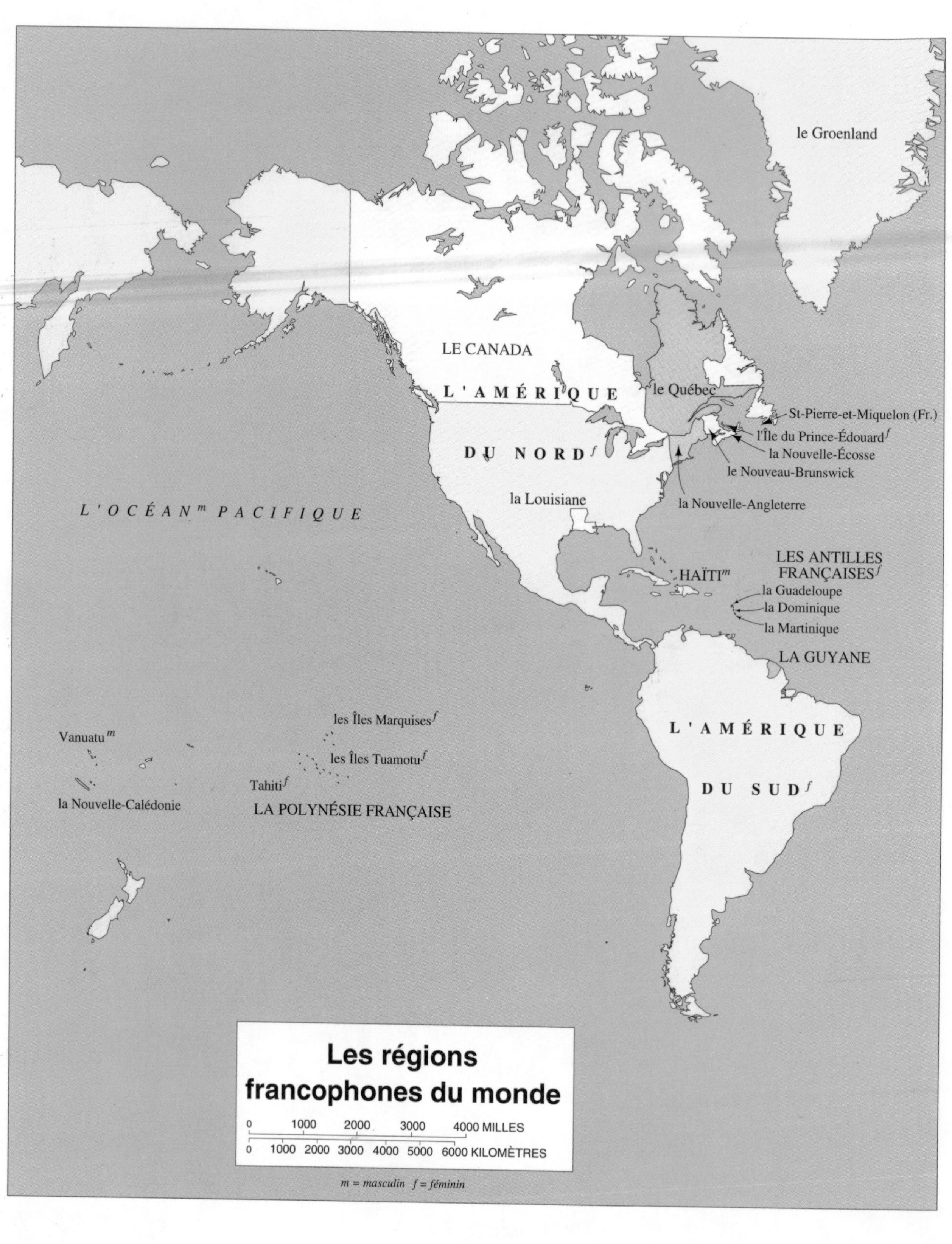
le Groenland
LE CANADA
L'AMÉRIQUE
DU NORD f
le Québec
St-Pierre-et-Miquelon (Fr.)
l'Île du Prince-Édouard f
la Nouvelle-Écosse
le Nouveau-Brunswick
la Nouvelle-Angleterre
la Louisiane
L'OCÉAN m PACIFIQUE
HAÏTI m
LES ANTILLES
FRANÇAISES f
la Guadeloupe
la Dominique
la Martinique
LA GUYANE
L'AMÉRIQUE
DU SUD f
les Îles Marquises f
Vanuatu m
les Îles Tuamotu f
Tahiti f
la Nouvelle-Calédonie
LA POLYNÉSIE FRANÇAISE
Les régions
francophones du monde
0 1000 2000 3000 4000 MILLES
0 1000 2000 3000 4000 5000 6000 KILOMÈTRES
m = masculin f = féminin